D1246982

ANNALS OF THE

NEW YORK STAGE

VOLUME XIII

[1885–1888]

ADA REHAN AS KATHARINE, THE SHREW

From a Photograph by A. Bassano, in the Brander Matthews
Dramatic Museum, Columbia University

ANNALS OF THE
NEW YORK STAGE

BY

GEORGE C. D. ODELL

VOLUME XIII
[1885–1888]

AMS PRESS
New York

Reprinted with permission from the edition of 1942, New York
First AMS EDITION published 1970
Manufactured in the United States of America

International Standard Book Number:
Complete Set: 0–404–07830–3
Volume 13: 0–404–07843–5

Library of Congress Card Catalog Number: 77–116018

AMS PRESS, INC.
NEW YORK, N. Y. 10003

CONTENTS

VOLUME XIII

BOOK TWENTY. SUPREMACY OF DALY'S THEATRE, 1885–1888

ILLUSTRATIONS

VOLUME XIII

ILLUSTRATIONS

ILLUSTRATIONS

ILLUSTRATIONS

ILLUSTRATIONS

ILLUSTRATIONS

ILLUSTRATIONS

ILLUSTRATIONS

ILLUSTRATIONS

ILLUSTRATIONS

BOOK TWENTY

SUPREMACY OF DALY'S THEATRE, 1885–1888

CHAPTER I

WALLACK'S, DALY'S, THE MADISON SQUARE THEATRE, THE LYCEUM, THE STAR, THE UNION SQUARE, THE FIFTH AVENUE, THE STANDARD, FOURTEENTH STREET THEATRE, CASINO, 1885–1886

WE left Wallack's Theatre at the end of a summer season by the McCaull Opera Company. The Black Hussar closed on August 15th, after fifteen weeks of apparent success. On Monday, the 17th, came the not felicitously named Chatter, adapted by Held and Jacobson from Millöcker's Die Näherin, familiar to German audiences in our city from the brilliant performances of Marie Geistinger. Chatter, I fear, did not duplicate, in English, its German acclaim; it gave way, on September 14th, to the ever-dependable Die Fledermaus, with, in leading rôles, Cottrelly, Rosalba Beecher, Mark Smith, DeWolf Hopper, Olga Brandon, Plunkett, Hoff, Charles Dungan and Jennie Prince. Two weeks of this revival led McCaull's artists, De Novellis still conducting, into the nebular regions of "the road." Miss Brandon, by that time, had left the force. The company contained excellent material, in parts, though it was not so brilliant, as a whole, as was the rival host at the Casino.

Wallack's was approaching its end as the home of the leading stock company in America; but two more seasons remained of that theatre as directed by Wallack, himself. The autumn of 1885 saw him beginning late and somewhat tentatively. While he hesitated, more light opera entered his new house. Viennese operetta and Gilbert and Sullivan, combined, had at last driven from its stronghold in popular favour that long-established darling of the boulevards, opéra-bouffe. Yet Maurice Grau, so long the captain of those French entertainers, tried once more, and almost for the last time, as it proved, to interest American playgoers in the obsolescent art.

On Thursday, October 1st, he introduced to America Mme. Judic, perhaps the most artistic representative of the species ever seen in this country. She began as Denise, in Mlle. Nitouche, by Hennequin and Millaud (music by Hervé), and was at once recognised by connoisseurs as a comedienne of the first rank. As the Herald repeatedly pointed out, she depended, not, like previous performers of this school, on winks and kicks and flirting of skirts, but on genuine comedy touches and sustained working out of character and situations. The company supporting her included old favourites like Mezières, Gregoire, Mme. Delorme and Mme. Vallot, and less known aspirants in Cooper, Salvator, Dupuis, Estiot and Vinchon, with Mmes. De Witt, Caro, Mirybel, Andrée and Jeanne Blanc. The opening piece continued through two performances on October 3rd. October 5th brought Lili, another Hennequin-Millaud concoction, with music by Hervé; in this Mme. Judic was Amélie and Antonine, with Cooper as Antonin, Germain as le Baron, Mezières as le Vicomte, Gregoire as Bonpan, Dupuis as René, Mme. Delorme as Mme. Bonzincourt and Mlle. Vallot as Victorine. On October 6th the new star made a big hit (at least with the discriminating) in La Femme à Papa, her leading support including Cooper, Gregoire, Mezières, Mlle. Vallot and Mlle. Tournyaire. This was repeated on October 7th, and Lili on the 8th and 10th (matinée); on the 9th, Niniche, by Hennequin and Millaud, with music by Marius Boullard, allowed the prima donna to display further reaches of her art.

The engagement, artistically, if not financially successful, wore to a close. La Femme à Papa, perhaps its best-liked offering, was repeated on October 12th and 13th; Mlle. Nitouche, on the 14th; and, on the 15th and 16th, came a revival of Le Grand Casimir, with Judic as Angelina, and with the American début of Alice Raymonde, as Ninetta. As Geistinger had done, Judic now switched from opera to comedy, and, on October 19th and 22nd, appeared as a delightful Cyprienne, in Divorçons; on the 20th and at the matinée on the 24th, she repeated Niniche, and, on the 21st, Lili; she gave the inevitable La Mascotte, on the 23rd, and departed, on Saturday, the 24th, with a benefit, in which she showed her versatility in the second act, each, of Niniche, La Femme à Papa and Mlle. Nitouche. Her departure must have caused former admirers of Tostée, Irma, Aimée, Théo and Paola-Marié to mourn the change in public taste. Such changes always distress conservatives, who cannot see that perfection passes almost as soon as attained.

THE WALLACK COMPANY; KYRLE BELLEW, 1885–1886

At last the aging Wallack entered his home, for so many months deserted by the muse of English comedy. Wallack's, under his management, was never again to be the Wallack's dear to older New Yorkers. Daly was forging forward with buoyant success, Palmer was for a while to make the Madison Square Theatre a vaunted home of drama, and — alas! — Wallack was standing dazed by the way things were going. Much missed, Osmond Tearle and Rose Coghlan had left the fold, and, though Gilbert, Edwards, Mme. Ponisi and Effie Germon remained, they were surrounded by younger colleagues, less accomplished than those of earlier years. Worst of all, Wallack seemed not to know whither to turn for new plays, and surfeited his refined

KYRLE BELLEW
AS CAPTAIN ABSOLUTE

SOPHIE EYRE
(PALACE OF TRUTH)

MADAME JUDIC
(OPÉRA-BOUFFE)

JOHN DREW—ADA REHAN

ADA REHAN—MISS DREHER
CHARLES FISHER

OTIS SKINNER

MRS. G. H. GILBERT AND
CHARLES FISHER

JAMES LEWIS

E. HAMILTON BELL AND
EDITH KINGDON

SARONY'S PHOTOGRAPHS (LOWER SIX) FROM THE MERRY WIVES OF WINDSOR

audiences with crude melodramas, quite unfitted to their tastes.   Those audiences really sought solace at Daly's — a momentous fact.

Nothing could have been more disastrous than the failure which began the new season, on October 26th — a piece by Mark Quinton, entitled In His Power.   In this Kyrle Bellew, a handsome, if not very virile leading man, made his début as Hubert Hastings, and, despite mannerisms and a curious walk, established himself in popular favour, which grew with the years that saw him entering on his maturity.   His father, J. M. Bellew, read to us in the '70s.   Sophie Eyre, who looked remarkably like Rose Coghlan, but who had only a modicum of Miss Coghlan's ability, also made her first appearance in New York (she had played elsewhere in America) as Marie Hastings, in In His Power.   And George Clarke entered the once sacred precincts as Eugene Scara, whose name gives him away as the villain of the piece. Others in the cast were familiar to Wallack *habitués* — Harry Edwards as Dr. Cameron, and William Elton and Effie Germon as Mr. and Mrs. Edward Walker.   Ivan Shirley played René and Austin Browne was Johnstone. A week of bad business shuffled this ghastly failure into oblivion.

Wallack, as usual with him in such emergencies, fell back on old comedy. The Rivals, on November 2nd, enlisted, in parts easily assigned by the reader, John Gilbert, Mme. Ponisi, William Elton, Kyrle Bellew, Annie Robe and Helen Russell, those two nice young girls whom we all admired despite their lack of supreme art.   Others in the cast were George Clarke (Sir Lucius), Dan Leeson (David), Ivan Shirley (Faulkland), C. E. Edwin (Fag), and Kate Bartlett (Lucy).   This classic, with a cast that still reads well, a half-century later, filled a fortnight at Wallack's, and was succeeded, on November 16th, by Mrs. Centlivre's The Busybody, not seen previously at Wallack's since the Charles Mathews season of 1871-72.   Now Gilbert returned to his former rôle of Sir Francis Gripe, but the others were all new to us: Bellew as Sir George Airy, Harry Edwards (fine actor) as Sir Jealous Traffick, Elton as Marplot, Shirley as Charles, C. E. Edwin as Whisper, Miss Robe as Miranda, Helen Russell as Isabinda, Kate Bartlett as Patch and Miss Blaisdell as Scentwell.   This charming relic from a vanishing past also ran an allotted two weeks.

Desperately Wallack resorted (November 30th) to the sort of melodrama that had recently brought profit to his theatre — Hoodman Blind, by Henry Arthur Jones and Wilson Barrett.   This fable, based on the resemblance of two sisters and a young husband's belief that the misdeeds of one (Jess) were attributable to his wife (Nance), carried us through many finely painted scenes by Philip Goatcher and Harley Merry, and moving performances by Kyrle Bellew as Jack Yeulett, the honest young farmer, and Annie Robe as the waif, Jess, and the wrongly suspected wife, Nance Yeulett.   John Gilbert, to strengthen the cast, played Mr. Lendon, murdered in the first act, and, with the same laudable purpose, Mme. Ponisi essayed a small part

[3]

quite beneath the level of her abilities. George Clarke was strangely cast as the villain. The complete distribution:

Jack Yeulett	Kyrle Bellew	Ephraim	John Germon
Mr. Lendon	John Gilbert	Abe Chawner	W. H. Pope
Mark Lezzard	George Clarke	Footman	Robert Snowden
Ben Chibbles	William Elton	Jelks	Edward Charles
Joe Swirrup	Harry Edwards	Nipper	Charles Daly
Kridge	Daniel Leeson	Nance and Jess	Annie Robe
Mad Willy	Ivan Shirley	Polly Chibbles	Kate Bartlett
Tom Lattiker	Harry Gwynette	Granny Quodling	Mme. Ponisi
Noah Quadling	E. T. Webber	Mrs. Chawner	Miss E. Blaisdell
Jim Dadge	C. E. Edwin	Liz	Marion Booth
Tomtit	Carrie Elberts	Mrs. Beevor	Jennie Elberts
Kit	May Germon	Kitty	Maud Matthews

I apologize for inflicting on my patient reader this long cast of a bygone era, but, after all, the authors of Hoodman Blind are of historical importance, and everything at Wallack's, however unworthy, must be attentively scrutinised.

Hoodman Blind left with the performance on Tuesday, January 19th. On the 20th, a revived The Guv'nor presented Gilbert as Butterscotch, George Clarke as Freddy, William Elton as Macclesfield, Harry Edwards as the MacToddy, Gwynette as Jellicoe, Ivan Shirley as Theodore, W. H. Pope as Vellum, Dan Leeson as Gregory, Annie Robe as Carrie, Helen Russell as Aurelia, Kate Bartlett as Kate, Miss Blaisdell as Barbara, and Mme. Ponisi as Mrs. Macclesfield. It carried through to February 15th, when Lester Wallack returned to his own stage in Valerie, a new play by David Belasco:

Walter Trevillian	Lester Wallack	Helena Malcolm	Sophie Eyre
Sir Everard Challoner	Kyrle Bellew	Valerie de Brian	Annie Robe
Xavier	Harry Edwards	Lady Bettly	Mme. Ponisi
George Alfred Bettly	Ivan Shirley	Julia Trevillian	Helen Russell
Dr. Rushton	Dan Leeson	Agnes	Kate Bartlett
Roberts	John Germon		

This was an adaptation from Sardou's Fernande, and ran for four weeks; Sophie Eyre, we observe, made in it her first appearance since the opening week of the season. In sooth, from aught that I could ever read in history, Miss Eyre had not been able to fill the place left vacant by the superb Rose Coghlan. At this place I mention a benefit of February 4th, arranged for the Actors' Fund by Wallack, Palmer and Daly, to take place at the theatres they controlled. For reasons I shall later adduce, I will describe this feat under discussion of the Madison Square Theatre.

On March 15th Wallack reverted to revivals. Home, on that evening, enlisted Wallack, of course, as Colonel White and John Gilbert as Mr. Dorrison, characters in which they had long been familiar; Harry Edwards was Montraffe, Ivan Shirley Bertie Thompson, Miss Eyre Mrs. Pinchbeck,

[4]

Helen Russell Lucy and Kate Bartlett (this year unusually busy) Dora. At the matinée, on March 20th, the bill was considerably strengthened by A Happy Pair, with Bellew and Annie Robe.   Home and A Happy Pair — what a brace of titles!   They continued in happy union till March 29th, when Wallack revived his antiquated Central Park, his Wyndham Otis being associated, as ever, with the Kerr Flamberry of Gilbert; other rôles fell to Elton, Shirley, Leeson, Sophie Eyre, Miss Robe, Miss Blaisdell and Kate Bartlett.   Meanwhile, on the afternoons of March 16th and 18th, George W. Cable, then a popular novelist, read his Grande Pointe; on the 17th he gave Posson Jone and a sketch from Dr. Sevier.   April 5th brought She Stoops to Conquer, revived for two weeks, with Wallack, Gilbert, Elton, Shirley, Leeson (Diggory), Miss Robe, Miss Russell and Mme. Ponisi — not the strongest cast for the play ever proffered by this once classic stage.   On April 11th (Sunday), F. Federici, of the Mikado company, took a benefit, Bellew, Wilder, Cottrelly, Laura Clement, Elsie Cameron among the volunteers.

The season of 1885–86 was, we shall see, a Gilbert and Sullivan season, entailing revivals of Engaged and Broken Hearts, and now, on April 19th, at Wallack's bringing out The Palace of Truth, with Elton as King Phanor, Bellew as Prince Philamir, George Clarke as Chrysal, Harry Edwards as Aristæus, Shirley as Zoram, Leeson as Gelanor, Mme. Ponisi as Queen Altimire, Annie Robe as Zeolide, Sophie Eyre as Mirza, Helen Russell as Palmis and Kate Bartlett as Azema.   With this dainty satire Wallack played the Viscount de Ligny, in The Captain of the Watch, assisted by Gilbert as Vanderpotter, F. Corbett (début) as de Courtray, Kate Bartlett as Katryn, and Helen Russell as Kristina.   The perplexed season closed on May 1st, with no high lights of achievement in its entire course, but with a fair degree of excellence scattered through its dragging weeks.   What it had needed was an interesting new play or two, such as Nancy and Company (at Daly's), Saints and Sinners (at the Madison Square), or One of Our Girls (at the Lyceum) — all soon to enter our list of bygone joys.   But, except for one week, later, at the Grand Opera House, these were Lester Wallack's last appearances on the New York stage — assuredly a thought to sadden the most frivolous.   From 1847 to 1886 had run his span of endeavour; with him, as has so often been said, departed the gay, carefree heroes of old comedy.   But he was in 1886 too old longer to look such parts — age had withered him, if custom had not staled, his not too infinite variety. His name is inseparably connected with the annals of the New York stage. I droop in spirit as I record for May 11th Charles W. Seymour's illustrated lecture on Mexico, with Turkey to follow, on the 13th.

Colonel John A. McCaull brought in his light artillery on May 3rd.   Before that date, however, a benefit for Selina Dolaro promised, for April 25th, a varied host in Isabelle Urquhart, Henrietta Markstein, Marshall P.

Wilder, Mary Stemmler, Emma Mabella Baker, Gustavus F. Hall, John A. Mackay, Lillian Russell, Sophie Eyre, Pounds, Harry Hilliard, Will Rising, &c. McCaull's first offering (May 3rd) was Don Cæsar, by Rudolph Dellinger, with a cast of favourites including Mathilde Cottrelly, Bertha Ricci, Genevieve Reynolds, Perugini, DeWolf Hopper, Edwin W. Hoff, Charles Dungan, and Mountjoy Walker, and with, as usual, Signor de Novellis conducting. As such things go, and especially as they went, this season, at the rival Casino, Don Cæsar was a failure; it gave up the struggle on May 28th, to be succeeded, on the evening of Saturday, May 29th, by The Crowing Hen, adapted from Audran's operetta, Le Serment d'Amour. Before that event, however, on May 9th, Joseph Howard, Jr., made his first appearance as a lecturer. In The Crowing Hen (named from an inn that figures in the plot), Mathilde Cottrelly played the Marquise who sadly interferes in the love affairs of a count (Perugini) and a peasant girl (Bertha Ricci), and Hopper and Herndon Morsell supplied fun as, respectively, Gavadeau and Grivolin. Celie Ellis was Marion, Charles H. Jones Martial, Josie Knapp Javotte, Kate Ethel Francine, and A. Manai Bel-Azur. Bessie Cleveland, Zoe de Vielle, Ida Bartelle, Grace Seavey, Agnes Bowen, Emma Miller and Rita Schrader filled parts in the vague world between chorus and principals.

From the Decoration Day matinée (Monday, May 31st), the Bijou Opera House, practically across Broadway from Wallack's, had been running Sydney Rosenfeld's version of Le Serment d'Amour, under title of The Bridal Trap. When I reach that piece in the discussion of the Bijou, I shall recount the story of the disgraceful street advertising in which both houses indulged, rather to the disadvantage of both. The Bijou version closed on June 26th, and the Wallack adaptation on July 10th. Meantime, on June 26th, Agnes Consuelo succeeded Madame Cottrelly as the Marquise. About this time (28th), also, Hubert Wilke and Rachel Booth replaced Perugini and Celie Ellis. McCaull, sadly in need of another Black Hussar, fell back, on July 12th, on a revival of Falka, with a cast including Bertha Ricci, Ray Samuels, Josie Knapp, Kate Ethel, Hubert Wilke, De Wolf Hopper, Harry Macdonough, George Boniface, Jr., Alfred Klein and Herbert Cripps. This closed the house on July 17th, but re-opened it, on August 2nd, for a four-weeks sojourn; Alice Galliard succeeded Ray Samuels as Edwige. August 30th brought Josephine Sold by Her Sisters, adapted by William von Sachs from Ferrier and Carré, with music by Victor Roger. In this Emily Soldene returned, after many years, as Mother Jacob; Louise Parker was Josephine, Mathilde Cottrelly Benjamine, and Eugene Oudin made his stage début as Montosol. De Wolf Hopper and Herndon Morsell completed the important members of the cast. This last contribution of McCaull's season carried on till Saturday, October 9th. I feel that the season had not been a glittering success, but, after all, it had lasted for more than five months, even though no Black Hussar had dashed boldly on the scene. On Sunday, September

[6]

12th, the artists of the company gave a concert for the Charleston sufferers, and, for the same victims, on the 26th, Herrmann and Mme. Herrmann appeared in magic, displaying the "marvellous illusion" of The Vanishing Lady. After being closed for two nights, the theatre reopened, on October 13th, for the beginning of the last season of Lester Wallack's management in New York.

DALY'S THEATRE, 1885–1886

It is a pleasure to turn from such melancholy thoughts to the brightness of Daly's Theatre, then (1885–86) beginning its seventh season with a programme that clearly indicated the glories of the future. The preliminary season, at that time expected in "stock" theatres, brought in (September 7th) the ever-welcome Mr. and Mrs. Florence, in Our Governor, which allowed Florence to prevaricate as Pinto Porterhouse Perkins, an American Munchausen, and presented the ebullient Mrs. Florence as Matilda Starr, an English authoress, occupied with looking, in America, after the flighty young Englishman, whose mother she had known for "yahs and chahs." The English accent of Mrs. Florence I still remember as fearfully and wonderfully made; Mrs. Florence must have been born funny. Others in the cast of Our Governor were Henry Holland as Robert Kingsley, Edwin Nalod as Captain Newman, Earle Sterling as the Hon. Beverly Outran, F. C. Wells as Dobson, Ethel Greybrooke as Mrs. Kingsley, Hattie Russell (sister of Ada Rehan) as Mrs. Monroe Jennings, and Minnie Radcliffe as Stella Perkins. Our Annals have chronicled worse casts and also better.

After a fortnight of this not very pronounced success, Florence assumed once more his famous Cap'n Cuttle, with Henry Holland as Dombey, Cyril Searle as Carker, Earle Sterling as Toots, J. H. Brown as Walter Gay, Ethel Greybrooke as Edith, Louisa Eldridge as Mrs. Skewton, Hattie Russell as Susan Nipper (Mrs. Florence did not appear during this week), and Miss Radcliffe as Florence. I regret that I did not see this revival. The Mighty Dollar was staged for the fourth and last week of the preliminary term, ending on October 3rd.

Daly's superb comedians returned, on Wednesday, October 7th, for a delightful season, opening in Pinero's lively farce, The Magistrate, produced under the supervision of the author. About this time, as we shall see, Henry Arthur Jones was in New York to direct, at the Madison Square Theatre, rehearsals of his play, Saints and Sinners. Students of the drama may be pardoned a thrill at the thought of the presence in our city in 1885 of those two gods of the machine of the "well-made" plays of the '90s. Well I remember, that season, the fun of The Magistrate, with the predicament of the respectable characters held up by rain in a restaurant beyond the legal hour of closing, the escape of the magistrate (Posket) and the trial, next morning, of the arrested offenders before the judge who had been

[7]

their partner in law-breaking — a judge (Lewis) whose wife (Miss Rehan) was among the defendants. And that wife's lie, in declaring that her son (Hamilton Bell) by a former marriage was only fourteen years old, when, in reality, he was nineteen and quite excusably in love with his governess (Edith Kingdon)! John Drew and Otis Skinner appeared as middle-aged, bewhiskered army officers caught by rain in the meshes of the early closing law. According to Judge Daly, Pinero had doubts as to Drew's being able to shift from his usual rôle of bright young lover to the peppery Colonel Lukyn, but Daly persisted in his choice, and Drew fully justified the faith of his manager.

The crowd of fashionable and literary folk on the opening night almost "rushed" the gates of the theatre, and this is the fine cast they applauded:

Æneas Posket	James Lewis	Achille Blond	Frederick Bond
Colonel Lukyn	John Drew	Sergeant Messiter	Augustus Yorke
Bullamy	Charles Fisher	Charlotte	Virginia Dreher
Captain Vale	Otis Skinner	Beattie	Edith Kingdon
Sergeant Lugg	William Gilbert	Popham	May Irwin
Cis Farringdon	E. Hamilton Bell	Agatha Posket	Ada Rehan

A finer cast probably could not have been found in Christendom. Hamilton Bell, who played the boy, was new to our stage, but he became a recognised figure in American life, first as an actor, later as a writer and as a stage director. It was he who discovered at All Souls College, Oxford, the drawing now generally accepted as Sir Christopher Wren's plan (1674) for the second theatre in Drury Lane; and years after his début at Daly's he designed some of the beautiful settings accorded revivals of classic plays at the ill-starred New Theatre in Central Park West.

Pinero, on the opening night of The Magistrate, made a speech before the curtain; doubtless he was gratified at the enthusiastic reception of his play. The seventy-fifth and last performance of the merry farce occurred on December 9th (matinée). On the 9th (evening) Daly revived an even merrier thing — his great success of the preceding season — A Night Off, with the entire original cast — Lewis, Drew, Skinner, Fisher, Leclercq, Bond, Mrs. Gilbert, Miss Rehan, Miss Dreher and Miss Irwin. During the run of this revival I was fortunate enough to see a performance of the farce, and I still recall it as one of the most delightful evenings I ever spent in the theatre. This was my first sight of the incomparable Mrs. Gilbert and my first experience with the wonderful *ingénue* accomplishments of Ada Rehan, whose Nisbe, in A Night Off, was the most perfect thing of its kind that I ever saw. The memory of that performance of the comedy cheered me through a long and painful illness that came on me at this time and wrecked my Freshman year at Columbia College.

A Night Off reached its final performance on January 13th. On Thursday, the 14th, Daly produced The Merry Wives of Windsor, the first of the Shakespearian revivals that for many years thereafter were to be imposing features of his theatre. We remember that, in 1872, he had put on The Merry Wives at his little Fifth Avenue Theatre, with Charles Fisher, Louis James, George Clarke, James Lewis, Davidge, Fanny Davenport, Fanny Morant, Sara Jewett and Mrs. Gilbert in the leading parts. He now proffered it with this cast:

Sir John Falstaff	Charles Fisher	Pistol	George Parkes
Ford	John Drew	Nym	John Wood
Page	Otis Skinner	Bardolph	H. Roberts
Slender	James Lewis	Jack Rugby	E. P. Wilks
Fenton	E. Hamilton Bell	Robin	Bijou Fernandez
Shallow	John Moore	Mrs. Ford	Ada Rehan
Sir Hugh Evans	C. Leclercq	Mrs. Page	Virginia Dreher
Dr. Caius	William Gilbert	Anne Page	Edith Kingdon
Mine Host	Frederick Bond	Dame Quickly	Mrs. G. H. Gilbert

Critical opinion was divided. Ranken Towse, of the Post, thought this and all of Daly's subsequent Shakespearian offerings too much tinged, not to say tainted, with the spirit of the German farces for which his house was famous. The Herald review of The Merry Wives implies that Mrs. Gilbert was the only member of the cast who acted with the authority of the older school; but Misses Rehan and Dreher looked lovely and acted with merry dash and sparkle. We know that, to a generation with memories of Hackett and De Bar, Fisher's Falstaff was never wholly acceptable. Daly had mounted the comedy with fine scenery and costumes, the dresses being vouched for in Sarony's numerous photographs of the members of the cast. He carried the production through the matinée on February 13th — thirty-five performances in all. James Lewis was out of the cast in late January. For self-protection, but reluctantly, I call attention to the fact that Allston Brown mistakenly sets down the first performance of A Night Off as October 9th and that of The Merry Wives as October 14th, as if Daly had staged the first three productions of his season within a period of about a week.

For reasons later to be stated, I leave for discussion that three-fold benefit for the Actors' Fund, arranged by Daly, with co-operation of Wallack and Palmer, to be carried out, on February 4th, at the theatres controlled by the three managers. I pass to the evening of February 13th, when Daly pursued the policy so agreeable to his patrons and himself, of restoring for a brief time his previous revivals of old plays. On that evening She Would and She Wouldn't, as Daly habitually printed it, came back, with Misses Rehan, Irwin and Jean Gordon and Fisher, Drew, Skinner, Parkes, Lewis, Gilbert, Bond and Wood, and with Edith Kingdon as a new Donna Rosara. With the Cibber piece Daly put on a trifle called A Wet Blanket, with Drew and Miss Rehan as the engaging protagonists. February 18th found The Country Girl again exerting her charms and her assumed innocence in the incomparable performance of Ada Rehan; the original group of Fisher, Drew,

Skinner, Parkes, Miss Dreher and May Irwin assisted. The accompanying farce was now A Sudden Shower, with Lewis and Mrs. Gilbert in the complications involved. This pleasing bill lasted through February 24th (matinée).

Daly's final production for this prosperous season was Nancy and Company, his adaptation of Halbe Dichter by Julius Rosen. The main theme involved the artistic union of Nancy Brasher, a would-be authoress, and Kiefe O'Kiefe, an author, in the writing of a work of importance. Needless to say, their continued meetings aroused the jealousy of Tippy Brasher, Nancy's husband. Two pairs of young lovers were forced to hide, I forget why, under sofa-covers and behind travelling bags, and Lewis and Mrs. Gilbert mingled nimbly in the general farcical confusion. And George Parkes had a silly-ass part of the kind he had portrayed, eleven years previously, in The Big Bonanza. May Irwin had her usual rôle of the knowing maid. The cast:

Ebenezer Griffing	James Lewis	Nancy Brasher	Ada Rehan
Kiefe O'Kiefe	John Drew	Mrs. Huldah Dangery	Mrs. Gilbert
Captain Renseller, U.S.A.	Otis Skinner	Oriana	Virginia Dreher
Sikes Stockslow	George Parkes	Daisy	Edith Kingdon
Tippy Brasher	William Gilbert	Betsy	May Irwin
Bell-Boy	John Wood		

As I write that cast, the company seems to me perfect for such pieces; I recall my utter joy in this performance. The comedy carried Daly to the close of his regular season on May 1st — seventy-seven times in all. On March 8th, a charity benefit revived Love on Crutches, which had been part of the triple joy offered at the Actors' Fund benefit, on February 4th. Daly offered for Lenten entertainment a series of five illustrated morning lectures by John L. Stoddard: Bonaparte from Corsica to the Throne (March 11th); Bonaparte from the Throne to St. Helena (15th); New Walks with Charles Dickens (18th); Mary, Queen of Scots (29th); Switzerland (April 1st). Ladies of refinement found this agreeable Lenten diversion (the Herald says that Mrs. Gilbert and Ada Rehan were regular attendants), and Daly offered a second and a continuous course of the talks, prefixing to them, on April 12th, a lecture on Spain. Switzerland ended the series on April 17th. Before the days of the cinema and before the deluge of ocean travel, these magic lantern views of foreign parts were excellently educational.

After short stays in Boston and Philadelphia, Daly and his company sailed for a second summer visit to London, and a first to the continent. His theatre was taken over, on May 3rd, by the best possible substitute for his departing actors — Rosina Vokes, fresh from a most successful season at the Standard Theatre, and in the same tripartite bill that there had enchanted our best playgoers — In Honour Bound, My Milliner's Bill and A

JAMES LEWIS—MRS. GILBERT
EDITH KINGDON—VIRGINIA DREHER

JAMES LEWIS—MAY IRWIN

OTIS SKINNER—JOHN DREW
EDITH KINGDON

JOHN DREW—ADA REHAN
GEORGE PARKES

SARONY'S PHOTOGRAPHS FROM NANCY AND COMPANY

Christmas Pantomime Rehearsal. Miss Vokes was without a rival in light comedies of that class. Who that saw it can ever forget her comic distress in My Milliner's Bill, with her incomparable singing of 'Is 'Art was True to Poll, and her delightful portrayal of Lily, in the delicious satire of that rehearsal? As at the earlier Standard engagement Miss Vokes's company included Weedon Grossmith, best of all representatives of the brainless nobleman, Courtenay Thorpe, Augustus Yorke, Brandon Thomas (a man of note, later author of Charley's Aunt), W. G. Elliot, J. Rolfe, Miss Farleigh, Leslie Chester and Agnes Miller — a company notable for refinement of manner, style and speech. It is a joy to remember it. No change of bill was required to the close of the Vokes season, on June 5th — a season of profit and delight to Daly and his loyal patrons.

MADISON SQUARE THEATRE, 1885–1886

It will be remembered that, for the first time since the early days of Hazel Kirke, the Madison Square Theatre had, in the summer of 1885, brought in visiting stars and their organisations to help New York forget the heat outdoors. John T. Raymond, in July, gave both In Chancery and For Congress. I suspect that the engagement was not wholly profitable. On August 3rd, C. W. Couldock followed, as Luke Fielding, in the very old-fashioned The Willow Copse, and was accused by the Herald of being as old-fashioned as the play. Nevertheless, he surprised critics by holding on till August 29th. Perhaps his good company had something to do with the success — Carrie Turner, Mr. and Mrs. Charles Walcot, Thomas Whiffen, Walden Ramsay, A. S. Lipman and Samuel Hemple.

Mme. Janish was to have opened, on August 31st, in Anselma, Leander Richardson's adaptation of Agnes, that Sardou play in which Agnes Ethel had starred in 1872. Miss Ethel (or Mrs. Tracy) enjoined Mme. Janish, but the latter finally achieved her desire, on September 7th, and inaugurated a run of Anselma with a good cast including Henry Miller, Max Freeman, Leslie Edmunds, W. J. Ferguson, John G. McDonald, H. S. Millward, G. H. Leonard, Gabrielle Du Sauld and Nettie Abbott. Surprisingly, the play ran till September 26th.

A. M. Palmer, now in control of the fortunes of this theatre, re-opened it, on October 5th, with a revival of the last-season success, Sealed Instructions. He had gathered a superb company, which in great part was to remain with him for several glorious seasons. In Sealed Instructions Agnes Booth returned to this theatre as Mrs. Haughton (originally played by Mathilde Madison). From the wreckage of the Union Square company, Palmer enlisted the lovely Maud Harrison (who succeeded Jessie Millward as Katherine), and J. H. Stoddart (now seen in Thomas Whiffen's former rôle of Benton). Herbert Kelcey fell heir to H. M. Pitt's rôle of Captain Haughton, yielding his former part of Guy Dunbar to Louis F. Massen. Members of the original cast remaining were Frederic Robinson (Lord Dorchester), W. J. LeMoyne (M. Dupuis), Walden Ramsay (Gerald Dunbar), Harry Hogan (Servant), Annie Russell (Ada), and Lena Langdon (Suzanne). H. C. De Mille was listed for Appleby (*vice* Fred Ross). It gives me extreme pleasure to contemplate the excellence of that cast and to revive the memory of its performance, which I thoroughly enjoyed from my front-row gallery seat. What a joy to be a boyish lover of the drama in that exalted position! Yet I remember that, to my surprise, the usually beautifully gowned Mrs. Booth and Miss Harrison wore dresses of a former era; perhaps they were unwilling to buy new clothes for what could be but a brief run for a play not new.

On Saturday evening, November 7th, Palmer presented, under direction of the author, Henry Arthur Jones's fine play, Saints and Sinners:

Jacob Fletcher	J. H. Stoddart	Uncle Bamberry	Frank Drew
Captain Fanshaw	Herbert Kelcey	Tom Marks	Alfred Becks
Ralph Kingsmill	L. F. Massen	Leeson	H. S. Millward
Samuel Hoggard	W. J. LeMoyne	Porter	Harry Hogan
Mr. Prabble	C. P. Flockton	Letty Fletcher	Marie Burroughs
Lot Burden	E. M. Holland	Lydia	Mrs. E. J. Phillips
Peter Greenacre	W. Davidge	Mrs. Partridge	Lizzie Duroy
Raddles	Walden Ramsay	Fanny Partridge	Marie Greenwald

This distribution, combined with that of Sealed Instructions, reveals the astonishing strength of the Palmer forces. E. M. Holland. Flockton, Davidge and Mrs. Phillips (she so long Palmer's colleague at the Union Square Theatre) were among the best stock actors in America. In this play Stoddart made a great hit as the clergyman who would not yield his honour in return for silence as to the dishonour of his beloved child; and the beautiful Marie Burroughs as the errant and repentant Letty greatly increased her artistic standing by her performance of the part. I once heard Henry Arthur Jones speak in the highest admiratioin of Stoddart's rendition of the great rôle of Jacob Fletcher. Saints and Sinners ended its run on February 22nd, having passed its hundredth performance on February 12th. How sadly Wallack must have eyed these long runs at Daly's, the Madison Square and the Lyceum!

As we know, New York and Brooklyn were beset by amateur actors, especially actresses. One group — perhaps the best in Manhattan — including Mrs. James Brown Potter, Alice Lawrence, Mrs. Walter Andrews, Edward Fales Coward, Prescott, Valentine Hall, Butler and Bedlow, gave, on December 28th and 29th (afternoons) at the Madison Square, where it had originally performed it, A Russian Honeymoon. An incidental dance brought in Mrs. Noel, Mrs. Lounsbury, Mrs. Wilber Bloodgood, Miss Caffery, Alice and Rita Lawrence, Valentine Hall, Frederic Satterlee, Goodhue Livingston, Charles Beekman, Fairfax Harrison and Richard Wainwright —

a list of names that will show how American New York society once was. Miss Lawrence also sang a song very prettily. The Misses Lawrence were accomplished young ladies.

Let me set down for February 4th a remarkable tripartite benefit for the Actors' Fund, which I have aleady twice briefly mentioned. The plan is said to have originated with Daly, with whom Wallack and Palmer co-operated. The Wallack company at two o'clock, began the afternoon, in their home theatre in Act II of The Rivals; at three o'clock, Palmer's company gave the second act of Engaged; at four o'clock, Daly's company did the last act of Love on Crutches. And so the merry round continued. The Madison Square Theatre at two o'clock offered Act I of Engaged; at three o'clock, Daly's Love on Crutches followed; and at four o'clock Wallack's actors gave the last act of The Rivals; Daly's began, at two o'clock, with Act I of Love on Crutches, followed, at three o'clock by Act III of the Wallack Rivals, and, at four, by the last act of Engaged. Wallack addressed the audience at Daly's, Palmer at Wallack's, and Daly at the Madison Square. Reserved seats sold at $2, but could be used at any one of the three theatres. At first glance this seems like an attractive novelty, but, after all, each audience feasted on scraps of plays. Yet, in that day of few successes, probably the majority of spectators had seen each of the plays involved, and to study the art, in one day, of the distinguished members of our three famous stock companies was in itself an experience worth craving, and the actors must have had fun scurrying, in make-up, from theatre to theatre.

I recorded the benefit in this place because the performance of Engaged was obviously a try-out in that Gilbert and Sullivan season. At any rate, it entered the regular bills, on February 23rd, with the glorious Agnes Booth as Belinda, tarts and all, with Maud Harrison as a delightful Minnie, Annie Russell as a perfect Maggie McFarlane, seemingly demure and inwardly selfish and self-seeking, Mrs. Phillips as Mrs. McFarlane, Kelcey as a surprisingly good Cheviot Hill, LeMoyne as an unctuous Mr. Symperson, Flockton as Belvawney, Frank Drew as McGillicuddy, Massen as Angus Macalister, and Marie Greenwald as Parker. Not for anything conceivable would I give up my memory of that priceless performance, the women of the cast being as near perfection as anything on the stage can be.

I go back to February 16th (afternoon), when Charles Roberts, Jr., read from Bret Harte, Coppée, Lewis Carroll, Owen Meredith and other now (1941) forgotten worthies; he read also on the 23rd and March 2nd. And I go forward with delight to another glorious memory of my youth — Gilbert's pathetic verse-drama, Broken Hearts, brought out, on March 30th, with Bronson Howard's charming Old Love Letters. In the latter, Agnes Booth renewed her earlier success as Mrs. Brownlee, assisted by the handsome Herbert Kelcey as Warburton. In Broken Hearts Maud Harrison was an exquisite Hilda, and Annie Russell's pathetic Lady Vavir was one of the memorable achievements of her earlier career.   LeMoyne also was excellent as the dwarf, Mousta, and Louis Massen a handsome Prince Florian, though one could have wished for him a greater degree of poetical fervour.   The cast was completed by Sara Estor as Lady Amanthis and Marie Greenwald as Lady Melusine.   This was a lovely production, lasting through April 17th.   On April 15th (afternoon), a benefit for Marshall P. Wilder promised an immense group, in Geraldine Ulmar, Marie Burroughs, Mme. Cottrelly, Bellew, Perugini, Harry Edwards, Pounds, Harry and Robert Hilliard, John Howson, &c.   The last offering of the regular season was Our Society, adapted by Clinton Stuart and Mrs. Verplanck from Le Monde où l'on s'Ennuie.   The cast of April 19th was delightful:

Philip Van Pelt	Herbert Kelcey	Sylvia Spencer	Annie Russell
Ferdinand C. Tupper	Walden Ramsay	Mrs. Ferdinand Tupper	Maud Harrison
Reginald Rae	W. J. LeMoyne	Mrs. Katherine Spencer	Mrs. E. J. Phillips
Socrates Browning	E. M. Holland	Mrs. Van Pelt	Virginia Buchanan
Senator Montgomery	W. Davidge	Constance Gray	May Robson
Hon. Reuben Carey	Frank Drew	Mrs. Aliburton	Lizzie Duroy
Mr. Starling	C. P. Flockton	Mrs. Browne	Marie Greenwald
Williams	H. S. Millward		

The season was so far advanced that Palmer could keep this bright play but two weeks on his stage; it closed, perforce, on May 1st, after having established once more the exquisite girlish charm of Annie Russell and the brilliant comedy talent of Maud Harrison.

On May 3rd, Richard Mansfield tentatively began here his career as a star, bringing from Boston a concoction of A. C. Gunter, entitled Prince Karl, a light summer show in which Mansfield not only acted but exhibited his powers of entertaining at the piano and in song.   He played the part of a prince become a guide, and by sheer force of personality carried the piece to success.   At first the cast included several members of the company of the Boston Museum:

Karl von Arhmien	Richard Mansfield	Sylvio	C. E. Boardman
Spartan Spotts	Charles Kent	Giuseppe	G. B. Bates
Cool Dragon	William Seymour	Pippo	William Malley
Howard A. Briggs	A. R. Whytal	Mrs. Daphne Lowell	Mrs. J. R. Vincent
Markey Davis	James Nolan	Mrs. Florence Lowell	Maida Craigin
Gustavus	H. P. Whittemore	Alicia Lowell	Helen Dayne

It is a pleasure to welcome to New York Boston's beloved "old lady," Mrs. Vincent; others in the cast will be recognised as having supported Booth, not very brilliantly, at the Fifth Avenue Theatre, in February preceding. Gradually, the Boston players went home.   The fortieth performance of the play, "altered and improved," advertised (June 14th) Effie Germon, Rillie Deaves, Joseph Frankau and Harry Gwynette in parts formerly played by Mrs. Vincent, Maida Craigin, "Willie" Seymour and Nolan.   Later on (June 23rd) Emma Sheridan and Beatrice Cameron, both new to the stage,

ANNIE RUSSELL
(BROKEN HEARTS)

MAUD HARRISON
(OUR SOCIETY)

MARIE BURROUGHS
(SAINTS AND SINNERS)

JOHN E. KELLERD
(HELD BY THE ENEMY)

RICHARD MANSFIELD
(PRINCE KARL)

PARKS—MISS KIDDER
(HELD BY THE ENEMY)

ARTHUR W. PINERO

MRS. J. R. VINCENT

HENRY ARTHUR JONES

were Alicia and Florence. And Cyril Scott, in August, was Spotts. The hundredth showing of Prince Karl was listed for July 30th, and the engagement closed on August 14th. During the summer, ladies in the audiences were served *gratis* with ices from Maillard's, just a few steps from the theatre, at the corner of Broadway and 24th Street. Old-time memories cause us to wonder if there has ever been ice cream so rich and delicious as that of Maillard, wondrous caterer for connoisseurs.

The beautiful little Madison Square Theatre could not be allowed to close. On August 16th, William Gillette brought to it (it had previously housed two of his plays, The Professor and Esmeralda) his very striking drama of the Civil War — Held by the Enemy. This was the first good play dealing with that catastrophe of our nation, and, like Gillette's later Secret Service, pictured the adventures and hairbreadth escapes of a Northern spy in a Southern scene. Southern ladies in a charming home, Confederate officers in love with the heroine, the heroine's promise to marry the mean man (I dislike to call him the villain) if he will say the reputed dead man is really dead, and the fine Northerner's compelling the mean one to release the girl from her promise — all this, with a comic subplot of a newspaper man and a Southern *ingénue* made of Held by the Enemy a stirring piece destined to continue until the more deft Secret Service drove it from the stage. It had been played in Brooklyn, on February 22nd, but the cast at the Madison Square had, as had that of Prince Karl, a Boston suggestion:

Major-General Stamburg........C. W. Stokes	Captain Woodford............D. J. Sullivan
Colonel Prescott............George R. Parks	Hinton......................J. H. Williams
Lieutenant Hayne............John E. Kellerd	Sentry........................Hugh Fuller
Fielding..............Melbourne McDowell	Clerk..........................W. H. Pope
Hathaway....................H. A. Moran	Mrs. McCreery...........Mrs. M. A. Farren
Thomas Henry Bean..........C. S. Dickson	Rachel McCreery...........Kathryn Kidder
Uncle Rufus...............Harry Woodson	Susan McCreery...............Louise Dillon

The Herald thought Miss Kidder's acting as Rachel was not quite up to her standard, but Louise Dillon was thoroughly delightful as Susan. It is interesting, by the way, to find Charles Dickson and Miss Dillon playing opposite, in comedy relief, as they were to do, two years later, so brilliantly, in The Wife. George R. Parks, a popular leading man in Boston, must not be confused with George Parkes, of Daly's Theatre. Held by the Enemy, a great success, held the Madison Square stage through October 23rd. The history of this theatre for 1885–86 is fragrant still in older memories.

Lyceum Theatre, 1885–1886

Since the Lyceum Theatre was, in two years, to become the home of a distinguished stock company, and since, in the season we are discussing, it had elements of the stock system, I will here introduce its record for 1885–86 immediately following the account of the three great stock companies I have just transcribed. Daniel Frohman opened the house on Tuesday, September 15th, with Steele MacKaye's version of Andrea (or Agnes), which he called In Spite of All. Curiously enough, we recall, another adaptation of the same play finally got itself acted at the Madison Square Theatre at about this same time. In the Lyceum piece Minnie Maddern achieved stellar rank as Alice Glendenning, and became one of a fine quartette including Eben Plympton as Carol Glendenning, Richard Mansfield as Kraft, and Selina Dolaro as Stella; John A. Lane, Joseph Frankau and William Payson also participated. The play, thus acted, achieved a minor success, running, I am surprised to find, till November 7th — a pleasing record for Miss Maddern, in her early stellar career.

On Tuesday, November 10th, Helen Dauvray assumed the management of the Lyceum, and brought out One of Our Girls, a very successful new comedy by Bronson Howard, a somewhat artificial story of the bright American girl breezily entering the home of French relatives whose family "is mentioned in Froissart." The daughter of this family has been sacrificed in marriage to a "noble" roué, and, after her flight to a lover, she is saved, as Professor Quinn says, by the device of Les Pattes de Mouche, wherein the brave American girl takes on herself the questionable situation arising. Miss Dauvray made a great hit as the American Kate Shipley, and was, if truth must be told, more delicately French in her method of acting than were some of the excellent players who in the cast surrounded her as French nobles. But the cast was remarkable:

M. Fonblanque	George F. DeVere	Dr. Girodet	Louis James
Captain John Gregory	E. H. Sothern	André	F. Williams
Comte de Crebillon	F. F. Mackay	Mme. Fonblanque	Ida Vernon
Henri St. Hilaire	Vincent Sternroyd	Julie	Enid Leslie
Duc de Fouché-Fonblanque	J. W. Pigott	Kate Shipley	Helen Dauvray

Miss Dauvray at once established herself as an artist of delicate charm, French, we thought, in approach. Perhaps the greatest hit of the piece was made by the young E. H. Sothern, who finally arrived at the height of popularity, which, soon, was to rank him among the most notable of our stars. His young English officer was delightful. I still remember that smiting of the French roué and duelist with the glove that rings like a clarion (pardon the incongruity of this simile) in my storehouse of recollected thrills. And the scene at the piano, with Miss Dauvray, and Miss Dauvray, herself, in the letter scene! The reader must study Falk's photographs of the actors in the play, admiring Miss Vernon's aristocratic poise, Enid Leslie's pretty girlishness, Louis James's distinction, Mackay's polished villainy and Vincent Sternroyd's (he was a newcomer here) manly bearing. And always Sothern and Miss Dauvray!

Happy the theatre that knows no change of bill! One of Our Girls

[16]

reached its fiftieth performance on December 12th; the hundredth night and souvenirs fell on February 15th. Breaking into this heartening run, J. W. Pigott, a member of the cast, brought out, on March 11th (afternoon) a comedy of his own, She Loved Him, a love that produced no offspring of subsequent performances. In this abortion, Charles A. Smiley made his New York début, and, I suppose, awaited results. Sophie Eyre and Louis James were announced. John Rickaby, manager of the theatre, died, after a long illness; Miss Dauvray, on March 4th, arranged a benefit for his widow, promising Maud Harrison, Stoddart and Massen, of the Madison Square company, in One Touch of Nature, A. P. Burbank, Marie Prescott, C. W. Couldock, and One of Our Girls. The Lyceum, like most of the leading houses of New York, was closed on Good Friday, March 23rd, but One of Our Girls piled up credit till April 5th, when occurred the hundred and fiftieth performance; and so on, to May 22nd, when the triumphant comedy closed with its two hundredth showing. How splendid and what a lesson for Wallack, struggling on with feeble dependence on old comedies and English melodrama; he evidently had but little faith in American plays. For a time, latterly, Sam Sothern temporarily replaced J. W. Pigott, ill, as Fouché-Fonblanque. May 24th brought Frank Mayo and Miss Kidder, in Nordeck, that rousing success at another theatre; it filled a fortnight at the Lyceum.

Star Theatre, 1885–1886

Leaving my favourite field of the stock companies, I arrive at the Star Theatre, certainly, since the passing of Booth's, the leading home of stars and important "combinations."   On July 4, 1885, ended there the second and last week of the Mexican Typical Orchestra, concerning which posterity has maintained a chilling reticence. On August 17th, Adelaide Moore, an English actress of no great importance, though fairly competent, began in Romeo and Juliet, this season to be a play of note in New York, with the rivalry of Mary Anderson and Margaret Mather. With Miss Moore were Atkins Lawrence as Romeo, Joseph Wheelock as Mercutio, Mason Mitchell as Benvolio, Archie Cowper as Tybalt, Leslie Allen as Friar Laurence, E. L. Tilton as Capulet, Charles Stanley as Peter, Clara Fisher Maeder as the Nurse and Octavia Allen as Lady Capulet — not a bad support, one supposes. Her second and last week Miss Moore began with three nights of The Hunchback (August 24th, 25th and 26th), and, on the 27th, played Rosalind, with Atkins Lawrence, W. J. Constantine, E. L. Tilton, Miss Loduski Young and Effie Germon in the cast. She then left New York, not to return till 1889, though she toured the country with I know not what success. The Herald found her pretty good, but quite unintelligible in diction.

[17]

ROBSON AND CRANE; MARY ANDERSON

On September 7th, Robson and Crane made an elaborate scenic revival of The Comedy of Errors, all new, and directed by Alfred Thompson — one of the most elaborate productions seen here, up to that time, of a Shakespearian comedy:

Dromio of Syracuse	Stuart Robson	Dr. Birch	W. H. Young
Dromio of Ephesus	W. H. Crane	Cupid	Bijou Fernandez
Duke	C. H. Riegel	Adriana	Selena Fetter
Ægeon	C. B. Hanford	Luciana	Kate McKinstry
Antipholus of Ephesus	William Harris	Phryne	Carrie Reynolds
Antipholus of Syracuse	C. Handyside	Æmilia	Annie Douglas
Angelo	H. A. Langdon	Blowsabella	Mrs. F. C. Wells
Balthasar	William Haworth		

This merry farce ran for five weeks, which is more, I fear, than it could do today, unless doctored tastelessly, as I recently saw it, at Stratford, or unless turned into a "comic" opera, as not long since in New York. The Robson-Crane revivals of The Comedy of Errors occupy modest niches in our gallery of fame.

The most exciting event of the season in America was perhaps the return of Mary Anderson, most beautiful of actresses. She had had two brilliant years at Irving's Lyceum Theatre, London, while Irving was in America winning acclaim for his superb scenic productions. She had been taken to the hearts of British playgoers and had won their esteem socially, if not wholly as an artist. Royal academicians designed for her exquisite costumes for her plays, and Irving's scenic artists set for her Romeo and Juliet and lesser pieces with all the beauty to which Lyceum audiences had become accustomed. On October 12th, then, this darling of the gods returned in a production of As You Like It, which she had studied for performance only a short time before at Stratford-upon-Avon. The cables had apprised us of this important event, and curiosity led into the Star, on that auspicious evening of the 12th, a host of eager witnesses. I myself sat enthralled in the first row of the family circle (or gallery). The company supporting Miss Anderson was almost entirely British:

Rosalind	Miss Anderson	Jacques du Bois	L. Gillespie
Orlando	J. Forbes-Robertson	Touchstone	J. G. Taylor
Jacques	F. H. Macklin	Adam	J. Kenneth Black
Banished Duke	Henry Vernon	Corin	H. Sainsbury
Duke Frederick	Sidney Hayes	Sylvius	T. C. Bindloss
Le Beau	Arthur Lewis	William	F. A. Gaytie
Eustace	Dawson	Celia	Zeffie Tilbury
Lewis	Evans	Phebe	Eloise Willis
Charles, the Wrestler	C. Stewart	Audrey	Mrs. John Billington
Oliver	J. A. Mulor		

Some of us wondered if it was merely acquired British snobbery that impelled the actress to import so many aids, none of whom, except Forbes-

LOUIS JAMES AND
HELEN DAUVRAY

EDWARD H. SOTHERN
AND HELEN DAUVRAY

EDWARD H. SOTHERN
AND HELEN DAUVRAY

LOUIS JAMES AND
F. F. MACKAY

HELEN DAUVRAY

F. F. MACKAY AND
HELEN DAUVRAY

ADELAIDE MOORE
AS JULIET

ROBSON AND CRANE
AS THE DROMIOS

J. FORBES-ROBERTSON
AS ROMEO

FALK'S PHOTOGRAPHS (UPPER SIX) FROM ONE OF OUR GIRLS

Robertson (his first appearance in America), Macklin, Taylor, Miss Tilbury (Lydia Thompson's daughter) and Mrs. Billington had more than average ability; of course the star was used to their ways and did not wish to train a new company of Americans.   And there was something top-lofty about her announcing herself only as Miss Anderson — *Mary* having been discarded in the years since she went away.   But what of Rosalind?   The Herald, on the 13th, thinks Miss Anderson's "manner is more refined, her diction is purer (though she still clings tenaciously to the Western 'r'); her voice, without losing any of its remarkable power, has grown more mellow. . . ." She was "at her best in the first act," beautiful in a dress of pink, "though the traitor speech was only a fine theatrical display."   How well I remember that tragic, eloquent outburst, perhaps not quite in Rosalind's character!   "When," says the Herald, Rosalind "came on in doublet and hose, she presented one of the loveliest pictures the stage has ever seen."   But she was "not successful in merging her individuality in the character."   The life and soul of the part were not there; furthermore, Orlando must have been very stupid not to see, at once, that this boy was not Ganymede, but in reality his very Rosalind.   William Winter (Shakespeare on the Stage) entirely disagrees with this estimate and pronounces Miss Anderson's Rosalind, except Ada Rehan's, the best he ever saw.   Yet he had seen Adelaide Neilson's and Helena Modjeska's.

Of course this engagement was limited from the first to six weeks.   As You Like It ceased its enchantment on October 21st; on the 22nd, Comedy and Tragedy, which W. S. Gilbert had written for the actress, was first seen in America, along with his Pygmalion and Galatea, in which Miss Anderson was always superb.   In Comedy and Tragedy, she gave a fine performance of the actress, Clarice, who must entertain her guests while her lover was fighting a duel with the nobleman-villain in the garden.   This sort of double-acting always takes an audience, and I remember well Miss Anderson's superb rendition of the part of Clarice in that tense episode.   And her joy when the lover enters through the door (or was it a window?) at the back! And Forbes-Robertson won all hearts in that little play.   He was also excellent as Pygmalion to the captivating Galatea of the star.   Others in the cast of Pygmalion and Galatea were J. G. Taylor as Chrysos, Joseph Anderson (brother of the star) as Leucippe, Arthur Lewis as Mimos, Rudolph Strong as Agesimos, Zeffie Tilbury as Cynisca, Mrs. Billington as an excellent Daphne, and Miss M. Ayrton as Myrine.   This pleasing double bill lasted through October, except for As You Like It, on the 31st, and re-appeared on November 5th and at the matinée on the 7th.   For November 2nd, 3rd, 4th, and 7th (evening) we were treated to the star's beautifully dressed Pauline, in The Lady of Lyons, with Forbes-Robertson as Claude, Macklin as Damas, Sidney Hayes as Beauseant, Mrs. Billington as the Widow, and Sainsbury and Mrs. Calvert as the Deschappelles.

The theatre was closed, on November 9th and 10th for rehearsals of Romeo and Juliet, elaborately produced on the 11th with the wonderful scenery by Irving's artists and the beautiful costumes designed by royal academicians. A lovelier series of pictures never greeted the eye, and Miss Anderson's successive costumes from the first in pale blue brocade, to the next in pink and pale green to the white clinging robe of death brought out her beauty in unforgettable radiance. The cast included Forbes-Robertson as the best Romeo I ever saw, Macklin as Mercutio, S. Hayes as Capulet, J. G. Taylor as the Apothecary and Peter, Vernon as Friar Laurence, Arthur Lewis as Benvolio, Bindloss as Paris, Joseph Anderson as Tybalt, Mrs. Billington as the Nurse, and Mrs. Charles Calvert (the Rumour of Rignold's Henry V) as Lady Capulet. This was the finest production of Romeo and Juliet that I ever saw, and the memory of it has dwarfed for me every subsequent performance of the tragedy; it made Margaret Mather's much advertised presentation of it, just round the corner at the Union Square Theatre, seem cheap and tawdry and violent to a degree. Mary Anderson's Juliet remained until her season closed, on November 21st. The London photographs of her, as Juliet, show how lovely she was. In 1934 I told her, at her home in Broadway, England, that my favourite photograph of her was that of Juliet, with the dagger; she gave me permission to say, in this part of the Annals, that it was also her favourite. Gladly, then, I reproduce it for the delight of my readers.

On November 23rd, Gustav Amberg presented at this theatre Friedrich Mitterwurzer, from the Imperial Theatre, Vienna, doubtless of some repute in his own country. Apparently to show his versatility, he began with a triple bill, consisting of Herzl's one-act Tabarin (in which he played the title-rôle), Bernstein's little Mein neuer Hut, and the familiar Das Schwert des Damocles. Members of the Thalia Theater dramatic company assisted, as well as Mathilde Madison, seen here in the preceding spring, in Sealed Instructions; she gave chief support in Mein neuer Hut. For November 24th and 25th, Mitterwurzer essayed the title-rôle in Iwan (by B. Aléxejew); Mathilde Madison came forth in the dual rôle of Marya and Elisawata; with Kugelberg as Fürst Waldimir, Possansky as Alexander, Frl. Schmitz as Anna Feodrowna, Walter as Pater Timofei, Rank as Wassiljewitsch, and, in other parts, Frl. Fanto, Frl. Berger, Frl. Becker, Frl. Lorenz, Frl. Schatz, &c. November 26th gave the star as Kean, with Mathilde Madison as Gräfin Helena, Kugelberg as Graf von Coefeld, Hitzigrath as Herzog von Devonshire, Walter as Salomon (confiseur), Frl. Schulz as Pistol, Frl. Grosse (début) as Anna, Rank as Darius (Theater-Friseur), &c.

Die Leibrente (by von Moser) on November 30th and December 1st, 2nd and 3rd, allowed Mitterwurzer to repeat a pretty success, in the character of Zippe, with Walter as Kerner, Frl. Schulz as Jenny, Possansky as Georg Harturg, Kugelberg as Schmoll, Adolfi as Kratzer, Frl. Schmitz as Gertrud,

MARY ANDERSON
AS GALATEA

MARY ANDERSON
AS ROSALIND

MARY ANDERSON
AS JULIET

MARY ANDERSON
AS JULIET

MARY ANDERSON AS JULIET

The upper portraits from photographs by Van der Weyde Light, London;
the portraits as Juliet by W. and D. Downey, London

&c. Twice on Saturday, the 5th, Die Leibrente held sway. And thus ended the fortnight's engagement originally planned at the Star; on December 7th, the new actor began a visit in the Thalia Theater.

MODJESKA; LAWRENCE BARRETT

This incursion of foreign art was followed, on December 9th, by The Black Hussar, which then began a four-weeks term, with the customary cast, Mathilde Cottrelly, Lilly Post, Marie Jansen, Mark Smith, Hopper, Edwin Hoff, George Boniface, Jr., A. W. Maflin, and L. M. Hall. The Herald of December 23rd informs us that Louise Lablache was replacing Lilly Post. The exquisite Helena Modjeska restored drama to the Star. On January 4th, and at the matinée on the 9th, she acted Camille, with E. H. Vanderfelt (début) as Armand, Leslie Allen as Père Duval, Kate Denin Wilson as Prudence, &c.; on January 5th and 8th she for the first times in this city acted Mary Stuart; As You Like It, on January 6th, 7th and 9th (evening) allowed one to compare her lovely Rosalind with that of Mary Anderson. In Mary Stuart, Mary Shaw was Elizabeth, Vanderfelt Dudley, Frank Clements Cecil, James Cooper Talbot, Robbins Howe Kent, Leslie Allen Sir Amyas Paulet, L. J. Henderson Mortimer, Erroll Dunbar Sir Andrew Melville, Kate Denin Wilson Hannah Kennedy, &c. According to the Herald the scene between the queens aroused tremendous enthusiasm. Modjeska's rendering of that scene indeed leaves me cold to more recent Mary Stuarts. Of course, in As You Like It, Clements was Jaques and Vanderfelt Orlando.

Modjeska began her second week with Adrienne Lecouvreur (January 11th); on the 12th and 13th she repeated Mary Stuart. A new offering for January 14th was Westland Marston's adaptation of Moreto's comedy, Donna Diana, a play long familiar to the German stage in New York. The cast:

Donna Diana	Modjeska	Don Diego	Erroll Dunbar
Don Cæsar	E. H. Vanderfelt	Donna Fenisa	Evelyn Shaw
Perin	Frank Clements	Donna Laura	Daisy Dorr
Don Gaston	James Cooper	Floretta	Kitty Wilson
Don Luis	L. J. Henderson		

As Donna Diana, Modjeska was charming as the proud noble woman who scorned love and her disconsolate suitors till Don Cæsar conquered her by her own tactics; pretending to despise her as she had despised others. She kept the light comedy going to January 22nd; on the afternoon of the 23rd she again acted Rosalind, and, on the evening of that day, she gave, for once only, her exquisite, poetic Viola, in Twelfth Night, with Mary Shaw as Olivia, Vanderfelt as Malvolio, Allen as Sir Toby, Clements as Sir Andrew, &c. Her last week began with As You Like It (January 25th) and Mary Stuart (26th). On the 27th she acted Odette, with Vanderfelt as Count

Clement, Clara Lipman (!) as Berangère, Clements as Bechamel, Kate Denin Wilson as the Baroness, Owen Fawcett as Narcisse, Mary Shaw as Juliette, and L. J. Henderson as La Hoche. This play finished her season, on January 30th. On February 18th she came back, in As You Like It, for a benefit of the Polish exiles. Louis James, Joseph Haworth, Harry Edwards and Effie Germon were to assist.

Edwin Booth began an engagement, on February 1st, at the Fifth Avenue Theatre; hence, as things had latterly gone, one might expect Lawrence Barrett on the same night at a rival theatre. Good policy or not? who knows? At any rate he began, on the 1st, at the Star Theatre, in an Anglicised version of Hugo's Hernani; his assistants were F. C. Mosley as Don Carlos, C. M. Collins as Duke of Sylvia, and Minna K. Gale as Donna Zanthe. The spectacle ran through February 16th; on the 17th, came Francesca da Rimini. Monday, February 22nd, restored to us Barrett's ever-admired Cassius, with W. E. Sheridan (specially engaged) as Brutus, Mosley as Antony, Ian Robertson as Cæsar, Isabelle Urquhart (believe an ye list!) as Portia, and doubtless patrician in appearance, and Miss Gale as Calpurnia. February 26th united David Garrick and Yorick's Love. The engagement closed, on the 27th, with Hernani (afternoon) and Juluis Cæsar (evening). One always wished, with Barrett, that he had possessed just that one bit of magnetism that would have carried him into the ranks of the greatest.

JUDIC; BOUCICAULT

I always dread the coming of opéra-bouffe, the constant changes of bill wearying me and my pen. Let me try to run off with least possible delay, if with but little coherence, the dates of Mme. Judic's performances now crying for attention: La Femme à Papa (March 2nd); La Grande Duchesse (3rd, and matinée, 6th); La Cosaque (4th); La Mascotte (5th); and 6th, Divorçons, with Verney's little opera, Josephine. From Tostée to Judic, what years, what irrevocable years, my masters!

March 8th introduced a week of The Guv'nor, by unoccupied Wallack actors and others — John Gilbert, Elton, George Clarke, Fred Corbett, C. E. Edwin (as the MacToddy), Theresa Butler, Josephine Bailey and Kate Bartlett. And now, on the 15th, Dion Boucicault drew the last success he was ever to win on our stage. The Jilt, a racing drama, had been running in Boston, and it came to the Star Theatre, with this cast:

Myles O'Hara	Dion Boucicault	Mr. Spooner	Donald Robertson
Sir Budleigh Woodstock	Henry Miller	Kitty Woodstock	Louise Thorndyke
Lord Marcus Wylie	F. M. Burbeck	Lady Millicent	Helen Bancroft
Colonel Tudor	John P. Sutton	Mrs. Welter	Mary E. Barker
Geoffrey Tudor	W. F. Williams	Phyllis	Bijou Heron
James Daisy	Frank Wright	Mrs. Pincott	Mrs. M. A. Pennoyer

Boucicault had provided an excellent comedy part for himself and a light breezy rôle for his young, new wife, Louise Thorndyke; and he had mixed tried melodramatic and comedy elements in a really exciting drama of men and jockeys and horses and villains and wives with a past. The cowboy pianist, aptly named O. O. Babel, who had never had a lesson in the art, played at the Star, on Sunday, the 14th.

The Jilt temporarily left the Star, on April 3rd, making way for the positively farewell visit of Mme. Judic. This lady was a very fine artist, but I once more dread the rapid changes of bill involved in the visit of any opéra-bouffe company. Let me huddle the details, with an eye to the goal: La Belle Hélène (April 5th, and matinée, 10th); La Roussotte, by Meilhac, Halévy and Millaud (first time in America (6th); La Périchole (7th, and matinée, 17th); Niniche (8th), La Mascotte (9th); La Cosaque (by request, evening of the 10th); La Vie Parisienne (12th); La Femme à Papa (13th); Divorçons (14th); benefit to A. Durand, for years connected with Maurice Grau, La Grande Duchesse and a monologue by Judic, Clary vs. Clary (15th); benefit of Judic (16th), with La Femme à Papa (second act), Josephine and Lili (second act); and La Jolie Parfumeuse (evening of the 17th). The poor financial returns for the season of this excellent artist were deplored by all who were capable of recognising fine talent. Judic was followed at the Star by a return week (April 19th–24th) of Boucicault and The Jilt, and that, in sequence by two weeks (April 26th–May 8th) of Fanny Davenport in her everlasting Fedora, with, as usual, in leading support, Robert B. Mantell, Eugene O. Jepson, Melbourne McDowell and Marie Sheldon. Edgar L. Davenport, the star's brother, was Désiré.

Palmer having given a perfect Engaged, an inferior group took possession of the Star, on May 10th, there to present the same satire, with Agnes Herndon as Belinda, Cedric Hope as Cheviot Hill, Alice Butler as Minnie, John Matthews as Symperson, Punch Robertson as Angus, Henry Dalton as Belvawney, Addie Cummings as Maggie, and Ethel Douglas as Mrs. McFarlane. Imagine this, after Agnes Booth and her superb associates at the Madison Square! The next week atoned, with a return of Mary Anderson in Pygmalion and Galatea and Comedy and Tragedy (17th), Ingomar (18th and 20th), The Lady of Lyons (19th, and matinée, 22nd), and As You Like It (21st), Pygmalion and Galatea and Comedy and Tragedy (evening, 22nd). To me, Mary Anderson of 1885–86 is an imperishable memory of utter delight.

The best of the season at the Star had passed. Harry Edwards, sterling artist, had a benefit there, on Monday, May 31st; with Mrs. John Drew, John T. Raymond, Marie Wainwright, Louis James, Kyrle Bellew, Osmond Tearle, Georgia Cayvan, Mrs. Bowers, Mme. Ponisi, Annie Robe and Couldock and Mansfield (fourth act of Prince Karl) in the amazing list of volunteers. On June 3rd a benefit for the widow of poor Bartley Campbell enlisted the company of The Little Tycoon, Myra Goodwin, Lillian Conway, Mrs. Bowers (in an act of Queen Elizabeth), W. J. Scanlan, Frank McNish, Helen Hooker in an act of Ingomar, W. Henry Rice, Mayo and Miss Kidder, in an act of Nordeck, and the second act of The White Slave (with Georgia Cayvan and Gustavus Levick). Two wonderful bargains these! A summer season began, on June 24th, with a new Millöcker operetta, The Maid of Belleville, the company including Alice Harrison, Roberta Crawford (substituted for Aimée, originally announced), Laurette Millard, Hattie Grinnell, Emma Duchateau, Herbert Archer, Frank David, Samuel Reed, Charles Coote, Ben F. Grinnell, &c. A failure, this piece was withdrawn on July 7th. The Star then went into darkness till the new season of 1886–87.

Union Square Theatre, 1885–1886

The Union Square, shorn of the glory of its formerly acclaimed stock company, began, on July 20, 1885, a season at times interesting, and often perplexed and precarious. On July 20th, Sydney Rosenfeld attempted to anticipate, as Miner's People's had done, ten days earlier, the D'Oyly Carte production of the great London success, The Mikado; in lack of international copyright, this was, then, the second signal of the seizure of the rights of Gilbert and Sullivan that had made 1878–79 the raging Pinafore season that it was. The first cast here of The Mikado included J. W. Herbert in the title-rôle, A. Montegriffo as Nanki-Poo, Roland Reed as Ko-Ko, Herbert Archer as Pooh-Bah, George H. Broderick as Pish-Tush, Alice Harrison as Yum-Yum, the pretty Belle Archer as Pitti-Sing, Lizzie Quigley as Peep-Bo, and Emma Mabella Baker as Katisha. The Herald next day described the offering as "wholly discreditable"; Roland Reed was the sole member of the cast who met requirements. Only one performance was given, since an injunction had been obtained. The same cast, practically, was brought back by Harry Miner, on August 17th, two nights before the Carte company gave the real Mikado at the Fifth Avenue Theatre. It lasted but two weeks — so much for non-ethical procedure. On August 26th, Frankie Kemble succeeded Alice Harrison as Yum-Yum.

The week of August 31st–September 5th presented A Brave Woman, with the J. M. Hardie-Sara von Leer company. On September 7th, James M. Hill assumed the management of the theatre, proffering A Moral Crime, by Elwyn A. Barnes and Morgan Bates:

Count d'Albert	Joseph Haworth	Mme. Fontaine	Flora May Henry
M. de Clare	Henry E. Walton	Totote	Charlotte de Musset
Father Dablon	H. A. Weaver	Mme. Girard	Carrie Jamison
M. Marius	J. W. Pigott	Marie	Genie Langdon
Jules Granot	E. H. Sothern	Mathilde	Marie Prescott
Sandois	Edwin Cleary		

MRS. BILLINGTON

HELENA MODJESKA
AS MARY STUART

ZEFFIE TILBURY

LOUISE THORNDYKE
AND DION BOUCICAULT

MARY ANDERSON
(LADY OF LYONS)

E. H. VANDERFELT

F. H. MACKLIN

JOSEPH ANDERSON

J. G. TAYLOR

Possibly to the surprise of all, this play achieved a mild success, running at the Union Square till October 10th, and transferring its thrills, on October 12th, for a fortnight, to J. M. Hill's other theatre, the Third Avenue.

MARGARET MATHER

And now the stage was set, and lavishly set, for the production which, perhaps, had been the cause of Hill's renting of the Union Square. He had become convinced that, in Margaret Mather, he had discovered a great actress, or at least a great actress in the making. Miss Mather was a striking person, with natural force and a powerful voice which spoke in accents unrefined and provincial. But she had great energy, ambition and courage. A person of no original culture, she came forth, on Tuesday, October 13th, in an elaborate staging of Romeo and Juliet:

Juliet	Margaret Mather	Benvolio	William Wilson
Romeo	Frederick Paulding	Escalus	F. A. Tannehill
Mercutio	Milnes Levick	Peter	F. W. Peters
Friar Laurence	H. A. Weaver	Apothecary	William V. Ranous
Tybalt	Edwin Cleary	Nurse	Carrie Jamison
Capulet	Harry Eytinge	Lady Capulet	Jeannie Harold

The scenery was by Voegtlin and Hughson Hawley; the dances by Novissimo; the vocal music was directed by W. D. Marks. The entire production was directed by Alfred Thompson, who had rendered similar aid to the Robson-Crane Comedy of Errors. No performance ever given in our city had been more insistently "publicised" than this; it became a sort of duty to see it. Miss Mather's Juliet, compared with Mary Anderson's, was simply commonplace, lacking in refinement and the breeding expected of a daughter of the Capulets; but its force was undeniable. The town talked of her wonderful rolling down a flight of steps, after the taking of the potion. If that was legitimate acting, so must have been Francis Wilson's fall, later in the same season, down the trick steps in Erminie. The fiftieth performance of Romeo and Juliet came on December 1st and the seventy-fifth on Christmas night. The run ended on January 2nd, certainly a great showing for a Shakespearian revival.

On Sunday, December 20th, Kate Field lectured on The Vice and Treason of Mormonism; on the 27th, she gave An Evening with Dickens. The house was closed on January 4th, re-opening on Tuesday, the 5th, with Leah, the Forsaken, in which Miss Mather as the hapless Jewish maiden forcibly delivered the famous curse, with Paulding as Rudolph, Levick as Nathan, Weaver as Lorentz, Cleary as Father Herman, Eytinge as Ludwig, Jeannie Harold as Madeline, Carrie Jamison as Mother Groschen, and Baby Wood as the child. The old play had unexpected appeal, running through January 30th. Meantime, Professor Latham, on January 10th (Sunday) delivered an illustrated Tour of the World, making Sabbath eves sacred

[25]

thereafter with Switzerland and the Rhine, with ascent of Mt. Blanc (17th); Ireland (24th), etc. On January 18th, illness forced Paulding from the cast of Leah, Cyril Searle replacing him, until January 22nd, when Edwin Cleary undertook the part.

On February 1st, Miss Mather began as Juliana, in The Honeymoon, with Levick as Aranza, Paulding as Rolando, Maud Peters as Volante and Jeannie Harold as Zamora. The strenuous excitement of this old comedy filled the final week (February 1st–6th) of Miss Mather's engagement, the length of which must have gratified her exceedingly. On February 8th, Carrie Swain, erstwhile of vaudeville, brought out a play by George R. Sims and Clement Scott, Jack-in-the-Box, with assistance of Ralph Delmore, Hugh Fay, Blanche Thorne (a promising actress often seen, that year), Walter Bentley, Julia Brutone, C. W. Bentley and McCullough Ross. February 28th found Kate Field again in possession, presenting a musical monologue, with W. Russell Case at the piano.

On March 8th, The Banker's Daughter, a glorious memory of this stage, returned with a cast far from glorious — Edna Courtney, Marion Earle, Harry Lisan (Strebelow), S. W. Glenn (Westbrook), C. W. Kidder (the Count), R. L. Tayleure (Harold), &c. According to the Herald, the men were "stilted to a distressing degree." When the four men stood in a row, "the audience felt like groaning," and "burst out laughing when Tayleure appeared." Recovering from the doldrums of the last month, the Union Square brought out, on March 16th, a comic opera by Alfred Thompson and Edward Solomon, afflicted with the title of Pepita, or, the Girl with the Glass Eyes:

Pepita	Lillian Russell	Curaso	Fred Solomon
Carmansuita	Alma Stuart Stanley	Gravolo	Fred Clifton
Juanna	Julia Wilson	Juan	George Middleton
Professor Pongo	Jacques Kruger	Maraquita	Carrie Jackson
Pablo	Chauncey Olcott	Pasquala	Lizzie Hughes

This cast is extremely interesting. Lillian Russell was then at the very height of her radiant beauty; Alma Stanley, also very handsome in a statuesque way, and Julia Wilson, so long the Little Tot of Joshua Whitcomb, added distinction to the show; Chauncey Olcott hitherto a minstrel performer, now made his stage début, and Jacques Kruger and Fred Clifton (the original Policeman, in The Pirates of Penzance) could certainly be depended on for any amount of fun. And the public responded commendably till the opera closed, on May 22nd. Latterly, Carrie Tutein had essayed the soubrette rôle, to be succeeded, on May 17th, by Mary Gay. On May 24th, McNish, Johnson and Slavin's Minstrels came in with a burlesque Little Fly Coon. Negro minstrelsy, in that season, was reviving, but two weeks now sufficed for this venture.

F. FEDERICI
(THE MIKADO)

ELSIE CAMERON
(KATISHA)

F. BILLINGTON
(POOH-BAH)

GEORGE THORNE
(KO-KO)

KATE FORSTER
GERALDINE ULMAR
MISS ST. MAUR

COURTICE POUNDS AND
GERALDINE ULMAR

FREDERICK PAULDING
AS ROMEO

MARGARET MATHER
AS JULIET

LILLIAN RUSSELL
IN PEPITA

FALK'S PHOTOGRAPHS (SIX UPPER) FROM THE MIKADO

FIFTH AVENUE THEATRE, 1885–1886

August 19th starts us off with the glorious production by the D'Oyly Carte company of the immortal Mikado, then visually, vocally and dramatically given the best performance to be heard in that harried Mikado season.   As when The Pirates of Penzance was first produced in 1879–80 at this same theatre the English manager engaged for the leading female rôle an American singer; the others, as in 1879-80, were from the British stage. And good they were, to a man and a woman:

Mikado	F. Federici	Yum-Yum	Geraldine Ulmar
Nanki-Poo	Courtice Pounds	Pitti-Sing	Kate Forster
Ko-Ko	George Thorne	Peep-Bo	Geraldine St. Maur
Pooh-Bah	F. Billington	Katisha	Elsie Cameron
Pish-Tush	G. Byron Browne		

This aggregation, with the beautiful setting and costumes, the authoritative Gilbert and Sullivan touch, outdistanced all competition, and practically carried through the season of 1885–86.   Courtice Pounds, "the vest pocket tenor," as he came to be called, at once became a matinée idol, and Thorne's antics convulsed his fastidious audiences.   On October 6th, Pounds, ill, yielded Nanki-Poo to Jeffrey, but soon returned to gladden the eyes and ears and hearts of his adorers.   Billington, ill, also left for a time, but returned on December 21st; his place had been supplied by a Mr. Edgar. The hundred and fiftieth performance of The Mikado fell on January 11th. On January 30th, the company, forced by previous contracts with Booth, left its familiar haven at the Fifth Avenue, and migrated for a month to the Standard Theatre, which in the autumn had offered a rival and inferior Mikado. On September 24th, Arthur Sullivan conducted a gala performance.

EDWIN BOOTH

Booth returned to New York, on February 1st, offering for a week his still admired, not to say venerated Hamlet.   He was supported, under the management of James M. Field, by members of the Boston-revered Boston Museum company, and a sorry, inadequate lot the Herald, for Booth's month of playing, declared them to be.   And who can wonder, with Charles Barron as a sepulchral Ghost, Annie Clarke, long past her youth, as the Queen, Charles Kent as Claudius, and Blanche Thompson as Ophelia?   J. B. ("Jack") Mason should have been a good Laertes, and W. F. Owen excellent as the First Gravedigger.   Alfred Hudson was Polonius.   According to the Herald, the receipts for the Saturday matinée were $1730, the largest in the history of the house.   To lighten his task, Booth, on the evening of the 6th, acted Iago.   On the 8th, 9th and 10th, Booth was King Lear; for the rest of the week he revived Brutus, with Kent as Sextus, Mason as Titus, A. Russ

Whytal as Aruns, Hudson as Valerius, C. S. Abbe as Claudius, James Burrows as Lucretius, Albert Lang as Collatinus, Louis Atkins as Horatius, Annie Clarke as Tullia, Blanche Thompson as Tarquinia, and May Davenport as Lucretia. This support was declared, by the Herald, to be "ludicrously unequal" to their tasks. Scattering features for the third week were Macbeth (imagine Annie Clarke as Lady Macbeth! on the 15th); Sir Giles Overreach (16th and 17th); Richelieu (18th, 19th and 20th). The final week brought The Fool's Revenge (February 22nd and 23rd); Richard III (24th and 25th, for the first time in several years with Booth, in the Colley Cibber version), and Julius Cæsar (26th and 27th). The Herald of February 27th asserts that "inefficient as Mr. Booth's support has been during his present engagement, the performance last evening may, without exaggeration, be set down as the very worst that has been seen here in many a year." Even Booth, splendid as he was as Brutus, was at times uncertain in his lines. J. B. Mason as Antony was the only good member of the supporting cast. I read this attack with sadness, but am consoled to remember that next season Lawrence Barrett was to take charge of Booth's tour.

The Mikado came back, on March 1st, for its two hundredth showing, and remained till April 17th, its two hundred and fiftieth performance. Its successor at the Fifth Avenue (April 19th) was The Little Tycoon, which had been successful at the Standard Theatre, and was now transferred to the apparently allied stage of the Fifth Avenue. The cast, as at the earlier production, included R. E. Graham, Will S. Rising, R. N. Dunbar, E. H. Van Veghten, Elma Delaro, Netta Guion and J. W. Daniels; but Annie Leaf was now Violet. This piece lasted till the Fifth Avenue closed for the season on June 26th. The Mikado had made that season simply glorious — The Mikado, the only new work of 1885 that has come down, fresh and lively, to our times and the only one that would stand the slightest chance of revival in 1941.

The Standard Theatre, 1885–1886

James Duff had intended to stage his first performance of The Mikado on August 19, 1885, the night of the opening of the rival Mikado at the Fifth Avenue. He was compelled to postpone this defiant gesture to Monday, August 24th, when a promising cast appeared:

Mikado	W. H. Hamilton	Yum-Yum	Vernona Jarbeau
Ko-Ko	J. H. Ryley	Pitti-Sing	Sallie Williams
Nanki-Poo	Harry Hilliard	Peep-Bo	Carrie Tutein
Pooh-Bah	Thomas Whiffen	Katisha	Zelda Seguin
Pish-Tush	A. E. Stoddard		

One would have expected satisfactory results from that aggregation; in fact, the performance, on the opening night, was tentative and wholly lacking in authority. Besides, the scenery and the costumes quite fell behind the beauty of the setting at the Fifth Avenue. Things improved as the season advanced, but Duff had failed in his purpose of equalling the success of his Pinafore and Patience. The engagement carried on till November 21st, when the company left for Chicago.

Nat C. Goodwin followed, on November 23rd, in The Skating Rink, by Robert Griffin Morris, one of those emphemeral, topical hodge-podges so popular since the days of The Tourists, etc. The cast:

Ronald Delaine	N. C. Goodwin	Clarence O'Dear	F. E. Morse
Erasmus	J. B. Radcliffe	Amelia Tubbs	Daisy Murdoch
Timothy	Henry V. Donnelly	Sallie Tubbs	Marietta Uart
Mickey	Edward F. Goodwin	Franchita	Lillian Fletcher
Philander	Major Newell	Matilda Squibbs	Helen Lowell
Ignus Fatuus	C. Fletcher	Phœbe	Hattie Schell
Hither and Thither	William Fletcher		

This was a stopgap for two weeks, till Lotta entered, on December 7th, in Little Nell and the Marchioness, with Carlyle as Dick Swiveller, P. A. Anderson as Quilp, Mahoney as Grandfather Trent, and Berte Cook as Kit. On December 14th, Lotta appeared in a version of Mlle. Nitouche, without, I am sure, suggesting anything of the delicate art of Mme. Judic. December 21st brought to us one of the delights of the winter, Rosina Vokes (returned after many years) and her English company of real ladies and gentlemen in three delightful little plays. In Honour Bound gave chief honours to Courtenay Thorpe, with Leslie Chester and Agnes Miller (Miss Vokes did not appear in this); My Milliner's Bill, was a delight, with Brandon Thomas and Miss Vokes (oh! the joy of her singing and acting in 'Is 'Art Was True to Poll); and finally came that exquisite bit of fooling, A Christmas Pantomime Rehearsal, acted by a company of brainless titled amateurs. No one who saw them can ever forget the vapid Lord Arthur Somersault of Weedon Grossmith, the Captain Tom Robinson of Brandon Thomas, the Lily of Miss Vokes, and the stately vapidity of Miss Carlingford as Lady Rosa Tralee, in velvet and an aristocratic manner. W. G. Elliot was admirable as Jack Deedes, author of the pantomime. W. R. Stavely was Sir Charles Grandison, and two exceedingly pretty girls, Leslie Chester and Agnes Miller, were Violet and May, respectively. No other plays were required during this highly successful engagement, which ended on January 16th. As we know, Miss Vokes carried those three delightful pieces, in the spring, to the aristocratic purlieus of Daly's Theatre.

On January 18th a refugee from vaudeville, Kate Castleton, entered the Standard with Crazy Patch, playing Sybilla Tubbs, assisted by L. R. Stockwell (as Jupiter Tubbs), Eddie Girard (as McGlue), J. N. Long, Willie Royston, John D. Gilbert, Esther Williams, Courtney Haviland, Elsie Graham and Ada Gilman. Much better fun came on February 1st, when John Stetson, who had hired the Standard, brought here from his Fifth Avenue Theatre, The Mikado, with his Japanese court intact, except that

Sebastian King was now Pish-Tush. After a month he transferred that delectable court to its former home at the Fifth Avenue.

Thereafter the Standard weathered clouds of uncertainty. Theresa Vaughn (a lovely woman, with a very sweet voice) and her husband, W. A. Mestayer, had the week of March 8th–13th, in their hodge-podge, We, Us and Company. On the 15th, we stiffened our sinews with the melodrama, Blackmail, with W. C. Cowper, Lawrence Hanley, James Wilson, Eleanor Moretti and Addie Plunkett in leading rôles. Two weeks of this suspense led, on March 29th, to a new and rather pleasing comic opera, The Little Tycoon (words and music by Willard Spencer):

General Knickerbocker	R. E. Graham	Teddy	Joseph Mealey
Alvin Barry	Will S. Rising	Violet	Carrie M. Dietrich
Rufus Ready	R. N. Dunbar	Dolly Dimple	Netta Guion
Lord Delphin	E. H. Van Veghten	Mme. Hurricane	Elma Delaro

The Herald states that many of the cast "acted with spirit, but sang with hollow untuneful voices or as remote from the pitch as they could well get." This concoction made a tempered hit, and, on April 12th, Marie Bockel succeeded to the part of Violet. On April 19th, Stetson exercised his manager-privilege and transferred The Little Tycoon to the Fifth Avenue Theatre. Barry and Fay, on that date, began at the Standard two weeks of Irish Aristocracy. I confess, to my shame as mere annalist, these last weeks at the Standard have not thrilled me with historical enthusiasm. Charles H. Hoyt's A Tin Soldier began on May 3rd, carrying to the end of the season on July 3rd. James T. Powers, Amy Ames and George C. Boniface, Jr., were in the cast; also Paul Arthur, Marion Elmore, Isabelle Coe and Fannie Batchelder.

FOURTEENTH STREET THEATRE, 1885–1886

Bartley Campbell's vaulting ambition o'er-leapt itself and fell into disaster and madness. He had leased the Fourteenth Street Theatre, apparently for the production of his own plays, but a preliminary season, on August 3rd, presented Myra Goodwin in Sis, a trivial concoction by E. E. Kidder. This dealt with a bad stepfather, a frightfully abused mother and a clever "Sis" to defeat one and save the other. A good cast introduced, in addition to Miss Goodwin, in what I hesitate to call the title-rôle, George Richards as Hickory Hawkins, Byron Douglas as Warren Wade, W. A. Paul as Granville Barker, Harry Dalton as Joe Barrett, Dickie Martinez as Mabel, Emma Maddern as Delia Dooley, Elizabeth Andrews as "Marm" Pepper, and Mrs. E. M. Post as poor abused Agnes Barrett. August 17th invited with Mixed Pickles, presenting J. B. Polk as star, supported by Julia A. Polk, Nellie De Vere Mortimer and Alexander Vincent. These Pickles were sour for two weeks.

W. H. HAMILTON
(THE MIKADO)

J. H. RYLEY (KO-KO)
ZELDA SEGUIN (KATISHA)

THOMAS WHIFFEN
(POOH-BAH)

HARRY S. HILLIARD
(NANKI-POO)

ROSINA VOKES
(MY MILLINER'S BILL)

S. WILLIAMS—C. TUTEIN
VERNONA JARBEAU

BRANDON THOMAS

LESLIE CHESTER

WEEDON GROSSMITH

On August 31st, Bartley Campbell, his brain teeming with plans and perhaps incipient madness, opened Bartley Campbell's Fourteenth Street Theatre (thus advertised) with Bartley Campbell's Stock Company in Bartley Campbell's new Mexican play, Paquita:

Hortense	Kate Forsyth	Dr. Delponte	C. P. Flockton
Paquita	Mary Mills	Victor	Ivan Shirley
Señora Maria	Ida Vernon	Philippe	Jerome Stevens
Zinari	Evelyn Granville	Stephano	Russell Bassett
Lucette	Eloise Willis	Padre	D. Van Deren
Dr. Manuel	F. de Belleville	Little Hortense	Bijou Fernandez
José Borosco	H. M. Pitt		

Unless my historical imagination deceives me, that is a good cast and should have carried even a fair play to success. Alas! Campbell fell on evil days. He had elaborately staged his Clio at Niblo's and that financial failure, along with the moderate returns on Paquita, involved him hopelessly in debt. The Herald for Sunday, September 13th, gives an account of his financial difficulties at both theatres, and the public could not have been surprised when, on October 3rd, his management of the Fourteenth Street Theatre closed.

Very different was the fortune of E. E. Rice, who, on October 7th, began a long run of his Evangeline, revised, and elaborately staged, with Fay Templeton as Gabriel, Irene Verona as Evangeline, Mollie Fuller as Eulalie, George K. Fortescue as Catherine, James S. Maffit as the Lone Fisherman, John A. Mackay as Le Blanc, Fred H. Frear as Dietrich and Annie Summerville as Hubert. For the fiftieth performance (November 19th) Rice conducted the orchestra, and, at the hundredth (December 31st), Dixey bounded on the stage, in his Adonis costume, and joined the dance at the end of the first act. Evangeline had never had so glorious a career as in this season. Toward the middle part of January, Fay Templeton left the cast, and was replaced by Mollie Fuller. On February 22nd, Irene Verona assumed the part of Gabriel, resigning her rôle of Evangeline to Forepaugh's $10,000 beauty, Louise Montague. And, by March 4th, George Schiller had replaced Mackay as Le Blanc. The two hundred and fiftieth performance of the jolly *farrago* occurred on April 30th. The last performance, on May 1st, was a benefit to the victorious Rice; Fay Templeton, Irene Verona and Mollie Fuller, in turn, enacted Gabriel; Louise Montague, Annie Summerville and Irene Verona followed each other as Evangeline.

A benefit for the widow of John Rickaby, lately deceased, brought in, one afternoon in early March, Robert Hilliard and Selina Dolaro, in the second act of Engaged; Marshall P. Wilder, Emma Carson (ballads), Dixey, John A. Mackay, Lillie Grubb, Burbank and J. S. Maffit (in The Comanches); and the second act of Evangeline, with Irene Verona, Louise Montague, &c.

It is a pleasure to think of that run of Evangeline and other heartening runs of 1885–86. Not so successful was Effie Ellsler, who, on May 3rd,

[31]

brought out Frank Harvey's drama, Woman against Woman, which she had tried elsewhere in the city, Now, as Bessie, she had the support of Frank Weston as John Tressider, Charles Foster as Philip Tressider, Arthur Howard as Sir Henry, Harry Davenport (young son of E. L. Davenport) as Gilbert Craven, W. C. Armstrong as Crank, Mattie Earle as Rachel Westwood, Mrs. E. L. Davenport as Deborah, Marjorie Bonner as Miriam and Florence Fields as Mary. According to Allston Brown, Miss Ellsler decided not to play a second week, and the theatre closed till May 17th, when Lydia Thompson, still shapely, though no longer exactly young, came back, after several years, appearing in her former success, Oxygen. The cast included Louis de Lange, Alexander Clark, Fred Darrell, Richard F. Carroll, Addie Cora Reed, Lillie Alliston, Ruth Stetson, Leila (*sic*) Farrell, Virgie Graves, Marion Langdon and Daisy Ramsden. The season closed on Monday, May 31st, Miss Thompson sailing next day for London. It will be remembered that her daughter, Zeffie Tilbury, had this year supported Mary Anderson; it will be seen, therefore that Miss Thompson was somewhat more mature than she had been in 1868, when she and her British blondes set young America, male, in excited raptures.

The Casino, 1885–1886

I will end this chapter of the leading theatres of New York with gales of laughter and merry airs from the comedians and singers of the Casino. That Moorish hall, in the summer and autumn of 1885, carried through its brilliant success of Nanon, beautifully staged and directed by Heinrich Conried and with the chic charm of Sadie Martinot (let the reader study Sarony's lovely photographs of her as Nanon) and the contrasting brunette beauty of Pauline Hall as Ninon de l'Enclos. W. T. Carleton, Francis Wilson, W. H. Fitzgerald, Harry Standish, Billie Barlow, Agnes Folsom and Rose Beaudet were other leaders in a cast that delighted the public heart. The scenery by Mazzanovich, Henry Hoyt and Harley Merry seemed very right to 1885. And of course the Casino roof garden, then a novel device, was a pleasing retreat, between acts or after the show; sweet music, flowery retreats and cooling drinks whiled away the summer hours. Rudolph Aronson there, on Sunday nights, led an orchestra in light, good music.

At the matinée, on Saturday, August 22nd, Miss Martinot fainted in Act I of Nanon, her understudy, Agnes Folsom, finishing the opera. The roof garden closed with a concert, on September 20th, but the charming Nanon continued in the theatre. On October 5th, Perugini succeeded Carleton as the Marquis d'Aubigne. And now Sunday evening concerts, still led by Aronson, called to the Casino auditorium. Good soloists participated: Teresa Carreño and Jules Levy (September 27th); Mae St. John, Adolph Glose and Levy (October 4th); Belle Cole, Mae St. John, Levy and Henrietta

Markstein (October 11th); Michael Banner (violin), Belle Cole and Lelo de Bernis (harp — October 18th). Mme. Judic was announced for November 1st, but failed to appear; Mae St. John took her place, with F. Gaillard, Levy and Celie Ellis helping to mitigate the disappointment of the audience. Judic came forth on the 8th, with Miss St. John, Banner, and Gaillard. The inducements of November 15th were Louise Lablache, Mlle. Litvinoff, Giannini and Del Puente, all of the Mapleson forces then struggling at the Academy against an indifferent public.

Nanon finally departed on November 14th. Its successor on the Casino stage was (November 16th) Czibulka's opera, Amorita, with this cast:

Fra Bombarda	Frank Celli	Amorita	Madeline Lucette
Castrucci	Francis Wilson	Perpetua	Georgie Dickson
Sparacani	W. H. Fitzgerald	Cechina	Agnes Folsom
Lorenzi	Harry Standish	Peppina	Billie Barlow
Count Asinelli	Alfred Klein	Fortebraccio	Rose Beaudet
Angelo	Pauline Hall	Anda	Evelyn Granville

I admit having left out a few names of fillers-in, chiefly pretty girls. But I must not omit Victoria Schilling, who had a very minor rôle, as an artist. Amorita, despite its pretty name, was not a great success. And the Sunday concerts grew less interesting; that of December 6th presented Belle Cole, Michael Banner, and Emma and Emilia Schneelock (vocalists). Madeline Lucette was still advertised for Amorita, on December 5th, but now Victoria Schilling, a very amateur, succeeded to the part; Miss Schilling's chief claim to distinction consisted in her having run away with the coachman (Ernest Schilling) of her father, the banker, Morosini. The papers were full of the story, irate, unforgiving father and all; the episode naturally carried Victoria to the stage, which I cannot say she ever elevated to heights beyond the reach, say, of Helena Modjeska or Mary Anderson. In mid-January both Miss Schilling and Pauline Hall were out of the cast of Amorita, but were expected to return on January 18th. A benefit for the Actors' Fund, on December 10th (matinée), promised Courtice Pounds, Pauline Hall, Aimée, F. Federici, Marshall P. Wilder, Michael Banner, Howard Paul, Victoria Schilling, Belle Cole, Levy, Francis Wilson and Aronson's orchestra.

On February 15th, under direction of the efficient Heinrich Conried, the Casino presented Johann Strauss's charming operetta, The Gypsy Baron. William Castle, formerly of "grand" opera, sang Sandor, with Francis Wilson as Kalman Zsupan (I hope Wilson behaved in pronouncing this name), Alfred Klein as Jozsy, W. H. Fitzgerald as Count Carnero, Furey as Ferko, J. Tibbetts as Michaly, Pauline Hall as Saffi, Letitia Fritch (*sic*) as Arsena, Mae St. John as Czipra, Georgie Dickson as Mirabella, Billie Barlow as Ottokar, Victoria Schilling as Bunko, Agnes Folsom as Sidi, Emma Hanley as Katinka, Rose Beaudet as Ilka, &c. Jesse Williams conducted. Pauline Hall was out of the cast in latest February. At the concert, on March 7th, we were promised the elusive Mme. Judic; Alice Raymonde and Minart (Grau's new baritone) were to assist. Judic was again listed on the 18th of April. Godowski, Aimée and Gaillard were stars at the concert on April 25th. The Gypsy Baron also, like Amorita, held the stage but for a comparatively short time. May 10th saw the first performance at the Casino of an opera that was to be the culminating success of the house. Erminie, founded on the old farce of Robert Macaire, was the first production at the Casino of a work by English authors. The book, by Harry Paulton, was set to music of a pleasing tuneful quality by Jacobowski, and for many years thereafter the operetta was good for revival and revival, here, there and everywhere. Francis Wilson and Daboll as the two rogues made immense hits, especially Wilson, whose fame to this day is closely associated with his amusing Cadeaux. The original cast:

Erminie	Pauline Hall	Marquis de Ponvert	Carl Irving
Cerise	Marion Manola	Eugene Marcel	Henry Pepper
Princess	Jennie Weathersby	Chevalier de Brabazon	Max Freeman
Javotte	Agnes Folsom	Dufois	Murry Woods
Marie	Victoria Schilling	Simon	A. W. Maflin
Delaunay	Rose Beaudet	Vicomte de Brissac	C. L. Weeks
Cadeaux	Francis Wilson	Sergeant	J. A. Furey
Ravennes	W. S. Daboll		

Except for Pinafore and The Mikado, no operetta success like Erminie had been known in New York; since there had been hesitancy about producing it, the management were left prostrate with astonishment. Soon the town was whistling the "catchy" tunes and buying Falk's photographs of the chief performers, particularly the amusing group pictures of the two comic rogues. The piece could have run indefinitely, but was forced by previous contracts to go touring (October 2nd) to turn over the Casino to — whom or what, think you? To Violet Cameron, who came to America to cash in on the notoriety involved in her life on and off the London stage. I am pleased to state that her engagement (October 4th–November 13th) was a complete failure. Erminie returned, on November 15th, for a resumed run of ten months.

IRENE VERONA
(EVANGELINE)

BARTLEY CAMPBELL

JOHN A. MACKAY
(LE BLANC)

MAX FREEMAN
IN ERMINIE

MARIE JANSEN
IN ERMINIE

MARION MANOLA AND
PAULINE HALL

FRANCIS WILSON
AND W. S. DABOLL
IN ERMINIE

E. E. RICE

W. S. DABOLL AND
FRANCIS WILSON
IN ERMINIE

CHAPTER II

NIBLO'S, BIJOU OPERA HOUSE, HARRIGAN'S, GRAND OPERA HOUSE, PEOPLE'S THEATRE, THE WINDSOR, THE THIRD AVENUE, THE MOUNT MORRIS, THE COMIQUE, THE COMEDY, FOREIGN LANGUAGES, METROPOLITAN OPERA HOUSE, ACADEMY OF MUSIC, VARIETY, ENTERTAINMENTS, MUSIC, 1885-1886

THE season now under review was not very interesting at Niblo's. It opened, on August 17th, with a spectacular Clio, an old piece of Bartley Campbell's, revamped and lavishly mounted:

Lucia (Clio)................Adele Belgarde
Didi......................Marion Elmore
Countess....................May Newman
Duchess.................Mrs. Charles Poole
Fabian.......................Frank Losee
Count Giovanni.............B. T. Ringgold
Spring.....................Tommy Russell
Pietro....................Thomas H. Burns
Paolo..........................Harry Rich
Marquis Mattu............Harold Forsburg
Prince Zeliah..................Harry Carter
King of France.............E. L. Davenport
Philippeaux......................Jay Hunt

Much stress was laid on the ballet, led by Adele Cornalba, and on an elaborate scene of an earthquake. With all these ingredients and the good cast, one might have expected a success; we know, however, that the failure of Clio and of Paquita at the Fourteenth Street Theatre dragged Campbell into irrevocable ruin. He and Gilmore, manager of Niblo's, kept Clio afloat till September 12th. On the 14th, Rose Coghlan, now a star, came in for two weeks of Our Joan, her company including Frazer Coulter, George F. Robinson, Florence Robinson, B. R. Graham, C. A. McManus, Luke Martin and Clara Flagg. Henry Chanfrau, on September 28th, tried to be as good as his lamented father, in Kit, the Arkansas Traveller. Thatcher, Primrose and West's Minstrels, in that year of reviving minstrelsy, began on October 5th in a show involving the burlesque Black Adonis.

Pretty May Blossom, on October 12th, still glorified Georgia Cayvan and Ben Maginley, assisted by Forrest Robinson, W. H. Crompton, Nestor Lennon, Eliza Logan, Frank Currier and Agnes Carter — very good "road" Madison Square. Wallack followed, on the 19th, in Rosedale, surely a voice from the past. With him were Harry Edwards, Annie Robe, Louisa Eldridge, Kate Bartlett and Elton. The Daly Brothers, in Vacation, finished October at Niblo's; on November 2nd, Thatcher, Primrose and West returned, their burlesque now being The Mick-ah-Do. Cora Tanner, on the 9th, brought in Alone in London, which, before the season ended, she was to play in many theatres in New York and Brooklyn; it was a good melodrama by Robert

Buchanan. James O'Neill in his everlasting Monte Cristo filled the fort-night of November 16th–28th; in his support were J. W. Shannon, W. H. Wallis, H. B. Bradley, S. Miller Kent, J. V. Melton, Howard Gould, Annie Bond, Elizabeth Robins and Marie Floyd.

After this scurry of the roving bands, we settled down, on November 30th, to a run of Kiralfy Brothers' musical spectacle, The Ratcatcher, or, the Piper of Hamelin. Hubert Wilke, in the title-rôle, was nearly the "whole show," but the immense cast included a few good names in Arthur Tams as Simpliciton Rumple, J. F. Hagan as Hans von Kronold, Julia Stuart as Hilda von Kronold, Mrs. G. C. Germon as Martha, Clara Lipman as Nettie, and Annie Boyd as Tina. If I were to adduce the many other names of that cast, the reader would admit that he had never heard of one of them. Allston Brown, in speaking of The Ratcatcher, recalls the piece on the same theme, with music by Neuendorff, which, some years previously, had been a success in German New York. It lasted at Niblo's till Thatcher, Primrose and West began a fortnight, on January 25th, featuring the Black Mikado, and, in the second week, Hughey Dougherty. The thrills of February 8th were provided by J. H. Wallick, in The Bandit King, with a bowie-knife combat on horseback, a quartet of acting horses — Charger, Raider, Texas and Arabian Jim, and an Irish donkey, Calamity Jane. What could be more equine and asinine for the drama? The White Slave was here, on February 15th, for two weeks, with a cast including May Newman, James J. Tighe (as Clay Britton), Emily Baker (as Nance), Thomas H. Burns (as P. H. Stitch), Mr. and Mrs. Frank R. Foster, Harry C. Vetterlein, Esther Lyon, and a singing quartet. A rise in acting values came with Clara Morris, who had just opened the New Windsor Theatre with the same company and practically the same plays. Her week at Niblo's gave Miss Multon (March 1st and 4th); Article 47 (2nd), The New Magdalen (3rd); Alixe (5th); and Camille (matinée, 6th)—all the plays by which she is now remembered. Since she would not play twice on one day, Niblo's supplied an extra attraction for Wednesday afternoon and Saturday evening. Affie Weaver, on the evening of the 6th, essayed Camille. W. H. Powers's Company entered, on the 8th, in The Irish Leaf, very Irish, with J. P. Sullivan as Murty, May Wolcott as Colice O'Brien, W. H. Powers and Grattan Phillips as bad villains; Delia Powers and Little Mabel also figured. On the 15th, the Templeton Company gave The Mikado, with local gags and very little Gilbert.

And, on March 29th, the expected happened; Niblo's again brought forth its specialty — The Black Crook, with Olga Brandon, of all people in the world, as Amina, Mrs. Selden Irwin as Dame Barbara, G. F. Peters as the Crook, De Gey as the Count, Ward as Grippo and Clifton as Rudolph. This venerable relic, thus resuscitated, lasted till the 24th of April.

On April 12th, the Herald advertised specialties by the Herbert Brothers (gymnasts) and the Mignani Family; also a ballet representation of Tennyson's Dream of Fair Women. April 26th brought W. J. Scanlan, in Shane-na-Lawn, a popular thing at various minor theatres, in 1886; it had two weeks at Niblo's, yielding the stage, on May 10th, to The Guv'nor and A Happy Pair, with Wallack's actors, including Bellew, John Gilbert, Elton, George Clarke, Harry Edwards, Dan Leeson, Annie Robe, Helen Russell, Kate Bartlett and Mme. Ponisi — pretty good for Niblo's at that time. McNish, Johnson and Slavin's Minstrels had the week of May 17th–22nd, and Henry Chanfrau, again in Kit, that of May 24th–29th. Ada Gray, in her inescapable East Lynne, was tearful for the week beginning on May 31st; "a fresh roasted played-many-times chestnut," the Herald calls the play. Bound to Succeed (by George Conquest and Henry Pettitt) began on June 7th; a cast, including Augustus Cook, James E. Wilson, Charles T. Hagan, Gus Reynolds, C. Morton Price, Lottie Blair, Nellie Pierce, and others failed to make the play justify its title. A reliable Uncle Tom's Cabin (with Mrs. Howard, Horace Weston, Amy Washington and the Magnolia Quartet) began two weeks, on June 14th, and gave the stage, on June 28th, to an equally antiquated Streets of New York, with George C. Boniface. I found no more of Niblo's for the season of 1885–86.

Bijou Opera House, 1885–1886

It was a relief to pass from that dull year at Niblo's to the very lively Bijou Opera House, where Henry E. Dixey, continuing in Adonis, went merrily along, all the summer of 1885, latterly with George K. Fortescue replacing Amelia Summerville as Rosetta, the simple mountain maid. But, on October 1st, Miss Somerville (*sic*) returned to the part she had made her own, and Adonis headed bravely to its four hundredth performance, which it passed (on October 2nd) to reach a four hundred and fiftieth, on November 20th. On November 2nd, new scenery and costumes freshened the proceedings. The five hundredth showing (January 7th) was made a great occasion for Dixey. Nothing ever produced in New York had run so long, and the actor's friends determined to make a night of it. Though prices were doubled, the theatre was packed, and, on due occasion, brother comedians rushed on the stage, disrupting the play, but delighting the audience. George Thorne, Francis Wilson and John A. Mackay, in their stage-clothes, scurried from the theatres in which they were playing, to shake Dixey's hand and wish him Godspeed. And, when this glad excitement had worn itself out at the Bijou, a Dixey ball at the Metropolitan glorified the hero with dancing, Gilmore's Band, Bernstein's Orchestra and unlimited jollity. A huge floral heifer, reminder of Dixey's part in Evangeline's heifer, was exhibited among the decorations and was, indeed, placed, on following evenings, in front of the Bijou Opera House, until souvenir-hunters stripped it to its wire anatomy. I like to think of that triumphant evening for the popular actor who was, alas! in subsequent years not so universally acclaimed. Adonis really was delightful fooling; I saw it many times, and never tired of it.

After the festal evening of the 7th, it was necessary to wait, with what patience one could command, for the six-hundredth showing, which arrived on April 16th. The following day, Saturday, the 17th, saw the last two performances of the great success. Dixey and his company transferred Adonis to London, beginning on May 31st, at the Gaiety Theatre; the venture was not the success that had been hoped for. I pass back to March 7th, when Leander Richardson discoursed on We Bohemians.

The Bijou was closed for the week of April 19th–24th (Holy Week), but re-opened, on April 26th, with a futile thing by William Gill, called Arcadia, which lasted only to May 15th. In the cast were Lizzie St. Quinten (first appearance, and next season to be enrolled at Daly's), Hattie Delaro, Hattie Richardson, Ada Boshell, Alice Hosmer, George Richards, J. S. Ransone, F. F. Ward, R. Macintyre, and Gill himself. On May 17th, Thatcher, Primrose and West began, their company including Billy Rice, Milton G. Barlow, George Edwards, Delhauer and Geyer (the Human Frog and the Dumb Fisherman), Griffin and Marks (tumblers), "Professor" Burton's dog circus, the Four Aces, the Crescent City Quartette, &c. Two weeks of these minstrels led (May 31st) to The Bridal Trap, adapted by Sydney Rosenfeld from Le Serment d'Amour. The cast included Roland Reed as Foutelard, Francis Gaillard as the Count, Laura Clement (new here) as Rosetta, Augusta Roche as the Marquise, Jennie Prince as Marion, Harry Mills as Gravelin, E. S. Grant as Martial and Paul Vernon as Bel-Azur. With that *dramatis personæ* in mind, the reader need not be told that this piece was derived from the same source as The Crowing Hen, then playing across the street at Wallack's. Allston Brown (iii, 284) relates a ridiculous strife that took place between Miles and Barton, lessees of the Bijou, and Colonel McCaull, at Wallack's. On June 17th, the Bijou pair put a stereopticon on the roof of their theatre and threw on the wall of Wallack's sarcastic jibes at The Crowing Hen. "When McCaull had recovered from his indignation," he procured calcium lights, and with their aid blotted out the stereopticon pictures. The next night, the Bijou aggressors were served with an injunction, preventing them from throwing views on the Wallack wall; they thereupon hung out a canvas on the Bijou itself, turning the stereopticon thereon. Theodore Moss and McCaull hired a building next to the Bijou and turned a stereopticon on that. The streets became packed with the usual crowds of New York idle. The scheme wore itself out in a very few days, and The Bridal Trap, which had been doing bad business, closed on June 26th.

This was a season of benefits, the causes of which are at times hard to discover; apparently people simply put themselves up for such profits as might accrue. John F. Donnelly made what he could, on Sunday, May 16th, from the efforts of Agnes Herndon (who recited both Teazles, in the quarrel from The School for Scandal), Will Rising, R. E. Graham, Elma Delaro, &c. Georgia Cayvan failed to appear. On June 13th, Frank Farrell's enlisted De Wolf Hopper, H. M. Pitt, Alice Harrison, Dora Wiley, Roland Reed, Francis Wilson, Minnie Maddern, &c. H. M. Pitt thus stood, on Sunday, June 27th, with a mighty host of volunteers — Alice Harrison, Celie Ellis, Isabelle Urquhart, Sara Lascelles, Harry Edwards (he seemed to be necessary to any benefit), Atkins Lawrence, George Fawcett Rowe, J. O. Barrows, Will Rising and George S. Knight. I hope they all appeared; as a matter of fact, Hopper, Pauline Hall and Alma Stanley, advertised, did not. On July 8th (afternoon), Daisy Murdoch had her name up for a similar benefaction, with a remarkable promise as to assistants — Roland Reed, The Maid of Belleville company, Pauline Hall, Marion Manola, Lena Merville, Emma Carson, De Wolf Hopper, Bertha Ricci, Mme. Consuelo, Jesse Williams, Signor de Novellis, Pauline Markham and Max Freeman; again let us hope that they appeared in unbroken phalanx. The Bijou was storm-centre for such functions.

Meantime, the house had resumed business, on June 30th, with Humbug, in which, as star, appeared Roland Reed, who, as Ko-Ko, had attained to reputation, of a sort, in a lesser Mikado. He now came forth as Jack Luster, with A. S. Lipman as Ned Ramsey, Augustus Cook as Dick Podds, Fred Hight as Jackson Luster, Fritz Williams as Albert Worth, S. W. Glenn as Jacob Bartz, Paul Vernon as a Servant, Joseph Gobay as Judge Shaw, Alice Hastings as Arminda, Loie Fuller (one day to be an international star in dancing) as Nettie, and Mary Myers as Mrs. Shaw. So far as the men are concerned, the cast was interesting, and it carried Humbug to August 14th. On August 16th, another failure came to the recent long home of Adonis. It had the attractive title of Soldiers and Sweethearts, and the authors were Owen Westford, Susie Russell (always rather hard to classify) with music by George Schleiffarth. The first two of these were in the cast, which otherwise included Charles Overton, Frederick Darrell, Charles Allison, Henry V. Donnelly, Sylvia Gerrish, Louise Edgar, Ragna Linne, Ada May Drew, Thomas Welch and Henry Leoni, not to mention a few young girls, usual fillers-in in such musical pieces. The lively Lena Merville replaced Susie Russell, on August 23rd, but nothing availed. The house was closed for renovation (week of September 6th–11th), to re-open, on the 13th, for what might be called the Nat Goodwin season of 1886–87.

Harrigan's Park Theatre, 1885–1886

Harrigan's for 1885–86 is the record of but three good runs and three long casts. The transcribing of long casts is to me a wearying task, especially when so many minor characters and actors are involved, but Harrigan's interminable *dramatis personæ* can be accounted for by the origin of his playmaking. He was a graduate from the halls of Variety, and the earlier sketches of his career were provided for Variety bills and were acted by members of the olio. Hence he came to realise the amusement value of character sketches, Irish, German, Italian, etc., and he continued them in the longer plays his later career evolved. And, as a glance at his casts will show, his actors were largely from the field of Variety, many of them engaged for "bits" or "turns" in the evening's entertainment. And a consideration of his history will reveal the fact that his company became as permanent as did the force at Daly's or Wallack's or the Union Square. His was indeed a "stock" theatre.

He began his new season on August 31, 1885, with a new and final version of Old Lavender, now turned into more of a play than were certain others of his successes, and the final working of an idea with which he had experimented for years. He evidently was very fond of the character of Old "Lav." The cast of the re-arrangement:

Old Lavender	Edward Harrigan	Henry Mercer	Richard Quilter
Smoke	John Wild	Jack Dingle	Peter Goldrich
Dick, the Rat	Dan Collyer	Pop Jones	G. L. Stout
Martin Reilly	M. J. Bradley	Mother Crawford	Annie Yeamans
John Filbert	Harry Fisher	Laura Coggswell	Stella Boniface
Philip Coggswell	E. A. Eberle	Sally Stacy	Amy Lee
Paul Cassin	H. A. Weaver, Jr.	Mrs. Heartsoul	Ada Farwell
Zolia Brown	George Merritt	Mrs. Guile	Annie Langdon
Gideon Guile	William West	Mrs. Stone	Emily Yeamans
Silas Longmetre	A. C. Moreland	Mrs. Mercer	Kate Langdon
Lascar Joe	James Fox	Mrs. Grenell	Della Stillwell
John Stone	Joseph Sparks	Mrs. Wilbur	Annie Hall

One might have been surprised to find in this democratic fold Stella Boniface, reared in the more delicate atmosphere of Wallack's; Eberle, Dan Collyer (in Tony Hart's old rôle), A. C. Moreland, Henry Weaver, Jr. (husband of Stella Boniface) and Amy Lee (daughter of Harry Watkins) also in this play made their first appearances with Harrigan. Dave Braham, without whom Harrigan's would not have been Harrigan's, provided cheer with "catchy" new songs — The Jolly Old Owls, Please to Put That Down, Sweetest Love, Poverty's Tears Ebb and Flow (a very popular one, this), and Get Up, Jack, John, Sit Down.

After a very pleasing success, Old Lavender gave way, on November 30th, to The Grip, which fastened itself on the stage till February 13th, with, in chief characters, Harrigan as Patrick Reilly, Wild as Captain Erasmus Pebble, Dan Collyer as Catherine O'Hallerhan, Bradley as Handsome Grogan, Weaver as John Clancy, Harry Fisher as Colonel Reilly, Goldrich as Roland Pebble, Moreland as Jay Evarts Spread, James Fox as Lucinda Pebble, West as Roscoe Walker, George Merritt as Tom Walker, Quilter as Lysander Hartley, John Sparks as Myles O'Brady, Stout as Captain Clancy, Joseph Sparks as Tim Mahone, Mrs. Yeamans as Rosanna Reilly, Miss Boniface as Rosalind Reilly, and Amy Lee as Carrie, and, in minor rôles, Ada Farwell, Emily Yeamans, Annie Hall, Adele (*sic*) Stillwell, Annie and Kate Langdon, Georgie Hawley, Charles Coffey, James McCullough, Thomas Ray, William Merritt, and Robert Snyder. It is an act of cruelty to force my pen into writing so huge a cast. On December 21st, the Seventh Regiment, always devoted to Harrigan, occupied 530 orchestra chairs. The Grip relaxed its hold, on February 13th.

The Leather Patch, on February 15th, revealed Harrigan as an undertaker, and involved the fun and confusion incident to concealing a will or some such document under a leather patch on the trousers in which a corpse was buried. A negro steals the trousers, and the hunt is on. In this not wholly pleasing plot figured Harrigan as Jeremiah McCarthy, John Wild as Jefferson Putnam, Collyer as Caroline Hyer (quite in the line of Tony Hart), Bradley as Airy McCafferty, James Fox as Linda Corncover, Harry Fisher as Judge Doebler, Moreland as Counsellor Delancy Wriggle, Goldrich as Levy Hyer, Quilter as Jemmy, the Kyd, George Merritt as Dennis Mc-Carthy, West as Dr. Noah Corncover, Joseph Sparks as Moses Levy, John Sparks as Roderick McQuade, Annie Yeamans as Madeline McCarthy, Amy Lee as Libby O'Dooley, Nellie Wetherill (late of the Union Square) as Mrs. O'Dooley, and, in lesser bits, Engel, McCullough, Charles Coffee (*sic*), Ray, Stout, William Merritt, Robert Snyder, Annie and Kate Langdon, Adele (*sic*) Stillwell, Emily Yeamans, Annie Landor, Ada Farwell, Annie Hall, Ray Bristoe and May Tromton. My exhausted pen collapses in thankfulness that, with casts of such inordinate length, Harrigan was called on for only three plays in that busy season. The Leather Patch held firmly till the close of the theatre, on May 1, 1886. My cast of it I derived from the advertisement in the New York Herald; it differs materially from that offered by Allston Brown.

GRAND OPERA HOUSE, 1885–1886

The Mecca of West Side playgoers from homes and boarding houses in the neighbourhood of Eighth Avenue and 23rd Street, opened, on August 24, 1885, for its now usual kind of season with weekly visits of stars and good combinations. The first offering was Mortimer Murdoch's play, A Brave Woman, with the James M. Hardie-Sara von Leer company. Storm Beaten, with Shook and Collier's company, followed on August 31st, which, on September 7th, yielded the stage to another Union Square feature, A Prisoner for Life, avalanche and all, with J. B. Studley and Inez Rochelle in the cast. Michael Strogoff, on the 14th, allowed audiences to continue the revel of melodrama, with Joseph Slayter, Clarence Wilkins, J. M. Francour, Edward Holst, J. L. Munger (men quite unknown to me) and Ida

Waterman and Florine Arnold (good actresses, both) in leading rôles. The essential ballet was arranged by Baptistin Ceruti. And Shadows of a Great City cast more gloom for the week of September 21st–26th.

Skies brightened perceptibly on September 28th, when Evans and Hoey, with Minnie French, began a week in Hoyt's lively A Parlour Match. But melodrama returned, on October 5th, when Cora S. Tanner began the second of several visits in New York with Robert Buchanan's Alone in London, which came to us by way of Boston, where indeed I saw it a few weeks earlier. For the week of October 12th–17th, Anselma and Mme. Janish, came, fresh from the Madison Square Theatre; on the 19th, Annie Pixley's M'liss enthralled her many admirers. She did an (for her) unusual thing, on October 26th, by bringing out a new play, Eily, which hardly survived its birth pains. Better fare replenished the feast, on November 2nd, when Fanny Davenport and Robert Mantell (he had rejoined her after a season's absence) began a week in the all-compelling Fedora. A Bunch of Keys, on November 9th, inaugurated a merry week that led gracefully to a return of dear Maggie Mitchell, perhaps no longer the elfin sprite of the '60's or even of the '70's, in a usual repertoire: Jane Eyre (November 16th, 17th and 18th, matinée); Lorle (18th, evening, and 19th); Fanchon (20th and 21st). Charles Abbott and Mrs. E. A. Eberle assisted her. A benefit for the Elks, on the afternoon of November 19th, brought a fine array, with Mary Anderson, in Comedy and Tragedy, and contributions from Maggie Mitchell, Lotta, Kellar, and members of the companies in Evangeline, Old Lavender and Adonis. I always like to think of May Blossom, with Georgia Cayvan and Ben Maginley; it was here for the week of November 23rd–28th; and one of my very favorite actresses, Kate Claxton, carried November into December (November 30th–December 5th) in her never-dying The Two Orphans, with Adele Waters, Mrs. Brutone, Charles A. Stevenson (now as Jacques), Lee (as Pierre) and Hoey (Picard).

I reluctantly check the flow of this narrative to state that Professor Cromwell for the entire season of 1885–86 gave, on Sundays and on certain afternoons, illustrated lectures of travel, doubtless pleasing to auditors who could never hope to indulge in such peregrine pleasure. Beginning on October 4th with St. Petersburg, Moscow and Constantinople, he journeyed successively to Paris and Versailles (11th), Ireland (18th), Homes of England (25th), the Rhine (November 15th), Switzerland and Mt. Blanc (December 6th), Great Britain and Ireland (27th), Jerusalem and the Holy Land (January 10th), etc. From these bones I shall ask the reader to construct the season-long monster. Of course many of the lectures were repeated as the season "dragged its slow length along." But national pride forces mention of his America, illustrated on January 24th, and Chicago and the Wild West, on February 7th.

Let me recur to drama, with (December 7th–12th) Aimée, Russell Bas-

J. L. CARHART

HATTIE DELARO

HENRY CHANFRAU

MAMIE FLOYD

ELIZABETH ROBINS

DAN COLLYER

HUBERT WILKE

W. J. SCANLAN

CLARA MORRIS

sett, Newton Chisnell and Charline Weidman, in Mam'zelle; Eleanor Moretti, in Her Atonement (14th); the McNish, Johnson and Slavin Minstrels (21st), with Charles W. Mitchell, pugilist, in classic poses; Gus Williams (28th) in George Hoey's Oh! What a Night, assisted by C. F. Tingay, C. E. Lothian, De Los King, A. W. Showell, C. E. Collins, Topsy Venn, Josie Loane, Florence Vincent and Anita Harris; and Janauschek (once regarded by Germans as the rival of Ristori) in Zillah (January 4th), Bleak House (5th, 8th, and matinée, 9th), Mother and Son (January 6th), My Life (January 6th, evening), Mary Stuart (7th), and Macbeth (evening, 9th) — a hard week, as any star of 1941 will admit. On January 11th, Sol Smith Russell began a week, in Felix McCusick (by J. E. Brown); in this, the star gave his songs and recitations, Miss O'Leary sang, and Lawton played the banjo, clogged and whistled — verily a high-class show. And Nat Goodwin's The Skating Rink (January 18th) may have been timely and funny, but it did not elevate its appeal to the brain of the auditor. William Gillette, with M. A. Kennedy, aroused uncontrollable laughter, on January 25th, in The Private Secretary.

February 1st revealed The Wages of Sin, illustrated by Eleanor Carey (missed since the break-up of the Union Square stock company), Charles Maubury, Emma Courtaine, Emma Cliffden, Susie Russell, Abbie Pierce, Viola Daily, Mark Price, W. C. Deal, Westford and Sackett, some of whom I cannot identify. Goodwin and The Skating Rink returned on the 8th. A benefit to Robert W. Fraser, on February 11th (matinée) enlisted Goodwin, Francis Wilson, Mrs. Bowers and Ida Vernon (these two in the big scene from Mary Stuart), Lillian Russell, Pauline Markham, the trio, Read the Answer in the Stars (with Cottrelly, De Wolf Hopper and George Boniface, Jr.), Dora Wiley, the Dare Brothers, and Fraser (his first appearance in six years) in a scene from Humpty Dumpty. This was verily a great offering in that season of many benefit bargains.

On February 15th, Salsbury's Troubadours gave Three of a Kind; on the 22nd, James O'Neill, as Monte Cristo, punished all his enemies; Hoyt's A Rag Baby relieved the tension, on March 1st, allowing Frank Daniels to cause laughter unlimited. Alone in London again saddened us, on March 8th, and Denman Thompson's Joshua Whitcomb made us, on the 15th, all truly rural. The Knights, in Over the Garden Wall, were, on March 22nd, still supported by the incredibly funny George Monroe, as Aunt Bridget. Lotta, on March 29th, began as Mlle. Nitouche, following, at the matinée, on April 3rd, with Musette. For her second week she offered The Little Detective (April 5th, 6th, 7th) and her new play, Larks (a name which she changed to Odd Tricks, given on April 8th, 9th and 10th), with C. H. Bradshaw, P. A. Anderson, Emma Hinckley, Adelaide Eaton and Elsie Gerome as chief support. Duff's Mikado group filled the week of April 12th, with the cast heard in 1885 at the Standard Theatre, except that Gustavus Hall was now the Mikado and Francis Gaillard Pish-Tush, Hamilton and Stoddard, first representatives of those parts having deserted to the American Opera Company. On April 19th, Effie Ellsler gave Woman against Woman; on the 26th, Robson and Crane began two weeks in The Comedy of Errors. Joseph Murphy and The Kerry Gow held the stage for the week of May 10th; Kiralfy's Black Crook, from Niblo's, awakened amaze for the week of the 17th. A sad leave-taking was that of the week of May 24th, when Lester Wallack acted for the last times in New York. For May 24th, 25th and 26th, he and his company from the home theatre gave Home and A Happy Pair; on the 27th, 28th and 29th, She Stoops to Conquer bowed the veteran from the stage. I saw the matinée performance on the 29th, and, like all youngsters since the beginning of time, I could not but feel the incongruity of Marlow's bashfulness in a Marlow so obviously mature. But the art was there, and it is pleasing to think that John Gilbert and Mme. Ponisi were in the support of their colleague of so many beautiful years. Others were Annie Robe, Helen Russell, Ivan Shirley, Dan Leeson and Ed Lamb (Tony). No one suspected that this would be Wallack's farewell to a public before whom he had appeared for so many decades; but farewell, alas! it was. The week of May 31st saw the return of The Private Secretary, with William Gillette, whose star was rising, as Wallack's set.

June went out of the Grand Opera House with George C. Boniface in The Streets of New York (week of the 7th); James Schönberg's play, Not One Word, with Henry Walton and the début of Katherine Ware (14th); Rose Lisle and Frederick Paulding (our erstwhile Romeo) in The Sea of Ice (21st); and (28th) Pat Rooney and his company, Katie Rooney, Herbert Brothers, the American Four, Nellie St. John, Hi Tom Howard and the Three Whitneys. They shut the season on July 3rd. During the later Sundays, Cromwell took his listeners to London, or Paris, or the Sunny South.

PEOPLE'S THEATRE, 1885–1886

I cannot help boring my reader to the point of exhaustion, as I carry him from one "combination" theatre to another, up and down and across the city and even in Brooklyn, with repetitions of the same organisations flitting hither and yon, with the same offerings more or less trite. But annals are annals and require thoroughness to the last degree of cataloguing.

Harry Miner's People's Theatre, in the Bowery, shall first arouse our scholarly conscience, and, if possible, our narrative zeal. On August 10th, it proffered that company, in The Mikado, which tried, a few nights later, to steal D'Oyly Carte's thunder, at the Union Square Theatre. This is news to the reader, as to me; we had both thought the Union Square venture the earliest in the realms of that particular piracy. The cast at the People's included Charles L. Harris (later a favourite at the Madison Square Theatre) as the Mikado, with Alice Harrison, Emma Mabella Baker and Roland Reed, as later seen at the Union Square. The Bowery, then, proffered New York its very first taste of The Mikado.

Barlow, Wilson and Rankin's Minstrels gave (August 17th) early warning of the revival, in 1885–86, of the black-face art; with the company were Thomas B. Dixon (tenor), James S. Adams and Thomas Baines— "wandering minstrels" they, to match Nanki-Poo of the preceding week. The "opening" of the theatre came, on August 24th, with The World. On August 31st, Thomas W. Keene played Richard III, with a support including Gustavus Levick (as Richmond), Eugene Moore (as Buckingham), John T. Malone and Louise Davenport. September 7th brought Storm Beaten, with E. K. Collier, Lizzie Hudson, Archie Cowper and Miss Wayland. Cora S. Tanner, on September 14th, began her itinerary of the city, in Alone in London. W. J. Scanlan, on the 21st, in Shane-na-Lawn, sang Peek-a-Boo, and acted at the head of a company including Marion Warren and Messrs. Tessler, Ogden and Reynolds; the 28th gave Michael Strogoff. Many of these attractions figured in the bills at the Grand Opera House. Nobody's Claim (October 5th) introduced Joseph Dowling and Sadie Hasson, names that echo like ghosts in the seats of my memory; Effie Ellsler, in Woman against Woman, had, on the 12th, the support of Frank Weston, Charles Foster and Mattie Earle. Oliver Doud Byron, on the 19th, ran on The Inside Track, and, on the 26th, Edwin Thorne disclosed The Crimes of Paris to a public that knew, too well, the crimes of New York. Mme. Janish, on November 2nd, transferred Anselma to a part of our city less fashionable than that in which she had first revealed it. Her Atonement, wearing well, came on November 9th, with Eleanor Moretti, Virginia Buchanan, M. J. Gallagher and Mr. Evelyn Evans. Lizzie Evans, on the 16th, ran Fogg's Ferry, that piece once shown by Minnie Maddern; with her were Steve Corey, Henry Scharf and Tillie Shields. F. C. Bangs, on the 23rd, revealed the sturdier tissues of The Silver King. And here, on the 30th, Fanny Davenport and Mantell brought to this Bowery theatre the higher eloquence of Fedora. For the Wednesday matinée, December 2nd, Maude Granger came all the way from Worcester, Massachusetts, to try a new piece, An American Marriage.

Let us hurry to the New Year, with Evans and Hoey, in A Parlour Match (December 7th); Lillian Lewis as Cora, in Article 47 (14th); the Standard Theatre Mikado (21st); and Effie Ellsler, in Woman against Woman (28th). What can I say about any of these pieces that I have not already reiterated to the utter weariness of my reader and myself? Having thus passed New Year's, let us hasten to Washington's Birthday, opening the record with A Bunch of Keys (January 4th); and continuing with The Wages of Sin (11th), Eleanor Carey and Charles Maubury illustrating; with The Sea of Ice (18th) starring Kate Claxton, Harry Lee as Carlos and C. A. Stevenson as the comic Barabas, both uncomfortably miscast in the support; with a new play, Blackmail (January 25th) enlisting Eleanor Moretti, W. C. Cowper and Charles Vandenhoff; with John A. Stevens (February 1st) in another new play, A Great Wrong Righted, in which his support came from Maud Miller, Loudon McCormack, Adelaide (*sic*) Stanhope, Emily Lytton, Harry Colton and W. P. Sheldon; with Gus Williams, in One of the Finest (February 8th); Frederick Warde in a week (February 15th–20th) divided, in order, among Virginius, Othello, The Lady of Lyons, Damon and Pythias, Richelieu, Ingomar and Richard III — a repertoire suggesting hard work and times even then long past. With him were Mittens Willett and Harry Aveling.

So here we are, expeditiously arrived at February 22nd, for Milton and Dollie Nobles, in Love and Law. March gales blew in, in succession, The Romany Rye (March 1st); Nat Goodwin, in The Skating Rink (8th); Mestayer and Theresa Vaughn, in We, Us and Co. (15th); The World again (22nd), with Hamilton Harris, Thomas Q. Seabrooke (on his way, upward in the world of the theatre, as Jewell, the Jew), Frank Harrington, Amelia Watts, &c.; and, beginning on the 29th, A Prisoner for Life, with J. B. Studley, Inez Rochelle, Sara Neville, C. L. Farwell, E. L. Tilton, T. H. Glenney and Martha Wren, an interesting cast, if not so good as that of the preceding season at the Union Square. May we so quickly evade the April showers of attractions grave and gay? April 5th presented Aimée, in Mam'zelle; in quick order followed Frank Daniels, in A Rag Baby (April 12th); William Redmund and Mrs. Thomas Barry, of Boston, in A Midnight Marriage (19th); and even again (26th), Cora Tanner, in Alone in London. And May went smoothly along with Tony Hart, in his recent success at the Comedy, A Toy Pistol (May 3rd); W. J. Kersteller's illustrated lecture on Japan (Sunday, May 9th); Gillette, in The Private Secretary (10th); Murray and Murphy, in Our Irish Visitors (17th); and (24th) George Clarke's new play, A Strange Disappearance, which failed, though acted by Henrietta Crosman, McCullough Ross, J. E. Henshaw, Marjorie Burke and George Clarke himself. Barry and Fay, in Irish Aristocracy, began on May 31st, yielding the stage, on June 7th, to One of the Bravest, acted by Charles McCarthy, William Cronin, J. B. Radcliffe, Georgie Parker, Donnelly and W. F. Doyle. Milton and Dollie Nobles, in The Phœnix (June 14th) preceded a new, much-heralded play, Zitka, brought out, on June 21st, with this cast:

Pierre Petrovsky	Gustavus Levick	Lotzky	John Armstrong
Petrof	Frank Roberts	Countess	Edith Crolius
Vladimir	Arthur Forrest	Mme. Marzoff	Rose Snyder
Dr. Marzoff	Hudson Liston	Sabina	Mrs. Gerald Eyre
The Czar	Henry Aveling	Nannie	Edith Jordan
General Omoroff	M. B. Snyder	Zitka Marzoff	Charlotte Behrens
Gribbos	Edward Coleman		

This posthumous play of William Carleton dealt with the effort of a betrayed girl to avenge herself on the noble seducer.   She plays the siren, captivates him, and, in return, is captivated, till the final curtain leaves everybody where the dramatist desired to place him or her.   A second week of the stirring romance closed the theatre, on July 3rd, for the season of 1885–86.   But we shall hear of Zitka, in the same theatre, on August 23rd, and elsewhere in subsequent years.

Windsor Theatre, 1886

We remember that, in November, 1883, the Windsor Theatre, formerly the Stadt-Theater, and described as the largest playhouse in the city, was destroyed by fire.   After more than two years it was re-opened, rebuilt, reduced considerably in size, and prepared for a renewed career of interesting presentations.   Clara Morris, still a luminary, though of somewhat diminished brilliance, was the first attraction, beginning, on February 8, 1886, as Miss Multon, supported by Eben Plympton as Maurice de la Tour, Bijou Heron (who had been one of the children in this play in 1876) as the stepmother, now, of those children, J. L. Carhart as M. Belin, Carl Ahrendt and Mrs. Farren as the Osbornes, Clara and Vivia Ogden as the children, Ada Crisp as Kitty and Marion Lester as Louise.   This tearful version of East Lynne was repeated on the 9th and 10th; on the 11th and 12th, Miss Morris was the fiery Cora, in Article 47, and, at the matinée on the 13th, she enacted the self-sacrificing Camille, Affie Weaver replacing her, in the evening in the tearful rôle.   The Madison Square actors who were not then employed in Saints and Sinners at the home theatre came, on the 15th, to the more democratic Bowery in the refined Young Mrs. Winthrop, with Agnes Booth in her original rôle of Mrs. Dick Chetwyn, Maud Harrison as Constance, Annie Russell as Edith, Frederic Robinson as Buxton Scott and Walden Ramsay as Douglas Winthrop.   February 22nd began a week of Louis Aldrich, in My Partner — the same star and play that had been performing the night of the fire in 1883.

Having thus prepared the house, I may now hastily introduce the not very novel weekly visitors for March and April: James O'Neill, in Monte Cristo (March 1st); Frederic Bryton, in Forgiven (8th); Harry Lacy and Louise Balfe, in The Planter's Wife (15th); Hero (22nd), with Oliver and Kate Byron, Harry B. Johnson, Charles Willard, Miss D. Delaro and Rose Leigh; The Ivy Leaf (29th); Georgia Cayvan and Ben Maginley (April 5th), in May Blossom; Storm Beaten, with Lizzie Hudson and E. K. Collier (12th); J. H. Wallick, in The Bandit King (19th); Rose Coghlan, in Our Joan (26th).   Gliding thus comfortably down the ways (not forgetting Sunday concerts that began on March 7th), we may move into the easy May waves, greeting such passing craft (if I may be permitted the expression) as Minnie Maddern (May 3rd) with In Spite of All; the Vaughn-Mestayer We, Us and Co. (May 10th); Annie Pixley, in M'liss (17th); Joseph Murphy (May 24th) in Shaun Rhue and (27th) in Kerry Gow; and Baker and Farron, of diminished appeal (31st), in A Soap Bubble. June 7th began a week of Peck's Bad Boy, with Master Harry Brooks as the Boy and H. Crandall as the Groceryman. On the 14th, The Colleen Bawn again excited pity and terror, with Marion P. Clifton, Emma Pierce, Miss Gwynne Cushman, Kate Mallon, Frank Drew, W. P. (sic) Cahill, W. S. Lyle, G. H. Leonard, and E. G. Holland, worthy souls of some of whom I know absolutely nothing. John W. Jennings (21st) enacted Christopher Blizzard, in Confusion. The Tourists in a Pullman Palace Car reminded us (June 28th–July 3rd) that it was near vacation-time and the season for closing theatres. But "Sir" Roger Tichborne, the "claimant," on Sunday, June 27th, lectured before such as chose to renew acquaintance with the famous lawsuit that nearly disrupted English opinion. Rose Levere attempted in early July to arouse interest in the "legitimate," with Leah (5th, 6th, 7th) and Romeo and Juliet (8th, 9th, 10th). She had surprisingly good support in Alexander Salvini, John A. Lane, L. F. Rand, Louis Barrett and Gussie De Forrest. Very different was the attraction for the week of July 12th–17th — the Leonzo Brothers with their dogs (Tiger, Lion, Panther and Spot), in the canine melodrama, Brother against Brother. On July 11th we had a concert for the Irish Parliamentary Fund, then exciting gullible Americans, and, on July 19th, began a week of true Bowery, with N. S. Wood, in Jack Sheppard. This closed the theatre till the next season began in August, 1886. If my patient reader objects to the likeness of the offerings at the Windsor to those at the Grand Opera House, I can only assure him that I am not responsible therefor; indeed he may brace himself for much such sameness in the records of the three theatres which immediately follow. And wait till he renews the good fight against monotony in Brooklyn across the bay!

THIRD AVENUE THEATRE, 1885–1886

The reader knows I will spare him no bones that I can exhume from a remote past; let him therefore prepare for more catalogues of ships that passed in the night. But really the Third Avenue Theatre offered in 1885 something more novel than did other "combination" houses. J. M. Hill began, on September 7th, with the interesting melodrama, Nordeck, detailing adventure and villainy in eastern Europe:

Waldemar Nordeck	Frank Mayo	Fabian	F. F. Mackay
Witold	J. M. Taylor	Ladislaw	W. H. Murdock
Franz Vogel	J. R. Furlong	Margaret	Stella Teuton
Count Morynski	G. F. De Vere	Princess	Emma Wilmot
Prince Leo	Edwin F. Mayo	Wanda	Kathryn Kidder

This piece, really a new and needed vehicle for Frank Mayo, so long dependent solely on Davy Crockett and The Streets of New York, carried Hill's theatre for five stirring weeks. On October 12th, Hill transferred from his other theatre, the Union Square, A Moral Crime, which had, perhaps unexpectedly, made a hit there; two weeks sufficed for Third Avenue. William Davidge, Jr., had succeeded Edwin Cleary, now in the support of Miss Mather, at the Union Square.

Another novelty began on October 26th, C. T. Dazey's drama, For a Brother's Life, with Newton Gotthold, J. J. Lessinger and other worthies in the cast. This fraternal sacrifice was paid in full on November 14th; on the 16th, little Ida Mülle came in with Dimples, surely a simpering title, even for that pretty Cupid of Orpheus and Eurydice of a year or two preceding. Mrs. Howard's Topsy, everlasting if not immortal, was "so wicked" in the week of November 23rd–28th, with Bijou Fernandez as Eva, W. Davidge, Jr., as Marks, and with, of course, the now expected plantation scene, featuring Horace Weston and jubilee singers of dusky hue, physically and vocally. Frank I. Frayne in Si Slocum (November 30th), M. B. Curtis, as Sam'l of Posen, with Albina de Mer and Florence Roberts (December 7th), Henry Chanfrau, in Kit, with Horace Weston supporting (14th), these were surely ancient gifts to proffer, just before Christmas. But Christmas week (December 21st–26th) considerably brightened the outlook, with Lester and Allen's Minstrels, including the O'Brien Brothers, Charles Sheffer and Harry Blakely, Lester and Allen, P. C. Shortis (banjo and violin), and with William Muldoon and John L. Sullivan, those two doughty muscular heroes, in "classic" poses. Scenes of Southern Life carried us, in imagination, down to Dixie before the war. This lively fantasy carried through to January 2nd — surely a happy New Year for all.

January and February, 1886, may have interested the Third Avenue of that time, but for residents near Fifth Avenue it was a time of staléd sweets. Tony Denier's Wild West Pantomime began (January 4th) the progression, a feature being Humpty Dumpty among the Indians, or, Buffalo Bill's Last Miss — possibly not so bad. Joseph J. Dowling, in Nobody's Claim (11th), Murray and Murphy, in Our Irish Visitors (18th) and A Hoop of Gold (25th) made a most unappealing January. But The Rajah, on February 1st, cheered us with promise of J. G. Saville in the title-rôle, with Rillie Deaves (of the original Madison Square cast), Ethel Brandon, Sedley Brown, Walton and Stokes in the cast. Ida Lewis, in The Banker's Daughter, promised on the 8th, was not given till the 10th; repairs to the house were needed. This disappointment past, we enjoyed (February 15th) the jingle of A Bunch of Keys, with Eugene Canfield and Marietta Nash (as Teddy) featured. Joseph Murphy filled the next week (22nd–27th) in Kerry Gow and Shaun Rhue, three days of each. The Mikado, by the Templeton Company, proved (March 1st–6th) that the real Mikado

[49]

was elsewhere — at the Fifth Avenue, in fact; Charles L. Harris (Mikado), George Broderick (Pooh-Bah), Emma Mabella Baker (Katisha), Jay Taylor (Nanki-Poo), Lucille Meredith (Yum-Yum), W. H. Seymour (Ko-Ko), William Gulberson (Pish-Tush), Hattie Starr (Pitti-Sing) and Selina Rough (Peep-Bo) were the interpreters for Third Avenue of the charms of this opera. The Colleen Bawn (March 8th), with Henry E. Walton as Myles, Cahill as Danny Mann, Jessie Lee Randolph as Eily, Marion Clifton as Mrs. Cregan, Emma Pierce as Anne Chute, with Kate Mallon and Messrs. Randel (*sic*), Magnus, O'Brien, Braham and Woods; Carrie Swain, in Jack-in-the-Box (15th); F. B. Warde, in a week (22nd–27th) devoted to Virginius, Ingomar, Richard III, Damon and Pythias and The Lady of Lyons — this March fare led to reviving Spring (March 29th–April 3rd) when The Shaughraun peeped unexpectedly from the bills; on the 5th, Lizzie May Ulmer was to have presented Dad's Girl, to all who could be attracted by so inane a title; instead, The Banker's Daughter came back to interrupt the duel in the snow. Neil Burgess was very funny, week of the 12th, in his great specialty, Widow Bedott; Gibson and Ryan, on the 19th, gave their version of Irish Aristocracy. And here, on April 26th, is the never-dying Hazel Kirke, with Lottie Blair as the heroine and Fenwick Armstrong as the unyielding father; we can only imagine the rest. Ada Gray came in East Lynne (May 3rd–8th); Milton Nobles, in Love and Law (May 10th, 11th, 12th) and in The Phoenix (13th, 14th, 15th), had his week and went his way; Only a Farmer's Daughter, with Blanche Curtisse (17th); Uncle Tom's Cabin (24th), with Mrs. Howard, of course; John A. Stevens in Passion's Slave (May 31st), with Henry Holland, G. L. Mason and Louise Balfe — these questionable artistic devices, led us, not very happily, into the flowery month of June. The Big Four Specialty Combination let in "Variety" (June 7th–12th) with the Big Four (Smith, Waldron, Martin and Haley), with Conroy and Dempsey, Hilda Thomas, &c. Rose Lisle, Frederick Paulding and W. F. Blande gave us, on June 14th, the venerable antique, The Sea of Ice; and Pauline Markham, the toast of the town in 1868, ended the season (June 21st-26th) in Camille and The Ticket-of-Leave Man (Allston Brown says in The Lady of Lyons). The season, beginning with better offerings, ended in the doldrums, with C. Erin Verner, in The Shaughraun (June 28th–July 3rd).

Mount Morris Theatre, 1885–1886

We must now journey, by street car or possibly by our own carriage, to the Harlem Mount Morris Theatre, at 130th Street and Third Avenue, near (if truth must be told) the stables of the street car line. There, on September 7th, Emma Hendricks began in Only a Miner's Daughter; we were still sentimental in 1885. Zozo, the Magic Queen, was the attraction on the 14th; on the 21st, A Russian Honeymoon gave us Alexander Fisher as the Shoemaker.   Really, I hesitate to invite my fastidious reader to such dubious entertainment.

And regretfully I must confess that my bulging scrip fails me, at times, in items for the Mount Morris.   The week of October 19th–24th appealed, with Hazel Kirke, but the 26th became far more vigorous with The Stranglers of Paris.   Edwin Arden, in Eagle's Nest, sounds promising for November 2nd–9th, but I rather fear that the new Harlem Theatre Comique, with far better attractions, drove the old Mount Morris to the wall, or (shall I say?) into the adjoining stables.   The week of November 30th–December 5th, however, found, at the Mount Morris, Lulu Delmay and George France, in Wide Awake and The Block Game.   On February 1st, Rose Levere began, in Leah, the Forsaken, assisted by H. B. Bell, Frank Tannehill, Hudson Liston, C. L. Graves, Kate Gilbert and Nellie Sanford (*sic*)—a sharp re-awakening for a sleepy house.   On Sunday, February 14th, Professor Latham, who had given illustrated lectures at the Union Square Theatre, now came to the Mount Morris, with Ireland — Charles Stewart Parnell.   On March 11th, the Herald informs us that this theatre is to be remodelled and turned into Williams' Opera House.   Evidently the Comique had driven it out of business.

Theatre Comique, Harlem

Evidently Harlem was awaking to a theatre-sense.   The old Elite Skating Rink, on the south side of 125th Street, between Third and Lexington Avenues, was changed, in 1885, to the Theatre Comique, operated by Josh Hart, and offered for 1885–86 a series of plays quite as good as those at the Grand Opera House, the Windsor or the People's — in fact frequently the plays were the same.   Harlem, if it were willing to wait, need not journey to the southward for entertainment.

The Comique opened very strongly, on October 19th, for a week of Fanny Davenport and Robert Mantell, in the all-compelling Fedora.   Thereafter followed offerings with which my reader has become only too familiar: Shadows of a Great City (October 26th), Effie Ellsler, in Woman against Woman (November 2nd), A Parlour Match with Evans and Hoey (9th), Cora Tanner, in Alone in London (16th), Eleanor Moretti, in Her Atonement (23rd), Rose Coghlan, in Our Joan (30th), and (December 7th) the American Four Combination.   December progressed with Nat Goodwin, in The Skating Rink (14th), Gibson and Ryan, in Irish Aristocracy (21st), Watson and McDowell, in Wrinkles (28th), and with no pain slipped into January, on the 4th, with the seasoned stand-by, The World.   Arthur Rehan's company, in A Night Off, on the 11th, interests me, as a Daly item, with Harry Hotto and Clara Fisher Maeder (Professor and Mrs. Babbitt),

Virginia Brooks (Nisbe), Helen Leigh (Angelica), Hardy Vernon (Jack), and Clarence Harvey (Harry Damask). Mr. and Mrs. George S. Knight followed (January 18th) in Over the Garden Wall, to give open sesame, on the 25th, to A Bunch of Keys.

Thus February came in, on the 1st, with Gillette, in The Private Secretary, and continued with My Partner (8th), acted by Louis Aldrich, Dora Goldthwaite, John E. Ince (Wing Lee), Charles Mason (Ned Singleton), Charles Stanley (Major Britt) and Emma Jones (Posie Pentland); with Kate Claxton, Stevenson and Harry Lee, in The Sea of Ice (15th); with George Parks (not Parkes) and Emma Vaders, in Siberia (22nd); and May Blossom (29th), still with Maginley and the charming Georgia Cayvan. The ubiquitous Mikado reached Harlem, on March 8th; and Gus Williams, in What a Night, on the 15th.

The Rajah came on the 22nd, and Neil Burgess, in The Widow Bedott, on the 29th. Frank Daniels, in A Rag Baby (April 5th), assisted by Fanny Rice, Mark Sullivan, Harry Conor and Edward A. Osgood (in the parody, Three Little Tramps from Jail); Mestayer and Theresa Vaughn, in We, Us, and Co. (12th); The Mikado (19th and 26th); Emmet, in Fritz in Ireland (May 3rd) — these well-known items carry us to the engagement of Maggie Mitchell, with The Pearl of Savoy (May 10th); Little Barefoot (11th and evening of the 15th); Fanchon (12th and matinée, 15th); Lorle (13th) and Jane Eyre (14th) — verily a busy week for the little actress. On May 17th, John P. Smith's Uncle Tom's Cabin presented Mr. and Mrs. G. C. Howard; the 24th brought Engaged, with Cedric Hope and Agnes Herndon; and the 31st presented McIntyre and Heath's Minstrels, once more to show the revival of the black-face art.

A benefit to the manager, Josh Hart, on June 22nd, gave the Madison Square Theatre company (M. A. Kennedy, Charles Coote, A. S. Lipman, Herbert Ayling, T. A. Wise, and Mrs. H. Charles), in Act I of The Private Secretary; the Harlem Männerchor; Lizzie Evans, Louisa Eldridge and H. Scharf, in an act of The Culprit Fay; acts of Devilled Kidney and The Henpecked Husband, George S. Knight, John E. Kellerd, Dave Reed, Napoleon Sarony, Sam Devere, W. T. Bryant and Lizzie Richmond, Smith and Rowland and Haines and Vidocq — pretty good for remote Harlem, but not comparable to benefit bills further south, in 1886.

COMEDY THEATRE, 1885–1886

Perhaps it is doing violence to topography to flit from Madison Square to the Bowery to Harlem and then return to the centre of the town for the season at the Comedy Theatre (Broadway and 29th Street). This house, formerly the home of the lamented San Francisco Minstrels, re-opened, remodelled and redecorated, on September 21st for a very long engagement of the magician, Kellar, who cleverly brought variety to his assistance in persons of the clever Tissots and Dora Wiley (songstress). The Tissots accompanied for many weeks of the protracted season. Harry Pepper and the Tissots were listed on October 12th. A Sunday concert (October 18th) promised Kellar, Eva Hewitt (cornet), Beatrix Hamilton and Edward Cameron. Morley's Fata Morgana and Harry Pepper were stressed on October 25th. James Blamphin and the Fata Morgana were offerings of December 7th. And Kellar triumphantly reached his hundredth performance on December 15th — surely a magical showing; he passed the goal of the hundred and twenty-fifth, on January 2nd.

This happy engagement carried into February. On Saturday, February 20th, Tony Hart, so long with Harrigan, came singly into the Comedy Theatre, with William Gill's nonsense, A Toy Pistol. That title was the name of a paper, it seems, and Hart played the part of Isaac Roast, the editor, with J. B. Mackie as Pie, his assistant, F. R. Jackson as the Veteran, John Rice as Greeley and Rossa O'Donovan, D. G. Longworth in the triple rôle of Ernest Seeker, J. Lancelot Hustler and Primrose Path, Annie Adams (mother of Maude Adams) as Dora M. Solfer, Mattie Ferguson as Miss Colorado and Miss Juliet, Bertie Amberg as Miss Chatter, Eva Granville as Gracie, Bijou Fernandez as Puck, and the sprightly Lena Merville as Subtly New and the Swell. Hart's friends made the opening night a riot; they applauded, yelled greetings as he first came on the stage and compelled him to stop the show and make a speech. Of course he said he was happy to be "back," and he predicted, truly, that the length of his visit would depend on the public response to the show. That response cooled perceptibly, and, we may regret to announce, Hart fired that silly Toy Pistol for the last time at the Comedy, in early April. Meantime, Marie Prescott turned the overburdened stage into a rostrum, lecturing, on Sunday, March 21st, on stage life, in Among the Stars. I always fear actresses bearing gifts in the shape of lectures.

A variety and minstrel show began on April 5th, featuring Charles and Ella Jerome, the Muhlemann Sisters and Joseph Muhlemann, Tim Murphy, George D. Melville, William Carroll, Ira and Mrs. Paine, the Forresters (in Going to the Masquerade), Nellie Parker and Florence Jordan. What would you, in those days of the diminishing vogue of variety? The scheme lasted but a week. On April 12th, Daniel Sully was listed for The Corner Grocery, a store heretofore set up usually at Tony Pastor's hospitable establishment.

EIGHTH STREET THEATRE, 1886

The former Johnny Thompson's Theatre pursued an uncertain course in 1886; chiefly, I suspect, it remained sadly dark. During the week of April 4th–9th, however, Bertha Welby appeared as Camille, with support none too brilliant in Louis Barrett as M. Duval, Henry W. Mitchell as Armand, J. V. Melton as Darville, Annie Bishop as Prudence and Susie Russell as Nichette. The following week was to feature Adelaide Thornton, in The Galley Slave. J. B. Studley followed (April 25th) in The Corsican Brothers, with H. G. Clarke as Château-Renaud, O. B. Collins as Montgiron, Jessie Lee Randolph as Emilie, and Laura Linden as Mme. dei Franchi.

For the evenings of May 9th–14th Ed J. Mack played Fagin, E. F. Gilpin Bill Sykes, Annie (Mack) Berlein Nancy, Bertie Willis Oliver Twist, and J. H. A. Rumey the Dodger; the Monday, Wednesday, Thursday and Saturday matinées allowed Miss Berlein to undergo the agonies of Leah, with Mack as Nathan. The last I found that year for this declining stage was Richard III, on May 16th, with D. H. Harkins (his glory, if not his avoirdupois withering — temporarily), O. B. Collins (Richmond), J. H. Fitzpatrick (Buckingham), Master Tommy Russell, young brother of the lovely Annie (Duke of York), Mrs. W. G. Jones (Elizabeth) and Marie Haynes (Anne). Harkins and Mrs. Jones, at least, knew how Shakespeare should be played.

THALIA THEATER, 1885–1886

This home of the Germans re-opened on August 24th, with an English-speaking company, in Bartley Campbell's stirring Siberia; August 24th began a fortnight of Shadows of a Great City.

Then Gustav Amberg began the regular season of German productions, devoting a large part of the term to light opera or to operetta, a form of entertainment best liked by his patrons. The opening performance (October 1st) was Czar und Zimmermann, with Otto Rathjens as Peter I, Eduard Elsbach as Peter Iwanow, Ludwig Ziehmann as Van Bett, Hannah Norbert-Hagen as Marie, Walter Hoffmann as General Leford, Franz Wackwitz as Lord Syndham, Ferdinand Schütz as Châteauneuf, Fanny Schegar as Wittwe Brown, Hermann Korn as ein Offizier, and Heinrich Habrich as ein Raths-diener. The reader knows that it is necessary for him to become acquainted with the company. Der Feldprediger, on the 2nd, was another old friend. But October 5th showed Der Weg zum Herzen (by Adolph L'Arronge); the cast will introduce members of the dramatic (as opposed to the musical) corps whom we must meet for the season. August Walter appeared as Franz Kern, Fabrikant; Elisabeth Hagedorn as Mathilde, his wife; Emilie Becker as Martha, his daughter by a former marriage; Fritz Kugelberg as his brother, the Commerzienrath Ferdinand; Selina von Krottnauer as Ferdinand's daughter, Anna; Eduard Possansky as Assessor von Schott; Fritz Hitzigrath as Assessor Fritz; Bertha Schulz as the sister of the last-named; Hugo Hasskerl as Sanders, Landswirth; Eugenie Schmitz as Babette, Dienst-mädchen bei Franz Kern; and Gustav Adolfi and Heinrich Habrich as servants of official importance. This Weg zum Herzen won its way to the hearts of audiences for the week of October 5th–10th, except that, on Friday, the 9th, Paul Lindau's Maria und Magdalena allowed Hermine Fanto to make her début as Maria, with Elisabeth Hagedorn as Magdalena, Possansky as Fürst zu Rothenthurn, August Walter as Graf Egg, Kugelberg as Werren, and Emilie Becker as Elly.

Thus we have gone through the serious business of introduction of actors; I may add that, while drama held the stage of the Thalia, the operatic contingent was giving operetta in Brooklyn. This branch of the enterprise returned, on October 12th with Nanon, Emmy Meffert (first appearance this season) filling the title-rôle, with Franziska Raberg as Ninon de l'Enclos, Ferdinand Schütz as d'Aubigne, Max Lube as Marquis von Marsillac, Otto Meyer as Ludwig XIV, Helene Delia as Mme. von Maintenon, Eduard Elsbach as Vicomte von Marsillac, and Bernhard Rank as the Abbé. This charming thing was repeated on the 15th. In Der Freischütz, on the 13th, Selma Kronold, later known here in English opera, made her début as Agathe, with Rathjens as Ottokar, Wilhelm Frank as Samuel, Wackwitz as Caspar, Otto Meyer as Kuno, Ferdinand Schütz as Max, and Hannah Norbert-Hagen as Ænnchen. Der Bettelstudent, revived on the 14th, stressed Max Lube, Emmy Meffert, Wilhelm Frank, Hermine Lorenz, Rank and Albertine Habrich. On October 16th, 17th and 19th, Der Postillon von Lonjumeau, which for many years had glorified Theodor Wachtel, introduced his son, Ferdinand, not, I fear so glorious. He remained, intermittently, throughout the season. His Chapelou, in Der Postillon, profited by the efforts, in other chief rôles, of Hannah Norbert-Hagen, Hermine Lorenz, Ludwig Ziehmann and Elsbach.

"Auf Verlangen," on the 20th, Die schöne Ungarin came back into the bills; on the 21st, Martha allowed Wachtel to show what he could do with charming melodies, and with a cast including Norbert-Hagen, Fanny Schegar, Hermann Gerold (Tristan) and Wackwitz (Plunkett). On the 23rd, Frl. Raberg sang Rosalinde, in Die Fledermaus. Der Raub der Sabinerinnen (by Franz and Paul von Schönthan), on which Daly had founded his delightful A Night Off, was staged at the Thalia, on October 23rd, and made a laughing hit:

Professor Gollwitz	August Walter	Emil Gross	E. Possansky
Friedericke Gollwitz	Eugenie Schmitz	Emanuel Striese	Bernhard Rank
Paula	Bertha Schulz	Rosa	Johanna Schatz
Dr. Neumeister	Fritz Hitzigrath	Auguste	R. Michaelis
Marianne	Emilie Becker	Meissner	Arthur Zolki
Karl Gross	Ferdinand Urban		

The reviews declared that the performance was excruciatingly funny, Rank, although all the parts were well played, receiving highest praise for his Striese, theatre-manager, played so well, also, at Daly's, by Charles Leclercq.

This Rape of the Sabines ran along merrily till November 14th. November 12th marked the twentieth performance and also the benefit of Rank. At the matinée on the 14th, it was joined by Die Verlobung bei der Laterne.

And then more operetta! Lori Stubel, sister of Jenny Stubel, our favourite of a few seasons earlier, made her début on November 16th, as Boccaccio, with Rank as Scalza, Edmund Fabbiani as Lotteringhi, August Walter as Lambertuccio, Eugenie Schmitz as Peronella, and Selma Kronold as Fiametta — apparently a good cast. November 17th presented Lori Stubel as Pauline, in Der Walzer König, with Rank, Walter, Frl. Delia and a tremendous supporting company; it ran till the 21st, inclusive. Boccaccio returned, on the 23rd, and, on Tuesday, the 24th, Das Glöckchen des Eremiten (Les Dragons de Villars) presented Hannah Norbert-Hagen, Rathjens, Wackwitz, Fabbiani, &c. This also had a run, ending its career on November 29th. Ein Blitzmädel, on November 30th and December 1st and 2nd, and matinée, December 5th, allowed the star of Lori Stubel once more to shine. Der Bettelstudent (December 3rd) led to Fatinitza, on the 4th and 5th, with Lori Stubel, Lube (Izzet Pacha), Rank (Vielosorum), Wackwitz (Graf Timofey) and Selma Kronold (Lydia). A good company this!

Let me hasten to insert the not very exciting information that, since October 11th, Sunday concerts had prevailed at the Thalia; on November 1st, Prince Lichtenstein's Zigeuner Kapelle supplied chief nutriment to the faithful. On December 7th and 8th, Mitterwurzer, having finished his fortnight in Broadway, came to the Bowery, in Carl Saar's adaptation of L'Assommoir, which he called Der Todschläger. Leaders in the cast were, besides the star as Coupeau, Fritz Hitzigrath as Goujet (Schmied), Eduard Possansky as Lantier (Hutmacher), Kugelberg as Mes-Bottes (Schmied), August Walter as Poisson, Rank as Bec-Sale, Anna Schlag as Sidore, Elisabeth Hagedorn as Virginie, Eugenie Schmitz as Mme. Roche, and Hermine Lorenz as Clemence. On the 10th, Mitterwurzer changed to Narciss, with Helene Delia as Maria Lescinska, Frl. Hagedorn as the Pompadour, Hitzigrath as Choiseul, and Mathilde Madison as Doris Quinault. Kean returned on the 11th, and Die Räuber on the 12th (evening), both cast about as earlier at the Star Theatre. Die Leibrente served for the matinée on the 12th. The concert on the 13th was for the benefit of the Thalia orchestra. Der Raub der Sabinerinnen came back on the 14th. Mitterwurzer's last two performances for the present were Narciss (15th) and Dr. Wespe (16th). For December 18th to 21st (Monday) we were treated to Papageno, a musical farce by Kneifel, with, in leading rôles, Walter, Frl. Schmitz, Hermine Fanto, Bertha Schulz, Hitzigrath, and Possansky, with all of whom we now have a casting acquaintance.

Christmas joys at the Thalia were varied. Wachtel, on the 22nd, restored Der Postillon von Lonjumeau, high notes, cracking whip and all; on the 23rd, Frl. Raberg, Frl. Meffert, Lube and Schütz returned in Der Bettelstudent. Christmas Eve (24th), as usual, shut the theatre. But Christmas Day brought, in the afternoon, for the children, Der gute Michel, oder das Binsenmännchen; every boy in the audience was to receive a present, and every girl a doll. The evening presented the expected Lumpaci Vagabundus. On Saturday, December 26th, Lori Stubel appeared as Fanchette, in Der Seecadet, Lube and Frl. Raberg assisting. A "Massen Concert," on the 27th, enlisted many of the theatre company. Der gute Michel charmed on several following afternoons, its career temporarily checked, on the 30th and 31st, by Schneewittchen. Lumpaci Vagabundus was the afternoon gift on January 1st, Das Binsenmännchen serving on the afternoon of the 2nd.

On the evening of January 2nd came Der Trompeter von Säkkingen, which was set down as by Emil Kaiser, after a poem by Victor Scheffel. It was mounted "mit vollständigem Chor, Orchester und neuer Ausstättung." In the cast were Wackwitz, Frl. Norbert-Hagen, Ludwig Ziehmann, Fanny Schegar, Ferdinand Wachtel, Rathjens and Selma Kronold. This good cast kept Der Trompeter going for several nights. On Sunday, January 10th, Adolf Bolgar's one-act Vom Fels zum Meer was part of a "Jubilæum" for the twenty-fifth anniversary of Kaiser Wilhelm. And, on January 11th, the Thalia staged Frau Direktor Striese, a sequel to Der Raub der Sabinerinnen, with Rank again as a comic Striese, Frl. Schmitz as the "Direktor" Striese of the title, with Emilie Becker and Bertha Schulz as their daughters, Hasskerl as Dr. Richard Bredow, Helene Delia as his aunt, Possansky as Oscar Clemens, Fritz Kugelberg as Carl Gross, Anna Schlag as ein Commis, Johanna Schatz as Minna, and Adolfi as Caspar. This novelty ran through January 16th. On Monday, the 18th and on the 20th, it united in the bills with Der Raub der Sabinerinnen. I wonder why "runs" were now comparatively so brief? On the 19th of January came Rosenmüller und Finke; on the 21st, Nanon; on the 22nd, for the benefit of Otto Rathjens, Der Trompeter von Säkkingen; on the 23rd, Der lustige Krieg, the second old-time operetta of the week. On Sunday, January 17th, a sacred concert, Das lachende New York, included Becker's Geschichte, Bei Wasser und Brod, and Aus Liebe zur Kunst — far from "sacred," methinks. A promenade concert, on the 24th, involved the laying of a new parquet (movable) floor for the dancing of those who listed.

The next week went entirely operatic: Der lustige Krieg (25th); Czar und Zimmermann (26th); Gasparone (27th); one hundredth Die Fledermaus (29th) and Die lustigen Weiber von Windsor (28th and 30th). The cast of Nicolai's operatic version of Shakespeare included Rathjens and Frl. Norbert-Hagen as Fluth and Frau Fluth, Walter Hoffmann as Reich, Hermine Lorenz as Frau Reich, Fabbiani as Spärlich, F. Wachtel as Fenton, Ludwig Ziehmann as Falstaff, and Selma Kronold as Anna. Surely they must have been amusing, if not overwhelmingly musical. January 31st had a concert for 8,000 striking or shut-out cigar workers. The first week of February merely juggled about previous contributions: Die lustigen Weiber von Windsor (February 1st and matinée, 6th); Der Seecadet (2nd); Der Raub der Sabinerinnen and Frau Direktor Kriese (3rd); Nanon (4th); Rosenmüller und Finke (5th); and Robert and Bertram (evening, 6th). On Sunday, February 7th, we had a Valentine Concert, with prizes. The 8th was an Historischer Theater-Abend, with Der Fahrent Schuler (1600); Der Mentor, oder ein weiblicher Hussar (1700) and Die lebendigtodten Eheleute (18–1900). Familiar repetitions figured till February 13th, when the Germans put on that devouring element, The Mikado:

Mikado	Max Lube	Yum-Yum	Emmy Meffert
Nanki-Puh	F. Shütz	Piti-Sing	Carola Engländer
Ko-Ko	Bernhard Rank	Püp-Buh	Martha Berger
Puh-Bah	Conrad Junker	Kati-Shah	Albertine Habrich
Pisch-Tusch	Otto Meyer		

I trust the changed spelling of the names of the characters in no way reduced the wit of the libretto. At any rate, the opera ran uninterruptedly to February 25th. On Sunday, the 21st, for Washington's Birthday, we had a "Feier" of serious import. A matinée of Nanon signalised the very day of the birth. On the evening of the 26th we celebrated the hundredth rendition of Nanon; on Saturday evening, Pech-Schulze had chief funmakers in Lube, Rank and Eugenie Schmitz. On Sunday, February 28th, the perplexed management resorted to selections from fourteen operettas, with the Thalia actors serving as they might.

The first week of March certainly provided variety: Pech-Schulze (1st); Der Bettelstudent (2nd); for the benefit of Hermine Fanto (3rd), Käthchen von Heilbronn; Die Fledermaus (Act I) and The Mikado (4th); Faust (5th), with Kugelberg (it was his benefit) as Mephisto, Hitzigrath as Faust, and Frl. Fanto as Margarethe. For the matinée, on the 6th, children were admitted free; the evening revived Das Volk, wie es weint und lacht. The concert of the 7th boasted of actors from Saxony, Berlin, Breslau, Stettin and Dresden (all of course members of the Thalia force), who were to give Das Fest der Handwerker. I suspect that the Thalia was hard up; its constant revival of ancient wares showed perplexity in the office. After Pech-Schulze, on the 8th, came, on the 9th, a revival of Figaro's Hochzeit, which with my memories of Emma Eames, Marcella Sembrich and other great exemplars of Mozart singing, I cannot imagine as satisfactorily given by the faithful cohorts of the Thalia. Whatever their success, they were Rathjens (Almaviva), Selma Kronold (the Countess), Wackwitz (Figaro), Norbert-Hagen (Susanna) and Carola Engländer (Cherubin). Parts of this immortal work figured in the Sunday concert on the 14th. Meantime for the benefit of Gustav Adolfi (March 10th) and again on the 13th, we had Mit Vergnügen and Die schöne Galathee; Frl. Schmitz's benefit, on the 12th, revived Der Schwabenstreich. And, on the 13th, Wachtel and Selma Kronold were heard in a revival of Das Nachtlager von Granada. Assuredly this restlessness betokens anxiety.

Again Mitterwurzer came to the rescue. On March 15th, his Richard III had the support of Elisabeth Hagedorn as Elisabeth, Bertha Schulz and Emilie Becker as the princes, Hermine Lorenz as Queen Margaret, Eugenie Schmitz as Duchess of York, Hermine Fanto as Anna, Kugelberg as Buckingham, Wilhelm Frank as Richmond, and Hitzigrath as Clarence — a striking cast. Thereafter Mitterwurzer offered usual parts for such a star: Dr. Wespe (16th), Narciss (17th), Die Räuber (18th), Die Journalisten (19th) and Hamlet (20th). As Hamlet, he was associated with Walter (Polonius), Hasskerl (Horatio), Hitzigrath (Laertes), Kugelberg (Claudius), Otto Meyer (der Geist), Lube and Rank (Todtengräber), Frl. Fanto (Ophelia) and Fanny Heller (Queen). For his last week, the star was Mephistopheles to the Faust of Hitzigrath and the Margarethe of Frl. Fanto (March 22nd); he was Bergheim, in Drei Bräute auf einmal, oder Ein Lustspiel (23rd). The 24th repeated, by general desire, Dr. Wespe, and, on the 25th Mitterwurzer acted Präsident Roquette, in Der Scheinheilige, oder Das Urbild des Tartuffe. I am impressed by the revival of the ancient custom of renaming old plays. A double bill of March 26th and 27th combined Bürgerlich und Romantisch with Die Schulreiterin. A matinée on the 27th, at reduced prices (another ominous sign), repeated Dr. Wespe. The bill for Sunday, March 28th, provided Lori Stubel, in Blitzmädel, a first performance of Die Auswanderer, and Lube as Dr. Peschke.

Mitterwurzer devoted three more nights to the waning season: Die Journalisten (29th), Der Scheinheilige (30th), and (31st) Der Winkelschreiber and Wahn und Wahnsinn (this last really Sie ist wahnsinnig, as the star's character, Sir Bernard Harleigh, shows). The Casino, as we remember, was at this time and before, producing with some success The Gypsy Baron; the Thalia, freed from stellar alliances, staged, on April 1st, what it was pleased to call the "original"— Der Zigeunerbaron. Leading parts fell to Eduard Elsbach as Graf Peter Hamonay, Rank as Carnero, Schütz as Sando, Carola Engländer as Arsena, Albertine Habrich as Mirabella, Fabbiani as Ottokar, Johanna Schatz as Czipra, and Franziska Raberg as Saffi; I omit the army of fillers-in. It ran successfully, at least continuously, I am pleased to say, through April 26th — perhaps the most encouraging run of the season. Guten Morgen, Herr Fischer, was part of the "sacred" concert, on April 4th; on Sunday, April 25th, nearly all the leading members of the company, including Lori Stubel, appeared for the benefit of Herren Rothenstein and Michaelis, whom I cannot, offhand, identify. Mitterwurzer, for August Walter's benefit, on the 27th, appeared in Wahn und Wahnsinn; Miller und Müller also was part of the joy. For Capellmeister John Lund, on the 28th, we had Nessler's Der Rattenfânger von Hamelin, with Wachwitz, Gerold, Elsbach, F. Wachtel, Rathjens, Frl. Lorenz and

[59]

Selma Kronold. Unlike the Ratcatcher of Hamelin, seen earlier at Niblo's, this Rattenfänger caught no bit of a run. Der Zigeunerbaron came back on May 1st, and the ever-homing Mitterwurzer, on the 3rd, gave Drei Bräute auf einmal and Mein neuer Hut. On the 4th, he appeared in von Moser's Reif Reiflingen, and on the 5th as Graf Thorane, in Der Königslieutenant. For the benefit of Ferdinand Schütz, on May 6th, the Genée-Millöcker opera, Die Jungfrau von Belleville, which in English dress failed on Broadway, tried its luck in the Bowery, with a cast including Lube, Emmy Meffert, Albertine Habrich, Bertha Schulz, Conrad Junker, Elsbach, Schütz, Fabbiani, Rank and as many others as comic opera in those days enlisted as fillers-in. Lori Stubel's benefit, on Sunday, May 2nd, presented her in acts of Prinz Methusalem, Drei Paar Schuhe, Blitzmädel, Boccaccio and La Mascotte. I wonder if she had set the East River afire with evidences of a flaming genius? On May 9th, the "sacred" concert presented a miscellany and Hochzeit bei Laternenschein.

The last week of the season entailed benefits: Rank's and Junker's (10th); Lube's (11th); that of the ushers and doorkeepers (12th); Elsbach's and Fabbiani's (13th) — Die Jungfrau von Belleville serving on all those occasions of anxious hope. Franziska Raberg, for her night (14th) depended on Der Zigeunerbaron. On the 15th, for the benefit of Amberg, acts of Die Fledermaus and Der Zigeunerbaron were preceded by Mitterwurzer in Ich werde mir den Major einladen. The Schluss-Concert, on Sunday, May 16th, was to benefit Theater-Agenten Stein and Brunell, and was to include Liederspiel am Hochzeitstag (by Jacobi).

The reader may agree with me in thinking this a dull season. Unending revivals of former productions of operettas gave the keynote for the term. Mitterwurzer (what an unfortunate name for international repute!) brought something of the dignity of tragedy and serious drama into the scheme, and Der Raub der Sabinerinnen and Frau Direktor Striese gave a touch of hilarious comedy in mid-season. Otherwise comic opera held the stage. Doubtless attendants thereon had a good time, but history is slightly bored with the record.

Lexington Avenue Opera House (Terrace Garden), 1885–1886

The years we are now traversing cut to the very centre of amateur acting in New York and Brooklyn; we are not surprised, then, to find overflow of the activity not only in the University Club Theatre but in the Lexington Avenue Opera House. In this last-named refuge, in early October (9th), the Greenwich Amateur Opera Company gave Iolanthe, proudly asserting, in its advertisements, that Sir Arthur Sullivan was expected to be present. Marion Booth was to be Iolanthe and Michael Morton Lord Chancellor. And now, under piloting of the Staats-Zeitung, we learn of a Russian Opera

Company, that gave here, on November 9th, Esther and Haman.   The deluge of Russian music is beginning.   The Russian Opera Company, on January 4, 1886, were to present Abramovitch's opera, Joseph und seine Brüder, a device that sounds Jewish.   The Dauntless Rowing Club was, I dare avouch, native enough, on December 7th, with its "entertainment" — whatever that may have been.

But something very professional, and exquisitely so, came, on December 12th, when, for charity, Young Mrs. Winthrop presented Agnes Booth, Maud Harrison, Annie Russell, Mrs. Whiffen, Frederic Robinson and Walden Ramsay.   Amateurism lurked in the Rival Dramatic Association and its acting, on December 18th, in Byron's Blow for Blow.   And in the offering of December 15th — the Yorick Club, in Withered Leaves and The Man with the White Hat, though on that occasion Lillian Cleves recited and Hortense Pierse sang.   A festival of the Sons of St. George makes January 26th sound romantic, though, so far as I could see, it contributed but little, if anything, to our story.   Though we always think of Terrace Garden as a German fastness, I found there for this season but two German exploits — the Männerchor festivity of February 16th, and that of the Quartett Club, Sängerflug, on March 8th.

Minor German Activities, 1885–1886

Let us be as brief as possible in chronicling German miscellany.   August and September, 1885, and later, call us hither and yon for beer and cool air. Künstler Halle, 167 Chrystie Street, with Grosses Concert und Gesang-Vorträge; Adam Gander's Palast Garten, 139 8th Street and 79 9th Street, inviting with the California Damen Capelle; the Harlem Bridge Garten, 129th Street and Third Avenue, with Annie Schober, Emma Marden and Marie Chlupsa; the Cafe Cosmopolitan, 1½ Second Avenue, with billiards and reading rooms; Café Saxonia, 64 Avenue A; Hamburger Halle, 186 Orchard Street; Deutsche Reich's Hall, Stanton and Eldridge Streets; Deutsches Casino, 14 Stanton Street, with Anna Bennholst, Mary Schmidt, Kittie Rodolphi, and Minnie Stoffer to entertain; Major Sauer's Atalanta Casino, "last station of the Sixth Avenue Railroad," and with Don Ferreyra to whistle like a flute; Bauer's Union Park, 133rd Street and the Boulevard; Elm Park and Löwen Park; Walhalla, 48–52 Orchard Street; the Felsen-keller, Foot of 5th Street and the East River; Germania Garten, 9 Second Avenue; Conrad Stein's Sommer-Garten, 517 West 57th Street, running through to 58th Street; Café Logeling, 239 East 57th Street; the Berliner Music-Halle, 153 Forsyth Street, with, as entertainers in latest October, Mlle. Rosa, der schöne Nicolaus Tyroleans, Martin Puchner, Marie Krause, Jennie Stanton, Billie Seden; Concert Hall Erholung, 13 Rivington Street, also with singers; the Jumbo Concert Halle, 206 Eldridge Street; all these resorts are advertised among the theatrical notices in the autumn Staats-Zeitung, and therefore percolate through these Annals.

The Harlem Bridge Garden seems most germane to our usual line of discourse; there, in early November, were appearing Louise Murio, Marie Schupsa (*sic*) and Daisy Norwood; in late November Dollie Foster, Charles H. Duncan and Marie Chlupsa enlivened the proceedings. We know, of course, that the Concordia Rooms, their glory withered, piped up, occasionally, in newspaper advertising, with neue Kräfte (August 30th). Sometimes a farce, as in former times, would close whatever show there was; Eifersüchtigen, for instance, on May 15th. The season closed on May 29th and 30th.

The Atlantic Garten, 50 Bowery, was always itself. Elsa Alberti, concert singer, was there for many autumn weeks, as well as the "beloved" Damen-Elite Capelle, C. Wolf directing the music of the place. Alvin Jaeger came forward, on November 2nd; Ignatz Conradi, a very movable attraction, was listed in mid-January, along with Theodor Hoch and the Damen-Elite Capelle.

My apprehensive reader need not be told that the Vereine and Männerchöre were busy all winter, too busy for my pen. But I shall cut and curtail to the limit of possibility. The Ausflug of the New York Männerchor to Roton Point, Connecticut, since it hastened away on September 2nd, possibly belongs to the season of 1884–85; perhaps there belongs, also, the concert in Washington Park, on Sunday, September 20th, of the Schule des New Yorker Turn-Vereins. The Germania Assembly Rooms, 291–293 Bowery, advertised two concerts for Sunday, October 4th, and breathlessly opened almost daily for varied functions in October. The Beethoven Männerchor Hall was also much in demand; there joyously gathered, on October 18th, the Rheinischer Sängerbund, all to celebrate its thirty-ninth annual Stiftungsfest; the Bremer Verein held the place on the 25th. The Schleswig-Holsteiner Verein, at Turn-Halle, on the 18th, gave, in its jolly course, Fritz Reuter's three-act Onkel Jacob und Onkel Jochen; on that same busy 18th, the Schützen-Lyra gathered in the Teutonia Rooms; there also November 9th found the Sängerrunde for Stiftungsfest, concert and ball. In my eagerness to attend (in spirit) that gala occasion, I almost forgot to tell the reader that October 25th brought the Bloomingdale Eintracht to these same rooms for a concert in which Minnie Dilthey and Carl Dufft participated. The Beethoven Männerchor Halle opened, on November 8th, for the Sing-Akademie. On November 15th, the twenty-fifth annual Jubilæum of the Kreutzer Quartett Club filled both halls of the Germania Assembly Rooms. The Beethoven Männerchor Hall served the Mainzer Carneval-Verein for its concert, banquet and ball, on November 22nd.

In its own hall, of course, the Beethoven Männer-Chor (*sic*), on November 15th, held a vocal and instrumental concert, with the aid of Minnie Dilthey, Carl Dufft and Max Spicker (director). Three items by Beethoven

[62]

and five by Abt constituted the bill of music. And, still on the 8th, the Mozart Männer-Chor (*sic*) held the Harmony Rooms, Essex Street. On November 22nd, in its own rooms, the Liederkranz gave a concert, with the aid of Rafael Joseffy. November 26th distracted with varied allurements: the Gesangverein Harmonia occupied Turnhalle, with, to assist, Frl. A. M. Britting, Hattie Chapel, W. H. Rieger, George Peters and others, their inducements including the comic operetta, Die Afrikanerin; the Ottersberger Verein was at the Teutonia Assembly Rooms; and the Wagner Harlem Männerchor summoned to the vague north, in Major Sauer's Atalanta Casino. On November 29th, the Germania Assembly Rooms gave two concerts.

The Helvetia Männerchor concert availed itself, on December 5th, of the services of Rosa Müller, Emil Meyer, Fritz Steins and Methfessel; the Teutonia Assembly Rooms housed the swelling joy; the Germania Assembly Rooms, on the 6th, took in the Veteranen Gesang-Verein (*sic*); on the 6th, also, the Schleswig-Holsteiner Verein gathered in Turnhalle. And now for the Carneval-Sitzungen! The Arion Society's, January 9th; those of the Mainzer Carneval-Verein, six in all, in January and early February; that of the Beethoven Männerchor, on January 17th. The Bund Hand in Hand greets us, on January 11th, with a ball in Mentge's Hall, Fourth Avenue and 87th Street; the New Yorker Zither Verein concert and ball was at the Beethoven Männerchor Hall, on the 16th. A Lady Washington Ball was German, on the 18th, at Harmony Hall; the Swiss Grutli Männerchor had a concert, with soloists, on the 23rd, at Beethoven Hall, and the 25th found the Schillerbund dancing in the Germania Assembly Rooms. Far different in kind were two lectures in late January: that of G. Bamburger, Principal of the Workingmen's School, who, at Turnhalle, proposed A School Reform; and that of G. von Hesse Wartegg, in Arion Hall, on Mexico und seine Zukunft. Some persons, less serious, may have preferred the mask ball of the Concordia Mixed Choir, on February 1st, in the Metropolitan Assembly Rooms, 61 East 4th Street. The big mask ball of the Arion Society invaded, on the 8th, the big Academy of Music. But the rival Liederkranz, the evening before, had its second concert with Mrs. Gerrit Smith, Emily Winant, Jacob Graff, Franz Rummel and George Prehn to assist; and its ball, on the 18th, at the Metropolitan Opera House.

Helene Wagner, on February 16th, read, from the Minnesang, the poem of Tannhäuser, engaging for the purpose the "Grosser Saal" of Steinway Hall. But nothing could check the epidemic of mask balls. The Gesang-Verein Harmonia was thus engaged, on February 15th, in the Teutonia Assembly Rooms; the Männerchor, on the 16th, at Terrace Garten; the Beethoven Männerchor, on the 18th; the Veteranen Gesang-Verein (*sic*), on the 25th, in the Germania Assembly Rooms, etc. Meantime, on the 21st, the Verein Concordia and the Verein Schwestern der Freundschaft joined for an evening

[63]

in the Harmony Rooms; on the 22nd, the Arion Quartett Club was in the Germania Assembly Rooms. February 28th tinkled with a zither concert "bei" Jacob Schloeder, 166 First Avenue. Harugari, with Arminia and Wilhelm Tell associates, celebrated its thirty-ninth annual Stiftungsfest, on March 7th, entering Walhalla therefor; the same heavenly refuge, on the 8th, received the Bremer Frauen-Bund, all for a calico ball. We were merry in Kleindeutschland. The Quartett-Club Sängerflug, went, on the 8th, to Terrace Garten.

Reader, what is a "blow-out" nur für Herren? Ask the Arion Society, which had one on March 6th, or the Beethoven Männerchor which held one on the 14th. March 7th opened Wendel's Assembly Rooms, West 44th Street, for the sacred concert and ball of the Quartett-Club Eintracht; Turn-Halle also hospitably welcomed, on the 8th, the twentieth Stiftungsfest, Abendunterhaltung and ball of the New Yorker Uhrmacher-Verein. Well, the Germans apparently love polysyllables and hyphenated delights.

Having thus re-introduced these busy *Vereine* of the distant past, I will now allow them silently to steal out of this chapter; the reader can imagine their Schluss-Concerte, their summer excursions to neighbouring harbours and woods, etc. The calico ball of the Lorelei Loge must, however, detain us, on April 10th, in the Harmony Rooms. The Harmonia concert, on the 11th, in Turnhalle, invited with Anna Britting and Jean Joseph Bott. And I fear we must renew acquaintance, on April 18th, at the Germania Rooms, with the Franz Abt Schüler; that same evening brought the Ulk Quartett Club, to Florence Hall, Second Avenue at 1st Street. Concerts we will not forgo: the third of the Liederkranz (April 18th) with the splendid Lilli Lehmann, Emily Winant, of the opulent voice, Ovide Musin, A. Silbernagel (tenor) and Max Treumann (baritone) — what a treat! also that of the Beethoven Männerchor (April 25th), with Lucy Osborne, Albert Paulet, Carl Dufft, and Max Spicker.

The closing season allows our fancy to waft our German citizens to outings in East Side Sänger Hall, 136 Pitt Street; to Carmansville Park, 155th Street, between Eighth and Ninth Avenues; to Conrad Stein's Sommer Garten, 58th and 59th Streets, between 10th and 11th Avenues; to Löwen Park; to Jacob Blank's Wintergarten, 100 Third Avenue, where, in May, Seppel Thaler and Minnie Lee appeared; to the Empire City Colosseum (formerly Jones Wood); to Fort Lee; to Staten Island; to Adam Geib's Park, 170th Street and Avenue A; to Karl's Park, 148th Street, near Third Avenue; to the Riverview Casino, Avenue B, between 87th and 88th Street; to the Felsenkeller, foot of 57th Street, at the East River; to Brommer's Union Park, 133rd Street and Willis Avenue; to South Beach Pavilion; to Bauer's West Brighton Casino, Coney Island; to Sauer's Atalanta Casino; to the Coney Island Casino; to Dobbins' Schützen Park, 50th Street and Third Avenue; to Rockaway Beach; to the Boulevard Hotel and "Waldchen,"

College Point; to Ridgewood Park; to Wendel's Elm Park; to Lang's Cosmopolitan Park, 169th Street and Tenth Avenue; to the Mikado, 62 Third Avenue; to Bowery Bay Beach; to Sand's Point; to Sulzer's Harlem River Park; to how many other rural retreats heaven alone knows. I ask my reader if he has any recollection of these pleasances of the '80s; if he has, he outwits me.

Having escorted German parties to these heart-warming resorts, I may call attention to the Neuer Volks-Garten, 231–233 Bowery, which, in late July, promised concerts by the Wiener Damen-Orchester, led by Marie Roller; the Geistinger Doppel Quartett vom Thalia Theater also appeared; and Eintritt was frei. George J. Kraus was Eigenthümer. I fear the worst for a future full of news my pen must report.

French Activities, 1885–1886

Except for the appearance of Mme. Judic, the French story for the year under discussion is hardly dramatic in our sense of the word. From the Courrier des Etats-Unis I glean a thin harvest of news.

The Société Belge de Bienfaisance, French by name, if not by nationality, starts the processional, on September 14th, with a *Fête Champêtre*, at Lion Park, with a *tir à cible* and other innocent amusements. L'Orphéon Français and La Lyre joined, on September 26th, in the same park for a "Pique-Nique," somehow amusingly spelled for English eyes. Meantime, 117 Bleecker Street advertised regularly its *Concert des Familles*, Pizzarello and his company figuring on September 12th; and Gaieté Gauloise, *"ancien Cercle des Familles,"* in West Houston Street, was likewise active in October. Heavier artillery was fired on November 8th, when, at Irving Hall, the concert and ball of L'Espérance enlisted Anna Trischet, C. Lyon and Andureau. November 21st found the Bataillon and Club des Grenadiers Rochambeau engaging Tammany Hall for a *"bal avec parade militaire,"* very stirring, no doubt. And the Gaieté Gauloise and 117 Bleecker Street still summoned in November and December. Louis Pizzarello was featured "Au Boeuf à la Mode" during those same dun days of the dying year. Tammany Hall opened, on December 13th, for a concert of l'Orphéon Français. At Everett Hall, on December 20th, the Société Israélite Française held a ball, and, on the 27th, the Société La Renaissance advertised in the Courrier a forthcoming Tour du Monde to be accomplished in eighty minutes. Lyric Hall, 21 South Fifth Avenue, was to house the feat, but *when?* And on December 31st, the New Year gift of the Société des Familles, at 117 Bleecker Street, was to include M. and Mme. Olivero, M. and Mme. Manoel, and Eugène, whom we may meet again before spring calls us to the open.

The Gaieté Gauloise was lavish in promise for January 2, 1886 — the Treizième Concert de Famille and a *"Tombola à la Fin de la Soirée."*

[65]

The Chimney Corner, which sounds English, though the Courrier advertises it as at "57 Ouest 25e Rue," promised, for January 1st, 2nd and 3rd, a concert with the much engaged and possibly engaging Louis Pizzarello. And — to end this phase of our subject — we learn, in January, that Joseph Marion was president of the Société des Familles, at 117 Bleecker Street, and that, on glad occasions, one found there a *"Grande Soirée musicale et chantante avec scènettes et nouveaux duos, suivie de bal. Entrée gratuite."*

And now we plunge madly into the season of the *"bal d'invitation, paré et masqué."* La Sincérité starts us on the dance, with its fortieth anniversary, on January 9th, at Irving Hall. The 11th found L'Amitié in the large spaces of the Academy of Music and Nilsson Hall; these same roomy quarters opened, on the 18th, for the ball of the Cercle Français de l'Harmonie, this latter event employing an orchestra under the ubiquitous Max Schwab, as well as Cappa's Military Band. The Tribe Huron, No. 35, of the Red Men, danced, on January 16th, at Tammany Hall; and at Irving Hall, on January 23rd, the Idaho Tribe, No. 36, did the same thing in devoted zeal. These events were, possibly, of a certain magnitude; but now, into this imposing January schedule creeps, perhaps with mouse-like timorousness, the *"Grand Bal à Grand Orchestre donné par la Société Philharmonique Latine"* — twelve musicians under direction of M. Codeluppi (*sic*). Fifteen cents admitted one, on January 10th, to 21 South Fifth Avenue, where the function passed into history. Very different from the twentieth annual ball of Cuisiniers — the French Cooks' Ball — launched, on February 2nd, at the Metropolitan Opera House, with *"Billet pour Cavalier et Dames"* fixed at five dollars! But there was a *"Grande Exposition Culinaire"* thrown in *gratis* (I suppose).

The Prospect Association evidently felt the need of much room for their prospecting on February 4th, and hired the Academy of Music, Tammany and Nilsson Halls, and engaged six orchestras to keep gaiety afloat (or should I say afoot?). La Concorde, on the 20th, confined its joy to the moderate spaces of Ferrero's Assembly Rooms, Tammany Hall. A cessation in dancing allows me to remind the reader of the continuing activities of the Gaieté Gauloise, and, of a concert, on January 21st, at Lyric Hall, South Fifth Avenue, by Louis Pizzarello and his troupe. On January 24th, the Société La Joyeuse, held its first *"soirée dansante"* in that same Lyric Hall. And, on February 6th, the Société Tessinoise de Secours Mutuel held a ball at the Teutonia Assembly Rooms. The Société des Familles, at Lyric Hall, on January 27th, held forth with Eugène Reval (*"comique excentrique de la Scala, Paris,"* evidently the beneficiary), M. and Mme. Olivero, M. and Mme. Manoel and M. Marion. And, on February 6th, a Pizzarello concert and ball employed the Oliveros and the Manoels, the last two, for the last time, in the one-act operetta, L'Amour et l'Appétit. I end the paragraph with note of the "conférences," at the University Club Theatre, of

[66]

Mme. Henry Greville, in French (evening of February 5th, afternoon of the 9th, and afternoon of the 16th) and in English (afternoon of the 12th). These talks were largely devoted to a glorification of Russian life.

By mid-February Pizzarello had gone to Theiss's New Alhambra Hall in 14th Street. The Gaîté (*sic*) Gauloise moved to Lyric Hall, in South Fifth Avenue, enlisting to their service M. and Mme. Manoel. But their deserted quarters, at 123 West Houston Street, were now occupied by La Renaissance "par des Fondateurs de la Gaîté Gauloise," with *"soirées musicales, chanteuses et dansantes, comme par le passé"* — all this on the word of Leon Berger, Président. Bleecker Street (117) still blandly advertised its Société des Familles. And Eugène Reval and les frères Plouviero made glad March visitors to 21 South Fifth Avenue.

Rather weary of this small fry, I hurry to the balls of March; for $2 a "monsieur et dames" could dance to Max Schwab's orchestra, on March 6th, at Fererro's Rooms, Tammany Hall, the occasion being the ninth *"grand bal paré et masqué,"* of the Association du Mardi-Gras. "Vive la Commune!" shouted the providers of the dance and concert, at the Germania Assembly Rooms, on March 21st, to celebrate the fifteenth anniversary of the Revolution of March 18, 1871. I am now forced back upon mere miscellany. La Superbe Cascade, 130 West 26th Street, F. Maurer, proprietor, showered (March 21st) the blessing of les Frères Thorino, "clowns et mimiques." For March 27th and 28th, 21 South Fifth Avenue promised for its "concert de famille" Eugène Reval, F. Lebrun (baritone), Papot (monologist) and Mme. C. Delavigne. For a large part of March Mme. Judic had been playing at the Star Theatre. And the American Opera Company, at the Academy of Music, had sung Lakmé, with Les Noces de Jeannette to follow in April.

The bill for April 4th, of the Renaissance, 123 West Houston Street, promised M. and Mme. Manoel (in M. Bloison), Le Mandarin (*bouffonnerie chinoise*), Sur les Bords de l'Ohio and Un Ménage d'Auvergnats. On April 10th, Mme. Henry Greville lectured, at the University Club Theatre, on Tourgeneff and Tolstoi; on the 15th, on La Vie Parisienne. La Lyrique, which the reader may identify, held the South Fifth Avenue Lyric Hall, on April 11th, with Mme. C. Delavigne, Reval, and Jacques Papot. The French are preparing to leave our Annals for 1885–86. A concert and ball of the Union des Sociétés Françaises on April 25th, at Ferrero's, Tammany Hall, cannot detain me; and, I fear, I shall not find it convenient to attend, on May 16th, at Irving Hall, the concert of Maurice Sallard and Pizzarello, even though the inducements are l'Orphéon Français, Ada Melrose, Nand'l Hofer, Conradi, Eschert and Ella Raimé. Lyric Hall, 21 South Fifth Avenue, a regular chameleon of a place, becomes in later May, a Grand Alcazar d'Été, with promise of a *"grand jardin couvert en cas de pluie."* La Société des Familles, 117 Bleecker Street, and the Renaissance, West Houston Street (this closing for the season on June 6th, with a benefit to G. Bosejour) — these minor activities may close for us the indoor amusements (French) of 1885–86.

But the great outdoors may for a moment hold our enthusiastic pen. The Société Française de Bienfaisance went, on June 17th, to Lion Park, 110th Street and Ninth Avenue, for the customary *tombola, jeux divers, illuminations* and a *grand bal*. And the interesting Pizzarello was disporting, on June 20th, at the Baby Elephant Hall, Surf Avenue, Coney Island. On July 14th the Union des Sociétés Françaises de New York held, at Jones Wood, a Fête Nationale de la République Française, with *jeux divers, tir,* a *grand bal de nuit,* orchestra of L. Conterno, *feu d'artifice* and *retraite aux flambeaux;* and all, mind you, for 25 cents admission. The Société Belge de Bienfaisance, which began for us the French chronicle for 1885–86, shall end it, with a *"fête champêtre,"* on August 16th, at Lion Park.

Italian Activities, 1885–1886

The faithful Eco d'Italia garners for the autumn of 1885, a rather plentiful harvest of Italo-American delight. I should, if I had found it in time, have recorded for the summer of that year the *Ottava Festa Campestre* of the Società di Sant'Antonio, held, on July 4th, at Union Park, 133rd Street, with L. Conterno directing the music. At the same park, on July 22nd, the tenth *Festa Campestre Annuale ("Pic-Nic")* of the Società Italiana Firenze di Mutuo Soccorso also employed the services of the frequently engaged Conterno. On August 4th, the Italian Rifle Guard di Mutuo Soccorso shot into, and for ought I know, shot in Wendel's Elm Park. Though my scheme does not force me to journey to Newark, I will, from international comity, accompany, in imagination, the Società Italiana Cavour di Newark, in its outing, on August 10th, in Voight Union Park of that neighbouring city.

We make, on September 14th, a renewed entry into foreign festivities. On that day we might have chosen, again in imagination, to attend the second annual excursion of the Società Italiana di M. S. di Brooklyn, in Schützen-Park, 50th Street and Third Avenue. A *Festa Campestre,* with *Banchetto e Ballo, "data dalla Società Patriottica Liberale Ticinese di New York"* caused participants, on September 20th, to ferry to Villa Castel, Grant City, Staten Island. Some might have preferred to escape the dangers of water-travel by waiting till the next day (September 21st), when a *Grande Festa Nazionale sotto gli auspici delle Società Unite di* New York, Brooklyn, Hoboken and Newark, held in Union Park, 133rd Street, necessitated merely travel by the still novel Elevated Railroad. Venturing to this sylvan retreat, one could have enjoyed *tiro al bersaglio, tombola,* and other harmless amusements, and might have wondered at the *Giuochi di Prestigio* of Professor Antonio Poletti, every one of whose *Giuochi* is listed in the advertisement of the Eco.

Personally, I feel it a relief to run to cover from the chill blasts of October. It is, therefore, a pleasure to invite the reader to Steinway Hall, on November 8th, when the Italian Societies of New York, Brooklyn, Newark and Hoboken gave (I must reproduce the solemn Italian) a *"Gran Concerto Serale a beneficio dei Colerosi di Palermo, sotto il Patroanio del Signor Conte di Foresta e del Comm. G. B. Raffo."* I wonder if the receipts lived up to that grandiloquence? But the dance led us from sad thoughts of the "colerosi." I do not know that zeal saltatory would have led us, on December 12th, to wander vaguely in search of Odd Fellows Hall, Hoboken, where the Società Unione e Fratellanza Italiana di Hoboken was featly to dance the merry hours away, but, on the 19th, we might have gone to Irving Hall, for the eleventh *Gran Ballo Mascherato della* Società Italiana Firenze di M. S. On the same 19th, the Germania Assembly Rooms took in the fourth annual ball of the Italian Rifle Guard, with Professor Davis directing the music. I cannot quite decide whether the admission fee, to this last pleasure, of 25 soldi sounds cheaper or dearer than 25 cents.

Shortage of files of the Eco, in the New York Public Library, now forces me, for 1886, to the Progresso Italo-Americano, a paper still (1941) in publication. I glean nothing from it for January, and the harvest for February is not rich. A concert at the Florence House (the Firenze, 65 West Houston Street?) begins for us, on the 4th, the journey through that chilly month; in that offering were listed Ella di Carlo, Mme. di Carlo, Marzo, Rotoli and Ferranti. On the 6th, at the Teutonia Assembly Rooms, the Società Ticinese di Mutuo Soccorso held its sixteenth *"ballo annuale"* — admission, *"per un signore e piu dame,"* cheap enough at one dollar; L. Conterno directed the music. On Sunday, February 7th, at the Germania Assembly Rooms, the Circolo Filodrammatico Italo-Americano gave a *"Grande Rappresentazione a beneficio del fondo sociale."* The plays included I Timidi (*commedia in uno atto*), I due Sordi (familiar to us in French) and Rival Tenants. In addition we were promised *"meraviglosi Giuochi di Prestigio"* by "Professor" Edoardo Lopez. A ball, with music by L. Conterno, ended the glad evening (or perhaps began the next morning).

March will keep us on the run, polishing our Italian as we go. For the sake of Figaro we will begin, on the 4th, at Tammany Hall, where, with music by C. Sanna, the Società Italiana di Barbieri held its first *"Gran Ballo Annuale."* Drama again raised its head on March 14th, when, in the Germania Assembly Rooms, the Circolo Filodrammatico Italo-Americano presented Bog Jargal, o la Rivolta degli Schiavi di San Domingo (a play in a prologue and five acts). After songs by interested parties, we had a farce, Il Campanello del Spoziele. L. Conterno, as usual, directed the music, and 50 cents admitted to all. But I fear this may have paled before

the *"Primo Gran Ballo Annuale delle Società Militari Unite,"* Vittorio
Emanuele II and Umberto I, held, on March 15th, in Irving Hall; certainly
before the twelfth *Gran Ballo Annuale* of the Legione Giuseppe Garibaldi,
on March 19th, at Irving Hall. Listen to the promises of this last: *"La
musica di 36 scelti professori sara diretta dal Capo Banda della Legione
Professor Paolo de Fina";* and *"Biglietto d'ingresso incluso l'Hat Check
(I love this), $2, ed ammette un signore e dame."* And the eighteenth
"Gran Ballo Annuale" of the Associazione Italiana del Tiro al Bersaglio e
Mutuo Soccorso (Guardia Colombo), on March 27th, sets our memories
working backward through the years in which we have been attending those
balls (eighteen, is it, or did we miss some of them?)! This one advertised
"Gran Tombola e magnifici Premi." The dancing would begin at nine
o'clock, and the institutional Luigi Conterno would direct the music therefor. For April only the 11th showers a blessing on our parched souls, and
that, I am pleased to say, is very germane to our subject. On that date the
active Circolo Filodrammatico Italo-Americano presented, at the Germania
Assembly Rooms, Il Fratello d'Armi, a drama in four acts, in verse, by Cav.
G. Giacosa. Then, after a declamation by some person unspecified in the
advertisement, we were faced with the incongruity of the negro sketch, The
Coal-Heaver's Revenge. Of course L. Conterno directed the music; 50
cents admitted, with 25 cents extra for *"sedie riservate."*

A festival *"in occasione dell'anniversario dell'entrata di Garibaldi in
Palermo"* was carried through, on May 24th, at Union Park, 133rd Street
and East River. A *Gran Tiro al Bersaglio con Premi* was inevitable; *"rap-
presentazioni del Circolo Filodrammatico Italo-Americano,"* also figured in
the proceedings. I am a bit puzzled by the promise that *"la Bandiera Nazionale offerta dalle signore Italiane verrà presentata alla Società in questa
occasione"*— puzzled because the notice does not make clear to me what
"società" received the "bandiera." In any case, Sanna directed the music.
At Tammany Hall, on May 29th, a *"Grande Torneo"* was to be staged between "Professor" R. Senac (*"la spada Americana"*) and Enrico Casella (*"la
spada Italiana"*). And G. De Grandi was to direct the music. The eleventh
annual *Festa* (Pic-Nic) of the Società Italiana di M. S. Firenze, was held,
on May 31st, at Kroebl's Hudson County Park, *"vicino alla Funiculare,
Hoboken."* L. Conterno and a *Tiro al Bersaglio publice* and an admission
of 25 cents were jumbled promiscuously in the advertisements.

We tread familiar, not to say sacred ground, on June 7th, at the Empire
City Colosseum, Jones Wood, when came the nineteenth *"Pic-Nic per la
Celebrazione dello Statuto, sotto gli auspici della Guardia Colombo"* — certainly a function we have often noted in the years preceding. June 15th
carries us to the now accustomed haunt, the Union Park, 133rd Street, there
to enjoy the *Prima Festa Annuale (Pic-Nic)* of the Società Militari Unite
Vittorio Emanuele II and Umberto I; and let us not overlook the important

fact that Sanna supervised the music. The Pic-Nic of the Società Mazzini di Mutuo Soccorso went to Elm Park, on June 22nd, there to enjoy the music of Luigi Conterno. Almost portentous in gravity of annunciation was *"il Primo Gran Pic-Nic Annuale della Società Militare Sant'Arsenio Italo-Americano di Mutuo Soccorso in New York,"* on July 19th, *"all' Union Park, 133ma Strada, East River,"* for the benefit of the Ospedale Italiano in New York. *"Gran tiro al bersaglio e gran tombola con premi di valore"* must have aroused the most lethargic. The Italian Rifle Guard di Mutuo Soccorso held, in this same Union Park, on August 7th, its *"Quinto Annuale Pic-Nic,"* with Luigi Conterno providing sweet strains of music.

Again I take the weary traveller to Newark, there to enjoy the *Gran Pic-Nic delle Società Unite Cavour e Fratellanza di Newark,* at Caledonian Park; this affair, on August 16th — of course with L. Conterno's music — was to provide funds for a statue of Cristoforo Colombo. The twelfth Pic-Nic of the Legione Giuseppe Garibaldi was to commemorate, on September 7th, the anniversary of the entrance of Garibaldi into Naples; Jones Wood Colosseum was deemed none too large to hold this Italian joy. With the "Gran Pic-Nic dato dai Gruppi dell' Associazione Internazionale dei Lavoratori," given on September 18th, in Held's Schützen Park, Astoria, Long Island, "a benefizio dei Prigioneri Politici," I leave the Italian activities in New York for 1885–86. *Tiro al bersaglio con premi,* and a *"gran ballo"* were part of the serious purpose of these "lavoratori" of the days before the almost universal "strikes" of 1941. In commemorating these activities of Italian-Americans, we must not forget that Tommaso Salvini was holding aloft, in that season here, the loftiest standards of Italian dramatic art.

METROPOLITAN OPERA HOUSE, 1885–1886

Wagner and German opera were to be strongly entrenched at the Metropolitan for a second flourishing season which drove Mapleson and his cohorts decisively from the Italian field at the Academy of Music.

Before that catastrophic defeat, however, the big new opera house was devoted to another Italian venture, a return engagement of the incomparable Tommaso Salvini, who began, on October 26th, a three-weeks visit, in his inevitable opening rôle of Othello, assisted, as usual of late, by an English-speaking cast, including Frank Little as Roderigo, W. A. Whitecar as Cassio, John A. Lane as Iago, Viola Allen as Desdemona and Augusta Foster as Emilia, a rather weak support for a star in any language apparently, says the Herald, "engaged to resist rather than support him." Othello was repeated on October 31st (matinée) and November 4th and 7th (matinée). On October 28th, Salvini gave King Lear, with Lane as Kent, A. Salvini as Edgar and Miss Allen as Cordelia. "The rest of the cast hardly tolerable," declares the Herald. Ingomar lightened the burden on November

2nd and 6th. The mighty Italian, on October 30th and November 9th, was overwhelming as The Gladiator (with Miss Allen as Neodamia, and A. Salvini as Flavian); and, on November 11th, 13th and matinée, 14th, he for the first times here gave Coriolanus, with the unconvincing support of actors already cited. The reader can imagine the compelling grandeur of Salvini's rebellious Roman; the reader also conjectures that Miss Allen was Virgilia, Mrs. Foster Volumnia, and Alexander Salvini Aufidius (his English not good).

And here at last are the serious Germans with their serious opera. Walter Damrosch, young and enthusiastic, who, at the time of his father's death in February last, had leaped into the saddle and finished the year's work laid out by that departed spirit, now had an important part in the arrangements for 1885–1886. Since Edmund Stanton, the manager for the Metropolitan stockholders, could not go abroad for artists, young Damrosch was delegated for that delicate service, and secured, on the whole, a good company; he prides himself, very justly, on four new artists he brought to America for that important season — Lilli Lehmann (of the Berlin opera), Emil Fischer, the eminent basso (from Dresden), Max Alvary, a poor vocalist, but a very handsome young tenor (from Berlin) and the great conductor, Anton Seidl, schooled in the Baireuth tradition and one of the most accomplished and magnetic leaders ever heard in America. The fame of those four musicians is still known to all except the most careless; their influence on the development of musical taste in this country cannot be over-estimated. Except for Alvary, they were artistic giants, and he was, later, the handsomest young Siegfried ever heard in New York.

The season opened, on November 23, 1885, with Seidl giving an inspiring orchestral rendering of Lohengrin, sung by Albert Stritt (a new tenor, not very good, but passable), Fischer, Alexy (the Herald) and (from last year's company) Auguste Seidl-Kraus (wife of the great new conductor), Marianne Brandt and Adolf Robinson (a fine baritone, as Telramund). I heard this performance, but had no idea that I was assisting at an historic occasion — the début in America of two men of great fame here from that season forward, Anton Seidl and Emil Fischer. Educated in the school of *bel canto*, I found the singing of Stritt, Frau Kraus and even Frl. Brandt strident and unpleasing; I had no further desire to go to the Metropolitan, but since early December ensnared me in a long illness, I had no opportunity, thereafter, in early 1886, to attend operas that I believe I should, under better health conditions, have essayed. On Wednesday, November 25th, and at the matinée, on the 28th, Lilli Lehmann made her first appearance in America, in an astonishing rôle for such a singer — Carmen, no less, which Minnie Hauk had made her own, and in which she had but shortly before appeared at the Academy. It was announced that Lehmann had sung the part fifty times in Berlin. In viewing this astonishing début-choice of Frl. Lehmann, we must remember that she was known in Germany as a coloratura soprano (she had been the Forest Bird, in the first Siegfried, at Baireuth) and never sang Isolde or any of the Brünnhildes till she did so in her glorious career at the Metropolitan.   I was interested in the account of her début, in the Herald of November 26th: She "won an unqualified triumph.   Her voice is of phenomenal range . . . of smooth and even quality throughout, of extreme brilliancy in the upper register and full of warm, sensuous color. No other songstress combines the excellence of the Italian method with the earnestness and sincerity of the German school as does Frl. Lehmann.   The ornate passages of the two arias in the first act were given with delightful ease and fluency, and as the music progressed and grew more dramatic the artiste sang with a strength and splendor no other singer here has ever given it.   Dramatically her Carmen differs in every respect from that of Miss Hauk.   She is full of repose, never skipping or prancing about the stage or flouncing her skirts. . . . Before the first act was over the judicious and groundlings alike agreed that a superb singer and an excellent and unconventional actress had come to the Metropolitan Opera House."   Alvary was "the handsomest Don José that has ever been seen here, but his singing was very unequal . . . at times he sang woefully flat."   Frau Kraus the Herald thought "the best Micaela since Mme. Valleria."   And Seidl led impressively.   Carrie Goldsticker, an American of operatic experience in Germany, was Mercedes.   Lehmler, Kemlitz and Frl. Slach also sang.   Lehmann did not again sing Carmen in this city.   On Friday, November 27th, Eloi Sylva, a tenor from Russia, was John of Leyden, in Der Prophet, of course with Frl. Brandt as Fides, with Frau Kraus as a poor Bertha, Alexi as Oberthal, and Kemlitz, Kaufmann and Lehmler as the Anabaptists.

On November 30th, Lilli Lehmann for the first time in her life sang Brünnhilde, in Die Walküre, with Stritt as an unsatisfactory, weak-voiced Siegmund, Seidl-Kraus overweighted, according to the Herald, as Sieglinde, Frl. Brandt as a superb Fricka, Fischer, in bad voice, as Wotan, a part in which to this day (1941) he stands unrivalled in memory, and Lehmler as Hunding.   Lehmann's voice, if it lacked the clarion call of Materna's, "glorified the music" as Krehbiel (Chapters of Opera) declares.   The cries of Act II "were fairly brimming with eager, happy vitality.   The noble dignity" of her scene with Siegmund, was "transformed into a sympathetic woman" as the scene progressed.   Walter Damrosch, who led the orchestra, was declared by the Herald to be too inexperienced for the task.   At later performances Seidl succeeded him.   On December 2nd and 4th, the Metropolitan produced Goldmark's Die Königin von Saba, a success of at least ten years in Vienna and elsewhere in Europe, and which enjoyed, during 1885–86 at the Metropolitan, the astonishing record of fifteen performances.   Lilli Lehmann won chief honours in the pretty part of Sulamith, though Frau Krämer-Wiedl, a large woman and an artist not so great as her avoirdupois would lead one to expect, did well enough as the Queen. Frl. Brandt, true artist, essayed the small part of Astaroth. Others were Stritt as Assad, Fischer as the High Priest, Robinson as Solomon, and Alexi (*sic*) as Baal. Extraordinary spectacle helped materially, in the success, and New York opera-goers had never seen anything to match the excitement of the sand-storm in the desert. Repetitions filled further nights till the company, to our surprise, stopped the New York season, to give two weeks to Philadel-phia. These repetitions were Die Walküre (matinée, December 5th); The Queen of Sheba (7th, 12th, matinée, 14th and 16th); Der Prophet, greatly improved, with Lehmann as Bertha (9th); and (11th) a repetition from last year, at least, Tannhäuser, with Sylva, Robinson, Fischer, Alvary (Walther), Lehmler (Biterolf), Kemlitz (Heinrich), Frau Kraus, Anna Slach (Venus) and Ida Klein (Shepherd). December 18th brought another Lohengrin, and the 19th, the last day of the "preliminary season," another matinée of the all-conquering Queen of Sheba. In this opera, on December 16th, Frl. Brandt resigned her small rôle to Miss Goldsticker. On the 7th, "she sang her small scene with a tremolo that was positively painful," says the Herald. On the 7th, Frau Kraus temporarily replaced Lehmann, "weaken-ing the cast materially," says the Herald critic, and at about this time Staudigl was Solomon.

I avail myself of the fortnight's absence of the company to state that the concerts of the Oratorio and Symphony Societies, under Walter Damrosch's directing and therefore, naturally, given at the Metropolitan, I have, as usual, discussed each under its own heading, at the end of this chapter. On January 4th, returned from their outing, the singers gave the first perform-ance in this country of Die Meistersinger, a performance for which the orchestras had for years prepared our public. The cast of the opera on that first night included Emil Fischer, unfortunately in poor voice, in the part he has made his own in our operatic history, Hans Sachs, Stritt as Walter (there have been better Walters on that stage), Staudigl as Pogner (and better Pogners there), Lehmler as Kothner, Otto Kemlitz as Beckmesser (the tiresome), Dworsky as Vogelsang, Emil Sänger as Nachtigal, Hoppe as Zorn, Klaus as Eisslinger, Langer as Moser, Doerfler as Hermann Ortel, Weber as Hans Schwartz, Anlauf as Foltz, Krämer as David, Auguste Seidl-Kraus, whose obesity, according to the Herald review, was "beginning to assume alarming proportions," as Eva, and the ever-willing, ever-dependable Frl. Brandt as Magdalena. The Herald assures us that Seidl conducted with magnificent results. Tannhäuser (conducted by Damrosch and with Lehmler succeeding Fischer, indisposed), on the 6th, and Die Meistersinger on the 8th, filled the other evenings of the week. The Queen of Sheba was splendidly dressed for the matinée, on the 9th. Die Meistersinger (11th and matinée, 16th), Die Walküre, now conducted by Seidl (13th) and the everlasting Queen of Sheba (15th) made a comfortable week for

FRAU KRÄMER-WIEDL

FRAU SEIDL-KRAUS
AND EMIL FISCHER
(DIE MEISTERSINGER)

MITTERWURZER

ALBERT STRITT
(LOHENGRIN)

LILLI LEHMANN
(BRÜNNHILDE)

EMIL FISCHER
(WOTAN)

ANTON SEIDL

MAX ALVARY

ELOI SYLVA

all concerned. The following nights repeated Lohengrin (18th), Queen of Sheba (22nd) and Der Prophet (matinée, 23rd). On the evening of the 20th, Faust, injudiciously cast, presented Lehmann as Gretchen (not one of her best parts), Stritt, Robinson, Fischer, Frl. Brandt (Siebel, and terribly miscast) and Carrie Goldsticker (Martha). This assignment effaced no memories of Nilsson, Scalchi, Campanini, Novara and Del Puente, who had opened the Metropolitan, on October 22, 1883, with this very opera.

Let us hurry to the end, with Faust (January 25th, 30th — matinée — and February 1st, and with Anna Slach replacing Frl. Brandt), Queen of Sheba (27th), Die Meistersinger (29th, February 3rd, and matinée, 6th), and Rienzi (February 5th), with Sylva as Rienzi, Frl. Lehmann as Irene, Fischer as Steffano, Frl. Brandt as Adriano, Robinson as Paolo Orsini, Lehmler as Raimondo, Kemlitz and Sänger as Roman Citizens, and Ida Klein as the Messenger of Peace. The management had promised, for that season, Die Götterdämmerung, and Rienzi is the Wagner they gave us instead! They repeated it, on February 8th and 10th, with Tannhäuser (with Kraemer-Wiedl succeeding Frau Kraus), on the 12th, and Lohengrin again for the matinée, on the 13th, and still again on the evening of the 19th. The Queen of Sheba again held court on the 24th, and (matinée) on March 6th. What a hit! Rienzi figured and postured, February 17th, 20th (matinée), 27th (matinée) and March 1st. Lohengrin sailed in and out, on February 19th, and Die Meistersinger, evidently no such success as had been The Queen of Sheba, wrangled on the 22nd. On the 26th, Faust again held forth in German style. On March 3rd, Lehmann was Venus, in Tannhäuser, thereafter one of her most popular rôles; on March 5th Die Walküre had its last performance. The Herald of February 24th throws strong light on the "extra" chorus of the opera. They were paid in tickets for performances and "struck" because enough tickets were not forthcoming!

This ended the opera season, leaving me wondering why, in a time alleged to have been devoted to Wagner and the new cult, Die Walküre and Die Meistersinger, not to mention the earlier Wagner operas, had, each, so few performances, compared with the never-ending repetitions of the ephemeral Queen of Sheba. With this disturbing thought which seems to require re-writing of the histories, I pass to the balls that danced out the wintry nights at the Metropolitan: the Dixey ball (January 7th); that of the Veteran Firemen's Association (January 12th); that of the Palestine Commandery, No. 18, K. T. (January 14th); the annually awaited fashionable Charity Ball (19th); the Old Guard Ball (21st); the Patriarch's Ball (26th); the French Cooks' Ball (February 2nd); Union Boat Club (February 9th); the Purim Association Charity Ball (11th); the Liederkranz Ball (18th); that of the Sparkling Coterie (March 8th); and possibly others that escaped

[75]

me. Eagerly I return to concerts. On February 23rd, a testimonial to Emma C. Thursby promised assistance from Sylva, Staudigl, Richard Hoffman and Walter Damrosch and orchestra. Two nights later (February 25th) came a concert for the Baireuth Fund, and, on the 27th, one for the benefit of the opera chorus. In the former, appeared Seidl, Walter and Frank Damrosch, Lehmann, Kraus, Brandt, Stritt, and an orchestra of 114 from the Metropolitan, Philharmonic and Symphony orchestras, playing the Good Friday Spell, the Funeral March from Die Götterdämmerung, etc.; Lehmann sang the Liebestod, which no one since her time has ever sung so superbly, and she, also, with Kraus and Brandt, gave the trio of the Rhine Maidens. For the benefit of the chorus, on the 27th, we had Sylva, Fischer, Alvary, Seidl, and a performance of Max Bruch's Fair Ellen, with Lehmann, Robinson and chorus. A "monster" concert, on March 2nd, for the German Polyklinik, promised Lilli Lehmann, Fischer (he did not appear), Stritt, Frl. Brandt, Robinson, Charlotte Walker (sic), W. H. Fessenden, Alonzo Stoddard, Helen Campbell, Lillian Russell (she was at least advertised), F. Rummel, Michael Banner, the Arion Society and (to tinkle down lightly) the New York Zither Club. Heinrich Conried was organiser. On April 12th, the American Opera Company, then struggling for permanency at the Academy of Music, came to the rival establishment with (in aid of the Masonic Hall) a performance of Lohengrin. On April 26th, John Stetson began a fortnight of The Mikado, with a huge orchestra, with a big spectacular setting, and with Mary Beebe, Marie Stone and Marie Cerbi, Alice Carle, George Olmi, Brocolini, J. W. Herbert, Stanton, and a chorus of 200 selected from twelve Mikado companies. This excitement, after a brief run, closed the Metropolitan for 1885–86.

ACADEMY OF MUSIC (NEW YORK), 1885–1886

The fading glory of the famous Academy of Music finally died out in the year we are reviewing. Fashion now patronised the Metropolitan; the newly rich who had built that house, because, it was said, they could not hire boxes at the Academy, now had the proud satisfaction of renting boxes to the very aristocrats who had excluded them from the enchanted circles at the older temple of song.

Mapleson, who had revived Italian opera in New York and had restored Adelina Patti in New York's delighted admiration, came back, in 1885, with that singer and that opera which had helped to establish him in 1878–79. Carmen, on November 2nd, opened his season, with Minnie Hauk (her first appearance in three years) and Del Puente in the parts they had made their own; Mlle. Dotti, whom we could not escape, sang Micaela, Ravelli, always a delightful singer, was Don José, Cherubini was Zuniga, Caracciolo Il Dancairo, Rinaldini Il Remendado, and Mlle. Bauermeister, later a mainstay of minor rôles in opera, and the respected Mme. Lablache were Frasquita and Mercedes. Surely that was, except for Mlle. Dotti, a worthy cast; but 1885 was not 1878. In view of recent happenings at the Metropolitan, Mapleson's second offering (November 4th) was antiquated to a degree — the venerable Il Trovatore, with Giannini (as Manrico), the excellent De Anna (as Conte di Luna), Cherubini, Rinaldini and De Vaschetti, Mme. Lablache (as Azucena), Mlle. Bauermeister, and a new Felia Litvinoff (as Leonora). And that is a good cast of the second rank. But Mapleson, to the disgust of his subscribers, was forced to give the same opera on his third night (November 6th); his coloratura importation, Alma Fohström, announced for Lucia, on that evening, became inconveniently indisposed. At the matinée (November 7th) Carmen again exercised her witchery.

Mlle. Fohström finally sang Lucia on November 9th, with Giannini and De Anna in support. She was a pretty, blonde, slim Norwegian, with a pretty, blonde, slim voice, agile in coloratura, and quite unable to eclipse the memory of Patti and Gerster and Sembrich in the same rôle. Of course, her second rôle (November 13th) was Amina, in La Sonnambula, with the promising support of Ravelli, Del Puente, Mlle. Bauermeister and Mme. Lablache. Between these two familiar manifestations, the pretentious L'Africaine enlisted, on November 11th, Giannini, De Anna, Cherubini, Rinaldini, Vetta, Caracciolo, Mlles. Dotti, Bauermeister and Minnie Hauk. It was repeated for the matinée, on the 14th. Carmen re-emerged on Monday, the 16th. Quite out of the general tune was Robert G. Ingersoll, who, on Sunday, November 15th, discoursed on Myth and Miracle. Canon Farrar, let me anticipate by saying, gave, on Thursday, December 3rd, his Farewell Thoughts on America, a topic that must have appealed to the discouraged Mapleson.

But Mapleson carried on with La Favorita (November 18th) for the début of a useless Mlle. Pervini, assisted by De Falco and De Anna (the last-named winning all the honours). Fra Diavolo was announced for Friday, November 20th, with Ravelli, De Falco, Del Puente, Cherubini, Caracciolo, Mme. Lablache and Mlle. Fohström; and again for November 23rd and 27th. Lucia was the mitigated joy of the matinée on the 21st. The evening of the 21st brought a benefit for Del Puente who, it seems, had suffered financial losses. He sang Don Giovanni, with Ravelli as Ottavio, Cherubini as Leporello, Rinaldini as Massetto, Litvinoff as Anna, Bauermeister (!) as Elvira, and Minnie Hauk as Zerlina, not the best cast ever vouchsafed the immortal work. By this time prices of admission had been reduced to $3 and $2 for seats in boxes, with $2 top in the body of the house.

On November 19th, the Academy stage held a performance — described by the Herald as a "comedy" and very funny in its bad acting — of Romeo and Juliet, with Mlle. Bianca and Alfred Young as the lovers, Mrs. F. (sic

[77]

in the Herald review) G. Jones as the Nurse and Garrett W. Owens as Mercutio. From a note in the Herald, I suspect that the Mrs. Jones was our
old Bowery friend, Mrs. W. G. Jones. I cannot identify the other players.
The last week of the opera (poor Mapleson!) provided Fra Diavolo (November 23rd and 27th), Don Giovanni (25th) and Faust (matinée, 28th,
with Hauk, Giannini, De Anna and Cherubini). This collapse is pitiable.
Mapleson utilised his singers in a Sunday night concert — December 6th.
On December 19th, Mme. Murio-Celli and her pupils, Arditi leading, gave
scenes, in costume, from Faust, Ernani and Il Trovatore, and, on a stage
recently glorified in that opera by Patti and Scalchi, the first and second
acts of Semiramide with Marie Engle and Marie Groebl. Minnie Dilthey,
Florence Conron, Giannini, Lablache and others appeared. On the 21st,
real art came in, with Salvini in The Gladiator — a benefit for the New York
Exchange for Woman's Work; but something less notable was Leonora
Hussey's Leah, the Forsaken, revealed on December 10th. And the in-
domitable Mapleson put up a last fight. On December 19th (matinée) he
staged Maritana, with Ravelli, Del Puente, De Anna, and Mmes. Lablache,
De Vigne and Fohström. Sunday evening (20th) found Hauk, Fohström,
Ravelli, Giannini and Del Puente leading the embattled hosts in a concert.
And, on December 23rd, a benefit for the harassed manager brought the first
performance in New York of Massenet's opera, Manon, with Minnie Hauk,
Giannini and Del Puente in the leading rôles, and with, in smaller parts,
Rinaldini, Cherubini, Foscani, De Vaschetti, Bieletto, Mmes. Bauermeister,
Lablache and De Vigne. Mapleson's company had remained loyally by
his side in months of dire uncertainty. And they now accompanied him
on a tour of the country. The Herald, on December 24th, cruelly states that
Mme. Hauk "feels that her voice is not what it once was, and seems to take
greater delight in the dramatic . . . part of her rôles. Her Manon was
acted with grace, piquancy and strong intelligence, but was sung in tones
that were forced, harsh and unmusical. She would do well, too, to abandon
any embellished passages, for which her voice is now utterly lacking in
flexibility."

American Opera Company, 1886

Before bringing more opera into the Academy, I pause to say that I elsewhere include, each under appropriate headings, the concerts of the Philharmonic Society and Theodore Thomas's series of forty-eight popular
concerts. But I here record Tony Pastor's holiday festivals, on November
26th (Thanksgiving) and December 25th; he brought his company from
next door. And the few remaining balls left here by the all-engrossing
Metropolitan: that of the Elks (January 14th); that of the Cercle Français
de l'Harmonie (18th); that of the Arion (February 8th).

And now I will introduce a venture that promised much for the future.

[78]

HELENE HASTREITER

ALMA FOHSTRÖM

SIGNOR RAVELLI

JESSIE BARTLETT DAVIS
PAULINE L'ALLEMAND

MINNIE HAUK AS MANON

EMMA JUCH
AS EURYDICE

SIGNOR DE ANNA

WILHELM LUDWIG
(FLYING DUTCHMAN)

FRANCESCO GIANNINI

The American Opera Company, organised with Mrs. Jeannette B. Thurber and other enthusiasts as sponsors, and with Theodore Thomas as musical and artistic director, would, it was hoped, bring in, for permanent custom, opera in the vernacular, presented with great orchestral and choral improvements, with beautiful staging, and with artists in complete artistic ensemble, if not of individual brilliancy. Most of these promises were fulfilled for a long first season (January 4th to April 17th), but in no way would the business management seem less astute than in arranging scheduled performances on the same dates as those at the Metropolitan. Thus the very first bill of the new venture was posted for the night of the first hearing in America of Die Meistersinger. I can hardly imagine anything more unfortunate. That opening night (Monday, January 4th) presented for the first time here Goetz's opera, The Taming of the Shrew, with Pauline L'Allemand as Katharine, Kate Bensberg as Bianca, A. E. Stoddard (recently Pish-Tush, in The Mikado) as Hortensio, W. H. Fessenden as Lucentio, W. H. Lee as Petruchio, E. J. O'Mahoney as Grumio and John Howson as the Tailor — a distribution suggestive, in spots, of comic opera. Well, the Goetz work was a kind of comic opera, and no harm would have been done if Pauline L'Allemand, a high, coloratura soprano, had not been slightly miscast as the dark-voiced Shrew. As usual in opera in English, the diction of the singers was declared by the Herald to be indistinct; perhaps it improved in repetition of the opera on the 6th and at the matinée on the 9th. The company met with far greater success, on Friday, January 8th, when it brought out Gluck's Orpheus and Eurydice, for the introduction of a noble contralto, Helene Hastreiter, who made a hit second only to that of Lilli Lehmann at the Metropolitan; Emma Juch was the Eurydice and Minnie Dilthey the Cupid. The management, in this production, justified its boast about staging; it gave a magnificent setting for the work which readily lends itself to such decoration. This novel beauty, with the success of the two leading singers, carried the opera through thirteen performances — certainly a record for a town accustomed to frequent changes and few repetitions in the opera season.

The American company sang frequently in Brooklyn, closing the New York house on such visits — January 11th and 18th for instance. Meanwhile the two operas already produced lasted in New York for a second week — Orpheus (13th and matinée, 16th) and The Shrew (15th). Lohengrin, on the 20th, introduced William Candidus, a tenor once popular in Kleindeutschland, as Lohengrin, with Emma Juch, Mme. Hastreiter, Myron W. Whitney, A. E. Stoddard and E. J. O'Mahoney in parts easily assigned. The production was proudly advertised as costing $30,000. I hope its ten performances resulted in a profit, for the investors. The League of Amateur Dramatic Societies (Brooklyn, New York and Jersey City) revealed, on January 21st, that they were not so good in Saratoga as Daly's actors had been in 1871. Orpheus filled another matinée, on the 23rd, and Lohengrin once more came down the river, on the 25th. On the afternoon of that day, a testimonial to Henry A. Thomas revealed well-known painters and illustrators actually painting, sculping, etc., before enraptured auditors. The Magic Flute, on the 27th, enlisted Pauline L'Allemand as the Queen, Emma Juch as Pamina, Minnie Dilthey as Papagena, Candidus as Tamino, Howson as Monostatos, Stoddard as Speaker of the Temple, Whitney as Sarastro, Hamilton (also from the Standard Mikado) as Papageno, May Fielding (lately at Daly's), Charlotte Walker and Helen Dudley Campbell as the Three Ladies, and Anna Phelps, Charlotte Maginnis and Addie Frank as the Genii. Somehow that cast does not awaken sparks in my imagination; it had only six performances.

I cannot afford space for the dates of the numerous repetitions of this "noble experiment"; I pass, therefore, to Nicolai's tuneful Merry Wives of Windsor, brought out, on February 5th, with Pauline L'Allemand and Jessie Bartlett Davis as the Wives, merry indeed, as it proved, with May Fielding (how odd!) as Anne Page, William Hamilton as Falstaff, Stoddard as Ford, Whitney as Page, Fessenden as Fenton, Howson as Slender, and O'Mahoney as Dr. Caius. This attained to nine performances, one of the higher lights of the season. Repeated on February 10th, 12th, 15th, and 20th (matinée), it granted the stage, for the matinée on the 13th and on the evening of the 19th, to Lohengrin and the interesting swan. Orpheus again went through Hades to the Elysian Fields, on the 17th and the afternoon of the 22nd; on this last holiday the Academy closed for the evening. The Rival Association broke in, on February 25th, with Richard III, for the benefit of the Grant Monument Fund. The last week of February provided, in opera, The Magic Flute (24th), The Merry Wives (26th) and Lohengrin (27th, matinée). The next novelty was Délibes's opera, Lakmé, March 1st, 3rd and 6th (matinée) evidently (judging from its eleven performances) the second ranking success of the season. Pauline L'Allemand had in it opportunity to show how high and brilliantly her voice could soar, and Stoddard had dramatic and vocal opportunity as Nilikantha. The young men who caused the woe were Candidus and W. H. Lee. Others in the cast were Charlotte Walker, Helen Dudley Campbell, May Fielding, Jessie Bartlett Davis (Malika), and W. H. Fessenden. W. Hock directed the elaborate spectacle. March 5th restored Orpheus to an admiring public. Lakmé suffered and sang her high notes again on March 8th, 12th, and 13th (matinée), with The Merry Wives intervening, on the 10th. This narrative of ours is becoming very monotonous.

Another venture sailed into the repertoire, on March 17th — The Flying Dutchman, with William Ludwig (first appearance) in the title-rôle, Whitney as Daland, Whitney Mockridge as Erik, Fessenden as the Steersman, Helen Dudley Campbell as Mary, and Helene Hastreiter, oddly enough, as Senta; this was repeated on March 22nd (with Emma Juch as Senta) and at the matinée on the 27th.   Meantime, on the 24th, the last production of the season gave a double bill, Massé's Marriage of Jeannette, with L'Allemand and W. H. Lee, and Délibes's ballet, Sylvia, with Theodora de Gillert as leading danseuse.   On March 21st (Sunday), a benefit to Leonard Grover, in that year of benefits, provided a host of volunteers, including Lilli Lehmann, Pauline Hall and Lillian Russell (what a trio!), Colonel Ingersoll, Jessie Bartlett Davis, M. W. Whitney, Courtice Pounds, Agnes Herndon, George Thorne, Elsie Cameron, Carrie Swain, Letitia Fritch, Harrigan, John A. Mackay, Francis Wilson, Tony Hart, Marshall P. Wilder, Sophie Eyre, Tony Pastor, and others.   What a host!

I love opera, but this season has almost worn me out; fortunately it closed on April 17th, with repetitions of the works already presented.   The Flying Dutchman ended all, at the matinée on the 17th; it had been sung seven times as against five showings of the double bill.   This season was among the most promising in our operatic history.   After all speculation has failed concerning its potentialities, we are left merely with the saddening reflection, If only — !

A benefit to John A. Mackay (I cannot see why he had one) brought promise for the afternoon of April 22nd, of participation by Alice Harrison, Max Freeman, Aimée (she was to do Act II of Divorçons), R. C. Hilliard, Pauline Hall, H. S. Hilliard, Mae St. John, Victoria Schilling, Rosina Vokes ('Is 'Art was True to Poll), Elsie Cameron and George Thorne (these two in The Stage-Struck Lover), Harry Kernell, Vernona Jarbeau, Tony Hart, and Tim Cronin.   The high spice of the performance was a scene from Macbeth, with Henry Dixey as the Thane and Mackay as Lady Macbeth. Funny?   Certainly to a friendly audience.

The most impressive event of the season at the Academy was a joint engagement of the two greatest tragedians then in the country — possibly in the world — Salvini and Booth.   In Othello, on April 26th, they were, of course, Othello and Iago, with Mrs. D. P. Bowers as Emilia, Marie Wainwright as Desdemona, Alexander Salvini as Cassio, Couldock as Brabantio, Barton Hill as the Doge, G. W. Wilson as Roderigo, John A. Lane as Montano.   This was repeated on April 28th and May 1st (matinée).   On Friday, April 30th, Salvini graciously acted the Ghost, to the Hamlet of Booth, still with the support of Mrs. Bowers, Miss Wainwright, Couldock (Polonius), Barton Hill (Claudius), Alexander Salvini (Laertes), Lane (Horatio), and Wilson (Gravedigger).   There was much talk about a bad fall of Booth, in the big scene, on April 28th, with Salvini; the management explained by stating that Booth was ill, and suffered a dizzy spell; the world's wagging tongue attributed the fall to too much drink; in fact, Salvini, in his reminiscences, says the same thing.   Admirers of the tragedian were shocked and grieved; and certain newspapers did much to spread the sad report.

[81]

In 1885–86, it was benefits, benefits all the way and all the time; I admit that the epidemic mystifies me. There must have been much procurable money in sight. The New York Lodge No. 1, B. P. O., Elks, had its benefit-bout, on May 2nd, at the Academy, with advertised volunteers in Elma Delaro, Elsie Cameron, George Thorne, Hilda Thomas, Flora Moore, Federici, F. Billington, Harry Kernell, Jacques Kruger, Will S. Rising and Harry Kennedy. But the audience was small and the programme went awry. May 6th was to enrich the Bartholdi Pedestal Fund through the efforts of an extraordinary group (if they all appeared); Mrs. James Brown Potter, A. P. Burbank, the Venetian Mandolin Quartet, Mme. Roberti, Kyrle Bellew, Burr McIntosh, Helen Dauvray, Fanny Davenport (she was to sing La Marseillaise), Mme. Fursch-Madi, &c. For the Polish Fund, on May 8th, the Chevalier de Kontski presented his opera, The Sultan of Zanzibar, with a cast including Isidora Martinez, Ida Corani, Richard, Vicarino, P. Clech and H. Rykers. From Mapleson and the American Opera Company to this! No wonder the Academy closed for the season! But it opened again on May 23rd, to allow John E. Cannon to see how ardently the public would pay for his benefit, which promised Nat Goodwin, Tony Hart, John A. Mackay, Tim Cronin, James Powers, Marie Salvotti, Elma Delaro, Marion Elmore, Amy Ames, Dora Wiley, Addie Cora Reed, Will Rising, R. E. Graham, Gus Bruno, and George C. Boniface, Jr.

TONY PASTOR'S, 1885–1886

The week of July 6th–11th found Pastor's pretty little theatre under control of Daniel Sully, who then presented Frank Jones and Alice Montague, fresh from "Variety," in Si Perkins, or, the Girl I Left Behind Me. The next week (July 13th–18th) gave us J. H. Farrell's musical farce comedy, Funny Valentines, not much of a valentine and not very funny. The cast included Misses Earle Remington, Lena Cole, Dolly Warren and Kate Ferguson, along with Odell Williams (later a very popular comedian), J. Joseph Fields, W. E. Hines and the author. Julius Volger and Paul Ritter wrote the music. Edward R. Lang's musical comedy, Scheming, had the week of July 20th and three weeks thereafter. On August 10th, Ezra Kendall began in A Pair of Kids, or, Which Is Which? very poor stuff, according to the Herald; yet it lasted for three weeks. On August 31st, R. E. Graham entered as Brother Max, assisted by Lizzie Fletcher, Bella Vivian, William Moore, Baby Wood and Little Aggie. The offering of September 7th propounded Whose Can It Be? leaving the answer to Lillian Lewis, Marie Muloch, Miss Palmo, Richard M. Carroll and his sons, Richard F. and Edwin H. The play itself was part of the Carroll progeny. The Carrolls were funny enough to ask that question through October 3rd. On the 5th, Ella Wesner began, in The Captain of the Queen's Own, a pretty title, in

[82]

which she had the assistance of T. H. Glenney, Will J. Mack, Ed J. Connelly, Richard Lyle, Virginia Ross, Mamie Bernard, Cora Lyle, and Edna Lewis. Things began to look up, at Tony's.

And here, on October 19th, is Tony at Home, with strong support in Three St. Felix Sisters, May Arnott, the American Four (Pettingill, Gale, Daly and Dailey), Mr. and Mrs. Harry Watson ("Dutch"), Hilda Thomas and Sheehan and Coyne (Ashbox Inspectors). The farce was Dunderbock in a Fix, or, Life in a Tenement. October 26th brought in Charles Diamond, Dan Hart, Devlin and Mullaly, the Twilight Quartet, the Four Shamrocks (Conroy, the Dalys and Thompson), William Carroll and Juan A. Caicedo ("high-wire artist"). Of course Tony sat at the head of the table. The Howard Athenæum Specialty Company brought in, on November 9th, a touch of Boston, with Sam Devere, Lina and Vani, Pavallio (*sic*) and Roussillion, Sweeney and Ryland, Sharpley and West, A. W. Filson and Miss Lee Errol, Cronin and Wild, James F. Hoey, and the farce, No Trespassing. For November 23rd were promised the American Four, Frank and Lillian White, the four Schrode Brothers (circus acts) the three St. Felix Sisters, George Murphy (once of Murphy and Shannon), Harry Thorne and Maggie Willet, Mabel Sterling and the De Bar Brothers (human serpents).

Lizzie Evans, on November 30th, began in The Culprit Fay, followed on December 4th by Florette. On December 7th she presented Fogg's Ferry, with herself as Chip, the Ferry Girl, E. R. Marsden as Gerald White, Will D. Ingram as Bruce Rawdon, Henry Scharf as Fogg, the Ferryman, Charles Drake as Judge Norwood, Mamie Tucker as Blanche Norwood, Tillie Shields as Mrs. Fogg, Rose Bradbury as Martha and Steve Corey as Still Bill. Why had Tony's Variety gone astray? George Murphy's Pleasure Party, in Rudolph's Ambition, consisted (December 14th) of William Carroll, Sheehan and Coyne, "Professor" Abt (Grecian mystery), Jennie Bartine, George Reynolds (negro act), Sam Lang and Dollie Sharpe, Toner and Frobel, Wiley Hamilton and J. Arthur Doty. And dolls were given away at the Tuesday and Friday matinées — ominous sign! The specials for December 28th–January 2nd were Lottie Elliott (skipping rope act), the Gilmore Sisters, Charles Raymond (one-legged dancer), E. J. Connelly, Virginia Ross, Smith and Weston ("musical mokes"), Jeppe and Fannie Delano (these two in The Bashful Lover), Sanders and Dean (negro comiques), and the Durell Twin Brothers — all with Tony himself.

With Tony (January 4th–9th) a vast host included Queen Vassar (début in America), Hawkins and Collins (in The Two Doctors), William Carroll (banjo), Frank H. and Lillian White, Harry Morris ("Dutch"), Le Clair and Russell, the Three Gregory Brothers (acrobats), Lillie Western ("greatest of all musical experts"), and Maggie Willet, in The Fool of the Family ("performed by her over 1000 times"). For January 11th we had the American Four, Queen Vassar, Catherine Nelson's trained pigeons, Henriette,

[83]

Charlotte and Clementina St. Felix, George Homer and Georgie Lingard, Thorne and Maggie Willet, Schmidt Brothers and George Murphy ("Dutch"). Tony and his company combined with the Kernell company to the end of a perfect joy (January 18th–23rd); the high lights were Flora Moore, the Sisters Coulson (from England), W. T. Bryant and Lizzie Richmond, the Lamartine Brothers, Harry La Rose, Bryant and Saville, Lillian Markham (balladist), the McShane Brothers (midget acrobats) and the Kernells (in The Half-Way House). January went out (25th–30th) with the Dare Brothers ("greatest bar act in the world"), Mlle. Alberta ("Australian marvel" — a wire-walker), Billy and Alice Payne (musical act), Maud Beverly, Queen Vassar, René (sensation dancer), Jennie and Arthur Dunn, Bingham (ventriloquist and magician), Frazer and Allen, and Harry Morris's travestie, The Dutch Actors.

February began (1st–6th) with Flora Moore, Catherine Nelson, Queen Vassar, Dan Mason and Dan Hart; continued (8th–13th) with Callan, Haley, and Callan, Newcomb and Hassan, the St. Felix Sisters, Frank and Lillian White, Kitty O'Neil, George F. Moore ("the man with 100 faces"), Emma Bretto, Neil Smith's dogs, Harry Thorne, W. H. Melville, Frank White and Maggie Willet (these four in After the Opera Is Over); carried on (15th–20th) with W. Carroll, the Muldoon Quartet, Charles Raymond, Smith and Weston, Morello Brothers (head-balancing), Dick Morosco and Kitty Gardner (in The Schlum Family), Robert Hewlette ("floating wire equilibrist"), Tony, and Harry Thorne and Maggie Willet (in Midnight Marauders); and ended (22nd–27th) with Pastor, Mlle. Attilie, Coulson Sisters, Leroux and Wilton, Powers Brothers, Eva Lester, Leonard and Mullen and W. F. Harbeck — rather a weak conclusion to February's high-swelling tale.

The week of March 1st–6th was lively, with Charles Fostelle (as Mrs. Partington), Mlle. Georgia ("Female Hercules"), Dan Kennedy and Lottie Allen, Lillie Western, George E. Homer and Georgie Lingard, Frank Moran, "Professor" Howell's Dog Circus, Tony Pastor and a comic No Mikado, or, the Japanese Prima Donna. John T. Kelly ("That Man from Galway") John H. Byrnes and Miss Helene, Frank H. and Lillian White, the Three Romalo Brothers, Cuponti (Hindoo juggler), Leopold and Bunnell (sic), Major Burke (lightning drill) and May Arnott's Mystic Cabinet made March 8th–13th agreeable to the audiences; March 15th–20th tried to please with Harry and John Kernell, Bryant and Lizzie Richmond, Queen Vassar, Parker's Dog Circus, Mlle. Nelson's birds, Tim Murphy, the Clipper Quartette, and A Fourteenth Street Flat (with Harry Kernell, W. T. Bryant and Lizzie Richmond) — decidedly an outstanding bill. And very interesting, also, was the offering of March 22nd–27th — Lina and Vani (acrobats), Hilda Thomas, Chevalier Ira Paine ("recently knighted by the King of Portugal"), Mrs. Paine, James F. Hoey, Sam Devere, Sharpley and West ("with their musical cabinet and comic dogs"), Ed H. Sheehan and Ada Hulmes, Sweeney and Ryland, Parillo (*sic*) and Roussillion, and No Trespassing (with Sam Devere and Hilda Thomas).

Assuredly bills brightened as the season waned. The fare for March 29th–April 3rd included Mr. and Mrs. Harry Watson, Marie, Sophie and Joseph Muhleman ("Swiss Song Birds"), William Harbeck ("man serpent"), Charles Raymond ("unipedal [!] dancer"), Harry Thorne and Maggie Willet (in My Mother-in-Law), Mlle. René (dancer), Dan Hart and Nelsoni (Japanese juggler). Harry Sanderson's benefit, on the afternoon of April 8th, promised Lillian Russell, Jennie Yeamans, Elma Delaro, Fred Solomon, Jacques Kruger, John Wild, R. E. Graham, Harry Fisher, A. C. Moreland, Dan Collyer, J. S. Maffit, Robert Fraser and Tim Murphy — verily a glittering host. The week of April 12th–17th provided Tony, Henry Morris, the St. Felix Sisters, the Dare Brothers, Hines and Remington, Leopold and Bunnell (*sic*) and the Tissots; a large group of Shriners attended on the 13th. Harry Kernell and his company took possession, on April 19th, for a week of Harry La Rose, Arthur Johnson, Flora Moore, Queen Vassar, the Coulson Sisters, the three Phanlons (acrobats), John and Nellie Healey and Bryant and Saville, not to forget the farce, The Half-Way House. McIntyre and Heath's Minstrels, a new magnet in those times, came to Pastor's on April 26th, contributing factors including Hi Tom Ward, Delhauer and Geyer, the Barlow Brothers, Harry Earle, Woods and Connor, Harry Armstrong, Dave Christy, F. A. Howard and De Witt and Kerwin.

Variety finally leaving the post, Dan Sully came in, as usual, for a summer season. His imperishable Corner Grocery began on May 3rd and continued to June 12th. On June 14th, the Weston Brothers (Sam and Morris) presented Our Minstrel Boys, with Frank Girard, Percy Meldon (*sic*), Charles Foster, Bella Moore, Annie Wood and Lillie La Verde; no one of these occupies a niche in the hall of fame. Daniel Sully's new play, Daddy Nolan, entered, on June 21st, to achieve four weeks of business. Mrs. Neuville and her son, Augustin, "the boy comedian," possessed the week of July 26th–August 1st, with a double horror, The Boy Tramp, or, the Maniac Mother. This atrocity held the heated stage for a second week, ending on August 7th. Something almost equally unpleasing began on August 16th, The Mikado "by females," including Florence Richards, Maggie Dean, Nannie Roman, Aline Copp, and, surprisingly, Jennie Reiffarth and Clara Thropp. One male participated. And Sully came back, with The Corner Grocery (week of August 23rd–28th) and Daddy Nolan (August 30th–September 4th). On September 6th, George H. Adams showed The Missing Link (by Arden Smith and Edwin Arden, with music by Charles F. Ditmar). There were specialties by Adams, P. Toma Hamilton, Maude White, Frank Gibbons and Pony Seneca. Aaron Woodhull, in Eli Wheatfield, came on September 13th; on the 20th, On the Sahara brought in Alice

Crowther, Hattie Saphore, Nellie Pierce, Fannie Forrester, Harry Wilson, Charles H. Marrell, J. M. Martin, M. M. Jones and Frank E. Dunn, and this very tiresome September fainted into October (September 27th–October 2nd) with Dan Kelly, in The Shadow Detective. I admit to a feeling of profound joy in leaving the precincts of Pastor after that summer of (to me) ineffable boredom.

ORIENTAL THEATRE, 1885–1886

The Jewish theatre at 113-113½ Bowery, site of the former Bowery Garten, was active during the season we are recording. On Thursday, October 1st, the Harvard Theatre Collection shows, it presented Fanatic, or, the Two Kune Lemels, a comedy in four acts and eight scenes by Goldfaden, with Lateiner as Pincheseel; Mrs. Borodkin as Rifca, his wife; Mrs. Goldstein as Carolina; Silberman as Max, her lover; Borodkin as Kolman, a matchmaker; Mrs. Silberman as Libele, his daughter; Carp as Schulemunu; and Chaimovich as Kune Lemel, his son — all actors familiar from the preceding season. Silberman and Carp were the managers, and, on October 9th and several later October evenings, they gave Esther and Haman, an historical opera in four acts and nine tableaux, by Josef Lateiner, with Carp as Aschasuerus, Mrs. Chaimovich as Esther, Mrs. Silberman as Naomi, Silberman as Mordechai, Adler as Hathoch, Chaimovich as Haman, and Lateiner as Cherbonah; other parts fell to Mrs. Borodkin, Miss Fischer, Miss Rahukin, Miss Simon, Wachtel, Simon, Stern, Jacques, Mrs. Ernestina, Rosenthal and Borodkin.

January 18th, 20th, 22nd and 23rd (Saturday), brought The Jewess, adapted by Lerner from the opera. The cast included Silberman as Eliezer, Mme. (sic) Goldstein as Rachel, Carp as Cardinal Bronye, Avramovitz as Prince Leopold, Mme. Chaimovitz as Princess Yevdovkye, Adler as Rodsiera (commandant), Chaimowitz (sic) as Albert (general commandant); minor rôles were filled by Wachtel, Lateiner, Borodkin, Mmes. Silberman and Borodkin. The Phantom, or, the Demon in the Ruins, a comic opera in five acts and eleven scenes, by Lateiner, sounds far from comic in its dramatis personæ, with Adler as Chave, an aged fanatic Jewess; Mrs. Chaimowitz as Amalia, her grand-daughter; Silberman as Leon, her lover; Wachtel as Folik, his servant; Lateiner as a disguised Rabbi; Chaimowitz as Yekel, his sexton; Mmes. Borodkin and Silberman as the two wives of the Rabbi; Carp as a Fiendish Spirit; Mrs. Silberman as an Angel; and Mme. Borodkin as the Dead Daughter. This same small, devoted band of actors appeared, on February 10th, in The Usurer, a comedy with songs and dances, by Scheikewitz. The last of their activities for that season met by my research was The Spanish Inquisition, also by Scheikewitz. Something of the secret of this play may be gathered from the dramatis personæ: Karp (sic) was

[86]

Fulton, a secret Jew; Mme. Chaimowitz Isabella, his wife; Lateiner Adman, their son; Mme. Goldstein Jacqina, their daughter; Silberman Pedro, her lover; Miss Muchnik Gabriel, as a child, and Carp Gabriel as a man; Mme. Silberman Erina, his daughter; Chaimowitz Mendes, a priest; Adler Felix, a wealthy merchant; Wachtel an Inquisitor "in Chef"; and Mme. Borodkin a servant.

NATIONAL THEATRE, 1885–1886

Deserted by its fellow German-American institutions, the Volksgarten and the Bowery Garten, the National, at 104 Bowery, struggled on, in 1885–86, to uphold "Variety" in its former German fastness. The Harvard Theatre Collection, I am pleased to inform my voracious reader, has a complete file of bills for the season.

August 31st–September 5th seems not over-interesting in its lure: T. C. Parker (character songs), Frank and Fannie Davis (in The Old Veteran), Fitz and Webster (in Bud's First Visit to the City), and "Professor" F. Davys's Marionettes. But plays were killing "Variety." The bills for that week ended with Cyril Searle (why had he sunk?) as Pierre Michel, with Mamie Wallace as Rose. The week of September 7th–12th provided Carlisle (prestidigitateur), Harry McAvoy and Emma Rogers (in Love in a Horn), Thomas H. Ward and Con R. Lynch, Wade and Mack and, to conclude, George Morton (in His Sin). The olio of September 14th–19th presented the Hanley Brothers (Charles and Ed — acrobatic song and dance), Lottie Elliott, Mr. and Mrs. W. J. Conway (in Summer Comforts, or, Chestnuts in the Woods), and Ella Wesner. The concluding play, Our Shop Girls (by Jerome Stansill) had a cast including Sam Roberts, Alf Wallace, Dulany (sic), E. J. Holland, Marston, W. J. Conway, C. and M. Hanley, Mamie Wallace, Edith Crolius, Mrs. Conway and Alice Raymond. The Ainsleys (John and Harry, Southern negro act), Jeppe and Fannie Delano, John W. Leslie and Hen C. Clark (in Samples), and the Four Shamrocks were but olio, on the 21st, to the drama, Only a Miner's Daughter (with Emma Hendricks). How completely drama, especially melodrama, dominated the bills may be seen in the week of September 28th–October 3rd, when Mamie Wallace and George S. Grey, in The Child Stealer, capped an olio embracing Charles Roach and Ada Castleton (in The Latest Craze), the Three Franklins (John, Lillie, and James, in Irish Pastimes), the Delanos (in The Hunter), Keating and Sands, and Valjean (juggler). I must admit a fair interest in September at the National.

Jake Russell (pantomime clown), Sheridan and Flynn, George A. Booker and Maude Leigh, Crowley and the three Lorellas led the way (October 5th–10th) to J. J. McCloskey's play, Poverty Flats, with Harry Clifford as Tom Flynn, Wallace Jackson as Joe Mercer, Dulaney (sic) as Tim Black·

burn, who shot Sandy McGee, and Mamie Wallace as Gracie, the lily of Poverty Flat. I hope the reader from a study of the bills already cited sees the kind of play patrons of the National enjoyed; also that the theatre employed regular players for its rousing melodramas. But think of Fanny Herring (week of October 12th–17th) as Topsy, with George Allen as Uncle Tom, William Moore as George Harris, Dulaney (*sic*) as Legree, A. A. Wallace as St. Clair, Harry Clifford as Phineas Fletcher and Gumption Cute, Mamie Wallace as Eliza and Cassy, Carrie Wallace as Eva, and May Preston as Miss Ophelia! This must have overshadowed the short olio involving Harry Edwards and Daisy Kernell, Minnie Lee, and the Four Diamonds — Nat. W. Haines, John T. Ward, Robert J. Richmond and W. S. Sedgwick, in The Darkey's Wedding.

But even in those, her early days, nothing could eclipse Maggie Cline (here for October 19th–24th), along with Lillie Western, W. G. and Fannie Everett (these two in A Husband Wanted) and with strong concluding attraction in N. S. Wood, dividing the week among The Boy Scout, Nan, the Newsboy, and The Boy Detective. The week of October 26th–31st stressed Professor A. L. Gleason and his five trained dogs, Fields and Leslie (The Two Irish Barristers), Thomas A. Lord and Jessie Cunningham (in The Tutor), the St. Felix Sisters (in Rehearsal in the Wood) and ended all with Jesse James, in which appeared William Lee and his horse, Charger. November 2nd–7th began the bills with Cort and Murphy, in The Editors; passed to Dan Hart, Frank and Fannie Davis, and Harry Rogers, and ended with J. H. Grover, in I. O. U., supported by George Lascelles, Marston, Mamie Wallace, Dulany (*sic*), Lew Fowlks, May Preston and Fannie Davis. Karoly Ordey, Dan Kennedy and Lottie Allen (these two in Two of the Upper Ten), Jennie Engel and the Horseshoe Four prepared us, during the week of November 9th–14th, for a poisonous Lucretia Borgia, with T. W. Hanshew, Mamie and Alf Wallace and other minor giants.

The trained goat, Woodside, bucked in (November 16th–21st) with "Professor" Charles White to direct; Charles Roach and Ada Castleton again exposed The Latest Craze; the Four Comets (Hawley, John E. Walsh, Walter Manning and Thomas Williams); the Three Franklins — what more could one desire to lead to Wide Awake, with George France as Sam Buster and Lulu Delmay as Danger? This thriller began in New York, in 1855 and ended in Arizona, in 1870. "Professor" Hampton and his performing animals joined the faculty for November 23rd–28th; Harry Le Clair and W. J. Russell followed, in A Practical Joke, and C. W. Barry closed the show in the well-known Escaped from Sing-Sing. November passed into December (30th–December 5th) with the Whitings, George F. Kaine (Dutch and Hebrew songs and dances), the Four Shamrocks, and William Cattell (in Micaliz). Olio was almost fading from the bills, to make room for full-length plays. For December 7th–12th I can list only Nettie Carlyn, George

Beauchamp and Ward and Lynch; but I can invite the reader to share my surprise at finding The Danites as final attraction, with Marie Wellesley, William E. Sterling and the dogs (Sultan, Caesar and Monarch), Harry Mitchell, F. F. Varnum, George Fisher, Jennie Baringer and Rose Manning. And overtopping all, on December 14th–19th, was The Creole (Article 47), with Emma Hendricks as Cora, Mamie Wallace as Marcelle, Harry P. Kily as George, E. W. Marston as Potain, Charles Ray as Victor, and Dulaney (*sic*) as De Rives. But the olio was good, with the Four Diamonds, Lottie Elliott, Mel Reed (shadowgraphs) and three St. Felix Sisters (Clementina, Henrietta and Charlotte, in Our Birthday Party, introducing selections from The Mikado). Eugene Ward, a footless dancer, somehow made his way into the theatre for Christmas (December 21st–26th), with Frank Lester, Farrell and Jennie Leland, as fellows in the olio; and again Uncle Tom's Cabin figured, with Laura Alberta as Topsy, J. U. Randal as Uncle Tom, Mamie Wallace as Eliza, and W. Mamie (a female George Spelvin?) as Cassy. Joe Allen (in A Sister's Oath), the Horseshoe Four, McAvoy and Emma Rogers, "Professor" Harry Campbell and Miss Bertie Hastings (double-voiced vocalist) saw the old year out and the new year in (December 28th–January 2nd)—I must say, with no brilliant allure. For January 4th–9th, the Du Rell (*sic*) Twin Brothers, Maggie Cline, the Gilmore Sisters (Drusie and Carrie), and Manning and Drew were counted on to hold the audiences till Gustavus Clarke came on in Monte Cristo.

The plays thus far presented might have been seen, a few years earlier, at the old Bowery Theatre; surely "Variety" was backing up its efforts tremendously with drama. And here, for January 11th–16th, comes Frank I. Frayne, in Si Slocum, with the dog, Jack, Annie M. Read, Baby Etta, Little Clara V. Frayne, Master Franky Frayne, Maude Leigh, George Booker, Blanche Read, Mr. and Mrs. T. C. Medinger, Andy Amann, &c. In view of that weighty matter, who could have cared that the "olio" consisted of J. J. Jones ("champion rifle shot of the world"), George A. Booker and Maude Leigh (in Assurance) and Andy Amann ("the German King")? And how impatiently (January 18th–23rd) must one have sat through the "turns" of Max Hugo (Sports of Ancient Egypt), Lillie Western ("the musical wonder — performs on two banjos at once"), Gleason and his five dogs, John F. Byrne and Miss Helene, when, just ahead, Rose Lisle was to play the protean lead, in A Union Heroine, with George C. Jordan as Gilbert Butler, Pete Johnson and Fritz Oppenheimer; W. T. Dulany (*sic*) as Harold Marston and the Quaker, Ephraim Hardpan; Carl H. Anderson as Euphrates, "true blue though black"; A. A. Wallace as Sam Vinton, and Henry Dunbar as General Pemberton. I can almost see that play. And one could have seen, in Brooklyn, a few weeks earlier, Burr Oaks, given at the National (January 25th–30th) with David Higgins as Jester Judkins, supported by the Wallaces, Dulaney (*sic*), Cattell, &c. The olio preceding presented

Jessie Carl (song and dance), the Three Franklins, and Ed Smith and Charles Weston ("comedians, vocalists and instrumentalists"). February 1st–6th gloried in the Three Royal Russian Athletes, Alexander Wilson (ventriloquist), Jerry Hart and Beatrice Leo (in a burlesque, French Opera), John F. Leonard and John K. Mullen (Irish punsters and singers) and in Charles Thornton in Tried for Treason, or, Back from the Grave — surely thrills for all.

Percy Meldon, on February 8th, began a week as Frederic Marston, in Sin's Penalty, a title good enough for a "talkie" of 1941; Conroy and Dempsey, Al W. Filson and Lee Errol, Rosina, Howard and Fox, and Cora and Nora ("birds of melody") enriched the olio. "Professor" Charles Moore's "School of Educated Dogs," Harry Rogers, Fannie and Frank Forrester (these two in Going to the Masquerade), and Charles and Carrie Moore (American skaters) kept patient the audiences of February 15th–20th, till Arizona Joe, "the Shooting Star," appeared in Black Hawks, with "three beautiful mustang ponies." The mere players were Henry Spencer, A. Clayton, H. Fisher, G. W. Watson, W. T. Johnson, T. F. Thomas, May Harrington, Mabel Sterling and Libby Kirk. Cuponti (Hindoo juggler and equilibrist), Al W. Filson and Miss Lee Errol, the Electric Three, and the Four Shamrocks preceded (February 22nd–27) A. C. Gunter's Two Nights in Rome, with Horace Lewis as Benedetti, Mamie Wallace as Antonia, Irene Arlington as Evelyn, Alf Wallace as Gerald, and William Cattell as Herr Franz. Hattie Westcott (songs of the day), the Dolan Brothers, the Delanos, and the Four Comets were introductory (March 1st–6th) to The Hunchback of Paris (The Duke's Motto), with Gustavus Clark (sic) as Lagardère, C. William as Æsop, W. Manning as Peyrolles, Fannie Delano as Blanche de Caylus, and Evelyn Knapp as Blanche de Nevers. If this keeps on, we must regard the National as a real theatre. Edward Hanford, in his own play of Partners in Crime, ended the bills of March 8th–13th; preceding olio included Layman ("facial mimic"), Mr. and Mrs. Joe Allen (in Terpsichorean Mania), Hawkins and Collins, and the Clipper Quartet (F. T. Ward, Alfred Hart, George F. Campbell and Robert McIntyre, in A Sour Mash). Hereafter, I serve notice, I shall adopt the spelling quartet, and abide by it.

The attraction for March 15th–20th was the Sid C. France Grand Double Specialty and Comedy Company. Ma, Look at Him enlisted Bob Allen, Ada West, Frank Keenan and Thomas Bryant, followed by Virginia Ross and Ed J. Connelly (in specialties) and the Brantfords (Tom and Bertie, in Fritz's Return). Then came France as Buckskin, in The James Boys, or, the Missouri Outlaws, with Frank Keenan as Jesse James, Thomas Brantford as Frank James, Robert Allen as Bob Ford, Maud Hillman as Jenny Sommers, Bertie Brantford as Mrs. Greyson, and Ada West as Eliza Jane Green. This second James play of the season interests those who saw The Missouri Legend of 1938. Charles Weston (late of Weston and Hanson),

[90]

J. W. Hampton's performing animals, Rosina, Ashley and Hess and Harry Le Clair and W. J. Russell (in The Stage-Struck Chambermaids) were precursors in the bills of March 22nd–27th, of Augustin Neuville and Mme. Neuville, in The Boy Tramp, or, the Maniac Mother, a violently-named piece elsewhere exhibited in 1885–86.   March 29th–April 3rd gave us "Professor" C. W. Giovanni and his performing birds, George W. Callahan (ventriloquist), the Braham Brothers (Abe and Lew, in Shadowgraphs), the Virginia Trio (Turner, Udell and Pearce, in Sundown), and, for concluding play, John W. Ransone in a revised version of Across the Atlantic.   April 5th–10th started the show with Hotel de Beans (James C. Vincent, T. F. Thomas, George W. Watson and Miss Ollie Collins), continued with Master Belzac (on the invisible wire), the Three Franklins, Dan Regan (late of Marlow and Regan — banjo), and Catherine Nelson and her birds, and ended with a return visit of Arizona Joe, in Black Hawks, now supported by "four beautiful mustangs," performing dogs, twenty-four drummer boys and one hundred people on the stage.   A big show!   I pass in wonder to April 12th–17th, with J. F. Hoey and Lillie Western, Sweeney and Ryland, and The Stranglers of Paris, acted by Frank Tannehill (as Jagon), Emily Franklin, Mamie and A. A. Wallace and Dulany (sic).   April 19th–24th I also succinctly record with Foreman and Ida Meredith (in Lawn Tennis), Frank Evans and Joe Coyne (in Full of Excitement), Ramza and Arno (horizontal bar) and a return visit of George France and Lulu Delmay, in Wide Awake. A return of George Morton, in His Sin, ended the bills for April 26th–May 1st, the olio including Harry Steele (in Ups and Downs of an English Swell at the Skating Rink), R. M. Carroll (in The Bowery Dancing Master), and the Big Four (Smith, Waldron, Cronin and Martin).   Only Dan Hart and his dog Gip preceded (May 3rd–8th) John A. Stevens's play, Unknown, that too well known item in our Annals.   In this Lottie Church was Bessie Merribright, with Wright Huntington as Harold Merribright, the unknown, Walter Fletcher as Jack Salt, Edward Knott as Albert Stormking, Milton Aborn as Dr. Brinkton, Gus Blancke as Arnold Tyson, George W. Woods as Jimmy, Agnes Roselle as Louise and Virgie Melville as Annette.   Obviously some visiting stars brought their own support.

May 10th–15th restored the regular company —Dulany (sic), Bart, A. A. and Mamie (three Wallaces), E. W. Marston, &c., in support of Will S. Marion, in A Desperate Game.   Also in the bill were R. M. Carroll (in Mortar and Bricks), Ottilie (in her popular statue of Liberty Enlightening the World), Kokin Segowa ("Jap" juggler) and the Horseshoe Four (in Dramatic vs. Variety).   Harry La Rose (revolving globe) started the bills for May 17th–22nd; also appeared Frank Lester, F. H. and Lillian White (in Past, Present and Future), and Manchester and Jennings (as The New York Aldermen).   The bills ended with Lucky Ranch, a Tale of the Yosemite, with W. M. Paul as Dionysius O'Malley and Mrs. Paul as the Mexican Florilla. Charles H. Stanley and Lizzie Conway, the Braham Brothers, Lottie Elliott and Valjean led the way (May 24th–29th) to Bartley Campbell's play, '49, once acted by Mr. and Mrs. McKee Rankin. At the National, Maud Miller was Carrots, and Loudon McCormack '49; others included Frank Ambrose, Alf Wallace, Dulany (*sic*), Bart Wallace, E. W. Marston, Mamie Wallace and Lizzie Conway. The Sid C. France company returned for May 31st–June 5th, with Ma, Look at Him, Virginia Ross and E. J. Connelly, Fritz's Return, and France dividing the concluding play successively in the week with Marked for Life, Dead to the World and The James Boys. June 7th–12th began summer with John Carroll (topical vocalist), Mlle. Zittella (*sic*), Matt Flynn and Minnie Lee, De Witt and Kirwan (*sic*), Frank Bush, and East Lynne (with Mamie Wallace!). The next week (14th–19th) is not very interesting, with Donnelly and Drew (in The Irish Strangers); Farrell and Jennie Leland (in Love in a Hammock); Dave Marion and Minnie Belle (change and character artists), Lester and Williams and Dick Gorman (in My Hebrew Friend). June passed by (21st–26th) with Harry Woodson (as the aged negro), Will O. Petrie and Maggie Elise (in Passing the Toll Gate), Keating and Flynn (acrobatic breakneck), McAvoy and Emma Rogers (in Stimulation) and Mortimer Murdoch, in his own play of Hoop of Gold, thus cast:

Sammy Wetherwick	Mortimer Murdoch	Richard Wrench	A. A. Wallace
Tilly	Annie Clybourne	Henry Bullion	Bart Wallace
Ruth Bullion	Mamie Wallace	Dr. Hartland	Harry Maitland
Lizzie Lovegrove	Emma Rogers	Scotty	E. W. Marston
Diamond	Maggie Elise	Welsher Humm	W. T. Dulany

Mabel Myrtle (vocalist), Lamont Trio, Lizzie Mulvey and Belle Clifton, McIntyre and Heath — these specialists were prelude to the thrills (June 28th–July 3rd) of Called to Justice, with Charles G. Craig, Charles H. Mestayer and J. de Gey. July 5th–10th provided as hostages to the heat James F. Hoey (in Gaglets), Charles Sanders (*sic*) and Lillie Burdell (in Mugs and Sally), Fox (the bird man), the Clipper Quartet (A Sour Mash) and the drama, The Two Slaves, with C. E. Marshall as Zingara, a greaser, and Edith Crolius as Zola and Albert, the slaves. The Halls (James and Miss Frankie), Sheridan and Flynn, Lester Howard and John and Emma Whitney, and the Four Emperors of Music (Ed Howard, Frank Russell, Billy Seeley and Jack Talbert) led to the excitement (July 12th–17th) of Will S. Marion's dramatisation of Called Back, which he entitled Love and Reason:

Gerald Maynard	Will S. Marion	Horace Greyson	John Whitney
Gennaro	E. F. Nagle	Pauline Lloyd	Edith Crolius
Walter Maynard	Bart Wallace	Rosa Maynard	Alice Newton
Tornelli	W. T. Dulany	Mary Downs	Emma Whitney
Julian Lloyd	Lester Howard		

Two weeks of Around the World in Eighty Days began on July 19th, with Marston as Passepartout, and W. J. Fleming as Phileas Fogg. Charlie Schilling gave a "turn" in the first week, but absolutely no Variety interfered with the drama in the second week. This carries us comfortably to the week of August 2nd–7th, when the Brantfords, George W. Woods, Marion and Belle, and J. P. Sullivan and Charles T. McCarty (in The O'Gradys) served as prologue to the swelling tale of Grizzly Adams, Hunter of the Sierras, with, in leading rôles, Mattie Goodrich, Harry W. Mitchell, and the Indian pony, Ginger Blue. For August 9th–14th, patrons tried to forget the heat with Charles De Bar, Nat Haines and Will Vidocq, Fred J. Huber and Kitty Allyne (in Pleasant Dreams) and Walter S. Sanford and T. J. Meagan— these two stars of The Italian Convict.

London Theatre, 1885–1886

Let us continue our Bowery journey with a year's visit to the London Theatre. The season at this firmly established house began, on August 29, 1885, with Reilly and Wood's Comedy and Specialty Company, Pat Reilly and Alfred Wood, proprietors. John F. Byrnes and Miss Helene were grandly described: "he is the best male dancer extant," and "she can give her associate 100 points and discount him dancing, and there you are!" Florence Miller, put down (or, should I say, swallowed?) as "a sort of musical cocktail," followed, and in turn yielded the stage to Mr. and Mrs. Conway (in Summer Comforts); the Two Virtos ("just from Spain" — a musical act); The Three Herbert Brothers (gymnasts and acrobats); Pat Reilly; J. E. Henshaw and May Ten Broeck (in Yes, My Dear); Petrie and Fish; the Woods (four in number); Reno, Regina and Reilly, with John F. Byrnes (rapid crayon cartoons); and Election Day (with Larry Tooley, John D. Griffin, and the elephant, Alice)—these completed the glittering array.

This attraction continued for the week of August 31st–September 5th, and was succeeded (September 7th–12th) by The Man Trap (with Henshaw, E. D. Gooding, W. J. Conway and May Ten Broeck), Annie Dunn and Rosa Mack (in Dudeens), Leonard and Mullen, Dan Kennedy and Lottie Allen (in Nigs of the Upper Ten), Mr. and Mrs. Conway (in A Lawyer in Search of Clients), William Gaylord ("defies laws of gravitation"), Arthur and Jennie Dunn (in Only a Joke), Charles H. Sheffer and Harry Blakely (in The Wrong Girl), the Four Luciers (J. R., C. N., Lucier and Rosalie), John F. Leonard and John K. Mullen, and the farce, Match-Making.

Beginning in the week of September 14th–19th, the London offered the Consolidated Gaiety and Lilly Clay's Company, component elements of which were Marie St. Aubyn, Louise Bliss, Ada Barton, Elsie Hall, Clara Coleman, the La Porte Sisters, Victoria North, Mattie Bliss and Julia de Bertrand (apparently a rosebud garden of girls in a "Musical and Vocal Soirée");

Alice Townsend, the Metropolitan Four (Louise Bliss, Lida Moss, Palma Schröder and Gertie Keith), Antonia ("queen of the slack wire") and "first production in the United States" of The New Adamless Eden, with all these women. Evidently there were no men in the force. The next week (21st–26th) provided the Four Diamonds (Nat W. Haines, Robert J. Richmond, John T. Ward and W. S. Sedgwick), Frank Melrose (one-legged gymnast), Mai Conway (singer), Henshaw and May Ten Broeck (in Deception), Frank Lester (black-face), De Croix (on the invisible wire), Howe and Doyle ("dancing kings"), J. W. Myers, the Jackleys, Crowley, and Bachelor's Hall (with members of the olio). M. B. Leavitt's Double Specialty Company (September 28th–October 3rd) turned out to be no better than Joe J. Sullivan (in Just Over and in The Blighted Bachelors), the Martell Brothers, Elsie De Vere, Charles H. Stanley and Lizzie Conway (in Periwinkle's Return), Manchester and Jennings (in The Aldermen), John and Louisa Till's Marionettes), Mollie Wilson, Andy and Annie Hughes and William F. Carroll — fairly good, even so. For October 5th–10th we were bidden to a feast involving Earle (equilibrist), Burke Brothers (Jim and Dan), Shannon and Emerson, A Dress Rehearsal (with Henshaw, May Ten Broeck, the Conways and Gooding), Tony Farrell and Jennie Leland, Hyde Buckingham and Lizzie Aldine ("champion male and female rifle shots of America"), Charles Raymond (one-legged pedestal clog), the Horseshoe Four, and Murphy's Dream, with John E. Murphy, Phil Mack, George Shannon (George Murphy no longer of that quartette), and Harry Emerson.

October 12th–17th provided Cort and Murphy (in The Editors), Kitty Randolph (Irish male impersonator), "Professor" A. L. Gleason and his dogs, Millie Lottie ("aerial queen"), George Beauchamp ("England's greatest eccentric vocal comedian"), Harry Budworth and Nellie Brimmer (in Stray Tips), the Lamont Trio, the Four Comets (Frank Hawley, John E. Walsh, Walter Manning and Thomas Williams), Whitfield ("man with a hundred faces"), Charles Raymond, and Grabber and Snapper (with Budworth, Henshaw, Nellie Brimmer, May Ten Broeck, &c.). The Rentz-Santley Company became, if one may believe careful mamas, a bit dangerous for our sons (October 19th–24th) with A Gay Bal Masqué and The High Card Oh! The troupe included May Howard, Kitty Love, Marie Sherman, Mlle. Zitella, Mat Flynn, May Clinton, and Georgie Blake. Kernells' Own Company was more masculine (October 26th–31st) with Bryant and Saville, W. T. Bryant and Lizzie Richmond, Florence Matthews, Harry La Rose, Harry and John Kernell (Sidewalk Conversation), Annie Suits, the Lamartine Brothers, the Coulson Sisters, and the concluding Half-Way House. This combination became familiar to us at Miner's theatres. November 2nd–7th presented at the London Arthur O'Brien and Katie Morris (in Above Her Station), Isabel Ward, Le Clair and Russell (in A Practical Joke), Bobby Newcomb (in An Evening Party), Clark and Williams (Pull-

BILLY CARTER   McINTYRE AND HEATH   JOHN HART

THE JULIANS   QUEEN VASSAR   MAY HOWARD

TIM MURPHY   HARRY BLAKELY   FRED HALLEN

man Palace Porters), P. C. Shortis ("elegant musical act"), Lottie Elliott, and Murphy's Wedding (with Murphy and Mack, Henshaw, Conway, &c.). The Murphy and Wells Pleasure Party seems new to me and my gasping reader (November 9th–14th), its offerings including Fun on the Rail, or, the Deacon's Daughter and the Dude Actor (with Lillie Hamilton, Roger Dolan, Wiley Hamilton, George Lavender, Ed Gallagher, Theodore Price and Belle Dolan), the "Wonderful" Shaw, Mr. and Mrs. Conway (in Girls Will Be Girls), Golden and Drayton (in Rabbit Hash), Malvina Renner, Dolan and McCarty, Henshaw and Ten Broeck (in Interviewing an Actress), and the concluding Rudolph's Ambition (with George Murphy, Malvina Renner, &c.). This Murphy was once of Murphy and Shannon.

Henshaw and May Ten Broeck, evidently regularly employed at the London, began the bills for November 16th–21st, with Yes, My Dear; following came Frank Livingstone (equilibrist), Kittie (*sic*) Sheppard, Muldoon and Magee, Somers and Walters (banjo, songs, etc.), Sawdust Bill (with some of those just named), Kennette ("who leaps from the roof to the stage"), the Horseshoe Four (in The Actor's Family) and Bradley's Luck (with Mullen and Magee and other willing souls). And here we are at the close of November (23rd–28th), thankfully responding to Thanksgiving, with Mr. and Mrs. Conway (in Bilkins, the Butler), Dan Hart and his dog, Gip (in A Man's True Friend), Sheehan and Coyne (Irish), Ten Broeck and Henshaw, Nellie Parker, Earle ("classic equilibrist"), John C. Harrington and Arthur Johnson, Jerry Hart and Beatrice Leo (in the sketch, French Opera), James O'Hearn, the Morello Brothers, P. C. Shortis ("musical prince"), Valjean, and Looney, the Wrestler (with Sheehan, Coyne, &c.). November gloom settles on my spirit as I realise how many nonentities my conscientious pen is resurrecting and "eternising." And especially do I feel dejected at my ignorance of the quality of Davene's World-Renowned Allied Attractions, flaunting their fame before our bewilderment (November 30th–December 5th) with an opening Our Lawn Party, six lady Swiss bell-ringers and the Criterion Quartet, Billy Lyons, Mlle. Natta (we have heard of her), the Female Comedy Four (Misses Capitola Forrest, Alice Smith, Marie Nelson and Annie Livingston), John and Henry Ainsley (Southern negro types), Frank Lester, Valvo, George and Marie Nelson, Maud (*sic*) Beverly (*sic*), Le Clair and Russell (Stage-Struck Chambermaids), the French Troupe Davene, and the burlesque La (*sic*) Petit Zao (acted by many of the "world-renowned" specialists just brought to the admiring gaze of my reader).

I pass into bleak December (7th–12th), hoping to enjoy the "turns" of Tom and Maud Morrissey ("Irish"), John W. Leslie and Harry C. Clark (in Samples), Andy Gaffney ("American Hercules"), Murphy and Mack (in The McMullen Family), the Conways (in Summer Comforts, or, Chestnuts in the Woods), Carter ("the American Jap"), Smith and Waldron ("late of the Big Four"), the Julians (Rose and Martin — athletic), Bingham (ventriloquist, and Murphy's Christmas (with Murphy, Mack, Henshaw, Ten Broeck, the Conways, and, in place of Murphy and Shannon — Smith and Waldron). With the exception of McAvoy and Emma Rogers (in Jealousy) I am not retrospectively attracted to the offerings of December 14th–19th: Charles A. Frazer and Joe M. Allen (in Arrival of Cousin Cal, "musical instruments," etc.), Rosina (male impersonator), Roseland and Millie May (in Mixed Ale), Gussie and Katie Hart (sketches, songs, dances), William Harbeck (India-rubber boy), the Crimmins Brothers (Mike and Danny, in Fun on the Quiet), the Four Herbert Brothers (Fred, Edward, Charles and James, acrobats), and a burlesque Nanon (with Le Clair, Russell, May Ten Broeck, Emma Rogers, the Conways, Henshaw, Rosina, &c.). Reilly and Wood's Comedy and Specialty Company (December 21st–26th) celebrated Christmas with A Terrible Night (Ten Broeck, Henshaw and the regulars), Ella Wesner, John F. Byrnes and Miss Helene, Pat Reilly, Petrie and Fish, Florence Miller, Ramza and Arno (horizontal bar), the Woods (vocal and instrumental), Hawkins and Collins (The Two Doctors), Reno, Regimi (sic) and Reilly (in combination with Byrnes, in crayon cartoons and caricatures), and Larry Tooley and John D. Griffin (in Election Day). This combination (in name, at least, it began the season here, in August) appeals to my antiquarian taste. The New Year came in less brilliantly (December 28th–January 2nd), with the Cooper Brothers (acrobatic breakneck song and dance), Bessie Bell, the Three Franklins (John, Lillie, James, in Irish Pastimes), Mr. and Mrs. Conway, the Virginia Trio (Turner, Udell and Pearce), W. J. Mills (ventriloquist), Little All Right, Robert and John Winstanley (dancers) and Thomas O'Brien and Mattie Redding, all ending with Poor Grubb (Henshaw, Ten Broeck, Gooding, &c.).

Early January (4th–9th) gave Eh! What Is It? or, Deaf as a Post (with Dave Oakes), Gibbons ("the man snake"), Joe Redmond and Ada Clifton (in 'Twas the Other Feller), Andy Collam (sic), Sheehan and Coyne (Ashbox Inspectors), Henshaw (Scene in One), Pickert and Mayon, Oakes and Boyd, the Lamont Trio (Albert, Madame and Master John), Arthur and Jennie Dunn, and the regulars, with Sheehan and Coyne (in Grogan's Reception). January 11th–16th gave Smith and Weston, "Professor" Charles White and his goat, Woodside, Avery and Moulton (gymnasts), Harry Morris, Gallagher and West, Silvo, Hawkins and Collins, Charles Raymond and a return of Poor Grubb; no one of these worthies has come down, in repute, to 1941. Rather better would seem to be the aggregation of January 18th–23rd: Florence Jordan (vocal), Alfred Liston, John Hart (in Eh! What Is It?), the St. Felix Sisters (Clementina, Henrietta, Charlotte), Carter, Frank and Fannie Davis (in Maloney's Night On), Gregory Brothers (double horizontal bars), Harrington and Johnson, and a concluding Oh! I'll Do Well Here (John H. Conroy, James L. Dempsey, Frank Davis, May

Ten Broeck and Henshaw). Kernells' Own Company returned, to usher January from the stage, with many of the entertainers they offered in latest October; but Lillian Markham and Hughes and Magrew were added. I shall not urge the reader to attend, in imagination, the offering for February 1st–6th — May Adams's Chinese Minstrels and Burlesque Company and Gus Hill's Mammoth Novelty Company, though the Female Chinese Minstrels appeared "in the grandeur of Chinese costumes," and Gus Hill (the noted club-swinger) appeared along with Fred Russell and Dollie (sic) Foster, Landis and Ward, Alma Bellina (operatic songs), Jennie Meade (song and dance), the Lamonts and Lillie Allen. I am a bit repelled by The Girls of Sheol, concluding farce. February 8th–13th is to me not very alluring, with Harry Bryant and Polly Holmes (in Dumps, the Drummer), Hughes and Vidocq (acrobats), the Conways (again in Girls Will Be Girls), Earle, John Hart, Clark and Williams, the Horseshoe Four, Mack and Curdy (with a mechanical trick donkey), Leroux and Wilson (bar performers) and Fizz! Bang!! Boom!!! (acted by John Hart, Henshaw and Ten Broeck).

Possibly February 15th–20th brings up the average: Abt and his Grecian Mystery, Maggie Weston (male impersonator), Retlaw and Alton, Henshaw and Ten Broeck (in Diamond Cut Diamond), John Hart (in Divorce), Healey and Sanders (sic — clog), Conway (in latest comic songs) O'Brien and Redding, the Julians (acrobats), Hawkins and Collins, and Jim Crow Alive (with Hart). And believe, if you can, Kernells' Own Company came back (for February 22nd–27th), with Bryant and Saville, Bryant and Lizzie Richmond, Harry La Rose, the Kernells, and for new lure, McShane Brothers, Queen Vassar, and Muldoon's Picnic. And other returning troupers were M. B. Leavitt's Double Specialty Company, seen here on September 28th, but now adding to many of the former visitors Lottie Elliott, Dick Morosco and Kitty Gardner, Valjean and Sam Weston, William B. Wood and Maurice Weston, bringing the evening to a close, with J. J. Sullivan (in Maloney's Visit to America).

The entertainers now came, not as separate entities, but as combinations more or less conglutinated. The Ida Siddons Burlesque and Specialty Company of March 8th–13th offered Our Picnic (with Ida Siddons, J. J. Keating, Ned West and Press Eldridge), Miss Lou Sanford (sic), Constantine and West (in The Thespians), Lizzie Mulvey and Belle Clifton, the Six Dashing Drum Majors, the Mikado Trio (Lou Sanford and the Bartlett Sisters), the Three Herbert Brothers, the Fascinating Four (Lizzie Mulvey, Belle Clifton, Vede Mansfield and Sadie Long, in Quaker song and dance), and Keating and Sands, Miss Siddons and H. Constantine, in Prince Faithful. Another combination I do not regret missing was that of March 15th–20th, the Rentz-Santley Company, with a Gay Bal Masqué (Lulu Mortimer, Kitty Love, Jennie Melville, Mary Sherman, Annie Wells, Georgie Blake, May Howard, Billy Chace, Billy Buckley, &c.) and olio turns by Zitella, Matt

[97]

(*sic*) Flynn, Kitty Love and May Clinton, Nellie and Pearl Inman and May Howard, all ending with The High-Card-Oh! or, the Joys of Japan — only slightly like the Mikado, even if inspired by it. This aggregation had been here somewhat earlier. Another return visit was that of the Gaiety and Lilly Clay's Consolidated Comique Burlesque Company (22nd–27th), with the same girls, and Emma Thall, Catherine Nelson, Antonio, the Julians, and The New Adamless Eden. For the next three weeks more individualistic groups prevailed: Harry Morris, Gooding and the Conways (in The Clockmaker), Nellie Parker, Hughes and Magrew, Henshaw and Ten Broeck (Diamond Cut Diamond), John F. Byrnes and Helene, Howard and Fox (jig and reel), the acrobatic Three Phanlons, Roger Dolan and Dennis McCarty ("Milesian Bards"), Harry Morris ("Dutch"), Dan O'Brien and Willy Edwards (pyramids of tables, somersaults, etc.) and the Conways (in Bachelor Hall) — this the bill for March 29th–April 3rd); Charles Gregory, the "Great" Crowley, C. H. Baker and J. A. West (in Music and Fun), Mr. and Mrs. Conway (in Scroggs' Sanctum), the "American Jap," John Hart (in Three A. M.), Dick Carroll ("first time in the Bowery in years," in The Tutor of Terpsichore), the three St. Felix Sisters (in selections from The Mikado), Manning and Drew, Gregory Brothers and Pompey's Patients (with John Hart, Henshaw, Gooding, &c.) — the lure for April 5th–10th; and Frank Livingstone, John Hart (in Am-u-let), Kitty (*sic*) Sheppard (*sic*), Thomas H. Ward and Con R. Lynch, Arthur and Jennie Dunn, Sheffer and Blakely (The Wrong Girl), Mr. and Mrs. Ira A. Paine, Conroy and Dempsey, and a repetition of Poor Grubb — lo! the feast of April 12th–17th.

I wish for the reader's sake (and mine) I could go more rapidly, but conscience doth make a bore of my pen. The Great Australian Company, seen at Miner's during the season, was scheduled for April 19th–24th, giving familiar artists in Harry Loa and Willie Ruge, Andy and Annie Hughes, Billy Carter, the Four Luciers, Topack and Homer (*sic*), the Austin Sisters (aerial artists) and Mlle. Aimée ("the human fly"), Baldwin and Miles ("the German Senators") Annie Hart, Rinklets, or, the World on Rollers (with Frank Vern, and Tom Volt, "England's greatest laughter-makers"), &c. Also familiar were (April 26th–May 1st) Le Clair and Russell (in that same old Practical Joke of theirs, but now expanded to a long play, with Nellie Germon, Nellie Parker, William J. Sully, William A. White and Ed Clarence to assist). Also John and Nellie Healey were in the bill. May 3rd–8th glittered as it might with Frank Hilton (contortionist), Daly and Edwards (black-face), "Professor" Fox (imitations of birds), Henshaw and May Ten Broeck (in Deception and in Mistakes), Harry Woodson, C. Ed Foreman and Ida Meredith (in Lawn Tennis), Leonzo (Japanese juggler), Ed H. Sheehan and Ada Hulmes, Wilmot and Sewell, &c.

The Rentz-Santley Company, formerly a spring growth at Tony Pastor's, now came to the London for three weeks, in one or more of which appeared

Dutch Daly, Georgie Blake, Nellie and Pearl Inman, Kitty Love, May Clinton, Lulu Mortimer, E. H. Sheehan and Ada Hulmes. High-Card-Oh! re-emerged, and May Adams's Chinese Fête and Burlesque Company again enchained the Bowery (May 31st–June 5th), with Fanny Lewis, George W. Wills, John B. Wills, May Adams, Foster and Hughes, Ward and Lee ("Irish"), Lizzie Whitehill, and Our Girls (with May Adams and an immense cast). If I could only go more expeditiously with caution and desire for completeness! Well, June 7th–12th, was hot with the Horseshoe Four and Joe J. Sullivan's Consolidated Shows; Frank and Fannie (*sic*) Davis, Hattie Westcott (songs), John and Nellie Healey, J. J. Sullivan (in The New Policeman), McAvoy and Hallen, Kokin Segowa (*sic* — "greatest of living jugglers"), Fred Roberts, the Horseshoe Four (in Dramatic *vs.* Variety), and Maloney's Awful Night (with Sullivan) — not much in quality, methinks. And, except for the "Irish Queen" — Maggie Cline — the entertainers for June 14th–19th send few thrills to the seat where fond memory lies — Alice Townsend, Harry Edwards and Harry Kernell, Mlle. Monti ("cantatrice"), J. G. Griffin ("Irish"), Lida Moss (song and dance), Rice and Barton, and Don Dudedoo (with Alice Townsend, Marie Rostelle, Lida Moss, Griffin and many women). What would burlesque be without the frailer sex? Mlle. Georgie's Burlesque and Specialty Company, when it presented, for June 21st–26th, Coney Island, or, the Floating Minstrels, answered that question with a cast including May Adams (now again a mere hired artist), Fannie (*sic*) Lewis, Lillie (*sic*) Morris and many more. In the olio were Billy Kaye, the Forresters (Fannie and Frank, in Going to the Masquerade), Donnelly and Drew, Fred Russell (Chinese impersonator), Mlle. Georgia ("Samson, with iron jaws"), McAvoy and Hallen, and The Turkish Seraglio (with May Adams and many others).

Let us hasten through June 28th–July 3rd, with greetings for E. B. Fitz and Katherine Webster (in Musical Chips), Conroy and Dempsey, Sheehan and Ada Hulmes, the Big Four (Smith, Waldron, Martin and Haley, in Barnyard Frolics), Charlie (*sic*) Ross (comedian and mimic), Sheffer and Blakely (The Wrong Girl), Fred Matthews (grotesque dancer), Dolan and McCarthy, and Early in the Morning (with the Big Four, Ada Hulmes, &c.). These are old friends. The great holiday (July 5th–10th) brought in The Pleasure Party (management of George H. Wood), presenting as a long play, Rudolph's Ambition (with George Murphy, Al W. Decker, Charles E. Fisher, Gus H. Smith, Drew Fisher, Polly McDonald, Bessie Osborne, &c.). The only vaudeville came between acts, Gibbons and George H. Wood supplying it. Hume and Wesley's Big Specialty Company occupied the week of July 12th–17th, participants being Dick Hume, "Professor" H. M. Braham ("known as the Great Vim," balancing trapeze, ventriloquism, etc.), Ada Melrose, George Spence and Minnie Sartelle (*sic*), Wesley Brothers, Tom Ward (Fun in the Kitchen) and the farce of

That Don't Go, with Hume, the Wesleys, Braham, &c. Beaven's Big Burlesque Company followed (July 19th–24th), with McAvoy and Hallen, Booker and Leigh, Gus Hill, the La Verde Sisters, Gertrude Nora, Alfred P. Beaven and many girls. A burlesque Mikado figured. July 26th–31st brought back as a long play, A Practical Joke, now with Le Clair and Parker. And the last week of the season (August 2nd–7th) flickered out with A New Adamless Eden, with Lilly Clay's Gayety Company. Maggie Cline was in it, also the Ross Sisters, the La Porte Sisters, Vede Mansfield, Eva Stetson and Alice Townsend.

Miner's Theatre, Bowery, 1885–1886

Once again the Harvard Theatre Collection summons to the banquet at Miner's East Side house; I must, perforce, describe — possibly in wearisome detail — the proffered delights. From August 31st to October 3rd, in dizzying confusion past our vision the management whirled "Professor" Abt and His Wonderful Grecian Mystery, Daisy Norwood, Frank and Clara Mara, Duncan (ventriloquist), W. G. and Fannie Everett (in Seeking a Wife, by Frank Dumont), the Howard Sisters, W. T. Bryant and Lizzie Richmond, Charles and Ed Hanley (in acrobatic song and dance), Pete Shaw, the "justly-famed" Horseshoe Four (in The Actor's Family), George F. Moore ("the man with 100 faces") and Sheldon and the dramatic-olio actors in Married in Haste — all this for August 31st–September 5th; for September 7th–12th, Pat Rooney's New York Star Combination, including Thomas Dayton and Josie Granger (in Blackmail), the Great Hi Tom Ward (in Fun in the Kitchen), Harry Woodson and Laura Bennett, Pat Rooney, Keating and Flynn, the Ramblers (Lester Howard and John and Emma Whitney, in Rehearsal in the Parlour, and, to end the bills, Who Owns the Baby?), Katie Rooney, the O'Brien Brothers, and the Four Emperors of Music (Howard, Russell, Weeks and Talbert or Talbot). The Silbons and "their own Great Company" showed their greatness (September 14th–19th) in Dr. Pro-tem (with Sheldon, James M. Bradford, J. R. Lewis, Nellie Sandford and L. Crolius), Jennie Schumann (vocalist), La Petite Pauline (on a slender silver thread), Leopold and Bunell (*sic*), Hume and Jennie Lindsay, Ada Melrose, Imro Fox (illusions), Gorman Brothers, the Silbons (aerialists) and the concluding spectacle, The Yellow Dwarf (with Bunell, Leopold, the Gormans, Dick Hume, Kate Victoria and Ada Melrose).

Courage, reader! we are more than half way through September. Girding our weary faculties, we digest the offering for September 21st–26th — John Russell and Lulu Arlington (in Mulcahey's Flirtation), Danny Daly and Florence Edwards (in Kuriosities), Fanny (*sic*) Lewis, Lillie Western, Budworth and Brimmer (in Tidbits), Murphy and Miles, Wills and May Adams, Billy Carter, Major Burk (*sic*) and Maude Beverly (*sic*), Garry

Hopper and Carrie Hall (in Secret Service), the Seven Venetian Troubadours, the Star Athletes (Kenyon, Jerome and the King Sisters), and, for concluding farce, The Irish Shoemaker (with J. H. Russell, Nellie Sandford, Bradford, Posner, and L. Crolius).   If the diligent reader is impatient to discover the personnel of the Appleton and Randolph Novelty and Burlesque Company, he may attend Miner's in the week of September 28th–October 3rd, to witness Sheldon, the abiding (in A Quiet Little Home), Kitty Wells (character and change artist), Ben Gilfoil and Irvin Bush (in Street Scenes in Washington), Mlle. Cappalini ("star dancer in boys' costumes"), Maggie Cline (thrice welcome to my dazed pen), John and Nellie Healey (in the Ethiopian, Dat Offspring), Mlle. Emilie Tournour (*sic* — invisible wire), Joe Hart, Fannie (*sic*) and Frank Forrester, T. G. Ducrow (in The Crazy Jester), and the six Elliotts ("premier bicyclists").   The long bill ended with a burlesque Mikado, with Irvin T. Bush in the title-rôle, Maggie Cline as Ninki-Poo (*sic*), Ben Gilfoil as Ko-Ko, Joe Hart as Pooh-Bah, John Healey as Pish-Tush, Fanny (*sic*) Forrester as Yum-Yum, Jennie Shepherd (*sic*) as Pitti-Sing, Kitty Wells as Peep-Bo, Nellie Healy (*sic*) as Katisha, and with a Japanese ballet, led by Gilflo and Hartilini, "Japanese premiers." Another burlesque of the reigning Mikado came in the next week (October 5th–10th) when Hallen and Hart's First Prize Ideals ended their bill with My-Card-Oh, Frank Bush as Nincumpoop, John Russell as Bah-Pooh-Bah, George Hallen as Push-Push-Tush, James Russell as Kat-with-Claw, Katherine Webster as Sing-a-Sing, Jennie Miaco as Peek-a-Boo, Enid Hart as Yum-Yum, and Fred Hallen as Ko-Ko and Co.   I hope this was as funny as it sounds.   In addition, the olio (most of that cast had "turns" in the olio) presented Fox and Van Auken (on the three silver bars), James McAvoy, Ottilie (very popular) and Nelton (Egyptian juggler).   Of course the favourite Russell Brothers were featured in the olio.

October 12th–17th huddled, in rapid succession, "Professor" Fred Davys's Marionettes, Viola May, Will C. Matthews and Nellie Harris (these two in Fragments), Gibbons and Doyle, William Carroll (banjo), the Three Franklins (in Irish Pastimes), Master Tommy (in songs), W. T. Bryant and Lizzie Richmond, Max Hugo (Egyptian juggler), Hughes and Magrew ("formerly of the Four Eccentrics"), Marco ("serpentine wonder"), and Porter and La Montagne, all ending in The Pet of the Circus (with Dave Foster, Artie Hughes, David Roche, John Foye, N. Sanford [*sic*], L. Crolius, J. R. Lewis and Dave Posner).   Up to this date, we observe that Miner's bills ended, in the old way, with farces or short sketches, in contrast to those at the National, which gave almost the whole evening to a long play sometimes plucked from the heart of recent Broadway successes.   The week of October 19th–24th, at Miner's, gave us merely Dominick Murray, in his familiar Escaped from Sing Sing, his support including James L. Edwards, Charles Saunders (*sic*), Frank Roberts, B. F. Hendricks, Edith Crolius and

Alice Newton. For this relief, thanks and ever thanks! Alas! the next week (October 26th–31st) plunged us again headlong into a thicket of names that ultimately must clog an interminable index. Sheldon (in The Secret Panel), Lillian Markham (contralto), Al W. Filson and Miss Lee Errol (in The Same Old Story), T. J. Cronin and William Wild (songs and dances), G. Donald Melville (juggler), Sweeney and Ryland (in Cross Walk Talk), Lina and Vani ("wonders of the world"), Sam Devere, Sharpley and West, Pavillio (*sic*) and Roussillion (gymnasts), and James F. Hoey (burlesque ventriloquial act). No Trespassing, the concluding farce was solemnly declared to have been "written for De Vere (*sic*) by Frank Dumont, and duly copyrighted, 1885." In it, Devere played Bogumil Schreiner, a German photographer, and the olio, just cited, supplied actors for his support.

Thus with excessive detail, we have rushed October from the calendar. And November began (2nd–7th) with R. G. Austin's Great Australian Novelty Combination, offering Miner's permanent Sheldon, in In Hot Water, H. Loa and W. Ruge, Mlle. Rosalie ("queen of song"), Andy and Annie Hughes (in The Masquerade Party), Billy Carter, William J. Mills (ventriloquist), the Austin Sisters, and Mlle. Aimée ("the human fly"), George Topack and J. Horner, Annie Hart, the Four Luciers, and, for that time of craze for Skating Rinks, the concluding farce of Rinklets, with the famous Russian skaters and members of the olio. November 9th–14th assembled an interesting group, in Pickert and Mayon, Jeppe and Fannie Delano (Flirting under Difficulties), Mr. and Mrs. Lacy, Wills and May Adams, the Tissots, Daisy Norwood, Lillie Western, Mr. and Mrs. Harry Watson, George F. Moore, the American Four (in Fun in a Beanery), Karl Michels and Dan Lacy (in Casey the Fiddler). I must hurry through remaining November with (16th–21st), W. G. and Fanny (*sic*) Everett, the Howard Sisters, the Jeromes, Ward and Lynch, Lillie Allen, the Paynes (Billy and Alice), Kenyon, Jerome and the King Sisters (four athletes, as we remember — do we?) Petite Kitty, "Professor" John White and his dogs, the Twilight Quartet (J. W. Hodges, William Moore, J. Hines and R. B. Marston), and the three Purvises (Johnny and his two donkeys); and with (23rd–28th) the returning Seven Venetian Troubadours, and Davys's Marionettes, as well as George Homer and Georgie Lingard, the Marion Brothers (Charles and John), Matt Green and James Marco, Senator Frank Woodson, the three Lorellas, Dave Reed, "Adam Forepaugh's $10,000 Trick Elephant, introduced by the distinguished clown Charles McCarty," Dick Baker ("songs and crayon drawings of distinguished people"), "Professor" Al Lawrence's Prismatic Fountain, and A. H. Sheldon (in Two Detectives). November 30th–December 5th) gave plenty, such as it was, in M. E. Nibbe and May Vernon (in You'll Miss Your Mother When She's Gone), Alice Brooks (vocalist), Fred Barth and Master Tommy, Farrell and Leland, Harry Kennedy (he, at least, was good), Mr. and Mrs. Joe Allen (Terpsichorean

Mania), Tim Murphy, very, very welcome to me (in imitations of actors), Foster and Hughes, Master Belzac, Toner and Frobel (horizontal bar), Pete Shaw, the Muldoon Quartette (*sic*), Catherine Nelson and her birds, and the Three Schrode Brothers. I do not know whether to regard this richness as a blessing or a blight; but my pen knows.

Adah Richmond's Burlesque Combination (Thomas Canary, manager) held the week of December 7th–12th, Miss Richmond playing Princess Is-a-Belle, in The Sleeping Beauty, surrounded by a bevy of (may we suppose?) beauties in Ettie White, Ruby Marion, Jennie Sinclair, Kitty Raymond and Marion Langdon, and by some degree of comic talent in W. B. Cahill, George Rareshide, Ed J. Connelly, Virginia Ross, Maud Webber and Amy Boshell. Incidental to the piece appeared Weber and Fields, E. H. Talbot (*sic*), Duncan, and the four "acrobatic marvels," Dan O'Brien, Ed and Frank Rice and Dick Morosco. December 14th–19th looked toward Christmas with Sheldon (in Jack, the Hackman, No. 44), Charles H. Duncan and Ada Laurent, Sanders (*sic*) and Dean, the Delanos (in The Bashful Lover), Howe and Doyle, the Coopers, F. H. and Lillian White (The New Coachman), Louis Wesley, Marco, the American Four (in Scenes in a Beanery) and Karl Michels. And Christmas week (21st–26th) hung on the tree of our desire Minnie Lawton, Kenyon and Jerome (on the high perch), Tim Murphy, Mr. and Mrs. Harry Watson, John Walsh, "Professor" Al Lawrence's Prismatic Fountain (if a fountain can be hung on a tree), William Carroll, the Three Lorellas, Ed H. Sheehan and Ada Hulmes, Kenyon, Jerome and the King Sisters, Johnny Purvis and his two performing donkeys, "Professor" Wallace and Mlle. Loraine's Le Salon du Diable. Verily, "Variety" boasted more "professors" than, in those days, we might have met on a college campus. We enter the New Year (December 28th–January 2nd) with another back-breaking load of talent — Collier Brothers, Charles T. and Lizzie Anderson (The Old Rustic Bridge), George and Marie Nelson, Kitty O'Neil (the ever welcome), Binney and Murray, Daisy and Charles Belmont (banjo, song, dance), J. W. McAndrews (whom, also, we always gladly greet), René, the Martens Trio, the "Great" Crowley, the Three Schrode Brothers, Tim Murphy, one day to star in Hoyt farces (now in imitations of popular actors and brush drawings of well-known men), "Professor" W. Hampton and his dogs, monkeys, cats and geese, and Purvis, with his two donkeys. Children should have enjoyed this animal kingdom, but they would have been too young to wonder why Hampton with that collection of beasts and birds should be a "professor" in the faculty (I confess I know no university professor who could train a menagerie), and why poor Purvis, with two donkeys, should remain only "Johnny" — a mere tutor, so to speak.

The attraction for January 4th–9th included some performers whose names still (1941) endure; in fact, the entire group is interesting: "Professor" Abt, Daisy Norwood, Mr. and Mrs. Dan Lacy (these in I was Here First — a real "Mr. and Mrs." argument), René, George Homer and Georgie Lingard and Gallagher and Gannon. The Great Crowley merits a sentence for his programme tag: "This gentleman has been a puzzle to the community at large as to his sex. He outwomans a woman." Others in that bill were Major Burk (*sic*), Houssabura Sam, Flora Moore, Weber and Fields (in their "Rough Songs, Dances and Eccentricities"), Charles Diamond, the Four Diamonds (Nat W. Haines, Robert J. Richmond, John T. Ward and James G. Brevarde), the Three Albion Brothers, and Dan Lacy (in Casey, the Fiddler). Even without that "puzzle" of Crowley, this was truly a remarkable bill, even into our own generation (1941). And January 11th–16th, though not so interesting for later students, promises well, with Abt, Maud Webber (serio-comic), Lefavre (juggler), W. C. Matthews and Nellie Harris (in Fragments), Fred Wenzel ("the funny little Dutchman," in Slattery's Boarding House), Ned Thatcher and Ada Adair, the Muldoon Quartet (Richard Harris and William Mack, tenors, Arthur Harris, baritone, and C. A. Green, bass), the Whippler Twins, John F. Byrnes and Miss Hellene (*sic*), Dick Baker, Leopold and Bunell, Marietta Myers (on a silver thread wire), Hughes and Magrew and Ed Baldwin. I feel as if I were watching an army passing by, with occasional returns of the same persons, as in a stage procession.

The great host of January 18th–23rd comprised Frank and Clara Mara, John and Nellie Healy (*sic*, as the aged darkey and a wing dancer), Nubar Hassan (slack wire), the Marion Brothers, Robert Gilfort (equipoise), Nellie Parker, F. H. and Lillian White, returning (in The New Coachman), A. O. Duncan (ventriloquist), Cooper and Lovely, Dave Morosco and Kitty Gardner (in The Schlum Family), Newcomb and Hassan, George W. Allen, Barnum's Gladiators, the Gilforts (Robert and William, in gladiatorial feats), "Senator" Frank Woodson, Clint Williams and his educated bear, and a concluding Around the Block, with Sheldon, David Roche, J. R. Lewis, Nellie Sandford, L. Crolius, and recruits from the foregoing olio. The Silbons returned (January 25th–30th) with apparently a new force, W. Wibberly, Don Antonio's Roman Studio (acrobatic feats), Hume and Lindsay (in Clipper Ads), the Gilmore Sisters, the Silbons, Wesley Brothers, Ten Arabs, Madge Aiston, Don Ferreyra, and Kate Victoria (in Cupid). February began (1st–6th) with Davys's Marionettes, Daisy and Charles Belmont, Pickert and Mayon, William Carroll, Gussie and Katie Hart (songs, duets, medleys, dances), Thomas H. Ward and Con R. Lynch, the Paynes, George F. Moore, the American Four (in That's What I Thought), Toner and Frobel, and olio and regulars in A Day and a Night Off (with compliments to Augustin Daly?). For February 8th–13th, Hallen and Hart's First Prize Ideals returned, their most interesting contribution being The Two Off'Uns, with James Russell as Louise, John Russell as Mme.

[104]

Frontyard, Katherine Webster as Henriette, Miss Dorina as Mary Ann, George Hallen as La Sault and Pepper, Polly McDonald as Jack (Ranking) Frontyard, E. B. Fitz as the Chevalier, Frank Bush as Pierre, Dorina as the Countess de Liners, somebody's mother, Rigoli as La Flower, and Joe Hart as Count de Vinegar. The sagacious reader knows that all these had done "turns" in the preceding olio; but he must be told that Hallen and Enid Hart also did their duty by their own olio and that Fox and Van Auken went through their $5,000 challenge act on three silver bars. And in all solemnity I edify the reader with the programme note regarding James McAvoy and George Hallen: "Originality is paramount with these salta-torial mimics and prolific entertainers, whose quick and perceptive minds are replete with laconicisms of a nature to cause the most sedate and morose auditor to succumb with unstained [*sic*] hilarity." It is interesting, also, to find Joe Hart in this company of Hallen and Enid Hart; a few years later he becomes the Hart of Hallen and Hart, in Later On.

The Howard Athenæum Specialty Combination came from Boston (February 15th–20th) to show the Bowery acts it already knew, with Ed H. Sheehan and Ada Hulmes, Sweeney and Ryland, Sheffer and Blakely, Hilda Thomas (singing My Love is a Sailor Lad, Sally in Our Alley, The Cows are in the Clover, etc.), Lina and Vani (now set down as brother and sister), Sam Devere, Sharpley and West, Pavillio and Roussillion, James F. Hoey and No Trespassing (revised, and with Sam Devere). Week changes to week in Miner's, entirely different, yet similar in befuddlement for the reader. February went out (22nd–27th) with the Hogan Brothers (in The White-Eyed Kaffirs), Arthur Dunn and "his charming sister," Jennie, Foster and Hughes, Robert Gilfort, the Du Rell (*sic*) Twins, Fannie (*sic*) Lewis, the Muldoon Quartet, Shedman's Dogs and Monkeys, Petite Kitty, Barnum's Gladiators, the Ventinis, the Three Schrode Brothers, &c. And March blew in (a cheap way of putting it, but anything for "Variety") with (1st–6th) Ed Baldwin, Manning and Drew, Gallagher and Gannon, Luke Brant and Rose Vernon, C. A. Frazer and J. M. Allen, John Walsh, Dorina and Rigoli, Newcomb and Hassan (juggling), the Russian athletes (Fredericks, Gloss and La Van) and The Rival Car Conductors (by the regular company of the house).

Reilly and Wood's Great Specialty and Comedy Company filled the week of March 8th–13th, with Sheridan (in Anatomy), Florence Miller, Fields and Hanson, McAvoy and Emma Rogers (in Stimulation), Pat Reilly, Ramza and Arno, the Wood Family, Reno and Reilly (crayon cartoons and caricatures), Will O. Petrie and Fish, C. T. Ellis and Clara Moore, and the farce of Senator McFee, acted by the olio. Pat Rooney's New York Star Combination brought (March 15th–20th) familiar friends almost as in the visit of September 12th. The following week (22nd–27th) also gave us familiar friends in W. G. and Fanny (*sic*) Everett (in A Husband Wanted),

Matt Green and James Marco, Howe and Doyle, Harry Kennedy, George Murphy, Jennie Leland and Tony Farrell (in Butler and Maid), William Carroll (banjo and songs), F. H. and Lillian White (in Past, Present and Future), Tim Murphy (imitations), the American Four, Doddretti, and Schmelzlein's Companions (George Murphy, Roche, L. Crolius, &c.). March finally gave up (29th–April 3rd) with Delmore and Wilson (Ethiopians), Daisy Norwood, George Homer and Georgie Lingard, Mr. and Mrs. Dan Lacy, Charles and Annie Whiting (in The Soldier's Return), Charles and Ella Jerome, William Carroll, the Four Shamrocks (Conroy, Daly, Thompson and Daly, in Fun among the Tenants), Layman (facial mimic), Shedman's Dogs and Monkeys and the Four Powers Brothers. It softens the asperities of March to come on so many familiar names. The regular actors began the bills for April 5th–10th in Where's Anthony? Then followed the Raynor Brothers (Harry and Joe), Joe Byron and May Blanch (in Stage-Struck), Charley Ross (mimic and vocalist), Harry Steele (comedian and skater), Maud (*sic*) Beverly (*sic*), Leopold and Bunnell (*sic* — musical eccentrics), A. O. Duncan (ventriloquist), Rice and Barton, the Three Milo Brothers (gymnasts) and A Dutchman's First Visit (with J. C. Moore, F. W. Sanford, Lewis, Roche, Posner and L. Crolius). April progressed (12th–17th) with "Professor" Charles Moore's dogs, John H. Russell (Irish comedian), Burke Brothers (James and Dan), Ed Giguerre (boy warbler), Fannie Beane and Charles Gilday (welcome!), Maude (*sic*) Beverly, W. T. Bryant and Lizzie Richmond, Prince Pharaoh ("a puzzle to Europe"), René, the Ventinis (hat-spinners), Charles Diamond, D. B. Emery and Laura Russell, the Three Romalo Brothers (Walter, Frank, Oscar — acrobats), Charles and Carrie Moore and Our Next Candidate (with J. H. Russell). The week of April 19th–24th brought a third visit of Hallen and Hart's First Prize Ideals, new faces including Isabel Ward, John T. Kelly, George Murphy, Charles Fox and Flora Wheeler. The show ended with a big group in Irish Stew. Another combination — Harry Watson and Alfred McDowell's Comedy Company — gave us (April 26th–May 1st) nothing new in Master Tommy, in F. H. and Lillian White (The New Coachman), but introduced novelty with Wrinkles. No matter what special travelling combinations arrived, Sheldon and the regulars opened or closed the bills with a farce — The Telephone (April 19th) and Devilled Kidney (26th).

The entertainers for May 3rd–8th were Mlle. Loraine (*sic* — Le Salon du Diable), John and Edna Vidocq, Gussie and Katie Hart, Nellie Hague, the People's Four (Fred J. Huber, William and Alice Payne and Kitty Allyne), Marietta Myers (wire and revolving globe), John Carroll (topical and comic vocalist), the American Four again (in Scenes in a Beanery), "Professor" Wallace (bird man), "Professor" Al Lawrence's Prismatic Fountain, and F. J. Huber (in Kidnapped). Fred Davys's American Marionettes, in Scenes from Humpty Dumpty, led the way (May 10th–15th) to Master

Belzac, Sharpley and West, Maggie Cline, the Four Shamrocks (in Trouble-some Tenants), Weber and Fields (in Teutonic Eccentricities), Catherine Nelson, the Four Schrode Brothers (George, John, William, Henry, "classic acrobats"), and The Wrong Man in the Right Place (with Dick Morosco, J. R. Lewis, David Roche, John Foye and Nellie Sandford).   Sheldon came back (May 17th–22nd) in Getting Rid of a Cousin, followed by Herbert Crowley (female impersonator), Lew Roseland and Millie May (in Mixed Mail), Paul and Frank Hamlin (in knockabout song and dance), Larry and Lizzie Smith (in Love Letters), Nellie Parker, Fannie Beane and Gilday, Ed Giguerre, the Sisters Coulson, Dave Reed, Rice and Barton, Hamlin, Newcomb and Hamlin and The Arrival of Gilbert.   May 24th–29th had Sheldon, in $10,000 for a Hero, Lillie Morris (songs), Mlle. Natta, Pickert and Mayon, John J. Lessenger (in Pipe de Whistle), Matt Green and James Marco (as usual, in Quarter to Nine), J. F. Hoey, Ellis and Clara Moore, Harry Kernell, Latta and Lynch, Wilmot and Sewell (unicycle, acrobats, trapeze), and Karl Michels — verily a remarkable group.

May 31st–June 5th brings us thankfully into summer, granting us Charles Crosby and Viola Wray (in Remnants), James H. Hammond (acrobatic trick and triple dancer), the Days (Harry and Daisy, in Gera-niums on a Lark), Daisy Norwood, Glenroy Brothers, Dave Marion and Minnie Belle, Andy and Annie Hughes, Nat Haines and Will Vidocq (in Jackson's Recruits), Bryant and Lizzie Richmond (in Imprisoned), Lester and Williams, P. H. Thurber (equilibrist) and Rival Car Conductors (with the regulars).   Val Simpson and Minnie Russell (skating), Harry Edwards and Daisy Kernell (in A Summer Day), Patrick Miles, Young Ireland and E. H. McHugh (first appearance in America), Morosco and Kitty Gardner (in The Schlum Family), Eddie Magee, Arthur and Jennie Dunn, Annie Hart, John Walsh, the Three Ronaldos, the Four Emperors of Music, and the concluding A Dime Museum Drama, with Dick Morosco, Nellie Sandford and the regulars made June 7th–12th simply indigestible for delicate ap-petites — there was too much of it.   The old farce, The Clockmaker's Hat (with Sheldon) began the bills for June 14th–19th, and yielded the stage to George H. Adams's Humpty Dumpty among the Indians, which latter had specialties by Al Fostelle ("Dutch" musical king), Florence Emmett, Cooper and Lovely, and Adams's "beautiful trick pony, Seneca, valued at $5,000." Howard and Fox and Frank Hilton (contortionist) also figured.   "Profes-sor" Gormon (sic) with his "wooden-headed family" opened the bills for June 21st–26th, followed by Delmore and Wilson (in The Birthday Sur-prise Party), W. C. Matthews and Nellie Harris (in Oddities), Billy Carter and Mr. and Mrs. Joe Allen (in Terpsichorean Mania), Ed and Charles Hanley, Frank B. Sheridan and Joe F. Flynn (in Matchlets), Valvino (Ven-ezuelan star, in equipoise, juggling, etc.), Flora Moore, the Four Luciers (three brothers and one sister, Joseph, Rosalie, Charles and Alfred, playing

[107]

forty different instruments), and Who Owns the Fence? (with Gildersleeve, Nellie Sandford, Lewis, &c.). The bills for June 28th–July 3rd gave Sheldon (in Dodging for a Wife), Ned West, Daly and Edwards (in Kuriosities), Lottie Gilson, Fannie Beane and Gilday, Moore and Sanford ("Dutch"), Frank Lawton, C. Ed Foreman and Ida Meredith (in Lawn Tennis), Heffernan and McDonald (Irish), Howe and Doyle (dancers), Layman, and F. W. Sanford, J. C. Moore, Crolius, Posner and J. R. Lewis in Servants by Legacy. July 5th–10th was in heated holiday mood with Thomas A. Lord and Jennie Cunningham, Albert Virto, David Foster and Artie Hughes, Tom Brantford (in A Little of Everything), Marion and Belle, Marietta Myers, Frank Lester (black face), the American Four (in That's What I Thought), Carlisle (prestidigitateur), and the farce of School Boy Days (with Artie Hughes and David Foster).

We are getting on, painfully but surely, to the end of the season. July 12th–17th brought the Christie Brothers (in Froliques), Larry and Lizzie Smith, Weber and Fields and Master Frank (he gave imitations of actors), C. T. Ellis and Clara Moore, Maud Beverly (thus hereafter, I shall spell her names), the People's Four (in Perkins' Musical Party), George W. Earle (Irish-American bagpiper) and Paddy Miles (Irish jig, reel, etc.), Emery and Russell (silver bells and cornets), P. H. Thurber and the closing farce of Home Comforts. For the week of July 19th–24th, the manager promised Wally De Forrest and Dick Gorman (in High Times on the Mississippi), Roseland and May (in Mixed Mail), Frank Hewitt (instrumental, on violin, cornet, piccolo, "clarionette" and Burmese hautboy), George and Marie Nelson, Capitola Forrest, G. Donald Melville ("grotesque and comique juggler"), the Electric Three, the Ventinis, the Three Ronaldos (sic), Les Froliques Parisienne (sic) and George Nelson (in The Statue Lover). I am amazed at such prodigality, but hurry to the end of July (26th–31st), with Lefavre (legerdemain, in The Mysterious Bartender), George W. Barlow (eccentric German comique), Thomas H. Ward and Con R. Lynch, the Inman Sisters (Nellie and Pearl), Andy and Annie Hughes (in Teddy's Misfortune), Master Tommy, Bryant and Lizzie Richmond (in Opera Buffers), Annie Hart, the Four Shamrocks, Glenroy Brothers (vocalists and dancers) and the regulars, with Ward and Lynch, in a concluding farce. How could such extravagance pay?

The offering for August 2nd–7th included Dave Reed, Mrs. Reed and Eugenie Reed (in Hydrophobia), the Collier Brothers, Queen Vassar, Crosby and Wray, Mr. and Mrs. Dan Lacy (in I Was Here First), John Walsh, Dick Morosco and Kitty Gardner, the Four Powers Brothers, and Morosco's Casey, the Fiddler. And, utterly dazed, I close with the offering of August 9th–14th, including Eugene Revillo, Lillie Morris, Fannie (sic) and Frank Forrester (in Masquerade in an Alchemist's Library), Heffernan and McDonald, McAvoy and Emma Rogers (in Dick's Sweetheart), Ada B. Burnett, Green and Marco, Rosina (little male impersonator), Idaletta and Wallace (water queen and man fish), Wilmot and Sewell, and Irish Life (with E. J. Heffernan and Charles McDonald).

Will the reader, for his own satisfaction, count the number of acts and performers at this Miner's for 1885–86, and check the returns and divagations observed in his investigation of such activities? I confess I have not done so, but I am in a hurry to reach Miner's Theatre in Eighth Avenue.

MINER'S EIGHTH AVENUE THEATRE, 1885–1886

The new season at this house began in the week of August 24th–29th, with James Marco and Sam White (in The What Is It? or, the Troubles of a Coloured Gent in the Woods), Master Belzac (impersonations of Bobby Gaylor), Burke Brothers (James and Dan), Daisy Norwood, John and Stella Cooper (in Diversifications), Billy Carter, Duncan (ventriloquist), Kitty O'Neil, Frank Lewis, the Horseshoe Four (in The Actor's Family), Catherine Nelson (trained birds and dogs), and The Secret Panel (played by F. J. Huber, Robie, Decker, James Burke, Kitty Allyne and Daisy Norwood). Several of these appeared next week at Miner's Bowery. At the Eighth Avenue, week of August 29th–September 5th, we had Porter and La Montagne (trick and acrobatic skating), La Petite Kitty, Mlle. Natta, Weber and Fields, Kenyon and Jerome (*la perche equipoise*), Joe J. Sullivan (Irish), Dave Foster and Artie Hughes, Charles and Bly Harris (in Lee's Brewery), The Tissots (in Living Pictures), Annie Hart, the Four Star Athletes (Kenyon, Jerome and the King Sisters), the Four Diamonds (Nat Haines, Robert J. Richmond, John T. Ward and James G. Brevarde — a different group, often in that season), and The Two Tramps (with Huber and Robie). September 7th–12th huddled into a big bill "Professor" Abt, the Howard Sisters, W. G. and Fanny (*sic*) Everett (in A Husband Wanted), Collier Brothers, Charles Duncan (motto vocalist), Harry Budworth and Nellie Brimmer (in Stray Tips), Major Burk (*sic*), Pickert and Mayon, Lillie Western, Loa and Ruge, W. T Bryant and Lizzie Richmond, and Umbrellas (with Kitty Allyne, Huber and Robie and others of the regular dramatic company).

Most of the performers listed above appeared at about this same time at Miner's Bowery Theatre, never, however, *en bloc,* from house to house; Pat Rooney's New York Star Combination, at Eighth Avenue, September 14th–19th, was practically the same that went to the Bowery the week preceding. Reilly and Wood's Comedy and Specialty Company (September 21st–26th, in Eighth Avenue) comprised Florence Miller, John F. Byrnes and Miss Helene, Pat Reilly, the Wood Family (Harriet, Julia, Frances and Albert — a musical family), Petrie and Fish, the Two Virtos, Reno, Regina and Reilly, and Larry Tooley and John D. Griffin, with the regular actors (in Election Day).   And September 28th–October 3rd brought in the Silbons and their troupe, as seen two weeks earlier in the Bowery, even to The Yellow Dwarf; and the Appleton and Randolph Novelty Burlesque Company, of October 5th–10th, had shown just the week preceding at the Bowery house, Mikado burlesque and all.   The only difference in all these cases was that, instead of Sheldon, Nellie Sanford and the rest, in the Bowery, in opening or closing farces, Huber, Robie and Kitty Allyne performed a similar service in Eighth Avenue — The Watch Dog (September 28th) and A Matrimonial Spectre (October 5th).   The week of October 12th–17th congregated a new host in Garry Hopper and Carrie Hall, Harry d'Alberti (juggler and equilibrist), Fannie Lewis, Beattie and Bentley (black-face—"kings of contortion and legmania"), Jeppe and Fannie Delano (in Flirtation under Difficulties), Karl Michaels (*sic*), Lulu Delmay, Mr. and Mrs. John Burton, the Seven Venetian Troubadours, the Horseshoe Four and the regulars in An Awful Pickle.   The next week (October 19th–24th) restored hope to my weary pen by bringing in the group, Filson, Lee Errol, Cronin and Wild, &c., exactly as seen on the 26th, in the Bowery, except that Where's Anthony?, the opening piece, employed Huber, Robie and the West Side regulars.   And October died (26th–31st) with Huber in He Got Her, and Dominick Murray in Escaped from Sing Sing, cast exactly as on the 19th–24th, at the Bowery retreat.

And here (how can I ever be sufficiently thankful?) for November 2nd–7th come Hallen and Hart's First Prize Ideals, burlesque Mikado and all, exactly as at Miner's Bowery on October 5th–10th, except that the opening farce was Papa's Clock (by the Eighth Avenue regulars).   A novel attraction followed (November 9th–14th) with Kernells' Own Company, including George Beauchamp, Bryant and Saville, Charles Banks, W. T. Bryant and Lizzie Richmond (in Opera Buffers), Annie Suits, Lamartine Brothers, Coulson Sisters, and the farce Half-Way House (by Frank Dumont, and with the Kernells, W. T. Bryant and Charles Banks in the cast).   The Acme Variety Company filled the week of November 16th–21st, proffering Mr. and Mrs. John Burton, Thomas A. Lord and Jennie Cunningham (in Jinks, the Tutor), Cort and Murphy (in The Two Commercial Drummers), Will C. Matthews and Nellie Howard (in Fragments), the Hanley Brothers (Charles and Ed, in song and dance), Mr. and Mrs. Lacy, the Tissots, the "Great" Crowley, the American Four, and the concluding Golden Days (by Huber, Decker, &c.).   For November 23rd–28th we had the Coopers, Carroll and Ward (in Going Back to Arkansaw), Wills and May Adams, the Paynes (Billy and Alice), the "Three" Purvises (Johnny and his two donkeys), the Howard Sisters, Mr. and Mrs. Harry Watson, Thomas H. Ward and Con R. Lynch, the Horseshoe Four (in The Actor's Family) and Huber, Robie, &c. (in B. A. *vs.* A. D. T.).   An annoying circumstance is that several of these performers appeared during the preceding week in the Bowery, but not as an entire group; hence the necessity of listing them again in time so approximately near. And the same thing applies to the company of November 30th–December 5th, many of whom can be found at the Bowery in times contiguous: "Professor" Fred Davys's Marionettes, La Petite Kitty, W. G. and Fanny (*sic*) Everett (in A Husband Wanted), the Durell (*sic*) Twin Brothers, Lillie Western, Leslie and Clark, George Homer and Georgie Lingard, and William Carroll, with a concluding Larks, Sparks, Barks (Huber, Allyne, Decker, &c.). Adam Forepaugh's $10,000 trick elephant, Pickaninny, also appeared, with Charles McCarty to direct.

Just as the reader began to fear endless repetition, I can ease his scholarly mind by informing him that the Great Australian Novelty Company brought to Eighth Avenue (December 7th–12th) precisely that aggregation which it had exhibited in the Bowery a few weeks earlier, except of course, for the opening farce, The Skeleton Witness (by the local regulars). And Adah Richmond's Burlesque Company, seen the week of December 7th–12th in the Bowery, moved (December 14th–19th) to the West Side house, with exactly the same performers in The Sleeping Beauty, and with, in the olio, Weber and Fields, E. H. Talbot, the Marion Brothers (Charles and John, in The Finest) and the Three Lorellas. And Clara Thropp, not unknown, was in The Sleeping Beauty. Again we sink into the morass of names, many of them to be found in those weeks at Miner's Bowery. For December 21st–26th, we tried to catch the holiday mood with the Seven Venetian Troubadours, John H. Russell ("eccentric Irish comedian"), Budworth and Brimmer, the Delanos, Charles A. Frazer and Joe M. Allen, Lottie Elliott, the Three Albion Brothers, Pete Shaw (female impersonator), Dick Morosco and Kitty Gardner, the American Four (in Fun in a Beanery), Catherine Nelson and, to conclude, The Broadway Line. And we might have retained the holiday spirit (December 28th–January 2nd) in attentively watching Lew Roseland and Millie May (in Mixed Mail), Charles Duncan, Christie Brothers (Arthur and Frank, in Froliques), Minnie Lawton, Kenyon and Jerome and the King Sisters, William Carroll, "Professor" Wallace (man-bird), Dave Reed, Matt Green and James Marco (in their usual Quarter to Nine), Maggie Cline (bless her hearty style!), the Four Comets (Frank Hawley, John E. Walsh, Walter Manning and Thomas Williams) and Eh! What Is It? (with Huber, Robie and Kitty Allyne).

I can only rush pell-mell through early January. For the 4th–9th our dazed faculties apprised Garry Hopper and Carrie Hall (in Secret Service), George Beauchamp, Master Tommy, Hughes and Magrew ("the Short and Long"), Robert Gilfort (equipoise), J. W. McAndrews, A. O. Duncan (ventriloquist), Mr. and Mrs. Harry Watson, Howe and Doyle ("terpsichorean art"), the Three Lorellas, Barnum's Gladiators (the Gilforts—Robert and William, athletic) and the concluding Eighty Winks at New York, or, Seeing the Elephant. Does the reader note the dramatic content of many of the

[111]

team acts of these years, and also the local flavour in many of the farces—survival, perhaps, of the negro minstrelsy of an earlier date? But let us on with January 11th–16th, pouring a cornucopia of vaudeville into our receptive laps: Sam Lang and Dollie Sharpe (in The Reporter), Major Burk, the inescapable Daisy Norwood, the Three Franklins (John, Lillie and James, in Irish Pastimes), Charles Diamond (Milanese minstrel, harp soloist, song and dance), John and Nellie Healey, Nellie Parker, F. H. and Lillian White (in The New Coachman), Flora Moore, the Four Shamrocks, the Marion Brothers, and The Growlers, or, the Adventures of a Fresh Young Man (with Huber, Decker, Robie, Kitty Allyne, Charles and Ella Jerome, John Healey, Sam Lang, Charles and John Marion, Charles Diamond and Major Burk). If my gentle reader does not think that an amazing post-Christmas cornucopia, I must take the liberty of disagreeing with him. Reilly and Wood's Comedy and Specialty Company, seen here on September 21st–26th, came back for January 18th–23rd, with Florence Miller, Pat Reilly, the Wood Family, Larry Tooley and John D. Griffin (these two now in Muldoon's Trip to Coney Island), and Petrie and Fish still in the corps. But, to the best of my knowledge, McAvoy and Emma Rogers, Norm Carr and Dan Tourgee (in Ah! there, Professor, with various musical instruments), Ramza and Arno ("funny horizontal bar performance"), Reno and Reilly (crayon cartoons), and Hawkins and Collins were new accretions. The Eighth Avenue regulars acted Cummings, or, the Other Fellow. January ended (25th–30th) with Will C. Matthews and Nellie Harris (in Oddities), George and Marie Nelson, Houssabura Sam, William Carroll, Tony Farrell and Jennie Leland, Rose and Martin Julian (contortion), Thomas H. Ward and Con R. Lynch, Clint Williams ("better known as Grizzly Williams") and his educated performing bear (Clint, oddly enough, was not listed as "Professor"—perhaps he thought "Grizzly" a more distinguished title), the American Four (in its favourite That's What I Thought) and the concluding Law vs. Lunacy (of course by the regulars).

When the Silbons returned, on February 1st–6th, their company had suffered almost a complete change from its fall enrollment; its features now included Dick Hume and Jennie Lindsay (as before), Don Antonio's Roman Studio ("a troupe of male and female marble gems, introducing wonderful tumbling, acrobatic feats, and living pictures"—rather pleasing, one thinks), the Gilmore Sisters, Charles Eastwood (imitations of Fritz Emmet), the Silbons (aerialists), Harry Rogers, ten Arabs, the "great clown," W. J. Rollins, Don Ferreyra ("the only man flute") and the concluding Cupid, or, Cinderella Red Riding Hood (with Kate Victoria, Madge Aiston, Eastwood, James and John Wesley, Carrie Gilmore, Eddie and C. Silbon, Ida Victoria, &c.). The mere regulars of the theatre began the bill in Two Americans in Paris. The Howard Athenæum Star Specialty Company presented exactly the same bill, for February 8th–13th, that it gave, the follow-

[112]

ing week, to Miner's Bowery patrons; the regulars, here, began proceedings with Love's Sacrifice. Kernells' Company (February 15th–20th) presented Lillian Markham, Byant and Saville, Harry La Rose, Queen Vassar, W. T. Bryant and Lizzie Richmond, the Lamartine Brothers (Joe, John and Paul, acrobats), the Coulson Sisters ("champion rope dancers"), the Kernells (in Sidewalk Conversations, and in Half-Way House). For February 22nd–27th, Hallen and Hart's First Prize Ideals returned, with The Two Off'Uns and the gladsome olio seen two weeks earlier in the Bowery. March 1st–6th provided the "Three" Purvises, Fannie Lewis, the Belmonts (Daisy and Charles), René, Clark and Williams, Harry Kennedy, Arthur and Jennie Dunn, the Hogan Brothers, Charles T. Ellis and Clara Moore, the Four Schrode Brothers (George, John, William and Henry, acrobats), and Huber and the regulars (in Stew in a Box). Except for these regulars, we might be reading a history of Miner's Bowery. This impression carries us through the familiar—thrice familiar—names of March 8th–13th: Luke Brant and Rose Vernon ("eccentric comedian, and England's dashing serio-comic"), the Coopers (John and Stella), Nellie Hague, Manning and Drew (banjo, songs, dances), the Three Royal Russian Athletes (Fredericks, Gloss and La Van), John Walsh ("Irish patriotic and motto"), Mr. and Mrs. Lacy, Frazer and Allen (in Arrival of Cousin Joe), Tim Murphy (as The Actor, with imitations of noted actors), the Horseshoe Four and Barnum's Gladiators (the Gilforts); and, for that matter, through the equally well-known group of March 15th–20th: W. G. and Fanny (sic) Everett, La Petite Kitty, Charles Diamond, Tony Farrell and Jennie Leland (in Butler and Maid), William Carroll, Matt Green and James Marco (still keeping the clock at Quarter to Nine), George F. Moore, the American Four (in The Primrose Family) and George Murphy and the regulars (in Rudolph's Ambition, or, the Dutchman Who Desires to Be an Actor—that old, popular theme).

It is pleasant "going," with Pat Rooney's New York Star Combination (March 22nd–27th), including many of the performers of earlier visits at either Miner's, but with the Jackley Wonders (J. H. Jackley and Prince Flatow), Don Stirk and William H. Zeno (flying trapeze) apparently new to the group. Reilly and Wood's Comedy and Specialty Company (March 29th–April 3rd) also brought much of its former array, though "Chevalier" Ira Paine and Mrs. Paine, with their rifles, hit the bull's eye of popularity; they were returned from six years in Europe and were, it was alleged, engaged at $350 per week. Sanders and Dean (in Jubilee Day) began the bills for April 5th–10th, and Huber and the regulars ended them, in Three Scratches. Between those limits, came Charles and Annie Whiting, the three Romalo acrobats, Layman (facial mimic), Thomas Carter and Lizzie Anderson (in The Old Farm Gate), Billy Gallagher and Johnny Gannon, Mr. and Mrs. Joe Allen, the Four Comets, and Shedman's dogs and monkeys—material familiar to us. Hallen and Hart's First Prize Ideals made another visit

[113]

(April 12th–17th), with the Russell Brothers, John T. Kelly, George Murphy, McAvoy and Hallen, and others as recently at the Bowery Miner's. For April 19th–24th, "Professor" Abt, Daisy Norwood, Ed Baldwin, the Du Rell (*sic*) Brothers, Mullen and Magee ("Man of Nerve"), Beane and Gilday (in Love Letters), Louise Clements, Roger Dolan and Dennis McCarthy, Lillie Western, Bryant and Lizzie Richmond, Ada Laurent (transformation dancer), the Four Powers Brothers (roller skaters), and Huber, Robie, &c. (in The Country Visitor) must have made the audiences feel that they were welcoming old, tried friends. April 26th–May 1st gave the Ventinis, Moore and Sanford (German specialty), Charley Ross (mimic and vocalist), the People's Four (Huber, Kitty Allyne and Alice and William Payne, in Perkins' Musical Party), Howe and Doyle (dancing kings), Frank Evans and Joe Coyne, Henshaw and May Ten Broeck (in Diamond Cut Diamond), D. B. Emery and Laura Russell ("musical stars"), and Hotel Runners' Ball (with Huber, J. C. Moore, Robie, &c.). Henry Watson and Alfred McDowell's Comedy Company started May (3rd–8th) with Haines and Vidocq, Watson and McDermott (in Wrinkles, with W. R. Green, M. J. Thomas, James Powell, Alice Watson, Annette Zelna, and Clara Washburn). This was a long play — a rarity with Miner. William F. Cooper and John A. Lovely ("kings of song and dance"), Mr. and Mrs. Dan Lacy, Charles and Ella Jerome, Harry Steele, Master Tommy, John and Edna Vidocq (in A Rehearsal), Gussie and Katie Hart (Harmony's Electric Duo), Fannie Beane and Charles Gilday, F. H. and Lillian White, and Lacy (in Casey, the Fiddler) constituted a bill for May 10th–15th, excellent in large part, somewhat dubious in smaller proportion.

The Martinetti Brothers' Pantomime and Novelty Company brought (May 17th–22nd) a trace of novelty, even though their concluding Jocko, the Brazilian Ape, must have been to most of the audience a long-familiar offering. Ignacio and Alfred Martinetti and Edith Murillo were chief mimes, but their cohorts included Layman (the man with a hundred faces), the Three Phanlons (athletes), McAvoy and Hallen, Jennie Miaco, the Gronotski Brothers (burlesque quadrille), Joe Hart, and Harry Emerson and George West (in The Rival Brewers). This reads well, and braces our sinews for May 24th–29th: Dave Marion and Minnie Belle, Daisy Norwood, Larry and Lizzie Smith, Dave Reed, Harry Edwards and Daisy Kernell (in A Summer Day), Sweeney and Kearney, Charles and Ed Hanley, John Carroll, Arthur and Jennie Dunn, Rice and Barton, Marietta Myers (wire and revolving globe) and the final farce, The Arrival of Gilbert (acted by members of the olio just cited). And now we progress into summer (May 31st–June 5th), with Larry and Lizzie Smith, Lillie Morris, John and Nellie Healey, Annie Hart, Farrell and Leland, John Walsh, the Three Ronaldos (*sic*), Harry Kernell, Mlle. Natta, Karl Michels, and the farce, The Pet of the Circus (also with members of the olio). Evidently Huber, Robie and the regulars had departed.

The offering, as June advanced, grew less interesting: Lew Roseland and Millie May, Lizzie Smith, Charles Crosby and Viola Wray (these two in Remnants), Matt Green and James Marco, Thomas A. Lord, C. T. Ellis and Clara Moore (this happy pair always welcome), Lottie Gilson (she also a favourite), Nat Haines and Will Vidocq, P. H. Thurber (equilibrist), Wilmot and Sewell (comic athletes) and Larry Smith and others (in The Happy Family)—all this for June 7th–12th; Val Simpson and Minnie Russell, Larry Smith and Arthur Stiles (in Political Coons), Tom Brantford ("the Electric Light of German Comedy"), Patrick Miles and Young Ireland, E. H. McHugh, the Forresters (Fanny and Frank, in Going to the Masquerade), James F. Hoey, Andy and Annie Hughes, the Four Emperors of Music, and The New German Man (with Larry and Lizzie Smith, Brantford and Arthur Stiles)—the not glittering array for June 14th–19th; George H. Adams (in Humpty Dumpty among the Indians, exactly as at Miner's Bowery, during the preceding week) aiming to attract for June 21st–26th. Kersands' Minstrels (real negroes) held the stage for June 28th–July 3rd, contributors to the joy including Billy Speed, Billy Wilson, Charles Johnson, Billy Kersands, Wallace King, Frank Mallory, Harry Thomas, and Billy and Charles Washington.

Despite the lapse in attractiveness, in June, at the Eighth Avenue Miner's, we may agree, I think, that, in general, the offerings at this and its sister establishment in the Bowery eclipsed in interest those at the older London Theatre.

Harlem Pavilion, 1886

Le Clair and Russell start the fun for June 7th–12th with A Practical Joke. The next week brought the Fannie Beane-Charles Gilday Collars and Cuffs Company. Mr. and Mrs. Alfred Miaco, in the week of June 21st–26th, presented the never-failing Humpty Dumpty; with them were Donna Stickney (slack wire), Billy Wilson (Silence and Fun), Frank La Rosa (flying rings), Annie Cushman (song and dance) and George Burnell (*sic*— roller-skater). Gibson and Ryan's Company, in the week of June 28th–July 3rd, introduced us to Irish Aristocracy. For the holiday week of July 5th–10th, Dick Gorman appeared in his frequently-seen Conrad, or, the Hand of a Friend; in his support were Thomas Doyle, Spencer Pritchard, Frank Crane, Esther Lyons and Ada Boshell.

A treat of July 12th–19th was the Davene Specialty Company, presenting headliners well-known in vaudeville—Lew Baker (in a negro act), Tom and Henrietta Murray and their dogs, Billy Lyons (female impersonator), Marie and George Nelson, Capitola Forrest, De Forrest and Gorman, the Davenes (William and Lotta), and the concluding farce, Casey, the Piper.

[115]

July 19th–24th presented Hume and Wesley's Specialty Company, comprising Imro Fox (legerdemain), Tom Ward (Fun in the Kitchen), Vim (*sic* — in feats of strength and ventriloquism), Wesley Brothers (John and James — blackface), Ada Melrose, Spence and Sartelle (on musical instruments) and, to end the sport, That Don't Go. Rather big attraction was that of July 26th–31st — J. J. Sullivan and the Horseshoe Four's Specialty Company, Charles H. Stanley (songs), Cooper and Lovely (also with songs), the Horseshoe Four (the Love Sisters, F. B. Carr and J. J. Quinlan, in The Actor's Family), Billy Payne (musical instruments), and Joe J. Sullivan (in Maloney's Visit to America). This was a bill good enough for the London or for Miner's, far to the south. Similar commendation might be given to the offering of August 2nd–7th — Winnett's European Sensation and H. M. Parker's Dog and Cat Circus; besides Parker, we had Queen Sarbro ("ladder of life"), Eurardo (trapeze), John Devoy (songs), Frank and Fannie Davis, Marco (contortionist) and Layman (impersonations of prominent people). Evidently the Pavilion was improving. Thomas and Watson's Comedy Company offered (August 9th–14th) a cosmopolitan group in Weber and Fields (now big boys and big stars), Frank Livingstone, Roseland and Millie May, Estelle Wellington, Kittie (*sic*) Sheppard (*sic*), Fitz and Webster, and (to conclude) A Surprise Party. The next week (August 16th–21st) was equally appealing, with Sheehan and Coyne, John Walsh (Irish songs), Lena and Lew Cole (in Love Taps), Hattie Westcott (songs), Frank La Rose (*sic*), Daly and Edwards (blackface), George W. Earle and Paddy Miles (songs and bag-pipes). The farces of Gilhooley's Misfortunes and Grogan's Reception, seen the first of the week, were changed, on Thursday, to The Crowded Hotel and Our Stage-Struck Daughter. The guests for August 23rd–28th were also highly esteemed in the Bowery — Lester and Williams, the Big Four, the La Verde Sisters, Conroy and Dempsey, Gus Bruno and Arthur Dunn. For the last roses of summer (August 30th–September 4th) travelled to the Harlem Pavilion Thomas Carter and Lizzie Anderson (in The Old Farm Gate — she "a clever whistler"), Emma Alfredo and Master John Lamont (horizontal bar), Frank and Fannie Davis (in Maloney's Night On), Dave Oaks (in The Darkey's Strategy), Lamont Trio (athletic act), Alfred Liston (musical act), Billy and Alice Payne, and the after piece, John L. Sullivan. The following week presented Edith Sinclair, in A Box of Cash. A heavy storm, on September 12th, damaged the Pavilion, but it re-opened on Monday, September 13th, for a week of Thomas and Watson's Dramatic and Specialty Company, and, says the Clipper, "to a packed audience." The lure consisted of acts by the proprietors of the show, George Pancoast, W. H. Bryan and May Jennings, R. G. Knowles (in Conglomeration), Estelle Wellington, and the play, The Two Wanderers. Judging from their failure to achieve reputation down to our times, I should fancy that most of these performances were themselves storm-beaten.

Since autumn weather soon forced the Pavilion to fold its tent and steal away, I will continue its campaign of 1886 to the close in October. The entertainers for September 20th–25th were Thomas and Watson and Estelle Wellington (their second week), Foreman and Stevens (in Lawn Tennis), Steve and Addie Lamont (trapeze), Minnie Lawton (musical act), Dick Morosco and Kitty Gardner (in The Schlum Family), Fields and Hanson and Martin and Collins (blackface). A benefit to Wilson, the proprietor of the place, in that week, had the aid of Mina Geary; Weber and Fields, announced, failed to appear. G. F. France, the manager, had a benefit on the 25th. September bowed to October (27th–October 2nd) with a presentation of Kelly and Murphy and Foster and Hughes's International Star Specialty Company. They began with the sketch, The Baby Elephant, and gave good measure in "turns" by Fannie Lewis (topical songs), William McMahon (songs and witty sayings), Maud Beverly, Frank Lester, and Dalton and Watts (songs, dances and one-armed sparring). For October 4th–9th, we were treated to Mattie Goodrich (in Grizzly Adams), with the Delmanning Brothers as Ben Whiteside and Melinda Peachblossom. W. J. Sully's Comedy and Specialty Company struggled, under the Pavilion, October 11th–16th, against the chill of October air; on the 18th, Davene's Allied Attractions began a week, with Mlle. Lotta (trapeze), Latta and Lynch, Capitola Forrest, Maud Chatwood, De Forrest and Gorman and Sheehan and Coyne. And the last week of the place (October 25th–30th) brought back Thomas and Watson, who revived the once-famous Here She Goes and There She Goes.

Huber's Prospect Music Hall, 1885–1886

As Variety relaxed its stranglehold on the Bowery, it stretched grasping fingers northward. Huber's Prospect Concert Garden, 106-108 East 14th Street, allured, all through the summer of 1885, with cooling drinks and soothing draughts of music mixed with "vaudeville." In earliest July, 1885, it advertised the Crescent City Quartet and Charles Noble, Jack O'Keefe, F. W. Oakland, Will Raymond (of Primrose and West's Minstrels), Pauline Harvey and John Williams—names that have not hurtled through future ages. The week of September 7th–12th provided James Taylor (English comique), Marietta Myers, J. M. Wood, Maurice Tallard, Minnie Schult, Eva St. John and Ada Alexander. This was the re-opening of the season. September 28th–October 3rd listed Adele Roselle, Fannie Lewis, Pickat (sic) and Mayon, Emma Meyers, J. L. Hudon, Minnie Schult and A. L. Gleason (with his dogs). Minnie Schult, Budworth and Miss Brimmos (sic) added to the zest of late October evenings. November 23rd became quite like a night at Pastor's or Miner's, with Fenton and Sharpley, Gus Hill, Jennie Engel, Minnie Schult, George Beauchamp (eccentric), Amy Nelson and Lillie

Forrest. I am beginning to be alarmed at thought of the future. But perhaps Bessie Gilbert's cornet may set me wondering, in December, why one of what used to be called the female sex should ever play the cornet or, for that matter, the 'cello.

GUNTHER'S PALM-GARTEN THEATER, 1885–1886

Thanks to the Staats-Zeitung we can enter in spirit Gunther's Palm-Garten Theater (14th Street near Third Avenue), and for the entire season appraise its bill of fare. There, for the week of August 31st–September 5th, appeared Victoria Martell and Alice Brooks, Adele Martinetti (dancer), Murphy and Miles ("Gentlemen from Kerry"), Joe Lewis ("das Wunder der Gymnastie"), Dave Martin and Knowles ("Neger Comic"). In the week preceding we tried, perhaps successfully, to admire Ada Melrose, Emma Jones, Jennie Cunningham, Thomas Lord, the Schane (sic) Brothers ("die kleine Boxer") and James B. Radcliffe. October 26th listed Sam Roberts (baritone), Signora Rinaldi (soprano), Crowley ("male prima donna"), John B. Wills and May Adams and Mr. and Mrs. Burton. Adele Martinetti, Foster and Hughes and the Collins Sisters carried the banner into early November. On the 11th of November Frank and Fannie Davis, Ella Raimé, Julia Wilson, Adele Martinetti, Sam Roberts, John Devoy, and the "Nachspiel," One Dollar for a Kiss, sounded promising and provocative. The week of November 30th–December 5th bore the names of Arthur O'Brien and Kate Morris, Ella Raimé, Helene Duval, Lena Cole and Minnie Lawton, Sam Rogers and Harry Lawton, along with Lillie (sic) Hall's burlesque, Hassanbad. In mid-December Gunther's flourished with Lillie Hall, Alwine Renner, Ella Raimé, Fred Bryant (cornet), May Arnott, Alice Drayton, Billy Bryant and Len Bloom. At last we are meeting old acquaintances. Those listed in early January were Lillie Hall, Minnie Lee, Hattie Wescott (sic), Kittie Wells, Ignatz Conradi, Billy Bryant, Annie Devere, and Dave Martin. The burlesque Ixion also figured on January 2nd. The week of January 25th–30th had a burlesque Pygmalion and Galatea, acted by Agnes Carle (Galatea — or Galathée), Hamilton Nichols (Midas), Ada Melrose (Ganymed) and Paul Vernon (Pygmalion). In the olio were Alfred Liston and Mr. and Mrs. Morrissey.

In earlier February we garnered the talents of Signora Monti, Gallard (basso), Agnes Carle, the abiding Ella Raimé and Arthur Cook. A kind of Princess of Trebizonde was here during the week of February 8th–13th. February 22nd boasted of Ada Melrose, Gallard, Florence Latelle, Nellie Hamilton and Lillie Bailey, Paul Vernon, Lawlor and Lang, &c. Let us pass into March, on the 8th, expecting to hear or see Mat Chatwood, the Thaler Trio of Tyrolean singers, Ella Raimé, Ada Melrose, Maurice Gallard and Paul Vernon. At the end of that blustery month we were cheered with promise of Charles Diamond, Frazer and Allen, Ada Devere (soubrette), Ignatz Conradi, Gallagher and Gannon, Sabra Lonsdale (English songs) and Elsa Alberti. Surely Gunther's is looking up. April 12th–17th gave us Annie Suits, the abiding Ella Raimé, Sabra Lonsdale, the Laverne Sisters, the Burke Brothers, Frazer and Allen and the clever Charles Diamond. During the next week, newcomers were Baker and West, Mlle. Bessie (in An Arabian Night's Dream), Robinson (ventriloquist), Watson and West, &c., Annie Suits, Ella Raimé and the Laverne Sisters (Bella and Carlotta — proudly set down as "die Königinnen der Luft"). I perforce skip to May, with Mlle. Grévain, Mlle. Bessie (*sic*), Diamond, Robinson, Frank Bush, the La Vernes and Master Belzac inviting to the show. As May passed into June, Sharpley and West, Alice Grévain, Adele Roselle and Frank Lester headed the attractions.

The Brothers McShane were advertised, in latest June, as "the smallest boxers in the world." June 21st–26th gave us Arthur and Jennie Dunn, Steve and Addie Lamont and Bertha Marshall — a promise that leaves me cold. For July 23rd, Gussie Hart, Dan Hart, James F. Hoey and Marco (contortionist) tried to make us forget cruel summer's heat. Hoey, Gracie May and Harry Rogers also tried. For earlier August, the Palm-Garten entrusted that delicate obligation to Marie and J. Martens (cat duet), Hattie Westcott, Greenbaum (magician), Gussie Braasch and Sheridan and Flynn. Gussie Braasch ("die schwebende Jungfrau, in Engel's Traum"), C. Ed Foreman, Lizzie Whitehill ("das reizende Baby"), and Gussie and Kate Hart were among the wonders of latest August. Whatever his opinion of the worth of Gunther's Palm-Garten, the reader may thank the Staats-Zeitung for the items here laboriously transcribed for his information.

THEISS'S NEW MUSIC HALL, 1885–1886

Theiss's New Music Hall and Alhambra Court, 14th Street near Third Avenue, for Sunday, August 30, 1885, announced two "grand sacred concerts," with Albert Eschert (director), Della Torra (Berlin chansonnette), Josephine Schroeder and a comic Herr Grose-Craff (certainly a comic name). Della Torra became a fixture; Emil Müller joined her in the announcements for October 5th–10th. In November the Herald advertises Jules Levy and his cornet as sources of musical delight; perhaps Variety had flown to warmer climes. I found no more for this elaborately named hall till April, when Albert Eschert, Pizzarello (French "Komiker") and Adele Martinetti were advertised in the Staats-Zeitung; Amalia Martin was an acquisition of the 10th. Thereafter I found no notice of the place; perhaps the management did not care to advertise. Perhaps this German-sounding record should have been placed under the German division of our work.

[119]

University Club Theatre, 1885–1886

This little theatre, clinging, as it were, to the life-line, had a rather busy season. A French performance for charity, on January 7th, enlisted Mrs. Wilber Bloodgood, Elsie De Wolfe (two queens of the amateur stage), Geraldine Reed, W. G. Heath and Mr. Le Maistre; the plays were L'Été de St. Martin and La Soupière. The Normal College Alumnae, on January 22nd acted a farce, possibly to the satisfaction of all concerned; those energetic Alumnae were at it again, in early March, with An Amazon Success. February 3rd (afternoon) brought Kitty Berger's concert, Anna Bulkley Hills, Michael Banner and William H. Lee, of the American Opera, assisting. In the evening of that day, some amateurs of the Dramatic Social Club acted The Wedding Day.

A midnight performance, on March 3rd, was for the benefit of Selina Dolaro and brought a striking array of talent in Francis Wilson, Sophie Eyre, Edward Solomon, Lillian Russell and Geraldine Ulmar. A novelty of the show was that the performers sat in the audience and passed thence to the stage to do their "turns." On the 4th, Clara Spence was here, assisted by Henrietta Beebe, Mr. and Mrs. Gerrit Smith and W. H. Beckett. On the 13th, an impressively-named Colonna Istria gave the first of three Lenten Soirées Dramatiques, presenting La Goutte d'Eau (by Jacques Normand) and En Wagon (by Verconsin). John Fiske, on March 17th, began a series of four lectures on the Civil War, with maps, pictures, etc. George Riddle was to recite on the afternoons of April 1st and 8th. April 15th (afternoon) brought Mme. Henry Greville, with La Vie Parisienne. On the evening of April 15th Moncure D. Conway made us serious with his lecture on The English in India and Australia. He had lectured here, also, on April 1st and 8th. The Harvard students, on the 12th, acted Papillonette.

The contribution of April 22nd (evening) was Moncure D. Conway's lecture on The English Church and the Question of Disestablishment — a question far more important than any amateur acting. Frank P. W. Bellew, "known as Chip," gave on the 29th, Chips from a Workshop, with Fannie and Little Mattie Johnson serving (perhaps?) as chips. A testimonial to A. S. Baralt made May 3rd important (at least to him).

The Amateur Comedy Club, 1886

To its own section I relegate performances at the University Club Theatre of the Amateur Comedy Club, Incorporated, a club which was a feature of New York social life for many, many years thereafter. We saw its initiation, in that time of the craze for amateur acting, in February, 1885. Now, fully organised, the company began its long and amateur-honorable career with what it set down as its second and third performances (January 9th

[120]

and 11th, 1886). The bill presented The Anonymous Kiss (a one-act come-dietta by J. A. Woodward), the actors including H. Chauncey, Jr., Elisha Dyer, 3rd, Samuel Parsons and Misses Marian Sharpless and Ruth Lawrence; also The Trial of Tompkins (a farce in one act by Thomas J. Williams), with a cast including Alexander T. Mason, Robert Sturgis, Henry S. Blake and Misses May Burke and Cornelia Van Auken. The fourth performance (February 6th) of the ambitious group likewise gave us two pieces—A Misunderstanding (by Mrs. Walter S. Andrews) and Peacock's Holiday (a two-act farcical comedy by Herman C. Merivale). In the former appeared Frederic D. Weekes, Evert Jansen Wendell (one of the most devoted theatre-lovers that ever lived), Samuel Parsons, Mrs. Andrews and Miss Van Auken; the players in the second were Robert Sturgis, Elisha Dyer, 3rd, H. Chaun-cey, Jr., A. T. Mason, Miss Van Auken and Miss Katherine (Kitty) Brady. On April 27th and 28th, a double bill gave A Cup of Tea with E. J. Wendell, Stephen G. Williams, Meredith Howland, Jr., and Elsie De Wolfe (later on the professional stage); also Withered Leaves (a one-act comedy by Fred W. Broughton), with a cast including A. P. Montant, R. Sturgis, Charles E. Boynton, Henry S. Blake, Mrs. Samuel L. Post and Mrs. Wilber A. Blood-good. The Amateur Comedy Club, one sees, consisted of gentlefolk plucked bodily from the social register of the time.

On February 11th, the Greenwich Literary Society proffered the amateur-loved The Doctor of Alcantara, with Eugene Clark (sic), M. Cooper, Miss O'Keefe, Nina Douglas, Mrs. Griggs, George C. Pearce and Charles Hetzel. The Crib Club of the upper city gave here, on February 23rd, a minstrel show of (to me) unknown quantity and quality. On February 25th, the Arlington League of Amateurs acted Hazel Kirke. On March 26th, Bertha Grosse appeared in the everlasting Deborah. And, on April 5th, the Central Turn-Verein attempted Krieg im Frieden (The Passing Regiment). March 31st brought the Manhattan Turn-Verein, with the Columbia Amateur Club, in a Theater-Vorstellung—a promise of some vagueness. The New-York Männerchor held here, on Easter Monday, April 25th, a "Grosse musikalische Abendunterhaltung," which, in effect, may have been as big as it was poly-syllabic. Certainly promising was the Jubilæum of Fritz Fichtner, on April 18th, with assistance from Henrietta Markstein, Letitia Fritsch and Helene Weingarten.

May 23rd staged an Abendunterhaltung by Thalia Theater actors; this for the benefit of Theodor Urban. Members of the Thalia force were at it again, on June 18th, with Unser Präsident, Das Versprechen hinter'm Herd and Verlobung bei der Laterne—good, light stuff for summer.

Koster and Bial's, 1885–1886

The popular establishment, Koster and Bial's, was offering, on July 6, 1885, a burlesque of La Belle Hélène, the Martens Trio and the Herbert Brothers; Ella Wesner was stressed for Sunday, July 12th. La Belle Hélène was still going, as August lapsed toward September; but a burlesque of the Casino Nanon, called Na-Non, came forth on August 31st. Latest August featured, also, the Yang Yings (Stuart, Emile and Katey), in Idiosyncrasies. Na-Non and nine Bedouin Arabs were advertised on September 21st; shortly thereafter Mlle. Rose and Master Julian ("acrobatic wonders") enlivened the careless auditors. Could these be the later-famous Julians? The first appearance of Prince Lichtenstein's Hungarian Gypsy Band fell on October 4th; on the 5th, we learned that Harry Le Clair was Na-Non. Maud Oswald (flying rings), Alice Raymond (cornet) and the Julians (Rose and Martin) also figured in the bill. Laura Burt and the Hungarian Gypsy Band combined to allure, on the 13th. Louise Lester (soprano) and Herr Conradi (tenor) figured on Sunday, November 1st.

Of course there must be a burlesque Mikado. This duly appeared, on November 2nd, with Paul Bown, Murry Woods, Louise Lester, Fred Warren, Laura Burt, Sophie Hummel, Georgie Parker, Louise Fox and Carrie Gould, and it continued until I wearied making notes of it for my bulging scrip. The Tissots, Liberati and P. C. Shortis were stressed on November 29th; for Sunday, December 13th, Ella Wesner, the Lucier Family and The Mikado (burlesque). With these, on December 21st, Laura Burt and Eva Hewitt peeped from the advertisements. The week of December 28th–January 2nd was rich with promise of Flora Moore, William Carroll, A. O. Duncan (ventriloquist), Bessie Gilbert, nine Venetian Troubadours and — The Mikado. For January 25th we were summoned by Alice Grévain ("comique eccentrique"), Pete Shaw, Ella Wesner, Flora Moore, Alfred Liston, Laura Burt, Louise Lester, The Mikado and selections from The Gypsy Baron. Ella Wesner and Louise Lester were now features of the house.

The Martens, Vienna Duettists and the Hungarian Gypsy Band performed on February 15th. For the 22nd, a long-promised Princess of Trebizonde, Fata Morgana and Ella Wesner were the lure. That Princess, with Louise Lester, Laura Burt, Agnes Earle, William Paul Bown and Fred Warren in the cast, divided honours, on March 1st, with the Dare Brothers. We passed into April with very little change, and, on the 12th of that uncertain month found Louise Lester's benefit to decide on. Later April revived Trial by Jury and Pinafore. Ixion was the cry for May 10th and some weeks later. An "opera," Students of Heidelberg, and Liberty Enlightening the World (we were then excited about the Bartholdi statue) joined in the bills for July 5th–10th. Ixion was still rolling up a run, on July 19th; on August 2nd, a burlesque Venus and Adonis may have been intended to draw seekers of sensation; it was reconstructed by September 6th. Here I leave Koster and Bial's for 1885–86, decidedly pleased to depart.

EDEN MUSÉE; COSMOPOLITAN, ETC., 1885–1886

If Koster and Bial's was deemed a bit fast for gay New Yorkers, the Eden Musée, further down West 23rd Street was the Mecca of suburban visitors, who stared with amazement at the waxen effigies and shuddered with fear in the famous Chamber of Horrors. In July, 1885, this popular institution was advertising a replica of the Bartholdi Statue of Liberty, then firmly fixed in public imagination. On July 27th, "Our Dead Hero," Ulysses S. Grant, just deceased, was exhibited in wax. And in late August (24th) a "Grand Sacred Chamber" opened, with six pictures from the life of Christ. Sunday concerts were not considered too profane for the faithful Edenites. General McClellan and the late Cardinal McCloskey, in waxen image, faced the curious in earliest November. Later in that sombre month, Mary Anderson, recently at the Star Theatre, was shown in waxen beauty as Galatea; and Ajeeb, chess automaton, excited wonder. And by December 1st, Helen Dauvray figured (in wax) in One of Our Girls. Surely the Musée kept up to date. Death reaped a harvest of notabilities at that time, and the Musée was busy, providing waxen effigies of the victims. The late W. H. Vanderbilt was added to (so to speak) the morgue, on December 14th. But Little Linda Da Costa was a living voice in later December — perhaps a Christmas gift to sadly ruminant visitors. Indeed she had been there on November 7th — for children.

However life-like and moving the effigies in the collection, they could not move. Remaining as they did, they necessitate my recording of only what was new. Pasteur, operating on a child, was a cheerful addition in January; in February Ferdinand de Lesseps was shown, explaining the Panama Canal — to his children! who must forsooth have become somewhat weary of the subject, long before the Eden Musée set them up as models of filial behaviour. A "life-like figure" of the late John Kelly was added, in June, to the waxen morgue.

The Cosmopolitan Skating Rink, at Broadway and 41st Street, began, on July 27th, concerts by the Mexican National Band, under direction of Encarnacion Payen; they faded out before New York knew what was happening. As a skating rink the Cosmopolitan also cut a poor figure. Here, on January 26th, Jacob Schaefer and Maurice Vigneaux began a billiard contest, 3,000 points for a stake of $5,000 — perhaps not so much like easy money as it sounds. These two heroes advertised another combat for 3,000 points in blocks of 600 points, this time (March 9th to 13th) for a considerably reduced purse — $2,000.

On February 13th, the hall was advertising the European Circus; Stick-

[123]

ney and Odell were stars of the show, in late February, and, beginning on March 1st, Mlle. Lottie took her Slide for Life. In April, Professor Gleason held the stage in exciting acts of taming intractable fiery horses. In May, the Japanese Village that had for a time set up in Madison Square moved to the Cosmopolitan. That was a Japanese year, if ever we had one.

MINOR RESORTS, 1885–1886

Fortunately we can tread the primrose path with very few steps. The Haymarket, Sixth Avenue and 30th Street, which mothers feared for their young sons, was set down throughout the year in the Herald, as "Bijou of Terpsichore — Sociable Dansante"; it began every night at nine its promenade concert, and whoever listed could, by paying twenty-five cents, enter and enjoy the festal scene. But admission was free to the Cremorne Garden, in 32nd Street, near Broadway, with its "Palace of Mirrors. 75 Pretty Barmaids." So ran the slogans of these resorts throughout 1885–86.

Harry Hill's was more muscular and less suggestive in Herald advertisements. There, on Sunday, August 23, 1885, appeared the Excelsior Quartet, in Jubilee Songs, again exciting wonder as to why this sporting establishment turned on Sundays, to that kind of entertainment. Southern Jubilee Singers also on the 27th and on October 4th caused tears and wonder over the cups. Variety of wonderment brought in, on Sunday, February 15th, a concert and Gibbons, the "man snake"— very different from the concert, on May 2nd, by the Twilight Club. But January 1st was big with promise of two grand athletic and variety performances — wrestling, pool, boxing tournament, prize waltzing for ladies, etc.

GLOBE DIME MUSEUM, 1885–1886

The reader perhaps does not realise how hard it is to find details of very minor activities of the amusement world; of course they did not usually advertise in reputable journals. If it were not for the matchless Harvard Theatre Collection, I know not where I should have discovered the programmes of all those Bowery theatres of "Variety" with which for some years back I wearied the diligent student. To Harvard, likewise, I am indebted for two bills for the Globe Dime Museum, 298 Bowery. There, on December 28, 1885, appeared, in sequence, Allie Adams, F. Madden (jig and reel), William Morton ("Irish"), Thomas Fairview (European songs), and, in the farce, Pepper's Ghost, a "stock company"; also were provided "Professor" King ("paper King"), Broncho Johnnie ("government scout and broncho rider"), and a "Second Annual Convention of Old Maids." Though within a short distance from the London and Miner's, this Museum, it would seem, was artistically miles away. On February 15, 1886, Darwin's Missing

Link, Krao, the Monkey Girl, set the customers thinking and possibly feeling, surreptitiously, their own classic features.   In addition, the bill provided Clint Williams, Beaucamps (*sic*), Dolly Masters, Harry W. Bernard and the cheery concluding attraction, Edward Atkins, in his own play, Happy Joe, the Telegraph Boy.   We all know that theatrical offerings "ascend by base degrees" to Edwin Booth as Brutus or as Hamlet.

STEINWAY HALL, 1885–1886

The reader may well view with apprehension the complexities of the season's programme at Steinway Hall; but he knows well that he must be informed.   I should hesitate to assert that this hall housed concerts rather more imposing than those at Chickering Hall; suppose we see.

Two concerts, on Sunday, November 1st, start us in the month of sodden, fallen leaves.   In the afternoon, Frank Van der Stucken proffered the first of four orchestral concerts, his reliable assistants on that occasion being Christine Dossert and S. B. Mills.   The evening function was a Musical and Literary Entertainment, given by the Livingston Association, for the benefit of the Sir Moses Montefiore Fund, with, as performers, the Beethoven Männerchor, the New York Zither Club Verein, Ida Klein, J. Kerch (bass), Nahan Franko (violin), Emanuel Moor (pianist), and F. Michel and G. Schlesinger (elocutionists).   On the afternoon of November 6th, W. Waugh Lauder gave a piano recital, severely handled by the Herald reviewer.   For the benefit of the Palermo Cholera Sufferers, a concert, on Sunday evening, November 8th, promised co-operation of the Italian Societies of New York, Brooklyn, Newark and Hoboken, Cappa's Seventh Regiment Band, Juliette Corden, Liberati, Del Puente, Giannini and Alexander Salvini.   On Monday, the 9th, the Chinese Sunday School Mission carried us even farther afield, ethnologically, with a concert involving Carrie Hun-King, Nahan Franko, and a group I challenge the reader to identify — T. Ratwing (charming name), Adolf Glose, Nettie Dunlap, and E. Stellini.   For the Grant Monument Fund, a benefit, on November 10th, still kept us in the racial realm; the Astor Place Coloured Tragedy Company gave Othello, with B. J. Ford as the Moor, J. A. Arnoux as Iago, and Eloise Molineux as Desdemona. This has a familiar ring.

November 17th, 24th and December 1st were to be important with joint concerts of Ovide Musin and August Hyllested, a Danish pianist.   Meantime, on November 15th, Van der Stucken's second Sunday concert proffered, as soloists, Francesca Guthrie and August Hyllested.   On November 18th, one might have heard in concert Therese Heilner, Edmund Neupert and Van der Stucken with his orchestra.   On the 20th, Jeanne Franko gave a concert, assisted by Carolina Zeiss and others.   On the 21st (afternoon) we lovingly set back the clock to give a testimonial concert to H. C. Timm, president of the Philharmonic from 1844 to 1861; Theodore Thomas, Richard Hoffman, Emma Juch, Helen Dudley Campbell, the Meigs Sisters, Charles H. Thompson (tenor) and A. E. Stoddard were advertised. Timm, once a digital proficient, was lavish in performing on the piano; he played the first movement of Beethoven's C minor concerto, and, with Hoffman, parts of Mozart's Concertina in E-flat, for two pianos. November 22nd promised the Greeley North Pole Expedition, illustrated by Behre and Kohler.

On November 24th, Juliette Corden sang at the Musin-Hyllested matinée, Jennie Miller serving on December 1st. November 30th found Edward Mollenhauer's pupils nervously showing what they could dare and do. The Van der Stucken afternoon of the 29th promised Edmund Neupert and Holst Hansen. Señor Carlos Sobrino's piano recital, on December 3rd, availed itself of the valued assistance of Ovide Musin and Ida Cortada. On the 5th, Florence Mangam (soprano) gave a concert, with a fine group including Anna Bulkley Hills, Ovide Musin, Christian Fritsch, F. Remmertz and E. Agramonte — perhaps the most imposing group, thus far, of the season. F. E. Bristol's concert, on December 9th (afternoon), included the second act of Martha. Lilly Post, May Fielding, Minnie T. Seligman (remember the name!), Michael Banner, J. Williams Macy and Sophie Flack were among the participants. On the 12th, 19th and 28th, William Courtney and the Courtney Ladies' Quartet officiated, and, on the 13th, Van der Stucken again wielded the baton, with, as soloists, Mrs. E. Dexter (soprano), Carl Dufft (baritone) and A. Lambert (pianist). On the evening of the 14th, Steinway Hall opened its platform to Ida Serven ("singing reader"), Laura A. Collins, Ella M. Crocker (what would nonentities be without initials of middle names?) and the St. George's Glee Club. The Gotham Art Students took the hall on December 16th, with Harriet B. Clarke, Jeanne Franko, Carolina Zeiss, Ida Corani (sic), Gustav Bley, Holst Hansen, W. H. Lawton, and the Tipaldi Mandolin Quartet. And, on the 17th, Eugenie de Roode Rice joined the season's endless procession of pianists, with Miss Omagh Armstrong and Van der Stucken's orchestra in support. On the 18th, Adele Margulies and Thomas's orchestra appeared. The People's Concert Society, on the afternoon of December 20th, offered a free concert, promising the appearance of Theodore Thomas and his orchestra. On the 21st, Jean Joseph Bott opened the house, with Juliette Corden and Wilhelm Mueller (violin) to swell the pæan of joy. Marie Selika gave a concert, on December 22nd, and then returned to the obscurity from which she came. Aptommas, on the afternoon and evening of December 30th, harped beautifully, with Manx airs figuring in the programme.

Mrs. W. H. Sherwood rendered a piano recital, on the afternoon of January 13th, Villa Whitney White (soprano) co-operating. Master Bernhard Sisheimer (violinist), a pupil of Richard Arnold, presented himself, on January 14th, Annie Tanner, Sarah B. Anderson and Emanuel Moor aiding and abetting. On the 19th, the Bergen Star Concert, "coloured talent," Adelaide Smith, Flora Batson, Sam Lucas and the Walker Male Quartet, stormed the citadel of public regard; on the 23rd, Edward Mollenhauer's The Passions had the assistance of Julia Stark, who read the poem and of Minnie Dilthey, who sang. Michael Banner's concert fell on January 26th. On the 28th, the annual concert of the Frauenverein enlisted Mme. L'Allemand, Charlotte Walker, W. H. Fessenden, A. E. Stoddard, Kitty Berger, Richard Arnold, E. A. Lefebre and F. Q. Dulcken. Carlos Sobrino's, on the 29th, proffered Carl Dufft and Henry Pinzi; on the 30th, Alexander Lambert called to his aid Van der Stucken's orchestra. At another session, on the 31st, Wagner's The Love Feast of the Apostles enlisted Max Alvary, Ida Klein, Minnie Dilthey, J. J. Bott (violin) and the Germania Club of Newark. Van der Stucken's fifth Novelty Concert invaded the hall on February 2nd (evening), with Christine Dossert, W. H. Lawton, F. Remmertz. A. Victor Benham, announced, could not appear.

A testimonial to Carl Alves came, on February 17th, with the assistance of Adolph Hartdegen and two former pupils of Alves—Agnes Florence and Kate Nuffer. On the 19th, John Lavine was similarly honoured. The Teacher's Association (Wilber F. Hudson, president) took the hall, on the 22nd (afternoon), and invited with lure of Henrietta Beebe, W. H. Lawton (her husband), Harriet Webb, and Laura A. Collins. A concert for the Minerva Home for Cash Girls (worthy charity!) gave us, on the 23rd, Hortense Pierse, Marie Bowen, G. Becker, Carl Levinson and our old friend, G. G. Rockwood. The 25th offered a benefit for the German Emigrant Home, the participating artists being Charlotte Walker, Frank Kaltenborn, Jacob Graff, E. Schenck ('cello) and the choir of St. Matthew's Church, Hoboken. Outstanding events were the piano recitals of Franz Rummel, returning to an expectant public. On February 26th, Emilio Belari's concert of his pupils was to present Isabelle Urquhart (later the stately beauty of Casino operettas) in selections from La Favorita; I never thought of this singer as having prepared, possibly, for "grand" opera. And, we remember, she played Portia, that very week, in Lawrence Barrett's revival of Julius Cæsar. The evening of the 27th found Master Friedberger, fourteen years old, playing the violin; in his programme were Franz Remmertz, Carrie Goldsticker and the ubiquitous Michael Banner. An Old Folks Concert edged its way into this careful hall, on March 2nd. A. Victor Benham advertised quite unnecessary piano recitals for March 9th and 13th; illness had prevented his appearance, on February 2nd, at this hall, with Van der Stucken's orchestra.

How glorious the "concert artistique" of March 8th, with Lilli Lehmann, F. Rummel and Ovide Musin, Gustav Hinrichs directing! A matinée, with these celebrities, was listed for March 20th. And now the esteemed Mme. Fursch-Madi announced three concerts for March 18th, 24th (matinée) and April 1st. Adele Margulies, Jacques Bouhy and F. Bergner assisted. Madeline Schiller, whom we are glad to greet in that season of too many pianists, announced matinées for March 27th and April 10th. But I must go back (so hard is it to keep a straight path, chronologically, in this terribly complicated record) to a Gilmore concert, on March 15th, and a concert, arranged by Joseffy, for the German Press Club, on the 21st. At the last-named function were to appear Emma Juch, Anna Eschenbach, Fannie Hirsch, Candidus, Dufft, von Inten, Dulcken and the Standard Quartet Club. The Press can always count on good support from artists. On the evening of March 30th, Helen Hopekirk made another pianist for our collection. And all for excitement I end the paragraph with A. O. Babel, the Texas Cowboy Pianist, who on March 12th and 13th (matinée) was to play from 1,200 selections, improvise, compose and "play with marvellously brilliant execution." Yet he had never received any instruction! Pianistic pugilism, says the jocose Herald.

Mlle. Florenza d'Arona announced English ballad concerts for April 7th and 12th, at which were to appear Charlotte Walker, J. N. Pattison, Carl Sanger and the Courtney Quartet (7th) and Ida Klein and Christian Fritsch (12th). At a concert on the 6th, David Bimberg came forth. The Arion concert of April 18th enlisted Van der Stucken, Louis Maas (of Boston — pianist), Marie Groebl, C. Fritsch, Heinrich and Remmertz. Just to let the reader know, I will say that Carlos Sobrino, on April 14th, played Rubinstein's Concerto in E minor and Mendelssohn's in D minor, with Rafael Navarro directing an orchestra. Adele Margulies, Pauline L'Allemand and Leopold Lichtenberg united, on the 17th. The Virginia Jubilee Singers exemplified, on April 20th, an art then dwindling in appeal, except in Uncle Tom's Cabin. On the 24th, Holst Hansen, August Hyllested, Marie Gramm, Sam Franko and Emil Schenck possessed the platform for what should have been a "nice" concert, Scandinavian in flavour. Under the patronage of Mme. Murio-Celli, in latest April (29th — afternoon) appeared Mme. Sacconi, De Anna, W. H. Rieger, Marie Groebl, Christine Rosswog and Carlo (sic) Sobrino. And Jerome Hopkins re-emerged on April 28th. On the 30th, the New York Operatic Club appeared, under direction of Chevalier Filoteo Greco. But livelier than these final outpourings of genius nonplussed was the Annual Irish and Musical Festival of the Gaelic Society, on April 27th, with Carrie Hun-King, Fred Harvey and Carl Levinson. After the concert, the Seanachas was celebrated in Tammany Hall.

CHICKERING HALL, 1885–1886

The first I find for this attractive hall is a charity concert (Saturday afternoon, October 3rd) arranged by Mlle. de Nogueiras, daughter of the Portuguese minister at Washington; she sang in such contralto tones as she could muster. With her were Christian Fritsch, Miss Homer, Adolph Hartdegen, Gerrit Smith (organ) and Herman (piano). The Fisk Jubilee Singers were here on October 19th, 20th and 22nd. S. N. Penfield began, on October 20th, a series of ten organ recitals; on the first afternoon his assistants were Louise Pyk (soprano) and Richard Arnold. The Venerable F. W. Farrar, Archdeacon of Westminster, delivered three lectures that I should like to have heard: Dante (October 26th); Browning's Poems (28th); and The Talmud and Its Authors (30th). Edward J. O'Mahoney, (basso) gave, on October 27th, a concert, with, as assistants, Hattie Clapper, Ollie Torbett, Miss Hallenbeck and William Courtney.

The Chevalier Antoine de Kontski, much in evidence that season, began, on October 30th, a series of six piano matinées; Frl. Kitty Berger (zither) then made a tinkling début in America. The Raymond Sisters and Harry Hilliard also appeared. Frederick Archer, on November 2nd, began his series of organ recitals, with Annie Louise Tanner, Whitney Mockridge and Kitty Berger as co-adjutors. And, on November 5th (evening) and 7th (afternoon), Emma Nevada, who never quite conquered her fellow-countrymen, displayed her arts of *coloratura,* to the applause of her hearers; with her were Edmond Vergnet (tenor), Carlo Buti (baritone), Luigi Casati (violin), Gustav Levita (pianist) and Paolo Giorza (director). The reader surmises the importance of the concert from the unimportance of the participants.

The Archer organ recital of November 9th, had, as soloists, Carolina Zeiss (much in demand), Carl Levinson and Carl Venth. Dora Becker (violin) was another November actuary (9th, evening), with, to assist, Marie and Edward Groebl, Robert Goldbeck, Rusack and G. W. Colby. Of course the "recitalists" grimly pursued their way. Penfield's third occurred on November 3rd. At his fourth (November 10th) we heard Emma Watson Doty (soprano) and Josephine Ware (pianist). De Kontski's second concert (November 13th) enlisted Marie Havely (soprano), Carl Levinson (baritone), Carl Bayrhoffer ('cello) and W. E. Taylor (accompanist). A benefit for St. John's Guild made charitable and possibly interesting the evening of November 14th; Helen Dudley Campbell, Louis Blumenberg ('cello), Paul Clech (baritone) and Emma Juch contributed to the spell. Bradford Recitals of the Polar World—The Greeley Expedition—changed the tone, on November 16th; another Bradford Recital, on December 1st, was devoted to Norse Ruins.

November 17th brought the first concert of the New York Philharmonic Club, with Anna (*sic*) Louise Tanner and S. B. Mills to strengthen the inducement. The St. George's Glee Club sounds promising for November 19th, with Henrietta Beebe, George and Maud Morgan, Corinne Flint and Caryl Florio. On the 21st Kate Field lectured on Social and Political Crimes in Utah, possibly proclaiming thereby her succession to the moral

[129]

heritage of Anna Dickinson. On November 26th, F. and H. Carri had to begin a series of six violin concerts, aided on that date by Gertrude Luther, Carl Bayrhoffer and F. Derschuch. De Kontski's third recital (November 27th) provided variety with Harriet Avery, A. L. King and Frederick Archer. The Henrietta Beebe Quartet (Miss Beebe, Sarah Barron Anderson, William H. Lawton and Carl E. Martin) sounds delightful for November 28th, especially as Pergolesi's Stabat Mater was in the programme. The evening of the 27th bristles with the names of the Mendelssohn Quintet Club of Boston, Mmes. Trischet, de Bremont and Feurdent, and Messrs. Clech, Vicarino, Mesnier, and Marshall P. Wilder. Radio addicts of 1941 and later will be interested to learn that this concert was sponsored by the Ammoniaphone. Robert Goldbeck (pianist) came alertly on the platform (November 30th) with Nita Carieta and J. Meyer as assistants, none too promising. The Penfield recital, on December 1st, proffered F. and H. Carri, W. H. Stanley and Mrs. Tonceda. The inducement for December 3rd at the Musurgia concert seems attractive — Ella Earle, one of the best of our church and concert sopranos, and the New York Philharmonic Club. The hall was busy on December 5th. In the afternoon, La Petite Louise Marguerite, "the miniature Patti," was presented, in concert, with Emily Winant, Harriet Webb, the Henrietta Beebe Quartet; the evening was, to intelligent souls, rather trying, with Aunt Polly Bassett's Singin' Skewl, which never "let out" or let up. A banjo concert, on the 9th, leaves me cold, though Marshall P. Wilder somehow was fitted into the proceedings. De Kontski's assistants on December 11th were Dora Hennings and Dora Becker — gifts by name, if not by nature; on the 19th he proffered Carolina Zeiss and F. Carri.

On December 10th, Kate Field lectured on Eyes and Ears in London. Goldbeck, on the 11th, presented in concert himself, Marie Havely, Helen Ludington, and Edward and Henry Mollenhauer. Adelina Puerari had a concert on the 20th. S. N. Penfield was busy at Christmas time. His organ recital, on December 22nd (afternoon) provided Anna Trichett (*sic*) and F. W. Jameson, in addition to his own art; and on the 23rd, he directed the first of three concerts of the New York Harmonic Society, with performances of Bach's cantata, Thou God of Israel, and Leslie's The First Christmas Morn, the soloists being Emma Watson-Doty, Eva Kennedy-Laurie, William Dennison and Carl E. Dufft. On the 21st, came the Bank Clerks' Glee Club, in concert. On the evening of the 22nd, the second concert of the Carri Brothers called in the aid of Laura Carroll Dennis, C. H. Clarke and Penfield. The second concert of the New York Philharmonic Club, on January 5th, had, as soloists, Blanche Stone Barton (soprano) and Richard Arnold. On the 7th (afternoon) De Kontski, Belle Cole, F. Jameson and Frederick Archer appeared; in the evening the St. George's Glee Club came in, accompanied by Hortense Pierse, Michael Banner, H. R. Humphries (a member of the club), and Caryl Florio. On the 8th, the Greenwich Amateur Opera Company again assailed The Mikado, who never made the punishment fit the crime of such assailants. In this case the perpetrators were Charles A. Hetzel, George C. Pearce, J. Williams Macy, Eugene Clarke, Misses H. M. O'Keefe, Alice Mersereau, E. Brett and Henrietta Griggs, one or two of them not unknown to our history. An Amateur Minstrel Show on December 28th had, perhaps, prepared the way for this amateur Mikado.

Robert J. Burdette, lecturing, January 11th, on The Diligent Man, diverted us for a moment from the excess of music everywhere. But we hastened back, on January 18th, 22nd and the afternoon of the 23rd for more piano recitals, this time by William H. Sherwood; Dora Becker and Effie Stewart appeared at first. And De Kontski was at it again, on the 20th, with Emily Winant, Dora Hennings, Alice Archer, Courtney, Jr. Sam Franko had a concert on the 27th, aided by Jeanne Franko, Mrs. Hartdegen and Holst Hansen. A voice from the past calls, on January 30th; a testimonial to J. R. Thomas, "composer of Cottage by the Sea, Beautiful Isle of the Sea, and 'Tis but a Little Faded Flower," was to enlist George and Maud Morgan, S. B. Mills, Imogene Brown, G. Maeder, Mrs. S. B. Anderson and the St. George's Glee Club. And here is another suggestion of advertising methods of 1941: on January 25th, at Chickering Hall, for the Dry Goods Mutual Benefit Association appeared Ella Earle, Anna Bulkley Hills, Orlandini, the Weber Male Quartet, Max Jägerhuber and Marshall P. Wilder—certainly a good group. On February 4th came the second private concert of the Musurgia Society, Chapman conducting, with the New York Philharmonic Club, and with W. H. Rieger, E. C. Bailey, C. J. and E. Bushnell and Marie Groebl as soloists. A concert for the Loan Relief Association, on February 8th, presented Emily Winant, Hortense Pierse, F. W. Jameson, Silas G. Pratt, James Hazard Wilson, the Weber Quartet and the Philharmonic Club, a group decidedly worth hearing.

The concert of the Philharmonic Club, on February 9th (evening), called in Richard Hoffman, Marie Le Clair and Richard Arnold—two standbys of the years. In the afternoon, Mme. Greville appeared in an entertainment postponed from an earlier date. John B. Gough, on the 11th, delivered his Blunders. The February 19th concert of F. and H. Carri relied on the assistance of Effie Stewart, Max Bendheim and Hugo Bialla. An Eisteddfod was celebrated by the Welsh, on the afternoon and evening of February 22nd. The Orpheus Glee Club was here, on the 24th, with Mary Garlichs (piano) and Anna E. Mooney (soprano). St. George's Glee Club, on the 25th, invited with Blanche Stone Barton and Master Macfarlane. The Herald of February 22nd advertises six lectures on foreign countries, by the Reverend Dr. Maynard, but it fails to specify the dates thereof. I must admit that I remain calm in face of the announcement, for February 27th (evening) of a concert given by Arthur Voorhis (pianist) and George Lehmann and Carl Wenzel (violinists); Belle Cole and Albert Greenhalgh (accompanist) were to assist. In my haste, I neglected to invite the reader to the first concert in America (February 15th) of Louis Melbourne, with help from Virginia Rider (pianist), Effie Stewart, Laura Carroll Dennis, Isabella Stone, Dora Becker, Hortense Pierse, W. H. Lawton and the Courtney Ladies' Quartet—an imposing array.

Thus February passed from things living to things beyond recall. On March 2nd, George W. Cable, at 11 A.M., repeated his story of Grande Pointe. March 11th brought Barnby's Rebekah, sung by Anna Triechet (*sic*), R. H. May, Carl Dufft, and with G. W. Morgan officiating at the organ. The Philharmonic Club, on March 9th, engaged Ella Earle and Caryl Florio. For the fifth concert (March 16th) of F. and H. Carri, Harriet Avery and Bareuther were engaged. I always approach with imaginative delight the organ and harp recitals of G. W. and Maud Morgan; my pleasure is increased, on March 18th, by the participation in the concert of my favourite Meigs Sisters. On the 19th, Mme. Henry Greville lectured on Parisian Life in All Its Phases. Kate Field came back on March 26th, with The Vice and Treason of Mormonism, passing specifically, on the 27th, to Polygamy in Utah. This sounds very like the voice of Anna Dickinson. On March 27th (evening), George Riddle read A Midsummer-Night's Dream, Walter Damrosch, an orchestra, and the chorus of the Oratorio Society assisting. Courtice Pounds, the beloved Nanki-Poo, started the April showers of blessings, with a concert in which were to appear Geraldine Ulmar, Mae St. John, Hattie J. Clapper, Kyrle Bellew, Ivan Shirley, Federici, George Thorne, R. H. Warren, Frederick Archer and F. Billington —a host indeed. The 7th of April brought a concert of the pupils of that fine singer of long, long ago—Cora de Wilhorst-Raucourt; professional assistance came from G. W. and Maud Morgan and the inescapable de Kontski. W. H. Rieger's concert, on the 8th, lured (or tried to lure) with promise of Miss Groebl, Wenzel Robach, Miss Douglas, E. F. Bushnell, and a chorus of sixty, directed by W. R. Chapman. On the afternoon of that day, the organ and harp recital of G. W. and Maud Morgan had, as soloists, Alice Keller and Laura B. Phelps; the last Morgan recital, on April 15th, relied on additional aid from Rachel Chandler (soprano) and Selina Lilliendahl (harpist). The last Carri recital (April 13th) advertised assistance from Kate de Jonge, F. Remmertz, Christian (*sic*) Bareuther and Max Liebling. The harmonious and melodious Meigs Sisters, on April 16th, called upon the aid of de Kontski.

The Boys' Reading Club was to profit, on the 17th, from a performance by the Lenox Hill Vocal Society of Massenet's oratorio, Mary Magdalen, with, as soloists, Isidora Martinez, Fred Harvey, George Prehn and Josephine Le Clair; on the next evening Eli Perkins discoursed on Wit, Humour, Philosophy, Truth—surely a heavy contract to be fulfilled in an hour or more. Another lecturer, in German this time, was holding forth in the devoted Chickering Hall. On April 2nd, he spoke of Schuld und Strafe; on the 20th his topic was Dichter und Charactere; on May 11th, it was Romantik. On April 26th, H. R. Humphries, a fading voice, tried a concert, with the aid of Blanche Stone Barton, Mrs. R. C. Rogers, Michael Banner, S. B. Mills, George Prehn and St. George's and the Banks Glee Clubs. For old times' sake I hope the house was filled. Eduardo Marzo's pupils made their bows on the 27th. On the 30th (afternoon), John L. Wheeler lectured on The Fall of the Confederacy. Mr. and Mrs. Courtney's pupils also tempted fate, on May 3rd. The New York University Glee Club sang merrily and lustily, on May 4th, for the benefit of the lacrosse team. A testimonial, on May 11th, to Phipps and Edwards, amusement agents, was to enlist Harriet Avery, Harry Hilliard, Charles Roberts, Jr., A. P. Burbank, Clara Spence and many others. The New York Harmonic Society, on the 12th, presented, in addition to itself, Richard Hoffman, Hattie Clapper, Miss Hallenbeck, Dennison, Dufft and Phiney — all for the benefit of the Bartholdi Fund. The afternoon of May 13th found William Ordway Partridge reciting Julius Cæsar, I know not before how many auditors; but Maud Morgan harped. I should think that the evening of that day would have assembled many to hear Maud Powell, Fannie Hirsch, Minnie Swayze (reader), O. R. Steins, Alexander Lambert and the Hatton Male Quartet. And young ladies would have taken their indulgent parents, on the 14th, to hear the Yale College Glee Club. And the very next evening (15th), the Princeton and Columbia Glee Clubs united in an effort to convince a similar audience that college life was indeed a merry thing. And it was! The afternoon of the 14th proffered the second recital of Mme. de Roode-Rice. May 20th found Beatrice Strafford in a "grand dramatic performance." A farewell testimonial to Del Puente congregated, on May 28th, the wreckage of Mapleson's hopes, in Alma Fohström, Marie Engle, Marie Groebl, Mme. Lablache, Giannini and Vetta. On the 29th, S. B. Mills and others appeared for the Refuges for Homeless Women. James S. Burdett's benefit, on June 24th, at last allowed us to leave for 1885–86 this hall of many musical hopes and possibly, at times, of achievements, carrying with us memories of the performers on that occasion — the Misses Schneelock, Kate Fitch, Carrie Ray, the Weber Male Quartet, the Venetian Mandolin Quartet and D. W. Robertson (musical glasses). Or would it not be wiser, perhaps, just to forget most of them over the long summer?

Minor Miscellany and Music, 1885–1886

There remain but a few scattered entertainments, musical or otherwise, to enter into the record. The summer ended in 1885 with Gilmore still celebrating his Jubilee at Manhattan Beach and with Pain's brilliant and spectacular fireworks, Last Days of Pompeii, also awaking wonder and amaze. Levy and his cornet had been at Bauer's West Brighton Casino. Failing these, one could go to a concert of the St. George's Glee Club, on August 3rd, at Long Beach. Cappa held a musical festival, at the Hotel Brighton, Coney Island, on August 26th, 27th and 28th, afternoons and evenings. The Hanlon-Lee Races, at Rockaway Beach (August 22nd), and at Manhattan Beach (September 5th), kept New York and its neighbours excited, even if the theatres were closed. And the great international Yacht Race, between the Genesta and the Puritan, baffled by a light wind on the first day, but with the Puritan winning on September 16th, and thus keeping the America's Cup where it had been for so many years!

Thus summer lapsed into golden autumn. For minor joy, we might go to the Manhattan Skating Rink, 59th Street and Eighth Avenue, which opened, on October 19th, with an exhibition by R. J. Aginton. At Masonic Hall, Sixth Avenue and 23rd Street, began, in November, a Crazy Quilt Show, which carried on for weeks with, as special inducement, a $5,000 quilt. Few of my readers will have passed through that raging epidemic of the '80s, when all sorts and oddments of silks and satins were cut into fantastic shapes, sewed together and embroidered between pieces by, as I know, frequently very pretty embroidery designs invented by the maker of the quilt. Well, foolish as that may sound to 1941, it was better, *me judice*, than the utter hard negations of these, our later troubled years.

Henrietta Markstein, according to the Herald of November 2nd, was to perform, on November 5th, at the Idiot Asylum on Randall's Island, and a week later at the Almshouse on Blackwell's Island. My reader wonders what mental derangement induces me to put those items in our record. On November 6th, a Chrysanthemum Show opened at Horticultural Hall, West 28th Street. On the same day, Diacount and Lundberg skated at the Manhattan Rink. November 12th found the Jubilee Singers of Fisk University at the 13th Street Presbyterian Church (between Sixth and Seventh Avenues). Steck Hall, 11 East 14th Street, housed, on November 28th, a concert by the Standard Quartet Club (Herrmann, Roebbelin, Schwarz and Bergner), with S. B. Mills to assist. This was the first of four projected concerts of chamber music; another came on January 23rd. The Coliseum Skating Rink (107th Street and Lexington Avenue) had, since November 11th, been calling for custom.

And here is something entirely like radio procedure of later years. Paul Steinhagen was to give (November 24th, at 3) a piano recital, at the Grand Bazaar, 20 West 14th Street, where holiday goods were displayed. And "you are cordially invited and will be presented with a complimentary ticket for the Prize Piano (Behr Brothers)." Well! On the 27th, Victor Kuzdo, Mme. Krielsheimer and W. Lowitz were at Steck Hall. A Norwegian concert, on November 28th, at Irving Hall, was to present Edmund Neupert

[134]

and Albert Arveskaug, and end with a ball. At Madison Square Garden, as November whirled out of the calendar, a model of a Japanese Village seemed very appropriate in that year of the Mikado craze; it remained for weeks. The Southern Jubilee Singers were, on December 8th, at the Broome Street Tabernacle, and, on the 9th, something equally innocuous and less exciting —Aunt Polly Bassett's Singin' Skewl, at the Church of the Strangers. I ask again, Were we ever so innocent? On December 11th and 12th, Dolly, a skating horse, was sliding about at the Manhattan Rink. December 14th revived Hazel Kirke, at Turn Hall Theatre, the Phœnix Lyceum being responsible agent. An Old Folks Concert, on December 17th, made less sacred the Union Tabernacle, in 35th Street.

The reader has been anxiously awaiting news of the Mendelssohn Glee Club. I will reward his patience with the concert of December 8, 1885, at which appeared Mrs. Gerrit Smith (soprano) and Carl Faelten (pianist). The feature of the programme was King Olaf's Christmas; for February 16, 1886, the Club availed itself of the assistance of Ella Earle, Francis Fischer Powers, the New York Philharmonic Club, Emilio Agramonte and Harry Rowe Shelley. The twentieth anniversary of the society was duly celebrated on April 27th, with music selected from compositions in honour of the event, including Gilchrist's Journey of Life, from the poem of William Cullen Bryant. Henrietta Beebe lent her valuable aid to the ceremonies.

On January 3rd the Crescent Club, in their rooms, over Koster and Bial's, West 23rd Street, gave a musical and dramatic entertainment; the 11th found the Thomas Jefferson Association at Ferrero's Assembly Rooms. On the 15th, in Lyric Hall, the Choral Union burst into song, P. La Villa directing. The Seventh Regiment Glee Club sang at the Armoury, on January 30th; the Regiment as a whole, tendered, on February 6th, a benefit to its band leader, Cappa, with, as soloists, Florence Mangam and Cholmeley-Jones, and with a chorus of 100 from L'Espérance and L'Helvétienne. A panorama of the fight between the Merrimac and Monitor was set up, in late January at Madison Avenue and 59th Street, and there it stayed for months. The Free Baptist Church, 25th Street, between 7th and 8th Avenues, gave, on January 30th, a concert that intrigues me, with the wonderful Meigs Sisters, whom I always admired, Anna Bulkley Hills, James A. Metcalf (baritone), Frank Lincoln (humourist) and James E. Taylor (elocutionist). And at that time, a great World Clock was ticking away at 34 East 14th Street.

On February 1st, Miss Wickham read, at the fashionable Hotel Brunswick, A Blot in the 'Scutcheon. She appeared there again on six very select occasions. Frequently Browning was her quarry, though, on February 8th, Dante Gabriel Rossetti came into court. But there was something far more robust about Patrick S. Gilmore, who, on February 14th, at Madison Square Garden, gave two monster concerts with 150 performers, for the Parnell

[135]

Parliamentary Fund; W. H. Stanley, Levy and Belle Cole were soloists. A dog show, sponsored by the Westminster Kennels, was also robustly audible, beginning on February 8th, at Madison Square Garden. On February 19th, S. N. Penfield directed, at Lyric Hall, a concert of the New York Choral Union, assisted by Pauline Adele (soprano), Laura Carroll Dennis (contralto), Edward Schultze (tenor), Adolphine Kallnitz (piano) and Disney Robinson (bass). On February 22nd, at the Metropolitan Opera House Concert Hall, the New York Trio (Bernhard Boeckelman, pianist, Sam Franko, violin, and Adolph Hartdegen, 'cello) tried its luck. With Kate S. Chittenden at the organ, they gave the Vorspiel to Tristan und Isolde, arranged by Julius Sachs. Annie Louise Tanner sang songs by Mozart and Schubert. At the Grand Opera House Concert Hall, on February 26th, some kind person or persons gave a benefit for William S. Rogers (conjuror) and his sister, Virginia. But let us retrogressively dance, on January 12th, at Irving Hall, with the Hebrew Ladies' Benevolent Society; or on the 11th, at the Opera Ball Masquerade, Madison Square Garden.

The Herald of March 6th says that Princeton students gave The Rivals last night and would repeat it tonight; but it fails to state where these rivals of Wallack's actors were to play this great Wallack specialty. Perhaps it was in Princeton; at any rate, it was to pay off the baseball debt. A. Victor Benham was listed March 9th (afternoon) and 13th (evening) for piano recitals that the town assuredly did not need. On March 14th, at the Church of the Holy Innocents, Rosa d'Erina and the Cæcilian Society sang the Stabat Mater. The fourth and last Standard Quartet Concert invaded Steck Hall on March 20th. About this same time (April 6th) some unknown persons gave a benefit, in Masonic Temple, for Mrs. C. L. Brocklebank.

Barnum demands a paragraph to himself. His Circus entered Madison Square Garden, beginning on the afternoon of March 31st, with Arabs, Millie Christine (the two-headed girl), Chang ("the Chinese Colossus"), a Marimba band, the infinitesimal Lucia Zarate, giants, giantesses, &c. And Jumbo was exhibited, "with his ivory bone skeleton standing beside him." There was, of course, no Barnum but Barnum; he rose to great heights, on April 19th, when he advertised "Alice, the Affectionate Widow of the Lamented Jumbo — just from London."

Tableaux by Society Girls for Charity — how extremes meet in this world! William M. Chase and Carroll J. Beckwith arranged them from celebrated pictures, with Misses Jeanne Barrowe, Edith Draper, Mary and Martha Otis, Caroline Duer and others; the Metropolitan Opera House Concert Hall housed this loveliness on April 7th. Loveliness of other kinds was featured, on April 6th and 7th, in the Flower Show displaying in Nilsson Hall. Lillie Berg's concert, on April 8th, in the Hotel Brunswick Ballroom, assembled an interesting aggregation, in Donald De V. Graham, de Kontski,

Dora Becker, Kitty Berger, Sarah Cowell and C. B. Hawley. The Metropolitan Opera House Concert Hall (or Assembly Rooms) housed, on April 15th, the ambition of Mrs. Aldred J. McGrath, whose concert promised the aid of Constance Howard, Richard Arnold, James Aitken, Metcalf McGrath (her husband) and twelve choir boys. On the 15th and 16th, Aunt Polly Bassett held "skewl," in Grace Methodist Church, 101st Street, near Ninth Avenue. In the Hotel Brunswick Ballroom, on April 17th, appeared Anna Bulkley Hills (contralto of St. Bartholomew's Church), Ella Earle and Theodore J. Toedt (both of the same superb choir), Franz Remmertz, Francis F. Powers (baritone), Ovide Musin and Carl Walter (piano), certainly one of the best concert aggregations of the busy season. An entertainment in that same ballroom (April 27th and 29th) presented Pictures from A Dream of Fair Women. On April 18th, at their club rooms, the Liederkranz held a concert, with notable artists in Lilli Lehmann, Emily Winant, Ovide Musin, Treumann and Silbernagel. Gilmore, on the 26th, united with the Twenty-second Regiment in effort to swell the fund for the Bartholdi Statue. And May 4th, 5th, 6th and 7th set up, at Madison Square Garden, a dog show sponsored by the Westminster Kennel Club. At Irving Hall, for five evenings from May 11th, a pool contest for the championship of America and $1,000 enlisted Albert M. Frey and James L. Malone. Virginia Pervini, who had failed dismally in the autumn with Mapleson, had a concert, on May 22nd (evening) at the Metropolitan Opera House Concert Hall, with Emma Roderick, Signor F. Toldo and George D. White (baritone) standing by in equal lack of renown.

But here is summer breaking on us, on May 31st, with the opening of the new Central Park Garden, 59th Street, Boulevard (our modern Broadway) and Eighth Avenue. There and then our recently retired Adolf Neuendorff began a season of nightly concerts, leading an orchestra of sixty in just such summer night programmes as one might expect. We must not, however, overlook Miss Clyde Ralston, reciting her own versification of Ingomar, on one of those balmy nights (May 31st), at Spencer Hall, 14th Street. And lo! to the puncturing of the conceit of our year 1941 that thinks itself so original with its caravan stages, here, says the Herald of June 11th, Comic Opera under canvas has opened at 34th Street and Second Avenue. And, to rival the panorama of The Merrimac and Monitor, a cyclorama of The Battle of Vicksburg (Grant had died but recently) was declared by the Herald of June 12th to be now open at Seventh Avenue and 55th Street. Both these visions of bygone strife ran through the summer of 1886.

The outdoor spaces began to call. On June 17th, the French Benevolent Society enjoyed itself at Lion Park, 110th Street and Ninth Avenue. One could, by that time, take the charming ferry sail to Staten Island, where, as we shall see, provision was made for enjoyment, with Buffalo Bill's Wild West, or with popular concerts at St. George. At Manhattan Beach, Pain's new spectacle, The Burning of Moscow, seemed very wonderful to the imagination of the parents or grandparents of the flaming youth of 1941. And baseball raged at the Polo Grounds. Indoors, however, one might have attended, on July 17th, at Madison Square Garden, a dress parade of the 69th Regiment, "for Parnell and Gladstone"—Parnell then being weighed in the balance. And far down town at 317 Bowery, the Alexander Museum was exhibiting Steve Brodie, the Newsboy, "who jumped from Brooklyn Bridge, 140 feet." Verily, 1886 had its heroes. A Firemen's Tournament possessed West Brighton Beach, on August 18th. And the expected, perhaps eagerly awaited Gilmore Jubilee began to call on August 20th, with promise of the Anvil Chorus played by the famous band and two batteries of artillery. On the sound and fury of that mighty achievement, we may leave the music and miscellany of 1885-86.

Philharmonic Society, 1885–1886

Theodore Thomas began the Philharmonic season with a rehearsal and concert, on, respectively, Friday afternoon, November 13th, and Saturday evening, November 14th. The programme included Weber's Euryanthe overture; a symphonic prologue, Othello (new), by Arnold Krug; Maud Powell, in Max Bruch's concerto, No. 1, for the violin; Scherzo Capriccioso (first time), by Dvorak; and Beethoven's Eroica Symphony—a list still potent to draw in 1941, only in the opening and closing members. On December 11th and 12th, Thomas conducted Mozart's Symphony in G minor; the esteemed Mme. Fursch-Madi followed with Ah! perfido; the Mendelssohn overture, Melusine, led to Mme. Fursch-Madi's singing of Forth the Eagle Hath Flown (by St. Saëns); and the concert ended with a Symphony in C minor (new) by Xaver Scharwenka. January 8th and 9th provided Dvorak's new Symphony in D minor; Faelten in Schumann's A minor piano concerto; the overture to Gluck's Iphigénie in Aulis, and Haydn's Symphony No. 3 in E-flat.

For February 12th and 13th, Thomas prepared Brahms's Tragic Overture; Schumann's Second Symphony in C major; Liszt's Symphonic poem, Orpheus; and, from Die Götterdämmerung, Morning Dawn, Siegfried's Journey and Siegfried's Death—a programme quite desirable in 1941. The offering of March 12th and 13th provided Bach's Suite No. 2, in B minor; Helene Hastreiter, in Haydn's Ariadne auf Naxos; Bernhard Scholz's new Symphony in B-flat, op. 60; Liszt's Mignon, sung by Mme. Hastreiter; and Berlioz's overture, King Lear. With how much of that programme is 1941 familiar? a lesson for 1941 in connection with its own vaunted novelties. The last of the season brought (April 9th and 10th) a Beethoven night, Emma Juch singing the Egmont music, Josefify playing the fourth piano concerto, and the Ninth Symphony, which Damrosch and the Symphony Society had performed only a week before. Thomas's soloists came from his American Opera Company — Emma Juch, Helen Dudley Campbell, Candidus and A. E. Stoddard; the Brooklyn Philharmonic chorus laid the vocal foundation. The Herald review of the rehearsal states that Louise Pyk sang the Egmont solos — and indifferently.

Thomas Popular Concerts, 1885-1886

We saw how hard work with German opera and two musical societies broke down Leopold Damrosch, in 1884-85; in the season of 1885-86 Theodore Thomas would seem to have toiled even harder. In addition to conducting the Philharmonic concerts and the exacting new American Opera performances, he carried through at the Academy a succession of twenty-four popular concerts every Tuesday evening, and an equal number of Thursday matinées presumably inaugurated as Young People's Concerts.

I cannot exhaust the patience of my pen and my reader, by recording details of those forty-eight interesting sessions. Thomas, we may be sure, supplied only worthy music, though not, of course, much of the more profound character expected in Philharmonic concerts. But since personality counts as much on the platform as on the stage, I will unroll before the reader's eyes a list of the soloists who passed in procession through the twenty-four weeks involved in the gigantic scheme. Beginning on November 3rd, that month of falling leaves presented, in succession, Mme. Fursch-Madi, Emma Juch, Joseffy, Marie Van, Richard Hoffman, Maud Powell, Franz Remmertz, Emily Winant, A. Hartdegen, Emma Juch again (November 24th), Max Heinrich, and Joseffy (a second time, matinée, 26th). A Berlioz night (December 8th) presented Mme. Fursch-Madi; Carl Faelten, a new pianist, was to appear, on December 10th (afternoon). December 15th promised Emma Juch, in Egmont music; also Hoffman, Schmidt and Hartdegen in a concerto for piano, violin and 'cello. Felix Bauer, 'cello, appeared on the afternoon of the 17th. Hartdegen came again on December 22nd, and Joseffy on the 24th. On January 5th, the sonorous Myron W. Whitney, and, on the 19th, the bird-like Pauline L'Allemand delighted. Carolina Zeiss intervened, on the 10th.

For January 12th and 21st Joseffy once more delighted; I do not know much about the soloists for the 14th — Blanche Stone Barton (soprano) and C. Hildebrandt (violin of Thomas's orchestra). But we are pleased to greet Madeline Schiller, on the afternoon of February 4th, and Franz Rummel, on the evening of the 9th. February 16th was to offer Jacques Bouhy (singer) along with Joseffy (in a Mozart concerto). Bouhy finally appeared on March 2nd; he had been ill on February 16th. On the 23rd of February Candidus sang Siegmund's Love Song and Julius Sachs's Serenade. A third "request" matinée, on the 25th, brought compositions by Bach, Mendelssohn,

Beethoven, Wagner, Liszt, Rubinstein, Schumann and Boccherini. Helene Hastreiter (March 9th) and M. W. Whitney (11th, matinée) showed how closely related were Thomas's interests. Joseffy and S. S. Sanford, on March 16th, vied in pianistic art. Just to vary the scheme, I will announce that composers for March 30th were Spohr, Svendsen, Brahms, Liszt and Délibes (a new scène du bal). Mrs. R. Chase appeared. At the twenty-third evening concert (April 6th), Pauline L'Allemand sang airs from The Marriage of Figaro and Lakmé. The series — an exhausting procession — ended on Tuesday, April 13th, and matinée, April 15th.

SYMPHONY SOCIETY, 1885–1886

Walter Damrosch's connection with the German opera naturally led him, as conductor of the Symphony Society, to carry its concerts into the Metropolitan Opera House. The first rehearsal (November 6th) and concert (7th) gave Beethoven's Pastoral Symphony; Liszt's By the Waters of Babylon, sung by Marianne Brandt, with violin and harp obbligato; the Vorspiel to Parsifal; Raff's Walpurgis Night; an aria from Euryanthe, by Frl. Brandt; and Liszt's orchestration of his fourteenth Rhapsodie Hongroise. The Herald, on the 7th, complained of "a listlessness, a lack of life, of spirit and of color" in the orchestral performance, that "distorted the music almost beyond recognition." The Witches' Sabbath of Raff was "as tame as a young lady's literary coterie," and the Rhapsody of Liszt "would have put gypsies to sleep." Consequently, it was a "great relief when that noble artist," Frl. Brandt, came forward and sang "gloriously." Of course we must remember that Walter Damrosch was, in 1885, hardly more than a boy, just starting on his long and honourable career.

Bruckner's Symphony in D minor (first time) began the next programme (December 4th and 5th); Eloi Sylva followed with Handel's Sound an Alarm; an air de ballet from Gluck's Iphigénie in Aulis, Mendelssohn's Fingal's Cave, an aria from Nero, by Sylva, and the finale to Das Rheingold surely filled the cup to overflowing. The January gifts (15th and 16th) were the Egmont overture; Schubert's Die Allmacht, with Miss Goldsticker; Lalo's Rhapsodie and Scherzo (new); Spohr's Ninth Concerto for violin (with Miss Dube, of Louisville, Kentucky); Leopold Damrosch's Festival Overture; and Raff's Im Walde. Walter Damrosch always was a good programme-maker.

February 5th and 6th brought Berlioz's La Damnation de Faust with, as soloists, Medora Henson Emerson, Max Alvary, Max Heinrich and Herr Sänger. The programme of March 5th and 6th contained several novelties: the Goldmark overture, Penthesilea; Fuch's Serenade, for string orchestra; and Nichol's Scherzo. Franz Rummel played Rubinstein's piano Concerto in D minor; and Schumann's Symphony No. 1 completed the offering.

Beethoven's Ninth Symphony ended the season, on April 2nd and 3rd, with Mrs. Ford, Miss Groebl, Stanley and Heinrich as soloists. Preceding this mighty work, Liszt's Manfred was played, following a reading from Byron's poem by George Riddle. I may end with the statement that the Herald, as the months advanced, softened its asperities regarding Damrosch's conducting. After the rehearsal, on March 5th, the reviewer finds it "pleasant to modify the opinion which was expressed" at the beginning of the season. Damrosch was "not yet a master of his art, but the prospect which seemed so dreary and unpromising at the beginning of the season assumes a brighter and more hopeful view."

Oratorio Society, 1885–1886

The concerts (and rehearsals) of the Oratorio Society, for reasons potent in the case of the Symphony Society, were held in the Metropolitan Opera House. On November 18th and 19th, Damrosch produced the Messe des Morts and Apotheosis, by Berlioz, with the new Max Alvary as soloist. In view of the acclaim which my younger readers have heard heaped upon Alvary (certainly his good looks blinded many to the bad faults of his singing—eyes against ears, as it were), it gives me a certain amount of respect for my own judgment (I heard him many times) to read in the Herald, on November 19th, that, in the Requiem, at the rehearsal, he had to battle, in the Sanctus, against two obstacles—first, "the memory of Campanini's splendid delivery of the music," at the Damrosch Festival, "in May, 1881," and "the other, the nervousness attending his first appearance" in the music. "His voice is strong and of good quality in the lower and middle registers; his high notes, however, were most unpleasantly forced yesterday and not true to the pitch." The sextet of the Requiem was "the least satisfactory portion of the concert." The voices, unaccompanied, "did not blend"—the singers being Miss Van, Miss Goldsticker (what a name!), Alvary, Dworsky, Colletti and Sänger.

The expected Messiah, on December 18th and 19th, utilised more German singers from the Metropolitan—a handy arrangement for all concerned, whatever the English one might hear from Lilli Lehmann, Marianne Brandt and Josef Staudigl; but Whitney Mockridge, the tenor, might be depended on, in that respect. The Herald thought that the ladies, avoiding the dramatic, were rather too calm.

The Herald now atones for its strictures on Damrosch's conducting, in the first Symphony concert, by declaring that, in oratorio music, he is "thoroughly at home, and in this field at least he is likely to win for himself an exalted position."

Damrosch, on March 3rd and 4th, announced Parsifal in concert form, with Marianne Brandt ("who created the part of Kundry, in Baireuth"),

[141]

Alvary, Fischer, Lehmler, and Max Heinrich (as Amfortas). Among the flower maidens were Ida Klein and Marie Groebl. That surely was an event to enrapture the steadily increasing band of Wagnerites; but the performance, at the matinée was unsatisfactory, with Alvary unable to appear, and Kraemer trying to take his place.

FRANK DANIELS   LOTTA   PRIMROSE AND WEST

CHARLES L. DAVIS   FLORA WALSH   CHARLES MAUBURY

AMY AMES   JAMES O. BARROWS   G. C. BONIFACE, JR.

CHAPTER III

BROOKLYN, WILLIAMSBURGH, QUEENS COUNTY, STATEN ISLAND, 1885-1886

THE dramatic fare provided by the various communities of Long Island now gathered to the motherly bosom of the Greater New York will seem perhaps less appetising than a connoisseur might desire. Brooklyn, for instance, was but a ferry-ride or a bridge-crossing from Manhattan and accepted, apparently with due thanks, second helpings from the richer feast across the bay. To be sure, Brooklyn in 1885–86 was used with a certain determined policy as a trying-out place for new dramatic offerings, but only one of these (the Gillette Held by the Enemy) ever gained a place on the more carefully scrutinised tables across the bridge, in the region of Broadway. On the contrary, Brooklyn and Williamsburgh accepted the same staled sweets of melodrama and musical comedy which gratified the taste of playgoers in the Bowery, in Third Avenue, in Eighth Avenue and in Harlem. The reader of these veracious Annals may expect, in consequence, to feast in Brooklyn on viands much the same as those on which he was dyspeptically nourished in his visits to the cheaper combination houses in Manhattan.

Park Theatre, Brooklyn, 1885–1886

By priority of service, Colonel Sinn's Park Theatre demands priority of treatment in our chronicle. Redecorated and advertised as "the handsomest theatre in Brooklyn," it re-opened, on August 31, 1885, with J. B. Polk and Julia Polk, in Mixed Pickles, a spiced condiment that turned sour, here and in Manhattan, though Polk's personal popularity kept it from absolutely spoiling in the presentation. A novelty, Burr Oaks, succeeded as it might, for the week of September 7th–12th, with a cast of utter insignificance, including David M. Murray, Annie Barclay, Cryptic Palmont, J. W. Reynolds, E. E. Hullfish, Jr., Joseph Brennan, Walter Anderson, Julian Reed and John Holmes. Imagine that group at Wallack's or Daly's! Peck's Bad Boy, with John J. Williams in the title-rôle, was expected to suffice for September 14th–19th. On September 21st, Cora S. Tanner came forward in Robert Buchanan's machine-made melodrama, Alone in London, supplying villains, a noble hero, a street-waif, a maiden struggling in the swirling waters, and final happiness for all the good people in the *dramatis personæ*. I saw this play in Boston, a few weeks earlier, and New York and Brooklyn were to see it again and again, before 1885–86 passed from the theatrical calendar. Herbert Archer, later famous in the parts of sleek, oily villains, appeared, in this piece, in that sort of rôle, and his wife, very pretty Belle Archer, was the sympathetic street boy in need of help. Miss Tanner, as the heroine, made so great a hit that she soon emerged as a star and married her manager, the redoubtable Colonel Sinn. In the Brooklyn production also were Walter Reynolds and Grace Hathaway. Perhaps the most essential members of the cast were the stage-hands who manipulated the elaborate scenery. After a week of this melodramatic woe, the tension was relieved (September 28th–October 3rd) by Louis Harrison and John Gourlay, in Skipped by the Light of the Moon.

We changed our style and our language, next week, when the Thalia Theater Opera Company came from the Bowery, its home, for a week of tuneful gayety: The Black Hussar (October 5th, and matinée, 7th); Czar und Zimmermann (6th); The Beggar Student (evening, 7th); Nanon (8th and 10th); and Boccaccio (9th). To find the casts, look under the heading of the Thalia Theater. Clio, from its stormy career at Niblo's, transferred its earthquake to the Park (October 12th–17th), bringing the New York cast, the best seen thus far at the Park — Adele Belgarde, Marion Russell, May Newman, Mrs. Charles Poole, Frank Losee, B. T. Ringgold, Thomas H. Burns, and Harold Fosberg (sic). John T. Raymond, seen so recently before at the Madison Square Theatre, devoted October 19th, 20th and 21st, to For Congress, and 22nd, 23rd, 24th, to the ever-welcome Colonel Sellers. Another Madison Square delicacy finished October at the Park (October 26th–31st) with Mme. Janish in Anselma, supported, as in New York, by Henry Miller, Max Freeman, W. J. Ferguson and Gabrielle Du Sauld — names which still ring pleasantly in older ears.

Again variety was subserved (November 2nd–7th) with the jolly A Bunch of Keys, chief executants being Eugene Canfield, Marietta Nash and George Lauri. And once again (9th–14th) the never-dying taste of Madison Square goodness emerged in May Blossom, presented by Daniel Frohman, with Georgia Cayvan, Ben Maginley and W. H. Crompton to awaken tears and laughter. Aimée, in Mam'zelle, had the next week (November 16th–21st), except when, on the 20th and 21st, she substituted the clever Divorçons. Fanny Davenport, with Robert Mantell, devoted to Fedora the week of November 23rd–28th; and November passed into December with the sweet ministrations of Maggie Mitchell, all the week (November 30th–December 5th) dancing the shadow dance of Fanchon, except when, on December 3rd, The Pearl of Savoy yearned in splendour for her native hills, or when, on the 5th, Little Barefoot untied the string, thereby proving she would make a suitable wife for the none too brilliant hero. Once more, I congratulate Sinn and his patrons on the excellent variety of his menu for

[144]

a month. Certainly the Park bills, though not new, were palatable and easy to digest.

And here, on December 7th, Robson and Crane began a week of their spectacular Comedy of Errors, recently seen at the Star Theatre, New York. Annie Pixley followed for three nights (December 14th–16th) in Fred Marsden's new play of Eily, her support including M. C. Day, T. M. Hunter, Donald Harold, Robert Fischer, Maurice Drew, Dollie Pike and Blanche Moulton; but, so far as Miss Pixley was concerned, the public wanted only M'liss, and that trustworthy provision ended her week (December 17th–19th). N. C. Goodwin, in The Skating Rink, satirised the skating craze of the times, for the week of December 21st–26th, preparing the way for the holiday mirth (December 28th–January 2nd) of McNish, Johnson and Slavin's Minstrels. Reader, look back over that autumn chronicle for the Park Theatre and see how many of the attractions you might have enjoyed; I can select several for myself.

Any lover of the theatre would eagerly have attended the plays of earliest January, given by Lawrence Barrett and his interesting support — Minna K. Gale, F. C. Mosley, Ben G. Rogers: Richelieu (January 4th); Francesca da Rimini (5th); Much Ado about Nothing (matinée, 6th); Yorick's Love and David Garrick (evening, 6th); Hamlet (7th); The King's Pleasure and The Wonder (8th); and Julius Cæsar (9th). That list of plays I respectfully submit to pampered stars of to-day (1941) who sacrifice themselves to a season's "repertory" of two or three pieces — generally modern in scope. Naturally, after that serious week, Sinn relaxed the nerves of his patrons (January 11th–16th) with something light and frothy — Mr. and Mrs. George S. Knight, in Over the Garden Wall, their efficient support including John Rice, James Maas, George W. Monroe, Charles Sawtelle, Rosita Worrell (Mrs. Knight had been Sophie Worrell) and Mary E. Barker. On the afternoon of January 15th, a benefit for the Elks promised Margaret Mather, in an act of Leah; the Knights, Estelle Clayton and Murray and Murphy in acts of their season's plays; Kellar, R. C. Hilliard, Billy Barry, Marshall P. Wilder and Griffin and Marks — a goodly array. But Sinn bade us be serious again (18th–23rd) with Charles C. Maubury and The Wages of Sin, cheering us with the return (25th–30th) of Nat C. Goodwin, in The Skating Rink.

And here comes (February 1st–6th) what was proclaimed to be the "first authorised" performance (whatever that might mean) of The Mikado — that raging epidemic of 1885–86. The company thus "authorised" was McCaull's:

Mikado	C. W. Dungan	Yum-Yum	Bertha Ricci
Nanki-Poo	Harry Macdonough	Pitti-Sing	Cecilia Ellis
Ko-Ko	Digby Bell	Peep-Bo	Nellie McCartee
Pooh-Bah	Charles Plunkett	Katisha	Laura Joyce Bell
Pish-Tush	Hamilton Adams		

[145]

We shall soon see Brooklyn infested with mushroom Mikados of all degrees of efficiency; this one, except for Digby Bell and his wife, seems to me somewhat lacking in attractiveness. At this very time, the Criterion Theatre, with a rival Mikado, was making Brooklyn recall the multiple Pinafores of 1879. McCaull retained the Park Theatre for another week, presenting therein a second wing of his army (De Wolf Hopper, Mathilde Cottrelly, George C. Boniface, Jr., Louise Lablache, Marie Jansen and E. W. Hoff — decidedly a stronger group), in The Black Hussar. After so much joyousness, we were invited to a week of the exquisite Modjeska, with the varied repertoire then expected of a visiting star: Donna Diana (February 15th), Odette (16th), Mary Stuart (17th), As You Like It (18th), Adrienne (19th), Camille (20th, afternoon), and Twelfth Night (20th, evening). Reader, I must take you in imagination to all those choice performances, Odette alone excepted. A bit weary, physically, with that busy week, we might be pardoned for ignoring Sinn's offering of February 22nd–27th, Kate Castleton, in Crazy Patch, even though her support included Ada Gilman, John D. Gilbert, Eddie Girard, Esther Williams and L. R. Stockwell, a good aggregation.

We know how large was the excellent company of A. M. Palmer at the Madison Square Theatre, and how few of them were employed in Engaged, then current at that home theatre. But actors engaged for the season cannot be allowed to enjoy their salaries without a working return. Palmer, therefore, began at the Park, on March 1st, a production of Sealed Instructions, for which he engaged Mathilde Madison, in her original part, since played by Agnes Booth. Others in the present cast were Frederic Robinson, Walden Ramsay, E. M. Holland, E. M. Royle, J. H. Stoddart, Lin Hurst, Harry Hogan, Marion Russell (as usual substituting for her more richly gifted sister, Annie) and Marie Burroughs (in the part created by Jessie Millward and more recently taken over by Maud Harrison). I wish I might have seen this Brooklyn cast, to compare it with the two earlier assignments, both of which I saw. I pass with this sigh of regret to laugh heartily at A Rag Baby, played here (March 8th–13th) by Frank Daniels, Julian Mitchell, Mark Sullivan, Harry Conor, Fanny Rice, Flora Walsh, Helen Reiner, Clara Lane and Nettie Lyford — each with a bit of a niche in our theatre-history. I believe I shall forgo the offering of March 15th–20th — Ezra Kendall, in A Pair of Kids. W. T. Carleton, who had encountered legal trouble in getting on the road with Nanon, brought that charming operetta to the Park (March 22nd–27th) with a support including Louise Paullin, Alice Vincent, Clara Wisdom, Josephine Bartlett, Charles H. Drew and Joseph S. Greensfelder.

Thatcher, Primrose and West's Minstrels made merry the week of March 29th–April 3rd, some of their funny men including Billy Rice, Luigi dell'Oro, and Barney Fagan. A Prisoner for Life, with J. B. Studley, E. L. Tilton,

C. L. Farwell, T. H. Glenney, Inez Rochelle, Sara Neville, Henrietta Irving and Martha Wren, drew us back (April 5th–10th) into the realm of the serious. And another Mikado—the Templeton group, recently rivalling at the Criterion the McCaull company, then at the Park—came to the Park for the week of April 12th–17th, and doubtless scored its usual success. Alice Harrison, who had been Yum-Yum with this group when, the first in the field, it had presented The Mikado at the People's Theatre in New York, now followed it at the Park (April 19th) for a week of Hot Water, her support including Charles S. Dickson, Frank Girard, Frank David, Dora Stuart, Ida Toucy, Helen Sedgwick, Charles Allison—a list somewhat akin to the mediocrities of the early fall in Sinn's Park. The funny band who came out on April 26th, in Hoyt's A Tin Soldier, fills one with nostalgia for a merry time long since past—James T. Powers, Amy Ames, George C. Boniface, Jr., Marion Elmore, Paul Arthur, Flora Walsh, James H. Dyer, Isabel Coe, Gus Hennessey, Fannie Batchelder and William Taylor. What a list, most of them just beginning to make their way!

And equally glorious to an old-timer was Evangeline (May 3rd–8th), fresh from the Fourteenth Street Theatre, with Irene Verona, Louise Montague, Annie Summerville, G. K. Fortescue, James S. Maffit, George Schiller and George Mason. Boucicault, in his recent success, The Jilt, filled the week of May 10th–15th, still supported by Henry Miller, F. M. Burbeck, Fritz Williams, Louise Thorndyke, Helen Bancroft, Mary E. Barker and Bijou Heron. Lester Wallack's Company—Gilbert, Mme. Ponisi, Annie Robe, Kyrle Bellew, Helen Russell, and all the rest—followed for a week (May 17th–22nd) in comedy acting such as the Park had seen but rarely that season. Charles L. Davis, in Alvin Joslin, decidedly let us down from Wallack standards for the week of May 24th–29th. The last week of the season (May 31st–June 5th) vainly tried to interest us in George Clarke's play, A Strange Disappearance. I will close this house for the summer, with a benefit to Harry Kennedy, at which Edward Lamb and George R. Edeson acted Box and Cox; Leonard Grover and Leonard Grover, Jr. gave a scene from the former's Our Boarding House; R. C. Hilliard and Frank Losee did the duel scene from Led Astray; Fred Warde declaimed the curse from Richelieu; and a generous olio enlisted John Henshaw and May Ten Broeck, Billy Barry, &c.

BROOKLYN THEATRE, 1885–1886

The Brooklyn Theatre next demands attention; occasionally the brilliancy of its stars may have outshone that of Sinn's constellations at the Park. The two houses re-opened on the same evening, August 31st. W. A. McConnell, set down as lessee and manager of the Brooklyn, began rather feebly with Around the World in Eighty Days, acted by Helen Tracy, L. J.

Spencer (Phileas Fogg), William Richardson (Passepartout), and with the usual spectacular effects and Mlle. De Rosa as *prima ballerina*.   Incidental to the play were the Mignani Family as Parisian street-singers and Mons. Arnold ("wonderful grotesque").   Edward Hanlon, Wallace Ross and George W. Lee, whose feats in rowing then occupied space in the newspapers, were "expected" to be present on September 1st.

T. W. Keene brought in tragedy for a changeful week; Richard III (September 7th, 8th and 9th); The Merchant of Venice (matinée, 9th); Hamlet (10th and 11th); Romeo and Juliet (matinée, 12th); and Macbeth (evening of the 12th).   Honestly, I do not know what to predicate for the offering of September 14th–19th — John Howson and Louise Lester, in Putting on Style, with Charles Coote (an amusing actor), Ed Cameron and Carrie Wallace in support.   I fear time has buried this effort beyond hope of recovery.   Rose Eytinge, a waning attraction, entered on September 21st, in Niagara (by E. E. Kidder); other parts were entrusted to Ada Gilman, Laura LeClaire, Lillian Lee, Henry Dalton and Charles Stanley.   That Niagara soon washed completely over the dam.   Thatcher, Primrose and West's Minstrels (September 28th–October 3rd) boasted of — besides the three leaders — Billy Rice, George H. Edwards, Barney Fagan, H. C. Talbot, Burt Shepard, Chauncey Olcott (observe!), J. P. O'Keefe, and Julius Whitmark, names that, except for Olcott, I can read without increased pulse-beats. The burlesques offered were Polo on Skates and (as a bow to Dixey) The Black Adonis.   And assuredly I am calm in face of Madame Boniface, the offering of the first three days of the week of October 5th–10th, and of Niniche, given on the last three days.   Madeline Lucette, Will S. Rising, Charles F. Lang and Mme. de Fossez led the players.

Up to this time the Brooklyn had offered but meagre pittance to its patrons.   But things looked up, on October 12th, when Rose Coghlan, first real star of the season at this house, produced Our Joan, with support from Frazer Coulter, B. R. Graham, Charles A. McManus, Luke Martin, George Deyo, George F. and Florence Robinson and Emma Hagger.   The upward tendency was again noticeable (October 19th–24th) when Effie Ellsler, also a charming actress, presented Frank Harvey's play, Woman against Woman, assisted by Frank Weston (her husband), Charles Foster, Mason Mitchell, Harry Davenport, Mattie Earle, Marjorie Bonner and Mrs. E. L. Davenport, a support more brilliant, I fancy, than Miss Coghlan's.   Roland Reed in Humbug (October 26th–31st) need not detain our scholarly aspirations; neither need The Shadows of a Great City (November 2nd–7th) though we know that, in it, Annie Ward Tiffany, Nelson Wheatcroft, George R. Edeson and Edna Carey probably gave good account of themselves.   On Sunday, November 8th, Ingersoll discoursed on Myth and Miracle.   And here, at last, is a great star — Joseph Jefferson, who, on five days (November 9th–13th) gave The Cricket on the Hearth and Lend Me Five Shillings, submitting, for the two performances on the 14th to the expected demand for Rip Van Winkle; in his company were Robert L. Downing, William Herbert, May Wolcott (whom I remember as a charming, pretty actress) and Lillian Lewis. The Brooklyn had at last got into its stride. Lotta, beloved of Brooklyn playgoers, was here for the week of November 16th–21st, presenting Mlle. Nitouche, with, in support, Charles H. Bradshaw, Frank Carlyle, Adelaide Eaton and Emma Hinckley. For Saturday evening (21st) she restored Musette to a public that loved it. Evans and Hoey released laughter (November 23rd–28th) in A Parlour Match; and Gus Williams possibly did the same thing (November 30th–December 5th) in Oh! What a Night. Topsy Venn in this latter piece doubtless contributed to the public joy. Similar entertainment was provided (December 7th–12th) with Mestayer and Theresa Vaughn, in We, Us and Co., seen everywhere that season in Greater New York. I know nothing of The Tigers, brought out with John T. Kelly (December 14th–19th) and with help from Dan Mason, Barney Reynolds, A. Haywood, Edwin Foy (have we met him before?), Sadie Scanlan, Julia Elmore, and the delightful Lena Merville.

As a Christmas gift to the City of Churches and (may I say?) of Theatres, Harry C. Miner, yearning for worlds to conquer, outside the field of Variety, took over the management of the Brooklyn Theatre, and, as evidence of good intention, brought out (December 21st–26th) David Belasco's play, La Belle Russe, a sort of Forget-Me-Not thing which Rose Coghlan had made vital, a year or two before, at Wallack's. Now, in the Brooklyn cast, Sophie Eyre, who had been brought from England to succeed Miss Coghlan at Wallack's, and who, despite her looking like the gifted Rose, simply could not replace her, attempted the title-rôle, with help from Newton Gotthold, J. W. Jennings, Henry Talbot, Fred Goldthwaite, S. DuBois, Mary Hill, Maud Hill and Miss E. Lewis—certainly not a brilliant array. But next week Miner amply atoned, with the beautiful Mary Anderson, then the most beautiful star in our firmament, in a delightful repertoire: Pygmalion and Galatea and Comedy and Tragedy (December 28th, 30th and January 1st); As You Like It (29th and matinée, January 2nd); The Lady of Lyons (31st, and January 2nd, evening). This seems to bring the joy of the season to a head.

And a distressing drop seems to me The Devil's Auction, spectacularly held during the week of January 4th–9th. Lost ("by a Cleveland journalist") also seems feeble for January 11th–16th, particularly as the actors were of but slight consequence—Miss Ramie Austen, Dore Davidson, Bessie Bernard, J. H. McGrath, John Burke, and fifty children to sing nursery rimes. I am pleased to have missed this show. But any one would have enjoyed the benefit matinée of January 12th, at which were promised Henry Dixey, Clara Louise Kellogg, John A. Mackay, Hattie Schroter, Anna Winch, Ivan Morawski, H. S. and Robert Hilliard, Whitney Mockridge, Francis

Powers, Franklyn Reglid, &c. Echoes from a profitable past floated in with the revival (18th–23rd) of My Partner, with Louis Aldrich, Dora Goldthwaite and John E. Ince; and pleasingly the past came back (25th–30th) with The Sea of Ice, now acted by Kate Claxton and Charles A. Stevenson. Thus January passed out, I must say not overwhelmingly important at the Brooklyn, making one dubious (February 1st–6th) concerning Blackmail, by and with W. C. Cowper, his associates in the cast including James Wilson, Lawrence Hanley (a handsome actor), Eleanor Moretti, Addie Plunkett and the dependable Virginia Buchanan. Many, doubtless, were pleased, when Margaret Mather, having just finished her lengthy and highly advertised engagement at the Union Square, came to the Brooklyn Theatre for a week of the "legitimate": Romeo and Juliet (February 8th and 11th); The Honeymoon (9th); Leah (10th and 12th); The Lady of Lyons (matinée, 13th); and Macbeth (evening, 13th). If this talented but crude young woman could give to her characters the force required, certain of the elegance and refinement would be out of her reach. William Gillette, in The Private Secretary, delighted during the week of February 15th–20th, with the assistance of an admirable group of players — Frank Tannebill, Jr., T. A. Wise, Herbert Ayling, Maud Haslam, Maud (sic) Giroux, and Fanny Addison. A venture similar in intent followed during the week of February 22nd–27th — Pinero's farce, The Magistrate, acted not so brilliantly, I fancy, as in its autumn run at Daly's. At the Brooklyn the cast included Charles Leclercq, Ed. Lamb, Hart Conway, Hamilton Bell, Fred Bond, Jean Gordon, May Sylvie and May Brookyn.

Emma Abbott, not recently prominent in our record, began March with opera: The Bohemian Girl (March 1st); The Mikado (2nd, 5th, and matinée, 3rd); Mignon (evening of the 3rd); La Traviata (4th); Martha (matinée, 6th), and Il Trovatore (evening, 6th)— an ambitious schedule. The Ratcatcher (March 8th–13th) was as like its Niblo performance as Hubert Wilke and the others could make it. A pleasing change came (15th–20th) with Saints and Sinners, J. H. Stoddart, Marie Burroughs, E. M. Holland, Lizzie Duroy and Davidge acting the parts they had filled during the long run of the piece at the Madison Square. Other characters now fell to Frederic Robinson (in LeMoyne's part), Walden Ramsay, Harry Holliday, Mrs. Whiffen and Marion Russell (she never had a chance to act at her home — the Madison Square). So this was the second company partly of regulars from Palmer's theatre that Brooklyn had welcomed during the run of Engaged at the Broadway house. Of course one could not expect a manager to allow expensive members of his corps to eat up their salaries in idleness; nor, I believe, did the actors wish to do so. Dagmar was played (March 22nd–27th) by Louise Balfe, Frank Losee, Ralph Delmore, Mason Mitchell, Matt and Rose Snyder and Eliza Long, an earnest, if not a brilliant, group. And here is still another Madison Square offering — the fifth at this theatre and the Park—The Rajah, acted (March 29th–April 3rd) by J. G. Saville, E. L. Walton, Norman Campbell, Sedley Brown, C. W. Stokes, Rillie Deaves (in her original part), the ever-flitting Marion Russell and Mrs. Sol Smith. Tony Hart brought (April 5th–10th) A Toy Pistol, two interesting members of his cast being Annie Adams (mother of Maude Adams) and Minnie Dupree (a better ingénue than some who have succeeded her in that line of parts).

Thus far the Brooklyn Theatre had escaped The Mikado (except for three performances by the Emma Abbott singers); for the week of April 12th–17th it presented the raging element with Alfa Norman, James Parkes, Ellis Ryse, W. W. Morton, Miss Martinez, Annie Maxwell and Alice Jones —an aggregation in which I recognise only a name or two I ever met before —or since. In this same week the Templeton Mikado was at the Park Theatre; Brooklyn must have been Mikado-mad. A charming change came (April 19th–24th) with Rosina Vokes and her delightful English company in the triple blessing—In Honour Bound, My Milliner's Bill and A Christmas Pantomime Rehearsal—one of the glories of my youthful years. And blessings on Engaged, our sixth gleaning (April 26th–May 1st) from the Madison Square Theatre treasure-house, with Agnes Booth (not then acting at the home establishment) in her great part of Belinda Treherne, with Robert C. Hilliard, specially engaged, for Cheviot Hill (*vice* Herbert Kelcey, then in Our Society, at the Madison Square), with Frederic Robinson, rather "out of it" this season at the Madison Square, L. F. Massen, Mrs. Whiffen, E. M. Holland, and Ethel and Olga Brandon! And One Touch of Nature, preceding the Gilbert satire, presented Stoddart in his well-known and well-liked rôle, with Marie Burroughs succeeding to Maud Harrison's usual character. Until I came on these Brooklyn performances of Madison Square plays, I had always wondered what the members of Palmer's company were doing when not engaged in the current production at the Madison Square. And I am pleased to find dear Mrs. Whiffen in so many Brooklyn casts.

Murray and Murphy, in Our Irish Visitors, filled the week of May 3rd–8th, and J. K. Emmet, happily returned, in Fritz in Ireland, that of the 10th–15th. Tony Hart came back (17th–22nd), in A Toy Pistol. The "last week of a brilliant season," so advertised, presented once more Gillette in The Private Secretary. I rather hate to go back (afternoon of May 7th) for a benefit for the widow and child of Kenward Philp, at which was promised a generous array of volunteer talent, in Clara Morris, the Brooklyn Sängerbund, the New York Sketch Club (Napoleon Sarony, Henry Thomas, Albert Operti, and others, in Rapid Sketches, to be sold from the stage for the benefit fund), Harry Kennedy, the St. Felix Sisters and W. E. Hines (in Our Birthday, introducing selections from The Mikado), bits from A Tin Soldier, and so forth.

[151]

GRAND OPERA HOUSE, BROOKLYN, 1885–1886

The third playhouse of Brooklyn began its new season on Saturday, August 29, 1885, with something important, the Russian drama of Nordeck, in which Frank Mayo at last had found a rôle suited to his unquestioned ability and allowing him to put aside, for a time at least, his somewhat antiquated Davy Crockett and Badger. In Nordeck Kathryn Kidder made a hit as the proud heroine and by it started on a career of some interest in our theatre. F. F. Mackay had a familiar part as the man of intrigue. As we know, Nordeck soon journeyed from Third Avenue, New York, to the aristocratic purlieus of the Lyceum. The first Mikado to assail the happy Brooklynite came for the week of September 7th–12th, with part of that company which had launched it in New York — Charles Harris, Frankie Kemble, Jay Taylor, Hattie Starr, J. Herbert, Alice Butler, Paul Bown (*sic*), George H. Broderick, J. M. Francis and Emma Mabella Baker. This company shifted its personnel from visit to visit. The Breadwinner, adapted from Cormon and Dennery's La Belle du Faubourg, reverted (September 14th–19th) to a remote past, with Loduski Young, R. E. Graham, Joseph B. Gordon and Walter S. Sanford to speed it on its way. That article safely pigeon-holed, we may pass (September 21st–26th) to Nobody's Claim, starring J. J. Dowling and Sadie Hasson, and pass into another month (September 28th–October 3rd) with Storm Beaten, acted, as usual this season, by Edmund Collier, Octavia Allen, Joseph P. Winter, Archie Cowper, L. F. Rand, Charlotte Wayland and Lizzie C. Hudson (an actress I always liked).

The Romany Rye, another standby of melodrama, proffered (October 5th–10th) Victory Bateman, Belle Douglas, Lizzie Creese, John T. Burke (as Jack Herne), O. B. Collins and Charles Jackson, a cast good but not glittering. Oliver Byron, who seems to have dropped, this season, his middle name of Doud, introduced (October 12th–17th) "for the first time in America," an English strenuosity, The Inside Track; in his company were Kate Byron (his wife, and Ada Rehan's sister), J. P. Johnson, Charles Howard, Fred Warren, Harry B. Hudson, J. M. Hart, Charles Young, Lisle Leigh and Dollie Delaro — certainly a cast that would have seemed, in the main, strangers to Broadway. Kate Claxton, bravely struggling to escape from the bonds of The Two Orphans, brought to Brooklyn, on October 19th, the last-season *quasi*-success, Called Back, herself playing the heroine to the Gilbert Vaughan of C. A. Stevenson, and the Macari of Alexander Salvini; Burr McIntosh (an excellent comedian in a limited range of parts), H. A. Thomas, Frank Stevens, Preston Moore, Maida Craigin, Mrs. Mary Dowron, aided. Certainly the record of the Grand Opera House will overweight if not overwhelm the index of this volume with names of players of no importance. This will be seen from a new play of Charles Gayler, which sent October (26th–31st) into the void — Lord Tatters, acted by Dan Maguinnis, J. L.

Morgan, W. E. Hines, J. W. McGrath, Charles Drake, Miss Earle Remington, Mrs. Nelson Kneass and Virginia Wellington.   Such a cast must have
made fastidious Brooklynites rush over to Wallack's or Daly's to renew
acquaintance with the familiar.

And now (November 2nd–7th) began an amusing contest.   Phyllis
Denohr, adapted from Hugh Conway's novel of Dark Days, re-introduced
Charlotte Thompson, along with Fanny Barry Sprague, Lizzie Masters,
Marion Clifton, Kate Magnus, George F. Learock, William Yearance, J. C.
Padgett, Julian Magnus, Sylvia Miller and Charles Lorraine.   Another
dramatisation of Dark Days came to the Criterion Theatre in the following
week.   W. J. Florence brought us back to the familiar and the good, with a
week (November 9th–14th) of No Thoroughfare, making the visit all
Dickens, with Dombey and Son for the matinée on the 11th.   In his support
were F. C. Wells, Earle Sterling, Henry Holland, Hattie Russell (another
sister of Ada Rehan), Lillie Eldridge and Minnie Radcliffe.   The Grand
Opera House went back (November 16th–21st) to the inconsequential with
Vacation, a trifle about Yale and Harvard boys and Vassar girls — the kind
of thing beloved of the films in 1941.   In it appeared the four Daly brothers
(Thomas, William, Robert and Dan), Lizzie Derious, Pauline Batchelder
(sic), Lizzie Daly, Julia Smith and W. Derious.   George and William Hanlon made glad Thanksgiving week (November 23rd–28th) with Fantasma,
bringing in their train the juvenile prodigies, Alice and Frances Hanson, as
well as Alexander Zanfretta and Kate Davis.   The World (November 30th–
December 5th) certainly could not have set the solid earth afire, as acted by
Charles Chapelle, Frank Harrington, W. G. Melville, Amelia Watts and
Laura Alberta.   If such minor lights continue to darken our path, this book
will become, I fear, an index et praeterea nihil.

Rather better, however, was the distribution — at least in two respects —
of another melodrama from the Wallack treasury — The Silver King — with
F. C. Bangs, Grace Thorne, Samuel Verney, Horace Vinton, James Vincent
and Frank Dayton.   On December 9th we had a benefit for the Actors' Fund,
in which participated F. C. Bangs, Frank Mayo, Tony Hart, Charles Pope,
Effie Shannon (whom we are glad to meet), Lizzie Evans, Gertie Granville
and many more.   Boucicault's After Dark gave us (December 14th–19th)
King Hedley and Verner Clarges, of both of whom I have heard, and
Alfred H. Warren, Elsie Grey, Nellie Donald and Ida Sollee, complete
strangers to me.   Surely Brooklyn was expected to take any actors, so long
as they could remember their lines and not fall over the stage furniture.
Ida Mülle, "cute" at least, appeared on December 21st for a week of Dimples,
and Edwin Varrey, S. S. Block and Eugenia Carr abased themselves to her
support.   Frank Mayo and Miss Kidder returned (December 28th–January
2nd) in Nordeck.   This production and one or two others were, to me, the
sole redeeming features of the autumn and early winter at the Grand Opera

House—a theatre, it seems to me, somewhat lower in artistic values than the Park or the Brooklyn. Probably there were too many theatres in the City of Churches.

A Mountain Pink, all about the South and moonshiners, was the very provincial offering for January 4th–9th, and the cast is hardly worth resurrecting from oblivion — Bella Moore, George Hanna, Ruth Hawkins, Ellerslie Gilpin, M. J. Kennedy, Louis Eagin, Katharine Walsh, T. M. Hardy, W. Baker, Clara Douglas, T. E. Fraun, and A. H. Gilbert, most of whom were probably ambitious souls desirous of inscribing their names on the scroll of time. Well, at least they will be buried in the cemetery of our index. I never heard before of one of them. Henry Chanfrau, unfamed son of a well-known father, appeared (January 11th–16th) in that father's famous character of Kit. This at least was an improvement, as perhaps was Lizzie Evans, in Fogg's Ferry, the production of the following week. The Ivy Leaf (January 25th–30th) introduces us to other strangers whom we are not anxious to meet — J. P. Sullivan, F. E. Dunbar, W. J. O'Donoghue, T. F. O'Malley, Dan McCarthy, May Wolcott (she was no stranger) and Delia Powers, constituting a leaf from the Irish directory. In the Ranks brought (February 1st–6th) R. Fulton Russell, William H. Stuart, George S. Fleming, Josie Batchelder, Alice Butler and Connie Thompson, possibly good enough for "the road," but hardly good enough for a theatre so near Broadway. A Great Wrong Righted was the uplifting title of John A. Stevens's effort, produced on February 8th, with J. W. Thompson, Harry Colton, C. A. Nichols, W. P. Sheldon, Loudon McCormack, Minnie Dupree, Emily Lytton and Adelaide (sic) Stanhope constituting a cast only two women and a man or two of whom ever even chipped their names in enduring brass. Sad, sad the tale of thwarted hopes! On Sunday, February 14th, a concert presented Cappa's Seventh Regiment Band, Belle Cole, Laura B. Phelps and T. N. Currie — all for the Parnell Fund.

But here comes Joseph Murphy, brightening February 15th, 16th and 17th, with Kerry Gow, and the three following dates with Shaun Rhue — something to be moderately thankful for. And I welcome gladly the mirth of Salsbury's Troubadours in Three of a Kind (by E. E. Kidder); Nellie McHenry, John Webster, Nate Salsbury and W. S. Daboll were personalities, not merely names for the cemetery of an index. And The Shaughraun may have been endurable, even for memories of the great Wallack casts, with (March 1st–6th) Henry E. Walton (as Conn), E. T. Webber, T. D. Frawley, W. E. Wilson, Verner Clarges, Miss Meroe Charles, Clara Henderson, Irene Ackerman and Mrs. Charles Peters. The Grand Opera House leaned to melodrama; The Romany Rye returned on March 8th, with J. O. Barrows and O. B. Collins. Lydia Thompson, survivor of her own "blondes" of long ago, came back (March 15th–20th) in William Gill's Oxygen, seen somewhat later in New York; with her were Ruth Stetson, Annie Sutherland, Lelia Farrell, Louis de Lange, Richard Carroll and Alexander Clark, all of some note in the realm of extravaganza.   Also light in spirit was Crazy Patch, enlisting (March 22nd–27th) Carrie Swain, Edwin Foy, Verner Clarges, S. Philleo, Paul Thomas, Harold Russell, Thad Shine, Newton Dana, Fannie Austin, Julia Brutone, and Adelaide Arthur.   If I ever emerge from the welter of names through which I stumble and nearly fall in this record of the Grand Opera House, I shall sacrifice a white bullock to the god of things that ought to be more interesting.

The Dalys in Vacation save my time for the week of March 29th–April 3rd; Proved True, by and with Mortimer Murdoch, discreetly withheld, in the Eagle of April 5th–10th, names of supporters of that wandering star. Edwin Arden, in Eagle's Nest, depended (April 12th–17th) on the assistance of Charles Macklin, George W. Mitchell, Alf Beverly, Horace Jones, Emily Spencer and Sarah McVicker (she at least was a rather good actress.)   Storm Beaten again excited for the week of April 19th–24th.   And here, finally, comes (April 26th–May 1st) the paragon of the period, the sequel (by Denman Thompson and George W. Ryer) to Thompson's successful Joshua Whitcomb.   This epoch-making piece, The Old Homestead, fated to be the outstanding rural drama of the ages and one of the most successful plays of all time, had, in this, its early stages, an excellent cast including Thompson (as Uncle Josh — an outstanding characterisation in our stage history), George A. Beane, Walter Lennox, Sr., Walter Gale, Chauncey Olcott, Charles Kruger, Jennie Christie, Rosa Cooke, Alice Logan, Minnie Luckstone, Annie Thompson and Rachel Booth.   One imagines that more than its allotted week might have profitably engaged this work, but previous contracts doubtless prevented extension of time.   At any rate, we are surprised to learn that the next visit lasted for three weeks.   This brought forward Edward Harrigan, with Mrs. Yeamans, Stella Boniface, Amy Lee, Wild, Collyer and all the merry host in Old Lavender (May 3rd–8th); in The Grip (10th–15th); and without Miss Boniface (17th–22nd) in The Leather Patch.   Brooklyn always liked Harrigan.   Milton and Dollie Nobles, in Love and Law (May 24th–29th) led the way for Not One Word (May 31st–June 5th), with a cast including H. E. Walton, James F. Dean, J. E. Wilson, Leslie Edmunds, Mrs. Charles Peters, Hester (sic) Lyons and Katharine Ware.   This play, by James Schonberg almost closed the season at the Grand Opera House; June 7th–12th, however, dragged along, with The Baron, a musical comedy by H. M. Pitt; he and J. O. Barrows headed the cast.   On July 14th, a benefit to George W. Sammis brought together R. C. Hilliard, J. Frank Dallon and others, in a programme including Villikins and His Dinah.

CRITERION THEATRE, BROOKLYN, 1885–1886

Sitting quietly at my desk in 1938 I had the temerity to suggest that, in 1885–86, Brooklyn had too many theatres to provide good entertainment for the good people of the town. In sheer derision of any such idea, a new Criterion Theatre threw open its doors, after customary delays in getting ready, on October 26, 1885, with an offering very stately, compared with the season's major programme at the Grand Opera House. Lester Wallack, on this auspicious 26th, gave his undying Rosedale, with a cast partly composed of Wallack actors — Edward Lamb, Annie Robe, H. Gwynette, Kate Bartlett, George F. De Vere, Little May Germon, W. H. Pope and Louisa Eldridge. This seemly ceremony having rolled into the irrevocable past, James O'Neill, Elizabeth Robins, Annie Boudinot, Marie Floyd and J. W. Shannon dedicated the week of November 2nd–7th to the equally undying Monte Cristo. On November 9th, the management brought out, in opposition to the work of last week at the Grand Opera House, Hugh Conway and Comyns Carr's adaptation of Conway's novel, Dark Days, with Walter Spekeman and Felix Pitt in leading rôles. A Moral Crime, after a bit of success at the Union Square, came to the Criterion for the week of November 16th–21st. The offering for the next week, In the Swim, was stated to be a Sydney Rosenfeld adaptation from the German; the cast included H. M. Pitt, Charles Bowser, Fred Lotto, Victor Harmon, Mrs. Sol Smith, Rillie Deaves, Marion Russell, Mercedes Leigh and Ella Hunt, some of whom in this season depicted for Brooklyn the comic situations of The Rajah. Clay Greene's Forgiven (November 30th–December 5th) served Frederic Bryton and Miss Sydney Armstrong, with T. J. Herndon, Alfred Follin, Frank Russell, Henry Matthews, Clara Goldsby and Louise Reming — two good players surrounded by persons of no note whatever.

But of great note was the offering of December 7th–12th — Rosina Vokes and her London company, in In Honour Bound, My Milliner's Bill, and an adaptation of F. Anstey's The Tinted Venus. This last could not have satisfied; I never heard of Miss Vokes's trying it elsewhere. The Parvenu was announced for the last days of the week. Certainly the Criterion was taking a leading place in Brooklyn theatricals. The offering of December 14th–19th fills me with joy — the seventh Madison Square play we have met this year in Brooklyn, and probably the best of the seven. Young Mrs. Winthrop, in that week, employed many of the best members of the Madison Square company, out of the current Saints and Sinners in the home theatre — Agnes Booth (again Mrs. Dick Chetwyn,) Maud Harrison, Annie Russell, Frederic Robinson (as Buxton Scott) and Walden Ramsay (as Douglas Winthrop). Mrs. Whiffen enacted her original rôle of Mrs. Ruth Winthrop and E. C. Boyle was Herbert. The Templeton Mikado — Charles Harris, Lucille Meredith, &c. — made Christmas cheer (December 21st–26th); and

[156]

for December 28th–January 2nd, Minnie Maddern gave In Spite of All, with Mlle. Nadier, Lillian Wallack, Susie Curtis, Joseph Frankau, Geoffrey Hawley and Cyril Scott — a cast of diminished glory as compared with that seen a few weeks earlier in New York.

Charles Gayler's play, The Bohemian, "written for Colonel John L. Burleigh," presented (January 4th–9th) Burleigh, G. Morton Price, Spencer Pritchard, Randolph Murray, C. J. Tiernan, Edward Prince, men unknown to me, with a quartette of women I know — Agnes Herndon, Constance Murielle, May Waldron and Addie Plunkett. So it happens at times. Estelle Clayton, a pretty woman, appeared next (January 11th–16th), in Favette. Brooklyn amateurs were excited during the week of January 18th–23rd, when Robert C. Hilliard, one of Brooklyn's most cherished amateurs, made his professional début in the lamented Montague's favorite play, False Shame. A good company rallied to his support — Carrie Turner, H. Everard, T. J. Herndon, Walter Eytinge, F. M. Burbeck, Cedric Hope, George Reed, Nellie Yale, Kate Meek and Ethel Kyle. Furthermore, the Mohican Club was to attend on Monday, the Gilbert Amateur Society on Tuesday, and the Kembles on Wednesday — surely a great "send-off" for any man. After that mad, glad excitement, it must have seemed tame (January 25th–30th) to hear C. W. Couldock, in the antiquated The Willow Copse, even though he was supported by Eugenie Blair, Sydney Cowell, A. S. Lipman, James Taylor, Samuel Hemple and Raymond Holmes.

Well, The Mikado (February 1st–6th) was modern enough, with the Templeton Company once more assaulting the public purse; Harris, William H. Seymour (Ko-Ko), Jay Taylor, Lucille Meredith, Emma Mabella Baker and Hattie Starr were now chief wearers of the Japanese costumes. Far from the mood of this specialty was the repertoire of Frederick B. Warde: Damon and Pythias (February 8th, 9th, 10th); Ingomar (matinée, 10th), and Virginius (11th, 12th, 13th). He had good support, I assume, in Henry Aveling, John E. Kellerd, and Mittens Willett. The Templeton artists took another week (February 15th–20th), in The Mikado, proving that, whatever New York had thought of them in August, 1885, Brooklyn liked them during many scattering winter weeks. From the standpoint of American drama, the Criterion produced (February 22nd–27th) the most important item of the year — William Gillette's Held by the Enemy, that exciting drama of the Northern spy caught in the meshes of Confederate discipline, with accompanying story of the lovely Southern girl wooed by the Northern hero and the young Confederate soldier. These three leading rôles were played respectively, by Carrie Turner, Robert Hilliard (substituting for Arthur Forrest, ill) and A. S. Lipman. H. M. Pitt filled the important rôle of the army surgeon, John Woodard was the faithful negro, Charles Bowser the comic journalist, Bean, and Louise Dillon a delightful representative of the ingénue, which always remained her part. Nellie Taylor, William Yearance, E. H.

Barron also appeared. As we know, Held by the Enemy, with a greatly changed cast, was successful in late summer, 1886, at the Madison Square Theatre.

March began with a week (March 1st–6th) of Engaged, then current at the Madison Square Theatre. At the Criterion, Robert Hilliard, evidently much in demand, was Cheviot Hill, and the clever Ada Dyas, not recently seen, must have been good as Belinda Treherne; others were Henry Dalton (as Belvawney), Fred Chippendale (as Symperson), J. E. Nagle, Jr. (as Angus), Burr McIntosh (as Magillicuddy), Olga Brandon (as Minnie), Elizabeth Andrews (as Mrs. McFarlane),· Sadie Morris (as Parker), and Sydney Cowell (once more as Maggie). Adelaide Moore, who swam into our ken in early fall at the Star Theatre, now came to the Criterion with full classic repertoire: As You Like It (March 8th and 12th); Romeo and Juliet (9th and 13th); The School for Scandal (matinée, 10th), The Hunchback (evening, 10th); Ingomar (11th), and (matinée, 13th) The Lady of Lyons. The Eagle preliminary notice asserts that, unlike Mary Anderson, a Southerner, who this year had not visited the South, Miss Moore, a foreigner, had successfully toured that region; furthermore her exotic beauty reminded one, especially as Juliet, of the lamented Adelaide Neilson. Well, Adelaide Moore was no Anderson or Neilson, though doubtless she did her best. A much greater artist, Clara Morris, came forth in much the same plays with which, a month earlier, she had dedicated the new Windsor Theatre in New York: Article 47 (March 15th and 17th); Miss Multon (16th and 18th); Alixe (19th); and Camille (matinée, 20th). Her chief support, Eben Plympton, appeared at the Wednesday matinée as Belphegor, in The Mountebank. He did not appear on the evening of the 19th, Gustavus Levick succeeding him. Ada Gray had the next week (March 22nd–27th), of course in East Lynne. Her dresses were declared to be very beautiful.

After this concession to drama, the Criterion reverted (March 29th–April 3rd) to the inevitable Mikado, this time by the Philadelphia Church Choir Company (yet the group had been seen, at the Lexington Avenue Opera House, under an entirely different name):

Mikado	Charles A. Hetzel	Yum-Yum	Emma Henry Thomas
Nanki-Poo	George C. Pearce	Pitti-Sing	Alice Mersereau
Ko-Ko	Charles H. Parsons	Peep-Bo	Marie Dennison
Pooh-Bah	Eugene Clarke	Katisha	Henrietta Griggs
Pish-Tush	Malcolm Cooper		

Verily this is becoming something too much; we ourselves shall need to devise some form of punishment to fit the crime of all these Mikados. But Brooklyn apparently could not get enough; the Philadelphians remained a second week (April 5th–10th). On the afternoon of April 2nd, a charity matinée promised co-operation of Burbank, Frank Lincoln, Alfred Cammeyer, Harriet Webb, the New York Madrigal Quartet (Emma Henry Thomas, Clara

J. T. BURKE
(ROMANY RYE)

GRACE THORNE
(YOUTH)

ANNIE WARD TIFFANY
(SHADOWS OF A GREAT
CITY)

MAIDA CRAIGIN

ADELE BELGARDE

SYDNEY ARMSTRONG

JOSEPH MURPHY

GEORGE W. MONROE
(MY AUNT BRIDGET)

W. H. SEYMOUR

Stutsman, George C. Pearce (*sic*) and William Thomas). And equally non-theatrical were the illustrated lectures (how epidemical was becoming that form of dissipation!) of Charles W. Seymour, filling April Tuesday afternoons with Spain (6th), Mexico (13th) and Turkey (20th). In regular course, The Lily of Yeddo, an oriental fantasy of the Eighteenth Century, by George Fawcett Rowe, bloomed uncertainly in the parterres of April 12th–17th; Henry Dalton, Alfred Follin, Frederick Paulding, George D. Fawcett, Carl Ahrendt, George Fawcett Rowe, Margaret Leighton, Emma V. Sheridan, Jane Stuart (later well-liked in W. H. Crane's company) and Elizabeth Andrews could not instil enough life into The Lily of Yeddo to transplant it to the more chilling critical clime of New York. Aimée was here for a week of Mam'zelle (April 19th, 20th and 21st) and Divorçons (22nd, 23rd, 24th). Disaster fell on the next venture, a Gilbert and Sullivan season under management of Robert Grau. Patience (April 26th–May 1st) listed Dora Wiley, Alice May, Alice Vane, W. H. Seymour, J. C. Armand, Eugene Clarke and H. L. Rattenberry. For the following week, these artists promised The Pirates of Penzance. The Eagle of April 6th announces the abrupt termination of the engagement; Robert Grau seemed never to achieve anything like the success of Maurice Grau. On Monday, May 10th, the serviceable Robert Hilliard and Carrie Turner were rushed in, in Led Astray; a really excellent cast included also Frederic de Belleville, Mrs. Charles Poole, Mrs. Sol Smith, Jessie Williams, Josie Bailey, Frank Losee, Sedley Brown, H. W. Montgomery (who had been in the original Union Square cast of 1873), Fred May and William Booth. In The Matchmaker, by Edmund Roderick Terry, of Brooklyn, appeared (May 17th–22nd) James O. Barrows, Mrs. Sol Smith, Tessie Butler, Alice Brooks, Kate V. Tousey, Charles B. Welles, Frederick Paulding, R. J. Dustan, Adele Clarke and W. B. Barnes — a good spring cast. This was the last of the Criterion for 1885–86; the Eagle for later May dates advertises that the house may be rented for a day, a week or a month by worthy organisations. I am not sure that the Criterion had not given the most interesting season of that theatre-year in Brooklyn.

ACADEMY OF MUSIC, BROOKLYN, 1885–1886

How better can I induct the eager reader into the mysteries of that temple of sacred delights — the Academy of Music — than by inviting him to a week (September 14th–19th) of that roving Mikado, whose cast continued to change as it roved, and that now was headed by Charles L. Harris, Harry Pepper (Nanki-Poo), Frankie Kemble and Hattie Starr? "Positively the last week" of this aggregation began on the 21st. Very different in kind were the illustrated lectures of J. L. Stoddard: Napoléon from Corsica to the Throne (October 1st); Napoléon from the Throne to St. Helena (October 5th); Dickens Nights (October 8th); Mary Queen of Scots (12th); and

[159]

Switzerland (15th).   And different also the offerings for Charity (October 14th, 16th, and matinée, 17th) of J. M. Hager's historical show.   The Great Republic.   On October 19th, for the benefit of the Y.M.C.A., Archdeacon Farrar lectured on Browning's Poems; this seems an odd choice of subject for the visiting clergyman.

Not until November 19th may I again invite to the royal Academy; on that evening, the almost defeated Mapleson offered Carmen, with Minnie Hauk, Ravelli, Del Puente and others of the recent New York cast.   The Philharmonic programmes, beginning on November 20th and 21st, I shall, as usual, record under their own appropriate caption.   Edwin Booth filled at the Academy a week in his accustomed rôles: Richelieu (November 23rd); Iago (24th); Hamlet (25th); Ruy Blas (matinée, Thanksgiving, 26th); The Fool's Revenge (evening, 26th); Macbeth (27th); Hamlet (matinée, 28th); and The Apostate and Katharine and Petruchio (evening, 28th).   Times were indeed changing when this actor would play eight times a week; how weary he must have been when Sunday allowed him to forget the tragic pall!

On December 8th, Dudley Buck directed a concert of the Apollo Club. Mapleson came back (December 10th) with Fra Diavolo, sung by Ravelli, Del Puente, Alma Fohström, Caracciolo, Mme. Lablache, and Cherubini, with Malvina Cavalazzi leading the ballet; on the 17th, he contributed Maritana, with Ravelli, Del Puente, De Anna, Mmes. Lablache, De Vigne and Alma Fohström.   The Amaranth Society was here, on December 16th (14th, according to the Brooklyn Times), but I shall treat the amateur performances of the year under separate heading.   Mapleson's singers, homeless, appeared, on December 22nd, in Faust, Giannini substituting for Ravelli, announced, and other parts falling to De Anna, Cherubini, Lablache, De Vigne and Fohström.   Poor Mapleson and poor singers, apparently lost to patronage in Manhattan!   I pass, with that sad sigh, to Salvini, who gave, at the Academy, on Christmas night, Coriolanus, and, on the 26th, Othello. And I end the last four months of 1885 even as I began them at the Academy, with The Mikado, this time sung for a week (December 28th–January 2nd) by the Duff Opera Company.   The principals were as at the Standard Theatre in preceding weeks, except that Gustavus Hall was now the Mikado, Francis Gaillard Pish-Tush and Lulu (sic) Tutein Peep-Bo.

Everybody likes the young, and therefore we may venture, on January 7th, to hear the Yale Glee Club, doubtless unhampered by the cares that beset crabbèd age.   The German opera singers, seemingly securely settled at the Metropolitan Opera House, did not, as far as I have discovered, invade Brooklyn in 1885–86; but Theodore Thomas, inaugurating what all hoped would prove a permanency, in the American Opera Company, brought to Brooklyn all the operas that loyal band produced at the New York Academy. He began, on January 11th, with The Taming of the Shrew, cast as in the sister city, following, on the 18th, with Helene Hastreiter and Emma Juch in

[160]

Gluck's enchanting Orpheus and Eurydice. The first annual ball of the Brooklyn Volunteer Firemen's Association, on February 1st, employed Cappa's popular Seventh Regiment Band, the Emerald Ball, green and Irish as could be, following on the 3rd. February 6th found Thomas's New York cast of Lohengrin in Brooklyn, and the 8th proffered a big Kirmess Festival, with Brooklyn boys and girls dancing to the strains of Lander's orchestra. When before have I thought of a Kirmess, that popular diversion in my boyhood days? Before I can answer that question, I am hurried to the Brooklyn Library Lectures — two recitals with stereopticon — given by the explorer, William Bradford, on The Wonders of the Polar World, exploited on February 11th and 18th, and again on the 26th! On February 15th, Mrs. James Brown Potter and her group of gifted amateurs appeared in their favourite Russian Honeymoon — of course for charity, that god of the amateur, in fact the sole excuse, often, for his public appearances. Henry Mollenhauer's College of Music (professors and pupils) boldly stormed the Academy on February 20th. On the 25th, the American Opera Company gave The Merry Wives of Windsor. The masquerade ball of the Brooklyn Sängerbund deflected our interest, on February 22nd, to our dancing feet; but Gluck's Orpheus, on March 11th, returned us to the saner issues of head and heart.

On March 18th, the American Opera mounted Lakmé; on the evening of the 22nd came a concert by the startling group of Lilli Lehmann, Ovide Musin, Franz Rummel and Emanuel Moor. The Marriage of Jeannette and Sylvia, by the unwearied Americans, came on March 27th, and The Magic Flute worked its spell on the afternoon of March 31st. The Brooklyn season of this devoted band ended on April 15th, with Lohengrin ringing down the curtain on their hopes and fears. On April 5th, Georgia E. Weld made her professional début as a singer. On April 12th, Frank Van der Stucken directed an orchestral concert, aided by Christine Dossert, Dr. Mandeville (violin), Edmund Neupert (piano) and Henry S. Brown (bass). The Duff Mikado, which hovered restlessly round the Academy, entered again on April 19th. And Ossa was reduced to a wart when, on April 26th, the Jerome Association of St. Francis College acted The Shaughraun, and when, on the 27th, the St. Francis Literary Society presented the Irish drama, Loughmore. An amateur Mikado, on the 28th, exploited Alice Mersereau as Yum-Yum, Laura Groves as Katisha, George C. Pearce as Nanki-Poo and J. W. Macy as Ko-Ko. I love The Mikado, but my pen is utterly weary of its peregrinations and permutations in 1885-86. And fancy Hazel Kirke, with the Leonardis Society, St. Francis Academy, acted in sheer juvenility, on May 3rd!

The sixth reception of the seventh season of Entre Nous came, on April 28th, in the Assembly Rooms, Ida Terhune, the Philharmonic Quartet and

Miss Gammon assisting. On May 4th, the Apollo Club gave Dudley Buck's cantata, The Voyage of Columbus, and, on May 6th, the Amphion Musical Society, the Cecilia Ladies' Society and the Orpheus Glee Club of New York, all directed by C. Mortimer Wiske, their regular director, presented Joseph Barnby's Rebekah.

Hyde and Behman's, Brooklyn, 1885–1886

I wish I might dismiss this important theatre by stating merely that the artists and "turns" for the season now under our scalpel were very like those enjoyed across the river at the London Theatre or at either or both of Harry Miner's. Of course my reader expects information far more specific; on his own head recoil the boredom that may result from a careful perusal of the following conscientious record! I hasten to state that my history is founded on notes printed every Sunday in the Brooklyn Eagle; the theatre did not advertise in that trustworthy sheet during the week. The Sunday notes also vary in fulness of delivery; hence my narrative at times grows thin.

The popular theatre re-opened, on September 7th, with an aggregation not up to winter exaction — Bedouin Arabs, Elsie Devere, the Horseshoe Four, the Delmanning Brothers, Farrell and Leland, and the Four Shamrocks (Hogan, Brown, John J. Sullivan, &c., in Malony's Trip to America). A burlesque Mikado, in the week of September 14th–19th, boasted of a ballet with Bonfanti, Cæsarini and Cappelini. The Hallen and Hart Prize Ideals began on the 21st, Mlle. Ottilie being part of the attraction. And Tony Pastor, not yet ready to return to his home in Manhattan, filled the week of September 28th–October 3rd, with a fine host — the American Four, Harry and John Kernell, Mr. and Mrs. Harry Watson, Hilda Thomas, Harry La Rose (athlete), P. C. Shortis (mimic) and E. H. Talbot (grotesque acrobat). The Pat Rooney combination, with Katie Rooney and Keating and Flynn, firmly fixed October (5th–10th) in the schedule.

Thus far, we see, travelling Variety had possessed the hall; now, on October 12th, the "regular season" opened, with William Barry, late of Barry and Fay, as stage-manager, a post he held for the season. On October 26th he began a week with an imposing group — the Imperial Dragon "Japs," Vern and Volt (fancy skaters), the Four Comets (in Fragments), Charles Raymond (one-legged clog dancer), John B. Wills and May Adams, Bessie Bell (operatic vocalist), Leslie and Clarke, Billy Barry, John A. Teale, Edith Sinclair and Edward M. Favor — these last two becoming fixtures for several weeks. The lure for November 2nd–7th included Billy Barry, Crossley and Elder, Harry Morris (German sketches), the St. Felix Sisters, Little All-Right (in a slide for life) and a farce, Car Conductors. Variety seemed to be having difficulty in keeping upright on its own legs; a dramatic company, headed by Dominick Murray, gave, for November 9th, Escaped from Sing

Sing; on the 12th, Murray changed to A Great Crime.   James L. Edwards and Clara Otis were in the bills for that week.

The Mikado of Brooklyn, by J. J. McCloskey, had (November 16th–21st) a big cast, including Billy Barry, Dave Oakes, George H. Wood, Ed Favor, Frank M. Gibbons, Harry C. Dietz, Charles C. Barrett, J. A. Kavanagh, Edith Sinclair, Grace Everett, May Stuart and Charles Fostelle; these were noted in the Eagle, but I suspect that some of them merely filled the olio.   At any rate, it is an interesting aggregation.   Billy Barry, in His First Racket, headed the bills in the week of November 23rd–28th, with an excellent olio including Harry Kennedy, Amanda and Jules Tissot (cat duet), the Martens trio, Charles and Annie Whiting (in The Professor), Charles and Ella Jerome (in Burlesquing), Edith Sinclair and Favor.   For succeeding weeks newcomers were the Austin Sisters (gymnasts), Topack and Homer (breakneck song and dance), Annie Hart (serio-comic), Mlle. Rosalie (ballads), a quartet of Russian skaters; Murphy's Pleasure Party (December 7th–12th), with the Lorellas, the Four Diamonds, George Murphy, E. H. Sheehan and Ada Hulmes, Gordon and Grey, Jennie Satterlee, Johnson and Cooper (acrobats), Wiley Hamilton; the company of Watson, Quinlan and Carr (December 14th–19th), including Flora Moore, Silvo (English equilibrist), the little McShane Brothers, Mr. and Mrs. Harry Watson, Leslie Brothers (acrobats), the Horseshoe Four, and Jesssie Boyd — the concluding farce of Blinks and Jinks enlisting Barry, Jennie Satterlee, Dave Oakes, Gracie Clarke, &c.   A Banker's Escapade involved Barry and George H. Wood (December 21st–26th), the huge accompanying olio presenting Sheehan and Coyne, Henry McAvoy and Emma Rogers, Charles and Ella Jerome, Wade and La Clede, George Murphy, Helen Courtland, Jennie Satterlee, Grace Clark, Wiley Hamilton and L. C. Lingard.   The houses on the Bowery could not surpass this glittering host.   Let us pass into 1886 with (December 29th–January 2nd) the American Four (Pettingill, Gale, Daly and Dailey), Howe and Doyle ("dancing kings"), St. Felix Sisters, Barry, George H. Wood, the Jeromes, J. Vogler and his orchestra and Abt's illusions.

Marinelli, the "human snake," was the only feature listed in the Eagle for January 4th–9th, but much ado was made concerning his contortions; a prophecy was in order for the week following — Brooklyn in 1986, or, a Hundred Years Hence.   A version of Pink Dominos, by George H. Wood, was tested for January 18th–23rd; the olio of that week boasted of our favourite Kitty O'Neil, Amelia Waugh (in the character of an old woman), Turner and Vail (acrobats), Hughes and Magrew, the important Queen Vassar, &c.   Obviously Barry, Dave Oakes, George Murphy, the Jeromes, Wiley Hamilton and Jessie Boyd were regular fixtures in the bills.   Mulcahy's Aspirations, week of January 25th–30th, started a series of Mulcahy adventures of a kind made popular by Harrigan's Mulligans.   February 1st–6th listed the "second" week of Mulcahy's Nomination, which leads me to infer that his Aspiration had been quickly gratified. The olio of this latter week presented the Muldoon Quartet, Conroy and Dempsey, Gallagher and West, the Crimmins Brothers (song and dance), the Gregory Trio (gymnasts) and the Four Diamonds. Mulcahy's Excursion took place (February 8th–13th) and was listed as "second piece in that series," thus settling our doubt as to Aspiration becoming Nomination. Marinelli was stressed in this week.

Political satire evidently underlay the contribution of February 15th–20th — The Brooklyn Penal Code, with Billy Barry as Judge Michael Clancy, George H. Wood as District Attorney Bridgeway, and Charles Jerome as Jerry Steinberg; this sounds akin to 1941. The olio in the same bill included Mollie Wilson, the Electric Three (Callan, Haley and Callan, in The Moonlight Masquerade), Pete Shaw, Farrell and Leland, the Kernan Sisters and Frank H. and Lillian White. For February 22nd–27th we had Stirk and Zeno (gymnasts), Bedouin Arabs, Billy Maloney and Mabel Gray (sketch artists), Harry Steele (roller skater), Lynwood Sisters (transformation dancers), and Civil Service Examination (with Barry and Wood) — evidently a good bill. The Hallen and Hart Ideals returned for March 1st–6th, presenting Fox and Van Auken, Frank Bush, Polly McDonald, Joe Hart, John and James Russell and the burlesque, The Two Off'uns. The Rentz-Santley Novelty and Burlesque Company, always eyed askance by purists, gave us, for March 8th–13th, May Howard, Georgie Blake, Billy Buckley, Billy Chace, Mlle. Zitella and a burlesque Mikado. I gladly dismiss this group, to welcome (March 15th–20th) Charles T. Ellis and his clever wife, Clara Moore, who brought with them the Wood Family Juvenile Quartet, Hawkins and Collins, Petrie and Fish, Fields and Hanson, Florence Miller and John T. Kelly (as Senator McFee). The Eagle stressed nothing for March 22nd–27th except Billy Barry and William F. Carroll, in Irish Aristocracy. An enormous host atoned (March 29th–April 3rd), with Pat and Katie Rooney, Lester Howard, John and Emma Whitney, the Jackley Wonders (acrobats), Tom Ward ("the only rival to Frank McNish," in Silence and Fun), Leonzo (Egyptian juggler), Dan Keating and John Flynn ("Ethiopians"), Thomas Dayton (impersonator), the Musical Emperors (Howard, Russell, Weeks and Talbot) and A Red-Hot Stove. Living through that lengthy bill, we arrive, somewhat exhausted, to the offering of April 5th–10th: Fannie Beane and Charles Gilday (whom we always welcome), the Musical Kings, the Clipper Quartet, Fred C. Bryant, George H. Wood, Ada Melrose, George Murphy, C. Ed Foreman and Ida Meredith, and Parker's dogs. McIntyre and Heath's Minstrels were old acquaintances (April 12th–17th); and a grand coterie of friends old and new followed (April 19th–24th) in Hilda Thomas, Pavillio and Roussillion (acrobats), James F. Hoey, Sheffer and Blakely, Ed H. Sheehan and Ada Hulmes, Sharpley and West and Sweeney and Ryland; I cannot imagine that the reader will cherish memories of the farce—No Trespassing. The names piled up as the season waned; April 26th–May 1st filled the bills with the Horseshoe Four, W. T. Bryant and Lizzie Richmond, John and Louisa Till and their marionettes, Manchester and Jennings, Valjean (Egyptian juggler), Charles Stanley and Lizzie Conway, Joe J. Sullivan, B. F. Hodges, Martell Brothers (acrobats) and the farce, Maloney's Visit to America. I begin to wish that Hyde and Behman's would close.

Tony Pastor, having ended his season in New York, brought (May 3rd–8th) a pleasing aggregation, in the Tissots, the St. Felix Sisters, Helene (comedy negress), John F. Byrnes (crayon artist), the Electric Three (Callan, Haley and Callan), William E. Hines and Miss Earle Remington, and Leopold and Bunell (comic musicians). The Australian Novelty Company next entered the hospitable theatre; for May 10th–15th they provided Mlle. Aimée (human fly), Harry Kernell, the Lucier Family, the Austin Sisters ("aerial"), the Russian skaters, Andy and Annie Hughes, Frank Verne (sic) and Tom Volto (sic), Topack and Homer, Annie Hart, William Carter (banjo), Mlle. Rosalie ("polite queen of song")—all this array closing with a farce, Rinklets. An Adamless Eden, frowned on when I was young, stopped the shows at Hyde and Behman's for 1885–86. Except that (why I can't imagine) an elaborate benefit for James Hyde, manager, and Henry W. Behman, treasurer, occupied the afternoon and evening of May 31st. Volunteers included Hallen and Hart, Harry Kennedy, Sheffer and Blakely, McIntyre and Heath, J. F. Hoey, Sheehan and Holmes (sic), Tommy Granger, Maggie Cline, Bryant and Lizzie Richmond. Annie Hart, Kitty O'Neil and many more.

STANDARD MUSEUM, BROOKLYN, 1885–1886

The place thus listed is difficult to classify; perhaps it was, at least at times, a home of plays with accompanying vaudeville. At times it advertised only plays. And there, certainly, found refuge a number of former stars of Broadway, now reduced to cheap houses in the suburbs and outlying districts. Such a one appeared at the Standard at the opening of the season, on August 31, 1885—Pauline Markham, no less, in 1868 "the toast of the town," whatever that may mean. Her play was called Dolly's Luck. Performances were given twice daily (September 7th–12th) when Lottie Blair played Hazel Kirke, with Fenwick Armstrong as the implacable Dunstan. I hope I may bring the reader quickly to his journey's end, with N. S. Wood, in Nan, the Newsboy (September 14th–19th); The Unknown (September 21st–26th), and (September 28th–October 3rd) Reed Birds, with Dave Reed, Jerome and King Sisters, Frank and Fannie Davis, Tableaux Soleil of Professor Davis, Master Tommy (motto singer), the Big Little Three (Mack and Holbrook, Lottie Russell), and the farce, Between Two

Fires. However cheap the price of admission, this company, except for Dave Reed, would seem to me to be worth it — perhaps. Our Shop Girls, the offering of October 5th–10th, no doubt was tearful and informative. Sam Roberts was in some way figuring in the establishment. And here comes back the delight of the Bowery, N. S. Wood, in The Boy Detective (October 12th, 13th, 14th) and The Boy Scout (15th, 16th, 17th). Just as we were getting on rapidly, our progress was checked by The Block Game, or, Playing to Win, with the Museum company and George France. Also at every performance appeared Matsada and Ogoray (Japanese athletes), Rosina, Dan Hart and his dog, and John Manning ("king of the air"). Moths flew into the breach (October 26th–31st) with Helene Adell, Sara Lascelles and D. W. Eagle.

More talented contribution brought (November 2nd–7th) Frank I. Frayne, in Si Slocum; less known to me was Ethel Tucker, in Queena (9th–14th), and, for that matter (16th–21st), Viola Rosa, with Edward Lang, in Scheming. I am surprised to find at this humble home of the drama, The Creole (Article 47), acted (November 23rd–28th) by Lillian Lewis, Wilton Lackaye and W. H. Allen. Crimes of a Great City (November 30th–December 5th) let us into early winter, with Mamie Wallace and Alfred A. Wallace as leaders; an olio provided W. J. Hampton's trained animals, T. F. Thomas, George W. Watson, Kittie and Nellie Howard, Charles H. Duncan (topical songs), &c. The "vaudeville" at the Museum seems to me about as good as the plays it accompanied; in other words, good for those who could not afford seats for higher-priced and better houses. For instance, what shall we say of Dick Gorman, in Conrad, or, the Hand of a Friend, tried in the week of December 7th–12th? or of A Hoop of Gold (14th–19th), with Beatrice Leib and Arthur Moulton? or of Helene Adell, in The New Magdalen (21st, 22nd, 23rd) and in The Two Orphans (24th, 25th, 26th)? or, indeed, of Burr Oaks that had not stuck in the repertoire, of the earlier season, of higher-class theatres, and now ended the year at the Museum (December 28th–January 2nd)? We observe that, since our last volume, Helen Adele has become Helen Adell; possibly, before we know it, she will again be Adele.

The Colleen Bawn had (January 4th–9th) possibly the least distinguished cast these Annals afford for it, in T. F. Thomas, Elsie La Miere, Bart W. Wallace, Gus Striker, Alexander Fisher, Amy Lionel, Kate Mallon, J. U. Randal, Charles O'Brien, and Fred Post. Has the reader ever heard of any of them? A Box of Cash, a musical burletta, presented (January 11th–16th) two recruits from Hyde and Behman's, in Edith Sinclair and E. M. Favor, as well as J. V. Arlington, J. C. Kline and T. F. Thomas. But here are two whom we have found in more elegant surroundings — J. M. Hardie and Sara von Leer, who came forth (18th–23rd), in A Brave Woman; like all others visitors to the Museum, they must play twice a day. And, of all people in the world, D. E. Bandmann, far voyager in theatreland, gave a week (January 25th–30th) of the "legitimate," twice daily, acting, in this order, Don Cæsar de Bazan (twice), The Merchant of Venice, The Lady of Lyons, Hamlet, East Lynne, Dora, Othello, The Hunchback, Narcisse, Romeo and Juliet and Richard III. It seems incredible. And still another relic from a far-off happier past—Fanny Herring—gave Little Buckshot (February 1st, 2nd, 3rd) and The French Spy (4th, 5th, 6th). This sad ending merits the tear of sympathy and charity. Poor Fanny!

We must admit that fare at the Museum distinctly improved when (February 8th–13th) The Galley Slave enlisted Frank Roberts, T. D. Frawley, James Bevins, Virginia Marlowe, Mrs. Frank Evans, Annie Helen Blancke, Rose Snyder, J. P. Keefe and Fred Lawrence. The Pavements of Paris (15th–20th), and The Banker's Daughter (22nd–27th) brought February out with a certain distinction. George W. and W. J. Thompson had the week of March 1st–6th, divided evenly between The Gold King and For a Life. Clara Lloyd, with W. H. Rightmire, also cut her week (March 8th–13th) evenly in two, assigning the parts respectively to A Romance of a Poor Young Girl and The California Detective, or, Life in Two Great Cities. Those plays seem just the kind of thing that would be liked by those who like that kind of thing. But here, on the 15th, for three days came Only a Farmer's Daughter, and, on the 18th, for three more, Only a Woman's Heart, titles that merit tears of pity, even a half-century later. Lottie Blair and Fenwick Armstrong returned (March 22nd, 23rd, 24th) in Hazel Kirke, and (25th, 26th, 27th) in The Child Stealer. Our Boys (with J. W. Jennings) had half of the next week (March 29th–April 3rd), and The Long Strike the second half. Monte Cristo (April 5th) brought back "Alf." A. Wallace and Mamie (also a Wallace). And more people familiar in our walks through the cheaper theatres came forth (April 12th–17th), when Without a Home presented Minnie Oscar Gray and W. T. Stephens, with J. B. Brown, Robert Neill, W. H. Danvers and Lizzie Hunt. The ever-desired N. S. Wood returned (19th–24th) in Jack Harkaway, and the Hall, Devoy and Knowles Comedians at least gave us something new (26th–May 1st) in Odds and Ends, or, Alphabetical Fun, a rather intriguing pair of titles.

The Irish in plays were ever travelling, if only for a short distance. Muldoon's Trip to Brooklyn enlisted, for May 3rd–8th, Harry La Rose, Bryant and Saville, the Coulson Sisters, Kitty Sheppard and Frank Livingstone (weight-balancer). And here (May 10th–15th) is the everlasting novelty, Uncle Tom's Cabin ("with a double company"). A big bill for May 17th–22nd gave The Government Scout, by and with Edward Akins, assisted by Estelle (sic) Crolius and G. W. Watson; the olio gave Conroy and Dempsey, the Novelty Quartet, Steve and Addie Lamont, Signor Manola (man serpent), Polly McDonald (skipping rope) and E. Clarence Worrall ("child cornetist"—horrible!) The end was drawing near when (May

24th–29th) James Harrison and W. H. Stuart proffered "the beautiful temperance drama," Ten Nights in a Bar-Room. Lucky Ranch, a tale of Yosemite, was the contribution (May 31st–June 5th) of Mr. and Mrs. W. M. Paul, assisted by T. F. Thomas and George W. Watson. June 7th–12th brought George Murphy, under management of George H. Wood, in Rudolph's Ambition; and the Mestayer Company of Comedians followed (14th–19th). On June 16th, G. W. Watson kindly took a matinée benefit; and we may take a rest from the Standard Museum, which I have found, in its more democratic way, rather interesting.

ZIPP'S CASINO, 1885–1886

The concert hall of Zipp's Casino, Elm Place, would be open to the public, quoth the Eagle, on the evening of September 12, 1885; the "regular season" would begin on Monday, September 14th. Millie St. Clair and Charles Storms and the Otremba Band figured in the following week (21st–26th); October 5th–10th boasted of Adele Martinetti, who continued to dance for weeks, and Marie Rembach, whose name soon passed from Eagle columns. Later October gave Emil Müller, Minnie Lee and Annie Schober, along with Otremba's Band; Louise Murio and Minnie Lee were heralded in early November. Thereafter the Eagle wraps us in silence till December 7th–12th, when Brandl and Katzer (Vienna duettists) and Johanna Wagner ("international serio-comic"—portentous) did as they might. Georgie Marsh and Annie (sic) Raimé figured in the following week; Adele Martinetti, Malvina Renner and Otremba (in the week of December 21st–26th), and Lulu Delmay (for January 4th–9th).

The Eagle now carries me to January 18th–23rd, to hear Ignatz Conradi (Tyrolean warbler) and Elsa Alberti, and then retains silence till February 1st–6th, when the Caldwell Sisters were to do their "turn." Herr Schulze and Frl. Müller, North German duettists (February 8th–13th); Malvina Renner and Georgie Marsh (15th–20th); Hattie Howard (soprano) and Annie Schober (mezzo — 22nd–27th); a Vienna Ladies Orchestra (March 1st–6th); Della Torra and Ida Krause (vocalists — March 8th–13th); the continuing Ladies Orchestra (22nd–27th) — these delectabilities lead me to Spring, with none of the exhilaration that re-awakening Nature usually excites. Elsa Alberti begins April, and, after silence that my readers may regret, the Eagle for May 10th–15th promises Ella and Annie Caldwell (sopranos), Mlle. Messenek (violinist — as for weeks past) and Herr Lowe (xylophonist), an array that makes one willing to stay at home. With this uncharitable thought, I leave the Casino for the season, merely remarking that it was opened for Sunday concerts.

SUMMER PAVILION, BROOKLYN, 1885–1886

We remember that the Summer Pavilion, Flatbush Avenue and Fifth Street, was offering, in latest August, 1885, the not novel Uncle Tom's Cabin; for September 7th–12th, an entertainment listed as Parlour Matches invited with the Vidocqs (John and Miss Edna), Carrie Lloyd, Mark Ryder and Frank George. On this site, perhaps in the Pavilion itself, a Permanent Circus, the Nick Roberts-Gardiner Shows, held sway (May 3rd–15th) with Leon de Leon (silent clown) and the Snow Brothers among the performers. The last week of this excitement provided, among other acts, Parker and his dogs, and George Melville, the clown, in The Dumb Waiter.

Then the Summer Pavilion Theatre re-opened (May 24th–29th) with the Metropolitan Star Opera Company, in The Chimes of Normandy, with Louise Lester, Emma Elssner, Annie Ross, Julia Earnest, Lottie Laselle, W. T. Raymond, J. C. (*sic*) Campbell and Kirtland Calhoun, declared by the jubilant managers to be the "grandest cast ever appearing under canvas," the "largest and handsomest summer theatre in the world." As Friday's Summer Pavilion Theatre, at prices of 10, 20 and 30 cents, the place offered The Mascotte (June 7th, 8th, 9th) and Olivette (10th, 11th, 12th). Louise Lester, Georgie Knowlton and Charles J. Campbell led the starry hosts. Perhaps business was poor; at any rate, a "grand Whitney piano" was, at the close of the season, to be given to the person holding the largest number of reserved seat coupons (50 cents) "over Nos. 1 to 90." The contest was to begin on the 7th. The Shaughraun, with Henry E. Walton and "the same company that appeared in March at the Grand Opera House," held the Pavilion for June 14th–19th, with C. Erin Verner as Conn and Aïda Doranzie as Moya. The attraction for June 21st was The Mikado, with Bessie Gray (or Grey) as Yum-Yum; on June 28th Lenox, Welch and Rice's Minstrels boasted of Hughey Dougherty and the Weston Brothers. Con O'Grady (July 12th–17th) brought to the Pavilion Gustave Frankel, W. G. Gilmore, Annie Ware and Emily Kean.

August 2nd began two weeks of The Mikado, with T. M. Holland in the title-rôle, Gerard Coventry as Nanki-Poo, George Gaston (a wandering fire) as Ko-Ko, Mack Charles as Pooh-Bah, J. R. Oakley as Pish-Tush, Bessie Grey as Yum-Yum, Miss E. Waite as Pitti-Sing, Miss Lascelle (*sic*) as Peep-Bo, and Tillie McHenry as Katisha, not to mention a chorus of "24 fresh young voices." August proceeded with Pinafore (16th, 17th, 18th) and The Chimes of Normandy (19th, 20th, 21st). I caught no more echoes from this bower of bliss.

AMATEUR ACTING, BROOKLYN, 1885–1886

The Eagle, I regret to state, is defective for this season in announcements and reviews of acting by amateurs. I found in it, for instance, no record of the activities of the stately Kemble Society, and only three for the revered Amaranths. Doubtless many other functions, highly important to the perpetrators, eluded my vigilant search. Fortunately, the Brooklyn Times occasionally comes to our assistance; for November 11th, it provides, at the Athenæum, a performance of Love's Sacrifice, Ira H. Moore as Matthew Elmore, J. H. Arnold as Paul Lafont, J. J. Jackson as Eugene de Lorme, Paul Dater as St. Lo, Stella Elmore as Margaret, and Annie Culver as Herminie. The Amaranths, pride of Brooklyn, began their season, on November 16th, at the Academy of Music, with Love, or, the Countess and the Serf, presenting their esteemed John C. Costello as Huon, Helen Dayton as the Countess, and, in other rôles, S. G. Frost, B. R. Throckmorton, W. B. Vernam, Alfred Young, Ada Austin, Ada Woodruff and Kate Ten Eyck, names as familiar to us as those of professional actors. It would have been interesting to compare these amateurs with members of Wallack's and Daly's companies. When, on November 25th, Company C, 13th Regiment, gave a reception, a playlet, Enlisted for the War, or, the Home Guard, itself enlisted a cast of actors familiar to our researches in Amateurland — M. J. Colligan, M. J. McKenna, J. J. Moran, Adolph Meyer, Jennie Dyas, Ella Healey, Katie Leibold and others. This I glean from the Brooklyn Times, a source which also furnishes news of the Clio Dramatic Society invading the Athenæum, on December 3rd, with Naval Engagements, waged by William R. Groth, George McEvoy, William C. Fleming, Joseph Ewyatte, Sarah Hughes and Emma Keerey. St. Peter's Dramatic Association had no fear of The Pirates of Penzance, whom (or which) they assailed, on November 25th and 26th, in St. Peter's Academy.

For the performance by the Arcadians of Our Boys (Athenæum, December 10th), I am indebted to a notice in the Brooklyn Times; the cast included C. T. Catlin and George W. Cogan as the Champneys, father and son; W. T. Harris, Jr. and Adam Dove as the elder and the younger Middlewicks, respectively; May Herbert as Violet and Amy Zell as Mary; Nellie Clayton as Clarissa Champneys; and Ida L. Waller as the irrepressible Belinda. And now the respected Kemble Society, so exclusive, so elusive to research, emerges once more in the Brooklyn Times, with a performance, on December 15th, in the stately Academy of Music, of The Merry Wives of Windsor, only a very few weeks before Augustin Daly revived it with all the resources of his theatre. Did the Kembles thus anticipate by accident or design? At any rate, they cast the comedy with their best actors:

Sir John Falstaff	J. H. Bird	Dr. Caius	W. Macfarlane
Shallow	John Smithson	Host	Gerald Ainslie
Slender	Deane Pratt	Mrs. Ford	Elita Proctor Otis
Fenton	A. J. Macaulay	Mrs. Page	Annie L. Hyde
Ford	Douglas Montgomery	Anne Page	Lizzie Wallace
Page	E. J. Wilkins	Mrs. Quickly	Mrs. Parkhurst

[170]

Thankful for this information I proceed.   On December 16th, No Thorough-fare was presented at the Academy of Music by the Amaranths, with Charles Heckman (Obenreizer), Ada Austin, Ada Woodruff, Antonio Perez, A. H. Marquis, Charles Young, Charles Bellows, Jr., Percy G. Williams, Ida E. Williams, Mrs. G. H. Parkhurst, A. P. Vredenburgh, Franklin Norris, George W. Hermance, S. G. Frost, and J. C. Costello (*sic*) — names that undoubtedly meant much to "nice" Brooklyn residents on or near the Heights.   The Athenæum began to offer a series of dramatic entertainments; on December 21st it proffered Micaliz, with William Cattell.   At the Academy, also, the Gilbert Dramatic Society, on January 6th, appeared in Villikins and His Dinah (with Darling, Dr. Cantrall, Kimball and Bertie Cecil) and in The Snowball (with Pauline Willard, May Herbert, Hattie F. Nefflin, H. J. Stokum, John W. Noble, Charles H. Canfield and Theodore Baldwin).   The third performance of the fourth season of the Arcadian Society enriched January with Love Wins, proved in their serious amateur way by C. T. Catlin, Harry Peckham, W. T. Harris, Jr., Will E. Horton, Amy Zell, Flor-ence Harris and Nellie Clayton.   The Brooklyn Dramatic Society, on Janu-ary 19th, invaded the Athenæum with Comrades, participants being James J. Byrne, William J. Mullin, Elijah J. Malloy, John T. O'Grady, Lizzie Wal-lace, Lizzie Healey and Emily Caldwell — a rather Irish Brooklyn, one suspects.

From New York, on January 22nd, came Mrs. James Brown Potter and her amateur colleagues, in The Old Love and the New, which suggests The Banker's Daughter in the days of its youth.   The Amateur Opera Association, at Remsen Hall, on January 29th, included Laura S. Groves, Winifred Rogers, George L. Ellard (whom we know), Samuel Swazey, John G. Hall and Edward W. (*sic*) Bray (whom also we know).   Minnie Dorlon, pupil of Gabriel Harrison, offered her mite.   The Brooklyn Euphonia Singing Society gave, on February 9th, at the Athenæum, an amateur per-formance of a kind I am unable to designate.   Lost in London, on February 17th, again brought forward, at the Academy, the almost professional Amaranths, with B. R. Throckmorton as Gilbert Featherstone, J. C. Cos-tello and Ada Woodruff as the sorrowful Armroyds, Percy G. Williams as Blinker, the tiger, Virgil Lopez and A. H. Marquis as his fellow-servants, Mamie Sloat as Tillie Dragglethorpe, and Elise Fiedler as Florence, the maid.   The Amaranths did things in style; on this occasion Cappa's Seventh Regiment Band played in intervals of the acting.   They repeated this offer-ing, on March 1st, for the Sons of St. George.   The Melpomene Society, on February 19th, held a "stag racket," featuring the omnipresent Robert C. Hilliard, Frank (*sic*) Bowne, E. O. Jacobson, Knudsen (prestidigitateur), Judge Greene, F. C. Randall and Pearce (piano).   On the 19th, also, the Booth amateurs gave Father and Son, at the Athenæum, with T. H. Kane, M. E. O.'Neil, W. M. Caldwell, John Hanan, W. J. M. Cahill, E. J. Carr,

G. P. Cavanagh, Nellie Keating, Emma Londwersick (*sic*), Emily Caldwell and many more.

Turn Hall, Eighth Street, South Brooklyn, provided, on February 16th, harbourage for the Washington Dramatic Association, in The Octoroon (amateurs that year tended to melodrama, perhaps because it is easier to do than high comedy). In the cast were Pauline Demonet (Zoe), William Hawkins (Wah-no-Tee), Joseph P. Briody (George Peyton), J. D. Harrison (Salem Scudder), A. J. Tybring, Charles J. Briody (McCloskey), J. P. Nolan (Sunnyside), J. J. McDermott, M. J. Hanlan, P. H. Cosgrove, George Parkson, Jennie Parson (Paul), Fred H. Storms, John F. Pundt, Thomas J. McGreal, Miss E. J. Kellogg (Mrs. Peyton) and Sadie Mortimer (Dora). I pity my poor pen as it needs to write the names of all those Brooklyn amateurs; would they had been satisfied just to be "nice" young men and women in good society! The Widow Hunt, at the Athenæum, carried us to another part of Brooklyn, to see (and, if possible) admire the Arcadian Dramatic Society, with H. J. Stokum as Felix Featherly, Frederic (*sic*) W. Bowne as Icebrook, James Jordan Darling as Major De Boots, Edward Morris as Traps, Ida Darling as Mrs. Featherly, Mrs. Charles Bellows, Jr., as Mrs. De Boots, and Ida Woodruff as Mrs. Swansdown.

Courage, reader! even amateurs cease upon the spring with no pain. The Dunreath Society did its best, I suppose, on March 4th, at the Brooklyn Irving Hall, with The Loan of a Lover and The Chimney Corner, participants being Gilbert Young, Charles A. Missing, William Wilson, Daniel M. Peters, Viola Young and Jessie Neale, C. H. Beale, R. A. Saul, W. H. La Zelle, F. W. Shipman, B. F. Darland, Nellie Horton and Emmie Chester. Brooklyn Amateurs, on the 5th, took to the Academy The Iron Chest (which Booth had recently revived) and Ici On Parle Français, with Harry J. Stokum, Charles T. Catlin, M. Delgado, H. H. Gardner, J. C. Cordello (*sic*), S. de Lissner, Virgil Lopez, Ada Woodruff, Mamie Sloat and Lizzie Wallace. March 16th announced Worth a Struggle, by the Melpomene Dramatic Society, who invaded the Athenæum in persons of Fred C. Randall, Jennie Cochrane, Frank J. Oliver, Thomas C. Bell, Lizzie and Georgie Wallace, William Dunbar, W. M. Campbell and Ella Starr. By good luck I came, in the Brooklyn Times, on a performance, at the Academy, by the Amaranth Society, of the ever-interesting Diplomacy, with A. P. Vredenburgh as Orloff, J. C. Costello as Stein, Wallace Grant as Julian, Charles Heckman as Henry Beauclerc, Charles Bellows, Jr. as Algie, Harriet Lawson as the Marquise de Rio Zares, Harriet Webb (later on the professional stage) as Zicka, Madge Longstreet as Dora, Mamie Sloat as Lady Henry Fairfax, and the obliging Ada Woodruff as Mion. She seems to have been willing to play any part, large or small. Perhaps I should list elsewhere, though I do not, Nellie Doute, who, on March 25th, appeared at the Athenæum, in The Orphan of Geneva; she was a pupil of Gabriel Harrison, who supported her. Long in

[172]

advance, it was announced that Julia W. Reid, an amateur, would act The Banker's Daughter, on Easter Monday afternoon, at the Criterion Theatre. Did she?

Two farewells for the season must have wrung the emotional sensibility of amateur Brooklyn. On April 13th, the Kemble Society said goodbye, in the Academy of Music, till the season of 1886–87 might once more set their ambition on the wing. Their offering was The Lancashire Lass, played by Julia W. Reid, Matilda Davis, Douglas Montgomery, A. C. Munn, H. H. Gardner, Anna M. Kerr, E. J. Burke, J. C. Wilson, T. G. Frost, George R. Lamb, James C. Lamb, Frank Cuddy and J. Nethersole, whose names I quote, with thanks, from the Brooklyn Times. That same serviceable paper allows me, on April 15th, to wave a fond farewell, for the season, to the Amaranths, reviving, at the Academy, May Blossom, with Ada Woodruff (in the title-rôle), George E. Barnett (Tom Blossom), J. C. Costello (Steve Harland), B. R. Throckmorton (Richard Ashcroft), Percy G. Williams (Uncle Bartlett), Mrs. Ida E. Williams (Deborah), Mrs. Charles Bellows, Jr. (Millie) Bijou Fernandez (little May, as played by her at the Madison Square), and, in smaller parts, A. H. Marquis, H. T. Hall and W. B. Vernam.

A "grand dramatic entertainment," contents unspecified, was at the Music Hall, on May 6th; on the 7th, at the Athenæum, the Brooklyn Dramatic Society once more assailed the long-suffering Hazel Kirke. For charity, on May 11th, the Melpomene Dramatic Society brought to the Academy The Crushed Tragedian, under its original title of The Prompter's Box; the cast included W. T. Harris, Jr., W. M. Campbell (De Lacy Fitzaltamount), Deane Pratt, Samuel C. Austin, Charles E. Le Barbier, Fred Randall, Ernest O. Jacobson, Charles T. Catlin, Frank Norris, J. D. Nairn, Master Fred Porter, Lizzie Wallace, Mabel McCoy and Jennie (sic) Cochrane. I hope some of the amateurs in this section may be alive to thrill at reading their names along the line. On the 11th, also, the veteran amateur, at the Athenæum, benefited, let us hope, by performance of A Happy Pair and Toodles, Mr. and Mrs. George Woodruff appearing in the former, and Faulkner and Marion Sackett in the latter. For good measure, Ira H. Moore ended the bill as Havresack, in The Old Guard. From this spring board, it was but natural for Moore, on May 25th, to dive into a benefit at the Athenæum, with The Merchant of Venice and Delicate Ground, Harry M. Noble and Mrs. Elmore assisting.

I almost envy the intrepidity of amateurs. J. H. Arnold, on May 14th, entered the patient Athenæum, as Bertuccio, in The Fool's Revenge. I know not what deft new touches he supplied to Booth's great character, but I know that the Boo' ﹏ Dramatic Society supported him to the extent of the abilities of T. H Kane, J. Bateman, W. F. Wells, H. Egard, John Olsen, Paul Dater, Fannie Rorke, Mrs. Stella Elmore, Randa Florence, Dulcie Durant and Miss A. Culver. St. Peter's Dramatic Association, on May 26th and 27th, repeated The Mikado, in St. Peter's Academy Hall. They had

[173]

done it at an earlier date, in April. This ends it, so far as my weary eye found amateurism in the Eagle or the Times, for my weary pen.

BROOKLYN MUSIC AND MISCELLANY, 1885–1886

The Brooklyn Turn-Verein held, as August, 1885, left the calendar, a Sommernachtsfest at 200 Court Street, that old meeting-place of Germans. Roller skating obsessed America in this year, and therefore my reader will expect to attend all sorts of exhibition skating in the Palace Rink, Clermont Avenue, the Heights Roller Skating Rink, the Fifth Avenue Skating Rink, etc. Will he also excuse me from wearisome repetition on this theme, throughout this already overcrowded narrative of Miscellany? That favour granted, I note the Union des Sociétés Françaises de Brooklyn, which, on September 12th, held, at Broadway and Washington Park, Brooklyn, a festival and *bal de nuit*.

With this concession, also, I pass to September 28th for a contest, at De Kalb and Classon Avenues, between the W.A.C. Team and the St. Regis Indian Lacrosse Team. On that same 28th, Music Hall was transformed into a Temple of Mysteries, with Hoffman's European Wonders: Beulah, the mystic marvel; the Lucier Family of musicians; Mlle. Ellani, in operatic selections; Pasha, the automatic cornetist; and an illusory Lady Downing's Clever Capture. The Fisk Jubilee Singers were at Plymouth Church, on October 26th; on the 31st occurred at the College of Music, Livingston Street, the first of a series of private chamber music soirées by Henry Mollenhauer. Jerome Hopkins was tirelessly at the Music Hall, on the 27th; on the 29th, Henrietta Beebe and W. H. Lawton sang at Historical Hall; and at this time it was announced that Harry Rowe Shelley would soon begin a series of organ recitals at the Church of the Pilgrims.

At the Brooklyn Tabernacle, on November 4th, Sauahbrah gave an illustrated lecture on India; at his second lecture he was associated with Belle Cole and D. G. Lawson (humourist). R. J. De Cordova, on the 10th, possessed Arcanum Hall, Fulton Street and Bedford Avenue, with the easily digested humour of The Dyspeptic Club of East Pietown. Daniel Doherty, on November 17th, in The Y.M.C.A. Hall, Bond Street, near Fulton, spoke on Orators and Oratory; on the 19th, the same hall graciously welcomed the Fisk Jubilee Singers. Reverend Charles R. Treat, on the 24th, filled the same hall with his illustrated talk on From Amsterdam to Waterloo; and the same date found the indefatigable Fisk singers at the Throop Avenue Presbyterian Church. And (still on that eventful 24th) Jerome Hopkins's Young Philharmonic was at the Athenæum, with, among other manifestations, his "comic opera," Taffy and Old Munch. Far preferable to me would have been the concert of the Washington Avenue Baptist Church, on the 26th, when were to appear Emma Thursby, Emily Winant, A. L. King (tenor), Chevalier de Kontski and Albert Greenhalgh (piano). This is almost metropolitan. At the Tabernacle were promised R. J. Burdette (November 30th); Wallace Bruce, orator (December 7th); and Helen Potter (December 14th). Y.M.C.A. Hall, on December 1st, gave sterling attractions in A. P. Burbank and the Meigs Sisters, happy memories of my happy youth.

Eli Perkins, on December 2nd, in the same hall, expounded The Philosophy of Wit and Humour—more than Schlegel or Coleridge had been able successfully to do. On that same evening, at Music Hall, Dr. Greene began a course of four illustrated lectures on medical subjects—some "for ladies" only, others only "for gentlemen." "For young men only" were the Moody and Sankey services, beginning on December 8th, at the Y.M.C.A. Rooms, with a male chorus of fifty men, led by George C. Stebbins, to drive home the lessons. On the 7th, the Entre Nous Society reception occurred in the Academy Assembly Rooms. On the 9th, the Bergen Star Company (coloured) was at Music Hall; and, on the 10th, in the same hall, came an annual banjo concert and Marshall P. Wilder. A new organ at the Clinton Avenue Congregational Church was inaugurated at this time with playing by Samuel P. Warren, Henry Eyre Browne, Harry Rowe Shelley and Francis Taft— assuredly a music dish to set before a king. And Alma Fohström and Mlle. Svenbladh, from Sweden, held, on a contiguous date, the ever receptive Historical Hall. On the 10th, Penelope was sung at Knickerbocker Hall, by the Comic Operetta Company.

Dr. McGlynn, the Catholic priest round whom debate raged hotly, lectured on Sunday, December 13th, at the Church of St. Ambrose; a date on which Moody and Sankey said good-bye at Association Hall. Far different in tone and spirit was the Complimentary Promenade Concert held, on the 16th, at the Armoury of the Twenty-third Regiment. It does not interest me to learn that, on the 14th, Luigi Monti, at St. James Church, lectured on Victor Emmanuel; or that, on the same date Helen Potter read at the Tabernacle, Schermerhorn Street; or that, in Christmas week, at Music Hall, appeared one Maria Selika (successor to the Black Swan) and S. W. Williams. On the 17th, at Knickerbocker Hall, appeared Hortense Pierse, F. C. Bowne, R. C. Hilliard, Florence Lethridge and D. W. Robertson (tumbleronicon). This gets us neatly out of 1885.

A test *séance* by John Slater, on January 4th, came to Conservatory Hall, Bedford Avenue and Fulton Street; on the 5th, Jerome Hopkins's Young People, with Taffy and Old Munch, possessed Historical Hall, that auditorium, on the next night, opening for the Pastime Glee Club. John B. Gough lectured at the Y.M.C.A. Rooms, on the 13th, on Powers that Be. On the 12th, the Brooklyn Schützen-Corps were at Sängerbund Hall, and in a house, 310 Clermont Avenue, Ida K. Hinds, at a date contiguous to these exciting events, recited from Tennyson and Owen Meredith, both still revered in 1886. William S. Roberts, on January 13th, 14th and 15th, promised to give at Everett Hall, 398 Fulton Street, mind reading and cabinet manifestations. Very much less abstruse was a great bicycle contest, on the 14th, at the Fifth Avenue Roller Skating Academy; and decidedly more spiritual, in an entirely different sense, the second chamber music concert, at the Brooklyn Conservatory of Music, postponed from January 13th to the 20th. Harry L. Sands, prestidigitateur, and Fred Chase were at St. Peter's Chapel, on the 19th; that same date (19th) found Professor Nathan Sheppard at the Y.M.C.A. Hall, with a stereopticon lecture on Dickens. January 20th was doubly blest with the first of a series of five organ recitals, by Harry Rowe Shelley, in Plymouth Church, Alfred Cammeyer (banjo) assisting, and with the nineteenth chamber music soirée at Historical Hall, Minnie Landis (contralto) serving as soloist. And January 23rd also doubled its delight: at Packer Institute Chapel appeared Helen Potter, Clementine Lasar Studwell, S. Lasar and Harry Loomis; at Historical Hall, Ida Mollenhauer and Carlos Sobrino engaged in a concert for two pianos. The Brooklyn Männerchor, on the 28th, sang at the Sängerbund Hall; on the 28th and 29th, Professor Greene lectured, at the Athenæum, on Physical Culture, and, on the 30th, a review at the Thirteenth Regiment Armoury revealed the young soldiers doubtless in an exemplification of that very culture; it was a benefit for Harvey Dodworth, bandmaster. At this time, Robert Goldbeck was giving musical recitals at Groschel's Conservatory of Music, State Street.

We must retrace our weary steps to January 25th for three inducements: a sacred concert at the Church of the Incarnation, Ormond Place; a choir festival in St. Paul's Church, Clinton and Carroll Streets; and the dizzy delight of the Hanoverian Family — a saxophone band, a silver cornet band and a banjo band — along with the Shaffers. This combination was down for the week of January 25th–30th at Irving Music Hall, 182 Gates Avenue. Professor James L. Farley began, on February 5th, a series of Friday afternoon readings; but Professor R. L. Cumnock anticipated him in that sport by doing the same thing, on January 29th, at the Y.M.C.A. Hall. Perhaps it would have been only civically polite to attend the concert of the Chicago Schubert Quartet, on February 2nd, at the Y.M.C.A. Hall, even though such courtesy forced us to miss the scenes in costume given on the same date, at the Everett Assembly Rooms, by the Mexican Opera Company. On February 3rd, the Shelley-Cammeyer organ recital at Plymouth Church availed itself of further aid in the singing of Francis F. Powers. A children's carnival in costume, held the Brooklyn Rink, on the 6th (afternoon). Mme. Maguille (soprano), on February 9th, in Plymouth Church called in for help Leland T. Powers (elocutionist), Harry Rowe Shelley, Giuseppe Vitale (violin and mandolin), V. Fanelli (harp), and P. L. Villa (accompanist). February 11th presented, at the Washington Avenue Baptist Church, Scarecrows and Cherubs (a good title), with Isabel Rockwell (soprano), Eleanor

[176]

Hooper (violin), James S. Burdett (humourist), H. E. H. Benedict (organ), John Hyatt Brewer (conductor) and the Boylston Glee Club; this sounds rather pleasing.   Meantime, on the 10th, the twentieth chamber music soirée brought to Historical Hall. Henry Rusack (tenor), Mrs. Groschel Chadick (piano), Edward Herrmann (violin), Leonore Schenck (violin), Manuel Knauth (viola) and Emil Schenck ('cello).   None the more intelligent for considering those forgotten names, I revel, imaginatively, in the Brooklyn Charity Ball, held on the 11th, at the Palace Rink.   Professor William G. Sumner, of Yale, still cherished in memory by the now thinning ranks of Yale students of that far-off time, lectured at Art Association Hall, on the 12th, on Defensive Taxes; this severe diet was furnished to the Revenue Reform Club.

Waning February brought stimulating enjoyment.   At Unity Church, Classon Avenue, on the 15th, Edward Everett Hale read his story, In His Name; on the 16th, at Y.M.C.A. Hall, we had Methods of the Magicians, illustrated.   Gabriel Harrison, relic of an interesting past, gave with his pupils, at the Athenæum, a "reception," which I cannot describe.   Priscilla Whittingham, with her charming name, read, on the 18th, at Washington Street M.E. Church; on the same evening, at the Central Congregational Church, a remarkable concert promised Ella A. Earle (a delightful soprano, as I remember), Francis F. Powers (baritone), Charles Herbert Clarke (tenor), Charles Roberts, Jr., Harry Rowe Shelley, and the Dudley Buck Quartet.   The 18th was almost too busy for staid Brooklyn.   William Ordway Partridge, at a place I could not learn, read (heaven knows why!) Julius Cæsar.   The Princeton Glee Club was youthful and free, on the 20th, at the Long Island Historical Hall, and, at the Simpson M.E. Church, on the 22nd, Sauahbrah, a native Burmese, gave, in native costume, an Oriental Entertainment.   And still oriental was Yan Phon Lee, at Y.M.C.A. Hall, on the 23rd, with China, Its Manners and Customs.   Mme. Henry Greville, on February 25th and March 3rd, held audiences at the Y.M.C.A. Hall.

In that hall, on February 22nd, March 1st and 11th, John L. Wheeler gave The Civil War, Illustrated.   March 1st also enriched the schedule with Francis F. Powers, Grace D. Rider (elocutionist) and Miss Weidenback (soprano), at the First Reformed Church, Joralemon Street; but we waited for March 2nd to enjoy, at Avon Hall, Bedford Avenue and Halsey Street, J. S. Burdett, J. Walter Clark and the Avon Piano Quartette (sic).   On the 2nd, less inciting was a concert to Edith Tuttle, given, at Historical Hall, with aid from New York in the Urania Glee Club and the choir of St. Patrick's Cathedral.   The Camp Fire and the Trail brought to the Everett New Assembly Hall, Fulton Street and Gallatin Place, on March 8th, Captain Jack Crawford, "late chief of the Scouts," with Corporal Tanner to preside.

A busy March 9th left us distracted as between a testimonial to Rose Horwitz, at Sängerbund Hall, and Leland T. Powers's "rendering" of David

[177]

Copperfield, at St. Peter's Chapel, along with Miss R. A. Potter (contralto), the Misses Mackey (pianists), Henry S. Brown (bass), and H. E. Hutchinson (organist). If the evening was March at its most blustery, I believe I had just as soon have read David Copperfield before the fire in my library. Taylor, "the world's greatest illusionist," began, on March 15th, an engagement at Music Hall, an auditorium occupied, on the 12th, by Leon Florestan, who read bits of The Merchant of Venice, Hamlet and Phèdre — obviously a classical Florestan. The Arion Singing Society, on the 16th, held Turn Hall, Meserole Street. At Historical Hall, on the 17th, a concert involved Harriet W. Schrotter (sic), Belle Elliott, Ivan Morawski, Bignardi (tenor), Giuseppe Vitale (violin) and Fanelli (harp). The inescapable Jerome Hopkins, on the 22nd, presented, at Historical Hall, his Young Philharmonic and his oratorio of Samuel. Let us hope he enjoyed a paying audience — a devout wish for many of the offerings catalogued in this veracious chronicle. The 22nd also gave to the willing, at the Nostrand Avenue M.E. Church, the Dudley Buck Quartet, Antoinette Cooke, Susie L. Tooker (where had she been this season?), A. P. Burbank and John Hyatt Brewer — not so bad, and not so very good. It might have been fun, on March 20th, to hear the Amherst College Glee Club, at the Central Congregational Church (Hancock Street); and some doubtless enjoyed looking at Count and Countess Magri (the former Mrs. Tom Thumb) who began, with their company, on March 29th, at the Athenæum. All, I believe, would have been pleased to hear Donald G. Mitchell (Ik Marvel), on March 23rd, at Y.M.C.A. Hall, on Johnson and the Men of His Time. On March 31st the "Peak Sisters" went through their act, whatever it was, in Plymouth Bethel.

At Plymouth Church, a scheduled evening of A Midsummer-Night's Dream, to be read by George Riddle, with Walter Damrosch conducting Mendelssohn's music was, according to the Eagle, "withdrawn." Francis Fischer Powers's fifth annual concert, advertised in this too, too busy season, promised for the Memorial Presbyterian Church, Seventh Street and St. John's Place, Jean Herrick (soprano), Adah Foreman (contralto), Charles Herbert Clarke, Harry Rowe Shelley, and John H. Brewer, along with the Meigs Sisters and the Dudley Buck Quartet — a group to arouse pleasing anticipation. Let us on with April, trusting that its showered blessings may not submerge us. If fond of that sort of exhibition, we might have gone, on April 6th, to the Athletic Tournament of the Varuna Boat Club, proffering, at Music Hall, a contest between Jack Dempsey (middleweight champion of America) and John McAuliffe (champion lightweight), with Joe Deming of Williamsburgh exhibiting the finesse of muscle. If this did not interest us, perhaps we should have enjoyed, on that 6th, Frank Lincoln, on The Humorous Side of Life, at the Y.M.C.A. Hall, especially as the Ricca Venetian Mandolin Quartet was to aid in cheering us. Passing by the Crescent Athletic Club Exhibition, on April 5th, at the Music Hall, we

[178]

find Robert R. Raymond reading, on the 13th, at Packer Institute, and Count and Countess Magri still at the Athenæum.   On the 14th, at Plymouth Church, Viola Gilbert was to be Mary Queen of Scots, with scenery, sculpture, piano, tableaux, guitar and violin, something of an undertaking.   On a crowded 15th, the New York University Glee Club sang at the Throop Avenue Presbyterian Church, and, at the Marcy Avenue Baptist Church were Tillie T. Crane, the busy Dudley Buck Quartet, Vitale, Fanelli and Marshall P. Wilder—rather good, I suspect.   A Japanese Feast, on April 16th, illuminated and decorated Summerfield M.E. Church with, in that Mikado year, lanterns, umbrellas and fans.   Edward Everett Hale, on the 21st, read his My Double, at the Second Unitarian Church, Fred Steins singing. From the Courrier des États-Unis I learn that l'Union polonaise de Brooklyn gave, at Baumgärtner's Military Hall, on April 25th, a *"soirée musicale et dramatique."*   T. De Witt Talmage raised his voice on April 27th, in his own Tabernacle, on Making Things Go, additional attractions including Henry Eyre Browne ("first time in concert" playing the organ with kettledrum attachment), Laura Groves (contralto) and Maude Thorburn (mezzo). At the Palace Rink, from the 26th, Wilmot and Sewell, "from Barnum's Circus," rode bicycle and unicycle, without, so far as I can discover, lightening the sorrows of the world.   And what thinks my austere reader of Mlle. Hernamston's Female Megatherians and Burlesque Blondes, opening on April 27th and 28th, at the Music Hall? Let us get out of these continuous April showers of, generally, mediocre quality, by attending two glee club concerts: that of the Pastime Glee Club, with Harriet Schroter (April 29th) at Historical Hall; and that of the Columbia College Glee Club (April 30th) in the same hospitable auditorium.   Vocal also was our entrance into May, on the 3rd, with Arthur Lilley, English elocutionist, at Historical Hall.

At the Church Edifice, Pierrepont Street, Albert S. Caswell, on May 5th (or 6th, according to the Brooklyn Times), directed a concert of the Brooklyn Cecilian Society, with, as aids or soloists, Alice M. Judge (organ), H. E. H. Benedict (piano), Beulah Caswell (piano), Jay Nova (violin) and Harriet Schroter (soprano).   In the Hanson Place Baptist Church, on the same evening, were gathered Miss E. M. Crocker (soprano), Jennie Figgis, Misses E. Seymour and M. Spitzer (contraltos), Edward Descamps (tenor), S. H. Holland and E. Campbell (basses), R. P. Jarman (piano), W. Bloomfield Goate (*sic*—accompanist) all doubtless doing their best for music, while, in the same programme, Charles Roberts, Jr., did his bit for elocution. May 12th brought to the Y.M.C.A. Hall an illustrated lecture on Rome, brightened with singing by Emma Howson and the Schubert Glee Club. The Church on the Heights, Pierrepont Street, held a concert, on the 15th, with contributors quite unknown, except for U. C. Burnap; and reader, how well known is he, even to our diligent research?   Mme. Melville's "closing reception," on May 18th, at the Brooklyn Institute, may have caused a pang

[179]

to hearts just packing up for a summer at the shore or in the mountains. May 20th found the Orpheon Vocal Society at the Tompkins Avenue Congregational Church, intent on giving a testimonial to George C. Stebbins; George W. and Maud Morgan, Isabel Rockwell, William Courtney and Louis Schmidt (violin) constituted a pleasing group.   On the 28th, John F. Rhodes (violin) and the admirable Henrietta Beebe, with Miss Hoch and W. H. Lawton, attracted, I should hope, to Historical Hall.   Let us escape from May, on the 31st, with the benefit concert of Bianca Martini, who gathered to her aid, in Y.M.C.A. Hall, Carlo Snignaroli (*sic*), Francesco di Martini, Laura Phelps, Olivia Barberie (*sic*) and Charles E. Pratt.   The printers, like some radio announcers of 1941, obviously had difficulty with foreign names.

The Symphonia Society, on June 2nd, tried to justify its claims, at the Church of the Good Shepherd.   Strawberry festivals on lawns and in churches now informed visitors that Brooklyn was still a bit provincial. But June 9th broke out in varied miscellany: May Frances in readings at the College of Oratory, Meeker Street; a Strawberry Festival, music, etc., at Plymouth Church, with Carrie Hun-King, Catharine McNeill (contralto), Ollie Torbett (violin), Adolph Glose (piano), Ross David (tenor) and Helen Mar (sketches)— raspberries, I submit, rather than strawberries of musical lusciousness.   On this event I thankfully would leave Brooklyn Miscellany for 1885–86, except that I put here an announcement in the Eagle of June 9th that an Irish drama, Shoo-it-Ach (which sounds like a jest) was playing at the Athenæum, with C. B. Grant, J. J. Tighe and Emma Loraine, names that may reach to that part of the reader's mind where vague memories dwell.   Of course neighbouring beaches and Staten Island invited with spectacle and allurements I have cited at the close of New York Miscellany for 1885–86; Gilmore's Jubilee, beginning on August 12th, was for several days a Mecca for lovers of the loud music his band provided.   And Zipp's Elm Place Casino was nearer the inclination of tired stay-at-homes.   But, for the edification of my French readers I cite the Fête Nationale Française held at Washington Park, Broadway, near East New York, by the Union des Sociétés Françaises de Brooklyn, on July 24th, with a pique-nique, tombola, ball, etc., a continuation of a similar event, a short time earlier, in the same park.

PHILHARMONIC, BROOKLYN, 1885–1886

Musicians must have marvelled, in 1885–86, at the incredible activities of Theodore Thomas.   Not only did he conduct, in New York, six Philharmonic concerts, with their preliminary public rehearsals, forty-eight popular concerts, and carry on three months and more of strenuous labours with the American Opera Company, but also, in Brooklyn, in addition to many visits of that company, he conducted for the Brooklyn Philharmonic six concerts and rehearsals and eight popular concerts. The man was, apparently, indefatigable; it was believed that he was desperately striving to establish here a permanent orchestra—a dream he never realised.

The Philharmonic began its season with a rehearsal (November 20th) and concert (21st) at the Academy of Music. The programme consisted of Berlioz's overture, Benvenuto Cellini; Beethoven's Fourth Symphony; Spohr's violin concerto, No. 9, op. 55, with Maud Powell; the Introduction and Finale to Tristan und Isolde; and Liszt's symphonic poem, Festklänge. The orchestral Tuesday matinées began on December 3rd, working through to a finish, on April 6th. The Christmas regular concert (December 19th), proffered The Messiah, with, as soloists, Emmy Fursch-Madi, Charlotte Walker, Emily Winant, Eloi Sylva and Myron W. Whitney. The Eagle trenchantly remarks that Mme. Fursch-Madi's work proved that one may be very good in opera, but not so good in oratorio—a fact that many opera singers have failed to realise. In regular sequence, on January 15th and 16th, the Philharmonic played Beethoven's Leonore, No. 3; Dvorak's Symphony in D minor; Götterdämmerung excerpts (Morning Dawn, The Rhine Journey and Siegfried's Death); and, with Paul Tidden assisting, Schumann's Concerto in A minor.

The society proffered (February 26th and 27th) Schubert's Symphony, No. 8, in B minor; Beethoven's Concerto for piano, violin, 'cello and orchestra, with Richard Hoffman, Louis Schmidt and Adolph Hartdegen; and Berlioz's Symphonie Fantastique. Let us not forget that the Tuesday popular matinées continued. The Philharmonic programme for March 19th and 20th provided Dvorak's cantata, The Spectre's Bride, and Raff's Die Tageszeiten (for piano, chorus, piano and orchestra). Engaged in the proceedings were Helene Hastreiter, Wilhelm Ludwig, Whitney Mockridge and Franz Rummel—a generous supply of good soloists. The esteemed society ended its season (April 16th and 17th) with the Passacaglia of Bach (which Stokowski's Philadelphians of these, our years, have played so gloriously); Schumann's Symphony in B-flat; the King Lear overture of Berlioz; Liszt's Mephisto Waltz; and Lilli Lehmann in the big scene-arias from Armide and Fidelio.

NOVELTY THEATRE, WILLIAMSBURGH, 1885–1886

If Brooklyn partook of second helpings from the Manhattan stage, Williamsburgh either waited for dramatic delicacies till they had been tested by Brooklyn or, at rare instances, tried the confection before the western section of the city had ventured to test it. Let us enter the Novelty Theatre, in Williamsburgh for proof or disproof of this thesis. The house opened, on August 31, 1885, with The World, as seen later in Brooklyn, with a cast

[181]

including Hamilton Harris, Frank Harrington, W. T. Melville, W. J. Leonard, John Sutherland, M. J. Jordan, Amelia Watts and Laura Alberta. The next week (September 7th–12th) provided The Hoop of Gold, followed (14th–19th) by Burr Oaks, fresh from its Brooklyn try-out of the week before. A more novel offering was that of September 21st–26th, German Luck, acted by the former stars of vaudeville, Charles T. Ellis and Clara Moore. W. J. Scanlan, another recruit from "Variety," enlivened the week of September 28th–October 3rd, with his recent success, Shane-na-Lawn. James O'Neill's permanent offering of Monte Cristo started October (5th–10th) safely on its course. His support included J. W. Shannon, Elizabeth Robins and Annie Boudinot. And Lester Wallack in his permanency, Rosedale, continued the good work (October 12th–17th), his associates including Kate Bartlett (as always, for Rosa Leigh), Annie Robe (as Lady May), William Elton, George F. De Vere, Harry Edwards (as Myles McKenna), Louisa Eldridge, Mrs. Selden Irwin (as Lady Adela), Mrs. Fred Williams — good players all.

For a Brother's Life, a specialty by C. T. Dazey, from the Third Avenue Theatre, tried Williamsburgh for the week of October 19th–24th, with Newton Gotthold, S. S. Block, L. Hanley, Madge Butler, J. J. Lessenger and Florence Elmore. It was succeeded, next week, by John T. Raymond, in For Congress (26th, 27th, 28th), and In Paradise (29th, 30th, 31st), with Bessie Hunter, Leonora Bradley, J. B. Eversham, Frank Lane, Lew Baker. Roland Reed, with Madge Carr and Augustus Cook, in Humbug, carried on the funmaking (November 2nd–7th) yielding the stage (9th–14th) to the graver humours of A Moral Crime, with Marie Prescott and Joseph Haworth. Appropriately enough, as to title, Her Atonement followed (16th–21st), Eleanor Moretti and Charles Mason driving home the hard lesson. A different military company appeared each night. M. B. Curtis and Albina De Mer then lightened the scheme with Sam'l of Posen (November 23rd–26th) and Spot Cash (27th–28th). Fantasma, with the Hanlons, began the winter (November 20th–December 5th), with Fanny Davenport and Mantell to continue (December 7th–12th) in their chronic Fedora. Joseph Murphy, in his equally inevitable Kerry Gow, got into the heart of winter (December 14th–19th), the chilly journey advancing (December 21st–26th) quite appropriately as to the skies, but inappropriately as to the Christmas season, with Dark Days (acted by Emily Sheridan, Felix Pitt, E. Grace, F. Terry and Walter Spekeman). Then, out of this gloomy feast, brightly for the holiday spirit came (December 28th–January 2nd) Tony Denier's Humpty Dumpty. And the Duff Opera Company, from the Standard Theatre, New York, treated Williamsburgh (January 4th–9th) to the all-conquering Mikado.

Thus, with the aid of a mere catalogue, I have carried my patient reader to the week of January 11th–16th, when, if he agrees with me, he will prob-

[182]

ably decline to partake of the offering of Murray and Murphy, in Our Irish Visitors; but, if he wants an evening of merriment without psycho-analysis, he will not miss A Bunch of Keys, with Marietta Nash and Eugene Canfield, the attraction for January 18th–23rd. And all must rejoice to welcome (25th–30th) the quaint (there is no other word for him) Sol Smith Russell, in Felix McCusick, a poor play, I fear, though Miriam O'Leary, Frank Lawton and H. L. Meery (*sic*) tried to make it "go." February 1st–6th brought the W. H. Powers Company, in The Ivy Leaf, an Irish play, with evidently an Irish cast, including J. P. Sullivan, W. J. O'Donoghue, Dan McCarthy, T. F. O'Malley, May Wolcott (recently with Joseph Jefferson) and Mabel O'Malley. The stirring scenes were Eagle's Crag, the Lakes of Killarney, and the revolving Ivy Tower.

The February round of pleasure continued (8th–13th) with In the Ranks; (15th–20th), J. H. Wallick, in The Bandit King; and (22nd–27th) Katherine Rogers, in Leah, the Forsaken. Miss Rogers, like Rose Eytinge, was passing into the ranks of the less desirable stars; age had withered their attractiveness. But Kate Castleton, in Crazy Patch, tried to prove (March 1st–6th) that she was young enough to please the fickle crowd. And surely Georgia Cayvan's May Blossom (8th–13th) was dewy-fresh as the connotation of the title of the play. A Rag Baby also (15th–20th) was new enough and lively enough for even the most juvenile auditor. I leave the reader to decide concerning Lizzie May Ulmer, in Dad's Girl, the offering of March 22nd–27th. McCaull's Opera Company, with Digby and Laura Joyce Bell, gave to the joyful Novelty (March 29th–April 3rd) its second Mikado of the season. And Dan Sully, in The Corner Grocery, made the Novelty, on April 5th, closely akin to Tony Pastor's, in Manhattan. Louise Balfe, in Dagmar, leaves me indifferent for the week of April 12th–17th, though Frank Losee, Matt and Rose Snyder, Mollie Revere and Spencer Harrison supported her. Tony Hart brought (19th–24th) A Toy Pistol to his numerous admirers. And Effie Ellsler, in Woman against Woman, ended the month (26th–May 1st) with a touch of necessary seriousness.

Let us traverse earlier May at the Novelty with McIntyre and Heath's Minstrels (3rd–8th); The Long Strike (10th–15th), with J. C. Padgett and Rose Osborne; and leave the theatre for the summer with a performance of the long-suffering Hazel Kirke, acted on Monday, May 17th, by the veriest amateurs, the Leonardis Society of St. Francis Academy.

LEE AVENUE ACADEMY OF MUSIC, WILLIAMSBURGH, 1885–1886

This theatre, facing a busy season, was opened for public inspection, on Saturday evening, August 29, 1885, and started the term, on the 31st, with the Carrolls, in Whose Can It Be?—In Three Guesses, certainly an unpretentious inaugural, with Lillian Servis, Marie Mulock, Edwin Warren and

Harry Horn. And Charles L. Davis, in Alvin Joslin, appeals with no greater force (September 7th–12th) to the historical fancy. Estelle Clayton, in Favette, rather improved the prospects for September 14th–19th, and The Breadwinner became a necessity for September 21st–26th. It was by Charles Overton, from Dennery and Cormon; the cast included R. E. Graham and Loduski Young. The first impressive offering of the Novelty came on September 28th, when Cora Tanner started a week of her breadwinner, Alone in London.

I can easily lead the reader through the joys of October: Clio, with Adele Belgarde and Adele Cornalba (5th–10th); The Romany Rye, as in Brooklyn (12th–17th); Rose Coghlan (first star of importance) in Our Joan (19th–24th), with Frazer Coulter, Georgine Flagg and C. A. McManus; and Kate Claxton (the second interesting star) in Called Back (26th–31st). In this Kate Claxton was Pauline, Maida Craigin Mary, C. A. Stevenson was Gilbert Vaughan, Ralph Delmore Macari, Clay M. Greene Arthur Kenyon, and Burr McIntosh Anthony Marsh—an interesting cast. The reader chooses from this list his own incitements for visits to the Lee Avenue; he will, perhaps, have seen all of them, recently, in Brooklyn. Much of the same principle holds good in November: Oliver and Kate Byron, in The Inside Track (2nd–7th); Shadows of a Great City (9th–14th) with Annie Ward Tiffany, G. R. Edeson, Edna Carey, Nelson Wheatcroft; Evans and Hoey, in A Parlour Match (16th–21st); and Aimée (interesting survival from *opéra-bouffe*) in Mam'zelle, all the next week, except Friday, the 27th, when Divorçons made an evening wholly French in spirit. Prospects were, we observe, improving at the Lee Avenue Academy. Mme. Janish, in Anselma, filled the week of November 30th–December 5th; Frank Mayo, in Nordeck, that of December 7th–12th; the Templeton Opera Company, with Harris, Jay Taylor, W. H. Seymour, George Broderick, Emma Mabella Baker and Lucille Meredith, in The Mikado (that of the 14th–19th); Daly's A Night Off, with Mrs. Maeder, Hotto, and a Brooklyn girl, Virginia Brooks, the week of the 21st–26th; and Siberia, with Emma Vaders and George R. Parks (not George Parkes of Daly's) ending one year and beginning another (December 28th–January 2nd). My pen rather enjoys this method of cataloguing, rendered possible by the reader's knowledge of most of the productions involved, a knowledge acquired in his careful study of Brooklyn theatres in times wholly contiguous.

Our faculties sharpened by such careful study, we may cheerfully enter January, 1886, at the Lee Avenue, with Mestayer and Theresa Vaughn, in We, Us and Co. (4th–9th); Thatcher, Primrose and West's Minstrels (11th–16th); and the Thalia Theater company in a week (18th–23rd) devoted, successively, to Nanon, The Black Hussar, Czar und Zimmermann, and The Beggar Student. Just as we had imagined that the house was intending to brighten all the dark days of winter with such merry entertainment, it dashed our hopes (January 25th-30th) with The Wages of Sin; but it revived them (February 1st-6th) with Mr. and Mrs. Knight in Over the Garden Wall.

Serious also was the offering of February 8th-13th — the veteran Couldock, in the veteran relic, The Willow Copse, and serious, not to say momentous, was the visit of the much-heralded Margaret Mather, in Romeo and Juliet (February 15th), with The Honeymoon, Leah, The Lady of Lyons and Macbeth, following in a busy week. Then what, my masters? Gus Williams, in Oh! What a Night, and oh! what a merry ending (February 22nd-27th) for the never merry month of February. A Sunday concert actually sent that bitter month hurtling into March; the Seventh Regiment Band, the Spanish Students, Michael Banner, Clara Spence (elocutionist), William Sherwood ("king of pianists") and Misses Schneelock ("wonderful soprani") made Williamsburgh gasp at the *richesse* provided.

May Newman and James J. Tighe, in The White Slave, held the week of March 1st-6th; and more fun bubbled in the following nights (8th-13th) with the Salsbury Troubadours in Three of a Kind, except on March 12th, when they gave Tom, Dick and Harry. Nat Goodwin's The Skating Rink continued the merry round (15th-20th), yielding the stage (March 22nd-27th) to A Prisoner for Life, with J. B. Studley, E. L. Tilton, C. L. Farwell, T. H. Glenney, John Swinbourne, W. S. Quigley (our old "utility" at the Union Square), Inez Rochelle, Sara Neville, Henrietta Irving and Martha Wren, a remarkably good "combination" troupe, certainly so far as the men were concerned. On March 28th, the Cowboy Pianist showed Williamsburgh how well (or ill) one could play without instruction; but Blind Tom or Cowboy what mattered it, so long as the public would pay and wonder?

The second week of the Templeton Mikado was proudly flaunted in the advertisements for April 5th-10th; but the next week (12th-17th) again became entirely "legitimate" and serious, with F. B. Warde in, successively, Virginius (to this old "classic" he had become devoted), Richelieu, Damon and Pythias (also devoted to this), Ingomar and Richard III. And how may we bid Time roll backward in his flight, to enjoy (April 19th-24th) the venerable Uncle Tom's Cabin? Doubtless, nice old ladies, who had enjoyed Eliza and Uncle Tom and Little Eva, far back in 1853, escorted their grandchildren now to watch their reactions to the venerated relic. With this comforting assurance we may pass (April 26th-May 1st) to Edmund Collier in Storm Beaten, and renew our acquaintance (May 3rd-8th) with another antiquity, Kit, the Arkansas Traveller, now put before us by the son of the original Kit. And here (May 10th-15th) is something more of a venerable flavour — Arrah-na-Pogue, with, if one may believe it, the handsome Irishman, Charles A. Stevenson, as Shaun the Post, the last part in which one could ever have expected to see him. Perhaps Stevenson was becoming weary of some of the plays in which his wife, Kate Claxton, had so often appeared with him. Engaged, frequently emergent, in 1886, entered the Lee Avenue Academy (May 17th–22nd) under the ministrations of Cedric Hope and Agnes Herndon. Louise Litta and Ralph Delmore, in Chispa (May 24th–29th) send me coldly into summer.

Rose Levere came to the Lee Avenue (May 31st–June 5th) in Leah (which, alas! Margaret Mather had sent cursing through the season). The supporting cast was worthy of Broadway — Alexander Salvini, F. A. Tannehill, L. F. Rand, Elmer Grandin, Hudson Liston, Harry Pratt, Gussie De Forrest, Nina Freith, Laura Johnson and Mrs. Gilroy. This dismisses us from that theatre until the season of 1886–87 calls us once more to gird ourselves for whatever fate may bring. But who can leave these houses though girt and hatted? Certainly not we, who wait for the benefit, on June 12th, to J. H. Berger, manager, for which we had promised appearances of C. A. Stevenson, Rose Levere, Lillian Lewis, Fred Warde, Fred Bryton and Lucille Meredith. And Caleb L. Woglum, business manager, gathered his friends for his benefit, on June 17th. Reader, let us hurry away, lest some other ambitious souls summon our unwilling feet to other benefits.

PEOPLE'S THEATRE, EASTERN DISTRICT, 1885–1886

The People's Theatre, Montrose Avenue and Leonard Street, may be traced for this season in the columns of the Brooklyn Times. It was a very humble servant of the muses.

We were informed, in late August, that the house would open, on September 2, 1885, "thoroughly redecorated and improved," with Louis A. Phillips as manager. The first attraction I find for it was Michael Strogoff, played for the week of September 21st–26th, by Charles L. Andrews's Company, including Francoeur, Wilkins and Cecile Rush (as Marfa); that was, in fact, set down as the "opening." For September 28th–October 3rd, Minnie Oscar Gray and W. T. Stephens, with their dogs, presented a play with a touching title — Without a Home. Then the People's fell (October 5th–10th) to the lure of the devastating Rentz-Santley Company, with Mat Flynn, Marie Sherman, Billy Buckley, Mlle. Zitella, Georgie Blake and many others, in The High-Card-Oh, or, Joys of Japan. The house followed the suggestion of female burlesquers for October 12th–17th, Sallie St. Clair's Lady Artists and Goldie and Steele's World of Novelties providing, as headliners, Gus Hill, Karoly Ordey, Nellie Hague and Joe Mealey.

Hallen and Hart's First Prize Ideals figured in the next week (19th–24th), with E. B. Fitz and Katherine Webster, McAvoy and George Hallen (blackface), Fred Hallen and Enid Hart, Mlle. Dorina and Rigoli, and My-Card-Oh! For October 26th–31st Applegate and Randolph's Specialty Company stressed the Silbon Family and the Elliott Family (bicyclists). The Stranglers of Paris (November 2nd–7th) presented Newton Beers as Jagon.

[186]

For November 9th–14th, Edwin Arden scaled the familiar excitements of Eagle's Nest. Then the house reverted (16th–21st) to its best-liked "Variety," with the Howard Athenæum Company, strong in Sam Devere, Pavillio and Roussillion, James F. Hoey, Miss Lee Errol and Al W. Filson and Lina and Vani. For November 23rd–28th, Dominick Murray offered his thrice-familiar Escaped from Sing Sing. Again "Variety" possessed the stage (November 30th–December 5th) with T. H. Winnett's European Sensation, including Six English Acrobats, "Professor" Gleason's dogs, Morosco and Gardner, Mlle. Lottie ("Mexico's meteoric star"), the Rice Brothers ("horizontal kings"), "Senator" Frank Woodson, Lillie Bailey, and Dick Morosco's comedy, Fitts!

We can easily traverse the wilds of December: the Gibson-Ryan Company, in Irish Aristocracy (7th–12th); Helene Adell's New York Park Theatre Company (herself, Sara Lascelles, Edith Bird, O. W. Eagle, John T. Walsh and Edgar Waterman) in Moths (14th, 15th); The Two Orphans (16th, 17th); A Night in Rome (18th–19th); The Great Australian Novelty Company (21st–26th), with Billy Carter, Andy and Annie Hughes, the Austin Sisters, Topack and Horner (sic); the Luciers, Annie Hart, and Rinklets (sic); and Chrisdie and Zeltner's Pantomime and Specialty Company (December 28th–January 2nd), featuring Mlle. Nelson (sleight of hand), Gallagher and Ryan, and Leopold and Wentworth. J. J. Dowling and Sadie Hasson filled the week of January 4th–9th, with Nobody's Claim, and Silbon's Cupid Comedy Company that of the 11th–16th, its specialists including Four Silbons, Kate Victoria, Ten Mahdi Arabs, W. J. Rollins, the Wesley Brothers, Madge Aiston and Don Ferreyra. Harley Merry's play, Argonauts of '49, presented (January 18th–23rd) E. J. Brittain, Frank D. Allen, D. J. Sullivan, C. M. Roblee, J. F. Ryan, Charles Ray, Josephine Merry, Adelaide Roselle and Elsie White. Reilly and Wood's Comedy Company bowed out January (25th–30th).

The first week of February (1st–6th) provided Pelletreau's Specialty Company, for the benefit of the widows of G. Metternich Post No. 22, G.A.R. The following week (8th–13th) was interesting, with George C. Boniface as Badger, in The Streets of New York. February 15th began a lively week of Hallen and Hart's First Prize Ideals, proffering Fred Hallen and Enid Hart, Fox and Van Auken, Frank Bush, Joe Hart, Jeannette Dorina, Polly McDonald, E. B. Fitz and Katherine Webster, James McAvoy and George Hallen, and John and James Russell (in The Two Off'uns). The Howard Athenæum Star Specialty Company filled the last week of February. Louis A. Phillips's Star Company, for March 1st–6th supplied Al W. Filson and Lee Errol (in An Off Night), the athletic Phanlons (Lewis, Robert and Wash), Fanny and Frank Forrester and Foster and Hughes, Kitty Drew and "Professor" J. W. Hampton. The People's, carrying on in "Variety," presented, for March 8th–13th the Kernells and their company.

[187]

The next week, however, reverted to drama, with King Hedley's Company, in After Dark. March 22nd–27th brought Henry Watson and Alfred McDowell's "absurdity," Wrinkles. The Romany Rye bloomed in the week of March 31st–April 3rd, yielding the stage, for April 5th–10th, to A Mountain Pink, a flower of the suburbs, with Laura E. Dainty. Frank Evans, once prominent in The Galley Slave, filled the week of April 12th–17th, as Corporal Antoine, in The Soldier's Trust. After those weeks of drama, the management, for April 19th–24th, changed to Leroux and Silvo's World's Minstrels. And Tony Pastor, then on his summer travels, came (April 26th–May 1st) to the People's, with a fine group, including himself, the Dare Brothers, the Tissots, Byrnes and Mlle. Helene, Harry Morris, Callan, Haley and Callan (the Electric Three), Leopold and Bunell (*sic*), and Hines and Earle Remington. This was a combination worthy of the best theatres.

May 3rd–8th was devoted to S. Draper's Double Uncle Tom's Cabin Company; the following week exploited Blanche Curtisse, "the famous Vassar beauty," in Only a Farmer's Daughter—that near-classic of the cheaper theatres. The last night of the season, May 17th, offered The Two Orphans, as a testimonial to Bertha Grosse and Ludwig Steingade. I am not sure that this record of the People's is worth the trouble and expense involved in preparing it. But I add the contribution of early June—J. J. Dowling and Sadie Hasson, in Nobody's Claim.

PELLETREAU'S GRAND MUSEUM, 1885–1886

Pelletreau, Bruce and Company's Grand Museum, 166 Grand Street, between Fourth and Fifth Streets, Williamsburgh, opened on Saturday afternoon, September 12th, with Lottie Church, in her favourite, Unknown. The establishment boasted also of a museum, menagerie and aquarium. Entrance for the opening was "free to all." Of course Unknown was made known for the week of September 14th–19th. On the 21st, N. S. Wood began a melodramatic week, in The Boy Scout.

Pelletreau and Bruce's Refined Specialty Company and The Surprise Party, or, Muldoon's Trip to Brooklyn, I cannot find it in my heart to regret having missed (October 5th–10th), nor, indeed, can I avoid feeling the same lack of sympathy (12th–17th) for the Boston Novelty Company. On the 19th, the Leonzo Brothers, with their dogs, Tiger and Lion, began in The Planter's Child; Muldoon's Second Trip, or, the Working Girl, may, on October 26th, have been a "song of social significance," with T. F. Thomas, James Marlow, and Ada Clifton. Then ho! for November 2nd–7th, when George France gave his popular A Block Game; for the 9th–14th, Frank I. Frayne proffered Si Slocum. Surely these are acquaintances from many theatres along our route. Sheehan and Coyne, May Arnott, Jessie Boyd and Earle (equilibrist) were among the "Variety" list for November 16th–21st. I confess utter ignorance of the worth of the wares of the Lang Comedy Company, in Edward R. Lang's play, Scheming—the lure for November 23rd–28th. In the cast figured the author, with B. F. Grinnell, James Mulligan and May Smith. The following week was Ethel Tucker's, and she bravely cut it into two equal parts, with Queena and The Two Orphans sharing the spoils of patronage; Leslie Miller, B. McDonough, S. J. Wheeler and Mrs. E. Wilde assisted.

The next week (December 7th–12th), must have been exciting for customers who might not have cared for Shakespeare. Mamie Wallace and Alf A. Wallace, long in "stock" in the Bowery, now brought to the Grand Museum three days of The Crimes of a Great City, and three of Jesse James, with the "original" James horses—Jack and Hero. Little boys would have revelled in this latter show. Wellesley and Sterling's Company, in The Danites, also glorified the untutored West, for the week of December 14th. Burr Oaks (December 16th–21st) did as it might, with a cast including Percy Meldon, Milton Higgins, David Higgins, Josie Crocker, Lillie Loomis and Louise Galloway. I rather think that I have heard, somewhere, of two of these performers. But even my most careless reader has heard often of the attraction of the next week (December 28th–January 2nd)—Sid C. France, in Marked for Life; also of that of January 4th–9th—Bartley Campbell's Galley Slave.

A Hoop of Gold bound together the nights of February 1st–6th, yielding the stage (February 8th–13th) to Arizona Joe, the Shooting Star, in The Black Hawks. Three dogs and three mustang ponies added a touch of verisimilitude to that bald and exciting melodrama. This perversion of Pooh-Bah's classic phrase lands us into a presentation of The Mikado (February 15th–20th), executed by the National Opera Company. Any Mikado in that first season of its American triumph! The Colleen Bawn was saved (February 22nd–27th) from the watery grave prepared by villainy. And The Pavements of Paris were digested (March 1st–6th) by devourers of melodramatic thrills. The next week gave us "the young American actress," Ethel Tucker, in evenings, successively, of Queena, East Lynne and The Pearl of Savoy. This sounds like something too provincial even for Williamsburgh. For March 22nd–27th John Jennings brought three performances each of Our Boys and The Long Strike.

March 29th–April 3rd gave those who accepted the gift Brower's Thespian Family and two evenings each of The Chimes of Normandy, The Mascot and Olivette. For April 5th–10th, we had John W. Ransone in his unvarying Across the Atlantic. April 12th–17th brought the Original Coloured Georgia Minstrels, and the 19th–24th promised Kate Claxton's Called Back, with the "Union Square Theatre Company." I wonder if this could have been the Called Back, sponsored by Miss Claxton, which I saw at that far-off time in Newburgh, with Sara Jewett in the leading rôle? For April 26th–May 1st, what was listed as the Union Square Company gave Only a Woman's Heart. Dan A. Kelly and Joan Craven, in The Shadow Detective, filled the week of the 3rd. A. C. Gunter's play of Vendetta was at Pelletreau's during the week of May 10th–15th, and another divided week gave us (17th–22nd) Joseph Keane in, successively, Rip Van Winkle and Mrs. Partington. The week of May 24th–29th allowed Louise Arnott to present four plays in succession — East Lynne, The Two Orphans, Leah, the Forsaken, and The Little Detective. Throughout the country, at that time, little towns in their "opera houses," were offered exactly that kind of dramatic nourishment. A benefit to Robert Bruce, on June 7th, gave us Micaliz. The week previously (May 31st–June 5th) had thrilled customers with the vengeful progress of Monte Cristo. A supplementary season is indicated by the appearance here, in early July, of Henry Belmer's Jesse James Company, the play "founded on facts given by the reformed outlaw, Frank James." For July 14th–19th, Western Justice, by Geoffrey Woodruff, had a cast headed by James K. Keane.

PHILLIPS'S SUMMER PAVILION, 1886

Phillips, closing, at least temporarily, his People's Theatre, at Montrose Avenue and Leonard Street, moved his hopes to Phillips's Summer Pavilion, at Montrose and Union Avenues — surely not far from his sister camp. There, with tent to flap in summer breezes, he began, on May 24th–29th, with the Martinetti Brothers' Pantomime and Specialty Company, Albert Martinetti reviving the venerable Jocko, the Brazilian Ape. The Four Shamrocks Specialty Company (June 7th–12th) stressed Dave Conroy, John Daly, Dan Lacy and Mike Thompson, Irish as the shamrock they personified. We conserved our geography, in the week of June 14th–19th, when O'Brien Brothers' Specialty Company turned green the landscape, but we switched our *locale* June 21st–26th, with the Pleasure Party, "supporting the greatest German dialect artist living" — George Murphy, whom we shall always remember as of the team, Murphy and Shannon. May Adams's Comedy Company and Japanese Fête were cool in array for the torrid week of June 28th–July 3rd. And 10 cents and 20 cents allowed the public to enter and behold.

Hume and Wesley's Big Specialty Company began, on July 5th, another week of unadulterated "Variety," and Miaco's Humpty Dumpty and Specialty Company began another, on the 12th. Fannie Beane and Charles Gilday, in whom I am always interested, filled the week of July 19th–24th, in Collars and Cuffs. T. H. Winnett's European Sensation ended July (26th–31st). W. A. Davene's Le Petit Zoa (*sic*) started August on its humid way (2nd–7th), and Lester and Williams's Parlour Match Company, with the "original Innocent Kidd," followed in due course for a week (August 9th–14th). Subsequently came (August 16th–21st) The Tourists in a Pullman Palace Car; the Acme Novelty Company and the Gem Pantomime Company dividing the week of the 23rd–28th. The American Specialty Company followed (August 30th–September 4th), Louis M. Frey profiting from a benefit tendered by Louis A. Phillips. The People's Theatre was again in operation and Phillips closed the Pavilion, betaking himself to winter quarters snugly roofed.

WILLIAMSBURGH MISCELLANY, 1885–1886

My reader knows, as well as residents of the suburb, exactly the kind of entertainments provided, in those seasons, for Williamsburgh outside the theatre precinct.

Merely noting the Plattdeutsches Volksfest, of August 30th and 31st, and September 1st and 2nd, at George Grenauer's Ridgewood Park, and the re-opening, on September 1st, of the Palace Rink, Clermont Avenue, with "new floor and decorations, and electric lights," we arrive at the ninth Annual Schwaben Volksfest (September 20th to 23rd) also at Ridgewood Park. More in our field was the humourist, Von Boyle, at the First Presbyterian Church, South Fourth and Sixth Streets, on September 29th. Similar semi-interest attaches to the concert and reception, on November 9th, of the Amphion Society, in its rooms, Clymer and Division Streets, with Ivan Morawski, J. Lambert, the Courtney Ladies' Quartet, and S. Rose ('cello). At the New England Church William Courtney, with the Courtney Ladies' Quartet, announced concerts on November 18th and 25th and December 9th; this awakens my first excitement for the autumn in Williamsburgh miscellany. I pass by a concert of fourteen men and twenty-six boys directed, on November 26th, by E. H. Ducharme, in the Sunday School Building of the Old Bushwick Church, and also, on the same date, the Hannibal A. Williams entertainment in the Ross Street Presbyterian Church. But I have been so starved for music that I am induced to journey, on December 1st, to the South Bushwick Reformed Church, to hear the Brooklyn Glee Club, led by E. J. Fitzhugh, with assistance from the excellent Clementine Lasar Studwell, Blanche Fitzhugh (piano) and Louis J. Cornu (violin). And, on the 2nd, other treasured friends appeared at the First Presbyterian Church, South Sixth Street — Priscilla Whittingham, Hector Toulmin (violin) and David Drewry (tenor). That same beneficent 2nd brought J. S. Burdett to the Central Baptist Church, South Fifth and Eighth Streets. And the fair for some time operative in the new Armoury of the 47th Regiment closed, on the 2nd, having made, according to the Greenpoint Globe, a profit of $6,000 — much money, in those innocent days.

The Star Course of Lectures, at the Lee Avenue Congregational Church, was a five-fold allurement: Kate Field, An Evening with Dickens (December 7th); Colonel L. F. Copeland, Snobs and Snobbery (December 14th); A. P. Burbank, with Jefferson's Rip Van Winkle (21st); J. S. Burdett and Robertson, with his tumbleronicon (28th); and Frank Lincoln, The Humorous Side of Life (January 11th). Dwight L. Moody and Ira D. Sankey, those precursors of the Salvation Army in the effort to redeem errant man, were at the Y.M.C.A. Rooms from December 8th to 13th. On the 10th, one could have heard, at the Lee Avenue Church, Will Carleton's reading from his own poems, or, at the Ross Street Presbyterian Church, the Fisk University Jubilee Singers. Williamsburgh should have crowded the Bedford Avenue Reformed Church, on December 16th, to welcome Emma Thursby, once identified with that church, though now (1885) not quite in the prime of her powers. With her were Dora Becker (violin), A. L. King (tenor), Robert Goldbeck (piano) and Charles E. Pratt (accompanist). I prefer this to an Amphion concert (December 14th) or to the Columbia Germania Chor, at Turn Hall, Meserole Street (December 20th). On December 28th occurred, according to the Brooklyn Times, a performance by the St. Vincent de Paul Literary and Dramatic Association of two farces, A Public Benefactor and New Brooms Sweep Clean, acted by Arthur S. Somers, J. Delaney, P. F. Craddock, Mary and Angela White and Nina Drummond. Knickerbocker Hall housed the show.

On January 8th, the Lee Avenue Congregational Church became secular with readings by Nella F. Brown and saxophone performances by F. E. Lefebre (all Lefebres took to that belching implement of torture). At about this same time All Souls Church, South Ninth Street near Fourth, allowed the Reverend Dr. Maynard to give an illustrated and historical lecture on Switzerland, all for the benefit of the Industrial School Association. But let us not forget the Zoellner Masquerade, on January 8th, at Turn Hall, Meserole Street; we need not attend, merely because we remember. In the parlours of the Amphion Society, on February 2nd, C. Mortimer Wiske directed a concert of the Cæcilia Ladies' Vocal Society, with Mrs. Peter Bell, Miss Costello, J. H. Haaren and Walter (*sic*) Gunn serving as soloists. And the Brooklyn Times announced that Wiske would give a series of Sunday night concerts in the Old Armoury, Bedford Avenue and North Second Street. The first of these would fall, on Saturday, February 6th, with J. H. Haaren, Walter (*sic*) Gunn, Mrs. A. K. Decevee and Mrs. Carpenter. The second, on the 14th, presented Maggie Mitchell, Fred Harvey, Max Bendheim (baritone), Madden (violin) and Ella Joslyn. A masquerade ball of Daniel Webster Council, No. 516, A.L. of H. was danced, in Winter's Teutonia Hall, to the strains of Bauer's 32nd Regiment Band. I greatly prefer the offering of February 16th, at the Lee Avenue Congregational Church, where were promised Settie Blume and Nella F. Brown (those valiant elocutionists), Dora Becker (violinist), the New York Madrigal Quartet (Emma

Henry Thomas, Clara Stutsman, William Thomas and George Sturges), Harry E. Arnold (pianist) and J. M. Loretz, Jr. (organist). This same hospitable church became, on February 25th, a sanctuary for the Grand Council, Royal Arcanum, with an offering of Jennie D. Grant (soprano), John Hill (baritone), Charles Roberts, Jr., John M. Turner, and the Hatton Glee Club, except for Roberts, hardly worth the journey to the church. The Brooklyn Rink celebrated Washington's Birthday by matching Nate Clark of Brooklyn against E. L. Maddocks of Boston.

Another concert of C. Mortimer Wiske occurred in later February, in Grand Army Hall, late 47th Regiment Armoury, co-adjutors including Edna Day (soprano), Marie Le Clair (contralto), F. R. Treasure (baritone), C. W. Madden (violin) and A. M. Fuentes (flute—and somehow a singularly appropriate name, in sound, for a blower into a flute). On February 22nd, this same hall housed bicycle, athletic games, and drills. February 22nd provided numerous incitements to leave home: Professor J. W. Moore lectured at Grace English Lutheran Church, on From Sumter to Appomattox; the Reverend Henry A. Powell lectured at the Lee Avenue Congregational Church; and, at the South Second Street M.E. Church, an entertainment of the Young People's Association netted the tumbleronicon of D. W. Robertson, the zither of H. J. Schmalix, the humour of J. S. Burdett, and the talent (whatever it was) of Hortense Pierse. February 23rd brought to the Ross Street Presbyterian Church C. Mortimer Wiske, with a double quartet including two Wiskes and F. R. Treasure; a choir of sixty voices; A. M. Fuentes (flute), F. Koch (viola), Carl Heim and C. Madden (violins), and George D. Holston (viola).

St. John's M.E. Church, on March 1st, opened its doors and its shrine to George Riddle, "prince of elocutionists," who read Come Here, that war-horse of Janauschek; the choir of the church also sang. The Brooklyn Times lists for March 1st, a performance by the young men of St. Thomas Dramatic Union of Kathleen Mavourneen, with F. N. Gomez, J. Tweed, J. J. Breen, J. F. Connellan, J. J. Sullivan, Miss C. McDowell, Clara Edgar and many more. The place of execution escaped me. In those days the Germans possessed Turn Hall for the expected masquerades, the Williamsburgh Sängerbund, and the Arion holding forth on different evenings. The Brooklyn Rink, on March 3rd, pitted the art "skatorial" of Charles Walton against that of Nate Clark; on the 6th, it held a Valiquet Reception, whatever that was. The Cæcilia Ladies Vocal Society held, on the 9th, the Lee Avenue Congregational Church. March 12th brought Chaplain McCabe to the Central M.E. Church, South Fifth Street, near Driggs, there to deliver his well-worn lecture, The Bright Side of Life in Libby Prison. The Young People's Association of the busy Lee Avenue Congregational Church provided, for March 22nd, Priscilla Whittingham, Mlle. Floretta (soprano), W. H. Bartels (tenor) and the Hungarian Gypsy Band. Captain Jack Crawford, on a contiguous evening, gave, for the Camp Fire and the Trail, his The Veteran and His Grandson. A chapel in Wilson Street, between Bedford and Lee Avenues held, during the week of March 29th–April 3rd, a Bazaar of Nations. And, on March 30th, at the New England Congregational Church, Major W. P. Halsted gave his Personal Recollections of the War. On April 4th, at Baumgärtner's Military Hall, came a concert by the Arion Quartet Club.

The Old Bushwick Church comes, on April 7th, into the chronicle with a Grand Potpourri Concert; it was repeated, by request, on the 12th. The United Singers (German) of Brooklyn held a Sängerfest, at Ridgewood Park, on Pfingst-Sonntag und Montag. On the 14th, the Williamsburgh Sängerbund was at Turn Hall, Meserole Street. April 15th brought to the Central Baptist Church, South Fifth Street, a concert of Emma Wilkinson, whom we are pleased to hear again. The Presbyterian Church, South Fourth Street, invited, on April 19th, with Priscilla Whittingham and the Hon. E. Carswellon, in Laughter. On an evening in late April, Hon C. H. Russell talked, in St. John's M.E. Church, on Gladstone. A tableau and statue entertainment in early June brightened the Lee Avenue Congregational Church. To that sanctuary the Greenpoint Globe attributes a five-days musical festival, beginning on June 7th, under the beneficent guidance of Jerome Hopkins. Strawberries were now ripe, and were served with musical and literary embellishments, on June 9th, at the Lee Avenue Congregational Church and, on the 10th, at the Central M.E. Church. The Bushwick Sunday School, on the 16th, had a Mikado Strawberry, Apron and Necktie Festival; and the Cook Street M.E. Church, at Bushwick Avenue and Cook Street limited its call merely to berries and ice cream. On July 7th and 8th, the ever-busy Lee Avenue Congregational Church launched a Grand Fruit, Floral and Ice Cream Festival, with an Old Folks Concert. Those men and women, young and old, took their church life simply and seriously.

I may now pass to that other manifestation of lives not too complex— the summer outing. The fifth Grand Annual Bundes Schützenfest of the Germania Schützenbund took place on July 4th, 5th and 6th, at shadiest Ridgewood Park; but the Brooklyn Caledonian Club was very Scotch, on the 5th, at Myrtle Avenue Park. Even before these glad events, on June 26th, to be exact, the Improved Order of Red Men of Kings County held a picnic at Broadway and Washington Park. The Times and the Eagle advertise Coney Island, Long Branch and other cool retreats. August 29th, 30th and 31st and September 1st stationed the tenth annual Schwaben Volksfest in Grauer's Ridgewood Park; this same bosky retreat, on September 5th, 6th, 7th and 8th, held the joy of the Plattdeutscher Volksfest-Verein of Brooklyn and its vicinity. The theatres were now re-opening, and all we lovers of open spaces could do was sail to Staten Island, for Buffalo Bill's Wild West, at Erastina.   Even that closed on September 25th.

GREENPOINT, 1885–1886

When this division of the Eastern District of Brooklyn began to recover from the debauch of excursions hither and yon that had, during the summer of 1885, assailed its solid respectability, it went into an ecstasy of the roller-skating madness then infesting the country.   The Long Island City Star advertises two establishments that catered to the phrenetic bliss.   The Manhattan Roller Skating Rink, on Greenpoint Avenue, announced for September 28th the facile Diacount and Lundberg, and, for the 30th, Lillie Lewis, who, as we shall see, was making a tour of the rinks.   On October 5th and 10th, Frank Melrose, the one-legged skater, awakened pity and amaze, and, on the 7th, Frank and Fannie Harrington whirled round the circle; they returned to an eager public, on October 19th and 20th.   On the 19th, also, Mlle. Titiens, "queen of the cornet," blew thrillingly through that unwomanly implement of torture.   But I go back to October 12th to greet the appropriately-named Speedwells, and to the 15th, to admire, once more, Jennie Houghton, "queen of the rink."   November 2nd brought a Polo Contest, between the Atlas of New York and the Manhattans of Greenpoint.   Leo ("tumbleroniconist") was bright beacon on November 4th.

Here I leave the Manhattan, to picture the delights of Elliott and Odell's Greenpoint Roller Skating Rink, which opened, on Monday, October 5th, with star exhibitions by Lillie Lewis and Porter and La Montagne.   A Calico Carnival, on December 3rd, will allow us to depart, gracefully and economically, from this scene of rolling exuberance.   Having thus, in one clustered, feverish record, given account of that madness of 1885, I pass to more intellectual nourishment provided for Greenpoint across the river.

This drastic procedure allows me to ignore opening balls at Germania Hall and Eckford Hall, and to attend the concert, on October 17th, of the popular Fisk Jubilee Singers, at Association Hall (Manhattan Avenue, near Calyer Street).   A concert and entertainment opened, on October 28th, the Christian Church of the Evangel; on the 29th, the Reverend J. F. Riggs spoke, in the Reformed Church Chapel (Kent Street), on Curiosities of Literature.   I can only ask my perplexed reader to remember that October, in any small suburban community, provides a lean harvest of professional entertainment; the excitement preceding the November elections is sufficient to warp the nerves of local politicians and voters.   But, having survived the trying experiences of Election Day, Greenpoint pulled itself together with an aftermath of November and December festivities of a serious character.

My male readers would hardly revel in the thought of a fair, which began, on November 16th, at Smithsonian Hall; but they might be mildly interested,

[195]

on that same 16th, in a lecture at the Orchard P. M. Church, of W. D. Thompson, on Seven Weeks on Sea and Land — an account of a cruise in those days long anterior to the cinema. The Java Street Church of the Ascension broke out in a festal celebration of three days. On November 24th, it invited with a Promenade Concert (which seems to me rather secular for a churchly edifice); on the 25th, came a Kettledrum (again a provision seemingly sub-religious); and, on the 27th, it promised tableaux, songs, recitations and Annie (or Anne) Mooney, a well-liked singer. This brings us to the 25th of November when, at Smithsonian Hall, the St. Anthony Council, No. 104, of the Catholic Benevolent Legion, offered a concert and Harry C. Boniface's melodrama, A Year Ago Today, with the scene laid in Riverdale, New York, and acted by Boniface and members of the Brougham Literary Union of New York, including A. C. Bracton, James O'Farrell, J. H. Gorham, Edward J. Capper, Freddy Fox, Nellie Flemmer, Olive Morandel and Lizzie Nailier (*sic*) — as undistinguished a group as one can imagine. A concert also edged itself into the proceedings, two men of the name of James and Charles O'Neill being among the participants. A double inducement of Thanksgiving (November 26th) consisted of the Fisk University Singers, at the First M.E. Church, and an Old Folks Concert, in the Tabernacle M.E. Sunday School. In the utter paucity of the record, Greenpoint could but look forward to a concert for a night in December, when its own Apollo Union was to function in Smithsonian Hall; even so, fulfilment of this promise was deferred to January.

December featly stepped out of the path of Christmas shcppers. The Misses Mooney gave a concert, on the 7th, at their home, 115 Java Street. On the 9th and 10th, at the First Baptist Church, Noble Street, a Little Old Folks Entertainment must have seemed sweet and artistic to an audience of fond mothers. The Canonicus Tribe, No. 64, held Smithsonian Hall, on the 14th, for an entertainment and reception of red-men import. M. F. Vallette, in those chill December evenings, was giving illustrated lectures, at the Evening School, 22 Java Street. The Reverend W. H. Boole, husband of the militant prohibitionist of later years, Mrs. Ella Boole, added to the gloom, on one dark pre-Christmas evening, by lecturing, at the M.E. Tabernacle, on What I Saw in Kansas. Fewer than a hundred, according to the Long Island City Star, attended. December 16th found the Junior Choir of the Church of the Ascension in the new school building in Java Street, acting Bachelor's Hall and two scenes from The Mikado.

January brought brighter entertainment. On the 4th, the concert of the Apollo Union, at Smithsonian Hall, invited with promise of Lena Bungert, the Apollo Quartet, Charles P. O'Neill (singer), John F. Skelly (humourist), and Professor Keil, who, in the Star review, "manipulated the piano, in the difficult selection, Poet and Peasant." On the 7th, the children of the Church of the Ascension did, I know not what, in the Parish House, in Java Street;

and the Young Bachelors of Greenpoint, on the 9th, gave a ball, in Smithsonian Hall. In the Noble Street Presbyterian Church, on January 14th, a concert was to assemble Greenpoint's own Annie Mooney, Neva Hall, of Utica ("one of the most talented cornetists of the State," whom the Mikado should have punished, along with the "lady novelist"), the Orpheus Glee Club of Brooklyn, and two boy vocalists, Freddie Voss and Asher Stanley. January 18th at last brought something germane to our subject, if only mildly so. In the Parish House of the Church of the Ascension, the curiously-named Alta Dramatic acted Give Me My Wife. This charity affair utilised the services, in song, of the ubiquitous Annie (or Anne) Mooney and of the pleasingly-named Frank R. Treasure. On the same date, the second annual ball of the Seminole Club danced away the hours at Smithsonian Hall. And something dramatic graced Turn Hall (Meserole Street), on the 20th, when the State Convention Committee of Sons of Veterans and the Lexington Dramatic Association and Company C, 13th Regiment, presented Enlisted for the War, with a cast including M. J. Colligan, M. J. McKenna, J. J. Moran, Adolph Meyer, James A. Kerwin, John White, P. M. Colligan, Ella Healey, Jennie Dyas, and Kate Liebold (or Leibold), some of whose names seem familiar to my studious reader. At Eckford Hall, on the 25th, the Greenpoint Burns Club celebrated the hundred and twenty-seventh anniversary of the poet. I end this by no means thrilling paragraph with the statement that the Noble Street Presbyterian Church advertised a course of People's Lectures, running from January 21st to March 18th, given by reverend and worthy gentlemen all engulfed, a half century later, in the waves of time.

I pass into February, on the 3rd, hoping that the Christian Church of the Evangel may revive the drooping season with the Madison Glee Club and two "dialogues"—of course plays camouflaged under that innocuous name—and acted by Lizzie Germain, May Hamilton, Lena Harrison, Emily Miller, Libbie Floyd, Minnie Christie, Araminta Fenwick (striking name) and Hattie Depew. February 9th found R. V. Young Post, No. 20, Sons of Veterans, at Smithsonian Hall. Heroes Ancient and Modern was the theme of a discourse by the Reverend George L. Alrich (*sic*), on February 17th, at the Reformed Episcopal Church of the Redemption. Boker's difficult play, Francesca da Rimini, employed some modern amateur heroes, on February 18th, the cast embracing, at Smithsonian Hall, Mortimer J. Ashton (Lanciotto), Walter Hawley (Paolo), William L. Garrison (Malatesta), G. W. Bailey, Jr. (Beppo Pepe), Maude Storey (Francesca), and Jessie Storey (Ritta). We shall soon find a Jessie Storey on the professional stage. February 22nd revered the Father of his Country with the ball and concert, at Smithsonian Hall, of the Shipwrights' Mutual Relief and Benefit Association and with W. P. Halsted's lecture, at the Kent Street Reformed Church, on Personal Recollections of the War, with battle views, all lightened by the singing of Hattie Schroter.

[197]

Something happened to skating rinks, not only in Greenpoint, but through-out the country; young people no longer wished to roll along on skates. The Manhattan Skating Rink that had so bravely begun in September, adver-tised, for the week of March 1st–6th, the ever-recurring Oliver W. Wren Company, in a succession of Rip Van Winkle, Enoch Arden and The Two Orphans. The following week, except on Thursday, March 11th, gave us Cool Burgess, in variety and a Burlesque Mikado. On Thursday, the Olive Leaf Lodge tendered a benefit to Leonard Smith, who had lost his sight by the explosion of an ammonia tank. I come back to the Germans, with the masquerade ball of the Frohsinn Singing Society, on March 6th, at Koch's Broadway Hall. On March 17th, Professor Cromwell, hero of countless illus-trated lectures in New York, came to the Manhattan Rink, with A Trip Round the World, following it, on the 29th, at Smithsonian Hall, with Ireland. March 18th allowed the Young People's Association of the Christian Church of the Evangel to offer a concert with Nettie McEwen (soprano), Jennie Van Velsor and Julia Stamper (elocutionists), and John W. Stalker (xylophone); Maddison Morton's farce, At Sixes and Sevens, also, as Carlyle might say, got itself acted. In my eagerness to reach this delectable offering, I neglected to invite my reader to attend, on March 15th, at the Tabernacle M.E. Church, a concert with Annie Mooney, J. Leslie Gossin, J. W. Stalker, Josie Bassett, Julia Stalker, Professor La Rue and Alice Cook The First Methodist Church, on April 5th, was rich with the art of H.E. H. Benedict, the Handel Quartet, Helen Ames, Nellie Stearns, Libbie Bennett and Wilbur Rushmore.

April 6th brought to Association Hall Professor A. G. Waring's Magical Entertainment; the 18th found at St. Anthony's Church a rendering of the greater magic of Rossini's Stabat Mater. A double blessing transfigured the evening of April 21st: for the testimonial to M. F. H. Smith, organist, the Tabernacle M.E. Church promised the co-operation of Annie Mooney, Laura Groves ("late of the Kellogg Concert Company"), D. W. Robertson (tum-bleronicon), H. J. Schmalix (zither), J. Williams Macy (humourist) and Smith himself as, doubtless, a willing director; at the Reformed Church, Kent Street, appeared Nellie Zoble, Julia Stalker and Ernest Bann (violinist). On the 22nd, a benefit for a "widow lady" was to enlist H. F. Roberts (violinist), Jessie Woodruff, Hattie Brazier, John W. Stalker, and Sophie and Minnie Christie, Smithsonian Hall being the sanctuary of these wandering birds of passage. Murphy's Mastodon Minstrels endeavoured to lighten the strain, on April 24th, at the Manhattan Rink.

May 6th called us once more to that rink, for a benefit to Kate Simpson, at which were to appear Zachary Taylor (still another violinist), Charles H. Patterson, Amy Terry, Louise Scannell and George Law, all, I believe, un-known to my pen. The columns of the Star now began to bristle with an-nouncements of excursions and strawberry festivals, all dear to the suburban heart. But May gave a few final gasps, before the indoor season expired.

At the Parish House of St. Anthony's Church, the Leonardis Dramatic Society acted, on May 4th and 5th, Enlisted for the War and Our Boys. On the 24th, the Church of the Ascension gave a concert in the Parish House, with those tireless executants, Anne (*sic*) Rooney and Charles P. O'Neill, and with bigger lure in Julie de Ryther (*sic*). The second act of Il Trovatore was very metropolitan for modest little Greenpoint. The Herbert Family, on the 26th, gave, at Manhattan Rink, a Minstrel and Variety Entertainment; on the 28th, the Barbara Frietchie Post was at G. A. R. Hall, with music and dramatics. And May died out of the calendar, on the 31st, with the Reverend Newland Maynard lecturing, at Smithsonian Hall, on the ever recurrent, burning question of Ireland. The Knights of Tara Association sponsored this function. I end the chronicle with the return to their former home of Greeenpoint of the delightful Meigs Sisters, who appeared in concert, on June 1st, in the Parish House of the Church of the Ascension, Java Street. After that, excursions and ice cream and strawberry festivals enticed Greenpoint from home and porch.

FLATBUSH AND ITS NEIGHBOURS, 1886

On an evening in April, a testimonial to Miss C. McDowell, of the heavy Brooklyn amateur brigade, mounted on the stage of Turn Hall, Eighth Street, between Third and Fourth Avenues (was this address New York City or South Brooklyn?) another Hazel Kirke, with the beneficiary as Hazel, supported by S. G. Frost (who also directed), J. C. Costello, E. A. Slattery, J. J. Breen, J. J. Sullivan, Miss M. Wallace and Miss L. Bendit. This striking treasure I dig from files of the Brooklyn Times.

LONG ISLAND CITY AND ITS NEIGHBOURS, 1885–1886

The Two Orphans, by the Wren Comedy Company, suffered on September 28, 1885, at the Astoria Assembly Rooms; Wren was Pierre and Picard and Mrs. Wren the pitiful Louise. Merrily the Astoria Skating Rink opened, on September 24th, with "Professor" E. W. Franke and Lulu Billard, the latter as the Dandy Dude on Rollers—an amusing idea. And the Arlington Rink, at Hunter's Point, was, in October, blithely rolling along. The Star Athletic Club, on November 23rd, gave a concert and a farce, The Wig Maker. New Mexico and Its History served L. Bradford Smith, late Chief Justice of New (?) Mexico, as topic for discussion, on December 14th. On the 11th, he had lectured in St. Paul's Church, Woodside, on The Pueblo Indians. December 18th brought to Knickerbocker Hall the ball of the Eckford Club. And December 29th, at the Astoria Assembly Rooms, shivered toward 1886 with Kate Percy as Fanchon, Oliver Wren as Landry and Didier (he seemed to enjoy doubling parts) and Mrs. Wren as Madelon.

[199]

The Newtown Choral Union, on the 24th, held the Newtown Association Hall, with the aid of Ida Wing (pianist), J. Baumeister (reader), L. Wetzler (violinist) and Fred Randall (singer). With the reader's permission, I will here affix two items I discovered in the Long Island Daily Star, after the printer had set up the foregoing list. "Professor" Edward Earle (equilibrist) was, on November 5th and 7th, at the Astoria Rink. And, on December 16th, at the First Reformed Church, Astoria, in a "testimonial" to R. Fletcher Nevins, appeared Mrs. E. Kearney (contralto), S. H. McClintock (tenor), Carl Dufft, Will Hunt (baritone), and (long before Peter Pan was acted) Flora Bell Tinker (soprano).

January 19th found Chaplain McCabe at the M.E. Church, Astoria, of course with his inescapable Bright Side of Life in Libby Prison. Aside from this, January seems to have warmed its sentiment with church "socials" in private homes. On February 15th, the St. Lawrence Young Men's Union gave, at Athletic Hall, a benefit for St. Patrick's Church. Among the performers were Isabella Scott (piano), Lucy Ryan (soprano), Theresa Kerwin (soprano), Charles Jarvis and James Judge. A play, Harvest Storm, enlisted W. J. Patterson, C. Connors and E. S. Murphy; and The Mischievous Nigger ended the show. February 22nd brought to the East Avenue Baptist Church Lillian F. Wells, Edward G. Jardine (organ), J. L. Ewell, Lena Wolfe (sic) and Charles S. Jardine. Some of these names seem to awaken faint chimes in my memory. A "Hare and Hounds" was run, on Washington's Birthday, in Woodside.

A literary and musical entertainment, by Will Hunt, precentor of the First Reformed Church, Astoria, fell on February 22nd, with Harriet Webb, Herr H. A. Plate (violin), H. Marum (piano), and H. R. Nevins (accompanist). This seems hardly worth waiting for, so many wintry weeks. Nor should I advise a journey to Woodside, on the 23rd, for a concert in the First Baptist Church involving the Orpheus Glee Club, Nettie Carman, W. H. Weeks, Mamie Andrews (reciter), the Peake (sic) Sisters and others. This may have occurred on the 16th; the Greenpoint Globe is hazy as to the date. The Reformed Church, Remsen Street, Astoria, proffered a pleasing programme, on February 26th, with Marie S. Bissell, Sarah Barron Anderson, W. H. Stanley (English tenor), Oscar Steins and Marshall P. Wilder, with William E. Taylor (accompanist). Many balls were danced through in March, but a musical and dramatic entertainment of the Star Athletic Club slipped into Athletic Hall, on the fourth. Then on with the dance! The tenth annual masquerade of the Ladies' Assistance Association (German-American, I take it, for Ladies' Aid Society), on March 8th, at Scher's Assembly Rooms; the ninth annual ball of the Kronprinzessin Victoria, No. 1, on the 15th, at the Astoria Assembly Rooms; the invitation ball of the Ancient Order of Hibernians, Division No. 3, on March 16th, in the same Astoria Assembly Rooms — these were some of them.

[200]

But other amusements? Even so far back as February 23rd, a concert of the Choir of the Church of the Redeemer, Astoria, in the Sunday School Room, called into service Priscilla Whittingham and the Rotzoll Double Quartet. And drama came in for a week (March 1st–6th), with the Wren Comedy Company in Fanchon, Rip Van Winkle, Enoch Arden and The Two Orphans, Oliver W. Wren, of course, appearing in all. Admission to all parts of the house was held at 15 cents. On March 4th, the Mount Carmel Literary Association availed itself, in the Astoria Assembly Rooms, of the services of Professor J. R. Bennett, Thomas Richards (Lancashire clog), Master Edwards ("musical wonder"), H. Lukin and R. Smith, in a farce, Charles Wilson (banjo), Barney McPhillips (Irish comedian, vocalist and dancer), and Yorkville Young Men, in The Mischievous Nigger. March 27th staged a benefit to Edwin W. Frake, at the Astoria Roller Skating Rink. But, on March 15th, one might have journeyed to the Presbyterian Chapel, Newtown, there to appraise the singing of the Newtown Choral Union.

On April 3rd, the Mascotts, described by the Long Island Star as "a popular social organisation," gave what the same paper calls "a charming reception," at the Astoria Assembly Rooms. The First Reformed Church, Dutch Kills, showed, on the 13th, a stereopticon exhibition by G. A. Perrine; a concert of the Astoria Männerchor and the Gesangverein Frohsinn came to pass, on April 24th, at Koch's Broadway Halle. I skip a kindergarten entertainment, on April 29th, at St. John's P.E. Sunday School, in order to arrive more quickly at Mr. and Miss Bassett's Singin' Skewl, on May 1st and 3rd, at Arlington Hall. The second annual Summernight's Festival of the Richard E. Kane Association, dared the weather, of May 5th, at Kane's Park, Blissville. The Young People's Society of Christian Endeavour stayed indoors (in Arlington Hall) for a fair, on May 12th and 13th. Some sort of entertainment enlisted Misses Laws and Wright, Isberg, Anable (sic) and Kelty, Hemstis and Bostwick and Mrs. Haff (elocutionists), and banjo playing by G. F. Herbert and Edward Watkins, of Greenpoint. I admit it seems ridiculous to put these trifling amateurs in the same volume with Edwin Booth, Salvini and Ellen Terry.

May 23rd promised two ceremonies: Memorial Services, in the evening, at Arlington Hall, in Hunter's Point, under the auspices of the Benjamin Ringgold Post, No. 283, G.A.R.; and the first of a series of Sunday concerts to be given at Pete Hall's Concert Hall, at Laurel Hill, announced coadjutors including Jack Hennessey, John Carroll (motto singer), Jerry Sullivan, and George Millis ("London's lion comic"), every one of whom would, I think, be astonished to find himself eternised in any book of 1941. I pass out of May, on the 30th, when the "Club" of Hunter's Point held a picnic, in Schwalenberg's Jackson Avenue Park. And here is June 30th, with a lecture by Dr. Greene, of New York, at Arlington Hall, on Rome, Egypt and the Holy Land—illustrated, of course. The same hall, on June 25th, gave a lecture by Professor Kersteller, Ph.D., on his oxy-hydromicroscope; also was worked in A Tour through England and Ireland, *via* the Midland Railroad. Robbins' Circus and Museum was in Long Island City, on August 7th. Except for that, July and August advertised, in the Star, only picnics and excursions. The record for 1885–86 is not of enthralling interest; but of "social significance" is the "Pic-Nic," on September 18th, of the "Lavoratori," held in Astoria. The full significance may be gleaned from my account of the function under the heading of Italian Activities.

Flushing and Its Neighbours, 1885–1886

Flushing was become rather lively—a bit of a centre for minor shows. On September 16th, Moynaham's Crocheron House stressed the Bayside Festival; then Oliver W. Wren, on the 30th, played Enoch Arden, under the auspices of the Empire Hose Company. There's rural 1885 for you! October 13th brought to the Flushing Opera House (with Guzman) Mrs. G. Luther, Allan Latham and the Philharmonic Quartet of Brooklyn. There must have been intervening joys, but the Flushing Journal admits us not thereto; actually it carries us, on November 10th, to Grace Chapel, Whitestone, for the performance, by the Whitestone Dramatic Association, of Woodcock's Little Game. But the Flushing Opera House, on December 8th, was very ambitious, with an Historical Pageant of America, from the Landing of Columbus to the Present Time—and with pictures, mind you!

Fire companies were at the fore. The Mutual Engine Company, on December 17th, gave a minstrel entertainment, with, according to the Journal, "every seat occupied." Well, fire laddies were, in those days, a social feature in little towns; village maidens were proud to attend their dances or their shows. In December, on chilly, darksome evenings, the Attalia Society held meetings in houses of members, and Christmas festivals, of course, gladdened staid church interiors.

And here we are, already in Flushing January. On the 13th of that cold month, amateurs were in Roslyn Hall, in Bread Upon the Waters; it was "to be repeated soon." Whitfield, "humourist and facial contortionist" made faces at all who attended, on January 18th, at the Opera House; for charity, on the 25th, the Willets Point Dramatic Club, gave at the same hall, Sterling Coyne's A Widow Hunt. And all this while Knab's Skating Rink gave Whitestone a sliding happiness. The Opera House, on February 10th, offered Frank Lincoln's The Humorous Side of Life; the Kelpies, a banjo and guitar club, participated. The humorous side of life seems to me delightfully uppermost in the announcement of the same auditorium for February 17th—Naval Engagements "by four military gentlemen from Willets Point and two Flushing ladies."

A comic opera, Seven Times One, written by Charles S. Clark and arranged by Francis P. Hamlet, both of Hempstead, and acted there on February 10th, came to Flushing Opera House, on March. 8th. Two nights later, the New York University Glee Club, sang in the same hall, before an audience of about forty persons (saith the Journal). And, on the 15th, Cornucopia Lodge, No. 563, F. and A.M. presented Marshall P. Wilder, Lottie Vandeveer (singer) and the Venetian Mandolin Quartet. Fancy, all that in gusty March! Perhaps satiated with amusement, Flushing waited till April 28th, when the Opera House once more offered Frank Lincoln, with Josie Nimnao (soprano), A. E. Gosling (pianist) and Mrs. M. Ackerly Drew (soprano) — all for the benefit of St. George's Brotherhood. A lecture in earlier May, by the Hon. L. Bradford Smith, The Pueblo Indians, reduced the Opera House to the normal dignity of a little town.

The Mutual Engine Company was again in evidence, on May 25th, presenting, at the Opera House, the Bassetts in Bric-a-Brac ("as at the Bijou Opera House, New York"). And June 21st and 22nd brought the Drummond Family and Harry Shotwell (negro delineator), with Baby Pinky "in a new rôle." She was to sell tickets in a store, on Saturday, the 19th. For the third season on Long Island, the New Shows Museum, on July 26th, was proffering Frank A. Robbins and Ira Payne ("the master shot of the world"). We must not forget that residents of Flushing could easily reach New York or Brooklyn for plays — real plays by real actors; especially the ladies could attend matinées at Daly's or Wallack's or the Madison Square, and reach home in ample time for dinner (or would it be supper?).

Jamaica and Its Neighbours, 1885–1886

Frank A. Robbins's New Shows and Menagerie came to Jamaica, on August 1, 1885, with Charles W. Fish, Mlle. Alma ("woman fly"), Ahnetta (Hindoo snake charmer), a herd of elephants and unicycle and bicycle contests. The afternoon performance was omitted, because of a funeral in the village. The Two Orphans blessed the Jamaica Opera House, on October 7th, with Oliver Wren and his Comedy Company, and under auspices of the De Grauw Hose Company. Obviously, on Long Island, firemen were trying to kindle pleasure in the drama. Abbey's Double mammoth Uncle Tom's Cabin Company held the Opera House, on October 13th, with two uniformed bands, one coloured, one white, with bloodhounds, two Topsys and two Markses. On the 14th, for the benefit of the Reformed Church Sabbath School, the Puritan Quartet of Brooklyn, Eva Davis, child elocutionist from Jersey City Heights, John Jones, elocutionist of Brooklyn, and others cooperated to the joy (I trust) of their neighbours in Jamaica.

The Jamaica Rink was now open, on Tuesdays, Thursdays, and Saturdays, with music. The Meigs Sisters (Hattie and Jennie, sopranos, and

Edith and Florence, altos), who had delighted Jamaica on June 3rd, came again on November 11th, accompanied by the Brooklyn reader, Louise Johnson. We all enjoyed the singing of the Meigs quartet. On December 14th, in Town Hall, a big group included Lena Bungert (soprano), Hattie Snow (pianist), H. J. Clarke (humourist), William D. Spearman (tenor), George H. Kilmer (baritone), Charles H. Campbell (basso) and the Philharmonic Male Quartet of Brooklyn. On December 31st, Oliver Wren, that wandering soul, gave, afternoon and evening, Fanchon, the Cricket; bad weather brought a bad house, but Fanchon sang the then very popular In the Gloaming. The Opera House, of course, was scene of this faded joy. It was the scene also of the activities of the Virginia Coloured Minstrels, "composed mostly of coloured gentlemen of our village," who gave a concert on January 21st. There was some town opposition, but the performance, before a large, orderly audience, was declared by the Democrat, to be "fine." When the group returned, on February 17th, one of the best singers, because of a sudden blindness, was absent, and the paper now described the offering as "very poor."

Meantime, the village had had opportunity to appraise the Crescent Band, of home talent, then beginning a career with a concert on February 10th; and Taylor, illusionist, advertised sessions for February 12th, 13th and 15th, at the Opera House. March began its wild career, on the 3rd, with the private theatricals of the Jamaica Sängerbund, held in their hall at John Distler's Atlantic Garden. At Association Hall, Richmond Hill, on the 5th, "Professor" D. W. Robertson played the tumbleronicon, and W. B. Green, humourist and dialect reader, did what he did. But, on March 11th, Kate Field in Town Hall lectured, as she often did in larger centres, on The Mormon Monster, her point being that, now we had abolished slavery, we must, as a nation, be (if I may so put it) Siegfried to this Fafner. On April 7th, a Mother Goose entertainment (the Democrat does not say where) called in the aid of Jamaica's own Adela Rankin. Under T. R. Davenport's direction the Presbyterian Church Choir, on the 11th, showed Jamaica what it could do for the glory of the town. And, on April 15th, the Tennessee Jubilee Singers were due. A Singin' Skewl of school children, with Mr. Bassett (Jedediah?) amused, on April 16th and 19th.

May 6th found the proud choir of the Presbyterian Church ensconced in Town Hall, to show what Davenport had been able to make of it. On the 12th, a benefit to Eddie Phillips once more brought to the Opera House the Virginia Coloured Minstrels, with assurance that Raymond Wilson, whose temporary blindness had kept him from the last concert, would positively appear. Better were it, as the poets say, to attend a concert on that same 12th, of the Richmond Hill Christian Association, which promised the art of Rilla Bronson, Lena Bungert, Mrs. George T. Mulford, Priscilla Whittingham, Ross David, Melvin A. Bronson (baritone), and William F. Bron-

[204]

son (basso).   Reserved seats for this luxury came high — 75 cents, in fact. Nourished on thought of that pleasure, Jamaica might wait for the second concert, on May 26th, of its gradually coagulating Crescent Band — becoming a source of community pride.

June began the hunt for excitement, on the 10th, with the entertainment, at Shiloh Baptist Church, of the Amateur Concert Company of Jamaica. And highly successful was the strawberry festival and entertainment, on June 11th, in the M.E. Lecture Room; believe if ye may, the profits were $40!   On June 23rd, church choirs assembled at the Mineola Fair Grounds, what there to do, the bewildered reader may conjecture as well as I.   "Professor" Ballard, connected with the school system of Jamaica, had started an H. and H. (Health and Happiness) Association among his young charges; what more natural, then, than to exhibit them in Town Hall, on June 24th and 25th, in Three Little Kittens?   I do not see why we should attend the Cedarhurst Steeplechase, on July 5th; and I cannot echo the plaint of the Democrat, on July 13th, that no picnic has gone from the village in that year.   The paper probably rejoiced in the Picnic and Summer-Night Festival of the Jamaica Sängerbund, held on August 16th (afternoon and evening) in Distler's Park.

Staten Island, 1885–1886

With the New York Herald as guide, we may safely ferry twice to the charming Staten Island: At the Pavilion Hotel, West Brighton, on September 17, 1885, Rosa d'Erina was announced to sing Music of the Nations, her assistants being Professor Vontona (*sic*) and Bessie Byrne (reader); love of sport and open air might have induced us to visit the Staten Island Cricket Grounds, there, on October 10th, to watch the lacrosse game between Montreal, "champion of the world" and our own New York heroes undismayed.

And now the Richmond County Sentinel, again so called, shall be our guide.   On September 28th, the Rock Band Concert summoned to Griffith Hall, Port Richmond; the same auditorium, on October 17th, presented Dick Hunt's Dramatic Company, in Lady Audley's Secret, with Helen Hooker, Miss A. Hutchinson, Minnie Waldo, Bella Bell, David Woodbury, Charles Johnson and Dick Hunt.   I still find it difficult to believe that anything so provincial could be found so near Broadway.   November 14th proffered two incitements: the Fisk University Jubilee Singers at the First Baptist Church, New Brighton; and a concert in the German Club Rooms, Stapleton, with Carl Dufft (baritone) and pupils of Signor Giuseppe de Grandi.   Would either be worth the long ferry trip, on a chilly evening?   But, of course, if one lived on the Island, with nothing else to do!   The more intellectual features of early winter appeared in the "literary entertainments" announced for St. John's Church, Clifton: George William Curtis's lecture on Dickens

(December 3rd), and three by Dr. Eccleston — Our Great Empire on the Pacific (December 10th), St. Paul's, London (17th), and Philip II and the Invincible Armada (January 14th). On January 7th, Miss Bennett was down for Studies in Chaucer. A rather bleak time on the Island!

The Staten Island Vocal Society, on January 6th, at the German Club Rooms, invited with promise of Marie Tuck (soprano), Charles Herbert Clarke (tenor), James A. Metcalf (baritone) and the New York Philharmonic Club. It was only a week (January 13th) till the same rooms opened for an amateur performance of Vice Versa; Edward Fales Coward, whom I always think of with the greatest pleasure, recited between the acts. Parabola Hall, on February 3rd, housed the masquerade ball of the Staten Island Liederkranz; and February 11th and 12th, with a matinée on the 13th, were doubtless pretty, at Roe's Hall, West New Brighton, with tableaux, statuary, pictures and pantomime, directed by G. B. Bartlett of Boston, who seemed, in those years, to make the journey easily from Boston to New York. The masquerade ball of the Staten Island Quartet Club (March 1st) and the Charity Ball (March 3rd) both found hospitable refuge in the German Club Rooms. The Medora Minstrels went, on March 8th, to Roe's Hall.

A tableaux entertainment exercised, on April 8th, the Young People's Association of the First Presbyterian Church, Stapleton. From the excitement of this, we leap, on April 29th, to hear the Olympian Club, in New Men and Old Acres, and, on May 8th, to the Lyceum, New Brighton, to test the Melpomene Association, in Snowed In, by John E. Wylie, Jr. Of course, in good weather, Staten Islanders could ferry to New York or Brooklyn for real "shows" by real actors. Hence, perhaps, the slenderness of dramatic fare in their home precincts. They fared rather more sumptuously in music, on May 6th, when Miss (Ella?) Earle appeared with the Staten Island Vocal Society; possibly, also, on June 1st, at the concert of the Choral Union, when at Trinity M.E. Church, West New Brighton, soloists included Nellie Hillyer (pianist) and Lila Benedict (soprano). As to the talent of these two ladies history has preserved discreet silence. Whatever the gain from those concerts, we could, on May 31st, have danced at least in Hugenott, at the concert and dance in the Pincus Summer-Resort Hotel. A lacrosse tourney at St. George Grounds may have been exciting, on June 5th.

Summer, in 1886, was really exciting, with Buffalo Bill's Wild West Show, all noise and tumult, opening on June 28th, at Erastina Woods, Mariner's Harbour, and continuing, with whoops and Indians and brave horsemen till September warned that it was time to close. And, if this was too much for more delicate sensibilities, at St. George, "popular concerts by the seaside" began on June 30th, with illuminated fountains, and Cappa's Seventh Regiment Band (at times). On Saturday, August 7th, the riches were sufficient, I should judge, to draw many heated New Yorkers and Brooklynites to the enchanted isle — the Seventh Regiment Band, Julie de

[206]

Ryther (*sic*), the boy soprano, George Bauer, and the Young Apollo Club. But the playhouses began to resume, in both the big cities just mentioned, and Staten Island ceased to call from across the bay; not, however, before the model Japanese Village had set up on the St. George Grounds. And at St. George, in the week of August 16th–21st, the Young Apollo Club and Rosa d'Erina united in song for good islanders.

CHAPTER IV

WALLACK'S, DALY'S, THE MADISON SQUARE, THE LYCEUM, THE STAR, THE UNION SQUARE, THE FIFTH AVENUE, THE STANDARD, THE FOURTEENTH STREET THEATRE, THE CASINO, 1886-1887

THE McCAULL OPERA COMPANY, in possession of Wallack's stage for the summer of 1886, moved away, on October 9th, when Josephine for the last time was Sold by Her Sisters. The stock company of the theatre began, on October 13th, the final season of Lester Wallack's management in a city that had grown to look on him as an indispensable institution in its pleasures. Alas! like all institutions, he and his company had become outmoded and passed away.

It was largely, we remember, a matter of plays; the old comedies no longer attracted, and the freshness of repertoire at Daly's and the Madison Square left Wallack bewildered and helpless. This was apparent in his choice of opening play for the new season. He had brought from England Henry Hamilton, a young actor of no distinction, whose adaptation of Moths had won success in 1883, and, on October 13th (the opening night), he produced another piece from the same pen — Harvest, dealing in a prologue with the heartless abandonment by a young man of a deceived girl and her baby boy and in the body of the play with the scornful refusal of the woman, now grown old, with her devoted boy a man, to allow the careless seducer to make her an "honest" woman. That theme was used, later, by Oscar Wilde, in A Woman of No Importance and by St. John Ervine, in The Magnanimous Lover.

The company that interpreted this ephemeral thing included Kyrle Bellew as Noel Musgrave, May Germon as his little son Geoffrey, Herbert Kelcey, returned to the fold, as Captain Tressider, Harry Edwards as Hamish, and Annie Robe as Brenda Musgrave. This was the assignment for the prologue. In the play all, except Little May Germon, carried on in the same parts, except that the deceived Brenda was now known as Mrs. Marston, with Creston Clarke, son of J. S. Clarke and nephew of Edwin Booth, as Roy, her son. Others were Hamilton, the author, as Bevil Brooke, Helen Russell as Nora Fitzgerald, Katherine Rogers as Miss Macleod, and Carrie Coote, a pretty novice, as Lettice Vane. To those who remembered the glorious Wallack company of previous years this was hardly a strong cast, but, looking back from the vantage point of 1941, I am somewhat impressed with it. I saw the performance on October 13th, and, inexperienced as I

[208]

was, I found the play thin and uninspired.   I chiefly remember the beautiful
scenery by Goatcher (Wallack always provided about the best scenery of
his time) and a certain dignity in the acting of Annie Robe in the latter part
of the play.   Katherine Rogers, once a notable actress, had grown haggard
and uninteresting; but we must remember that her rôle was insignificant.   I
have not the slightest recollection of Creston Clarke (in that play), or of
Henry Hamilton (in any play).   Kelcey, all that season, was overshadowed
by the handsome Kyrle Bellew.

On the afternoon of Election Day (November 2nd) we were invited to a
performance of Jack, a play by Mrs. Harry Beckett, with Eben Plympton as
Jack ("as played by him in London"), E. J. Henley as Noel Blake ("as
played by him in London"), E. Valentine as Teddy, and, in other parts,
John Howson, Lillie Alliston, May Gallagher, Harry Edwards and Helen
Russell.   Unlike certain other plays brought out that season in special
afternoon productions, this one we shall meet again.   As to the regular company of the theatre, its Harvest closed on November 3rd.   The following
evening (Thursday), we were summoned to Robert Buchanan's dramatisation of Tom Jones, which he called Sophia:

Tom Jones	Kyrle Bellew	Fothergay	S. DuBois
Squire Western	Harry Edwards	Gamekeeper	James Shannon
Partridge	Charles Groves	Sophia	Annie Robe
Mr. Allworthy	W. J. Constantine	Miss Western	Mme. Ponisi
Blifil	E. J. Henley	Lady Bellaston	Katherine Rogers
Square	Daniel Leeson	Molly Seagrim	Carrie Coote
George Seagrim	Creston Clarke	Mistress Honour	Kate Bartlett
Farmer Copse	W. H. Pope	Dorothy	Evelyn Granville

That cast seems better in retrospect (1941) than in actual performance
(1886).   The play must have been the thing that brought failure, or, at
best, only partial success.   Charles Groves made in it his first appearance
since he played in New York, several seasons previously, in Evangeline.
I remember him well as Partridge, especially in the scenes with Kate Bartlett.   Strive as I may, I cannot recall anything more of the performance
except the utter improbability of Katherine Rogers's Lady Bellaston and
the make-up of Creston Clarke as George Seagrim.   But, in 1886, I did not
dream that, so many years later, I should be writing this harrowing con-
fession of forgetfulness.   Was it, I wonder, my fault?   I certainly recall,
vividly, the two great successes of that season in New York — Daly's revival
of The Taming of the Shrew, and Palmer's magnificent production of Jim,
the Penman.   Sophia held the stage of Wallack's till December 7th.

Meantime, like so many theatres of that period, Wallack's opened frequently for extra-theatrical entertainments.   On Sunday evening, November 7th, a benefit for Stanley McKenna promised participation of Mme.
Trebelli, Ovide Musin, Giannini, Mme. von Januschowsky, Steele MacKaye,

Tim Murphy, Loie Fuller, Jessie Bartlett Davis, Mme. Fabris, Julie de Ryther, Lionel Brough, "Jolly" Nash, &c. I cannot vouch for the appearance of all. For November 10th we were promised a second performance of Jack. On December 8th, Hamilton being here to direct, a revival of Moths brought this cast:

Raphael de Correze	Kyrle Bellew	Vere Herbert	Annie Robe
Lord Jura	Herbert Kelcey	Lady Dolly	Fanny Addison
Prince Zouroff	E. J. Henley	Fuchsia Leach	Helen Russell
Duke of Mull	Henry Hamilton	Princess Nadine	Mme. Ponisi
Ivan	S. DuBois	Duchesse de Sonnaze	Sadie Bigelow

Sadie Bigelow, a useful actress, and Fanny Addison, a delightful one, were specially engaged for the revival. One gathers an idea of the way in which Wallack's company had changed since 1883, by reflecting that, of the cast of 1883, only the utility S. DuBois re-appeared in 1886; gone were Rose Coghlan, Tearle, Gerald Eyre, Caroline Hill and Flora Livingston. I learn from the Herald of December 11th that Helen Vane, an English actress imported by Wallack for heavy rôles, had been ill ever since her arrival. Wallack paid her salary while here, and her passage to New York and back. He never saw her while she was here. She sailed for home in early December. With the splendid success of Daly with American players, one can but marvel at Wallack's persistent habit of importing English actors, often, it must be admitted, of inferior talent.

Moths, as I remember it, went with a swing. Fanny Addison was delightful as the volatile Lady Dolly Vanderdecken, and Henley was a very convincing villain. A post-Christmas gift (December 27th) was that Wallack specialty, The School for Scandal, in which John Gilbert, the matchless Sir Peter, made his first and very welcome appearance of the season, with Harry Edwards as the usual excellent Sir Oliver and Mme. Ponisi as the best of all Mrs. Candours. Others in the cast were far below the standard of former seasons: Kyrle Bellew a rather self-satisfied and effeminate Charles, Herbert Kelcey very uncomfortable as Joseph, Annie Robe, pretty and quite inadequate as Lady Teazle, Hamilton as Sir Benjamin, Henley as Crabtree, Groves as Moses, Leeson as Rowley, Herbert Ayling as Trip, Carrie Coote as Maria, and Sadie Bigelow as Lady Sneerwell. Of course, some of these interpretations were not really bad, but none of them could compare with the elegance of former casts at Wallack's. But, I am pleased to say, the classic comedy held the stage through January 26th — a good showing and, I hope, a profitable one. During a few of the later performances, Annie Robe was compelled by illness to relinquish her rôle to Helen Russell, who, I need hardly inform the reader, eclipsed no memories of Rose Coghlan's delightful Lady Teazle.

On January 27th, Wallack staged another of those crude English melo-

ANNIE ROBE
(DOMINIE'S DAUGHTER)

KYRLE BELLEW
(HARBOUR LIGHTS)

ANNIE ROBE
(SCHOOL FOR SCANDAL)

CARRIE COOTE
(WALLACK'S THEATRE)

HELEN RUSSELL

KATE BARTLETT
IN SOPHIA

CRESTON CLARKE

CHARLES GROVES
IN SOPHIA

E. J. HENLEY

dramas that, for several years, now, had caused his judicious patrons to grieve. This time it was Harbour Lights, a confection in many scenes by George R. Sims and Henry Pettitt, a compilation involving, as usual, virtue beset by villainy and ultimately winning the girl. This was the cast:

Lieutenant Kingsley	Kyrle Bellew	Detective Wood	David Shelly
Mark Helstone	Herbert Kelcey	Detective Pull	Alfred Perkins
Captain Nelson	Harry Edwards	Dora Vane	Annie Robe
Nicholas Morland	E. J. Henley	Lina Norton	Helen Russell
Tom Dossiter	Charles Groves	Mrs. Chudleigh	Mary E. Barker
Jack Lirriper	D. Leeson	Peggy Chudleigh	Carrie Coote
Frank Morland	Creston Clarke	Bridget	Miss E. Blaisdell
Dick Hockaday	Herbert Ayling	Mrs. Helstone	Alice Grey
Captain Hardy	W. S. St. Clair	Polly	Evelyn Granville
Solomon	W. H. Pope	Fisherwoman	Enola Grant
Harbour Master	J. W. Totten		

This stirring, if inelegant piece, mounted with fine scenery, carried through to March 12th, covering the middle period of a not impressive season. On February 2nd, Wallack's, for the first time in its history, began to fall into the fashion of midweek matinées. On that date and for several following Wednesdays it presented Lester Wallack's last revival of his famous theatre's classic, The School for Scandal, drumming up patronage and his own courage by advertising it with its "unapproachable" cast. As things were then going, perhaps it was. Other outside activities entered; Fred Lyster had a benefit, on Sunday, February 20th, with the help (advertised) of Dora Tilla, Ethel Corlette, Harry Edwards, Haydon Tilla, Michael Banner, Mark Smith, C. B. Bishop, Isabelle Urquhart, Lillie Grubb, Alice J. Shaw (the whistler), Kyrle Bellew, Marie Jansen, Alonzo Hatch, Pauline Hall, Marie Salvotti, Tony Hart, Lizzie Hughes, John Ince and John McWade. Since the papers often failed to review such complimentary "testimonials," I am left to wonder if, as on this occasion, all of the glittering host of volunteers appeared. W. Irving Bishop, the mind reader, had the evenings of Sunday, February 27th and March 6th. March 17th found Rose Osborne giving a matinée of Frou-Frou, with D. H. Harkins, John Howson, Fred G. Ross, Helen Corlette, Sibyl Johnstone, Tommy Russell, and Mary E. Barker as a support none too brilliant.

Old Heads and Young Hearts was listed to succeed Harbour Lights, on Monday, March 14th. John Gilbert's illness forced deferment, and Moths fluttered in, instead, to the extinguishment of those Lights; it ran through the evening of March 22nd. Charles H. Burnham, long connected with Wallack activities, had a benefit on March 20th, when were promised Bellew, Pounds, Edwards, D. H. Harkins, Federici, J. T. Powers, W. J. Ferguson, Nellie McHenry, John Jolly Nash, Elsie Cameron, Abramoff, and the Ruddygore orchestra. On March 24th, Wallack did, for him, an unusual thing—he produced an American play, David D. Lloyd's story of New York in the

[211]

time of the British occupancy, a rather dainty trifle entitled The Dominie's Daughter. Like Held by the Enemy, its theme concerned a girl of one belief in war (American) and two officers of the army in possession (British), one a brave gentleman, the other rather unscrupulous, and both in love with the sweet maid. When the dominie's son, of the revolutionary force, is caught hiding in his sister's room, both British officers assume he is the girl's lover, with demands by the baser of them as the price of his saving the refugee. Of course, since this was a comedy, all ended happily. The cast included the excellent Harry Edwards as the Reverend John Van Derveer, Kyrle Bellew as the fine Captain Dyke, Herbert Kelcey as Major Barton, Creston Clarke as young Robert Van Derveer, Groves as Hiram Brown, Miss Robe as the unhappy Molly Van Derveer, Mme. Ponisi as Aunt Kezia Beekman, Helen Russell as Dorothy Beekman, and Miss Blaisdell as Ann Stryker. This was the last new piece ever brought out by Lester Wallack, and one is pleased to find it a suitable though fragile ending to his long career. It ran through the evening of April 16th.

And still the stage harboured extraneous matter. On Sunday, March 27th, George Fawcett Rowe emerged from obscurity in A Picnic among the Crocodiles. A testimonial to Maze Edwards, on April 3rd, promised participation by Myra Goodwin, Lillian Conway, Adah Richmond, Louise Paullin, Jennie Yeamans, Amy Lee, Emma Carson, Vernona Jarbeau, Julie de Ryther (sic), Alice J. Shaw, F. de Belleville, Robert Hilliard, D. H. Harkins, and many more — a goodly array, if all appeared — and many of them did. And, on April 17th, Harry Edwards gave a matinée promising, as assistants, Clara Barton, Henrietta Maurer, Maze Edwards, F. Federici, Francis Walker, Carrie Coote, Osmond Tearle, Kyrle Bellew, Henry Vandenhoff, J. E. Kellerd, Harriet Webb, and many more. And Colonel Milliken's benefit on April 24th, offered Loie Fuller, Pat Rooney, &c. I may now return to normal, on Monday, April 18th, when John Gilbert, recovered from serious illness, at last appeared as Jesse Rural, in the delayed revival of Old Heads and Young Hearts. With him were Edwards, Bellew, Kelcey, Groves, Leeson, Creston Clarke, Annie Robe, Mme. Ponisi and Helen Russell. The last week at its own home of the famous organisation, as under the independent management of Wallack, came irrevocably with Old Heads and Young Hearts (May 2nd, 4th, 6th, and 7th, matinée) and The School for Scandal (evenings of May 3rd, 5th and 7th). On Saturday, May 7th, therefore, Lester Wallack left his theatre with a performance of the comedy that all to this very day (1941) most closely associate with its great fame.

On the afternoon of May 5th was acted a much discussed drama of Robert Louis Stevenson and W. E. Henley — Deacon Brodie, or the Double Life. In this, E. J. Henley, brother of the half-author, W. E. Henley, made a powerful impression as the devilish Brodie. The full cast:

[212]

Walter Leslie	Eben Plympton	Rivers	T. G. Patten
Deacon Brodie	E. J. Henley	Old Brodie	W. H. Pope
Ainslie	F. F. Mackay	Doctor	John Lewis
Moore	Charles Groves	Mary Brodie	Annie Robe
Hunt	Luke Martin	Jean Watt	Carrie Coote
Smith	Charles Coote	Mother Clarke	Ella Chudler
William Lawson	F. Everill	Servant	Florence Eber

This powerful play will re-appear in our annals. I will, in order to say good-bye to Wallack's Theatre under Wallack, carry the company to Daly's Theatre, where, on May 16th, they began two weeks in The Romance of a Poor Young Man. As if eulogising a famous corpse, I give the full cast:

Manuel	Kyrle Bellew	Louis	J. W. Totten
Dr. Desmarets	John Gilbert	Henri	S. DuBois
Bevannes	Henry Hamilton	Marguerite	Annie Robe
Laroque	E. J. Henley	Mme. Laroque	Mme. Ponisi
Yvonnet	Herbert Ayling	Mme. Aubrey	Fanny Addison
Nouret	W. H. Pope	Mlle. Helouin	Helen Russell
Alain	Charles Herbert	Louise	Miss E. Blaisdell
Francois	H. W. Perry	Christine	Carrie Elberts

The passing of Lester Wallack from the history was simply epochal. The last night of The Romance of a Poor Young Man (May 28th) might well be taken as the end of a brilliant era in the annals of the New York stage.

And what could more fittingly mark the treading of the new age on the departing era than what followed the now defunct stock company on the stage of Wallack's? According to Allston Brown, Wallack, on May 10th, transferred to Theodore Moss, so long connected with Wallack's Theatres, the lease of the house, for a period of ten years, at an annual rental of $10,000, Moss to pay all interest on mortgages, ground rents, taxes, assessments and water rents, until the expiration of the lease. Moss also was to have the right to keep the name "Wallack's Theatre," a right he soon abrogated. But what was the attraction under the new tenant? Well, one similar to that of previous years in summer. The McCaull Opera Company began, on May 9th, with a revival of The Black Hussar, the cast including Mathilde Cottrelly, Marion Manola, Celie Ellis, Hubert Wilke, De Wolf Hopper, Edwin W. Hoff, Alfred Klein, and Jefferson De Angelis, with De Novellis to direct the music. This pleasing show ended its run with two performances on Decoration Day, yielding the stage, on May 31st, to a revival of Falka, the cast composed of Cottrelly, Manola, Ellis, Grace Seavey, Wilke, Hopper, Harry Macdonough, De Angelis, Carl Irving and Alfred Klein, many of whom had figured in the opera at the Casino.

Admirers of this sturdy organisation may have been surprised to find it opening with two revivals, good though they were. A novelty came, on June 13th, in André Messager's opera, Jacquette, with Klein as the Duke of Parma, Marion Manola as Countess Bianca, Hopper as Chevalier Pomponio, Wilke as Perpignac, Carl Irving as Grabosson, Mme. Cottrelly as Jacquette,

[213]

Celie Ellis as Bettina, De Angelis as Girafo, Harry Macdonough as Cadet, and Grace Seavey as Carlo. Girls (pretty, I suppose) in small parts, were Tillie Frank, Leona Clarke, Rose Murallo, Louise Cox, and Annetta Hall. I fear this was a disappointment; it closed on July 2nd — a rare experience for McCaull and his popular artists.

What was wrong with the venture? On July 11th, the house re-opened, after a *relâche* of a week, with Indiana, sung during the season at the Star Theatre, and with Marion Manola, Laura Joyce, Digby Bell, John Brand and Jeff De Angelis in the leading rôles. The Beggar Student revived memories from July 25th. Evidently McCaull had been caught unprepared with novelties. On August 22nd, however, he gave Bellman, which had, earlier in the season, graced the German Thalia. In English, Wilke sang Carl Bellman, Hopper was Elvegaard, Macdonough was Otto Funk, C. W. Dungan Kolmodin, Jeff De Angelis Clausen, Laura Joyce Bell was Tronda and Marion Manola Countess Ulla; H. A. Cripps, Josie Knapp, and Carl Irving participated. Nowak directed. This carried through the closing night of the opera season, on October 8th. On October 11th, Henry E. Abbey began a stock season — the last with Wallack actors that Wallack's was ever to know. Times were indeed changing.

DALY'S THEATRE, 1886–1887

The regular actors of this, then the most popular theatre in America, had played very successfully in London and the English "provinces," and now returned for one of the most impressive seasons they and their manager ever experienced. Daly usually began the fall term with a comedy of no great importance, his sole purpose being, apparently, to re-introduce the company to their adoring public, and save for later productions what he hoped would be more memorable matter. This plan he carried out to perfection in 1886–87.

The opening comedy (October 5, 1886), adapted from the German of Blumenthal, Daly called After Business Hours, and leading members of the force had good parts:

Tommy Chipper	James Lewis	Mrs. Tommy Chipper	Mrs. G. H. Gilbert
Richard Brandegee	John Drew	Angelina Zipperoff	May Irwin
Septimus Trim	George Parkes	Mrs. Cline Kreesus	May Sylvie
Peter Raritan	Charles Fisher	Miss Breezie	Jean Gordon
Shoumoff	T. Patten	Doris Brandegee	Ada Rehan
Little Arabella	Nellie Liscomb		

One missed, on that first night, Virginia Dreher, Otis Skinner, Charles Leclercq (all to appear later in the season) and Edith Kingdon, who had recently married George Gould and retired from the stage. Perhaps Daly himself may have been surprised to find this piece running forty-eight times; its last performance fell on November 15th.

Its successor on that well-graced stage was a comedy adapted by Daly "from a new source," Albin Valabrégue's Bonheur Conjugal, which Daly named Love in Harness (he loved to get *Love* in his titles), and brought out on November 16th. This charming play, one of the delightful memories of my youth, presented in scenes of refinement and with beautiful up-to-date costumes for the ladies of the cast, almost the full strength of the company:

Julius Naggitt	James Lewis	Rhoda Naggitt	Virginia Dreher
Frederick Urquhart	John Drew	Jenny Joblots	Miss Hadley
Jeremiah Joblots	Charles Fisher	Antoinette	Jean Gordon
Charley Hoffman, M.D.	Otis Skinner	Myrtilla	Lizzie St. Quinten
Schlagg	William Gilbert	Susan	Grace Filkins
Keyes	Frederick Bond	Una	Ada Rehan
Mrs. Joblots	Mrs. G. H. Gilbert		

I wish I could reproduce for the reader some of my delight in that charming production; all I can do is to reproduce Sarony's photographs of a chief scene or two from the play. Fortunately that photographer has handed down to posterity all the scenes and characters of Daly's long career of success.

The last performance of Love in Harness (its seventy-third) occurred on January 17th. The following evening, Tuesday, January 18th (Daly was fond of first nights for Tuesdays) brought the most important production, thus far, in the manager's career. We have seen him gradually feeling his way toward productions of the classics (She Wou'd and She Wou'd Not, The Country Girl, The Recruiting Officer, and The Merry Wives of Windsor) and now we find him climaxing the series with the first performance in this city of the complete Taming of the Shrew, Induction and all. The cast must again be set down in full:

PROLOGUE

A Lord	George Clarke	Huntsmen	Patten, Ireton, Murphy
Christopher Sly	William Gilbert	Players	Bond, Wood, Miss Hadley
A Page	Master W. Collier	Hostess	May Sylvie

PERSONS IN THE COMEDY

Baptista	Charles Fisher	Grumio	James Lewis
Vincentio	John Moore	Nathaniel	Hamilton
Pedant	John Wood	Philip	Ireton
Lucentio	Otis Skinner	A Tailor	George Parkes
Petrucio	John Drew	Katharine	Ada Rehan
Gremio	Charles Leclercq	Bianca	Virginia Dreher
Hortensio	Joseph Holland	Widow	Jean Gordon
Tranio	Frederick Bond	Curtis	Mrs. G. H. Gilbert
Biondello	E. P. Wilks		

I need hardly inform the reader that this was the first appearance for many years with Daly of the once recalcitrant George Clarke; he now remained with that company till Daly's death in 1899. It was also the first appearance here of Joseph Holland, youngest son of the comedian, George Holland, of long ago at Wallack's. The reader observes that Daly gave the part of Curtis to a woman (Mrs. Gilbert) and, knowing that *ch* is pronounced *k* (and *c* like *tch*), in Italian, he carefully spelled the tamer of the shrew Petrucio.

The staging of the comedy (and Daly presented it as a comedy, not as a farce) was, for that time very magnificent, though 1941 might regard it as too realistic. A set of early Italian furniture, gilt with red damask upholstery, was imported for the interior scene in Baptista's house; the last scene was a gorgeous reproduction of a banquet, in the style of Paul Veronese, with Lizzie St. Quinten very prettily singing Bishop's Should He Upbraid, to the splendidly clad guests. Of course the acting was the chief allurement. Ada Rehan reached the peak of her fame in the rôle of Katharine; I believe I may say that her stormy entrance as the shrew, with her flaming red hair and her rich dress of superb mahogany-coloured damask, was the most magnificent stage-entry I have ever seen. And her change from shrew to loving wife was an exquisite bit of acting, placing Miss Rehan among the great artists in dramatic history. Probably this was her finest impersonation. John Drew's Petrucio (*sic*) was a worthy associate, and Miss Dreher, Skinner, Holland and Bond were delightful in the restored sub-plot of the wooing of Bianca. And little E. P. Wilks gave memorable help as Biondello.

Thus cast and thus staged, the restored Taming of the Shrew entered on a heartening run of one hundred and twenty-one performances, a proud record for that or any day. The only break in this starry record came in John L. Stoddard's usual Lenten morning lectures. This year he gave two separate series, Course B (March 8th, 15th, 18th, 23rd and 25th) merely repeating the talks and pictures of Course A (March 7th, 14th, 17th, 21st and 24th). The Shrew was tamed for the hundredth time, on April 13th. After the performance, at twelve o'clock, Daly gave a "little supper" of celebration, to some fifty guests, including the theatre company, General Sherman, Mark Twain (who made a speech), Lester Wallack (who also spoke), Elihu Vedder, Horace Howard Furness, William Winter, Bronson Howard, and many more. On March 18th and at the matinée on the 19th, Miss Rehan was out of the cast, Virginia Dreher playing Katharine and resigning Bianca to Jean Gordon. Miss Rehan returned on the 20th. On the afternoon of April 18th, for charity, Ada Rehan, Fisher, Drew and Skinner gave The Country Girl, Mrs. Gilbert, Lewis and others supplementing in A Woman's Won't. The Shrew was tamed for charity, on the afternoon of April 25th, and the glorious production reached its final (one hundred and twenty-first) performance on April 30th, ending what may have been Daly's most successful season, artistically and financially. As we know, the Wallack actors, forced to resign their own stage to the McCaull Opera Company, crossed the street to Daly's Theatre for a fortnight (May 16th–

FINAL SCENE IN THE TAMING OF THE SHREW
From a Photograph taken in Daly's Theatre, 1887

SCENE FROM LOVE IN HARNESS
Virginia Dreher, Charles Fisher, Mrs. Gilbert, Ada Rehan

28th) of The Romance of a Poor Young Man. The correspondence preceding this visit may be read in Judge Daly's life of his brother. The theatre remained closed from May 28th to October 5th; a brick proscenium wall, twenty-four inches thick, was, during the summer, built between stage and auditorium.

MADISON SQUARE THEATRE, 1886–1887

Held by the Enemy was a genuine success at the beautiful little Madison Square Theatre; we saw it produced there on August 16th, and may attend its last performance for the present on October 23rd. In early October a new act had been introduced, changing the setting from the tent to the house. The theatre was closed for the following week, re-opening on Monday, November 1st, with one of the greatest triumphs in the history of the New York stage. This was Sir Charles Young's very ingenious social drama, Jim, the Penman, dealing with the life of a forger who mingled with the "best" people and was finally identified by his wife, who realised that it was he who had separated her from an earlier lover, whom she meets years later, and who gives her the letters apparently written by her which had caused him to leave her and, indeed, England. Palmer cast the play to perfection from the ranks of his superb company (he had first tried it in the preceding summer in the Western trip of his actors):

James Ralston	Frederic Robinson	Mr. Netherby	H. Holliday
Louis Percival	H. M. Pitt	George	Herbert Millward
Baron Hartfeld	W. J. LeMoyne	John	Henry Hogan
Capain Redwood	E. M. Holland	Nina (Mrs. Ralston)	Agnes Booth
Lord Drelincourt	L. F. Massen	Agnes Ralston	Maud Harrison
Jack Ralston	Walden Ramsay	Lady Dunscombe	Mrs. E. J. Phillips
Mr. Chapstone	C. P. Flockton	Mrs. Netherby	May Robson
Dr. Pettywise	William Davidge		

I need not inform the reader that Mrs. Booth, as Mrs. Ralston, achieved one of the mighty successes of her splendid career. Throughout the earlier scenes she bore herself with the dignity of a woman of the world beset by perplexing problems; but in the scene of pantomime where she is reading and examining the letters she never wrote, her silent acting, with her successive thoughts mirrored in her face, was among the most notable bits of stage business I have ever witnessed. It became the talk of the town, rivalling in prestige Ada Rehan's great performance, later in the season, of Katharine. Those two were, to me, the outstanding features in the New York theatre for 1886–87. E. M. Holland, as the detective, Captain Redwood, always pretending to fall asleep in company, made a distinct hit that advanced him mightily in public estimation and in professional standing. I very much admired Maud Harrison and Walden Ramsay as the attractive young Ralstons and handed to LeMoyne a meed of praise for his masterly

[217]

portrait of the detestable crook, Hartfeld. Those were the finest performances in the play, but all the parts were well done. It was one of the triumphs of Palmer's career as a manager.

Jim, the Penman, ran steadily, except for two nights later to be noted, up to and including April 30th — six months in all. Its permanence allows us to chronicle ephemeral incidents of the season. Palmer had announced a series of special matinées for the trial of new plays by American authors — assuredly a commendable purpose. The first of these was offered on the afternoon of November 18th — a dramatisation by W. D. Howells of his novel, A Foregone Conclusion. The conviction of that time that a successful novelist could not write a good play was amply justified by this effort. The Times review asserts that one act of Jim, the Penman, was worth all five of the Howells drama, and I dare say, except for literary values, the Times was right. Palmer gave good support from his actors, including Alexander Salvini as Don Hippolito, the priest who falls in love with the lively American girl, Florida Vervain (Marie Burroughs), a fine impersonation of an unpleasing part. Louis F. Massen played Ferris, E. M. Holland John Billings, Mrs. Phillips was Mrs. Vervain and May Robson the Italian servant. Small parts fell to Herbert Millward and Marie Greenwald, neither of whom, so far as I know, ever was entrusted with a big part. But they also serve, etc.

Sidney Woollett, much admired, gave a series of six Monday morning readings or recitals, beginning on January 3rd, at 11:30. Elaine, on that poetic occasion, led the way to Guinevere (January 10th), The Passing of Arthur (17th), Philip Van Artevelde (24th), King John (31st) and The Tempest (February 7th). The second Author's Matinée (January 11th) presented a comedy by Brander Matthews, that devoted lover of the theatre. Dealing with the perplexities of a girl whose father was a gambler of ill repute, Margery's Lovers was declared by the Herald to be a success. Palmer cast it excellently:

Commodore Brevoort	C. P. Flockton	Mrs. Webster	Mrs. E. J. Phillips
Lieutenant Alden	Louis F. Massen	Bobby Webster	Walden Ramsay
Lewis Long	E. M. Holland	Sara Webster	Lena Langdon
William Blackwall	J. H. Stoddart	Count de Sarazue	Alexander Salvini
Margery Blackwall	Marie Burroughs	Sophie	Marie Greenwald

This play had some performances elsewhere, but Palmer never put it in his regular bills. Meantime, on January 13th and 14th (afternoons) a group of amateur players, whom we have met before and shall frequently meet again, came into the cozy little Madison Square, with a rather interesting programme, all, of course, in dear charity's name. In A Mouse Trap (could this be Howells's farce?) appeared Elsie Anderson De Wolfe (later a professional actress, before she became a decorator) and Edward Fales Coward, probably the best amateur actor of his day. The farce of Weeping Wives

[218]

WILLIAM GILBERT   CHARLES LECLERCQ   CHARLES FISHER

JOHN DREW   ADA REHAN   JOHN DREW

FREDERICK BOND   VIRGINIA DREHER   JOSEPH HOLLAND

SARONY'S PHOTOGRAPHS FROM THE TAMING OF THE SHREW

followed, with Mrs. Oliver Sumner Teall (a distinguished lady and a talented amateur), Alice Lawrence, Coward, Walden Ramsay (of the Madison Square), and W. F. Johnson.   Mrs. Charles Dennison (Mathilde Madison) then gave a monologue, and Courtenay Thorpe (of Miss Vokes's company) recited.   The cast of the concluding Tea at Four enlisted Mrs. Dennison, Lucie Coffey, Laura Sedgwick Collins, Alice Lawrence (a talented girl), Howard Martin, Alfred Young, Valentine G. Hall, Edward Fales Coward, Henry Gallup Paine, Courtenay Thorpe and Charles T. Thomas.   This is veritably a group from the Social Register.

The hundredth performance of Jim, the Penman, duly fell on February 7th.   Thence we skip a full month to Sidney Woollett's second series of recitals, on March 10th, 17th, 24th, and 31st, his choice ranging from Enoch Arden, The Northern Farmer and Elaine, through Hiawatha and The Courtship of Miles Standish, to shorter bits by George R. Sims, Burns (Tam O' Shanter), Adelaide Anne Proctor, Parnell and Oliver Goldsmith.   The world was young in 1887 and, perhaps, happier and better.   Professor Lanciani was down for a series of four lectures on Rome, beginning on March 25th, at 4 o'clock.   And George Fawcett Rowe was promised for the afternoon of March 16th, with A Picnic among the Crocodiles.   I failed to find details of this scheme; but lectures on foreign scenes were everywhere in New York in 1886–87.   On March 28th, Agnes Booth, ill, was out of the cast of Jim, the Penman, her understudy, Annie Mayer, having the difficult task of satisfying a disappointed audience.   On April 4th, both Mrs. Booth and Miss Mayer (or Mayor) were ill, and the manager, perforce, closed the theatre.   Caroline Hill (Mrs. Herbert Kelcey), who had played the part in the tour of the company during the preceding summer, haughtily refused to play it in the emergency that confronted the former manager of herself and Kelcey.   If Mr. Palmer wished her services, he should hire her for the season, indignantly proclaimed the lady.   Mrs. Booth returned to the cast on April 5th, but, on that night, LeMoyne was summarily dismissed from the company, apparently (according to the Herald of the 6th) because he had signed for next season with Daniel Frohman, for the Lyceum Theatre. LeMoyne indignantly told the Herald reporter that Palmer made no contracts with his actors; Stoddart, in his book, says the same thing, at least as regards his own association with the manager.

For April 14th was advertised a complimentary testimonial to Walt Whitman, who was to deliver his lecture on Abraham Lincoln; it was scheduled for the twenty-fifth anniversary of Lincoln's assassination.   On the 18th, Palmer took his company to Washington, to play Jim, the Penman, before President Cleveland and other dignitaries.   The receipt of $3,100 was given to the Actors' Fund.   On the evening of the 18th, Charles Roberts, Jr., read in the Madison Square J. H. McNoughton's Indian poem, Onnalinda.   This, of course, varied for the actors whatever tedium may have

[219]

accrued from the long run of Jim, the Penman. On the afternoon of April 25th, Miss Wickham was to read The Flight of the Duchess ("Browning's humorous poem") and The Statue and the Bust. Admission was to be at $2, with no reserved seats. The next Author's Matinée brought, on April 28th, a dramatisation by George Parsons Lathrop and Harry Edwards of Tennyson's then dearly loved Elaine:

King Arthur	H. M. Pitt	Dumb Servitor	C. P. Flockton
Sir Torre	L. F. Massen	Harper	H. Holliday
Lavaine	Walden Ramsay	Guinevere	Marie Burroughs
Gawain	Robert Hilliard	Elaine	Annie Russell
Launcelot	Alexander Salvini	Llanyd	May Robson
Friar	H. Millward	Roselle	Marie Greenwald
Lord of Astolat	Harry Edwards		

This, the only one of the tested authors' plays, reached the goal of a production in regular repertoire, but not till the next season. When I saw the play, in 1888, I felt that nothing could be sweeter or more poetic than Annie Russell's Lily Maid of Astolat, and nothing less regal than the Queen of pretty Marie Burroughs. Actors accustomed to prose do not readily pass to poetry. The run of Jim, the Penman, ended on April 30th. On May 2nd, Our Society, which had been so greatly enjoyed at the close of the preceding season, was revived, with Annie Russell, Maud Harrison, Mrs. Phillips, Virginia Buchanan, Marie Greenwald and Walden Ramsay in their original rôles; but E. H. Vanderfelt was now Philip Van Pelt (vice Herbert Kelcey), Frank Rodney was Reginald Rae, and Jennie Eustace (a very good actress) was Constance Gray. The charming comedy ran for four weeks, ending on May 28th.

The trial of plays at matinées became a veritable trial for our pen. On May 13th A Game of Chance (by Louis Ludovici, from the German) enlisted M. A. Kennedy, W. A. Clarke, J. H. Brown, H. A. Moray, Percy Williams, Alice Crowther, Mary Myers, Marion Russell and Adele Clarke —surely as undistinguished a group as ever trod that stage. The afternoon of May 19th gave us Selina Dolaro's play, Fashion, with Annie Robe as Dora, Mathilde Madison (Mrs. Dennison) as Adelaide Lapierre, Belle Archer (a rising young actress) as Marion, Eben Plympton as Captain Denalguez, John T. Sullivan as Philip Valnay, E. J. Henley as Baron Sarcey and Harry Edwards as M. Pierson—surely a very distinguished group. This was played at Wallack's, in the next season. And, on May 24th, Linda Dietz, who had been absent from our stage since 1879, attempted to re-establish herself in New York after a good career in the St. James's, the Haymarket and the Court Theatres, in London. Alas! she could not do it, and never, thereafter, did she win back the position she gave up when she departed from our shores.

She made her re-entrance in Fair Fame, Clinton Stuart's adaptation of Denise, a play by Dumas, which Clara Morris, two seasons earlier, had failed to make attractive. Miss Dietz was far from being an emotion. actress of the power that part required. The cast of Fair Fame:

Margaret Preston	Linda Dietz	Captain Farquhar	Frank Rodney
Mrs. Preston	Mrs. E. J. Phillips	John Preston	J. H. Fitzpatrick
Ada Dennison	Lilla Vane	Sir Thomas Dry	Rowland Buckstone
Lady Dry	Virginia Buchanan	Thompson	Harry Hogan
Lady Clara	Mathilde Madison	Lord Elsmore	E. H. Vanderfelt
Hugh Stanton	Walden Ramsay		

This performance ended the special matinées for 1886–87; one sees that the output had hardly warranted the labour entailed. One pities Mrs. Phillips, Mathilde Madison, Miss Buchanan, Walden Ramsay and Vanderfelt for the hard work they had been called on to do. I regret to say that Allston Brown lists Fair Fame a year late, assigning it to May 24, 1888.

RICHARD MANSFIELD

The Palmer actors closed their season on May 28th, and, on Monday, May 30th, the rising Richard Mansfield, who, in 1886, had played a long summer engagement at the Madison Square, returned for a similar venture in 1887. He began, on May 30th, in his successful Prince Karl, with a support including the veteran Clara Fisher Maeder (the lovely Clara Fisher of 1827), Johnstone Bennett, Anne O'Neill (her first appearance on any stage), Beatrice Cameron (one day to be Mrs. Mansfield), Joseph Frankau, Cyril Scott (a delightful light comedian), John Parry, Harry Gwynette and Charles Eldridge. The five hundredth performance of Prince Karl (in the week of June 13th–18th) found the little theatre decorated with ferns and flowers. Starting on that flowery path, the lively play ran till, on July 11th, Mansfield presented a piece by himself, entitled Monsieur, in which he acted a starving musician, who fainted from hunger in performing his duties. Mansfield in those days could do such things perfectly and his Monsieur lightly carried through the hot nights of summer, with this cast:

Alice	Beatrice Cameron	Ezra J. Golden	D. H. Harkins
Mrs. Golden	Josephine Laurens	Morton Saunders	Joseph Frankau
Mrs. Pettigrew	Anne O'Neill	Popples	Harry Gwynette
Mrs. Morton	Helen Glidden	Mount Vernon	John Parry
Sally	Johnstone Bennett	André R. M. de Jadot	Richard Mansfield
Tom Vanderhuysen	J. T. Sullivan		

The sensation of Mansfield's season came on September 12th, when he brought out T. R. Sullivan's dramatisation of the then widely-read Dr. Jekyll and Mr. Hyde of Robert Louis Stevenson — a piece brought out, the spring before, in Boston. Mansfield's changes from one character to the other were almost instantaneous, and, in the last act, with Jekyll turning in horror from the fate he had brought on himself, Mansfield's acting reached a height of tragic melodramatic intensity that I have seldom, if ever, seen equalled. No other actor of his time could have approached him in the part. The first

[221]

appearance of Hyde, looking through the open French window, in genuine green stage moonlight, was the most horrible thing I ever saw. It left me limp, and the entire play so worked on my sensibilities that I was actually afraid to go home in the dark; and so was everybody who saw the play. Mansfield introduced into the story Dr. Jekyll's love for Agnes Carew (who does not appear in the original story) and that love made all the more frightful Hyde's appearance at the window, intent on violating the girl. The supporting cast included John T. Sullivan as Gabriel Utterson, D. H. Harkins as Dr. Lanyon, H. B. Bradley as General Sir Danvers Carew, C. E. Eldridge as Inspector Newcomen, Harry Gwynette as Poole, Thomas Goodwin as Jarvis, Katherine Rogers as Mrs. Lanyon, Helen Glidden as Rebecca Moor, and Beatrice Cameron as Agnes Carew. The gruesome, fascinating horror ran till October 1st, and established Mansfield in the front rank of actors. On October 3rd, the regular Madison Square Company returned in a revival of Jim, the Penman.

LYCEUM THEATRE, 1886–1887

We all kept an appraising eye, at that time, on the beautiful little Lyceum Theatre, as if, prophetically, we foresaw its glory in the decade of the '90s. It re-opened, on Saturday evening, September 18, 1886, with The Main Line, or Rawson's Y, an Idyl of the Railroad, by Henry C. De Mille (whose fame was then beginning) and Charles Barnard (whose fame in the theatre hardly ever began):

Lawrence Hatton	J. B. Mason	Sam Burroughs	Henry C. De Mille
Colonel Hatton	Charles Overton	Prairie Flower	Dora Stuart
Zerubbabel Puddychump	F. F. Mackay	Dora Van Tyne	Lillian Richardson
Addington Spline	Raymond Holmes	Positive Burroughs	Etta Hawkins
Jim Blakely	Ralph Delmore		

The names of some of the characters indicate an eye theatrical, rather than an eye on the object, but good actors were in the cast, though the women, except for the comic Etta Hawkins, produce in me no thrill in the seat where memory sits enthroned. The play ran through October 16th, and lived, through the season, in the "combination" houses. W. H. Crompton, engaged for the part of Burroughs, was prevented by illness from appearing on the opening night; Henry C. De Mille replaced him. Crompton soon returned to the cast.

MISS FORTESCUE, HELEN DAUVRAY

The more important autumn term began on Monday, October 18th, with the New York début of May Fortescue, a rather pretty English girl who had become known to some Americans through her breach of promise suit, in 1885, against Lord Garmoyle. She began, here, in the first production we had seen of W. S. Gilbert's play of Gretchen. As the deceived and suffering

Below.
AGNES
BOOTH

MAUD HARRISON
L. F. MASSEN—W. RAMSAY

W. J. LE MOYNE AND
F. ROBINSON

GROUP FROM THE FIRST ACT
Standing: C. P. Flockton, L. F. Massen, F. Robinson, H. Holliday
Sitting: Walden Ramsay, Mrs. Phillips, May Robson, E. M. Holland, Agnes Booth,
Davidge, Pitt
SCENES FROM JIM, THE PENMAN, 1886-1887

Gretchen her support included Frederick Terry (brother of the great Ellen) as Faustus, Charles Sugden as Mephisto, Charles Overton as Gottfried, W. H. Crompton as Anselm, John Findlay as Dominic, J. B. Booth, Jr. (son of Agnes Booth) as Friedrich, Kate Hodson (a good actress) as Martha, Helen Fortescue (sister of the star) as Lisa, Marie Floyd as Agatha, Lillian Billings as Bessie and Grace Hall as Barbara.

Something kept this venture afloat for three weeks — perhaps curiosity to see the fair litigant had its effect in audience-building. On November 8th, however, Miss Fortescue, whose face somehow fitted the part, appeared as Gilberte, the thoughtless wife, in Frou-Frou. My reader could, almost blind-folded, assign the characters among the star's assistants: Sugden as de Sartorys, Fred Terry as de Valreas, Crompton as Brigard, and Kate Hodson as Baroness de Cambri. The rest of the cast was not imposing for playgoers with memories: John Findlay as Baron de Cambri, Hardy Vernon as Pitou, Grace Hall as Pauline, and Alice Crowther as Louise. Frou-Frou also yielded a run of three weeks, and, on November 29th, the young actress began her final week with a production of King René's Daughter and Gilbert's ever-welcome Sweethearts. In the former play, she was, of course, the blind Iolanthe, with Terry as Count Tristan, Crompton as King René, Kate Hodson as Martha, Hardy Vernon as Sir Geoffrey, Charles Overton as Eben Yahia, John Findlay as Sir Almeric, &c. Charles Sugden, Findlay and Miss Fortescue played the leading parts in Sweethearts. This bill carried through a week — Miss Fortescue's last in the annals of the New York stage. She left the city for a tour of other cities, telling the Herald reporter that she was proud to have filled a longer consecutive engagement in the metropolis than had any other English star. After all, that was a feat.

On Sunday, November 28th, Dr. Baralt illustrated Masterpieces of Ancient and Modern Art; on December 5th, Beauties of Art and Nature. The stereopticon was everywhere in evidence. The Lyceum closed on December 6th, and revived, on Tuesday, the 7th, One of Our Girls, with Miss Dauvray, Ida Vernon, Enid Leslie, E. H. Sothern, George F. DeVere, and J. W. Pigott in their former rôles. Joseph E. Whiting succeeded Louis James as Dr. Girodet, and J. G. Saville replaced F. F. Mackay as the icy Comte de Crebillon. Other parts fell to Frank Rodney, as Henri, William Payson as Pierre, and Gus Brooke as André. Evidently One of Our Girls had run its course. It was succeeded, on December 20th, by that specialty of Wallack's Theatre, A Scrap of Paper, with, I fear, a cast not quite the equal of Wallack's in 1879:

Prosper Couramont	E. H. Sothern	Louise de la Glacière	Ellie Wilton
Baron de la Glacière	J. E. Whiting	Mathilde	Enid Leslie
Brismouche	J. W. Pigott	Mlle. Zenobie	Emma Skerrett
Anatole	Rowland Buckstone	Mme. Dupont	Clara Douglas
Baptiste	William Payson	Pauline	Nadage Dorée
François	Gus V. Brooke	Suzanne	Helen Dauvray

[223]

I am pleased to find Ellie Wilton in that aggregation, and surprised, as usual, to meet once more Emma Skerrett, who had come out at the old Park Theatre, more than forty years previously. Time spares or takes away as it will. The William Payson of this and following casts was William Payson MacKaye, son of Steele MacKaye; he died very young.

The Lyceum became a favourite haven for those really good amateurs who, at this time, acted for charity (of course, and not for personal glory!) in those dear old days of the '8os. On January 6th they came to this theatre with Sugar and Cream (acted by Alice and Rita Lawrence, Edward Fales Coward and Valentine G. Hall — possibly the sugar and cream of the group); two scenes from The Hunchback, with Elsie Anderson De Wolfe as Helen, and Edward Fales Coward as Modus; and Delicate Ground, with Coward (how good he was!), W. F. Johnson and Mary R. Perkins. Beginning on January 4th, Sarah Cowell, once inconspicuous in the Union Square Theatre and later to be famous as a reciter of Browning's poetry, advertised for the Lyceum a series of four Tuesday afternoons, beginning a fine career; her programmes were miscellaneous and far below the austerity of her Browning days. And may I anticipate by saying that Hjalmar H. Boyesen, then a well-known novelist and a Professor of German, in Columbia College, lectured at the Lyceum on Byron (March 8th), Keats (14th), Browning (21st), and Swinburne and Late Lyrists (28th)?

Playgoers had been anxiously awaiting what was expected to be the crowning event of Miss Dauvray's season and a leading feature of the New York season as a whole. After the great acclaim in 1885–86 of Bronson Howard's One of Our Girls, it was only to be expected that his new play would achieve something of the same success. In that hope Miss Dauvray had commissioned him to write a play for her theatre, and much preliminary announcement had awakened the eager curiosity of playgoers. After unforeseen delay, the comedy was produced on Tuesday, January 11, 1887, and achieved one of the most disastrous failures in theatrical history. Miss Dauvray had provided a beautiful woodland setting, with real waterfall (had she noted the similar scene in The Rajah?), a violent thunder shower, and, of course, appropriate interior sets in the Adirondack region. The audience, all expectancy at first, finally sat in limp boredom, as the play progressed. The Herald, next day, ruthlessly asserted that "the best thing Miss Dauvray can do for 'Met by Chance' is to take it off for a certainty." When she "gave Mr. Bronson Howard an order for a new play she bought a pig in a poke with a vengeance." History requires that I record the cast of Met by Chance that met with such extreme mischance:

Dr. Harrington Lee	E. H. Sothern	Wilson	William Payson
Edward Dudley Talford	F. Rodney	Hope Rutherford	Ellie Wilton
Dudley Bretton	J. G. Saville	Lucy Rutherford	Enid Leslie
Charlie Hartwell	J. W. Pigott	Aunt Mary Hartwell	Emma Skerrett
Macdonald	J. E. Whiting	Stella Van Dyke	Helen Dauvray

[224]

The last performance of this ghastly failure occurred on January 29th. One must pity the plight of the ambitious, brave Miss Dauvray; one also wonders if a success for Met by Chance might have established her with some degree of permanence in the New York theatre. I fear, however, it settled whatever aspirations she may have had in that direction. As soon as possible she got ready Charles Reade and Tom Taylor's always welcome Masks and Faces, which she produced, on January 31st, with this cast:

Sir Charles Pomander	J. E. Whiting	Lysimachus	Daisy Dean
Ernest Vane	E. H. Sothern	Pompey	Master Stevens
Colley Cibber	Joseph Wilkes	Call Boy	Master Brown
Triplet	John Howson	Mrs. Vane	Ellie Wilton
Quin	George F. DeVere	Kitty Clive	Enid Leslie
Snarl	J. G. Saville	Mrs. Triplet	Isabella Preston
Soaper	Frank Rodney	Maid	Miss Bertie
Burdock	William Payson	Roxalana	Bijou Fernandez
Colander	Walter Osmond	Peg Woffington	Helen Dauvray
Hunsden	G. V. Brooke		

Miss Dauvray should have been a good Woffington, though not so exuberant, joyous and finally affecting, as the beautiful Rose Coghlan, who, on February 7th, played it at the Union Square Theatre.

Miss Dauvray carried the charming comedy through March 5th, with what public response I cannot say. On March 7th she tried anew with Walda Lamar, in which she played a fiery Russian actress, called on to make a final sacrifice; it had, quoth the Herald, "bits like Article 47 and Camille." I must, for completeness of detail, quote the cast:

Paul de St. Germain	A. Salvini	Romanville	J. W. Pigott
André de Latour	E. H. Sothern	Joseph	Gus Brooke
Count de Valdaure	J. E. Whiting	Adèle Regnier	Adeline Stanhope
Chevalier de Monval	J. G. Saville	Duchesse de St. Germain	Ida Vernon
Vladimir	William Payson	Louise de Valdaure	Enid Leslie
Richard	G. B. Clayton	Mme. de San Die	Percy Haswell
M. Lecocq	George F. DeVere	Blanche	Carrie Lewis
Dr. Varney	Lin Hurst	Justine	Nadage Dorée
Baron von Rosenfeld	James Bell	Walda Lamar	Helen Dauvray

We pass to special features of the Lyceum season. Backward to February 10th (afternoon) we cast an eye and an ear to a reading by Courtenay Thorpe, whom some people admired. The New York School of Acting, including Laura Sedgwick Collins, Elsie Lombard, W. C. Bellows and Vida Croly, performed on the afternoon of March 23rd what was announced as "the first time in America" of Les Précieuses Ridicules; I wonder? The pupils also showed their genius in scenes from airy trifles like Adrienne Lecouvreur and Leah, the Forsaken; what will aspiring youth not attempt? I will follow this query by bringing forward a matinée, on April 15th, of those amateurs whose work we are assaying in these, our annals. After a performance, on that gala 15th, of Brander Matthews's This Picture and That, with Mathilde Madison, Henry Miller and Joseph Brennan, they acted

[225]

Two Strings to Her Bow (adapted by Mrs. Burton Harrison from the French); in it appeared Henry Gallup Paine, Ada Webster Ward, Alice Lawrence, Edward Fales Coward, Alfred Young and Harold Harrison, under direction of the youthful David Belasco. This combination causes us to think once again of the dear old days.

Helen Dauvray's stellar journey closed with The Love Chase, that once popular device of Sheridan Knowles. Her Constance was praised by the critics and must indeed have had something of the elegance once imparted to the rôle by actresses like Mrs. Hoey and Laura Keene. But I am sure that young Sothern's Wildrake could have effaced no memories of Lester Wallack. Of course such parts died with Wallack. The support in The Love Chase, on April 11th, included J. E. Whiting as Trueworth, Frank Rodney as Waller, Charles Wheatleigh as Sir William, William Payson as Neville, Ida Vernon as the Widow Green, Adeline Stanhope as Lydia and Percy Haswell as Phœbe. Are these Lyceum nights our first acquaintance with the charming Miss Haswell? When The Love Chase ended its run on April 30th, Miss Dauvray left the Lyceum forever, and Daniel Frohman picked up the reins for a brilliant career of management that was not to close for considerably more than a decade.

He began, on Tuesday, May 3rd, with E. H. Sothern (practically a star) in The Highest Bidder, a farcical comedy which the skillful Maddison Morton had put together for E. A. Sothern, who had never acted it. Its first cast here is interesting as showing the beginning of Frohman's companies soon to flower for years thereafter either in support of E. H. Sothern or as the resident stock company of the winter season in the theatre:

Lawrence Thornhill	J. W. Pigott	Parkyn	W. A. Faversham
Bonham Cheviot	W. J. LeMoyne	Sergeant Downey	W. Payson
Sir Muffin Struggles	Rowland Buckstone	Bill	Maurice Clyde
Sir Evelyn Graine	Herbert Archer	Rose Thornhill	Belle Archer
Joseph	Walter Bellows	Mrs. Honiton Lacy	Alice Crowther
Jack Hammerton	E. H. Sothern	Louise	Vida Croly

Verily the new generation was knocking at the stage-door, and the Lyceum readily opened to their signal. Percy Haswell, Belle and Herbert Archer and William Faversham are here shown in their beginnings; Vida Croly was daughter of the then well-known "Jennie June," but candour forces the statement that she never reached any heights in stage-history. The Highest Bidder was delightful, with Sothern in his usual mood of perturbed perplexity, making love (the turnstile scene with Belle Archer was charming), foiling villainy (in person of Herbert Archer), befriended by the unctuous Cheviot of LeMoyne, and triumphing in the hilarious auction scene that his inherited business forced him to carry on. LeMoyne, we see, had, after his ejection from the Madison Square Theatre, found at the Lyceum a haven from which, for several years, he was not to wander at all. And most perfect

FRED TERRY

MISS FORTESCUE

CHARLES SUGDEN

ANNE O'NEILL

RICHARD MANSFIELD
(JEKYLL AND HYDE)

JOSEPHINE LAURENS

ALEXANDER SALVINI
AND HELEN DAUVRAY
(WALDA LAMAR)

ENID LESLIE

EDWARD H. SOTHERN
AS WILDRAKE
(THE LOVE CHASE)

he was in The Highest Bidder; his part might have been written for him. Allston Brown states that Pigott, on July 9th, retired from the cast, Arthur Elliott taking up his rôle on the 11th. The Highest Bidder closed for a few weeks during the heat of summer (July 18th–August 20th), but resumed on August 22nd. Long before that a benefit (May 13th) to Mlle. Malvina, teacher of dancing, provided the New York School of Acting in The Cape Mail, with Grace Kimball, Laura Collins, Alice Ferris, and E. P. Stevenson; the turnstile scene from The Highest Bidder; and The Circus Rider, with William Payson, Cyril Scott and Elita Proctor Otis. William Payson (MacKaye) had figured in all the Lyceum bills since Miss Dauvray began her season in December.

I close the Lyceum record for 1886–87 with account of a benefit, for Bijou Fernandez, on the afternoon of June 7th, when was given something that sounds remote from that stage — Peggy, the Fisherman's Child; and the cast also sounds remote from our recognition — S. Miller Kent, Henry Holland, Marion Russell (Annie's pretty but not very interesting sister), Helen Windsor, Marion Erle, John Germon, Joseph Conyers and Harry Mack. Who in the world are they? 1887 might have asked, though we today (1941) could identify the first three.

STAR THEATRE, 1886–1887

With the Lyceum, I close the account of the four most interesting theatres in New York of that season — the homes of splendid stock companies. I pass thence to what had once been the leading "stock" theatre of America — Wallack's, at Thirteenth Street — and had now, as the Star Theatre, become the leading haven in New York for visiting stars and "combinations." Its array of stars across the theatrical heavens of the autumn of 1886 was most impressive, nay, let us admit it, brilliant.

After a fortnight of Lester and Allen's Minstrels, closing on August 21st, Lawrence Barrett, our most ambitious classicist, began the inspiring procession, on August 30th, with Yorick's Love, which he repeated on the 31st, September 1st, and at the matinée on September 4th, with, as usual with him, a good support. As Yorick his assistants were Minna K. Gale as Alice, Miriam O'Leary as Dorothy, Newton Gotthold as Master Heyward, Charles B. Welles as Edmund, S. E. Springer as Master Walton, Charles M. Collins as Master Woodford, and the reliable Ben G. Rogers as Gregory. Richelieu (September 2nd), Hamlet (3rd) and Julius Cæsar (evening of the 4th) completed his first week. In these plays new actors were Frederick Vroom, C. S. Abbe, and Minnie Monk. The second week involved the moving Francesca da Rimini (September 6th and 7th, and matinée, 11th), Hamlet (which Barrett could never refrain from playing, 8th), Richelieu (which also obsessed him, 9th), and The Merchant of Venice and David Garrick (evenings

[227]

of the 10th and 11th). His deeply affecting performance of Harebell re-emerged on the 13th, 14th, 15th, and 16th, (with a matinée on the 18th); Yorick's Love and David Garrick made a new combination for the 17th; and Richard III, with which one does not associate Barrett, came on Saturday evening, September 18th. The fourth week advanced with Richelieu (20th); The Merchant of Venice and The King's Pleasure (21st); Francesca da Rimini (22nd, and matinée, 25th); Julius Cæsar (23rd); Hamlet (24th); and, to close a very interesting, and, I hope, profitable engagement, Yorick's Love and David Garrick (evening of the 25th). In reading such a repertoire, one cannot but highly respect Barrett, the nearest approach this country had, in catholicity of dramas and in careful production, to Henry Irving, in England. And American authors of repute — Howells and Boker — were in his list.

Genevieve Ward; Wilson Barrett

Another American player, but mostly resident abroad, followed Barrett, on September 27th, at the Star. This was Genevieve Ward, who never seemed quite to capture the admiration of her fellow-countrymen; perhaps a hard, if technically efficient style and personality detracted from her charm. She presented herself, on September 27th, in Sydney Grundy's adaptation of Scribe's Un Verre d'Eau, which he called The Queen's Favourite. Miss Ward, of course, played the Duchess of Marlborough, with W. H. Vernon, fresh from England, as Henry St. John, D. G. English as Masham, John Wilks as De Torcy, Percy Winter as an Officer, Gertrude Kellogg as Queen Anne, and Eleanor Tyndale (*vox et praeterea nihil* in our record) as Abigail. The critics praised this effort of Miss Ward, but the public did not wildly flock to see it. A week sufficed for that glass (I fear) of water, and, on October 4th, Miss Ward reverted to the rôle with which her later fame is associated — Stéphanie de Mohrivart, in Forget-Me-Not, assisted, of course, by Vernon as Sir Horace Welby, English as Barrato, J. W. Summers as Prince Maleotti, Miss Tyndale as Alice Verney, and Miss Kellogg as Mrs. Foley. After a week of this, Miss Ward departed for a tour of the open spaces. What had happened to bring back this distinguished American for a bare fortnight?

A pretentious, very pseudo-classic thing followed, on October 11th, in a play by W. G. Wills (usually a good playwright) and Henry Herman (known as a constructor of melodrama). Claudian, their joint handiwork, had won success in London, largely because of its scenery and spectacular effects, and Wilson Barrett, an athletic and rather handsome actor, who had made his way up from The Silver King to a much discussed Hamlet (discussed because it was so different and, if the truth must be whispered, so *queer*) had achieved in its chief rôle undisputed stardom. Naturally, with an eye to Irving's success in America, he came hither to show us the splendours of his Claudian,

[228]

both play and part. He opened at a top price of $2 in orchestra and front balcony, and found that it did not pay. Claudian, a native of long, long ago, in a country where they wore pretty oriental clothes, was, in the prologue of the play, a very sad, bad rogue, who wickedly pursued maidens, and, as it happened, killed a holy hermit, who cursed him with immortality and a power to possess any wish of his heart, that wish invariably plunging him into uttermost woe. Barrett brought with him a regiment of players, and this was the cast of Claudian:

PROLOGUE

Claudian Andiates............Wilson Barrett	Symachus.....................S. M. Carson
Holy Clement................Charles Fulton	Seriphon......................W. A. Elliott
Theorus...................H. Cooper Cliffe	Demos..........................H. Evans
Zosimus........................H. Bernage	Sorana......................Alice Belmore
Volpas.....................Langley Russell	Caris.......................Evelyn Howard
Captain of the Scythians............Aubrey	

CHARACTERS IN THE PLAY

Claudian....................Wilson Barrett	Rhadamantes........................Warren
Almida.......................Miss Eastlake	Edessa......................Lily Belmore
Alcares.....................Austin Melford	Threna.....................Miss Medway
Belos......................George Barrett	Clia.......................Miss Thompson
Thareogalus.................Charles Hudson	Galena........................Alice Cooke
Agazil........................J. H. Clynds	Hera..........................Lila Garth

In very minor rôles were utilised G. Maxwell, Howard, Belton, Miss Woode, Miss Wilde and Mr. Percyval. The papers spoke of some hissing on the first two nights because Charles Hudson seemed to be ridiculing, in voice, manner and gait, the mannerisms of Henry Irving. A later item in the Herald told us that the actor, without offence, had comported himself in London in exactly the same way. That difficulty smoothed away, Claudian went its allotted course, astonishing by its great scene of an earthquake, which tumbled down buildings and columns in indiscriminate ruin, though the Herald says that the audience plainly saw the wires that let down those props of the solidly constructed masonry. The same paper calls the play tiresome and declares that Barrett, though "a large, well-built man with heavy features" and looking his part, "failed to make a strong, artistic impression." His voice was "monotonous." And Miss Eastlake, who had been acclaimed, was certainly no Ellen Terry. And, finally, according to Allston Brown, the vaunted earthquake was not so good as that recently seen at Niblo's in Clio. As a youth, I saw this Claudian, and was impressed. A few years later Barrett, in other parts, made on me no impression whatever. A matinée of Claudian was given, on October 20th, for the sufferers from the Charleston earthquake — earthquake to earthquake, as it were. The three-weeks engagement closed on October 30th. For the matinée, on October 23rd, Barrett presented a triple bill of Chatterton, A Clerical Error (by Henry Arthur Jones) and The Colour Sergeant.

[229]

Booth; Jefferson; Robert Downing

The great Edwin Booth returned, on November 1st, in his favourite Hamlet. With him were Charles Barron as the Ghost, and, as I remember, a very sepulchral, hollow-voiced spirit, Emma Vaders as a colourless Ophelia, Carl Ahrendt as Polonius, John T. Malone as the King, Augusta Foster as the Queen, Charles B. Hanford as Horatio, John T. Sullivan as Laertes and C. S. Abbe as Osric. On Saturday evening, November 6th, before a crowded house, we had The Fool's Revenge. This play was repeated on Monday, November 8th, but illness prevented Booth's appearing again till November 15th, when he re-emerged as Iago (one of his less vigorous rôles) for three nights; and for the matinée, on the 20th; Richelieu finished that week (November 18th, 19th, 20th). The last week of this engagement offered Hamlet (November 22nd, 25th, and matinée, 27th); Iago (Thanksgiving matinée, 25th); The Fool's Revenge (23rd and 26th); The Merchant of Venice and Katharine and Petruchio (24th and evening, 27th). I then saw Booth for the first times in my life, as Hamlet, Richelieu and Bertuccio; I still retain vivid pictures of his magnificent art, and that, too, despite the general inadequacy of his support. Who could forget the high lights of his Hamlet, the threat to launch the curse of Rome, in Richelieu, or the marvellous dance of the tragic Bertuccio? and the beautiful voice and superb reading?

He was followed at the Star by the most finished, the most natural comedian I have seen — Joseph Jefferson. This great artist appeared, on November 29th, as Rip Van Winkle, supported by George W. Denham, Edwin Varrey, W. A. Whitecar, Lin Hurst, Lizzie Hudson (a charming actress, in the not very charming rôle of Gretchen), May Wolcott (also very sweet) and Dora Leslie. This famous thing I then saw during that season at the Star; also the double bill which followed it, on December 13th — The Cricket on the Hearth and Lend Me Five Shillings, with Jefferson, of course, in his matchless renditions of Caleb Plummer and Mr. Golightly. In the former of these comedies the support included Lizzie Hudson as Bertha, May Wolcott as Dot, George W. Denham as Tackleton, and Jefferson's sister, Cornelia Jackson, as a marvellous Tilly Slowboy. I can never forget her extraordinary performance, or the humour and pathos of Jefferson's Caleb.

On December 20th, something less perfect arrived, in person of Robert Downing, who brought the Forrestian tradition in Forrest's favourite play of The Gladiator. In support of his Spartacus, Downing proffered Henry Aveling as Phasarius, Frank Lane as Crassus, Mittens Willett as Senona, Gail Forrest as Julia, and brawny William Muldoon as the Fighting Gaul. John Swinbourne, Charles Nevins, Royal Roche and L. A. Wagenhals also participated. Spartacus fought his way for two weeks, and yielded the stage, on January 3rd to Lillian Olcott, who carried northward the elaborately

[230]

spectacular Theodora, which she had proudly exhibited, during the autumn, at Niblo's. She remained two weeks. On the afternoon of January 13th came a benefit to John Howson, at which were to appear Nat Goodwin, in an act of Turned Up; Francis Wilson and Mark Smith, in a scene from Erminie; Michael Banner, in a violin solo; John Wild, some Sioux Indians, Alexander Salvini (in an assaut d'armes with Senac), Willis Sweatnam, Charles Roberts, Jr., in specialties; Fred Warde, in a scene from Virginius; and a new play, The Violin Maker of Cremona, in which appeared Howson, Hudson Liston, Marie Jansen and J. H. Gilmour — verily a rich offering. Miss Olcott left the house on January 15th.

We are conscious of waning interest in the offerings of the next few weeks at a theatre which began the season with such promise. John A. McCaull's Opera Company, of which I admit I am somewhat tired, entered the house, on January 17th, with Indiana, a new work by H. B. Farnie, with music by Audran. Leading rôles fell to Lilly Post as Indiana, Laura Joyce Bell as Lady Prue, Annie Meyers (sic) as Nan, Adine Drew as Maud, Digby Bell as Matt o' the Mill, George Olmi as Lord Dayrell, Edwin Hoff as Philip Jervaux, Ellis Ryse as Sir Mulberry Mullet, and H. A. Cripps as Peter. I doubt if it was any better than it sounds; it remained for three weeks. A charity benefit, on Sunday, January 30th, promised Harry Edwards, Kyrle Bellew, E. J. Henley, Cottrelly, Oudin, Mrs. Edwin Hoff, Laura Joyce, De Wolf Hopper, Digby Bell, Louise Parker Oudin, Marshall Wilder, Marie Jansen, &c. On February 7th, Salsbury's Troubadours gave The Humming Bird:

Mr. Joseph Brass	Nate Salsbury	Sally Styles	Nellie McHenry
Augustus Honeymoon	George Backus	Mrs. Honeymoon	Leonora Bradley
Robert Rackett	John Webster	Matilda Fullalove	Marie Bockel
Jerry McLaughlin	F. B. Blair	Biddy	Emma Gilbert
The Tramp	F. Bowman		

The merry band got three weeks out of this nonsense. And we passed from this winter era of unimportant things with Lorraine, which the ever-recurrent McCaull's Opera Comique Company presented, on February 28th, with a cast including Mathilde Cottrelly, Gertrude Griswold, Alida Varena, Emily Soldene (imagine!), Josephine Knapp, Perugini, De Wolf Hopper, G. Olmi, Herndon Morsell, Harry Standish, and others. Adolf Neuendorff conducted. After all, this is not the McCaull group lately seen in Indiana. On March 3rd, according to Allston Brown, Perugini, ill, surrendered his rôle to Herndon Morsell; Gertrude Griswold, also ill, had given her part to Josephine Knapp. Despite this ill fortune, Lorraine carried on through March 12th. The libretto was by W. J. Henderson, the score by Dellinger.

SARAH BERNHARDT; WILSON BARRETT; DION BOUCICAULT

The house resumed its accustomed dignity on March 14th, when, after an absence of six years, Sarah Bernhardt, most famous actress of her time, came forth in the part that Sardou had written for her — the fiery, ill-fated Fedora. With her were Philippe Garnier as Loris, Angelo (who had been her leading man here in 1880–81) as de Siriex, Mlle. Malvau as Olga, and, in other rôles, Mme. Vallot, Mme. Fontanges, Fraisier and Fornier. I seem to have seen many things, that season, at the Star Theatre. Certainly, even as a sophomore at Columbia College, I could not have been foolish enough to miss this Fedora. Who could ever forget the wail that swept through the theatre when Bernhardt's Fedora realised that her lover had died, behind those closed doors? And the golden voice and the tragic intensity of the succeeding scenes! Yet the Herald felt a lack of perfect simplicity that marks great art. Fedora was given throughout the week, except on the 17th, when Frou-Frou replaced it, and, on the evening of the 19th, when La Dame aux Camélias again became very French and very tragic. The second week of the engagement proffered Le Maître de Forges (21st and 26th), Fedora (March 22nd, 25th, 26th), Frou-Frou (23rd), Adrienne Lecouvreur (24th), and La Dame aux Camélias (matinée, 26th). The third week (March 28th–April 2nd) was devoted entirely to the sensational Théodora, which proved conclusively that these Sardou horrors demanded for their perfect representation the perfect art and the fiery outbursts of the matchless Bernhardt. Yet Fanny Davenport, acting that week at the Grand Opera House dared to give a special matinée of her Fedora for the supreme Bernhardt, who promised to attend! Bernhardt gave a special matinée of Théodora, on March 31st.

With this brilliant engagement ended, the Star opened, on April 4th, for Wilson Barrett's much-discussed Hamlet, with its odd readings, its attempt to make Hamlet and his mother very youthful, and with a re-arranged text. His melancholy Dane was associated with the King of Charles Hudson, the Ghost of J. H. Clynds, the Polonius of Austin Melford, the Laertes of Cooper Cliffe, the Horatio of Charles Fulton, the Osric of Langley Russell, the Gravedigger of Frank Emery, the Ophelia of Miss Eastlake, and the Queen of Mrs. Belmore. According to the Herald, his Prince was "manly, sonorous, does not make time-worn points — makes ingenious ones," but it "wants color, flexibility, augustness and spirituality"— all of which might have been said, in 1938, of the Hamlet of Maurice Evans. I refer the reader to William Winter's analysis of Barrett's Hamlet (Shakespeare on the Stage, Volume I). Barrett repeated Hamlet, on April 5th, and, on the 6th, brought out Clito, a sort of foster-brother to Claudian, by Sydney Grundy and Wilson Barrett himself. It ran for a week, and gave way, on April 13th and 14th, to a revival of Claudian; Hamlet graced April 15th and 16th (matinée), and the engagement closed on the evening of the 16th, with The Lady of Lyons, Barrett, of course, playing Claude to the Pauline of Miss Eastlake.   Perhaps I should say that, in Clito, Barrett assumed the leading rôle, with Miss Eastlake as Helle, H. Cooper Cliffe as Glaucias, Austin Melford as Theramenes, J. H. Clynds as Xenocles, Charles Fulton as Dares, S. M. Carson as Atys, W. A. Elliott as Corax, Percyval as Aelius, Lila Garth as Irene, Lily Belmore as Chloe, Miss Medway as Selena, Alice Belmore as Neona, and Miss Byron as Libya.   I am glad to bid these parting guests godspeed on their journey home.   They had not ignited the East River or the Hudson, whatever they may have done to the Thames.

Dion Boucicault, much of his glory withered, entered the Star, on April 18th, in Kerry and Fin McCool, the latter, as it proved, a reworking of Belle Lamar, which had failed several years before.   His company included Georgia Cayvan, Helen Bancroft, Louise Thorndyke (his new wife), W. J. Ferguson, Fritz Williams, J. C. Padgett, Dan Maguinnis and others — a good aggregation.   But Fin McCool was a ghastly failure, and was speedily withdrawn.   The Jilt replaced it on April 23rd.   Boucicault, poor man, fell ill, and the Herald of April 30th (Saturday) announced a cessation of playing at the Star.   On May 2nd, the veteran actor returned in his ever-useful The Shaughraun, supported by W. J. Ferguson as Kinchela, H. J. Lethcourt as Captain Molineux, Louise Thorndyke as Claire, and Marion Elmore as Moya.

Unfortunately benefits beset our path.   R. M. Carroll was down for one, at this theatre, on April 21st.   On May 10th (afternoon) C. W. Couldock benefited, on the fiftieth anniversary of his stage début.   The bill was really superb.   The third act of Hamlet enlisted Edwin Booth, Charles Barron, Carl Ahrendt, John T. Malone, T. L. Coleman, Emma Vaders and Augusta Foster, in rôles they sustained in November at this theatre; the screen scene from The School for Scandal gave Fanny Davenport, John Gilbert, Robert Mantell, J. H. Barnes (Joseph) and S. DuBois; then, in order, followed a recitation, by Couldock, of Trowbridge's The Vagabonds; the quarrel scene from Julius Cæsar, with Lawrence Barrett, John Malone, Ben G. Rogers, &c.; and the third act of The Rivals, with one of the best casts ever seen in the play — Joseph Jefferson, Mrs. John Drew, James O'Neill (Sir Lucius), Kyrle Bellew (Jack), G. W. Denham (David) and Annie Robe (Lydia).   No wonder the price of orchestra chairs advanced to $3; and no wonder the receipts were $5,000.

I pass, rather reluctantly, from that glittering promise to Charles Puerner's The Pyramid, brought out on May 16th, with Frank David as Ramses XXVII, Addie Cora Reed as Rhea, Witt as Abdul, Harry Hilliard as Albert Leroy, Paul Arthur as William Dodge, Helen Standish as Tai, Rosa Cook (or Cooke) as Hatasu, Ellis Ryse as Sabako and Herbert

B. Chesley as Memphis. I never heard or read a word as to the delectability of this show, but it lasted for at least four weeks.

The final curtain for that season fell on something of note. Sarah Bernhardt came back, on June 15th, in Fedora; on the 16th, and at a matinée, on Friday, the 17th, she triumphed anew as Théodora; and, for her benefit, on the 17th (Friday), she played Doña Sol, in Hernani. The receipts for that night, says the Herald, were $2,838.50. She sailed for home, on Saturday, the 18th, and carried with her, again according to the Herald, the satisfying thought that her American tour had cleared for her the comfortable sum of $300,000. With her departure, the Star put out its lights for the season.

UNION SQUARE THEATRE, 1886–1887

It is difficult to think of the theatre once so brilliantly directed by A. M. Palmer in its new phase as a home for itinerant stars and "combinations." Its season of 1886–87 began on September 20, 1885, with an engagement of the once so popular Aimée, queen of opéra-bouffe, as a star in an English comedy, appropriately named Mam'zelle; the cast could not have quickened the pulse of anticipation. Aimée as Toinette and as Fleur de Lis was assisted by Thomas H. Burns as Tarleton Tupper, A. del Campo as Lionel Leslie, John Marble as Bob Pritchard, Newton Chisnell as Colonel Hiram Foster, Clara Baker as Mrs. Tupper and Jennie Williams as Mary. Lester Victor, Collin Varrey, W. L. Browning and J. Charles filled in. Allston Brown states that he and Simmonds were managers of the show; how could he expect to attract with such a company? On Tuesday, September 28th, Aimée came forth in the title-rôle of Marita, adapted by Barton Hill from Victorien Sardou. Most of the support just cited appeared in the new play, and, in addition, Emma Skerrett, Ada Laurent, George A. Ketchum and G. J. Henderson were the most conspicuous of several recruits to the service. Marita was a dire failure, and, after three performances, retired in favour of Mam'zelle, which finished the engagement, on October 2nd. Doubtless some regretted the passing of the former sprightly singer of Offenbach into the dubious broken English of Mam'zelle.

CLARA MORRIS; FANNY DAVENPORT; MODJESKA

Three actresses of fame on the American stage followed, successively, in an effort to maintain their once acknowledged pre-eminence. Clara Morris, acclaimed in the '70s and earliest '80s as the greatest American actress, had latterly become a travelling star with an almost unbreakable repertoire, and with her mannerisms hardened into something less appealing than of yore. But tears still flowed copiously in her moments of extreme emotion. She began now (October 4th), in a part, Miss Multon, which had, in 1876, been

[234]

Below:
E. H. SOTHERN

E. H. SOTHERN AND
BELLE ARCHER

E. H. SOTHERN AND
W. J. LE MOYNE

SOTHERN—LE MOYNE—BELLE ARCHER—H. ARCHER—R. BUCKSTONE
B. J. FALK'S PHOTOGRAPHS FROM THE HIGHEST BIDDER

her supreme success on this very Union Square stage. With her were Henry Miller, Bijou Heron (the original child, Jeanne, of the cast, ten years before, but now grown up into the rôle of Mathilde), H. B. Phillips, Mollie Revel, Kate Denin Wilson, Joseph Brennan, and Sara Lascelles. Miss Multon was repeated on the 5th and 6th; Article 47 came on the 7th and 8th, and Camille at the matinée on the 9th. Rowland Buckstone was in Article 47. Miss Morris would not act twice in one day; therefore, on Saturday evening (the 9th) her company acted Engaged for such as cared to attend.

Fanny Davenport, a competent actress and still a handsome woman, if not the beautiful girl of ten years earlier, was moved to escape from the thraldom of Fedora, and, on Tuesday, October 12th, staged an ambitious revival of Much Ado about Nothing, for her first attempt at Ellen Terry's great rôle of Beatrice. To those who remembered Irving's production of the comedy, the cast was not impressive:

Benedick	J. H. Barnes	Conrade	Edmund Pembroke
Don Pedro	B. R. Graham	Balthasar	Thomas Mellor
Claudio	Wilton Lackaye	Friar	John Sutherland
Don John	George Morton	Seacoal	J. F. Deheany
Leonato	J. F. Dean	Hero	Genevieve Lytton
Antonio	W. J. Hurley	Ursula	Alma Aiken
Dogberry	Harry Hawk	Margaret	Mary E. Hill
Verges	Frank Willard	Beatrice	Fanny Davenport
Borachio	Erroll Dunbar		

It will be remembered that, in 1874, Barnes had played Benedick to the Beatrice of Adelaide Neilson; neither then nor in 1886 did he make a hit in the part. Miss Davenport had in recent years played Rosalind, Viola and Imogen, without the poetic charm required; she now attempted the sparkling Beatrice, without a greater degree of success. Of course she dressed the part beautifully and staged the comedy with some good scenery and costumes, but I fear she was not wholly encouraged by the result. I saw the production, but it failed to print itself, except vaguely, on my memory. According to the Herald, the largest theatre party on record attended on an evening in this engagement; it came from Bloomingdale's store.

At the close of her second week, on October 23rd, Miss Davenport carried the venture on the road. If I remember her Beatrice and the entire offering only faintly, I have the most vivid memory of Modjeska's Rosalind, which was shown again on October 25th. That was one of the glories of the American theatre. What her Rosalind may have lacked in raillery and youthful buoyancy it made up in gentle humour, grace, poetry or even at times pensive charm, attributes just a little beyond the reach of Fanny Davenport. Modjeska easily transcended all phases of technical efficiency, of which, indeed, she was past mistress, and arrived into a realm of poetic and spiritual beauty that few have reached. And this in spite of her foreign accent which one must admit detracted from utter enjoyment of her Shake-

[235]

spearian interpretations. Her Rosalind, which I saw in that engagement, was bewitching and exquisite as no other Rosalind in my experience has been. She brought with her, as usual, a very satisfactory group of actors. Maurice Barrymore, a very handsome, manly actor, then in his prime, was the best Orlando I ever saw, Grace Henderson was a charming and pretty Celia, and William F. Owen was, as he ever was, a perfect Shakespearian clown, in Touchstone. These were the outstanding features of the cast, but Charles Vandenhoff as Jaques, Hamilton Bell as Le Beau, William Haworth as Oliver, James L. Carhart as Adam, Ian Robertson (brother of Forbes Robertson) as Sylvius, Howell Hansell as Corin, Robert Taber as Amiens, James Cooper as the Banished Duke, Albert Lang as Frederick, Laura Johnson as Phebe and Clara Ellison as Audrey must not be overlooked in an appraisal of the cast. The delightful comedy, thus pleasingly presented, ran for two weeks; for November 4th, 5th and 6th, Twelfth Night was billed, but withdrawn in favour of the successful As You Like It. I glow as I think of that glorious presentation of love in the Forest of Arden.

At this time we were led to believe that Modjeska desired to acquire a permanent footing in New York, with long seasons devoted to new and standard plays. Would she had succeeded in that noble ambition! The Union Square was closed for two nights in preparation for the production of The Chouans, a dramatisation by Paul Potter of Balzac's Le Dernier Chouan, ou la Bretagne en 1799. It was a stirring drama of mystery, fighting, spies, danger, etc.— the usual accompaniments of melodrama, with the hero and the heroine involved in misunderstanding and final happiness. Modjeska put it forward (November 10th) with great care and with, in general, a good cast:

Colonel Hulot	James L. Carhart	Gibot	Howell Hansell
Captain Gerard	Robert Taber	Priest	Albert Mario
Sergeant Beaupied	Robert Burnaby	Coupeau	Charles B. Kelly
Corentin	Charles Vandenhoff	Footman	Joseph Leon
Marquis de Montauran	Maurice Barrymore	Countess de Kersac	Grace Henderson
Baron de Guenic	Albert Lang	Princess de Rohan	Miss Siddonell
Count de Beauveau	Hamilton Bell	Jeanne	Laura Johnson
Major Brigant	Frank Lyman	La Babette	Mary Shaw
Bellereau	James Cooper	Francine	Clara Ellison
Pille-Miche	William Haworth	Mme. de St. Cyr	Mary Fraser
Marche-à-Terre	Ian Robertson	Marie de Verneuil	Modjeska

It is interesting to find in this company Mary Shaw, Grace Henderson and Robert Taber, then at the beginning of their careers. The regard for Modjeska and the stirring qualities of The Chouans, kept the play on the boards for a few weeks; but Modjeska did not retain it in her repertoire. I remember it, somehow, as I might remember the perfume of a delicate flower.

The week of December 6th–11th brought Modjeska's exquisite Viola, in Twelfth Night, incomparably the loveliest Viola I ever saw. The reader conjectures correctly that Barrymore was Orsino, Hamilton Bell Sebastian, Grace Henderson Olivia, Mary Shaw Maria, W. F. Owen Sir Toby, and Vandenhoff Malvolio.   The last week of the engagement (December 13th–18th) brought Daniela, Felix Philippi's play, in an English version by William von Sachs and E. Hamilton Bell.   The plot is almost identical with that of Pinero's His House in Order.   Let us bid farewell to the company in this play, with Barrymore as Egon, Hamilton Bell as Baron von Bergen, Ian Robertson as Dr. Nordon, Vandenhoff as Ferdinand Arndt, Owen as Felix Fliederbusch, Howell Hansell as Brauer, Robert Burnaby as Fritz, C. B. Kelly as Wilhelm, Modjeska as Daniela and Grace Henderson as Toni von Lexow.   Most regretfully did I see the charming actress depart; her Rosalind, her Marie de Verneuil and her Viola were to me, a youth, revelations in acting — incomparably the most poetic impersonations that, up to that time, I had seen.

Margaret Mather; Rose Coghlan; Richard Mansfield

The house, closed for December 20th, opened, on December 21st, with a return engagement of the forcible, if not elegant or finished art of Margaret Mather.   She began in Leah, the Forsaken, with Milnes Levick as Nathan, Frederick Paulding as Rudolph, O'Kane Hillis as Lorentz, Harry Eytinge as Dr. Ludwig, Jean Harold as Madalena, Hattie A. Saphore as Mother Groschen, Helen Glidden as Sara, &c.   After Leah's last curse (December 25th), Miss Mather reverted (27th) to the truculency of Juliana, in The Honeymoon; thus she saved for her last two weeks the sweetest morsel of her repertoire — Romeo and Juliet, with, of course, Levick and Paulding in their former rôles.   What this performance lacked in delicate or tragic beauty, it made up in physical force.

A curious novelty was presented on January 17th, in the début of one Helen Hastings in a piece called Pen and Ink.   With her were J. H. Clark, Henry E. Walton, J. Daily, Eugene Jepson, William A. Faversham (as Dick), S. Fox, Ida Jeffreys, Helen Corlette and Annie Ware.   With Jepson and Faversham we were soon to become well acquainted; but the others!   Yet Miss Hastings kept her venture afloat till Saturday, January 29th.   How did she do it, in a community that always demanded good actors?   And a very favourite actress, Rose Coghlan, began, on January 31st, in a repertoire made up of old comedies in which she had won acclaim at Wallack's.   Her opening bill consisted of London Assurance, in which for the first time, then, I first saw that exuberant, unique comedienne.   In the support were Charles Walcot as Sir Harcourt, J. H. Gilmour as Dazzle, A. S. Lipman as Charles, Mrs. Walcot as Grace, &c.   The beauty, dash and sparkle of Miss Coghlan "got me" as it had conquered so many before me; the only adverse criticism as a youthful devotee that I could make was that her entrance, with the

[237]

hunting speech, was not quite so brilliant as had been that of Ada Dyas, which I had seen a few years previously. But I never lost, from that time forward, my extreme admiration for Rose Coghlan. On the 7th, 8th, and 9th of February, she was the buoyant Peg Woffington in the ever-popular Masks and Faces of Reade and Tom Taylor, a piece which, we remember, Helen Dauvray was playing at this very time in the Lyceum Theatre. I saw Miss Coghlan's Peg, but not Miss Dauvray's and have no doubt that for effective acting I made the wiser choice. For February 10th, 11th and 12th, Miss Coghlan changed to As You Like It, which I regret not having seen. Her support in Masks and Faces included J. H. Gilmour as Pomander, Lipman as Ernest Vane, Mrs. Walcot as Mrs. Vane and Maude Peters as Kitty Clive; it was repeated during the week of February 14th–19th. For the matinée, on the 16th, however, Miss Coghlan was listed to act Pauline, in The Lady of Lyons.

Richard Mansfield followed, on February 21st, in his successful Prince Karl, his support now including Effie Germon, Emma Sheridan, Adelaide Emerson, Beatrice Cameron, Joseph Frankau, Cyril Scott, Albert Roberts, Harry Gwynette, Charles Eldridge and Joseph Burnett. On February 27th, for a benefit for John M. Morton, journalist, actor and author, a host of volunteers included Mrs. D. P. Bowers, Rose Coghlan, Nellie McHenry, Nate Salsbury, John G. Webster, Helen Bancroft, Ethel (sic) Corlette, D. H. Harkins, Eben Plympton, much in demand, George Thorne, Abramoff, Herbert Archer, and G. F. De Vere. Bessie Byrne, the elocutionist, gave, on March 1st, a matinée performance of Leah, the Forsaken, an elocutionary part indeed; her cast included O. H. Barr, James R. Smith, Maurice Pike, Anna Archer and Carrie Jamison. I wonder who attended?

AGNES HERNDON; JANAUSCHEK; ANNIE PIXLEY

Mansfield closed, on March 12th, and, on the 14th, Agnes Herndon, ambitious, but never quite attaining, presented The Commercial Tourist's Bride, certainly an unattractive title; and silly beyond words are the names in the *dramatis personae*:

Violet Granville Smith......Agnes Herndon		Wing Wing..............Jacques Luckstone	
O. N. Time.....................Frank Lane		Sam...........................W. F. Loftus	
B. Innocent Smith.......William C. Sampson		Rose E. Flour...........Beverley Sitgreaves	
Philip True..................George Cohill		Lucy..........................Daisy Lyon	
B. B. Catcher..................C. W. Travis		Camilla Celeste.............May Thompson	
Tip.....................James McCormick			

I should be ashamed to inscribe that cast were it not for the presence in it of William Sampson and Beverley Sitgreaves, one day to be valued adjuncts to any cast. Miss Herndon remained till April 9th, proving that the attraction of The Commercial Tourist's Bride must have been stronger than one

ROBERT DOWNING
(THE GLADIATOR)

EMMA VADERS

WILLIAM MULDOON
(THE FIGHTING GAUL)

MISS EASTLAKE

WILSON BARRETT
AS CLAUDIAN

WILSON BARRETT
AS HAMLET

MRS. LANGTRY AND
SARAH BERNHARDT

SARAH BERNHARDT
(THÉODORA)

GEORGE BARRETT
IN HOODMAN BLIND

would suspect. On April 11th, Fanny Janauschek, no longer a stellar magnet, came to the Union Square as Meg Merrilies, which she doubtless acted with much of the eerie power associated with the part. This was launched as a very special venture, but it departed, on the 23rd, leaving hardly a wrack behind.

Annie Pixley, who had tried before to vary the monotony of constantly playing M'liss, found something suitable at last in A. C. Gunter's play, The Deacon's Daughter. In this she played (April 25th) Ruth Homewebb, with Ed Temple as Malatesta, Robert Fischer as Squire Hiram, P. Redmond as Amadie, M. C. Daly as Isaiah, George Backus as Charles, W. G. Regnier as Irving, Annie Douglas as Mrs. Homewebb, Annie Barclay as Mrs. Brown, and Irene Avenal as Mary. Though I doubt if that list of players would have attracted me (and in reality I did not see the play), The Deacon's Daughter ran for six weeks, closing on June 4th; Miss Pixley gave a professional matinée on May 17th. On Sunday evening, May 22nd, Augustus Heckler (can the reader identify him?) had a benefit, at which volunteers advertised included Edward Mollenhauer, C. R. Thorne, Sr. (imagine!), Gus Williams, Harry Hilliard, Newton Gotthold, Ruby Brooks, Pauline Hall, Emma Carson, Loie Fuller, Julia Wilson, Addie Cora Reed, the Tipaldi Mandolin Club and The Old Homestead Quartette — a goodly promise. The Herald review mentions only a few of those celebrities. On the 29th, Jerome Hopkins's oratorio of Samuel was the lure. On June 12th occurred a benefit for the Workingmen's Free Library.

Two sturdy graduates from vaudeville closed a very interesting season at the Union Square. Murray and Murphy, in an enlarged Our Irish Visitors, came in, on June 6th, and did not leave till July 9th, proving once more that summer audiences are not too fastidious. The show began in a curious way, advertising that admission on the first night would be free to "the profession" and, on the second, free to the newsboys. No money would be taken till Wednesday, June 8th. Furthermore, the piece had "no literary merit, no plot." Such engaging candour possibly set the venture on its weeks of success. The cast included Murphy as McGinnis, Murray as Gilhooley, Helena Hardenberg as Mrs. McGinnis, Annie Lewis as Dorothy, Addie Boos as Mrs. Gilhooley, and, in other parts, Percy Lorraine, Charles Young and James Reilly. Well, success to their nonentities! and so farewell for 1886–87 to the Union Square Theatre.

Fifth Avenue Theatre, 1886–1887

The third of the leading "combination" and "star" houses, the Fifth Avenue, also provided for its patrons a number of interesting attractions. It started the new season, on September 6, 1886, with the well-known The Kerry Gow, in which Joseph Murphy had the assistance of certain players whose fame has not seeped down to 1941 — Belle Melville, Edward White, Maurice Heppard, W. J. Sheean, F. W. Sackett and John S. Murphy. This lasted for a fortnight. September 20th was a gala night. On that auspicious date Henry E. Dixey, returned from an engagement not altogether triumphant in London, greeted his devoted followers here in Adonis, with Amelia Somerville (*sic*), Howard and Alice Arnold (Artea) in support. Howard gave a new burlesque of Boucicault as the Shaughraun, and the piece was brightened here and there with novel features; but intrinsically it was the old Adonis, and that was what, for the next two weeks, delighted adherents of the original play.

Mrs. Langtry; Gilbert and Sullivan

If these preceding attractions were somewhat off the line of expected Fifth Avenue offerings, the third attraction was quite of the Fifth Avenue standard. Mrs. Langtry, still beautiful to those who thought her beautiful (and some preferred the classic features of Mary Anderson), returned for her third American tour, presenting, on October 4th, A Wife's Peril, in which, as Lady Ormond, she was still supported by the talented Charles Coghlan as Captain Bradford. Kate Pattison, a good actress, was Lucy Ormond. After two weeks this comedy gave way (October 18th) to a careful and beautifully dressed revival of The Lady of Lyons:

Pauline	Mrs. Langtry	Deschappelles	H. A. Weaver
Claude Melnotte	C. F. Coghlan	Landlord	G. Raiemond
Colonel Damas	F. A. Everill	Gaspar	Herbert Ackhurst
Beauseant	Joseph Carne	Mme. Deschappelles	Mrs. Charles Calvert
Glavis	Sidney Herbert	Widow Melnotte	Kate Pattison

Whatever one's questioning about the perfection of the features of the Jersey Lily, one admitted that, in her old-time dresses as Pauline, she was radiantly beautiful; and, though, at that time my judgment may have lacked mature wisdom, it seemed to me that she acted convincingly in all phases of her character. The Herald critic calls her "the best Pauline" he had ever seen; and he had seen Julia Dean, Eliza Logan, Mrs. Mowatt and Jean Davenport. Coghlan as Claude was superb, and all the company gave perfect support. Does one note the name of Sidney Herbert, later and for many years a pillar of the company of Daly's Theatre? That Lady of Lyons, still a pleasing memory to many, closed on October 30th.

And then Gilbert and Sullivan were restored to the stage they had brightened in 1885–86, and with the same opera. The Mikado, on November 1, 1886, retained but two of the earlier cast, Geraldine Ulmar and Courtice Pounds. New contributors to the Japanese joy seem less striking than those of the year before; they were Brocolini as Pooh-Bah, J. W. Herbert as Ko-Ko, and N. S. Burnham as the Mikado, Joseph C. Fay as Pish-Tush, Agnes Stone as Pitti-Sing, Edith Jennesse as Peep-Bo and Alice Carle as Katisha.   They may have been good, but posterity has not been informed of the fact.   Whatever the excellence of the revival, it lasted but three weeks.   On November 22nd, came a production of Princess Ida, the original performances of which at this very house had been far from a popular success. The new cast:

King Hildebrand	Brocolini	Scynthias	L. W. Raymond
Hilarion	Courtice Pounds	Ida	Geraldine Ulmar
Cyril	Phil Branson	Lady Blanche	Alice Carle
Florian	Stuart Harold	Melissa	Agnes Stone
King Gama	J. W. Herbert	Psyche	Helen Lamont
Arac	Joseph C. Fay	Sacharissa	Edith Jennesse
Guron	N. S. Burnham		

New York has never admired this work, or, rather, it has never loved it. The music is scholarly, but to me, as to many, it lacks melodic charm; it is not inspired, certainly not inspiring.   And Gilbert made nothing intensely bright or witty out of Tennyson's fantasy.   The present revival left us on December 11th.   This Gilbert and Sullivan flurry (The Mikado and Princess Ida) could not have been inspired from the throne in the Savoy, London; it seems to me a "scratch" company that gave the operas.

ROBERT B. MANTELL; RUDDYGORE

Those who saw Robert Mantell only in his later years, when he roamed the country in Shakespearian repertoire, must go back in imagination to 1880–90, when he was a very handsome blond young Englishman, with an admirable gift in heroic or romantic plays, a gift with which he largely helped Fanny Davenport's success in Fedora.   Now, in 1886, he was beginning his career as a star, and New York had opportunity to appraise him in that capacity when, on December 13th, he presented himself at the Fifth Avenue as Raymond Garth, in a romance by John W. Keller, called Tangled Lives.   A very good company assisted, with Eleanor Carey as Helen Garth, Effie Shannon ("looking sweetly pretty," according to the Herald) as Edith Ainsley, Nelson Wheatcroft as Josephus Howson, and with W. F. Blande, Louisa Eldridge, Kate Stokes, Helen Windsor, B. T. Ringgold and R. J. Dustan in other rôles.   Surprisingly, this piece continued to January 29th, when its fiftieth performance closed the run.   January 31st brought the impressive survival, The Marble Heart, which actors of that heroic school always loved.   Mantell's hero, of old time and of the present, was supported by Eleanor Carey as the heartless one, Effie Shannon as Marie (this is the first time I ever saw the very young and very pretty Miss Shannon, whom

[241]

I have seen with admiration ever since) and Nelson Wheatcroft as Volage.
The persisting popularity of Mantell (remember his good looks!) carried the
old play for two weeks. The long engagement from December 13th astonishes me. Eben Plympton, also a popular actor, followed, on February 14th,
in Jack, that comedy by Mrs. Harry Beckett, which he had tried at matinées,
in the autumn, at Wallack's Theatre. This play, derived from Augier's
La Pierre de Touche, was thus cast:

Jack Beamish	Eben Plympton	Withers	Jacques Martin
Noel Blake	Charles Kent	Jenkins	F. Hodson
Major Spott White	Myron Calice	Madge Heskett	Georgie Drew Barrymore
Sebastian Smythe	John Ince	Lady Blanchemayne	Virginia Buchanan
Teddy Sprott	W. G. Gilmore	Baby Blanchemayne	Josie Hall
Bertie Ffolliott	J. B. Hollis	Mrs. Bunn	Adele Clarke
Mr. Smylie	John Archer		

This was probably but a stop-gap of a week, to fill time to February 21st,
when D'Oyly Carte's company, seen in last year's Mikado, came, almost
intact, from London to give the eagerly awaited Ruddygore (sic), or, the
Witch's Curse. George Thorne was the perplexed Robin Oakapple, Courtice
Pounds a delightfully dashing Richard Dauntless, Geraldine Ulmar a very
demure Rose Maybud, and Kate Forster and Fred Billington a wonderful
pair as Mad Margaret and Sir Despard Murgatroyd. To these and to
Federici as Sir Roderick fell some of the wittiest lines Gilbert ever wrote,
and the chorus of professional bridesmaids also came in for a large share
of the plaudits. Other members of the cast were Elsie Cameron as Dame
Hannah, Aïda Jenoure as Zorah, Amy Augarde as Ruth and S. King as
Old Adam Goodheart. It would be difficult to say why this operetta failed
to duplicate the success of The Mikado; certainly some of the situations are
deliciously droll, and the debate which convinces the ghosts that logically
they could not have died at all is for sheer fooling the funniest thing Gilbert
ever wrote. Perhaps the music, charming as it is, was not quite so clear
and sparkling as Sullivan had often written. Whatever the cause, Ruddygore was withdrawn on April 9th, after a respectable run, but certainly
not a glorious one. In March, for a time, both Federici and Elsie Cameron
were ill and out of the cast. The reader notes the spelling, Ruddygore, which
prevailed during this engagement; in England it became Ruddigore.
Mr. and Mrs. McKee Rankin (Kitty Blanchard) came, on April 11th,
in Clay Greene's play of The Golden Giant, in which, as Alexander and
Bessie Fairfax, they were supported by Robert Hilliard as Jack Mason,
Charles Stanley as Bixby, Nestor Lennon (a pleasing young actor) as Duncan LeMoyne, J. Winston Murray as Max Wayne, Daisy Dorr as Ethel
Gray, Louise Dickson as Mrs. Boggs, Ollie Berkeley as little Jack, Luke
Martin as Flynn, &c. The advertisements also promised Ah Wing Sing,

ROSE COGHLAN
AS PEG WOFFINGTON

ANNIE PIXLEY

MRS. CHARLES CALVERT
AS MME. DESCHAPPELLES

HELENA MODJESKA
AS VIOLA

MAURICE BARRYMORE
AS ORLANDO

HELENA MODJESKA
AS ROSALIND

MRS. LANGTRY
(THE LADY OF LYONS)

MRS. LANGTRY
(A WIFE'S PERIL)

MRS. LANGTRY
(THE LADY OF LYONS)

"the first real English-speaking Chinaman on any stage." After two weeks of this, Mrs. Langtry came back (April 25th) in Tom Taylor's delightful Lady Clancarty (as she, a female star, billed it):

Lord Clancarty..............C. F. Coghlan	Sir John Friend.............Sidney Herbert
William III....................F. A. Everill	Clink.......................W. Lennox, Jr.
Earl of Portland....................H. Rich	Princess Anne.............Miss A. Sutherland
Lord Woodstock..............Joseph Carne	Lady Betty Noel..............Kate Pattison
Lord Spencer................H. A. Weaver	Susannah.....................Miss Calvert
Sir George Barclay............Kenneth Lee	Mother Hunt................Mrs. C. Calvert
Robert Hunt..............George Raiemond	Lady Clancarty...............Mrs. Langtry

Again I salute one of the engrossing performances of my youth. Mrs. Langtry closed in this play on May 11th, and, on the 12th, 13th and 14th (the last of her engagement) reverted to her charming Pauline, in The Lady of Lyons. Doubtless there had been greater Paulines, from Helen Faucit's day down through the decades, but few more pleasing to look upon. On May 23rd, Lillian Olcott and her travelling caravan (few theatres had escaped the show, that season) entered the Fifth Avenue for a week of Theodora. After that week of the sensational piece, the theatre closed for the season.

STANDARD THEATRE, 1886–1887

The Standard re-opened, on August 16, 1886, with hope, doubtless, of success on familiar lines. A piece by Charles H. Hoyt, with music by Edward Solomon, could, presumably, be depended on to make its way for weeks, if not months. And Duff provided a wonderful combination in Lillian Russell and Tony Hart, with other excellent artists in support. And yet it failed! Under title of The Maid and the Moonshiner, it had this cast:

Bourbon Miller..............John E. Brand	Rev. Mr. Thayer.............Fred Solomon
Upton O. Dodge.................Tony Hart	Pomp........................John Hogan
Colonel Peyton.............James Radcliffe	Honora Lee....................Elma Delaro
Captain Bryton Beach........Joseph Armand	Leonora.....................Carrie Tutein
Captain Monmouth Beach......G. Wilkinson	Marguerite....................Annie Leslie
Captain Ivan Suwarrow.......A. L. Nicholas	Violetta.....................Queen Vassar
Captain Fahrbach..............F. Boudinot	Virginia.....................Lillian Russell

Edward Solomon conducted the orchestra. But nothing availed, and after two weeks, the expensive thing failed. From August 28th, the Standard remained closed till Saturday, September 25th, when it began the season with A. C. Gunter's drama, A Wall Street Bandit, dealing, in prologue and play proper, with the financial distresses in 1837 and 1857. The long and interesting cast follows:

[243]

Weston Minton	Charles Wheatleigh	Ethel Wayne	Bijou Fernandez
Justice Sharkey	Robert McWade	Patience Mawley	Fanny Addison
Joshua Joab Jinks	Charles Bowser	Annie	Marion Russell
Dr. Ralson	Frank Losee	Mattie	Edith Bird
Broadstretcher	Lysander Thompson	Katie	Little Ollie
Stephen Mawley / J. Edison Shocks	W. J. Ferguson	Gentleman Jimmy	J. H. Farrell
		Ethel	Georgia Cayvan
Jonathan Wayne / Johnny Graham	Atkins Lawrence	Marion Longdale	Sadie Bigelow
		Katie Morton	Anna Boyle
Jonathan Wayne, Jr.	Tommy Russell	Patience O'Flynn	Fanny Addison

There are good names in that cast; all the characters except Shocks and Johnny Graham down through Katie (Little Ollie) appear in the prologue, and many of them (some under different names) in the play. By the way, the talented Miss Cayvan was wandering from theatre to theatre so uncertainly that one longs for 1887–88 when she was to take her place permanently as the leading lady in Daniel Frohman's Lyceum Theatre Company.

A Wall Street Bandit flourished till October 16th. Henri Rochefort's play, L'Irlandaise, translated into A Daughter of Ireland, endured a precarious existence of one week (October 18th–23rd) in its hectic story of Irish rebellion, stern officers, patriotic lady incurring great danger for the cause of all that material famous since The White Horse of the Peppers. In it appeared an excellent group of players, including Georgia Cayvan (Una), Sadie Bigelow (Lady Edith), W. J. Constantine (Lord Hastings), Robert Hilliard (Sir Richard Sweeney), Hardy Vernon, Alfred Follin, Charles Brandt, W. H. Pope, Frank Kemble and Charles Hawkins.

The passing of this failure left the Standard dark till October 30th, when The Jilt hurried in, with Boucicault, Miss Thorndyke, and a "London" company, including H. J. Lethcourt, Frank Norcross, J. B. Hollis, Fritz Williams, Herbert, Mary Barker, Miss M. Bannister, Maude Mowbray, and (says Allston Brown though not the Herald) Helen Bancroft. The Jilt departed on November 13th, and, on Monday, the 15th, a risky venture started—Hamlet, so to speak, without Hamlet. Rosina Vokes was, on that night, to have made her re-entrance for a lengthy engagement. Illness kept her from the stage for several weeks, and the management presented the star's charming company of refined English comedians, without the star. They gave In Honour Bound, A Pantomime Rehearsal, and a new Cousin Dick. In the last-named piece Gordon Dalzell was Richard Dalson, Helena Dacre Constance, Mabel Millett Florence, and Geraldine Dalzell Mary. In A Pantomime Rehearsal, Courtenay Thorpe, Weedon Grossmith, Helena Dacre, Mabel Millett and Agnes Miller (she in Miss Vokes's part) made merry as they could without their leader. The bill for November 22nd substituted, for Cousin Dick, the short play of A Little Change, retaining In Honour Bound and A Pantomime Rehearsal.

This triple bill faded out after the performance on Monday, December 6th. December 7th brought back to an eager public the buoyant

Rosina Vokes, "at her post again," in Pinero's farce, The Schoolmistress. This play, dealing with the antics of some schoolgirls while the schoolmistress is away, had some lively scenes, involving a supper party arranged by the girls, for a schoolmate just married, with, of course, the unexpected return of the mistress, and her own secret marriage to a silly neighbouring lordling. It carried the engagement through January 8th. I remember my youthful delight at the scene of the pudding. More guests than were expected arrive at the party, with resultant drain on the food supplies. The girls are warned to decline any pudding, and, of course, do so; but the men suspect there is something wrong with the sweet, and also decline. As the farcically small dish was passed about the board, no one taking any of it, the laughter in the audience was simply hilarious, one touch of the familiar making us all kin. The farce had been done in London by the ebullient Mrs. John Wood, and was produced here by permission of Augustin Daly, who seems to have controlled for America all of Pinero's farces. The cast of The Schoolmistress is appended:

Hon. Vere Queckett	Weedon Grossmith	Jeffray	J. Rolfe
Rear Admiral Rankling	Mr. Elliot	Mrs. Rankling	May Carew
Lieutenant Mallory	Gordon Dalzell	Miss Dyott	Helena Dacre
Mr. Saunders	T. Roberts	Dinah Rankling	Mabel Millett
Reginald Paulover	Courtenay Thorpe	Gwendoline	Geraldine Dalzell
Otto Bernstein	Malcolm Bell	Ermyntrude	Agnes Miller
Tyler	Charles Rivers	Jane	Margaret Trelawney
Goff	R. Charles	Peggy Hesslerigge	Rosina Vokes

I recall the stately Helena Dacre as the schoolmistress, the silly ass of Weedon Grossmith and the natural comedy touches of Miss Vokes; the girls were extremely pretty.

The farce was not, I suspect, a great success. On January 10th, Miss Vokes changed to The Baron's Wager (by Sir Charles Young, author of Jim, the Penman), A Double Lesson, by B. C. Stephenson — in which she and Miss Dacre were delightful, and the ever-welcome A Pantomime Rehearsal. On January 19th, the Rehearsal was succeeded in this bill by My Milliner's Bill; later in the week In Honour Bound replaced The Baron's Wager. The last week of the engagement progressed from In Honour Bound, My Milliner's Bill and A Double Lesson (February 7th and 8th), to The Schoolmistress (9th and 10th) and the best triad of all — In Honour Bound, My Milliner's Bill and A Pantomime Rehearsal. On February 14th, Sol Smith Russell began an engagement in Cal Wallace's play, unfortunately named Pa:

Perkimen Guinney	Mr. Russell	Mrs. Rymer	Mattie Ferguson
Raymond Dawsey	Fred P. Marsh	Hope	Virginia Nelson
A. Spartacus Hubbs	Frank Lawton	Sybil	Emily Bancker
Sydney Bumpps	Fred P. Ham	Beatrice	Emma Hagger
Captain Startle	Albert H. Warren		

[245]

The three girls who end the cast were pa's daughters. And how fast the new generation crowds on us! Here is Emily Bancker, to join Effie Shannon and other débutantes of that busy season. On February 21st, J. K. Emmet, almost as bright as ever, came forward in Fritz, Our Cousin German; Helen Sedgwick assisted. Few actors had ever been more popular than Emmet; his personality, his songs and his smile carried Fritz through April 2nd — a cheering exploit.

The theatre was closed during Holy Week (April 4th–9th) and re-opened on April 11th with von Suppé's opera, A Trip to Africa:

Titania	Lillian Russell	Sebil	Bessie Cleveland
Fanfani Pasha	J. H. Ryley	Buccametta	Zelda Seguin
Antarsid	Eugene Oudin	Tessa	Louise Parker
Miradillo	C. W. Dungan	Hosh	J. E. Fox
Pericles	John E. Nash		

During the week of April 25th–30th Madeline Lucette and Frank Boudinot were in the cast. This attraction closed on May 14th, yielding place (16th) to a revival of Gasparone, with Lillian Russell, Zelda Seguin, Madeline Lucette, Oudin, F. Gaillard and J. H. Ryley. Evidently the taste for German operetta was waning; McCaull and Duff were reviving, rather unsuccessfully, successes of previous years. And now Duff turned to Gilbert and Sullivan, producing, on May 30th, the delightful Iolanthe, with Lillian Russell, Mrs. Seguin, Florence Bemister, Bessie Cleveland, Dungan, George Appleby, Nash, Boudinot, and, of course, Ryley (as the Lord Chancellor). Even this, despite Lillian Russell's beauty and her lovely voice and Ryley's unique comic ability, won but two weeks from reluctant public purse-strings. On June 13th, came Japanese Tourists, in The Antipodes. For their second week these Orientals advertised Little All Right and Miss Hannah "with the Tiny Feet." But the Herald carries no Standard for that week.

FOURTEENTH STREET THEATRE, 1886–1887

At the former Lyceum Theatre, in Fourteenth Street, we find, on September 6th, a feeble opening with David Milton Higgins's play, Our Rich Cousin:

Cynthia	Georgia Cayvan	Tom Merrygold	T. J. Herndon
Florence Robbins	Louise Muldener	Sim	William Richardson
Winona Melrose	Fanny Addison	Zed	Milton Higgins
Martha	Mrs. Sol Smith	Theodore Zahn	W. J. Ferguson
Will Styles	A. S. Lipman		

The really excellent cast was wasted on a poor play; again I express sympathy for Georgia Cayvan, exploiting her talent, since May Blossom, in one failure after another. Two weeks of Our Rich Cousin led to another misfortune, an effort of Henrietta Chanfrau once more to win the favour she had enjoyed in the '60s. On September 20th she staged Sir Charles L. Young's drama, The Scapegoat, and engaged an interesting support, including Stella Boniface, Helen Bancroft, Horace Vinton, Myron Leffingwell, Henry A. Weaver, Jr., Lewis Baker, Sidney Drew, and Harry Clifford. Two weeks ended this venture.

Mrs. D. P. Bowers; M. B. Curtis; Denman Thompson

The worthy Mrs. D. P. Bowers, one of the best of the grand school then departing from our stage, began a month's engagement in a repertoire composed of relics from a vanishing day. On October 4th, 6th (matinée and evening) she appeared as Mary Stuart, in Edmund Falconer's version of the play; with her were Joseph Wheelock as Douglas, John A. Lane as Mortimer, Mark Lynch as Leicester, Fanny Gillette as Elizabeth, and Alberta Gallatin as Catherine. On October 5th, 7th and 9th (matinée), Mrs. Bowers gave her striking performance of Elizabeth; Friday night brought Lucretia Borgia and The Jealous Wife, and the busy and impressive week ended, on Saturday night, October 9th, with Macbeth. In the last-named tragedy, Wheelock was Macbeth, Lane Macduff, and, of course, the star showed her own art as Lady Macbeth. Having thus satisfied her taste for the tragic "legitimate," Mrs. Bowers devoted the greater part of the next fortnight (October 11th–23rd) to her impressive Lady Audley's Secret, the first break coming at the matinée on the 23rd, when Mrs. Bowers (advertised now as "the worthy successor of the great Cushman") must have been a mature and stately Camille. On the evening of the 23rd, she repeated Lucretia Borgia and The Jealous Wife. For her last week, the distinguished actress mingled parts from her repertoire in rapid progression: Elizabeth (October 25th and 29th); Mary Stuart (26th, 28th, and matinée, 30th); Camille (matinée, 27th); Lady Audley's Secret (evening, 27th); and Macbeth (evening, 30th). After this exhibition of versatility, she departed, honoured, I hope, with fulness of financial returns.

The theatre then entered on a remarkably prosperous term, which gives my pen a welcome relief. On November 1st, M. B. Curtis, whose Sam'l of Posen had been a success for the last few years, found another money-maker in a play dealing with stock-speculation and bearing the taking title of Caught in a Corner. With him were his wife, Albina de Mer, C. A. McManus, and Vincent Sternroyd, this last-named last year in One of Our Girls. This piece caught the fancy of a public, itself devoted to speculation and frequently caught in a corner, and it ran to a fiftieth performance, on December 17th, and continued merrily till Christmas night, certainly a fine holiday gift for all concerned. In November, I learn from

Allston Brown, J. W. Rosenquest bought E. G. Gilmore's interest in this theatre. Samuel Colville, Gilmore's partner, had died in August, 1886.

A brief stopgap from December 27th to January 8th, brought Mr. and Mrs. George S. Knight, in their familiar Over the Garden Wall; their support included Edwin Foy, Charles Frew, James Quinn (succeeding George Monroe as Our Own Bridget) and the St. Felix Sisters. This last engagement causes us to ponder on the rapidity with which the popular farcical nondescript shows of that time abstracted from "Variety" some of its best performers.

And now, on January 10th began a twenty-weeks respite for my pen. On that auspicious date, Denman Thompson, also snatched from "Variety," and an excellent actor withal, brought out his reworking of the Joshua Whitcomb theme and started the unending triumph for The Old Homestead, certainly the most famous of all rural plays:

Joshua Whitcomb	Denman Thompson	François Fogarty	Frank Martin
Cy Prime	George A. Beane	Len Holbrook	C. M. Richardson
Happy Jack	Walter Gale	Aunt Matilda	Louisa Morse
Henry Hopkins	Walter Lennox	Rickety Ann	Annie Thompson
Reuben Whitcomb	T. D. Frawley	Annie Hopkins	Virginia Marlowe
John Freeman	Frank Thompson	Nellie Freeman	Lillian Stone
Frank Hopkins	Alfred Swartz	Maggie O'Flaherty	Minnie Luckstone
Judge Patterson	Gus Kammerlee	Mrs. Hopkins	Venie Thompson
George Hopkins	Albert Barnes	Nellie Patterson	Leonore Willard
Eb Ganzey	J. L. Morgan	Mrs. Murdock	Mrs. Owen Marlowe
Pat Clancy	Frank Mara		

That is certainly a long cast, but it satisfied easily satisfied Americans who sat through the play time after time. The realistic farm scenes, the scene in the supposed elegant drawing room of Mrs. Hopkins, in which Uncle Josh's rustic habits quite "shame" the hostess before her "elegant" guests, the moving scene before Grace Church at night, with its lighted windows and the voices of its choir reaching to the street, with the tramp, Happy Jack, superbly played by Walter Gale, and Uncle Josh's miraculous finding of his wandering boy, all this material, carefully adjusted to audiences that like the simple and the good, led us to a happy concluding act on the comfortable old farm at Swansea, where no one was going to worry any more. Rickety Ann and Cy Prime were laughable enough for any mind not too self-centered and intraverted. I doubt if troubled 1941 would find the play so enjoyable. But we may be thankful for the twenty-weeks cessation from labour it provided, in 1887, for our conscientious pen. The hundredth performance, on April 12th, must, of course, be noted, and the last performance on June 4th.

June 6th presented a new piece by Lawrence Marston, called The Hypocrite, a sort of Othello-Iago-Desdemona device in which a vengeful octoroon almost wrecks the happiness of Edward Walton and his wife. The cast, it will be noted, employed several Wallack actors, including Osmond Tearle, happily returned to his admiring public:

Edward Walton	Osmond Tearle	Archibald	Tony Farrell
George	Newton Gotthold	Edith Walton	Annie Robe
Richard Singleton	Herbert Kelcey	Grace Coutraire	Miriam O'Leary
Barney Elliott	Charles S. Dickson	Martha	Marie Bates
Dr. Vernon	Harry Courtaine		

Two weeks sufficed for this crudely written play, and, despite the remarkable cast, it closed the house on June 18th.

THE CASINO, 1886-1887

We left the popular Casino, on October 2nd, when the big hit, Erminie, because of previous contracts, was forced to retire. Violet Cameron, niece of Lydia Thompson, came into the house, on October 4th, in The Commodore, a version by H. B. Farnie of Offenbach's La Creole, and one of the worst failures in the history of the Casino. The company was brought from England by the Earl of Lonsdale and thus disported in the new production:

Captain René	Violet Cameron	Sabord	Miss Clyde Howard
The Commodore	Lionel Brough	Antoinette	Edith Brandon
Maître Garble	Sidney Brough	Zoe	Constance Loveby
Maître Babble	Edward Marshall	Berthe	Frances Lytton
Baupré	H. Tomkins	Lolotte	Nelly Woodford
Frontignac	John Barnum		

Minor parts fell to Misses G. Austin, B. Burrows, Evelyn Vale, Violet Dashwood, Julie Conteur and Lillie Russell; Michael Connolly conducted.

Miss Cameron had acquired considerable notoriety, in the theatre and in her life off-stage, and, for a time, curiosity led people (but not in large numbers) into the auditorium. But The Commodore could not be boosted into a success. The advertisements on October 10th were somewhat strident: "Notwithstanding malicious reports to the contrary, the Casino is filled nightly with fashionable and delighted audiences to witness Miss Violet Cameron's charming impersonation of Captain René, in The Commodore." Notwithstanding this blatant proclamation, The Commodore sailed out, on October 23rd.

On Monday, October 25th, the English visitors changed to Kenilworth, with Miss Cameron as Earl of Leicester, Miss Loveby as Raleigh, Julie Conteur as Sussex, Edith Brandon as Amy Robsart, Alice Lethbridge as Janet, John Barnum as Queen Elizabeth, Sidney Brough as Tony Foster, Edward Marshall as Mike Lambourne, and Lionel Brough as Richard Varney. This was better than The Commodore, but not good enough to outweigh the distaste for Miss Cameron and her offerings. To the relief of all, she closed her engagement on November 13th, and sailed for England on the 25th. Her last week here reverted to The Commodore; she spent the week of November 15th at the Brooklyn Theatre.

[249]

I regret to say that, for that time, the Casino continued its policy of Sunday night concerts. The first of these for the season presented (September 26th) Mae St. John, Belle Urquhart and the Armanini Mandolin Quintet. That quintet played again on October 3rd, and Belle Cole sang Wagner's Albumblatt and Jules Levy's cornet gave The Lost Chord and Aronson's My Darling Waltz. These same entertainers figured on the 10th; but, with the Armanini five, on the 17th, newcomers were A. P. Burbank and the Sappho Male Quartet. Evidently a lull followed in this aspect of Casino activities.

And now Erminie returned, November 15th, to its desecrated shrine. The cast stood thus:

Erminie	Pauline Hall	Eugène Marcel	Henry Hallam
Cerise	Belle Thorne	Chevalier	Max Freeman
Javotte	Marie Jansen	Marquis de Ponvert	J. A. Furey
Princess	Mrs. G. C. Germon	Dufois	Fred Clifton
Delaunay	Alma Varrey	Simon	A. W. Maflin
Marie	Sadie Kirby	Vicomte de Brissac	C. L. Weeks
Cadeaux	Francis Wilson	Sergeant	Charles Parr
Ravennes	Mark Smith		

Jesse Williams directed the orchestra. From the cast we met in May, one noted the absence of W. S. Daboll, Jennie Weathersby and Marion Manola. This revival ran steadily till September 17th, 1887.

Sunday concerts took on unwonted splendour when, on November 21st and 28th appeared great singers from the Adelina Patti troupe — Sofia Scalchi, Mme. Novara, Galassi, Guille and Novara, probably the finest group, vocally, ever heard in that theatre. Arditi conducted. Another great contralto, Trebelli, and Ovide Musin exalted the concerts on December 5th and 12th. Snow and cold reduced, on the 5th, the attendance. Thenceforward I find a lacuna in the record of Sunday concerts; certainly the Casino could not hope to equal some of the glorious Italians they had recently presented.

I may thus revert to Erminie, with the statement that, in mid-January, the statuesque Belle Urquhart was listed for the part of Cerise. On January 20th (afternoon) a benefit for the Actors' Fund promised the second act of Erminie, R. C. Hilliard, Lilli Lehmann and Adolf Robinson, in a duet, John A. Mackay, Georgia Cayvan, Mme. Cavalazzi, Loie Fuller, R. B. Mantell, a scene from The Hunchback (with N. C. Goodwin and Estelle Clayton), Rosina Vokes, in A Double Lesson, and a scene from Investigation, with Harrigan, Wild and Mrs. Yeamans. Such an offering, if carried through, should have packed the theatre. The three hundredth performance of Erminie was duly celebrated on April 12th. On Sunday, April 24th, Patti's company then singing at the Metropolitan, a group of noble singers were at the Casino concert — Scalchi, the incomparable, and Guille, Galassi, Del Puente, Vicini and Abramoff; the group on May 1st

GERALDINE ULMAR
IN RUDDIGORE

KATE FORSTER AND
F. BILLINGTON

COURTICE POUNDS
IN RUDDIGORE

COURTENAY THORPE

AGNES MILLER

HELENA DACRE

F. A. EVERILL

JOSEPH CARNE

CHARLES F. COGHLAN

included Scalchi, Guille, Vicini, Del Puente, Miss Groebl, Novara and Mme. Novara. June 2nd was luminous with the four hundredth Erminie (at least so announced, though I can't see how they could have piled up a hundred performances since April 12th); the four hundred and fiftieth was announced for July 21st. Louise Sylvester, once our favourite at Wood's Museum, had latterly succeeded Mrs. Germon as the absurd Princess; in later June, Fanny Rice succeeded Marie Jansen as Javotte, Miss Jansen leaving for a holiday of a few weeks, and returning on August 29th.

CHAPTER V

NIBLO'S, BIJOU OPERA HOUSE, HARRIGAN'S, GRAND OPERA HOUSE, PEOPLE'S THEATRE, THE WINDSOR, THE THIRD AVENUE, POOLE'S, THE COMIQUE, FOREIGN ACTIVITIES, METROPOLITAN OPERA HOUSE, ACADEMY OF MUSIC, MINSTRELSY, VARIETY, ENTERTAINMENTS, MUSIC, 1886-1887

THE historic Niblo's re-opened for its fifty-third season on Saturday evening August 21, 1886, with a revival of the Kiralfy Around the World in Eighty Days. Needless to report, spectacle and dancing were the main features of the show; Clara Qualitz led the ballet. Chief actors were Beatrice Lieb as Aouda, Joseph Slayter as Phileas Fogg, Arthur Moulton as Passepartout, Henry W. Mitchell as O'Pake, Claude Brooke as Fix, Ed Mortimer as Arthur Mayburn, J. Wakefield as Foster Jones, and Ricca Allen as Nakahira. If these were the principals, very minor indeed must have been the minor players. Business for the three weeks of the visit was, according to Allston Brown, excellent.

LILLIAN OLCOTT AND THEODORA

This theatre still served as a home of scenic splendour. Its next attraction had been written up, excitedly and at great length, in the papers for several weeks before September 13th, when it was finally offered to an excited public. This was Sardou's sensational Théodora, written, as we knew, for the great Bernhardt, and now produced by Lillian Olcott, a young actress of whom few playgoers had ever heard until she then emerged in the gorgeous trappings of the wicked Roman empress. She or her backers had expended great sums of money on scenery and costumes and accoutrements and there can be no doubt that the result was a most impressive and possibly an artistic spectacle. Supporting the ambitious star, in chief rôles, were J. H. Gilmour as Andreas, Hudson Liston as Justinian, J. H. Rennie as Belisarius, J. Wirt Kail as Marcellus, George Gaston as Nicephorus, Carrie G. Vinton as Antonina, and Laura Phillips as Tamyris. A host of minor players assisted in the slight parts with which Sardou packed his dramatis personæ. For the benefit of harried readers, I pause to explain that Théodora, when acted in English, became Theodora, without a trace of French accent, acute or otherwise.

Though Miss Olcott was no Bernhardt, hardly indeed more than a rather

[252]

handsome amateur, she kept Theodora on the large stage of Niblo's through October 23rd and re-appeared in it, as we know, in various theatres during the following months. A big show but a different followed on October 25th, when Thatcher, Primrose and West's Minstrels brought in, as assistants to the name-stars, Billy Rice, George H. Edwards, George W. Powers, Ed Marble, H. C. Talbert, Griffin and Marks, Delhauer and Grover, Banks Winter, Burt Shepard and many more. During their second week they advertised Theodora in Cork, which was speeding the departing guest with a vengeance. Bartley Campbell, though departed, lived on in his spectacular Siberia, which came back, on November 8th, for two weeks. James O'Neill, with his ever-living Monte Cristo, entered on November 22nd for another fortnight of melodrama in fine scenery; J. W. Shannon and Grace Thorne still supported.

Mrs. Langtry

It is difficult for me, even though I saw her there in this very engagement, to think of Mrs. Langtry and her refined appeal, in the Niblo's of 1886–87. Yet here she came, on December 6th, in a production of Enemies, a new play by Charles Coghlan, which one might have expected her to launch near Madison Square. A story of conflicting interests between unfriendly rivals, Enemies was cast to the full strength of Mrs. Langtry's very good company:

Lord Dunderby	G. Raiemond	Daft Willie	Walter Lennox, Jr.
Arthur Blake	Sidney Herbert	Shaw	E. Mortimer
Sir Manvers Glenn	F. A. Everill	Mr. Dornton	G. Raiemond
Colonel Anderson	Newton Dana	Aunt Anne	Mrs. C. Calvert
Captain Glenn	Joseph Carne	Mrs. Lawler	Kate Pattison
Peter Darvel	H. A. Weaver	Rose Heeley	Miss Calvert
Richard Darvel	C. F. Coghlan	Margaret Glenn	Mrs. Langtry

Very small parts fell to Messrs. G. S. Stevens, Chambers, Burton, E. Shelly, S. J. Browne, and W. Spencer and Miss Brunel. Though I saw this play, I remember nothing about it except that the night outside was very cold, and that I sat in the balcony, to the side. And I seem to recall a picture of Mrs. Langtry in a becoming winter costume. And that is all I can get from a reluctant past; such a result leads me to infer that the public was right in dooming the comedy to failure. After two weeks, Mrs. Langtry reverted (December 20th) to her charming Lady of Lyons, which sufficed till her departure on January 1st.

Evangeline gaily started the new year (January 3rd), with Irene Verona (Gabriel), May Stembler (Evangeline) and Maffit as the Fisherman. Evans and Hoey (January 10th) prolonged the hilarity with a week of their unextinguishable Parlour Match. Then Niblo's restored (January 17th) its pet attraction, The Black Crook, with, as leading dancers, Clara Qualitz, Mlles. De Rosa and Newman, and, as incidental diversion, Arnold, D'Alvini,

[253]

the Mignani Family, and the Siegrist Brothers (acrobats). Mere actors were not specified in Herald advertisements, but even without such adventitious help, the youthful veteran wrung another five weeks from an insatiable public. Let social philosophers ponder well the inferences involved. Thatcher, Primrose and West's Minstrels returned, on February 21st, now accompanied by Fred W. Millis (the Australian ventriloquist), and offering a burlesque, Our National Opera, or, Thomas *versus* Trouble, with Billy Rice and Burt Shephard (*sic*). At this time newspapers were full of accounts of trouble in the National (late American) Opera Company, so bravely launched in 1886, and now (1887) headed toward the rocks, with Thomas, Mme. Fursch-Madi and Emma Juch as chief storm-centres. Cora Tanner, in Alone in London, caused tears and thrills (February 28th–March 5th) and before one knew it, Frank Daniels, in A Rag Baby (March 7th–12th) restored the reign of mirth. I hardly know what The Ivy Leaf accomplished (March 14th–19th). The White Slave (March 21st–26th) boasted of a "wonderful rain storm of real water"; May Newman, Frank Roberts and Frank Drew headed the cast. Washington Irving Bishop, on Sunday, the 20th, made a "farewell" appearance.

Robert Downing, stalwart and Forrestian (at least in intent), brought (March 28th) The Gladiator to a house that, in Forrest's time, had loved it well; William Muldoon was still the fighting Gaul. But that tragic experience passed into the recent Niblo progress of hilarity when, on April 4th, A Tin Soldier carried along the increasing vogue of the Hoyt formula in farce. And lo! on the 11th, once more The Black Crook came home, with Qualitz, De Rosa, Arnold, the Tissots, the Siegrist Brothers and A. O. Duncan (ventriloquist); but actors the advertisements entirely ignored. Again the unaging relic won three weeks of excited approval.

LAWRENCE BARRETT AND RIENZI

On May 2nd, Lawrence Barrett, our most farsighted and ambitious, if not our greatest tragedian, produced with care and reverence another seldom-acted play, Mary Russell Mitford's tragedy, Rienzi, adapted, I learn, by Steele MacKaye. Barrett devoted much attention to the spectacular possibilities of the piece (were the stage requirements his reason for selecting Niblo's?) and brought it out with this carefully trained cast:

Rienzi	Lawrence Barrett	Camillo	S. E. Springer
Stephen Colonna	B. G. Rogers	Alberti	Charles Koehler
John Ursini	C. M. Collins	Paolo	J. M. Sturgeon
Angelo	Charles B. Welles	Tommaso	Jameson Lee Finney
Savelli	Frederick Vroom	Claudia	Minna K. Gale
Frangipani	Kendall Weston	Lady Colonna	Minnie Monk
Torelli	J. W. Albaugh, Jr.	Leila Savelli	Miriam O'Leary
Leonardo	W. M. Stuart		

[254]

MRS. OWEN MARLOWE

MRS. D. P. BOWERS
AS QUEEN ELIZABETH

DENMAN THOMPSON
(OLD HOMESTEAD)

VIRGINIA MARLOWE

WALTER GALE
(HAPPY JACK)

LOUISA MORSE

LIONEL BROUGH
AND SIDNEY BROUGH

VIOLET CAMERON

ANNIE THOMPSON

The revival lasted three weeks, and, for his fourth, Barrett went back to established favourites: Yorick's Love (May 23rd, and matinée, 28th), Francesca da Rimini (24th and matinée, 25th); Hamlet (evening, 25th); The Merchant of Venice and David Garrick (26th and 27th); and Richelieu (28th, evening). I fear these four weeks may have been rather above the grasp of patrons habituated to The Black Crook.

Mr. and Mrs. McKee Rankin, on May 30th, brought to Niblo's their recent The Golden Giant, fresh from an engagement at the Fifth Avenue Theatre. It had three weeks accorded at Niblo's and gave way, on June 20th, to Travers House, the cast of which, perhaps from a mistaken sense of duty, I transcribe:

Sir Reginald Travers	J. T. Sullivan	Stella / Valerie	Adele Belgarde
Elliott Adair	Forrest Robinson	Mrs. Emery	Carrie Jamison
John Bland	Nelson Wheatcroft	Sarah Swaggers	Frankie McClellan
Mr. Bills	Kenneth Lee	Maria	Elizabeth Andrews
Father Antonio	Howard Coveney		
Lady Travers	Adeline Stanhope		

The last week of this fortnight closed the house for the season, on July 2nd. Niblo's was a declining force in our theatrical chronicle; it had become very far down town.

BIJOU OPERA HOUSE, 1886–1887

The Bijou, for the better part of two seasons had been a Dixey fastness. Nat Goodwin determined to make of 1886–87 there a Goodwin season. He succeeded. He began, on September 13th, with a very amusing burlesque by Yardley and Stephens — Little Jack Sheppard:

Jonathan Wild	N. C. Goodwin	Jack Sheppard	Loie Fuller
Blueskin	C. B. Bishop	Thomas Darrell	Rose Leighton
Sir Roland Trenchard	E. F. Goodwin	Mrs. Sheppard	Jennie Weathersby
Kneebone	Frank Currier	Winifred Wood	Addie Cora Reed
Mendez	F. T. Ward	Polly Stanmore	Lelia Farrell
Wood	A. Hart	Edgewood Bess	Helen Sedgwick
Captain Cuff	Ida Van Osten	Kitty Kettleby	Mabel Morris

According to Allston Brown, William Yardley, one of the authors of the burlesque, made his début, on November 15th, in the part of Blueskin. This merry fooling lasted through December 10th — a run of about ninety performances. With it, for much of the run, we had a skit, The Vanishing Lady, an item treated on various stages. On December 11th (Saturday night) Goodwin appeared in a double bill, Turned Up and Those Bells. In the first of these he was Caraway Jones, an undertaker, and, in the second, he gave his well-known imitation of Henry Irving — one of the most easily imitated of actors.

This bill lasted Goodwin till, on January 24th, he appeared as Lorenzo,

[255]

in The Mascot, with Lillie Grubb as Bettina, Lelia (*sic*) Farrell as Fiametta, Flora Irwin as Frederic, C. B. Bishop as Rocco, Stuart Harold as Pippo, E. F. Goodwin as the Doctor. A. Kerker directed the music. According to the Herald, the company, on the night of February 9th, after acting, took the 11:30 train for Boston, was to have supper on the way, would arrive in Boston at 7 o'clock on the morning of the 10th, be breakfasted by the Mayor and others, then, at eleven-thirty o'clock give two acts of Turned Up at the Elks' Benefit, in the Boston Theatre, and arrive again in New York in time for the evening performance. Somehow the actors in this and in similar exploits seemed to feel there was a lurking glory that might redound to their fame. This familiar specialty — The Mascot — closed on the 26th of February, The Skating Rink beginning, on the 28th, with Goodwin, Lillie Grubb, Loie Fuller, Lillie Alliston, Jennie Reeves, Lillian Fletcher, Bishop, J. W. Ransone, E. F. Goodwin, J. Canfield, C. Fletcher, W. Fletcher and H. De Witt in the merry-go-round on rollers. Allston Brown tells us that, on March 24th, Mrs. Goodwin (Eliza Weathersby) died. An attempt was made to stage The Mascot, but ultimately the audience was dismissed. On the next night, The Mascot was staged, with A. W. F. McCollin in Goodwin's part. The house was closed on the 28th, 29th and 30th.

On March 31st, Goodwin returned in Big Pony, or, the Gentlemanly Savage, by A. C. Wheeler (Nym Crinkle), with music by Edward I. Darling. For this American item the reader demands the cast:

Big Pony	N. C. Goodwin	Billy the Stag	Otto Wilkins
Don Filibusto	C. B. Bishop	Inez	Lillie Grubb
Sancho Mendingo	Stuart Harold	Marie	Loie Fuller
Lieutenant Arlington	Henry Moulton	Sagastina	Estelle Mortimer
Sergeant O'Glory	E. W. Leon	Oo-ka-how-ya-yah	Dolly Delroy
Polecat Pete	E. F. Goodwin	Un-ka-ki-yi	Madge Perry
Mustang Mike	H. C. De Witt	So-ro-sissi	J. Laurence
Gopher Joe	Robert Vance	In-ki-tink-i-mink	H. Dye

This sounds silly, but it ran into April. For his last week (April 25th–30th), Goodwin revived Little Jack Sheppard. From September through April he fulfilled his promise of making 1886–87 a Goodwin season. A benefit to John F. Donnelly, on April 10th, promised Goodwin, Bishop, John A. Mackay, Sweatnam, the Kernells, R. C. Hilliard, Sam Devere, Charles Dickson, Vernona Jarbeau, Federici, Jennie Yeamans, Loie Fuller, Ida Mülle, &c. On Sunday, April 24th, F. Federici, of Mikado and Ruddygore fame, gave a concert at the Bijou, with assistance from a heterogeneous group comprising Ida Corani, Rose Leighton, Queen Vassar, Robert Hilliard, A. P. Burbank, Harry Braham, Lester and Williams, Gus Kerker, Max Freeman and many more. And Henry E. Dixey, on May 2nd, became partner of Miles and Barton, in the management. And he came "home again," on that date, for more than a month of the never-failing Adonis. The eleven hundredth performance of the delightful nonsense was announced for June 11th. Herrmann began a fortnight of mystification, on June 6th, so I am in doubt as to how that epoch-making Adonis performance occurred on the 11th. On Tuesday, June 21st, Minnie Maddern began in Howard Taylor's play, Caprice, with which she closed the Bijou on July 9th; her company included William Morris, T. J. Herndon, Charles Stanley, Cyril Scott, Percy Brooke, F. A. Tannehill, Charles Webster, Harry Reeves, J. S. Madero, F. W. McClelland, Odette Tyler (later a favourite in Charles Frohman's companies) and Lulu Klein. This is not the most brilliant list of names my pen has inscribed.

HARRIGAN'S PARK THEATRE, 1886–1887

The company of Edward Harrigan was almost the most permanent stock company in the city; its membership varied but slightly from year to year. And the authorship of the plays produced varied even less — they were all by Harrigan himself.

The new season began on August 23, 1886, with a revival of Investigation, with Harrigan as D'Arcy Flynn, John Wild as Leander Tuck, Dan Collyer as Lorenzo Hogan, M. J. Bradley as Oscar Onderdonk, Harry Fisher as Orion Overhoe, William West as Mr. Hop Sing, Annie Yeamans as Belinda Tuggs, Amy Lee as Sarah Tuggs, Emily Yeamans as Mrs. Onderdonk, and, in other parts, George and William Merritt, John and Joseph Sparks, Richard Quilter, Peter Goldrich, Charles Sturges, G. L. Stout, Annie Langdon, Nellie Wetherell (now so spelled, and once of the Union Square company) and many more.

This revival served merely to bring the beloved actors before their admiring friends. Its successor, The O'Reagans, came forth on October 11th (postponed from the 4th) with this cast:

Bernard O'Reagan	Edward Harrigan	Earnest Strike	W. West
Silas Cohog	John Wild	Bernard O'Reagan, M. P.⎫ Bill Scailey ⎬	...Joseph Sparks
Lulu Cohog	Dan Collyer		
Darrell Kilhealy	M. J. Bradley	Bedalia McNeirney	Annie Yeamans
Herman Krouse	Harry Fisher	Kate McNeirney	Amy Lee
Paddy Kelso	John Sparks	An Unfortunate⎫ A Ballet Girl ⎬	Annie Langdon
Charley Dreams	George Merritt		
Ludlow Philkins	P. Goldrich	Mrs. Kehoe	Nellie Wetherell
Stevie McAleir	R. Quilter	Sylvie Dreams	Emily Yeamans

Among many minor adjutants were Charles Sturges, Charles Coffey, G. L. Stout, Joseph Davis, James McCullough, William Merritt, Kate Langdon, Annie Hall, Florence Hastings and several others utterly unknown to later generations. The O'Reagans, though not a memorable or outstanding Harrigan success, nevertheless achieved a run of sixteen weeks before it departed on January 29th.

On January 31st Harrigan was ready with another novelty, McNooney's Visit, in which, as Martin McNooney, he had the assistance of Wild as Ely

Umstead, Dan Collyer as Clara Grizzle, Bradley as Lionel Mellow, Fisher as Judge Holzweizer, Mrs. Yeamans as Norah Gilmartin and Amy Lee as Adèle Spoonful (Harrigan could not rival Augustin Daly in utterly appropriate but credible names for his characters). All the rest of the large company, including Quilter and Goldrich, John and Joseph Sparks, the Langdon girls and Emily Yeamans, filled parts of less importance. This piece ended its career on April 16th; though they had respectable runs, neither of Harrigan's new plays of 1886–87 rivalled in success some of his best plays. I learn from the Herald that, on February 14th, Harrigan's friends, the Seventh Regiment, "let loose" at a performance of McNooney.

Cordelia's Aspirations, one of the most famous of the Harrigan-Mulligan series was revived on April 18th and continued till the close of the regular season on April 30th. Harrigan and Mrs. Yeamans, needless to say, were again Dan and Cordelia, and Dan Collyer succeeded to Tony Hart's old rôle of Rebecca Allup. Wild, Fisher, Bradley, Goodrich, Amy Lee, Nellie Wetherell (now sic) and the customary phalanx of familiar faces cheered the regular patrons and by them were cheered in turn. And so good-bye for the season to friends tried and true!

On May 2nd, The Gypsy Baron came, under direction of Heinrich Conried, into these unaccustomed quarters. The company included Laura Bellini, Harry De Lorme, Taglieri, Gustavus Hall, Jacques Kruger, Marion Singer, Lydia O'Neill and "Jennie" Reiffarth. The visit was very short, and Harrigan's soon closed for the summer. But how unified the record of the theatre, and how simple to transcribe! Two benefits, however, clog our path. On the afternoon of May 19th, the family of the late minstrel, William Welch, profited, I hope, through participation of scenes from The Highest Bidder, The Kindergarden and Kit, and bits by Harrigan, Gus Williams and Annie Yeamans. Henry Dixey was to take tickets at the gate. And a benefit to Billy Birch, poor fellow, enlisted (May 26th) Dockstader, Frank Mayo, Mr. and Mrs. Rankin and others.

Grand Opera House, 1886–1887

The reader will tire, I fear, of the story of proceedings for this season at the six theatres now to be discussed — cheaper "combination" houses, each opened, generally for a week in turn, to stars and companies, often very good, though not the very best or most acclaimed at the moment. Worst of all, cross-reference will show that an attraction listed at one of the houses will re-appear at another, and then journey to Brooklyn or Williamsburgh, bringing into our narrative an almost sickening monotony. The reader may skip what wearies him, but a poor, conscientious annalist must plod along.

Let us open the west-side Grand Opera House, on August 23, 1886, with McNish, Johnson and Slavin's Minstrels — negro minstrelsy, as we know,

[258]

CLARA QUALITZ

LILLIAN OLCOTT
(THEODORA)

LOIE FULLER

N. C. GOODWIN
AS JONATHAN WILD

LAWRENCE BARRETT
AS RIENZI

LAWRENCE BARRETT
AS RIENZI

J. H. GILMOUR

SARA JEWETT

LELIA FARRELL

having acquired a new popularity. A week of Frederick B. Warde whirled us to the opposite extreme of theatre with a rapid succession, in order, of Virginius (August 30th, September 3rd), Julius Cæsar (August 31st), Ingomar (matinée, September 1st), Richelieu (evening of the 1st), Damon and Pythias (2nd), The Lady of Lyons (matinée, September 4th) and Richard III (evening of the 4th). The next week (September 6th–11th) brought something humorously different, with Frank Daniels, in A Rag Baby, that new kind of hilarious farce; and spectacle succeeded (September 13th–18th) in shape of Kiralfy Brothers's Sieba. In the cast were Misses Lieb and Hunter, Mrs. Irwin, the four Miss Allens, and Messrs. Slayter, Bartholomew, Denham, Bonner, Moulton and Mason. James A. Herne's play, The Minute Men (20th–25th) gave patrons the opportunity to ponder on how many kinds of dramatic entertainment one could enjoy in a month's attendance at one theatre. Hoodman Blind, seen the season before at Wallack's, came now (September 27th–October 2nd) laden with melodrama and fine, realistic scenery, and with a good cast headed by Joseph Haworth and Sydney Armstrong in the rôles played at Wallack's by Kyrle Bellew and Annie Robe; others were Augustus Cook, Sidney Howard, M. B. Snyder, Bessie Bernard and Rose Snyder. Tony Pastor, not yet ready to return to his home in Fourteenth Street, brought still another form of amusement for the week of October 4th–9th; with him were Leopold and Bunnell (*sic*), Catherine Nelson with her birds, Master Belzac (prestidigitateur), John F. Byrne and Miss Helene, Callan, Haley and Callan, Flora Moore, Dare Brothers, and the Viennese grotesques, Steff and Trepp. If one thinks that Tony had often been surrounded with more glittering hosts, let him remember that the brightest talents in Variety had been drafted into the service of the raging musical farces like A Rag Baby and all that Charles H. Hoyt and others were producing for the delight of an indulgent public. Evans and Hoey, in A Parlour Match (October 11th–16th) will show the inquiring reader exactly what I mean.

The variety of entertainment offered to patrons of the Grand Opera House, that autumn, is a lesson to us of what changes in kind the theatre can offer. Here (October 18th–23rd) comes, on the heels of the shifting pageant of the weeks preceding, the first comic opera of the season, Conried's Company, in The Gypsy Baron, with Laura Bellini, Lydia O'Neill, Jacques Kruger and Gustavus Hall. And dignified drama, direct from the region of Broadway, ended October, when Genevieve Ward, in Forget-Me-Not (October 25th to 28th) and in The Queen's Favourite (29th) revealed the sharply-etched talent that was hers.

For the benefit of the Actors' Fund, on the afternoon of October 29th, a fine array was enlisted: Frederic Bryton, in an act of Forgiven; Marshall P. Wilder; Wilson Barrett and Miss Eastlake, in Chatterton; Maud Harrison as Helen, and N. C. Goodwin as Modus, in a scene from The Hunchback; the third act of Moths, with Miss Fortescue, Kyrle Bellew and Henry Hamilton; a song by Lucille Meredith; and Genevieve Ward in an act of The Queen's Favourite. The public responded to the sum of $3,000. And, since I have thus drifted from the regular bills at the Grand Opera House, I may report that, throughout the season, beginning on October 10th, Professor Cromwell gave Sunday night illustrated lectures, transporting his hearers to foreign or even domestic scenes now (1941) familiar to every one, either by means of the cinema or by personal experience: Scotland (October 10th); Brussels, Antwerp, Waterloo (17th); The Sunny South, Charleston Before and After the Earthquake (31st); Amsterdam (November 7th); Paris of Today (14th); Cologne and the Rhine (21st); London (28th); Chicago and the Wild West (December 5th); Paris Today (December 19th); Rome and Southern Italy (26th); The Homes of England (January 9th); Around the World (16th); Chicago, repeated (23rd); and Paris again (30th). Here I leave him, in the lap of winter. But I go back to the afternoon of December 9th, when a benefit to the New York Lodge, No. 1, B.P.O. Elks promised rare enjoyment with stage contributions by Wilson Barrett and Miss Eastlake, Helen Dauvray and company, the Madison Square company, Louis James and Marie Wainwright, Nat Goodwin, Marguerite Fish (once Baby Benson), Harrigan's company, Dockstader's, Loie Fuller and M. B. Curtis.

Let us return to drama, if only with Gus Williams, in George Hoey's Oh! What a Night (November 1st–6th). The Silver King (November 8th–13th), yielded the stage (15th–20th) to A Bunch of Keys, with Eugene Canfield and Marietta Nash, that, in turn, making way (22nd–27th) for a return of Conried's Gypsy Baron. Shadows of a Great City (November 29th–December 4th) enlisted W. S. Harkins, Thomas Lytton and Helen Rand. I record the performances of December 6th–11th with a tender regret, since they mark the last appearances on the New York stage of the lovely Sara Jewett. She had retired, we remember, in 1884–85, when the Union Square stock company, with which her fame was connected, went out of existence. Illness prevented her from working, and now Kate Claxton engaged her for a week in The Two Orphans, which they had played together in the palmiest Union Square days of 1876. "Mature, but impressive orphans" the Times review called them, now, in 1886, and impressive to me they were as I watched them, one of an audience not very large, on an evening in this week's engagement. Miss Jewett was not sure of her lines, but her exquisite charm remained, and I am glad to have been there to bid her good-bye, though, of course, I then thought it was merely *au revoir*. She lived, in poor health, till 1899. The other members of that Claxton-Jewett cast of The Two Orphans included Charles A. Stevenson and James L. Edwards.

Entirely divergent entertainment followed (December 13th–18th), in the Kiralfy Around the World in Eighty Days, featuring, as at Niblo's, Clara Qualitz, Arnold and the popular Newman. Oliver and Kate Byron (December 20th–25th) excited with The Inside Track, and Annie Pixley (December 27th–January 1st) exhibited the thrice familiar blandishments of M'liss; with her were Davenport Bebus as Juba Bill and Samuel Reed as Templeton Fake. Members of the Madison Square Theatre company not employed in the current bill on the home stage presented the beautiful Saints and Sinners (January 3rd–8th), with J. H. Stoddart, Marie Burroughs, W. J. Ferguson and Sydney Cowell (then passing into the interpreting of middle-aged women). Thatcher, Primrose and West's Minstrels disported during the week of January 10th–15th; and Lillian ·Olcott as Theodora found haven here for the next (17th–22nd). Joseph Haworth returned (January 24th–29th) in Hoodman Blind. Cora Tanner, in Alone in London, offered similar thrills for January 31st–February 5th. Mme. Janauschek, whom I always pity as a relic not quite placed in the theatre of that day, had a customary week of repertoire with Bleak House (7th, 10th, and matinée, 12th); Mary Stuart (8th and 11th); Mother and Son (matinée, 9th), Marie Antoinette (9th, evening) and Macbeth (evening, 12th). The Lights o' London (February 14th–19th) featured Harry Lee and Helen Weathersby; and (21st–26th), Monte Cristo featured James O'Neill, unless indeed in that case it was the other way about. A Tin Soldier (February 28th–March 5th) passed into smiling (?) spring with a laugh. And Hubert Wilke, in Kiralfy's The Ratcatcher, charmed audiences, if he did not carry them away or march them out, in the week of March 7th–12th. W. J. Scanlan, in Shane-na-Lawn (week of March 14th–19th) did in an Irish way exactly what J. K. Emmet, in Fritz, did in a German way. He sang his own ditties and smiled and won all hearts. C. C. Maubury (21st–26th) showed The Wages of Sin.

Far more to the liking of fastidious tastes was the attraction of the following week, Fanny Davenport, in Fedora (March 28th, 31st, and matinées, March 30th and April 2nd); The Lady of Lyons (inspired by Mrs. Langtry's, March 29th); The School for Scandal (April 1st); and Oliver Twist and London Assurance (evening, April 2nd). Forgiven (April 4th–9th) employed F. Bryton, Blanche Thorne, Marie Bingham and Harry Harwood; and Held by the Enemy (11th–16th) awakened tense excitement. And Hoodman Blind came for a third visit (18th–23rd) still with Haworth, Miss Armstrong and the cast first seen here in the autumn. Evangeline, ever popular and doubtless missed, came back (April 25th–30th) with special engagements of George Thorne and Vernona Jarbeau, leaders, the year before, in the rival Mikados that tore the town in twain. Biggest and best star of the season was Joseph Jefferson (May 2nd–7th) in the never-failing Rip Van Winkle, timeless in the decades. Herrmann, the magician, was here for the week of May 9th–14th; the following week brought Joseph Murphy, in The Kerry Gow (May 16th, 17th, and matinée, 18th); and beginning on

[261]

May 18th, evening, a new piece by George Fawcett Rowe, entitled The Donagh:

Lantry Killaly..............Joseph Murphy	Phil Slattery.................W. T. Sheehan
The McBride....................H. D. Byers	Piper.....................Bernard Delaney
Dorsey McMurragh..............O. J. Loring	Kate McBride.................Belle Melville
Dennis...................Maurice Heppard	Rose Coonan....................Alfa Perry
Terence Killaly.................Fred Sackett	Mrs. Killaly.................Marion Clifton
Arthur McBride................G. R. Boaler	Peggy...........................Ella Baker
Mike Coonan.................John Murphy	

Reading that list of names is almost like reading inscriptions on tombstones in a country churchyard. Well, here we are at last—The Black Crook, fresh from Niblo's, for May 23rd–28th.

Rose Coghlan, the radiant, came into the Grand Opera House, supported by her colleague of the last of the great years at Wallack's—Osmond Tearle. It must have been delightful to follow them through their week: Peg Woffington (May 30th, 31st, June 2nd and 4th); The Lady of Lyons (also inspired by Mrs. Langtry's? matinée, June 1st), London Assurance (evening, June 1st) and The School for Scandal (June 3rd). Auditors could compare the buoyant and beautiful Miss Coghlan with the beautiful and more placid Fanny Davenport in some of these same comedies, as presented a few weeks earlier on the same all-embracing stage. George C. Boniface and his likable daughter, Stella, followed (June 6th–11th) in the frequently trod Streets of New York, she somewhat out of her Wallack line as Alida Bloodgood. Another Frank Mayo specialty emerged for the week of June 13th–18th, when Edwin F. Mayo tried to duplicate his father's success, in Davy Crockett; Loduski Young was the heroine saved from the villain and the wolves. In Hazel Kirke (June 20th–25th) appeared C. W. Couldock, W. J. Ferguson, May Wheeler (Hazel), Ada Gilman, Frank Carlyle (Carringford) and W. H. Crompton (Aaron Rodney). Henry Chanfrau, another son trying to walk in his father's footsteps, finished the season at this house (June 27th–July 3rd) in his father's famous play of Kit, the Arkansas Traveller. His support included Alice Bancker, J. R. Carey, Odell Williams and Little Birdie Black. For the matinées, on June 29th and July 3rd, was advertised American Grit.

I resume peregrinations with Cromwell, just to apprise the reader of the powers of the magic lantern, in those days before the cinema: Moscow, St. Petersburg and Constantinople (February 6th); Berlin (13th); America, Our Home (March 6th); Gems of Art and the Alhambra (April 10th); Within a Mile o' Edinboro' Town (17th).

People's Theatre, 1886–1887

The pattern of the seasons at these cheaper "combination" theatres is about the same from house to house; only the component items differ. The

[262]

People's Theatre, Harry Miner's fastness in the Bowery, re-opened, on August 23, 1886, with the play that had closed it in early July—Zitka. The cast included Charlotte Behrens, Adeline Stanhope, Victoria Reynolds, Marie Whittingham, J. Leslie Gossin, Frank Evans, George A. Robinson and John Walsh. Edmund Collier, become Forrestian, filled the week of August 30th–September 4th with Jack Cade and Metamora. James A. Herne and Katharine Corcoran Herne followed (September 6th–11th) in his new play, The Minute Men. Blackmail followed (13th–18th), with Carrie Rose and W. C. Cowper. Shadows of a Great City (September 20th-25th) enlisted Helen Rand, Annie Ward Tiffany, W. S. Harkins, George R. Edeson and W. W. Allen. A Rag Baby allows us to laugh (September 27th–October 2nd) with thankful enjoyment; Frank Daniels, Harry Conor, W. F. Mack and Bessie Sanson (once of the Vokes forces) were chief funmakers.

Ada Gray had at least something new for her in A Ring of Iron (October 4th–9th), and Effie Ellsler (11th–16th) something older, in Woman against Woman. The theatre began, on the 10th, a series of Sunday Illustrated Lectures, with Erminic on Napoleon and Moscow. A Wall Street Bandit, from the Standard Theatre, enlisted (18th–23rd) W. J. Ferguson, Robert McWade, Charles Bowser and Anna Boyle. John A. Stevens (25th–30th) ended October with A Great Wrong Righted, and Kate Claxton, Charles A. Stevenson, Alice Leigh, James Edwards, Dollie Pike and Joseph A. Wilkes began November (1st–6th) with the inescapable The Two Orphans. We became rather educational, during the week of November 8th–13th, with Robson and Crane, in The Comedy of Errors, but lapsed (November 15th–20th) to melodrama with The Silver King. For this performance were advertised a "double stage and revolving scenery"—a suggestion that "intrigues" my modern spirit. Frank Mayo, in Nordeck, brought romance into the week of November 22nd–27th, the star's support including Alice Lorimer as Wanda, Alice Fischer as the Princess, St. Martin as Fabian and J. H. Taylor as Witthold. Thereafter in weekly sequence followed (November 29th–December 4th) Held by the Enemy, with Kathryn Kidder; Gus Williams, in Oh! What a Night (December 6th–11th); Tony Hart, in Donnybrook (13th–18th), assisted by Belle Stokes and Carrie Tutein; and Evans and Hoey, in A Parlour Match (20th–25th). Something of higher reputation came with Fanny Davenport, who divided the week of December 27th–January 1st between Fedora and the double bill of London Assurance and Oliver Twist, a bill that indubitably called for great versatility.

Edmund Collier, with Sara Neville and a group of Sioux Indians, came back (January 3rd–8th) in Metamora. Joseph Haworth and Sydney Armstrong (10th–22nd) suffered through the agonies of Hoodman Blind, which visited, as we know, the Grand Opera House thrice in that season; it had the unique distinction of staying two weeks at the almost invariably one-week stand at the People's. The Private Secretary, with William Gillette and

[263]

A. M. Palmer's company, filled the week of January 24th–29th, A Tin Soldier, with James T. Powers, following for January 31st–February 5th. J. K. Emmet was bright star of February 7th–12th. The Mestayer-Theresa Vaughn combination filled the week of February 14th–19th, of course in We Us and Co., followed, with no logical reason (21st–26th) by Maubury's haunting refrain of The Wages of Sin. Robert Downing, still accompanied by William Muldoon, devoted the week of February 28th–March 5th to the then dying Gladiator. March 7th began a week of Milton and Dollie Nobles, in Love and Law (first half of the *semaine*) and The Phœnix (second half). On the 14th, John A. Stevens introduced Passing Shadows, his support including Louise Balfe, Emily Lytton, Harry Eytinge, C. B. Hawkins and Addie Cummings; it was advertised as revised from the author's play, Her Second Love. After fulfilling its allotted six days, it resigned the stage to Aimée, in Mam'zelle (March 21st–26th). Mrs. D. P. Bowers then came for a week in her accepted parts: Elizabeth (March 28th and 29th and April 1st); Mary Stuart (March 30th); Macbeth (31st); Lady Audley's Secret (matinées, March 30th and April 2nd). I end the paragraph by stating that ubiquitous stereopticon travel lectures occasionally, that winter, made sacred Sunday evenings at the People's. On March 20th, Frank E. Hipple spoke on The Dominions of the Czar and the Condition of the Jews in Russia and Poland — a theme suggestive of our dire European troubles in 1938–41; on March 27th he discoursed on Ireland, Past and Present. On April 10th his theme was Germany and the Rhine.

And here is Hoodman Blind again (April 4th–9th); what a vogue it had in the minors! Conried's singers in The Gypsy Baron, also very popular, at least frequently seen, filled the week of April 11th–16th with music and mirth. And, of all things in the world, the elegance and lace-like precision of Mrs. John Drew, the elder, came to the Bowery, on April 18th, as Mrs. Malaprop, in The Rivals, her daughter, Georgie Drew Barrymore playing Lydia, her son, Sidney Drew, enacting Bob Acres, J. H. Fitzpatrick Sir Lucius, and Newton Gotthold Jack Absolute. That should have made a delightful week. The Main Line came for the week of April 25th–30th, with, of course, Etta Hawkins in the comic lead, and with Dora Stuart, Hague, De Mille, Allen, Mills and Conway. The popular Scanlan, in Shane-na-Lawn (May 2nd–7th) was assisted by Lillian Clarke, Kitty O'Shea (as the child), and Laura Wilson (as the Witch). James O'Neill, in Monte Cristo (May 9th–14th); Lillian Olcott, in Theodora (16th–21st); Goodwin, in Little Jack Sheppard (23rd–28th) behold the events of a varied May! May 30th began a week of On the Rio Grande. For two weeks (June 6th–18th), Frank Mayo played The Royal Guard (by Mayo and John W. Wilson, authors of Nordeck). In this reminiscence of Dumas, Mayo was D'Artagnan, Edmund Collier Athos, David Hanchett Porthos, George Frederick Nash Louis XIII, Henry Bergman Richelieu, Miss Clyde Harron Anne

[264]

of Austria and Katherine Rogers Lady de Winter—an astonishing cast to find so far from Madison Square or Thirtieth Street. And will the reader note his meeting with Nash and Bergman—strong men of the near future? Robert McWade, in Rip Van Winkle (June 20th–25th) closed what must have been to regular patrons of the house an interesting season, some items of which were, even to Broadway taste, decidedly attractive.

WINDSOR THEATRE, 1886–1887

Again we try to solve the pattern of a "combination" house. The Windsor Theatre, 43-47 Bowery, began the season of 1886–87, on August 16th, with Fred B. Warde in his latterly favourite rôle of Virginius; this he repeated on the 17th and 20th, piecing together a week of repertoire with Ingomar (matinée, 18th); with Damon and Pythias (evenings of the 18th and 21st); Richard III (19th) and The Lady of Lyons (as an easy matinée offering on the 21st). All this sounds like a fading dream of times in the '60s. The melodrama, Youth, seen five years earlier at Wallack's, came to the Windsor (August 23rd–28th), with Agnes Proctor, Mary Mills, King Hedley, W. A. Paul and Harry Woodruff. More thrills ran along the following week (August 30th–September 4th) with A Prisoner for Life, involving Frances Field, Marie Vernon, Nellie Cross, O. B. Collier, James Jackson and Charles Farwell—as unfamed a group as posterity might puzzle over. And almost equally undistinguished was the cast of The White Slave (September 6th–11th), with May Newman, Frank Drew, F. S. Russ (sic), and Frank Foster.

Thus far, the record for the Windsor, that season, is not shining. Something rather better came (September 13th–18th) when Frederic Bryton, with Blanche Thorne, gave the omnipresent Forgiven; Harry Harwood, Henry Bergman and Marie Bingham, were, as we learned at another theatre, in the cast. Lost in London brought more melodrama (September 20th–25th) with Newton Beers, Phœbe Don and Miss Randolph heading the cast. Mr. and Mrs. George S. Knight, in Over the Garden Wall, held the week of September 27th–October 2nd; they were still accompanied by the St. Felix Sisters and Edward (sic) Fay (sic). Something very dignified entered for the next week, in person of Mme. Janauschek, in her familiar plays: Mary Stuart (October 4th, and matinée, 9th); Bleak House (5th and 7th); Mother and Son (matinée, 6th); Marie Antoinette (evening, 6th); Henry VIII (8th); and Macbeth (evening, 9th). I wonder what we should think, in 1941, of a series of classic plays staged in so fortuitous a manner. And another week of repertoire followed, when Clara Morris, fresh from a brief stay at the Union Square, brought the same company and about the same plays to the Windsor: Article 47 (October 11th, 12th); The New Magdalen (13th, 14th); Miss Multon (15th); and Camille (matinée, 16th). Accord-

[265]

ing to Allston Brown, Mary Shaw took up the cough and the tears of Camille on the evening of the 16th. We remember that Henry Miller and Bijou Heron were in Miss Morris's company. Our Boarding House began a week, on October 18th, with Charles Stedman as Gillipod and W. L. Clark as Elevator.

May Blossom, with Ben Maginley as star, filled the week of October 25th–30th, allowing us to enter November (1st–6th) with Oliver and Kate Byron, in The Inside Track. I regret that I cannot inform the reader specifically about Phosa McAllister or her company, which held the week of November 8th–13th, in Taken from Life. Storm Beaten we remember from its Union Square history; it came to the Windsor for November 15th–20th, and gave way (November 22nd–27th) to A Bunch of Keys, which in turn moved out for Annie Pixley (November 29th–December 4th) in M'liss, of which she must have grown somewhat weary. Louis James and Marie Wainwright brought still another week of what may have begun to seem an over-familiar repertoire: Virginius (December 6th, 7th, 11th, and matinée, 8th); Hamlet (evening, 8th); Othello (9th); The Merchant of Venice and Katharine and Petruchio (10th); and Romeo and Juliet (matinée, 11th). With them were F. C. Mosley, F. C. Huebner and Kate Meek. James, like Warde, Downing and other members of the tragic group, never quite entered the realm of the immortals. Siberia followed (December 13th–18th) with Adele Belgarde, George Nash, Stella Teuton and Forrest Robinson. Christmas week (December 20th–25th) gave the rich, if very familiar, gift of James O'Neill, in Monte Cristo, and passed into the New Year (December 27th–January 1st) with Tony Denier's Humpty Dumpty, Fred W. Millis, ventriloquist, serving among the special performers.

Candour compels me to admit that the autumn at the Windsor was far from impressive. I pause to chronicle a testimonial (December 26th) to Henrietta Markstein, at which were to appear Tim Murphy, Harry Kennedy, Mabel Stephenson, Marie Cahill, Carl Lanzer and others. On Sunday, January 2nd, appeared there, for some purpose unknown to me, Harry Pepper, John E. McWade, Jolly Nash, Carrie Tutein, the Misses Stanley, Adolphe Glose and Carlo de Serag. On a cold evening, such as January 2nd may have been, I should have preferred, to that group, a good book by a fire. The business in the theatre, for January 3rd–8th, was The Romany Rye, with Victory Bateman and John Burke. The ambitious Fred B. Warde presented, for the week of January 10th–15th, Leonard G. Outram's new play, Galba, the Gladiator; Eugenie Blair was Neodamia, Miss Wood Fulvia and Mrs. Herman Flavia, a trio of graces that leaves me cold and guessing. And George C. Boniface, as Badger, in The Streets of New York cannot lure me (January 17th–22nd) from my fireside to the ill-cleaned sidewalks of the town. I have not been able to learn the charms of W. H. Powers's company in that elusive play, The Ivy Leaf, and I can-

[266]

not in midwinter (January 24th–29th) go 'way 'way down to 43 Bowery to discover what they really were. Having carefully avoided in prehistoric days the offerings of James H. Wallick, I believe I will pass over, by mere mention thereof, his performance of The Cattle King (January 31st–February 5th). Harry Lacy, in The Planter's Wife, sounds more promising for the week of February 7th–12th, especially as Edna Carey played the troubled heroine. Surely those last few weeks at the Windsor sank considerably below the offerings of the People's, farther to the north in the Bowery.

Cora Tanner was here, February 14th–19th, in Alone in London, assisted by C. G. Craig, W. A. Sands, Laura Le Claire and Ada Dwyer. Effie Ellsler followed (21st–26th) in the equally familiar Woman against Woman, and with a better company, including Mrs. E. L. Davenport, Frank Weston, Mattie Earle, Mary Sanders and Archie Boyd. The Daly Brothers, in Vacation (February 28th–March 5th) hardly exalted the Windsor's prestige, nor, probably, did Charles Bowser (March 7th–12th) in Howard Coveney's piece, Dollars and Dimes, the cast of which included Helen Blythe (whom we had not recently seen), Blanche Plunkett, Alice Grey and J. F. Brien. We, Us and Co., with Mestayer and Theresa Vaughn, drew laughter in the week of March 14th–19th, and probably set agog the minds of auditors for the fooling (21st–26th) of Thatcher, Primrose and West's Minstrels, with Millis and the skit, Our National Opera.

Almost the only really superior attraction seen that season at the Windsor came in the week of March 28th–April 2nd, when the distinguished Genevieve Ward appeared in Forget-Me-Not. April 4th–9th supplied Fantasma, with William Hanlon, Alexander Zanfretta and Kate Davis leading. The Ivy Leaf must have been better than I had supposed; it had another week, beginning on April 11th. But I know that audiences never tired of Evans and Hoey, in A Parlour Match, lighted once more for April 18th–23rd. And Joseph Murphy also delighted ever, with The Kerry Gow and Shaun Rhue, which divided (into equal parts) the week of April 25th–30th. And the undiscourageable Mme. Janauschek brought, on May 2nd, that Meg Merrilies which she had tried at the Union Square Theatre; it was advertised as with Bishop's music. And Clara Morris also returned to raise the standard with Miss Multon (May 9th, 10th); Article 47 (11th, 12th); The New Magdalen (13th); and Camille (matinée, 14th). The company acted Engaged at the Wednesday matinée, and a special bill, on Saturday evening. Those "off" performances in a Clara Morris season must have entailed sad loss to the treasury. Edmund Collier, who had tried to be Forrestian, became, for April 16th–21st, his former melodramatic self, in Michael Strogoff. Her Atonement was paid in the week of May 23rd, and, for May 30th–June 4th, Edwin Arden again essayed Eagle's Nest. The Lights o' London made familiar going, in the week of June 6th–11th, with Archibald Foster, William Lee and Helen Weathersby. Arizona Joe, the Shooting

Star, sufficed for June 13th–18th, and Henry T. Chanfrau, in Kit, for the following week (20th–25th). A comedy by Colonel Joseph Nunez, of Louisville, entitled False Steps, was brought out, on June 27th, under supervision of F. F. Mackay, the cast including Harry Rich, J. H. Fitzpatrick, C. H. Bradshaw, Lester Victor, Gus Hennessey, Hattie Russell (sister of Ada Rehan), Ada Deaves, Belle Shreve, Amy Ames and Frances Sumner. "Old Bowery Favourites" were advertised, in July, including Joseph P. Winter, Charles Foster, J. B. Brown, Maurice Pike, Mrs. W. G. Jones and Millie Sackett. Their ancient fare consisted of La Tour de Nesle and An Irishman's Home (4th, 5th); Waiting for the Verdict and The Staff of Diamonds (6th, 7th); Nick of the Woods and Cartouche (8th, 9th); and, with N. S. Wood, Jack Sheppard (11th, 12th, 13th); The Boy Detective (14th, 15th); and The Boy Scout (both performances, 16th).

THIRD AVENUE THEATRE, 1886–1887

This theatre in Third Avenue re-opened, on August 16th, 1886, with "Professor" Bristol's trained horses. Dignified as "Bristol's Equine Wonders," the steeds pursued their career for two more weeks. Murray and Murphy, in Our Irish Visitors, were here for September 13th–18th, possibly foreseeing, even thus early, their six-weeks run, in the same play, next summer, at J. M. Hill's other house, the Union Square Theatre. Josephine Cameron, of whom, I suspect, the reader has never heard, unless, like me, he saw her, in his boyhood, in a small city — Josephine Cameron appeared as Camille (September 20th, 24th and 25th); as Parthenia, in Ingomar (21st, and matinée, 22nd); and in East Lynne (22nd, 23rd, and matinée, 25th). According to a Herald review, she and her company "turned Camille into a farce." The audience laughed at it; she was very "plump" — a handicap to Camille whatever it may be to Violetta, in La Traviata. Miss Cameron may not again cross our range of vision. Bertha Welby, who never reached the heights, followed, also in repertoire: Oliver Twist (September 27th, 28th and 29th); The Martyr Mother (September 30th, October 1st, 2nd). Her Nancy was supported by Ida Ward as Oliver, Julian Magnus as Fagin, John Hazelrigg as Bill, George Le Claire as the Dodger, all uniting, according to the candid Herald, in "a poor performance." I fear we must not expect too much in this democratic theatre.

The Lillian Conway Comic Opera Company was here, October 4th–9th, in The Grand Duchess and, later in the week, in Fatinitza. I cannot imagine Mrs. Conway's daughter in these works or in such surroundings; neither of the Conway sisters had fulfilled the hopes of their native Brooklyn. With her, in this venture, were Charles F. Lang and the funny Jeff De Angelis. Edwin Arden, in his popular Eagle's Nest, came for a week beginning on October 11th, and Joseph Murphy, for October 18th–23rd, with, as usual,

[268]

three days of Kerry Gow and three of Shaun Rhue. I am delighted to welcome (October 25th) Neil Burgess for a week of Vim, but look somewhat askance at Daniel Bandmann, who filled the week of November 1st–6th with a repertoire including Hamlet, The Merchant of Venice, East Lynne, Othello, Romeo and Juliet, Narcisse and Richard III. I doubt if utmost finish of detail could characterise plays juggled about in such rapid changing. The following week (November 8th–13th) was to have brought Louise Rial, in Fortune's Fool. T. J. Farron, once of Baker and Farron, seems to have substituted, in A Soap Bubble; Gracie Emmett was in the cast. F. B. Warde, whom I cannot so highly regard, in these, his starring days, as in his fine years at Booth's, gave a week (November 15th–20th) divided into performances of Virginius, Richard III, a double bill of Shylock and Petruchio, Claude Melnotte and Ingomar. And, for the week of November 22nd–27th, Murray and Murphy returned, in Our Irish Visitors.

Let us pass into winter and (December 6th–11th) greet Louis Aldrich, in the reliable My Partner, noting with interest the name of T. M. Hunter, the Boston actor, for the part of Clay Britt. Dominick Murray, once again in democratic circles, was at the Third Avenue, in the week of December 13th–18th, in his perennial Escaped from Sing Sing. The Long Strike, also an undying asset, filled the holiday week of December 20th–25th. And, on December 21st, the theatre passed from the control of J. M. Hill to that of H. R. Jacobs, who figured for years in the name of the theatre—thenceforward known as H. R. Jacobs' Third Avenue Theatre. He signalised his entrance into the management by reducing admission to 15, 25, 35, 50 and 75 cents. Beginning on December 27th, Shadows of a Great City followed this Christmas transfer of property, and the offering of January 3rd–8th seems quite in line with reduction of admission prices—Zo-Zo, the Magic Queen; Blanche Curtisse, George H. Adams and Louis Farrell led the cast. A Bunch of Keys, however, for the week of January 10th–15th carries us back to "normalcy."

These catalogues of offerings at the "combination" houses are easy to set down, but rather boring to read. Frank Mayo in Nordeck restored (January 17th–22nd) to this theatre one of its salient successes of the previous season. When The World began the week of January 24th–29th, prices of admission were reduced to 10 and 20 cents, of course for the less desirable seats. What was wrong with Jacobs? Another of those Wallack melodramas—The Silver King—awakened terror (January 31st–February 5th).

I found no more for this theatre in the Herald. Allston Brown states that in the season after Jacobs took charge appeared Ada Gray, in Taken from Life, Pauline Markham, May Blossom, Pat Rooney, My Aunt Bridget, Her Atonement, Michael Strogoff, Peck's Bad Boy, The Black Thorn, Uncle

[269]

Tom's Cabin, Inshavogue, and Hicks and Sawyer's Minstrels, the season closing on June 25th.

POOLE'S (LATE ABERLE'S) THEATRE, 1886–1887

The theatre in Eighth Street, once directed by Jacob Aberle and since operated unsuccessfully under different names, re-opened hopefully, after a long silence, on September 6, 1886. John F. Poole directed it for that season, advertising it as "an entirely new and elegant theatre" and announcing admission charges for $1.00 in the orchestra, 75 cents for the parquet, 50 cents for orchestra circle and balcony and $10 and $6 for boxes. He gave an interesting, if not a particularly "elegant" season.

The opening attraction was the popular W. J. Scanlan (now habitually so spelled) in Shane-na-Lawn, by James C. Roach and J. Armory Knox ("Texas Siftings"). The name of the piece and the personality of the star would apprise us of the kind of harmless Irish work this was; if not, the *dramatis personæ* may aid us to understand:

Shane-na-Lawn	W. J. Scanlan	Buckley	C. R. Webster
John Power	J. B. Turner	Agent Dillon	Albert Morrell
Gerald Power	George W. Deyo	Captain Fitzgerald	H. L. Cleveland
Squire Redmond	Sidney B. Ellis	Rose Redmond	Lillian Lee
Harry Redmond	Charles Dade	Peggy O'Moore	Marion Warren
Mat Kirwin	George W. Barnum	Mrs. Power	Mrs. W. G. Jones
Ronald	Gus Reynolds	Moll	Mrs. J. B. Turner

I need hardly say that the period of the play was 1790, under the Grattan Parliament; and furthermore I hazard the conjecture that the reader never before heard of any member of Scanlan's supporting cast except the highly respected and institutional Mrs. W. G. Jones. For his last week (October 4th–9th) Scanlan played Larry O'Flynn, in The Irish Minstrel, with S. B. Ellis as Robert Wynbert and Lillian Lee as Nellie Cregan.

I am surprised to find Lotta in this remoter district, for the week of October 11th–16th; her vehicle was The Little Detective, and with her were Harold Courtney, Fred Lennox, Bert Coote, P. Augustus Anderson, James A. Mahoney, J. O. Le Brasse, Josie Sheppard, Sara Manypenny and Julia Wheeler, certainly as insignificant a band as ever supported the dimming radiance of this once so brilliant star. Frederic Bryton followed, on October 18th, for a fortnight of Forgiven; his support included Harry Harwood, Henry Bergman, Charles S. Titus, Frank Russell, Blanche Thorne, Marie Bingham and Jessie Storey — at last something like a cast of interest to us of later days. W. T. Bryant and Lizzie Richmond, snatched from vaudeville, filled the weeks of November 1st–13th, in George Hoey's concoction, Keep it Dark. And now I regret to inform my long-suffering reader that Poole's fell into the devastating practice of Sunday illustrated lectures on travel, similar, I suppose to those proffered by the Grand Opera House;

Professor De Morgan was the perpetrator and began on Sunday, November 14th, with Ireland, following, on the 21st, with Windsor Castle and The Tower of London. The Holy Land was the theme on December 26th — quite appropriate for Christmas. Life and Scenes in the Life of the late General John A. Logan oddly intermixed with the scheme on January 2nd. Let us leave De Morgan's talks and pictures on January 9th, with Paris, the Magnificent, merely premising that they continued for weeks.

The stage-offering for November 15th–20th was Roland Reed, in Humbug; on the 22nd, A Wall Street Bandit, ranging the town, arrived for a week at Poole's, with a cast diminished from its original Standard glory, and including H. W. Bradley, William Richardson, Charles Bowser, Atkins Lawrence, W. L. Denison, J. W. Summers, George Morton, J. H. Farrell, Hannah Welter, Louise Dickson, Ethelyn Friend, Edith Bird, Anna Boyle and Cora Macy. Louis Aldrich, in My Partner, added a touch of the familiar and the good to the week of November 29th–December 4th. And My Aunt Bridget scattered mirth broadcast in the following week (December 6th–11th):

Bridget McVeigh	George W. Monroe	Dora Blazor	Minnie Richardson
P. Alton McVeigh	John C. Rice	Polly Glyder	Josie Devoy
Jack Treyser	E. J. Ratcliffe	Abby Shrinker	Mrs. E. M. Post
Joe Nervy	W. H. Leary	Nellie Ryder	Polly Casey
Tompkins Blazor	F. W. Holland		

I intensely dislike male impersonators of women who aim to look and be like women; but impersonators like George Monroe and Neil Burgess, who give rough hints of feminine traits in a make-up and a comic dress that suggest the woman without too much verisimilitude, I greatly enjoy, I suppose because the effect is broadly farcical and not at all "pretty." George Monroe, in his way, was a genius.

The Silver King (December 13th–18th) brought to Poole's Carl Haswin and Eleanor Moretti as the unhappy Denvers, Sam H. Verney as the faithful Jaikes, G. Morton Price and Gracie F. Wade as the villainous Skinner and Olive, W. Athold White as Eliah Coombe, &c. During the week of December 20th–25th, Pat Rooney exhibited Pat's Wardrobe ("first times in New York"). James M. Ward, who, it was said, was making "his first appearance in New York in eleven years," presented (December 27th) another of those then frequent Irish plays of political and sentimental interest, interspersed with an occasional song —The Red Fox:

Rody McCaura	James M. Ward	Sir John Adare	Wright Huntington
Mave Carolan	Carrie Clark Warde	Tony Grimes	J. P. Sullivan
Lady Ann	Mary Young	Lanty Lawler	W. A. Lavelle
Lady Adare	Ida Clayton	Dan Davron / The Magistrate	Charles Manly
Peggy Carolan	Mrs. W. G. Jones		
Norry Davron	Daisy Fletcher	Bob Jones	T. L. Reilly
Captain O'Neal	Horace Vinton	Servant	Fred Stone
Sir W. Luttrell	G. Morton Price		

[271]

Ward kept The Red Fox at Poole's for two weeks. The theatre did not close, with this engagement; Allston Brown made an error in saying it did. A. H. Woodhull, in Eli Wheatfield, filled the week of January 10th–15th. This and succeeding attractions Brown erroneously assigns to the next year, 1888.

January 17th brought The Kindergarden (*sic*), by Robert Griffin Morris, with Stanley Macy and Laura Dinsmore as stars, and, in support Benjamin F. Grinnell (our former friend "Benny"?), Fred S. Sanford, E. A. Archer, George Bruening, Fred Mendoza, Blanche Seymour, Clara Lloyd and Nellie Bowers. With all these inconspicuous names to record, I look apprehensively at the giant index looming on the horizon. At all events relief pertains in the fact the Kindergarden continued for three weeks. Edna Courtney followed (February 7th), in The Banker's Daughter. For February 14th–19th, Frankie Kemble appeared in Sybil, a Romance of Dublin Lights, a piece put together by Clay M. Greene. In this, as Sybil, she was supported by Harry B. Bell as Brown Madder, Geoffrey Hawley as Horace Paxton, William Herbert as John Dart, W. J. Constantine as James Benson, Richard M. Carroll as Crooked Mike, E. H. Thayer as Mark O'Donnell, Emily Maynard as Rachel Pendleton, Annie Evelyn as Grace Pendleton and Little Ada Terry as Bessie. The following week (February 21st–26th) introduced a sudden transition to variety, with Katie and Gussie Hart, in The Rising Generation, James B. Ratcliffe (*sic* — negro songs), Murphy and Miles, Hubar Hassan (juggler and tightrope), Conchita (song and dance), Barrett and Loraine, Harry Braham (character vocalist), Lester and Williams, the Caldwell Sisters, the Harvey Brothers, and a concluding farce, New York Nowadays.

Variety dominated the bills for February 28th–March 5th, with Hampton's Animal Circus, Booker and Leigh, T. J. Ryan, King Sisters, Herbert Crowley, the Delmanning Brothers, the Caldwell Sisters and with Radcliffe in City Life, or, the Uncrushed Tragedian. The variety troupe of March 7th–12th is, however, specified in that trusty journal, the Herald: John Hart, the Lamont Trio, Howe and Doyle, C. E. Foreman and Ida Meredith, Alexander Wilson, Harley (*sic*) Brothers, Gallagher and West, Edward Earle, Kitty Wells, J. B. Radcliffe (*sic*), Harry Pierson and Harry Rowe.

Ada Gray was here for two weeks (March 21st–April 2nd) in her expected East Lynne; Camille, with Bertha Welby and H. W. Mitchell, served for the performance on April 4th and the rest of that week. The price of admission had now sunk to 10, 20 and 30 cents. The Galley Slave held the week of April 11th–16th, and A Celebrated Case, involving, as we know, another galley slave, that of April 18th–23rd. In the latter stirring play, James F. Crossen was Jean Renaud, George J. Maddox the villain, Marion A. Erle Adrienne, Laura Linden Madeleine, and J. L. Mason O'Rourke. J. B. Studley in The Corsican Brothers (April 25th–30th); The World (May 2nd–7th), with Frank Evans, Frank De Vernon, Dollie Norman and Ellen Cummens (as Mabel); Annie Berlein and Gilpin, in Leah, for the matinées and Oliver Twist for the evenings (May 9th–14th); D. H. Harkins, like Studley, once with Augustin Daly, in Richard III, with Tommy Russell as the Duke of York (May 16th–21st); The Banker's Daughter (23rd–28th); William Cullington, in For Congress (May 30th–June 4th) — this congregation of varied pleasures will carry us comfortably, at reduced rates, toward the close of the season. A benefit, on the afternoon and evening of June 3rd, for the Relief Fund of the Volunteer Firemen's Association of New York, provided For Congress and G. W. Thompson as Mose, in New York as It Was. A hot June week (6th–11th) heated the audience with Ten Nights in a Bar-Room, with the veteran E. W. Marston, and with George Maddox, J. L. Mason, E. J. Mack, Louis Barrett, Adelaide Thornton, Little Eva Pollock and Fannie Burt driving home the lessons involved. The last week of the season brought in N. S. Wood, with The Boy Scout of the Sierras (June 13th, 14th), Life and Adventures of Jack Sheppard (15th, 16th), and The Boy Detective (17th, 18th). George W. Thompson, W. D. Chalfin, Joseph P. Winter, James J. Tighe, Charlotte Waylord, and Nellie Maskell assisted him in transferring the Bowery to Eighth Street.

THEATRE COMIQUE, HARLEM, 1886–1887

Our journeys to the Comique, in Harlem, will result in offerings so like those we have registered for "combination" houses to the south, that, to a great extent, we shall merely wear our rue with a difference of dates. Let us then not expect much novelty.

Hallen and Hart's Vaudeville Combination spread antidote to the summer heat outside (September 6th–11th) with Jennie Yeamans, Julia Wilson, Harry Kernell, Fox and Van Auken, the Russell Brothers, McAvoy and Hallen, Eugene B. Sanger and Thomas Rooney. Ada Gray, ever roaming from theatre to theatre, arrived on the 13th for a week, in A Ring of Iron. Two weeks followed of Irish drama. Joseph Murphy, in The Kerry Gow, began on September 20th; and Kate Claxton followed, on the 27th, for a week as Arrah Meelish, in Arrah-na-Pogue, a part I am surprised to find her playing; Charles A. Stevenson was Shaun the Post, and Floride Abell was Fanny Power. I am really surprised. October brought Neil Burgess, in Vim (4th–9th); Emmet, in Fritz, Our Cousin German (11th–16th); Effie Ellsler, in Woman against Woman (18th–23rd); and Arthur Rehan's company, in Nancy and Co. (25th–30th) — a rather good selection.

November began (1st–6th) with Hanlon's Fantasma; continued (8th–13th) with Held by the Enemy; Charles A. Gardner (15th–20th) in Karl, the Pedler (sic); Hart's Elite Novelty Company, including Hilda Thomas and Georgie Parker (22nd–27th) and lapsed into winter (November 29th–December 4th) with Roland Reed, in Humbug. J. B. Polk, in Mixed

[273]

Pickles, filled the week of December 6th–11th; and dear Maggie Mitchell, not quite so attractive as in her youth, brought memories of the '60s and '70s with a rapidly changing repertoire (December 13th–18th) of Little Barefoot, Lorle, Jane Eyre and Fanchon. Genevieve Ward, travelling in the hinterland of Broadway, was here (20th–25th), with Vernon, in Forget-Me-Not. And 1886 passed into the new year (December 27th–January 1st) with Evans and Hoey, in A Parlour Match. This catalogue is easy, if not particularly enthralling.

Let us courageously enter 1887, with John T. Raymond (January 3rd–8th) in David D. Lloyd's comedy, The Woman Hater — our first novelty for that season in Harlem:

Samuel Bundy	J. T. Raymond	Tom Ripley	Lewis Baker
George Dobbins	J. B. Eversham	Mrs. Lucy Joy	Helen Tracy
Professor Mulbridge	W. Cullington	Mrs. Walton	Octavia Allen
Dr. Lane	Harry Pierson		

Poor Raymond, ever seeking a new Colonel Sellers, and never finding it! Three weeks of fun are ahead: Neil Burgess, in Widow Bedott (January 10th–15th); William Gillette, in The Private Secretary (17th–22nd); and Mr. and Mrs. George S. Knight, in Over the Garden Wall (24th–29th). Ben Maginley, in May Blossom, changed the key for the week of January 31st–February 5th; his support included Mary Hamilton and Joseph Adelman, not among the theatre's most shining lights. The Main Line, with James Neill, Dora Stuart and Etta Hawkins (February 7th–12th); McKee Rankin and Mabel Bert, in The Danites (14th–19th); The World (21st–26th) lead us by familiar paths to February 28th–March 5th, when Rose Coghlan entered in her charming repertoire, recently seen at the Union Square. In addition, on the 28th, she played in A Scrap of Paper, with Walcot as Prosper. The company of William Redmund and Mrs. Thomas Barry divided the week of March 7th–12th between René and A Midnight Marriage; and Richard Mansfield (14th–19th) delighted with the vagaries, the blandishments and the accomplishments of Prince Karl. Another downtown success flitted northward for the week of March 21st–26th — M. B. Curtis, in Caught in a Corner.

Mme. Janauschek shall end March (28th–31st) and begin April (1st–2nd) with her impressive repertoire seen so frequently of late — Mother and Son, Bleak House, Marie Antoinette and Mary Stuart. The month of showers proceeded with Tony Denier's Pantomime Company (April 4th–9th); Arthur Rehan's Company for a return engagement of Nancy and Co. (11–16th); W. J. Scanlan, in Shane-na-Lawn (18th–23rd); and Alone in London (25th–30th). May 2nd–7th brought the Templeton Opera Company, and, on the 6th, a benefit to Josh Hart, the manager of the Comique. The repertoire consisted of The Mikado, Giroflé-Girofla, and The Mascot, Hattie Starr, C. L. Harris and Edward Chapman being in the casts. There-

[274]

after, the month of flowers brought forth The Main Line again (9th–14th); Rose Coghlan and Osmond Tearle (16th–21st), in The School for Scandal, London Assurance and Peg Woffington; J. M. Ward, in Inshavogue (23rd–28th); and Fantasma once more (30th–June 4th). I found no more for this busy mart of plays, in 1886–87, till June 17th, when occurred a benefit at which was to appear Magistrate St. John, "who has been in the British provinces."

THALIA THEATER, 1886-1887

The last season but one of Gustav Amberg in the Thalia (formerly the Bowery) Theater began on October 1st (Friday) with a revival of Lortzing's pretty Undine, with Selma Kronold in the title-rôle, Lucie Colmar as Bertalda, Ferdinand Schütz as Ritter Hugo, Otto Rathjens as Kühleborn, Otto Meyer as Tobias, Carola Rennen as Marthe, Eduard Fischer as Pater Hellmann, Eduard Elsbach as Veit, and Hermann Gerold as Hans. This innocuous offering came again on the 2nd, and on Monday, the 4th. On Sunday, the 3rd, a "sacred concert" ended with 1733 Thaler, 22½ Silbergroschen—not the most sacred thing in my repertoire of memories.

From this time forward Amberg vied with the Casino and the Bijou Opera House in presentation of operetta and light entertainment. On Tuesday, October 5th, he reverted to Der Zigeunerbaron, for the first appearances of Carl Friese (as Kalmar Zsiepian), Fritz Schnelle (as Sandor) and Adam Lellman, as Ottokar); others in the cast were Albertine Habrich, Emmy Meffert, Johanna Schatz, Louis Prätorius, Eduard Hirsch, Hermann Gerold and Selma Kronold, the last-named to be, one day, in productions in English. A novelty of October 6th was Don Cæsar, an operetta by R. Dellinger, with the début of Alexander Rüdinger as der König, with Eduard Elsbach as Don Fernandez, Carl Friese as Don Manudo, Albertine Habrich as Donna Uraca, Sophie Offeney (début) as Don Cæsar, Gerold as Hauptmann Martinez and Paula von Varndal (début) as Pueblo. Except for a matinée of Undine, on the 9th, and Die Fledermaus, on the 15th, with the new and important Sophie Offeney as Rosalinde, Don Cæsar ran till Saturday, the 16th. On Sunday, October 10th, the Thalia began a series of weekly Sunday visits to Wareing's Opera House, Hoboken, Der Zigeunerbaron being their first offering, with Don Cæsar following there on the 17th. The Thalia, on the 17th, promised a Blumen-Concert, with ten thousand roses, and the farce, Aurora in Oel.

The Thalia was now in its stride of old operettas. "Auf allgemeines Verlangen," Nanon, on the 18th and 19th, presented Emmy Meffert as Nanon, Adolf Link (als Gast, a guest who remained practically throughout the season) as Marquis von Marsillac, Carl Witt (début) as Hector, Ada Bergen as Frau de Maintenon, F. Schütz as Marquis d'Aubigné, Otto Meyer as Ludwig XIV, Sophie Offeney as Ninon de l'Enclos, Johanna Schatz as Frau von Frontenac, Lucie Colmar as Gräfin Houlières, &c. Der Feldprediger, on the 20th, gave us Link as Heidekrug (*sic*), and, on the 21st, Die Fledermaus had Max Lube as Frosch, Link as Frank, Schütz as Gabriel, Frl. Offeney as Rosalinde, and Johanna Schatz as Adele. A busy week ended with a matinée of Die Fledermaus, on the 23rd, and Der lustige Krieg, in the evening.

Lovers of serious drama must have wondered when these waves of frivolity were to recede; alas! they were not to do so. Link, who seems to have reached the star-rank, gave Die Fledermaus, on the 25th, and Robert und Bertram, on the 26th and 27th. A Bartholdi-Festival, on the 28th, in that age of excitement about the Statue of Liberty, gave appropriate tableaux and a revival of Der Raub der Sabinerinnen. Then, on the 29th, Hundert Jungfrauen (Les Cent Vierges), Brandes's operette, grouped Conrad Junker as Sir Jonahan, Bernhard Rank as Brididick, Link as Anatol, Sophie Offeney as Gabriele, Friese as Rumpelmeyer, Johanna Schatz as Eglantine, Hugo Hasskerl as Crockley, Rudolf Sinnhold as Thompson, August Walter as ein Konstabler, &c. And all hundred virgins figure in the cast, each with her stage name and the name of the actress impersonating the part. Frankly, I cannot believe that a hundred girls appeared in that chorus of Hundert Jungfrauen. This was Amberg's first pretentious offering of the season, and it ran for many nights. On Sunday, October 31st, a concert involved Enrico Ducenzi, a tenor to appear frequently that winter in New York, Mlle. A. Jawianska, Link and Friese, and ended with Die Hanni weint und der Hansi lacht, with Offeney, Rüdinger, Friese and Schnelle.

On the evening of November 5th, a benefit for the German Press Club presented Marianne Brandt, Emma Juch, Bertha Pierson, Pauline L'Allemand, Ducenzi, and others. Except for that interruption Hundert Jungfrauen ran steadily through November 6th, and re-appeared, on the 9th, for several other performances. On Monday, November 8th, Link appeared in Der Verschwender, Ein altes Weib also figuring in the bill. Drei Paar Schuhe, that former success of Marie Geistinger, introduced, on November 11th and 12th, Link, Friese, August Walter, Rank, Rüdinger, Junker, Hasskerl, Frl. von Varndal, Frl. Offeney, and Johanna Schatz. Robert und Bertram, in that year of the success of Erminie, may have been a profitable matinée offering for November 13th. On Sunday, November 14th, Ada Melrose, Julius Grünbaum and Ada Dore appeared; the farce was Wenn Frauen sparen.

Neuendorff's Der Rattenfänger von Hameln was revived on November 18th, and became the second long-lived production of the season; it ran continuously through December 1st, yielding the stage on December 2nd, 3rd and 4th, to Adolf Link, that long-remaining "Gast," in Goldonkel.

[276]

Monday, December 6th, brought an interesting Gastspiel. Marguerite Fish, whom we met as a child (Baby Benson), but who had since won, it was alleged, success in Vienna, came forth, in her native land, in Der Glücksengel, a musical farce, by Leon Treptow, with music by Ralba. In her support, on the 6th, were August Walter, Lucie Werner, Hermann Korn, Hugo Hasskerl, Carl Witt, Anna Regan, Reinhold Bojock, Bernhard Rank and Lena Wassmann, almost entirely a new group; Amberg's regulars may have carried their art to other centres.

After three nights of Der Glücksengel, Frl. Fish sought the opposite region with Der Teufel im Schloss, by Louis Fuchs. In this, on December 10th, she was Baron Archibald, and Fanny Heller and Ludwig Steingade joined, in the support, those already mentioned for Der Glücksengel. On Sunday, December 12th, the regular company came back in concert. Frl. Fish had been announced to depart on the 11th, but she must have been successful enough to be retained. On the 12th, the management excitedly cried, Sie bleibt da! sie sind da! and she blithely enacted Ein Taugenichts. The next week brought repetitions of autumn offerings: Der Rattenfänger von Hameln (13th); Hundert Jungfrauen (14th); and Die Fledermaus (15th). Anna (or Ada?) Namm, who was no more important than her name sounds, appeared, on the 16th, in Raub der Sabinerinnen; Der Rattenfänger again tried to catch the dollars, on the 17th. For the matinée, on the 18th, Marguerite Fish returned, in Ein Taugenichts, Der Raub der Sabinerinnen also figuring in the bill. For the celebration of the hundredth anniversary of the birth of Carl Maria von Weber, Amberg, on the evening of the 18th, revived one of the master's least notable works, Preciosa, with a huge cast, including Anna Namm as Preciosa, and many of the regulars. Marguerite Fish appeared at the concert, on the 19th, and Heimliche Liebe ended the bill with romantic suggestiveness.

Christmas week offered varied gifts: Preciosa (20th); Raub der Sabinerinnen (21st); Robert und Bertram (22nd); Einer von unsere Leut' (23rd and 24th), with Link as Isaac Stern; Der Rattenfänger (matinée, 25th); and (evening of the 25th) Das Volk wie es weint und lacht. The week of December 27th–January 1st gave old-fashioned German attention to children; the afternoons of the 27th and 28th were devoted to Schneewittchen; those of the 29th and 30th to Der gute Michel, oder das Binsenmännchen; that of the 31st to Humpty Dumpty and Marguerite Fish, in Heimliche Liebe; and that of January 1st to Lumpaci Vagabundus. The evenings of that week gave, in succession, Der Bettelstudent, Nanon, Der Zigeunerbaron, Czaar und Zimmermann, Der Feldprediger, and Pech-Schulze.

In reviewing this autumn season at the Thalia, one can only regret the absence from it of anything stimulating to the imagination; and I fear the new year will bring but little to change our estimate of Amberg and his cohorts. An interesting revival, on Monday, January 3rd, was but a flash

[277]

in the pan. Nessler's light opera, Der Trompeter von Säkkingen, was to figure in two seasons at the Metropolitan; Kaiser's opera of that name reached
the Thalia stage on the 3rd, with a cast including Hermann Gerold, Selma
Kronold, Otto Meyer, Albertine Habrich, F. Schütz (who seems to have
been an acceptable tenor), Otto Rathjens, Lucie Colmar, Eduard Elsbach
and Camilla Clairmont, an aggregation of ability. This was the concoction partaken of, a year ago. On Tuesday, Die Banditen was advertised as
from Millöcker's Gasparone, "neu arrangirt." Sophie Offeney was Carlotta,
with Friese as Nasoni, Conrad Junker as Sindulfo, R. Sinnhold as Erminio,
Schütz as Benozzo, and Emmy Meffert as Cora. Link as Isaac Stern, in
Einer von unsere Leut' filled the evening of January 5th.

Drama, without songs, real drama, though of a sentimental flavour, began on January 6th, when Else Hofmann, a much, a violently advertised
actress, made her début in the well-worn Dorf und Stadt, following it, on
the following evening, with Die Hagestolzen and Sie hat ihr Herz entdeckt.
At reduced prices, Der Feldprediger held the fort, at the matinée on the
8th, Dorf und Stadt, in the evening, allowing the public once more to
appraise the talent of Frl. Hofmann. Die Grille, on Monday, the 10th,
presented this new star as Fanchon, Adele Eichberg (new to us), as
Mutter Barbeaud, Bojock as Vater Barbeaud, Hugo Hasskerl as Landry,
Felix Schnelle as Didier, Ada Namm as Madelon, and Fanny Heller as die
alte Fadet. On the 11th, Frl. Hofmann continued, with Die Hagestolzen and
Feuer in der Mädchenschule; she repeated Dorf und Stadt, on the 12th. On
the 13th, a new Conrad l'Allemand came forth in Ehrenschulden, and Frl.
Hofmann touched comedy, in Cyprienne (Divorçons). As Cyprienne the
briefly-sojourning Frl. Hofmann said farewell, on the 14th. On Saturday,
the 15th, Amberg produced Die Meininger in New York — "grosse komische
Burleske mit Gesang und Tanz." This frivolous, if amusing nonsense ran
— fortunately for my pen — through February 1st, with Rank as ein Theater-
direktor, Frl. Heller as seine Gemahlin, Bojock as Lerche, Frl. Schatz as Frl.
Lehmann, Walter as Busch, Hitzigrath as Herzog, Lube as Er, Hasskerl as
ein fremder Herr, and, in other rôles, Witt, Frl. Eichberg (sic), Burghardt
and Junker. I must set down the German note: "Zeit—jetzt." For Sunday, January 16th, Lube and Rank, excellent comedians, contributed to
the "sacred" concert specialties, the former with Wie baut man ein deutsches
Theater, the latter with a Ballade von der Sparlingsmald. The Three
Phoites were stressed for Sunday, January 30th.

Up and down the amusement columns of the Staats-Zeitung Amberg
flashed notes of the "grosser Erfolg" of his precious Meininger in New York,
arousing wonder as to whether business was bad. Adolf Link, who seems to
have been a popular loadstone for Amberg, gave, by request, on February
2nd, his apparently well-liked Einer von unsere Leut'. Then, on February 3rd, we were favoured with another sop of lightsome entertainment, an

[278]

extensively advertised "operette," Der Vagabund (by W. West, with music by Carl Zeller), employing in its cast Max Lube, Sophie Offeney, Cora Cabella, H. Hasskerl, Rüdinger, Johanna Schatz, F. Schütz, Adolf Link, Ada Bergen (*sic*), Adele Eichberg (*sic*), Cäcilie Alma, Hermine Lorenz, Franz Klosczinski, Hermann Korn, Eugen Kubach, John Beroni, Wilhelm Burghardt and Eduard Hirsch. The worst thing about writing these German casts is the foreknowledge that but few of the members will appear in the following year; I assume that government control in the "Vaterland" prevented their return.

Der Vagabund held the stage through February 16th. On Sunday, February 6th, we were regaled with "Viel Vergnügen" — to wit, the Clipper Quartet, Layman ("the man with a hundred faces"), Siegrist, and the farce, Monsieur Hercules. The two-weeks runs accomplished (practically) by both Die Meininger in New York and Der Vagabund, were followed (February 17th) by another success of similar calibre, a light concoction of Mannstädt and Steffens, entitled Der Stabstrompeter, with all the principals so often mentioned in the cast, even including Ada Namm, whose indeterminate name continues to bleat through our solemn pages. With but one interruption Der Stabstrompeter ran through March 7th — nearly three weeks in all. Sunday, February 27th, found Maximilian Lichtenstein here with his violin. On March 1st, the operatic corps went to the Academy of Music, there to give, for the benefit of the German Policlinic, Der Vagabund; on that evening, the Thalia staged Hasemann's Töchter. Adolf Link returned, on the 8th, in Der Vagabund, following, on the 9th, in Die Fledermaus. On Sunday, March 13th, appeared the Clipper Quartet, and a child of three-languaged description — Petite Josie, Kleine Josie, Little Josie — "die einzige und die beste."

EMIL THOMAS

The German theatres always depended for main strength on their resident "stock" companies; yet we remember many a season was glorified by the engagement of stars. Far back, in the '60s, we met Bogumil Dawison and Frau Methua-Scheller; in more recent times we had had Marie Geistinger, Friedrich Haase, Carl Sontag and Sonnenthal. Now, in the latter nights of 1886–87, Amberg introduced a star of comedy, in Emil Thomas, who made his bow, on March 10th, in Von Schrot und Korn, a Volksstück mit Gesang, by C. Niedt, with music by Gabriel. As Wulkow, Thomas was supported by Junker, Ada Namm, Hermine Lorenz, Hitzigrath, Fanny Heller, Lucie Werner, Ada Bergen, Paula Büchner, Frida Brede, Hasskerl, Ludwig Steingade, Johanna Schatz (seldom absent from any cast), Carl Witt, Hedwig Buschmann, Louise Lindau, and Mary Schlag. This play ran through Saturday, March 12th, yielding the stage, for the matinée on that day, to Die Fledermaus. Inspector Bräsig served Thomas for the

[279]

14th and 15th; on the 16th he appeared in both Der Vater der Debutantin and 1733 Thaler, 22½ Silbergroschen; on the 17th and 19th (matinée) he returned to Von Schrot und Korn. He showed his versatility by acting, on the 18th, Gottlieb Weigelt, in Mein Leopold, and, on the 19th (evening), Hasemann, in Hasemann's Töchter. On Sunday, the 20th, in the concert, he appeared with Link and Lube.

The star had a very busy week, beginning on Monday, March 21st, with Inspector Bräsig. On the 22nd, a "Feier" for the ninetieth birthday of the Emperor Wilhelm, brought Des Königs Befehl, with Thomas as Friedrich II (alter Fritz). "Auf allgemeines Verlangen"—a useful request, very often —Thomas repeated, on the 23rd, Der Vater der Debutantin and 1733 Thaler, 22½ Silbergroschen. Mein Leopold (March 24th) preceded Der Aktienbudiker (25th and 26th), with Thomas as August Knötsche. The next week began (March 28th) with a double bill, Des Königs Befehl and 1733 Thaler, 22½ Silbergroschen; with Link as Gast, Rank and Thomas, Der Registrator auf Reisen must have been very amusing, on the 29th and 31st, and April 4th, Thomas playing Cæsar Wichtig. Hasemann's Töchter (March 30th), and Thomas in both Der Vetter and Dr. Peschke (April 1st) lead us inevitably toward the close of the season.

Soll und Haben, Julius Rosen's four-act comedy, presented (April 5th, 6th and 8th) Thomas as Sebastian, with, in other parts, A. Walter, Hermine Lorenz, Lucie Werner, Ada Namm, Fanny Heller, C. Junker, Steingade, Bojock, and Johanna Schatz; Der Vater der Debutantin and Dr. Peschke filled the bill on the 7th. Hasemann's Töchter (afternoon) and Der Registrator auf Reisen (evening) were the lure on the 9th. Monday, April 11th, brought So sind sie alle (Posse mit Gesang, by W. Mannstädt and A. Willer) with Thomas as Püpke and his wife, Betty Damhofer (début) as Grete; this was repeated on the 12th, 13th and 14th. For the 15th we had Luftschlösser, revived with Thomas and Betty Damhofer, evidently an attractive pair—at least the best the Thalia could provide. Der Registrator auf Reisen was matinée fare, on the 16th, and Luftschlösser the evening delight.

Betty Damhofer was part of the "last concert but one," of the season. The "last" appearances of Thomas and Frau Damhofer brought Luft-schlösser (April 18th); Der Registrator auf Reisen (19th); Inspector Bräsig (20th); Einer von unsere Leut' and Guten Morgen, Herr Fischer (21st); and, for the 22nd and 23rd, Die schöne Helena, with Betty Dam-hofer as Helena, Thomas as Calchas, Link as Menelaus, and Ferdinand Schütz as Paris. For the matinée, on the 23rd, Thomas repeated Der Vater der Debutantin and 1733 Thaler, 22½ Silbergroschen. Die schöne Helena caught the popular fancy; it was repeated on the 25th (for the benefit of Link) and 28th. On the 26th came, a Fest-Vorstellung und Uhland-Feier, with two of Uhland's poems (Das ist der Tag and Des Sänger's Flucht) and

[280]

Gedicht von Uhland, with lebende Bilder; Thomas and Betty Damhofer also repeated Luftschlösser. Frau Damhofer, on the 27th, gave Endlich hat er es gut gemacht and Versprechen hinter'm Herd. Two extra performances of Die schöne Helena, on Saturday, April 30th, allowed the star-pair to leave the Thalia with, I trust, a feeling of satisfaction at success achieved. Sunday, May 1st, brought the 25 jahriges Bühnen-Jubiläum of August Walter, with promised co-operation of Elise Patti-Rosa, Helene Doenhoff, Adolf Neuendorff, Otto Kemlitz (of the Metropolitan opera), Steindorff (of the Trebelli company), Schütz, Adolfi and Junker.

Adolf Neuendorff, who had failed as theatre-manager, in 1883, still kept busy in the amusement-world. On Monday, May 2nd, he brought out an opera, Prinz Waldmeister, with Rank as Professor Kluggescheidt, Conrad Junker as Justinius, Johanna Schatz as Ursula, Gustav Adolfi as Martin, Anna Heineck (new) as Marie, Schütz as Anton, Steingade, Witt and Korn as Students, and (as allegorical figures) Hitzigrath as König Feuerwein, Lucie Colmar as the Prinzessin, Georgine von Januschowsky as Prinz Waldemar, Helene von Doenhoff as Bruenessel, Hasskerl as Graf Neckar, and Pauline Büchner as eine Elfe. This ran for two weeks; that is, through the matinée on May 14th. The last week used it for benefits to Rank (May 9th); Frl. von Januschowsky (10th); the ushers and doorkeepers (11th); the treasurer, Emanuel M. Schwarz (12th) and Neuendorff (13th). The season closed, on the evening of Saturday, the 14th, with a benefit to Gustav Amberg, who had directed one of the lightest repertoires ever presented in this city, in a German theatre. The programme for his benefit comprised Eine vollkommene Frau, Aus Liebe zur Kunst, the second act of Die Raüber (the only Schiller vouchsafed in 1886–87 to his auditory), and Die schöne Galatea (*sic*).

The operatic force of Amberg went almost immediately, as we shall see, to Terrace Garden, for a summer season such as Germans, as purveyors, loved to give there, and, as audiences, loved to take. The advertising, for a time, took us into the open at 58th Street, but the actors seem to have suffered a nostalgia (a pretentious word I dislike to use) for the heated interior of the home-theatre in the Bowery.

Consequently, on May 30th (Pfingst-Montag) Adolfine Ziemaier-Modjeska came to the Thalia in her Terrace-Garden hit, Gillette von Narbonne. On June 13th, we find the Thalia opened by the magic key of Blaubart, with, as Boulotte, Adolfine Ziemaier-Modjeska, who had been singing, with apparent success, at Terrace Garden. Others in the cast were old friends, at least for the past season—Junker, Albertine Habrich, Selma Kronold, Hasskerl, Rank, Steingade, F. Schütz (as Blaubart), Adolfi, Heinrich Habrich, and several young women. On June 18th, Der lustige Krieg introduced Cäcilie Hecht, then at Terrace Garden, with Albertine Habrich,

[281]

Max Lube, Frau Ziemaier-Modjeska, and F. Schütz, the indispensable; there was no performance, on these evenings, at Terrace Garden.

TERRACE GARDEN, 1886-1887

We begin the season at this festival site with performances, on October 13th, 14th and 15th, of Blaubart, by what the Staats-Zeitung advertises as a "neue Jüdische Operetten Company aus Rumänien," under direction of Künstler Mogulesko and Finkel (sic). And I still quote the boastful German tag: "Diese Truppe besteht aus 10 Damen und 20 Herren die als Künstler in Europa wohl bekannt sind." This group we shall meet, hereafter, in two theatres in the Bowery. The Yiddish drama had definitely arrived; in fact, as we know, the Roumanian Company was here in June, 1886. On October 16th, 18th and 19th, it continued with The Coquettish Ladies, a "new comical Russian Polish operetta," by Shaikevitch. On October 17th, the Social Männerchor held the Garden.

The mask-ball of the New York Männerchor made gay the Garden on February 15th (tickets, $2); that of the Central Turn-Verein celebrated Washington's Birthday with holiday cheer. And the ambitiously-named Verein für Kunst und Wissenschaft forgot its head, temporarily, on February 19th, in favour of its masks and its dancing feet, I hope in utter enjoyment of the occasion. On March 26th, the Standard Society entertainment provided M. P. Wilder, Linda Da Costa, Clara Spence, Arencibia, and the Strebe Brothers.

In the summer of 1887, Gustav Amberg leased the Garden, from M. Heumann, then the responsible Eigenthümer. There, as soon as his Thalia season closed, Amberg brought his actors. On Friday, May 20th, he began with Die Fledermaus, interpreted by F. Schütz, Georgine von Januschowsky, Conrad Junker, Lucie Colmar, Gervini, H. Hasskerl, B. Rank, Johanna Schatz, Gustav Adolfi and Hermine Lorenz. In the outer airy garden, the Ninth Regiment Band, directed by Luciano Conterno, played popular music. This all sounds attractive. Die Fledermaus ran two nights, followed, on Sunday, the 22nd of May, by the expected "sacred" concert.

On Monday, May 22nd, came the début of Adolfine Ziemaier-Modjeska, in Audran's operetta, Gillette von Narbonne. As Gillette, the star was supported by Junker as König von Neapel, Schütz (surely an overworked man) as Prinz Olivier, Kemlitz as Graf Roger, Hasskerl as Richard, Rank as Gristardin, Selma Kronold as Rosetta, and Adolfi as der Dorfrichter — a cast quite able, I suspect, to hold its own with any assembled by Aronson or McCaull. Gillette ran through May 28th, and, on the 30th, transferred to the more heated spaces of the Thalia Theatre. Its run, at Terrace Garden, ended on May 31st. On June 1st, La Mascotte presented Frau

[282]

Ziemaier-Modjeska as Bettina. Success carried The Mascotte through Saturday, June 4th, and it ran all the week of June 6th–11th. A benefit (matinée, June 4th) to Frau Ruscha Michaelis proffered Hochzeit bei Laternenshein, Eine vollkommene Frau and Die schöne Galathée (*sic*). The first appearance of Cäcilie Hecht (June 13th) was as Arsena, in Der Zigeunerbaron, with Rank, Schütz, Albertine Habrich, Lube, Sinnhold, Frl. Schatz and Selma Kronold in leading rôles. Nanon, on June 20th, presented Frau Ziemaier-Modjeska in the title-rôle, with Johanna Schatz as Ninon, and with Lube, Schütz and Rank in the forefront of the supporting army.

On June 24th, the third Stiftungsfest of the German Press Club promised Ida Klein, Minnie Dilthey, Wilhelm Hock, Marie Hock (début in New York), the Beethoven Männerchor, and the Thalia actors in both Aurora in Oel and Zehn Mädchen und kein Mann. Der lustige Krieg (June 21st) and the farewell (June 24th), in Pariser Leben, of Adolfine Modjeska carry us to a whirling month of one piece after another flashing across our fevered vision. These manifestations of managerial perturbation I will proceed to blind the reader withal: Der Zigeunerbaron (June 27th, and July 7th and 23rd); Der Bettelstudent (with Cäcilie Hecht and Selma Kronold, June 28th, July 4th, July 19th and 28th); Boccaccio (June 29th and 30th); Der Rattenfänger von Hameln (July 1st); Der Feldprediger (July 2nd, 5th); a Fest-Concert (Sunday, July 3rd) with Er ist taub and Lott' ist todt; Czar und Zimmermann (July 6th); Giroflé-Girofla (July 8th, 26th and 27th); Fatinitza (July 9th, with Paula von Varndal in the title-rôle, Adolfi as Timofey, and Selma Kronold as Lydia—repeated on the 12th and 21st); Die Fledermaus (July 15th and 25th); Der Seecadet, with Paula von Varndal as Fanchette (July 16th and 18th); at the "concert" (July 17th), Einer muss heirathen and Wenn Frauen sparen, a pretty combination of titles, and quite in keeping, "Jeder Dame ein Souvenir"; Gasparone, with Selma Kronold as Carlotta and Frl. Hecht as Cora (July 22nd); and, for the benefit of Capellmeister Paul Steindorff (July 29th), Der Freischütz. The season closed, on July 30th, with Der Freischütz (Act II), Guten Morgen, Herr Fischer, and Die Fledermaus (Act II). The cast of Der Freischütz included Frl. Kronold, Frl. Hecht and Ferdinand Schütz (as Max). The reader's eye, missing certain dates in that connotative catalogue, will remember that, on the few occasions when Terrace Garden moved, so to speak, to the Thalia, with its actors and its goods and chattels, no performances took place in 58th Street. Similarly Terrace Garden was closed on July 13th and 14th, when the Thalia company went to the Ocean Theatre, Long Branch, to present, successively, Der Zigeunerbaron and Der Feldprediger. I do not know why there was no performance in the cool Garden, on July 20th. From August 1st, there were merely Garden Concerts and Promenades, with the orchestra from the Thalia Theater.

OTHER GERMAN ACTIVITIES, 1886–1887

Perhaps I had better group the activities of the busy Vereine. The Germania Assembly Rooms, 291-293 Bowery, hospitably opened for many of these, but we began the progress, on October 13th, with the opening ball at Wendel's Assembly Rooms, far over in West 44th Street. On the 17th, a triple inducement distracted Kleindeutschland: in the Columbia Club House, 52 Lexington Avenue, the Columbia Zither Trio and the Columbia Zither Verein tinkled the happy hours away; the Arion Concert, in Arion Hall, St. Mark's Place, enlisted, under direction of F. Van der Stucken, Charlotte Walker, Dora Becker, Emanuel Moor and Franz Remmertz; and the Beethoven Männerchor gave, in their hall, their concert, with Ida Klein, W. H. Rieger and Carl Dufft. After that outburst, it seems rather flat to record the dance of the Allemania Council, on the 18th, in Wendel's Assembly Rooms.

Then the Germania Assembly Rooms gathered their toll of German enjoyment. The ball of the United German Brothers danced out the evening of October 21st. The double entry for October 23rd confuses my conscientious pen; both Thusnelda Loge, No. 726, R.L.H., and Hand in Hand, No. 1, are down in the Staats-Zeitung for balls, on that date, in the Germania. Possibly the rooms were divisible, or, possibly, the two societies united. The Bremer Verein held the place on October 24th; and, at a date I could not discover in the Staats-Zeitung, the Gesangverein Oesterreich held a Stiftungsfest, Liedertafel und Ball, assistants including Ernestine Grott, the New York Zither Verein (why were Germans so addicted to the zither?) and the Kreutzer Quartett Club, with G. Bachmann's orchestra as musical base.

The Germans, as we know, selected Sundays not only for rest, but for fun. Hence, if, on October 31st, they did not attend David Bimberg's concert, in Nilsson Hall, they might have gone to the Germania Assembly Rooms, for a concert of the Verein Franz Abt Schüler, or, haply, to Wendel's Assembly Rooms, for the concert and ball of the Turn-Verein (*sic*), Bloomingdale. Thus we reach Sunday, November 14th, and the "Feier des 38 Stiftungsfeste" of the New Yorker Sängerrunde, held in the Teutonia Assembly Rooms; in this appeared Frau Dr. Steiger (soprano), W. Bartels (tenor), F. Kohler (violin), and W. Bascet (piano), without, I admit, causing the slightest stir in my imagination, except that I am amused by the humourless tag of "Frau Dr." for a soprano singer.

Becker's Hall, 147-149 West 32nd Street, now leaps (November 14th) into the arena, with a "musikalische Unterhaltung" of the Loreley Männerchor, Louis See directing, and Conrad Heinemann singing bass. The Kreutzer Quartett Club's twenty-sixth annual concert came, on the same 14th, in the Germania Assembly Rooms, as did the twenty-sixth Stiftungs-

[284]

fest, Concert and Ball of the Mainzer Carneval-Verein, in Beethoven Männerchor Hall, 210 East 5th Street. The New York Männerchor ball and concert fell at this time, with Helen Dudley Campbell, F. Bergner, Augusta Marschall and Carl Dufft to assist in the music. I pass to an interesting November 20th, with allegiance divided between a Schweizer Bazar, for the Swiss home, held in Irving Hall, and the concert of the Theodor Körner Liedertafel, in Turn-Hall. On the 21st, the Beethoven Männerchor indulged in its "erste Abendunterhaltung." The Liederkranz concert, on November 26th, was a stately affair, with Max Bruch's Achilleus, sung by Henrietta Beebe, Emily Winant, Carl Zobel (tenor), Max Treumann and Max Heinrich, an array of soloists far above the usual German offering. On the 5th of December, Liederkranz Hall, 111-119 East 58th Street, allowed us to enter "frei," to hear Dr. Theodor Barth, of Berlin, on Das moderne politische Deutschland. With a sense of familiarity, on that same 5th, we learn of the Germania Assembly Rooms and their offering of the Bloomingdale Eintracht, with Hedwig Marcus (alto), J. Hanauer (tenor), C. Klaus (tenor), C. Heim (baritone), Adolf Hartdegen ('cello), and Wilhelm Busch (accompanist); the familiarity, I hasten to add, arises from the rooms, not from all the artists involved. Those well-known rooms summoned again, on December 16th, when the Beethoven Doppel Quartett Club played as it might. On the 19th, the Columbia Zither Trio once more displayed its musical prowess, in the Columbia Club House. Christmas Day instituted the Kinderfest of the Beethoven Männerchor.

Theiss's New Music Hall and Alhambra Court began to infest columns of the Staats-Zeitung with boasts of a Monster Orchestrion; mechanical music was then a novelty. The Männer-Gesang-Verein Arion, thus trebly hyphenated, starts us on our January quest, with its first Carnevalsitzung (on the 8th), "mit Damen." On the 9th, the Mainzer Carneval-Verein (thus hyphenated) began a series of three evenings, the others listed for February 6th and 20th. The "Kickers," with ball and banquet, were, on January 12th, in the Germania Assembly Rooms. The columns of the Staats-Zeitung were then bristling with advertisements of dances—especially masked balls, almost a religion in Kleindeutschland. But let us not forget the Carnevalsitzung—that of the Eichenkranz, on January 15th, in Beethoven Hall, or that of the Beethoven Männerchor, on the 16th. The Schillerbund danced in masks, on January 31st, in the Germania Assembly Rooms, and not extravagantly at one dollar "für Herr mit Dame." The Sängerrunde, also on the 31st, had its ball in the Teutonia Rooms. But, even before that, on the 23rd, the Schwäbischer Sängerbund made its mask-attack on Beethoven Hall. The Frauen-Verein concert of January 26th I have treated in notice of Steinway Hall.

February clustered masked gayeties in (I suppose) entrancing delight. On the 3rd of that gloomy month, the Prospect Association, as we know,

[285]

carried on, in dance and masks, at the Academy of Music, Tammany Hall and Nilsson Hall; no cheap affair this, with tickets at five dollars, with hat-check included. February 7th carries our curiosity far to the north, to enjoy, at Sulzer's Harlem Casino, the dance of the Harlem Eintracht. On the 9th, the Teutonia Lodge Ball went through, for aught I know, successfully and happily, in Teutonia Hall, The Uptown Gardner's (*sic*) Horse Troop, whatever that may have been, had the customary masked ball, on February 9th, in Wendel's Assembly Rooms. On the 10th, the great Liederkranz ball utilised the vast spaces of the Metropolitan Opera House, as, on the 17th, did that other outstanding club, the Arion; nothing small about those aggregations! The Veteranen Gesangverein (*sic*) masked and danced, on the 12th, in Turn Hall. The Schwäbischer Sängerbund, on February 14th, held either a second or a deferred masked-ball in Beethoven Männerchor Halle; but the Eichenkranz maskers danced, on that night, in the roomier spaces of the Academy of Music. The Teutonia Assembly Rooms, on that same saltatory 14th, were deemed spacious enough for the masked-ball of the Gesang Verein, Harmonia. On the 17th, Concordia Lodge, No. 290, masked and footed a joyous measure, in Wendel's Assembly Rooms.

At this time the Deutscher Gessellig-Wissenschaftlicher Verein von New York continued to hold, in Arion Halle, discussions less heavy, I hope, than their own distinguishing name. A concert for the German Emigrant Home, on February 17th, I have treated under caption of Steinway Hall. So on with the dance, till there isn't a mask left on sale in Kleindeutschland! The Maskenball of the Theodor Körner Liedertafel danced its way, on February 19th, in the New York Turn Hall. The Marschner Männerchor went, on February 19th, to the Concordia Assembly Rooms, for the reader guesses what — a Maskenball. February 20th found Kleindeutschland rampant in gayety: The Loreley Männerchor chose Wendel's Assembly Rooms as a suitable place in which to hide their joyous faces in masks. The Gesangverein (*sic*) Arminia, however, approximated to a contemporary custom, in its calico dress ball, on the 20th, in Beethoven Hall. And on that same hectic 20th (it was Sunday in stern New England usage) we had two Stiftungsfeste raising their head in midst of all the dancing elsewhere: that of the Manhattan Schützenbund in Suppe's Harmony Rooms (135-145 Essex Street); and the fourth and last Carneval-Sitzung of the Rheinische Carneval-Gesellschaft, at 1393 Second Avenue.

The Helvetia Männerchor, on the 21st, went back to masks for its Swiss dance, in the Teutonia Assembly Rooms; on the same date the Turn-Verein (*sic*) Bloomingdale, in Wendel's Assembly Rooms, danced, to the comfortable feeling that tickets "für Herr und Dame" cost only one dollar. The Harlem Männerchor, on the 21st, took possession, in masks, of Sulzer's Harlem Casino, and danced the happy hours away. Under caption of Terrace

[286]

Garden (I wish these functions did not so hopelessly overlap) the reader will find mention of the activities of the New York Männerchor (February 15th), the Verein für Kunst und Wissenschaft (February 19th) and the Central Turn-Verein (February 22nd).

February 22nd found the Hebrew Sheltering Guardian Society of New York offering the first reception in the Children's New Home, Grand Boulevard and 150th Street. But Kleindeutschland still kept whirling like mad in dance and masks. The New York Sing-Akademie had that kind of enjoyment, on February 26th, in Turnhall (*sic*) and for almost nothing — 50 cents für Herr und Dame! I suspect that the cost was trifling (at least for a man of means) when, on the 27th, the Hamburg Verein went to Walhalla, in Orchard Street, for its ball. And cheap, also, the tickets for the Maskenball of the Bund deutscher Frauen, on the 28th, in Turn Hall (*sic*) — "tickets 25 cents per person." That is as low in price as tickets sank for maskèd pleasure — at least in these annals.

Reader, again I confess to utter weariness over this record of long-past pleasure. I include it merely because of its historical significance; these things loomed large in certain sections of our cosmopolitan city. March allows us to relax our diligent research. The Maskenball (I have grown to hate that word) of the Heinebund occupied, on March 2nd, Lyric Hall, at Sixth Avenue and 42nd Street. The concert and ball of the Männer-Gesangverein Liederfreund held, on March 19th, the well-known Concordia Rooms. The 27th divided allegiance between the meeting, in the Germania Assembly Rooms, of the Walter Scott Loge, No. 402, and the third Abendunterhaltung, in Beethoven Halle, of the New York ZitherVerein. On that 27th the Staats-Zeitung publishes an advertisement for the Germania Assembly Rooms, showing every date filled for April. The Arion concert, for April 5th, is listed under Steinway Hall.

At last the Vereine shifted from dance to music. The thirty-ninth Stiftungsfest, Concert and Ball of Harmonia fell on April 10th, in Turn-Halle, with assistance from Master Willie Ford, Frl. Anna Kasche and Bernhard Vierlich, three from the past whom I fear the reader cannot identify. On the 10th, also, the Beethoven Männerchor held forth, with the aid of Angelica Müller-Spess, whom I cannot place in her proper niche, with Carl Steinbuch and H. W. (*sic*) Rieger. This Männerchor, on the 17th, listed more notable soloists in Ida Klein, Mme. Dory Burmeister-Petersen (pianist), W. H. (*sic*) Rieger (tenor) and Carl E. Dufft. In Beethoven Halle (im Kleinem Saal), on that 17th, the Zither-Schule of Edmund Himmler gave a concert that may have pleased lovers of the instruments involved; and, since I am on that subject, I may here apprise the reader that, on April 24th (Sunday), the Germania Assembly Rooms opened for a zither concert and ball, presumably for the benefit of "Professor" J. Eberle. Of course Sunday was to the Germans in New York a day of pleasure; the Liederkranz concert, on the 24th, brought in, as soloists, Agnes Huntington (later of brief acclaim in comic opera), Ida Klein (who never quite made the opera grade), Anton Schott (a heavy voice from the Metropolitan Opera House), Fannie Hirsch, and the gifted, youthful Adele Aus der Ohe. This function occurred in the Liederkranz Rooms in East 58th Street. In Beethoven Halle, also on the 24th, the Schwäbischer Sängerbund held an Abendunter-haltung.

The Denkfeier von Ludwig Uhland, a poet much celebrated by Germans in 1887, was duly observed by Uhland Loge, No. 735, on April 27th, Wendel's Assembly Rooms opening for the event; on the 27th, the Arion and Lieder-kranz Societies joined, in Steinway Hall, to observe the same sad-glad birth. The Palestrina Verein of New York, on the 27th, entered Turn-Halle, in Fourth Street, there to sing Schiller's Die Glocke, with soloists not highly distinguished, in Lilly Kompf, Otto Löbner and Carl Dufft.

And now approaching summer carried the Vereine hither and yon, far and near in excursions, excursions, excursions. These I will not detail, embark or entrain, except to say that the Mozart Männerchor, on July 2nd, 3rd and 4th, took a far-flung "Ausflug" to Niagara Falls, with tickets at fifteen dollars per person; that the Beethoven Männerchor sped, on July 16th and 17th, to Lake George and Saratoga; and that, on September 10th, 11th and 12th, the New Yorker Sängerrunde indulged in a "grosse Sängerfahrt nach Wilkesbarre, Pa." Well, happy trip to each and every one! Let us end this too lengthy record with the Cannstatter Volksfest, on September 11th, 12th, and 13th, at Wendel's Park, Union Hill, and with the Plattdeutsches Volksfest, also at Union Hill, New Jersey, on September 22nd, 23rd, 24th. Another Cannstatter Volksfest took possession, on September 18th, 19th, 20th and 21st, of Sulzer's Harlem River Park. Through the summer, Klein-deutschland, if it wished, could join Americans, in visits to Staten Island or to neighbouring beaches.

OTHER GERMAN PLAYS, 1886–1887

The reader is doomed to a meagre harvest of plays, aside from the Thalia supply. The Concordia, 28 Avenue A, went its accustomed way, its Sunday "sacred" concerts ending, as usual, with a farce. Successively I found it advertising, as a closing relish, Bleib bei Mir (October 10th); Der Ursprung des Korbgebens (October 17th); Die Eifersüchtigen (October 24th); So zahlt man seine Schulden (October 31st); Selbstmord aus Liebe (December 19th); Der Goldonkel (December 26th, and a good title for Christmas). A Gala-Vorstellung und Ball, for the birthday of John Bender, made joy, somehow, on April 6th.

The Central Turnhalle, 66 East 4th Street, opened, on October 24th, for a concert and ball of the Gesangverein Schillerbund, soloists in the concert

[288]

including Fannie Hirsch, Master O. Sturm, G. Feist, F. Althaus, G. Breit-haupt, H. Martels and C. Fuchs, who may have been good, despite the fact that oblivion has engulfed all except Miss Hirsch. A Theater-Vorstellung of the Central Turn-Verein gave us, on October 25th, Gebrüder Bock, a Volksstück in three acts. A dramatic season was advertised, beginning on December 12th; alas! without specifications. Bürgerlich und Romantisch emerged, on April 4th.

Minor German Resorts, 1886-1887

Perhaps *minor* is not the word, except as regards omission of our main quarry—drama; certainly, as regards beer and German good-fellowship, several of them were of major interest.

The Atlantic Garten, 50 Bowery, by long usage, takes precedence. A Damen-Kapelle was advertised in early October; also Max Abramovitz and Emil Grosé-Graff (genannt Flick und Flock) and G. Wolf, whose name means nothing to me. Frederic N. Innes (trombone) and A. Liberati (cornet) with the "beliebte" Damen-Elite-Kapelle made impressive the week of November 29th–December 4th; Innes was featured in early January, and then we were thrilled, I suppose, by Liberati's Militär-Kapelle. In latest May, the management advertised a newly-engaged Damen-Kapelle, Elsa Alberti and Ignatz Conradi ("tenorist"). In mid-June, Marie Roller's Damen-Kapelle and Elsa Alberti and Conradi filled the brimming cup of delight (with beer).

The Neuer Volks-Garten (231-233 Bowery) "alles neu!" was striving, perhaps, to take the place of the old resort, at 113 Bowery. On Sunday, October 17th, it advertised the Wiener Damen-Orchester, with Marie Wolker (*sic*); also Nand'l Hofer, Schwarz and Weiss (surely no accidental collocation of names), Fred Lion (*sic*) and (most important) "Eintritt frei!" The place throughout the autumn advertised, with vigour, two Sunday concerts; the Staats-Zeitung does not specify the ingredients of the Circe-cup then offered. An Ungarische Damen-Kapelle could come from almost any European country—Spanish, Hungarian, Austrian; Nand'l Hofer, that travelling star, and a Tyrolean group also appeared. In later May, this resort was advertising music and beer, a combination irresistible to Germans; also the manager announced the "Grosse Wieder-offnung der prachtvollen Palast Musik-Halle und des offenen Sommer-Gartens. Verzügliche Musik und Gesang."

Künstler Halle, 165-167 Chrystie Street, sends a scanty trickle of news through our chronicle; earliest October opens it for Gesangsvorträge. Seppel Thaler and Rosel Rainer were here, on December 14th, with Joseph Stritter. In mid-June, Der Rattenfänger von Hameln pursued the quarry, with assistance from "Doctoress" Mary Rembach, Frl. Bade, Frl. Salma, Frl. Berndorf and Herr Stritter; I apologise for including in the chronicle these absolutely negligible names.

The first note I retrieved for Walhalla, 48-52 Orchard Street, was announcement, for October 10th, of the fourteenth Stiftungsfest of the Beverstädter Plattdeutscher Club. The opening ball came on October 21st. At Deutsche Reichs-Halle, Stanton and Eldridge Streets, mid-October boasted of Frl. Tilly, Frl. Somer, Frl. St. Clair, Frl. Louise and Frl. Engel, not, I fancy, the supreme artists of the world. A. Gander's Bier Palast was offering, for Sundays in October, a "Grosses Concert und Gesangsvorträge." And the opening ball, at Wendel's Assembly Rooms, 334-344 West 44th Street occurred on October 13th. Other festivities in this place will be found under caption of Other German Activities.

I merely mention other seats of German amusement: Conrad Stein's Summer Garden, with a Sunday concert (October 17th); Major Sauer's Atalanta Casino, last station of the Sixth Avenue "Hochbahn," with (October 17th) Pauline Hoffer, F. W. Bent (cornet) and Nussbaum (xylophone); Sulzer's Harlem River Park and Casino (126th Street and Third Avenue). The last of these I mention in the list of Other German Activities.

The Café Cosmopolitan, at 1¼ Second Avenue, provided, for the idle-minded, billiards, Schach and a Lese-Zimmer; I do not know that Empire Hall, Third Avenue near 40th Street, could do more for weary man. This Cosmopolitan pleasance must not be confused with the Cosmopolitan Park and Casino, at 169th Street and Tenth Avenue, Highbridge. Since I am so far north, I may as well journey to W. Urback's Morrisania Park and Hotel, at 170th Street and Third Avenue, just to see if it is worth my reader's attention with a view to a possible visit. W. Geib's Grove Hill Park, 161st Street and Third Avenue, was solemnly declared, in the spring of 1887, to be "der schönste Sommer Vergnügungsort für Gesangvereine, Regelclubs und Logen"; for aught I know, it may have been. Inability to answer that question leads me, on July 3rd, to the Felsenkeller, 57th Street and East River, which on that day (Sunday) gave two concerts.

French Activities, 1886–1887

Again I invite the reader to accompany me on a journey through the files of the Courrier des États-Unis. We begin rather early, with a visit to Frank's Hall, 173 West Houston Street, a place familiar to us, in 1885–86, under various guises and disguises. On July 18, 1886, it promised the *"premier grand concert d'été, suivi de bal,"* participants being M. and Mme. Manoel, Mendel (tenor), Baumont (artiste dramatique) and Herman (pianist). For August our Courrier points the way to no entertainment specifically French, and we must wait till September 18th. when Lion Park opened for a continuation of the July 14th celebration of the Union des Sociétés Françaises de New York.

A concert and ball at Ferrero's Rooms, Tammany Hall, was sponsored, on October 23rd, by l'Orphéon Français, l'Helvétienne, L'Espérance, the Union Chorale of Newark and the Jura Männerchor. Aside from this firmly based festivity, October summoned to trifling pleasures. On October 4th, the Bijou Café (*ci-devant Theiss*), 61 West 14th Street, announced a concert, with Mlle. Grévain and an orchestra of *Dames Parisiennes*. The Renaissance, 123 West Houston Street, re-opened, on October 10th, proffering M. and Mme. Olivero, Paul Pizzarello (*fils*), MM. Decheno and Arnould (*sic*) and Mme. Paul. On the same evening, at Poujade's Lyric Hall, 21 South Fifth Avenue, the concert and ball for Professor F. Groux enjoyed the co-operation of the Orphéon Français and the Association Musicale Française. The Concert des Amis Réunis, at 117 Bleecker Street, on Sunday, October 24th, was the *"inauguration des Soirées Musicales et Dansantes de la saison d'hiver."* And entrance was free. La Superbe Cascade, *"la seule existant aux États-Unis,"* advertised at this time that *"Amateurs de chant qui voulront faire partie de la Societe, La Gaieté,"* might apply to the California Hotel. Finally, Saturdays and Sundays in late October and early November found concerts and balls waging at or by the Hotel du Commerce, 117 Bleecker Street. Lyric Hall, 21 South Fifth Avenue, retained the services of M. and Mme. Manoel, Paul Pizzarello, Roussel and Herman. The Manoels appeared in tiny playlets, such, on November 14th, as Fleuriste et Typographe. The places listed in this paragraph carried on, about as above, till 1886 lapsed into 1887.

Such scant treatment of their activities permits me to start the season of balls. On November 25th (Thanksgiving Day) the Grenadiers Rochambeau celebrated with fête, concert and ball the third anniversary of the foundation of the *bataillon*. 21 South Fifth Avenue welcomed the guests, for the admission fee of 25 cents, for *"cavalier et dames, vestiaire compris."* L'Espérance was to go, on December 5th, to Irving Hall, for its fourteenth concert and ball, calling for help on Fannie Hirsch, L. Kap, F. Rucquoy, Carlos Sobrino, the Tissot Family, and Max Schwab's orchestra. From an advertisement in the Courrier of December 10th, this event was deferred to a date to be announced, *"par suite de la stricte application de la loi du dimanche."* The Orphéon Français "played safe," in selecting a week-day, December 8th, for its sixteenth *bal paré et masqué*, held at Tammany Hall. The Cercle, La Française, at this time, went to Poujade's Lyric Hall, for a concert and ball, involving the aid of the Manoels (in L'Amour et l'Appétit), Arnoux (*sic*), Paul Pizzarello, Henry Kohn and Herman. On December 12th, and again on January 9th, the Manoels, let me say in passing, acted, at Poujade's, La Lune de Miel. On Sunday January 2nd, the Cercle, La Française, gave a Grand Concert et Bal, with M. Marius making his *rentrée*,

[291]

and with the Manoels in a one-act "operette." And *"les amateurs sont admis cordialement"*; others paid an extravagant entrance fee of five cents. That same festive January 2nd found the association, Aux Amis Réunis, at the Hotel du Commerce, 117 Bleecker Street, with a liberal promise of Mme. Darelli (later made more weighty as Darelly), Mlle. Adrienne, and Toto Carabo (*"par un artiste sans rival"*). And one might reflect with satisfaction on the assertion that *"le piano sera tenu par Mlle. Plantier"*— a good name, if one greeted it, in English, from the significance of the first syllable. Entrance to this show, with tombola and ball to boot, was *"libre."* This same group, on January 16th (Sunday) lured to the Hotel du Commerce, with the art of Mme. Darelli, Mlle. Aimée, and MM. Marx (*sic*), Bertall, Pizzarello, Albert and Corneille. The chief attraction was Bibi, l'Enfant de l'Amour, acted by Mme. Darelli and Marx (Max?).

Having thus done my duty by the little amusements in the "Colonie Française de New York," let me pass to the major festivities of the dance. The whirl began with the *"bal paré et masqué* of L'Amitié," footed featly, on January 10th, in the Academy of Music and Nilsson Hall. The Red Men, comprising *"les tribus"* Huron, No. 35, Ontario, No. 38, and Sioux, No. 56, buried the hatchet, appropriately, in Tammany Hall, on the 15th of January, the ever busy Louis Conterno furnishing the music. It required all the space of the Academy of Music, Irving Hall and Nilsson Hall, to hold the joy of the Cercle Français de l'Harmonie, on the gay evening of January 17th. And more Red Men—*la Tribu* Idaho, No. 36, I. O. R. M. took their initials and their insignia, on January 22nd, to Irving Hall, to dance to the rhythms of Conterno's orchestra. On January 29th, Irving Hall housed the seventeenth annual ball of the Société Tessinoise de Sécours Mutuels. The 29th, also allowed the Union des Patrons Boulangers to dance in the Teutonia Rooms. Having thus got into the swing of the dance, I will, with the reader's permission, carry the record into February, beginning, on the 1st, at the Metropolitan Opera House, with the eagerly awaited and not over-prim Bal de Cuisiniers. On the 3rd, the Prospect Association hid behind masks and danced, to the tune of five dollars admission, at the Academy of Music, Nilsson Hall and Tammany Hall. The Grand Bal du Mardi Gras, *paré et masqué*, crowded on the heels of these foregoing pleasures, promising, for February 5th, at Tammany Hall, a *"Grand Cortège Burlesque,"* a *"surprise aux dames,"* and music by E. Gomer's orchestra. La Concorde, on February 19th, went modestly to Ferrero's Rooms, Tammany Hall, to dance in costumes and masks, to the appealing strains of Conterno's band. On that same 19th, the Union Alsacienne and L'Espérance Société Chorale gave a *"grand bal,"* in the Teutonia Assembly Rooms. Washington's Birthday opened Everett Hall, 31-35 Fourth Street (between Broadway and the Bowery) to the happiness of children. Then and there, at two in the afternoon, the Union des Sociétés Françaises de New York, held, for the benefit of their Salles d'Asile, a *"Grand bal d'enfants, paré et travesti, offert aux enfants de la colonie française de New York."* For children entrée was *"gratuite"*; maturity paid 25 cents *"per personne."* Another function by the same group for the benefit of the same "Salles" held Ferrero's Assembly Rooms, on April 11th. But this is anticipating, and I go back to Sunday, March 20th, to record "Vive la Commune! the sixteenth anniversary of the Revolution of March 18, 1871." This was held in the Germania Assembly Rooms and charged 25 cents for a *"ticket de famille."*

I fear I have worn out my reader, head to foot, by this record of French dancing. In thus grouping the festivities of Terpsichore, however, I have cleared the way for the chronicle of Thalia in resorts, it must be said, of no exalted dramatic consequence. I resume with the offerings of the Cercle, "La Française," operative, apparently, chiefly on Sundays, at Poujade's Lyric Hall, 21 South Fifth Avenue. The benefit of A. Bertall there, on January 20th, promised appearances of Adèle Martinetti, Mme. Talvar, M. and Mme. Manoel, and MM. Sablon, Mendel and Arnoux. These, except for Miss Martinetti, were listed for evenings in later January and in earlier February, little farces, acted generally by M. and Mme. Manoel, including Une Marine à la Vapeur, La Leçon de Musique, Le Serment d'Horace, Un Charcutier dans les Fers and La Lune de Miel. Besides the Manoels, participants in the bills were Bertall, Herman, Mendel and the popular Arnoux, this last-named "comique" to follow us for years in our journey through cheap palaces of wine and song.

La Leçon de Musique must have been popular; Mme. Darelli and M. Marx gave it, on January 29th and 30th, in the rival establishment, Aux Amis Réunis. This company, on February 5th, proffered Les Deux Prix de Vertu, with Mme. Darelli and M. Germain, and Bibi, l'Enfant de l'Amour, with Mme. Darelli and Marx (*sic*). This last-named farce and Chez un Garçon, both with Mme. Darelli and Marx, had held the stage on January 23rd; assisting artists then in the bill were Mlle. Lee, Pizzarello, Raoul, and Corneille. The last I found for this company was a bill for February 12th, repeating La Leçon de Musique and Les Deux Prix de Vertu. In fact, the two rival organisations seem to have amalgamated. As the Cercle "La Française," they proffered, at Poujade's, on March 20th, a group of entertainers comprising Mme. Darelli, Manoel, Mendel, Arnoux, Pizzarello and Herman; on the 27th and also on April 3rd they gave La Leçon de Musique, with Manoel and Mme. Darelly (*sic*). Les Troubadours Ambulants, in later April was in no way, I take it, allied to the popular Nanki-Poo. Then, one paid 15 cents to enter, with an additional dime for the tombola. For May 1st and 5th, Mme. Darelly was Jeannette and Manoel was Pierrot, in Sous Louis XV, ou Un Coq en Jupons.

Another May flower was the California Hotel, 130 West 26th Street — an address which will haunt our later journey; for the present, it suffices to say that it now announced *"Continuations des soirées dites 'La Gaiete Française,'"* rich with the *"premiers débuts des inimitables Tartampion, Armand, Fery and Merdigo,"* surely a pretty dish to set before King Public. We next hear of Mme. Darelly, on May 26th, when she comes forward at Clarendon Hall, 114-118 East 13th Street—a place from which we shall never wholly escape in years that follow. On that 26th of May she was of a numerous band, embracing Mme. Bageard, Manoel, Max (*sic*), Roussel, M. and Mme. P. Debuchy, and la Société Espagnole, La Barretina. But, of the farces offered, two at least had pursued us from hall to hall; the three given were Bibi l'Enfant de l'Amour, Un Duel sans Témoins, and La Leçon de Musique. This advertisement in the Courrier des États-Unis was the last I found for anything French-dramatic in minor halls in 1886–87.

But what is so rare as a "pique-nique" in June or July, with merry *sociétés* gathering in leafy grove or on shady lawn? Ours shall be the privilege of taking bird's-eye views of these celebrations for the summer of 1887. Beginning with the *Fête Annuelle d'Été* of the Société Française de Bienfaisance, held in Lion Park, on June 23rd, a fête with Max Schwab's orchestra, and with the expected *tombola, jeux divers, concert* and ball, we pass readily to the celebrations, on July 14th, of the Fête Nationale de la République Française; these were carried through by the Union des Sociétés Françaises de New York, at the Harlem River Park, 127th Street and Second Avenue, and by the banquet, ball, concert and *assaut d'armes,* of the Ligue des Sociétés Françaises at Terrace Garden. On August 25th, the Société Française de Bienfaisance seems to have held another *Fête Annuelle d'Été* (or perhaps it was the event of June 23rd deferred), with promises of Schwab's orchestra, *tir, concert* and *tombola;* Lion Park again was scene of the festivities. I end with the Grand Pique-Nique and Fête de Nuit, held, on August 27th, in Washington Park by the Société Générale Suisse. Of course the genuine riches of the French season in New York were supplied by the visits of the incomparable Sarah Bernhardt.

ITALIAN ACTIVITIES, 1886–1887

Let us start the Italians on their joyous round, with two festivities to commemorate Columbus and his discovery of this perplexed and perplexing hemisphere. According to the Progresso Italo-Americano, the Guardia Colombo, on our Columbus Day, celebrated, at Sulzer's Harlem River Park, the *"Scoperta d'America,"* all for the benefit of the Italian Hospital. For the benefit of the New York Hospital, October 12th proffered a Gran Pic-Nic Italiano *"sotto gli auspici delle Società Italiane Militari Unite, coll' intervento delle Società Spagnuolo, Ungheresi e Francesi"*—this at Brommer's Union Park, 133rd Street, to celebrate the *"Scoperta d'America."* The Italian Rifle Guard held its fifth annual ball, on December 18th, at the

[294]

Germania Assembly Rooms; L. Conterno, as usual, furnished the music. At Irving Hall, on January 29, 1887, came the seventeenth *Ballo Annuale della Società Ticinese di Mutuo Soccorso.*

The file of the Progresso Italo-Americano furnishes but little besides dancing of "Società" for the winter of 1887. Nevertheless, on February 20th, at the Germania Assembly Rooms, Bowery, the Circolo Filodrammatico Italo-Americano gave a benefit for the Garibaldi Monument in New York. The first part of their programme presented Un Episodio della Rientrata dei Guelfi in Firenze, ovvero l'Arcano della Vendetta, a *"dramma tragica in 5 atti di* F. Castelvecchi." Pellacani then played a flute-solo; the dialogue, Il Nome di Garibaldi, was recited by the *"figli della Signora Argia Calarsi";* and a "Gran Ballo" ensued, with music by "Professor" R. Codeluppi. 25 cents admitted, and 25 cents additional procured one a reserved seat. A *"Preavviso del Monumento a Garibaldi"* in New York brought a *"Gran Festa"* and ball *"de fondo per il monumento,"* all on the happy night of February 26th, in Tammany Hall; at midnight the Liberati band was to play *"una grande serenata."* Otherwise, the ubiquitous Luigi Conterno was to supply dance music for those who attended at the rate of one dollar *"per un signore ed una signora."* And, since Garibaldi so much occupied the minds of Italo-Americans, in 1887, I will end the paragraph with the thirteenth annual ball of the Società Legione Giuseppe Garibaldi, danced, on March 21st, at Irving Hall, when one dollar admitted *"un signore e più dame."*

Very cheap would seem the entrance fee, on March 14th, to Irving Hall, for the second annual ball of the Società Italiana Guardia Vittorio Emanuele II; then 50 cents allowed *"un signore e più dame"* to dance to the music provided by "Professor" Carmine Sanna. I cannot believe that the Italians in New York amused themselves so sparingly as the files of the Progresso Italo-Americano compel me to think; and I should be sorry to believe that my eye missed items in the paper. At any rate, I am forced to leap to May 1st, when the Circolo Filodrammatico Italo-Americano gave a benefit (I could not discover where) for the victims of the earthquake in Liguria. La Rivincita, a four-act comedy by Tebaldo Ciconi, was played by A. Nanetti, Lina Metella, Signora Burron, L. Pensa, L. Zumbo, R. Guidone, I. Delicati (what a name to act up to!), P. Mattly, A. Lio, L. Sambruna, S. Bono, F. D. Malzone, Burron, Staiano, A. Sambruna and Carro. In the intermezzo, Icilio Delicati was to declaim a poem by Alessandro Gatti. And the eagerly awaited *"ballo"* was to be danced to music furnished by Sanna. May 24th took us to the open, far north to Sulzer's Harlem River Park, for the *Gran Festa Campestre della Società Reduci delle Patrie Battaglie;* it also took Carmine Sanna northward to supply music for the festivities. But Luigi Conterno, so often tried and (I hope) true to pitch, furnished music for the dance at Kroebel's Hudson County Volks Park, Hoboken,

[295]

whither, on May 28th, the Società Firenze de Mutuo Soccorso of New York betook itself for *"tiro al bersaglio,"* and kindred joys. And, after one had ferried thither, 25 cents admitted to the Elysian fields of joy unconfined.

June, from aught I could recover from files of the Progresso, was niggardly in providing amusements. On the 22nd of that month of rosy charm, the Società Mazzini (di Mutuo Soccorso) went to Brommer's Union Park, 133rd Street and Third Avenue, for whatever fun or pleasure they could derive from open air, music, fireworks, *tiro al bersaglio* and I know not what besides. But July did better for the Italo-Americans. On the very first day of that torrid month, the Guardia Vittorio Emanuele II, held its twentieth *"Gran Pic-Nic Annuale,"* in that same Union Park, far to the north of Union Square. Music by the "Capo banda dell' Associazione Professor A. Sanna" incited to happiness as did *"gran tiro al bersaglio con premi di valore"* and *"gran giuochi diversi."* I hope the reader agrees with me that it would be wicked to translate into English that thoroughly Italian promise of joys to come. The Italian societies were invited to share, on July 14th, the picnic of the French societies, to celebrate the anniversary of the fall of the Bastille. On the 26th, with similar patriotic fervour, the *Gran Festa Campestre delle Società Italiane Unite* commemorated the *"supplizio dei Martiri Italiani, Emilio e Attillio Bandieri e loro compagni."* Union Park, 133rd Street, again sheltered the company, and Luigi Conterno furnished the music required.

On August 17th, the first *Festa Campestre* of the Società Italiana Principe di Napoli of Brooklyn, betook itself to Schützen Park, 50th Street and Third Avenue; but to Brommer's Union Park, on August 27th, went the Italian Rifle Guard for its sixth annual "pic-nic," inducing the willing Luigi Conterno to accompany them in their flight. This same much-occupied Brommer's was scene of the thirteenth annual "pic-nic" of the Legione Giuseppe Garibaldi, on September 7th; that happy event was in commemoration of the twenty-seventh entry of Garibaldi into Naples. Professor P. De Fina supplied the musical accompaniment to this function of the "legione." On September 29th, the Società Italiane di New York, Hoboken, Brooklyn and Newark united, in Brommer's park, to commemorate the entrance of the Italian troops into Rome; the profits were to go to the fund for erecting an Ospedale Italiano and also for the benefit of the fund of the Società Italiana di Beneficenza. Luigi Conterno was again called into requisition for whatever music the occasion demanded. September passed from our ken, on the 29th, with the second annual "pic-nic" of the Società Militare Torquato Tasso, held in Sulzer's Harlem River Park, with music by "Professor" G. Peluso, "Capobanda della Società."

Metropolitan Opera House, 1886–1887

I will begin, if I must, with an opera by Harley Newcomb—The Hermit of Cashel—produced mostly with children, on October 7th, for the Grant Monument Fund. The German opera, apparently strongly entrenched at the Metropolitan, began its third season, on November 8, 1886, with the great success of the preceding year, The Queen of Sheba, with, in leading rôles, the best of the artists of that season—Lilli Lehmann, Marianne Brandt, Max Alvary, Adolf Robinson and Emil Fischer; the part of the Queen was sung by Frau Herbert-Förster, wife of the 'cellist and later most popular composer, Victor Herbert, who played, that year, in the Metropolitan orchestra. The new Queen was better in voice than her predecessor, and far less ample in person; nevertheless, she was not more than a satisfactory routinière. Herr Heinrich was Baal Hanan. This opera had been given fifteen times in the preceding season, but four satisfied the demand for 1886–87.

On the second night of the subscription, November 10th, Albert Niemann, a celebrated tenor for thirty-five years in Germany, made his début here as Siegmund, in Die Walküre, a part he created in Bayreuth in 1876. It is not too much to say that he made musical history in New York. His voice was worn by years of service and probably had never had the sensuous beauty of the voices of Campanini and Ravelli; but he used it as the medium for great dramatic utterance, colouring it to fit all moods, and utterly abandoning the *bel canto* of the Italian school. He was a great actor, and as Siegmund his heroic figure, his blazing eyes, his declamation of the text were a revelation to his audiences. From the first night he became the idol of the intense partisans of the German school of singing actors. With him in Die Walküre, on the 10th, were Lilli Lehmann (who could sing beautifully and dramatically) as Brünnhilde, Frau Seidl-Kraus (who couldn't) as Sieglinde, Marianne Brandt as Fricka and Gerhilde, Fischer as Wotan, and George Sieglitz as Hunding. Among the Valkyries were Frl. Better, Januschowsky, Franconi, Meyer, Klein and Escott and Frau Kemlitz. This opera was sung again at the first matinée (November 13), and, oddly enough, in view of the craze for German opera, only once again in the course of a long season. Of course Seidl was at the helm for all the great music-dramas of Wagner.

Aïda, the offering of the third night (November 12th) was very German Verdi, as one might have expected from the cast—Frau Herbert-Förster, Frl. Brandt, Frl. Better, Herren Zobel (new, as Rhadames), Robinson, Fischer (Ramfis), Sieglitz (King) and Kemlitz (Messenger). The concerts of the Philharmonic, Symphony and Oratorio Societies, all held that year in the Metropolitan, I shall treat separately, as usual, each under its own heading. Aïda came again on November 15th and 20th (matinée). Der

Prophet, on November 17th, allowed Niemann to show his dramatic gifts as John of Leyden; Lilli Lehmann as Bertha, Frl. Brandt as a great Fides, Dr. Basch (Germans love titles) as Oberthal, and Alvary, von Milde and Sieglitz as the gloomy Anabaptists, completed an efficient cast, which gave this opera on four subsequent occasions. The Golden Cross (Das goldene Kreutz) of Brüll, made another novelty for November 19th, with Seidl-Kraus as Christine, Frl. Januschowsky as Therese, Alvary as Gontran, Fischer as Bombardon and von Milde as Nicholas. The ballet of Vienna Waltzes formed part of the bill on that evening and on three subsequent performances — all conducted by Walter Damrosch, and very tamely, according to the Herald of November 20th. Mme. Cavalazzi led the dance.

Repetitions of this double bill (November 22nd and matinée, 27th) and Der Prophet (24th) allowed time, on the 26th, for Tannhäuser, of course with Niemann, Lehmann, Seidl-Kraus, Ida Klein, Fischer, Robinson and Alvary. The last Aïda fell on the 29th. On December 1st came the great sensation, the revelation for musical New York — the first performance in America of Tristan und Isolde, with Niemann and Lehmann as the lovers, Robinson as Kurvenal, Fischer as King Mark, Marianne Brandt as Brangäne, von Milde as Melot, Otto Kemlitz as ein Hirt, Max Alvary as the Seemann and Emil Sänger as the Steuermann. From that first performance the tide of admiration for the opera has risen, till now (1941) Tristan und Isolde, with a satisfactory cast, is perhaps the manager's best bid for an overflowing audience.

The Herald, on December 2nd, gives hardly a half column in review. "The score . . . is possibly the most perfect thing that Wagner ever wrote. Never before has the quintessence of passion been painted in tones so startlingly brilliant and at once so true. . . . The whole score . . . is a constant passage from beauty to beauty." In the performance the first place went to Seidl and the orchestra. "Nor has Fräulein Lehmann ever shown what a magnificent dramatic singer she is as she did last evening" (this was her first performance of Isolde). Niemann "looked" Tristan, but his singing was not so good in the second act — that terrific test for a tenor, thought to be impossible till Jean de Reszké, years later, showed us how easy it was for a great vocal and dramatic artist. The Herald also thought Frl. Brandt, though painstaking, "not at all herself. Only the 'Wachruf' . . . is deserving of warm praise." Tristan und Isolde became the musical hit of the season, receiving eight performances before the German opera closed. Yet let us remember that, in 1885–86, The Queen of Sheba mounted to fifteen renderings; it came again, by the way, on December 3rd. Der Prophet, with Damrosch conducting, was given at the matinée on the 4th. Tristan (6th) and Tannhäuser (10th) allowed Niemann to strengthen his hold on popular appreciation. On the 8th and matinée, 11th, the management had the Germanic idea of mounting the most French of operas — Faust, with Alvary, who never could sing in the French or Italian style, or indeed in any style, in the title-rôle, Lilli Lehmann as a rather mature Gretchen, Fischer as Mephistopheles, Robinson as Valentin, Frl. Franconi as Siebel, and Frl. Mayer (*sic*) as Martha. The reader knows that this cast was conscientious, and, except for Lehmann and possibly Fischer, quite out of the spirit of the work; its third and last performance fell on the 17th. The Queen of Sheba (December 13th), with Frl. Franconi replacing Frl. Brandt, led to Lohengrin (15th) with Niemann, not a very golden-voiced Knight of the Swan, Sieglitz as the King, Dr. Basch as Telramund, Frau Herbert-Förster as Elsa, Frl. Brandt as Ortrud, Max Heinrich as the Herald; Niemann was good, and in the best voice he had yet displayed. Tannhäuser served for the matinée on the 18th. Christmas week repeated Tristan und Isolde (20th and 24th), the double bill (22nd), and The Queen of Sheba (matinée, 25th). During the next week (December 27th–January 1st), the Metropolitan gave no performances.

This pause allows me to glance back at Augustin Daly's annual benefit for the Roman Catholic Orphan Asylum, held on November 23rd, with the usual two bills. In the afternoon, Modjeska and Maurice Barrymore gave an act of Adrienne Lecouvreur, the Wallack company one of Sophia, the Daly actors one of Love in Harness, Harrigan's one of Investigation and the Thalia force a bit of The Ratcatcher of Hamelin. Nat Goodwin, Dockstader and Frank Bush appeared in specialties. In the evening, J. H. Stoddart and Marie Burroughs, not in the current bill at the Madison Square, gave One Touch of Nature; the Rosina Vokes players performed the delightful Pantomime Rehearsal; Daly actors not employed in Love in Harness—Charles Leclercq, May Irwin, Joseph Holland, May Amber, John Wood and May Sylvie—contributed the amusing A Woman's Won't; and Mme. Valda, Blanche Stone Barton, von Milde, Tony Pastor, Jules Levy and Lizzie St. Quinten appeared in special features. This bill began with Ada Rehan and John Drew in A Wet Blanket; and the Highland Schottische from The Passing Regiment employed Mrs. Gilbert, Miss Rehan, Miss Dreher, Miss Bleecker, Parkes, Drew, Skinner and Bond.

This delightful interval now past, I recur to the serious business of the German opera. After their week's holiday, the singers, on January 3rd and 7th, presented Goldmark's opera, Merlin, which, I may say at once, failed to achieve the success here of his Queen of Sheba. The cast:

King Arthur	A. Robinson	Viviane	Lilli Lehmann
Mordred	Otto Kemlitz	Bedwyn	Rudolph von Milde
Gawain	Max Heinrich	Glendower	Sieglitz
Lancelot	Dr. Basch	Morgana	Marianne Brandt
Merlin	Max Alvary	Demon	Emil Fischer

The four maids of Viviane were impersonated by Frl. Better, Klein, Franconi and Mayer. Tannhäuser, with Niemann, again emerged on January

5th and Lohengrin, at the matinée on the 8th. Merlin had two more performances on January 10th and 15th (matinée), with Tristan und Isolde on the 12th, and, on the 14th, a striking revival of Fidelio, in which Niemann's Florestan again showed how great a singing (or should I say, declaiming?) artist he was. The Herald, next day, asserted that "derisive laughter" greeted Frl. Brandt as Leonore (she was a very plain woman and perhaps the boy's dress was not becoming). Laughter from a box threw the singer into consternation, in her duet with Niemann, and Seidl stopped the performance till order was restored and the tearful Brandt recovered her composure. This unpleasantness was thrashed out in the papers. When Fidelio was repeated, on the 19th, Lilli Lehmann, beautiful and glorious in voice and vocal style, sang Leonore and created a profound impression, so great an impression indeed, that Fidelio was given again at a special performance, on February 3rd. Henry E. Krehbiel, in his Chapters of Opera, states that the average receipts of those three Fidelios exceeded even the average returns for Tristan und Isolde, supposed to be the hit of the season. In Fidelio, I may say, Fischer sang Rocco, Robinson Pizarro, Seidl-Kraus Marcelline and Kemlitz Jacquino. On January 17th, Niemann, who was leaving before the end of the season, sang his last Lohengrin, Frau Seidl-Kraus reverting to Elsa; Die Meistersinger had, on the 21st, its first performance of the season (I wonder if it was as popular then, as Wagnerites of New York, fifty years later, maintain); Alvary for the first time sang Walther, Basch Beckmesser, and Fischer, Seidl-Kraus and Brandt the parts they had assumed in the preceding season. Fidelio (19th) and Tristan und Isolde (matinée, 22nd) completed a week German as German could be. And on the wave of that accomplishment I stop to record balls, now moved irreparably from the Academy of Music to this larger, more conveniently situated hall. January 20th brought the Charity Ball; January 27th that of the Old Guard; February 1st, the French Cooks' Ball; February 10th, the Liederkranz masquerade; the reception and drill of the Palestine Commandery, K.T., on February 8th; and the Purim Ball, on March 10th. So on and off with the dance!

Niemann's last Tannhäuser fell on January 24th, his last Tristan but one on the 26th, and his last Prophet at the matinée on the 29th. Whatever cheerfulness came in that week of farewells was injected by Die Meistersinger, on the 28th. January 31st brought back Anton Schott, whose truculent and ungallant behaviour had been an unpleasant feature of the days following the death of Dr. Damrosch, in 1885. He came forth in a showy revival of Rienzi, which, like Der Prophet, Merlin and Die Meistersinger, enjoyed five performances before the season closed; he had, of course, been engaged to take up the heroic rôles soon to be dropped by Niemann. With him, in Rienzi, were Lehmann, Brandt, Robinson, Fischer, and, to lead the dance, Mme. Cavalazzi. Die Meistersinger (February 2nd), Fidelio and the Vienna Waltzes (3rd), Lohengrin (4th), with Schott as a poor swan-knight, and Die Meistersinger (matinée, 5th) carried the season on.   Monday, February 7th, brought the farewell of Niemann, of course as Tristan. Krehbiel (Chapters of Opera) doubts "if the history of opera in New York discloses anything like a parallel to the occasion" (the great farewell to Marcella Sembrich certainly exceeded it, but that was two years after Krehbiel's book was published).   Despite cold rain and slushy walking outside, the house was crowded, orchestra seats bringing from ten to fifteen dollars each; "delegations" came from Boston, Philadelphia and Cincinnati Niemann "husbanded his vocal resources in the first act, but after that both he and Fräulein Lehmann threw themselves into the work with utter abandon, such abandon, indeed, as made some of the prima donna's friends tremble for her voice."   After the two singers had responded, at the end of that act, Niemann came out alone to cheers, "while a laurel wreath, bearing on one of its ribbons the significant line from 'Tannhäuser,' 'O, kehr zurück, du kühner Sänger,' was handed up to him."   The close of the third act climaxed the scene with a speech of thanks (in German) from the departing tenor.

After that excitement, the season settled down to "normalcy," with Rienzi (9th), Merlin (last time — 11th), and Rienzi again (matinée, 12th). On the 14th, Schott replaced Niemann as Siegmund, in Die Walküre, which, as we remember, he performed in the original Metropolitan cast in 1885. The last new production of the season came on February 16th and at the matinée on the 19th — Masaniello (or La Muette de Portici, or Die Stumme von Portici, just as the reader prefers).   In this, of course, Mme. Cavalazzi mimed Fenella, Schott was Masaniello, Janouschowsky (sic) certainly not a scintillant Elvira, with Fischer, Alvary, Frl. Franconi in other rôles.   It was given again but once.   The season thenceforth went on to the close with repetitions: Rienzi (18th), Tannhäuser (21st), with Frau Herbert-Förster, Schott, Fischer, Basch (as Wolfram), Lehmann, and Januschowsky as the Shepherd, Der Prophet (23rd); Die Meistersinger (25th, with presentation of a large loving cup worth a thousand dollars to Seidl); and a concluding matinée, February 26th, of Rienzi with Schott, Lehmann and Brandt in accustomed rôles.   Like the reader, I wonder that Alvary, in his first two seasons in New York, had been entrusted with so few important rôles.   His success as Siegfried, next year, changed all that.

NATIONAL OPERA (LATE AMERICAN), 1887

Immediately after the departure of the Germans the American Opera Company, which had made so good a record in 1886 at the Academy of Music, entered the Metropolitan for a season considerably curtailed from that of the preceding year.   It had changed its name to the National Opera

Company. The troupe had had, apparently, a rather tempestuous experience on the road. The Herald published, occasionally, accounts of disagreements between Theodore Thomas, Mme. Fursch-Madi and Emma Juch; the negro minstrels had turned the disturbances into a timely skit. When the company began, on February 28th, at the Metropolitan, Mme. Fursch-Madi was not in the roster and things wore to a conclusion, it would seem, in something like peace.

The season began with The Flying Dutchman, sung by Wilhelm Ludwig, Emma Juch, M. W. Whitney, Charles Bassett (Erik), Mathilde Phillipps (Mary) and W. H. Fessenden (Steersman); the high seriousness of the Germans may not have been over-emphasised in the American rendition of this essentially German work, but some of the cast, Whitney and Emma Juch, particularly, knew how to sing. The Huguenots (March 2nd) reintroduced Pauline L'Allemand as the Queen, Jessie Bartlett Davis as the page and Candidus as Raoul, and gave us a rather good Valentine in a new Bertha Pierson. Others were Ludwig (St. Bris), A. E. Stoddard (de Nevers) and Whitney (Marcel). I remember this performance with pleasure, though I have since heard far greater aggregations in that opera. Faust, on the 4th, presented Bassett, Ludwig (Mephistopheles), Stoddard, Emma Juch, Jessie Bartlett Davis (Siebel) and Mathilde Phillipps (Martha). The matinée, on March 5th, bravely essayed the spectacle, drama, song and dance of Aïda; Miss Pierson was Aïda, Mme. Van Zanten Amneris, Candidus Radames, Whitney Ramfis, Hamilton the King and Ludwig Amonasro.

The casts of that first week allow us to see just what to expect for the rest of the season. Lakmé, on March 7th, introduced Mme. L'Allemand, Bassett, Stoddard, W. H. Lee, Jessie Bartlett Davis and Mathilde Phillipps (as Mrs. Benson). On the 9th another Aïda led (11th) to The Marriage of Jeannette and Coppelia (first time). In the former sang L'Allemand, W. H. Lee, G. W. Williams and Kate Oesterle; the dancers in the latter were Marie Giuri, Felicita Carozzi, Mamert Biboyran and Cammerano. Gustav Hinrichs conducted. The Flying Dutchman again indulged in gloom and death, at the matinée on the 12th. At last, on March 14th and 16th, we were treated to the oft-promised and long-expected Nero of Rubinstein:

Nero	W. Candidus	Terpander	W. H. Lee
Julius Vindex	W. Ludwig	Poppaea	Bertha Pierson
Tigellinus	A. E. Stoddard	Epicharis	Cornelia Van Zanten
Balbillus	M. W. Whitney	Chrysa	Emma Juch
Saccus	W. H. Fessenden	Agrippina	Agnes Sterling
High Priest	} W. Hamilton	Lupus	Pauline L'Allemand
A Centurion	}		

Nearly the entire company, one sees, participated in this costly production; Mlle. de Gillert led the ballet. On the 17th, Coppelia and Massé's Galathée were given for charity — the Société Française de Bienfaisance profit-

[302]

SELMA KRONOLD

FERDINAND SCHUETZ

MARGUERITE FISH

ADELINA PATTI
(1886-1887)

ALBERT NIEMANN
(TRISTAN)

FRAU HERBERT-FOERSTER
VICTOR HERBERT

GIULIA VALDA

MME. JANAUSCHEK
AS MEG MERRILIES

WILLIAM DAVIDGE

ing. Repetitions of Lakmé (18th) and Faust (matinée, 19th—twenty-eighth anniversary of the first performance in Paris) carried us into the fourth week of the uphill fight, with Nero (21st and 25th), Galatea (*sic*) and Coppelia (23rd), and Martha (matinée, 26th). The fifth week merely repeated Nero (28th), Martha and, first time, Rubinstein's Bal Costumé (30th), and Sylvia (last year's hit) and Galatea (April 1st). Nero, at the matinée, on April 2nd, saw Rome (and hopes) burn.

Adelina Patti, 1887

To me the great feature of the season at the Metropolitan came with two weeks of Italian opera given by Adelina Patti and the admirable singers who had accompanied her on a concert tour through American and Mexican cities. The concerts in the autumn of 1886, at the Academy of Music here, I shall describe under the caption of that venerable institution, so long the New York home of opera. Though the complete Wagnerite would expect me to proclaim my first hearing of Tristan und Isolde as my supreme musical experience of 1886-87 (and it was an experience not to be forgotten), I re-assert that the coming of the matchless Patti in opera was to me the ultimate in the year's musical enjoyment. Let me say to the shocked Wagnerite that I have, since 1887, heard very many performances of Wagner's great love-tragedy, but I have never heard any Patti but Patti; again to quote Mme. Sembrich, "when you speak of Patti, you speak of something that happened only once."

The diva began her six performances, on Monday, April 11th, in her favourite entrance-rôle of Violetta, in La Traviata. Her support included Vicini, rescued from the autumn fiasco of the Valda opera at the Academy, Galassi, the resonant baritone, so long a favourite here, Abramoff (as il Medico), Corsi (Gastone), Migliara (as il Barone) and Mlle. Valerga. An enormous audience hailed the great soprano. Educated by the Germans on the dramatic possibilities of opera, the Herald admitted that Mme. Patti's acting was lacking in fervour, but "Vocally she is beyond compare in the part. . . . Every time Mme. Patti appears anew . . . her voice seems to have grown richer and stronger, more mellow and more sensuous. And her art of controlling this voice, of making it obey the intentions of the singer at every turn, is even more wonderful, if possible, than the voice iself. . . . The Libiamo and the Ah fors e lui were matchless vocal achievements. In the latter aria (one of Mme. Patti's 'chevaux de bataille') the broad recitative as well as the succeeding trills, runs, shakes, scales descending and ascending, and every slight embellishment, were given with such ease, such spontaneity, such grace, such elegance of expression and such intoxicating beauty of tone as no other singer now before the public is able to impart to it."

[303]

Semiramide, on the 13th, united the incomparable art of Patti and Sofia Scalchi, in the most perfect singing New York, possibly, ever heard. It was ravishing, as always, and it was the last time these two superlative artists ever sang that opera together in New York. Some unpleasantness had developed, on the recent tour, and the association of the two singers ended forever, so far as New York was concerned, with the short season I am trying to discuss. The other parts in Semiramide fell to Novara (Assur), Abramoff (Oroe) and Migliara (l'Ombra di Nino). Faust, on the 15th, enlisted Patti, Scalchi, Valerga, Vicini, Del Puente (who had not appeared in the concert tour) and Novara (always good as Mephisto). Though Vicini was only acceptable as Faust, this was a memorable performance, hardly to be equalled till the de Reszkés and Emma Eames (or Mme. Albani) revived the opera in 1891–92. Shortly before this American tour, Mme. Patti, always anxious to increase her repertoire, had undertaken the difficult part of Carmen, presenting it on the stage of the little theatre in her Welsh castle of Craig-y-Nos. The cable messages had made us dubious about this experiment, and experience of the event proved that our doubts were well-founded. Mme. Patti was not an actress, such as Minnie Hauk had been in Carmen, and, worst of all, the music was too low for her heavenly voice; and there was no opportunity for display of the remarkable *coloratura* singing one expected in any Patti performance. Perhaps one should say that the attempt was ill-advised; but ill-informed persons who like to assert that this greatest of vocalists was not a musician should observe this, only one of numerous similar attempts, that she was ever making to increase the range of her interpretations. The cast of Carmen included Gertrude Griswold as Micaela, and not a notable one, Vicini, Del Puente, still the incomparable Escamillo, and Novara as Zuniga.

After this lapse, Patti went back (April 20th) to an evening of simply dazzling singing in her own part of Lucia de Lammermoor. Her singing of the mad scene was (I heard it) of intoxicating beauty and set the vast audience wild with excitement. There was no Patti but Patti. The little but clarion-voiced Guille was Edgardo and Del Puente Aston. The sixth and last performance of the too-brief fortnight gave us (matinée, April 23rd) Martha, with Patti, Scalchi, Guille and Novara. I wish my younger readers could have attended.

I heard every one of those six performances, and the memory of them (even of the Carmen of glorious voice, at least) is one of my precious possessions. I love to think back on them. And the public, which the Germans had been "educating" for three years, responded in a manner somewhat disconcerting to the complete Wagnerite. According to Krehbiel (Chapters of Opera) the receipts for the six performances were nearly $70,000. I remember that when, in the mid-morning of the first day's sale, I went to the box office for seats for the six performances, the line of buyers coiled like

[304]

a serpent in the lobby of the opera house, stretched up to the corner of Broadway and 40th Street, and in single file down to the corner of 40th Street and Seventh Avenue. I never saw anything like it before or since. But the public had now reached, regarding Patti, something like the excitement formerly obtaining in regard to Jenny Lind. After all, there was no Patti but Patti. And, as it turned out, it was the vogue of this artist in the spring of 1890 that finally ousted German opera from complete possession of the Metropolitan. The sensational success of the original schedule led to an announcement of two final Patti nights, on May 11th and 13th. On the 11th, when she was to repeat Lucia, the diva, alas! was ill, and the audience dismissed. She fulfilled her engagement for the 13th, appearing in bits of La Traviata, Martha (second act) and Aïda (third act). Nicolini was Alfredo and Radames, as hard to tolerate as ever, in recent years.

Duty compels me to go back to April 14th for a matinée benefit arranged by Augustin Daly and A. M. Palmer, for the New York Catholic Protectory. The programme promised A Conjugal Lesson, with George Clarke and Rose Eytinge; Prince Paul Esterhazy's Orchestra and Munczi Lajos; the Madison Square Company, in Act III of Jim, the Penman; Wilson Barrett in a recitation of Gone with a Handsomer Man; Francis Wilson and Mark Smith, in a scene from Erminie; Wallack's Company in the first act of The Dominie's Daughter; Helen Dauvray, in the third act of The Love Chase; Harrigan and his company, in an act of Investigation; Miss Rehan, Drew and Fisher in a scene from The Taming of the Shrew; and J. C. Duff's Company (Lillian Russell and Oudin), in a scene from A Trip to Africa—really a remarkable offering. On the evening of June 21st, the reader will be amused to find the opera house given over to a strawberry festival and concert of the Young Men's Hebrew Association. According to the American Hebrew, tickets at one dollar "entitled to refreshments."

ACADEMY OF MUSIC (NEW YORK), 1886–1887

The former abode of fashionable opera and of the finer concerts began a season not yet wholly bereft of music with, on October 4, 1886, a lecture by Justin McCarthy, M.P., in aid of sufferers from the Charleston earthquake. This was followed by a sort of operatic earthquake in the purlieus of the house itself. On October 18th, the Angelo Opera Company started an engagement in Petrella's old-fashioned Ione, with a libretto drawn from The Last Days of Pompeii. The cast, of whom few of us had then heard, included Francesco Giannini (a relative of Dusolina Giannini of the 1930s), Pogliani, Greco, Pinto, Cosmi, and Mmes. Mestress, Valerga and Bianchi-Montaldo. A rather melancholy evening resulted. Luisa Miller, on the 20th, introduced more aspirants in Eugenio Vicini (who played in the next spring in the Patti opera), Lalloni, Bologna, Greco, Giulia Valda, Mlles.

[305]

Prandi and Valerga. Let us hope the audience liked what they received. I Lombardi, more very early Verdi, followed on the 22nd, with Giannini, Pinto, Corsi, Migliara, Conti, Mme. Correri, Mlle. Valerga and Matilda Ricci. The Herald records that this was simply "awful," and that Mlle. Ricci was hissed for a thoroughly bad, amateurish performance. Luisa Miller tried to attract hearers at the matinée on the 23rd. A Sunday concert, on the 24th, allowed Mlle. Prandi, Mlle. Ricci, Mlle. Groebl, Vicini, Pogliani, Mme. Correri and others to sing as they might.

One observes that Angelo disinterred the bones of long-buried works, chiefly by Verdi. That composer's I Due Foscari, announced for October 25th, was postponed to the 27th, and Un Ballo in Maschera was substituted, with Giulia Valda (Miss Julia Wheelock, an American and part backer of the scheme) in the pretty rôle of Oscar, the page. In the florid music of this part she revealed a light, pleasing soprano voice capable of considerable *fioriture;* remaining rôles were entrusted to Mme. Mestress (Ulrica), Mme. Bianchi-Montaldo (Amelia), Giannini, Lalloni, Pinto, Bologna, Greco, Cosmi, and Melli. In I Due Foscari, finally produced on the 27th, one might have heard Miss Valda, rather overweighted by the tragic rôle she essayed, a new Eugenio Salto, Bologna, Pogliani, Melli and the ever-useful Ida Valerga. Rigoletto was scheduled for October 29th, but Miss (or Mme.) Valda's illness caused a substitution of I Lombardi. Ione was the matinée offering on the 30th.

Another concert came on Sunday, October 31st, and Un Ballo in Maschera ended the unfortunate venture, on Monday, November 1st. L'Ebrea (La Juive) was announced for the 3rd, with Giannini and Bianchi-Montaldo, and Rigoletto, with Mme. Valda, for the 5th. Neither performance was given. Very acrimonious interviews with the warring backers, Angelo and Mme. Valda, were printed in the Herald, but all was over between them, as managers; and between them and would-be auditors. The venture was dead.

I may now go back to Tuesday, October 26th, when a reception and concert to the French Delegates was proffered by the Cercle Français de l'Harmonie, at which were to officiate Mme. Fursch-Madi, Mme. Trebelli, Ovide Musin, Adele Margulies and Frank Van der Stucken. And a glory descended on the house when, on November 18th, Adelina Patti—"positively her farewell tour"—appeared on the stage of her former triumphs. Henry E. Abbey was again her manager and he engaged, to accompany her, three of the finest singers then known to New York—Sofia Scalchi, Antonio Galassi and Franco Novara. The only newcomer was Albert Guille, a diminutive French tenor, with a high, powerful voice, which enabled him to join, in the first concert, with Galassi and Novara, in the famous trio from Guglielmo Tell. The plan of entertainment consisted of a concert part, in which the singers appeared in their best operatic airs; the evening ended with an act from a favourite opera that did not require a chorus or a ballet.   Mme. Erminia Novara, Mme. Giuditta Galassi and Carlo Orlandini were advertised as of the force, but, so far as I can find or remember, they appeared only in Sunday night concerts at the Casino.   Luigi Arditi, beloved of generations, conducted.

On the opening night, Semiramide allowed Patti and Scalchi to renew their great triumphs in Rossini's melodious and brilliant arias and in the glorious duet.   That my memory of this performance does not exaggerate its exquisite perfection I can prove by a review in the New York Times of November 19th: "Never was the great soprano in better voice. . . . The voice was the same . . . perfectly even and true and of exquisite quality . . . no feathered songster sings with slighter effort, and no bit of mechanism that man could contrive could possibly perform its functions with more absolute precision.   Between Mme. Patti as an executant and the best singers of the age no comparison whatever can be established. . . . Mme. Scalchi was in as good form as Mme. Patti, and her rich tones and facile vocalization called forth almost as hearty plaudits as did the soprano's matchless achievements."   As to Semiramide: "It is unnecessary to dwell upon all these performances; their like is not to be enjoyed from any other source, and with the two songstresses concerned in last night's representation, 'Semiramide' will pass away."

I have dilated sufficiently as to the glory of Mme. Patti, in my account of her operatic appearances in April, 1887, at the Metropolitan.   Now I merely record that, on Saturday afternoon, November 20th, she and her gifted colleagues sang beautifully, after their concert, the garden scene from Faust.   I shall never again hear the music of Margherita and Siebel sung as exquisitely as Patti and Scalchi sang it.   Those two concerts proving extremely successful, Abbey arranged for two more, which ended, respectively, with a repetition of the scenes from Semiramide (November 29th) and the second act of Martha (December 1st) — this with Patti, Scalchi, Guille and Novara.

Let me call attention to The Acharnians of Aristophanes, played, on November 19th, by students of the University of Pennsylvania, a feat of Greek that few university students of 1941 could accomplish.   The Herald flippantly styled the play a "Greek chestnut."   On December 5th, Anna Eva Fay and a company of English mediums performed "in broad gaslight."   Tables were to "float in air," and spirit hands were to "answer any question."   A testimonial to Jules Levy, "about to go abroad," promised for Sunday, December 12th, Rudolph De Cordova, Camilla Urso, Georgia Weld, D. H. Harkins, the Ricca Mandolin Quartet, Francis Walker, Marshall P. Wilder, H. M. Pitt, Mme. Vogrich, Alexander Salvini, Nat Goodwin, Edward O'Mahoney, Maurice Barrymore, Haydon Tilla, S. B. Mills and the beneficiary and his cornet.   And, on December 25th, Tony Pastor, as

[307]

usual for the Christmas holiday, went a short distance from his theatre to the big Academy for what he called his Jubilee.

The Academy was almost abandoned as a scene for balls, but L'Amitié Société Française, danced in masks there and in Nilsson Hall on January 10th; the Cercle Français de l'Harmonie there held its reception and ball on January 17th. On February 3rd, the Prospect Association Mask-Ball got itself danced, and, on the 10th, for the benefit of the Morton Commandery, No. 4, K.T., the Amaranth Society of Brooklyn acted The Two Orphans. The Eichenkranz Mask-Ball fell on Februay 14th. Something more in our line came, on February 17th, in aid of a fund for a new La Salle Institute of the Christian Brothers. George Clarke directed, and, in the afternoon presented Harrigan and his company in part of McNooney's Visit; Grace Golden, by permission of Max Maretzek, sang La Farfalla, by Celli (is this Grace Golden's first appearance in our Annals since, as Mlle. Goldoni, she sang in the Italian opera, of 1883–84, at the Metropolitan?); Helen Dauvray gave a French chansonnette; Daly's company acted A Woman's Won't; Dockstader's Minstrels appeared in The Old Kentucky Home; Joseph F. Nugent recited, Ella Davis sang, and Gilmore's Band played; and Box and Cox ended the bill, with William Gilbert, George Parkes and May Irwin. In the evening the galaxy included Lizzie St. Quinten, the New York Male Quartet, Stoddart and Marie Burroughs (in an act of Saints and Sinners), Georgia Weld (of Plymouth Church Choir), Hortense Pierse, Grace Golden (in an aria by Verdi), Max Maretzek, selections from Buffalo Bill's Wild West, Annis Montague and A Conjugal Lesson (with George Clarke and Rose Eytinge). Tony Pastor held another "Jubilee," on Washington's Birthday, bringing to the Academy a "triple bill by three companies." And here, on March 27th (Sunday) came the company from Koster and Bial's. And quite at the opposite pole was the discourse, on March 29th, by the Reverend Edward McGlynn, whose differences with his superiors in the Church of Rome were then exciting much public interest. His lecture, on the 29th, was called The Cross of a New Crusade. Sarah Bernhardt gave, on April 16th, a special matinée of Théodora. A benefit to T. S. Burlew, on the evening of April 19th, presented New York and Brooklyn amateurs, in Othello — no less; Garrett W. Owens essayed Iago.

Far more important was the offering on the afternoon of April 21st — a testimonial to William Pleater Davidge, in commemoration of his fiftieth year of active service on the stage. The programme included P. C. Shortis and the quartet, Rieger, Davis, McWade and Garland, from Dockstader's Minstrels; the screen scene from The School for Scandal, with John Gilbert, Kyrle Bellew, Herbert Kelcey and Annie Robe; Janauschek, in the death scene from Meg Merrilies; Davidge's colleagues from the Madison Square Theatre — Stoddart, Holland, Robert Hilliard, Massen, Holliday, Millward

[308]

and Marie Burroughs—in the third act of Saints and Sinners; Davidge in an address to the audience; Mr. and Mrs. Rankin in an act of The Golden Giant; Loie Fuller; Carrie Coote in songs; and The Wandering Minstrel, with Davidge, Henry Hallam, Flockton, Holliday, Mrs. Phillips, Marie Greenwald and Vernona Jarbeau. Harry Edwards was to deliver an address "suitable to the occasion." At the time we wondered that Augustin Daly, in whose companies Davidge had once been so prominent, took no part in this testimonial.

According to Allston Brown, the Academy property was sold, on April 27th, at auction, for $300,000, subject to a mortgage of $195,000; "it comprised about ten lots in the very heart of the city." A few years later it was sold to W. P. Douglas for $325,000. "The property was sold subject to a mortgage to secure the payment of $195,000 to the executors of John Schenck. Mr. Douglas, by a mortgage recorded Aug. 30 borrowed $300,000 from the Connecticut Mutual Life Insurance company, to enable him to buy the property."

The glory of the Academy departed in 1886–87. It opened, on September 19, 1887, as a "combination house."

Tony Pastor's, 1886–1887

Tony Pastor, still reaping the harvest of the road, continued to rent his theatre in 14th Street to such as would pay. Charles Tingay and Harry Thayer, in Our Strategists, were in possession for the week of October 4th–9th; Frank I. Frayne, in Mardo, the Hunter, was there during the following week, John V. Melton and Eugenie De Forrest assisting. Bertha Welby, as Nancy Sykes, followed for October 18th–23rd.

"Tony Pastor at Home" was the jubilant cry of October 25th–30th, the home-coming gladdened with engagements of Jolly Nash ("laughing comique of England"), Frank Bush, Isabella Ward, Hilda Thomas, Cardello and Vidella (silver bars), John F. Byrnes (sic) and Miss Helene, George Murphy, Antonio von Gofre and Ardel ("the clown and the frog") and Fisher and Lord.

November began (1st–6th) with Hawkins and Collins (in a negro sketch), Thomas J. Ryan (late of Kelly and Ryan, in Terry's Brothers), Mons. and Mme. Julian (acrobats), Ada Melrose, Capitola Forrest, Cardello and Vidella, and Till's Marionettes; continued (15th–20th) with Annie Whiting (trombone—odd for a woman) and Charles Whiting (cornet), Heffernan and McDonald, Ben J. Miles and Harry Kelly, Bryant and Saville, George Murphy, Georgie Parker, Florence Kellogg, John T. Kelly (in McCann's Night Off), the Harvey Brothers, and the Mephisto Orchestra, an electric contrivance operated by Miss Dot d'Alcorn, to sounds of drums, thunder and lightning, hail, etc.—"involving twenty-eight miles of electric

[309]

wire"; carried on with (22nd–27th) John T. Kelly (in That Man from Galway), Joe Hart, Adams, Casey and Howard, Cheevers and Kennedy, Cummings and Orndorff, the Stanley Sisters, the three Caron Brothers, Frank Bush, George Murphy, Flora Zanfretta and Isabella Ward; and passed into winter (November 29th–December 4th) with the Julians, Pastor (in his song of The Prodigal Son), Ashley and Hess (the Jumbo Policemen), Griffin and Marks ("funny tumblers"), Hilda Thomas, the Tissots, Fred Matthews, Lizzie Hughes, Connors and Collins and Estelle Mortimer.

Let us see (December 6th–11th) a "local comedy" by E. D. Gooding and Dave Oakes (sic), entitled Married Life, acted by Gooding, Ida Meredith, C. Ed Foreman, Georgie Parker, Lester Howard, Capitola Forrest, Dave Conroy, Micky Thompson, Morton Emerson and Dave Oaks (sic). The Gilmore Sisters, Conroy and Thompson, the Rixford Brothers, Till's Marionettes and Emerson and Reynolds figured in the olio. Dolls were given away at the matinée on Tuesdays, December 14th and 21st. For the week of December 13th–18th we might have seen the Lucier Family (three brothers and a sister), the O'Brien Brothers (acrobats), Florence French (serio-comic), Harry M. Parker's Dog Circus, O'Brien and Redding, Harry Hewlette ("magic wire"), Harry Thorne and Maggie Willet and the genial Tony, himself. For the following week, our Christmas cheer (20th–25th) came from the Clipper Quartet, Ada Melrose, Von Gofre and Ardel (sic), Isabella Ward, George M. Devere, the Four Schrode Brothers (George, John, William and Harry), Frank Bush, George Murphy and George T. Melville. And we greeted the new year (December 27th–January 1st) in the company of Burton's Dog Circus, Lester Howard, Thomas J. Ryan, the Martens Trio, Leopold and Bunnell (sic), Rose and Martin Julian, Heffernan and McDonald (sic), Lottie Elliott, Lenton Brothers, Nellie Hoyt, and Tony Pastor and Lester Howard's farce, A Red Hot Stove. All these performers from late October to early January were doubtless good, but somehow they lack, to me, the glamour attaching to several former "Variety" favourites then (in 1886–87) drafted into the service of musical farce or regular comedy or comic opera — Nat Goodwin, Francis Wilson, May Irwin, Lillian Russell, "Jimmy" Powers, J. K. Emmet, W. J. Scanlan — to mention only a few.

The week of January 3rd–8th provided a large array, in Muldoon's Picnic (with James K. Gibson as Muldoon and Samuel J. Ryan as Mulcahy), Lizzie Parker, Helene Mortimer, Lillian Markham, George M. Devere, Frank Howard, the abiding George Murphy, Mattie Yore, and the Donkey (the original "Jerry"). The olio presented Tony Pastor, Prince Segowa, Adams, Casey and Howard, P. C. Shortis and Mamie Learned, Tom and Bertie Brantford and LeFavre and Gale. Certainly Tony was a liberal provider. Again (January 10th–15th) he invited to a bountiful table — the Great Three Phoites (in the pantomime, A Night of Terror); Mlle. Phoite as the Flying Mephisto ("in which she will fly about like a bird"); Tony Pastor, Rice and Barton,

[310]

Georgie Parker, Shedman's trained dog and fire brigade, Homer and Lingard, and Alice Harvey. The week of January 17th–22nd provided the Clipper Quartet (Ward, Hart, McIntyre and Campbell), another visit of Cardello and Vidella, of Ada Melrose and of Lester Howard. Andrew Gaffney (cannonball performer), Carrie and Edward de Hasse (*sic*), Mr. and Mrs. Joe Howard (in A Quiet Villa), Scenes on the Mississippi and Tierney and Wayne helped to swell the pæan of joy. Dinkle and Maginty's Racket (with Murphy as Dinkle and Griffin as Maginty), Lizzie Hughes, Jolly Nash, the Julians, the Romalo Brothers, the Gilmore Sisters, Harry Thorne and Maggie Willet, and Von Gofre and Ardel were the amazing host of January 24th–29th. On the 24th the hundredth night of the season was duly celebrated with souvenirs. For January 31st–February 5th, Tony provided, for his loyal guests, Marinelli ("anatomical puzzle"), Ralph Terry's Shadowgraphs, the Blondin Donkey ("walks the tightrope"), Marzello Brothers ("clowns on the bar"), Sheffer and Blakely, Billy Carter and Leroy and Flynn. In spite of his attractive feasts, Pastor found it necessary to reduce admission to 25 cents — to be "up to the times." Catherine Nelson, Nellie Eddy, Madame Langtry and Pat Rooney, Lizzie Daly, Lillie Allyn, Katie and Gussie Hart, Cuponti (juggler), George Murphy and others were the liberal offering for so slight a cost.

"The Kernells' Own Grand Company" held the fort in the week of February 14th–19th, their group including Baggesen ("the human corkscrew"), Mme. Eichlerette's performing donkeys, the Horseshoe Four (Carr, Quinlan and the Love Sisters), Frank H. and Lillian White, Conway and Leland, Tommy McShane and Little Dixie, Queen Vassar, Professor Abt's Grecian Mystery and Joe J. Sullivan (in O'Grady's Awful Night) — not so very "grand," after all.

The week of February 28th–March 5th proffered Sam Erwin Ryan (in Irish Luck), the Orion Trio, Isabella Ward, Frank Bush (these two regularly recurring through the season), Topack and Steele, J. W. McAndrews (welcome, old friend!), the Victorellis, Burton's Dog Circus, Campbell's Voyage around the World, and Tony Pastor (of course). The Boston Athenæum Company began a week's visit (March 7th–12th) with the Great American Four (Joseph Pettingill, Peter Dailey, Pete Gale and Tom Ardel — this four seemed of late always to be changing its composition), Chevalier Ira Paine and Mrs. Paine, William Carroll (black face and banjo), John E. Henshaw and May Ten Broeck, James F. Hoey, Anna Boyd, Conroy and Dempsey, Polinski Brothers ("England's greatest grotesque comedians") and Leroux and Wilton (gymnasts) — a "grander" group, I should think, than the Kernells' "Grand" Company of two weeks before. I plod through the week of March 14th–19th with May Howard, the Livina Brothers (slack wire), Valjean, Marie Gilchrist, Jessie Boyd, Dave Oaks (*sic*), Lenton Brothers (hat spinners), John A. Toole and the Winstanley Brothers — a group not inspiring to imagination a half-century later; in fact careless time has engulfed most of them. The elegantly-curiously named Miss St. George Hussey re-emerged for March 21st–26th, in company with Tom and Bertie Brantford, Adams, Casey and Howard, P. C. Shortis and Miss Learned, Lottie Elliott, Ida Ranier, the Wingfield Brothers, Leonzo (juggler) and mine host, Tony. The Kernells, Frank Bush, Joe Hart, the Three Phoites, the Julians, Georgie Parker, William De Bar, and A Night of Terror called custom for April 4th–9th. The following week (11th–16th) provided the "Grand Italian Ballet Troupe" (Mlle. Olga, *première*), C. T. Ellis and Clara Moore, Catherine Nelson, F. H. and Lillian White, James Tierney, Dave Wayne, Frank Girard, the McShane Brothers (midgets) and Charles Seamon (in Ridiculous). Familiar faces, for April 18th–23rd, were three St. Felix Sisters, the Clipper Quartet, Le Clair and Russell, and the Ladies Martens, and less familiar Baldwin and Daly ("Zulu Twins"), the Thompson Sisters and the Dare Brothers.

Charles A. Young, in Karl, the Pedler, was here for April 25th–30th, with David B. Young, Thomas F. Fitzgerald, Robert McNair, Robert V. Ferguson, Eva Byron, Marion May and Emily Kean — as undistinguished a cast as I have ever recorded. Gus Hill's World of Novelties filled the week of May 2nd–7th, with Mlle. Alberta ("who walks the walls"), Weber and Fields ("knockabout comedians"), Vidocqs (John and Edna), Sheridan and Flynn, Estelle Wellington, Booker and Leigh, Mlle. Anna ("female Hercules"), Lottie Gilson (gladly welcome, I suspect), William Wyckoff (aerial), Gus Hill ("champion $10,000 club swinger") and William F. Carroll's comedy, Two Old Sports. Verily that was a host!

"Variety" departed, leaving the stage (May 9th–14th) to William J. Thompson's thriller, The Gold King, or, a Life's Prisoner, acted by George W. and W. J. Thompson and the dogs, Hero and Hector. A realistic quarry scene, the lock step and the escape from prison were factors in the excitement. Monroe and Rice, in My Aunt Bridget, relieved the tension and loosed laughter for May 16th–21st. The next week (May 23rd–28th) veered to Hicks and Sawyer's Consolidated Coloured Minstrels; we see that lovers of minstrelsy were becoming adherents of realism — they demanded black performers, not, as formerly, merely black-face. Well, here on May 30th, for a week, comes "the Queen of Laugh-Makers," Frances Bishop, "prettiest and brightest star on the American stage," if we may believe the advertisements, in "the funniest of all funny plays," Muggs' Landing; she remained two weeks. Another Man's Wife sounds involved for June 13th–18th, with Edna Courtney, Press Eldridge, Julius Scott, Charles Drake, Percy Meldrum, Charles Phillips, Minnie Kissells and Emma Pollock to solve the problems of the story. Sarah McVicker, in Plasir, Queen of the Miners, followed (June 20th–25th) and J. W. Jennings, in Bijah Frisby, carried on for June 27th–July 2nd; his company included Queen Vassar, Lizzie Hunt and J. B.

Brown. I judge that times were good; the theatres seemed very reluctant to close for the season. Pastor's kept open with Sam'l of Posen (July 4th–9th); Callan, Haley and Callan's Electric Three Minstrels (11th–16th); Harry and John Kernell, in Two Fine Ducks (18th–30th), Joe Hart, Katie Hart, Gussie Hart, Sol Aiken, Miss La Verde, Charles Smith and George Hoey being in some way concerned with the show.

Let us carry Pastor's through hot August, with Kathleen Roland, unknown to later fame, supported by T. A. Wise, later very well known, in Desperate Straits (August 1st–6th); Joseph Palmer, in Widow Bedott (15th–20th); A Grass Widow (22nd–27th), with Owen Westford, Julius Kahn, Lucie Russell and Mrs. E. L. Fernandez; and Josie Devoy, in Boarding School (August 29th–September 3rd). Here we may leave the house for 1886–87.

ORIENTAL THEATRE, 1886

The "grand reopening" of the Oriental Theatre, the former Bowery Garten, 113 Bowery, occurred in mid-October, 1886. A bill for October 16th, in the Harvard Theatre Collection, is labelled "second time," for Emigration to America, a "musical drama" by Joseph Lateiner. The cast included Lateiner, S. Borodkin, Max Carp, Mme. Heine (Chaimovich), Moses Silbermann (*sic*), Morris Heine (Chaimovich), E. Silbermann, Joseph Wachtel, N. Rosenthal, S. Adleb (*sic*), G. Courage, Frank and Nathanson. The scenes will give an idea of what was afflicting the minds of these actor-refugees: (1) The Outrage upon the Jews in Balta; (2) The Departure—on (*sic*) the Cemetery; (3) She will go to America; (4) Jerichom's Home; (5) Nihilist—Railroad Station in Balta; (6) Revenge in Constantinople; (7) Burglary rife; (8) The Sacrifice of the Child—Muskovitz's Home in New York; (9) Pedler—Ludlow Street; (10) The Unexpected Guest—a Wedding Hall. One might laugh at the naïvete of the scheme, unless the underlying pathos choked his mirth. According to programme pronouncement, the theatre had been made over in twenty-eight days.

Thanks to complete files of the weekly American Hebrew, in the New York Public Library, I can carry the reader's imagination to the Oriental Theatre for many weeks to come. Two "historical operas" by Goldfaden start November, 1886, on its course: Sulamita (November 1st and 6th), and Bar Cochba (3rd and 5th). Lateiner's "historical operetta," Joseph and His Brothers, was listed for November 8th and 13th, and, for the 10th and 12th, The Inquisition of Spain, by Schaikevitch, with music by Joachim Kurantman. This last was repeated on the 16th, for the benefit of New York Lodge No. 43, O. B. A. Schaikevitch became a leading play-builder for this venture; he was responsible, as author, for The Orphans (November 17th) and Der Jüdische Poritz (19th). But Joseph Lateiner wrote Esther and Haman, produced on November 15th and 20th. Repetitions of Joseph and His Brothers (November 22nd and 27th), Sulamita (23rd, for the benefit of Rothschild Lodge, No. 5), and Bar Cochba (24th) were ancient joys compared with (November 26th) Lateiner and Kurantman's revived opus, Emigration to America, a piece of familiar sound and connotation to us of 1941. Thence Fanatic, or, the Two Kune Lemils (December 1st), The Usurer (3rd) and Sulamita (4th), led to the novelty, Der Neder in the Temple, or Rabbi Akiba with His 24,000 Scholars, an historical opera in five acts by Schaikevich, with music by Kurantman. This successfully ran through the weeks from December 6th to the 3rd of January, inclusive; except that Sulamita was played, on December 7th, for the benefit of the Down-Town Ladies' Benevolent Hebrew Association, and Emigration to America, on December 21st, for the benefit of the Jewish Immigrants' Protective Society. On January 3rd, Der Neder served for the benefit of Mrs. Heine (Chaimovich). The reader may thank the American Hebrew for this valuable information. Peter Cooper Lodge benefited on January 4th; benefits abounded in the programme of the Oriental, generally on Tuesday evenings. Schaikevich or Schaikevitch — the reader must decide as to the proper spelling.

I hurry through January with (5th, 7th, 8th) Der Jüdische Poritz; The Gambler (10th, 12th, 14th and 15th); The Orphans (11th, for the Franz Joseph Lodge); The Gambler again (17th, 19th, 21st and 22nd); Fanatic, or, the Two Kune Lemils (18th, for the benefit of Davis Lodge, K. S. B.); Joseph and His Brothers (24th, for the benefit of Mrs. Karp Goldstein); and Sulamita (31st). Repetitions of Fanatic, The Neder, Esther and Haman and Bar Cochba filled the cold evenings of February 1st to 5th, inclusive. Then comedy held the evenings of February 7th, 9th, 11th and 12th, in shape of Zillah, or Saved by Their Child, another perpetration of Schaikevich. This could not have been liked; it disappeared, leaving the stage for The Usurer (also by Schaikevich), restored on February 8th; Emigration to America (14th, for the benefit of Mrs. Borodkin); Der Neder (15th, for the benefit of Kurantman, its composer); The Gambler (16th); Sulamita (18th); Joseph and His Brothers (19th); Menachim Ben Israel (22nd, for the benefit of a poor widow); Maternal Love (23rd); and Der Neder (24th, for the benefit of the Kaiser Franz Joseph Kranken-und-Unterstutzung-Verein).

Another novelty made important February 25th and 26th — The False Partner. On the 27th (Sunday) came a concert for the Jewish Choral Union. The evening of the 28th provided Brandele Kasak and a concluding Der Katar. Emigration to America seemed to be a favourite for benefits; it was repeated, on March 1st, for a charity, and, again on the 3rd, for the Passover Relief Association. Der Dibik supplied novelty on March 2nd. Bar Cochba (March 4th), Sulamita (5th) and Der Neder (9th, for Mrs. Carp's benefit)—there, reader, is all I found in the American Hebrew till March

18th and 19th, when, for the first times, came David Ben Jesse, or, the Successor of King Saul, an historical opera, in five acts, by Joseph Lateiner, with music by J. Kurantman, and arranged by Professor J. Schwenseck. This had, in the course of time, many repetitions; immediately it was repeated on March 21st, 24th, 25th, 26th, 29th, 30th, 31st and April 1st. The Fanatic came again on the 23rd. For her benefit, on March 28th, Mrs. Heine (Chaimovich) proffered Joseph and His Brothers. Thus the American Hebrew dismisses us for 1886–87; at least I found no more in that paper for the Oriental. But the Roumania Opera House (see *infra*) continued blithely for some weeks longer.

National Theatre, 1886

The last remaining German-American fastness of vaudeville in the Bowery carried through the autumn of 1886, still under the management of Heumann; by January, 1887, it became the seat of Jewish entertainments. Thenceforth, for a time, the National was known as the Roumania Opera House.

The season, before that change, began on August 28, 1886, with a fairly good group, comprising Sanford and Shannon (in a German skit), Ada Melrose, John and Lea Peasley and Valjean. The culmination of joy came with the thrills of the play, Micaliz, with William Cattell as star, and with a support including W. T. Dulany, E. W. Marston, Alf A. Wallace, May Preston, Mamie Wallace, Ada Melrose, and E. E. McFadden.

September 6th–11th was specifically announced as a "gala" week. Entertainers included Lawrence M. Donovan, "the latest Brooklyn Bridge jumper," with Ada Melrose, Harry J. Campbell and his "tableaux soleil," Al Fostelle and Florence Emmett (*sic*), Dalton and Watts ("one-armed song and dance"). The bill concluded with The Danites, played by Loudon McCormack as Sandy, Harry Pratt as the Chinese laundryman (his original character), Alf A. Wallace as the Parson, and, in other rôles, E. W. Marston, W. T. Dulany (*sic*), Mamie Wallace, Ada Melrose and Florence Emmett. Gold-Dust Dave, with George Morton, thrillingly closed the bills for September 13th–18th, the preceding olio listing the Sans-Souci Quintet, George Earle and Paddy Miles, Frank and Fannie Davis, and the Hogan Brothers. Obviously melodrama was in the ascendant, as in the latter years of the old Bowery Theatre; A Sister's Oath, for September 20th–25th, allowed Joe Allen to enact several rôles. But the olio also presented favourites in Valvino, Frank and Fannie Forrester, the Twilight Quartet, and Mason and Titus. September merged into October (27th–October 2nd) with Lottie Church in Unknown, ending a programme that presented, in olio, Phillips and Wood, Alfred Liston and Frank Majilton. The fact that, Harvard files for these variety theatres becoming scattering and thin, I am now dependent on notes, sometimes scanty, in the Clipper, will explain why I cannot furnish that fulness of information for vaudeville which my diligent readers doubtless crave. No daily paper which I have consulted supplies the desired advertisements or notices.

The strength of the National regular "stock" company is shown when, for October 4th–9th, David Higgins and Miss Castleton appeared in Burr Oaks; the regulars, in support, included Alf A. Wallace (who also was stage-manager), Dave Roche, W. T. Dulany (*sic*), E. W. Marston, Charles A. Mack, Mamie Wallace, Carrie Wallace and Bessie Hollis. These people remained till the National expired at the close of the year. The olio for that first week of October provided Lottie Elliott and the Sans-Souci Quintet. Harry Rogers, announced, failed to appear, at least on the 4th. Fanny Herring, in Little Buckshot, began the week of October 11th–16th. Two Sunday concerts, on the 17th, were to provide George Beauchamp, Roach and Castleton, May Howard, Edward Barry, Carrie Brower, W. H. Burk (*sic*) and Ella Raimé. Barry's name may have been *Edwin*.

Edwin Browne, in Good as Gold, was the main feature of October 18th–23rd, his assistants including George C. Jordan, C. Smith, H. Sullivan and Jennie Browne, along with regulars tried and true, in Roche, Marston, Wallace, and Mamie and Carrie Wallace. Harrington and Sullivan, Smith and Rowland and the farce of Senator McFee were contributed in the olio. Terry's Blunders, with Thomas J. Ryan and the stock actors, inaugurated the pleasures for October 25th–30th, and W. M. Paul, in Lucky Ranch, ended them; mid-"turns" were supplied by Edwards and Ashford, Billy Bryant, Lou Merritt, and Tom and Bertie Brantford. I huddle in rapid survey the delights of November: Catherine Nelson, Master Belzac, Manning and Drew, Martin and Conners (*sic*), the Montgomery Five, the mystery of The Vanishing Lady, and the enthralling sensation, The Crimes of a Great City, with Wallace, Roche and the regulars (1st–6th); Hawkins and Collins, Marietta Myers, Thomas and Watson, Ida Rainer (*sic*), and The Two Wanderers (8th–13th); One Hundred Wives, with a cast including Joseph Herman, James K. (*sic*) Keane, Marston, Wallace, Roche, W. H. Burke, Bessie Hollis and Mamie Wallace, and preluded by vaudeville "turns" of Lenton Brothers, Murrill and Bellini, George Beauchamp, and W. H. Burke (15th–20th); Edward Kirwan (*sic*), Fisher and Lord, the Unique Quartet, and The Pavements of Paris, with Harry Belmer (22nd–27th); and just a long play, The New World, launched for November 29th–December 4th, by Charles Manley, May Preston, Mamie and Alf Wallace, and other worthies from the regular staff.

And now I devote to the obsequies of the National Theatre one final, tearful paragraph. The mortuary December began (6th–11th) with a lively "turn" by Jolly Nash, in a sketch called Come In; Al Reeves also functioned, and Edith Sinclair and Ed M. Favor presented A Box of Cash, declared by the Clipper to be the well-known The Corner Grocery. The following week (December 13th–18th) displayed the massive muscular development of Karl Michels, the art of Rosina, and The Gold King, with G. W. and W. J. Thompson digging the rich nuggets of popular approval. And what more appropriate Christmas gift could be offered to the Bowery than (December 20th–25th) Fanny Herring as Topsy, in Uncle Tom's Cabin? relayed by the art of Campbell's Tableaux Soleil (a show, I hope, better than its French), Harry Blake, and the Stanley Sisters. Dominick Murray, in Escaped from Sing Sing and Le Favre and Gale's Specialties rang down the curtain (December 27th–January 1st) for Heumann. The Clipper of January 1st states that he had "disposed of his rights" in the house to M. Goldman, Louis Levy and Ludwig Roth, who would take possession on January 3rd, and, on the 7th, introduce the Roumanian Opera Company, for four performances a week.

ROUMANIA OPERA HOUSE, 1887

As the Roumania Opera House ("früher National Theater") the Staats-Zeitung informs us, 104-106 Bowery opened, on January 7th (Friday) with Raichi, oder die Judenverfolgung in Frankreich ("historische Operette in 5 Akten und 10 Bildern"). It was repeated in the afternoon and in the evening of January 8th. The providers were set down as "Die Neue Jüdische Operetten-Truppe aus Roumania," Mogulesko and Finkel, directors; a group we met, in mid-October, at Terrace Garden. The bill for Friday, January 14th, and Saturday afternoon, January 15th, comprised Die Italientischen (sic) Sanger (sic) and Zehn Mädchen und kein Mann. Blaubart again ruled the evening of the 15th. The actors in these pieces included Mrs. Finkel, Finkel, Kessler, Feinman, Mogulesko, Nechankus, Weinblatt, Abramson, Mrs. Edelstein and Schwartz.

On Tuesday, February 1st, a benefit for Chevra, Degel Machic Menvin (I believe I copied this accurately from the constricted Gothic type of the Staats-Zeitung) gave us something so little Yiddish as La Périchole; Blaubart, on the 2nd, was, I take it, also French-Yiddish. But Sulamita, on the 4th, and Die Coquetten Dame, on the evening of the 5th were, I assume, quite in the Yiddish vein. Blaubart again appeared for the matinée on the 5th.

Beginning on Monday, February 7th, we had a run of Die Vorschwörung und der Process in Tioza Gozlar; it was given on the 7th, 9th, 11th and 12th. Tuesday, February 8th, portrayed Der Petersburger Student (for the benefit of Joshua Lodge, No. 90), and the matinée, on the 12th repeated La Perichola (sic). March 14th, 16th, 18th, 19th and 21st were thoroughly racial, with Bar Cochba, oder die letzten Tage Zions (book by Goldfaden and music by Mogulesko and Finkelstein). And the Kostenaufwand was $5,000! On

[317]

the 22nd, we had Raschi; on the 23rd, The Conspiracy of Tisza Eslar; on the 26th, The Trial of Tisza Eslar. Thus the Tioza Gozlar of February 7th changes its spelling (if it was the same thing), in two weeks. The reader cannot imagine the perplexities involved in such erratic variations.

From the American Hebrew we gather the flowers of early spring: Bar Cochba (March 26th); Bal Tschiva (28th); The Exile in Siberia (29th); Sulamita (30th); The Two Kuni (*sic*) Lemils (31st); The Student of St. Petersburgh (April 1st); La Perichola (*sic*—April 4th); Ten Girls and No Man, The Italian Singers and Matches (6th); Jehuda and Israel (April 15th and 16th); Dr. Almasado, or, the Jews in Sicily (April 18th and 20th).

Though the Staats-Zeitung fails us at this point, the American Hebrew fortunately takes up the refrain and announces, for April 18th and 20th, Doctor Almasado, or the Jews in Sicily, a work by Goldfaden. Thenceforward we had Jehuda and Israel (April 22nd and 23rd); a "sacred" concert (Sunday, the 24th); Sulamita (25th); The Orphans (27th); and, for the benefit of the conductor, Finkelstein (on the 28th), Don Joseph Abarbanel, an historical opera, in four acts, by Horowitz. This had several repetitions—on May 11th, for instance, as a benefit for the Talmud Tora Association. On May 10th, came another novelty, The Ruined Banker, for the benefit of its author, Horowitz. Jehuda and Israel was featured in the benefit, on May 12th, for Queen Esther Lodge, A. S.

I hurry to the end of the season, listing The Ruined Banker (May 13th and 14th); La Perichola (16th); Jehuda and Israel (17th, for the benefit of G. Kessler); Raschi (*sic*—May 18th); Don Joseph Abarbanel (19th, for the benefit of the Russian Charity Society); The Coquettish Ladies (27th); The Jewess (28th); a sacred concert (29th); a benefit (30th) for the comfort of Louis Levy, manager, and proffering bits of Sulamita, Jehuda and Israel, and of both The Conspiracy and The Trial of Tisza Eslar. The season closed (May 31st) with a benefit to T. Weinblatt, Bluebeard serving as the farewell offering.

The National Theatre having thus been servant to Jewish manipulations, since January, 1887, re-emerged on June 6th under the management of George A. Henderson, and with such English as was provided by the Charles Guinness Company, in Fun in a Grocery. For June 13th, we were promised A Shadowed Crime. Alas, promise, and for aught I know, fulfilment, runs out at this point, in the Clipper.

London Theatre, 1886–1887

The autumn glory of August 30th–September 4th, at the London Theatre, comprised the Edward R. Lang Company, in Scheming, the cast including Lang, Harry Mills, Charles Frey, William A. Lang, Viola Rosa, Carrie Brower and Lizzie Hughes, a catalogue of ships that sailed in the night and

AL REEVES

THE BIG FOUR
AND BILLY EMERSON

BILLY LESTER

WEBER AND FIELDS

LOTTIE GILSON

C. T. ELLIS
CLARA MOORE

CHARLES V. SEAMON

BOBBY GAYLOR

JULIA WILSON

quickly disappeared. Better were Luigi dell'Oro and John Kernell, props of the olio.

The Clipper promises, for the week of September 6th–11th, a rather attractive list, with Emma Alfredo and John Lamont (in a horizontal bar performance), Estelle Wellington (song and dance), John and Nellie (*sic*) Healey, Jack Burgess and J. J. Bagley (sparring), the Stanley Sisters (vocalists from California), Dave Oaks (*sic,* throughout the season) and E. D. Gooding (in a comedy act), E. H. Talbot (in Silence and Fun), J. H. Cummings and Harry Orndorff, the Lamonts (acrobats), and Whose Baby Is it? (with Larry Tooley, Dave Oaks, Gooding, &c.). Gus Hill's Company entered for the week of the 13th–18th, proffering Five Japanese Ambassadors, Mlle. Anna ("feats of jaw strength" — a description that sets one thinking), Dollie Foster, Weber and Fields, Lottie Gilson, Gus Hill (in his act with the clubs), Haines and Vidocq, Mlle. Alberta (on the wire), and Two Old Sports (with Frank Sheridan, Will and Edna Vidocq, J. F. Flynn, &c.). Daniels and Manchester's Night Owls Company filled to overflowing the cup of September 20th–25th, opening with Paris Life, proceeding with "turns" by Manchester and Jennings, May Howard, Lizzie Mulvey and Belle Clifton (dancers), a scene of Lovely Women ("eight young ladies in concerted change act"), E. D. Gooding, Emma Juteau, and a showy concluding A-Donis (set down as by H. M. Pitt!), with Louise Dempsey in the title-rôle, Pauline Batchellor as Venus, May Howard as Squire Fizzle, and, in lesser parts Larry Tooley, Lester Howard, Robert Manchester and John Jennings. The cooler fall evenings (and afternoons) of September 27th–October 2nd brought familiar and warming talent in Kitty O'Neil, Frank Bush, H. M. Parker and his dogs, Bryant and Saville, Martin and Connors (*sic*), Edward Leslie, Monsieur Cheltra (contortion), Florence French, and McCann's Night Off (with Dave Oaks, Charles Crosby, E. D. Gooding and Florence Zanfretta). One easily grants the superiority of the offerings at the London to those at the waning National.

For October 4th–9th, the stock actors began with Stratagem, leaving the stage for successive efforts of Nellie Rosamond (singer), Gordon and Lick, Mack Sullivan, Antonio von Gofre and Ardell (*sic*), O'Brien and Redding, Topack and Steele (*sic*), Booker and Leigh and John T. Kelly (this last-named in Irish farce). The Rentz-Santley Company began its ministrations (October 11th–16th) with Our Yachting Party and ended with a burlesque of Erminie (Our Minnie). In the course of the proceedings appeared Sanford and Wilson, Billy Buckley, W. J. Conway, the Inman Sisters, the Dashing Vivandières ("six pretty young ladies in fine costumes"), Lillie May Hall, the Vanishing Lady Trick, Georgie Blake and Valjean — assuredly a list far more respectable in all ways than that of earlier years for this company. Dr. A. Davis, adept in mystery, began the bills for October 18th–23rd, to be followed by the (to me) greater mystery of a "lady-cornetist"—Alice Raymond, with Leoni and Nelson, Jessie Boyd, Miles (*sic*) Morris, Harry Kelly, the Winstanley Brothers, and Our Irish Boarder, acted by John T. Kelly, Gooding, Flora Zanfretta, &c. October passed from the London (25th–30th) with a genial olio comprising Till's Marionettes, Julius Tournour, Annie Brightstein, De Forrest and Gorman, Billy Lyons, Latta and Lynch, Capitola Forrest, John Sheehan and M. Coyne, &c.

The Night Owls came back to flutter through the week of November 1st–6th. For the 8th–13th the London must have dazzled its patrons with the aggregate charms of "Professor" H. J. Campbell's Tableaux Soleil, Helen Courtland, Jerome May's Banjo Quartet, Cardello and Vidella, Harry Bruns (*sic*) and Carrie Monroe, Leslie and Hardman, Connors (*sic*) and Collins, Conroy and Dempsey and the farce of Senator McFee (with John T. Kelly, Gooding, Oaks and Flora Zanfretta). November wore on (15th–22nd), with offerings of Moulton and Francis, the Parker Twin Brothers, Leopold and Bunell, Mr. and Mrs. W. J. Conway (in Scroggs' Sanctum), Alexander Wilson (ventriloquist), Ashley and Hess, Kitty O'Neil, Fisher and Lord, Isabel Ward, Rose and Martin Julian (brother and sister), Frank Bush, and the farce of The Boodler's Rest, with Gooding, Leopold, the Conways, Dave Oaks and Jessie Boyd. The music of J. H. Smith's accordion launched the bills for November 22nd–27th, and the bone-solos of Frank Emerson nearly ended them. Between these musical freaks appeared Estelle Wellington, Andy McKee, Flora Franks (from California — her début), and the Three Comets (Frank Hawley, Walter Manning, and Bob Richmond). Juan Caicido (*sic*) performed on the wire, Lester Howard and the Leech Brothers did what they could, and A Red-Hot Stove warmed the hearts of the departing guests.

A curious feature of November 29th–December 4th was the "First Company under the Auspices of the Universal Amusement League," under charge of Joe Allen — an announcement that suggests the unionism of much later years. In the corps were Frank and Fannie Forrester, William Devere, Coffee Brothers, Kitty Shepard (*sic*), Hanley Brothers, Phil Gibbons, Homer and Lingard, Dave Marten (*sic*), Frank Livingstone, William and Alice Payne, W. B. Moseley, Lou Merritt, Edwards and Ashford and Mr. and Mrs. Joe Allen — a good group, if not a notable. T. H. Winnett's American and European Sensations must have had some difficulty (December 6th–11th) in justifying their name, since the combined talents were no more "sensational" than Thomas J. Ryan, Catherine Nelson, Fred Roberts, Von Gofre and Ardell, McAvoy and Hallen, John and Nellie Healey, Master Belzac and the farce of Terry's Blunders. The features of December 13th–18th were J. G. Fletcher, Gallagher and West, Imro Fox, Foreman and Ida Meredith, Tin-pan Fields, Bryant and Saville, Harry Rogers, Green and Marco (in 8:45), and Jolly Nash; the farce of The Baron's Double engaged Oaks, Gooding and Jessie Boyd. The Ida Siddons Mastodon Burlesque Company took Christmas week (December 20th–25th) with A Strike in the Harem engaging Ida Siddons, Pauline Parker, Clara Willoughby, Julia Edmonds, Fannie Delano, Estelle Moore, Ethel Thornton, Susie Russell, Maude (*sic*) Beverly (*sic*) and others. This delectability was followed, in order, by Edward M. Ryan (German act), the Stanwood Sisters, Jeppe and Fannie Delano, Mlle. Lamont, Professor J. W. Hampton (with his dogs, geese, etc.), the Lamont Trio, and the Southern Quartet (James, Justin and Charles Bentley, and Herbert St. John). All this, I learn from the bill at Harvard, was offered for 15 cents admission, 10 cents to the gallery, 25 cents for the balcony and orchestra circles, 75 cents for a seat in a box, and $6 or $8 for an entire box. Kelly, Murphy, Foster and Hughes's International Star Company (December 27th–January 1st) was larger in name than in personnel, since its stars were only Frank and Fannie Davis, Harry M. Parker and his dogs, William McMahon, Lillie Morris (dancer), Billy Wilson, Adams, Casey and Howard, the aerial Stirk and Zeno and Pete Shaw. Such a holiday gift would not have attracted me from Daly's or Wallack's.

January pursued its chilly course with (3rd–8th) Harry Le Clair and W. J. Russell, in A Practical Joke; with (10th–15th) Andy Gaffney, Myles Morris, the Donaldson Brothers (contortionists), William Melville, P. C. Shortis (banjo), Whitfield, the Julians, Silvo, Lester Howard, and Schoolcraft and Coes (these two in their long-popular Mrs. Didemus' Party). Gus Hill's Company (17th–22nd) was undeniably strong in its enrollment of Sheridan and Flynn, Dollie Foster, Gus Hill, John and Edna Vidocq, Smith and May, Lottie Gilson, Haines and Vidocq, and the Barretta Sisters; many of these ended the bill in the cast of Two Old Sports. Other names of popular appeal called (January 24th–29th) to the enthusiastic when Harry C. Bryant, Polly Holmes, Maggie Meredith, Cardello and Vidella, Connors (*sic*) and Collins, St. George Hussey ("fresh from her bridal holiday"), J. W. McAndrews, T. F. Grant, Joe Hart, Jennings and O'Brien, Mr. and Mrs. Joe Allen and Billy and Alice Payne comprised a list that astonishes me today, a half-century after the event. I can only say that I wish I might have been present to appraise all the talent involved. January 31st–February 5th showed, however, some effects of the frosty season in the group of Corrlea (*sic*) and Castor (trapeze), Baughman and Aldine (rifle shooting), Conroy and Thompson, De Witt Cooke, Ed. H. Sheehan, Estelle Wellington, the Lenton Brothers, Isabel Ward, Cheltra (at last I have discovered how to spell the name of this contortionist), John and Nellie Healey and Frank Bush. Yet, after all, as that list reaches its climax, it achieves something like vaudeville excellence.

The increasing band of companies presided over by ambitious females was represented in the following week (February 7th–12th) by the combined Lillie Hall's Burlesque Company and Fannie (*sic*) Bloodgood's Specialty

[321]

Company. These two ladies appeared in Oxygen, with Charles Fostelle (female impersonator), Mlle. Zitella, Montie Collins, Larry Smith, Ada B. Burnett, and Allie Smith. "Turns" were forthcoming from Fannie Bloodgood and Allie Smith, from Ada Burnett (songs), Zitella, Dave Oaks (*sic*) and Jessie Boyd, the California Quartet (T. B. Dixon, William Mack, H. Stanley and William Thatcher), the Davenport Brothers, and, best of all, from the inimitable Maggie Cline. The Big Four Specialty Company attracted (February 14th–19th) with the regulars, Dave Oaks, Jessie Boyd and John A. Toole, in a farce, followed by Florence French, Dan Hart, Georgie Parker, Hines and Earle Remington, Harry Rogers, Joe Hart, Schoolcraft and Coes, Luigi dell'Oro, and the Big Four (Smith, Waldron, Haley and Martin) — an astonishing list. The Rentz-Santley Company brought familiar lure for February 21st–26th) chiefly stressing Mlle. Dorst and Monsieur Oreste, set down as "dancers of the French sensational style." Marinelli's Company, with which we are familiar, carried us into windy March (February 28th–March 5th).

An Adamless Eden, an idea then devastating our theatres, filled the week of March 7th–12th, with Alice Townsend, Rice and Barton, the La Porte Sisters, Dora Hart and Vede Mansfield. The Night Owls, doomed to considerable popularity in the halls, returned on March 14th, with, as the Clipper states, Agnes Earle in the rôle formerly "so artistically filled" by May Howard, but otherwise the cast about as lately seen — surely a comfort to the faithful. The Big Four came back (March 21st–26th) with a new contingent — Billy Birch (poor Billy, once so master of his fate in the San Francisco Minstrels), Joe Hart, Roach and Ada Castleton, Moulton and Dashway (their first appearance in several years in the Bowery), Till's Marionettes and J. W. Myers. The Kelly, Murphy, Foster and Hughes Company (March 28th–April 2nd) was topheavy as to title, but rather good in some details — Ward and Lee, Lottie Elliott, Frank Bush, Isabella (*sic*) Ward and Mlle. Lottie. The Rentz-Santley troupe again (April 4th–9th) brought a touch of spring and pulchritude to weary males of the Bowery. I pass with relief (April 11th–16th) to the return of Gus Hill's Company, with Frank and Grace McClane, Weber and Fields, Estelle Wellington, the Vidocqs, the Barretta Sisters, Booker and Leigh, Minnie Schult, Shedman's Animal Circus, and, of course, the nimble, athletic Hill, himself. Dave Oaks and John A. Toole, formerly of the stock, now launched (April 18th–23rd) a company of their own, including the Hanley Brothers, De Witt Cooke, Keating and Barton, Minnie Lee, Frank H. and Lillian White, Imro Fox, Annie Hart, J. J. Keating (formerly of Keating and Sands) and Adolph Seeman. And lo! the Night Owls returned, on April 25th, for two weeks — a fortnight of relief to my weary reader and my weary pen. And further relief accrues from the return of Lillie Hall and Fannie (*sic*) Bloodgood with (May 9th–14th) about the same cohorts that appeared with them a few

[322]

weeks previously. And the Rentz-Santley combination carried on the return *motif* (May 16th–21st), opening with Our May Party, proceeding to The Dashing Vivandières, and thence to The White Hussar (a burlesque of The Black Hussar) and employing Henshaw and May Ten Broeck (in Diamond Cut Diamond), Sanford and Wilson, Mlle. Dorst and Oreste, Louise de Luisi, Victoria North, Amy Wells, Lulu Mortimer, Pearl Inman, Georgie Blake, Carrie Wentworth, Gertie Keith, Lida Moss, Billy Buckley and Tommy Dayton. The second and last week of this female effulgency (May 23rd–28th) added the male talent of Add Ryman ("his first appearance in the Bowery for several years"). For May 30th–June 4th the London offered Anzo, John and Nellie Healey, Imro Fox, El Niño Eddie (from the long ago), J. W. Myers, Hanley Brothers, and several Zanfrettas (Alex, Leo, George and Emma).

Sam T. Jack, making his way to a certain importance in vaudeville, kindly provided a two-weeks visit of Lilly (*sic*) Clay's new Adamless Eden, with Alice Townsend still leading the amazons and a few males (Rice and Barton and Lester and Allen). In the second week of the delectability Maggie Cline brought in a touch of genuine Irish humour. These female organisations must have been more innocuous than they sound. Ida Siddons's Company, for instance (June 20th–25th) enlisted such utterly reputable players as Flora Moore, Ella Wesner, and Maude (*sic*) Beverly (*sic*); the company also included Lida Moss, Frank Lester, the Southern Quartet and the Wesley Brothers. "House Company," as mere aggregations without title came to be called, presented us, successively, from June 27th through July, Edwards and Kernell, William McMahon, Wilson and Brevarde, Fields and Hanson, Annie Hart, James F. Hoey (one of the best in vaudeville), Frank Livingstone (also very good), the Melrose Sisters ("first appearance as a team for years"), Frank Bell, George Murphy, the Lamont Trio, Hines and Earle Remington, Achmed-Ali-Bey (illusions), the Glenroy Brothers, John Daly and Annie Devere, Fitz and Webster, Marshall's Troupe of Japanese Tourists, Petrie and Elise, Conroy and Thompson, Otis Shattuc (*sic*), Daniel J. Hart, Harry Woodson, Laura Bennett, Baldwin and Daly, John W. Myers, Sam and Hannah Holdsworth, Connors and Collins, El Niño Eddie, Mr. and Mrs. Joe Allen and Press Eldridge.

When a titled organisation (Duncan Clark's Company) broke the bonds of August (1st–6th) the phalanx was not impressive, with Millie Barretta, Harry West, Charles J. McKlosky (*sic*), Catherine Nelson, Frank and Mamie Sheppard (*sic*), Keating and Flynn, John R. Harty, Mollie Wilson, Nina (high kicker), Lew Baker, Bruns (*sic*) and Monroe. One sees that the performers were so little known, that the programme-maker could not spell their names. Sam T. Jack now became manager of the place and naturally brought in Lilly (*sic*) Clay's Colossal Gaiety Company, which may have been gay (August 8th–13th) but does not seem very colossal in talent, with

[323]

Rice and Barton, Sidney Euson, Sadie Norwood (statuesque posings), Sabra Lonsdale (skipping-rope dance), Irma von Rokay (*pas seul*), La Porte Sisters, and (the only delight to me in the list) Maggie Cline. The second and last week of this aggregation (August 15th–20th) substituted Annie Hart for the ebullient Miss Cline and Keating and Flynn for Rice and Barton. The London then closed for a week of cleaning and renovation.

Miner's Theatre, Bowery, 1886–1887

The week of August 28th–September 4th, in Miner's Bowery pleasance, seems to me to have a hollow ring, with entertainers so little known as Billy and Alice Payne, Williams and Brannon (*sic*), Ed C. Lovett, Dick Carroll, Dave Reed (well-known these two), Conroy and Dempsey, Cooper and Lovely and Professor Wallace.

Thereafter, as we pass from the National to the London, to Miner's in the Bowery, we realise that the artistic barometer rises. September 6th–11th, in the last-named temple, flung wide the gates of opportunity with William Mitchell and Claudia Lorraine, Edward Andrew Glover, Lew Roseland and Millie May, Heffernan and McDonald, Charles and Annie Whiting, Carlisle, Tom and Bertie Brantford, Frank Lewis, Valvino, Sam Devere, and the Sheerans. The week of September 13th–18th presented Austin's Australian Novelty Company, preceded by the stock actors of the house, in The Latest Patents. Charles A. Loder (German dialect), Frank and Paul Hamlin, Retlaw and Alton, the Lynn Family (Harry, Lottie and Jennie — in Avarice), Charles T. Ellis and Clara Moore, the Newcomb Trio (dancers), Mlle. Aimée (human fly), the Austin Sisters in somersaults, forward and back, and the farce of Hot Rods — behold the lure for the lovers of variety! Marinelli's Cosmopolitan Congress, from September 20th to the 25th, was found to include the Marzellos, May Templeton, Billy Carter (banjo), Charles and Ella Jerome, James Reilly (as the Flower Girl), Sheffer and Blakely, the Blondin Donkey, Fields and Shepherd (*sic*) and Ralph Terry. The stock actors of the theatre began the show with The Lion and the Lamb, and they and olio "headliners" ended the proceedings with Widder De Arcy. The Reilly and Wood Company was not very distinguished (September 27th–October 2nd) with Burt Watson, Ed Kelly, Chrissie and Phil Sheridan, Adele Wilson (gyrations on a silver globe), Florence Miller, Bobby Gaylor, Fields and Hanson, and The Two O'K.'s.

October 4th–9th also sank in importance of offering, with the Four Powers Brothers, George H. Murphy, the Three Franklins, Manning and Drew, Idaletta and Wallace, Wilmot and Sewell, William Melville, Ada Clifton, Rosina and W. H. Burke. Harry Kernell's Specialty Company, seen the week before at Miner's Eighth Avenue Theatre, now journeyed (11th–16th) to the south-eastward, chief constituents being Kernell, Lou

Merritt, Professor Abt, Edwards and Ashford, Frank H. and Lillian White (in Past, Present and Future), the Horseshoe Four, Conway and Leland, and Baggesen ("the human corkscrew"). The Howard Athenæum Company had (October 18th–23rd) as chief attraction the inimitable American Four (Pete Dailey, Pete Gale, Joseph Pettingill, and William Daly) in Scenes in a Restaurant. Other popular members were Retlaw ("human Ophidian"), McAvoy and Hallen, John E. Henshaw and May Ten Broeck. The month went out, at the Bowery, with (October 25th–30th), "Professor" Wallace, Master Rogers, Frank and Fannie Forrester, Edward A. Glover (*sic*), Thomas Carter and Lizzie Anderson, George Beauchamp, Harry Kennedy, Rice and Barton, the Four Schrode Brothers, Homer and Lingard, &c.—a mixed bill with some excellent features.

Mistaken Identity started the list for November 1st–6th, the cast including the regular actors of the house—A. H. Sheldon, J. R. Gildersleeve, J. R. Lewis, Dave Posner, George Williams, Nellie Sandford and Louise Crolius—names long familiar to our Annals; Hallen and Hart's company filled the olio. Well known to us also were the guests of November 8th–13th— "Professor" Cameron, Charles H. Duncan, Dick Carroll, Robert Gilfort, Minnie Lawton, Wenzel and Morris, Albert Virto, John Mayon, Green and Marco, Smith and Rowland, the Gilforts and the Caron Brothers. The stock company, with Sheldon, opened the festivities for November 15th–20th, with The Secret Panel, disclosing, so to speak, the Hughes Novelty Company, Ada Melrose and George Jackson (roller-skater) being added to the list. The Harvard bill advertises for November 22nd–27th Hattie Belle, Al Reeves, Professor Al Lawrence's Prismatic Fountain, Fred Matthews, the Tissots (Amanda and Jules), Ed C. Smith and Jessie Carl, Howe and Doyle, Nelson D. Hadley (Barnum's Drum-Major, in uniform), the Ventinis, Keating and Flynn, the King Sisters and Woodside, the trained goat, so often butting into our story. The Montgomery Five included Kennedy, Newman, Hayden and Ryan, "headed by P. J. Shields, America's champion Zouave driller." For the week of November 29th–December 4th, patrons were asked to appraise Morton and Coleman, Dave and Lizzie Foy, Minnie Kaine, Sanders and Dean, Georgie Parker, Shedman's dogs and monkeys, Jim and Dan Burke, Charles and Annie Whiting, Carlisle, the Three Franklins, Lottie Elliott, the Luciers, and Dick Morosco and Kitty Gardner— verily an overflowing cornucopia.

Such riches induce us to enter December with cheerful confidence, only to be baffled by less glittering names for the week of the 6th—Lew Roseland and Millie May, Edward Barnell, Lizzie Hughes, Alna Don Janata and her snakes, Somers and Walters, George and Marie Nelson, the Caron Brothers, the Powers Brothers, the Morello Brothers (fraternities to the fore) and Hayward and Moore. If not particularly brilliant, some of the visitors for December 13th–18th were at least known to our inquisitive pen—Till's

[325]

Marionettes (always good), Charles H. Duncan (character vocalist), Vanola (Mexico's "greatest wonder"), Fred Barth, Marietta Myers, Mr. and Mrs. Dan Lacy, the Glenroy Brothers, the Caron Brothers, the Three Romalo Brothers, the Winstanley Brothers, Capitola Forrest, Loa and Ruge, Frank Venetta and Hattie Adams, with a concluding farce of Judge Duffy's Substitute. After all, we may be thankful if we always encounter entertainers so good. Christmas week (December 20th–25th) showered the blessings of George Laible, the Gilmore Sisters (Drusie and Carrie), "Professor" Fox (imitator of birds and animals), Carter and Anderson, Burt Ransom ("Premier banjo manipulator in the world"), Wilmot and Lester, Charles and Jennie Welsh, Miles, McHugh and Ireland, the California Quartet (T. B. Dixon, William McAlone, C. F. Stanley, W. S. Belknap), the Gilforts, Razor Jim (with A. H. Sheldon) and The Outcast. We note how these variety hosts writhe into ever-varying combinations, like figures in a kaleidoscope. And Wilmot was "late of Wilmot and Sewell," and Lester "late of Lester and Pressey." The New Year offering (December 27th–January 1st) included Daisy Norwood (according to the Clipper she had just become a mother), Edward A. and Marie Glover, Harry Kennedy, Susie Wilde, W. H. Burke, Dick Carroll, Fannie Beane and Charles Gilday, Manning and Drew, Clint Wilson and Maggie Brevarde, Valvino, Frank Lewis, Hewlette, Nelson D. Hadley, and the Four Schrode Brothers, verily an astounding cornucopia.

Marinelli's Company returned to New York for January 3rd–8th, presenting Leroy and Flynn, Hilda Thomas, Billy Carter, Sheffer and Blakely, Charles and Ella Jerome, Maggie Bursell, the Marzellos (*sic*) and Ralph Terry, some of whom had accompanied him in his visit in September. We learn from the Clipper of January 15th, that the theatre was undergoing improvements, to the utmost luxury of which I must admit the reader. The proscenium arch and the supporting pillars were decorated in gold, bronze and pink — surely an odd conglomeration; and the boxes "look bright with tasty paper, and new draperies hung on nickeled bars add elegance to the unique papier-mache (*sic*) ceilings of the boxes. The side-walls of the parquet and balcony have been papered. The ceiling is to be elaborately frescoed. New footlights and a protection-bar now add to the stage-effects." I hope this grandeur added to the enjoyment of the bill provided (January 10th–15th) by Reilly and Wood's Company, with Roach and Castleton, Fred C. Bryant, Jolly Nash and Bobby Gaylor. I confess to being impressed by the notable aggregations found at this leading Bowery hall. Familiar faces greeted addicts in the week of January 17th–22nd — Dave Reed, Mrs. Reed and Eugenia of that name, Lizzie Hughes, Georgie Parker, Maud Beverly, John and Louisa Till, George Murphy, Clark and Williams, the Electric Three, Charles White and his goat, Fred Matthews, O'Brien and Redding, the Tissots and the King Sisters — verily *multi* and *multum*. Harry Kernell's Company, last week at Miner's Eighth Avenue Theatre, came to the Bowery house for January 24th–29th, the Bowery stock appearing in A Quiet Little Home.   J. R. Lewis and J. R. Gildersleeve, of that stock, had, at this time, a joint benefit at Turn Hall.   From a week at the Eighth Avenue establishment, likewise, the Hallen and Hart Company came south-eastward (January 31st–February 5th) with only Frank Bush absent from the roster.

The two following weeks (February 7th–19th) allowed us to study the "turns" of Karl Michaels, Minnie Lawton, Dick Devlin, the Collins Sisters, the Forresters, Ed H. Banker, Howe and Doyle, Sam Devere, Carlisle, Lester and Williams, Dick Morosco and Kitty Gardner, the Morello Brothers, J. W. Hampton and his performing animals, and George Melville (all these in the first week), and (in the second) Tom and Bertie Brantford, the Three Franklins, Clint Wilson and Maggie Brevarde, Keating and Flynn, the Four Emperors of Music, H. M. Parker and his "canine circus," the Albion Family, Wilmot and Lester and the Gilforts.   The Howard Athenæum Company, fresh from the Eighth Avenue house, made glad the week of February 21st–26th.   Austin's Australian Novelty Company met spring half-way (February 28th–March 5th), especially stressing Aimée, "the human fly," and Bruns (sic) and Monroe.   The bill for the Actors' Fund, on March 3rd, netted $475.   March wore on with a week of "Professor" Wallace, Hattie Belle, Sanders and Dean, Lillie Allyn, Alna Don Janata and her snakes, Howard and Fox, Clint Williams and his performing bear, Philo Nathans and his canines, and Doddretti; and a week (March 14th–19th) of Roseland and May, John Carroll, Thomas Carter and Lizzie Anderson, Ed C. Smith and Lizzie Carl, Marietta Myers, the Days, Heffernan and McDonald, W. H. Burke, Shedman and his dogs, and the Four Diamonds.

Hallen and Hart were back (March 21st–26th) with an excellent support in George F. Moore, the Russell Brothers, Fox and Van Auken, Polly McDonald, Bryant and Lizzie Richmond, Lester and Allen, George Beauchamp, Ella Wesner, May Howard, Hawkins and Collins, &c.   March gales passed into April breezes (March 28th–April 2nd) with the Reilly and Wood Company, ever welcome, the purveyors of mirth now including Kelly and Watson, Phil and Chrissie Sheridan, Adele Wilson, Chris Kitchie (sic), Florence Miller, Bobby Gaylor, the Orion Trio, Mlle. Forgardus, the Mignani Family, Mlle. Costello, D'Alvini, the Nelson Family and Pat Reilly.   Miner served always a liberal banquet.

Successively through April came a host in Daisy Norwood, Dave Hanson and Mamie Hayman, Fred Wenzel, Musical Dale, Dick Devlin, Frank H. and Lillian White, the Gilforts, the Gilmore Sisters, Ada Laurent, and the Schrode Brothers, with a Teutonic afterpiece (April 4th–9th), employing Fred Wenzel, Nellie Sandford, Louise Crolius, J. R. Lewis and J. R. Gildersleeve — the "stock" of the feast; Valvino, Master Rogers, Sully and Nellie Germon, P. H. Thurber, Edward Kirwan (sic), Martin Julian, the King

Sisters, the La Rose (*sic*) Brothers, Sam Devere, the Four Powers Brothers, Till's Marionettes, Charles H. Duncan, Bryant and Saville, Leonzo, Topack and Steele (*sic*), Gallagher and West, Tom and Bertie Brantford, and the Four Tourists (J. F. Campbell, Lou F. Shaw, Maggie Edwards and Lizzie Haywood), Smith and Hoey, the Forresters, Rogers and Fields, C. Ed Foreman and Ida Meredith, the Lamont Trio, Lester and Williams, the Three Comets, Charley Banks and the Four Emperors of Music.

The New York Clipper, strong in vaudeville advertisements, loads us down with the burden of May flowers. I will catalogue the names that threaten to break the back of my index. The first week (May 2nd–7th) provided Fred Morphet, Ida Ranier, Virto, Leonard and Hart, Dick Carroll, Mr. and Mrs. Joe Allen, Heffernan and McDonald, the Big Little Four (Buckley, Coyne and the Callan Brothers), Hewlette (*sic*), Glenroy Brothers, Monsieur Bellac and Mlle. Aouda (equilibrists, musical bottle specialists, etc.) and Karl Michaels. May 9th inaugurated a week of James H. Hammond, Matthews and Lynch, Professor Wallace, Florence French, Adams, Casey and Howard, and the trio of Callan, Haley and Callan. Latter May (16th–28th) carried on with, in succession, Ed Banker, Lefavre, the Collier Brothers, the Ventinis, Sam Devere, the Days, the Love Sisters, Frank Clayton, and Miles, Ireland and McHugh, Fannie Lewis, George Murphy, Edward Kirwan (*sic*), the Marion Brothers, Lottie Elliott, the very popular American Four and the Three Rinaldos (*sic*). Again I comment on the excellence of the banquet. Karl Michels is now Michaels.

From May 30th to the 2nd of July, kaleidoscopic shiftings of talent brought weekly visits of, in order, Revillo, Ed Giguerre, Charles and Lillie Weston, Ward and Lynch, the Big Little Four, Marietta Myers, Lester and Williams, W. H. Burke, the Four Tourists, Loretto, George C. Marshall, Rogers and Fields, Tom and Minnie Flynn, Lottie Gilson, Capitola Forrest, Ned Hanson and Marie Hayman, Billy Carter, Henshaw and May Ten Broeck, Alexander Davis, Ed Slocum, Will C. Matthews and Nellie Harris, the Cecilia Quartet (Will Walling, Arthur Cook, W. R. Ridgeway, Harry W. Roe), Foster and Hughes, Sheehan and Coyne, La Petite Kitty, M. G. Pettingill, the Hogan Brothers, the Morton Brothers, Heffernan and McDonald, G. W. Callahan, Lang and Viola Rosa, Marion and Belle, Pusey and Lester, Ed H. Banker, the American Four, Valvino, George W. Barlow, Fannie Lewis, John Carroll, Fannie Beane, Conroy and Thompson, Haines and Vidocq, and Adams, Casey and Howard. Never, I believe, have I compiled a paragraph so undisputably a mere heap of bones.

I feel that summer heat is drying the meaty content of the bills. July 4th–9th piled up a huge offering in Professor Wallace, Clara Purvis, Sheridan and Flynn, George W. Earle and Paddy Miles, Nellie Anderson, the Four Tourists (Joseph F. Campbell, Lou F. Shaw, Maggie Evans, and Lizzie Haywood), Edward Barnell (*sic*), Lottie Gilson, Thomas J. Ryan

[328]

and May Richfield, all ending with a farce employing Dick Morosco, J. R. Gildersleeve, J. R. Lewis, Dave Posner, Nellie Sandford and Daisy Norwood (successor in the stock of Louise Crolius). The name of the farce, Dr. O. B. Careful has lost for 1941 some of its original humour. The bill for July 11th–16th offered familiar friends in Beane and Gilday, Lew Baker, Frank Lawton, Lester and Williams, Imro Fox, John Walsh, the Cecilia Quartet and Loa and Ruge. July crowded toward its close, proffering (18th–23rd), Marion Brothers, De Forrest and Sanders, E. H. Banker, Tommy Nolan, Isabel Ward, Foster and Hughes, Annie Hart, the Whippler Twins, Jennie Pickert, Virto, Hewlette, Frank Bush; and (25th–30th), Larry Tooley, Dick Carroll, the Delmanning Brothers, Billy Carter, Ward and Lynch, Florence French, Dick and Ida Cummings, C. Stockman, and the interesting Rose and Martin Julian.

Only August remains for this crowded season. For its first week (1st–6th) it lured with promise of Will C. Matthews and Nellie Harris, Revillo, Smith and Rowland, Ada B. Burnett, La Petite Kittie (*sic*), the Four Emperors of Music, the Days, Tom and Minnie Flynn, Van Leer and Barton, and Add Ryman. Later dog-days (8th–13th) made us forget the heat inside and outside of the theatre with Leonard and Hart, George C. Marshall, Al Fostelle and Florence Emmett, Annie Boyden, Saunders and Burdell, Leech Brothers, Carter and Lizzie Anderson, Miles, Ireland and McHugh and another three, Callan, Haley and Callan. I hurry to the close, with (August 15th–20th) Lillie Morris, Charles and Lillie Weston, James M. (*sic*) Hammond, Alexander, George, Leo and Emma Zanfretta, William McMahon, H. M. Parker and his dogs, and A Chapter of Accidents (with the regulars); with (August 22nd–27th) Mr. and Mrs. Dave Reed and their daughter, Eugenia, Roseland and May, the Morton Brothers, John E. Drew (accomplished dancer), Lottie Gilson, George Earle and Paddy Miles, Morosco and Kitty Gardner, the King Sisters (Nellie and Rosie), and Till's Marionettes; and, finally and thankfully, with (August 29th–September 3rd) Ed H. Banker, Fannie Beane and Charles Gilday, Bethel and Coles, John Carroll, Matthews and Lynch, Heffernan and McDonald, Farnum Brothers, "Professor" Wallace, John E. Drew, and "Professor" A. Matthews and his troupe of goats, this last an idea none too sweet. I feel that I have most conscientiously whirled the embarrassed and dizzy reader through a complete cycle of fifty-two weeks at Miner's in the Bowery, without, I fear, perceptibly clarifying his moral and spiritual outlook.

MINER'S EIGHTH AVENUE THEATRE, 1886–1887

The West-Side Miner's re-opened, on August 23rd, with Weber and Fields, Master Fran (imitations of German actors), Eugene Revillo (Fun and Mystery), George W. Earle and Paddy Miles, George and Marie Nelson,

Capitola Forrest, Sheridan and Flynn, the Four Powers Brothers and Fannie Beane and Charles Gilday. Whatever glitter attended the week of August 30th–September 4th accrued from the "turns" of A. O. Duncan, Harry Steele, Kelly, Murphy and McMahon, Delmore and Wilson, Frank Hewitt, Marion and Belle, James and Dan Burke, the Inman Sisters, Donald Melville, and the Four Comets (Frank Hawley, Bob Richmond, Walter Manning and Thomas Williams) — an array less glittering, methinks, than obfuscating. But who am I to adjudicate?

We must expect to find a certain reciprocity in bills between Miner's two theatres; indeed what could be more natural or more advantageous for the performers? The week of September 6th–11th gave the Eighth Avenue stage to William Carroll, John and Lea Peasley, Gus Hill, Wilmot and Sewell, the Wesley Brothers, Maude (sic) Beverly (sic), Ward and Lynch, Frank Lester, Dave, Eugenia and Mrs. Reed, Crosby and Wray, Ada Burnett, and the concluding farce of Married Mashers — rather vulgarly named even for that new slang of "mashers." September 13th–18th brought the group seen the week previously at Miner's Bowery — Mitchell and Claudia Lorraine, Roseland and Millie May, Edward A. Glover, &c. But the regular actors of the West-Side house — Fred J. Huber, Louis Robie, Al W. Decker and Kitty Allyne — ended the show with Two Old Pards. And the attraction for September 20th–25th, Austin's Australian Novelty Company, had been seen the week before at the Bowery Miner's; the only difference was that the Eighth Avenue regulars acted "45." I found no bill for September 27th–October 2nd, at the uptown house.

Harry Kernell's Specialty Company filled the bills of October 4th–9th, the roster practically identical with that at the Bowery house in the week following. October 11th–16th began the offerings with Kitty Allyne, Robie and Huber, in Where's Anthony? and continued with Hallen and Hart's Company, including the hilarious Russell Brothers, Fox and Van Auken, Julia Wilson, Lester and Williams, George F. Moore, and the Fletchers (Charles, William and Lillian, roller-skaters). I have recorded more interesting aggregations. The Vanishing Alderman and Reilly and Wood's Company sufficed (I hope) for October 18th–23rd. And the excellent company from the Boston Howard Athenæum disported in the week of October 25th–30th, as in the preceding week at Miner's in the Bowery. And most of the performers for November 1st–6th had been seen in the week preceding in the house downtown — Professor Wallace, Charles H. Duncan (character songs), Delmanning Brothers, Homer and Lingard, Fred Matthews, Rice and Barton, the Forresters, Topack and Steele (sic), Valvino and Harry Kennedy. The title of the concluding play amuses one — The Mild West, by and with F. J. Huber. Hughes's American and European Novelty Company graced the bills of November 8th–13th. And the Clipper and Harvard both fail me for the following week. But bravely to the fore come in (November-

[330]

ber 22nd–27th) Albert Virto, Lew Roseland and Millie May, Fred Barth, Sanders and Dean, Clint Wilson and Maggie Brevarde, Ronaldo Brothers, Leslie and Hardman, the Gilfort Brothers, and Miles, McHugh and Ireland, old friends all. And observe the fraternal bonds in the bill for November 29th–December 4th — the Glenroy Brothers, the Powers Brothers, the Morello Brothers, the Caron Brothers and the Winstanley Brothers, along with Mr. and Mrs. Edward A. Glover, Thomas J. Ryan, Hulette (sic), &c.

That bill seems interesting, as does that of December 6th–11th — Doddretti, Charles and Annie Whiting, Manning and Drew, George Beauchamp, the Ventinis, Keating and Flynn, the Franklins, J. W. McAndrews (not recently seen) and Shedman's dogs and monkeys. On the 11th, I learn from the Clipper, Robie and Huber were "called to the footlights and presented, each, with a fine silk umbrella, by a Mr. Kaufman, an admirer of these gentlemen." This is touching, and consoles me for my inability to find Eighth Avenue offerings for the week succeeding. But I can assure the anxious reader that the semaine of December 20th–25th brought Christmas cheer in the engagements of Mr. and Mrs. W. J. Conway, Charles Seymour, Ada Byron, Minnie Kaine, Howard and Fox, Emerson and Clark, Ida Ranier (sic), Wenzel and Morris, the Tissots, Fannie Beane and Charles Gilday, and in the farce of Senator McFudd (sic). Very familiar to our pen were, also, the New Year visitors (December 27th–January 1st) — Karl Michaels, James and Dan Burke, Cardello and Vidella, Wilmot (late of Wilmot and Sewell) and Lester (late of Pressey and Elder), C. H. Duncan, Foreman and Meredith, Hines and Earle Remington, and Woodside, the goat. Somehow these frequent re-appearances of artists and the decrease in houses presenting vaudeville lead me to hope that, in consequence, the indexes of my future volumes will bulge somewhat less oppressively.

Kelly, Murphy, Foster and Hughes exhibited their company for the week of January 3rd–8th, and Marinelli brought in his for the week beginning on the 10th. For January 17th–22nd, Harry Kernell and Company began with the Eighth Avenue stock actors in The Watch Dog, and presented successively Queen Vassar, Professor Abt, Herr Grais, Frank and Lillian White, the Horseshoe Four, Mlle. Eichlerette, Conway and Leland, and Baggesen. The following week presented Hallen and Hart and their company, including George Beauchamp, Polly McDonald, Tierney and Wayne, Frank Bush, the Three Carons, George F. Moore and Bryant and Lizzie Richmond. Reilly and Wood's Company, for January 31st–February 5th lost the services of the Nelson Family; one member was under age and the Society for Prevention of Cruelty to Children felt called on to be cruel only to be kind. Fred Bryant was engaged to fill the gap in the programme. All these three last-named combinations transferred, we remember, in weeks immediately following to Miner's in the Bowery. A "house" group, for February 7th–12th, included Lefavre, Murphy Brothers, George and Marie Nelson, Robert

[331]

Gilfort, Johnny Carroll, the Albion Family, J. P. Sullivan ("first appearance in this house for several years"), the D'Alve Sisters, Harry Kennedy, the Brantfords, Edward Kirwan (*sic*) and the Gilforts—a fine group. The Howard Athenæum Company, which always gives my pen a thrill of Boston, came, on February 14th, with the Brothers Poluski, (comical gymnasts), the clever Anna Boyd, Conroy and Dempsey and many more.

For February 21st–26th, the generous management proffered Carlisle, Minnie Lawton, John and Nellie Healey, Sam Devere, Howe and Doyle, Roach and Castleton, Lillian Wood, Leopold and Wentworth, Charles A. Loder, J. G. Fletcher, Gallagher and West, and Tracy and Eagan. From February 28th to March 19th scurried across our fevered vision, in succession, "Professor" Wallace, Ed H. Banker, Billy Gallagher and Ada Devere, Manning and Drew, Dave and Lizzie Foy, Rixford Brothers, Keating and Flynn, Clint Wilson and Maggie Brevarde, the Clipper Quartette (*sic*), Austin's Australian Novelty Company (this group for March 7th–12th); H. J. Campbell's Tableaux Soleil (a Voyage around the World in Twenty Minutes), Dave Reed, with his wife and daughter (in Hydrophobia, or, a Dish of Reed Birds), Sanders and Dean, Harry Edwards and Daisy Kernell (in A Summer Day), the Three Comets (Frank Hawley, Walter Manning and Bob Richmond, in Twenty Minutes in a Cyclone), James H. Hammond (acrobatic trick and triple dancer), Adams, Casey and Howard (comedians, instrumentalists and vocalists), Eugene Ward ("the only footless dancer in the universe"), Till's Marionettes, and Seven Miles (concluding farce, with Huber, Robie and Kitty Allyne). This is an astonishing aggregation.

Kelly, Murphy, Foster and Hughes's cumbrously named troupe filled the week of March 21st–26th, with W. J. Sully and Nellie Germon, William McMahon, A. L. Gleason and his dogs, Dick Morosco and Kitty Gardner, Adele Martinetti, Sam Devere, C. Ed Foreman and Ida Meredith, and Billy Wilson. The Big Four Company, as last week at the London Theatre, moved to the nor'-nor'west for Miner's customers in the week of March 28th–April 2nd. Reilly and Wood's Company returned, on April 11th, with Bobby Gaylor, D'Alvini, Mlle. Forgardus (with her trained pigeons), Chris Kitchie (contortionist), Three Brothers Altoff (acrobatic musical grotesques), the Mignani Family (five Parisian Musical Street Pavers), Mlle. Costello, Mlle. Sheridan, Kelly and Sheridan, in an illuminated terpsichorean spectacle. I found no record, either at Harvard or in the New York Clipper, for activities at the Eighth Avenue for the weeks of April 4th–9th and April 18th–23rd. I hope the reader regrets this loss more sincerely than I do. I can tell him that the bill at Harvard for April 11th promises, for the week of the 18th, Gus Hill's World of Novelties, and The Golden Boom.

April 25th–30th proffered a less engaging host in Vennetta (*sic*) and Adams, Latta and Lynch, Minnie Lawton, Roach and Castleton, Delmanning Brothers, the Brantfords, the Four Tourists, Leslie and Hardman, &c.

[332]

Andy Hughes's American and European Novelty Company began the bills for May 2nd–7th, with Mrs. Brown Presents (acted by Huber, Robie, Decker and Kitty Allyne), and proceeded to the main business of the show with the Archmere Sisters (Helia and Ollie, in English and Italian selections), Andy and Annie Hughes (in Masquerade Party), Al Reeves (banjo), John and Lea Peasley (in Etiquette), Billy Lester and Paul Allen, Edward Leslie (mimic), Hawkins and Collins, Dave Marion and Minnie Belle, and ended with Sim Dimpsey's (sic) Visit (played by Lester and Allen, Collins and Hawkins and Al Reeves). That reads like an attractive offering. The programme for May 9th–14th was very like that of the preceding week at Miner's Bowery. The week of May 16th–21st also has a familiar ring with the names of the Hanley Brothers, Annie Hart, Keating and Barton, DeWitt Cooke, Herr Schlam, Frank and Lillian White, Howe and Doyle, Minnie Lee, O'Brien and Redding, El Niño Eddie, and Conroy and Thompson.

The last week of the season (my pen is grateful) brought (May 23rd–28th) John E. Henshaw and May Ten Broeck's Consolidated Stars, including Will C. Matthews and Nellie Harris, Dave Foster and Artie Hughes, Frank and Fannie Davis (in Maloney's Night On), Howard and Fox (dancers), Dick Morosco and Kitty Gardner (in The Schlum Family), Loretto (in Silent Pastimes), the Three Electrics (Callan, Haley and Callan), Henshaw and Ten Broeck (in Diamond Cut Diamond), and the concluding farce, The Two Tramps (with the ever-faithful Huber, Robie and Kitty Allyne, in conjunction with Dick Morosco). And thus we leave Miner's in Eighth Avenue, consoling ourselves with the promise of its re-opening on August 22, 1887, redecorated and cleaned for our admiration and our comfort.

Harlem Casino, 1886–1887

The closing of the Pavilion Theatre, on October 30, 1886, left Harlem, says the New York Clipper of November 6th, "without a variety house." But confirmed Harlemites could be gratified by a belated announcement in the same journal for November 20th that the Harlem Casino, on Second Avenue, opposite 127th Street, opened, actually on the 5th, with an aggregation consisting of Marietta Myers, George F. Kaine, Keating and Flynn, the Stanwood Sisters, Minnie Kaine, the O'Brien Brothers and "Professor" Charles Young. Thomas and Watson were set down as managers, and A. F. Higgs, "late treasurer of the Harlem Pavilion," also served and waited for customers — 1,500 for the floor space, and 500 more for the balcony.

Something went wrong. The Clipper, on December 4th, bears the sad tidings that the place was closed, on November 29th, "by the mayor's orders." Like the Clipper, I wonder why. But the answer came in the paper for December 18th, whereby we learn that the house, "after considerable trouble with the Building Department and the theatrical laws," resumed,

[333]

on Monday, December 13th. Thomas and Watson could not appear, but those who had patiently waited were regaled with M. G. Pettingill and his dog, Daly and Devere, J. Tournour, Sanford and Taylor, Stanford, Shedman's Dog and Monkey Circus, Herr Schlam, Ashley and Hess and the Stanwood Sisters — a rather mixed blessing, I opine. The next call I heard from the place was for the week of December 27th–January 1st, with Le Clair and Russell, in A Practical Joke. For January 3rd–8th, the Clipper ruefully remarks that cold weather lessened the attendance. A good embattled host defied the besieging cold — Mr. and Mrs. Joe Allen (Terpsichorean Mania), Amy Arlington, C. Ed Foreman and Ida Meredith (in Lawn Tennis), Sheehan and Coyne (Our Irish Home), Nelson Hadley (lightning drum-major) and the farce, A Looking Glass Tragedy. For January 10th–15th enthusiasts were promised The Enchanted Clock, Kitty Sheppard (sic), the Brantfords, John and Nellie Healey and Frank Livingstone — all aristocrats from the Bowery.

The May Adams Burlesque Company brought, for January 17th–22nd, its pulchritudinous array, in A Japanese Fête and allied confections. Forced by the silence of the Clipper to skip a week, I carry the eager student to January 31st–February 5th, when the familiar Kelly, Murphy, Foster and Hughes Company gave their own specialties and provided "turns" by Lillie Morris, Fannie Lewis, the Morellos, &c. Again, the Clipper failing me, I leap to the week of February 14th–19th, to bring back May Adams's "troupe of female beauty," male and female entertainers including J. J. Nugent, Marietta Myers (slack-wire), Fannie Lewis, J. B. Wills and May Adams (in Larks), C. J. Fox and T. F. Watson, Dan Polk, Antonio von Gofie (von Gofre? contortionist, and a singularly suitable surname for one of that species), Frank Fisher, von Gofie's (von Gofre's?) assistant, and, appropriately for female burlesquers, Fun in a Boarding School, and Girls of Sheol. May Adams seems to me to have fallen from her former estate, but possibly her finances were improving.

The reader must be prepared for lapses in continuity of record. Either the Clipper failed to report, or my eye missed tiny notes in the columns of the paper. March 7th–12th, in any case, seems to offer a poorer host in the Martin Brothers, Phil Gibbons, Hogan and Mowbray, Harry Rogers, Adams, Casey and Howard, and Del Fuego. I found no more for 1886–87.

Harlem Pavilion, 1887

The Harlem Pavilion, in the summer of 1887, seems to have pursued a precarious path toward obliteration. The Clipper promises, for June 20th–25th, the Big Four Specialty Company, which began, on Monday, "to a packed tent." Entertainers were Rosa Lee, Woodson and Bennett, the Davenport Brothers, Conroy and Dempsey, Monsieur Bushnell, and the farce, Troubles of a Village Barber. The week of June 27th–July 2nd provided the opening farce of The Baby Elephant, Kate (*sic*) Gardner (*sic*), John Daly and Annie Devere, M. G. Pettingill, the Marion Brothers, Hi Tom Ward, Lillie Morris, Fannie Lewis (a very migratory lady), the Lamont Trio, and a concluding Razor Jim (charming title!). A holiday bill for July 4th–9th gave varied delight with Jack Farrell and Jack Hopper (in a "fistic display"), Conroy and Thompson, Kittie Sheppard, George Earle and Paddy Miles, Queen Sarbro, George Shannon and Pete Gardner, George Wood, and the farce Sawdust Bill (also a truly refined title!).

Then our faithful Clipper informs us that the Pavilion, "after having been closed for five weeks," re-opened, on August 8th, for a week of Larry Tooley, Ada B. Burnett, Taylor and Russell, the O'Brien Brothers, the seemingly ubiquitous Keating and Flynn, Edwards and Kernell, and Sheridan and Flynn. The next week enraptured Harlem with the ministrations of Sheehan and Coyne (Ashbox Inspectors), Connors and Collins, Fitz and Webster, Queen Sarbro, Kittie Zanfretta (song and dance), Lillie La Verde, Saunders and Burdell (Dutch) and Our Old Home — really a good bill for the faithful. May Arnott's Devil's Own Minstrel Company enlisted in its diabolical army harmless persons like Emma Alfredo, Sheridan and Flynn, Victoria North, Fannie (*sic*) Sandford (*sic*), Polly McDonald, Cooper and Lovely, &c. The Sculptor's Studio and The Old Sports were coagulating features for these diverse talents. On August 27th, when the show began, the Clipper pitied the poor performers; rain dripped through the canvas, down on the stage and the performers.

E. R. Lang's Brother Bill Company filled the week of August 29th–September 3rd; a miscellaneous group for September 5th–10th included Annie Hammond, Mary Harris, Roe Beam, Lottie Howard, the Aarons, Arthur Dunn, Artie Hughes and Hen Clark, and Frank La Rosa, only a few of whom waken echoes in my memory. A rather poor company may be gleaned as harvest for September 19th–24th — James Neary, Nellie Thorne, Charles Emmett (*sic*), Rose Sydell (*sic*), Bertha Marshall, José Rodriger, Rose Cameron, Matthews and Lynch and Dan Hart. With this the Pavilion disappears for the summer of 1887.

GUNTHER'S PALM GARTEN, 1886–1887

Gunther's Palm Garten, in 14th Street, near Third Avenue, became something of a "variety" stage. There, on or about October 4th, were Morris and Wenzel, the Burke Brothers, Ada Henry, Sanford and Taylor, Mamie Sheppard, Fred Lyon, Charles de Bax and Malvina (juggler). Frank Girard was director of amusements. Subsequently in October and November appeared Rosa Lee, the Laverne Sisters, Thomas Carter and Lizzie Anderson, Charlotte Laverne (trapeze), Charles and Thomas O'Brien, Ada Clifton,

Harry Rogers, Jules Tournour, the Brothers Hogan, Gracie Sherwood, Marie Richard, Ella Arlington, Virto, West and Ward, König and Venus, Ella Raimé, John Mayon, and others, of course in successive groups, not all together. The week of November 29th–December 4th inaugurated a run for The Queen of Love (the reader's guess is as good as mine as to the quality of this offering), with Jessie Warner in the title-rôle, assisted by Kittie Randolph, Annie Granger, Charles Phillips and Dave Martin. Later December brought visits from Miss Abrams, the Sisters de Babian (*sic* — who had been here previously), Mlle. Raimé, and Charles Bowen. Early January still flaunted The Queen of Love, and added Charles Young (ventriloquist), Roach and Castleton, Kittie and Mabel de Fabian (*sic*), C. B. Walsh (juggler), Frank Girard and James H. Hammond. For mid-January we were called to see Ada Henry, Kittie Wells, Mlle. de Babien (*sic*), Morphet (magic), J. G. Fletcher, Billy Bryant and Charles H. Phillips.

Jacob Blank's Winter-Garten, 1886–1887

This cool-sounding resort, at 100 Third Avenue, lured, in early October, with promise of a Spanish Damen-Kapelle. Two concerts, directed by Carl Otremba, called on a Sunday, in mid-December (19th). Leaping, for lack of matter, to mid-February, I recover from a reluctant past the names of Adele Roselle, Ella and Annie Caldwell; there was a "grosses Concert täglich." The place was now advertised as at 132–136 East 13th Street. On February 14th, specifications of anticipated pleasure listed Mons. and Mlle. Morell, Miss Roselle, Conradi, Elsa Alberti and the ever-roaming Nand'l Hofer, of the intriguing name.

Huber's Prospect Music Hall; Harry Hill's, 1886–1887

I ask the reader to descend with me into the feebler offerings of Huber's, 108 East 14th Street. There, on October 11th, were appearing the Olympia Quartet, Smith and Rowland, the Stapwood (?) Sisters, Annie Wildermuth, Minnie Schult, the Unique Quartet, Carrie Brower, &c. Later in the autumn I gather from the columns of the Herald the names of Marron and Murphy, Josie Gosland, Rosa (or Reca) Murilli, Annie Rinaldi, Tom Haywood and Maggie Moore, Rosina Whitty, Minnie Kaine, Smith and Rowland, Leary and (always) Minnie Schult. This carries us to November 8th. November 22nd–27th provided Edward Percy, Ned Hanson, Master Edward Percy, Mamie Hayman, Pearly May, Kate Percy, John Judge, Martin Brothers and Minnie Schult; and the Oyster House and Restaurant were a "specialty" of the establishment. Several of these remained for the next week, when Charles H. Duncan and Kittie Clifford were new. From December 20th, the place ceased to specify in the Herald its choice attractions.

[336]

I thankfully report that the Cremorne and the Haymarket passed through the new season with precisely the same slogans they had used the year before. Harry Hill's on Sunday, October 3rd, promised the Georgia Jubilee Singers—a form of art to which Hill was addicted. In December the place advertised a "ball and shadow dance." And, in mid-February, the proud boast was "Oldest Sporting Resort in the City. Open every night. Ball and Shadow Dances."

MINOR VARIETY, 1886

In late September, 1886, the Clipper was advertising a highly-named Alexander Musée, 317 Bowery, with N. Morris as manager. The French Spy and variety were promised for September 20th–25th; for the next week Edwin Blanchard thrilled with The Rover's Bride, and Billy Kersands, from the negro companies, provided musical entertainment. At this point, the Clipper flies away from the Alexander, leaving my reader and me in the lurch.

The Globe Museum boasted for October 11th–16th of Colonel Steer and wife, Little Goma, Herr Schlam, Musical Carson, Will H. Ryan and Edward Atkins, and a stock company including Charles Seabert and Jan and Fannie Everett. Imagine the hopelessness of being in the stock company of a dime museum! For November 1st–6th, the Globe advertised English Jack, the frog-eater, Edward Atkins in his border drama, Wild-Cat Rookie, the Waif of the Mines, with Fannie Everett in the title-rôle. Next week we were to see An Honest Hebrew.

EDEN MUSÉE, 1886–1887

For months preceding the opening of the season we are now traversing, Prince Lichtenstein's Gypsy Band had been playing to the wax figures and their guests at the Eden Musée. New wax images in late October were of the Chicago Anarchists, then exciting national horror. All kinds of novelty were flourishing at that time in New York—big pictures, like Munkacsy's Christ before Pilate; and now, in later November, the Eden Musée was advertising the "great success" of Benjamin Constant's picture, The Storming of Constantinople. And here, too, in that world of wax, was Ajeeb, the "chess phenomenon," not to mention Prince Lichtenstein's Hungarian Gypsy Band. And now came an excitement strenuously worked up by press notices—the arrival of Munczi Lajos—certainly an intriguing name—to conduct in picturesque fashion that last-named band. The Musée was closed—public take notice!—on December 6th, for a private reception to the celebrity. But, on the 7th, all who could crowd in were welcomed to

[337]

the first public concert of the great man. From that time forth, for weeks, Munczi Lajos and the Gypsy Band held rural visitors enthralled. Well, we all find Hungarian music haunting and arresting. An orchid show, opening for a week on March 1st, brought something exotic among the wax figures exhibiting. Some Japanese jugglers, in Mid-April, were sharing honours with Munczi Lajos. And a flower show bloomed from April 26th to May 1st. O'Brien and Parnell, in late May, joined the company who only stood and served in wax.

KOSTER AND BIAL's, 1886–1887

During the week of August 30th–September 4th, Hicks and Sawyer's Minstrels were the visitors — and rather odd visitors in kind — at Koster and Bial's. Venus and Adonis were perhaps, from September 13th, more attractive in name than in reality. The week of September 20th–25th swung decisively into the realm of "Variety," with May Hazelton ("tenor"), Anna Boyd (who was a long time fighting her way up to her position of later years), Ella Wesner, Layman ("the man with 100 faces"), Edward A. Glover, Tom Brantford and Venus and Adonis. The illusion of The Vanishing Lady, then awakening speculation in other theatres, was advertised at Koster and Bial's for some weeks after October 4th. Nat Goodwin was burlesquing it, with his Little Jack Sheppard, at the Bijou. This week of October 4th–9th was announced as the last of Venus and Adonis, and the first of Mlle. Dorst and M. Oreste (celebrities of no celebrity whatever, till then, in our town).

Nat Goodwin again, by inference, entered the proceedings on October 11th, when a new Jack Sheppard burlesque presented Ella Wesner as Captain Jack Sheppard, Anna Boyd as East River Bess, James B. Radcliffe as Jonathan Wild, a detective, and, in other parts, Gustav Adolfi, Vincent Hogan, Lillie La Verde and Miss Chip Howard. This thing continued for weeks. With it, on October 18th, was associated another burlesque, inspired, I suppose, by Mrs. Langtry's success as Pauline Deschappelles — a scene from The Lady of Lyons, with Lizzie Kelsey and Newton Carlisle. The Jolly (John) Nash, the Musical Paviors, Margarethe Gross, Ella Wesner, Anna Boyd, Lillie La Verde, Radcliffe and Captain Jack Sheppard filled, on November 8th, the cup of joy to overflowing. The Armanini Mandolin Quintet, The Vanishing Lady, Ella Wesner and Radcliffe (in Captain Jack Sheppard), united to please in the week of November 29th–December 4th. The Lucier Family, Captain Jack Sheppard, M. Choufleuri, with Anna Boyd, Radcliffe, and Adolfi and Ella Wesner, still as Captain Jack Sheppard, carried Koster and Bial's into the new year (December 27th–January 1st). The Harvey Brothers also contributed.

[338]

The Tissots, Frederick W. Millis (Australian ventriloquist), Hattie Howard and M. Choufleuri were stressed for January 16th. And (24th–29th), Jack Sheppard, Millis and The Vanishing Lady came again to the fore. The organisation was moving from the old quarters. The week of February 21st–26th finds the Concert Hall, 23rd Street, "to let for a term of years."

I do not know why Koster and Bial's moved to the Academy of Music on Sunday, March 27th and on subsequent occasions, And they ceased to advertise thenceforth their house in 23rd Street. On the 27th appeared Louise Searle, Radcliffe and the Martens Family. The license of the house, I learn from the Herald, had been revoked, or at least not renewed.

MADISON SQUARE GARDEN, 1886–1887

The Horse Show, since beloved of fashion, was featured for the week of November 1st–6th, 1886, at the big "garden" in Madison Square, horses and richly dressed fair ladies sharing the admiration of visitors. Buffalo Bill's Wild West, which had thrilled Staten Island, in the summer of 1886, moved into the Madison Square Garden, on November 24th, as a "Grand Drama of Civilisation," by Steele MacKaye, even then beginning his career as a maker of huge spectacles that in many ways anticipated the reach of Hollywood. Nelse Waldron invented the mechanical devices of the show. Of course Buffalo Bill and Nate Salsbury were still gods of the machine. This ran into later February. On Sunday, January 23rd, the town was invited to hear the last words of Michael Davitt in America. Everything came to us in those days, especially if there was something to gain. Custer's Last Rally was, in February, part of the Wild West Show. The exciting spectacle left, on February 22nd; but the hundredth night of it was celebrated on February 9th.

On February 24th, Gleason began again to tame horses; this he did for six nights only. And, on March 14th, entered the show of shows — Barnum and Forepaugh's combined collection of wonders. The "human-like elephant," John L. Sullivan, King Theebaw's Hairy Family, William Henry and Agnes Beckwith (swimmers), the Silbons, Blondin, Jumbo ("as in life"), Oudo (aerist), Mme. Garetta and her fifty doves and pigeons, and sixty trained elephants were the gist of the adventure. The last week of the great show (April 18th–23rd) stressed Captain Paul Boynton, "the lone navigator"; John L. Sullivan; King Theebaw's Hairy Family from Burmah; W. H. and Agnes Beckwith (swimmers); Blondin, the horse walking the tightrope; "Dear Old Jumbo's" likeness and his big skeleton; the Silbons, champion midair athletes, &c. A dairy cattle show (May 10th–14th) seems hardly urban; but I suppose the Westminster Kennel Club's Dog Show of May 3rd–6th would satisfy some city-dwellers.

[339]

Summer always brings big shows in city or by seashore. On June 13th, at Madison Square Garden, began a spectacular H. M. S. Pinafore, with a real boat on real water, a grand ballet of children as midshipmen, and a drill of marines. The cast included Charles Coote as Sir Joseph, Gustavus Hall as the Captain, Harry Hilliard as Ralph, Henry C. Peakes as Dick Deadeye, John Clarke as Bill Bobstay, Little Lottie as Tom Tucker, Emma Henry as Josephine, Sylvia Gerrish as Hebe, Dell Kellogg as Buttercup, and Robert Fraser (duplicating his Lone Fisherman of Evangeline) as the Silent Marine. G. B. Snyder served as musical director. The Herald review flatly declared that, in the vast Garden, nothing of Pinafore was seen or heard.

On August 15th, this was declared to be a "true summer-garden," with popular concerts, Gustav Hinrichs leading an orchestra of sixty. Much Wagner figured in the programmes; why not, with Wagner practically in possession of the Metropolitan Opera House? One evening was devoted to Die Meistersinger. Lafayette's birthday (September 6th) brought a programme of French music; the 7th was rhythmic with ballroom music. The 8th provided selections from Tannhäuser and Der fliegende Holländer.

DOCKSTADER'S MINSTRELS, 1886-1887

Dockstader's Minstrels began, on Friday, September 17th, with a merry and a musical group comprising Harry Pepper, Charles Heywood, Cool Burgess, José (alto), Joseph McWade, and Lew Dockstader as leaders. A song by Sydney Rosenfeld, He Didn't Know when to Stop, was featured, and Dockstader began at once with two timely skits, Dixey's Return and The Obelisk. And, on September 27th he got after Goodwin's Little Jack Sheppard with a long-continuing Little Black Sheppard. The advertisement in the Herald, for October 10th, proudly boasts, "No lithographs, no posters, no handbills, no deadheads — advertised only in the newspapers." Those who were boys in 1886 will remember that, for hanging theatre-posters in their store windows, shop-keepers received cards of admission (no seat coupons attached) for so obliging the managers of a given show thus advertised. Knowing persons could buy those admission tickets for about 25 cents each, and, by tipping a willing usher in the theatre another silver quarter, secure for 50 cents a good $1.50 seat in the orchestra for any play that was not doing a sell-out business. I suppose that is the sting of Dockstader's "no handbills — no deadheads."

A new Held by the Hennery parodied, beginning on October 18th, Gilette's popular Held by the Enemy; Dockstader, Dave Reed, Welch, Moreland, McWade, Cronin and Garland comprised the cast. A burlesque Bartholdi Statue, divided, on the 25th and later, the honours with Held by the Hennery. Miss Fortescue's Frou-Frou was next victim (November

8th–13th) with Fru-Fru *à la* Fort S. Q. "Compliments from Mrs. James Brown Potter," Howard Paul and Bartholdi Statue were advertised on the 15th. The Aqueduct, or, Days and Nights of Labour, was another timely skit, on November 29th, with Dockstader, Mack, Cronin, French, Garland, Pepper, Casey, Adams and Welch to supply the necessary fun. Of course Erminie must run the gauntlet and did so, on December 18th and for nights thereafter, in Our Minnie, with José, Pepper and McWade in chief command; The Fifth Avenue 'Bus was in the same bills. And, equally of course, Jim, the Penman, bowed the head, on January 17th, in Jim, the Pieman, with Dockstader as Captain Deadwood, Moreland as James Hailstone, McWade as Percy Louisville, Maxwell as Baron Hatfelt, French as Lord Dwellincork, Billy Sweatnam (one of the stage's funniest) as Weina, and José as Ag, her daughter. This concoction ran for weeks. On January 10th, Thomas Much-Mad Eh! or National Opera Troubles feebly worked into its title a pun on the name of the angry Fursch-Madi! February 7th–12th must have been hilarious, with a dash at Daly's Taming of the Shrew and with Willie Buffalo's Wildest West. These two delectabilities continued through the week of February 14th–19th, in union with Mr. Bishop Washington Irving Dockstader (The Curtain of the Mind Lifted), E. H. Talbot (*sic*) in Nobody Home but Me, and Tobogganing at Tuxedo (continued). Tobogganing and W. Irving Bishop's Mind Reading were, at that time, new forms of public insanity. Surely Dockstader was kept busy to keep up with the times.

The specialties for February 28th–March 5th were Our Harbour Lights (a hit at Wallack's), Songs of Der Vaterland, Tobogganing at Tuxedo, and The Taming of the Shrew (the last-named, doubtless, an admirable medium for knockabout comedians). On Sunday, March 13th, was to come A Complete Exposé of Bishop's Tricks, by Charles Howard Montague, city editor of the Boston Globe; for the week of March 14th, the minstrels offered Songs of Ireland and Sarah Heartburn, in Camille. And, with Barnum and Forepaugh in town, Bay Rum and Four Claws was inevitable for March 21st–26th, and, indeed, for the following week. And April 4th–9th, in The Old Bedstead, cast an eye at The Old Homestead, then in its thirteenth week of success; The Boodle Jury and Bay Rum and Four Claws accompanied in the bills. For their last week (April 25th–30th) the minstrels offered Our Minnie, Our Bartholdi Statue, etc.

Beginning on Tuesday, May 3rd, Robert Griffin Morris's absurdity, The Kindergarden, which ran for a time at Poole's, came to Dockstader's, with Charlie McShane as Sweet Willie, Mendoza as the Widow Magee, Misses Geoffreys, Bowers and Seymour as the three Disgraces, and Rheta Mann as Ivy; it lasted through June 18th. Ezra Kendall, in A Pair of Kids, had the weeks of June 20th–July 9th; Arthur and Jennie Dunn were featured. Extreme heat closed many houses on that fatal 9th of July.

STEINWAY HALL, 1886-1887

We enter Steinway Hall, on October 31st, for the first Sunday concert of our old friend, Adolf Neuendorff, who then presented with his orchestra Carlotta Pinner and Auguste M. Fischer (pianist). Neuendorff's second concert (November 7th) featured Helen Dudley Campbell and August Spanuth (whose last name probably sounded all right to himself; he played the piano). On December 4th, Carlotta Pinner came forward with a concert. And the Ragan Illustrated Lectures made December illuminating and instructive with The Heart of America (December 4th); Through Old Mexico with a Camera (11th); and Yosemite and the Yellowstone (20th); Ramblings in Spain and Morocco (27th). How this kind of thing was growing in our "cultural" life!

Emilio Belari and his pupils operated on December 9th, but, in the afternoon of the 9th, Edmund Neupert's pupils also appealed for praise. Anton Seidl, quick to catch at opportunity, announced for December 23rd, January 29th and February 26th a triad of Symphonic Soirées, doubtless ardently desired by his rapidly growing host of admirers. At the first he presented, as soloists, Albert Niemann and Adele Aus der Ohe. But we must notice the Arion concert, on December 19th, with Anna Lankow, Ovide Musin and Remmertz, and Michael Banner's concert, on December 21st; this violinist, I fear, played too often for the good of his purse. The American Hebrew of December 31st states that the hall was crowded, "on Wednesday last," for Raggan's (sic) illustrated lecture on Switzerland.

Steinway Hall either opened less frequently, or my eyes caught fewer notices in the frightfully torn and disintegrating files of the New York Herald, a condition inseparable from the use of wood-pulp paper. On January 4th, Jerome Hopkins brought in his Young Philharmonic. Benham, the pianist, advertised four historical pianoforte recitals, from Bach to Chopin, falling due on January 17th, 19th, 21st and 22nd. And the first American Symphony Concert, directed by William Wolf Lowitz, came on the afternoon of January 18th, with solos by Ella Hersey (soprano), Belle Cole and David Bimberg (violinist). The concert of the Frauen-Verein, on January 26th, promised Ida Klein, Sarah Cecil, Miss Garrigues, Ovide Musin, Fred and Oscar Steins, and Armin Schötte (organ), with the sonorous Arion, directed by Van der Stucken. At Seidl's second concert (January 29th) appeared Mme. Trebelli and Ovide Musin. Washington Irving Bishop, the mind reader, mystified on February 7th and 11th.

And we all must be interested in the first New York concerts of the since thrice-famed Boston Symphony Orchestra. Seventy-five strong, under the conducting of Wilhelm Gericke, it appeared on February 14th, March 2nd and March 31st. The programme of the 14th was exceedingly conservative, including the Oberon overture, Handel's Largo, Beethoven's Concerto for violin, played by Franz Kneisel, and Beethoven's Fifth Symphony. It began, of course, a big chapter in our musical history. February 15th found Jerome Hopkins's Young Philharmonic here. On the 17th, for the benefit of the German Emigrant House, appeared Sarah Cecil, Paula Belz, Mary Garlichs, Michael Banner, J. Blamphin (harp) and F. Dulcken. The New York Banks' Glee Club were at Steinway Hall on February 21st, with Blanche Stone Barton, W. C. Macfarlane (organ), and H. R. Humphries, their conductor. A concert tendered (March 3rd) to Isidora Martinez, prior to her departure for South America, was to be impressive, with Cappa's Seventh Regiment Band, Fred Harvey (tenor), Alma Dell Martin (contralto), Charles Steinbuch (baritone), S. B. Mills, Edward Mollenhauer, Emilio Agramonte, and selections from Verdi's new opera, Otello. February 22nd brought a testimonial to George F. Bristow, featuring Ida Klein, Liberati and C. Florio.

Seidl's third soirée (deferred) presented (March 1st) Marianne Brandt, Frau Seidl-Kraus and Karl Bärmann (pianist). The programme ranged from the Eroica to the Kaisermarsch. And, on the very next evening (March 2nd), the Boston Symphony Orchestra returned, with the overture to Anacreon, Lilli Lehmann singing Ocean, Thou Mighty Monster, with a Liszt Rhapsody, and Brahms's Second Symphony (this, according to the Herald, "exquisitely played"). March 5th found A. Dorer's pupils, in concert; Adèle Aus der Ohe played a piano recital, on March 14th; but Abramoff, the basso, was there, on the 9th, with S. B. Mills, Kitty Berger, Anna Bulkley Hills, and the ubiquitous Michael Banner. And Edmund Neupert's third pupils' concert graced the 8th. At the third concert of the Boston Symphony Orchestra (March 31st) appeared Rafael Joseffy. On March 26th and 30th, audiences may have enjoyed piano recitals by Mme. Dory Burmeister-Petersen.

The Arion Society concert, on Sunday, April 3rd, presented Van der Stucken, Marie Gramm, Toedt, Remmertz and Miss Aus der Ohe. A concert, on the 14th, was piously tendered to Carl Alves, by his pupils. April showered but few blessings into this dignified home of music. I would not classify as blessings the song recitals, on May 5th and 10th, of the explosive Anton Schott, late Siegmund at the opera; Marie Garlichs assisted. On the afternoon of April 13th, T. Lahodny, "zither soloist to the Czar of Russia," made auditors wonder why he had travelled so far on so slender an offering; Levinson, Belle Cole and Kitty Berger assisted. Signor G. de Grandi, "professor of singing," showed, on April 23rd, how well or ill he could sing. And another dubious venture, in that time, was the concert of the Chopin Club (twenty-four members) directed by Lillian B. Peters, with help from Charlotte (*sic*) Pinner, Ollie Torbett (violin), Harry A. Foresman (baritone), Hartdegen, Dannreuther and Otto Kruger (accompanist). On April 19th, Marshall P. Wilder said good-bye for the season. The Banks' Glee

[343]

Club again disported, on April 29th, led by Humphries, and assisted by the Meigs Sisters, Georgine Dressler (violin), Miss Mary Garlichs (pianist), Master Macfarlane (organist), Carl Dufft and Charles Roberts, Jr. Some of this was probably good.

CHICKERING HALL, 1886–1887

We begin our season's attendance at this busy mart of music and general entertainment, on the afternoon of September 7, 1886, there to appraise the Armanini Mandolin Quintet, an organisation that will invite rather frequently in subsequent concerts. On September 20th, Sarah Cecil, a Kentucky girl, appeared in concert, in a benefit for the Charleston sufferers, with Isidora Martinez, Claude W. Madden (violin), Adolf Glose (piano) and the Weber Male Quartet. Miss Cecil was to give a matinée, it was stated, on the 25th, for the Charleston Sufferers, and was to appear at Parepa Hall, on an evening in later September. John C. Freund, on September 28th, gave at Chickering Hall a lecture on Before and Behind the Footlights. And at about this time a group of coloured people presented a concert for the sufferers from the Charleston earthquake.

October 21st found Helen Maguille (*sic*) in concert, aided by Emily Winant, Coletti, Hasselbrink and Signor Arencibia. At three o'clock, on October 27th, Emanuel Moor ventured on a piano recital, with Sam Franko's violin in co-operation. And on October 30th Sarah Cecil again came forth, with Henrietta Beebe and the Dannreuther Quartet of Buffalo. And now Rudolph De Cordova, of London, and cousin of our own R. J. De Cordova, recited Broken Hearts, that tender fantasy acted the preceding season at the Madison Square Theatre; this treat was advertised for November 3rd, but the Herald states that the audience was bored. The Concordia Club gave a concert on the 31st of October. On November 4th, Frank Van der Stucken conducted the first of six symphonic concerts; on November 9th, he inaugurated a series of three matinées. On the evening of the 4th he enlisted the valuable assistance of Richard Hoffman, Helen Dudley Campbell, Max Heinrich and the Ladies' Chorus of the Choral Society. On the 19th, he presented Heinrich, Jessica Haskell Fuller, Hoffman, &c. The Carri Brothers also moved in terms of six evening recitals, beginning on November 16th (evening), also adding two matinées to their programme. With them, on the 16th, appeared Bareuther ('cello), Marian Macdaniel (*sic*) and B. B. Young. Robert Goldbeck's concert, in mid-November, presented Henrietta Beebe, Mrs. S. B. Anderson, Carl E. Martin, Dora Becker (violin) and S. N. Penfield (organ). On November 9th came Robert James Lee's lecture, The Tower of London. Robert G. Ingersoll, on the 14th, delivered A Lay Sermon and Helen H. Gardner also spoke on Pulpit, Pew and Cradle. The Douste Sisters opened a series of four piano recitals on November 16th (afternoon). On the 22nd, Frederick Archer began his eighth season of organ recitals, assisted by Hattie Clapper, Michael Banner and Alice Archer (reader). Richard Hoffman's piano recital filled the afternoon of the 23rd. Piano recitals in abundance! The New York Philharmonic Club gave its first concert for the season, on the evening of the 23rd, with Mrs. Emil Gramm, Paul Tidden and Emil Schenck. Emanuel Moor's second piano recital was listed for the evening of the 24th, Helen Dudley Campbell assisting.

An abundance of organ recitals! John White's series began on November 26th (afternoon); Jessica Haskell Fuller and Alexander Lambert assisted. The evening of the 26th found Robert James Lee lecturing on Through London with Dickens; and Ed Heron Allen announced for Saturday afternoons, November 27th, December 11th and 18th, and Tuesday afternoon, December 28th, The Science of Cheirosophy or Modern Palmistry. Henry M. Stanley, African Explorer and Governor-General of the Congo Free State, spoke on the evening of the 29th, on My Journey across Africa; on the afternoon of December 4th his theme was African Travels, Explorations and Works, illustrated with maps, pictures of the Congo River (7,000 miles in length) and his travels through the dark continent. Pretty interesting, I should say! On November 30th, afternoon, H. G. Tucker, of Boston (piano), and Richard Arnold (violin) were to appear; on December 7th, the Douste Sisters. Tickets for the two concerts could be had for $1.50. On the evening of the 30th, the New York Vocal Society proffered the first of its three concerts with the Mendelssohn Glee Club of Boston, A. E. Greenhalgh and Master W. C. Macfarlane (organ).

The Herald of November 28th bears notice of three concerts to be given in Chickering Hall by a new Beethoven String Quartet — Gustav Dannreuther, Ernst Thiele, Otto Schell and Adolf Hartdegen; unfortunately the paper does not list the dates. The second, on January 29th, enlisted Holst Hansen and Edmund Neupert. Will C. Macfarlane gave his second organ recital (I did not catch the first) on the afternoon of December 2nd, aided by Josephine Macpherson (soprano) and Cordelia Dougherty (pianist). On the evening of the 2nd, the Orpheus Glee Club concert employed Hattie Louise Simms and Michael Banner. Emilio Agramonte's recital (afternoon of December 8th) presented Gertrude Franklin, Carl Dufft, Emily Winant and Carlos Hasselbrink. The evening of the 9th proffered Van der Stucken's second symphonic concert, with, as soloists, Ella Earle, Anna Bulkley Hills, Theodore Toedt, Max Heinrich, Alexander Lambert and the Choral Society, the best group so far listed for that hall in 1886–87. In the afternoon of the 9th, Hermann Carri, alone, gave a piano recital. And ye gods! here is another pianist — Josephine Ware — exhibiting her art on the afternoon of the 14th, her associates being Helen Dudley Campbell, Hartdegen and Gustav Dannreuther. The second Carri concert (December 17th) celebrated the Beethoven anniversary with an all-Beethoven programme; Effie Stewart (soprano), Rusack (tenor) and Bareuther ('cello) participated. But let us not forget a benefit (December 11th) for the Gymnasium Fund of the College of the City of New York, at which were to appear the glee club and quartet of the college, with Marshall P. Wilder, Charles Roberts, Jr., Misses Martino (*sic*), Rosswog and Griswold, and George W. Morgan — worth attending. December 18th brought a benefit to the venerable Stephen Massett. For Sunday, the 19th, we had James Bowie's Pictoria, a morsel the reader may be able to digest. Emilio Agramonte's second Wednesday matinée (December 22nd) promised Isidora Martinez, Anna Bulkley Hills, Madeline Schiller, Jules Jordan (tenor) and F. Remmertz — decidedly worth attending. The evening before (21st) witnessed the pleasing social excitement of the New York Banks' Glee Club, doubtless pleasing to wives and mothers and sweethearts of the members; the afternoon of the 21st allowed Ed. Heron Allen to speak on Palmistry. Sunday, the 26th, was just one day late for the Christmas gift of a concert by Paula Buchheim (piano) and Minnie Dilthey, with Arencibia and Michael Banner assisting.

The evening of January 4, 1887, brought the second concert of the New York Philharmonic Club, with brave assistants in Annie Louise Tanner, Richard Hoffman and Richard Arnold. E. Agramonte's third matinée (January 5th) also provided artists of note in Gertrude Franklin, Antonia Henne, Francis F. Powers, S. B. Mills, Carlos Hasselbrink and C. and E. Schmidt. January 6th (evening) invited with Max Bendheim (baritone), Effie Stewart, Michael Banner and Emanuel Moor, again a promising aggregation. Dora Valeska Becker (violin) was also advertised for that evening. On the 11th, a Brooklyn girl, Auguste Fischer (piano) and Victor Herbert ('cello) played in concert. Van der Stucken's third concert (January 13th) enlisted Marie Van, Ovide Musin and W. H. Sherwood. The 14th found Goldbeck and Dell H. Thompson in concert union — not an appealing pair to me. The 19th was busy, with (afternoon) Agramonte's fourth concert with, to me, the attractive quartet (promised) of Ella Earle, Emily Winant, Theodore Toedt (he was too ill to appear), and Carl Dufft, a group suggesting the choir of St. Bartholomew's Church; and, in the evening, a group comprising Settie Blume, Michael Banner, John M. Loretz, Jr. and Max Liebling (accompanist). Addie Birdsall's concert, postponed from January 12th, was promised for the evening of the 22nd. A gap in time brings us to January 27th, when amateurs acted Second Thoughts (with E. F. Coward, Alice Lawrence and May Perkins), scenes from The Hunchback (with Coward and Elsie De Wolfe), and Sugar and Cream (with Alice and Rita Lawrence, Coward and Valentine G. Hall). On January 28th (evening), Arthur H. Mowbray gave an illustrated lecture on The Wonders of India.

The New York Philharmonic Club devoted February 1st to a concert, with, as aids, Ella Earle, S. B. Mills and Eugene Weiner. Van der Stucken's second matinée on February 4th, enlisted Isidora Martinez, Miss Groebl, Rieger (tenor), Dr. Martin and Mme. de Roode (pianist). William H. Sherwood felt induced to give two concerts (evening of February 4th and matinée, 5th), with Mrs. Otis Lockwood, and Chevalier B. de Salas (Cuban violinist); methinks one might have been enough with that list. And Sherwood stopped playing, at the first, to allow the talkers to stop. On the evening of the 5th George Riddle read A Midsummer Night's Dream, with Frank Damrosch directing the Symphony Society Orchestra, and the Normal College Alumnae Choral Society doing its bit to justify the title of Shakespeare's comedy. Sophia Priestley's interesting old-fashioned name was posted for a concert on the evening of the 7th, to be assisted by the busy Miss Martinez and the busy Michael Banner and some of her own pupils. Miss Martinez did not appear, and Belle Cole substituted. The second concert of the New York Vocal Union was to occur on the 8th.

I must carry the polite reader to a few mediocre exhibitions. On February 16th, at 7.45 o'clock, occurred the 139th concert of the Grand Conservatory of Music, West 23rd Street. I do not know a thing about Wenzel A. Raboch, who played the violin, on the 17th. But I do know Marie Salvotti, a testimonial to whom, on the 18th, promised co-operation from Anna Bulkley Hills, Coletti, Christian Fritsch, William E. Mulligan, Richard Arnold and the Gounod Vocal Society of E. Agramonte. On the 20th, Frank E. Hipple, whom we heard that winter in Bowery lectures, came forward in Chickering Hall with an illustrated lecture, From London Bridge to Windsor. The fourth symphony concert of Van der Stucken, on the 26th, provided Berlioz's The Trojans in Carthage, sung by Marie Gramm, Marie Groebel (*sic*), Fannie Hirsch, William Dennison, F. Remmertz, Prehn, Max Alvary and a chorus of 150. Charles Roberts, Jr. read, and Van der Stucken led an orchestra of sixty. Certainly that sounds interesting. In haste to arrive at this goal, I almost forgot to note the fourth Carri concert of February 22nd, when Miss L. Seymour and Bareuther were to be soloists; also Emanuel Moor's third recital, on the 24th. Hipple was again at it, on Sunday, the 27th, this time with the never-failing theme, The Land of the Cæsars. March 1st brought another concert of the New York Philharmonic Club.

George Riddle, on March 2nd, read for the Free Home for Incurables, associates in charitable endeavour being Adele Aus der Ohe and a double quartet from the Mendelssohn Glee Club. The afternoon of the 3rd proffered G. W. and Maud Morgan in organ and harp recital, with Minnie Dilthey to assist in song. The last concert of the Beethoven String Quartet (March 5th) promised Fannie Hirsch and Paul Tidden. I am interested in what follows. On the afternoon of March 7th, Courtice Pounds, the tenor of the D'Oyly Carte Company, came forth in concert, assisted by Lilli Lehmann (of all people in the world), Kyrle Bellew and Max Vogrich;

[347]

"pretty girls"—they all adored Pounds—"abounded," according to the Herald, in the audience. He and Lilli Lehmann sang simple English duets. The fourth and last concert of the New York Philharmonic Club occurred on March 8th. On the 7th (evening) Josephine McPherson (*sic*) had a concert, assisted by Michael Banner, James Poznanski and Master Walter McPharlane (*sic*). Once more for the Free Home for Incurables, George Riddle, on March 16th, read Manfred, Walter Damrosch conducted an orchestra of fifty, and Ida Klein, Hattie Clapper and a chorus from the Oratorio Society sang. Van der Stucken's fifth symphonic concert, on the 17th, provided Julie Rivé-King ("first appearance in New York in four years"), J. K. Paine's Prelude to Œdipus Tyrannus, and (by request) a repetition of The Trojans in Carthage. The 18th was jolly with the Princeton Glee and Banjo Clubs. A decline in sonority attends us in Hortense Hibbert's concert, on the 28th, several nonentities participating.

April supplies a thin list of entertainments. The Orpheus Glee Club, on the 14th, called in the aid of Ella Earle and John Wilson (baritone). Mlle. Atala Ramlek, "pianist to the Khedive of Egypt," came forward, on April 23rd, assisted by Gustav Dannreuther, the Henry Finze quartet, &c. On the 18th, I learn from the Herald, Michael Banner's concert drew a small audience; I dare say many of those I have just listed were amply able to accommodate all who attended. But fond friends and nice girls doubtless turned out, in force, on the 22nd, for a concert of the Yale Glee and Banjo Club; the dear old times! On the afternoon of April 19th, Eduardo Marzo's pupils showed what they could do, and possibly what they could not do. Fannie Bloomfield assisted Van der Stucken, at his last concert of the season, on the 23rd. And Madeline Schiller, bound for Australia, gave farewell matinées on the 22nd and 26th. The afternoon of the 27th gathered in Chickering Hall Charlotte Walker, Helen Dudley Campbell, Whitney Mockridge and the New York Philharmonic Club; for the evening of that day, Mr. and Mrs. McKee Rankin sponsored the first recital in New York of the music of Edgar S. Kelley, for Macbeth; Van der Stucken conducted the orchestra and chorus. For the 30th we were promised Esther Jacobs and Carrie Hun-King. And let us not forget the concert of the New York Vocal Union, scheduled for the 26th.

The earlier days of May gathered roses of custom while they might. On the 3rd, at 11 o'clock A.M., Sarah Cowell read Onnalinda, "the sensation" of London, and was to repeat it, on the 6th and 7th. On the afternoon of the 3rd, a benefit for St. Joseph's Hospital tried to win cash (and I don't see how it could be done) with the appearance of Juliet Wells (contralto) and T. J. Mapes ("illustrator of the Stoddard lectures"). And the evening of the 3rd exhibited pupils of Mr. and Mrs. Courtney. On the 5th, a testimonial to Samuel Edwards promised Edith Wendell, the Schneelock Sisters, Alice Shaw (the whistler), Mabel Stephenson, Harry Hilliard, S. B. Mills,

Leslie Gossin, Charles Roberts, Jr., A. P. Burbank, Tipaldi Brothers and the Weber Male Quartet. This evening function was preceded, in the afternoon, by Mrs. Rosalie Chase's concert, at which appeared Hattie Clapper, Miss Berger, Lambert, Jameson, Walker, Hartdegen, Morgan, Colby and Coward. According to the Herald, the audiences for both occasions were "slim."

A benefit to the Martens Ladies (Marie Martens-Emes and Emma Eisner), on the afternoon of May 13th, advertised the appearance (and only a few of them appeared) of Aimée, Lillian Conway, A. P. Burbank, Del Puente, Novara, Abramoff, and Kyrle Bellew. On the 9th, Bill Arp (Major Charles H. Small) lectured on Dixie Now and Dixie Then; and a Banjo Tournament made the 10th very tinkling. The Columbia College Glee Club sang, on the 13th, for the benefit of the Baseball and Athletic Association. And St. Mary's Glee Club was here (evening of May 26th), with, to assist, Mrs. Gerrit Smith, Gordon Cleather, Hartdegen and Miss Le Clair (singer). I found no more for Chickering Hall in that season; much that I unearthed seems to me to have been fittingly buried by a judicial public.

Minor Music and Miscellany, 1886–1887

Major entertainments and concerts have already been chronicled under suitable captions in theatres, opera houses and concert halls; it remains but to list smaller functions of the season. The cyclorama of The Battle of Vicksburg continued far into the winter. Cappa's Band Concerts in the Mall concluded on October 10th (Sunday). And the ninth month of the panorama, The Merrimac and the Monitor, started in earliest October, and, like The Battle of Vicksburg went far into 1887. For the weeks of October 11th–30th, "Professor" Gleason tamed horses in the Cosmopolitan, Broadway and 41st Street; Long Island's "Pet Kicker" was in the quarry. We ourselves might have been tamed by the spell of music, on the 17th, by the Arion Society (in their rooms), Dora Becker, Charlotte Walker, Remmertz and Emanuel Moor. On the afternoon of October 17th, Henry George read in Nilsson Hall. A chrysanthemum show held the Cosmopolitan Hall in the week of November 1st–6th, and left it, on November 8th, to Orrin Brothers and Benito Nichols's Aztec Fair and Mexican Village, which continued for four weeks. On November 18th, J. S. Burdett and a stereopticon called to Association Hall; but, on the 9th, Edward Mollenhauer's violin recital hopefully opened Steck Hall.

Munkacsy's big painting, Christ before Pilate, began to be shown at the Tabernacle, 23rd Street, on November 19th, and, thanks to clever advertising and "publicity," remained for many months to the delectation of visitors who would not have known the difference between Raphael and Tintoretto. Far less imposing, I ween, was the performance of the Livingston Literary Society of a three-act drama, Daniel Dawison, by Frederick Michel, who acted the principal part. Turn Hall housed the event, on December 3rd. S. P. Warren had resumed his organ recitals at Grace Church. On the evening of December 2nd, Sam Franko's String Quartet gave a concert in an unusual place — the foyer of the Academy of Music. Mme. Vogrich assisted. The quartet consisted of Franko, Boewig, Schenck and Hartdegen. And great excitement prevailed, in mid-November, when Munkacsy arrived on these strange shores, possibly to see if his big picture was properly hung. At Steck Hall, on November 27th, the Standard Quartet Club gave a concert, assisted by Mrs. Sophie Groschel Chadick. The quartet comprised Herrmann, Roebbelin, Schwarz and Bergner; and this was its ninth season. At Association Hall, December 7th, Mr. and Mrs. Henry Vandenhoff read. On December 9th, in the Metropolitan Opera House Music Hall, we had recitals by Sarah Cowell and Robert H. Hatch.

Following my usual custom (good or bad as it may be), I will group the concerts of the Mendelssohn Glee Club, stating that, on December 7, 1886, the soloists were Giulia Valda and Ovide Musin; on February 15th, Adele Aus der Ohe and Max Heinrich; and, on April 19th, Mr. and Mrs. Henschel. On this last date appeared, also, a quartet of 'cellos and an orchestra of string players.

The Amateur Comedy Club, strangely intermittent in public appearances, gave, on December 17th and 18th, the seventh and eighth performances of its career. At the Metropolitan Opera House Concert Hall, their offering, on those dates, included Sunshine, a one-act comedy by F. W. Broughton, and Anything for a Change, another one-act comedy, this one by Shirley Brooks. The first presented Alexander T. Mason, Frederic D. Weekes, Henry S. Blake, Elsie De Wolfe and Madeline Letterman. The second enlisted H. L. Cammann, Stephen G. Williams, Edward P. Sperry, Samuel Parsons, Emily Binsse, Kathleen Emmet (these two alternating as Mrs. Honeyball) and Clara Wright.

A "coloured" performance of The Lady of Lyons was spoken of in the Herald of December 11th; but the paper fails to specify the place where (as Latin grammars put it). A. A. Anderson was Claude, Bertie Towey Pauline, Jeanie A. Wanamaker Mme. Deschappelles, and David B. Meyer Glavis, other characters unlisted. The Mexican Village and Aztec Fair, recently seen in the Cosmopolitan Hall, returned, on December 21st, to Broadway and 28th Street; there for a long time thereafter it mystified homespun and unilingual Americans by nominating itself El Teocalli. John F. Rhodes, on December 28th, gave, at Steck Hall, the first of two violin recitals. And Gerrit Smith was giving Saturday afternoon organ recitals at South Church, 21st Street and Fifth Avenue. On December 28th, at the Lexington Avenue Opera House, some amateurs acted Faint Heart never Won Fair Lady and The Loan of a Lover. Our gifted amateur group, on the same evening, were at the Metropolitan Opera House Concert Hall, acting Drifted Apart, with

[350]

Elsie De Wolfe and Edward Fales Coward; A Poetic Proposal, with Lucy E. Coffey, Rita Lawrence, T. Francis Sykes, Valentine G. Hall and Frederic R. Satterlee; and Sugar and Cream, with Alice and Rita Lawrence, Edward Fales Coward and Valentine Hall. Let us leave amateurism for the moment with a visit to that same Metropolitan Concert Hall, on January 7th, there to see the Columbia College Dramatic Club in The Two Buzzards and My Turn Next; and gladly do I name the actors—Valentine G. Hall, Sidney Harris, Meredith Howland, Jr., Robert C. Sands, Richard T. Wainwright, Douglas Farley Cox, Frank C. Warren, John C. Wilmerding, Jr., James E. Warren, Robert Lee Morrell and Loyd E. Warren. On the same evening, Company F, 22nd Regiment, acted Ours, at the Lexington Avenue Opera House, with a few professionals to assist—Laura Alberta, Frank Oakes Rose, Florence Roberts, George Gaston, David P. Steele, Hattie Saphore, J. L. Saphore and J. Leslie Gossin.

Here I diverge from American interests to some lectures, scheduled in the American Hebrew to be given, in Temple Beth-El, before the Young Men's Hebrew Association. Ex-Consul Peixotto was to speak, on January 5th, on What Shall We Do with Our Immigrants?—certainly a vital topic to this day (1941). Bad weather, on the 5th, caused postponement of the discourse. On January 10th, in the same series, Reverend H. S. Jacobs was to tell What It Means to Be a Jew; the 17th was to hear Dr. Richard Gottheil's account of A Pilgrimage to an Ancient Shrine; on the 24th, the Reverend Dr. Alexander Kohut was to expound The Genius of the Talmud. That sequence of talks should (if given in English) have interested Americans as well as Hebrew-Americans.

Madeline Schiller, "by permission of Mrs. Sylvanus Reed," at 5 East 53rd Street, was to give piano recitals on January 25th and February 1st and 8th; they were "necessarily postponed." And a new sensation—Toboggan Slides—started in the week of January 10th–15th, at the Polo Grounds. "A grand winter carnival" it was to be, with the Seventh Regiment Band to keep the blood a-tingling. On January 18th, the Columbia College Glee Club was at the Young Men's Institute, Bowery. On the same night the Sam Franko String Quartet was again in the foyer of the Academy of Music. As one who saw Edwin A. Abbey's charming illustrations of She Stoops to Conquer, as they came out in Harper's Magazine, I am interested to learn that in late January the drawings were on exhibition at the National Art Galleries, along with Kenyon Cox's pictures for The Blessed Damozel. New York was not a barren waste, in 1887.

The Standard Quartet Club again held Steck Hall, on January 29th, and yet again on February 26th. On the 28th, H. V. Le Maistre began six recitations from Molière, Le Bourgeois Gentilhomme starting the series. On the 30th, a Liederkranz concert provided Helen Dudley Campbell, Musin and Silbernagel. "Professor" Carpenter began, on January 31st, in the Grand

[351]

Opera House Hall, a very long visit, with exhibitions of mesmerism. And Edward Mollenhauer's third violin recital occurred on February 8th, in Steck Hall; on the 4th, Mrs. Wilson's concert, in the Mendelssohn Glee Club Rooms, presented Ella Earle, Miss Bissell, Mrs. Raymond (Annie Louise Cary), Dennison, Beckett, Powers, Hartdegen and others. Miss Cary sang in a trio with Miss Bissell and Dennison; the Herald declared her voice and style were as fine as ever. Mr. and Mrs. Henry Vandenhoff read, on the evening of the 7th, in Association Hall. The New York Vocal Society sang in Lyric Hall, on the 18th, the Choral Union anticipating, in the same hall, on the 15th, with Francis F. Powers, Mabel Stephenson, Auguste Fischer and Alexander Salvini. On February 20th, the Queen Esther Ladies' Society made merry at Nilsson Hall. Sam Franko's New York String Quartet again possessed (February 24th) the foyer of the Academy and were aided by the excellent Rafael Joseffy. Anna Bulkley Hills's concert came, on February 21st, in the Mendelssohn Club Rooms, her assistants being Ella Earle, Madeline Schiller, Miss Berger, T. J. Toedt, Remmertz and Agramonte — all from the front ranks of resident musicians. On February 23rd, the Lexington Avenue Opera House held a concert for Washington Lodge 19, I. O. B. B., at which Max Maretzek, Adele Aus der Ohe and Michael Banner played, and acts of Martha and Faust enlisted Juliette Corden, Carrie Morse, Spigaroli and Abramoff.

Old London Street, a representation as real as possible of the thing named in the title, opened, on February 26th, in the walls of 728-730 Broadway, which had once been Daly's temporary Fifth Avenue Theatre and later, until destroyed by fire, Harrigan and Hart's Theatre Comique. Far to the north and almost out of reach of my not too energetic pen, the Harlem Choral Club concert fell, on March 1st, at the Pilgrim Church, Madison Avenue and 121st Street. On March 3rd, Ella Earle and Max Heinrich sang in Metropolitan Opera House Hall. Carpenter and Mesmerism were still (March 7th–12th) at the Grand Opera House Hall. Verily, New York, in 1887, was simply mad for excitement. On the afternoon of March 10th, Anton Schott gave a second song recital — where? The Social Twenty, according to the American Hebrew, on March 23rd, acted Among the Breakers, annexing thereto a reception and ball. The *locale* was not divulged by the paper.

By April 4th the inevitable had happened; the Old London Street became Ye Olde London Streete, thereby possibly advancing its commercial value. In late April Charles Heywood was singing in Old London Street. The Early Dance and Comedy Circle gave, on April 25th, at the Vienna Ball Room, East 56th Street, The Captain of the Watch, with W. S. Whitmore, H. H. Gardner, Frank Thayer, Pauline Willard and Hattie Nefflin, now redeemed by a prying pen from oblivion. And Adrian Primrose had a concert, on the 29th, at Steck Hall, assisted by Miss McDaniel, Miss Hibbard and Jameson. At the Old London Street, on May 15th, Rosa d'Erina appeared in concert. Lilly Runals, a Western prima donna, sang on May 22nd. But I must go back to May 3rd, when, at Bloomingdale, our favourite amateurs acted Sugar and Cream, and Mrs. Bloodgood and E. F. Coward gave Peace at Any Price.

The outer spaces began to call. Paul Baur's West Brighton Hotel, Coney Island, by mid-May summoned with an orchestrion concert; but our old friend, Philip Phillips, in latest May, gave at the Y. M. C. A. Rooms, Round the World in a Chariot of Song, with "finest views." And the Herald of May 27th warned "only four days more of Christ before Pilate." At Paul Baur's West Brighton Hotel, on May 30th and later, Jacob Bauer's 32nd Regiment Band gave two concerts. It was there again on June 5th. And, on that same Decoration Day, there were boat-races at Bowery Bay. The Herald for June 6th–11th advertises Pain's new fireworks spectacle — Sebastapol — to be given nightly at Manhattan Beach; the new seating capacity of the amphitheatre was 20,000. And Kiralfy's Fall of Babylon began, on June 22nd, at St. George, Staten Island. Pain, for the Queen's Jubilee, arranged a wonderful display of fireworks, in New York Bay, at St. George, Staten Island. And Adam Forepaugh's New Olympia began on June 28th, at Erastina, Staten Island. Glen Island opened on June 23rd.

Philharmonic Society, 1886–1887

Theodore Thomas, ensconced this year in the Metropolitan Opera House, and always busy, began with the Philharmonic, on November 12th and 13th, presenting Beethoven's Leonore Overture, No. 3; Schumann's First Symphony; a scene from Rubinstein's Nero, sung by Emma Juch and Wilhelm Ludwig; Bruckner's Seventh Symphony (new). The rehearsal and concert on December 3rd and 4th gave Schumann's overture, Genoveva; Beethoven's Eighth Symphony; the finale to Die Götterdämmerung, with Lilli Lehmann — the season before she sang it at the Metropolitan; and Tchaikowsky's new Manfred Symphony. For January 14th and 15th, the programme included Schubert's Symphony, No. 8, in B minor; La Fauvette, by Grétry, sung by Laura Moore; Brahms's new Fourth Symphony, a month after the Symphony Society had played it; Berlioz's song, The Unknown Land, with Laura Moore; and Liszt's Die Ideale. The Herald found the rehearsal listless, and Miss Moore's songs antiquated and uninteresting.

The next pair of concerts (February 18th and 19th) gave Beethoven's Fourth Symphony; his concerto No. 2, in B-flat, played by Joseffy; and St. Saëns' new Symphony in C minor. March 18th and 19th began the delights with Mendelssohn's Symphony No. 4, in A major, continued with Beethoven's Septet, op. 20, and ended with Rubinstein's fourth Symphony. April 7th (*sic*) and 9th ended the season with a new Symphony in E minor,

[353]

by Alberto Franchetti, whose opera of Asrael began all that woe of the last season (1890–91) of German opera at the Metropolitan; Adele Aus der Ohe then played Weber's Concertstück, and the concert concluded with the ever-reliable Seventh Symphony of Beethoven.

Since Thomas of the Philharmonic conducted the Thomas Popular Concerts, I will affix those functions to the preceding account. The number of those concerts was reduced to eight evenings and eight matinées. Thomas must be away with the moribund National Opera, and not only gave fewer concerts but allowed a long interval of time — he being then in other parts of the country — to elapse between the earlier concerts and the last.

The first evening concert fell on Tuesday, October 26th; at the first matinée (October 28th) Emma Juch sang. The composers for the evening of November 2nd were Tchaikowsky, Wagner, Liszt, Berlioz and Schytte; Laura Moore sang; Pauline l'Allemand was soloist, on the afternoon of November 4th. After a long interval, the third evening gave (February 22nd) selections from Schubert, Wagner, Liszt, Beethoven (the Egmont music), Dvorak, and Wagner. Emma Juch and Ludwig sang. Joseph Morse, harpist of the orchestra, was soloist at the matinée on the 24th. Adele Margulies assisted on the evening of March 1st, and Max Bendix (violin) on the afternoon of the 3rd. A "request" programme, on March 8th, brought compositions by Wagner, Bach, St. Saëns, Liszt, Rubinstein and Handel; Max Bendix again appeared. Joseffy was bright star on the afternoon of the 10th. Paul Tidden played on the 15th, and the 17th brought another "request" programme. March 22nd and 24th fulfilled their functions in the Thomas scheme, and the eighth night and day thereof fell on March 29th and 31st. The 29th was a Beethoven occasion, with Myron W. Whitney as soloist. To a great extent, we see, Thomas had drawn his soloists from the National Opera.

SYMPHONY SOCIETY; ORATORIO SOCIETY, 1886–1887

Young Walter Damrosch, inheriting most of the artistic interests of his lamented father, began the season of the Symphony Society, at the Metropolitan Opera House, with the rehearsal and concert of November 5th and 6th; the programme consisted of Arthur Bird's Symphony No. 1 (new); a violin serenade by Leopold Damrosch, played by Ovide Musin; songs with Anna Lankow (soprano); and Tchaikowsky's Capriccio Italiano. On December 10th and 11th came Brahms's Fourth Symphony (new); George Riddle read A Midsummer-Night's Dream and Misses Klein and Franconi and the ladies of the Oratorio Society participated in Mendelssohn's music. January 7th and 8th gave us Beethoven's Second Symphony; a suite for 'cello and orchestra, by and with (carefully note!) Victor Herbert; Wagner's

Waldweben; Chopin's Concerto in E minor, played by Adele Aus der Ohe; and Liszt's symphonic poem, Tasso — surely a programme to remember.

The fourth programme (February 11th and 12th) was interesting if not wholly beautiful; Weber's overture to Oberon; Airs de Ballet by Gluck; von Bülow's Der Sänger's Fluch, from Uhland's ballad; Rubinstein's Ocean Symphony, then so popular; Marianne Brandt, in airs from Cosi Fan Tutte and Leopold Damrosch's Sulamith.   For March 11th and 12th Walter Damrosch provided Toccata by Bach; Schumann's Fourth Symphony; Tchaikowsky's Serenade for String Orchestra; Adele Aus der Ohe, playing Liszt's Concerto, No. 1, in E-flat; and, for stirring close, The Ride of the Valkyries. The last pair of concerts (April 15th and 16th presented Berlioz's Romeo and Juliet, with the assistance of the chorus of the Oratorio Society; in addition, the overture to Coriolanus and the chorus, Awake! from Die Meistersinger.

The Oratorio Society ventured, on November 17th and 18th, on Israel in Egypt, engaging, as soloists, Marie Van, Marie Groebl, Dr. F. Mandeville (tenor), Carl E. Martin and George Prehn (bassi).   Let us remember the part played by the ladies of the society in the Symphony Society's rendering, on December 10th and 11th, of A Midsummer-Night's Dream. December 29th and 30th brought the accustomed Messiah; the soloists were Henrietta Beebe-Lawton (now so announced), Emily Winant, Dr. F. Mandeville and (oddly enough) Herr von Milde, a minor singer from the opera. Liszt's Christus was the third offering of the Society; on March 2nd and 3rd, its solo interpreters were Ella Earle, Hattie Clapper, Max Alvary and Max Heinrich.   All these concerts were given at the Metropolitan Opera House.

CHAPTER VI

BROOKLYN, WILLIAMSBURGH, QUEENS COUNTY, STATEN ISLAND, 1886-1887

THE theatres in Brooklyn and Williamsburgh continued to be merely parts of a circuit which included the "combination" houses in New York already written up in the preceding chapter. I need, therefore, only to repeat, in most cases, the record previously set down for stars and combinations seen in the larger town across the river. The reluctant reader will feel that his trips to Brooklyn and Williamsburgh are as tedious as a twice-told tale.

Colonel Sinn's Park Theatre began the new season on August 23, 1886, for a week of Frederic Bryton, in Clay M. Greene's Forgiven; the cast, of good material, included Blanche Thorne, Marie Bingham, Jessie Storey, Harry Harwood, Henry Bergman, Charles S. Titus, James Russell and Louis Martel. The week of August 30th–September 4th provided McNish, Johnson and Slavin's Minstrels, with, in addition to funny Frank E. McNish (Silence and Fun) and Bob Slavin, Frank Howard, John H. Davis and Fox and Van Auken. Richard Mansfield, in Prince Karl, filled the week of September 6th–11th, his support including Joseph Frankau, Harry Gwynette, Cyril Scott (then at the beginning of his bright career), Beatrice Cameron, Emma Sheridan and Effie Germon (now gone forever from her long home at Wallack's). Aimée also revived memories of her reign in opéra-bouffe, in her English comedy, Mam'zelle, her company comprising (September 13th–18th) Newton Chisnell, John Marble, A. Del Campo, Clara Baker and Jennie Williams—not a glittering host. Frank Daniels, in A Rag Baby, enlivened the week of September 20th–25th. The William T. Carleton Company, in Nanon, showed (September 27th–October 2nd) how casts can deteriorate by taking to the road; with Carleton now were Alice Vincent, Clara Wisdom, Josephine Bartlett and Charles H. Drew.

Lawrence Barrett, recently at the Star, New York, was the next attraction, with rapid changes of repertoire: Richelieu (October 4th); Francesca da Rimini (5th, and matinée, 6th); Hamlet (6th, evening); Julius Cæsar (7th); The Merchant of Venice and David Garrick (8th); Yorick's Love (matinée, 9th); and Richard III (evening, 9th). I should like to have seen every one of those productions. Thatcher, Primrose and West's Minstrels (October 11th–16th) dispersed the tragic gloom of Barrett's visit. And Annie Pixley tried (18th–23rd) The Deacon's Daughter, several months before she produced it at the Union Square Theatre. Conried's artists, in The Gypsy Baron, neatly ended October (25th–30th). Fanny Davenport filled

[356]

the first nights of November, with Much Ado about Nothing (1st); her favourite double bill of London Assurance and Oliver Twist (2nd, 6th, evening); The School for Scandal (3rd and 5th); and Fedora (4th, and matinée, 6th). So soon after her New York production, had she practically abandoned her expensive revival of Much Ado about Nothing? Her former leading man, Robert B. Mantell followed, for a week of Tangled Lives, his notable success, later, at the Fifth Avenue Theatre. Rose Coghlan, radiant and buoyant, held the week of November 15th–20th, with a repertoire not widely different from Miss Davenport's — The School for Scandal, The Lady of Lyons, London Assurance, As You Like It and Peg Woffington; Frederic de Belleville supported. All the attractions thus far listed for the Park were seen at some time during the season in New York.

The McCaull Opera Company divided the week of November 22nd–27th evenly between their summer offerings at Wallack's — Josephine Sold by Her Sisters and The Crowing Hen. Edwin Booth then raised the standard with Richelieu (November 29th, December 2nd); Hamlet (November 30th and matinée, December 4th); Iago (December 1st); Shylock and Petruchio (December 3rd); and The Fool's Revenge (evening, 4th). Another favourite, Maggie Mitchell, trod the familiar and pleasing round of The Pearl of Savoy, Little Barefoot, Fanchon and the newer and not successful Maggie, the Midget — except for the last-named, a pleasing list for December 6th–11th. F. B. Warde followed in classic dramas (December 13th–18th), succeeded for Christmas cheer (20th–25th) by Mr. and Mrs. George S. Knight, in Over the Garden Wall. And Dixey, in Adonis, augmented the gaiety for the new year (December 27th–January 1st). Certainly Sinn gave his patrons a richly diversified feast. The tone changed when Genevieve Ward and W. H. Vernon began a week with Forget-Me-Not (January 3rd, 4th, 5th and 6th), following (7th and matinée, 8th) with The Queen's Favourite; and closing (8th, evening) with Nance Oldfield and His Last Legs. Lawrence Barrett returned (January 10th–15th) in his careful and elaborate revival of Miss Mitford's Rienzi, which he produced, on the following May 2nd, at Niblo's. The cast at the Park was exactly the same as in New York.

Evangeline effaced that tragedy with mirth and melody (week of January 17th–22nd); and A Bunch of Keys (24th–29th) still kept bleak winter warm with merriment. The Main Line transported us (January 31st–February 5th) into more serious situations, the operetta, Indiana, once more (February 7th–12th) driving out gloomy winter. It is a great pleasure to greet Modjeska (14th–19th), in a repertoire larger than that we recently enjoyed at the Union Square; Frou-Frou, As You Like It, Camille, Mary Stuart, The Chouans and Twelfth Night — surely a busy week for actress and auditors. Cora Tanner (Mrs. Sinn) repeated for the week of February 21st–26th, the never-failing Alone in London; Eleanor Lane and Maggie Holloway were in her support. M. B. Curtis, with his new Caught in a Corner, filled the next

[357]

week (February 28th–March 5th), except at the matinée on March 2nd, when Washington Irving Bishop mystified. And here comes (March 7th–12th) what many, doubtless, had been waiting for—Wilson Barrett in Claudian; for the matinée, on the 12th, he offered the triple bill of The Colour Sergeant, Chatterton and A Clerical Error. Dion Boucicault followed (March 14th–19th) in The Jilt; in this, Georgia Cayvan replaced Louise Thorndyke, suddenly ill. Helen Bancroft and Julia Stuart also appeared. A Tin Soldier (March 21st–26th) introduced a merry, romping band in James T. Powers, George C. Boniface, Jr., Paul Arthur, W. H. Jordan, Isabelle Coe, Clara Lane and Ada Deaves. Sol Smith Russell, in Pa, came for the week of March 28th–April 2nd, and Marguerite Fish, for the following week, in Our Wedding Day; Marguerite Fish, let me remind the reader, was once Baby Benson. With her now were Sidney Drew and A. H. Woodhull. Brooklyn always loved Lotta and, I hope, gave the aging girl big welcome in The Little Detective (April 11th and 16th); Nitouche (12th); Bob (13th and matinée, 16th); and Little Nell and the Marchioness (14th and 15th). We note the absence of Zip and Musette from that list. Evangeline came back (April 18th–23rd); W. J. Scanlan followed (25th–30th), in his very popular Shane-na-Lawn; and Herrmann's prestidigitation and magic made May 2nd–7th a mystifying experience. The Wallack company were here in their specialties Old Heads and Young Hearts (May 9th, 12th and matinée, 14th); The School for Scandal (May 10th and 13th); and The Romance of a Poor Young Man (11th and 14th, evening). This was the week prior to their farewell fortnight at Daly's Theatre. Nat Goodwin, in Little Jack Sheppard, followed (May 16th–21st), and Dockstader's Minstrels almost finished May (23rd–28th). For the week of May 30th–June 4th Cora Tanner tried Fascination, or, the Way We Live, a play by Robert Buchanan; in this, in the double rôle of Lady Madge Slashton and Charles Marlowe, she was assisted by Lionel Bland and Virginia Buchanan as the Duke and Duchess of Hurlingham, Minnie Conway as Rosa Delamere, Carrie Coote as Arabella, Hal Clarendon as Lord Islay, Augustus Cook as Hon. Sam Slashton, P. A. Anderson as Count La Grange, Edwin Percival as Vane, Charles Coote as the Reverend Mr. Colley, and Robert Edeson as Earle Sparks and Captain Windsor. Rosina Vokes, in The Schoolmistress, and in other comedy pieces must have delighted lovers of refined fun (June 6th–11th). The bill changed nightly. And possibly box-office returns may have delighted William G. Sammis, the treasurer, who took a benefit, on June 13th, proffering Lillian Olcott, in the third act of Theodora; the third act of The Lady of Lyons, with Minnie Conway, A. S. Lipman and Fred Conway; and songs or specialties by Lillian Conway, Jennie Yeamans, R. E. Graham, J. A. Mackay, &c. Evidently the Conways were offered as magnets to Brooklyn that once so loved them. This season at the Park seems to me rich in promise; I trust it was also remunerative to Sinn.

[358]

BROOKLYN THEATRE, 1886–1887

What innumerable stars and "combinations" flitted in ever-shifting arrangement before the eyes of playgoers in the theatres of that time! The Brooklyn Theatre re-opened late, offering Robson and Crane in The Comedy of Errors, supported (September 20th–25th) by Harry Langdon, Clarence Handyside, William Harris, Selena Fetter, Alice Brown, May Waldron and Georgie Dickson. Zitka, by William Carleton — a play we had not expected to encounter again — came to this theatre for September 27th–October 4th, with Adelaide (sic) Stanhope, Frank Evans and F. O. Savage.

Effie Ellsler, in Woman against Woman, filled the week of October 4th–9th; the Madison Square Theatre that of October 11th–16th, in Our Society. The Kiralfy Brothers' Around the World in Eighty Days was the spectacular offering for October 18th–23rd. J. K. Emmet, in Fritz, Our Cousin German, probably delighted the less critical, during the last week in October (25th–30th). The evening of the 30th H. C. Miner, the manager, devoted to a benefit for the Homeopathic Hospital; the Kemble Dramatic Association acted The Road to Ruin. James A. Herne, in The Minute Men (November 1st–6th); Aronson's Casino singers and comedians, in Erminie, dispossessed by Violet Cameron from their home theatre (November 8th–13th); Violet Cameron (15th–20th); Mrs. Langtry, Charles Coghlan and her company, in A Wife's Peril (November 22nd–27th); and in The Lady of Lyons (November 29th–December 4th); A Parlour Match (December 6th–11th); Eben Plympton, in Jack (13th–18th); Held by the Enemy (20th–25th); Hoodman Blind, with Joseph Haworth (December 27th–January 1st) — thus in very compendious arrangement I reach 1887, advising the reader, if he seeks details, to study the records of "combination" houses in New York, where I have meticulously set down the details he is seeking.

R. L. Downing, in The Gladiator (January 3rd–8th); William Gillette, in The Private Secretary (10th–15th); Arthur Rehan's Company, with Carrie Turner, Harry Hotto and Clara Fisher Maeder, in Nancy and Company (17th–22nd); Lillian Olcott, in Theodora (24th–29th); Hoodman Blind again (January 31st–February 5th); Mestayer and Theresa Vaughn, in We, Us and Co. (February 7th–12th); James O'Neill, in Monte Cristo (14th–19th); Miss Fortescue, in Gretchen, etc. (21st–26th); Charles Maubury, Etelka Wardell and Florence Vincent, in The Wages of Sin (February 28th–March 5th); the Salsbury Troubadours, in The Humming Bird (March 7th–12th); Gus Williams (with C. F. Tingay, C. E. Lothian, Emma Pierce, Henrietta Irving, Topsy Venn and De Los King) in Oh! What a Night (14th–19th)— this compendious treatment of staled sweets gets me to an engagement of Margaret Mather (21st–26th). Her full repertoire included London Assurance and the mad scene from Faust, The Honeymoon, Romeo and Juliet, As You Like It, The Lady of Lyons, and Leah, the Forsaken; she was be-

[359]

ginning to lean more to comedy, one notes. This solid fare was followed (March 28th–April 2nd) by the everlasting absurdity, The Black Crook. Mr. and Mrs. McKee Rankin, in The Golden Giant (April 4th–9th); Sarah Bernhardt in Fedora, Frou-Frou, Camille, etc. (April 11th–16th); a benefit for the Elks (afternoon of the 15th); The Gypsy Baron (18th–23rd); Mrs. John Drew, in The Rivals (25th–30th)—behold April in a nutshell! I must, however, before closing the season at the Brooklyn cite the very interesting support for Mrs. Drew's incomparable Mrs. Malaprop, in The Rivals. Her son, Sidney Drew, was Bob Acres and her daughter, Georgie Drew Barrymore, Lydia Languish, with Leslie Allen as Sir Anthony, J. Newton Gotthold as Jack, J. H. Fitzpatrick as Sir Lucius, Fred Ross as Faulkland, and Alice Mansfield as Lucy. It will be seen, from the omission of Julia, that Mrs. Drew was using Jefferson's abridged version of the comedy. And I cannot pass by the benefit (afternoon of April 7th) for the family of John D. Nolan; promised participants included George Werrenrath, Henrietta Markstein, Maggie Mitchell (the singer), Kate Cavannah, Elsie Cameron, Federici, George Thorne and M. P. Wilder.

GRAND OPERA HOUSE, BROOKLYN, 1886–1887

Brooklyn, in 1941, might well look back with envy at the rich variety of plays it enjoyed more than fifty years earlier. The Grand Opera House re-opened on Saturday evening, September 11th; Knowles and Morris, the managers, then proffered Clio, with Adele Cornalba leading the ballet, and with a cast including John L. Burleigh, John L. Marshall, Odell Williams, Winfield Willard, Sibyl Johnstone and Pauline Taty. This attraction was followed, on September 20th, by Kate Claxton, in Arrah-na-Pogue, supported by Charles A. Stevenson as Shaun the Post, Floride Abell as Fanny Power, Alice Leigh as Katty, and Joseph Wilkes as Michael Feeny. John A. Stevens, in A Great Wrong Righted, was assisted by Lizzie McCall, Mr. and Mrs. Theodore Hamilton, T. J. Martin and Clarence Heritage. This filled the week of September 27th.

Joseph Murphy, for the week of October 4th, presented Kerry Gow and Shaun Rhue, equitably alloting three days to each; Belle Melville supported. Denman Thompson, on the 11th, began two weeks of his new play The Old Homestead, its first appearance in our neighbourhood; we remember its long run, in the months following, at the Fourteenth Street Theatre. The Mikado succeeded it, for the week of October 25th–30th, with part of the cast soon to revive it at the Fifth Avenue Theatre—Geraldine Ulmar, Agnes Carle, Agnes Stone, Edith Jennesse, Brocolini, Roy Staunton, J. W. Herbert, &c.

The Ivy Leaf, which always puzzles me, began November (1st–6th). Fantasma was bright and cheerful for the week of November 8th–13th, and

The Romany Rye thrilling for the week following (15th–20th), with John Burke and Victory Bateman.   Roland Reed, in Humbug, may have caused gratitude in Thanksgiving week (November 22nd–27th).   The aging Dominick Murray came (November 29th–December 4th) in From Prison to Palace — a new play that never had a chance to grow old.   Phosa McAllister, for December 6th–11th, presented her usual Taken from Life; the following week (13th–18th) Louis Aldrich gave his more than usual — his institutional — My Partner.   Frank Mayo then entered for a week (December 20th–25th) of the popular Nordeck.   Mayo, on December 27th, began a week of a new adaptation of The Three Guardsmen, possibly the version seen later in New York as The Royal Guard; in his support were Alice Fischer as Lady de Winter and Nettie Van Sickle as Queen Anne.

The Dalys, in Vacation, or, Harvard vs. Yale, may (January 3rd–8th) have amused college boys still loitering after their Christmas holidays at home.   Newton Beers, for January 10th–15th, appeared as Job Armroyd, in the harrowing Lost in London; Jessie Lee Randolph was the wandering one.   I am surprised to find how assiduously the spirit of Edwin Forrest walked abroad.   Fred Warde and Louis James, not to mention Robert Downing, were striving to perpetuate his heroic repertoire, and here is Edmund Collier, no stranger in the struggle, giving us a week devoted to Metamora (January 17th to 21st) and Jack Cade (for both performances of the 22nd).   The Lights o' London (24th–29th) also dealt with weighty matter, illuminating the art of Messrs. Rexford, Foster and Kelly (the Eagle does not blazon their given names) and Helen Weathersby.   I fear that Daniel Sully, in Daddy Nolan, represented (January 31st–February 5th) something of a drop in the cultural barometer; but February, one admits, is a cold month.

And I look askance at the offering of February 7th–12th — Frankie Kemble, in Sybil — a Romance of Dublin Lights; with her were Harry Bell, Geoffrey Hawley (an attractive young actor), R. M. Carroll (variety veteran), William Herbert (ever-recurring), W. J. Constantine, Annie Evelyn, and Emily Maynard — certainly an interesting group.   A Ring of Iron (February 14th–19th), a thriller by Frank Harvey, introduced Ralph Delmore (whom we shall frequently meet), Charles Barringer, Henry Mack, Frank Crane, Miss Angie Griffiths, Violet Campbell, Jennie Satterlee and Ellen Downey.   Bartley Campbell's Siberia (February 21st–26th) had, for a travelling combination, an unusually good cast in Forrest Robinson, George Frederick Nash, Lawrence Eddinger, John Dailey, C. W. Butler, Adele Belgarde, Frankie McClellan and Stella Teuton, every one of whom is familiar to us.   Princess Ida (February 28th–March 5th) presented practically the artists seen, earlier in the season, at the Fifth Avenue Theatre — Roy Staunton, Phil Branson, Joseph Fay, J. W. Herbert, E. J. Clony, V. Holland, Helen Lamont, Alice Carle, Edith Jennesse and Agnes Stone; but, of course, the two most popular members of the Fifth Avenue cast — Miss Ulmar and Courtice Pounds — were trying, in New York, to make Ruddygore the success it could not, then, become.

The reader, perhaps, is growing tired of The Main Line; he must, I fear, take it for the week of March 7th–12th, fortifying himself with expectation of the familiar pleasures of the next week. Then the ever-welcome Mr. and Mrs. Florence gave us The Mighty Dollar (March 14th–15th); Our Governor (16th and 18th); Dombey and Son (17th); and The Ticket of Leave Man (19th). For the matinée, on the 19th, they presented The Flirt, a new play which failed to win popularity, with Florence as Sylvester Sparks, and Mrs. Florence as Diana Lovington. Neil Burgess, who always delighted me, was funny (March 21st–26th), in Vim, his Mrs. Puffy being supported by Leslie Edmonds, Joseph Palmer, George W. Stoddart, Adolph Jackson, Albert Horn, May Taylor, Clara Stoneall and May Dargon. After all, Frankie Kemble, in Sybil, may have been better than I supposed; she returned for the week of March 28th–April 2nd. Again I shudder for the size of the index as I write the names of the nonentities who, during the week of April 4th–9th, revived Anson Pond's play, Her Atonement; Edith Clayton, Alice Crawford, Jean Delmar, Minnie Dean, A. H. Hastings, Frank Harrington, Graham Crawford, Will M. Dell, Emile La Croix, Bunt Cellers, Daisy Dean and M. J. Gallagher were they, and only Jean Delmar and Hastings strike chords in my remembrance. Evans and Hoey, in A Parlour Match (April 11th–16th); Patti Rosa, in Bob and Zip (18th–23rd), and in Zip and Bob (25th–30th) — these things, lively and undignified, lead us to three weeks of what Brooklyn playgoers devotedly loved — a visit of Edward Harrigan and his New York company, Wild, Collyer, Mrs. Yeamans and all, in a succession of his winter successes: The O'Reagans (May 2nd–7th); The Leather Patch (9th–14th); and Investigation (16th–21st). On that three-weeks wave of enthusiastic excitement, we may well leave the Grand Opera House for the season of 1886–87, thankful for some really excellent entertainment mitigated by somewhat more dubious delights.

CRITERION THEATRE, BROOKLYN, 1886–1887

We have now reached the Criterion, a more hazardous venture for manager and audience. It opened, on September 20th, with Viola Allen as Florell, in a play by W. C. Cowper, entitled Talked About; in her company were her father, C. Leslie Allen, her mother, and Florence Roberts and Hart Conway. Neil Burgess, in Vim, made merry the week of September 27th–October 2nd.

The offering for October 4th–9th was Louise Rial, in Fortune's Fool. Boston's highly respected Mrs. Thomas Barry, with William Redmund, then or later her husband, tried to capture Brooklyn (11th–16th), in A Cure for the Blues; I hazard the conjecture that they did not annex the City of Churches to Boston; their company included Amelia Watts, Clara Douglas, William Fairbanks, Frank Norcross and Carrie Hale. May Blossom, with Ben Maginley, filled the week of October 18th–23rd. Lillian Conway, with her opera company, returned to her girlhood home (October 25th–30th), presenting, in succession, The Grand Duchess, Chimes of Normandy, The Pirates of Penzance and Fatinitza, and retiring in favour of Minnie Maddern (November 1st–6th) in Caprice. Edwin F. Mayo and Loduski Young were here (November 8th–13th) in Frank Mayo's Davy Crockett. Catherine Lewis, no longer a popular favourite, and Donald Robertson tried, for November 15th–20th, an ineptly named My Mis'es. And the ever-recurrent Templeton Opera Company came, for November 22nd–27th, in their expected Mikado, which had outlived better performances of the Gilbert-Sullivan masterpiece. Arthur Rehan's Nancy and Company filled the week of November 29th–December 4th, with Carrie Turner in the Ada Rehan part. The Mexican Typical Orchestra, and Winnie Vance followed (December 6th–11th), with a concert on Sunday, the 12th. December 13th–18th brought back the mild pleasure of The Rajah, with W. A. Clarke in the lead. Louis James and Marie Wainwright were here in Virginius, Hamlet, Much Ado about Nothing, Julius Cæsar and other classics, in the week of December 20th–25th; Fanny Davenport's recent Beatrice had started something—or was it Ellen Terry's? December 27th–January 1st brought Stanley Macy and Laura Dinsmore, in The Kindergarden, that success of the following summer at Dockstader's. It seems to have closed the Criterion, a less pretentious theatre, which, on January 8th "was turned into a minstrel house," managed by Frank Bixby. The last week of this enterprise began on February 28th. During its occupancy we had John Hart (for several weeks), Harry Pierson, Billy Chace, A. J. Talbot, Harry Constantine, the Winstanley Brothers (clog), the Hanley Brothers (acrobatic song and dance), the farce of A-Merry-Can Uproar (poor Theodore Thomas!); Connors and Collins, Latta and Lynch, the Martin Brothers, C. W. Williams, Eddie Fox, Emmerson (sic) and Clark, Frank Livingstone (head balancer), Ashley and Hess, Walling, Roe and Demarest, John W. Byron, and, as stage director, E. D. Gooding. This carries us to January 31st, and prepares us then for Dan Hart and his singing dog, Howe and Doyle (clog), Talbot and Chace (still abiding), May and Kunkleman (banjo) and John Hart, in The Black Statue. Green and Marco, Bryant and Saville and Chace and Talbot (now in this order) were featured for February 7th–12th. The next week stressed E. D. Gooding's Black Mikado—My-Card-Oh!—with Charles Heywood as Yum-Yum; Till's Marionettes, P. H. Thurber, John Hart, Talbott (sic) and Chace, Eddie Fox and his violin filled the olio. My-Card-Oh lasted through February 21st–26th, when the Lenton Brothers entered the bills. Frank Bixby was rather pathetic in announcing the last week of

[363]

his minstrels (February 28th–March 5th); some one had leased the house, and he must depart. He consoled himself with a benefit, on March 3rd.

George O. Starr was the enterprising lessee, and, on March 7th, he installed in the Criterion a comic opera company that weathered the gales of that blustery month, lasted through April showers and bloomed into May with a repertoire of old operas that could have seemed novel to but few. The chief performer was Frank Deshon, who began March (7th–12th) as Lorenzo, in The Mascot, supported by May Duryea, Maggie Baxter, Charles Osborne, Harry Rattenberry, Kirtland Calhoun, Eugene Harvey, May Douglas and Julie Ernest, none of whom, except Rattenberry, has heretofore entered our hall of fame. Starr's idea was to provide weekly changes of bill, and with that intent he marched on with (March 14th–19th) The Chimes of Normandy — Deshon as Gaspard; Olivette (21st–26th); Billee Taylor (28th–April 2nd), with Deshon as Barnacle and Zuzel (*sic*) as Eliza; Pinafore (April 4th–9th); Giroflé-Girofla (11th–16th), with Deshon as Bolero and Louis Nathal as Mourzouk; The Princess of Trebizonde (18th–23rd), with Deshon, Osborne, Zazel (wire-walker), May Duryea, May Douglas and Alice May stressed in the announcements; The Mikado (April 25th–30th), with Deshon as Ko-Ko, and Alice May as Katisha; Audran's The Golden Hen (May 2nd–7th); Patience, with Deshon as Bunthorne (May 9th–14th); and revivals of The Chimes of Normandy (16th–21st) and Olivette (23rd–28th). The venture ended with these revivals, leaving me surprised that it could have carried through so many weeks. We perceive that the Criterion had had a precarious season, with great uncertainty of purpose. Perhaps Brooklyn had too many theatres. But the Criterion persisted hopefully (May 30th–June 4th) with Ezra Kendall, in A Pair of Kids, Arthur and Jennie Dunn and the Olympia Quartet assisting.

ACADEMY OF MUSIC, BROOKLYN, 1886–1887

This respected auditorium began its season with a brief visit of the once all-compelling, emotional Clara Morris, now sixteen years past the night of her sensational début, with Daly, in 1870. Her offerings for 1886 were very usual with her: Article 47 (September 22nd); Miss Multon (23rd); The New Magdalen (24th), and Camille (matinée, 25th). Brooklyn was still very loyal to this mistress of emotional appeal. The Stoddard Illustrated Lectures began on September 30th, with Napoleon III and the Fall of Paris; Queen Elizabeth followed on October 4th, and Charles Dickens and His Travels, on the 9th. Peter the Great (11th) and Egypt and the Nile (14th) ended a series that sounds rather good. The ill-starred Angelo Italian Opera Company came from the New York Academy, on October 21st, with the thin offering of Ione, or, the Last Days of Pompeii, sung by Giannini, Pogliani, Pinto, Mestress, Valerga and Bianchi-Montaldo.

Amateur Actors

The Brooklyn Academy for the season we are reviewing was beset by that favourite product of the Brooklyn social mill — amateur acting. The Kemble Society — one of the very best of these organisations — gave there, on October 26th, The Road to Ruin, with Annie Hyde as the Widow Warren, Lizzie Wallace as Sophia, Julia Goldzier as Jenny, Martha Witter as Mrs. Ledger, H. H. Gardner as Old Dornton, Douglas Montgomery as Harry, W. P. Macfarlane as Goldfinch, T. C. Bell as Sulky, Thomas T. Hayden as Milford, Deane Pratt as Silky, and, in minor rôles, M. J. Benjamin, E. O. Jacobson, George R. Lamb, Franklyn Norris, W. T. Angel and Frank Cuddy. We shall meet these aspiring spirits again, before the season ends. This performance was for the benefit of the Kemble library; it was repeated, we remember, on October 30th, at the Brooklyn Theatre, for the benefit of the Brooklyn Homœopathic Fund. The Brooklyn Philharmonic began its season on October 29th and 30th; the activities of that venerated organisation I shall treat under separate heading. Inured to the activities of amateurs, the reader will attend, on November 2nd, Watts Phillips's play, Not Guilty, acted by the Gilbert Dramatic Society, with a cast including William B. Vernam, Adam Dove (a guileless name), Charles T. Catlin, W. W. White, Harry M. Noble, W. T. Harris, Jr., G. H. Beuerman, Pauline Willard, Grace Clark and Clara Knowles. The Academy reverted to musical uses, on November 8th, with a charity concert involving the Dudley Buck Quartet, the New York Philharmonic Club, Eugene Weiner (flute), Miss McCollum and Francis Fischer Powers. Personally, I shall remain away from C. H. Rivers's Annual Exhibition, on November 16th; and my reader, if he prefers simple pleasures, may avoid the exhibition of November 22nd–27th — Lillian Olcott, in the sensational Theodora. On the 30th, the Long Island Historical Society sponsored a lecture by Henry M. Stanley — would I might have attended!

And here are more amateurs. The famous Kemble Dramatic Society once more emerged, on November 29th, with the old Wallack play, The Veteran, presenting Charles Rohlfs as Colonel Delmar, Douglas Montgomery as Leon, H. H. Gardner as Eugene, W. C. Pruden as Belmont, Charles D. Pratt as Mortier, Albert Meafoy as Mustapha, Annie L. Hyde as Mrs. McShake, Marie Bowen as Blanche, Marie Lamb as Amineh, and C. J. Wilson as the absurd Ofl-an-agan. Minor parts fell to C. D. Oxley, Thomas F. McGirr, Wallace Barton, Frank Norris, W. T. Angel, George R. Lamb, W. D. Preston, Charles Corwin, Frank Cuddy, Eugene Morton, Julia W. Reid, Genie Robinson, Gertrude Conran, and Emma Rite (*sic*). Certainly I am doing my duty. And I persist along the path — no primrose path, believe me! — with the Amateur Operatic Association, which, on December 16th (postponed from the 9th), assailed the difficult Iolanthe, with C. H.

Parsons as the Lord Chancellor, William C. Kimball as the Earl of Mount Ararat, S. L. Swazey as Tolloller, Edward Campbell as Sergeant Willis, John Hill as Strephon, Miss Edgeworth Starritt as the Fairy Queen, Mrs. A. Mesereau (*sic*) as Iolanthe, Mrs. L. P. Wilks as Phyllis, and with Misses H. C. Jackson, Clara Crooks and Bessie Rathburn (*sic*) as, I hope, pretty and tuneful fairies.

America being ever fair game for foreign propaganda, especially in 1886–87 for Irish propaganda, Justin McCarthy came forward, on December 11th, with a lecture on Ireland and Her Cause. Mayor Whitney, of Brooklyn, Seth Low, Mayor Grace, of New York, and Henry Ward Beecher were advertised to attend. In the Academy Assembly Rooms, on the 13th, the Entre Nous group held its second reception. December 21st promised Manfred, with George Riddle, Walter Damrosch and 250 voices from the Oratorio Society of New York. The Kemble Society, on December 22nd, staged an appealing thing—A Dickens Night. In the huge cast of real people and of those in the dream appeared J. Smithson as Bob Cratchit, Albert Meafoy as Peter, Bob's eldest son, Jennie Cochrane as Mrs. Cratchit, Mrs. Parkhurst as Mrs. Fizziwig, and Thomas C. Bell as Scrooge. The year ended with something professional—seven performances in English by the National Opera Company, sponsored by the financial backing of Mrs. Thurber and the musical direction of the sorely-tried Theodore Thomas. Mme. Fursch-Madi, a storm centre, had not yet erupted from the organisation, and, on the opening night, Monday, December 27th, she appeared in The Huguenots, with Pauline L'Allemand, Jessie Bartlett Davis, Candidus, Stoddard (De Nevers), Ludwig (St. Bris) and Whitney. The cast of Faust (December 28th) included Emma Juch, Jessie Bartlett Davis, Mathilde Phillipps, Bassett, Ludwig (Mephisto) and Stoddard; Gustav Hinrichs directed. Cornelia Van Zanten, from Holland, was, on the 29th, Amneris to the Aïda of Fursch-Madi, the Radames of Candidus, the Ramfis of Whitney, and the Amonasro (light, I suspect) of Stoddard. Arthur Mees conducted. The Bal Costumé of Rubinstein and Massé's Galatea combined on the 30th. One wondered why, on the 31st, the new Bertha Pierson sang Elsa, instead of Emma Juch, who was so satisfactory in the part. But Fursch-Madi and Emma Juch were both part of the temperamental disturbance then shaking the company to the very end of its endurance. On that 31st, Candidus was as good a Lohengrin as his limitations permitted, Van Zanten, Ludwig and Whitney completing the cast. The opera again allured to the matinée, on January 1st, and a double bill of Sylvia and The Marriage of Jeannette, on the evening of that holiday.

On January 10th, the J. C. Duff Comic Opera Company, from the Standard Theatre, New York, began a week of A Trip to Africa, advertising, as principals, Lillian Russell, Madeline Lucette, Vernona Jarbeau, Zelda Seguin,

ADELE CORNALBA

EDWIN ARDEN

BERTHA WELBY

J. W. JENNINGS

MRS. BARRYMORE
ETHEL—LIONEL—JACK

W. T. CARLETON

CARRIE TURNER

EMMA SHERIDAN

ELEANOR CAREY

Harry Hilliard, J. H. Ryley, Robert Boudinot, Charles Dungan, and Signor Campobello. The Amateur Operatic Association, on the 11th, held a reception, in the Assembly Rooms of the Academy, providing, in addition, Dell Thompson (reader), Laura S. Groves, Mrs. E. J. Grant and the Brunswick Quartet. January 25th brought Anton Seidl's orchestral concert, with assistance from Ovide Musin and Mme. Trebelli. A testimonial to Robert C. Hilliard, Brooklyn's favourite amateur turned professional, was advertised as tendered by Mayor D. D. Whitney and many other prominent citizens (I can't see why); it promised, for the afternoon of January 28th, participation by Nat Goodwin, John A. Mackay, Joseph Haworth, the ever-obliging Michael Banner, Marshall P. Wilder (also ever-willing), Harry Kennedy, Henry Hallam, John Howson, Anna Bulkley Hills, W. G. Elliot, Weedon Grossmith, and the third act of Saints and Sinners, with J. H. Stoddard, Marie Burroughs, R. C. Hilliard (as the bad officer), Louis Massen, Charles Coote and H. S. Millward. February found people dancing; on the 3rd, came the Mask Ball of the Prospect Association. The afternoon of the 4th, staged a benefit for the Actors' Fund, A. M. Palmer directing, and bringing from his Madison Square Theatre Agnes Booth and the others in the third act of Jim, the Penman. Brooklyn theatres supplied the other attractions — acts of Daddy Nolan, The Main Line, Alone in London, and vaudeville acts. The evening of the 5th was devoted to the Carlisle Indian School, with one hundred Indians of thirty different tribes. The annual ball of the Brooklyn Volunteer Fire Association was pretty elegant, on the 7th, going to the royal Academy and hiring Cappa's Seventh Regiment Band to set the joy in motion. The Amphion Society of the Eastern District came westward, on the 8th, with, as soloists, Helen Dudley Campbell and Charlotte Walker. On the 14th, for St. Valentine's Day, we became patriotic and nostalgic with Life Scenes and Tableaux of the Rebellion by Veterans of the War, assisted by the Hatton Glee Club, Annie Lockwood Poole, Charles H. Marcy (piano) and Deverill's orchestra. And here again is the Kemble Society, presenting, on February 18th, Robertson's somewhat antiquated play of Home, with Mrs. James S. MacCoy as Mrs. Pinchbeck, Mamie Dickinson as Lucy, Annie Wallace as Dora, Douglass (sic) Montgomery as Colonel White, H. H. Gardner as Mr. Dorrison, and William E. Wilson as Captain Mountraffe.

The Amateur Association of Brooklyn, on the 17th, sang Maritana, and, on the 21st, the Brooklyn Sængerbund indulged in the German specialty of a Masquerade Ball. The cast of Maritana included Emma Thomas, Charles H. Parsons, Laura S. Groves, J. T. Brennan and J. W. Macy. The National Opera Company, poor, wandering souls, began on March 3rd, a succession of five Thursday performances, coming from their temporary home in the Metropolitan Opera House. Martha was their first offering, with Pauline L'Allemand, Charles Bassett, Stoddard and William Hamilton (as Sir Tristan). Carl Venth's first popular orchestral concert, on the 7th, invited with promise of Marianne Brandt, Daisy Bowerman (a twelve-year-old violinist) and Mrs. Lydia Kunz-Venth. Except for Frl. Brandt, this aggregation leaves one guessing. On the 10th, the disintegrating National Opera sang Faust, with Emma Juch, Ludwig, Bassett, Stoddard, Jessie Bartlett Davis and Mathilde Phillipps. The aspiring Amaranths, on March 9th, gave Boucicault's never very popular Forbidden Fruit, with Harry T. Hill, Percy G. Williams, R. B. Throckmorton, G. H. Beuerman, William Phelps Macfarlane, Frederick Bowne, A. H. Marquis, Charles H. Turner, Mark Meyer, Ella Greene, Ida E. Williams, Elise Louis and May Halbert holding aloft the banners of the society. In the Assembly Rooms of the Academy, the Entre Nous Dramatic Society held a reception on March 11th. The third National opera was The Flying Dutchman with Bertha Pierson (again why not Miss Juch?), Mathilde Phillipps, Ludwig, Whitney, Bassett and Fessenden. Nero, announced for production on the 24th, could not be got ready, and Lakmé was substituted, with, of course, Pauline L'Allemand, and, in a small part, Amanda Fabris, sister of Emma Juch; Nero came in all its splendour, on the 31st. Meantime, on March 15th, the Kemble amateurs played Tom Taylor's fading Plot and Passion, entrusting leading rôles to Matilda Davis, Julia Goldzier, William E. Wilson, H. H. Gardner, J. H. Wilson, Douglas Montgomery, A. J. Macaulay, M. Delavante and T. J. Stuart. The Times, which generally praises amateur efforts, states that "the performance was given with that smoothness which too seldom characterizes the efforts of amateurs, and was fully up to the standard of the Kemble. Everybody knows what that is." The audience was "brilliant." On the 29th, the Brooklyn Choral Society appeared in a concert. And I must not forget a repetition of Iolanthe (March 23rd) by the same cast as to leading singers that so proudly produced it earlier in the season — the cast from the Amateur Opera Association.

April was more prodigal in blessings. The pupils of St. Francis College gave, on the 12th, The Maid of Erin, and, on the 15th, The Irish Agent. On the 16th came the much advertised Stevens lecture, Around the World on a Bicycle. The 18th found the Kemble Society playing willingly, for its benefit, The Follies of a Night (with Annie Burt Phelps, Julia Ledger, Bamburgh, William C. Wilson and T. C. Bell), and Two Can Play at that Game (with Mrs. Matilda Davis, Douglas Montgomery and J. C. Costello). The amateurs were running to cover; but the Amateur Opera Association kept up its courage, on April 23rd, with The Musketeers. And the Gilbert Dramatic Association, on the 20th, presented She Stoops to Conquer, with Charles T. Catlin as Hardcastle, Adam Dove as Young Marlow, Charles Canfield as Hastings, W. T. Harris, Jr., as Tony, H. Lindemann as Diggory, Pauline Willard as Kate, &c. And, under the auspices of the Thirteenth Regiment, No Thoroughfare, on the 22nd, enlisted amateurs from the Amaranth, the

[368]

Gilbert, the Melpomene and the Booth. I revert to a lecture, The Cross of a New Crusade, delivered at about this time, by the much-discussed Reverend Edward McGlynn, and to another Amphion concert, with Fannie Hirsch, on April 21st. Henry Ward Beecher, perhaps Brooklyn's most institutional personality, died on March 8, 1887, and almost immediately his fellow-citizens started a movement to raise funds for a fitting statue or memorial of the great preacher. On May 5th, the Academy housed an entertainment by T. J. Mapes, "illustrator of the Stoddard lectures," and singing by Juliet Wells (contralto). For this purpose also, the Amateur Opera Association, on May 12th, sang Maritana. I close with the second private concert (May 31st) of the Brooklyn Choral Society.

HYDE AND BEHMAN'S, 1886–1887

For the history of this, the leading "Variety" theatre of Brooklyn, I am indebted to such items as the Eagle injects into its notes and reviews of amusements of the town. By this means, I learn that Lester and Allen's Minstrels began the season (August 30th–September 4th) and that, for the week of September 6th–11th, the management provided Charles T. Ellis and Clara Moore (a pair I am always pleased to meet), Aimée ("the human fly"), the Austin Sisters (flying trapeze), the Lynn Family ("from England"), Paul Hamilton (song and dance), Charles A. Loder, Annie Hart and Retlaw and Allen. Marinelli, "the human snake" satisfied, during the next week (13th–18th) the desire for contortion. For September 20th–25th a large group consisted of the "Only" Leon and Cushman, William Carroll (banjo), Harrington and Johnson, Kitty O'Neil, Sheehan and Coyne (Irish), Mollie Wilson, Till's Marionettes, Topack and Steele (*sic*), Frank Lewis, Edwards and McKeever, Henri d'Albert (card manipulator) and the Davenport Brothers (acrobats). Kernell's Novelties occupied the house from September 27th to October 2nd; the Rentz-Santley combination followed (October 4th–9th). The week of October 11th–16th made merry with the Nelson Family, Caccobatic Golinas ("human serpent"), Kelly and Woods, Misses Costello and Sheridan (clog), Fields and Hanson, and Florence Miller. The Hallen and Hart Company possessed the week of October 18th–23rd, presenting the popular Russell Brothers, Julia Wilson, Lester and Williams, Fox and Van Auken, and the exquisite art of George F. Moore ("who makes 28 faces at the audience," most of whom, probably, could make only one face back). Manchester's Night Owls came next (October 25th–30th); the Eagle cries specific news of the component owls — Jutan (*sic*), Pauline Batchellor, Louise Dempsey, May Howard, Manchester and Jennings, Irwin Bush, John Dunn, and a new Adonis burlesque.

Sam Devere's Big Show began November (1st–6th); and Tony Pastor followed (8th–13th), with Leon and Cushman ("mock operatic," as one would expect from Francis Leon, once so popular as ministrel "prima donna"), Frank Bush, Stebb (*sic*) and Treppe, Isabella Ward, Catherine (bird trainer), Winstanley Brothers (concertina and dance), Gofre and Ardel (gymnasts) and Peterson and Rice (dancers). Tony, we know, was ever a liberal provider. Jolly Nash was star entertainer for November 15th–20th. A very host glorified Thanksgiving week (22nd–27th): William Conrad and his performing elephant, Parker's dogs, McAvoy and Hallen, Cordello (*sic*) and Vindella (*sic*), the Lucier Family, Alice Gleason, Laura Lee, Harry Allen, the Four Schrode Brothers, the Martens and Leon and Cushman (in Our Thanksgiving Dinner). Silence in the Eagle forces me to December 13th–18th, when Hyde and Behman offered Harry Kennedy, Frank Lewis, Cuponti (juggler), Hines and Remington, Lamartine Brothers, Susie Wilde, Luigi dell'Oro and Heffernan and McDonald. Again the Eagle fails me, and I finish the year (December 27th–January 1st) with Hyde and Behman's Minstrels, including Billy Birch, Luke Schoolcraft, William Conrad and his clown elephant, Tom Thumb. Lillie (*sic*) Hall's Burlesque and Fannie (*sic*) Bloodgood's Specialty Company began the new year (January 3rd–8th), with Maggie Cline, Charles Fostelle, Mlle. Zitella, and the burlesque, Oxygen.

Sam Devere came back for the week of January 10th–15th; in the next week (17th–22nd), "snakes twine round" Alna Don Janata, but without such cincture appeared Thomas Ryan, Harry Graham, McIntyre and Heath, the Dare Brothers (horizontal bar), the Four Emperors, Jeppe and Fannie Delano and Schoolcraft and Coes. Dot D'Alcorn's electric organ, Edward Earle (magic barrel), Tom Bradford, Manning and Drew (banjo and dances), John B. Wills and May Adams figured for January 24th–29th. January 31st–February 5th boasted of Baggesen ("human corkscrew"), Harry Kernell, Joe J. Sullivan, the Love Sisters, Mlle. Eichlerette and her monkeys, Frank and Lillian White and Queen Vassar—in some respects an improved allotment. The Howard Athenæum Star Company February 7th–12th stressed Isabella Ward and Retlaw ("the human snake"). How they loved contortion! Ralph Terry's Shadow Pictures, Charles and Ella Jerome, Billy Carter, Swift and Chase (*sic*), Hilda Thomas and Alice Temple were headliners for February 14th–19th; and for the next week (21st–26th), Jolly Nash, Mlle. De Granville's iron jaw, the Clipper Quartet, McAvoy and Hallen, Parker and his dogs, Wilmot and Lester, and the King Sisters—on the whole a good list. The Night Owls came back for February 28th–March 5th.

Tony Pastor's Company (March 7th–12th) included himself, Le Clair (*sic*) and Russell, Kitty O'Neil, Rose and Martin Julian, the Romalo Brothers, May Howard, Topack and Steele, Hi Tom Ward, Silvo, Childs and Maeder, and Jennings and Pratt. Hallen and Hart's Company (14th–19th) was also good—Ella Wesner, Bryant and Lizzie Richmond, the Carons,

Hawkins and Collins, Polly McDonald, George T. (*sic*) Moore, Donald Melville, Fox and Van Auken, "Mephisto" and the Russells.   The Rentz-Santley Company of March 21st–26th included Dorst and Oreste (fantastic dances), Sanford and Wilson (minstrel sketch), Billy Buckley and Tommy Dayton (in a comedy), Valjean (juggler), the Inman Sisters (wooden-shoe dancers) and a burlesque of Erminie — seemingly now a purged and innocent show.   The Australian Novelty Company (March 28th–April 2nd) introduced Mlle. Aimée (ceiling walker), C. T. Ellis and Clara Moore, Sharpley and West, the Lynn Family, the Austin Sisters (Aimée was one of these), the Hamlins, Bruns and Monroe, Retlaw and Alton, Frank Vern, the Newcomb Trio and Annie Hart.

Let us begin the April maze (4th–9th) with Adolph Seeman (conjuror), Bedouin Arabs, Kennette (gymnast), Moulton and Dashway (bars), the St. Felix Sisters, the McShane Brothers, Manning and Drew, Frank Girard, Dave Oaks (*sic*) and Jessie Boyd.   Ida Siddons's New Burlesque Company included (April 11th–16th) Flora Moore, the Melrose Sisters, the Southern Quartet, Maud Beverly, the Parisian Dancers, Frank Lester, the Wesley (*sic*) Brothers, Lizzie Hall, Thorpe and Castellat, &c.   Patrons of Hyde and Behman's saw many, if not always great, performers.   Reilly and Wood's Show next offered its riches, on April 18th–23rd, with the Nelson Family (acrobats), the Mignanis, Bobby Gaylor, the California Four, Chisikitchi, Mlle. Forgardus, the Altoff Brothers, Florence Miller, Adell (*sic*) Wilson and Pat Reilly — a show that would not appeal to pickers and choosers in "Variety."   And what did April offer on its departure (25th–30th)?   Mlle. Alberta and the Barretta Sisters (wire-walking and sliding), Mlle. Anna ("female Hercules"), Pritchard, Smith and Way (dancers), the Vidocqs, Sheridan and Flynn (Irish comedy), Estelle Wellington, Lottie Gilson, Weber and Fields (German comedy) and Gus Hill ("champion club swinging") — an interesting group.   Back for May 2nd–7th came Lillie (*sic*) Hall's Burlesque and Fannie (*sic*) Bloodgood's Specialty Performers — Fostelle, the Davenport Brothers, the California Quartet, Natta and Monte Collins and the concluding Oxygen.   Dot D'Alcorn (*sic*) also returned (9th–14th) with her electric instrument; in the company were Lester and Allen (no longer at the head of a ministrel band), Hawkins and Collins, John and Lea Peasley, Andy and Annie Hughes, Edward Leslie, the Archmere Sisters and Al Reeves.   Hyde and Behman's was still going, from May 16th to 21st; after that, the Eagle remains quiet concerning the place.

STANDARD MUSEUM, 1886–1887

The Standard Museum, a rather indeterminate hall, opened, on Saturday evening, August 28th, with a special performance, N. S.· Wood figuring on the stage and general jubilation filling the auditorium.   Wood continued for two weeks (August 30th–September 11th) in his usual pieces, The Boy Detective, The Boy Scout of the Sierras, etc. The Shadow Detective, with Daniel A. Kelly and Joan Craven filled the week of September 13th–18th.

Queena was the elegantly-named offering for September 27th, Ethel Tucker being the star; and an enterprising star, since, during her week, ending on October 2nd, she was to appear in Leah, Fanchon, The Two Orphans and The Ticket of Leave Man, surely derelicts of bygone decades. The Boy Tramp entered for October 4th–9th; even farther stretched the journey of John W. Ransone (11th–16th), in Across the Atlantic. Micaliz was here (18th–23rd), with "two tons of scenery," and with William Cattell as star — Cattell protesting in a letter to the Eagle that though, if he were a Jew, he would be proud of the heritage, nevertheless he was not, as the Eagle had announced, of Jewish descent. Personally, as I never heard of the man before, I remain strangely unmoved by his protestation. Ten Nights in a Bar-Room provided gloom for October 25th–30th; into that week also the Eagle crowds a performance by W. J. Fleming of Phileas Fogg, in Around the World in Eighty Days. The energetic Standard was giving two "shows" a day. The Leonzo Brothers and their canine actors devoted early November (1st–6th) to the thrilling The Dog Spy. The World, acted by I know not what ambitious souls, carried November (8th–13th) to a star engagement of the unyielding Daniel E. Bandmann, supported by the former comic opera beauty, Louise Beaudet, in The Corsican Brothers (15th), Hamlet (16th), etc. The Eagle records are confusing, because so meagre.

Arizona Joe filled Black Hawks (November 22nd–27th) with enough shoutings and shootings to gratify the most eager readers of Beadle's Dime Novels. Perhaps he shot "drama" off the stage; at any rate, the Eagle cries no further Standard wares till December 13th–18th, when "Variety" possessed the house, with Kokin Segowa (Mephistopheles cabinet of juggling and mystery), Carlisle, May Arnott, J. W. Hampton and his dogs, Homer and Lingard, H. J. Campbell and Gibbons and Harty (sic). This sort of entertainment continued (December 20th–25th), with Morosco and Gardner, Thomas and Watson, the Three Franklins, Billy Bryant, the Kingford Sisters and the Coloured Twilight Quartet. But "drama" returned, with Crimes of a Great City (December 27th, 28th, 29th) and Burr Oaks (30th, 31st, January 1st). I ought to regret my inability to supply the names of the actors; probably my reader rejoices that I cannot. But I am pleased to meet in this welter of unimportant things the familiar Fannie Louise Buckingham, in the thrice-familiar Mazeppa (January 3rd–8th); even N. S. Wood, returning (10th–15th) with his also very familiar Boy Scout and Boy Detective. I do not know Horace Lewis, but I know too well his medium (17th–22nd), The Count of Monte Cristo. The Standard Museum was a cheap theatre and it certainly provided shopworn goods. Lewis, for the second half of his week gave Two Nights in Rome. The week of January

24th–29th provided The Ranch King, with J. D. Clifton, May Treat and performing dogs; and February came in (January 31st–February 5th) with the ancient sorrows of Bertha, the Sewing Machine Girl. Possibly some of the auditors read The New York Weekly, in which Bertha originally plied that machine. After all, I am not sure that Bertha actually stitched, as announced the week of January 24th; on the 31st the Eagle merely announces, for the Standard, Edward Earle and Donald Melville.

I am surprised to find at the Standard two more delicate delights from the Madison Square Theatre repertoire: Young Mrs. Winthrop (February 7th, 8th, 9th) and Hazel Kirke (10th, 11th, 12th). George and Ada Morton revealed His Sin (February 14th–19th) and the Eagle cruelly remarks of Morton, "His Sin consists in producing the play." As to the week of February 21st–26th the Eagle leaves me in the dark (please remember that I am indebted to notes in that paper for my information); but Without a Home (February 28th–March 5th) restored to my memory Minnie Oscar Gray, W. T. Stephens and their clever dog actors. Sheehan and Coyne, the "original ash-box inspectors," fresh from "Variety," came (March 7th–12th) in a sort of Harrigan piece, Grogan's Elevation, one scene of which represented Shantytown by Moonlight — surely something poetical for the proletariat. Loudon McCormick (sic) appeared, on March 14th, in '49, and, before the week ended, in The Danites and The Black Diamond; I fear he was no McKee Rankin; his company included Edwin Clifford, George Mortimer, H. M. Perrin and Charles Crolius — names that mean to me nothing at all. The week of March 21st–26th brought in a versatile Louise Arnott, in Fun on the Bristol, Leah, the Forsaken and The Little Detective. And the undying, venerable Under the Gaslight again brightens this murky narrative (March 28th–April 2nd) with a cast including Mr. and Mrs. Clinton Hall, Frank Bell, Ward and Lynch, Charles T. Nichols, Eugenia Carr, Henrietta Floyd and Lizzie Newell, if indeed those minor lights could illumine anything.

Mixed pleasures were the lure on April 4th–9th: Leonzo Brothers and their dogs, Bryant and Saville, and Captain N. H. Chittenden, showing his Alaska Indian Village. The Tourists in a Pullman Palace Car stopped here for the week of April 11th–16th, accompanied by Julie ("ceiling walker"), Morello Brothers and Kirke and Clarke. April 18th–23rd brought a third visit of N. S. Wood, in successive renditions of Jack Sheppard, The Boy Scout, and Nan, the Newsboy. A note in the advertisement for his last day gives the only gleam of humour I have found in this dreary story of the Standard Museum. "He will give his photographs to the lady patrons and will then sail for Europe" — surely a discreet departure, not to say escape. I ask the reader to remember the early days of Wood — his début as Hamlet, his short career at Wallack's, his too ready decline to the Bowery, and this ending at the cheap Standard Museum; it saddens me. A Western play, Checkered Life, introduced (April 25th–30th) Edith and Charles Crolius, the former of whom we have long known and the latter of whom we recently met in this very Standard. Metropolitan Minstrels opened May (2nd–7th), accompanied by Blatt, "the iron-muscled cannonball catcher," who caught the deadly missiles as shot from a cannon—a feat not new, but ever thrilling. The following week (9th–14th) brought Joseph J. Sullivan, in The Black Thorn, his support including Spencer Pritchard, Evelyn Knapp, and the non-Jewish William Cattell. "I can no more" for this home of cheaper drama; in fact I can only apologise for drowning my reader's fancy in its shabby history. Of course any reader, unless his research-instinct is incurable, may blithely skip the record.

Brooklyn Museum, 1886–1887

Uffner's Brooklyn Museum and Art Gallery, Fulton Street and Flatbush Avenue, and therefore the old Music Hall, opened on November 22nd, with two entertainments daily and with curiosities galore in the Barnum-like museum proper. On the stage John W. Jennings played Christopher Blizzard, in Confusion, associate players being Hal Clarendon, Horace P. Harrison, Aimée Hercht, and Fannie Fuller. As Uffner, Robbins and Co.'s Brooklyn Museum, the place advertised for November 29th–December 4th, James F. Crossen, in A Celebrated Case. Constance Hamblin, long out of first-class theatres, was here for December 6th–11th, offering, for daily matinées, East Lynne, and, for evening entertainment, its French cousin, Miss Multon. On December 13th The Private Tutor began a week's sojourn, and then I discover that Sylvester Bleeker, of the long ago was superintendent of the Museum. In The Private Tutor, according to the Eagle, appeared Fred Long, Evelyn Evans, E. L. Lawrence, Helen Mortimer and Marion Russell, faintly praised by the Eagle as "thoroughly up in her lines." The cast, in the Brooklyn Times, is entirely different. Our Goblins, or, Fun on the Rhine, now, of course, without Francis Wilson, but with Charles Tyrrell and Beatrix Hamilton, was joy-contriver for Christmas week (December 20th–25th). The following holiday week (December 27th–January 1st) brought Welch and Thomas's Operatic Minstrels, in Fayette Welch, Bobby Newcomb, Frank Moran, Eugene and Collard. Tripartite pleasure for January 3rd–8th presented minstrels, Schlam, the wizard, and Davys's Royal Marionettes (marionettes seem ever to have been "royal"). Welch and Thomas's Minstrels were named in the bills for January 10th–22nd (two weeks), and component factors were Charlie Reynolds and our old watermelon man, J. W. McAndrews. At a venture, one might choose this Museum in preference to the Standard, just discussed.

One of the Bravest, with no actors advertised, played twice daily during the week of January 24th–29th; yet somehow the Eagle works in reference

[374]

to Lillie Hamilton, Charles McCarthy, William Cronin (as the Irish woman) and H. S. Parker.   W. H. Rightmire brought in, for January 31st–February 5th, The Two Wanderers "with specialty stars in new acts."   We almost hit the region of the stars (February 14th–19th), with Edwin F. Mayo, in Davy Crockett.   The place evidently wandered vaguely to a new policy — or perhaps no policy.   Announced (February 21st–26th) as J. W. Randolph's Brooklyn Museum, it offered George Murphy (once of Murphy and Shannon) and Jennie Elbon, in Rudolph's Ambition, just another of those amplified vaudeville sketches.   The Wall Street Bandit, with Atkins Lawrence (a good-looking man who never achieved) came in for February 28th–March 5th); with him were Harold Forsberg, Anna Boyle and Florence Stover.   The Brooklyn Musée (*sic*) offered for March 7th–12th, Pauline Harvey as Yum-Yum, in The Mikado.   Yet a Dog Show, sponsored by the Argosy Kennel Club, occupied, during that week, some portion of the building.

"Variety," not of the best class, but good in its way, gave us, for March 14th–19th, Gilfort Brothers, Miranda and Celeste, Morosco and Gardner, M. G. Pettingill and his dogs, the Forresters, Daly and Devere, Julia Wilson, Ray Wilson and Billy Robinson.   The Stranglers of Paris thrilled for March 21st–26th; Alfred and Laura Miaco, in pantomime (March 28th–April 2nd) effaced from our minds all that Parisian horror.   More "Variety" held thoughtless minds (April 4th–9th) with Catherine Nelson's dogs and birds, Belzac (slack wire), Fostelle and Emmett, Harry Rogers, the Stanwood Sisters, the Elwood Brothers, John Devoy, and Shepard (*sic*) and Whitney. Gilfort's Big Novelty Show and the Robinson-St. Clair Dramatic Company in Ben Bolt constituted the attraction for April 11th–16th.   And Uncle Tom's Cabin (18th–23rd) almost closed the house.   On Sunday, the 24th, the Eagle stated that the Museum "closed its doors last night for the season. It is rumored that the attempt to carry on this place of amusement has resulted in heavy loss."   But the management struggled on for another week (April 25th–30th) of Uncle Tom, Eva, Eliza, the ice and the pursuing villains and hounds.   And Peck's Bad Boy, by the Guinness Company, tried its fate for May 2nd–7th, and that really closed the house on a precarious season.

BROOKLYN ATHENÆUM, 1886–1887

The Athenæum, that season, like the Academy of Music, was haven for amateur actors; but so many entertainments, musical and otherwise, used its stage that it becomes a suitable subject for a separate essay.   On September 28th, Ira H. Moore, the manager of the house proffered, for the benefit of the sufferers from the Charleston earthquake, a performance by amateurs of Love's Sacrifice.   I leap thence to November 5th for a Kirmess given by the Guild of St. Paul's P. E. Church.   More amateurs reported, on November 17th, when the Arcadian Dramatic Society gave Hazel Kirke, with S. G. Frost as Dunstan of the iron will, J. C. Costello as the rather careless Arthur, E. A. Slattery as Pittacus Green, J. J. Breen as Aaron Rodney, J. J. Sullivan (could this be Joe J. of that patronymic?) as Met Miggins, Ada Austin as Hazel, Molly Riely (*sic*) as Mercy Kirke, and Miss K. T. Lee as Dolly.

The Booth Dramatic Society, for its second play of the season (I did not find the first), acted (November 30th) Wybert Reeve's drama, Parted, presenting therein William H. Masterson. F. E. Armstrong, G. E. Van Nostrand, W. J. McCahill, William M. Caldwell, George P. Kavanagh, N. W. Kellock, Fanny Rorke, Miss L. F. Healey and Miss E. Landwersick (*sic*). Thick and fast they came. The Melpomene Society, on December 2nd, revived Charles Reade's adaptation from Tennyson, the pastoral Dora, with John F. Dyer as Farmer Allen, Thomas T. (*sic*) Hayden as William, S. C. Austin as Luke, Ida Leon as the child, Lizzie Wallace as Dora and Georgie Wallace as Mary Morrison. I am interested to see that these amateurs passed from one society to another; after all, I suppose, they were all friends in a friendly city. On December 8th, the Dunreath Dramatic Society gave War to the Knife, with Louis A. Adams, George F. Corby, George H. Dickinson, F. W. Shipman, D. M. Peters, Jennie Nagle, Ella Moores (*sic*), Nellie Gurney and Sadie Hodgson as contestants in the struggle. December 10th found the Fenelon Literary Society playing Clouds, with P. C. Gibbons, M. E. O'Neil, A. Somers, M. J. Colligan, Ida Wachholder, Kitty Kelly and many more trying to prove their histrionic ability. And December 12th (Sunday) was devoted to Alabama Jubilee Selections by the Rainbow Quartet, an illustrated lecture somehow fitting into the scheme. But the 22nd whirled us back to dramatics, with the Nautilus Boat Club's performing of McBeth. Harry F. Waring had the title-rôle, L. Firuski was Lady McBeth, John A. Pollack Banquo, Marcus Donnally (*sic*) Malcolm, and Henry W. Sched McDuff. The Booth Dramatic Society, on January 11th, actually tried something new — Sydney Rosenfeld's play, The Ulster, acted by McCahill, Masterson, Kavanagh, T. T. Hayden, W. F. Wells, J. T. Nicholson, Misses K. Kelly, F. Rorke, E. Landwersick and L. F. Healey. The Brooklyn Times lists for middle or later January a performance by the Leonardis Dramatic Society of Our Boys, with M. J. Savage, E. J. Haverly, W. J. O'Leary, M. J. McKenna, J. A. Kerwin, D. J. Farrell, Annie O'Neill, Katie Leibold, Maggie McKenna and Mamie Courter, a group seen, according to the same paper, in early December, at Knickerbocker Hall.

The Melpomene group were here again, on January 24th, with My Fairy of the Glen (acted by Ernest O. Jacobson, Frank Norris, Frank J. Oliver, Jennie Cochrane and Lizzie Wallace) and Box and Cox (with William M. Campbell, Fred C. Randall and Annie Hyde). On February 21st the Mel-

[376]

pomene was to stage The Guv'nor. February 15th again saw the Booth Dramatic Society, this time in Mrs. Walthrop's Boarders, the leaders of the cast being W. F. Wells, W. J. McCahill, Edna Wallack and Libbie Healey. "Professor" Townsend, mesmerist, had the entire week of February 21st–26th. One of three things may account for the lacuna now impending: Lent may have caused the amateurs to repent; or the Eagle may have ceased to note their activities; or my eye may have failed to catch in the ragged wood-pulp file of the Eagle, in the Public Library in New York, items that I desire for March and April. At all events I must wait till March 29th for the Melpomene double bill of One Touch of Nature, with Charles Rohlfs and Marie Lame (in the rôles so often played by J. H. Stoddart and Maud Harrison), supported by Frank J. Oliver and William Mitchell Campbell; and Chiselling, a one-act farce by Joseph H. Dilley, acted by Thomas T. Hayden, Albert Meafoy, Ernest O. Jacobson, Jennie Cochrane and Lizzie Wallace. April 6th found the Arcadians here, in The Felon's Bond, signed and sealed by J. J. Breen, George T. Janvrin, J. J. Carboy, John F. Connellan, William M. Caldwell, James Luddy, J. J. Sullivan, Alice Raymond, Christine McDowell and Miss M. Caldwell. Like the quality of mercy, these long catalogues of amateurs are more blessèd to give than to receive. On April 12th, Ira H. Moore and other non-professionals tried to benefit E. F. DeNyse, with The Merchant of Venice. The Arcadian, on the 13th, gave The Dumb Witness, with Messrs. Breen, Janvrin, J. J. Carboy, Alice Raymond, players listed for performance, in the Athenæum just a week previously.

On the 15th, the Odette Society turned for the first time to dramatics and gave Lady Odette, written for the society by Arthur J. Westermyr (sic), leading parts falling to the author, H. H. Tilford, E. S. Greene, O. R. Robinson, E. P. Smith, F. B. Hyde, C. A. Alger, Mrs. M. M. Goldzisher, Nellie Garner and Nellie Hawkins. I almost faint with apprehension of the way in which the amateurs' names will weigh down the index of this volume. But I must persevere, recording the performance of the Leonardis Association "of the Eastern District," on April 20th — May Blossom, with M. J. McKenna, J. J. Moran, Jr., W. J. O'Leary, E. J. Haverly, Annie O'Neill (as May), Sarah Curran, Kate Leibold, &c. And April 27th was very amateur-dramatic, with St. Paul's Lyceum doubling David Garrick and The Golden Farmer. This ends my knowledge of that outbreak of amateurism in 1886–87 at the Athenæum, except that the Brooklyn Times announces, for May 4th, the Arcadians, in Hazel Kirke.

HISTORICAL HALL, 1886–1887

Historical Hall, the auditorium in the building of the Long Island Historical Society, at Pierrepont and Clinton Streets, became increasingly im-

[377]

portant as the scene of lectures, concerts and other sources of intellectual or musical pleasure; in fact, in such regards it seemed to supplant the Athenæum, which, as we know, had become a seat for amateur actors. Sarah Cecil began the season at this hall, on September 27, 1886, her concert also promising Isidora Martinez, Adolph Glose, Claude W. Madden and the Weber Male Quartet. The silence of the Eagle, thereafter, leaves me in doubt, until November 4th, when came a Peak Sisters entertainment, with Laura B. Phelps (violin), Grace D. Rider (elocutionist) and a ladies' quartet —surely a harmless evening's worth. On November 17th, Minnie C. Dorlon presented herself as an elocutionist, supported by Mrs. E. J. Grant (soprano), the Brunswick Quartet and Robert Thallon (accompanist). On the 22nd, Professor Darwin G. Eaton lectured on The Sandwich Islands. Laura B. Phelps (violinist) gave (December 2nd) the first of a series of "classical and popular matinées," her assistants including Clementine Lasar, Maud Morgan and F. V. Davies. The evening of the 2nd surrendered the stage to a piano recital by Carlos Sobrino, with Henrietta Beebe singing. On the 6th, Paul Tidden played the piano, in selections from Schumann, Chopin, Tchaikowsky and Liszt. Annie L. Walker's concert, on the evening of the 7th, passed into musical history (or limbo), her assistants including Maud Thorburn, J. Williams Macy, Mr. and Mrs. J. W. Parson Price, &c. And so we approach Christmas, with a prayer to Santa Claus.

Thus far the offerings of the hall were not of compelling interest. The first concert of the Brooklyn String Quartette (*sic*) occurred on December 15th, proudly announcing the members as Carl Otremba, Albert Arnheim, Ludwig Penzkofer (he was "from the Court theatre, Munich") and Ernest Reineccius. Tillie Crane assisted. On the 16th, Carlos Sobrino and Carl Dufft provided the musical feast. Augusta (*sic*) M. Fischer's piano recital was scheduled for January 4th; and the 6th brought the second concert of Laura B. Phelps. For the Franklin Literary Society, at this time, Charles H. Hodges, "of the New York Bar," attempted A Vindication of Richard III. The Groschel Conservatory Instructors announced for January 10th a Chamber Music Soirée, with aid from Henry Rusack (tenor), Mrs. S. Groschel Chadick (piano), Edward Herrmann (violin), Miss E. Bryan (piano), Manuel Knauth (viola) and Emil Schenck ('cello). Really, if the hall could provide nothing more alluring than its offerings thus far in 1886–87, I am almost sorry I opened it to my reading public. Georgia Weld, on January 18th, began a series of four concerts, displaying to the Eagle a "bad vibrato." With her were Julie de Ryther (*sic*), Atherton Furlong (a tenor who never advanced very far), and Francis Walker (bass). Miss Weld's second concert was listed for February 1st. On January 3rd, Laura Phelps made her third effort, with support from Edith Wendell (soprano), William T. Angel (baritone), E. L. Phelps (flute) and H. E. H. Benedict (piano); her fourth came duly on February 24th, with Miss

[378]

Wendell, A. S. Caswell's Cæcilian Chorus, and Walter Haan (piano). Perhaps four were enough.

Offerings at Historical Hall went in series. The Froebel Society came forth in five concerts for the building fund of the Froebel Academy; the dates were to be March 7th, 15th, 19th, 24th and 31st. On the last date, Mr. and Mrs. Emil Gramm and A. Hartdegen were to appear. H. O. C. Kortheuer's concert, announced for March 9th, was postponed to April 20th; the poor man was ill. Stewart L. Woodford lectured, on March 14th, on the ever-during character of Lincoln. The pupils of A. Arnold's Conservatory of Music displayed their talents, native and acquired, with Marie Gramm and Emil Schenck to make notable for them their evening of March 23rd. The Yale Glee and Banjo Clubs were here on April 13th. Alexander Lambert (pianist) and Hélène Maigille came for April 29th. April 30th brought the Columbia College Glee Club, and May 3rd was devoted to the efforts of Lillie Tavernier, J. Williams Macy and others even less known. With that feeble clutch on the life-line, the hall sank into the desuetude of summer.

ASSOCIATION (Y.M.C.A.) HALL, 1886–1887

Perhaps Association Hall (Bond Street, near Fulton) may restore our drooping spirits. It first summons, by Eagle advertisements, for November 2nd, when appeared the New York Philharmonic Club, assisted by Annie Louise Tanner. Robert James Lee's Illustrated Historical Lectures began, on November 22nd, with Lights and Shadows of London; his Through London with Dickens followed on the 29th, and The Tower of London, on December 6th. On November 30th, Reverend John Kir, D. D., "of Ireland," metaphorically crossed the Channel from Lee and London, and lectured on Ireland and Irishmen at Home; Henry Ward Beecher was to preside and speak. On December 8th, Annie Teresa Kemp (elocutionist) gave a concert, with Annie Louise Tanner, Abbie A. Kemp (pianist) and Eugene Weiner (flute). The Mendelssohn Quintette (*sic*) Club of Boston performed, on December 7th, with, as soloist, Alice Ryan (soprano). Boston had sent to us, in other times, more enticing gifts.

February 1st introduced the Schubert Quartet, and, so far as I could learn from the Eagle, began a month's reign of silence. On March 1st, the New York Philharmonic Club again performed, announcing its members as Richard Arnold, Friedhold Hermann, Emil Schenck, Eugene Weiner, Philip Farber and August Kalhof (*sic*). Henrietta Beebe was soloist. Viola Gilbert's Illustrated Tableaux and Songs on Mary, Queen of Scots, brightened (I hope) the evening of April 21st; on the 27th, Mrs. S. Sager Wiener lectured on A Moral Revolution, and "the celebrated Victor B. Wiener, the young pianist, will render some choice selections." Who possibly could

[379]

have bought tickets for that family party? The Bryant Literary Society brought in a notable group, on April 21st, in Ella Earle, Anna Bulkley Hills, Arthur D. Woodruff (tenor), Francis Fischer Powers, Michael Banner and Harry Rowe Shelley. I am interested in the effort, on May 5th (evening), of George Edgar to give Bible Readings from Bethlehem to Calvary, with 75 reproductions of famous pictures; interested merely because I remember when Edgar tried to be a tragic actor (or rather, an actor in tragedy). May 9th brought Phillips's Around the World in a Chariot of Song; and a "powerful lime light" was to illustrate songs and tour. Well, that excitement allows me to leave, for 1886–87, the hospitable Association Hall.

MISCELLANY, BROOKLYN, 1886–1887

The scattering entertainments of Brooklyn may be quickly dismissed. Zipp's Casino, Elm Place, re-opened on September 13th, and thereafter, throughout the season, provided for customers concerts (especially on Sunday nights) with a Ladies' Vienna Orchestra, occasional soloists, Ada Melrose, Miss P. Harvey, &c. The Palace Rink (Clermont Avenue, near Myrtle) opened, by request, on October 14th and 16th, causing me to wonder what had happened to the former craze for roller skating. And, on October 16th, in City Hall Square, was exhibited a Battle of Gettysburg, in a specially constructed pavilion; it remained throughout the winter, rivalling, perhaps, the popularity of a similar panorama in Manhattan.

Now we may inaugurate the round of entertainments in churches and minor halls by the incitement of October 20th, when the Old Bushwick Union held forth in concert in the Sunday School Room of the Old Bushwick Church (just on the borders of Williamsburgh). The Greenwood Literary Club, at about this time was to perform — the Eagle states not where — The Colleen Bawn, all for the benefit of South Brooklyn Catholic Schools. On October 21st a concert at Plymouth Church involved Eleanor Hooper (violin), Charlotte Welles (organ) and Alice Milne (soprano). The Brooklyn Männerchor invaded Sängerbund Hall, on October 27th, with a concert and ball, Minnie Dilthey, Carl Dufft and Fritz Handel (tenor) singing; this was to benefit the Charleston Sufferers. On the 25th, at the Columbia Conservatory of Music, Bedford Avenue and Fulton Street, Dr. Eugene Thayer, "one of the ablest of Boston Musicians," was to attempt to establish his claims to that proud title in the first of four free organ recitals. Harry Rowe Shelley's organ recitals were also operating, his first aided by Charlotte Welles and the popular baritone, Francis Fischer Powers; at Shelley's second recital, November 8th, he was assisted by Whitney Mockridge and Charlotte Welles (piano). But some hearts leaped up when they beheld St. Peter's Dramatic Association, at St. Peter's Academy, honour Gilbert and Sullivan with The Mikado (November 8th and 9th) and The

Pirates of Penzance (November 10th and 11th). Brooklyn should, I repeat, have been designated the City of Amateurs. Mid-November found, in St. Peter's Chapel, Reverend Lindsay Packer, lecturing on Ireland. At the Tabernacle, on November 25th, appeared the Courtney Quartet, Mrs. Josie Cook (piano), J. Williams Macy (humourist and buffo) and Claude W. Madden (violin).

That 25th (it was Thanksgiving) was busy. Will Carleton, then a popular poet, occupied the pulpit of the Summerville M. E. Church (Washington Street and Greene Avenue) with his lecture, The Chain of Success. The Washington Avenue Baptist Church (Washington and Gates Avenue) also piously opened for a concert with Laura S. Groves (contralto), Mrs. Henry Firth Wood (elocutionist), Maud Morgan, the Young Apollo Club, W. H. Rieger (tenor), Michael Banner and H. E. H. Benedict — a surprisingly able group, really something to be thankful for. The Eagle of November 26th bears tidings of illustrated lectures by Professor Crosswell (Cromwell, undoubtedly) to be given every Wednesday evening at the Baptist Church, Pierrepont and Clinton Streets). It also cites a U. S. Grant literary and dramatic entertainment and ball, providing the ineffable novelty of Robert Macaire and a host of amateurs in singing, reciting, etc. On December 2nd, a new organ opened at Dr. Cuyler's Church, Marie Van, J. H. Brewer, Miss Wilkinson, &c., assisting. And the Palace Rink began, on December 7th, the exhibition of an Aztec Fair and a Mexican Village, with a Mexican Fandango Orchestra to thrill us along the spine.

The Washington Avenue Baptist Church opened, December 9th (this time for the Mission Light Society) with promises of Clementine Lasar, Francis Fischer Powers, Marshall P. Wilder, Rosa King, Frank Slocum and Mattie Perry. Dr. Mary A. Allen lectured at various churches during the week of December 13th–18th. On the 13th, the Amaranth Society, in their parlours in Court Street, gave an informal reception, presenting Miss Gammon and Dell Thompson (readers), &c. At the New York Avenue M. E. Church Will Carleton, on December 14th, repeated The Chain of Success. St. Paul's Lyceum, on December 20th and 21st, gave Richelieu, as rehearsed by George Becks; on the 27th, St. Anthony's Young Men's Union, Parish Hall (Greenpoint), staged Caught by the Cuff and Barney, the Baron. The New Year furnished George William Curtis's lecture on Wendell Phillips (January 4th, at the Second Unitarian Church, Clinton and Congress Streets); the New York University Glee Club (January 7th, Unity Church, Gates Avenue and Irving Place); the Sängerbund (at Sängerbund Hall, January 10th), assisted by the Meigs Sisters, Neuendorff's orchestra, William Bartels, and W. Groschel, leader of the choir — this being the twenty-fifth and jubilee concert and ball of the Bund; the Clio Dramatic Society, in Better than Gold (January 12th, at Rivers's Academy); a concert by the Kofler Ladies' Quartet (in mid-January, at the Franklin Avenue Presbyterian Church); the Emerald Ball (January 18th, at Jefferson Hall, Adams and Willoughby Streets); an Athletic Tournament of the Varuna Boat Club (January 22nd, at Sängerbund Hall); and Albion W. Tourgee, author of the much-discussed A Fool's Errand, in a lecture on The Uses and Abuses of Dirt (Washington Avenue Church, January 31st). On that 31st, also, the Brooklyn Quartett Club had a masked ball, at Sängerbund Hall. The new year was busy, if not highly important.

Except for the Stiftungsfest and Schwesternfest of the Brooklyn Lessing Loge, No. 608, in Sängerbund Hall, in February (early) and except for entertainments cited under other captions, I found nothing for February until Washington's Birthday burgeoned in bliss of anticipated pleasures. At the Tabernacle we were to hear Henry Eyre Browne (organ) Peter Ali (cornet), Laura S. Groves, Dell Thompson (elocutionist), Benjamin Wechsler (violin), R. H. Mayland (flute) and the Perry Brothers (hand and sleigh bells); Miss Anna Morgan, of the Chicago Conservatory, and Lillian Blauvelt (violin) were to possess the pulpit of the New York Avenue M. E. Church; and Edward Everett Hale was to lecture, at the Brooklyn Institute, on The Human Washington. Gettysburg was still in City Hall Square. On March 10th, as I learn from the Progresso Italo-Americano, the Società di Mutuo Soccorso of Brooklyn held its fifth annual ball, at Sängerbund Hall, with Luigi Conterno to supply the music.

During the week of March 14th–19th, Lillie Devereux Blake, once prominent in the conflict, spoke, at Conservatory Hall, on Woman Suffrage; A. W. Gleason also spoke, and Dell Thompson, May Hall (singer) and Nettie Boell (pianist) contributed their quota of entertainment. On the 16th, A. P. Burbank, in the First Reformed Church, gave A Life for Love (founded on A Tale of Two Cities); Minnie Ashton and Mrs. Flocken sang. At Sängerbund Hall, on March 21st, the Brooklyn Turn-Verein danced in masquerade. At the First Baptist Church, Clinton and Pierrepont Streets (Brooklyn's very religious neighbourhood), March 30th brought a concert to Eleanor B. Hooper, at which ready aid was promised from Marie Van, Charlotte Welles, Francis Fischer Powers, S. B. Mills, A. Hartdegen and the Dudley Buck Quartet—rather good, one thinks. On April 1st and 16th, J. M. Loretz, Jr., gave organ recitals, for fifteen cents admission, in the North Reformed Church, Clermont Avenue, near Willoughby. Francis Fischer Powers, on point of departure for Europe, appeared at the Pierrepont Street Baptist Church, in company with Miss McCollom (mezzo), Ella Earle, Anna Bulkley Hills, Michael Banner (the inevitable), Harry Rowe Shelley, Emilio Agramonte, Reinhold L. Herman (director) and members of the New York Mendelssohn Glee Club. At least that starry host was promised in preliminary advertisements. Certainly Brooklyn furnished a rich supply of amateur actors and "elocutionists"—somewhat in excess of the demand, one might conjecture. But the Barnum and London United Shows (April 25th–

30th) may have brought welcome variety, at Putnam and Sumner Avenues. And Zipp's Casino, still operative, was probably not super-intellectual in allure.

April departed with showers of blessings, such as they were. On the 21st, the First Reformed Church, Bedford Avenue and Clymer Street, for the benefit of the Eastern District Dispensary and Hospital, advertised an address by Seth Low and music by Ella Earle and Daisy Bowerman (a young violinist). The Clarendon Literary Union, on the 25th, acted Single Life, with, in chief rôles, Peter J. Farrell, James J. Powers, Maggie Caldwell, Sarah Taws, Aggie Farrell and Thomas J. Bohen. The Melpomene Society, also on the 25th, held its last reception, at Rivers's Academy; and the same fated evening found the Halcyon Opera Association at Meserole Turn Hall, and the Brooklyn Quartett Club at Sängerbund Hall, with Dora Friedel, W. Bartels and Frl. Mickel to assist. On the 27th, at the home of Mrs. Robert Goodwin, Montague Street, Lillie P. Berg's concert enlisted brave aid in Sarah Cowell and Francis Fischer Powers. And, at the Everett Assembly Rooms, on the 29th, Mme. de Fere's pupils and friends held forth in Lightheart's Pilgrimage and other adventures. I feel that this narrative, like Julius Cæsar, has the falling sickness.

The Adelphi Academy, on the afternoon of May 7th, must have amused whoever liked that sort of thing with Aunt Polly Bassett's Singin' Skewl; but we were more mature, on the 9th, in Sängerbund Hall, with a concert involving (at least by promise) Ida Klein, and several Mollenhauers — Ida, Henry ('cello), and Louis (violin), with Robert Thallon (accompanist). At St. Malachi Hall (Atlantic and Smith Avenues), the Young Men's Catholic Lyceum Association acted The Tricky Wig and David Garrick. Far better entertainment, me' judice, came, on an evening in the week of May 23rd–28th, when, at Remsen Hall, a testimonial to Clementine Lasar-Studwell promised appearances of Ovide Musin, the Meigs Sisters, Whitney Mockridge, Francis Fischer Powers (still not on his way to Europe) and Robert Thallon. With F. Stevens's Bicycle Trip, on the 26th, at the North Reformed Church, I fly from Brooklyn Miscellany for 1886–87, though I must call attention to an early June Fête and Flower Market, in Pierrepont Park, Brooklyn Heights, entrance to which could be reached through the residence of Mrs. S. B. Chittenden, 18 Pierrepont Street. The Boylston Glee Club, the 23rd Regiment Band, the Columbia Zither Trio, and a German Peasant Booth rewarded the patrons — altogether a homelike festivity. On July 14th, at Ridgewood Park, the Union des Sociétés Françaises de Brooklyn celebrated.

A Plattdeutsches Volksfest held sway, August 14th, 15th, 16th and 17th, in Ridgewood Park; there, on September 11th, 12th, 13th and 14th, a Schwaben Volksfest appealed to natives of Swabia. And the Italian influence was in the ascendant, on August 17th, when the Società Italiana

[383]

Principe di Napoli, of Brooklyn, crossed, for its first Festa Campestre, to Manhattan and the Schützen Park, at 50th Street and Third Avenue.

Brooklyn Philharmonic, 1886–1887

Orchestral concerts are the one form of entertainment that, I believe, show improvement (1941) over similar offerings of 1886. Yet were the Philharmonic concerts in New York and in Brooklyn attractive in that earlier day. The Brooklyn Philharmonic, directed by Theodore Thomas, began with the rehearsal and concert of October 29th and 30th, proffering the Second Symphony of Brahms, a Symphonic Prologue to Othello (by Arnold Krug) and Beethoven's Fifth Symphony. Pauline L'Allemand sang an air from Rubinstein's Dæmon and one from Weber's Inez de Castro. A long delay, possibly due to Thomas's activities with the National Opera Company, forced us to wait till December 17th and 18th, when a Liszt Memorial brought his St. Elizabeth, sung by Emma Juch, Anna Lankow, Max Heinrich, Franz Remmertz and J. Allen Preisch. The programme for January 17th and 18th included Mozart's G minor Symphony, Schumann's in C major, and Joseffy in a Rubinstein concerto.

Lilli Lehmann magically brightened the programme of February 12th, with Schubert's Gretchen am Spinnrade and the finale of Die Götterdämmerung (a year before she sang in that opera at the Metropolitan). The orchestra at this concert performed Schubert's Rosamunde overture and Beethoven's Eroica. For March 11th and 12th, Thomas gave the first American performances of Rubinstein's Paradise Lost, with, as soloists, Laura Moore, Mme. Van Zanten, T. J. Toedt, A. E. Stoddard and Myron W. Whitney; though he was not getting on very well with the National Opera, he could draw, for his concerts, on the principal singers of that diminishing venture. The final programmes were "request," and the reader may learn therefrom something of the composite taste of the patrons of the society. In order we heard Beethoven's Pastoral Symphony; the Introduction and Finale of Tristan und Isolde; Liszt's Hungarian Rhapsody, No. 2; Serenade for String Orchestra (by R. Fuchs); and the Ball Scene from Berlioz's Romeo and Juliet — rather an odd assortment. But the six concerts must, as a whole, have been enjoyable.

Lee Avenue Academy, Williamsburgh, 1886–1887

We proceed to the Eastern District of Brooklyn by means of the Lee Avenue Academy, become, in 1886, the leading playhouse of that neighbourhood. It formally re-opened, on August 30th, for a week of Frederic Bryton, in Forgiven. Aimée, in Mam'zelle and Divorçons filled the week of September 6th–11th. J. M. Hardie and Sara von Leer acted (13th–18th) A

Brave Woman; and Celia Alsberg and Lewis Morrison appeared (20th–25th), in Faust and Marguerite. On Thursday, September 23rd, they were advertised to revive Measure for Measure. The White Slave served (September 27th–October 2nd), with May Newman, Marie Hilford, Marie Bates, Frank Foster, J. Weldon, Fred Ross and Charles White.

M. B. Curtis was here for the week of October 4th–9th, in his new Caught in a Corner, which had not yet achieved its New York success of later autumn. The cast included Albina De Mer, C. A. McManus, and Vincent Sternroyd. A Rag Baby, with Frank Daniels, followed (October 11th–16th) and, after that (18th–23rd) Edmund Collier in a succession of Jack Cade, Damon and Pythias, Metamora and Virginius — a Forrest repertoire without Forrest. The Carleton Opera Company rendered, for October 25th–30th, the engaging Nanon, Evangeline, the heifer, the Lone Fisherman and Le Blanc following for November 1st–6th. W. J. Scanlan in Shane-na-Lawn (November 8th–13th); Held by the Enemy (15th–20th); John A. Stevens, in A Great Wrong Righted (22nd–27th); the Zoellner Männerchor (Sunday, the 28th), led by Arthur Claasen, and presenting Carl Steinbuch, Ida Klein and Wilhelm Bartels (tenor); Rose Coghlan in As You Like It (29th, 30th, and matinée, December 1st); The School for Scandal (evening, 1st); London Assurance (2nd); Peg Woffington (3rd, and 4th); and The Lady of Lyons (matinée, 4th); Frank Mayo, in Nordeck (December 6th–11th); A Tin Soldier (13th–18th) with James T. Powers, George C. Boniface, Jr., Flora Walsh, Amy Ames and Ada Deaves — a very good cast; The Shadows of a Great City (20th–25th); F. B. Warde in repertoire, Emmie Wilmot, once of "Variety," playing Queen Elizabeth, in Richard III (this engagement for December 27th–January 1st); Annie Pixley for a week (January 3rd–8th) evenly divided between The Deacon's Daughter and M'liss — lo! reader, I find this curtailed account, rendered possible by the frequent appearances of those attractions, hither and yon, in New York and Brooklyn, very, very easy for my so-often too conscientious pen.

On the Stage (January 10th–15th), E. E. Kidder's farce, presented Leon and Cushman in an effort to reach the stellar grade. Evans and Hoey, in their ever-ready A Parlour Match (January 17th–22nd); Cora Tanner, Maggie Holloway, Leonard Grover, and C. G. Craig, in Alone in London (24th–29th); Thatcher, Primrose and West's Minstrels (January 31st–February 5th); this assortment of bargains made the winter less dull for Williamsburgh. On February 6th, Arthur Claasen gave in the Lee Avenue Academy his second symphony concert, with, if we can believe it, Adele Aus der Ohe and Max Alvary to assist. The Good Friday Spell, from Parsifal, a suite from the Sylvia of Délibes and Beethoven's Pastoral Symphony comprised the programme. Certainly the Eastern District was moving, culturally, toward the Western.

Margaret Mather, then at the height of her renown, such as it was, came

[385]

to the Academy with many incitements: London Assurance and the mad scene from Faust (February 7th and matinée, 12th); The Honeymoon (8th); Romeo and Juliet (9th); As You Like It (10th); The Lady of Lyons (11th); and Leah (evening, 12th), just the repertoire seen, in March, in the Brooklyn Theatre. The Main Line followed, fresh from Brooklyn, on February 14th–19th, with Etta Hawkins, Flora Willis and Harry L. Allen; the author, H. C. De Mille, played Jim Blakely. The Sparks Company, in A Bunch of Keys, included (February 21st–26th) Eugene Canfield, Marietta Nash, Sally Cohen, George Lauri, Murphy, Bell, and Misses Stanhope, Bell and Hart. The Templeton Opera Company officiated, during the week of February 28th–March 5th, in Giroflé-Girofla, Lucille Meredith, Ed Chapman, Alice Vane and J. C. Armand participating in whatever glory accrued. Williamsburgh need not journey to New York for theatrical entertainment.

And here again, on March 7th, something notable came to Williamsburgh, with Mrs. Langtry in A Wife's Peril, followed later in the week by The Lady of Lyons, and, on Saturday evening, by Pygmalion and Galatea. The following week (14th–19th) sank back to Hoodman Blind, which was, throughout what is, in 1941, the Greater New York, displaying remarkable vitality and popularity. In how many theatres was it shown in 1886–87? Richard Mansfield, in Prince Karl, again raised the tone (21st–26th). W. H. Powers, with The Ivy Leaf entered the lists (March 28th–April 2nd), followed (April 4th–9th) by Beatrice Lieb, in Infatuation, her rather capable support including John E. Ince, William Harcourt, Morton Price, Harry Woodruff and Grace Kimball, these last two emerging into their later fame. We, Us and Co. (April 11th–16th), I need hardly inform the reader, brought big W. A. Mestayer and the charming Theresa Vaughn. Tony Hart had the week of April 18th–23rd, in Donnybrook ("from the Brooklyn Theatre"). Herrmann deceived every one (April 25th–30th) with his clever prestidigitation. Erminie, on May 2nd, began an exciting week, with a company including Addie Cora Reed, Belle Thorne, Georgie Dennin, Mary Stuart, Fannie Daboll, Mamie Sutton, G. W. Wade, George Appleby, Samuel Reed, A. W. Maflin, and, as the thieves, W. S. Daboll (so that is why he had left the Casino!) and Solomon — a distribution distinctly inferior to that then current at the Casino. Fanny Davenport came for a week, beginning with Fedora (May 9th, 11th, 13th, and matinée, 14th) and continuing with The School for Scandal (10th), Much Ado about Nothing (12th), and her favourite closing bill of London Assurance and Oliver Twist (evening of the 14th). That impressive engagement ended the season at the Lee Avenue Academy; during its progress Williamsburgh had seen many of the best attractions then in America, all, indeed, except the very best. But I hold back the eager reader with announcement of a playing, on May 16th, of Robert Macaire, by St. Patrick's Literary Society. The Irish amateurs seemed frequently to select venerable relics for their shows.

[386]

NOVELTY THEATRE, WILLIAMSBURGH, 1886–1887

The Novelty, once the leading playhouse of the Eastern District, had sunk in artistic importance. It fell into the control of F. F. Proctor, whom we have known for several seasons as F. F. Levantine, of the vaudeville team of Levantine and Earl. He reduced the admission and strove to make the house entirely "popular." Matinées were advertised for Tuesdays, Wednesdays, Fridays and Saturdays. His attraction for the week of September 6th–11th was The Silver King, with Charles A. Haswin and Eleanor Moretti. The Streets of New York carried on in melodrama (September 13th–18th) with George C. Boniface as Badger. Youth, also from the same region of the drama, excited during September 20th–25th. I wonder why cheap audiences relish thrills and sensations in plays; but we must be fair and admit that Youth and The Silver King had, not many seasons before, enthralled polite Wallack congregations.

James A. Herne was at the Novelty, for October 27th–October 2nd, in his play of The Minute Men, in which he enacted Reuben Foxglove, Mrs. Herne Dorothy and H. M. Pitt Lieutenant Smollett; Josephine Benn also appeared. For October 4th–9th, we had Only a Farmer's Daughter; October 11th–16th went on with melodrama, in J. Z. Little's version of The World (more Wallack *in parvo*). James Claessen, in The Banker's Daughter, filled the week of October 18th–23rd; and Edwin Arden, in Eagle's Nest, "screamed," according to the Eagle, "for gore and revenge" — this Hamlet cry occurring for October 25th–30th. Surely the Novelty had served its patrons with very hot dishes; Marinelli's Cosmopolitan Congress, however, changed the course (November 1st–6th), preparing visitors for the relish of November 8th–13th — The Pulse of New York, to wit. Taken from Life may have been exciting (November 15th–20th); certainly the provision for the 22nd–27th must have roused thunders of applause — Without a Home, acted by Minnie Oscar Gray, W. T. Stephens, and, as the Eagle states, "dogs and several rounds of cartridges." But Ben Maginley, in May Blossom, restored us (November 29th–December 4th) to something like sanity. The attraction for December 6th–11th was Mattie Vickers, dividing the week between Jacquine and Cherub; and, for the 13th–18th, One of the Bravest. P. F. Baker, formerly of Baker and Farron, gave that team's former success, Chris and Lena, John Kernell somehow working into the show for December 20th–25th. Zo-Zo, the Magic Queen, makes me dubious for December 27th–January 1st; Peck's Bad Boy leaves me cold in the cold winter week of January 3rd–8th.

W. C. Cowper's play of Blackmail carried on (January 10th–15th) with a cast including Cowper, Alice Harrison, Carrie Rose, Archibald Cowper and Frederick W. Strong. A Wall Street Bandit, with Atkins Lawrence, Anna Boyle, Porter J. White and J. W. Summers invited during the week of

[387]

January 17th–22nd, Newton Beers, in Lost in London, following for the week of the 24th–29th. Edwin F. Mayo, in Davy Crockett, held the door against the wolves (January 31st–February 5th); Under the Gaslight (February 7th–12th) enlisted Mercedes Malarmi (*sic*), Ada Boshell, Clinton Hall, John A. Toole, William Woodall, Thomas H. Ward, Charles T. Nichols and Frank Bell. This assignment, at least in part, we met later at the Standard Museum. James H. Wallick, in The Cattle King (February 14th–19th); Daniel Sully in The Corner Grocery (21st–26th); the Howard Athenæum Company, with Pettingill, Gale, the Dalys, James F. Hoey, Chevalier Paine, Henshaw and Ten Broeck and others (February 28th–March 5th) — these ancient delights waft us to March 7th–12th, when Tony Farrell and Gustave Frankle (*sic*) revived Skipped by the Light of the Moon. Charles A. Gardner, in Karl, the Peddler (March 14th–19th); Mugg's (*sic*) Landing, with Frances Bishop and Alfred McDowell (21st–26th); Milton Nobles, in Love and Law (March 28th–30th), and in The Phoenix (March 31st–April 2nd) — that succession of inducements shows a rising tendency in the Novelty. John A. Stevens's play, Passion's Slave, aroused us (April 4th–9th), and Tony Denier's Humpty Dumpty carried us into a far different realm (11th–16th). The Wilbur Opera Company transported us even farther from melodrama in a week (18th–23rd) of The Merry War, Three Black Cloaks, The Mikado, Fra Diavolo, Giroflé-Girofla, and The Mascot. The brave souls who attempted that large repertoire were J. E. Conly, H. James, Alfred C. Whelan, Susan Kirwin, Fatmah Diard (a product of cheap Italian opera) and Julian Christian.

Her Atonement (May 2nd–7th) led in all seriousness to Tony Pastor and his company, Harry and John Kernell, Joe Hart, the Julians, Frank Bush, Topack and Steele, Georgie Parker, the Hart Sisters, William De Bar and Isabella Ward, who rang down (so far as I could discover) for the season (which had improved as it progressed) at the Novelty.

People's Theatre, Brooklyn, E.D., 1886–1887

The People's Theatre in the East presented, on Saturday evening, September 4, 1886, J. J. Dowling and Sadie Hasson, in Never Say Die, a play by Edward A. Locke; this filled the week of September 6th, and gave way (13th–18th) to Frank I. Frayne, in Mardo, one of the performers being Ingersoll, "the largest lion in captivity." Shook and Collier's A Prisoner for Life stressed (September 20th–25th) the "great avalanche scene." Passion's Slave ruled the stage from September 27th to October 2nd. The Brooklyn Times advertises no casts. October progressed with Edwin Browne, in Good as Gold (4th–9th); H. C. Miner's Zitka, with Gustavus Levick, Charlotte Behrens and Adelaide (*sic*) Stanhope (11th–16th); Henry Chanfrau in a week (18th–23rd) divided between Kit, the Arkansas Traveller and The

Octoroon; and (25th–30th) with a variety group including Harry Kernell, Baggesen (a human corkscrew), Conway and Leland, Herr Graïs, Mlle. Eichlerette, Sam Ryan, "Professor" Abt and Frank H. and Lillian White — an array decidedly good.

With this taste of "Variety," customers were treated (November 1st–6th) to more of the same sort of feast, furnished by the American and European Novelty Company, including Lolo, Sylvester and Lola ("first appearance in America"), Annie and Andy Hughes, the Archmere Sisters, Edward Leslie, Harrington and Johnson, Marion and Belle, and Booker and Leigh. And still more and very good (November 8th–13th) — Hallen and Hart's First Prize Ideals, listing the Russell Brothers, the Three Fletchers and their skating dog, Julia Wilson, and Fox and Van Auken (horizontal bar performers). A change came (November 15th–20th) with Fisher and Herman's Comedy Company, in A Cold Day, or, the Laplanders. Appropriately as to title, Storm Beaten followed (November 22nd–27th), but Monroe, Rice and Company ended November (29th–December 4th) with the gales of laughter always aroused by their My Aunt Bridget. Out of the glamorous past of the Lydia Thompson days came Pauline Markham, then struggling to "carry on," with (December 6th, 7th and 11th) The Two Orphans; with (December 8th, 9th and 10th) The Ticket of Leave Man; and with (matinées, 7th and 10th) East Lynne. As a boy I once saw this former "toast of the town" as Louise, in The Two Orphans. Formerly queen of burlesque, she could not efface my recollections of Kate Claxton in the same part. N. S. Wood divided the week of December 13th–18th between The Boy Scout of the Sierras and The Boy Detective; let us not forget that he was in the original cast of Diplomacy, in the palmy days of Wallack's. Dominick Murray, once in Hazel Kirke, at the Madison Square Theatre, now (December 20th–25th) played seven characters, in Escaped from Sing Sing, his support including James P. Fleming, T. J. Jackson, George B. Miller, P. F. Hendricks, Theresa Newcombe, Mamie Parker and Clara Otis — only one of whom (Miss Newcombe) has ever floated into my consciousness.

I regret that I cannot supply the casts of The Romany Rye (December 27th–January 1st), or of Miaco's Humpty Dumpty (January 3rd–8th). Le Clair and Russell, on the 10th, began a week of their popular A Practical Joke, and the Kelly, Murphy, Foster and Hughes Company, which we have so frequently met, filled the week of the 17th–22nd. Even more familiar (24th–29th) was George C. Boniface, in The Streets of New York, or, indeed, the Big Four Specialty and Comedy Company of January 31st–February 5th. Edwin R. Lang's Comedy Comiques, in Scheming, may have pleased in the drear week of February 7th–12th, and the European Novelty Company in that of the 14th–19th. And now, perhaps to rouse very young customers, male, the People's provided a fortnight of female burlesquers — Lilly (*sic*) Hall's Burlesque Company and Fannie (*sic*) Bloodgood's Specialty Com-

[389]

pany, for the week of February 21st–26th, and May Adams's Burlesque and Specialty Company for February 28th–March 5th. Obviously "Variety" was in the ascendant. Thomas J. Ryan and Kelly and Ryan's Bards of Tara Combination filled the week of March 7th–12th, and Lilly Clay's Gaiety Company of Ladies Only, in Opera di Camera, that of March 14th–19th. And the Original Big Four Comedy and Specialty Company (returning for March 21st–26th) yielded the stage (March 28th–April 2nd) to the Unique Specialty Company.

I fear the People's Theatre had fallen to the lure; reading its history for those weeks is like traversing the Bowery from theatre to theatre. April revelled in "Variety." Kelly and Murphy, Foster and Hughes's International Star Company returned for the week of April 4th–9th, and the Rentz-Santley bevy of beauty brightened (I hope) that of the 11th–16th. Foreman and Kennette's Electric Novelty Company (18th–23rd) ignites in me no spark of recognition. But I respond immediately to Austin's Australian Novelty Company, with (April 25th–30th) the "peerless" Austin Sisters, and Mlle. Aimée, the "human fly." Louis A. Phillips, the manager of the People's, provided his "Own" Company, for May 2nd–7th, and (May 9th–14th) the People's Star Company, whoever they may have been. Lilly Hall and Fannie Bloodgood came back (May 16th–21st) with all their pulchritudinous array, and remained for a second week (the last of the season). Phillips transferred his allegiance, for the summer, to the Pavilion, Montrose and Union Avenues. Perhaps, at the People's, "Variety" had conquered drama, but it was better in its sphere than, perhaps, the earlier dramatic offerings had been in theirs.

GRAND MUSEUM AND THEATRE, 1886–1887

The week of October 4th–9th proffered the Leonzo Brothers, in The Dog Spy, and, later, in Brother against Brother. Oliver Twist, on the 11th, presented John Hazelrigg as Bill Sykes, Julian Magnus as Fagin, George De la Claire as the Dodger, J. H. Hayes as Bumble, Bertha Welby as Nancy, Kathleen Rowland as Rose, Hattie Worth as Mrs. Corney, and Ida Ward as Oliver. An American Marriage came later in the week. Fannie Louise Buckingham rode the week of October 18th–23rd, in her favourite hobby, Mazeppa. The Pavements of Paris were trod (October 25th–30th) by Harold Forsberg (sic) and Inez Rochelle, a lady, according to the Brooklyn Times, "of rare beauty and undoubted dramatic genius." And there were promised twelve hundred cubic feet of special scenery.

Colville's Original The World filled the week of November 1st–6th, D. E. Bandmann and Louise Beaudet that of the 8th–13th, and Arizona Joe, in Black Hawks, that of November 15th–20th. The Martyr (from the same source as the play of that name, next year, at the Madison Square) began a

[390]

week on the 22nd, with a cast including Mr. and Mrs. Frank Evans, May Estelle, Sadie Dean, W. H. Bokee, Kate Estelle and W. C. Sampson.   I pass to December 6th–11th, when was exhibited a "wonderful mechanical city," and Lottie Church divided the week between the tripartite joys of Unknown, River Pirates and Trix.   Either this house advertised sporadically in the Brooklyn Times, or, thanks to the ragged condition of the files to which I had access, my eye failed to discover certain items.   For either or both of these causes I can find nothing till the week of December 20th, when The Ranch King introduced Harry B. Clifton, May Treat, Harry Adams, and Beth Summerville; then to the week of December 27th, when began Against the Stream, with Frank Aiken, Irene Worrell-Holton, W. J. Holton and Genevieve Rogers; finally to January 3rd–8th, when Barlow Brothers and Frost Minstrel Company invited custom.   On Sunday, January 9th, a "sacred" concert may have edified.   The Davene Specialty Company exploited also (January 10th–15th) Thomas and Watson's Comedy Company and the Wallace Dramatic Company — a triple joy of, to me, dubious significance.   For January 17th–22nd we were offered, not only the European Specialty Company, but the fast-fading glory of Fanny Herring, as Topsy for the first half of the week, and as the French Spy, for the second half.   Two performances daily gave a clue to the quality of the offering.   The Georgia Coloured Jubilee Singers appeared on Sunday, the 16th.   The Cardello and Victorello Company was here for January 24th–29th; also Horace Lewis, in Dan'l Druce.   Dick Gorman, for February 14th–19th (I jump against my will) divided six days between My Hebrew Friend, and Conrad, or, the Hand of a Friend.   Edith Sinclair (sic) arrived for February 21st–26th, in A Box of Cash.   The Stranglers of Paris entered, on February 28th, with "a carload of elegant scenery."   The D. E. Bandman-Beaudet Combination brought almost a carload of plays for the week of March 7th–12th; the evenings were devoted, in turn, to Dead or Alive, A Woman of the People, Richelieu and Othello; the matinées gave, successively, Dead or Alive, The Duke's Daughter, Kathleen Mavourneen and Romeo and Juliet.   Gilfether and Scott's Combination presented, for March 21st–26th, A Messenger from Jarvis Section.

George Morton, in His Sin, filled the week of March 28th–April 2nd, and, if we may believe advertisements, "Sir Roger Tichborne, Bart. will stand at the door, every evening, as Mr. Morton's business representative," and "Lady Tichborne will sing and dance in the play."   There, surely, is drama within drama.   A Checkered Life was, as to title, very congruous, as the offering for April 4th–9th.   And, for April 11th–16th, we sank easily into the fooling of the Metropolitan Minstrel Show.   Admission to this palace of dramatic art was set down at 10 cents.   I found no further cry of goods from the Grand Theatre till May 2nd–7th, when Fanny Herring divided a week between Little Buckshot and Leah, the Forsaken.   These last days of

[391]

the once popular Bowery favourite leave me very sad, with rumination on the tragedy of life. Plasir, Queen of the Miners, with Sarah McVicker, may have been amusing, for May 9th–14th. Again I must skip a week, arriving, on May 23rd–28th, at A Box of Cash. Arizona Joe, in Black Hawks, thrilled along the week of May 30th–June 4th, and George Middleton, in Shadowed Crime, along that of June 6th–11th. I can supply only titles for sultry summer: Lucky Ranch (June 13th–18th); True Irish Hearts (June 20th–25th); Good as Gold (June 27th–July 2nd). Here my packet of news gives out, except for a visit (July 11th–16th), of Oscar R. Gleason, "king of horse-trainers," a king not unknown to our Annals.

PHILLIPS'S PAVILION, 1887

The Summer Pavilion of Louis Phillips into which I inducted the reader for 1886, began its kindly ministrations in the week of May 30th–June 4th, with a curiously named The Twelve Cranks; for June 6th–11th we were treated to the Lester and Williams Specialty Company. Dick Morosco and Kitty Gardner's Specialty Company provided the frothy repast of June 20th–25th, and the Nelson and Lenton Pantomime Company that of June 27th–July 2nd. The Brooklyn Times stops, at this point, our entry to the tent.

WILLIAMSBURGH MISCELLANY, 1886–1887

The Greenpoint Globe allows us to become one of seven thousand, who visited, on October 6, 1886, the new Armoury of the 47th Regiment, in Marcy Street. With a puckish humour Williamsburgh began its new season of miscellany with a summons to Our Little Folks' Concert, held, on October 11th, at the South Second Street Church. Under the auspices of Mansfield Post, a concert and hop, on October 20th, enlivened Grand Army Hall. The same evening harassed us with necessity of deciding whether or not we should go to Knickerbocker Hall to see the Leonardis Dramatic Association perform Miriam's Crime, with Charles A. Webber, Matthew J. McKenna, Michael J. Colligan, John J. Moran, Jr., Francis S. Leibold, Annie O'Neill and Maggie McKenna showing how well Irish-American youth could act. And I am wondering now (1941) if the Annie O'Neill of the cast was the young, pretty actress of that name, admired just a short time later in professional companies. And the next evening forced upon us a choice between Professor Spedon at the Central M. E. Church (South Fifth Street) and a Young People's Association concert at the South Third Street M. E. Church, the latter function offering "Professor" James De Witt and Son (violinist), Charles Price (cornet), Miss E. C. Wolf, J. L. Ewell and W. Washburn. In view of the attractions offered, I am not sure that I might not have chosen to remain at home and read a book. I might also have decided not to hear, on October 29th, the Reverend George E. Reed's lecture, at the Central M. E. Church, on Prairie, Ranch and Geyser. This same Central Church was again geographically educational, on November 4th, with Reverend I. J. Lansing's Lecture on The Glaciers of the High Alps. On November 8th, the Amphion Society held, in their rooms, a "ladies' night," with the Meigs Sisters, Mrs. M. H. Leonard (contralto), Mrs. F. M. G. Emerson (reader) and Miss Rogers (violinist). On the 12th, "Professor" S. T. Ford gave readings that were re-assuringly "select." But November 8th found Chaplain McCabe, at the South Third Street Church, still harping on The Bright Side of Life in Libby Prison — his one and only theme, apparently. Williamsburgh, on an evening in the first week of November, welcomed in Turn Hall a visit of the Thalia Theater troupe, acting Hanni weint und Hansi lacht, as well as Die schöne Galathée; in the casts were Frl. Offeney, Rüdinger, Schnelle, Friese, and Paula von Varndal.

Music, heavenly maid, ventured into the arena, on November 16th, at the First Reformed Church, Bedford Avenue and Clymer Street, Minnie Walsh Ashton being the ministering priestess. With her were Laura Phelps (violin), Keila Engel (contralto), Carrie Louise Ray (elocutionist), George Ellard (tenor), and J. Allen Freeman (bass) — not a bad group. On the 17th, J. Williams Macy and Alfred E. Pearsall joined artistically in St. John's M. E. Sunday School Room. In the same church, on the 25th, appeared the Rutgers College Glee Club and C. F. Underhill (humourist). I see no reason for including notice of a fair, on November 16th, 17th, 18th and 19th, at the Lee Avenue Congregational Church; I therefore pass it by, to cite the blessings of Thanksgiving, November 25th. Alfred E. Pearsall, on that glad day, was again humorous at the Central M. E. Church; the Leonard Street M. E. Church and the Bedford Avenue M. P. Church, just modestly announced concerts, trusting, I suppose, to their respective congregations to oil the financial involvement; C. Mortimer Wiske, too, too much with us, was at the New England Church; and the Old Bushwick Sabbath School Building resounded to the thrilling music of the T. S. Dakin Drum and Flute Corps. This attraction drummed and whiffled again, on the 30th. On the 20th, also, the Ross Street Presbyterian Church promised a concert, with Carrie S. Wall (elocutionist), Minnie Walsh Ashton (soprano), Mrs. Peter Bell (contralto), Sarah E. Harris (pianist), W. F. Tooker (tenor), E. S. Swalm (baritone) and E. H. Harrison (organist). The Christian Social Union made, on the 29th, an "evening of music and mirth"— the latter, I hope, not caused by the former (music). A concert and ball of the Orpheus Association gladdened Turn Hall, on the 29th. At this time, the Reverend H. A. Powell began, in the Lee Avenue Congregational Church, the first of three scheduled lectures. The Williamsburgh Plattdeutscher Club, on Thanksgiving Night, gave a ball in the Eastern District Palace Hall. On December 6th or 7th (the Eagle and the Times

[393]

differ as to the date), the Leonardis Dramatic Society gave Black Sheep, with W. J. O'Leary, M. J. Savage, E. J. Haverly, Jr., Annie O'Neill, Katie Leibold, Maggie McKenna, and Mamie Courter.

We were roused, on December 6th, in Grand Army Hall, by the annual ball of the DeWitt Clinton Drum Corps, enjoying it, perhaps, so much that we could hardly keep awake, on the 7th, at the concert of the Young Apollo Club, with James S. Burdett, at the First United Presbyterian Church, at South First and Rodney Streets, or at the concert, also on the 7th, at the New England Church, by the Cæcilian Society. And George Riddle, on an evening at that season, read at St. John's M. E. Church. For December 9th, the First Baptist Church, Lee Avenue and Keap Street, proffered a lecture by Reverend H. M. Gallagher, on the attractive theme, Men of Mettle. Knickerbocker Hall, on December 15th, provided Marshall P. Wilder and several singers, chiefly sopranos; on the next evening that hall staged a testimonial to E. H. Ducharme, choirmaster of St. Mark's. On December 21st, the Reformed Dutch Church (I hope this was in Williamsburgh) gave, according to the Greenpoint Globe, an organ recital by the Jardine Brothers, one of whom (E. G.) played The Storm, "with a marvellous fidelity to nature." The Garroters, Howells's amusing farce, was acted, on December 22nd, in the Chapel of All Souls Universalist Church, South Tenth Street.

The holidays now lessened outside activities, except Christmas entertainments, chiefly by children, in churches; the South Second Street M.E. Church, for instance, rendered, on Christmas Day, the cantata, Immanuel. St. John's M. E. Church, Bedford Avenue and Wilson Street, devoted December 27th to C. E. Belton's lecture on Re-united Germany, or, Heroic Louise. All Souls' Church, South Ninth Street, near Bedford Avenue, turned to music, with Ella Cory, Mrs. Peter Bell, Winifred Rogers (violin), Mrs. Joshua Youngs (soprano), Haaren (tenor) and Harrison (organist). On January 14th, Maria Parloa began, at Knickerbocker Hall, a course of lectures on cooking—surely a useful theme. And, on January 15th, the 47th Regiment gave a band concert and reception at its new Armoury, Marcy Avenue and Lynch Street. On the 24th, at St. John's M. E. Sunday School Hall, C. T. Winchester re-evoked An Evening in London, One Hundred Years Ago. February 3rd found two of the leading churches in rivalry: at the Ross Street Presbyterian Church, Professor S. M. Spedon held forth on Characters and Characteristics, and, at the Lee Avenue Congregational Church, a man set down as "the greatest living humourist" may have felt himself weighed down by the tag. February was very busy in allure. On the 3rd, the Union des Sociétés Françaises de Brooklyn gave a ball at Teutonia Hall, Harrison Avenue. For the 9th, the New England Congregational Church provided a Peak Family Entertainment; and the Lee Avenue Congregational came back, true to form, on the 10th, with Minnie Ashton, Miss Hollis, Ewell and Wandell. But the 9th carried the Brooklyn Liederkranz to Turn-Hall, there to dance. The treat of the 14th, at the New England Church, included the St. Cæcilia, Wilhelm Bartels and Helen Maigille. On the 15th, Harriet C. Keatinge, M.D., lectured to ladies only, at the Lee Avenue Congregational Church (I suppose this tabernacle sometimes held religious services) on Health, and How to Keep It, surely an important topic for men as well as "ladies"; at the Ross Street Presbyterian Church, on the same date, the Reverend Archibald McCullough, D.D., took auditors From the Alps to Vesuvius. The 17th was too busy for choice; to which entertainment shall we rush? The DeWitt Clinton Commandery and Company K, 47th Regiment were in the fine new Armoury of the 47th; the Arion Ball was danced at Turn Hall; and, at St. Paul's Evangelical Lutheran Church, South Fifth and Rodney Streets, Reverend Miller Hageman gave Bird Songs, translated into English, Albert S. Caswell plying the organ, and Annie Walker serving as soloist.

I begin to fear that February will exhaust my willing pen, but I push it forward toward March. Company G, 47th Regiment, and the Bidwell Greys gave, on February 21st, a concert and reception, doubtless delectable to their gentle lady friends. This brings us to Washington's Birthday, which was full to bursting, with activities chiefly German. The masquerade ball of the Schwäbischer Sängerbund danced itself into history at Turn-Hall; the masquerade of the James A. Garfield Bund, No. 23, was, I surmise, merry at Winter's Teutonia Hall. A "grand patriotic entertainment with tableaux" enlisted, at old Bushwick Sunday School Hall, William A. Buckley and Little Ida Bell Travis; Calvary Church, Marcy Avenue and South 9th Street, held a Hard Times Scrabble (I hope my omniscient reader knows what this was), the Reverend C. L. Twing elucidating with Siftings and Cinders, or, Twenty Minutes with the Ash Barrel. Somehow I believe those people, so far back from 1941, must have been as human as the Greenwich Village of today fancies itself to be. I close February 22nd with a Tea Party and Martha Washington Reception, at the Lee Avenue Congregational Church; but I re-open that church, on the 24th, for a "Grand Valentine Festival." The Ross Street Presbyterian Church was really brilliant, on the 24th, with the Courtney Ladies' Quartet (Carrie Hun-King, Ida Haring, Lizzie Seymore, and Mrs. Arthur C. Taylor), with D. W. Robertson (verrephone) and Maud Budworth (accompanist). As February ended, Professor J. H. Warwick had an evening at the Ainslie Street Church, assisted by Mr. and Mrs. S. Neal, in Life Shadows, or, an Evening with the Poets of Many Lands. And the Greenpoint Globe, of February 26th, assures us that the Robert Emmet Association of Williamsburgh had engaged John Boyle O'Reilly as orator, for the anniversary of Emmet's death.

The Drummond Family emerged, on March 1st, at Knickerbocker Hall, after an absence, which I cannot regret, of two years; on the 6th, A. E. Pearsall was humorous at the Ross Street Presbyterian Church. Some-

[395]

where, on the 3rd, occurred a concert to Tillie Jones, under the auspices of Mme. Cappiani. The Young People's Association of St. John's M. E. Church gave, on March 7th, their closing entertainment, assisted by Mr. and Mrs. Henry Firth Wood (elocutionists), George Emrich (zither), A. A. Day (whistler) and Harry E. Arnold (organist). This leads to a triple venture of March 10th: the Gypsy Ball, at Turn Hall, of the Friedrich Gluck Quartet Club; the twelfth ball of the Williamsburgh Plattdeutscher Club, at Winter's Teutonia Hall; and a concert at the Lee Avenue Congregational Church, with Carrie Louise Ray, Marion Wilcox (soprano), Belle Cole, William Courtney, J. Allen Preisch (bass), E. A. Lefebre (saxophone), Herr Ludwig (saxophone), Frank Taft (organ), William B. Stone (accompanist), and Lawrence Bogert (manager). And Miss Parloa continued her lectures on cooking. On the 18th, at Turn Hall, Inshavogue was acted by the Roja Dramatic Corps of the St. Mary Literary Union.

The Hooper Street Free Baptist Church devoted March 23rd to an illustrated lecture, Sights and Scenes in Many Lands. The South Third Street M. E. Church must have searched for nonentities in arranging its concert for March 31st, succeeding, if that was the purpose, in a list including Genevieve Johnson McGregor, Miss Wolf, Frank Jones, James Dougherty, James De Witt and James De Witt, Jr. (violinists, these two, whom we have met before), Arthur Houghtman (sic), Miss Dale, Lillie Smith (elocutionist) and Benjamin Dale (cornet). This list I cite as the outstanding "booby prize" of 1886–87. April 4th assembled, in the New England Church, Mrs. Peter Bell, Carrie Rowbotham (soprano), H. Lehmann (tenor), Edward Hyde (bass), Frank Post (violin) and Gertrude Homan (reader). Could this last-named be Little Gertie Homan, who made a hit, subsequently, as Bootle's Baby? On Easter Monday, the 11th, Company A, 47th Regiment, the Kings County Wheelmen and the Sewanhaka Boat Club held a full dress reception at the Armoury. The Euterpean Concert Company, on that same 11th, stationed itself in the old Bushwick Sunday School Hall. All Souls' Chapel did for us lovers of American drama an interesting thing when, on April 13th or 14th (my papers again differ as to the date), it played The Sleeping Car, by the then acclaimed W. D. Howells; A Dress Rehearsal was part of the show. April 20th also furnished food for thought in a concert at Grand Army Hall (Bedford Avenue and North Second Street) proffered by the Mansfield Post Band, assisted by Minnie Dilthey, William Jaeger, the Schwäbischer Sängerbund and the Herman Soehne Männerchor. This rather makes the entertainment of the Irving Social Club, on the 21st, at Knickerbocker Hall, pale its ineffectual fires; also the testimonial, in the same hall, on the 25th, tendered by his pupils to F. W. Zaulig, though in this last function were promised Ottilie and The St. Felix Sisters. But possibly, on the 20th, Carrie Wall's reading of The Cricket on the Hearth made Knickerbocker Hall an interesting retreat in Williamsburgh. And this hall, in April, housed, for an evening, the minstrel show of the Lyceum Union.   Musical Vespers, on the 24th, at the Church of the Transfiguration, enlisted Minnie Ashton, Mrs. Spitzer Flocken and a large chorus.

Stewart L. Woodford, then a highly esteemed citizen, lectured, on April 25th, on Young Men in History, surely an alluring topic for the audience in St. John's M. E. Church.   Possibly akin in thought was a lecture at this time, in the Lee Avenue Congregational Church, Colonel L. F. Copeland there speaking on Handsome People.   The Eastern District Dispensary and Hospital held, on April 27th, a thirty-sixth anniversary at the First Reformed Church, Bedford Avenue and Clymer Street.   An address by ex-Mayor Seth Low, the Amphion Orchestra, led by C. Mortimer Wiske, and Daisy Bower- man ("the wonderful girl violinist") figured in the promise.

May releases the hold on my pen.   The 12th of that flowering month found, at the Puritan Church, Lafayette and Marcy Avenues, T. De Witt Talmage lecturing on Old Times and New.   The First Baptist Church, Lee Avenue and Keap Street, presented, on the 16th, Around the World in a Chariot of Song, with óur old friend, Philip Phillips, "the singing pilgrim," and "six hundred colossal views."   On May 24th Temple Beth Elohim, in Keap Street, provided a notable array in Henrietta Markstein, Maggie Mitchell, Mrs. Conner ("*née* Priscilla Whittingham"), Julia O'Connell (alto) and others.   The race for entertainments in 1886–87 is nearly run.   Early in June opened the Lee Avenue Congregational Church for a Fruit and Flower Festival; the columns of the Brooklyn Times teem with advertise- ments of excursions hither and yon.   But, on June 20th, at the 47th Regi- ment Armoury, Company G and the Christ Church Society engaged in a tennis tournament, and, on July 4th, the Brooklyn Caledonian Club betook itself to Myrtle Avenue Park.   With the Queens County Fair, at Mineola, Long Island, on September 27th, 28th, 29th and 30th, I leave Williams- burgh for 1886–87.

GREENPOINT, 1886–1887

I wish I could offer an appetising feast of amusements for that season in Greenpoint; I fear my desire will be balked.   The dramatic entertainment of St. Anthony's Young Men's Union, at St. Anthony's Parish House (Leon- ard Street) would not, probably, have been entirely convincing to habitués of Daly's or Wallack's.   Nor can I vouch for the excellence of an entertain- ment, on November 9th and 10th, at the Reformed Episcopal Church of the Redemption.   The Church of the Reconciliation, beautifully-named, in the impressively-named Noble Street, opened, on November 10th, for readings by the strikingly-named Blanche L. Friderici; among many associated with her were Jessie Crowell and Miss A. Bullock, in piano duets.   The second annual ball of the Columbian Club made November 24th light and bright, in Smithsonian Hall; possibly the 25th (Thanksgiving) pleased auditors with the literary and musical entertainment of the Sunday School of the Tabernacle M. E. Church.

I can only blame my over-conscientious pen for afflicting readers with such small-town detail. Slightly more interesting is the promise, for December 1st and 2nd, at the Parish House of the Church of the Ascension; then and there, under A. Forwood Bower, the children of the Sunday School were to give Schoeller's cantata, New Year's Eve, and a tit-bit called Uncle Sam's Welcome to All Nations, with a tableau of Liberty Enlightening the World. December 15th blossomed in triple incitement. A concert at the First M. E. Church (Manhattan Avenue, near Java Street) was directed by Charles W. Wernig, "formerly leader of the 23rd Regiment Band, now of the New York Seventh Regiment Band"; the Celtic Association annual ball came at Eckford Hall; and at Bartholdi Hall (late Manhattan Rink) the Court Shamrock danced at the entrance fee of 50 cents. The reader observes that I have not taken him to a single skating rink in all this mad Greenpoint gayety; and now here is Manhattan Rink turned into Bartholdi Hall, advertised as "suitable for receptions, concerts and lectures." How are the mighty fallen!

I begin the Greenpoint record with these imposing items, rather than with an antecedent notice in the Greenpoint Globe of October 23rd, a notice which states that "there will probably be no more roller skating rinks of any prominence open in the city [Brooklyn or Greenpoint?] this winter. All the large buildings formerly used by the rollers are now employed for other purposes." That farewell to the once so popular excitement should awaken a philosophic tear. But what could more characteristically fit the American harvest festival than a Pumpkin Pie Sociable, on December 8th, in Banner Lodge, Greenpoint, or, for that matter, than a Mum Tutti Frutti Sociable, on December 15th, in the Noble Street Presbyterian Church? These solitary notices are all I gleaned from the Greenpoint Globe, a paper that so much might have loaded my pilgrim's scrip for the year we are traversing!

The year passed out with a sputter. December 27th brought into Smithsonian Hall a children's entertainment, Thirty-One Operetta Company, with "Professor" Wernig directing the orchestra. At the Parish House, Java Street, on the 31st, the Peek (sic) Sisters ("27 of them from Pike's Peak") went through the device of trying to amuse by rustic simplicity; Marindy, Sukey Jacinthy and similar names were designed to amuse sophisticates of Greenpoint. As the year died, the busy St. Anthony's Young Men's Union again acted, in the Parish House, Caught by the Cuff and Barney, the Baron, being their quarry.

The reader observes that my Greenpoint gleanings for 1886–87 have thus far been meagre. The Long Island City Star furnishes a slim harvest for January. On the 19th of that bleak month, in the Parish House, Java Street, the Reverend D. Henry Miller, D.D., formerly pastor of the Noble Street

[398]

Baptist Church, lectured on the provocative theme, Marriage Customs of the World.   Eckford Hall, on the 25th, found the Greenpoint Burns Club commemorating the hundred and twenty-eighth anniversary of the poet.   And, on the 31st, at Parish Hall of St. Anthony's Church, Professor Turner lectured on An Evening in Ireland, supplementing with over a hundred stereopticon views.   Bartholdi Hall advertised, for February 10th, 11th and 12th, Grand Cosmoramic Views, by Professor L. Schultz; a George Cooke benefit concert competed, on the 11th, at Association Hall, with Nellie Stearns, Jessie Woodruff and many others of no note.   February 21st offered, at Bartholdi Hall, the concert and ball of the Shipwrights' Mutual Benefit and Relief Association; and The Ticket of Leave Man, played by the busy St. Anthony's Young Men's Union, at Parish Hall.   Two events of this trying month which I cannot definitely date were the ball, at Association Hall, of the German Ladies' Society of Greenpoint, and an entertainment, at Armoury Hall, 116 Calyer Street, of Nathan Hale Council, No. 2; at this latter function appeared Lottie Rennert, Minnie Hauff, Lizzie Hancock, Mrs. M. Herbert and J. A. Craig.   The First Methodist Episcopal Church, Manhattan Avenue, between Java and India Streets, launched, on February 23rd, a concert by the choir of the church.   Finally, for the week beginning on February 28th, Bartholdi Hall gave nightly showings of Grant's Diorama of the Civil War.

This brings us unscathed out of winter into a slender March, which yielded but three items to my research in the Star.   The Celtic Association, on the 4th, celebrated, at Smithsonian Hall, the hundredth anniversary of Robert Emmet.   May, James and Charles O'Neill, and Sarah Smith participated.   The very busy St. Anthony's Church had a benefit, at Parish Hall, on March 17th, providing a musical and dramatic entertainment; and something *extra*-mural, came, on the 30th, at the Tabernacle M. E. Church, when we were edified by the ministrations of Alfred E. Pearsall (musical humourist) and the Lambert Children (instrumentalists).   April provided a more generous offering, beginning on the 1st, at Smithsonian Hall, with a concert of Lillian and Elsie Anderson, Professor Bogert, James De Witt and others.   At Bartholdi Hall, on April 6th, that perplexing Rock Band Concert Company, of London, brought "music in stones."   The Christian Church of the Evangel, on April 13th, gave the time-worn Mrs. Jarley's Waxworks, the Young People's Association sponsoring and repeating the show on the 28th.   On April 18th, Canonicus Tribe, No. 64, proffered, at Smithsonian Hall, a vocal and instrumental concert; and, about this time, the Greenpoint Turn-Verein held a concert at Turn Hall, Eagle and Franklin Streets.

Something really worth while was announced for April 25th, at the Noble Street Baptist Church, with artists of more than merely local repute in E. G. Jardine, Grace Haskell, Carrie Couch, Marshall P. Wilder, Daisy Bowerman and Belle Cole.   The Church of the Ascension, on April 28th,

[399]

advertised a Kirmess, to be held at the Parish House, Java Street, with a "Country Store" to amuse the not very urban Greenpoint. My last item was launched on May 30th and 31st, at the Parish Hall, when the Choir of St. Anthony's Church sang Pinafore, with A. J. Dowling as Sir Joseph, Louis Reynolds as the Captain, John O'Neill as Ralph, John Flynn as Deadeye, Mrs. William Schilling as Josephine, May O'Neill as Hebe and Sarah Smith as Buttercup. I am beginning to know Miss Smith and all the O'Neills.

The thinness of Greenpoint amusements will be understood, if we but reflect on the village characteristics of the place. I found, in the Long Island City Star of August 15, 1887, a picture of the town life which explains much: "A drove of steers created intense excitement in Greenpoint this Monday afternoon, running wildly through the streets, overturning everything that came in their way. Two men and two boys were tossed by the mad brutes, and one old woman was badly trampled upon. The police gave chase to the animals and succeeded in killing one of them. Another was driven into the river. The others were captured late the same afternoon." There is drama for us, but of a kind that could be portrayed only by the cinema. We remember that animals ran through lower Broadway, in the early days of the Park Theatre; somehow I keep hoping that Greenpoint also will establish a theatre and justify my investigation of its feeble dramatic infancy.

FLATBUSH AND ITS NEIGHBOURS, 1886–1887

The record for this little child of the maturing Brooklyn grows more and more scanty. The Greenpoint Globe, of November 13th, speaks, with some humour, of a Harvest Home Festival, held, on October 31st, in the Williams Avenue M. E. Church, Flatbush. Vegetables of all kinds were piled on the pulpit and in other sacred precincts of the temple, meant, as the speaker or presenter remarked, for the preacher—possibly, I infer, as part of his salary. The speaker then branched into the dangerous domain of humour, remarking that some of the vegetable riches would go to the sexton, a man to whom every parishioner would ultimately be indebted for safe bestowal— I suppose in the grave. The orator thought, by the laughter of his audience, that he had made a hit; he had; indeed, inadvertently—the sexton was a woman!

The South Brooklyn Turn-Verein and South Brooklyn Schau-Turnen doubtless interested Turners and their friends, in mid-April, in the Turn-Halle, near Fifth Avenue, South Brooklyn.

LONG ISLAND CITY AND ITS NEIGHBOURS, 1886–1887

Queens County might almost have been taught to believe there was only one actor in the world—Oliver W. Wren. He came, inevitably, to start

Long Island City on its amusements for the new year, appearing in the Astoria Assembly Rooms, on September 13th, as Salem Scudder, in The Octoroon, supported by Mrs. Wren as Zoe, George Sands as Wahnotee and Therese Allston as Dora Sunnyside.   The bill also included The Toodles.

October 12th opened the Sunday School Room of the Church of the Redeemer for the first of a series of concerts by the choir of the church, under direction of W. O. Wilkinson, choirmaster and organist.   Listed to appear were Emma Brazier (pianist), Mrs. Charles Beebe (soprano), C. T. Steele (tenor), Kunstler (violin), and Tornwald (cello).   An equally undistinguished group figured in the concert of the Excelsior Cricket Club, in October, at Island City Lodge — Arthur Wilson, John J. Ling, Fred Smyth, Maggie House, Lulu Bevington, Mrs. Bevington, Louis Reynolds and Joseph J. Hogerty.   And the National Base Ball Club of Blissville had a variety and athletic exhibition, on October 18th, at McGilvery's National Assembly Rooms, Blissville.   Something more germane to our theme came on October 25th and 26th, with the visit of Dan Nash's Hibernicon Comedy and Specialty Company to Prospect Hall, Dutch Kills.   On November 4th and 5th, a Singin' Skewl amused Steinway.

For November I found in the weekly Star merely notes of balls, masquerades and "socials."   On December 9th, the Astoria Presbyterian Church announced an evening of Egypt and the Egyptians.   And the Star of December 16th fails to specify the date of a concert tendered to Walter O. Wilkinson by the choir of the Church of the Redeemer; in this appeared Kittie Coates (a local celebrity, as we know), Mrs. E. H. Dexter, Emma Brazier, E. H. Dexter (tenor), Dr. Rumbold (baritone) and Holden (reciter).   A charity ball by the Astoria Aid Society made December 31st gay in the Astoria Assembly Rooms.   One can only wonder at the paucity of entertainment in Long Island City, until one reflects on its proximity to New York, with its wealth of plays and music.   January 10th, however, had dual entertainment: the Till Family, at the Second Methodist Church, and a Rock Band Concert, in the same hall, apparently, employing "instruments never before seen or heard in this part of the country."   January 12th found another concert in the Church of the Redeemer, this time with Blanche Field, Grace Avery, F. L. Green and Paul Primier (in feats of prestidigitation).   Masquerade balls were rampant, in that winter in the Astoria Assembly Rooms and in Arlington Hall; but "bobbing" sent sleds merrily down the snow on Presbyterian Hill.   Yet the Dramatic Club of Astoria found time to prepare, for January 26th, in the Assembly Rooms, Which Is Which? acted by W. V. Draper, F. E. Havemeyer, V. W. Dubois, Agnes Taylor, Sarah Stuart and Margaret Lathrop; the Club, according to the Star, was composed of "many of the leading residents of the upper ward." The Kronprinzessin Victoria Ball made pleasure, on January 31st, at the Astoria Assembly Rooms.

[401]

February 2nd was devoted, in the Astoria Assembly Rooms, to the Astoria Athletic Club, with Mrs. Jarley's Waxworks and a one-act comedy. And St. John's Episcopal Church, on the 3rd, put on an elaborate Mrs. Jarley's Waxworks. In the Chamber of Beauties we had Julia Green as Queen Elizabeth, John Gosman as Sir Walter Raleigh, Grace Avery as Lady Jane Grey, Mrs. W. G. Neubauer as Queen Eleanor, Florence Bostwick as Fair Rosamond, John Talbot as Richard, &c. In The Chamber of Horrors Addie Smith was Catherine Parr, E. West an Elderly Naval Man, W. G. Neubauer Henry VIII, Ada Brown the Old Lady Who Died Dancing at 122, and Hattie White Charlotte Corday. Evidently those young persons of 1887 knew more history than, I fear, some of their descendants could muster in 1941. But balls and dances, then, as now, and ever, whirled through the dark nights of winter. The chapel of Trinity Methodist Episcopal Church, Astoria, veered us from the saltatory, on February 6th, with what the Star grandly calls "an elegant and recherché entertainment," involving Kittie Coates, Professor Braddick (*sic*), A. S. Beebe, and two "reciters" — Mrs. D. W. Van Wagenen and Richard A. Purdy. The Star lists this same group, in the same place, for April 6th. The Star Athletic Club reception held Arlington Hall, on February 9th, and the seventh anniversary of Allemania Lodge, on the 21st, brightened Germania Hall. And Washington's Birthday was to open the First Reformed Church, Astoria, for a concert of the Astoria Choral Society. And the Long Island City Lyceum, on February 28th, was shelter for the reading of five ambitious souls — F. S. Macintosh, Miss R. Gillert, Vernon P. Lanphear, Susie Topping and Laura Van Riper. I found nothing for March except the Astoria Männerchor Ball, on the 7th, at the Astoria Assembly Rooms. According to the Greenpoint Globe, the Newtown Choral Union, with Rundall and Baumeister, performed on February 26th, in the Newtown Association Hall.

This leaves a clear field for April. On Sunday, the 3rd of that month, St. Mary's Church rendered Mercadante's oratorio, The Seven Last Words of Our Saviour on the Cross; soloists were Tillie G. Harley, Rose Dempsey, P. J. Longbran and J. P. McKeever. Parts of Rossini's Stabat Mater employed L. J. Cornu (violin), V. H. Kelly (tenor), Minnie O'Connor (soprano), and F. R. Treasure (baritone) whose recurring name is actually treasure-trove to me, wandering in the morass of unfamiliar names. Under the leadership of J. William Suffern, the Astoria Vocal Union, on April 5th, invaded the Presbyterian Church, Astoria, dragging at its chariot wheels soloists so little known (to me) as Mrs. Suffern, William Brook, E. K. Conant, Miss L. Frazee and Miss Decker. On the 7th, the Dutch Kills Reformed Church ventured on a literary and musical show. I welcome A. P. Burbank to the realm of the well-known, on April 12th, at the Astoria Assembly Rooms, and, on the 13th, sink once more into the waves of amateurism provided, in the same rooms, by the minstrel entertainment of the Astoria and Steinway Combination.

On May 5th, at the home of F. H. Burke, a "dramatic reception" resulted in Pillicoddy, acted by Mr. and Mrs. G. H. Beardsley, Mrs. Striker, Mr. and Mrs. F. H. Burke, and in recitations by Edith and Anna Striker. Then dancing! The Astoria Choral Society possessed, on May 11th, the over-worked Assembly Rooms, soloists including Master I. Wessell, W. Oscar Faustan, Signor N. Norrito (clarinet), H. Perella (cornet) and Kittie Coates, evidently a favourite on the Island. The Star of May 20th states that the Star Combination, "which recently gave a very successful entertainment at the Astoria Assembly Rooms, is about to pay a visit to Steinway." Thence-forward I can invite my reader merely to strawberry and ice cream festivals (in June), or (in June, July and August), to excursions hither and yon — to Bowery Bay Beach, Schwalenberg's Park, Hillmeyer's Pavilion, Rockaway Beach, Pleasant Point, Shippen Point, or up and down the Hudson.

FLUSHING AND ITS NEIGHBOURS, 1886–1887

The Flushing Journal invites to but few entertainments in the autumn of 1886, and those of minor interest. The Startle Variety Troupe of Glen Cove gave at the Hall an entertainment and ball for the benefit of St. Mary's Church — this merely to begin the season, let us say. On September 7th, the Frohsinn Society of Long Island City journeyed to College Point, for what purpose my faithful Journal does not state. But I will give the reader one of the best contradictions in terms when I state that the Merry Com-panions gave at Turn Hall, College Point, on October 2nd, Ten Nights in a Bar-Room; they were to give another entertainment at Turn Hall, on Feb-ruary 12th. When the Boston Ideal Comedy Company ventured into Flush-ing, on November 25th, they had no audience — so they left! Let us re-member that residents of Flushing could easily travel by rail and ferry to New York for any play the metropolis was then offering.

At Whitestone roller skating began again, in January, at Knab's Hall. And, since our survey roams from village to village, we may roam to Willets Point, where, as we know, were stationed a Battalion of Engineers, U.S.A. In previous seasons we were privileged to attend some amateur theatricals arranged by the gallant corps. For 1886–87, I can merely reproduce from the Greenpoint Globe, of January 8, 1887, a rather pretty account of the post, with the "little church on the reservation" and a "good band." There are frequent theatrical performances, and "many of the officers display con-siderable dramatic talent." A glee club has been organised and "other amusements are indulged in that relieve the monotony of military life." This is cheering intelligence for kind civilians, and possibly sounded more attractive to wandering Islanders than the cantata of Esther, given, on

February 2nd, at the Hall, Roslyn; or, for that matter, than the show put on (February 17th) by the Mutual Engine Company, and declared two days later by the Journal to have been "poor." The Julian Comedy Company advertised for the entire week of February 21st–26th at the Opera House, Flushing — the company, declares the Journal, that appeared last fall under the title of the People's Theatre Company. Probably more in touch with human needs was Miss Parloa's lecture (afternoon of March 30th) on Marketing — best cuts of meat, etc. On April 1st, Dwight L. Elmendorf, in the same auditorium, lectured on A Trip Across Our Continent. I end the paragraph, as I began it, with busy Whitestone; a concert and ball, there, at Deppe's Hall, enlisted the Willets Point Band.

The Long Island Democrat (Jamaica) of April 19th states that the Julian Comedy Company took in $700, during the preceding week in Flushing. April 20th (or thereabouts) brought to the Flushing Opera House an amateur performance of Plot and Passion, L. E. Quigg being among the actors. A "chilly reception," according to the Journal of the 16th, greeted, on April 14th, at Bryant Hall, Roslyn, the singing of a band of Jubilee Singers. I leap to June 1st for the Alpha Trio (Charles H. Little, humourist, and the Perry Brothers, musicians) at the Flushing Opera House. On July 7th, the New York Comedy Company was to be at the Whitestone Village Hall; the audience was so small (three men, a boy and a woman) that only a partial performance was tendered. But the Arion Society of New York, eight hundred strong, were at Sands Point, on Sunday, August 5th. And I end August, on the 29th, and leave Flushing for 1886–87, with Abbey's Uncle Tom's Cabin Company, at the Flushing Opera House, on that date, with two brass bands, one white, one black. And, warns the Journal, this organisation "has no connection with a company billed to appear in Flushing, two or three weeks ago, which broke up at Mount Vernon." I speak, however, of the Harvest Home, beginning on August 31st, at the Crocheron Bayside House; and pursue Oliver Wren, from Turn Hall, College Point, on September 1st, to the Hall, Roslyn, on the 3rd, where he was to give Sweethearts, for the benefit of the Rescue Hook and Ladder Company. I am almost ashamed to offer my urban readers a record so suburban for 1886–87 in Flushing, so near Broadway.

JAMAICA, 1886–1887

How could we more characteristically open a season in any Long Island village than with a performance of Uncle Tom's Cabin? Let us then, start Jamaica on its merry campaign with Abbey's Double Mammoth Uncle Tom's Cabin Company, with its two bands, one white, one coloured, in uniform, its two Topsys, its two Markses, its Genuine South Carolina Jubilee Singers, its Æsthetic Trained Donkey, Oscar, "the smallest Shetland Pony in the world,

[404]

Edison's Electric Parlour Light, and a street parade by day." That mad, glad excitement convulsed Jamaica, by anticipation, on August 27, 1886; and yet, alas! the Democrat assures us that the show was poor—only about half the play was given, and, not till the jubilee singers appeared, was the audience pleased. This apprises us of the kind of entertainment deemed good enough for rural communities in 1886. After that disappointment, Jamaica, so far as I discovered, had merely Alderman Distler's Harvest Home Festival, on September 15th, at his Atlantic Garden, and a Festival, on the same day at Mineola.

But Harley Merry, whose name was better than his theatrical fortunes, opened, in East New York, his Bijou Theatre, with promise of weekly changes of bill. On October 18th, he and Mrs. Merry began at their theatre (on the site of the late Academy of Music, Atlantic and Vermont Avenues) with The Argonauts of '49. For the week of October 25th, Kathleen Mavourneen and Turn Him Out constituted the pabulum of joy; but, alas! November 1st brought in the New York Star Company, and the venture went up, so far as Democrat advertisements inform us, with Gregon's Elevator.

That side issue disposed of, I may recur to October 18th (or possibly it was the 11th) for a visit, to the Opera House, of Dan Nash and Company, a Panorama of Ireland being part of the show. Town Hall, on the 25th, housed an entertainment of the Bryant-Robertson Combination, which once before we greeted in Jamaica, tumbleronicon and comic humour combined. November 22nd provided, under management of Mrs. Kate Howe, music by the Crescent Band (at last established), with tableaux, recitations and other harmless delights. J. Bassett, of the Singin' Skewl, was here, on November 29th, in something called Bric-à-Brac (then a popular word in household decoration). The issue of the Democrat for November 23rd had mentioned, without assigning date or place of perpetration, a recent concert of the Knights of Temperance, with Kate Aymar, the Bartholdi Association, William J. Rand, and Carl Faust (violin). The "Original People's Theatre," on December 2nd, invaded the Opera House with matter no less antiquated than Fanchon, supplementing it with That Husband of Mine. For the 3rd, they promised Hazel Kirke. They were to stay a week, but, since the Democrat was printed only on Tuesdays, I cannot follow them through their semaine. But I know that the Democrat liked Hattie Arnold as Fanchon.

The third popular concert of that pride of the village—the Crescent Band—was scheduled for December 7th, at Town Hall, with assistance from Marshall P. Wilder and J. W. Jones (tenor). Jamaica bestirred itself to buy tickets for the Manhattan Refined Minstrels (by Jamaica boys), listed for December 16th, at the Opera House; actually 180 tickets were sold before ten o'clock on the first morning of the sale! Then sleighing and

[405]

skating drove out entertainments cabined, cribbed, confined in opera house or concert hall. Not till February 3rd did the Democrat summon us within doors; then the Boyd Concert, whatever it was, invaded Town Hall. And February 9th found the Jamaica Sängerbund giving private theatricals at Distler's. Washington's Birthday was duly celebrated, at the Opera House, by a Minstrel Troupe from Hyde and Behman's, Brooklyn. The night before that patriotic day found the Active Social Club very active indeed, at the Opera House with a triple bill of plays — A Tender Attachment, Wanted, a Male Cook, and the burlesque operetta, Il Jacobi. I could not discover where, on March 9th, Miss Cavannah, contralto of Plymouth Church, and the Brooklyn Male Quartette sang; but it was the Opera House that, on March 31st, opened for Theodore Drury's Concert Company, including Misses M. Bell, M. Schoot, Brown and S. Bercer (sopranos), Miss J. Allen (contralto), E. Shaw (tenor), Tazzer (baritone) and Miss St. Clair (piano). I hope the reader knows (I don't) whether these artists were our villagers or residents of communities more remote. April 30th, May 4th, 7th and 11th staged the Rockaway Steeplechase, allowing me to race past church fairs, festivals of fire companies and other rural incitements chronicled in the Democrat.

At the home of Mrs. Sayres, on May 11th, souls on amusement bent could have enjoyed, if possible, the musical and dramatic entertainment provided by Laura Brenton, Mrs. Jesse Browne, Jr., Miss and Mr. Meynan, A. K. Gardner, G. B. Sayres, W. S. Crane, Mrs. P. J. Bernhard, W. H. Mills, Miss E. Sayres and Mamie Carey, some of whom may re-appear in this, our village lay. "Professor" T. R. Davenport was proud of his Presbyterian choir. He displayed its talent, on May 25th, at the Opera House, and allowed us to become acquainted with Mr. and Mrs. T. J. Armstrong, Mr. and Miss Fosdick, Lora Ludlum (a vaguely haunting name) and Jesse Browne, Jr., "stage manager." Because the Democrat failed to inform me, I cannot tell where Miss Westover's class acted, on June 8th, something called A Dress Rehearsal; but I can end with a flourish by listing for June 20th a visit to the Opera House of Beers and Johnson's Minstrels. One of my friends says that, in the far-away '80s, one entered Jamaica by a very dusty road; that dust gathered thickly over the record, for those years, of amusements in the village.

STATEN ISLAND, 1886–1887

The Buffalo Bill Wild West which shook Staten Island to its heart of heart, in the summer of 1886, folded its tents like the Arab and left the island to its fate, on September 25th; it opened, later, as we know, in the Madison Square Garden. On September 11th, at the German Club Rooms, Stapleton, Abbey's Double Mammoth Uncle Tom's Cabin Company appeared, trailing clouds of glory in a pack of man-eating bloodhounds, two comical musical Markses and two Topsys. Later in the season, Flushing and Jamaica, as we know, endured the impact of this thriller, or something, at least, of similar name. Erheiterung, on the 16th or 23rd of October (the Richmond County Sentinel leaves me in doubt as to the exact date), held its opening concert and ball. A Diet Kitchen Housewarming, on October 26th, at Grant and Van Duzer Streets, brought in the aid of Maud Morgan, Florence Havelock Keeling (violinist), Mrs. Stephen D. Stephens (contralto) and Fred W. Jameson (tenor). In the afternoon a Harvest Home Fair was timely and, I hope, enjoyable.

A Turn Verein Gymnastic Exhibition, at Turn Hall, Stapleton, on November 14th, cannot hold us, fifty years after the event. But I must detain the reader with an account in the Sentinel of December 18th, which celebrates the twenty-fifth anniversary of Erheiterung, "composed of wealthy and influential Germans." The occasion involved performances of Eine möblirte Wohnung and Hans und Hanne. In the former appeared Otto Lindmann, Frau Luise Knudsen, Frau Therese Gräf, Otto Heyn, and A. G. Funk; the latter involved Carl Prahl, Frau Friedericke Wermerskirsh and Fritz W. Gräf. Hans und Hanne had been given twenty-five years before, when Erheiterung started, and Prahl had taken part in it then. Verily a celebration!

A black Mikado, directed by H. J. Tyndale, was a novelty of January 8th, at the German Club Rooms; in later February came the Charity Ball. On March 22nd, George William Curtis lectured on Dickens, the Club Rooms of the Girls' Club in the Baltimore Flats, Central Avenue, housing the treat, which I wish I might have heard. And I also gladly should have attended on April 30th, at the German Club Rooms, a performance by our favourite group of New York amateurs. They began with Ahing-Fo-Hi, a play in one-act by Mrs. Charles A. Doremus, with a cast including Mrs. Wilber Bloodgood, William Bard McVickar, Henry A. Murray and Alexander T. Mason. Then, by permission of Henry E. Dixey, a scene from Adonis presented Frank C. Warren as Rosetta and Valentine G. Hall as Adonis, with It's English You Know; and James P. Hurst's comedietta, Sugar and Cream, ended the bill, with Alice and Rita Lawrence, Edward Fales Coward and Valentine G. Hall in their accustomed characters. Nervous Manhattanese might have timed their watches to the refrain, "The last train connecting for New York boat leaves Stapleton at 11.10"—soothing and comfortable indeed. On May 3rd more amateurs came in, with The Rose of Auvergne (Miss Mortimer, Messrs. Kershaw and Molyneux) and A Happy Pair (with Miss Babcock and Mr. Ebo Raynor—"who are being coached by Mr. Kyrle Bellew").

A marvel of that time—perhaps a rival to Pain's great spectacles at Manhattan Beach—was Kiralfy Brothers' huge show at St. George, under

[407]

the management of Erastus Wiman's Staten Island Amusement Company. This was The Fall of Babylon, presented on June 25th, "with one thousand performers," and with an expected weekly attendance of 20,000 — chiefly, needless to say, from New York and Brooklyn. The Richmond County Sentinel of July 2nd says, "Imagine a stage larger than a city block, fronted by a great wall of masonry, flanked by two turreted towers." The paper proceeds to describe the show in all its oriental splendour — Persian and Babylonian troops — Belshazzar's Palace — dancing girls — banquet — and all the accompaniment the Kiralfys knew so well how to supply. The Fall of Babylon became a sensation of the summer of 1887.

From that magnificence we pass to fireworks, on July 2nd, at Peteler's South Beach Pavilion, New Dorp; for the Queen's birthday, Pain arranged a great display of fireworks at St. George. Since the afternoon of June 28th, Forepaugh's New Olympia has been operating at Erastina. And, on July 7th, 11th and 14th, at Temperance Lyceum, New Brighton, J. H. Moore's choir gave the long-suffering Pinafore. With the Grand Fest of the Staten Island Quartette (sic) Club, held on July 28th, at Bechmann's Brewery, Clifton, I leave Staten Island for 1886-87.

CHAPTER VII

WALLACK'S, DALY'S, THE MADISON SQUARE, THE LYCEUM, THE STAR, THE UNION SQUARE, THE FIFTH AVENUE, THE BROADWAY, THE STANDARD, THE FOURTEENTH STREET THEATRE, CASINO, 1887–1888

WE carried the summer season of the McCaull Opera Company to its close, on October 8, 1887, with the last performance of a not very notable work, The Bellman. On Tuesday, October 11th, the last Wallack group ever to occupy the stage of Wallack's, so long famous as the home of the best stock company in America, began the last season of the house under its well-known name. Lester Wallack, as we saw, retired from the management at the close of the preceding season, and, for 1887–88, Henry E. Abbey, ever looking for new outlets for his restless activities, assumed control, with Maurice Grau as partner. Neither man had the tradition necessary to carry on Wallack's, the very home of tradition in the acting of high comedy. After an unsuccessful attempt, they gave up, in the spring of 1888. Lester Wallack died in September, 1888, and the theatre passed under the control of A. M. Palmer, who, much to the distress of older playgoers, changed the name of the house to Palmer's Theatre and began there, in October, 1888, what promised to be a most attractive season, with visiting stars of great distinction.

But this is anticipating. Let us, on Tuesday, October 11th, betake ourselves hopefully to the opening of the Abbey term. All were encouraged to discover that Osmond Tearle and Rose Coghlan were returning to the scene of their earlier triumphs and that John Gilbert and Mme. Ponisi would, later in the autumn, re-appear in favourite or newer rôles. The initial offering did not seem over-attractive—Sydney Grundy's comedy, The Mouse Trap, which proved to be a feeble attempt in the vein of Forget Me Not and other plays involving a mean, bad adventuress—a type of which the public was weary. In fact, as the Herald cruelly remarked, the trap was "furnished with cheese." The cast was compact:

Lord Normantower	Osmond Tearle	Kate Derwent	Rose Coghlan
Sir Peter Lund	Charles Groves	Beatrice Selwyn	Mrs. Abbey
Philip Selwyn	E. D. Ward	Mildred Selwyn	Enid Leslie
Tom Verrinder	Sam Sothern		

A glance suffices to show the inferiority of that cast to former assignments at Wallack's. New York had declined, in 1883–84, to accept Mrs. Abbey (then Florence Gerard) at her own estimate, and now was reluctant

[409]

to confirm her husband's attempt to establish her in public esteem; she was no successor to Stella Boniface or Annie Robe. E. D. Ward was a gentlemanly negligibility, though acceptable; and Sam Sothern was then of the nice-boy type. Enid Leslie was pretty, but colourless, in spite of her blonde complexion. The cast could, of course, have carried a good play, but, alas! The Mouse Trap was really uninteresting. I remember a fine entrance, in the second act, for Rose Coghlan, but as to what the entrance led to I have no recollection. In the first night audience were Mrs. Lester Wallack, Mr. and Mrs. Arthur Wallack, Kyrle Bellew (he was announced in the bills, but not appearing in the season, as a member of the company), Mr. and Mrs. John Gilbert, Charles Coghlan, Georgie Drew Barrymore, John Hoey and Effie Germon — possibly more of Wallack's in the audience than on the stage.

The Mouse Trap failed, and caught Abbey unprepared. On October 24th, he revived Caste, certainly no novelty and bearing a message quite unprovocative, in 1887, in democratic America. Rose Coghlan, of course, played Esther, Mrs. Abbey was a most uninteresting Polly, Mme. Ponisi, as usual, a dignified Marquise, Tearle a good D'Alroy, Groves an acceptable Eccles, Ward at his best as Hawtree, and T. W. Robertson, who had been imported to stage his father's plays, was Sam Gerridge. I saw this revival twice (I was then a student of the drama) and I enjoyed it; but the public did not respond and Caste followed The Mouse Trap into the limbo of Abbey's hopes.

On Tuesday, November 15th, another Robertson comedy, so popular in the prime of Lester Wallack — the innocuous but gently pleasing School — allowed Mrs. Abbey to essay Naomi Tighe, with Netta Guion (her first appearance here) as Bella, Louisa Eldridge as Mrs. Sutcliffe, Kate Bartlett as Tilly, John Gilbert (first appearance this season) as Dr. Sutcliffe, Tearle as Jack Poyntz (Wallack's famous part of yore), Ward as Lord Beaufoy and Charles Dodsworth (new) as Krux. A rosebud garden of schoolgirls included Effie Liston, Patrice Boucicault, Florence Estor, Annie Cadiz, Florence Waldram, Ollie Dickson, Enid Leslie, Helen Hosmer, Virgie Graves, Josie Hall and Maud Litchfield. It was hard to keep this School going. Its last performance came on November 28th. Caste had a special matinée on the 24th (Thanksgiving) and on the evening of the 29th. November 30th ended the fall with another revival, Forget-Me-Not, which Genevieve Ward, by legal procedure, had cut short, at Wallack's some seasons earlier, in the height of its success. It was now far from a success, though Miss Coghlan, Tearle, Mme. Ponisi and Harry Edwards resumed their original parts. J. W. Pigott assumed the rôle of Barrato, and Netta Guion that of Alice Verney. Miss Guion was lacking, as always, in magnetism and personality.

New York must always have something to be crazy about. That season

[410]

MRS. G. D. BARRYMORE   JOHN GILBERT   MARION MANOLA
(L'ABBÉ CONSTANTIN)   (L'ABBÉ CONSTANTIN)   (BOCCACCIO)

W. T. LOVELL   SAM SOTHERN   E. D. WARD

MRS. ABBEY   CATERINA MARCO   CHARLES DODSWORTH

it was young Josef Hofmann, a Polish child of ten, who played the piano with the brilliancy and imaginative power of the most accomplished adult. Before his début at the Metropolitan Opera House, he gave, at Wallack's, a private performance, on the afternoon of November 28th.   He played variations by Beethoven, some compositions of his own, and a Chopin nocturne and waltz.   He also improvised on a theme given him by Rudolph Aronson, from Aronson's waltz, Blue Eyes.   According to the Herald review, the child took it up "note for note, ennobled it, transformed it into a dozen different shapes, and occasionally raised it to truly Chopinesque heights."   On the wings of that melody we fly back to Forget-Me-Not, which struggled limply on till December 24th, a sad Christmas for Abbey.

On December 28th, a play by Selina Dolaro — In the Fashion — tried to change the fortune of the house.   We had seen this at special performances in the last season, at the Madison Square Theatre.   Osmond Tearle appeared as Captain Denalguez, Eben Plympton (specially engaged) as Philippe Valnay, Harry Edwards as Mons. Pierson, E. D. Ward as Baron Sarcy, S. DuBois as a Footman, Rose Coghlan as Adelaide Lapierre, Netta Guion as Clare Rimini, Lilla Vane (a rising young actress) as Marion Pierson and the inescapable Mrs. Abbey as Dora Valnay.   In mid-January Kate Bartlett succeeded Lilla Vane as Marion.   This was followed on Friday, January 20th, by an adaptation of that harmless French romance, L'Abbé Constantin, which school boys and girls and college youths read, at that time, in their French classes.   The novel, by Hector-Cremieux and Pierre de Coeurcille, was dramatised by the busy Clinton Stuart.   The almost inevitable result of the co-engagement of the independent Rose Coghlan and Mrs. Abbey, who was little more than the wife of the manager, came in connection with this production.   Some disagreement as to assignment of parts led to the departure of Miss Coghlan from the company, and temporarily Mrs. Abbey was monarch of all she surveyed in her husband's theatre. Minnie Conway (Mrs. Osmond Tearle), announced from the beginning of the season as a member of the company, assumed the rôle of Mrs. Scott, the clever Georgie Drew Barrymore, specially engaged, made a hit as the Countess of Laverdens, and Mrs. Abbey was a far from juvenile Cynthia Ray.   Other assignments included John Gilbert as the Abbé Constantin, in which he was superb — the last new character, by the way, that he ever created; W. T. Lovell (his first appearance) as Jean Daubray; Harry Edwards as Mons. de Larnac; T. W. Robertson as Paul de Laverdens; Charles Dodsworth as Bernard; Louisa Eldridge as Baroness de Leonelle; Mme. Ponisi as Suzanne; and Enid Leslie and Kate Bartlett as the Morin demoiselles, Angelique and Seraphine, respectively.   There, except for the absence of Tearle and Rose Coghlan, is the strength of Abbey's Company. But the innocuous prettiness of the play was rather tame in 1888, and, after a month, this much heralded thing joined the list of failures dramatised from

[411]

popular novels. I remember sitting through the piece, wondering why any one should have made a drama out of the story I had read, as a college sophomore, with no engrossing interest. But I greatly enjoyed the lively performance of Mrs. Barrymore. In late January E. D. Ward was substituted for W. T. Lovell. Compared with The Railroad of Love, across the street, at Daly's, L'Abbé Constantin seemed very futile.

LAST OF WALLACK'S; OLD COMEDIES

February 18th marked the close of this vaunted play and of Abbey's attempt to continue at Wallack's. He persuaded Miss Coghlan to return to the fold, doubtless at the price of the retirement of Mrs. Abbey, and induced Lester Wallack to supervise the revival of a series of old comedies, with which the thirty-six year history of Wallack's Theatre was to end. The series began, on February 20th, with London Assurance, presenting Tearle as Dazzle, Gilbert, of course, as Sir Harcourt, Harry Edwards as Max Harkaway, E. D. Ward as a not very interesting Charles, Dodsworth as Dolly Spanker, J. W. Pigott as Cool, Charles Edwin (returned to the fold) as Solomon Isaacs, Groves as Mark Meddle, Rose Coghlan as a very lively Lady Gay, Netta Guion as a tame Grace Harkaway, and Kate Bartlett as Pert. This cast, though I enjoyed the performance, was like a layer of unpredictable talent on a genuine Wallack base in Gilbert, Edwards, Tearle (not a priceless Dazzle), Miss Coghlan and Miss Bartlett.

Old Heads and Young Hearts followed, on February 29th, made notable by participation of Gilbert (the exquisite Jesse Rural), Tearle, Edwards, Miss Coghlan and Mme. Ponisi, in parts in which they had been so frequently admired, and made not so brilliant by E. D. Ward as Tom, Lovell as Lord Charles, Pigott as the Earl of Pompion, Groves as Bob, Edwin as Stripe, DuBois as a Groom, and Netta Guion as Kate. One could recall better casts in the Wallack's of former days. Preliminary announcements of these farewell performances had promised revivals of The Road to Ruin, The Rivals, and other classics which I, as a lover of the stage, had long wished to see; when, then, the third choice fell on Morton's Town and Country, I had a distinct impression of flatness, intensified by the performance. It was scheduled for Monday, March 12th, the night of the immortalised blizzard of 1888, and Wallack's, like most theatres of New York, except Daly's and the Star, where advance sales had been very large, was closed. On the 13th, Town and Country, very frost-bitten by time, if not by the blizzard, engaged Tearle as Reuben Glenroy (once a favourite part even of tragic actors), Ward as Captain Glenroy, Pigott (who had been frequently miscast) as the Reverend Owen Glenroy, Dodsworth as Ross, Gilbert as Kit Cosey, Edwards as Trot, Lovell as Charles Plastic, Groves as Hawbuck, Minnie Conway as the Hon. Mrs. Glenroy, Mme. Ponisi as Mrs.

Moreen, Louisa Eldridge as Mrs. Trot, Miss Blaisdell as Goody Hawbuck and Rose Coghlan as Rosalie Somers — a part in which, with her girlish flowing blonde wig and her simple country attire, this mature actress seemed to me quite absurd. And the play was so old-fashioned!

Let us hear the Herald of March 14th, as to the revival; I quote it for the general principles involved: "It is called on the programme the Wallack Company . . . it is nothing more or less than Mr. John Gilbert, last survivor of the old Wallack Comedy Company, and some ladies and gentlemen who have been for the last five to ten years connected with the company. . . . The fact is that only three persons upon the stage gave to the audience the subtle, almost inexpressible quality of an age of which little is known." They were "Gilbert, Edwards and Groves. . . . If this is true it is not to be wondered at that there was a flatness where there should have been sparkle and poses and attitudes where there should have been graces and delicate finesse. An old comedy is so much like an old wine that it cannot be tampered with, and . . . actors and actresses fitted for the 'society plays' of to-day are almost incapable of presenting the arts and graces of a century that will ever be famous for its gallantry, its sentiments, its phrases and its members, although very largely a mere social veneer."

March 22nd terminated the career of this ghost of a past glory. Almost equally time-worn was Money, revived on Friday, the 23rd, with Tearle in Wallack's great part of Alfred Evelyn, with Rose Coghlan as the absurd Clara Douglas, Gilbert as Benjamin Stout (in which I can still see him, in the scene of the reading of the will, tearing the mourning band from his hat), Edwards as Sir John Vesey, Groves as Mr. Graves, Ward as Captain Dudley Smooth, Pigott as Sir Frederic Blount, Dodsworth as Sharp, Mme. Ponisi as a heavy Lady Franklin, and Netta Guion, overweighted, as the sly Georgina. I do not cite many nonentities, male, who undertook very small characters, especially in the gambling scene. Money departed, on April 7th, to be succeeded, on the 9th, by something far more desirable, the ever-welcome She Stoops to Conquer:

Charles Marlow	Osmond Tearle	Jeremy	Charles Edwin
Mr. Hardcastle	John Gilbert	Stingo	Adolphus H. Shelley
Hastings	W. T. Lovell	Mrs. Hardcastle	Mme. Ponisi
Tony Lumpkin	Charles Groves	Kate Hardcastle	Rose Coghlan
Sir Charles Marlow	J. W. Pigott	Miss Neville	Netta Guion
Diggory	Charles Dodsworth	Dolly	Maud Litchfield
Muggins	S. DuBois	Barmaid	Fanny Bart

This refreshing shower of Eighteenth-Century humour lasted till April 17th. On the evening of the 16th, I saw the comedy for the second time. Harry Edwards, as stage-manager, came before the curtain and announced that apologies from Wallack's stage were very rare; that afternoon, however, Miss Coghlan, had fallen and sprained her ankle and could not appear. Minnie Conway took her place and supplied a competent, if matronly Miss

[413]

Hardcastle. Meantime, on the afternoon of the 16th, a benefit to Marshall P. Wilder promised volunteers in Joseph Haworth, Robert Hilliard, Mme. Valda, Alice Shaw, the whistler, Francis Wilson and Eugene Oudin. On the 18th of April came that specialty of Wallack's — The School for Scandal, as last of the farewell revivals:

Sir Peter Teazle	John Gilbert	Careless	W. T. Lovell
Sir Oliver Surface	Harry Edwards	Snake	Adolphus Shelley
Sir Benjamin Backbite	J. W. Pigott	Sir Harry Bumper	W. Hampshire
Charles Surface	Osmond Tearle	Trip	C. E. Edwin
Joseph Surface	E. D. Ward	Lady Teazle	Rose Coghlan
Crabtree	Charles Dodsworth	Mrs. Candour	Mme. Ponisi
Moses	Charles Groves	Lady Sneerwell	Sadie Bigelow
Rowley	W. J. Leonard	Maria	Enid Leslie

S. DuBois, long of Wallack's, served as Joseph's servant, and Alvin Robinson was servant to Lady Sneerwell. J. W. Pigott, says Allston Brown, was too ill to appear, matinée and evening, on April 23rd, and Albert Roberts acted Sir Benjamin. John Gilbert fell ill on the 27th and for a performance or two was succeeded, as Sir Peter, by Harry Edwards, J. W. Pigott acting as Sir Oliver. The last week of the famous Wallack company, or at least what remained of its former glory, brought London Assurance (April 30th and matinée, May 2nd); Old Heads and Young Hearts (May 1st); Money (2nd, evening); She Stoops to Conquer (May 3rd and 4th); and The School for Scandal (matinée and evening, May 5th). The company acted these same pieces, in the same order, during the week of May 7th–12th, at Sinn's Park Theatre, in Brooklyn, there leaving our cognisance forever. On the last night at the home theatre, John Gilbert lamented the taste of the public for "whipped syllabubs"; looking down the list of comic operas and extravaganzas then current in New York, one could only echo his plaint. At any rate, Wallack's was gone, and with it went some of the pleasantest recollections in the Annals of the New York Stage.

THE LADY OR THE TIGER? BOCCACCIO

John A. McCaull, on May 7th, brought in a comic opera based on Frank R. Stockton's much-discussed conundrum, The Lady or the Tiger? Sydney Rosenfeld made the libretto, none too satisfactory, and Julius J. Lyons provided music that Adolph Nowak, the conductor, could not galvanize into popularity. Phil Goatcher devised some attractive sets, and the cast promised well, with De Wolf Hopper as Pausanias, Jeff De Angelis as Menander, Eugene Oudin as Lamachus, Francis Gaillard as Theotychides, Madeline Lucette as Hilaria, Maud Wilson as Daroona, and Mathilde Cottrelly as the comic Polyxena. One knew not what to expect of the Irene of Caterina Marco (daughter of the elder Mark Smith) and found, as I did on the opening night, that one's dubious conjectures were verified. The funny

VIRGINIA DREHER
(HERMIA)

JAMES LEWIS
(BOTTOM)

JOSEPH HOLLAND AND
PHŒBE RUSSELL

JOHN DREW
(DEMETRIUS)

ADA REHAN
(HELENA)

OTIS SKINNER
(LYSANDER)

ALICE HOOD
(OBERON)

BIJOU FERNANDEZ
(PUCK)

EFFIE SHANNON
(TITANIA)

SARONY'S PHOTOGRAPHS FROM A MIDSUMMER-NIGHT'S DREAM

little Alfred Klein was first Ephor, four others of that rank including Lindsay Morrison, F. W. Kyle and Louis Schrader and A. Barbara. We all
expected some kind of answer to the question then agitating the public
mind and were astounded to see emerge from the door of the arena, not the
princess and not the tiger, but the comic old woman, played by Mme. Cottrelly. Furthermore, the opera as a whole, was not very funny, though,
needless to say, Hopper had moments of hilarious fooling. I turn with
relief, on the afternoon of June 7th, to a benefit for Robert Hilliard (though
I hardly see how he merited it), at which were promised Henry Miller,
Genevieve Lytton, Richard Golden, Louis Harrison, Eben Plympton, Hopper,
Isabelle Urquhart, Sylvia Gerrish, George S. Knight, James T. Powers, J.
S. Burdett, and Mrs. McKee Rankin (with Hilliard) in the second act of
The Golden Giant — a goodly array, if haply they all appeared. The Lady
or the Tiger? ceased to perplex, on June 30th.

The house re-opened, on July 16th, with Prince Methusalem, the cast
including Marion Manola (in the title-rôle), Annie Myers, Marie A. Sanger,
De Wolf Hopper, De Angelis, John J. Raffael, Lindsay Morrison, Alfred
Klein, H. A. Cripps, Josephine Knapp, Grace Seavey and Master Freddie De
Angelis. This tuneful work carried through till August 18th, a solace for
the solstice. Another revival graced the stage, beginning on Monday,
August 20th; this was Rudolph Dellinger's opera, Lorraine, with Oudin in
the title-rôle, Hopper as Gaspard, De Angelis as D'Effiat, Charles W. Dungan
as Louis XIV, Annie Myers as Olivier de la Tour, Cripps as Pierre, Marion
Manola as Madeline, Alice Galliard as Oudarde, and Josephine Knapp as
Louise de la Vallière, a cast of a few good principals and rather weak assistants.

This stopgap lasted about as long as could be expected, two weeks. Thus
far, McCaull's long season had not been a glittering success. On September
3rd, however, he finally reached the goal with a delightful revival of Boccaccio, Marion Manola singing the name-part, with Laura Moore as
Fiametta, Laura Joyce Bell as Peronella, Annie Myers as Isabella, Dungan
as Pietro, Edmund Stanley as Leonetto, and with almost the funniest trio
I ever saw (and I saw them twice in this revival) in Hopper as Lambertuccio,
Digby Bell as Lotteringhi and Jefferson De Angelis as Scalza. All in all,
that revival was one of the best performances of comic opera I ever attended. It continued merrily till McCaull ended his season on October 6th.
September 27th brought a benefit for the yellow fever sufferers in the South,
a charity that had many benefits that autumn in generous New York. For
this particular manifestation were promised Geoffrey Hawley, Digby and
Laura Joyce Bell, Mme. Cottrelly, Kyrle Bellew, and (in the balcony scene
from Romeo and Juliet) De Wolf Hopper as a bouncing Juliet and tiny
Marshall P. Wilder as the love-torn Romeo. That supposedly funny perversion was frequently given in those days; but I always felt very sorry for

[415]

the humpbacked Wilder, even though I admired him for bravely making the best of his deformity.

When the theatre began the next season, on October 8, 1888, its name had been changed to that of its new lessee, A. M. Palmer, and, as Palmer's Theatre, it, for a few years, held a prominent place in theatrical history.

DALY'S THEATRE, 1887–1888

If Wallack's had pursued a precarious course in these later years, Daly's had reached its apogée. The season of the revival of The Taming of the Shrew was certainly the most brilliant thus far in his career, and the year we now chronicle hardly sank beneath it financially and, in some respects, was even more delightful, artistically. During the summer clôture, a brick wall of twenty-four inches had been built between stage and auditorium.

The opening play (October 5th) was Dandy Dick, a farce by Pinero, satirising the sportswomen of England, Miss Rehan being Georgiana Tidman, a sporting woman and Dandy Dick being the horse expected to win. If her character was out of her usual line, John Drew's was more astonishing, that of "a wilted old military beau of dejected mien [I am quoting from Judge Daly], given to small 'at homes,' where he played a melancholy flute, accompanying Lieutenant Darby (Skinner) as first violin. A finished bit of deception was the simulated playing by Drew and Skinner to a piano accompaniment by Miss Shannon." Though Dandy Dick had only thirty-two performances, the importance of Pinero and of Daly's company prompts me to print the cast:

Dean of St. Marvells	Charles Fisher	Hatcham	Frederick Bond
Blore, his butler	James Lewis	Salome	Virginia Dreher
Sir Tristan Wardon	George Clarke	Sheba	Effie Shannon
Major Tarver	John Drew	Hannah Topping	Lizzie St. Quentin
Lieutenant Darby	Otis Skinner	Georgiana Tidman	Ada Rehan
Topping, constable	William Gilbert		

This was the first appearance at Daly's of pretty little Effie Shannon; and Daly, by his usual custom of improving players' names, changed Lizzie St. Quinten into a more aristocratic Lizzie St. Quentin. And, whatever the players thought, he always bettered in such changing. Having experienced his customary fate (except in the case of The Squire and The Magistrate) with Pinero, Daly, on November 1st, produced one of the most delightful things ever seen on his stage. This was The Railroad of Love, adapted by the facile manager from Goldfische, by von Schönthan and Kadelburg. On the first night Henry Irving and Ellen Terry occupied a box, and it may have been Miss Rehan's matchless acting in this play that brought forth Miss Terry's enthusiastic praise recorded in her Story of My Life. During the

[416]

run of the comedy Charles Dickens, the younger, then on a reading tour in the States, wrote, according to Judge Daly, "If Miss Rehan and Mr. Drew as Cousin Val and the Lieutenant do not make the greatest comedy success that London has seen for years I shall be very much surprised." Their acting certainly was acclaimed, later, in the British capital, though the play failed there! In this comedy, Phœbe Russell, another pretty girl, made her début, but never went so far as did her young colleagues, Kitty Cheatham and Effie Shannon. The cast of The Railroad of Love:

Val Osprey	Ada Rehan	Adam Grinnidge	George Clarke
Eutycia Laburnam	Mrs. G. H. Gilbert	Benny Demaresq	Otis Skinner
Viva Van Ryker	Phœbe Russell	Judge Van Ryker	Charles Leclercq
Cherry	Evelina Cooke	Truffles	E. P. Wilks
General Everett	Charles Fisher	Tom	John Wood
Lieutenant Everett	John Drew	Crusty	E. Ireton
Phenix Scuttleby	James Lewis		

Two bits from this charming play are fixed in my memory — both in Cousin Val's apartment in a later act. Mrs. Gilbert, as a thriving business woman from the country, arrives in town for a round of gaiety. She throws open the window, looks out on the street, takes a long breath of extreme satisfaction and cries with the crisp, sharp intonation that none but Mrs. Gilbert could effect — "There, smell that! not a particle of ozone in it!" She had received what all the year she had longed for — the smell of the big city. The other scene is that at the door between Miss Rehan and Drew. He had called on Cousin Val, and she had gone into an adjoining room to dress for the evening. Bidden to examine the photograph album on a table, he casually turns the pages till she calls from the adjoining room, asking him what he thinks of her photograph in the book. Taking the cue, he finds the picture, slips it into his pocket, and replies that there is no likeness of her in the album. She protests, comes to the door, sees what he has done, and in the silvery Rehan voice and with the inimitable Rehan smile, says in an aside (asides were permitted in those happy pre-Ibsen days), "The wretch!" Gladly I reproduce this scene at the door, in Sarony's photograph, which we all lovingly bought and cherished in that halcyon year.

A MIDSUMMER-NIGHT'S DREAM

I believe The Railroad of Love was the most exquisite modern comedy I ever saw at Daly's; the success it achieved is shown by the length of its run. The hundredth performance fell on January 23rd. It might have gone longer, but Daly, ever restless and now anxious to duplicate his Shakespearian triumph of the preceding season, removed from the stage The Railroad of Love, on January 30th, presenting, on the 31st, a very elaborate revival of A Midsummer-Night's Dream, far more beautiful than that of the same comedy which he had made, in 1873, at the Grand Opera House.

[417]

Henry Hoyt devised very impressive scenery, severely Greek in pillars and vistas for the palace of Theseus, and soft and dreamy for the wood of perplexity. Daly followed the custom of giving a moving panorama, this time of the return voyage from the enchanted wood to Athens. The actors did not look particularly comfortable sitting or standing in the stationary boat while the scenery slid by. It was not quite so bad as Wagner's device of having Parsifal and Gurnemanz pretend to be walking while their journey was represented by sliding representations of scenes from the hall of the Grail to more customary localities below.

The cast now supplied by Daly for Shakespeare's fantasy was possibly the best ever given in New York. We had naturally expected that Ada Rehan would follow her success as the shrewish Katharine with a similar picture of the hot-tempered Hermia; those who thus reckoned little knew their Daly or their Rehan. No greater proof of Miss Rehan's versatility could be devised than the contrast between her fiery shrew and her gentle, lovelorn Helena in the beautiful delicate-coloured Grecian dress. I still see her reclining on the couch, in the palace, as the curtain fell at the close of the first act. And Miss Dreher was excellent as Hermia. The perplexed and perplexing lovers were men of superb diction and gallant bearing in the persons of John Drew as Demetrius and Otis Skinner as Lysander. Joseph Holland was not very heroic as Theseus and the Hippolyta of the young Phœbe Russell was only a pretty girl in a pretty dress — certainly no Amazon at all. Virginia Dreher would have looked and acted the part much better, though she was more effectively cast for Hermia. Of course Charles Fisher was a stately Egeus, and Eugene Ormond a satisfactory Philostrate. There had been some question of whether the slim James Lewis, with his perky manner and light, chirping voice could successfully cope with Bottom, the tradition of which had been set in 1854 by the stout unctuous Burton and the richly comic Davidge. But, after all, who knows what Bottom should look like, or how his voice should sound? It is his conceit that counts and his utter ignorance of everything under the sun or in a play, and that ignorance and that conceit Lewis perfectly displayed. Anything funnier than his performance in the rehearsal of the tragedy and his Pyramus in the playing I cannot imagine. The Flute of William Gilbert ably seconded Lewis's efforts. Minor artisans of Athens were Charles Leclercq as Quince, Fred Bond as Snug, John Wood as Snout and E. P. Wilks as Starveling. Collectively their rendering of Pyramus and Thisbe was the most hilarious I have ever seen; almost the only endurable one. As to the fairy scenes Daly followed the then unbreakable tradition of assigning Oberon to a woman and Puck to a child; we have today (1941) grown beyond that custom. Alice Hood, as the Fairy King was merely a pretty girl, but little Bijou Fernandez managed to convey a sense of reality in the character of Puck. And Effie Shannon was delightful as Titania, and a picture of loveli-

[418]

OTIS SKINNER—MISS DREHER—ADA REHAN

OTIS SKINNER—MISS DREHER—ADA REHAN—JOHN DREW
SCENES FROM A MIDSUMMER NIGHT'S DREAM
From Photographs taken in Daly's Theatre, 1888

ness.   Lizzie St. Quentin (*sic*) sang the solo music, in the fairy scenes, scenes that with their soft foliage, their dreamy lighting and flitting fireflies, seem to my memory A Midsummer-Night's Dream indeed.   In the groups of sing-ing fairies were Augustus Sohlke (as Peas Blossom), Mamie and Katie O'Brien (as Cobweb and Moth), and Master Yorer (as Mustard Seed), Miss Sears, Evelina Cooke, Belle Wharton and many others.   Some of the attend-ants of the Court of Theseus later attained distinction on the stage, Hamilton Revelle, Jameson Lee Finney and Franklyn Reglid; Keller, Ireton and Murphy also stood near the throne of Theseus.

I have dwelt at length on this revival of the Dream because I believe it is the best within my experience of half a century.   I enjoyed it thoroughly in several hearings, whereas most later revivals in America or in England have seemed overwrought and drawn out (particularly in the comic epi-sodes) and therefore somewhat boring.   But, of course, I have never since met such a quartet of lovers as Drew, Skinner, Miss Rehan and Miss Dreher. It is rather incongruous that A Midsummer-Night's Dream should have been playing at Daly's during the period of the great blizzard of 1888; that theatre and the Star were the only two high-class theatres that gave performances on the terrible night of March 12th.   An explanation that I read in the Herald stated that the house (Daly's) had been sold out and that, to redistribute the tickets through the next few days, for which the house was practically sold out, would be too severe a tax on the staff.   Perhaps the same reason pre-vailed at the Star, where Irving and Miss Terry were filling an extraor-dinarily successful engagement.

A Midsummer-Night's Dream carried through till the end of Daly's season on April 7th — a term requiring only three productions — Dandy Dick (thirty-two times), The Railroad of Love (one hundred and eight) and the Shakespeare comedy (seventy-nine).   John L. Stoddard delivered two courses of morning lenten lectures on travels abroad, Course B duplicating the talks and pictures of Course A.   Course A began on February 28th and Course B on March 1st.   The subjects were Travels in Sunny Spain, Julius Cæsar and Rome, Splendours of the Pyrenees, Lord Byron and His Times, and Constantinople and Its People — rather interesting, one thinks.   At the close of his New York season, Daly took his company to London for an-other successful season.

ROSINA VOKES

No more agreeable substitute for our favourite company could be imag-ined than Rosina Vokes and her merry associates.   We came for a short time to regard this alternation as a regular institution.   After a gap of one week Miss Vokes appeared, on April 16th, with a delightful trio of one-act comedies.   In A Game of Cards, adapted from the familiar Partie de Piquet,

[419]

Felix Morris was the Chevalier de Rocheferrier and Ferdinand Gottschalk Mons. Mercier, with Morton Selten and Isabella (*sic*) Irving, a perfectly charming girl, as the young lovers. No one can ever forget Miss Vokes, as Lady Lucille Grafton, in The Circus Rider, going through the antics on the sofa, in her efforts to convince the young man that she really was the circus rider he had arranged to have stopped at his gate. With her, in the cast of this amusing piece by Mrs. Charles A. Doremus, were Courtenay Thorpe (the only member of her company whom I did not admire) as Lord Morton, Morton Selten as Lord Weldon, and the exquisitely funny Ferdinand Gottschalk as Latimer, Weldon's servant. Not to deprive the audience of things familiar, Miss Vokes ended the bill with A Christmas Pantomime Rehearsal, never long absent from her scheme:

Jack Deedes	Courtenay Thorpe	Lady Muriel	Mercedes Leigh
Tompkins	J. Rolfe	Miss Violet	Isabella Irving
Captain Tom Robinson	M. Selten	Miss May	Eleanor Barry
Sir Charles Grandison	F. Gottschalk	Miss Lilly	Rosina Vokes
Baron de Rataplan	Felix Morris		

One sees, with regret, that the character of the brainless English nobleman, with his re-iterated explanations of why he was late for the rehearsal (his cab had upset) — a part so superbly played by Weedon Grossmith — has been changed, I suppose to fit Felix Morris, into a French baron. He was never so funny as the inimitable original of Grossmith.

The success of this opening bill carried it through May 5th. On May 7th, S. Theyre Smith's Which Is Which? enlisted Morton Selten, Morris, Gottschalk, Miss Leigh, Miss Barry and Isabella Irving (who made a hit as Jane, the servant). My Milliner's Bill, the great favourite, allowed Miss Vokes to sing her marvellous His 'Art Was True to Poll, with Courtenay Thorpe as her disguised husband. A Double Lesson ended the evening's delights, Miss Vokes, as the burlesque actress, teaching Mercedes Leigh (as Lady Moncrieffe) what she needed to learn about acting and life, and Thorpe as Harry Fielding what his wife (the actress) knew about him. Other parts fell to Gottschalk, Morris and Isabella Irving as another maid. One sees where Miss Irving acquired the art of acting maids that led her, next season, to the delightful Susan, in Daly's revival of A Night Off. Miss Vokes's last week was devoted to A Game of Cards, My Milliner's Bill and Buckstone's ever-popular The Rough Diamond (played on May 22nd and 23rd); and Sydney Grundy's In Honour Bound (with Thorpe, Selten, Miss Barry and Miss Irving), The Circus Rider and The Rough Diamond (May 24th, 25th, 26th). The Rough Diamond gave us Thorpe as Sir William Evergreen, Selten as Captain Blenheim, Gottschalk and Miss Barry as Lord and Lady Plato, Felix Morris as Cousin Joe, and Miss Vokes, of course, as Margery. A season that passed from Miss Rehan and her splendid colleagues to Rosina Vokes and her delightful company would be impossible to match today (1941) for refinement, charm and exquisite grace. I may report that Miss Vokes closed Daly's, on the evening of May 21st, to take part, as a supernumerary, in the great Wallack benefit at the Metropolitan Opera House.

MADISON SQUARE THEATRE, 1887–1888

We remember that Richard Mansfield's extraordinary performances of Dr. Jekyll and Mr. Hyde closed, on October 1st, at this pretty little theatre in 24th Street. On Monday, October 3rd, the regular company returned with Jim, the Penman, cast as at the close of the last season, Alexander Salvini still taking the place of W. J. LeMoyne, then gone, not without ill feeling, to Daniel Frohman's Lyceum Theatre. The popular drama held the stage through November 9th. Meantime one of those trying authors' matinées — Angela — was tested on October 18th, with Henry Lee, F. M. Burbeck, F. A. Everill, H. A. Weaver, C. P. Flockton, J. Findlay, Alexander Salvini, Florence Windram and Genevieve Lytton vainly trying to make of it a "go" in the theatrical sense and not in the literal. Lee was co-author with L. Ottomeyer.

On Thursday, November 10th, Palmer produced an adaptation of D'Ennery's Le Martyre, which he called The Martyr, certainly not an exact translation of the French title. The new play had a silly theme of a devoted wife, pretending that her mother's illegitimate son is her lover; and why? to save her mother's reputation, forsooth! Conspiracy is part of the plot, exemplified by Salvini and the handsome Mathilde Madison; but best of all I remember was the return of the young daughter of the self-sacrificing wife, and her incredulous query when she learns of her parents' divorce. Annie Russell was simply exquisite in the part, and I still hear her wonderful voice in that query to her father, asking him what horrible thing he had done, to induce her mother to leave him. It was one of the few genuine touches in the play. The cast was truly remarkable:

Duc di San Lucca	C. P. Flockton	Mr. Smith	William Davidge
General Moray	H. M. Pitt	Giacomo	J. H. Findlay
Admiral de la Marche	F. Robinson	Footman	Herbert Ayling
Sir Ellis Drake	J. H. Stoddart	Mme. Moray	Agnes Booth
Annibale Palmieri	Alexander Salvini	Mme. de la Marche	Mrs. Phillips
Robert Bruel	L. F. Massen	Paulette	Annie Russell
Corporal Pichot	E. M. Holland	Claudia Palmieri	Mathilde Madison

It would be wonderful to have such a group of actors playing throughout a season, and season after season, in the New York of 1941; alas! I do not know where one could find, today, the artistic equivalents of Stoddart, Holland, Mrs. Booth and Annie Russell. Despite that glorious cast, The Martyr failed dismally and had its last performance on December 5th. We shall find Clara Morris using a version of the same play as part of her repertoire in this and following seasons; neither she nor her company could approach the excellence of the interpreters at the Madison Square. I saw both.

Elaine, that adaptation from Tennyson, by George Parsons Lathrop and Harry Edwards, which had been tried at an author's matinée, in the preceding spring, was put in the regular bill, on December 6th, with several of the same people in the cast:

King Arthur	Charles Overton	Dumb Servitor	C. P. Flockton
Lancelot	Alexander Salvini	Hermit Friar	William Davidge
Lord of Astolat	Frederic Robinson	Guinevere	Marie Burroughs
Sir Torre	Louis Massen	Elaine	Annie Russell
Sir Lavaine	Walden Ramsay	Llanyd	Minnie Seligman
Sir Gawain	E. M. Holland	Roselle	Marie Greenwald

This was set down as Miss Seligman's first appearance on any stage. The reader need not be told that the pretty Miss Burroughs was incapable of expressing the queenly bearing or the tragic sorrows of Guinevere, or that Annie Russell was simply perfect as the lily maid of Astolat. The tableau of the dead (Miss Russell) steered by the dumb (Flockton) as the barge wended its way to Camelot lingers in memory as one of the beautiful realisations of a poet's dream.

Of course this slender, poetic charm could not be expected to be aught but evanescent. It was succeeded, on January 16th, by Henry Arthur Jones's improbably romantic drama, Heart of Hearts, a play involving the theft of a priceless ruby by the returned convict (Flockton) who surrenders it to his daughter (Miss Burroughs), only to have her accused of the theft, thereby delaying her marriage to the nice Fitzralph boy (Louis Massen). The Fitzralph toploftiness was taken down a bit when it was discovered that Wilhelmina, of the clan (Mrs. E. L. Davenport) had married the butler (Stoddart). In view of all this, Lady Clarissa had to consent to the marriage of her son (Massen) to the butler's niece (Miss Burroughs). Why do I put in so improbable a tale? Merely to show the reader what 1888 tolerated, and to invite him, if he dare, to a query as to what his own age tolerates. Since, despite its absurdity, Heart of Hearts ran, surprisingly, through March, I will supply the cast:

Harold Fitzralph	Louis Massen	John, footman	G. S. Stevens
Marcus Latimer	Frederic Robinson	Lady Clarissa Fitzralph	Mrs. Phillips
Dr. Chettle	E. M. Holland	Wilhelmina Fitzralph	Mrs. E. L. Davenport
Daniel Robins	C. P. Flockton	Lucy Robins	Marie Burroughs
James Robins	J. H. Stoddart	Sibyl Latimer	Blanche Curtisse
Murch	John Findlay	Barton	Marie Greenwald
Jeweller's Assistant	W. H. Pope		

The little Madison Square furnished a perfect auditorium for special matinées. Palmer, on January 4th, offered the first of seven Wednesday afternoon concerts, with, on that day, Imogene Brown, Lizzie Macnichol, C. C. Ferguson (tenor), Laura Sedgwick Collins, Francis Walker (bass), and

W. E. Taylor (director).   On the 18th, an impressive group included Giulia Valda, Teresa Carreño, Anna Bulkley Hills, Wilbur Gunn (tenor), Francis Walker, and Albert Edward Greenhalgh (accompanist).   The fourth Wednesday (January 25th) gave us Michael Banner, Mrs. Bulkley Hills, Walker, with Miss Morse, Spigaroli, Bologna and Mme. Valda — these last four in the second act of Martha.   February 1st brought Biro de Marion, Wilbur Gunn, Arthur Oswald and Jeanne Franko.   Mme. Valda was again the bright star on February 15th.

Sidney Woollett also, beginning on January 16th, tried to brighten some wintry Monday afternoons, with recitals (from memory) of, in successive days, Enoch Arden, Elaine, The Passing of Arthur, Guinevere, The Merchant of Venice, Much Ado about Nothing and The Tempest.   Since we are in the realm of poetry, I pass to March 15th, when the Goethe Society of New York tendered to Henry Irving (could it possibly have been in recognition of his production of Wills's Faust?) a reception, with Parke Godwin presiding, and George William Curtis delivering the final speech.   Between these speeches, Irving delivered an address on dramatic art and Goethe.   A person of poetic imagination could revel in the list of famous men and women present at this ceremony.   I can mention only a few — Ellen Terry, Mrs. A. M. Palmer, Jennie June Croly, Mrs. John Bigelow, Mr. and Mrs. Robert Ingersoll, Judge Brady, Agnes Booth, Winifred Emery, Parke Godwin, Mr. and Mrs. Henry E. Abbey, Augustin Daly, Annie Russell and George Alexander.

On March 20th (afternoon), Mrs. Genevieve Stebbins Thompson gave a Delsarte matinée in a city grown somewhat weary of her theme.   Let us return to Palmer, whose season had not been enthralling.   On April 2nd, he met success, financial and artistic, with Robert Buchanan's adaptation of Daudet, which he called Partners.   In this piece Alexander Salvini won high acclaim as the trusting elder partner deceived in love and in business by the younger member of the firm.   The cast had much of Palmer's brilliancy, though, for the better part of his season, he had been unable to employ in the home theatre his two best actresses, Mrs. Booth and Maud Harrison, or at any time there his most famous actor, Charles Coghlan.   Let us see who carried Partners to a minor triumph:

Henry Borgfeldt	Alexander Salvini	Smith	W. H. Pope
Charles Derwentwater	Walden Ramsay	Servant	G. S. Stevens
Mr. Parr	J. H. Stoddart	Claire	Marie Burroughs
Algernon Bellair	E. M. Holland	Alice Bellair	May Robson
Mrs. Harkaway's Husband	H. Ayling	Mary	Kate Molony
Dr. Somerville	William Davidge	Lady Silverdale	Mrs. E. J. Phillips
Boker	John Findlay	Mrs. Harkaway	Mathilde Madison
Dickinson	C. P. Flockton		

As I approach the summer seasons at the Madison Square, I regret the passing of the Mallory custom of continuing a winter success — Hazel Kirke,

Esmeralda, The Rajah, etc.—straight through the hot months of summer. And Palmer must also have regretted it, since previous arrangements for his theatre and his company compelled him to withdraw Partners, on April 28th, in the height of its success.

His were not the only schemes that had gone awry. The burning of the Union Square Theatre had left its manager, J. M. Hill, with a homeless production on his hands. This was Sydney Rosenfeld's comedy, A Possible Case, and Hill finally placed it on April 9th, for three weeks at the Standard Theatre; thence, on April 30th, he transferred it to the Madison Square. In the Standard the cast was as follows; possibly a few minor characters were deleted in Madison Square:

Otto Brinckerhoff	M. A. Kennedy	Bridgeman	Charles Standish
Lawrence Gould	F. M. Burbeck	Willie Carter	Edward Smart
Allan Weeks	Robert Hilliard	Violet Mendoza	Genevieve Lytton
Señor de Vidas	W. H. Thompson	Ethel Sorrero	Dorothy Dorr
Cyrus A. Wishton	George F. DeVere	Mrs. Wishton	Louise Rial
Aurelio	Dan Leeson	Gladys	Lelia Wolstan
Dick Hertel	E. D. Tannehill	Juanita	Kate Oesterle
Gomez	Robert V. Percy	Kitty	Carrie Jackson
Pedro	James H. Browne		

It ran for five weeks at the Madison Square, leaving on June 2nd. Meantime, on the afternoon of May 10th (this date I have verified), trial was made of a comedy by the ambitious Mrs. Charles A. Doremus; under title of A Fair Bohemian, it had an excellent cast in Georgie Drew Barrymore, Kate Forsyth, Lilla Vane, Nelson Wheatcroft, Frank Burbeck, John T. Sullivan, Thomas Patten and D. G. Longworth. Any aspiring author might be proud of such a cast.

Richard Mansfield re-entered the Madison Square, on June 4th, presenting for the first week his amazing Dr. Jekyll and Mr. Hyde. On June 11th he began a far easier week, with his charming Prince Karl, following it, on the 18th, with the inevitable A Parisian Romance, in which he was assisted by D. H. Harkins, Beatrice Cameron, Johnstone Bennett, John T. Sullivan, Maude White, Mrs. Sol Smith, Beverley Sitgreaves, W. H. Crompton, Joseph Frankau and other good players. After two weeks of his enduring Baron Chevrial, Mansfield departed on the 30th of June.

Effie Ellsler came back to what one might call her New York home par excellence, presenting, on July 2nd, The Keepsake, adapted by the very busy Clinton Stuart from the Antoinette Rigaud of Raimond Deslandes. Miss Ellsler played Christine Leroy (Antoinette Rigaud), with Mrs. Hart Jackson as Mme. Bernardet, Frank Weston as Jules Leroy, the advancing E. H. Vanderfelt as Philippe de Clermont, F. C. Bangs as General de Prefond, May Wolcott as Marcelle, Walden Ramsay as Robert Lambertin, Harry Eytinge as Bernadet, John Findlay as Pierre, and Harry Hogan as Jacques. One can only wonder as to where, even though it was the summer holiday,

[424]

producers found such promising casts. And Irene, tested at a matinée on July 3rd, also boasted of some good interpreters in S. Miller Kent, H. M. Pitt, Charles B. Welles, Charles Bowser, Cyril Scott, Luke Martin, J. McDonald, George S. Stevens, Grace Henderson, Lillian Chantore and Evelyn Campbell. Though I suspect her Keepsake had not met Miss Ellsler's expectations, she persisted, and, on July 30th, staged Judge Not, a drama by the usually efficient Frank Harvey. In the cast were E. H. Vanderfelt as Philip Vane, Frank Weston as Brightside, F. C. Bangs as Lord Ferndale, Fred Corbett as Rupert Derwent, Mme. Ponisi, thrice welcome to Wallackians, as Lady Moreland, Helen Bancroft as Ethel, Miss Ellsler as Katherine Clare, Mrs. Hart Jackson as Lady Chalmers, Master Vanderfelt as little Philip, and Harry Hogan as the servant. After two poor weeks, Miss Ellsler carried this disappointment to other stages.

And then, to illustrate the law of averages, for the Madison Square, William Gillette, on August 14th, produced his really bright and entertaining comedy, A Legal Wreck, a piece just suited to the warm summer nights, and with it achieved success:

Cap'n Edward Swift.........Alfred Hudson	Mrs. Kimball...................Ida Vernon
Jonathan Mazey...............Sidney Smith	Olive Grey.................Nina Boucicault
Ed Smith....................George Fawcett	Edith Kimball...............Frances Graham
Henry B. Leverett............Boyd Putnam	Nancy Dunks.........Fanny Denham Rouse
Richard Merriam.............Sidney Drew	Mary......................Elsie Lombard

The Herald of September 10th or thereabouts informs us that Lilla Vane and Bertha Welby had replaced Nina Boucicault and Ida Vernon. The fiftieth performance was listed for October 1st; on October 18th, the play was given at a matinée for the yellow fever sufferers in the South. And A Legal Wreck departed on November 10th, having brought Sidney Drew into notice as a talented light comedian. The last record for the busy season is that of a special matinée on November 1st, when another *opus* of Clinton Stuart, Beauty Abroad, failed to capture us at home, though a good cast included William Morris, E. J. Henley, Walden Ramsay (one of my favourite actors), R. Peyton Gibbs, Cyril Scott, J. A. Wilkes, Harry Hogan, Isabelle Evesson, Mary Shaw, the ubiquitous Lilla Vane, Nina Boucicault, Mrs. Mary Barker and Linda Dietz, who could not regain the position she abandoned in New York in 1879, to win fame, if possible, in London.

LYCEUM THEATRE, 1887–1888

Having traversed with protracted patience, not to say pain, the summer history of the Madison Square Theatre, I take up, with pleasure, the briefer record for the Lyceum, that other pretty little house, about to begin its career as another high class "stock" theatre. And dear to our memories is the Lyceum and its splendid management by Daniel Frohman.

The house having closed, on July 16th, re-opened, on August 22nd, with the same attraction, The Highest Bidder, with Sothern, LeMoyne, Pigott, Archer, and Belle Archer in their former rôles, but with Fanny Addison and Kitty Wilson replacing Alice Crowther and Vida Croly. The run terminated on Monday, September 19th. On the 20th, Frohman produced The Great Pink Pearl, by R. C. Carton and Cecil Raleigh (the latter directing), casting it extremely well with members of the Sothern company and the new aggregation which was, within a short time, to establish itself as the permanent stock company of the house:

Prince Paul Penninkoff	Herbert Kelcey	•Albert	W. Davenport
Count Serge Keronine	R. F. Cotton	Commissary	Thomas Crane
Anthony Sheen	E. H. Sothern	Princess Penninkoff	Mme. de Naucaze
Patruccio	W. J. LeMoyne	Mary Turner	Grace Henderson
Valovitch	Herbert Archer	Jessie	Etta Hawkins
Lillicarp	Rowland Buckstone	Mrs. Sharpus	Violet Campbell
Watson	George Randall		

Editha's Burglar was given on the same night, with Sothern and Archer and that clever child, Elsie Leslie, beginning in it her remarkable career. For certain Wednesday matinées we were enlivened with The Highest Bidder and Editha's Burglar.

September 23rd brought a trial matinée of Mark Twain's The American Claimant, or, Mulberry Sellers Ten Years Later, with, if you can believe it, A. P. Burbank as Sellers. Mark Twain was a great genius, but he simply could not write plays. This emanation had been born two weeks earlier, in New Brunswick, New Jersey, and had been seen since in Rochester and Syracuse. The cast at the Lyceum included Burbank as Sellers, J. W. Pigott as Rupert de Bohun, William Royston as Lafayette Hawkins, J. Barnes as Mr. Simpson, Alice King Hamilton as Mary Sellers, Annie King as Mrs. Sellers, and W. H. Lytell as Aunt Sally, seemingly a feeble array. On October 6th (matinée), an ambitious aspirant — Evelyn Foster — tried to act Camille. This special matinée epidemic is driving me mad; its unimportance, artistically, is appalling.

THE WIFE

And now we find relief in the pleasant haven of an all-season run, our first for too long a while. Daniel Frohman, on November 1st (the first night of The Railroad of Love, at Daly's), introduced his admirably selected company, in a new drama by David Belasco and H. C. De Mille — The Wife. We find, in William Winter's Life of David Belasco, the latter's account of how he and De Mille, at Frohman's suggestion, wrote the play, starting with no idea of what it was to be, and working to devise characters to fit the actors in the new Lyceum stock company. The plot finally selected had been used

ALEXANDER SALVINI
MARIE BURROUGHS

ANNIE RUSSELL
AS ELAINE

ADA REHAN—JOHN DREW
(RAILROAD OF LOVE)

FELIX MORRIS
(A GAME OF CARDS)

ISABEL IRVING

ROSINA VOKES
(THE CIRCUS RIDER)

SIDNEY DREW

ELSIE LESLIE
(EDITHA'S BURGLAR)

F. GOTTSCHALK

successfully in such stage hits as Pique, The Banker's Daughter and Lady Clare — the marriage of a girl who loves one man to another whom she does not love, and the awakening of love for the husband, always a noble, self-sacrificing man, too dull to recognise his wife's changing attitude toward him. In The Wife the husband is particularly noble, but tortures himself with constant brooding on the thought of his wife's affection for the other man. The three 'angles of this shaky triangle were well played by Herbert Kelcey, Henry Miller and the popular womanly Georgia Cayvan. The comic parts added to the success of the play, the scene in which the cub lovers, enacted by Charles Dickson and Louise Dillon, smudge their faces in looking at an eclipse of the sun through smoked pieces of glass being especially effective. And Mrs. Walcot and LeMoyne revelled in their parts. Despite its lack of originality and literary charm, The Wife exactly suited the taste of 1887–88, and enjoyed the rare distinction of two hundred and thirty-nine performances before Frohman ended his season. To this outcome contributed the beauty and comfort of the little auditorium, to which fashion wended its way, the charming stage-sets and the excellence of the acting. We were happy in 1887–88, and did not expect our plays to be moral and sociological treatises; we merely asked that they be clean and interesting. With pleasure I set down the cast of The Wife:

John Rutherford	Herbert Kelcey	Helen Truman	Georgia Cayvan
Robert Grey	Henry Miller	Lucile Ferrant	Grace Henderson
Matthew Culver	Nelson Wheatcroft	Mrs. Bellamy Ives	Mrs. Walcot
Silas Truman	Charles Walcot	Kitty Ives	Louise Dillon
Major Putnam	W. J. LeMoyne	Mrs. Amory	Mrs. Thomas Whiffen
Mr. Randolph	W. C. Bellows	Agnes	Vida Croly
Jack Dexter	Charles S. Dickson		

The career of the play was diversified only by occasional special matinées so boring to my pen. Interesting, however, even to a jaded student, is the matinée given on December 8th. John H. Bird and Elita Proctor Otis rendered the quarrel scene from The School for Scandal; Blue and Cherry enlisted G. W. Nicholas, J. F. Conrad and Alice and Rita Lawrence; A Comical Countess presented Edward Fales Coward, Francis G. Landon, Frederic R. Satterlee and Mrs. Wilber Bloodgood; and Twenty Minutes under an Umbrella closed the proceedings, with Henry Miller and Miss Otis. I need not inform the reader that some of the best amateurs in New York participated in that programme. On December 23rd, the New York School of Acting showed what its pupils could do with the fourth act of The Winter's Tale and with Les Précieuses Ridicules. Harriet Ford, Vida Croly, George D. Fawcett, "Will" A. Buckland and Elsie Lombard took part. The hundredth performance of The Wife was scheduled for February 6th. But, before that glad celebration, F. F. Mackay lectured, under the management of E. E. Kidder, on The Metaphysics of Acting in Relation to Dramatic

[427]

Elocution; these portentous utterances were delivered on January 24th and 26th. Mackay's school of acting, later, became a feature in our city. The afternoons of February 23rd and 24th were given over to the Ladies' Amateur Orchestra, a quartet from the Rubinstein Club, and Contrast, a one-act emotional play from the French, acted by Kelcey, Faversham, E. F. Coward, Elsie De Wolfe, Mrs. W. Fellowes Morgan. On March 22nd, for the benefit of St. Mary's Hospital, Mackay acted Eccles, in Caste, a part of which he grew very fond; others were Charles S. Dickson, F. M. Burbeck, Charles Bradshaw, and two amateurs, Mrs. Postley and Mme. Belazzi. Far more significant was the hundred and fiftieth performance of The Wife, listed for March 26th. Henry Miller, having been loaned for the first performances of A Possible Case, tried, on the 26th, at the Brooklyn Academy of Music, his part in The Wife was taken up by William Faversham, who thus first comes forward prominently in our story, which hereafter will greet him many times. The house was closed on Good Friday night. And, on April 14th, Henry Miller resumed his rôle of Robert Grey.

On the afternoon of May 4th, Ernestine was acted for charity, the cast including, besides Henry Miller, Vida Croly and F. M. Burbeck, those ambitious amateurs, George W. Nicholas, Laura Sedgwick Collins, and Alice and Rita Lawrence. The Dead Shot also figured in the bill. A week later (May 11th), the bicentenary night of The Wife gladdened all hearts. The winning favourite finally closed, on June 16th, with its two hundred and thirty-ninth representation. William Winter (Life of David Belasco) tells us that Frohman, from the profits of the play, paid in full more than $50,000 owed to the Tiffany Studios. So pleased was everybody that Belasco and De Mille were commissioned to write (should I say, manufacture) another play for 1888–89; Lord Chumley accrued from that contract.

STAR THEATRE, 1887–1888

It seems natural to me to begin each season's annals with our splendid stock companies. They belonged to us, whereas the visiting stars and combinations belonged to America at large. In one case we owned, in the other we merely shared. For the season we are reviewing, I now take up the record of the best "combination" houses. By priority of accomplishment, the Star Theatre (once Wallack's), at Broadway and 13th Street, demands attention. It certainly, in 1887–88, offered the widest diversity of attractions, from Henry Irving to negro minstrelsy, farce and vaudeville. The season began, on August 22nd, with Abbey, Schoeffel and Grau as managers; McNish, Johnson and Slavin's Refined (!) Minstrels possessed the stage for a week. Held by the Enemy, on August 29th, presented Carrie Turner, Louise Dillon, Kate Denin Wilson, Henry Miller, William Gillette, Leslie Allen, Ben Graham and Melbourne McDowell, for what was set down for the five hundred and fiftieth performance in America, and the hundred and

[428]

fiftieth in England. The stirring drama remained at the Star, through September 24th.

Beginning on September 26th, Maurice Grau tried to show that French opéra-bouffe was not dead; he merely proved that it retained but very little life, especially without an Aimée, a Théo or a star of similar brilliancy. Le Grand Mogol began the season, with Julia Bennati, Guernoy (tenor), Mezières, Maris, Tony, Vinchon, Delafosse, and Mlles. Nordall, Caroli and Tournyaire. Mlle. Bennati surprised with a fine voice, but "lacked *élan* and *chic.*" Repeated on the 27th, 28th, and at both performances on October 1st, Le Grand Mogol yielded the stage, on September 29th and 30th, to Audran's opera, Serment d'Amour, in which Mlle. Mary Pirard made her début as Posette. With her were Mlle. Stani, MM. Stephan and Vinchon and others cited above. The familiar La Fille de Mme. Angot graced the evenings of October 3rd, 4th and the afternoon of the 8th, with Julia Bennati as Mlle. Lange and Mary Pirard as Clairette. Other available evenings regaled with Le Grand Mogol (last time, on the 5th), La Mascotte, with Mlle. Bennati (6th and 7th), and Serment d'Amour (evening of the 8th). The third week repeated these specialties (except Le Grand Mogol) until Friday and Saturday, when Fatinitza was turned from something very German into something not so very French, with Julïa Bennati as Wladimir.

Something more natural to our taste came on October 17th, when The Rivals presented Joseph Jefferson, Mrs. John Drew, Emma Vaders (not a very satisfactory Lydia), May Wolcott (Lucy), Edwin Varrey (Sir Anthony), Geoffrey Hawley (a pleasing Jack), Barton Hill (a sepulchral actor, as I remember him, as Sir Lucius), McCullough Ross (Faulkland), Thomas Jefferson (Fag) and George W. Denham (a perfect David). This refreshing delight lasted uninterruptedly through October 29th; Jefferson, for his last week, gave, on October 31st, November 1st, 2nd and 5th (matinée and evening) his exquisite Cricket on the Hearth and his amusing Lend Me Five Shillings. The Rivals came back for the evenings of November 3rd and 4th. On the afternoon of the 3rd Jefferson gave a professional matinée of The Rivals, attended by a glittering host, including Henry Irving.

HENRY IRVING AND ELLEN TERRY, 1887–1888

"Build thee more stately mansions, O my soul!" For the first times, after long, eager waiting, I was now to see the famous productions of Henry Irving. He returned, after an absence from us of nearly three seasons, and opened, on November 7th, in W. G. Wills's version of Faust, in which he had great success in London. Of course he brought with him all the stage settings and effects that had seemed so marvellous to London playgoers of that happy era, and also his entire staff of stage hands and his musical director, Ball. The cast of Faust included Irving, of course, as Mephistopheles, George Alexander as Faust, Miss Terry as Margaret, Charles Glenney, once of Wallack's, as Valentine, and Mrs. Chippendale as Martha. Incidental characters were played by Charles Harbury (Frosch), Haviland (Altmayer), Martin Harvey (Brander), S. Johnson (Siebel), Miss Mathews (Bessy), and Thomas Mead (the Witch of the Kitchen).

This wonderful thing was, I believe, the most impressive spectacle and the most engrossing performance I had, up to that time, ever witnessed. I knew by heart the reputation of the Irving productions and I approached Faust with the highest expectation of beholding the most complete stage-setting I had even imagined. Nor was I disappointed; from scene to scene this Faust carried me into a realm of enchantment. I had never before seen, nor have I since seen, settings so perfectly satisfactory as Irving's always were; the castles, town or village streets, cathedral closes or woodland scenes evolved by his matchless scene-painters, Telbin, Hawes Craven and the others, were the real thing — they looked like the survival of ages. A castle, on Irving's stage, looked as if its mighty stones had been piled up in pre-historic times. More than this, the actors were so thoroughly trained that they seemed to be actually the parts they played. And they wore their costumes with such becoming grace! From the moment Miss Terry entered the stage, as Margaret, she became pre-eminently my actress *par excellence*. In her artistic costumes she was not, I fear, a simple maiden; rather was she the personification of poetic charm. And how easily she passed from smiles to tears! George Alexander was a very handsome Faust, of melodious speech; but, of course, Irving dominated the scene with his nimbleness, his biting sarcasm and his expressive face that represented the very "spirit that denies." I doubt if I have ever seen a more magnificent stage-picture than the scene on the Brocken, with Irving standing high amid the bedevilment, whirling liquid fire with diabolical relish. Some of this may have been far from Goethe, but it was admirable Wills-Irving-Telbin. And let us not forget that, later in the season, the Goethe Society honoured Irving with that imposing reception in the Madison Square Theatre.

Since Miss Terry did not usually play twice in one day, Irving devoted his first Saturday night (November 12th) to The Bells and a sketch — Jingle — derived from The Pickwick Papers. The title-rôle, in this piece, exactly suited Irving's face and his mannerisms of speech and bearing. The cast will show the size of his company:

Mr. Pickwick	H. Howe	Fat Boy	Mr. Gurner
Nathaniel Winkle	Mr. Emery	Cabman	Mr. Graham
Snodgrass	Mr. Haviland	Bailiff	Mr. Armadale
Wardle	S. Johnson	Watchers	Lawson, Marion
Tupman	Charles Harbury	Post Boy	J. Allen
Nupkins	T. N. Wenman	Miss Rachel	Mrs. Pauncefort
Perker	J. Carter	Miss Emily	Miss Mathews
Sam Weller	Martin Harvey	Arabella	Miss F. Harwood
Job Trotter	Mr. Archer	Chambermaid	Miss Mills

[430]

MRS. WALCOT AND
CHARLES WALCOT

LOUISE DILLON AND
CHARLES DICKSON

W. J. LE MOYNE AND
MRS. WALCOT

HENRY MILLER—HERBERT KELCEY—NELSON WHEATCROFT

WHEATCROFT AND
GRACE HENDERSON

GEORGIA CAYVAN AND
HENRY MILLER

HERBERT KELCEY AND
GEORGIA CAYVAN

B. J. FALK'S PHOTOGRAPHS OF SCENES FROM THE WIFE

In The Bells appeared Irving, J. Carter, S. Johnson, Alexander (Christian), Haviland (Dr. Zimmer), F. Tyars (President of the Court), Mrs. Pauncefort, Miss Mathews (Suzel) and Winifred Emery (Annette). Faust was continued throughout the week of November 14th–19th, till Saturday evening, when Irving repeated his striking Louis XI, with Martin Harvey as the Dauphin (a very fine performance), Alexander as Nemours, and Winifred Emery as Marie. The record is delightfully simple, with Faust running till December 5th, with changes on Saturday nights to Jingle and The Bells (November 26th), and Louis XI (December 3rd). On the 29th, a performance of Faust (matinée) was advertised for the Beecher Statue Fund. Beecher had been a friend of Irving and Miss Terry. The last week of this delightful engagement gave us Faust (December 5th), The Merchant of Venice (6th, 7th, 8th, 9th, and matinée, 10th), with a double bill for the farewell, evening of the 10th, devoted to Louis XI, beginning with Act II, and the popular Jingle.

The cast of The Merchant of Venice was very much the same as that seen in 1884–85, with Irving as Shylock, Miss Terry as Portia, Tyars as Morocco, Alexander as Bassanio, H. Howe as the Duke, Wenman as Antonio, Winifred Emery as Jessica, Martin Harvey as Lorenzo, Helen Mathews as Nerissa, S. Johnson as Launcelot Gobbo, J. Carter as Old Gobbo, Haviland as Salanio, Harbury as Salarino, Archer as Tubal and Glenney (new) as Gratiano. That was the most perfect Shakespearian performance I had ever seen; setting, lighting, costumes, acting, and (except for Irving) delivery of the poetry—all were perfect. Never had I seen an actress of such poetic charm as Miss Terry, whether in the yellow brocade in Belmont, or in the scarlet robe and cap of the advocate. And what a radiant figure and what comedy technique in the moonlit garden at Belmont! All of Irving's mannerisms fitted into Shylock—a very human Shylock; and Bassanio's poetic speeches came like gold from the lips of the handsome Alexander. This performance was the high light of my playgoing up to December, 1887. Booth, of course, was a greater tragedian than Irving; but when had Booth been surrounded by such actors in so beautiful a setting? On the wings of that question, I record a benefit, on Sunday, December 4th, at which appeared Rose Coghlan, Osmond Tearle, Harry Edwards, E. D. Ward, Mme. Cottrelly, Marion Manola, Hopper, Digby Bell, H. Wilke, Oudin, &c.

JULIA MARLOWE; MR. AND MRS. FLORENCE

Julia Marlowe, who made her début in New York, on October 20th, followed Irving's brilliant engagement, beginning, on December 12th, with the part that more and more she preferred, and in which, perhaps, she was as good as any one then playing it, except, possibly, Mary Anderson. No successor to the Juliet of Adelaide Neilson had yet arrived, and has not appeared to this day (1941). Miss Marlowe brought a company that would have seemed better if it had not come so closely after the Irving actors. Joseph Haworth was Romeo, with Charles Norris as Mercutio, Leslie Allen as the Friar, Nestor Lennon as Paris, E. J. Ratcliffe as Benvolio, Howard Kyle as Tybalt, George Gaston as Peter, John Sutherland and Blanche Weaver as the Capulets, and Elizabeth Andrews as the Nurse. She repeated Juliet, on the 15th, and at the matinée on the 17th. On the 13th, Miss Marlowe played Parthenia. Her Viola, on the 14th and 16th, had the co-operation of Haworth as Malvolio, Blanche Weaver as Olivia, Katie Gilbert as Maria, F. J. Currier as Sir Andrew, Leslie Allen as Sir Toby, Kyle as Fabian, Gaston as the Clown, Charles Fyffe as Antonio, and Charles Norris as Orsino. According to the Herald, her Viola "to the eye was most bewitching; to the heart gently appealing; to the imagination, lacking in depth and variety, and to the mind sweetly monotonous." The engagement closed, on Saturday evening, with Ingomar.

Mr. and Mrs. Florence arrived, on December 19th, in a play they had long tried to make acceptable to their public — Jessop and Gill's Our Governor, once known as His Little Hatchet. Their company was good, or seemed so to me as I then saw it — Stella Boniface and H. A. Weaver, Jr., as Emma and Herbert Kingsley, Eleanor Lane as the scheming Mrs. Monroe, C. J. Bell as the Hon. Beverly Outran, Harry Pierson as Victor Newman, Belle Pierson as Stella Perkins, F. C. Wells as Dobson, Florence as the prevaricating Perkins, and Mrs. Florence in her hilarious impersonation of Matilda Starr, the English novelist, here to learn all about America, and incidentally to keep an eye on young Outran — "the dearest boy, I've known his mother for yahs an' chahs!" On December 24th, Florence played Cap'n Cuttle, with Stella Boniface as Edith, Clarence Montaine as Dombey, and Mrs. Van Deren as Mrs. Skewton. The Mighty Dollar filled the bill for the entire second week of the engagement, till Saturday, December 31st, when Dombey and Son again emerged.

HEDWIG NIEMANN-RAABE

New York was richly blest in that year, with foreign actors of distinction. Heinrich Conried, who had latterly been engaged in supplying the Casino with gems of German operetta, brought to America in 1887–88 two of the foremost German artists. This venture was quite distinct from the activities of Amberg, at the Thalia Theater. The first of Conried's stars to arrive was Hedwig Niemann-Raabe, wife of the esteemed Metropolitan tenor, an actress who, if no longer in her first youth, had much of the soft charm of youth, and rich supplies of versatility and technical equipment. She came forth, on January 2nd and 3rd, in Dorf und Stadt, following, on the 4th and 5th, with Ein Tropfen Gift, and, on the 6th and 7th (matinée and evening), with

ELITA PROCTOR OTIS

MISSES LAWRENCE
(RITA AND ALICE)

EDWARD FALES COWARD

JULIA MARLOWE
AS VIOLA

FRAU NIEMANN-RAABE

HOWARD KYLE
(1887-1888)

DAVID BELASCO

EDWIN VARREY AS
SIR ANTHONY ABSOLUTE

JOSEPH HAWORTH

Divorçons (Cyprienne). Her support, a very good one, included Arthur and Adolph Meyer, Frl. Auguste Burmeister, Julius Metz, Hermann Haack, Hugo Rantzenberg, Ottilie Genée (our friend of long ago), Moritz Moritz, Lilli Petri, Antonie Ziegler, Alexis Schönlank, Carl Müller and Gustav Kober —all, except Ottilie Genée, new in America. The second and last week presented Dora (Diplomacy, January 9th and 10th), with the star in the title-rôle and Antonie Ziegler as Zicka; Alexandra, by Richard Voss (11th, 12th); Andrea (13th and 14th, evening); and Lorle (Dorf und Stadt, matinée, 14th). The engagement Allston Brown sums up as "a complete artistic success and a financial disappointment to her manager, who was compelled to increase the price of seats, owing to his expensive contract with the star." I go back to Sunday, January 8th, when a benefit to John P. Smith, the veteran manager, promised Bill Nye, the Blossom Quartet, the Tissots, George S. Knight, Dockstader, M. P. Wilder, Robert Hilliard and Henrietta Markstein.

Something possibly inviting came on January 16th, with William Mestayer and Theresa Vaughn, in Check 44, or, Tobogganing. Their company was far from noteworthy, with Joseph A. Ott, Bernhard Dyllyn, Mary Gray, Marion Russell, Lillian Hamilton, Sol Aiken and W. H. Sloan. The Garnellas contributed specialties. Such as it was, this show kept going through February 11th, leaving the stage for a return visit of Frau Niemann-Raabe, who began, on the 13th, a series of five farewell performances; Francillon, by Alexander Dumas was seen for "the first time in America," on the 13th, 14th and 16th; Dora came back on the 15th, and Die Hagestolzen for the farewell, on the 17th. Heinrich Conried filled out the week, on the 18th (afternoon and evening) in his well-known Dr. Klaus. The chief support in Francillon came from Rantzenberg, Lilli Petri, Haack, Schönlank, Moritz Moritz, Heinrich Zilzer, Antonie Ziegler, Frl. Auguste Burmeister, &c. Prices of admission were reduced to the usual top charge of $1.50. I have an idea that the famous lady (famous in Germany) met with but slight response here because she was too mature to look like the parts she played; and her repertoire was far from stimulating even to patient playgoers. She may at least have enjoyed being here while her husband, Albert Niemann, was dominating the Wagner operas at the Metropolitan.

On February 20th, Irving and Miss Terry returned, presenting Olivia, W. G. Wills's drama founded on The Vicar of Wakefield. Miss Terry had been acclaimed in the title-rôle, as far back as 1876, and, in the spring of 1887 Irving revived it at the Lyceum Theatre, in London, himself making a success as Dr. Primrose. New York had been eagerly awaiting this performance and was enchanted with the result. Anything lovelier than that Olivia I never saw on the stage. I recall with delight the festivities in the Vicar's garden, ending with his revealing to Olivia the loss of his little fortune, the while, in the light of the setting sun we heard the distant church bells chime;

the scene of Olivia's farewell to her little brothers, a scene so pathetic that the audience was almost flooded with tears; the "big" scene with the despicable Thornhill; the great scene when the Vicar discovers his errant daughter; and the final return to the home, with a renewal of peace, if not of happiness. Miss Terry's Olivia was superb, running with greatest ease the gamut from smiles to tears, from tears to chastened merriment. The Vicar I always esteemed one of Irving's best parts, ranking with his Shylock, his Becket and his Louis XI. His beautifully expressive face fitted to perfection his ideal of the benevolent Primrose, and in all the varying scenes of the play he brought Goldsmith's creation visibly before us. George Alexander, in his handsome costumes, was a convincing Thornhill and Wenman (a first-rate actor) exactly right as Burchell. Other rôles, all, as I remember, beautifully played, fell to Haviland as Moses, Tyars as Leigh, H. Howe as Farmer Flamborough, Mrs. Pauncefort as Mrs. Primrose, Miss Coleridge as Polly Flamborough, Miss Mills as Phoebe, Miss Barnett as the Gypsy Woman, Miss M. Holland as Dick, Miss D. Harwood as Bill, and Winifred Emery as Sophia.

This exquisite production continued till March 3rd. Of course Miss Terry did not play on Saturday evenings, and, for the first two of those "off" nights, Irving appeared in his startling dual assumption of Lesurques and Dubosc, in The Lyons Mail. For those performances he engaged Linda Dietz to enact Jeannette, which Miss Terry had assumed here in 1883–84. Other parts were assigned to Alexander, Wenman, Archer, Mead and Miss Emery. He also gave this piece on Monday, February 27th. On Monday, March 5th, Irving reverted to his spectacular Faust, which he dropped for the evening of Saturday, the 10th, when his Louis XI again excited wonder and amaze. That Saturday, as I remember, was a sunny balmy day altogether assuring us that spring had arrived. And lo! on Sunday evening snow began to fall, and Monday, March 12th, brought the great blizzard, still (1941) an immortal theme for newspapers on the anniversary of the event. On the evening of the 12th, most of the first-class theatres closed, but the Star, like Daly's, gave a performance, and probably for the same reason — the house had been sold out. This leaves us undecided as to how, if an audience could not reach the theatre, the actors could. One of my friends told me, years later, that he was marooned, on the 12th, in the Hotel St. Denis, three blocks from the Star, on Broadway. Unutterably wearied of the confinement, he and another man struggled to the Star, were told there were no seats left, but that, if they bought "standing room," there would probably be vacant seats into which they could slip. Following this advice, they found more seats than occupants, and, for the only time in the engagement, Irving, in Faust, played to a "beggarly array of empty benches," which had, however, been paid for. On the 17th, he gave Jingle and The Bells. The Star Theatre was closed, on the evening of March 19th; Irving,

[434]

HENRY IRVING AS DR. PRIMROSE
ELLEN TERRY AS OLIVIA
From a Photograph by Window and Grove

HENRY IRVING AS MEPHISTOPHELES
(BROCKEN SCENE)
From a Drawing by J. Bernard Partridge

ELLEN TERRY AS MARGARET
From a Photograph by Window and Grove

GEORGE ALEXANDER AS THORNHILL
From a Photograph by Barraud

Miss Terry and their associates went, by permission of the Secretary of War, to give a performance, in costume but without scenery, of The Merchant of Venice, before the students of the Military Academy at West Point, something, I should suppose, for those students to remember to the end of their days.   He gave The Merchant, at the Star, on the 21st and 23rd, and Olivia, on the 22nd, and at the matinée on the 24th.   Irving's engagement closed, on March 24th, with Olivia.   Irving was the foremost English actor of his day, but it is noticeable that during this season he had acted in New York only one Shakespearian character — Shylock — and that not a leading figure in tragedy.

He was followed, for the week of March 26th–31st, by the Boston-esteemed Howard Athenæum Specialty Company — an incredible drop in importance, even with the Irwin Sisters, James F. Hoey and Pete Dailey, Rezene and Robini.   Herrmann's magic filled the week of April 2nd–7th. Even lower we sank, on April 9th, when the incredible James Owen O'Conor tried to act Hamlet.   Before I tell that shocking story, I must list a "monster concert," on the evening of Sunday, April 8th, when a "diamond champion whip" was presented by Richard K. Fox to James McLaughlin, "America's foremost greatest jockey."   Just why this presentation must be celebrated in a foremost theatre, I cannot imagine.   Vaudeville added variety to the occasion, promised volunteers including Maggie Cline, Harry Kernell, Frank Bush, Laura Lee, Polly Cusick and Beane and Gilday.

And now for O'Conor.   For some time before his emergence he had been advertising himself as a great tragedian, promising wonderful things when he appeared.   He was to come forth as Hamlet, and in the course of two weeks essayed Othello, The Merchant of Venice, Richelieu and The Marble Heart.   According to Allston Brown, Jessie Villers, on the opening night, played Ophelia, and Emmie Young, a daughter of Brigham Young, the Queen.   Following the performance of Hamlet, the Herald declared "the Prince of Denmark" was "indeed a melancholy Dane."   On the 12th, the same paper decided that O'Conor's Shylock "was too contemptible to be noticed in these columns."   I refer the reader to Allston Brown's account (A History of the New York Stage, Volume II) of the completely rowdy proceedings that soon developed in this fortnight of ill-judged endeavour. The audiences laughed and booed and yelled throughout the performances, calling to the ridiculous "actor," hardly listening to his pleas for quiet and to his threats of action by the police, etc.   In fact New York was again treated to the system which prevailed in the later days of the "Count" Joannes, including the casting on the stage of decaying vegetables.   I will spare my readers further details, merely reminding them that these things occurred in a theatre recently dignified by the art of Irving and Ellen Terry. O'Conor was said to be related to the famous jurist, Charles O'Conor.   He was evidently mentally unsound.   He gave a "professional" matinée of Ham-

[435]

let during his present melancholy visitation, but soon betook himself to a long engagement at Koster and Bial's. Only recently (1941), one of my friends reminded me of the later O'Conor saga, when, in a tour of the country, he played behind a wire netting to prevent contact with missiles thrown at him by rowdy auditors. Brockman's Monkey Theatre followed on a stage so lately given to "monkey-shines." It evidently pleased, for it remained from Tuesday, April 24th, through May 26th, always with the cheery note, "They play, laugh, cry, and do everything but talk."

Union Square Theatre, 1887–1888

The once so popular Union Square Theatre was entering its last months in the shape well-known to A. M. Palmer and his audiences of the '70s and early '80s. In February, 1888, it was entirely destroyed by fire, and the theatre that replaced it on the same site never acquired the impressive following begotten of The Two Orphans, The Banker's Daughter and other successes of the Palmer *régime*. That glory, however, had withered with the departure in 1885 of the remnants of Palmer's once famous stock company, and since then, the theatre had housed some productions of dubious artistic value.

The Henrietta

J. M. Hill opened his theatre, on August 29, 1887, with One Against Many, a new opus by A. C. Gunter, illustrated by John L. Burleigh, a star of no luminosity, Katie Gilbert, Effie Germon, Carrie Jackson, Dan Leeson, George F. DeVere, Alfred Klein, Franz Reinau, Albert Roberts, F. Goldthwaite, J. C. Tiernan and Redfield Clarke, whose combined talents carried it only for the four weeks ending September 24th. On September 26th Robson and Crane brought out the greatest success of their artistic partnership — The Henrietta, by Bronson Howard, who had, we remember, presented on this very stage his vastly-liked The Banker's Daughter. The play deals with the struggle for financial control in stocks between gruff, kindly Nicholas Van Alstyne (Crane) and his unscrupulous son, young Nicholas (Charles Kent), with the final emergence of Bertie, the Lamb (played by Robson) despised at first by his father, Van Alstyne, but who really masters the market by buying or selling on the flip of a coin. Large Lady Mary Trelawney (played by May Waldron) and her small suppressed husband, Lord Arthur (Lorimer Stoddard) added much fun not necessary to unravelling the main plot. A pair of young lovers, evidently then regarded as essential to any such play, fell to the lot of Robson, as the misguided Bertie, and Jessie Storey, who acted the nice Agnes Lockwood. Villainy was rampant in the efforts of Watson Flint (Henry Bergman) to implicate Rose Van Alstyne (Sibyl Johnstone) wife of young Nicholas, in "those" letters, showing the un-

[436]

worthiness of the husband she trusts; but Bertie burns the letters, and, in order to save Rose's feelings, nobly takes on himself the blame for all the misdoing.   And the utterly self-sacrificing Dr. Parke Wainwright (H. J. Lethcourt) is finally rewarded, in prospect, with the love of Rose, when the bad younger Nicholas dies of a melodramatic heart attack after his father discovers his villainy.   The feminine interest of the play was vested in the sagacious Mrs. Cornelia Opdyke (beautifully played by Selena Fetter), who cut the knot of the story by informing Rose of the unworthiness of her deceased husband, and thus allowed patient Dobbin-like Wainwright to succeed to the post of husband of Rose.   This mixture of plots, aside from the financial implications of Van Alstyne and his two sons, sounds very old-fashioned to 1941, but 1887–88 loved it all.   In telling the story I have omitted two minor parts—the Reverend Murray Hilton, played by F. A. Tannehill, Jr., and Musgrave, played by Louis Carpenter.

The company was about as satisfactory as any that had been seen for some time in special productions, and, if we had known it, offered a good example of what would happen in days when stock companies were no more. I can hardly think of a suitable cast for The Henrietta, in any one of the famous stock companies I have recently discussed.   A survival of the stock system at the Union Square came to us on the afternoon of December 15th, when occurred a benefit for the once charming actress, Sara Jewett, so long connected with the company, and now ill and, I assume, in straitened circumstances.   One might expect that, in those days of wonderful benefit-bills (compare the Wallack benefit of May 21st, in this very season), something of great attractiveness might have been arranged, for the need of an actress once so liked.   Instead, though appropriately enough, on the stage she had so long adorned, Miss Jewett's benefit introduced a play by Estelle Clayton, assuredly not a playwright of distinction.   A Sad Coquette had this cast:

Paul Mortimer	Eben Plympton	Little Bobby	Ollie Berkeley
Lord Lawton	George Holland	Lady Lawton	Louisa Eldridge
Sir Charles	William Faversham	Mrs. Higgins	Selena Fetter
Frederick West	Lorimer Stoddard	Selina (sic)	Loie Fuller
Hansel	Franz Reinau	Leonore Merritt	Estelle Clayton
Tramp	C. R. Dodsworth		

Not a single member of her old associates in the Union Square company, several of whom were now at the Madison Square, participated in this testimonial; I wonder why.   Of course Eben Plympton had played small parts at the Union Square before Miss Jewett's advent on that stage.   According to Allston Brown, the receipts were about $1,500.

Let us advance, on December 31st, to the hundredth performance of The Henrietta, a fine New Year gift for all concerned.   I hope the reader notices how many productions of that season passed the century-mark.   J. M. Hill gave, on February 1st, a reception to the Nineteenth Century Club, in which

Aurelio Cerulos, a Spanish pianist, made his début, associated with a cluster of theatrical and other celebrities — Joseph Haworth, Robert Hilliard, Alice J. Shaw, C. P. Flockton, Lillie Eldridge, M. P. Wilder and others less notable. The last few weeks of The Henrietta had been announced when, on February 28th, the interior of the theater was entirely destroyed by fire. The news-papers indulged in "sob stories" of the former glories of the house, recalling the names of all the lustrous members of Palmer's company. Almost ironi-cally, as New York might have asked itself what now it could do with one theatre fewer, the new Broadway Theatre, at 41st Street, long expected and long heralded, opened its doors to the public, in the very week of the passing of the Union Square. The older theatre perished on Tuesday, February 28th, and the new temple opened on Saturday, March 3rd. Could a coincidence have been timed more perfectly?

Fifth Avenue Theatre, 1887–1888

Except for two engagements during the season now reviewing, I need not long detain the reader in the Fifth Avenue Theatre of 1887–88. The house re-opened, on September 5th, with Allan Dare, dramatised from Ad-miral Porter's novel, Allan Dare and Robert le Diable; the production was supervised by McKee Rankin. Chief assignments in a large cast fell to Francis Carlyle as Allan, Wilton Lackaye as Robert le Diable, Louise Pom-eroy, who gave up trying to be a star, as Louise Morton, Agnes Proctor as Agnes Gale, Kate Moloney (sic) as Mary, Alice Fischer as No. 10, Jerome Stevens as Simon Gale, J. E. Wilson as Charles Gale and Mr. Morton, W. H. Thompson as Mungo Park and F. B. Conway, Jr. as George May. Many supernumeraries swelled the host, but large as the army was, it decamped on September 17th.

Mrs. Langtry; Mrs. James Brown Potter

The beautiful Mrs. Langtry, on the 19th, began a six-weeks engagement in another play taken from a much-read novel, F. C. Phillips's As in a Looking Glass, adapted to the stage by Frank Rogers. Mrs. Langtry had disagreed with her former leading man, Charles Coghlan, who, as we know, had transferred his allegiance to A. M. Palmer; she therefore engaged the popular Maurice Barrymore to lead her support in the new play. The cast:

Captain Fortinbras......Maurice Barrymore	Lord Benley..................W. Nicholson
Lord Udolpho Daysoy........R. C. Hilliard	Kalmuck...........................M. Jones
Count Dromiroff...............F. A. Everill	Lady Damer.................Hattie Russell
Sir Thomas Gage..............H. A. Weaver	Beatrice Vyse...........Katherine Florence
Algernon Balfour...............Louis Calvert	Florence....................Lillian Florence
Frank Fairfield.................J. B. Hollis	Lady Gage.....................Rose Roberts
Lord Slumberton.............Sidney Herbert	Felicie.......................Nadage Dorée
Mons. Camille.............George Raiemond	Lena Despard.................Mrs. Langtry
Major Roberts...........Walter Lennox, Jr.	

[438]

To one, like me, who remembers the stage of 1887, that seems an excellent cast, though my memory fails me as to how admirable each was in his or her part.   One thing I know is that Mrs. Langtry never was more beautiful or more superbly gowned than then as Lena Despard.   She moved gracefully and at times forcefully through the play, without exhausting the possibilities of the objectionable Lena Despard.   In those days it was a sort of dramatic duty to see Mrs. Langtry, and that duty was now performed for six weeks.   I must admit that, though I saw the production, I remember but little of it; yet I remember very distinctly other things I attended in 1887–88.

On October 25th (afternoon), Mrs. Langtry gave her play for the Actors' Fund.   And matinée girls must have been "thrilled" to learn that the ushers were to be none other than those "matinée idols," Kyrle Bellew, Osmond Tearle, Alexander Salvini, Courtice Pounds, Herbert Kelcey, Henry Miller, L. F. Massen and H. J. Lethcourt.

That other "society lady" turned professional, Mrs. James Brown Potter, for several years our most treasured amateur, came out, on October 31st, in Mlle. de Bressier.   There had been great public excitement, expeditiously fanned by the managers and by a public auction of seats and boxes for the opening night.   The company was not so good as Mrs. Langtry's, though it sufficed to show up a poor play:

Pierre Rosny	Leslie Allen	Georget	Sidney Drew
Jacques Rosny	Kyrle Bellew	Jean	Jacques Martin
Captain Grandier	J. F. Hagan	François	P. J. Reynolds
Captain Maubert	Fred W. Sidney	Mme. Rosny	Minnie Monk
Marius	Kenneth Lee	Nellie	Maida Craigen
Henri de Guessaint	Hart Conway	Aurelie	Genevieve Lytton
Etienne	F. B. Conway	Faustine de Bressier	Mrs. Potter

The play was declared by the Herald to be "wearisome"; I found it, also, quite easy to forget.   And Mrs. Potter was pretty, whereas Mrs. Langtry was handsome; a big difference.   On November 14th, the new star changed to Loyal Love, playing Inez, to the Donna Leonora of Maida Craigen (this lady also an amateur turned not very first-rate professional), the Pedro of Kyrle Bellew, the King of Harry Allen, the Sebastian of F. B. Conway, the Count di Luna of Hart Conway, the Louis of Sidney Drew, the Antonio of Jacques Martin and the Gonzales of Joseph Haworth (brought in, perhaps, to salvage the crew).   After one week of this, Mrs. Potter carried her art to other communities.   Among other things she needed a good play, even a sensational one, like As in a Looking Glass.   The engagements of Mrs. Langtry and Mrs. Potter were the two interesting oases I found, that year, in this theatre.   But Miss Craigin has become Miss Craigen.

Observe what followed — The Begum, a Hindoo Comic Opera, by Reginald De Koven and Harry B. Smith; and read aloud the names of the *dramatis personæ*, if only to wonder how the perpetrators could descend to

[439]

such cheap wit of the variety or minstrel stage. John A. McCaull's company, on November 21st, presented the offering, with this cast:

Begum of Oude	Mme. Cottrelly	Aminah	Marion Manola
Howja-Dhu	De Wolf Hopper	Naomouna	Laura Joyce Bell
Pooteh-Wehl	Edwin Hoff	Damayanti	Annie Myers
Klahm-Chowdee	Hubert Wilke	Tafeh	Josephine Knapp
Myhnt-Jhuleep	Digby Bell	Kahra-Mel	Nina Bertini
Jhust-Naut	Jeff De Angelis	Nougat	Grace Seavey
Asch-Khart	H. Macdonough	Bon Bon	Paula Franko

A. Nowak led the orchestra, and H. A. Cripps was stage-manager. A Hole in the Ground filled the week beginning on December 12th.

RICHARD MANSFIELD; ZÉLIE DE LUSSAN

Perhaps I spoke too hastily in selecting only two oases in the desert of this Fifth Avenue season. No engagement of Richard Mansfield could fail to arouse our interest. He began, easily, on December 19th, with Monsieur, his company including Beatrice Cameron, John Parry, Josephine Laurens (a trained actress who always bored me), Helen Glidden, Anne O'Neill, J. T. Sullivan, D. H. Harkins, J. B. Eversham and Harry Gwynette. Stronger fare came during the holiday week beginning on December 26th, Dr. Jekyll and Mr. Hyde, which sent us out of the theatre afraid to go home in the dark. This terrifying play continued through January 11th, and, for the 12th, 13th and 14th, the gifted actor reverted to his other melodramatic specialty, A Parisian Romance.

So he went his way, and, on January 16th, the Boston Ideal Opera Company presented itself in The Daughter of the Regiment, with pretty little Zélie de Lussan, long known as a rather pleasing concert singer, as Marie, and, in other rôles, Frank Baxter, W. H. Clark, Clement Bainbridge, J. C. Miron and Harriet Avery — an aggregation which did not then strike me as "ideal," nor does it now, more than fifty years later. This offering filled the first week, except on Thursday night and Saturday afternoon, when Carlotta Pinner sang Martha, with Helen Dudley Campbell, George Appleby and A. D. Saxon. For the second week of the visit, Zélie de Lussan tried Carmen (January 23rd, 25th, 27th) a rôle she some years afterward essayed with the Grau company at the Metropolitan Opera House in a vain effort to make the audience forget Emma Calvé. Her "ideal" support now was very bad, with W. H. Clark as Escamillo, a hopeless George Appleby as Don José, Ida Klein as Michaela, Helen Dudley Campbell as Frasquita. On January 25th, A. D. Saxon sang Escamillo. On the evening of the 24th and 26th (afternoon), we were blest with The Daughter of the Regiment, on the 26th with Martha, and, on the afternoon of the 28th, with that other glittering novelty, The Bohemian Girl. The Herald reviewer thought that Mlle. de Lussan's Carmen was "over-acted, restless, and in poor taste." The whole opera, as presented, "might have been enjoyed in Kansas City." The operas sung in this second week were to be repeated in the third. For the matinée, on February 4th, L'Elisir d'Amore was given, with F. H. Baxter (replacing Appleby, ill) as Nemorino, and Harriet Avery as Adina. The evening bill gave us Mlle. de Lussan and Alonzo Hatch, in The Daughter of the Regiment. Something like success came, on February 6th, with Victor, the Bluestocking, adapted from Bernicat's François le Basbleu. In this Mlle. de Lussan made a hit as Fanchette, a street singer, with Harriet Avery as the Countess, Helen Dudley Campbell as the Fortune Teller, Louise Edgar as Friquet, Harry Rattenberry as Victor, Clement Bainbridge as the Marquis, Fritz Williams (of all people unexpected) as de Florac, J. C. Miron as Sergeant Gruyère, and George E. Holmes as Bertrand. The Herald thought Rattenberry very bad. This was repeated on the 7th, 8th, 9th and 11th (matinée); on the 10th, Harriet Avery sang The Bohemian Girl; and the Ideals departed with Fra Diavolo, sung on the evening of the 11th. I have not been unduly delighted in writing the record of their month's activities. But it is easy to write of the visit of Herrmann, who began, on February 13th, two weeks of magic, D'Alvini and Mme. Herrmann accompanying.

On February 27th entered a play that should have been better than it was — Deacon Brodie, by Robert Louis Stevenson and W. E. Henley, tried the season before, at a matinée in Wallack's Theatre. Needless to say two such authors could not fail to write something original and striking, but somehow Deacon Brodie did not win the public, with this cast (not so good as that at Wallack's):

William Brodie	E. J. Henley	Old Brodie	Robert Bourchier
Walter Leslie	Charles W. Sutton	Doctor	Fred Beaumont
William Lawson	Edmund D. Lyons	Hamilton	Bruce Phillips
Moore	Edmund Grace	Mary Brodie	Mittens Willett
Smith	J. B. Hollis	Jean Watt	Carrie Coote
Ainslie	Edmund D. Lyons	Servant	Clara Lennon
Hunt	Henry Vernon	Mother Clarke	Ella Chudler
Rivers	James Sinclair		

On Friday and Saturday, March 9th and 10th, E. J. Henley played the graceless, flippant spendthrift Archie Boyeaut, in Fortune Hunters, assisted by Lyons, Sutton, Hollis, J. B. Baur, Miss Willett, Miss Coote and a Miss Stewart, who acted an old maid, Arabella Brown.

ROBERT MANTELL; CLARA MORRIS; LOUIS JAMES

Robert Mantell, striving to scale the heights, was to bring, March 12th, a new version of D'Ennery's La Dame de St. Tropez. Under the name of Monbars, it enlisted the star as Robert Monbars, Charles Mason as Laurent, Edward R. Marsden as de Meran, Archie Lindsay as the Marquis de Noirmont, B. T. Ringgold as M. Mouton, F. Chippendale as Dr. Daniel, Fannie (*sic*) Gillette as Diane, Eleanor Moretti as Blanche, and Lizzie Duroy. This was, because of the blizzard, postponed to March 13th; it ended its run on March 31st. March 28th tendered a benefit to Manager Charles Schröder and Treasurer P. H. O'Connor. On April 2nd, Clara Morris appeared in Renée de Moray, Clinton Stuart's adaptation of Le Martyre, a play which, in another form had failed, as The Martyr, at the Madison Square Theatre. Palmer's company had acted it beautifully, and in no part, including that of the star, was it as well done at the Fifth Avenue. Clara Morris, once a devouring flame of emotional acting, was in 1888 but a mannered shell of what she had been, and artistically her performance could not, for a moment, match the subtle, penetrating power of Mrs. Booth's. Her cast now included B. R. Graham as Count de Moray, Verner Clarges as Admiral de la Marche, Giles Shine as Antonio Palmieri, E. A. McDowell as Ernest Drake, W. C. Kelley as Claude Burel, Lilla Vane as Cecile de Moray, Mrs. C. Watson as the Duchess de San Lucca, Mrs. Octavia Allen as Mme. de la Marche, and Clara Morris as Renée de Moray. Miss Morris kept this piece in her repertoire for a year or more. At this time, it ran for two weeks, the actress being then able to play twice on Saturdays.

The last two weeks (April 16th–28th) of John Stetson's management of this theatre were devoted to an engagement of Louis James and Marie Wainwright. For the first of these weeks the stars appeared as Virginius and Virginia, in the sturdy old Knowles tragedy, their associates including F. C. Mosley (as Icilius), Charles D. Mackay (as Lucius), William Harris, Erroll Dunbar, H. A. Langdon, F. C. Huebner, Willis Granger, E. M. Hoyt, Harry Leighton, Kate Meek, and Miss A. Sarner. During the second week of their visit, the bills were Othello (April 23rd, 24th and 28th), and Much Ado about Nothing (25th, 26th, 27th, and matinée, 28th).

Helene, by Martha Morton, an author then unknown, but of later success, was the offering of April 30th, the cast including, among others, E. H. Vanderfelt, E. J. Henley, C. H. Bradshaw, Nick Long, Minnie Seligman, Jane Stuart and Blanche Weaver. The Herald handled the play very roughly, and was ungallant enough to say, "Miss Seligman was wretchedly poor." Later scribes were to give the author of Helene and Miss Seligman notices of a distinctly more flattering flavour. Helene was put on for only one evening.

Eugene Tompkins undertook the management and, in early May, presented Natural Gas, one of those frothy confections so popular in the days of the decline of the "legitimate." In the cast were Jennie Yeamans, May Yohe, the obstreperous Amy Ames, Katherine Howe, Henry V. Donnelly and Eddie Girard. John D. Gilbert was announced, but unable to appear, and, after a few nights May Yohe and her rôle were eliminated. No one involved could have guessed that in a few years May Yohe was to be the

MAY WALDRON

SIBYL JOHNSTONE

JESSIE STOREY

STUART ROBSON

SELENA FETTER

W. H. CRANE

CHARLES KENT

BRONSON HOWARD

LORIMER STODDARD

THE HENRIETTA, AT THE UNION SQUARE THEATRE

toast of London, was to become Lady Hope, and own and wear the famous Hope Diamond. Natural Gas had almost reached its fiftieth showing when it was withdrawn on June 16th.

BROADWAY THEATRE, 1888

The site of the variously-named amusement hall, on the southwest corner of Broadway and 41st Street was utilised for a big, handsome theatre — the Broadway — which served for years as a home of brilliant productions, usually spectacular musical shows. Allston Brown informs us that, early in 1887, James Bailey, of circus fame, started the enterprise, but soon re- tired, and Frank Sanger, T. H. French and E. Zborowski carried the scheme to completion. Zborowski owned half of the stock, the other two one quarter each. McElfatrick and Sons were the architects, and erected an auditorium seating seven hundred on the orchestra floor, four hundred and thirty-six in the balcony, two hundred and thirty-eight in the family circle (reserved) and four hundred and thirty-six (unreserved) — eighteen hundred and sixty-six seats in all. There was, besides, standing room for five hun- dred more. If Brown was right as to the number of seats in each section of the house, his total is surcharged by fifty-six seats. Perhaps he was includ- ing the seating capacity of private boxes, which he does not mention in his schedule. As I have stated before, the theatre opened (March 3rd), in the week which witnessed the destruction by fire of the Union Square Theatre; it is not surprising, therefore, to find the Broadway immediately advertised as not only the handsomest but the *safest* theatre in New York or indeed in the world.

FANNY DAVENPORT IN LA TOSCA

The opening attraction had been eagerly expected. Two of Sardou's sensational clever melodramas — Fedora and Théodora — constructed to the measure of Sarah Bernhardt, were already famous in New York, and the cable had informed us at only too great length of the success of the great French actress in La Tosca, who killed the villain with a carving knife. Miss Davenport was no Bernhardt, but she could give a competent, work- manlike impersonation of any rôle she attempted. She staged La Tosca magnificently, and engaged Frank Mordaunt, always good as a villain, for the heartless Scarpia, entrusting the tortured Cavaradossi to Melbourne McDowell, not a very good actor, who was soon to succeed Edwin Price in the rôle of her husband. Characters of less importance, though not negligi- ble, were entrusted to Harry Davenport (the star's young brother) as Ange- lotti, W. B. Murray as Attavanti, W. J. Hurley as Eusebe, Archibald (*sic*) Cowper as Trevilac, H. A. Carr as Capreola, J. H. Roberts as the Prince, Judith Berolde as Reine Marie Caroline, Eleanor Merron as Princess Or-

[443]

Ionia. Lower grades of utility were conserved by F. McDonald, J. Weldon, J. H. Williams, J. N. Abl, Bruce Hayes, May Haines, Olivia Tolme, Morris Flynn, W. S. Taylor, and Messrs. Moss, Turner, Miller, and W. Peters, verily a big pay-roll, unless some "doubling" lurked behind the screen of these very minor names.

The Herald review bitterly attacked the play for immorality and vulgarity, and returned to the charge on March 7th, with nearly two columns of specifications. Miss Davenport wrote a note complaining of unfair treatment, and enclosed a letter from Sardou that did not bear effectively on the controversy. Of course the theatre was closed, on March 12th, the night of the blizzard; it was dark again, on March 16th, when Miss Davenport was ill. Sunday evening, March 25th, brought the inauguration of Sunday concerts, with Campanini (not what he once had been), Mme. Scalchi (still magnificent), Metaura Torricelli (violin), Galassi, Corsini and Alfredo Gore (conductor). Gilmore's band made happy the night of April 1st; with it appeared Annie Louise Tanner, Carlotta Maconda, and Helene Mellini, three ladies in all that shining male host. But Tagliapietra also sang. Campanini, Scalchi and Galassi figured again on Sunday evening, April 8th.

The theatre was closed on April 30th and May 1st, for rehearsal of The Queen's Mate, Paulton's revision of Lecocq's La Princesse de Canaries, now brought out, on May 2nd, with Camille d'Arville, a charming singer and actress, as Anita, the beautiful Lillian Russell as Inez, Rose Leighton as Catarina, Hattie Delaro as Gomez, J. H. Ryley as Pataques, Harry Paulton a Inigo, W. H. Clark as Bombardos, F. Darrell as Pedrillo, and Harry W. Emmet as Guzman. In the last week of this engagement, Lillian Russell, on vacation, was succeeded, as Inez, by Lillian Grubb. The theatre closed, on June 30th, to re-open, on August 13th, with The Queen's Mate. I must state, however, that on Sunday evening, June 3rd, the wandering Campanini gave a concert here, assisted by Eva Tetrazzini, Marie Groebl, and Cleofonte Campanini. The Stabat Mater was performed "in its entirety."

STANDARD THEATRE, 1887–1888

The Standard also gloried, in this season, in a run of over a hundred nights; but not immediately. The season began, on September 12th, with a burlesque, The Arabian Nights, or, Aladdin's Wonderful Lamp, leaders in the long cast including George Clare as Haroun-al-Raschid, Loie Fuller as Aladdin, J. H. Ryley as the Magician and Chow-Vhow, Lena Merville as Kickapoo, Lillie Alliston as the Widow, Celie Ellis as the Princess, E. J. Connelly as Klub-Lubba, F. W. Holland as Ski-Hi, and Tom Martin as Tckiky-Nokra. I hope the reader is as weary as I of these silly attempts to make English-sounding names appear oriental in the spelling; if so, he will pardon my omission of a round dozen of very minor players—chiefly

[444]

MRS. LANGTRY
AS LENA DESPARD

ROBERT MANTELL
IN MONBARS

MRS. BROWN POTTER
AS JULIET

FANNY DAVENPORT
AS LA TOSCA

FANNY DAVENPORT
AS LA TOSCA

FANNY DAVENPORT
AS LA TOSCA

DONNELLY AND GIRARD

CAMILLE D'ARVILLE

ZÉLIE DE LUSSAN

women — in very insignificant rôles — especially as this offering died almost at birth, or a few weeks after. It was succeeded, on November 5th (the house having been closed from October 31st to November 4th), by Dorothy, a comic opera by B. C. Stephenson and Alfred Cellier, a work which had been tried in London, in 1886. Marie Halton made her American début as Phyllis, and started therewith a good, if short, American career, competing with, as Dorothy, the beautiful sweet-voiced Lillian Russell. Harry Paulton also first appeared, in this land of dollars, as Lurcher; Eugene Oudin, always dependable, was Geoffrey Wilder, John E. Brand, not living up to his early promise, was Harry Sherwood, and William Hamilton Squire Bantam. Others were F. Boudinot, J. E. Nash, Agnes Stone and Rose Leighton. Success of moderate strength carried this production through Saturday, December 17th.

The theatre remained closed for a week, opening, on Saturday, December 24th (a bad night, one would think), with the success of the Standard season, Steele MacKaye's drama of the French Revolution, called Anarchy, at its Buffalo première, but now rechristened Paul Kauvar. It was stirring melodrama as presented, under management of the Meech Brothers and Frank W. Sanger, with this cast:

Paul Kauvar	Joseph Haworth	Dodolphe Potin	Sidney Drew
Honoré Albert Maxime	Edwin Varrey	Carrac	George D. Fawcett
Marquis de Vaux	Wilton Lackaye	Bourdotte	Edward Coleman
General de la Roche	Nestor Lennon	Coujon	Edward M. Hurd
Abbé de St. Simon	B. F. Horning	Diane de Beaumont	Annie Robe
General Kleterre	Jerome Stevens	Nanette Potin	Louise Rial
Colonel La Hogue	Leslie Allen	Scarlotte	Lillie Eldridge

On January 23rd, Robert Hilliard took up the rôle of General de la Roche, and Adele Belgarde succeeded Annie Robe, who deserted the stage for marriage with Daniel Paine Griswold — something of a loss to the theatre. Joseph Haworth retired on February 18th, and, on Monday, the 20th, Steele MacKaye began as Paul Kauvar, possibly better in acting than as a figure of romantic charm. Carrie Turner, about the same time, assumed the appealing rôle of Diane — its third representative thus far. In earlier March, Edwin Varrey left Paul Kauvar, to join the company of Joseph Jefferson, resigning his part to another good actor, W. H. Thompson. Steele MacKaye was ill on March 14th and 15th (too much blizzard, perhaps) and Wilton Lackaye became the third Kauvar of the run. March 29th celebrated the hundredth showing of the stirring drama. At the matinée, on March 17th, Cora Dean was the fourth Diane. The run of the play ended on March 31st. Its reworking of the old material, lovers in danger, villains, sansculottes, swirling, shouting mobs led by the customary mad woman revolutionist, fascinated the public for the best part of a season and came back, later, into the friendly domain of the combination houses. It is the remarkable handling of the mob scenes, with Lillie Eldridge as the shouting terror, Scar-

[445]

lotte, that I chiefly remember from my visit to the play — those, and the appealing, womanly personality of Annie Robe, whom I never saw again. Oddly enough, Margaret Mather succeeded this mad festival with Romeo and Juliet (April 2nd, and matinée, 7th); The Honeymoon (3rd); As You Like It (4th); Lady of Lyons (5th); and Leah (6th and 7th).

In connection with the summer activities of the Madison Square Theatre, I spoke of J. M. Hill's wanderings with Sydney Rosenfeld's play, A Possible Case, which had been scheduled for performance at the Union Square Theatre. It came out, on March 26th, at the Amphion Academy, with a cast quite like that seen, on April 9th, at the Standard Theatre, New York, except that Henry Miller had been loaned to Brooklyn for the part of Lawrence Gould, played at the Standard by F. M. Burbeck. The Standard cast I have given in the history of the Madison Square Theatre, and may now leave the migratory play with the statement that it filled three weeks at the Standard before its exodus to the Madison Square. Its going left the stage free for a jolly two weeks of Neil Burgess, in Vim, supported by Frank J. Currier, T. D. Frawley, Adolph Jackson, May Taylor and Clara Stoneall. This episode ended on May 12th. For his last week, ending on the 19th, Burgess revived Widow Bedott.

The never-wearied Charles Gayler was author of Lights and Shadows, which began, on May 21st, with May Newman in the double rôle of Mary Bland and Mabel Milburn, and with Ida Jeffreys as Mme. Gerard, Mother Meg and Jeannette. Other competent players were Marjorie Bonner as Edith Broughton, J. H. Gilmour as Rufus Milburn, James Dunn as Judge Broughton, Augustus Cook as Archy Bleecker and James E. Wilson as Max Wilton. Jennie Williams, Emily Rickaby, John Hannon, M. H. Rawley, Fred Warren and a few others bore aid in smaller rôles. Beginning on June 11th, His Lordship employed good players, in H. M. Pitt, Charles B. Welles, Charles Bowser, Harry Hawk, Russell Bassett, S. Miller Kent, Mark Price, J. B. Hollis, Lysander Thompson, Lillian Chantore, Grace Thorne and Virginia Buchanan. By that time custom was invited with promise of a theatre "cooled by iced air." In spite of cast and air, the Herald states that the play fell "quite flat." It did not raise its head for a second week.

FOURTEENTH STREET THEATRE, 1887–1888

The popular theatre at Sixth Avenue and 14th Street, diametrically opposite that haven of delight for rural visitors, the big store of R. H. Macy and Co., opened again on August 30th with Harry Lacy, in The Still Alarm, a play which gratified his admirers for years thereafter. The Fourteenth Street Theatre was now largely, though not entirely, given over to thrilling or broadly comic pieces such as one would never expect to find at 30th Street and Broadway, where Wallack's and Daly's occupied corners diametrically

[446]

EUGENE OUDIN

MARIE HALTON

HARRY PAULTON

FANNY RICE
AS NADJY

KITTY CHEATHAM
IN ERMINIE

MARIE JANSEN
AS NADJY

HARRY LACY
IN THE STILL ALARM

WILTON LACKAYE
IN PAUL KAUVAR

JAMES T. POWERS AND
FRED SOLOMON

opposed.   And The Still Alarm, by Joseph Arthur, with its fire engine, its prancing horses, and its conflict between simple virtue and frowning villainy exactly suited a large part of the population — that percentage that in more recent times has devoured gangster plays.   The original cast of The Still Alarm follows:

Jack Manley	Harry Lacy	Jenkins	Thomas W. Ford
John Bird	Nelson Wheatcroft	Nozzle	Benjamin Deane
Willie Manley	Charles S. Dickson	Elinore Fordham	Blanche Thorne
Doc Wilbur	Jacques Kruger	Cad Wilbur	Blanche Vaughan
Franklin Fordham	E. A. Eberle	Mrs. Manley	Mrs. Selden Irwin
Joseph Jones	M. J. Gallagher		

The first act was set in Fordham's library; the second in Jack Manley's home, centre of virtuous activity.   The third act began in John Bird's (Gorman's) apartments at Fordham's, and carried us to the Central Fire Station, where the "still alarm" set in action the "beautiful twin Arabian horses, trained for this production by Harry Lacy."   Act IV, in three scenes, took us to Jack Manley's new home; to an ante-room at Fordham's; and back again to the setting of Scene I.   The play was directed by Ben Teal, and was, I repeat, only just across from Macy's great department store, where one could buy anything from an ice-cream soda to garments fit for a queen.

In spite of its instant appeal, this mad, glad thing remained, then, for only two weeks, but wait, reader, till spring follows in wake of the blizzard! On September 12th another of those indescribable concoctions of Charles H. Hoyt, then almost playwright in ordinary — very ordinary — to the American people, came to the theatre.   A Hole in the Ground, named with Hoyt's usual felicity, presented William Mack as a Capitalist, Otis Harlan (a clever entertainer) as a Romantic Young Man, George Richards as a Stranger, Alf M. Hamilton as a Commercial Tourist and also as a Roper-in for Centropolis Hotel, Frank Lawton as a Station Agent, W. Mack also as a Second Commercial Tourist and a Roper-in for Grand Union Hotel, W. H. Jordan as a Boy, anxious to be a R.R. man, Julian Mitchell (son of Maggie) as a League Base Ball Umpire, Dudie Douglass, Fannie Stevens and Irene Hernandez as Tailor-Made Girls, Helen Leslie as a Young Mother, Nannette Comstock (soon to be doing more serious things) as a Telegraphic Operator, Alice Walsh as a Tarrier and a Deaf Lady, Daisy Hall as another Tarrier and a Brat, Helen Leslie as a Tarrier and Flora Walsh (later, if not then, wife of Hoyt) as the Lady of the Lunch Counter.   If that list of characters is not as American as Coney Island or a football game of 1887, I do not know where to turn for anything more national; it explains fully Hoyt's attraction for the tired business man.   It was far from intellectual, but it was very good fun.   It left the Fourteenth Street Theatre, after four weeks of good cheer, on October 8th, but we shall fall upon, if not into, that Hole many times in our history.

[447]

Minnie Palmer, a great favourite if not much of an actress, entered on October 10th, in her well-known My Sweetheart, to which she joined J. P. Wooler's one-act The Ring and the Keeper. Oddly enough prizes amounting to $100 were promised to those who could find the greatest number of words in the name "Minnie Palmer" — $50, $25 and $5 to each of five lucky trailers in the exhilarating game. She filled an allotted two weeks, and, on October 24th, Mr. and Mrs. George S. Knight (Sophie Worrell) returned in Baron Rudolph, that not very successful play of Bronson Howard and David Belasco, which they had recently abandoned for more popular flippancy, in Over the Garden Wall. The present cast follows:

Rudolph	G. S. Knight	General Metcalfe	Charles Bowser
Nellie Dashwood	Mrs. Knight	Sheriff	Frank Colfax
Rhoda	Carrie Turner	Allen	G. D. Woodruff
Ernestine	Jane Stuart	Owen	Lin Hurst
Whitworth Lawrence	Frank Carlyle	Geoffrey Brown	Harry Woodruff
Judge Merribone	M. A. Kennedy	John Henry Thomas	William Sampson

As I read the casts of 1887–88, I reflect on how many good players were available for special productions; the exquisite finish of the acting of stock companies that had worked for years together could not be attained immediately by the best of actors meeting together for only a limited period. But, of this group in Baron Rudolph, William Sampson would one day be found at Daly's, and Harry Woodruff at the Madison Square, each remaining in his stock station for several years. It is especially to be noted that Charles Frohman directed this production of Baron Rudolph. On Sunday evening, November 6th, Charles W. Barry delivered an illustrated lecture on The Queen's Jubilee. These Sunday offerings of the theatres almost choke my pen and my narrative.

The Knights departed, on November 19th, and exactly what pleased the people entered on November 21st, Denman Thompson in the sweet, funny, innocuous, moving The Old Homestead. A concert, on Sunday evening, December 4th, was to present Harry Pepper, Clinton Elder, E. J. O'Mahoney, Carrie Tutein, Ollie Torbett, Arthur Oswald, Alice Coleman, and Paula Buchheim (child-wonder pianist). The Hanlons made a merry holiday time, beginning at the matinée, on Monday, December 26th, with Le Voyage en Suisse; according to Allston Brown, Emily Bancker, Snitz Edwards, T. H. Glenney and Edward Hamilton were in the show. How the new faces have come crowding in on us, during that autumn in the Fourteenth Street Theatre! The Hanlons stayed for a second week, ending on January 7th. The attraction for January 9th–14th leaves me colder than the air in the streets — McNish, Johnson and Slavin's Refined(!) Minstrels, though I think Frank McNish was very funny. Something of the newer style of entertainment entered on January 16th — Frank Daniels (a very funny man) in his new Little Puck; with him were Rillie Deaves, who had not sustained the standing

[448]

she won in The Rajah, and Bessie Sanson, who, years previously, tried to take the place of Rosina Vokes, and failed. The Herald cruelly remarks that she was as lively as a bottle of warm ginger ale. Little Puck was derived by A. C. Gunter from F. Anstey's popular story, Vice Versa, and A Fallen Idol. Annie Pixley held the next week, beginning on January 23rd, with The Deacon's Daughter, which bored some persons inexpressibly.

MODJESKA

It is rather surprising to find in this democratic house the aristocratic art of Helena Modjeska. She began, on January 30th, as Camille, repeating it at the matinée on February 1st and on the evening of the 2nd. As You Like It followed on January 31st with Eben Plympton as Orlando, Charles Vandenhoff as Jaques, Mary Shaw as Celia, and W. F. Owen as Touchstone, and at the matinée on February 4th; Donna Diana, a favourite of the actress, if not with her audiences, was delicately played on February 1st and 3rd. And, for the first time in New York, she gave, on the evening of February 4th, her beautiful Imogen, in Cymbeline. The cast is worth preserving:

Cymbeline	James Cooper	Iachimo	C. H. Vandenhoff
Cloten	W. F. Owen	Pisanio	Robert Taber
Leonatus	Eben Plympton	Queen	Sarah Blanche Gray
Belarius	S. E. Springer	Imogen	Helena Modjeska
Guiderius	Vincent Sternroyd	Helen	Grace Filkins
Arviragus	J. N. Long		

I remember with great delight Modjeska's Imogen; her beautiful rendering of the scene before the entrance to the cave was exquisite in its purity, its pathos, its expression of fear tempered with curiosity. It is one of the big Shakespearian moments in my storehouse of memory — one of the truly great bits of Shakespearian acting.

The second and last week brought (February 6th) another Shakespearian rarity — Measure for Measure, in which the great actress was magnificent as the pure, sorely tried Isabella; her support included William Morris as Angelo, Vandenhoff as Vincentio, S. E. Springer as Escalus, Robert Taber (one day to be husband of Julia Marlowe) as Claudio, Vincent Sternroyd as Lucio, T. L. Coleman as the Provost, James Cooper as Elbow, Tully Marshall as Froth, W. F. Owen as Pompey, Mary Shaw as Mariana, and Mrs. M. A. Pennoyer as Mistress Overdone. On the 7th and 8th (matinée) the star was Beatrice, to the Benedick of Plympton; on the 8th (evening) and 9th, she repeated her lovely Imogen; on the 10th, her charming Rosalind; and, on the 11th (matinée and evening) she was a perfectly artistic Juliet, rather too old for Juliet's age. I am pleased to say that I saw Modjeska in all of those impersonations, and still treasure almost photographic-phonographic records of her wonderful, finished art in all.

[449]

N. C. Goodwin, Roland Reed, Maggie Mitchell, Harry Lacy

On February 13th, the theatre went back to its more recent normal, presenting Nat C. Goodwin, in Turned Up and Lend Me Five Shillings; his company had some good material, in J. B. Mason, Charles Coote, Maud Haslam and Estelle Mortimer. I cannot vouch for T. H. Burns, E. F. Goodwin, Frank Morse, Lucy Escott, Marian Earle, Weevie (*sic*) Vivien (from vaudeville?) and Little May Richards, simply because I never heard of most of them before. Goodwin stayed for two weeks, yielding the stage, on February 27th, to Roland Reed, developing into a likable comedian, who proffered a new play by David D. Lloyd, The Woman Hater. Reed as Samuel Bundy, had the support of Harry A. Smith as Horace Mulbridge, Fred Hight as Dr. Lane, A. C. Deltwyn as George Dobbins, W. C. Andrews as Tom Ripley, Alice Hastings as Mrs. Lucy Joy, Annie Lewice as Alice Lane, and Bessie Hunter as Mrs. Walton. The Woman Hater lasted for three weeks.

Maggie Mitchell, now showing that she was not so young as in her halcyon '60s, brought to this theatre, on March 12th, a new play by Fred Williams, with music by Dave Braham. Probably the blizzard prevented production on the 12th. With the unpleasing name of Maggie, the Midget, it was kept on view for two weeks, except that, for the matinée on the 21st, the perennial Fanchon returned, and, for the afternoon of the 24th, Jane Eyre. And now, on March 26th, the Fourteenth Street Theatre entered on the easy luxury of a hundred-nights run. The Still Alarm returned, on March 26th, and settled into the house for that long stay, making of the stage a fire station indeed for its engine and Arabian steeds. Harry Lacy, E. A. Eberle, M. J. Gallagher, Thomas Ford and Benjamin Deane, as well as Blanche Vaughan and Mrs. Selden Irwin retained the parts they had played at the opening of the season, but Lizzie Hudson was now Elinore Fordham, Charles E. Lothian (*vice* Charles Dickson) was Willie Manley, Ralph Delmore (*vice* Wheatcroft) was John Bird at least part of the time, and Joseph Wilkes (*vice* Jacques Kruger) was Doc Wilbur. Or course Dickson and Wheatcroft had been gathered into the fold at the Lyceum Theatre. The fiftieth performance of the play fell on May 8th, and (so the management advertised) the hundredth on June 20th. The run ended on June 23rd, the hundred and fourth time The Still Alarm had aroused an audience.

The Casino, 1887–1888

There was much, probably too much, comic opera and musical comedy in New York in those years, but, on the whole, the most consistently enjoyable performances of such things occurred at Broadway and 39th Street, where the Casino was devoted to operètta exclusively.

The revival of the immensely popular Erminie finished the season of

TWENTY-THIRD STREET AFTER THE BLIZZARD (1888)
From a Print in the New York Public Library

THE UNION SQUARE THEATRE
From a Print in the Harvard Theatre Collection

1886–87, having carried on for a trifle over a year.   In the last performances Marie Jansen again appeared as Javotte.   The five hundredth showing was listed for September 6th.   The Marquis, adapted from Jeanne, Jeannette and Jeanneton, was produced on September 19th, with several leading members of the Casino's large company:

Marie	Bertha Ricci	Marquis de Noce	Mark Smith
Mae	Isabelle Urquhart	Prince de Soubise	Courtice Pounds
Jacquette	Sylvia Gerrish	Lagrenade	Max Freeman
Clorinde	Rose Wilson	Bailiff	Arthur W. Tams
Florine	Estelle Morris	Notary	Edgar Smith
D'Auberval	Rose Ricci	Chevalier	Henry Leoni
Franchette	Lucy Rivers	Courier	C. L. Weeks
Marion	Lillie Grubb	Briolet	James T. Powers

It is interesting to find in the cast Lillie Grubb, once the Talamea of Dixey's Adonis, and the English Courtice Pounds, beloved of all New York maidens, in 1885–87, as Nanki-Poo and Dick Dauntless.   And James T. Powers was featured by having his name placed emphatically at the outstanding position at the end of the cast.   And certainly Bertha Ricci, the statuesque Isabelle Urquhart and Mark Smith were well-liked by Casino audiences.

Yet The Marquis was no successor in popular acclaim to Nanon and Erminie.   Though its fiftieth performance was reached on November 7th, its career ended on December 3rd.   Meantime, on Sunday, November 20th, one of those concerts my pen dreads (dreads, because the chronicling of it and its fellows takes so much room in a crowded narrative) brought appearances of Teresina Tua (violinist), Franz Remmertz, Alexander Lambert and the Casino orchestra.   On Sundays, November 27th and December 14th, came Helene Hastreiter, Theodore Bjorksten, De Anna, Nettie Carpenter and Carbone, of the Josef Hofmann force.   On Monday, December 5th, the theatre produced Madelon, by Meilhac and Halévy, with music by Lecocq and adapted for this occasion by Max Freeman.   Lillian (sic) Grubb had the title-rôle, Bertha Ricci was Trompette, Miss Urquhart Pompanon, Sylvia Gerrish Jomine and Lucy Rivers Hernandez.   The leading men were Powers as Taboureau, Mark Smith as Rabicamp, Courtice Pounds as Jolivet and Tams as Filoufin.   Many pretty girls and competent actors, most of whom may be found in the cast of The Marquis, tried without avail to make a success of Madelon.   The opera passed into the void with the performance of January 14th.   The Herald declared that honours were divided among Miss Grubb, Smith and Powers; and Pounds, the idol of The Mikado, only two years earlier, "made a poor figure as Jolivet . . . sang in his usual lackadaisical style, his high collar voice giving out his notes as if muffins were his usual diet and he had just finished eating some."   This is distressing for admirers of the wandering minstrel of The Mikado.   Some good singing, however, came in on Sunday, the 11th, with Hastreiter, Bjorksten, &c.

Peace settled on the perturbed establishment when, on January 16th,

Erminie returned, with a cast now including Pauline Hall, Kitty Cheatham (her first appearance in our annals), Marie Jansen, Louise Sylvester, Francis Wilson, W. S. Daboll (restored to the part of Ravennes), Henry Hallam, Murry Woods and A. W. Maflin. What was set down as the seven hundredth performance of Erminie occurred on February 29th; of course that included the performances "on the road." During part of the winter Daboll was out of the cast, but, by April 9th he had returned. This extraordinary opera celebrated on May 12th, its two hundred and sixty-second performance (says Allston Brown) for this revival, its seven hundred and seventy-fourth at the Casino (?); and it had had four hundred and eighty-two on the road. I ask the reader to check for himself these astounding figures; I have my doubts as to the infallibility thereof.

For weeks before its production the press had teemed with announcements of the coming to the Casino of Chassaigne's opera, Nadjy, excitement culminating with a disagreement between Sadie Martinot, engaged for the title-rôle, and Richard Barker, the stage-manager, a disagreement that led to the precipitate departure of the irate lady. Marie Jansen made a hit in the part, but I never heard what Miss Martinot thought of that. The much-discussed work was heard, finally, on May 14th, with this cast:

Nadjy	Marie Jansen	Mayor	A. W. Tams
Princess Etelka	Isabelle Urquhart	Ladislas	A. W. Maflin
Angelia	Jennie Weathersby	Faragas	James T. Powers
Rakoczy	Mark Smith	Hildebrand	J. A. Furey
Count de Rosen	Henry Hallam	Julie	Edith Mai
Margrave	Fred Solomon	Katrina	Mai Chester
Konrad	Kate Uart		

Others who served, in minor capacities, were V. de Lacy, Florence Mellin, Nellie Buckley, Clara Varrey (sic) and Eugenie Maynard. Photographs of Marie Jansen, as Nadjy, in the abbreviated ballet skirts, were soon decorating the rooms of college students; also one noted the constant advarce of "Jimmie" Powers into the front rank of comedians where De Wolf Hopper and Francis Wilson had hitherto reigned secure. Nadjy ran through the summer, and between acts one could ascend to the roof garden, drinking, 'neath the stars or the moon, to the dulcet strains of the orchestra. The fiftieth time of Nadjy charmed on June 30th, and, on July 2nd, Fanny Rice was replacing Marie Jansen, then enjoying her holidays somewhere out of the heat of the city; one began, also, to buy photographs of Miss Rice in Nadjy's abbreviated costume. She was as clever as Miss Jansen, but not so pretty or so alluring. And, lo! the hundredth rendering of the successful operetta, on August 25th. A benefit for the yellow fever sufferers in the South, was tendered on the afternoon of September 27th, Nadjy being the sole attraction. The present run of the operetta ended on October 13th, but it was to come back, in the following season for another protracted visit, and with Lillian Russell as the Princess.

[452]

CHAPTER VIII

NIBLO'S, BIJOU OPERA HOUSE, HARRIGAN'S, GRAND OPERA HOUSE, PEOPLE'S THEATRE, THE WINDSOR, THE THIRD AVENUE, THE COMIQUE, THE COMEDY, METROPOLITAN OPERA HOUSE, ACADEMY OF MUSIC (NEW YORK), VARIETY, ENTERTAINMENTS, MUSIC, 1887–1888

THE season at Niblo's, far to the south, at Broadway and Prince Street, now proffered various attractions, only some of which would have been acceptable at Daly's or the Fifth Avenue. The term began on August 17th, with Lagardère, founded on the outworn melodrama, The Duke's Motto, and staged under the supervision of the Kiralfy Brothers. In this Maurice Barrymore, then, I believe, the best romantic actor in America, played Lagardère, Henriquez and Aesop, with Joseph Slayter as Gonzagues, Maurice Drew as de Chaverny, G. F. Nash as Philippe d'Orleans, F. Osborne as Duc de Nevers, Robert Fischer as Peyrolles, W. H. Bartholomew as Comte Navailles, Harold Fosberg (sic) as Cocardasse, W. H. Lytell as Passepoil, Helen Tracy as Blanche de Caylus, Mamie Floyd (somewhat later, the wife of Barrymore, and ever the daughter of W. R. Floyd, and never much of an actress) as Blanche de Nevers, and Helen Sedgwick as Pepita. The ballet included Clara Qualitz and Arnold Kiralfy. The run ended on October 15th, a creditable showing, though in the last few weeks, Barrymore had left the cast to fill engagements elsewhere. On October 16th, Robarts Harper delivered an illustrated lecture on Three Jubilees (Queen Victoria celebrating the fiftieth anniversary of her accession). Monday, the 17th, brought Denman Thompson, for a month of The Old Homestead, a never-failing joy to minds not too complex. November 14th began a week of Sweatnam, Billy Rice and Barney Fagan's "Progressive" Minstrels with, in the host, Frank Cushman, Harry Woodson, Charles Fostelle, Banks Winter, James Norrie, Nel Sonia, Manning and Drew, and Crawford and McKission. We cannot but be impressed by the way in which minstrel organisations had latterly taken to "the road"; what would George Christy or Dan Bryant have thought of this?

Jefferson, having pleased the upper city with The Rivals and The Cricket on the Hearth, came down to Niblo's, on November 21st, for a week of the undying Rip Van Winkle. Then another dramatisation of a novel extensively read took the stage and failed to win a lasting acclaim. Every one had read Rider Haggard's exciting story of She, and most of us wanted to see William Gillette and William Furst's stage arrangement thereof. Niblo's was closed on the 28th for rehearsal, and, on Tuesday, the 29th, the spectacular show and mystic shivers somehow missed the goal. In the first place, we wondered, who was Laura Clement, who played She-Who-Must-Be-Obeyed? F. F. Mackay, Wilton Lackaye, Charles Bowser, H. W. Frillman, Howard Coveney, George D. Fawcett, Loie Fuller and Fanny Addison also lacked, collectively, that glitter which compels a playgoer to hurry to the theatre to be enchanted by actors' efforts. And that was the public verdict. "She" reigned at Niblo's for only four weeks, and, on Monday, December 26th (matinée and evening) resigned the stage to a play named, under the circumstances, with a shade of irony, A Run of Luck. The cast of this Drury Lane melodrama, presented by Eugene Tompkins, was simply huge (Allston Brown prints thirty names) and, with the reader's permission I will "eternise" only the most important, as indeed the newspaper advertisements did:

Harry Copsley	Forrest Robinson	Daisy Copsley	Minnie Radcliffe
John Copsley	W. H. Crompton	Mabel Selby	Lillian Lee
Squire Selby	J. F. Dean	Aunt Mary	Mrs. W. G. Jones
George Selby	Fred G. Ross	Mrs. Willmore	Florence Robinson
Captain Trevor	Frank Losee	Mrs. Seymour	May Merrick
Charley Sandown	D. J. Maguinnis	Phoebe Wood	Marion Elmore
Jim Ladybird	Frank E. Lamb	Lucy Byefield	Grace Thorne
Joe Bunny	W. J. Wheeler		

Let us not forget that Grace Thorne was the daughter of the lamented Charles R. Thorne, Jr., and wife of the talented Frazer Coulter. The character of The Run of Luck may be gauged by one scene — The Meet and the Race — a Stud of Thoroughbred Horses and the beautiful filly, Daisy. Snapper Garrison, the jockey, was to ride, on January 9th.

The Run of Luck stopped on February 4th, making way for a week (6th–11th) of Thatcher, Primrose and West's Minstrels, a style of entertainment apparently popular at Niblo's. They were followed, on February 13th, by William Mestayer and Theresa Vaughn, in Check 44, or, Tobogganing, which had just finished four weeks at the Star Theatre. Of course the company was the same, and Richard and Robert Garnella were agile as Sniff and Snuff, respectively. The Boston Ideal Opera Company, fresh from the Fifth Avenue Theatre, began, on February 20th, with Zélie de Lussan as Zerlina, in Fra Diavolo. During their stay of one week they repeated the ancient fare of their uptown season — The Bohemian Girl, The Daughter of the Regiment, and The Elixir of Love, along with the more novel Victor, the Bluestocking. Cora Tanner, still Alone in London, filled the week beginning on February 27th, and, on March 5th, the migratory Herrmann began a week of magic. Some of those who shivered at his black magic may have shuddered, during the week of March 12th, when Daniel E. Bandman tore a leaf from Mansfield's book of success, and boldly undertook a performance

[454]

of Jekyll and Hyde.   He was supported by Dore Davidson as Utterson, E. P. Sullivan as the Reverend Mr. Howell, J. M. Colville as Dr. Lanyon, J. R. Smith as Inspector Newcomen, and Louise Beaudet as Sybil.   After this trial, Bandmann carried the play to the Academy of Music.   Robson and Crane, so unexpectedly ejected from their engagement at the Union Square, filled the week of March 19th, at Niblo's.   And Margaret Mather finished March, with a week of Romeo and Juliet, Leah, The Lady of Lyons, The Honeymoon and Macbeth, the kind of repertoire then passing out of the life of the stage.

Sardou's famous play, La Patrie, was reworked, under the name of Dolores, and elaborately staged, on April 2nd, at Niblo's, and won from the Herald the decision that it consisted "of five indigestible layers of Sardou sombreness, cemented by two pastes of Kiralfy lightness," but, admitted the critic, the new ballerina, Francescina Paris, was "a graceful, skilful and accomplished little dancer, possessing an attractive personality."   Leading players were Newton Gotthold as Count de Rysor, John T. Malone as Karloo, Eleanor Carey as Dolores, J. H. Fitzpatrick as Duke of Alva, W. F. Blande as La Tremouille, Max Figman as Jonas, Edward H. See as Vargas, Charles Gotthold as Miguel, Ricca Allen as Sarah Mattheson, and Annie Dunbar as Gudule.   It was an utter failure.   On April 16th, Evangeline restored us to the familiar, and, on the 23rd, the Dalys were here, in Upside Down.   On the 30th, William Gillette and Viola Allen appeared, in Held by the Enemy, James E. Wilson playing Colonel Prescott and Minnie Dupree the ingenuous Susan.   Clara Morris began, on May 7th, a week of her strangely successful Renée de Moray, and Kate Claxton followed, on May 14th, in The World against Her, a piece which the reader will meet in many places.   It now remained two weeks at Niblo's.

The season at the historic old house was nearly ended.   On May 28th, the Hallen and Hart company began a fortnight, with the American Four reunited, with Frank Bush, James F. Hoey, Leroux and Weston, Ralph Terry, Albert Clives and his acrobatic dog (Pretty Pet), John and James Russell, Ella Wesner and the Jackley Troupe.   Pat Rooney joined for the second week, as did Baggesen, Ferguson and Mack, Harry Kernell and the Big Four.   John P. Smith's Uncle Tom's Cabin, on June 11th, began a week, with Laura Burt as Topsy and Sutherland as Tom.   Summer was here, and Niblo's became entirely Bowery, on June 18th, with the Leonzo Brothers, in Brother against Brother, star performers being an English mastiff and the accomplished dog-actors, Tiger, Lion and Panther.   With the exit of that thrilling piece, Niblo's, on June 23rd, closed for the season.

Bijou Opera House, 1887–1888

The new season at this house began, on September 12, 1887, with Rice's Surprise Party, offering John A. Mackay, in A Circus in Town, by Edward Holst and Woolson Morse. The cast included Mackay, W. H. Hamilton, Paul Arthur, W. C. Mandeville, Thomas Lewis, Edward Holst, Adah Richmond, Hattie Delaro, Grace Wilson, Emma Hanley, Josie Hall, Evelyn Granville, and Richard Golden (as Bridget Montmorenci). A mere bit of froth, it was blown out by the equinoctial gales, on September 22nd. Friday, September 23rd, brought The Humming Bird, sponsored by Salsbury's Troubadours, including Nellie McHenry, John Webster, Louise Searle and Frank Blair; this also was a brief visitor, and winged its way out of the Bijou, on October 15th.

And now the theatre entered on one of those long runs so frequent in 1887–88. Closed, on October 17th, it re-opened, on the 18th, with The Corsair, a gorgeous production, with, according to the Herald, a silly book, and music by E. E. Rice and John J. Braham. We must scan the cast, remembering that Annie Summerville was a sister of Amelia Summerville, the funny fat Rosetta of the Dixey Adonis:

Conrad	Annie Summerville	Ali	Jennie Bartine
Birbanto	Frank David	Ahmed	Maud Waldermere
Seyd Pasha	Brocolini	Bachsheesh	David P. Steele
Syng Smaul	George A. Schiller	Mustapha	Harry Mahoney
Yussuf	Edward Morris	Medora	Louise Montague
Hassan	Carrie Behr	Gulnare	Clara Lane
Ganem	Kate Uart	Zuliema	Rosa Cooke

At a special matinée, on October 20th, made her first appearance in this city a young girl who was destined to take a high place in the history of the American theatre. This was Julia Marlowe, to call her by her stage name. She had made her début, at the age of twelve, under the name of Frances Brough, as Sir Joseph Porter, in a children's Pinafore company. After a scattering series of performances, she had, in New London, in April, 1887, acted Parthenia, as part of a three-weeks tour. And now, on October 20th, she came out, at the Bijou, in the same part, with a decidedly mixed support, including Frank Evans as Ingomar, George Nash as the Timarch, F. J. Currier as Polydor, Leslie Allen as Myron, Effie Wild as Actea, and Isabella Waldron as Theano. This cast I copied from the Herald review. The débutante was recognised as a young woman of great promise, not yet the equal of Rose Coghlan, Agnes Booth or Ada Rehan, the leaders of our superb stock companies.

Dixey, Miles and Barton, as proprietors of The Corsair, could settle back in comfort on the success of their offering. It ran on, without a ripple of discomfort, to its fiftieth performance, on November 28th, and thence to its hundredth, on January 9th, when souvenirs were given, in shape of albums of photographic views of the play. Annie Summerville had missed some performances of late, but she returned for this happy centenary. Miss Summerville had become mixed up in a divorce case that called her to Chicago, and like other pretty ladies she became ill under the strain, and Kate Uart sometimes replaced her as Conrad, the Corsair. But, with or without the lady of the divorce, The Corsair pursued its lucky way to its hundred and fiftieth representation, on February 21st and thence to its very close on March 17th. At some matinées in February, Clarence Worrall, the boy cornetist, pleased those who liked that sort of youthful exhibition.

March 19th brought an adaptation of Lecocq's Fleur de Thé, under the name of The Pearl of Pekin. This also was produced by E. E. Rice, and in it Louis Harrison, as Tyfoo, almost attained stellar rank, possibly because his associates were not of notable brilliancy—Alice Johnston, Irene Verona, Clarette Vanderbilt, Carrie Behr, Grace Wilson, Bertie Fisch, Philip Branson, Joseph W. Herbert, Herbert Charter and John Leach. Nevertheless, the piece reached its fiftieth showing, on May 7th, and, according to Allston Brown, the illness of Irene Verona, on the next night allowed Carrie Behr to sing Finette. The operetta closed on May 26th. Town Lots, or, a Paper City, by Herbert Hall Winslow, had a mere week, beginning on May 28th, with Jacques Kruger as the only member of the cast of any note whatever; the others were Charles Burke, Hattie Weems, Jean Delmar, Lizzie Winner (I have given up the effort to remember all the Winner girls), Caprice Van Lissa, Claire Harley and Gypsy Tattersall (from London). The Herald wittily observed that the best lines in the play were those cut short by the petticoats. On June 4th, Lost in New York, "a tank drama" engaged another inconspicuous cast in Patrice, Eugenie Lindeman, Florence Stover, May Atkinson, Mollie Lawton, Frank Dayton, George Wright, Walter Fessler and Thomas Wise, the last-named alone ever reaching any reputation on the stage. One week of this brought the season to a close, on June 9th. Two of its productions had apparently been successful, but even they hardly deserve resurrection in our review.

Harrigan's Park Theatre, 1887–1888

This rather unique house began, in September 12, 1887, a preliminary season, with John T. Kelly in a burlesque, The Wily West. I found no account of it or of the length of its stay. In the company were Gus Bruno, Ruth Daryl, Blanche Howard, the Delmanning Brothers and Annie Williams.

Harrigan's season began, on October 10th, with a revival of The Leather Patch, familiar faces being Harrigan, Wild, Collyer, Bradley, Joseph Sparks, Charles Sturges, Quilter, Goldrich, James McCullough, G. L. Stout, Annie and Emily Yeamans, Amy Lee, and Annie and Kate Langdon. Cordelia's

Aspirations, perhaps the best of the Harrigan sketches, came back on November 7th.

All this was but preliminary to the big production (November 22nd) of Harrigan's season, Pete, his play of Southern life, in which he made a great hit as the faithful negro servant, in a play of melodramatic incidents. The cast, as so often with Harrigan, was simply enormous, but I drive my weary pen through its mazes:

Pete	Edward Harrigan	Mate	James McCullough
Gaspar Randolph	John Wild	Auntie Charlotte	Dan Burke
Vi'let	Dan Collyer	Sampson Flyhigh	Joseph Williamson
Dr. Clifford	Frank E. Aiken	Enos Clinker	James Burke
Victor Lemaire	Harry A. Fisher	Rasmus	Robert Gordon
Colonel Coolidge	Marcus Moriarty	Susie Rivers	John Decker
Emanuel Shadrach	William West	Laz Fisheye	Robert Snyder
Alderman Brannigan	Joseph Sparks	Mary Duffy	Annie Yeamans
Squire Bainbridge	George Merritt	Mary Coolidge	Esther Williams
B. Jabez Bender	Charles Sturges	Mary Morgan	Lavinia Shannon
Major Steel	George L. Stout	Winnie Coburg	Amy Lee
Whyland Whipple	John Sparks	Mirandy	Annie Wilson
Hampton Bailey	Peter Goldrich	Little May	Katie Pattison
Ruth Callowfoot	Richard Quilter	Blossom Quartet	Gorman, Spearman, Dickson, Wrennie
Sunset Freckles	M. J. Bradley		

Guests at the Blossom Lady Hotel were portrayed by Annie and Kate Langdon, Emily Yeamans, Minnie Richards, Emma Leslie, Fanny Knight, Mattie Winn and Gertie Tuthill. Braham's songs were The Bridal March, Massa's Wedding Night, Heigho! Lingo Sally, The Old Barn Floor, The Stonewall Jackson, Slavery's Passed Away, The Old Black Crow, Where the Sweet Magnolia Grows, Let Us Wander in the Orange Grove Tonight.

If it was burdensome to inscribe that long cast of Pete, it is very easy to carry the play through the season. Lavinia Shannon's rôle in the piece was cut out, says the Herald of November 29th, in order to shorten the play. February 14th celebrated the hundredth performance of Pete. Some day the reader may be interested to count the very large number of plays that, in 1887–88, passed beyond the century mark — several of them very far. Pete arrived at the hundred and fiftieth goal on March 29th and finally stopped its run on April 21st. The last days were saddened by the death of Michael J. Bradley, so long connected with Harrigan. Allston Brown states that three weeks before his death, he ruptured a blood-vessel in his stomach, but continued acting in Pete, till March 28th. On April 23rd, Harrigan revived Old Lavender, a favourite with him, if not with his public; with it he closed his season, on May 5th.

GRAND OPERA HOUSE, 1887–1888

This popular "combination" theatre began its season, on August 22, 1887, with that ancient melodrama, Lost in London, proffering Newton Beers as

THERESA VAUGHN
(MRS. W. A. MESTAYER)

LAMB—MARION ELMORE
(A RUN OF LUCK)

JAMES A. HERNE
IN THE MINUTE MEN

MRS. JAMES A. HERNE

ANNIE SUMMERVILLE

ADELINE STANHOPE

W. A. MESTAYER

GO-WONGO MOHAWK

D. J. MAGUINNIS

star, and, in support, Jessie Lee Randolph, Sam Bernard (later so popular in farce) and Lauren Rees.   I should imagine that even addicts in attendance at the Grand Opera House would have waited for an offering more modern and brilliant.   Such an attraction was provided in full measure during the week of August 29th, when Jim, the Penman, that sensational success of the last fall and winter at the Madison Square Theatre, was played with the admirable Ada Dyas as Mrs. Ralston, H. M. Pitt in his original rôle of Percival, Joseph E. Whiting as the forger, and Evelyn Campbell as Agnes.   On September 5th, Robert L. Downing, trying to be a Forrest, began a week as Spartacus.   In the same tradition came Louis James and Marie Wainwright, on September 12th, 16th and 17th, in Virginius, and, on September 13th and matinée, 14th, in Ingomar.   They toned down, so to speak, on the 14th, and at the matinée, on the 17th, with Gretchen, and essayed Hamlet, on the evening of the 15th.   F. C. Mosley was their chief support, as later in the season at other theatres in New York and Brooklyn.   The cast of Hamlet included, besides the stars as Hamlet and Ophelia, Mosley as Laertes, Kate Meek as the Queen, F. C. Huebner as the King, F. C. Barton as the Ghost, Kittie Wilson (an unusual assignment for a woman) as Osric, Harry Langdon as Polonius, and E. Y. Backus, a good actor, as the First Gravedigger.

One always expected in those years a resurgence of the English melodramas that had flourished so vigorously, in the early '80s, at Wallack's or the Union Square.   The Lights o' London brought thrills to the Grand Opera House during the week of September 19th, with a lesser cast, including Sam Hemple, Fanny Denham Rouse, Lizzie Winner, Mason Mitchell, L. J. Loring, and Miss Carey and Virginia Thorne.   Harbour Lights continued the duty of illumination, beginning on September 26th, with an excellent cast, including E. H. Vanderfelt (who, in appearance, somewhat suggested Kyrle Bellew, the creator of the part at Wallack's that Vanderfelt now took up), Helen Weathersby, F. M. Burbeck, Augustus Cook, Sidney Howard and A. R. Whytal; this attraction remained a second week.   Mr. and Mrs. McKee Rankin followed, on October 10th, in their recently successful offering, The Golden Giant, Haskins and Miss Bigelow supporting.   The Rankins, we know, were not averse to melodrama; neither, I assume, is any playgoer who is not hopelessly tainted with the idea that every play must induce one to go out and reform the world.   Clara Morris, still a powerful attraction, presented, on October 17th and 18th, Article 47, with, in support, B. R. Graham, Walter C. Kelley, Octavia Allen and Mollie Revel.   At the Wednesday matinée, her company gave Our Regiment, not, I assume, before a large regiment of playgoers; in the evening, Miss Morris offered The New Magdalen.   On October 20th and 21st, she produced Renée de Moray, Clinton Stuart's adaptation of Le Martyre, thereby antedating the Madison Square staging of its version of the same absurd original.   For the matinée and

[459]

evening of the 22nd, the star reverted to her once famous character of Alixe, for which she had lost much of the required girlishness of appearance. After all the woes in the plays of the past few weeks, regular attendants at the Grand Opera House may have welcomed, on October 24th, the fun of Thatcher, Primrose and West's Minstrels, or, indeed, A Bunch of Keys, for the week of October 31st.

I must inform the reader that, beginning on October 30th, the persistent Professor Cromwell gave a series of Sunday evening illustrated lectures, that before spring bloomed in city backyards or in the larger spaces of city parks, carried auditors back and forth through most of the cities and countries of Europe, sometimes remaining in America, serving with talk and stereopticon the purpose that, today (1941), we depend on the cinema to fulfil — the purpose of making travelled persons of men and women who cannot afford to go far from home. On the 30th, we visited Ireland, and Sunday by Sunday, saw, thereafter, Stockholm, Rome, Seventy Wonders (what they were, I know not), San Francisco and the Far West, The Sunny South, Switzerland and the Alps, Three Strange Cities, The German Empire, America, Our Home (patriotic-sentimental, doubtless), London and the Jubilee. When Cromwell, on March 18th, gave again his Ireland, the audience was to be photographed "instantaneously" by Rockwood, the well-known photographer. This startling feat was accomplished on subsequent sacred Sunday nights. Cromwell continued, on successive Sundays, with Up and Down the Rhine, Paris, Italy, the Art Land, and Around the World in Eighty Minutes.

Meantime, I resume the voyage theatrical by bringing to the roomy stage and auditorium of the Grand Opera House Annie Pixley, who, on November 7th, began a week in The Deacon's Daughter. Something Forrestian again came, on November 14th, when F. B. Warde played Virginius, repeating it at the matinée on the 16th. He offered Galba, on the 15th and 18th; Gaston Cadol, a play of which I have no knowledge, on the 16th and at the matinée, on Saturday, the 19th; Brutus, on the 17th; and Richard III, as a farewell, on the 19th. Actors with repertoires worked hard, but their work gratified their ambition. Very different, but very amusing was A Parlour Match, with Evans and Hoey, for the week of November 21st. Held by the Enemy combined (November 28th–December 3rd) laughter and thrills in plenty. And, before an enormous audience, on the afternoon of Thursday, December 1st, a benefit for the Actors' Fund, under direction of A. M. Palmer, presented Henry Irving and company, Jefferson, Mrs. John Drew and company, Mrs. Potter, Fred Solomon, the McCaull Opera Company, Dockstader's Minstrels, the New York Madrigal Quartet, Harry Kennedy and Thomas J. Ryan. The receipts, we learn from Allston Brown, were $3,156.75. The house went back that evening, to its customary charge of 75 cents for a seat in the orchestra and so on, down, as it mounted to the gallery.

Jefferson, in Rip Van Winkle, was the standard attraction for the week of December 5th, and, if one may credit one's reading of the billboards, Mrs. Langtry and Barrymore, in As in a Looking Glass, for the week of the 12th. This big attraction was kept for a second week, and was followed, on December 26th, by N. C. Goodwin, in Turned Up and Lend Me Five Shillings. Gus Williams, in Keppler's Fortunes, started the New Year, on January 2nd. Jim, the Penman, with Ada Dyas and J. E. Whiting, returned, on January 9th; an engagement of Mr. and Mrs. Florence, listed for that week, by Allston Brown, was carried through at the Brooklyn Grand Opera House. Thenceforward we greeted four weeks of familiar pleasures: Kate Claxton and Charles A. Stevenson, in The Two Orphans (January 16th); Oliver Byron, in The Inside Track (23rd); Fanny Davenport, in Fedora, with Melbourne McDowell as Loris and Judith Berolde as the Countess (30th); and Richard Mansfield as Jekyll and Hyde, for the week of February 6th, except that for both performances, on Saturday, the 11th, he gave A Parisian Romance. Cora Tanner and Alone in London, were appraised for the week of February 13th, followed, on the 20th, by James O'Neill, in his everlasting Monte Cristo, that, in turn yielding the stage, on the 27th, to Frank Mayo, in The Royal Guard.

Then the Grand Opera House once more (March 5th) opened to Harbour Lights, that success of its autumn campaign; E. H. Vanderfelt, Helen Weathersby, Madge Carr, Augustus Cook and Burbeck led the cast. W. J. Scanlan, a pleasing person, on March 12th, began, unless the blizzard forced postponement for a night, a week of song and (I suppose) false romance, in Shane-na-Lawn; Hoodman Blind gave more melodrama, on the 19th, and had distinguished interpreters in Frederic de Belleville and Viola Allen. Evangeline, which we cannot long escape, danced in again, on the legs of the heifer, on March 26th; on April 2nd, Minnie Palmer began a week with what was gravely announced as the 2,013th performance of My Sweetheart. It must have been a task to keep count of that overwhelming series. Thatcher, Primrose and West were back for the week beginning on April 9th. West-side dudes and haunters of stage-doors (if the West-side possessed such appendices to the civic body) must have been enchanted by the offering of the week of April 16th—Dorothy, with the Standard Theatre cast, including Lillian Russell, Agnes Stone, Hattie Delaro, Rose Leighton, Eugene Oudin, John Brand, Harry Paulton and William Hamilton. Quite at the opposite pole of art was the Renée de Moray of Clara Morris, returning on the 23rd for a full week, except at the Wednesday matinée, when the company played Our Regiment. I cannot explain this recurrence for some years of Renée de Moray, in Clara Morris's repertoire. It was possibly due to the survival of the fame of her early days, in those later times when her emotional fervour had waned into a very mannered mechanism. Her performance in this particular play could not for a moment equal Agnes Booth's, which had not been able to keep the impossible play alive at the Madison

[461]

Square Theatre. This I said at the time (I saw both actresses in the part) and this in full memory of both I re-affirm more than a half-century later. I once admired Clara Morris intensely, but, in 1888, her mannerisms made me sad.

N. C. Goodwin returned, on April 30th, for another week of Turned Up and Lend Me Five Shillings. A Hole in the Ground (May 7th), still with Flora Walsh as the Lady of the Lunch Counter; the Herrmanns (May 14th); Kiralfy's Niblo failure, Dolores (21st); and Robert Mantell, in Monbars (28th) carry us to June 2nd and what was technically the end of the season. But we were not to be so easily dismissed. On June 4th an interesting summer season began, with Mrs. James Brown Potter (set down then, as ever, in her professional career, merely as Mrs. Potter) as Pauline, in The Lady of Lyons, her support somewhat like that of her fall season at the Fifth Avenue Theatre. Kyrle Bellew, a mannered actor, was Claude Melnotte. This play Mrs. Potter repeated on the 5th and 6th. On the 7th and at the matinée, on the 9th, she gratified her ambition by playing Juliet; Loyal Love was shown on the evenings of the 8th and 9th. Bellew supported as Romeo, Hart Conway as Mercutio, J. E. Kellerd as the Friar, Frank Lander as Tybalt, Jacques Martin as Peter and Minnie Monk, ever serviceable for any "legitimate" rôle, as the Nurse.

Called Back, on June 11th, employed good players in F. de Belleville, W. J. Ferguson (still as Macari), J. E. Kellerd, Robert Fraser, May Wilkes, Harriet Ford, Jennie Elberts and Little Carrie Elberts. Better still was the cast of The Banker's Daughter, in the week of June 18th, Herbert Kelcey and Georgia Cayvan appearing, as John Strebelow and Lillian, parts, by the way, very similar to those they had performed all the preceding winter, in The Wife. Others were Frazer Coulter as de Carojac, Robert Hilliard as Routledge, W. J. Ferguson as Phipps, B. T. Ringgold as Westbrook, J. W. Jennings as Brown, George Woodward (sic) as Babbage, Ethel Greybrooke as Florence St. Vincent, and May Roberts as Mrs. Holcomb. I wish I had seen that production. H. W. Montgomery, so long at the Union Square, appeared in a small part in both the revivals I have just mentioned. Uncle Tom's Cabin with Laura Burt as Topsy, let us down and out, for the week ending June 30th. On the whole, West-siders, reasonably regular in attendance for 1887–88, at the Grand Opera House, had many pleasing memories to enjoy, before the next season opened in August, 1888.

PEOPLE'S THEATRE, 1887–1888

The ambitious Harry Miner, long a force in the Bowery, re-opened his handsome People's Theatre in that section of the city on August 22nd, with Kate Claxton, in her still compelling The Two Orphans, with C. A. Stevenson as Jacques, Alice Leigh as La Frochard, Dore Davidson as Pierre, and Alice

[462]

Hamilton as Henriette. The Dominie's Daughter, the last new play Lester Wallack ever produced in his own theatre, he supervised in its staging for the week of August 29th, at the People's. J. K. Emmet, in Fritz, Our Cousin German, began a week, on September 5th.

Mrs. D. P. Bowers, on the 12th, offered something rather more novel, in Madame Crœsus, though it proved to be nothing but another version of Serge Panine, that ghastly failure at Daly's, in 1883. In her cast were Henry Aveling as Serge Panine, Mittens Willett as Nadia, Alice Fairbrother as Clarice, Carl Ahrendt as Michaud, Sidney Bowkett as Maurice, and William G. Beach as Pierre de la Rue. Mrs. Bowers was Mme. Desvarennes, so well played at Daly's by Fanny Morant. On the 14th, Mrs. Bowers retreated to the safer shelter of Lady Audley's Secret; the 15th found her in The Czarina, a tragedy by Oscar Leland, in which she played Catherine of Russia to the Peter the Great of Henry Aveling. On September 19th, Hoodman Blind carried us to the realm of the usual, and The Still Alarm signalled us through the week of September 26th. October slipped by with Herne, in Hearts of Oak (3rd–8th); Harbour Lights, for three weeks (10th–29th — an unusual stay in the Bowery). Held by the Enemy allowed October to pass into November, ending on November 5th. Meantime, even the People's broke out with the epidemic of Sunday lectures. On October 23rd, General John L. Wheeler gave an illustrated discourse on Great Battles of America; he seems to have repeated this on the 30th. On November 6th, he lectured on Great Battles of Our Civil War.

Sanger's Sparks Company, in A Bunch of Keys, opened the week of November 7th–12th, and Shadows of a Great City began a week, on the 14th, with W. A. Whitecar, Annie Ward Tiffany and Miss Clyde Harron; Mrs. McKee Rankin (without Rankin) brought The Golden Giant for the week of the 21st. A Hole in the Ground was funny, beginning on the 28th. The Dark Secret, with its scene of the Henley race, was very exciting, beginning on December 5th; it had just come from the big stage of the Academy of Music. Roland Reed, in Humbug, beginning on December 12th; Arabian Nights, with Lena Merville, Richard Golden, William Gill, Jennie Reeves and Bonfanti, following on the 19th; and Jennie Yeamans, in Clay M. Greene's play, Our Jennie, carrying us from December 26th-to New Year's Eve (December 31st)— these were the more or less frost-bitten offerings for the pre-Holiday season. Thatcher, Primrose and West's Minstrels began the New Year (January 2nd) and Emmet returned, on the 9th, for a fortnight of song and comedy, not quite so fresh as it had been, in Fritz, Our Cousin German; a matinée, on January 18th, was for the benefit of Mrs. Crowley, the wife of the imprisoned police sergeant.

Kate Claxton was to have brought out, on January 23rd, for the first time, Frank Harvey's play, The World against Her. Her father's death, caused Miss Claxton to postpone this opening till the 26th, the ever-ready

[463]

Two Orphans filling the first three nights of the week, with Sadie Dean and George Roberts taking the places of Miss Claxton and her husband, C. A. Stevenson. On January 26th, The World Against Her gave Miss Claxton a quasi-success that allowed her to escape from The Two Orphans, at least for a time. Allston Brown gives the cast for this story of a short-sighted wife who lets her husband and others believe the worst about her, then goes out into the world to endure the consequence of her self-sacrifice:

Madge Carlton	Kate Claxton	Gilbert Blair	A. H. Forrest
Lucy Danvers	Leslie Tillson	Harold Vernon	Payson MacKaye
Liz Markland	Maud Hosford	Robert Danvers	E. T. Hall
Jenny Clegg	Esther Lyon	Rob Millet	E. E. Egleton
Sally Millet	Alice Leigh	Dick Markland	R. Hickman
Annie	Little Daisy	Heslop	Theodore Williams
James Carlton	C. A. Stevenson	Thwaites	Ed Short
Simon Clegg	Palmer Collins	Ned	Master Frank Dean

This novelty filled the week of January 30th. Payson MacKaye must be the son of Steele MacKaye, who acted with Helen Dauvray at the Lyceum. The Silver King returned, on February 6th, and, on the 13th, came Frank Daniels, in Little Puck. Maggie Mitchell, during the week beginning February 20th, proffered, in succession, Fanchon, Jane Eyre, and Little Barefoot. A Tin Soldier, with Eugene Canfield, allowed February, from the 27th, to slip into the gales of March. James O'Neill followed, on March 5th, with the inevitable Monte Cristo, J. W. Shannon assisting as Noirtier and Howard Gould as Villefort; and Goodwin came, on the 12th, in Turned Up and Lend Me Five Shillings. Possibly the blizzard postponed the opening till the 13th. A Rag Baby, with Charles Reed as Old Sport, made funny the week of March 19th–24th. Hoodman Blind ended March (26th–31st), and Frank Mayo, with The Royal Guard, started April on its way (April 2nd–7th). But I must not overlook the benefit on Sunday, April 1st, of the Theatrical Mechanical Association, at which were promised Herrmann, Steele MacKaye, Robert Hilliard, Harry Fisher, Marion Booth, Dora Wiley, Daisy Norwood, Adah Richmond and many more. Harbour Lights returned on the 9th, and W. J. Scanlan (Peek-a-Boo), on the 16th, started a week in Fred Marsden's The Irish Minstrel — a product absolutely of its own time. Emmet for "German" songs, and Scanlan for Irish — each purveyor was declared to have composed his most popular melodies — Emmet the Lullaby and Scanlan the Peek-a-Boo, both still sung (1941). With Scanlan were Thaddeus Shine, J. B. Turner, Kate Blancke and Kitty O'Shea. On April 23rd, Edwin F. Mayo began a week's starring, in his father's great success, Davy Crockett. Charles T. Ellis, our former favourite in vaudeville, presented himself, on April 30th, in Casper, the Yodler, his wife, Clara Moore, assisting. James A. Herne's new play, Drifting Apart, with a setting on the New England coast, in a fishing village, was tried, not very successfully, on May 7th:

[464]

Jack Hepburne............James A. Herne	Hester..................Victoria Reynolds
Percy Seward...................H. M. Pitt	Mrs. Seward................Henrietta Bert
Silas........................C. W. Butler	Miss Stanley................Maude Jeffries
Harry......................James Oliver	Margaret...............Little Dot Winters
Alec.......................Phineas Leach	Miss Estabrook.............Lucille Pearson
Josh.....................Robert Alexander	Miss Fairchild.............Adelaide Nelson
Mary Miller.......Katherine Corcoran Herne	

I am surprised to find here, in a small rôle, the later well-known Maude Jeffries. Though Herne soon laid aside this play, it ran now at the People's for two weeks.

Lost in New York, for the week of May 21st, promised "a river of real water, an actual steamboat running at full speed, and all kinds of marine craft." This excitement, with the boat-race of some weeks before, in A Dark Secret, must have gladdened the hearts of New Yorkers, who could have seen all the water and boats needful for their welfare merely by walking or riding to any one of the waters surrounding our native isle of Manhattan. Dolores, that lost soul of two other theatres, came, on May 28th, to the People's. Scott and Mill's production of A Chip of the Old Block, which could be depended on to ring down any reluctant curtain, had a week beginning on June 4th, and another novelty (I am surprised to find so many novelties in a "combination" house) was launched on June 11th—Among the Pines, by W. R. and J. P. Wilson, with a cast including Eben Plympton, P. Augustus Anderson, John F. Ward, Thomas J. Herndon, T. L. Coleman, R. F. McClannin, Little Wallie Eddinger, Helen Windsor, Louisa Eldridge, Maggie Fields and Libby Noxon. Thus ended, on June 16th, Miner's season in his People's Theatre.

WINDSOR THEATRE, 1887–1888

That other Bowery theatre, built on the site of frustrated German hopes (the old Stadt-Theater) began its season, on August 15th, with a play by Nelson Wheatcroft, entitled Gwynne's Oath, with Adeline Stanhope (then or later Mrs. Wheatcroft) as Gwynne Archer, R. F. McClannin as Sir Pearce Parker, Herbert Archer as Harry Vesey, George R. Edeson as Jim Richards, Ernest Tarleton as Gussy Lambton, Wheatcroft as Richard Welbeck, Dan Leeson as Gilbert Archer, Emma Skerrett (for forty-odd years on our stage) as Miss Willoughby Parker, Isabella Irving (perhaps her début in our annals) as Bessy Smith, and Little Belle Ross as Pepe. That is an extraordinarily good cast to find thus far from a leading Broadway theatre, yet it remained but for a week. On August 22nd, Ezra F. Kendall began, in A Pair of Kids, Arthur and Jennie Dunn assisting. The White Slave, on the 29th, enlisted May Newman, Lulu Jordan, Harry Courtaine and R. J. Dillon, a quartet of some importance.

Zozo, the Magic Queen, with George H. Adams and Pauline Montegriffo, seems not very alluring, on September 5th, nor, on the 12th, did Newton Beers, in Lost in London, which had begun the season at the Grand Opera House, far to the northwest of the Windsor. And most unalluring was the offering for the week of September 19th, of James Carden, in Two Roads, supported by Miss Marston Leigh, Belle Stokes, and a cast whose every name has perished in the engulfing waves of time. Louis James and Marie Wainwright, who, two weeks earlier, had been at the Grand Opera House, now brought to the Windsor a standard repertoire including Virginius, Othello, Ingomar, Hamlet, and Romeo and Juliet. Frederic Bryton, in Forgiven, filled the week of October 3rd–8th; and, in the week of the 10th, Effie Ellsler in Woman against Woman, had the support of Archie Boyd, Frank Weston, Archibald Foster, Florence Fields and Mrs. Mary Myers—certainly no glittering array. Joseph Murphy, during the week of October 17th, gave his oft-revealed The Kerry Gow and Shaun-Rhue; but actually, on the 21st and 22nd, he offered a new play, The Donagh. Stella Teuton led the support. F. B. Warde followed for the busy week of October 24th–29th (Allston Brown unfortunately lists this visit for September 24th–29th), with a repertoire of Galba, Virginius, Gaston Cadol and Damon and Pythias; with him were Clarence Handyside, L. F. Rand, Eugenie Blair, Thomas E. Garrick, J. A. Ransome, William Stuart and Margaret Pierce—enough to make playgoers turn from the classics and rush to A Parlour Match or A Bunch of Keys. And that very thing they did! "Dainty Minnie Palmer," as she was advertised, was the attraction, for the week of October 31st, of course in My Sweetheart. The Hanlons' new Fantasma came on November 7th, and Clara Morris, on the 14th, for a week of, in succession, Article 47, Renée de Moray and Alixe, her company, at the Wednesday matinée, drawing an audience of some sort, for Our Regiment. W. H. Powers's combination, for the week of November 21st, hung The Ivy Leaf on the billboards, and the next week gave something as little interesting to my reader and me, Phosa McAllister, of the astonishing name, in Taken from Life.

A curiously mixed December provided The Pavements of Paris, with Leslie Miller, Edwin Travers and W. P. Brown (5th–10th); Jim, the Penman (12th–17th), with Ada Dyas and H. M. Pitt; J. H. Wallick, in The Cattle King (19th–24th); and Tony Denier's Humpty Dumpty (26th–31st). Much of this seems unworthy of the artistically advancing Bowery. And January improved but little in its offerings: Oliver Doud Byron and Kate Byron in The Inside Track (January 2nd); Mr. and Mrs. Knight (9th), for a week divided equally between Rudolph and Over the Garden Wall; the Hanlons, with Le Voyage en Suisse (16th); and, more to our taste, Jeffreys Lewis, in La Belle Russe (23rd and 24th), Forget-Me-Not (25th and 26th) and Clothilde (27th–28th). There was trouble on the opening night, and no play was given. Harry Mainhall was her chief support. Michael Strogoff, on January 30th, began a week, with Atkins Lawrence

[466]

and Florine Arnold, supported by Go-won-go Mohawk, an Indian girl, in the part of the gypsy, Sangarra.   Incidental attractions were Mlle. Eloise (dancer), Nelton (juggler), and Hewlette (wire-walker).   February and March proffered attractions so hackneyed that I need only to catalogue them like a schedule of articles of merchandise: The Lights o' London (February 6th), with Horace Vinton, Charles Patterson, Sam Hemple, Joseph Mitchell, L. J. Loring, Virginia Thorne, Helen Ottolengui and Fanny Denham Rouse; Annie Pixley, with M. C. Daly (13th), in The Deacon's Daughter; Evans and Hoey, in A Parlour Match (20th); the Dalys, in Upside Down (27th to March 3rd); the inescapable, but lively Evangeline (March 5th), with Fay Templeton as Gabriel and Bessie Tannehill as Evangeline; Cora Tanner, in Alone in London (12th–17th, possibly delayed by the blizzard, on the 12th); Daniel Sully, in Daddy Nolan (March 19th); and J. B. Studley (26th–31st), in a play by John A. Stevens, entitled A Great Wrong. Both star and author belonged to a day and a style that were passing.

The Salsbury Troubadours began April (2nd–7th) with The Humming Bird.   On the 9th, James M. Hardie and Sara von Leer began a week of On the Frontier.   The week of April 16th–21st belonged to the Howard Athenæum Star Specialty Company, so recently seen at the Star Theatre. The 23rd opened The Main Line, with actors whom I fear my readers cannot identify.   April 30th began a week's devotion to Passion's Slave.   Charles Erin Verner, another unknown star, brought in, on May 7th, Shamus O'Brien; I hope the customers were satisfied.

The offerings at the Windsor, since the New Year, and a month before, have seemed to me most unnoteworthy, inferior to those at the People's Theatre.   And see what follows — almost a revival of the spirit of the Old Bowery Theatre for a year or two before it became the Thalia.   Kate Purssell, another star whose fame has not survived, entered, on May 14th, for a week of Queen of the Plains, by Ned Buntline, with Ed Chapman, Pauline Parked (sic), Amelia Watts, John and Al Richard affording such help as their talents, if any, allowed.   And Rookwood, or, Turpin's Ride to York, on the 21st, went back, one imagines, to the Bowery of the '50s.   O. B. Collins played Turpin on the opening night and the 22nd, but was injured, falling from his horse, and thereafter W. H. Hamilton rode to York.   Collins's injury came in the advertised "leap over a donkey and cart, and over the turnpike gate," a feat which was supposed, in the play, to bring the death of the "gallant Mare."   Others in the cast were Edna Courtney as Lady Rookwood, Louis Glover as Ranulf Rookwood, A. H. Hastings as Luke, Ed Coleman as Jerry, T. J. Herndon as Peter Bradley, Louis Monico as Tom King, Nellie Sandford as Barbara, Rosita Worrell as Eleanor, and Nellie Donald as Sybil.   After this thrilling episode, the Windsor quieted down (May 28th) with a week of Charles L. Davis, in Alvin Joslin, passing thence to a week (June 4th–9th) of Under Cover, a play written for George

C. Boniface, in which he now appeared with his daughter, Stella, and her husband, H. A. Weaver, Jr., with Ed Tannehill, Carl Smith, May Stetson, Helen Corlette and Louise Rial. Edmund Collier gave a week (June 11th–16th) of a repertoire exactly such as Edwin Forrest might have offered twenty years earlier — Virginius, Jack Cade, Damon and Pythias, Julius Cæsar and Richard III. Forrest was dead but Louis James, Fred Warde, Robert Downing and Collier tried, not with complete success, to keep his spirit alive. John McCullough had come nearest to accomplishing that desired miracle, but McCullough alas! had himself passed from the scene. The Black Flag was listed for the week of June 18th. Dollars and Hearts, the last offering of the season (June 25th–30th), was the work of H. A. Du Souchet, and the cast was quite as undistinguished as the play itself, including, as it did, Lillian Brown, Elizabeth Andrews, Lillie Ramsden, George Woodward, W. Perkins, E. Warren, J. J. Farrell and A. Brüning, the last-named an admirable actor from Germany and one of the very few members of the company I ever heard of, before or since. The offerings of the Windsor had not averaged to the standard of those of the People's Theatre, not many blocks away on the Bowery. Frank Murtha of the Windsor had been outdistanced, artistically, by Harry Miner of the rival establishment. The last calls of the Windsor, for 1887–88, came on July 1st for a benefit to the family of the late Dr. William Dwyer, and, on July 2nd, for a benefit to the treasurers of the theatre, Theodore Meyers and D. J. Shelley, promised entertainers including Pauline Markham, Ryan and Carroll, the Clipper Quartet, Robert McIntyre, Gus Phillips and James Hoey. Yet, according to the Herald of July 17th, Blanche Walsh, daughter of ex-Warden Walsh, of the Tombs Prison, was, on August 3rd, to act there, as Desdemona, in Othello, "not her professional début," but all amateur. J. Gordon Emmons (Othello) and B. R. Throckmorton (Cassio) were to assist, and Stanislas Stange, the only professional, was to direct, and act Iago. Mrs. Childs was Emilia.

THIRD AVENUE THEATRE, 1887–1888

Since the Theatre Comique, in Harlem, was more in line, artistically, with the Windsor and the People's, it would seem appropriate to jump from those Bowery pleasances to 125th Street. In that journey northward, one must pass the cheap, popular theatre of H. R. Jacobs, at Third Avenue and 31st Street; what more natural, then, than to stop at this establishment and see what it was offering for the amelioration of East-side worries?

It began its new campaign on August 22, 1887, with Passion's Slave, not deigning, in the columns of the Herald, to name the interpreters. Edmund Collier filled the week of August 29th, with echoes of Forrest, in, successively, Jack Cade, Metamora and Virginius; matinées were offered on Monday, Wednesday and Friday, in this theatre of the people. Zitka sounds almost

[468]

babbling for the week beginning on September 5th; its chief interpreters, unknown to me, were Effie Clora as the Princess, and Mary Wheeler as Zitka. Frank I. Frayne, the incumbent for the week of the 12th, was familiar, and so was his offering, Mardo, and likewise his leading lady, Gussie De Forrest. S. R. Chester and the dog, Jack, also figured in the proceedings. Zozo, the visitor for September 19th–24th, should have been first cousin to Zitka, of September 5th. C. A. Gardner, in The New Karl, was in the bills for the week of September 26th, and Dowling and Sadie Hasson, in Nobody's Claim, for the week of October 3rd. Nothing but a desire for completeness would justify the inclusion of such items in our aristocratic annals.

Bartley Campbell's play, Clio, entered, on October 10th, and, on the 17th, the Wilbur Opera Company for a week of, in succession, The Merry War, The Grand Duchess and Giroflé-Girofla, offerings that I find it difficult to associate with Mr. Jacobs's theatre; the company gave four matinées in its crowded week. Edwin Arden, who had progressed from Broadway, where we found him in 1883, to the more democratic Bowery, came in, on the 24th, in his popular Eagle's Nest. James A. Herne's Hearts of Oak raised the standard, on October 31st; George C. Boniface, in The Streets of New York, brought in something familiar, on November 7th. Jacobs's own company filled the week of November 14th–19th, with The Wages of Sin, and Ben Maginley, seen not so long before in May Blossom, entered, on the 21st, in Inshavogue. Austin's Australian Novelty Company started the winter (November 28th–December 3rd), and Pete F. Baker, in Chris and Lena filled the week of December 5th, with Lutie (?) Miller as Lena. Under the Lash sharpened our frenzied melodramatic taste, on December 12th, with Walter S. Sanford as star. The stars, one notes, were as inconspicuous as many of the starry hosts of heaven. Hallen and Hart's First Prize Ideals added Variety in the scheme, on December 19th; and the Louise Arnott Company may have brought Christmas cheer, on December 26th, in Fun on the Bristol. For the New Year (January 2nd–7th) was offered the questionable delight of the Kimball Musical Company, in Mam'zelle. I feel almost as if I were attending "shows" in a small country town. Donnelly instituted popular Sunday concerts, giving us, on December 18th, Jules Levy, Edward J. O'Mahoney, Alonzo Hatch, Josie Hall, Victor Harris, and Louise Searle.

N. S. Wood, in The Waifs of New York, is more familiar to our pen; he visited the Third Avenue during the week of January 9th; J. H. Wallick followed, on the 16th, in The Bandit King. Her Atonement, on the 23rd, was somewhat out of key with those offerings of the preceding fortnight. Gussie De Forrest and Jean Delmar were in the cast. Corinne, in Arcadia, was here for three weeks (January 30th–February 18th); in the last week it was promised that she would "indulge in a prize-fight with the comedians of the cast." Corinne, at that time, was but a pretty, precocious child, and,

[469]

I suppose, to many this fistic bout would have seemed "cute," especially to playgoers in the Jacobs establishment. And here, on February 20th, comes another infant, the former Baby Bindley. Now announced as Florence J. Bindley, she was to move through the concentrated excitement of Dot, or, the Avenger's Oath. I submit this title to Hollywood — free of charge.

Harrison and Gourlay's Skipped by the Light of the Moon, did (February 27th–March 3rd) as it might, without the acting of Louis Harrison. Joseph J. Dowling and Nellie Page, on March 5th, introduced E. A. Locke's play, Never Say Die; boisterous fun entered, on the 12th, with Peck's Bad Boy. Perhaps the all-persuasive blizzard interfered with the opening on the 12th; at any rate, on the 19th, the house advertised that "Blizzard or no Blizzard," it would offer W. H. Bishop's Company, in Muggs' Landing, "a blizzard of fun and laughter." The Two Johns, with J. C. (Fattie) Stewart, filled the stage for the week of March 26th–31st. I hurry through April with Tony Denier's Company (April 2nd–7th); The White Slave (9th–14th), with R. J. Dillon, Helen Rand, Frank Drew, Georgie Dickson, J. J. Tighe, &c.; A Chip of the Old Block (16th–21st), with Robert L. Scott, Harry Mills and Ada Melrose; The Silver King (23rd–28th); and (April 30th–May 5th) Lost in London, with Newton Beers and Frances Field as the suffering Armroyds, Lauren Rees as Gilbert Featherstone, and Sam Bernard as Benjamin Blinker. Perhaps Bernard, from his later history, was the most important person seen in that season on the Third Avenue stage.

On May 7th, came another Dr. Jekyll and Mr. Hyde, perpetrator unheralded in the paper on which I rely for material. May 14th gave an eager auditory Frankie Kemble, in Sybil, with an unusually good support, for this theatre, in Harry B. Bell, Howard Kyle, W. J. Constantine, Margaret Hatch, and Annie Lockhart. The next week (May 21st–26th) was to have presented Lottie Church, in Unknown. On May 18th, however, the Department of Public Buildings closed the theatre. The building next door, at the corner of 31st Street, had been demolished, and the adjoining wall of the theatre, unsupported, was deemed unsafe. The resourceful Jacobs installed himself immediately in the Thalia Theater, which Gustav Amberg was leaving for his new theatre in Irving Place. These events I shall record under appropriate headings.

THEATRE COMIQUE, HARLEM, 1887–1888

I will now transport my reader to 125th Street, to let him see whether I was correct in assuming that the offerings of the Theatre Comique were of a higher grade than those at Third Avenue and 31st Street. After the variety show which opened the house, on September 5th, we waited patiently for the beginning of the regular season, on October 10th, with the ubiquitous The Lights o' London. Held by the Enemy, on the 17th, presented Mary

Mills, Minnie Dupree, Alice Grey, S. S. Block, J. J. Farrell, James Gardner, Sidney Bowkett, E. J. Holland, and the author, W. H. Gillette. Hoodman Blind came, on the 24th, with Frederic de Belleville and Viola Allen.

Myra Goodwin, fresh from vaudeville, held the stage (October 31st–November 5th) with Philopene, the fame of which has not descended to 1941 A.D. The Salsbury Troubadours, in The Humming Bird (November 7th–12th) prepared the way for Mrs. Langtry, who entered with A Wife's Peril (November 14th, 15th, 16th), As in a Looking Glass (18th and 19th) and The Lady of Lyons (matinée, 19th). Harlem must have been surprised. Arthur Rehan, brother of Ada Rehan, had secured from Augustin Daly the rights to Nancy and Company and Love in Harness; these he presented, each successively for half the week of November 21st–26th, with Carrie Turner and Harry Hotto, in parts originally played by Miss Rehan and James Lewis. The next week (November 28th–December 3rd) brought Kate Claxton and C. A. Stevenson, in The Two Orphans. Harbour Lights, with Vanderfelt, Helen Weathersby and Madge Carr, gleamed in the wintry nights of December 5th–10th; Thatcher, Primrose and West's Minstrels made cheerful the nights of the following week. The Weston Brothers, in their musical comedy, The Way of the World, leave me guessing as to the week of December 19th, but I am on firm ground (December 26th), with Jim, the Penman, and (January 2nd) with Mr. and Mrs. George S. Knight, in Rudolph.

The impression grows with the engagement of W. J. Scanlan, dividing the week of January 9th–14th, between Shane-na-Lawn and The Irish Minstrel; with Evans and Hoey, in A Parlour Match, with Minnie French as Innocent Kidd (16th–21st); with Frank Daniels, in Little Puck (23rd–28th); and with Leonard Grover's Lost in New York (January 30th–February 4th). Hoodman Blind (February 6th–11th), may not have been much, but Richard Mansfield, the most promising young actor then on our stage, came in (February 13th) for a week of Dr. Jekyll and Mr. Hyde, the strain of which he relieved, on Saturday evening. Daniel Sully, in Daddy Nolan, would unquestionably seem a let-down for the week of February 20th, as I fear, did Gus Williams, on the 27th, in Keppler's Fortunes. Dan A. Kelly, in After Seven Years, or, the Mystery of the Willows, was lenten fare, artistically, for the week of March 5th. Deacon Brodie was scheduled for the following week, a short time after it emerged at a theatre farther to the south in our city. The White Slave once more aroused pity, on March 19th, and Kate Claxton was here for the week of the 26th, in her recent production, The World against Her. April burgeoned with Murray and Murphy, in Our Irish Visitors (2nd–7th); the Herrmanns and D'Alvini (9th–14th); A Tin Soldier (16th–21st); Sydney Rosenfeld's A Possible Case, a novelty for Harlem (23rd–28th); and Joseph Murphy (April 30th–May 5th) in a week divided between The Kerry Gow and Shaun Rhue.

[471]

Julia Anderson, whose fame has not descended to 1941, came forth on May 14th, in Inez, or, a Wife' Secret (by Robert Johnston). Her co-adjutors were, with one exception, equally undistinguished — E. P. Sullivan, Louis Gifford, Charles Mortimer, Charles Herbert, Harcourt Vane, Hattie Hawley and Rose Stahl (the one exception to my withering comment, and known, later, much later, for her clever performance in The Chorus Lady). A benefit to Nat Roth fell on May 16th. Frank Mayo was star of May 22nd, 23rd, in Davy Crockett and for May 24th–26th, in The Royal Guard. The house was closed, on May 21st, to allow Mayo to take part in the Wallack benefit, at the Metropolitan Opera House. John A. Stevens, who seemed to be everywhere, appeared, on May 28th, in A Narrow Escape, just as we thought we had escaped for the season from the Comique. The Brockman Monkey Company were the feature of June 4th–9th, and Scott and Mills the features for the next week, in A Chip of the Old Block. I found no more for the Comique in the season we are so laboriously traversing.

POOLE'S THEATRE, 1887–1888

The former Aberle's Theatre, in Eighth Street, showed by its offerings how provincial was the neighbourhood to which it ministered. There, for one night only (August 22nd), it gave Monte Cristo, with H. G. Clarke, G. Maddox, Lulu Frieth and Laura Linden. For the week of August 29th–September 3rd, it proffered The Exile's Daughter (by C. L. Graves), with F. A. Tannehill, Bessie Clarke, Elsie Graham, Emma Fossette, S. J. Forhan, F. E. Cooke, J. S. Madero and George H. Whitman, only one of whom I ever heard of, before. For September 5th–10th, The Galley Slave did as it might with Adelaide Thornton as Francesca, David Murray as Sidney Norcott, Julian Magnus as the Baron, Sam Edwards as Franklin Fitts, and Margaret Lanner as Cicely Blaine — probably not a bad cast. The Pauline Harvey Comic Opera Company divided the week of September 12th–17th evenly between The Mascot and The Mikado, neither a novelty, one might suppose, in the hinterland of Eighth Street; the artists included Dan Packard, J. W. Sweeney, Henry Moulton, Clement St. Martin, Victor Hawley and Adele Reno, as to whose qualifications I plead complete ignorance. The Sea of Ice had (September 19th–24th) Joseph P. Winter as Carlos, E. W. Marston as Barabas, Edwin J. Mack as Raoul, Charles Drake as Jean Madoc, Blanche Mortimer as Louise and Ogarita, Mae (sic) Wentworth as Diane, and Laura Linden as the Countess, a cast somewhat suggestive of the Old Bowery's last days.

J. K. Tillotson's play, Lynwood, filled the week of September 26th–October 1st, with Adelaide Thornton, Edna Courtney, David Murray, G. Morton Price and others of very slight renown; admission was now held at 10 cents, 20 cents and 30 cents. What could we expect for that? Yet Ada Gray,

[472]

for that moderate fee, gave a week (October 10th–15th) of her undying, if not immortal East Lynne. The cast of Hazel Kirke (October 17th–22nd) included Estelle Mortimer, T. J. Herndon, Mamie Johnson, J. K. Mortimer and George Gaston (as Pittacus Green)—really a fair distribution.   Ten Nights in a Bar-Room sets us back (October 24th–29th) to the dark days of the mid-century; but In His Power was at least of newer thrills for the week of October 31st–November 5th, with David Murray, Francis Reinau, Lionel Bland and Estelle Mortimer.   Marked for Life, with Sid C. France, pleased patrons, no doubt, for the week of November 7th–12th; Dominick Murray's vehicle for November 14th–19th, leaves me helpless, since I never heard of it before or since; Right's Right was its austere title.   For Sunday, November 13th, we were to be entertained with Alfred H. Weston's 7,000 Miles in 7,000 Seconds—another dark secret, so far as I am concerned.

The Ticket of Leave Man (November 21st–26th) again carried us far back in memory, though W. J. Shea as Hawkshaw, and Mamie Johnson as Sam, are new to us in those rôles.   John W. Ransone, in Across the Atlantic, was viable for the following week; and most thrilling to Eighth Street must have been (December 5th–10th) Frank Tannehill as Jagon, in The Stranglers of Paris.   But think of One Million Dollars following that strangling, in the week of December 12th–17th!   In this strange interlude appeared Edith Hall, John Hazelrigg, Iram Peroult and Fannie Francis, the last-named being our old acquaintance of the late '70s or another of the same name. Sunday, December 18th, permitted Minnie Steinbricker, a lass of eighteen summers, to speak on Spiritualism.   Edifying!   Phosa McAllister, in Taken from Life, called custom in the week of December 19th–24th; One of the Bravest, also familiar to us in our visits to very minor playhouses, was the holiday offering of December 26th–31st, with Charles McCarthy, Lottie Blair, William Cronin, Ned Barry, Fred Jerome and others.   But the holiday largesse of January 2nd–7th must have caused the rafters (or their equivalents) to ring—William Madden's play, Round New York, with sparring (sparring, mark you!) by Jack Dempsey, Billy Madden and Denny Costigan. Lulu Delmay, J. C. Walsh and Lillie Morris acted.

This narrative is almost like that detailing attractions in cheaper Williamsburgh theatres; many of the same attractions appear on both sides of the East River.   For instance, Micaliz, or, the Double Life, seen in the week of January 9th–14th, with William Cattell and Evelyn Knapp!   Stanley Macy, in C.O.D., seems, for January 16th–21st, rather more fresh; in the cast were Gus Bruno, Emil Heusel, Barney McDonough, Tillie McHenry, Emily Northrop, Bessie Clarke (sic), Marie Cahill (of all people in the world!) and Gus Frankel.   A benefit, on Sunday, January 15th, to T. W. Moore, promised Lillian Conway, Henrietta Markstein, Flora Moore, Daisy Norwood, Harry Kennedy, Dutch Daly and many more.   If all appeared, it must have been a good show.   On January 22nd (Sunday) came another

[473]

illustrated lecture by "Professor" Alfred H. Weston. The week of January 23rd–28th presented A Hoop of Gold, with Mortimer Murdoch as Sammy Weatherick (*sic*), also with Harry Courtaine and Marie Hilford; Weston again lectured, on Sunday, the 29th, and, on the 30th, we began a week of Confusion, John W. Jennings playing Christopher Blizzard, with support from Lytton Baker, F. F. (*sic*) Webber and Annie Ware. Weston once more held forth (Sunday, February 5th), his theme being The Yellowstone; and he was to photograph the audience! It is observed that the same actors appear and re-appear frequently at Poole's, almost causing us to suspect that they formed a stock company for the season.

N. S. Wood, ever young, was here for the week of February 13th–18th, dividing the semaine equally between The Boy Detective and The Boy Scout; equally familiar (February 20th–25th) was Sid C. France, in Dead to the World. Weston's "last" lecture, on the 19th, had the mystifying title of Extracts. The Black Flag presented (February 27th–March 3rd) J. L. Ashton, Mrs. H. W. Mitchell, W. L. Gleason, and Hal Clarendon. And Ten Nights in a Bar-Room exercised its ancient spell and its warning for March 5th–10th, with George J. Maddox, E. W. Marston, Sam Edwards and Lucille Allen. D. A. Kelly, in The Shadow Detective (March 12th–17th); One of the Bravest (19th–24th); A Celebrated Case (26th–31st) carry me to April 2nd–7th, when The Colleen Bawn may have been new to the very young in the audience. Frank I. Frayne, in Mardo (April 9th–14th), Sam E. Ryan's Combination in The Long Strike (16th–21st), and Pauline Markham, in East Lynne (23rd–28th) were the rather faded flowers of April. Dan A. Kelly filled the week of April 30th–May 5th, with After Seven Years, or, the Mystery of the Willows.

Storm Beaten (May 7th–12th) enlisted Edwin Browne as Christian, Edward Summers as Squire Orchardson, H. P. Keene as Richard, Millie Pierce as Priscilla, Hattie Berleur (*sic*) as Kate, and Alice Mason as Dame Christianson. The Arabian Nights (May 14th–19th) had Louise Dempsey as the Princess, assisted by Josie Robinson Haywood, Louis Haywood and Al Decker. Uncle Tom's Cabin (May 28th–June 2nd) presented Adele Clarke as Topsy, Nonie Tucker as Eva, E. W. Marston as Marks, S. Pritchard as Uncle Tom and Jessie Lee Randolph as Eliza and Cassy. The Kindergarden enlisted (June 11th–16th) Stanley Macy, Fred Mendoza, Laura Dinsmore and Katie Hart. Muldoon's Picnic, with John and James Callan, was summery in suggestion for June 18th–23rd, and Our Strategists rather dubious for June 25th–30th, with Harry Trayer, Charles H. Titus, T. J. Branick, Charles Norris, E. J. Mack and Sol Aiken.

THALIA THEATER, 1887–1888

Amberg's last season at his established Thalia (the old Bowery) is generally conceded to be the most brilliant sequence of stars and plays ever given here in German, or, perhaps, in any other language. Only the best seasons in the best of our New York playhouses could be thought to equal it or surpass it. Great German actors appeared in the most important German plays, classic or romantic.

Yet the opening bill (Saturday, October 1st) gave no indication of the fine things in store. The season began with Fra Diavolo, in which Ferdinand Schütz sang the title-rôle, supported by Rudolf Sinnhold as Lord Koolborn, Jenny Boner (new) as Pamela, Eduard Elsbach as Lorenzo, Hermann Gerold as Matteo, Carola Engländer as Zerline, Carl Mühe (an important newcomer) as Giacamo, Max Lube as Beppo, and Otto Meyer as Francesco. I have no doubt these people gave a good account of the opera. In the concert, on Sunday, October 2nd, were prominent Selma Kronold, Johanna Schatz, Lube and Bernhard Rank, fine comedians these two for a "sacred" concert. Oscar Blumenthal's play, Ein Tropfen Gift, made a hit, on Monday, October 3rd, with Marie Hock, a successful new candidate as Hertha (Mme. Niemann-Raabe, later, played the part, at the Star Theatre). Others in the cast at the Thalia were Oscar Krüger as Lothar, Franz Hillmann as Prinz Karl Emil, Otto Meyer as Erwin, the returning Adele Palma as Liddy, August Walter as Graf Vahlberg, Rank as Geheimrath Fabricius, Theodor Wegern (new) as Oberst von Wendlingen, Franz Costa (new) as Baron Brendel, Anna Jordan (also new) as Baronin Breitenbach, and, in lesser rôles, Conrad Junker, H. Gerold, Hermann Korn and Eduard Hirsch. This reads like a fine stock company. Fra Diavolo was to be repeated on October 4th, but was replaced by Der Zigeunerbaron, and Familie Buchholz figured on October 7th and 8th with August Walter, Fanny Heller, Lucie Werner, Adele Palma, Anna Jordan, F. Hillmann, Junker, Costa, Rank, Lube, &c. With these exceptions, Ein Tropfen Gift ran uninterruptedly till October 15th, when came the début of August Junkermann. On the afternoon of the 15th, however, Alexander Strakosch, who was then reading about, promiscuously, appeared, with Die Wallfahrt nach Revelaar, of Heine. Eine vollkommene Frau also entered the bill.

AUGUST JUNKERMANN; HEINRICH BÖTEL

Junkermann's début, on the 15th, presented him as Inspector Bräsig, a part he frequently acted during his engagement. On Tuesday, October 18th, Junkermann appeared as Walter Boss ut Sielow, in Ut de Franzosentid (Aus der Franzosenzeit, adapted from Fritz Reuter). His support included August Walter, Albertine Habrich, Rank, Otto Meyer, Costa, Fanny Heller and Lucie Werner.   Gradually we are meeting all the members of Amberg's company.   The Reuter play was followed by Jochem Päsel, with Junkermann in the title-rôle, associated with Marie Hock, Fanny Heller, Oskar (*sic*) Krüger, and Anna Jordan.   This double bill was repeated on the 20th and 22nd (evening).   The predilection of Junkermann for Fritz Reuter plays indicates his quality as a character comedian in dialect parts.

An artist of wider appeal was associated with him during his present visit. This was a tenor, apparently of the school of Theodor Wachtel, that high-voiced tenor of the '70s.   Heinrich Bötel, the new star, came forth, on Monday, October 17th, as Manrico, in Der Troubadour, easily accomplishing the high notes of *Di quella pira*, and winning praise from both the German and the American press of the city.   With him were Emil Steger as von Luna (the German sounds funny to our Italian-accustomed ears), Jenny Boner as Azucena, Karl Mühe as Ferrando, and Frau Herbert-Förster (wife of Victor Herbert, and last year of the Metropolitan Opera) as Leonora. This opera was repeated on the 21st and on the afternoon of the 22nd.   It will be seen that the week of October 17th–22nd brought but two bills to the Thalia, interwoven into a pretty wreath of comedy and opera.   On Sunday, October 23rd, Strakosch read from Die Räuber and Der Erlkönig. The next week provided Der Troubadour (October 24th); Inspector Bräsig (25th), with Junkermann and Rosa Lesseur (début); Martha (26th and 28th, matinée, 29th), with Bötel, Selma Kronold, Jenny Boner, Karl Mühe (Plunkett) and H. Gerold (Tristan); and (27th) more Fritz Reuter with Dorchlauchtig (Durchlaucht), with Junkermann as Adolf Friedrich IV, other parts falling to Junker, Rank, Friese, Sigismund Störk, August Walter, Franz Costa, Johanna Schatz, Marie Kraft, Marie Hock and Fanny Heller. For the Sunday concert (October 30th) we were offered Wem sollen wir wählen?

Bötel's contribution for the following week was Wachtel's famous show-piece, Der Postillon von Lonjumeau, with assistance from Karl Mühe, Selma Kronold, Eduard Elsbach and Bertha Rabowska; this he gave on November 1st and 5th, with Martha serving as intermediary on the 3rd.   Junkermann, on October 31st and at the matinée, on November 5th, repeated the Reuter double-bill of the week of October 17th–22nd; on the 4th, he delved once more into the Reuter treasure-bag, and pulled forth Hanne Nüte, in the seven pictures of which he, as Snut, was aided by Rosa Lesseur (a lesser star), Johanna Schatz, Walter, Junker, Rank, Costa, Anna Jordan, Adele Palma, Otto Meyer, Lube and Gerold.   Bötel would introduce into an opera a song that would show off his voice; in Der Postillon, on November 7th, he sang Abt's Gute Nacht, du mein herziges Kind.   This favourite opera he sang again, on the 9th and 11th.   On the 8th, Hanne Nüte, and on the 10th, auf Verlangen, Inspektor (*sic*) Bräsig gave Junkermann a chance to rise above Bötel's sea of song.   For the matinée, on the 12th, he repeated

Dorchlauchtig ("Highness") and in the evening of that day appeared in Mein Leopold, of course as the stern parent. At the "concert" on the 13th, Junkermann did Onkel Bräsig, Einzug auf Pümpelhagen and Unsere Komiker.

Inspektor Bräsig came on November 14th, and at the matinée on the 19th. Junkermann brought variety into his rather monotonous repertoire by reviving (on the 16th) Hasemann's Töchter, and by producing, on the 18th, G. von Moser's play, Der Hypochonder. In the latter, he was Wirkenstock, Rentier; Marie Kraft was Emma, seine Frau; Marie Hock Asta, ihre Tochter; Lube Sauerbrer, Kaufmann; Fanny Heller was his wife; Adele Palma her daughter; Franz Hillmann was Arnold Reimann; Krüger Pieper; Paula von Varndal Lina; and other actors were Friese, Junker, O. Weber, Sinnhold, Walter, Rank and Anna Jordan—a faithful band. Alessandro Stradella, on November 15th, brought the début of Helene Livingstone as Leonore, with Bötel, of course, as Stradella. On the 17th, Bötel's hundred and fiftieth Trovatore was acclaimed. Der Postillon again snapped the whip and rode the high C's, on Saturday evening, November 19th.

Junkermann, for his benefit, on November 21st, gave a taste of his quality in four plays—Onkel Bräsig's letzte Stunden, Du drögst de Pann Weg, Ein Berliner Kreisrichter auf dem Wiener Juristentag, and Der Kapellmeister von Venedig; this bill was repeated on the 25th. Otherwise that week gave us Der Troubadour (22nd); Hanne Nüte (23rd); (24th—Thanksgiving afternoon) Aus der Franzosenkeit and Jochem Päsel; Der Postillon von Lonjumeau (24th, evening); and (matinée, 26th), Ein Tropfen Gift and Du drögst de Pann weg. For the evening of the 26th, the once-popular Die weisse Dame enlisted Bötel, Mühe, Selma Kronold, Carola Engländer, Jenny Boner and Sinnhold. Both Junkermann and Bötel found parting such sweet sorrow, and, I dare say, remunerative, that they established a series of farewells. Bötel's first farewell benefit, on Monday, November 28th, presented him in Der Troubadour (Act III), Martha (Act III) and Der Postillon von Lonjumeau (Act I)—each selection allowing him to emit high tones in stirring solos.

After the recurrent phases of the repertoires of the two stars, it is a pleasure to come on the novelty of November 29th—G. Kadelberg's comedy, Goldfische, the source of Augustin Daly's The Railroad of Love, and now produced with Daly's permission. The cast at the Thalia:

Joachim von Felsen	Otto Meyer	Adolf von Pochsaar	A. Junkermann
Erich	Oskar Krüger	Mathilde	Fanny Heller
Martin Winter	August Walter	Hans Roland	C. Friese
Emma	Adele Palma	Stettendorf	Conrad Junker
Josefine	Marie Hock		

Goldfische again swam into our ken on December 1st, 3rd (evening), 5th, 7th and 9th, and matinée, 10th. On December 2nd the two stars united to

[477]

the end, let us hope, of a perfect joy, Bötel giving acts of Die weisse Dame and Der Postillon, and Junkermann his distressingly long-named short pieces, Ein Berliner Kreisrichter auf dem Wiener Juristentag and Du drögst de Pann weg. This last-named, with Jochem Päsel, constituted Junkermann's contribution for the evening of December 6th, Bötel joining scenes from Der Troubadour, Stradella and the inescapable airs accruing. These conglomerated bills were offered with "keine erhöhten Preise" — perhaps to stimulate a sated public. For the matinée on December 3rd, Der Postillon again cracked the whip, without cracking the voice of Bötel. A change for Bötel occurred on December 8th, 10th and 14th, when he sang Raoul in Die Hugenotten, to the Valentine of Frau Herbert-Förster, the Queen of Frau Hovemann-Koerner, the Page of Jenny Boner, the St. Bris of Steger, and the Marcel of Mühe, a cast which, collectively, made no one forget the Nilsson, Sembrich, Scalchi, Campanini cast of 1884, at the Metropolitan. In fact, I suspect that the German names Der Troubadour and Die Hugenotten covered some German heaviness in these performances, despite the excellence of Bötel. Junkermann's farewell matinée came on December 10th; on the 13th, he repeated his popular Inspektor Bräsig. That concluded his long engagement; and Bötel departed with a benefit, on the 16th, with Die Hugenotten, and, parting with American dollars being such sweet sorrow, again on the 20th.

We returned to earlier principles, on December 15th, when Mathilde Cottrelly, by permission of John A. McCaull, began a short visit to her former haunts, in Geistinger's great success, Die Näherin, which, as Chatter, Cottrelly had recently sung in English. This she now repeated, in German, at the matinée on the 17th and on the evening of the 21st. Her former success, Boccaccio, enlivened the evenings of the 17th and the 22nd, and Die Fledermaus the evening of the 19th. Then Cottrelly left that scene for better things now imminent. A benefit for the Kinder-Unterstutzungs Gesellschaft covered two nights, with Goldfische (December 23rd) and Ein Tropfen Gift (24th). Monday, December 26th, celebrated Christmas with the twofold joy of Pech-Schulze (afternoon) and Der Bettelstudent (evening).

POSSART; GIERS

It must not be supposed that the encomiums heaped upon this season were begotten of the repertoire or the artists involved in the story which I have just chronicled for the autumn and early winter, 1887. Interesting that progress was, but the glory of the season came from the engagements of two great German actors, Ernst Possart and Ludwig Barnay, and of the excellent actress, Gertrud Giers.

Possart was the first of that impressive trio to arrive. He came forth, on December 27th, for an engagement that was to continue for over a hundred performances, involving representations of many of the best plays known to the German stage. His opening tragedy was Albert Lindner's Die Bluthochzeit, oder Die Bartholomäusnacht, in which he played König Karl IX, assisted by Fanny Heller as Katharina von Medici, Oskar Krüger as König von Navarre, F. Hausen as Heinrich von Anjou, Franz Costa as Alençon, Franz Hillmann as von Guise, Emanuel Lederer as Coligni and Emilie von Aichsberg as Margerethe von Navarre. The last two artists were new to the force, and they were to take an important place in the remaining activities of the season. Since Possart was not, at first, to play every evening, the 28th revived Der Freischütz, with Ferdinand Schütz as Max, Mühe as Caspar, Emil Steger as Ottakar, Selma Kronold as Agathe, and Cäcilie Hecht as Ænnchen. For his second night (December 29th), Possart gave the first of many performances of David Sichel, in Freund Fritz, his support including Krüger, Rank, Junker, Walter, Adele Palma, Friese, Fanny Heller and Marie Hartmann. This was part of a double bill, the other feature being Coppée's Der Strike der Schmiede, with Possart as Jean Everard.

Der Kaufmann von Venedig, on December 30th, allowed serious playgoers to compare the Shylock of Possart with that of Irving, visible in the same season at the Star Theatre. A student of today (1941) need not consult William Winter for an unprejudiced account of Possart or any foreign-language actor in any Shakespearian rôle; Winter simply could not conceive of Shakespeare in any language but Shakespeare's own. Needless to say, the famous critic found but little, except technical proficiency of method, to admire in Possart's Shylock or Lear or any other part deriving from Stratford-upon-Avon. The cast of the comedy embraced Emilie von Aichsberg as Porzia, Marie Hock (a charming actress) as Jessica, Adele Palma as Nerissa, Gerold as the Doge, Hillmann as Morocco, Costa as Arragon, Hausen as Lorenzo, Sinnhold as Tubal, Otto Meyer as Antonio, Krüger as Bassanio, Rank as Lanzelot Gobbo and August Walter (evidently a versatile man) as der alte Gobbo. December 31st gave a matinée of Schneewittchen and an evening repetition of Freund Fritz. Of course a "sacred" concert celebrated Sunday, January 1st.

For Monday, January 2nd, holiday provision included a matinée of Schneewittchen and Zehn Mädchen, and an evening Bluthochzeit. Freund Fritz (on January 3rd, 6th, and matinée, 7th) with Der Kaufmann von Venedig (on the 5th) made a busy holiday week for Possart; but, on the evenings of the 4th and 7th, he gratified his admirers, and they were many, with a triple bill including Björnson's well-known Ein Fallissement, with Coppée's short Schiffbrüchige and Berg's Unter dem Siegel der Verschwiegenheit. The cast of the Björnson play included Possart as Advokat Bevent, Emanuel Lederer as Djälde, Fanny Heller as Frau Djälde, Emilie von Aichsberg as Walburg, Marie Hock as Signe, Costa as Hamar, Rank as Jacobsen,

[479]

and, in other parts, Walter, Heinrich Habrich, Friese, Otto Meyer, Sinnhold, Junker, Gerold, H. Korn, F. Hausen and Eduard Elsbach. On January 12th, Possart played the sentimental Narciss. Otherwise the week of January 9th–14th gave repetitions, in this order, of Der Kaufmann von Venedig, Bluthochzeit and Freund Fritz, Possart appearing in all seven representations. For the following week he repeated Narciss (January 16th and 21st); Bluthochzeit (17th and 20th); Freund Fritz, with Eine Tasse Thée (18th and matinée, 21st), and the combination of three plays (19th). The constant repetition of a few plays in succeeding weeks seems a sort of novelty; but gradually Possart enlarged his repertoire, appearing, for instance, on January 24th and 28th, as Nathan der Weise. Otherwise he repeated the round of Der Kaufmann von Venedig (January 23rd), Freund Fritz and Eine Tasse Thée (25th and 30th), Bluthochzeit (26th and 31st), Narciss (27th and February 2nd), and the triple bill (matinée 28th). On February 1st and 4th, Des König's Befehl and Blaustrümpfe (Gelehrte Frauen) made an interesting combination. Narciss (2nd) and Nathan der Weise (3rd) rounded a busy week. The concert, on Sunday, January 29th, took advantage of the excitement regarding The Ring of the Nibelungen, and put on Unsere Götterdämmerung, with Lube, Rank, Friese and Junger. Ein Komiker Aventeuer, Wenn Frauen weinen and Man soll den Teufel nicht an die Wand malen also graced the bill.

Perhaps I wrong my reader in pursuing this path in such detail; but, after all, Possart was a great actor, and some few enthusiasts may wish the full history of this engagement. Let us, then, investigate his activities for another week: Nathan der Weise (February 6th); Des König's Befehl and Blaustrümpfe (8th); Freund Fritz and Eine Tasse Thée (10th). On the 7th, for his benefit, and again, on the 9th, he appeared as Richard III:

Gloster	Ernst Possart	Richmond	Franz Hillmann
Edward IV	Otto Meyer	Buckingham	E. Lederer
Elisabeth	Lucie Werner	Catesby	Rudolf Sinnhold
Prince of Wales	Marie Hock	Stanley	Conrad Junker
Duke of York	Adele Palma	Hastings	Hermann Gerold
Margarethe von Anjou	Frl. von Aichsberg	1st Murderer	Bernhard Rank
Duchess of York	Fanny Heller	2nd Murderer	Carl Friese
Anne	Elisabeth Hagedorn		

The Herald thought Possart not very good — too comical in the early scenes. The gallery actually laughed. The costumes were fine and the company good. On the 11th came Der tolle Wenzel, a "Posse mit Gesang," by Manstädt, with Friese, Lube, Rank, Adele Palma, and many, many more. Sunday, the 12th, adroitly mixed the magic of the volatile Mme. Fey and Homes, with Schiller's Lied von der Glocke. Possart, on the 13th and 15th, appeared, in Egmont, as Herzog von Alba and Vansen, with Frl. von Aichsberg as Margarethe von Parma, Oskar Krüger as Egmont, Lederer as Machiavelli, Julius Steger as Ferdinand, Otto Meyer as Wilhelm von

Oranien, Marie Hock as Clärchen, and, of course, many more in lesser rôles. Beethoven's music added to the solemnity of the occasion. The Herald thought the play a talky bore; and the audience was small. Richard III came again on the 14th, and Nathan der Weise, on the 16th. February 17th was set down as Possart's fiftieth performance, the Staats-Zeitung listing nine renditions of Bluthochzeit; eleven of Freund Fritz; five each of Der Kaufmann von Venedig, Nathan der Weise and Ein Fallissement; three each for Des König's Befehl and Richard III; and two for Egmont. On the 17th, to celebrate the half-century mark in his engagement, he appeared as Franz von Moor, in Die Räuber. For the matinée, on the 18th, Possart repeated Des König's Befehl and Blaustrümpfe; Richard III came in the evening. Die Räuber, on Monday, February 20th, was prelude in intensity to König Lear, given on February 21st and 24th, with care and attention to detail, with this cast:

König Lear	Ernst Possart	Edmund	F. Hillmann
Herzog von Burgundy	Franz Costa	Curran	Habrich
König von Frankreich	A. Werther	Der Narr	C. Friese
Albanien	R. Sinnhold	Oswald	Conrad Junker
Gloster	A. Walter	Goneril	Elisabeth Hagedorn
Kent	Otto Meyer	Regan	Emilie von Aichsberg
Edgar	Oskar Krüger	Cordelia	Marie Hock
Burgund	Hermann Gerold		

Der tolle Wenzel had two performances, on Washington's Birthday. On the 23rd, the energetic Possart gave a double bill of Die Tochter des Fabricius and Eine Partie Piquet, ending the week (Saturday, February 25th) with Die Räuber.

The benefit of Oskar Krüger, on February 27th, presented him as Othello, with Possart as Iago, Hillmann as Cassio, Friese as Roderigo, Frl. von Aichsberg as Desdemona, and Elisabeth Hagedorn as Emilia. This was repeated on March 2nd, the week otherwise providing King Lear (February 28th); Der tolle Wenzel (29th, for the benefit of Max Lube); Fabricius and Eine Partie Piquet (March 1st). On March 3rd (Saturday) Possart went to the Metropolitan Opera House, for a performance of Manfred, with all of Schumann's music, directed by Walter Damrosch. An account of this will be found under caption of the Metropolitan. On that evening, at the home theatre, occurred the "erstes Auftreten" of an excellent actress, Gertrud Giers, thenceforth to take a commanding position in the company. A large woman of commanding presence, not beautiful, she appeared as Maria Stuart, supported by Elisabeth Hagedorn as Queen Elizabeth, Oskar Krüger as Leicester, Lederer as Burleigh, Junker as Amyas Paulet and Adolf Werther as Mortimer. The next week was very interesting with (March 5th) Die Tochter des Fabricius and Eine Partie Piquet; Freund Fritz and Eine Tasse Thée (6th); Gertrud Giers as Deborah (March 7th); Die Räuber (8th); and (9th) Kabale und Liebe, with Lederer as Wurm and the Chamberlain,

Gertrud Giers as Lady Milford, Wilhelm Hoch (*sic*) as Präsident Walter, and Else Hofmann (new) as Luise Miller. Possart was to have appeared as Wurm and the Chamberlain but news of the death of Kaiser Wilhelm I caused him to mourn in retirement. On Saturday afternoon (March 10th) a beautiful balmy day, Gertrud Giers repeated Marie Stuart; in the evening, Die Bluthochzeit again gave Possart a favourite opportunity. Gertrud Giers was down for an appearance at the Sunday concert, on the 11th.

And thus we approach the never-to-be forgotten blizzard of March 12, 1888. Possart, on that evening, was to have repeated Manfred, as acted by him, on the 3rd, at the Metropolitan Opera House. I doubt if he braved the mountains of snow to reach the Thalia, only to perform before the meagre audience that could have reached the theatre. For the rest of that week in the beleaguered city, he was scheduled to act Kabale und Liebe (March 13th); Don Carlos (14th); Die Tochter des Herrn Fabricius (15th); and Faust (16th and 17th). The cast of Don Carlos included Possart as Philipp II, Emilie von Aichsberg as Elisabeth, Franz Hillmann as Don Carlos, Fanny Heller as Herzogin von Olivarez, Gertrud Giers as Prinzessin von Eboli, Oskar Krüger as von Posa, Wilhelm Hock (*sic*) as Herzog von Alba. According to the Herald, Ludwig Barnay, still disgruntled, I suppose, by the blizzard and Conried, was present as one of a small audience; the streets were still impassable for all except the sturdy. In Faust, Possart, of course, was Mephistopheles (Irving, at that time, was playing the part in the Wills version at the Star); Krüger was Faust, Hillmann Valentin, and Frl. von Aichsberg Margarethe. For the matinée, on the 17th, Frl. Giers repeated Deborah.

On Monday, March 19th, Possart could at last enact Manfred, to the sound of Schumann's music. I reproduce the cast, as advertised for the 12th:

Manfred	Ernst Possart	Astarte	Emilie von Aichsberg
Jäger	F. Hillmann	Nemesis	Anna Jordan
Abt von St. Maurice	A. Walter	Wassergeist	Selma Kronold
Manuel	Bernhard Rank	Feuergeist	Ferdinand Schütz
Hermann	C. Friese	Erdgeist	Otto Meyer
Queen of Alps	Lucie Werner		

In addition, Johanna Schatz, Marie Hartmann, Paula von Varndal and Jenny Boner were down as Schicksalsschwester, and Steger, Sinnhold and Gerold as Böse Geister. We see that many leaders of the company assumed very small parts for the glory of Byron (in German), Schumann and Possart. On the 21st, a performance occurred, in honour of the Kaiser, so recently deceased; part of Wilhelm Tell, curiously enough, figured in the programme—also Des König's Befehl. The performance began with Eine feste Burg and Die Wacht am Rhein. The week progressed with Kabale und Liebe (22nd); Die Jungfrau von Orleans, for the benefit of Frl. Giers

[482]

(23rd); and Faust (24th). In Die Jungfrau von Orleans, Possart was Raoul. The last week of March began (26th) with Die schöne Helena, for the benefit of Ferdinand Schütz, whom Possart's success had kept decidedly in the background of late. For the 27th, Faust again emerged. Heinrich Heine (with Possart as Hirsch) and Im Wahnsinn (with Possart as Graf Gaston) combined on the 28th; on the 29th, these short plays were joined by Die Schauspielerin (with Gertrud Giers, Adele Palma, Rank and Costa). This triple pleasure was repeated on the evening of the 31st. The performance in honour of Kaiser Wilhelm came again, on the 30th. And Die schöne Helena broke in, after that seriousness, for the matinée, on the 31st.

POSSART; GIERS; BARNAY

Ludwig Barnay, entirely frustrated temperamentally with his experiences under the management of Conried, entered the Thalia, on April 2nd, for a remarkable co-starring engagement with Possart and Frl. Giers. He began, on that night (it was Easter Monday) as Othello, with Possart as Iago, Hillmann as Cassio, Frl. Hermine Reichenbach as Desdemona, and Gertrud Giers as Emilia; on the 3rd, Barnay was Uriel Acosta, with Possart as Ben Akiba and Frl. Giers as Judith. Die Journalisten (April 4th, 6th, and matinée, 7th) enlisted Barnay as Bolz and Possart as Schmock. The supreme test came on the 5th, when Barnay, who seems, thus far, to have had the best parts, came forth as Hamlet, with Possart (was he, after all, a "character" actor?) as Polonius, Emanuel Lederer as the Ghost, Franz Costa as Horatio, Hillmann as Laertes, Junker as Rosencranz, H. Gerold as Guildenstern, Friese as Marcellus (a good actor in a very small part), Lube and Rank as the Gravediggers, Sinnhold and Frl. Giers as the royal pair, and Hermine Reichenbach as Ophelia. In Die Bluthochzeit, on the 7th, Possart was Karl IX and Barnay Navarra, with Frl. Giers as Queen Margarethe. This was to the scholarly Germans in town a week of transcendent delight. The Herald, however, on the 6th, thought Barnay's Hamlet a very inferior thing. It compared his performance with Irving's, and particularly Booth's. "There is no scene in the mighty tragedy in which Mr. Booth excels over another, and we know of nothing within the range of dramatic illustration so exquisite as when he looks into the swiftly deadening future to see the Providence which governs the fall of a sparrow and nerve himself against fate with the proud assurance that the readiness is all." "A Goethe Hamlet," whatever that may mean, is Barnay's. "A stormy, tempestuous and not in any way an agreeable Hamlet" was his. . . "There was no madness in this intense prince—simply fierce revenge; moody, savage revenge; a bearing of insolence, broken only by the slight touch of affection for Ophelia and the ever present devotion to Horatio." To William Winter (Shakespeare on the Stage), Barnay, as Hamlet, was "distinctly a failure." Oddly enough,

[483]

the absurd O'Conor was acting Hamlet at this time at the Star Theatre.

Of course, Sunday concerts continued to be very "sacred," at the Thalia; on April 1st and 8th, the much-advertised Sisters Saffi contributed to that pious effect. On April 9th, Barnay gave his favourite Kean, with Possart as Salomon, Krüger as Prinz von Wales, Elisabeth Hagedorn as Gräfin Helena, and Lucie Werner as Amy, in a big cast including Lederer as the Regisseur of the Covent Garden Theatre. Hamlet (10th) led to Die Memoiren des Teufels and Heinrich Heine, a double delight for the 11th and 14th; in the former piece, Barnay was Robert, and Possart Jean Gautier. The repertoire unrolled with relentless, frequent changes: Die Journalisten (April 12th); Nathan der Weise (13th); Kean (matinée, 14th); Uriel Acosta (Monday, 16th); benefit and hundredth performance of Possart (17th), with Der Kaufmann von Venedig (with Barnay as Morocco and Frl. Giers as Porzia), and Gelehrte Frauen; Die Journalisten (18th); Faust, with Possart as Mephistopheles, Barnay as Faust, and Frl. Reichenbach as Margarethe (19th); Othello (20th); Hamlet (matinée, 21st); Nathan der Weise (21st, evening); Die Räuber, with Possart, Barnay, Giers (23rd); Faust (24th); Hamlet (26th); Kean (27th); Barnay's benefit, with Wilhelm Tell (28th). On Wednesday, the 25th, Der Probepfeil was the only shred of anything novel or modern in that banquet of ancient drama; in it Possart was Rittmeister von Dedenroth, and Barnay Krasinski, the pianist. They say he played the piano very well. The week of April 30th–May 5th was gravely set down as the "last" of the three stars. The farewells began, on the 30th, with Barnay, in Ein moderner Barbar (he as Constantin von Horst), and with Possart in Freund Fritz. Thence we proceeded with Der Probepfeil (May 1st); Wilhelm Tell (2nd); Die Journalisten (3rd); Othello (4th); Faust (matinée, 5th); and Wallenstein's Tod (announced for the evening of the 5th). Having thus sadly traversed the nights of their farewell week, the stars began another, on May 7th, when a benefit to Stage-Manager Emil Hahn (and he had had a distracting season) brought again Der Probepfeil; Uriel Acosta (8th) was listed as the last appearance of Barnay, Possart assisting, and Narciss (9th) as the last "combination" of Possart and Giers. The benefit of Friese and Rank (10th) provided Possart in Doctor Klaus. For the 11th and 12th, Possart acted Napoleon. On the 14th, he repeated Dr. Klaus, and actually said good-bye, on the 15th, in the play which marked his début — Die Bluthochzeit. He sailed next day, according to the Herald, having appeared here in thirty-three parts including two monologues in character. His share of the $140,000 taken in during his engagement was $26,240, worth nearly three times what it would be today.

After his departure (all foreign stars, in those days quickly got away from this sordid land of dollars — dollars which they so despised), the Thalia finished its brilliant season with (May 16th) Der Raub der Sabinerinnen; Robert und Bertram (17th), for the benefit of the ushers and doorkeepers; Die Fledermaus (18th); and (19th) a benefit to Gustav Amberg, who had given so fine a season to New York playgoers. The occasion included Chefrenden, a three-act comedy, and All on Board, a one-act operetta by Zeig. The programme ended with an original review by Max Lube— Unsere letzte Saison, 1887–88. In this latter, we were treated to a series of scenes illustrative of the outstanding events of the season in Kleindeutschland's theatre. To revive the reader's memories, I will transcribe these events from Lube's catalogue; The Thalia Theater; August Junkermann's Gastspiel; Heinrich Bötel's hohe C; Possart's Besuch beim Präsident Cleveland (Possart had gone to Washington to meet the President); Kaiser Wilhelm's Trauerfeierlichkeit; New York im Blizzard; Gertrud Giers' Ankunft; Barnay im Thalia-Theater; Possart, Barnay, Giers unter einem Hut; Possart-Barnay Abschied. It is interesting to see the stress laid on Possart's hurried visit (February 28th–March 1st) to Washington, to call on President Cleveland. Call and comment are very German.

I regret to add to the solemn festival of great German plays greatly acted a coda of no great importance derivable from Sunday activities on the stage of the Thalia. On April 22nd, the German Press Club had there a benefit at which they promised appearances of the Arion Society, Gertrud Giers, Georgine von Januschowsky, Louise Meisslinger, Hermine Reichenbach, Joseffy, Possart, Barnay, the Thalia Theater company, and Adolf Neuendorff. The theatre was excited, on May 6th, by the appearance there of Die Original-Wiener Fechterinnen unter Leitung des Direktors und Fechtmeisters Prof. Johann Hartl. Such piling up of polysyllables ended in naming the nine Fechterinnen who were to fence away their talents on that sacred Sunday eve. They fenced again, on May 13th, for the benefit of Charles Stein, "ticket agent" of the theatre.

Immediately after the hegira of the Germany company to Terrace Garden, H. R. Jacobs, who had, as we have seen been forced from his instable Third Avenue Theatre, came to the Thalia, and made it a cheap house in art and in admission fees. On the stage so recently exalted by the art of great German actors, he began (May 21st–26th) with Lottie Church, in John A. Stevens' play, Unknown. After a week of this antiquity, he tried to awaken sympathy (May 28th) with True Irish Hearts, and (June 4th) thrills, with Arizona Joe. And Ada Gray (June 11th) brought tears to gentle eyes, with her never-dying East Lynne. Corinne, in Arcadia, lightened that woe, in the week of June 18th–23rd.

TERRACE GARDEN, AND LEXINGTON AVENUE OPERA HOUSE, 1887–1888

The opening banquet and ball, at this all-receptive resort, was celebrated on October 12, 1887; even two nights earlier (October 10th) the Central Turn-Verein der Stadt New York acted there, in Der grosse Wohlthäter, oder Soubretten-Streiche. The New York Männerchor concert fell on the evening of November 27th, and that of the Harmonia on the 24th. On January 23rd, the busy Central Turn-Verein held its expected ball; the masked ball of the Sängerrunde followed on February 1st, and that of the Eichenkranz on the 8th. Homes and Mme. Fey, exhibiting in many halls their mind-reading and spiritualistic marvels, finally reached Terrace Garden, on March 2nd and 3rd. On March 15th, the "Autocrats" acted £5,000, written for them by C. M. Stern; in the cast were C. Sentheimer, Mrs. Engelliard, S. J. Marks and Hattie Branden. On April 2nd, the Central Turn-Verein again moved into the Lexington Avenue Opera House, there to present Die Räuber, with Turner Ferdinand Göbel as Karl, and Turner Jakob Heinz, Senior, as Franz—a daring attempt, even for Turners. English-speaking amateurs ventured, on April 3rd, into this German fastness; there the Rival Amateur Dramatic Club staged Francesca da Rimini, quite as if Lawrence Barrett had never done it. A. M. Taylor was Lanciotto, J. W. Block Paolo, Fred Schaefer Malatesta, Frank Thonger Pepe and Helen Sweeny Francesca. I never thought of this tragedy as easy to act. Juliet Corson, who had earnestly lectured on Cooking with Gas, in the Metropolitan Opera House Assembly Rooms, carried the helpful message to housewives, on May 19th, in the Lexington Avenue Opera House. The Harmonia Gesangverein was here on May 21st.

And now the Lexington Avenue Opera House, which had been all things to all men and women, became, for the summer of 1888, permanently one thing—the home of the Thalia Theater opera company. This good band, which had been almost driven from home by the abiding success of Possart and Barnay, opened, on May 24, 1888, for what would seem to have been a charming season of Viennese operetta. And between acts one could enjoy the promenade music in the Garden. Preliminary announcements proclaimed that "Das Theater ist vollständig renovirt." Patrons of the Thalia who liked operetta and had had so little of it in the preceding winter could now cheer themselves by reading the cast of Die schöne Helena, which was sung on May 24th, 25th, 26th and 28th, with those dependable regulars, Ferdinand Schütz, Max Lube, Georgine von Januschowsky (my pen wishes her name were shorter for its necessary frequent transcribing), Marie Hartmann, Otto Meyer, Dutschka Lerma, Hermann Gerold, Bernhard Rank, Eduard Hirsch, Isidor Schraff, Franz von Metsch, Louis Prätorius, Marie Schlag, Hedwig Grünewald, and Ida Falz. On Tuesday, May 29th, Leichte Cavallerie employed many of these artists, in addition to Heinrich Habrich, Hugo Wichert, Valentin Hohmann, Josef Passhausen, Albertine Habrich, Anna Schlag, Rudolf Sinnhold and Vera Herrnkohl. The reader is now possessed of the personnel of the summer.

Boccaccio was announced for May 30th, and Die Fledermaus for the 31st. On June 1st, Marguerite Fisch (*sic* for the Germans—the former Baby

[486]

Benson) appeared in Treptow's operetta, Heimliche Liebe, and Lulu Klein was starred in Suppé's Die schöne Galathée. Frl. Klein disappeared after a night or two, but Frau Fisch (*sic*) repeated Heimliche Liebe, on June 4th and 5th, then in company with Leichte Cavallerie. On June 6th we had Flotte Bursche and Marguerite Fisch, in Taugenichts. For June 8th, Boccaccio again emerged, with von Januschowsky, Schütz, Rank, Lube, Walter, Albertine Rasch, Dutschka Lerma and Cäcilie Hecht; the 9th brought Prinz Methusalem, with, in leading rôles, Rank, von Januschowsky, Schütz and Marie Hartmann. On Sunday, June 10th, the "sacred" concert presented Pepi and Adolph, "die fidelen Wiener," whatever that may mean. The Casino, as we know, had dropped these Viennese operas, in favour of its everlasting Erminie, and now devotees of Strauss, Millöcker and the others could hear their works well done, in the cool spaces of the Lexington Avenue Opera House. Saturday, June 16th, gave Der Zigeunerbaron, and Monday, June 18th, Prinz Methusalem. Thence followed Der Feldprediger (June 19th), Der Zigeunerbaron (20th), Boccaccio (21st), and, by a switch to Offenbach, Pariser Leben (22nd–23rd) which I can never quite think of as La Vie Parisienne. The cast of this airy trifle, at Terrace Garden, included Lube as Baron Gondremark, Lucie Werner as Christine, Otto Meyer as de Gardesen, Sinnhold as Bobinet, Gerold as de Chaumières, Schütz as Jean, and von Januschowsky as Gabriele. I can hardly believe it, but Ilma di Murska, sad remnant of the glory of the early '70s, was advertised to sing at the Sunday concert, on June 24th. Fatinitza, with von Januschowsky, Cäcilie Hecht and Lube, came on June 27th and 28th, and Nanon brought us close to modern times, on the 29th and 30th.

Boccaccio (July 2nd) and Fatinitza (3rd) were all to the glory of Suppé, but Strauss came back, as a Fourth of July hint, with Der lustige Krieg. This popular piece was good for a few repetitions, as was Nanon. On July 10th, Giroflé-Girofla began a career which carried to July 16th and 17th. Orpheus in der Unterwelt was here, on the 18th, and The Mikado, on the 19th, started a run that lasted for more than a week, with Helene Dingeon as featured performer. Lori Stubel, Vienna soubrette, was heard in the week of August 6th–11th, the repertoire including Boccaccio, Prinz Methusalem, Fatinitza, Nanon, and (10th, 11th) Madame Angot. Under the caption of French Activities, may be found record of French visits to the all-receptive Garden (or Garten).

GERMAN ACTIVITIES, 1887–1888

As usual, our peregrinations in Kleindeutschland begin with the Cannstatter Harvest Home Festival, held at Sulzer's Harlem River Park, 127th Street and Second Avenue, on September 19th, 20th and 21st. After years of prowling among the Vereine, I believe I may justifiably curtail, for this

[487]

season, the record of their activities, except for functions of exceptional interest. Most of the organisations I so punctiliously followed in seasons gone by may be discovered, for 1887–88, advertising, in the Staats-Zeitung, their Stiftungsfeste, Carneval-Sitzungen and mask-balls, with occasional concerts; I shall limit my discussion, now, simply to these musical offerings, with notice of more important Abendunterhaltungen.

At the beginning, however, I cite three groups new to our story. They met, all three, in the Germania Assembly Rooms, 291-293 Bowery: the Liedertafel Egalité (October 9th); the Carl Sahm Quartett Club (also on the 9th); and the Druiden Liederhain (10th). I pass to Alexander Strakosch, who gave, on October 5th, a second subscription reading, at Irving Hall, with a third to follow, on the 7th. His first, on the 2nd (Sunday) was devoted to Julius Cæsar. On the 12th, he attacked Hamlet. This Strakosch was very active in the season now under review. Active also was Frau Hedwig Henrich-Wilhelmi, who lectured frequently, hither and yon. At the Central Turn-Verein Hall, 77th Street, between Lexington and Third Avenue, she lectured ("Eintritt frei") on Der Mensch das Produkt seiner Erziehung, which sounds serious indeed for a balmy night in early October — in this case, October 2nd. The earnest lady carried to the Harlem Turn-Verein, on October 20th, her exposition of Moralische Verantwortlichkeit. On that same 20th, lighter-minded gentry went to the opening ball at Walhalla. The night before (19th) occurred the Grosser Eröffnungsball, at Wendel's Assembly Rooms, West 44th Street. The Arion Quartett Club Concert and Ball, on November 6th, at the Germania Assembly Rooms, called in the assistance of Jacob Graff, Bechmann's Orchestra and Karl Pohl. And the Mainzer Carneval-Verein Concert and Ball occupied the Beethoven Männerchor Hall, on the night of November 13th. The Battery Park Concert Garten, 5 Battery Place, brings to our November record something of a desired novelty.

But it is practically impossible to escape a lady who is determined to lecture us into serious thinking. Here, on November 10th, the back of the Staats-Zeitung is almost broken by the weight of the polysyllables announcing "Deutscher Gesellig-Wissenschaftlicher Verein in New York — Versammlung, 239 East 57th Street. Vortrag der Frau Henrich-Wilhelmi — Die Ursachen der gegenwärtigen Frauensage." I wish the reader would attend that lecture and tell me about it. I suspect he would prefer the concert of the Liederkranz, in their hall, on the 19th, with Adele Aus der Ohe, and Frau Seidl-Krauss (sic), the works rendered being A. Goring Thomas's Die Feueranbeter and Liszt's Die Glocken des Strassburger Minsters. On the 20th, at the Germania Assembly Rooms, the Mozart Verein had assistance from Anna Britting, Louise Kull, George Prehn and H. Bersin. The Heinebund Concert and Ball (also on the 20th) at Wendel's Assembly Rooms, specifies, as soloist, Dora Friedel. For their concert, on

[488]

November 23rd, at Beethoven Männerchor Hall, M. G. B. Eichenkranz called in the aid of William Bartels, A. Wachs and Hannah Rosenberg.

I approach a busy November 27th; the Bloomingdale Eintracht, at the Germania Assembly Rooms; the Loreley Männerchor, concert and ball, at Wendel's; and the Schwäbischer Sängerbund (concert and ball) at Beethoven Hall, with Minnie and Charlotte Poland (in a piano duet). So life went on in Kleindeutschland, as the last November leaves blew along the streets.

Künstler Halle, Chrystie Street, advertised concerts for January 2nd, 3rd and 4th. I deliberately shut my gentle reader's eyes to the oft-repeated tale of the Carneval-Sitzungen of January, and the masked balls of the too, too energetic Vereine, that starred the wintry heavens. Perhaps I might call attention to the first "narrische Damen Sitzen" (which may have been more complimentary than it sounds) of the Rheinisch-Westphälisch Carnevals-Verein, held on January 7th, at Lenox Hall, 72nd Street and Third Avenue. At Künstler Halle, from January 19th, appeared Wolf Hirschberg, "der berümte Komiker aus Hannover." I always shrink from the necessity of transcribing the name, Deutscher Gesellig-Wissenschaftlicher Verein von New York (it is so long and so pretentious), but here it is again, on January 26th, inviting us to a lecture by Julius Auspitz, on Die Entwicklung des Eisenbahnwesens; and once more, on February 8th, for a Vortrag bei Wilhelm H. Hirsch, on Die ethische Grund-Idee in Wagner's Musik-Drama, Der Ring der Nibelungen — of course an effort to feed public excitement over the three Ring-dramas then heard for the first time consecutively in New York. That Grund-Idee is not yet quite fixed in our minds.

Passing by the Heinebund ball, on February 2nd, at Wendel's Assembly Rooms, I come to February 6th, 8th, 9th and 10th, at Beethoven Halle, where Homes and Mme. Fey exhibited their Modern Wonders; they were so successful that they returned for February 15th, 16th, and 17th, mystifying the credulous. The Vereine whirled in masked ball, in mid-February — the same groups that had done that for many seasons before. Feeling that I need not record these, I pass (February 28th) to the Stiftungsfest, Theater and Ball des Fünften Regiments Veteranen Verein, held in the Germania Assembly Rooms; Der liebe Onkel (Champagne and Oysters) employed Kierschner, Frl. Gerth, Lohmeyer, E. Spitz, Frl. N. Herz, Frl. Lohmeyer, and Frau R. Kierschner, names that I set down with the proud feeling of having done my duty.

I must carry the reader to Harlem, on February 13th, just to remind him that there is such a place, and to discover what he thinks of the entertainment of the Harlem Männerchor, in Sulzer's "two big salons," 127th Street and Third Avenue. Personally, I wish the Germans would get away from Third Avenue, to see if other regions of the city might not change them from German-Americans into Americans. On February 29th, the Columbia Zither Verein gave a concert, assisted by Mlle. E. Raimé. March 4th carried

[489]

the Harmonic Quartett (*sic*) Club to the Teutonia Assembly Rooms, for its first grand concert and ball. On March 8th, the inescapable Deutscher Wissenschaftlicher Verein, held, in the Vereins-Lokal, Café Logeling, 57th Street, its 212th Plenarversammlung mit Damen; Dr. F. Boaz, for so many years thereafter Professor of Anthropology in Columbia University, lectured on Die Ziele der Ethnologie. A concert of the Gesangverein Germania, in the Germania Assembly Rooms, availed itself, on March 31st, of the assistance of Frl. Hebe Herriot and Master Charles Burkhardt.

April 1st brought notice from two paradises: Jacob Blank's Winter Garden, 132 to 136 East 13th Street, proffered Frau Dr. Miller, Herren Coller and Kratz and (of all people in the world!) Minnie Dilthey, sunk from her former high hopes; and the Volksgarten, 231-233 Bowery, between Rivington and Stanton Streets, boasted of the California Damen-Orchester (Hedwig Jarabek, directrice), Hilda Rudolfi, "Professor" Emil Müller, Lillian Bailey and Charles Eschert. Thus spring set the summer going. On April 8th, Major Sauer's Atalanta Casino ("last station of 6th Avenue Hochbahn") advertised Della Dora, "Professor" Nusbaum (xylophone), Oscar Saul (cornet) and George Kauer (director). On that same Sunday (April 8th), J. Guterding's Walhalla (46-52 Orchard Street) was Germanically polysyllabic with a Humoristische-Musikalische Abend-Unterhaltung und Tanzkränzchen of the Harugari Liederkranz. Beside such weighty announcement, the evening of the Gesang-Verein Franz Abt Schüler, on April 8th, at the Germania Assembly Rooms, almost lapses into insignificance. But we could seek comfort at two new places crowding into our notice: Zeltner's Morrisania Park and Hall (170th and Third Avenue) and Cosmopolitan Park and Casino (169th Street and Tenth Avenue). I feel almost like a directory, as I thus enroll these pleasances of Kleindeutschland.

But April 12th takes us again to the Vereins-Lokale of the Deutscher Gesellig-Wissenschaftlicher Verein, in the Café Logeling, 239 East 57th Street. There and then Hugo Heinrich lectured on Die Kap-Colonie. April 15th perplexed with necessity of choosing between the concert of the Heinebund, with Carl Levinson, at Lyric Hall (723 Sixth Avenue) and the united efforts, at the Germania Assembly Rooms, of the Dramatischer Verein, Wir, the Franz Abt Schüler, Fidelia and the Bergischer Club—efforts from which was to emerge Schuster und Baron. The showery month calls, on the 21st, to Walhalla, for a concert of the Zither-Verein, helped by Wilhelm von der Au, G. Huth and J. Kolm, masters of the art. Since April 18th, "Professor" P. Schwiegerling had been exhibiting, at Beethoven Männerchor Hall, his Fantoches Marionetten. In later April and early May various parks and gardens were advertising in the Staats-Zeitung—Adam Geib's Grove Hill Park and Assembly Rooms (161st Street and Third Avenue); H. Sulzer's Harlem River Park, and also his Fort Lee Hotel and Pavilion; Brommer's Union Park (133rd Street and Willis Avenue, "one block from the Second

Avenue Railroad Station"); St. Nicholas Park Hotel (155th Street, between Eighth and Ninth Avenues); Wendel's Löwen Park, etc.

Having thus cleaned the docket, I may invite (May 5th) to the Schluss-Abendunterhaltung, Operette and Tanzkränzchen of the New York Sänger-runde, the Teutonia Assembly Rooms housing the celebration; and I may also record the performances in early May, at Sauer's Atalanta Casino, of Cora Arabella (certainly Sauer engaged sweet-named ladies), Nusbaum, and Oscar Saul. The Volksgarten, 231 Bowery, gave two concerts, on Sunday, June 3rd. At its two concerts, on that date, St. Nicholas Park Hotel promised the co-operation of Rosa Lee, Monsignor (*sic*) Montecello, Christian Schlebel (xylophone) and Charles Blank (cornet). I cannot but wonder at the way in which musical taste of frequenters of these paradises ranged from the tinkle of zithers and xylophones to the blare of a bold cornet.

City dwellers could now betake themselves to various suburban pleasure-grounds—advertised in the Staats-Zeitung: Schuber's Hotel and Restaurant (Seaside Station, Rockaway Beach); to the big spectacles, in Staten Island; to Paul Bauer's Casino, West Brighton, Coney Island; to the West Brighton Beach Hotel, Coney Island, with Levy's cornet in full blow; to the Silver Spring, Bowery Bay Beach; and, in lieu of such out-of-town excitement, one could, especially if he understood German, have a very good time at the operettas in Terrace Garten.

Atlantic Garten, 1887–1888

Let us tuck the record of Atlantic Garten in a corner by itself, beginning on Sunday, October 9th, with a "sacred" concert, involving Marie Roller's Damen-Orchester and Mrs. Peppi Sternheim (singer, and rather infor-tuitously named). Mr. Sternheim was here on the 14th, along with our old acquaintance, Max Abramowitz. The Roller orchestra remained for many weeks; in early November it was joined in the bills by Sepp'l Thaler's Tyroler Trio ("2 Damen und 1 Herr"). The "Character-Komiker," Arthur Fröhlich was here in late January, and for several weeks subsequently; this statement holds true, also for a long-abiding Emma Meyer. On Tuesday, May 8th, the Atlantic celebrated the fiftieth anniversary of its founding; Emma Meyer, Fröhlich, Max Bender and Hermann Williams helped in the festivities. This group was still here in latest May, joined recently by Fanny Geschandner (Tyrolean).

French Activities, 1887–1888

From this time forward in the history I am indebted for use of the files of the Courrier des États-Unis, to Mr. William M. Hewitt, former director of the paper, who kindly opened to my research the volumes that he controls; I herewith express my gratitude to him for this courtesy. I had spent a year in vain effort to find the files in various libraries throughout the city and the nation.

I dislike to start the record with the dance, an exercise to which our foreign-born citizens have, during the years, so persistently summoned me. The Société Chorale l'Espérance begins the round, on October 23, 1887, at the Lexington Avenue Opera House, with a concert directed by E. Vicarino, with Effie Stewart and Levinson as soloists; music for the inevitable ball that followed was provided by Max Schwab, past master of such assistance. On October 28th came the *"Premier Grand Bal Patriotique Alsacien-Lorrain,"* given by the "Société Colmarienne de New York." It celebrated, at the New Webster Hall, 11th Street (between Fourth and Third Avenues), the first anniversary of the inauguration of the Statue of Liberty and the founding of the society.

I pass to the Cercle La Française, which, on October 23rd, began its season at Poujade's Lyric Hall, South Fifth Avenue; providers of entertainment were Mme. Darelly (now invariably so spelled), Henri, M. and Mme. Olivero, Herman and Arnoux. Besides, we were promised a *"magnifique tombola."* Admission was held at 10 cents, giving rights to a *"billet de tombola."* Marius and Max (*sic*) joined those already mentioned, for November 6th, Mme. Darelly and Max supplementing with Les Deux Prix de Vertu. Advertisements for this palace of pleasure no longer appeared in the autumn Courrier. On Christmas Eve, however, we were summoned to a *"Grand Bal — ouvert toute la nuit."* And, for Christmas Day, for an admission-fee of 15 cents, Mme. Darelly and Max appeared in Un Coq en Jupons and La Leçon de Musique; les Olivero, père et fils, added to the attractiveness of the feast.

I go like the crab, backward, to the dances of autumn and early winter. December 3rd found Tammany Hall opening for the concert and ball of the Orphéon Français; Mme. P. Debuchy and Mme. A. Grévain assisted in the concert. Thence balls were operative in profusion: the twelfth grand ball of the Société Israélite Française, at Everett Hall (December 11th); the second annual ball of the Cuisiniers et Patissiers Italo-Suisse, with music by Cappa, of the 7th Regiment, at Irving Hall (December 10th); the second grand ball of the Union des Patrons Boulangers Français, in the Teutonia Assembly Rooms (December 17th); the bal paré et masqué of l'Amitié, at the Lexington Avenue Opera House (January 5th).

It is time to enter Poujade's Lyric Hall, to revive our fainting spirits with something definitely theatrical. The company installed there still (January 1st) included Marius, M. and Mme. Olivero, Arnoux, Mme. Darelly and Max, the last two offering, on that glad New Year's Day, Un Coq en Jupons and Bibi, l'Enfant de l'Amour. Les Deux Aveugles, so long a feature of our chronicle, began, on January 15th, a career of several weeks o' Sundays (the holy day only being advertised in the Courrier); Max and Arnoux, two very popular "comiques," played it.   The artists in the bills for those weeks included Mlle. Lafeuillade (chansonnettes), Marius, George, the Oliveros, Herman (grandly listed as "pianiste accompagnateur") Mme. Vanneste (*chansons nouvelles*), and Gachard (*chansonnettes comiques*). On February 5th came the début of Mlle. Lizzie (Tyrolienne).   She remained through February, Les Deux Aveugles groping toward an opportunity to close.

As far back as October 30th, À la Superbe Arcade, 130 West 26th Street, was advertising a *"Grand Concert d'Amateurs."*   It broke out, to the same strain, on January 1st and 2nd.   With title shortened to À la Cascade, a name by which we shall come to know it, only too well, in years to come, it announced, for March 10th and 17th, concerts and balls, *donnés par* la Société, Amis de la France.   Here I leave it, since sad duty calls me once more to take up the burden of the dance.

Surely the French were quite the equals of the Germans of New York in their passion for dancing.   February reeled from the calendar to this refrain: the ball of the Cuisiniers (February 2nd) at the Metropolitan Opera House; the eleventh concert and ball of l'Helvétienne (of course not geographically French), at the Teutonia Assembly Rooms (February 4th), a function made impressive by the *"présentation solennelle d'un drapeau offert par les dames";* the forty-first *"fête, bal paré et masqué"* of La Concorde, in Ferrero's, Tammany Hall (February 18th); the Union Alsacienne's *"grand bal d'invitation, avec le concours de l'Espérance,* at the Teutonia Assembly Rooms (also on February 18th); and (still the same 18th), the ball, at Irving Hall, of the Société Tessinoise; and the ball of the Union Chorale, at the Academy of Music (21st).   The second *"Grand Bal d'Enfants de la Colonie Française de New York,"* with *"les enfants des salles d'asile de l'Union des Sociétés Françaises de New York"* was a very Gallic feature for Washington's Birthday, at Everett Hall.   Entrée was *"gratuite"* pour les enfants, but 25 cents for adults, with *"vestiaire facultatif"* held at 15 cents. The masked ball of l'Harmonie ended the February round of such gayety, on the 27th, at the big Metropolitan Opera House.   I end this debauch of dancing, at least temporarily, on March 6th, when, in Irving Hall, La Sincérité provided a *"bal d'invitation paré et masqué* to the strains of Louis Conterno's orchestra; and, on the 10th, when the Mardi-Gras Association held its fourteenth masked ball, in Tammany Hall.

Once again Poujade's calls us to something connected, if only humbly and remotely, with the stage.   In that Lyric Hall, on March 3rd, the Brothers Templé, with Germain, appeared in Voiture à Vendre and the brothers alone, in Un Vilain Monsieur.   On Sunday, March 10th, Alice Grévain and Mme. Adrienne edified patrons of the salon; for the 24th Mlle. Grévain shared the bill with Faure, illusionist, in Thirty Minutes of Magic.   Mlle. Grévain was still the bright luminary through April 7th; on that Sunday we were treated to Un Jeune Homme Pressé. The benefit of Mlle. Lizzie, on March 29th, appealed through the "concours" of Adèle Martinetti and Mme. Maréchal (of the celebrated troupe, the Paravelli *"paveurs mélomanes"*). On April 8th, Mme. Désiré made her début; set down as *"chanteuse de genre,"* and *"immense succès,"* she was still holding forth on May 13th. She was still Mme. Désiré, on May 20th, but, on May 24th, Mlle. Nathalie Désirée, a name not unknown to our annals, had a benefit, with a large list of coadjutors in Mlle. Alice Grévain, Adèle Roselle, Hilda Rudolfi, and MM. Sablon, Max Poninski, Max, Gaston, and Arnoux, and M. and Mme. Olivero. For this supreme manifestation, admission was held at 25 cents, *"donnant droit à un billet de tombola."* The perplexing query as to whether Mlle. Nathalie Désirée was really Mme. Désiré is left unanswered when Mme. Désiré is again advertised for June 3rd. But, on June 9th, Mlle. Nathalie Désirée made her début "for this season, at Germania Garden and Germania Assembly Rooms, and she was bravely announced as *"la reine des chanteuses françaises."* Thereafter, Poujade's announced merely the opening of its *"jardin d'été, entrée 10 cents, donnant droit à un billet de tombola."*

I go to the rival hall, À la Cascade, California Hotel, 130 West 26th Street, which, on May 8th, was still advertising itself merely as the Café Concert d'Amateurs. Even so late as August 26th, the place was groping in the mist of such vague generalities; but we shall, in a few months, find it emerging in the clear light of specific announcements. I put here, for lack of better space, a charity benefit, on April 14th, at the Berkeley Lyceum, a performance of An Old Master and M. Choufleuri (this in French), with actors from the Social Register—Albert La Montagne, August Montant, Alice Lawrence, &c.

I have allowed my fancy to pirouette far beyond the bounds of the dance. I again greet Dame Terpsichore, on April 1st, when the Union des Sociétés Françaises intended to hold its seventh *"Grande Fête de Paques,"* at Tammany Hall, of course for the Salles d'Asile. The police interfered, under warrant of the Sunday law, and that Easter festivity was postponed. Perforce, Courrier advertisements failing me, I leap to June 9th, for a concert and ball, arranged by the Orphéon Français for the benefit of the Hôpital Français, Kasefang's Hall (26th Street and 7th Avenue) housing the charitable function. A benefit for this same hospital, on June 16th, was to gather, in Webster Hall, a large contingent of mediocre talent, in Nathalie Désirée, Fatmah Diard (of the New Orleans Opera), Adèle Roselle (*sic*), Anna Wallace, Mlle. Lafeuillade, Emile ("professeur de violon"), Albert Ross (pianist), Lowenthal (accompanist of the New Orleans opera), Fareux, Marius, Remog, Max and Arnoux—quite the cream of talent from the wine-halls.

The Bataillon des Grenadiers Rochambeau celebrated American independence, on July 4th, by a "Pique-Nique," at the Queens County Driving

[494]

LOUIS JAMES

FRANKIE KEMBLE

MARIE WAINWRIGHT

POSSART AS SHYLOCK

BARNAY AS HAMLET

EDNA COURTNEY

ERNST POSSART

JUNKERMANN

LUDWIG BARNAY

Park, Grand Street, Brooklyn. And the 14th of July opened the Harlem River Park, 126th Street, for the *"fête nationale"* of the Union des Sociétés Françaises, with a "Grande tombola au profit des Salles d'Asile." Conterno's orchestra sweetened the sacrifice. Lion Park, on that same 14th, was scene of mixed blessings in a concert by the pupils of Mlle. Viller, an *assaut d'armes* with R. Senac and one of his pupils—a demoiselle, be it noted. I pass, without reluctance, to August 18th, for the first grand "pique-nique des Peaux Rouges (Red Men!)," given, at Sulzer's Harlem River Park, by the Union des Tribus, "assisted by Dames of the Ponemah Council, No. 5, of New York." Votes for women, at last! The Bataillon des Gardes Lafayette went, on September 3rd, to Lion Park, for their eighteenth annual fête; and, nearly limp and gasping from a week's work on these French activities, I record, with joy the recessional hymn of September 8th, when, at Terrace Garden, a benefit for the École Maternelle was directed by Mlle. Viller, with the omnipresent Louis Conterno conducting the music. I say goodbye to the Franco-Americans till the next season finds me refreshed and revived. After a hard search for the paper for a year, this record is what I found in the Courrier for 1887–88.

Italian Activities, 1887–1888

We cannot better begin the season than with a remembrance of Columbus and his wonderful discovery of our hemisphere. On the 12th of October occurred at Brommer's Union Park, 133rd Street, the twentieth *"Celebra-χione Annuale della Scoperta d'America — sotto gli auspici della Società Militare Italiana"*— the Colombo Guard (*sic*). Before that, however, on October 8th, at Turn Hall Theatre, 66-68 East 4th Street, had occurred a benefit for "povera" Chiara Cignarale, who had, I learn from the Progresso, been condemned to death for the murder of her husband. The programme for this curious entertainment included Chiara, la Condannata a Morte, a four-act drama by Rocco Metelli; a farce, La Moglie Deve Segnire il Marito; and a concluding ball. Later in the file of the Progresso I found that Governor Hill, of New York, had saved Chiara's neck from the noose—at least temporarily.

There is something like drama to present to my dance-laden reader. Thenceforth, for the autumn and early winter of 1887 I must guide his weary feet through the mazes of the dance. The Italians here were beginning to interject English words in their mellifluous titles, as, for instance, in the *Gran Ballo Annuale del* Pleasure Club *Volontari d'Africa*, held, on November 28th, in Brooke's Assembly Rooms, with music by "Professor" B. Masino. December sped along with several such functions: the first ball of la Società Patriottica Liberale Ticinese di New York, at Lyric Hall, 723 Sixth Avenue (on the 3rd), with L. Conterno's music; the first annual ball

[495]

of the Società Nizza Cavalleria di Mutuo Soccorso, with music by Paolo de Fina, on December 12th, at Webster Hall, 119-123 East 11th Street; the sixth annual ball of the Italian Rifle Guard, held, on the 17th, at the Germania Assembly Rooms; and the thirteenth Ballo Mascherato e Civile of the Società Firenze, on the 19th, at Tammany Hall. I end the Italian or Italo-American year of 1887 with the concert, on December 22nd, at Chickering Hall, for the "Cholerosi" di Messina — a concert at which were to appear Teresina Tua, De Anna, Charles Graham, Bologna, Mme. Cortada, and a Mandolin Quintet. Yet, after all, 21 South Fifth Avenue, carried the Italians to December 31st for a ball to benefit the Scuola Palumbo and the victims of the earthquake of Calabria. With cholera and earthquakes Italy was sadly afflicted as 1887 slipped into the irrevocable past.

A Gran Ballo delle Tre Società Italiane Unite (Guardia Savoia, the Prima Società Reduci Patrie Battaglie Veterani, and Umberto Primo) was the sonorous announcement for January 7th, at Webster Hall; yet tickets for a *signore e una signora* cost only 50 cents, with an "extra" per signora, 25 cents — cheap, with Luigi Conterno again supplying music for the dance. That suffices us for early January; but later evenings of that bleak month were enriched by balls of similar pattern. On the 26th, at Webster Hall, the first annual ball of the Società Stella d'Italia was in commemoration of those who fell in Saati; "Professor" A. Gasiere directed the music. On the 28th, the Garibaldi Pleasure Club danced in Irving Hall. "Professor" G. de Grandi led us away from this saltatory prepossession to his vocal and instrumental concert on January 28th, in Chickering Hall, promised performers including C. Bologna, Miss L. Chapman (singer), Klahre, Miss S. Zorn, Miss M. Cornelius and Miss F. Meyer, collectively hardly worth the price of a reserved seat — one dollar.

Quickly we reverted to the dance: on February 14th came the *Ballo Civile e Mascherato* of the Associazione Fraterna Italiana *a beneficio del Monumento Garibaldi* — this in the Teutonia Assembly Rooms; on the 18th, the eighteenth annual ball of the Società Ticinese di Mutuo Soccorso, with music by the Seventh Regiment Band, directed by Cappa and his assistants; and, on the 28th, the *Gran Festa da Ballo della Società di Mutuo Soccorso* — a Rimembranza dei Caduti di Saati. The United Italian Societies of New York, Brooklyn, Newark and Hoboken danced, to the strains of Conterno's Band, on March 5th, in Tammany Hall, with admission at 50 cents *"per un signore e più signore."* The Guardia Vittorio Emanuele held its third annual ball, on March 14th, in Irving Hall; on the 19th, the Legione G. Garibaldi, under the auspices of the committee for the monument to Garibaldi, danced away its perplexities appertaining thereto, in Tammany Hall, one dollar being the admission fee, and Paolo de Fina leading two orchestras. A grand occasion, doubtless, but my pen will be pleased when that monument is erected and can pass out of our record. With this desire thus openly expressed, we may advance on March 22nd to Irving Hall, for the ball of the Società Italiane Militari Unite (Corona d'Italia and Dante Alighieri); and there we shall meet a new director of music — Germano di Matteo.

On May 30th (I leap thus far because the Progresso fails me in news) the thirteenth annual "Pic-Nic" of the Società Firenze di Mutuo Soccorso carried happy members to Brommer's Union Park, there to enjoy (for 25 cents, each) rural felicity and dance, to music provided by "Professor" G. Boccavecchia. And here once more is that hoped-for monument to Garibaldi; on June 4th, a *"festa campestre"* therefor was expected to be patronised by the family of the hero, and made joyous by *Gran Tiro al Bersaglio con Premi* and, in the evening, spectacular, with *Grandi Fuochi Artificiali* — in other words, by mere fireworks. July invited to the open spaces. On the holiday of the 4th, the twelfth "Pic-Nic" of the Società Sant' Antonio was duly celebrated in Kroebel's Hudson County Volk's Park, Hoboken; on the 12th, the Società Vittorio Emanuele II used the over-used Brommer's Union Park, with *"Gran Tombola di diversi oggetti di valore,"* and other sports, with dancing to Carmine Sanna's music. And the Hotel Caprera, at Clifton, Staten Island, provided the fifth banquet of summer for the Società Buontemponi (*sic*), Salute and Dollari, when, on July 22nd, that elaborately named aggregation ferried to the (then) charming isle across the bay.

A cheap Italian opera was holding forth in Turn Hall. Il Trovatore, on July 2nd, was, according to the Herald, to be sung by Signora Rosetti, Signorina Saffi, and Signori Butat, Bolli and De Ambrogio; on July 9th, Il Barbiere di Siviglia was due. July 26th repeated Il Trovatore. I found almost no news of this in the Progresso; but an advertisement in that paper invites to the eighth and last performance, on August 20th, when La Traviata was sung by Fatmah Diard as Violetta, Bolli as Germont, Bardini as Alfredo, Mlle. Viani as Flora and Annetta, and, in other rôles, Zaganelli, Gannio and De Ambrogio. I cannot supply further details until September 18th, when a "new company" for the autumn season rendered Lucia di Lammermoor, with Fathma (*sic*) Diard and E. Pasci as the hapless lovers, G. Bolli as Lord Hastan (*sic*) and L. Ambrogio, Zaganelli, G. Barberis, and Mlle. Viani in lesser parts. Scotto conducted, and one paid 50 "soldi" to enter the "platea," 25 for the "galleria," and 75 "soldi" for "sedie riservate."

Having thus, however inadequately, disposed of the operatic scheme, I revert reluctantly to August 13th and Union Park for the outdoor festivities of the Società Italiane Unite (Potenza, Lucania, e Stella d'Italia), with the expected *Tombola con premi di valore,* and with G. Matteo's music; thence, to August 15th and Roman Park, Astoria, for the *Festa Campestre* of the Fratellanza San Felese and the Politica Calvellese. The Progresso hardly varies the note of Italian amusements. Hence to Brommer's Union Park, on September 20th, went the Società Italiane Unite of New York, Brooklyn,

[497]

Hoboken and Newark, to commemorate the anniversary of the entrance of the Italian troops into Rome; "Professor" P. Peluso led the music of the festival. On the same day, and to commemorate the same victory, the Società Italiane Unite di Mutuo Soccorso di Brooklyn held Schützen Park, 59th Street and Third Avenue, trusting to the music led by Vincenzo Rosata to stimulate their patriotic fervour. With the picnic of the Società Militare Torquato Tasso in Washington Park, East 69th Street (I cannot supply the exact date) I leave the Italians for the year now so laboriously chronicled.

ACADEMY OF MUSIC (NEW YORK), 1887–1888

The Academy, so recently the shrine of opera and high-class concerts, presented, in the season now reviewing, a curiously mixed series of performances. To a house identified with the glory of Nilsson, Gerster and Patti, we were summoned, on September 8, 1887, for "America's farewell to her fistic hero, Jake Kilrain, prior to his departure for England, to meet Jem Smith." Charley Mitchell was in the show, also Senac, Gus Hill, Lester and Williams and many lights of "Variety." A. J. Murphy was manager when, on September 19th, A Dark Secret was revealed, with a Great Henley Regatta Scene — 5,000 cubic feet of real water. The cast was not remarkable:

James Norton	Harry Ashton	Cecil Raynor	Clarence Heritage
Jonas Norton	Joseph L. Mason	May Joyce	Dora Goldthwaite
Stephen	Hudson Liston	Nelly	Virginia Nelson
Martin Brooke	Frank Lane	Emilie d'Esterre	Gabrielle du Sauld
Arthur Loates	George Backus	Bessie Dickson	May Nugent

The fiftieth performance fell on November 7th, and the last on December 3rd. On October 3rd, Adeline Stanhope played May Joyce, replacing Miss Goldthwaite, Miss Stanhope was the first to take the "ducking" required by the plot; the audience howled with delight.

A benefit for the Elks, New York Lodge No. 1 (November 17th), promised the Brantfords, Nat Goodwin, A Hole in the Ground, Marianne Brandt (oddly placed in this group), Dockstader, George S. Knight (Act II of Rudolph), Fred Warde (last two acts of Gaston Cadol), James F. Hoey and "Pete" Dailey, and the Regatta Scene, from A Dark Secret. According to Allston Brown, Eugene Tompkins and Edward G. Gilmore took up, on November 28th, the reins of management. They offered, on December 5th, the Imperial Burlesque Company, in Arabian Nights, or, Aladdin's Wonderful Lamp. Participants included Mlle. Bonfanti (no longer so young as twenty years previously), Mlle. Dorst, Oreste and Master Sohlke. A Doll's Quadrille was danced by Lena Merville, Oreste, Dorst and Alice Stoddard. But the appeal was in the spectacle designed by Alfred Thompson — Crypt of Crimson Crystals, Parti-coloured Palace of Parasols, Dismal Swamp,

[498]

Market-Place of Boodle-Boo, and Home of the Lamp.   Yet, despite this scenic splendour (?) the piece ran only for two weeks.

The house was closed, during the week of December 19th–24th, in preparation ·for the joint engagement of Edwin Booth and Lawrence Barrett. The distinguished tragedians began, on December 26th, in an elaborate production of Julius Cæsar:

Julius Cæsar	John A. Lane	Metellus Cimber	L. J. Henderson
Brutus	Edwin Booth	Popilius Lena	Frederick Vroom
Cassius	Lawrence Barrett	Titinius	Jameson Lee Finney
Marc Antony	E. J. Buckley	Trebonius	Charles B. Hanford
Decius	Charles Collins	Cinna	Edwin Royle
Casca	B. G. Rogers	Portia	Minna K. Gale
Octavius Cæsar	Lawrence Hanley	Calpurnia	Elizabeth Robins

Very good names are in that cast, most of them associated with the last years of Booth and Barrett, now closing in on our dramatic horoscope.   The engagement under way was the first in which the stars were again to appear together, Barrett relieving the weary Booth of all the trials of management, rehearsals, etc.   Julius Cæsar ran for two weeks.

Mazulm, for which we might thank Imre Kiralfy, started its magic and machinery, on January 9th, and ran through March 10th, scant advertising depriving me of details, except for the names of Clara Qualitz, Arnold Kiralfy, Mlle. Newman (dancer), the Braatz Brothers and the Vaidis Sisters.   On March 5th, according to the Herald, Kiralfy announced the prizes for fourteen-year-old children for drawings of scenes from Mazulm.   A Sunday lecture, in early March, brought Dr. McGlynn before the Anti-Poverty Society.   On March 12th, the night of the great blizzard of 1888, Ludwig Barnay, the German tragedian, was to appear, with the company that had supported Mme. Niemann-Raabe, Kean being his initial rôle.   The storm prevented his appearance, but Kean was promised again for the 13th, and for the matinée on the 17th.   Uriel Acosta was advertised for the 14th and 15th, and Othello for the 16th and 17th.   The storm deranged this schedule, and Barnay did not appear till the 15th, when Kean effected his rentrée; it was repeated on Saturday afternoon, March 17th.   Othello (evenings of the 16th and 17th) completed what must for the star have been a disappointing and stormy week.   Ruffled pride figured in Barnay's attitude toward his manager (Heinrich Conried).

King Lear, on March 19th and 20th, enlisted Barnay in the title-rôle, Carl Müller as France, Alexis Schönlank as Burgundy, Reinhold Bojock as Gloster, Hugo Rantzenberg as Edmund, Arthur Meyer as Edgar, Moritz Moritz as the Fool, Antonie Ziegler as Goneril, Auguste Burmester as Regan, and Hermine Reichenbach as Cordelia.   The Herald did not like Barnay's Lear: "The German tragedian evidently thinks, with many other people, that King Lear was a good deal of an old fool, a great deal of an old bore,

[499]

and above all things a turbulent, violent old crank.   Never did those heart-less jades Goneril and Regan appear to have so much provocation for their acts as they did last evening."   On March 21st and 22nd, Barnay gave acts from Richard III, Wilhelm Tell and Julius Cæsar; Uriel Acosta returned on March 23rd and 24th, and Othello, at the matinée, on the 24th.   His Othello was, as before, associated with the Iago of Gustav Kober, the Cassio of Hugo Rantzenberg, the Roderigo of Arthur Meyer, the Desdemona of Frl. Reichen-bach, and the Emilia of Antonie Ziegler.   After this fortnight of fruitless activity, Barnay carried his wounded feelings to the Thalia Theater, there to enjoy a long success in a dual engagement with Possart.

Meantime, on March 22nd (postponed from the 15th) occurred a gigantic benefit for Tony Hart, ill, mentally and physically, and off the stage for-ever.   Frank Mayo and his company, including William Harcourt, D. Han-chett, Robert Neill, Alice Fischer and Frances Graham, gave an act of The Royal Guard; W. J. Scanlan, one day to know a fate like Hart's, was seen in an act of Shane-na-Lawn.   Specialties included "turns" by Arthur L. Oswald, Harry Edwards, Marshall P. Wilder, Marie Jansen, Dave Reed, John and Edna Vidocq, and others.   The pièce de resistance, as usual in such benefits, was a series of scenes from a tragedy — Julius Cæsar, acted by comic actors:

Cæsar	Charles Kent	Decius	Henry Bergman
Brutus	W. H. Crane	Casca	Frank Mayo
Antony	N. C. Goodwin	Trebonius	Osmond Tearle
Cassius	Stuart Robson	Popilius Lena	Robert Hilliard
Soothsayer	J. B. Mason	Metellus	Steele MacKaye
Flavius	Francis Wilson	Calpurnia	Selena Fetter

Maggie Mitchell was down for an act of Fanchon, and Pauline Hall was to appear; but I am not sure that these promises were fulfilled.

Daniel E. Bandmann, capitalising on the success of Richard Mansfield's Dr. Jekyll and Mr. Hyde, brought to the Academy for a week's visit, his version of the shuddering tale.   The National Opera Company then sang its own obsequies, with performances of Nero (April 2nd, and matinée, 7th), The Queen of Sheba (April 3rd), Tannhäuser (first time here in English, April 4th), Faust (5th), Flying Dutchman (6th) and Faust, replacing Lohengrin (7th, evening).   In Nero, leading parts were cast to Sylva, Lud-wig, Miss Poole, Miss Walker and Miss Traubmann; the leaders in The Queen of Sheba were Bassett, Bertha Pierson (Sulamith), Clara Poole (the Queen), Amanda Fabris (Astaroth), Vetta and Stoddard.   Faust employed McGuckin, Fabris, Stoddard and Vetta (Mephisto).

More opera came on April 16th, when Italo Campanini bravely pro-duced Verdi's much discussed Otello, recently staged with acclaim at Milan. Campanini, who had brought to this country a concert company, with which he had travelled extensively, utilised some of that force (Scalchi and Galassi) and invited his sister-in-law, Eva Tetrazzini, wife of Cleofonte Campanini, to America, to create for us the touching character of Desdemona. He also introduced, as Otello, a tenor, Marconi, who made a disastrous failure. Aside from these leading importations, the cast included the dependable Galassi as Iago, the popular Scalchi in the small part of Emilia, Jovine (*sic* in the Herald) as Roderigo, di Comis (new to us) as Cassio, Bologna as Lodovico, Maina as Montano, and Morelli as the Herald. The opera failed miserably; to this day, in spite of repeated hearings, New York has never enshrined Otello among its favourites, even when, in 1894, Tamagno and Maurel assumed their original rôles. And, in spite of our allegiance, in the late '80s, to Wagner opera, the Verdi masterpiece was not acclaimed as an opera of the future. Marconi's failure in the leading rôle was so complete that Campanini, no longer the clarion-voiced tenor of years gone by, took up the part from April 20th. The opera was accorded four performances a week till April 28th, when it disappeared for about two years from our repertoire. It was probably a colossal, disastrous failure for Campanini.

And what succeeded it, at the Academy? The Howard Athenæum Company, which served a week with, among others, Hoey and Dailey, the Irwin Sisters, Carl Hertz, the Brothers Fonti-Boni, Dutch Daly, Lizzie Daly, Rezene and Robini, Sweeney and Ryland, and Le Cocon. These served for the week of April 30th–May 5th. On Sunday, May 6th, Ossip Feldman was down for a *séance* of mind-reading and mesmerism, a popular device. Henry Lee's Company, on May 7th, began a week of Fergus Hume's The Mystery of a Hansom Cab, a piece known to us from our prowlings in Williamsburgh. The cast here was strong, including Henry Lee, F. C. Bangs, William Morris, W. S. Harkins, E. D. Lyons, Herbert Ayling, Bijou Heron, Helen Bancroft, Carrie Jamison, Marion Bond, and many others of less note. "A mass of dramatic rubbish," was the Herald verdict. Frank Mayo followed, on the 14th, for a week of The Streets of New York. Sunday, May 20th, brought a concert by Campanini, Tetrazzini, Miss Groebl and others. According to Allston Brown, a benefit, on May 27th, was for the building fund of the New York Press Club. The season closed (May 28th–June 2nd) with a week of Louis James and Marie Wainwright, proffering, in succession, Virginius, Othello and Ingomar. Their good company included William Harris, Erroll Dunbar, H. A. Langdon, F. C. Mosley, Willis Granger, E. Y. Backus, Kate Meek and Aurelia Sarner. Kellar was mystifying here, on Sunday, June 3rd. I end the record, as I began it, in September, 1887, with the fists of a fighter. A testimonial to John L. Sullivan, on June 4th, shut the eye of the Academy for 1887–88.

Metropolitan Opera House, 1887–1888

Passing by the Symphony and Oratorio concerts and also those of the Philharmonic Society, which I shall review under their own captions, I begin the new season of German opera (the fourth) at the Metropolitan, on November 2nd, with the last year's great success, Tristan und Isolde, presenting Albert Niemann, Lilli Lehmann, Marianne Brandt, Emil Fischer and Adolf Robinson again in the leading rôles, and with von Milde as Melot, Kemlitz as the Shepherd, Sänger as the Helmsman, and the popular Max Alvary in the tiny part of the Sailor. Seidl, of course, led the embattled hosts to victory. On November 4th, Alvary took the centre of the stage as Walter, in Die Meistersinger, Frau Seidl-Kraus being the Eva, Frl. Brandt Magdalena, Elmblad Pogner, Fischer Sachs, Kemlitz Beckmesser, von Milde Kothner, Hoppe Zorn, Ferenczy David and Sänger the Night Watchman. Fidelio, at the matinée, on the 5th, completed the serious Teutonism of the week, with Robinson as Pizarro, Fischer as Rocco, Niemann as Florestan, Kemlitz as Jacquino, Lilli Lehmann as Leonore, and Minnie Dilthey as Marcelline. Except for Lehmann, and possibly Brandt, Niemann and Fischer, those ambitious artists are today (1941) utterly dead to memory of those who heard them or to knowledge of any but the most exhaustive research-students. This happens when ensemble is rated above individual excellence. Of course the world today (1941) remembers Jenny Lind. Tannhäuser, on Monday, the 7th, enlisted Niemann, Alexi (as Wolfram), Elmblad, Alvary, Frau Seidl-Kraus, Frau Biro de Marion (as Venus) and Minnie Dilthey. On November 9th, Siegfried had its first performance in America, and in it Max Alvary, young and handsome, and with his voice still unfrayed by his bad German method, became, in his bare beauty, quite the idol of girl spectators, if not of judicious auditors. There is no doubt that his physical attributes had much to do with the immediate success of the opera, though Seidl's mastery of orchestra and stage must not be overlooked. The first cast included Ferenczy as Mime, Fischer as der Wanderer, von Milde as Alberich, Elmblad as Fafner, Lilli Lehmann as an incomparable thrilling awakened Brünnhilde, Frau Seidl-Kraus as a not very birdlike Forest Bird, and Frl. Brandt as an impressive, if not velvet-voiced Erda. For an Erda with such a voice we needed to wait till Frau Schumann-Heink arrived for the season of 1898–99. Siegfried was repeated on the 11th, and Tannhäuser at the matinée on the 12th.

I dislike to break the continuity of my theme, but must go back to Thursday, November 10th, when Italo Campanini came back in search of former glory with a concert company including Sofia Scalchi (who sang the great contralto air from Semiramide), Galassi, Baldini (tenor), Corsini, and Signorina Torricelli. Signora Elvira Repetto could not appear, and Adele Aus der Ohe, announced, did not. Campanini sang *Salve dimora* and Siegmund's love song, from Die Walküre, words and style Italian.   His voice was not what it had been, but his phrasing was impeccable.   The last Campanini concert (there had been a second, on November 12th, at Chickering Hall) was listed for the 15th, at the Metropolitan; artists cited above were to appear, in addition to Camille Gurickx and Alfredo Gore.   And a nervous Repetto revealed a high, shrill voice.   I can now revert to opera, with Siegfried (November 14th, and matinée, 19th), Der Prophet (16th) and Tannhäuser (18th).   The cast of Der Prophet included Niemann, Frl. Brandt, Biro de Marion (as Bertha), Robinson, Kemlitz, von Milde and Elmblad. In Tristan und Isolde, on November 21st, Louise Meisslinger succeeded Frl. Brandt as Brangaene and von Milde was Kurvenal; Lehmann, on the 25th, resumed her usual rôle of Bertha, in Der Prophet.   And, finally, after the unvarying gloom of all operas thus far provided, on November 23rd and matinée, 26th, came the lighter effects of Nessler's Der Trompeter von Säkkingen, which did not achieve much success with a cast including Louise Meisslinger, Frau Seidl-Kraus, Robinson, Elmblad, Ferenczy and Fischer— not a strong array for auditors with memories.   The next week gave Fidelio (November 28th), Lohengrin (30th, with Niemann, Seidl-Kraus, Brandt, Fischer, Robinson), Der Trompeter (December 2nd) and Siegfried (matinée, 3rd).

Etelka Gerster; Josef Hofmann

The Metropolitan had taken the place of the Academy of Music as a scene for impressive concerts.   Henry E. Abbey, who had so successfully managed the concert-tours of Christine Nilsson and Adelina Patti, engaged that other abiding favourite, Etelka Gerster, and was to present her, on November 22nd and 24th, with an excellent support in Helene Hastreiter, Theodore Bjorksten, De Anna, Carbone, Mme. Sacconi (harp), Nettie Carpenter (violin) and an orchestra of seventy-five, directed by Adolf Neuendorff.   The first appearance was deferred to Thanksgiving night, November 24th, and the result was tragic almost beyond belief—Gerster's voice was in ruins.   The Herald of the 25th tells the story:

> It is a sad, a hard duty to write it down—the voice was no longer a voice but a mere echo.   Its crystalline purity, its freshness, its limpidity are gone—quite gone.   She who in former times could not have sung out of tune had she tried, often deviated from the pitch.

She sang *Una voce poco fa, Connais-tu le pays* (as encore), the bolero from The Sicilian Vespers and the Fior di Margherita.   In this the voice sounded again "like sweet bells jangled, harsh and out of tune."   This misquotation may be charged to the Herald.   Abbey had also arranged for a concert season of the phenomenal young Polish pianist, Josef Hofmann, a boy of only ten years, who had created a sensation in Europe.   His first

[503]

concert, on November 29th (evening) presented him in what the Herald calls a "truly masterly" performance of Beethoven's C major concerto, with "plastic phrasing" and "decided rhythmical precision." Yet his playing showed individuality. The Rameau Variations (bravura) "brought down the house." The child also played compositions of his own, a berceuse and a waltz. Gurickx gave him a theme, on which the boy improvised variations. We remember that he did this in his début, earlier, in Wallack's Theatre. The youthful wonder played again on December 1st (afternoon) and 3rd (evening). On November 30th, the Herald declares that "certainly one has to go back to Liszt's boyhood to find a parallel for this case. Unless his musical training is fearfully mismanaged, the child is bound to grow up to be a great virtuoso. There is the material there, too, for something more — a great musician." I need not recall to the reader the complete fulfillment in later years of that prophecy. At the matinée, on December 1st, the boy played Beethoven's Concerto in C minor (No. 3), a Gavotte by Pirani, a Romance by Rubinstein, Le Bananier, a negro song by Gottschalk, improvisations on any theme given by a lady or gentleman in the audience, and the Capriccio in B minor, for piano and orchestra, by Mendelssohn. From the wreck of the Gerster fiasco, Abbey salvaged, in support of Hofmann, Hastreiter, De Anna, Mme. Sacconi, Miss Carpenter and Neuendorff's orchestra. These artists were to support him also on December 6th (afternoon), and December 8th (evening). Other concerts were announced for the evening of December 13th and the afternoon of the 15th. Casimir Hofmann, father and teacher of the boy, conducted one number.

There I leave for a time the marvellous child, and revert to the serious opera of the Germans. The Trompeter von Säkkingen (December 5th), Die Jüdin (December 7th, with Niemann, Alvary, Fischer, von Milde, Lehmann and Biro de Marion), Faust (December 9th, with a doubtful cast, including Lehmann, Meisslinger, Frau Göttich, Alvary, Fischer and Robinson), and Lohengrin (matinée, 10th) made somewhat brighter the week's offerings. The Herald, on the 8th, states that Niemann's Eleazar, in The Jewess, "demonstrated that he can still sing when he wishes and not merely declaim." Frl. Lehmann "sang beautifully," but showed "one fault which had better be noticed lest it become an incurable mannerism — *viz*., the singer's habit of sliding up occasionally to the high notes of her voice instead of attacking them honestly and fearlessly." This bad habit clung to the style of the great singer. The Herald also thinks that Mme. Biro de Marion's voice "will have to become an acquired taste." Walter Damrosch led the orchestra for Die Jüdin, as, indeed, he did for Faust and Siegfried. Die Jüdin was heard on the 12th and 17th (matinée), Faust, with the ballet scenes, often omitted in the past (December 14th), and, as we were beginning to wonder what had happened to Wagner, Siegfried (December 16th). The reader notes how seldom this opera, Die Meistersinger and Tristan und

Isolde had been sung, thus far, in the season.   And Die Walküre had not yet emerged in the bills.   I wonder if Wagner was quite so popular in that far-off time as enthusiasts would have us believe?   In other words, was he a cult?

While pondering that important question, we may note Hofmann concerts on December 22nd (evening), December 27th (afternoon), and 31st (evening).   The week of December 19th began with Der Trompeter von Säkkingen, and ended with it on the afternoon of the 24th.   Tannhäuser, for the 21st, with Louise Meisslinger as Venus, led to almost the first notable revival (December 23rd) of Euryanthe ever given in this city.   The cast included Frl. Brandt, Lilli Lehmann, Miss Dilthey, Alvary, Elmblad, Ferenczy and Fischer.   This was repeated on December 28th, and matinée, 31st; Sigfried's growing popularity was proved on the 26th (Kemlitz succeeding Ferenczy, ill, as Mime), and Lohengrin once more bade farewell to the swan, and later to Elsa, on the 30th.   I leave December in this temple of German song with a charity performance of Fashing Thursday in Venice, arranged by Carl Marwig and enlisting, on December 27th, "two hundred young society ladies and gentlemen."   And, since we have been thus deflected from opera, I may end the paragraph with Josef Hofmann, who appeared, on January 3rd, aided by Mme. Hastreiter, De Anna and the usual assistants.

The new year of opera began (January 2nd) with Tristan und Isolde (Fischer, ill, replaced by Elmblad, and Niemann practically voiceless and reducing the love duet to a solo by Lehmann), continuing with Faust (January 4th) and ending for the matinée on the 7th, with Euryanthe, which had not made the desired effect, possibly because Weber's music is harder to sing (I said *sing*) than Wagner's.   A novelty of January 6th was Spontini's old opera, Ferdinand Cortez, with Niemann as Cortez, Alvary as Alvarez, Fischer as the High Priest, Robinson as Telasko, Elmblad as Montezuma, von Milde as Morales, and Louise Meisslinger as Amazily.   The management made a spectacular production, with Mexican architecture and costumes, vast armies of supernumeraries, prancing (?) steeds, etc.   In spite of all this effort, the opera failed, and passed from the repertoire after performances on January 9th, 11th, and 14th (matinée).   The fact is that helter-skelter seekers of amusement in New York have no sense of historical significance in plays or operas, and will not sit through anything that does not entertain them.   Siegfried served on the 13th—its eighth performance.   Der Trompeter von Säkkingen re-emerged on January 16th, and, for the first times this season, Die Walküre, on the 18th and 21st (matinée).   Of course we again had the matchless Brünnhilde of Lilli Lehmann, a flaming tower of song; but, according to the Herald review, the staging was bad, the lighting wrong, Niemann apathetic, Fischer singing with effort, and Frl. Brandt (as Fricka) "not in the best of voice."   Perhaps the reviewer remembered the voices and style of Nilsson, Patti, and other representatives

[505]

of *bel canto*. In this revival of Die Walküre Frau Seidl-Kraus, of course, was Sieglinde, with Elmblad as Hunding, and, in the band of Valkyrior, Frl. Traubmann, Frl. Meisslinger, Frl. Brandt, Ida Klein, Minnie Dilthey, and Frauen Kemlitz and Göttlich and Frl. Miron. Ferdinand Cortez, announced for January 20th was not given, Robinson being ill; instead we had Fidelio, with Lehmann, Niemann and Fischer.

Once more I must shift the focus from opera, this time to the benefit, on January 19th, for the Roman Catholic Orphan Asylum. Directed by Augustin Daly, it provided, at the matinée, the Harrigan company in part of Pete; Lizzie St. Quentin (*sic*); J. K. Emmet in a scene from Fritz; Harry Paulton (in a comic lecture); Homer and Lingard; Helen Dudley Campbell; A. D. Saxon; and Daly's company in A Woman's Won't. In the evening, from 7.30, Daly's company gave an act of The Railroad of Love; Dockstader and the Virginia Trio appeared; Rose Eytinge and others were seen in A Conjugal Lesson; Mme. Fursch-Madi, Marianne Brandt, Whitney Mockridge, Tony Pastor, Leopold Jordan, Edward J. O'Mahoney and Arthur Oswald sang; and Daly's company ended the bill, with Little Toddlekins. Since I have again been deflected from the opera, I may pass to the season of balls, beginning on January 5th, with the Charity Ball, and on January 10th, with that of the 22nd Regiment; thence whirling to the twenty-fifth annual ball (January 12th) of the Sparkling Coterie; the Old Guard Ball (January 17th), the French Cooks' Ball (February 2nd), the thirty-fifth masquerade of the Liederkranz (9th), that of the Arion (on the 21st), that of the Cercle Français de l'Harmonie (February 27th). The Purim Charity Ball followed on the 28th. The 69th Regiment ball graced the night of March 16th, and that of Wine, Liquor and Beer Dealers the night of April 2nd.

This duty reluctantly performed, I revert to the opera, to record performances of Lohengrin (January 23rd) and Euryanthe (27th). Alvary appeared for the first time as Lohengrin, beardless, and in dazzling armour. Steger, from the Thalia, was a very weak Telramund. On January 25th was staged for the first time in our country Wagner's colossal conclusion to the story of the Nibelungen Ring—Die Götterdämmerung. In a season devoted, as this had been, to four other new and difficult productions—Siegfried, Der Trompeter von Säkkingen, Euryanthe and Ferdinand Cortez—the management deserved great credit for ending the season with this mighty achievement. I attended this first performance and I can still recall my bewilderment, lost as I was, in the ocean of sound poured forth by Seidl's orchestra and the ringing magnificence of Lilli Lehmann's voice. The Rhine maidens made, on me, an indelible impression, but, oddly enough, I have but slight recollection of Niemann's Siegfried, heroic as I have been informed that it was. Not until Jean de Reszké took up that mighty burden of song was the death of Siegfried even adequately sung in New York. Of course no one could be expected to evaluate Die Götterdämmerung on a first hearing, and, as it happened, I went to that performance quite unexpectedly and without proper preparation in study.   The cast, besides Lilli Lehmann as Brünnhilde and Niemann as Siegfried, included Robinson as Gunther, Fischer as Hagen, von Milde as Alberich, Auguste Seidl-Kraus as Gutrune, Sophie Traubmann as Woglinde, Marianne Brandt as Wellgunde, and Louise Meisslinger as Flosshilde.   The scene of the Norns and that involving Waltraute were omitted, and with Seidl conducting!   The tremendous opera was repeated on the afternoon of the 28th.

For two weeks of the later season the management took advantage of the public interest in the Nibelungen Ring.   Lacking Das Rheingold, which was to come in the next season, they gave two complete cycles of the three main dramas — Die Walküre (January 30th and February 6th), Siegfried (February 1st and 8th), and Die Götterdämmerung (February 3rd and 10th). For the matinée, on Saturday, February 4th, the less tempestuous sorrows of Lohengrin enlisted Alvary, Seidl-Kraus, Brandt and Elmblad (as the King).   A special matinée of Die Götterdämmerung was listed for February 16th.   This colossal tragedy was given also on February 13th, 16th (extra matinée) and 17th, with Lohengrin again mellifluously lightening the woe, on the 14th.   The season ended, on the 18th, with a matinée of Siegfried. On March 10th, a special performance of Fidelio was arranged for the last appearance in our opera of the able, conscientious Marianne Brandt; Alvary, Fischer, Sanger, Kemlitz and Seidl-Kraus sang the other rôles.   With Brandt and Niemann both gone, the Metropolitan for 1888–89 was bound to take on a decidedly changed aspect.   Because of the death of her Emperor, Frl. Brandt deferred her farewell to the 17th.

On March 3rd, Walter Damrosch, clearly a man of ideas, arranged, for the relief work of the Society of Ethical Culture, a performance of Manfred, with Schumann's music.   Possart, as Manfred, according to the Herald, "fairly sang his lines."   Frl. Schatz was one of the Fates, and Frl. Aichsberg Astarte.   The Herald, which had found Egmont, shortly before, at the Thalia Theater, "too too voluble," declared the performance of Manfred, as a whole, "not alone tedious and uninteresting, but positively depressing — devoid of dramatic interest."   "The music spoils the drama, and the drama the music."   Undeterred, Possart acted here, on March 26th, in Die Räuber. The Metropolitan, we see, had become practically a German theatre in New York.   April 11th and 12th danced Fashing Thursday in Venice.

One of the memorable events in the theatre-history of New York occurred on the evening of Monday, May 21st.   Wallack's Theatre had passed out of existence, a short time before, after thirty-six years of supremacy in American stage-life.   Lester Wallack was perhaps financially disabled, and, in any case, his retirement was very properly commemorated by the great benefit or testimonial arranged by Augustin Daly and A. M. Palmer.   When the time arrived, Daly, by previous contracts, had departed, with his company, for a summer season in London; the major part of the later management fell, therefore, on the capable shoulders of Palmer. For weeks before the great night, the papers ran exciting articles about the wonderful cast for Hamlet that was to astonish and delight us, and hope ran high as favourite names were suggested. I remember that Rose Eytinge was at one time promised for the Queen, and, at another, Mrs. D. P. Bowers; when the time arrived, Gertrude Kellogg, not so famous, played the part. The cast finally seen was a mixture of great names and unimportant:

Hamlet	Edwin Booth	Marcellus	E. H. Vanderfelt
Ghost	Lawrence Barrett	Bernardo	Herbert Kelcey
Claudius	Frank Mayo	Francisco	Frank Mordaunt
Polonius	John Gilbert	First Actor	Joseph Wheelock
Laertes	Eben Plympton	Second Actor	Milnes Levick
Horatio	John A. Lane	First Gravedigger	Joseph Jefferson
Osric	Charles Kohler	Second Gravedigger	W. J. Florence
Guildenstern	Lawrence Hanley	Ophelia	Helena Modjeska
Rosencrans	Charles B. Hanford	The Queen	Gertrude Kellogg
Priest	Harry Edwards	Player Queen	Rose Coghlan

As a whole that list of names is impressive. I read at the time that Booth insisted on having members of his company in parts with which Hamlet has most to do in the play; hence the presence of John A. Lane (a good actor), Kohler, Hanley, Hanford and Gertrude Kellogg, in rather important rôles, and the relegation to very small parts of Vanderfelt, Kelcey, Mordaunt, Wheelock and Levick, actors better and more famous than those just mentioned. It was a pity that only three persons associated with Wallack's Theatre — Gilbert, Edwards and Rose Coghlan — had speaking parts. And Frank Mayo was not a very good King, though he had that night closed the Theatre Comique, where he was to begin a week's engagement. Of course Booth and Barrett gave their customary high performances. But the hits of the evening were made by Modjeska, whose Ophelia was simply magnificent in the scenes of girlish perplexity and subsequent madness, and by Jefferson and Florence as the quaintest Gravediggers ever seen by anybody before or since. It has often been said that Booth, disturbed by his unusual surroundings, was merely walking through his part, till Modjeska's superb Ophelia, in the big scene with Hamlet, awoke him to respond with equally impassioned acting.

A great feature of the performance was the large number of famous players who served as supernumeraries. I cannot say that they were "stage-managed"; in the court scenes they simply moved about, trying to get into the lime-light. Rosina Vokes, particularly, as I remember it, maintained a front position regardless of those behind her. She had closed Daly's Theatre, where she was filling an engagement, Mayo, as I have said, closed the Comique, and Daniel Frohman had closed the Lyceum. From the long list of names, in the Herald review, I cull these, as the most famous group of "supers" I ever heard of: Mrs. McKee Rankin, Mme. Ponisi and Ada Dyas (these two inseparably connected with Wallack's), Kate Forsyth, Katherine Rogers, Minnie Maddern, Virginia Buchanan, Selina Dolaro, Nelson Wheatcroft, E. L. Davenport, F. F. Mackay, Ben Maginley, Amy Lee, Mrs. Barton Hill, D. H. Harkins, Isabella Irving, C. W. Couldock, Ferdinand Gottschalk, Harry Hilliard, Courtenay Thorpe, Owen Fawcett, Barton Hill, Ida Vernon, Dora Goldthwaite, May Brookyn, Charles Wheatleigh, Mrs. W. G. Jones, May Robson, Kate Bartlett, Mrs. Whiffen, Alice Harrison, &c., &c.   Members of the audience near the stage had great pleasure in recognising these celebrities.   I stood, for a time, behind the orchestra rail, where so often I later stood for opera; finally, I went to the dress circle or balcony (I forget which) and saw and heard as from a distance.   But to this day I can recall the exquisite Ophelia of Modjeska and the astonishing Gravediggers of Jefferson and Florence.

Wallack, who was lame and no longer able to act, was called before the curtain, and made, of course, a speech, in which he said (to great applause) that this was not his farewell to acting; if his rebellious knee would recover, he hoped to appear again in his favourite rôles (more applause).   Unfortunately, this hope was not fulfilled; Wallack died in the summer of that year, and, as has so often been said, with him died the gallant, rattling heroes of Sheridan and other writers of "old" comedy.   Allston Brown states that the profits for the benefit were $21,560.17, and that there were 3,950 persons in the house.

Tony Pastor's, 1887–1888

As we remember, various attractions, during the summer of 1887, occupied the hospitable stage of Pastor's.   For September 5th-10th, T. J. Farron (late of Baker and Farron), with Jennie Leland, gave A Soap Bubble.   The regular season of "Variety" presented, for September 12th–17th, Hallen and Hart's First Prize Ideals, ever one of the best vaudeville groups and at that time comprising, in addition to the popular Hallen and Enid Hart, themselves, Ralph Terry, Joe Hart, the Jackley Troupe, Frank Bush, Leroux and Wilson, Ella Wesner, the Russell Brothers, John E. Drew, Isabella Ward and the Arion Trio.   I should like to have seen these talented people.   For the week of September 19th–24th, Hicks and Sawyer's Coloured Minstrels introduced the Three Mallory Brothers, Walter Roberts, Harry Thomas, W. C. Harris's African Orchestra, and Downs, Thomas, Jackson and Jones ("greatest of quartets").   Gus Hill's World of Novelties was displayed during the following week; also a first-rate combination, it advertised Edward and Frank Price, Mlle. Alberta, Weber and Fields (in Crazy Dutchmen), Leslie and Hardman (blackface), Wesley Brothers, and Thompson and Conroy ("formerly of the Four Shamrocks").

Joseph J. Sullivan, in The Black Thorn, had, for October 3rd–8th, such support as could be rendered by Spencer Pritchard, John and Lea Peasley, Mamie Wallace, Carrie Wallace, Frank B. Carr, Joseph Davis, Alf Wallace and J. P. Turner. This cast illustrates the inroads of plays (of a sort) on the ranks of "Variety." The same lesson may be learned from the bill of October 10th–15th, when Sheehan and Coyne gave Grogan's Elevation, though the olio retained Polly McDonald, George Davenport ("Dutch"), Lillie La Verde, Fanny Gonzales, Ed Davenport and James Arlington. Harry Sanderson took a benefit, on October 17th.

Then, the week of October 24th–29th brought Tony Pastor "home," surrounded by a starry host including Little Tich, John T. Kelly, the Donnells ("from the St. James, London"), Rose and Martin Julian, Harry La Rose ("athletic expert from London and Berlin"), Tom and Bertie Brantford (with imitations of brass band, drum and cymbals), the Coulson Sisters (skipping rope), Albert Clives and his dog (from the Cirque d'Été, Paris), Rice and Barton (negro act), Musical Dale, Flora Zanfretta, and Harry Kelly — all ending in Our Boarders. The second week of this auspicious home-coming retained Little Tich, John T. Kelly (in Senator McFee), the Donnells, Flora Zanfretta, and Harry Kelly, and added Fannie Beane and Charles Gilday, William Carroll (banjo), the Harts (Katie and Gussie), the Ladies Martens, Rosina (male impersonator), and the Ventini Hat Spinners. For November 7th–12th, the list included Adam Forepaugh, Jr., the Herbert Brothers, Bessie Grey (sic — "elegant prima donna," whom we met in Brooklyn Pavilions), Millie Turnour, Morello Brothers (head balancers), Bartlett and Lorraine (sic), Braham Brothers (Shadowgraphs), Max Pettingill, Gracie May, and In Hot Water (with J. T. Kelly, Harry Kelly, George M. Devere and Flora Zanfretta). That was the last week of John T. Kelly and Little Tich. The Howard Athenæum Company presented (November 14th–19th) Le Cocon ("mysterious sensation"), James F. Hoey and Peter F. Dailey, Mlle. d'Alton, Rezene and Robini, the Brothers Fonti-Boni, Flora and May Irwin (re-united), Adams, Casey and Howard, C. Ed Foreman and Ida Meredith, and Lizzie Daly (dancer).

The week of November 21st–26th was not very interesting with its offering of Dan Mason, Keating and Flynn, Wood, Sheppard (sic) and Bryant, the Miller Brothers, the Electric Three (Callan, Haley and Callan), the Two La Roses and Tony, himself. After that rather lean Thanksgiving week, we journey toward Christmas with (November 28th–December 3rd), Ferguson and Mack, Thomas J. Ryan and Mai Richfield, Paul Hamlin, Ada Newcomb, Alice Smith, Fanny (sic) Bloodgood, John F. Burns (sic), Dave Oaks, Jessie Boyd, Will Harper ("unipodal acrobat"), Edward Kelly, Burt Watson, Phil and Chrissie Sheridan, Tony Pastor, and the comedy, After Two. For December 5th–10th, Harry Williams's Great Specialty Company, from the Academy of Music, Pittsburgh, displayed its wares in persons of Fontaine (wire-walker), the Three Sisters Lawrence (trapeze), Topack and Steele

SOPHIE TRAUBMANN

LOUISE MEISSLINGER

AMANDA FABRIS

JOSEF HOFMANN

MAX ALVARY
(SIEGFRIED)

JOSEF HOFMANN

MICHAEL BANNER

LESTER WALLACK

ANTONIO GALASSI

(*sic*), Frank H. and Lillian White, Charles L. Banks, Imro Fox, Conway and Leland, and Edegio, Campbelle (*sic*) and Nibbe.   Following December joys were (12th–17th) Andy and Annie Hughes, Pastor, Albert Clives, Juleine's Electric Organ, Rixford Brothers, Winstanley Brothers, the Parker Twin Brothers, Leonzo, Marion and Belle, Anne Boyden, and Huber and Kitty Allyne; and (December 19th–24th) Rose and Martin Julian, Miss Sylvester Cornish ("Brooklyn society contralto"), Sheridan and Flynn, Sandiland and Ruthden's (*sic*) Golden Statues ("beautiful living pictures in flaring gold and bronze"), Tom F. Gale, Leopold and Wentworth ("Barnum's greatest gymnasts") and, of course, Tony, himself.   All I can find for Christmas (December 26th–31st) is Andy and Annie Hughes, Max Pettingill, Dell'Oro, and Ashley and Hess.

But the New Year (January 2nd–7th) lavished rich treasures on the patrons of Pastor art: New Year's Calls (with May Adams, Fanny [*sic*] Lewis, John B. Wills and Dave Foster), the Four Schrode Brothers, the Tissots (cat duet). St. George Hussey, Parker's Mastodon Dog Circus, Frank and Fannie Davis (The Old Veteran), Bessie Grey (*sic*), Frank Cook ("the American Scot, in Scottish Games and Sports"), Tony Pastor's New Year's Carols, Harry Thorne and Maggie Willett (*sic*), the Westons (Charles and Lillie) and Nicodemus.   January wore on (9th–14th) with Mlle. Eichlerette's Monkey Show ("in which Pete, the Monkey Magician, catches a cannon ball"), the Pavanelli Troupe of five (from Paris), Herr Grais (juggler), the La Rose (*sic*) Brothers (trick tumbling), Fred Huber and Kitty Allyne, Ed C. Smith and Jessie Carl, H. J. Campbell's Tableaux Soleil, Maggie Willet and Harry Thorne, and a concluding An Uptown Flat.   Specialists for January 16th–21st were the Oura Japanese Troupe, W. F. Carroll, Homer and Lingard, Logrenia, Emilia (*sic*) Turnour (high wire), Rose Julian (contortionist), the Virginia Trio, and William Courtright ("Flewy Flewy").   Something mystifying featured the bills for January 23rd–28th, in Professor Frank ("expositor of black art") and Professor Klein's Theatre Universum; but open as day were W. F. Carroll, Musical Dale, the De Barr (*sic*) Brothers, Polly Cusick and Tony Pastor.   A change came (January 30th–February 4th) with the San Francisco Minstrels, including Billy Birch (sole relic of the former glory), Frank Moran, William (*sic*) Pickert, Dave Foy (*sic*), Ned Thomas and Arthur Johnson.   As usual a (*sic*) saves me through the mazes of "Variety" spelling of names; besides, it shows the reader the puzzles of the game.

Without explanatory hindrance the reader may revel in the purveyors of mirth and fancy for February 6th–11th — Lester and Allen, Sheridan and Flynn, Emily Eddy ("somersault artist"), Keating and Flynn ("knockabouts"), Polly Cusick (Irish vocalist), Fox (magician), an educated mule, and Winnie Johnson (banjo); also for February 13th–18th — Harry and John Kernell, the Luciers (Joseph, Charles, Fred and Rose), James McAvoy,

Allie Smith, Fanny Bloodgood, George, Frank and Sam Markoe, Queen Vassar and Jennie Miaco, a remarkable group. For Washington's Birthday Pastor arranged a "Grand Jubilee" and let himself go in verbal splendour. Thomas J. Ryan and May (*sic*) Richfield, led the way to Rose Julian ("the magnificent beauty, peerless in loveliness and grace, the only lady contortionist") and Martin, her brother, Maggie Cline, Harry Woodson and Laura Bennett, John and Nellie Healey, Huber and Allyne, Earle and Miles (Irish pipers and dancers) and the Ventinis. Certainly Tony's enthusiasm for that group was richly merited. And excellent was the aggregation for February 27th–March 3rd — Carl Hertz, from the Crystal Palace, London (with Le Cocon), James F. Hoey and Peter F. Dailey, emigrés from the American Four, Mlle. D'Alton ("London Beauty and Enchantress"), the Four Arabs, Sweeney and Ryan, and Flora and May Irwin.

This brings us to March 5th–10th, with Lester and Allen, Polly Cusick, Lou Sanford (*sic*), Lenton Brothers, Zublin, Canfield and Zublin (singers, dancers and musicians), Elmer Hanson (prestidigitateur), Richmond and Glenroy and Pastor. Not impressed with that offering, we proceed to March 12th–17th for the ministrations of Milt G. Barlow, Maggie Cline, John and Edna Vidocq, Dave and Mrs. Reed, Morphet (magician), Ida Abrams and John H. Byrne, a rich assemblage which encourages us to visit the attraction for March 19th–24th — Tierney and Wayne, John Daly and Annie Devere, Frank Bush, Alice Smith and Fanny (*sic*) Bloodgood, Isabella Ward, Queen Vassar, Millie Turnour, Hooley and Thompson (negro plantation act and soft shoe dancers), Tony Pastor and James F. Lamb (ventriloquist). For Harry S. Sanderson's annual benefit, on March 21st, many of these artists appeared, in addition to Harry Kernell, Dutch Daly, Maggie Cline, and the Martell Brothers. The offering for March 26th–31st included Annie Oakley, Little Tich, the Armstrongs, Beane and Gilday and Renane and Athos (grotesques).

Frank Bush's Own New Show was the feature for April 2nd–7th, including Eichlerette's Monkey Show, Herr Grais, Charles and Ella Jerome, Isabella Ward, George Homer and Georgie Lingard (in The Main Line) and La Rose (*sic*) Brothers. Pastor was now away from home, and was renting his theatre to visiting troupes. The Rentz-Santley Peerless American Burlesque Company entered for April 9th–14th, with Dolph and Susie Levino, George Murphy and Katie Wells, Charles V. Seamon, Lulu Mortimore (*sic*), Louise Leighton ("California nightingale"), James Sanford and Charles Wilson, Lillie May Hall, Marie Sherman, Lillian Markham, Lida Moss and Gertie Keith, Carrie Wentworth, Georgie Blake and William Kellogg; delectabilities of the show were Adam and Eve and Toe Bogganing. It is pleasing to pass thence (April 16th–21st) to Kernell's Comedy Company, in a three-act comedy, Two Fine Ducks, with Harry Kernell as Adam McFadden, collector for an instalment store, and James Rielly (*sic*) as Barney Flanagan, a lightning-rod agent, assisted by Rose St. Almond, Kate Hill, Lizzie and Allie Smith, May Templeton, John Guina (*sic*), Thomas and Charles McShane (*sic*) and Fanny Bloodgood.

April 23rd–28th found, at Pastor's, A Little Nugget, played by Sisson and Cawthorn's Company, enlisting Herbert and Joe Cawthorn (*sic*), Sager Mudgerly, Jr., George A. Payne, Oscar Sisson, Susie Forrester and Florence Dayton.   Charles A. Gardner in The New Karl, followed (April 30th–May 5th), supported by Earle Remington, Robert V. Ferguson, Frank Monihan, Marion May, James E. Nelson and Robert McNair.   The San Francisco Minstrels returned for May 7th–12th, poor Billy Birch in the lead, with the Manhattan Quartet, Frank Moran, Frank Dumont and J. M. Woods.   Listed as Frank Moran's San Francisco Minstrels, the group for May 14th–19th included Hughey Dougherty, Billy Birch, Harrington and Johnson, &c. Frank Dumont's burlesque, O'Conor's Othello, sounds funny, and quite in the old-time vein is Frank Moran's Steal the Alarm (with "Real Fire Horses, Real Engine, $100,000,000 challenge to all fire departments to equal them"). For May 28th–June 2nd, Muggs' Landing boasted of a cast including Alfred McDowell, Carlotta, W. J. Mason, J. R. Furlong, Charles T. Grilley, C. O. Richardson, Frank Smith, Rose Carroll and Kate Francis, not the most distinguished aggregation to be found in these Annals.   They kept the piece on the stage for a fortnight.

I find it in my heart to spare my reader a knowledge of casts so inconspicuous; but somehow, my over-conscientious pen, of its own volition, states that Going It, by Charles T. Vincent and Kenneth Lee, gave employment (June 11th–16th) to Verner Clarges, Owen Westford, Logan Paul, T. B. Butler, Susie Russell, Addie Eaton, Lottie Hyde, May Sherwood, and (of all persons in the world) St. George Hussey.   After all, that cast contains some names that we know well.   The Pastor canticle for 1887–88 ends here.

London Theatre, 1887–1888

From the New York Clipper I abstract a long list of names for August 29th–September 3rd, at the London Theatre.   Emily Soldene, known, ten or twelve years earlier, as a buxom singer in opéra-bouffe, was now reduced to the ranks of vaudeville and brought to the London, in The Fox Chase, in olio, and in an abbreviated version of her old success, Geneviève de Brabant, a company including J. H. Cummings, H. F. Orndorff, George B. Leslie, T. S. Dare, Jennie Leslie, the Stanley Sisters, Jennie Melville, Eva Stetson, Tierney and Wayne, Dare Brothers (horizontal bar), McAvoy and Hallen, and Ada Hall (Mrs. T. S. Dare).   Miss Soldene's costumes were declared by the Clipper to be "gorgeous."   Tierney and Wayne were the comical gendarmes in Geneviève de Brabant.   Gus Hill, as usual, brought, for September 5th–10th, a very interesting group, in Conroy and Thompson,

[513]

Amy Nelson, C. W. Williams (ventriloquist), Alberta, Minnie Schult, Leslie and Hardman, and Polly McDonald. According to the Clipper, Weber and Fields "did not quite break their necks, but at times it looked as if they would do so. Their rough song and dance turn, though boisterous, is highly acceptable." And Gus Hill "easily maintained his high reputation as a club swinger *par excellence*. His manipulations are both graceful and artistic, be the weight light or heavy. He tackles most kindly to those clubs about as large as himself and wields them with surprising ease." Finally, says the Clipper, "Alberta's and Gus Hill's ceiling act was a strong feature, and caught the house."

The London, we see, was making a fine start. The Early Birds Company carried on (September 12th–17th) with Lester and Allen (always popular), Add Weaver, Flynn and Zitella, Annie Hart, Bryant and Holmes (*sic*), P. C. Shortis (banjo), Adrienne Ancbau (*sic* — aerialist) and a burlesque *She*. These early birds were, oddly enough, succeeded, on September 19th–24th, by the Night Owls, crowded houses greeting them on their opening Monday. After the Chase introduced Victoria North, Pauline Batchellor, May Howard, &c. Manchester and Jennings, J. G. Fletcher, "Nine Lovely Women" (in the Owl Base Ball Nine), Delhaur and Debrimont, Harry Morris, Jutan ("handsomest aerial artist in the world"), and A-Donis Abroad, with Louise Dempsey, &c., comprised the bill. Sheffer and Blakely's Company, as last week at the Eighth Avenue Theatre, shed mirth in the London; Nellie Parker replaced Layman. The audience, afternoon and evening of October 3rd, says the Clipper, was "so large that breathing room was a positive luxury." When I state that the Rentz-Santley Company then began a week's ministration of culture and female charms, the reader will understand. Abe and Ben Leavitt and George W. Lederer, pilots of the craft, "come in," quoth the Clipper, "for no small praise." M. B. Leavitt, "has outdone himself in the organization of the troupe." Opening "turns" provided Lulu Mortimer, Marie Sherman, William Kellogg, Lida Moss, Sanford and Wilson, Charles V. Seamon, Fannie (*sic*) Bloodgood (leading the Broadway Mashers), Lillian Markham and George Murphy (late of Murphy and Shannon) and Katie Wells. A burlesque Adam and Eve enlisted Seamon as Satan, Marie Sherman as Adam, Fannie Bloodgood as Nervi, Georgie Blake as Berri Wall (then Berry Wall was New York dude *par excellence*), Lillian Markham as Mabel, Lida Moss as the Masher (a disgusting type of the '80s), Gertie Keith as Mamie, Minnie Farrell as Violet, Capitola Forrest as Bertha, Katie Wells as Sadie, and Lulu Mortimer as Eve. Because of ignorance I cannot place Sadie, Violet, Mamie, *et al;* if they were in or near the Garden of Eden, they added a touch of incongruity at which even 1941 may smile; and Berri (or Berry) Wall, that well-known figure of the long ago!

After all that excitement, the London brought in, for October 10th–15th, a rather dwindled attraction — Susie Byron, the Herbert Brothers (acrobats),

Crimmins and Doyle, Lillie Billington (male impersonator), J. A. Coleman (dancer), James and Frankie Hall, and enriched the bill with A Boy Wanted, acted by Dan Mason, J. A. Toole, Nellie Parker, G. M. Brennan and Mollie Bernard. William Hines and Dan Mason also gave The First of April. The Burglar Alarm awoke us, on October 17th–22nd, with Bob Harrison, Toole, Brennan and Nellie Parker, the olio thence proceeding with John and Nellie Healey, Nellie Parker, the Four Tourists (in Busted), the Morello Brothers (acrobats and equilibrists), W. J. Ashcroft ("one of the cleverest dancers seen here in many a day," says the Clipper, "the refinement of his art being strongly in his favor"). Domestic Difficulties, finally, may have been solved by Joe Campbell, Lou F. Shaw and Maggie Evans. I learn from the Clipper of October 22nd that Ashcroft had expected to appear on October 10th; a late train deferred his début to the 11th. Andy Hughes's American and European Novelty Company filled the week of October 24th–29th, with H. M. Parker and his dogs and cats, Marion and Belle (banjo, etc.), Mlle. de Granville ("Female Hercules"), Andy and Annie Hughes, the American Four (now transmuted into Pettingill, Gale, Haines and Ardell), Minnie Lee, the Martinetti Brothers, Willie Martell, the Davenport Brothers, Kennette (aerialist), and a final In a Fix. The Silbon Big Spectacular Burlesque Company (October 31st–November 5th) proffered Pendy, Nellie Parker, Harry Melville, Lucille Graves, Gallagher and West, the San Francisco Quartet (Grieves, Burton, Audrey and Talbot), the Four Silbons (aerialists), Bob Harrison, and The Yellow Dwarf (with Jessie Villers, Minnie Ross, Jeffreys Pendy, Kate Nicholls, Pendy, &c.).

An immense audience greeted the return, on November 7th, of the Night Owls — Belle Clifton, Delhaur and Debrimont, the Acme Quartette, Paris Life, the "Nine Lovely Women," and A-Donis. And Gus Hill's World of Novelties excites my retrospective interest for the week of November 14th–19th. High in the roster were Weber and Fields ("greatest of all versatile comedians — knockabout artists — in Crazy Dutchmen"), Hill himself, Alberta, Dan Hart, Amy Nelson, Minnie Schult, and C. W. Williams. I cannot thrill to the offering of November 21st–26th — Bob Harrison, J. A. Toole, Al Emerson and Nellie Parker, of the "stock," in Two Roses; Pat Doody and Con Daly; Sherman and Morrisey, Carr and Tourgee (musical mélange), Tom and Bertie Brantford, Byrnes and Helene, the Herbert Brothers, Karoly Ordey, and John T. Kelly, in Our Irish Boarder; of course, some of this was good. The Way of the World, in the week of November 28th–December 3rd, was in no way related to Congreve's brilliant comedy of the same name; in any case, the thesis was proved by the Weston Brothers (Morris and Sam), John Robinson, Dora Dean, Mary Bird, Mrs. W. J. Horton, Edward Bethel, Charles E. Fisher and Ed J. Webster, who, I suspect, would have had some difficulty in proving their own excellence, single or collective.

[515]

December progressed (5th–10th), with the regulars (in That Mighty Dollar), Mike Tracy and Hen Price, Mlle. Madeline (juggler), Gordon and Lick, Neil Smith and his "collegiate canines," Annie Boyden (songs), Albert Clives and his "petite canine wonder," Luigi dell' Oro, William and Lottie Davene ("aerialism"), and Dan Mason (in Dinkle and McGinty). And just as patrons may have begun to wonder if they were no longer to be electrified by the sensations of the fall season, back returned (December 12th–17th) the Emily Soldene Burlesque Company, re-enforced by George and Marie Nelson, and the Four Cards (May Adams, Fannie Lewis, J. B. Wills and Dave Foster — certainly a gifted quartette). Another return visit was that of December 19th–24th, bringing the Early Birds, with Lester and Allen to swell the attraction. The Mignani-Siegrist Company came for the holiday week of December 26th–31st, with gifts of Leonard and Flynn, Polly McDonald, Charles Harris and Nellie Walters, Valjean, J. A. Coleman (dancer), James Connors and Sam Collins (The Mashers), the Three Siegrist Brothers (athletes), Billy Carter ("banjoisms and timely effusions of song" — a tag truly fitting for immortality). The New Year dawned (January 2nd–7th) with P. J. Kenyon, Winstanley Brothers, Fayette Welch, Emerson and Clark, Minnie Lee, Huber and Kitty Allyne, the Harper Brothers, Mack (sic) Pettingill and his canine protegé, Jim, Sylvester Cornish, Kurtz (sensational juggler), Bartlett and Lorraine, and Much Ado about Nothing (with Willis Clark, Morton Emerson, Kitty Allyne and J. A. Toole.

J. J. Donaldson, Jr., manager of the London, provided a group of his own for January 9th–14th. After Robert Becker's orchestra had prepared the way, The Coopers enlisted Bob Harrison, Dan Regan (sic), Charles Mack, J. A. Toole and Nellie Parker. Subsequent delights included Sandiland and Ruthden's gold and bronze statues, Ned Farnon's songs and dances, Nellie Parker, Morlo (sic) and Reagan ("banjo effusions"), Lewis and Martin ("Ethiopian") and Walter Stanton and Miss Corn, in Farmyard Sketches. This does not excite my enthusiasm. But the Sheffer and Blakely Company, for January 16th–21st, brought dependable entertainers in Mme. Quitsch (and her *tableaux vivants*), Charles Eastwood (late of Crandall and Eastwood), Ashley and Hess, the Lenton Brothers, Kelly and Weston, George H. Wood, Hilda Thomas, Moulton and Dashway, Zano (on the wire), Adolph and Marie Seeman, Sheffer and Blakely and Conroy and Dempsey — a group worth going far to see. Hyde's Company, as seen, on December 12th, at Miner's Bowery, invited custom, for January 23rd–28th, at the London. Lilly Clay's Company, for January 30th–February 4th, gave Rice and Barton, the Four Cards (May Adams, J. B. Wills, Fannie Lewis and Dave Foster, in Summer Vacation) and The Little Devil's Revel. Smoothly ran the next week with Emerson and Clark (Much Ado about Nothing), Huber and Kitty Allyne, Alexander Wilson (ventriloquist),

[516]

Glenroy Brothers (bone solos), Lewis and Martin, Mike Tracy and Hen Price, Harry Fitzgerald and Ella Lewis, Smith and Carl (Autographs), Ira Paine and wife, and The Metropolis in Forty Winks.   Posterity is most interested in Sam Bernard, whose specialties, according to the Clipper, "were commendable and received endorsement to a large extent."   February 13th–18th enjoyed Gus Hill's Company — Conroy and Thompson, Alberta, Weber and Fields, the Sheerans, Thurber and Dubois, Lottie Rogers (a new vocalist), Marion and Belle, Swift and Chase, Walter Wentworth (his first appearance here in several years), and wrestling matches, with contestants changing every night (Hill and Martin Dempsey serving on Tuesday in that bout.)   Wrestling figured in the bills for February 20th–25th, when the Rentz–Santley "beauties" returned; then Matsada Sorakichi, a Japanese wrestler, was to meet several wrestlers during the week.

Female combinations were in demand.   The Lilly Clay Gaiety Company was in the ascendant for February 27th–March 3rd, the chief executants being the Four Luciers, Irma von Rokoy, the Excelsior Quartet (Primrose, Lonsdale, Davenport and Wilson), the La Porte Sisters, Mlle. de Granville ("Female Hercules"), Miranda Sisters, Alice Townsend and Rice and Barton — a group that pursues us through the season.   Another of James J. Donaldson, Jr's., own companies (March 5th–10th) set before us Schoolcraft and Coes, Ida Lillian Abrams, J. H. Byrne, Bryant and Hoey, and Kerrigan and McGonigle.   Then came March 12th, the day of the unsurpassable and impassable blizzard of 1888.   The London "for all of old Boreas," as it boasted, gave two performances on that day and throughout the week. The Night Owls officiated, with Belle Clifton and Lizzie Mulvey, May Howard, Pauline Batchellor, Robert Manchester (who did a single "turn," his partner, Jennings, being ill), Delhaur and Debrimont, and the burlesque, A-Donis, with Pauline Batchellor in the leading rôle.   And still sparring! Rice's Vaudeville Syndicate (March 19th–24th) strongly stressed bouts between Jack Dempsey and Denny Costigan, and passed to the gentler talent of Minnie Ross, T. B. Butler, the La Rose (*sic*) Brothers (acrobats and tumblers), John Walsh ("in taking vocalisms"), the Electric Three (in Clotilda's Birthday), Bobby Gaylor, the Four Cards and Richmond and Glenroy — surely a group worth sparring for.   The ever-recurrent Rentz-Santley bevy of beatitudes came yet once again (March 26th–31st), Evan Lewis, a wrestler, causing a row, on the opening night, by insisting that he be allowed to wrestle with Sorakichi, whereas the ethics of the situation debarred him, a Wisconsan, from entering into a contest for which none but natives were eligible.

After all the pulchritude and pugilism of that blustery March, April 2nd–7th was rather feeble with the offering of J. W. Hampton and his dogs, Kerrigan and McGonigle, Symonds and Hughes, Ed and Kittie Welch, Steve Sarsfield, Polly Cusick, Richmond and Glenroy, James Britton, Somers

[517]

and Walters and Huber and Allyne (in Seven Miles). Candour forces the admission that I never, previously, had heard of some of that host. The Hyde Company presented (April 9th–14th) Fred and Jennie Mackley, Imro Fox, Weber and Fields, Leopold and Bunell (*sic*), Heffernan and Mc-Donald, Kitty O'Neil, William McMahon, Flora Moore, Sam Devere and Jack McAuliffe — about the finest aggregation, *me judice,* seen that season at the London. The "Parson'" Davies Company sank below that standard, proffering, for April 16th–21st, nothing more notable than Blanche Boyer, Fitz Williams, Dunn and Mack, Charles Banks, Leonard and Mullen, Alice Raymond, and the Horseshoe Four. Best of all for those who liked such things were wrestling bouts between William Muldoon and Evan Williams. The Lilly Clay Gaiety Company, with The Little Devil's Revel, filled the warmer sessions of April 23rd–28th. And another return carried into May (April 30th–May 5th), with the Sheffer and Blakely company inviting custom through the efforts of the Tills, Bryant and Holmes (*sic*), Moulton and Dashway, &c. Hilda Thomas, announced, was too ill to appear. Fitzgerald's Early Birds gave us (May 7th–12th) Helene Mora, Franks, Marion and Flynn, Zitella, Maude Chatwood (song and dance), George H. Wood, Jolly Nash, the King Sisters, Tatali ("contortion act of the highest class, while sustaining himself on the flying rings"), and the burlesque of the not very popular She. Peter Rice's Syndicate, opening, on May 14th, to "standing room," proffered Jack Dempsey, Frank and Fannie Davis, Ed Giguerre, McAvoy and Rogers, Maggie Cline and Marie McNeil. Verily, we might stand and wait for those notabilities as, one by one, they flashed across the scene.

Who were the Boston Serenaders, of May 21st–26th? Schoolcraft and Coes, Tom Martin and C. F. Lorraine (in an introductory ministrel scene); the Boston Serenaders Quartet (George H. Coes, C. F. Lorraine, Charles Henry and A. D. Sinclair); and, as olio performers, Fred and Nellie Diamond, Harry LeClair and Edward Leslie, James McAvoy and Joseph A. Kelly (*sic*) — good talent, but not overwhelming. For May 28th–June 2nd, we were regaled with George Murphy (late of Murphy and Shannon) and Katie Wells, the Starr Sisters, Connors and Collins, Richmond and Glenroy, Franks and Marion, S. G. Beasley and Elmer and Mme. Ranson (prestidigitation). Lilly Clay's Gaiety Company, here again for June 4th–9th, presented the Four Cards, the Three Herbert Brothers, Alice Townsend and the Lamont Trio. The redoubtable Lilly Clay remained for a second week (June 11th–18th), ending the bills with an elaborate Robinson Crusoe. With the Lilly Clay group, for June 18th–23rd, appeared Irma von Rokoy, Leonzo, Amy Nelson, Bolton and Bradford, Maggie Cline, and Foster and Hughes; The Mash I Got (Mascot) may have been funny not without being vulgar, to parody Oscar Wilde's famous *mot* concerning Beerbohm Tree's Hamlet. And Lilly Clay's fourth and last week brought forward

(June 25th–30th) Bert Stanley and Gus Pixley, Lou Sanford, Hilton (contortion), and Harry LeClair and Edward Leslie (in A Society Star).   Sam T. Jack had managed the four weeks of the popular Lilly.

For July 2nd–7th, the London gathered Karl Michaels, Tommy Morrissey, John and Nellie Healey, Nellie Parker, Fred McAvoy, the Herbert Brothers, Tatali, and the farce, Sawdust Bill.   Progressively for the two final weeks of the season (July 9th–21st) we studied the art of Kelly and Murphy, Sam Bernard (pray, observe this rising man), Gibson and Welsh, Parker and his dogs, Leonard and Flynn, J. W. Myers, G. Donald Melville, Frank La Rose (sic), Emilie Peare, Webster and Barry, Wade and Mack, Mamie Conway, John Irving (Teutonic — new), Tatali, Lizzie Conway, Charles H. Stanley, Bertie Conway, Mr. and Mrs. Sam Lucas, Nellie ("instrumentalisms") and farces.   The theatre closed, on the 21st, to re-open, on August 11th, very greatly refurbished and redecorated, inside and out. The season just ended seems to me to have offered much interesting matter, possibly with a suspicion of too much Clay and Rentz-Santley.

Miner's Theatre, Bowery, 1887–1888

The Bowery Miner's passed without break from one season into another. We may resume our visits to the place during the week of September 5th–10th, to greet friends old and newer in William Melville, Nellie Brimmer, Ned Hanson and Mamie Hayman, Frank Clayton, Mme. Bell and her trained bear, Paul and Frank Hamlin, Kelly and Ashley, J. W. McAndrews (who lives on from volume to volume of these Annals), Lake and Lexington, Tex (cowboy fiddler), the Four Tourists, and the Newcomb Trio.   Hyde and Behman's Specialty Company, from Brooklyn (their "first city appearance"), with James Hyde, director, presented, for September 12th–17th, William McMahon, John and Edna Vidocq, Kelly and Murphy, Sam Devere, Richard Carroll and Flora Moore — talent not in the least confined to Brooklyn.   An opening sketch by Sheldon employed the stock actors of the house — A. H. Sheldon, J. R. Gildersleeve, J. R. Lewis, John Coffey, Dave Posner, Nellie Sandford and Daisy Norwood.   For September 19th–24th we appraised Master Gus Rogers, Edward Barnell (sic), Sheridan and Flynn, Taylor and Russell, and minor lights, in Annie Devere, Albion Brothers, Russell Williams (début in America), the Three Comets (Frank Hawley, Bob Richmond and John E. Welsh), the Three Franklins, and the San Francisco Quartet (Grieves, Ballinger, Talbot and Meader).

The popular Reilly and Wood's Company proved (September 26th–October 1st) to be an army, with Pat Reilly, the Nelson Family (acrobats), Bobby Gaylor, Robert and John Morrissey, Joseph Doner and J. Keating (song and dance), Adele Wilson's globe act, Chisikitchi (contortionist appropriately named), Florence Miller (songs), the Four Emperors of Music

[519]

(Howard, Russell, Seeley and Talbert), the Twelve Roman Gladiators (the Nelson Brothers and others), Mlle. Forgardus and her birds, and farces (The Irish Police Brigade and The Two O'Ks). The Marinelli Troupe, seen the week previously at the Eighth Avenue Theatre, came for October 3rd–8th, to the kindred house in the Bowery. October 10th–15th brought the Kernell Brothers' Company, including Jennie Miaco, Larry and Lizzie Smith, Solano and Fonti, Smith and Lord, Katie and Gussie Hart, Queen Vassar, Herr Grais ("with artistic manipulations") Harry and John Kernell (of course) Eichlerette and her trained monkeys (I cannot regret missing this high festival), the Luciers (musical mélange), the Lenton Brothers (acrobats), and Duffy's Blunders (with John Kernell and others). October wore on (17th–22nd) with George and Marie Nelson, Fannie Beane and Charles Gilday, Kelly and Ashley, Dick Morosco and Kitty Gardner, the Virginia Trio, George W. Earle and Paddy Miles, Layman, and H. J. Campbell's Tableaux Soleil — a list attractive to me, whatever the Bowery may have thought of it.

Harry Williams's Own Company was found (October 24th–29th) to include Edgelo (juggler — American début), Topack and Steel (*sic*), Frank H. and Lillian White, Imro Fox, Fontaine (wire performer), the Horseshoe Four (Ella and Josie Love, J. J. Quinlan and George W. Turner), Conway and Leland, and the Lawrence Sisters (Hattie, Jennie, Alice — aerial). The Howard Athenæum Company came (October 31st–November 5th) from the Eighth-Avenue Theatre, where it had entertained the week before. November 7th–12th allowed the Bowery to appraise George C. Marshall, Ainsley and Downie, John Daly and Annie Devere, Hassan and Whitby, Petite Kitty (*sic*), the Venetian Troubadours, "Professor" A. Matthews and his "herd of performing goats" (an exhibition I can afford to miss), Miles, Ireland and McHugh, Purvis and his "comical donkey," Rosina and the Zanfrettas. No wonder that, according to the Clipper, "the audience was of fair size" — only. Austin's Australian Novelty Company gave, as usual, increased pleasure for November 14th–19th. Emilie Peare, soprano, said by the Clipper to be a sister of Carrie Swain, made her début, and the bill promised LeClair and Russell (in A Practical Joke and in Married Mashers), Baldwin and Daly ("the Zulu Twins"), Edward Leslie, Ramza and Arno and the accomplished Rose and Aimée Austin (aerialists). According to the Clipper, Aimée, swinging back to back with Rose, turned a forward somersault from the flying bar, came up from underneath, and was caught by the hands of Rose. The next two weeks (November 21st–December 3rd) turned a double somersault with talent provided, successively, by Fred Morphet, J. H. Hammond, Harry Edwards and Daisy Kernell, Matthews and Lynch, Frank and Fannie Davis, the Cecilian Quartet, Burt Ransom, Harry Steele, William H. Burke, the American Four, Bedouin Arabs, Harry Deaves and marionettes, Florence French, Fred Barth, Kelly

[520]

and Ashby (*sic*), George W. Callahan, Dick Carroll, Frank Clayton, Keating and Flynn, the King Sisters, Bellac and Mlle. Aouda, the La Rosa (*sic*) Brothers, William Melville, and the farce, Everybody Eight Dollars Short.

The Hallen and Hart Company "as last week at Eighth Avenue" was here for December 5th–10th, and Hyde's Big Specialty Company for the following week with very attractive lure in the Vidocqs, Kitty O'Neil, Kelly and Murphy, William McMahon, Heffernan and McDonald, Sam Devere and Flora Moore — a list somewhat changed from that of the visit of Hyde and Behman in September. The last weeks of December (19th–31st) provided a week each of P. J. Kenyon, Polly Cusick (début), the Morton Brothers, Musical Dale, De Forrest and Sanders (*sic*), Wenzel and Morris, Fanny Sanford (*sic*), James Gray, the California Quartet, the Schrode Brothers, Emery and Laura Russell, William Carroll, the Tissots, the San Francisco Quartet (Grieves, Ballinger, Burton and Meader), John Fitzgerald and Dan Lacy, Fannie Beane and Charles Gilday, the National Four (Bryan, Morton and the Forrester Sisters), Rose and Martin Julian, the Virginia Trio (Dick Harris, Walter Manning, Thomas Williams), and "Professor" A. Matthews and his goats. In reading this list, I cannot but quote the comment of the old lady on the pie — "plenty of it, such as it is." The New Year gift (January 2nd–7th) also is a mixed blessing — Dave Reed, wife and daughter, the Albion Family, Edward and Caroline De Hass, Florence French, Charley Banks, Harry Deaves and his marionettes, the American Four, Matthews and Lynch, Dick Carroll, Petite Kitty and Valvino. Perhaps time has dimmed for 1941 some of the effulgency of those stars.

The Harry Williams Company returned for January 9th–14th; though Edgelo, Frank and Lillian White (now in On the Frontier) and Conway and Leland remained, Tom and Bertie Brantford, the Brothers Snow, who, according to the Clipper, "acrobated," Dutch Daly (concertina) and James S. Maffit (in The Comanches) were stressed in the bills. The Reilly and Wood Company also paid another visit (January 16th–21st), with only one change since it was last here; W. J. Ashcroft replaced D'Alvini. The Kernells likewise came back (January 23rd–28th), stressing James McAvoy and Hallen, Allie Smith and Fanny Bloodgood, Larry and Lizzie Smith (in Love Letters), and Marlow and Reagan — not a glittering array. The Howard Athenæum Company, a fourth returning wanderer, was almost a new force (January 30th–February 4th), with Harry Woodson and Laura Bennett, Vanola, Van Auken and Long, Wood and Sheppard (*sic*), Ryan and Richfield, Schoolcraft and Coes, the Gillette Family, Thornton and Lawler, Maggie Cline, Lester and Williams, and the Miner "stock" in The Lion and the Lamb, and Winkle's Fix (this with Dan Mason). For February 6th–11th, the Marinelli and Big Four Company was just as it was, on its former visit, except that P. C. Shortis was added. From February

20th to March 3rd, McCabe and Daniels, Loa and Ruge, Keating and Flynn, Saunders and Burdell (*sic*), Fitzgerald and Lacy, Herbert Crowley, the Paravelli (*sic*) Troupe, the Tissots and Three Franklins exercised their spell for the first week, and, for the second, A. Matthews and his goats, Roseland and May, George Kaine, the Four Tourists, Keating and Ardell, Frank and Fannie Davis, Minnie Kaine, the Paravelli Troupe and the American Four; good material may be found in that fortnight of variety.

The week of March 5th–12th enlisted H. J. Campbell's Tableaux Soleil, William Melville, Beane and Gilday (frequently recurring and ever welcome) Capitola Forrest (also seldom long-absent), Ned Hanson and Mamie Hayman, Gallagher and West, the Lamont Trio, Walter Stanton, &c. Despite the famous blizzard, Miner's opened, on that wild 12th, for a week of No. 11 Doolittle Alley (with Sheldon, Gildersleeve, Posner, Dick Morosco, Nellie Sandford, Charles Ludwig and Daisy Norwood) and treated to turns by Nettie Carlyn (song and dance), Herr Grais (juggling), Dave Oaks and Jessie Boyd (in A Little of Everything), Frank Clayton's Nonsense, Eichlerette, Kelly and Murphy, Parker's Canine and Feline Troupe, Johnny Purvis and his donkeys and a concluding Pleasant Companions. Reilly and Wood's Company, "with a make-up nearly new," exploited, for March 19th–24th, Booker and Leigh, La Rue Grove (baton drill), Adele Wilson, Pat Reilly, Bryant and Saville, the Horseshoe Four, the Nelson Family, Emerson and West, Healey and Jerry Keating and Pitrot. The Harry Williams Specialty Company saw March out (26th–31st) with Harry Kernell (John now absent), F. H. and Lillian White, the Brantfords, Conway and Leland, Shedman's Dog and Monkey Circus, Dutch Daly, Leopold and Bunell (*sic*) and "Professor" L. F. Klein's Panoramic Display — surely a good vaudeville venture. A benefit for the Actors' Fund fell on March 29th.

For the week of April 2nd–7th, my weary pen greets James H. Hammond, "Professor" Wallace, Hearne and McGill, Valvino, Thomas Flynn, the Gilforts, the Rogers Brothers (note this!), Kelly and Ashby, La Petite Kitty, the National Four (Frank Bryan, Gil Moulton, Nellie and Eva Forrester), and the Three Ronaldos (*sic*). The next week (April 9th–14th) advertised Minnie Lawton, Larry and Lizzie Smith, Leslie and Webber, Alexandre (*sic*) Wilson, the Zanfrettas, Tatsurgoro Hewlette, the American Four and the Morello Brothers, a group not too American in orthography. It would be simpler for our record if returning combinations retained the *personnel* of previous visits. Austin's Australian Novelty Company (April 16th–21st) was almost indeed a "novelty," with Marie McNeil (a "comely cornetist"), Vidocq and Gilson, Le Clair and Russell, the Bentley Brothers, Ella Wesner, Isabella Ward, the Southern Quartet, Wood and Healey and Frank Bush. But the wonderful Rose and Aimée Austin still ruled the air in their sensational performances on the flying rings. From April 23rd to May 19th an ever-changing weekly bill introduced

[522]

Mike Tracy and Hen Price, Charles and Ella Jerome, Sherman and Moris-
sey, Ramza and Arno, Frank and Lillian White (never long absent), Mamie
and Billy Williams, Bryant and Saville, the California Quartet, Eddie
Magee, Harry Woodson and Laura Bennett, the Ventinis, Herr Grais,
Charles H. Duncan, John Daly and Annie Devere, the Garden City Quartet
(R. E. and T. F. Callahan, C. B. Bryant, and C. F. Noble), the Four Cards,
Mlle. Eichlerette, Dave Reed and Family, Roseland and May, Clark and
Williams, Keating and Ardell, Carter and Lizzie Anderson, Capitola For-
rest, Imro Fox, Leonzo and (May 7th–12th), The Family Drug Store (with
Dick Morosco, Gildersleeve, Posner, Nellie Sandford and Louise Crolius),
George W. Barlow, A. O. Duncan, Charles McDonald (of Heffernan and
McDonald), Fitzgerald and Lacy, the Sheerans, Nat Curtis, Adams, Casey
and Howard, the Four Tourists and George Melville.   I wonder if that list
is worth the trouble of transcription to our record?

The week of May 21st–26th seems feeble with William H. Burke, the
Greene Brothers, Vidocq and Gilson, the Lucier Family, Tom Lewis and
Dave Oaks, George Laible and the Clipper Quartet.   The following week
brought Tommy Nolan, the Martells, Billy Carter, Frank and Lillian White,
John E. Drew, Valvino and Frank Clayton.   The final week of the season
(June 4th–9th) enriched attendant ears with Ella Wesner, Larry and Lizzie
Smith, George and Minnie Kaine, Fannie Beane and Charles Gilday, Adams,
Casey and Howard, Farrell and Wilmot, James F. Hoey and H. M. Parker's
dogs and cats — decidedly an improved list, worthy of the promise of the
preceding autumn.

MINER'S EIGHTH AVENUE THEATRE, 1887–1888

We begin, once more, our scholarly journeys to this West Side Palace
of Dainty Delights.   The new season opened, on August 22nd, with Alexander Davis, Dave Oaks, Jessie Boyd (these in farces, fore and aft of the
bill), Ed Kelly and Burt Watson, Fannie Beane and Charles Gilday, the
American Four (now composed of Pete Gale, William E. Hines, Nat Haines
and M. Hoyt — Gale the only one left of the famous group of yore), Parker
and his dogs, Billy Carter, and the Four Emperors of Music.   In a concluding Love vs. Deafness appeared Oaks, Louis Robie, Jessie Boyd, Burt
Watson, Ed Kelly, Charles Smith, &c.).   The house had, according to spring
promise, been "elegantly" redecorated.   And a programme note said "Smok-
ing not permitted.   A First Class Family Theatre, where Ladies and Children can enjoy with perfect comfort a Pure, Wholesome and Delightful
Entertainment."   Bravo, Harry Miner!

If the record of the following week was in the Clipper, I failed to find it.
For September 5th–10th Hallen and Hart's Company enlisted the Orion
Trio, Isabella (sic) Ward, Hallen and Hart, Leroux and Wilton (horizontal

bar), Joe Hart, Ella Wesner ("latest fall styles were betrayed becomingly and attractively," according to the Clipper), the Russell Brothers (in Two Irish Lillies — sic), Frank Bush, and the Jackley Wonders ("first appearance in this country in several seasons"). It takes no prophet to inform us that this was an admirable aggregation. I cannot so unreservedly praise the group for September 12th–17th — John A. Coleman, Tex, Hamlin and Hamlin, Heffernan and McDonald, Kelly and Ashby, Tom and Minnie Flynn, Ned Hanson and Marie Hayman, Annie Boyden and the Morton Brothers; yet there is some good talent there. On September 18th (Sunday), the Reverend Edward McGlynn lectured. The Sheffer and Blakely Company (September 19th–24th) included Mme. Quitsch (realistic views), Wylie and Sanford ("return after prolonged absence"), Moulton and Dashway, Sheffer and Blakely, Adolph Seeman and his Electra Illusion, Pavillio and Rousillion, Tony Ryan and Joseph A. Kelly. Our Bess, the afterpiece, enlisted William Wylie, Pearl Inman, Kate Sanford, Hilda Thomas, Harry Blakely, John Conroy, J. Dempsey, and Charles H. Sheffer (as Caroline Eliza). Surely this was, for variety, a glittering array. Marinelli's Cosmopolitan Congress and Big Four Company, despite its pretentious name, does not ring so grandly in the imagination of 1941 — Charles and Ella Jerome, François (drawings, caricatures and transparent glass drawings), Rosa Lee, Clark and Williams, Raffin and his pigs (enjoy this "turn" who might) and the Big Four (Smith, Waldron, Haley and Martin). According to the Clipper, Marinelli was "without doubt, at the head of his chosen line." Unfortunately, the reader and I cannot re-traverse the years to September 26th–October 1st of 1887, to verify this assertion.

Reilly and Wood's Company, as last week at Miner's in the Bowery came for October 3rd–8th to Miner's in Eighth Avenue; and Hyde's Big Specialty Company, as seen at Miner's Bowery, week of September 12th–17th, nibbled at custom for October 10th–15th, in the West-Side Miner's. Fair exchange between two theatres under one management, and pleasing to the actors withal! And the good work continued through the week of October 17th–22nd, when Harry and John Kernell moved their forces from the Bowery Miner's, where they had been the week before. My pen, fearful that this exchange system is becoming too easy for it, is checked by the coming, for October 24th–29th, of the Howard Athenæum Star Special Company, including C. Ed Foreman and Ida Meredith (in Lawn Tennis), Fonti-Boni Brothers, Sweeney and Ryland, Flo and May Irwin (alas! for May's departure from Daly's), Adams, Casey and Howard, Lizzie Daly (dancer), Hoey and Dailey's act, Carl Hertz (sleight of hand — "Vanishing Lady Out-vanished"). According to the Clipper, "the S. R. O. sign was out long before the curtain went up, and late comers were unable to get within the doors." The Irwin Sisters, after four years' absence from vaudeville, were "the hit of the show," but Hoey and Dailey's act "went with a dash." I

[524]

never was a patron of vaudeville, but to my fancy of 1941 that bill sounds fine. Harry Williams's Company was listed for October 31st–November 5th, but the Clipper cites no performers.

Gus Hill managed heavyweights in entertainers as easily as he juggled heavy clubs. During the week of November 7th–12th he manipulated a company including Rice Brothers, Amy Nelson, Conroy and Thompson, Leslie and Hardman, Dave Hart, Alberta, Weber and Fields, Minnie Schult, Edward and Frank Price, the Wesley Brothers, and C. W. Williams. The Andy Hughes Company, seen on October 24th, at the London Theatre, journeyed, for November 14th–19th, to the Eighth Avenue, minus Minnie Lee, kept by a sore throat from the bill. The next week (21st–26th) proffered Fannie Beane and Charles Gilday (whom I am always pleased to meet), Lewis Brothers, Sheridan and Flynn, Jessie Boyd and Dave Oaks, Professor Campbell, Newcomb and Hamlin, the Forresters, Frank Clayton, &c. Hallen and Hart's Company, with William Muldoon added, returned for the week of November 28th–December 3rd. For the next week (December 5th–10th) the Clipper specifies nothing except that the company was "clever."

I should not expect much from the guests of December 12th–17th — P. J. Kenyon, John and Nellie Healey, Dick Carroll, "Professor" Lamb, Herbert Crowley, Paddy Hughes and Nellie Oxford, the Electric Three, Kelly and Ashley, the Luproils (*sic*) and the Four Tourists. Fred J. Huber and Kitty Allyne were stressed in the bills for December 19th–24th, along with the Virginia Trio, the Morello Brothers, the Lamont Trio, the Tissots, John Daly and Annie Devere, Rob and Lulu Theis (*sic*), Al Emerson, Morphet, and the Glenney Brothers. Christmas week (26th–31st) gave "Professor" Morley's Fata Morgana, Ed C. Smith and Jessie Carl, Huber and Kitty Allyne, Paddy Miles and John E. Horoly (*sic*), Homer and Lingard, John Carroll, Ned Hanson and Marie Hayman, the Four Cards and the Schrode Brothers — a group with many of whom I am not sufficiently familiar to judge of their collective appeal. The Mignani-Siegrist Company, seen last week at the London Theatre, were the New Year's gift here, with Ashley and Hess as extra holiday attraction.

January 9th–14th brought old friends in John and Edna Vidocq, the Martell Family, Sharpley and West, Kitty O'Neil, Sam Devere, Flora Moore, Kelly and Murphy, Jack McAuliffe, William McMahon, and Heffernan and McDonald — Hyde's Company, to wit, and a big inducement to draw a crowd from the cold streets into a cozy auditorium. Harry Williams's Own Company moved, on the 16th, from Miner's Bowery. Reilly and Wood's Company were welcomed in the week of the 23rd–28th. The Clipper fails us for the week of January 30th–February 4th, but compensates with announcement for February 6th–11th of the Howard Athenæum Company No. 2. The Clipper again failing us, for February

[525]

13th–18th, it honourably acquits itself by going back on its traces to inform us, in the issue of the 25th, that Marinelli, the Big Four, François and his wife, and P. C. Shortis ("banjoisms") had been there for the week involved. For February 20th–25th, the excellent proffering consisted of the American Four, Beane and Gilday, Frank and Fannie Davis, Nellie Parker, the Winstanley Brothers, the Davenport Brothers, Roseland and May, Ed. Kirwan (*sic*), Dave Oaks, Louis Robie and Jessie Boyd. An incident of the evening of February 22nd was the fall of Michael Berrigan from the gallery to the balcony; he gashed his chin and had a bad shaking up — surely an anticlimax.

For the week of February 27th–March 3rd, the California Four, the Tissots, Foreman and Ida Meredith, Keating and Flynn, Miles and Hawley, Lester and Allen, the Schrode Brothers and John Daly and Annie Devere must have seemed like old friends, tried and true. Gus Hill's Company had the week of March 5th–10th. Another attempt to jump from the gallery to the balcony resulted successfully for the perpetrator (John Pratt) on March 3rd, but brought from the management the edict "Arrest anybody attempting the feat." For March 12th–17th Andy and Annie Hughes (in Katie's Surprise) were followed by Stirk and Zeno (mid-air), the Albion Family (William, Ettie and Edgar, in "acrobatic endeavours"), Bartlett and Lorraine (song and dance), Gallagher and West (blackface), Ned Hanson and Marie Hayman (songs and duets), Lou Sanford ("in vocal endeavours"), William and Alice Payne, A. G. Matthews and educated goats, Dorothy Brandon ("vocalisms"), and Healey and Saunders (in "terpsichorean exercises"). Best show of all would have been a gallery boy trying to translate into his accustomed speech, the magniloquence of those tags. March 19th–24th seems to me to have offered solid, familiar enjoyment with Mr. and Mrs. Joe Allen, the Lamont Trio, Beane and Gilday, Ed C. Smith and Jessie Carl (in Sunnyside Landing), Fitzgerald and Lacy, Lacy and Martin, Huber and Kitty Allyne, the Four Tourists (in Busted) and Parker's dogs and cats.

George Homer and Georgie Lingard, Ed H. Banker, James McAvoy, Huber and Allyne, James Richmond and Letha Glenroy, Paul and Frank Hamlin, the National Four (Frank Bryan, Gil Moulton, Nellie and Eva Forrester), the Newcomb Trio and Frank Bush for March 26th–31st, are like the egg — "excellent in parts" only. I found no record for the week of April 2nd–7th, but cheerfully submit, for April 9th–14th, Peter Rice's Syndicate and Vaudeville Stars, a lofty name for rather medium talent in Jack Dempsey, the Four Cards, the Electric Three, Farrell and Leland, the La Rose (*sic*) Brothers, John Walsh, "Professor" Abt, John Coleman, and Roger Dolan and Dennis McCarthy (Milesian Bards). Rather better seems the aggregation of April 16th–21st — Dave Reed, wife and daughter, in A Dish of Reed Birds, Belle Dolan (songs), Harry Kennedy, Leonard and

CORINNE

HUGH FAY
(OF BARRY AND FAY)

FANNY BLOODGOOD

MAGGIE CLINE

HELENE MORA

ANNIE OAKLEY

LEW DOCKSTADER

WILDER AS ROMEO AND
HOPPER AS JULIET

EMILY SOLDENE

Hart, Bryant and Saville, Leonzo, Larry Tooley, Frank and Fannie Davis, the California Four (Chrissie and Phil Sheridan, Ed Kelly and Burt Watson), all leading to The Hotel Runners' Ball.   Austin's Australian Novelty Company, so often seen and admired, was here for April 23rd–28th.   The "house" group for April 30th–May 5th included Nellie Van Auken, John and Nellie Healey, Frank Clayton, Lewis and Dave Oaks, Richmond and Glenroy, Charles Eastwood, Mike Tracy, Hen Price, the American Four (now Pettingill, Gale, Haines and Walsh), Andy and Annie Hughes, &c. The week of May 7th–12th gave the Murphys (Big and Little Nick), John Daly and Annie Devere, A. C. Rigby, the Ventinis, the Big Four (Smith, Waldron, Haley and Martin), Valvino, Charles and Ella Jerome, Ed Kirwan (*sic*) and the farce, A Horrible Night.   Less alluring seems the offering of May 14th–19th — Roseland and May, George and Marie Nelson, Huber and Allyne, Pickert and Mayon, Van Auken and Long, and English and McArthur.

The week of May 21st–26th presented Jack Hopper and "Professor" Clark (in sparring), Girard and Earle, Ed Giguere (*sic*), Sadie McGill and James Hearne, F. H. and Lillian White, Fitzgerald and Lacy, Leslie and Hardman, Minnie Lawton, and Lacy's sketch, Casey, the Fiddler.   The last week of the season (May 28–June 2nd) brought in P. J. Touhey (*sic*) and Charles J. Graham, Larry and Lizzie Smith, Thomas H. Ward and Con R. Lynch, Bartlett and Lorraine, James McAvoy, the Horseshoe Four and Foreman and Ida Meredith — surely a feeble ending for a season that had, on the whole, been strong in interest.

ROUMANIA OPERA HOUSE, 1887

While King Solomon's Judgment was pursuing a long run, in October and November, 1887, at the Oriental Theatre, the New York Herald advertises, on November 1st, a King Solomon for the Roumania Opera House (104-106 Bowery), with the cheering tags, "A Picture of Oriental Beauty. Great Success.   Houses Crowded.   Every Evening at 8."

NATIONAL THEATRE, 1888

The Jewish contingent seems to have deserted the theatre at 104 Bowery, and in the week of May 21st–26th, the Roumanian Opera House resumed its former title of National Theatre, with O. Heumann as director and Alf A. Wallace as stage manager.   They invited custom with Keating and Ardell, Ferguson and Mack, John Pendy, Tom Ward and Eddie Mack, Alf and Amy (*sic*) Wallace, Dave Robie, and Carrie Wallace — names once potent with National audiences.

Following weeks presented Dan Regan, the American Quartet, Bryant and Holmes (*sic*), M. B. Pike in Burr Oaks (May 28th–June 2nd); John and Nellie Healey, the Four Emeralds, Wenzel and Morris, Leonzo, and Shadowed Crime, with George W. Mitchell (June 4th–9th); Dan Hart and his "bright canine," H. J. Campbell and his Tableaux Soleil, and (June 11th–16th) A Box of Cash (with Ed M. Favor, Edith Sinclair, A. C. Favor, S. M. Favor, Eddie Coles and others); for June 18th–23rd, Edwin Browne's Good as Gold, with, in the olio, C. Ed Foreman and Ida Meredith, Le Clair and Leslie, and Ed Kirwan (*sic*); and (June 25th–30th) Joseph P. Winter's Daniel Boone, the Hero of Kentucky, the olio enlisting Roger and Belle Dolan, Alf A. Wallace, Edith Crolius, C. L. Farwell, Larry Tooley, Leslie and Hardman and Dave Roche — all familiar to the Bowery. And familiar were the participants for July 2nd–7th — Ward and Lynch, George A. Booker and Maude Leigh, Mme. Lavelle, George and Marie Nelson, George F. Kaine, Emma Alfredo, the Rogers Brothers, Minnie Kaine and Revillo, as good a group as the most exacting could demand.

The National was turning to plays. The Danites (July 9th–14th) had a cast including J. P. Winter, Alf Wallace, James Conners (*sic*), Harry Stone, Edwin Barry, Mamie Wallace, W. T. Dulany, Sam Collins, and Annie Devere; in the olio were some of these, with Lester and Williams. For the week of July 23rd–August 11th, the National was the only Bowery house open. The London Theatre re-opened on Saturday, August 11th, and Miner's in the Bowery shortly after. I found, thereafter, nothing for the National, except in playbills in the Harvard Theatre Collection. S. Levi was now listed as manager. For July 23rd–28th, came Hilton (acrobat and contortionist), Gilson and Welsh (songs), Lizzie Conway and Charles H. Stanley, John Walsh, George E. Atkins, and the play, A Checkered Life, with Mamie Wallace, W. T. Cattell, Stanley, C. Gilson, Alf Wallace and Mamie (?) Conway. The following week (July 30th–August 4th) provided Roach and Ada Castleton, M. J. and J. B. Murphy (in Commercial Drummers), Charles Kirke, the acrobatic Hilton, and John W. Ransone, in his favourite play, Across the Atlantic. The following weeks, through August 27th–September 2nd whirled before our eyes weekly visits of Conroy and Thompson, Rosina, J. B. Donovan and Lula Albright, Parker and his dog and cat circus, and George E. Atkins (in Texas Bill, the Ranchman — August 6th–11th); John Daly and Annie Devere (in Oddities), Fata Morgana, J. Herbert Mack and Lizzie B. Raymond (California sketch duo), and Martin Hayden as Jack Sheppard (August 13th–18th); the Collins Sisters, Frank Lester, the Maddens, Valjean, and Mr. and Mrs. W. M. Paul, in Lucky Ranch (August 20th–25th); and (August 27th–September 2nd) Frank Forrest, John C. Fox and Thomas F. Watson (in A Kitchen Match), S. G. Beasley, Connors and Collins (in The Mashers), and Ed Chrissie (in many rôles) and Lillie A. Hall (in Detected). A warning bell bids me ring down for the season of 1887–88.

[528]

ORIENTAL THEATRE, 1887–1888

In this home of Yiddish drama, I gather for the first two weeks of October, 1887, repetitions of plays seen many times during the preceding season: Bar Cochba (October 2nd); Emigration to America (4th); Sulamita (5th); The Orphans (6th); David ben Jesse (7th, 8th and 12th); and Maternal Love (10th). On October 11th, something less familiar came, in shape of The Katorznik of Siberia (by Schaikevich), with Schöngold in the title-rôle. Friday, October 14th, brought the first performance of a much-vaunted King Solomon's Judgment, which ran to the end of the month, except for October 25th, when David ben Jesse was staged for the benefit of King David Lodge, 44, O. B. A.

A gap in the files of the American Hebrew for earliest November forces me to November 7th, when Don Joseph Abarbanel re-emerged. On Tuesday, November 8th, Borman's benefit revived The Orphans. The Faithful Wife, a melodrama by Schaikevich, with music by Kurantman, was new, for November 9th, 11th and 12th, but, judging from absence of subsequent repetitions, not a conclusive success. For her benefit, on November 14th, Mrs. Heine (Chaimovich) reverted to Joseph and His Brothers; it was repeated on the 19th. Other November leaves were David ben Jesse (for benefits of lodges or charities, 15th, 23rd and 28th); Der Neder (16th, 29th and 30th—the last two for lodges); Emigration to America (18th); King Solomon's Judgment (21st, also on December 2nd); Uriel Acosta (22nd); and Esther and Haman (26th). In the midst of early December repetitions Fanatic came back, on December 14th, "for the benefit of a poor family." Beginning on the 16th, audiences were invited to appraise Moses in Egypt, an historical opera in five acts, with an epilogue, by Rubens Weisman and, of course, with music by the ever-serviceable Kurantman. This ran throughout the rest of December, except that, on the 25th, Heine (Chaimovich) proffered for his benefit, Emigration to America, that favourite of Jewish beneficiaries (and reasonably so), and that The Neder came back, on the 20th, and The Sorceress, on the 29th.

This record would be more interesting if I could supply casts and other details. Rather monotonous repetitions of works already cited for this year made January easy to traverse. From the record I cite merely the benefit of I. H. Finkelstein, who offered (January 4th) Joseph and His Brothers; The Dibik (January 5th and 20th); Maternal Love (10th); The Katorznik (11th); Brandele Kasak (12th); The Usurer (17th); The Gambler (18th), for the benefit of Mrs. Borodkin; The Chaluza (19th); Menachen ben Israel (21st); and The Faithful Wife (23rd). On the 25th. S. Kafkak took a benefit, with David ben Jesse, and Emma (sic) Raimé, product of variety, sang somewhere in the course of the proceedings. On Friday, January 27th, a novelty emerged, under the titles of The Child of Israel, or, Under the

Protectorate of Sir Moses Montefiore; Joseph Lateiner was the author, and, on February 13th, he offered the play for his benefit. On the 29th of February, Kurantman, the composer, and Kroll, leader of the music, used the piece for a joint benefit. I fancy these ambitious actors were none too prosperous; the frequency of benefits for lodges and charities leads me to believe that the beneficiaries simply hired the forces of the theatre to the mutual advantage of the parties concerned. But I hasten to say that The Child of Israel had many repetitions in the dark days of February. On February 1st Der Jüdische Puritz (*sic*) returned. On the 2nd, Mrs. Karp was Benjamin, in Joseph and His Brothers.

For February I go forward to mention Baum's benefit, on the 6th, with David ben Jesse; to The Spanish Inquisition (Febuary 9th); to C. Kreutzman's benefit, with Sulamita (15th); to J. Wachtel's benefit (23rd) with Emigration to America; to Esther and Haman (27th, "for the benefit of a poor family"); and (28th) to The Child of Israel, for the benefit of Solomon Lodge, No. 32.

March blew in one repetition after another; I feel justified in omitting these from the record, merely citing Mme. Heine Chaimovich's benefit, on the 7th, with her customary Joseph and His Brothers; Der Dibick (*sic* — March 23rd) and Der Jüdische Poritz (*sic* — 24th). The Mysteries of New York, "a grand operetta" by Joseph Lateiner, was promised for March 27th and 28th, and April 2nd and 3rd. I can only hope that Mme. Goldstein's benefit on April 4th, did not indicate, by the title of the piece offered — A Distressed Family — any condition in the fortunes of the beneficiary. On April 6th and 7th came the first performances of Supposed to Be Dead, a "comedy in 4 acts and 8 scenes," by Schaikevich. Performers included (in a playbill at Harvard) Courage, Mme. Borodkin, Mme. Goldstein, Miss Silberstein (a curious combination, the names of these two ladies), Schöngold (and this as a third!), Adler, Mme. Silberman (and lo! a fourth), Baum, Lateiner, Bervovich and Lehrer. S. Kroll still led the music. The American Hebrew, so far as I discovered, holds no more for the Oriental Theatre, in that season, after very early April.

ARMOURY HALL VAUDEVILLE THEATRE, 1888

Just as the passing of older variety houses encourages us to hope that the account of vaudeville will decrease in volume, new enterprises spring up in unexpected, generally humble, quarters. Thus Armoury Hall Vaudeville Theatre, 158-160 Hester Street, insinuates itself in the columns of the New York Herald of November 19th; it is "open for the season," with the Southern Minstrels, thirty men, women and children. From that reliable journal, the New York Clipper, I can bring tidings that, for the week of January 9th–14th, visitors were regaled with the combined ministrations of Frankie

[530]

De Forrest's Burlesque Company and Hunn and McIntosh's Minstrels. From this one bone we venture to reconstruct the mastodon. Viola May's Burlesque and Novelty Company filled the next week, apparently in the same tradition, *but* sacred concerts made holy every Sunday evening. More specific was the announcement of Maude Sylvester's Burlesque Company and Levanion's Star Specialty Company, which, for January 30th–February 4th, proffered Speed and Hunn, Edgar and Bartlett, Levanion and Mc-Cormick, Reed and Parker, and Charles Emmett (*sic*).

The idea of burlesque and female charms with native virtue clad as little as the law would allow was suggested by the next exhibition (February 6th–11th), when Josephine Walby's Burlesque Company was propped by Levanion and McCormick (whom we have met in better company), the Kane Brothers, Earle and Miles (also well-known in higher spheres), Frankie De Forrest (now reduced to the ranks), and the pantomime, Robert Macaire. The next two weeks subdued the "burlesque" element and advertised for at least one week each, and sometimes two, Kittie Burke, Eveline Florence, Jennie Brady, Billy Miles, Billy Speed, Hughes and Clark, the Jeromes, Lillie Ashford, the West Sisters, May Conditt, Van Leer and Barton, Artie Hughes, &c. Then back came the "burlesque" serpent (February 28th–March 3rd), with Mme. Kendall and her Blonde Burlesquers, including Kittie Burke, Viola May (reduced to the ranks), Kitty Williams, Lillie Levan, Lizzie West, Kate Cooper, Dan Collins and Dave Gratton (*sic*).

Not until April 2nd–7th did the Clipper yield further news of the Armoury Theatre; then it promised Georgie Marsh (in ancient and modern statuary, possibly a timid progenitor of the "strip-teaze" of the '30s), Stella Anderson (German nightingale), Lillie Devere, Georgie Leonard and the Burke Sisters. Many of the performers already listed re-appeared in the last two weeks of April, additions including Pete Gardner and Jimmy Petrie, Annie Riley, the Three Lucilles, Jennie Lindsay, the Dixon Brothers, May Mortimer, Pauline Scott and Sara. And Viola May and Frankie DeForrest were often in the crew of the popular ship, Burlesque. I found no more of this palace of dainty delights till I read in the Clipper of June 16th that the hall had been condemned and would be vacated shortly by order of the Board of Health. I do not know under what defects, architectural or otherwise, the Board was inspired to act.

Harlem Pavilion, Etc., 1888

For summers preceding we had sought the cool Harlem Pavilion, sometimes in danger of being wet by the rain that soaked through the tent. That pleasance passed, and, on May 5th, I read in the Clipper that a new Harlem Pavilion was "rapidly approaching completion" and was "expected to open on May 7th," with W. T. Dulany as business manager. And here is familiar matter from the Clipper of July 7th: a storm, on June 30th, closed the Mammoth Pavilion (a tent) at 130th Street and Third Avenue. I found almost nothing, this season, for Gunther's Palm Garten and Huber's pleasance, in Fourteenth Street.

MUSEUMS IN THE BOWERY, 1888

The Herald, of Sunday, April 22, 1888, has an article on this subject. It names five important museums on that much travelled highway — the Chatham Square, the Berlin Academy of Waxworks, the East Side Museum, the Globe Museum and the New York Museum, some of which we have occasionally met in our itinerary. The Sultan's Private Divan also receives attention in that article; this and the Berlin Academy of Waxworks sport the slogan — "For Men Only."

The New York Museum was declared to be a few doors north of the Sultan's Divan. According to the article in the Herald it offered a charming list of attractions — William Holmes ("who chews nails"), Major Herman (a drummer boy), Wesley Baum ("on whose cuticles were tattooed designs of all the animals"), and Little Henrietta Moritz ("an ugly dwarf."); J. W. Macready also acted The Slaves of Gotham. A few doors above the New York Museum was the Globe Museum. There Fanny Herring was acting in The Hidden Hand, doubling the parts of Capitola and the Newsboy. The reporter was saddened by this fact. "I had learned," he writes, "in my boyhood to regard Miss Herring as one of the greatest actresses the world had ever seen. . . . In those days she certainly reigned Queen of Thespis on the East side of New York, she rode in her carriage and lived in the best hotels. Now her manager informed me that she played for a small pittance, enough to keep her soul and body, seven times a day, every day except Sunday, between the hours of one and ten P.M." This is a worse tragedy than any the once popular Fanny had ever acted on the stage; I wonder what had brought her so low? I wish I had had sense enough, when I was a boy, to go into one of the variety houses to see this famous woman act, even in the days of her decline. The curious thing is that her name survives in theatrical history, when many actresses of higher fame have been engulfed in oblivion.

I can sympathise with the sympathy of this Herald scribe, in the fate of Fanny Herring. Well I remember how distressed I was, when in the '90s and beyond, once famous performers condescended to the lure of Proctor's or Keith's continuous vaudeville. Their glory withered, Rose Coghlan or Clara Morris came into those realms in one-act plays or condensations of their former successes; Emma Calvé and Sofia Scalchi, former idols of the opera, sang, in their later days for audiences that seldom if ever had heard them at their zenith. Of course the surroundings, back stage, were far superior to those poor Fanny Herring met in dime museums; but something of the same principle is involved—they did not leave the stage before their powers waned.

DOCKSTADER's, 1887–1888

Negro minstrelsy of the older type still struggled on, in Dockstader's (late San Francisco) minstrel hall.   This well-remembered site, at Broadway, near 29th Street, re-opened, on September 7, 1887, with a large force (and much larger than that ever employed by Birch, Wambold and Backus) including Carl Rankin, A. C. Moreland, Edwin French, E. N. Slocum, James Quinn (Queen?), Burt Sheppard (*sic*), Barry Maxwell, Perry and Magrew, Lew Dockstader, William Rieger, R. J. Jose, H. W. Frillman, L. Monico, J. H. Davis, Joseph Garland, W. S. Mullaly, and Masters Parr, Magar, Howard, Austin, Sloman and Henry.   Two skits bore the imposing titles of The Pneumatic R. R. to London, and, with an eye to Staten Island, The Fall of New Babylon.   The Swell Thing to Do was explained on September 19th, but The Fall of New Babylon still enriched the bills till October was in the ascendant.   On October 3rd, Dr. Freckle and Mr. Snide was far from Richard Mansfield.   October 10th was timely with Cleveland's Western Trip and Volunteer and Thistle and The Fall of New Babylon.   A rich collection of nonsense was that of October 24th–29th—The Corsehair, or, the Northerland Sisters, Cleveland's Trip, The Arabian Knights, or, Fun on the Old Homestead, and The Fall of New Babylon.   Few of my readers are old enough to remember the Sutherland Sisters, who used to brush their hair, reaching almost to their feet, in a window in 14th Street.

Of course Mrs. Potter, so recently translated from amateurism to the professional stage, could not escape.   On October 31st began Mrs. Blotter in Mlle. de Brass Ear, with Burt Shepard (*sic*) as Mlle. de Brass Ear, supported by Curly Bellows Dockstader.   With Irving's Faust the unique feature of the stage in November, of course the minstrels must produce a Black Faust; in it, from November 14th, appeared W. H. Rieger as Faust, M.D., A. C. Moreland as Enery Hirving Mephisto, H. W. Frillman as Valentine, Barry Maxwell as Siebel, James Quinn as Martha, and Burt Shepard (*sic*) as Marguerite.   This should have been funny; it was still stressed in early December.   For the week of December 12th–17th, we were promised Frank Howard, "author" of when the Robins Nest Again (how popular it was in those guileless '80s!), Only a Pansy Blossom, and Sweet Heather Bells; now, at Dockstader's, he was to sing a new Only a Blue Bell.   A burlesque on Josef Hofmann was inevitable, and it figured in this bill, as Josef Hofmann's Sister.   December 19th–24th brought the Madrigal Boys, Master Albert Weinstein (a musical prodigy) and a burlesque She.   For holiday merriment (December 26th–31st) Dockstader shook from the tree Buffalo Bill's Big Injun, The Modern Mother Goose (with himself) and Henrietta, an

[533]

Ethiopian afterpiece.   Frank Howard, W. H. Rieger and Bert Haverly were stars of January 2nd–7th; but then Hamlet, or, the Prints of New York, featured Dockstader as Booth and Carl Rankin as Barrett.   They must have had fun devising these parodies of current successes of the "legitimate" stage. January 9th gave us Anthony Cornstalk *vs.* Art.   Our Minnie, for January 16th–21st, probably did no damage to Erminie, at the Casino; Camel *vs.* Armuckle, or, a Jury's Estimate of K. M. Q. H. and K. leaves me groping for the basis of its fooling.   Billy Rice was advertised for January 30th–February 4th.

The week of February 6th–11th presented Pullman Car Porters (with Baker and Jones), Senator and Judge (with Billy Rice and Dockstader), and Eye-talian Uproar.   Mullaly and his orchestra, Frillman, Edwin French, R. J. Jose and W. H. Rieger still figured in the advertisements; also James Blamphin (harp).   For February 13th–18th, James Albert, "record breaker at Madison Square," was to appear at Dockstader's, "in the costume worn last week," in the walking match, at the Garden.   This was Dockstader's last attempt to win a reluctant public.   His season closed on February 25th. The world wanted bigger, if not better, minstrel bands.   Of course the house could not remain dark.   On February 27th, Corinne, then somewhat older than when she first broke upon our astonished vision, began an engagement, in Arcadia.   This device carried gaily through March.   On April 2nd, Jennie Kimball, mother of the young star, presented her as Edmond Dantes, in Monte Cristo, Jr.   In this rôle she was advertised, on April 9th, as "the brightest jewel in the coronet of art," but, on the 16th, she began her last week as Edmond Dantes.

Amanuensis, a play by John Lynd, employed, for April 23rd–28th, a cast including Mabel Sterling, Jennie Leland, Emma Maddern, Mattie Ferguson, Louise Sanford, Tony Farrell, Maurice Drew, W. E. Burton, W. P. Bown, and George R. Edeson, some few of whom we have met before.   Dockstader, Shepard and Grau resumed the management of the house.   We found, in the spring of 1888, Victoria Siddons trailing hopefully behind our caravan. Announced as the daughter of Mary F. Scott-Siddons and the great-grand-daughter of the immortal Sarah Siddons, she was about to play Rosalind, on April 27th, in the Berkeley Lyceum when the law stepped in with the warning that that auditorium was not licensed for regular theatrical pro-ductions.   Balked thus, the ambitious young lady hired the Cinderella house of Dockstader, and published advertisements of two performances daily on May 2nd, 3rd and 4th.   The table of luxuries included As You Like It (May 2nd), Pygmalion and Galatea and The Rose of Auvergne (May 3rd) and (May 4th) a new play by William Fearing Gill, entitled The Two Lives of Dr. Jekyll, with E. J. Henley.   With no excess of modesty the débutante promised "powerful attractions and great array of society and professional artists."   The advertisement in the Herald of May 1st states that the matinées of the 3rd and 4th would be held in the Madison Square Theatre; I found no fulfilment of that intention.

The Herald was cruelly waggish in its review of Miss Siddons's Rosalind, seeming to feel that she was very slender and made no attempt to disguise that fact by the arts of make-up and costuming. And it was not entirely a matter of physical "slenderness"—there was also "slenderness" of voice, of understanding of the character, etc. In fact the impersonation in no way resembled the "exquisite" Rosalind of Modjeska or that of the "sweet" Neilson; and the critic might have added, that of Miss Siddons's mother, whose Rosalind was still pleasantly remembered. The reader will find that Mrs. Scott-Siddons, on April 23rd, had introduced, as a pianist, her adopted son, Henry Waller ("Seraphael"), who also failed to reach the goal of popular acclaim. Thus, within a week, the fond mother saw her two children go down to defeat; verily, it is a wise mother who can accurately estimate the abilities of her young ones, and a bitterly disappointed mother who finds that she has overestimated them.

My excuse for going at such length into this minor tragedy is that it sets me wondering again as to why Mrs. Scott-Siddons, who had begun so brightly in America in 1868–69 (she was the most frequently photographed actress of that time), should have faded so quickly from our theatre. And yet, an English woman, she spent most of her time in America; I remember passing her in the street, occasionally—a distinguished looking lady. I never saw her act or heard her read.

KOSTER AND BIAL'S, 1887–1888

Koster and Bial's Concert Hall, in 23rd Street, possibly the late-century equivalent of present-day (1941) night clubs, was presenting, for September 12th–17th, the wholly respectable attraction of Victor Herbert and his orchestra of forty. Beginning on October 3rd, "a wonderful illusion" came, in Galatea; "a statue of stone becomes endued with life." This mystery soon invaded the variety halls; it remained awhile at Koster and Bial's. The hall, for October 24th–29th, plunged deeply into "Variety," with Polly McDonald, Byrnes and Helene, Ella Raimé, Emery and Laura Russell, Ada Jones and Lillie La Verde, all old friends of ours from one hall to another, in Varietyland. November and December brought profusion of gifts, successively, in Harry M. Parker's dogs, Bellac and Mlle. Claude (necromancers), Adolphine and Camille, Allie Smith, Fanny Bloodgood, Ella Raimé, Agnes Earle, Raynor Brothers, Tom Brantford, Hattie Howard, the Venetian Troubadours, Lillie May, Ella Wesner, Whitfield (man of 100 faces), Lawlor and Thornton, and Ellen Valeys.

Those last few names bring us to December 11th (Sunday), when a special assortment of headliners included Whitfield, Ryan and Richfield, Herr Rosner ("music by electricity"), Mme. Da Acosta, Harry Bryant, Regina Enelli, Theodor Hoch and Josephine Schroeder. Sandor Rosner's Electric Storm (by music) was specially stressed for December 19th–24th; rain, hail, wind, battles, rockets and bugles were promised shivering visitors. And they might thus shiver throughout December, though, from the 26th, "Professor" E. G. Johnson mitigated with mesmerism, and Alois Ploner's Tyrolean Troupe with music of their peculiar kind. Herr Richard Pitrot, "a living panopticon" was the (to me) inexplicable attraction of January 2nd–7th. He remained a second week (then set down as a mimic), Laura Lee (balladist) and Johnson (mesmerist) also figuring in the bill. For January 16th–21st, Koster and Bial's was a mere variety hall, with Mlle. Eichlerette's monkeys, Tex Bender (cowboy fiddler), Adele Martinetti, Laura Lee, Musical Dale, Mme. Bell and her trained bear, and Rosner's "Grand Electric Demonstration." Except possibly for this last curiosity, one could have seen all these performers, at a much cheaper rate, at Pastor's or in one of the Bowery halls of "Variety"; but I am not sure that one could have bought champagne in those resorts of a more plebeian populace. Herr Grais (juggler) was here in latest January, and Baggesen (human corkscrew) in early February.

Ferguson and Mack, Stone's Mysterious Cabinet, Laura Lee, Baggesen, Musical Dale, and Bertha Rigl (sic) were leaders for February 13th–18th. February 27th–March 3rd gave the Eddys, Pitrot, Ferguson and Mack, M. G. Pettingill and his dog, Valvino (master of equipoise), Adele Martinetti, Amy Boshell, Ella Raimé, Conradi, and Th. Hoch. The announcement for March 5th–10th is strong, at least numerically—Agnes Hallock, Luigi dell' Oro, Ignatz Conradi, Sepp'l Thaler's Tyrolean Trio, Theodore Hoch, Ferguson and Mack, the Tissots, James Irwin and Adele Martinetti. March 19th began an engagement of Schwiegerling's Theatre Fantoches—106 Marionettes. The next week (March 26th–31st) listed Leonzo (juggler), Wood and Sheppard, Gregory Brothers, Queen Vassar, Polly Cusick, Amy Boshell (new), Annie Will and Theodore Hoch. The group for April 2nd–7th was big enough for Pastor's—the California Brilliants, the Archmere Sisters ("youth, beauty, grace and talent"), Hamlin and Hamlin, Ramza and Arno (grotesque gymnasts), Fontaine ("prince of wire-walkers"), Charles Eastwood, Beatrix Hamilton, and Schwiegerling's Marionettes. The next week brought Frank Bush, Isabella Ward, Emilie Peare and Tom Brantford, to join many of those cited for April 2nd. But the Vienna Lady Fencers seem to me more like Koster and Bial's; they began in early May. Later on, we were treated to the American Lady Fencers; also to Josephine Hoffman, with "spook pictures." Leroux and Wilton (gymnasts) also slithered into the bills, and June 11th advertised, I am sorry to say, James Owen O'Conor, "the great tragedian"; he was lecturing, on Sunday, June 17th, on My Alphabet and Creed; on the 18th, he and Mrs. O'Conor acted scenes from

[536]

Romeo and Juliet, Hamlet and Othello.   On Sunday, June 24th, the incorrigible one lectured on Men, Women and Things.   La Cuenca, a "lady bull-fighter," made more fierce the heat of July evenings.

MADISON SQUARE GARDEN, 1887–1888

The big Madison Square Garden opened, on August 15, 1887, for a series of popular concerts, with John Lavine as manager and Gustav Hinrichs as leader of the orchestra.   A long jump carries us to December 14th, when the New York Poultry Exchange Show opened, and cackled and clucked the hours away.

A six-days walking match was to begin, at midnight, on February 5th, and end on the 11th.   Expected participants were Rowell, Cartwright, Albert, Hughes, Hegeman, Vint, Panchot, Hazael, Hart, Noremac and "fifty others."   The twelfth annual dog show of the Westminster Kennel Club ran from February 21st to the 24th, with promise of over 1,100 dogs on exhibition.   Barnum and Bailey's Circus opened, on March 12th, with enough adjectives and promises to inflame the imagination of the unwary, but with (at least in advertisements I can, in 1941, discover) no specification of performers in the air or on the tanbark.   But a "Real Wild Moorish Caravan," was, I suppose, pretty thrilling in the week of April 2nd–7th.   In the week of April 23rd–28th, this accumulation of joy was in Brooklyn, at Sumner and Putnam Avenues.   A circus of different design was frightfully pedestrian (May 6th–12th) in a six-day Go-as-You-Please, with Littlewood, Herty, Panchot, Cartwright, Noremac, Taylor, Vint, Day, Moore, Hughes, Hegelman (*sic*), &c.   I am tired of those names and their owners.   John L. Sullivan, "premier pugilist of the world," was to start the heroes on their way.

EDEN MUSÉE, 1887–1888

As September faded into October, 1887, the Eden Musée was still stressing Munczi Lajos and his orchestra and Ajeeb, the chess-mystery.   A. LeMoult's Flower Show was fragrant and charming for the week beginning on October 27th (Thursday).   The last two weeks of Munczi Lajos began on November 21st; but Ajeeb played on; new waxen groups included Custer's Last Battle and The Chicago Anarchists.   I wonder why waxworks are so prone to horrors?

With Munczi Lajos gone, the Musée tried to console visitors with Erdelyi Naczi and his Hungarian Orchestra, beginning on December 5th.   He was still here in early January, when, incongruously enough, a Realistic Indian Wigwam was lure for the quiet country visitors to these waxen solemnities. The History of Crime, in four scenes, was the delicate morsel of January 9th–14th with Erdelyi Naczi to entrance with Hungarian music.   Of course

[537]

Ajeeb still astounded those who could and those who could not play chess.

The Crown Prince of Germany and His Family were grouped as a new offering for early February; it but anticipated the cheerful (?) exhibition of later March — Emperor Wilhelm Lying in State. German expatriates in New York probably relished, with tears, this mournful message from home. Mid-February housed an orchid show. April 2nd began Ad. Kampf's Sensational Painting, the Ante-Mortem Statement. Why was this Musée, haunt of rural visitors, becoming so morbid?

I am pleased to pass, on April 11th, to something more cheering — a Butterfly Exhibition; but, almost at once, T. W. Shields's painting, Mozart Singing His Requiem forced us back to the thought of death. The Butterfly Show still fluttered in last days of April. Ajeeb was still centre of his mystifying circle. "Professor" J. Hartl (champion fencer) and nine Viennese lady pupils, on May 14th, began a rivalry with the Vienna Lady Fencers established recently at Koster and Bial's. The Surrender of Lee to Grant prevented visitors from becoming too gay, from mid-May into June.

OLD LONDON STREET, 1887–1888

This "quaint" representation of a picturesque past was still inviting the public, in the autumn of 1887. For early September, Edith Mason impersonated Poor Jo; Rosa d'Erina sang in the later days of that month. A Sunday concert fell on October 2nd, and then was advertised, "from Mme. Tussaud's," an image of Henry Ward Beecher.

Bunnell established, at this usually unlucky 728 Broadway, his Old London Museum, advertising a seal circus, midgets, giants, marionettes and vaudeville. October 17th began the transformation. The lure for October 31st consisted of Galatea (a very popular illusion everywhere) and Burmese Hairy Mascots. There were "three auditoriums, three shows." Submarine diving and Barnum's Aztecs were advertised on November 7th. A monkey show of thirty performers was Bunnell's next clutch (November 14th) at elusive prosperity. Willowthewhisperi was the elusive lure for late December. Thereafter Bunnell's Old London Museum escaped my eye eagerly searching through desperately ragged files of the New York Herald, in the New York Public Library.

STEINWAY HALL, 1887–1888

The staid and highly esteemed Steinway Hall offered, for this season, an interesting schedule of musical and intellectual entertainment. Not, however, till November 1st did my eye catch signs, in Herald advertising, of its re-opening, and then a concert by Mme. Fursch-Madi's pupils was the not over-tempting lure. On November 3rd, the Bergen Star Concert "of coloured talent" possessed the stage.   On the 7th, R. J. De Cordova was funny, with The American Mrs. Grundy, continuing, on the 21st, with That Dog Next Door, and, on the 28th, with Courtship and Marriage — serious themes all, subjected to platform humour.   The afternoon of the 14th allowed Mons. Douillet to display a limited ability in a piano recital.   Walter J. Hall's concert, on the 17th, engaged the assistance of Ed Herrmann (violin), Adolf Hartdegen and Dora Hennings.   November 24th enriched (?) the hearing with Russell Williams, Mrs. S. D. Teal (soprano), Willie Sullivan (reciter), Ferguson (tenor), the New York Madrigal Company, and three tested vocalists, in Imogene Brown, Lizzie Macnichol and Francis Walker.

Theodore Thomas continued to give in Steinway Hall his Symphony Concerts and his Concerts for Young People; these both started in early November, but I shall discuss the events in both series as a postlude to my chronicle of the activities of the Philharmonic Society.   This treatment allows me to reach November 29h and 30th, for Homes and Fey, anti-spiritualists.   I prefer to attend the first concert of Sam Franko's String Quartet, held on December 8th, with Victor Herbert ('cello), whetting thereby my desire for his subsequent concerts, on February 3rd and February 23rd.   Promised soloists were Adele Aus der Ohe, Rafael Joseffy, Max Vogrich and Charles Kaiser.   On December 10th forgathered Carrie Hun-King, Arencibia and lesser lights.   A truly big event was the first concert (December 14th) of a series of four promulgated by Wilhelm Gericke and his superb Boston orchestra.   His programme consisted of Weber's Overture to Der Freischütz, Liszt's arrangement of a Schubert funeral march, and Beethoven's Second Symphony — again a conservative message from Boston.   The orchestra, said the Herald, "possesses much of the finish and much of the perfect mechanism of the Thomas organization and some of the vigor of the Seidl orchestra.   If in point of individuality it is inferior to either, it is superior to both in . . . the beauty of tone and the unanimity of *attaque* and bowing in the strings.   Nowhere . . . outside of Vienna, is an orchestra so efficiently equipped or managed in this department."

With the reader's permission, I will carry this Boston history through the concerts vouchsafed us.   On January 9th we were treated to Mendelssohn's overture, Melusine; Schumann's piano concerto in A minor, with Adele Aus der Ohe; selections from Siegfried and Die Götterdämmerung; and Dvorak's Symphony No. 2, in D minor.   The third concert of these distinguished visitors provided (February 8th) the Egmont overture of Beethoven; a concerto for 'cello (Schumann), played by Fritz Giese; Danse Macabre, by Saint-Saëns; and Raff's Im Walde.   The fourth concert was listed for March 14th, but the musicians were "blocked" by the snow of the great blizzard of March 12th, and were forced to defer the visit till they were thawed out.   The concert finally took place on March 26th; a fine programme included Brahms's Third Symphony; airs from Armide and The Magic Flute; Krug's Sym-

[539]

phonic Prologue to Othello, played here, on January 13th and 14th by the Philharmonic Society; and the Vorspiel and Liebestod to Tristan and Isolde, Lilli Kalisch-Lehmann (now so announced) and her Paul Kalisch (an inoffensive tenor) were the soloists. I fear there is a drop in importance, on December 16th, with the New York Banks Glee Club and Blanche Stone Barton.

The afternoon of December 22nd tried to call music-lovers from their Christmas shopping with a concert by Emanuel Moor (his first piano recital) and Jennie Dutton. On January 11th (evening) Conrad Ansorge gave his first piano recital; on the 12th, H. H. Ragan lectured on The Yosemite and the Yellowstone — far less vividly, no doubt, than the silver screen can show them in 1941. The afternoon of January 17th brought Karl Klindworth's first piano recital to those who listed to hear his Beethoven programme. But January 15th was important for a combined Arion and Liederkranz concert (a benefit for the German Hospital), with notable soloists in Lilli Lehmann, Emil Fischer, F. Remmertz, Conrad Ansorge, Otto Oesterle (flute) and Max Bendix (violin) — the best array yet recorded for that season in either concert hall. Conrad Ansorge's second recital fell on the 18th, and Karl Klindworth advertised two more, on January 25th and 31st, playing Chopin and Liszt, respectively. Marie Biro de Marion was listed for January 25th (evening), in Steinway Hall; she sang Casta Diva (very badly) and an air from Der Freischütz. With her were Emilia Cosenza; Enrico Duzensi and Bologna. Conrad Ansorge was again on the platform on February 1st. The second "soirée" of Sam Franko's New York String Quartet, on February 3rd, availed itself of the help of Rafael Joseffy.

A concert for the German Emigrant Home, on February 9th, brought in a soprano with the astonishing name of Frances Schmittbrenner, as well as F. Remmertz, Emil Schenck, F. Dulcken and the Euterpe Club of Hoboken. February 10th (evening) and 11th (afternoon) must have awakened sad thoughts in the minds of the old admirers of Italo Campanini and Etelka Gerster. No longer in their vocal prime, Gerster, in fact, a ruined coloratura, these once idolised favourites appeared, on those dates, in concert; but pleasure unalloyed was derived from the singing of Scalchi and Galassi. Also we had Signora Torricelli, Baldini, Nannetti, Corsini, and (at last) Elvira Repetto. The greeting to Gerster was an ovation. The Kneisel Quartet of Boston, so long thereafter, our cherished possession, came to Steinway Hall, on February 11th, the busy Conrad Ansorge assisting. Sam Franko's third concert of his New York String Quartet gave us, in late February, interesting soloists in Conrad Ansorge and Victor Herbert. I cannot imagine why Mme. Petrelli thought she might profit by a concert, on March 2nd; Francis Walker, Dusenzi (sic) and several nonentities assisted. I can hardly account for a concert, on March 6th, involving Frederick S. Evans (piano), Damrosch's orchestra, Helene Eschenbach (soprano), Oscar Franklin Comstock (bass) and Robert Thallon (accompanist).

March 11th brought a twanging of the Vereinigten Zither-Verein. The competing elements (there was a prize) were the Hudson City Zither Club, the Uhu Doppel Quartett Club, the Philadelphia Zither Club, Herr von der Au, the Columbia Zither Club, the Max Albert Zither Club and the Beethoven Zither Club. I am pleased not to have attended. On March 17th and 19th, Barton McGuckin and William Ludwig, from the wreckage of the National opera, appeared in a concert of Irish music, and selections from Maritana, with Amanda Fabris, Attalie Claire, and John Cheshire (harp). Alexander Strakosch read here on March 15th. The Michael Banner concert of March 24th need not detain us. Loyal Germans commemorated the death of Kaiser Wilhelm in ceremonies on March 21st; Carl Schurz, John Bigelow, the Beethoven, Arion, and Liederkranz male choruses and Seidl's orchestra participated. For March 27th, Caryl Florio advertised a concert, assisted by Ella Earle, Ansorge and the Thomas orchestra. The Germans, finishing with Metropolitan opera, foregathered, on the 29th—Otto Kemlitz, Frau Herbert-Förster, Alvary, Max Heinrich, Emil Fischer, Ansorge and Victor Herbert.

April 1st (Sunday) gave us, if not an April Fool's Day, at least something not very brilliant, in a concert by Mme. Ladowiska Murray and a group of nonentities. The 4th of April opened the hall for the annual Feis Ceoil agus Seanachas (correct this who can!) of the Gaelic Society, with Carrie Hun-King, Edward J. O'Mahoney, William Courtney and Julia O'Connell (contralto) to thrill along the Gaelic musical line, and with T. F. Kerrigan (piper) to set the audience wild with delight. Another race was in control on April 5th, when Flora Batson, "queen of song" held court, supported by the "best local talent" and the Bergen Star Company of coloured performers. A concert for the Odd Fellows Home occurred on April 8th, given by the Eichenkranz, with Arthur Claasen and Conrad Ansorge; another, by Neupert's pupils, on the 9th; one by Lucie Mawson with Marie Gramm, on the 11th, and, on the 14th, another by the whistler, Alice J. Shaw, and the singer, Arthur Oswald. Many, in those days, wondered why any audience could be gathered to hear a woman, or, for that matter, a man or a child, whistle. The Arion concert, on the 15th, had the co-operation of Louise Meisslinger. April 17th found here the Courtney Ladies' Quartet, Mrs. Minna Sites (pianist), William Courtney, Arthur Severn ('cello), and Albert Greenhalgh (accompanist). For April 18th we were invited to the Banks Glee Club Concert, and, on the 19th, to Anna Marsh's concert, there to appraise the talents of Miss M. Cary Smith, M. Louise Kellogg and Mrs. A. Lorm (sopranos, all three), Anna Russell (mezzo), Miss Mattison, Louise Hoch (youthful pianist), C. Crespi (tenor), C. Bologna (bass), and

[541]

Nahan Franko. We have heard of the last two, at least. On the 21st, the migratory Ossip Feldman read minds.

This brings us to April 22nd, when a starry host illuminated the Liederkranz concert — Lilli Lehmann, Paul Kalisch, Maud Powell, Emil Fischer, Max Treumann and Reinhold L. Herman, to conduct the orchestra. On the 23rd, Mrs. Scott-Siddons, still haunting the town which nearly twenty years before had acclaimed her, sponsored a piano recital by her adopted son, Henry Waller, whom she had, some years earlier, presented under the killing name of Seraphael — a name sufficient to blight any career. Perhaps Mrs. Scott-Siddons thought the young man could duplicate the success of Master Josef Hofmann. He did not. On this frustrated evening, his mother-elect, now a handsome, dignified lady of middle age, gave, in a somewhat old-fashioned way, excerpts from Much Ado, Macbeth and Henry V. On the 24th, Nettie Carpenter and Gertrude Griswold, interesting young women, held a concert, along with Albert Gerard Theis. The 25th united a past age, in Maria Brainerd, with a present as represented by Emily Winant, the Meigs Sisters, A. P. Burbank, Caryl Florio and the Perry Brothers (bell-ringers). Albert Ross, Anna Russell, and Maude Teale did as they could, on the 26th. On the 30th, H. R. Humphries set up his concert, with Mrs. B. S. (*sic*) Barton, E. Colletti, Michael Banner, Mc. Farlane (*sic*), and the New York Banks Glee Club. Perhaps I should have stated that, on the 28th, Francis H. Dillon and others came out for charity.

CHICKERING HALL, 1887–1888

Let us open this pleasing place, on October 2, 1887, for an illuminated lecture by Professor Frederick Mooney, on Picturesque Ireland, with singing of Moore's songs by Ella Corrigan. On October 6th a lecture by Reverend Joseph Parker, of the City Temple, London, was Victorian to a degree in subject — Job's Comforters — Sympathy from Science. During the entire week of October 10th–15th was shown the Ulysseum (by William Voegtlin) illustrating the life of General Grant; sponsored by the Boston Art Association and the Grand Army of the Republic, the exhibition was for the benefit of disabled veterans.

On October 17th, Teresina Tua, violinist, appeared in this hall, and established a temporary reputation; with her were Alexander Lambert and William H. Sherwood (pianist). The lady played again, on the 19th, with Van der Stucken's orchestra. Other concerts of Signorina Tua fell on the 21st and at two o'clock, on the 22nd; Robert Goldbeck and Lambert assisted. On October 26th, the new star was ill, and unable to perform, but she came forward again on the 28th, and in the afternoon of the 29th, Max Heinrich and Lambert now serving as coadjutors. Her "last" two concerts were listed for November 4th and the afternoon of the 5th.

MAX O'RELL

TERESINA TUA

CHARLES DICKENS, JR.

ITALO CAMPANINI

LILLI LEHMANN
AND PAUL KALISCH

ADELE AUS DER OHE

C. CAMPANINI

EVA TETRAZZINI

WILHELM GERICKE

The younger Charles Dickens read, on October 25th, from his father's works, especially Dr. Marigold and Sergeant Buzfuz's Cross-examination of Sam Weller.   In the audience for that interesting occasion were Chauncey Depew, Napoleon Sarony, General W. T. Sherman, General Horace Porter, St. Clair McKelway (editor of the Brooklyn Eagle), Felix Adler and Reverend Robert Collyer, certainly a representative group.   The Herald, on the 26th, states that the reader was good, but had no magnetism, no sacred fire.   "He had no power, as had his father and Frances Anne Kemble, of changing his voice for different characters."   It seems so absurd to include a concert, on October 30th, for the examination of pupils of Theodore John's violin school, that I pass it by to arrive, on November 1st at the first of a series of lectures by Mrs. Longshore Potts (what a name!) from Great St. James Hall, London, on Health and Disease.   The younger Dickens, on the afternoon of the 11th read from David Copperfield, and also Bob Sawyer's Party.

Campanini and his concert company, heard, on the 10th, in the Metropolitan Opera House, came, on the 12th (afternoon), to Chickering Hall, Signora Repetto still unable to perform.   Very interesting were some American concerts given by Frank Van der Stucken.   At the first, on the evening of November 15th, were tried compositions by J. K. Paine, G. E. Whiting, L. A. Russell, E. MacDowell (symphonic poem, Hamlet), and Harry Rowe Shelley.   L. A. Russell's Pastorale was sung by Ella Earle and the Schubert Society of Newark; Carl Dufft sang G. E. Whiting's The Tale of the Viking; and Henry Holden Huss played, with orchestra, his own piano rhapsody.   The second concert (November 17th) included a singing by Corinne Lawton of an arioso from F. G. Gleason's Montezuma; Arthur Whiting's playing of his own piano concerto in D minor; and Dudley Buck's cantata, The Voyage of Columbus, with H. Brown, Stuart Coleville, J. Drill, H. Reddall, and the Apollo Club of Brooklyn.   In addition, there were orchestral pieces by A. Foote, A. Bird, Silas G. Pratt and Edgar S. Kelley. The next concert (November 19th) rendered compositions by Dudley Buck, E. Thayer, F. Van der Stucken, S. P. Warren and W. W. Gilchrist; soloists included Marie Gramm, W. H. Sherwood, Arthur Voorhis, T. J. Toedt, and the choir of St. Stephen's Church.   This impresses me as a remarkable demonstration, for that early date, of interest in American musicianship.   A fourth concert, on the afternoon of the 22nd, gave works by G. Chadwick, J. Beck, W. Burr, J. Paine, E. Sherwood, H. Rietzel and A. Foote; Effie Stewart, W. H. Sherwood and the Beethoven Quartet Club were to interpret; a fifth, on the 24th, honoured compositions by G. T. Strong, H. W. Parker, and E. Guirand interpreted by Henrietta Beebe, Charlotte Walker, Hattie Clapper, Max Heinrich, J. A. Preisch and F. Jameson.

On November 18th, Max O'Rell (Paul Blouet), author of John Bull and His Island, lectured, at Chickering Hall, on John Bull and Jacques Bonhomme. On the 21st, the Carri Brothers, with Miss B. Bracewell (soprano) and C. Bareuther ('cello), gave a usual concert, and, on the 25th, the Beethoven String Quartet, Ella Earle and Alexander Lambert held a concert. In aid of international copyright appeared, on November 28th and 29th, a number of American authors, reading from their own works, with James Russell Lowell presiding. The authors promised were George William Curtis, R. H. Stoddard, Mark Twain, Edward Eggleston, Charles Dudley Warner, W. D. Howells, Frank R. Stockton, George W. Cable and H. C. Bunner — names that recall the palmy days of Harper's and the Century Magazine at their very best. I go back to the afternoon of November 25th, when Major Pond presented, at Chickering Hall, Bram Stoker, M.A., so long the able manager of Henry Irving; Stoker lectured on Abraham Lincoln, as Viewed by an Englishman.

Edwin Klahre, on December 1st, invited with a piano recital; and, in those days, Ludwig Einstein's concert called for aid on Marie Gramm, Holst Hansen and the Beethoven String Quartet. The next night (December 2nd) was devoted to the Arimathean Society, which availed itself of the valued services of Ella Earle, Maud Morgan, Francis Walker, the New York University Glee Club, F. Taft (organist) and J. S. Burdett. December 7th heard the 156th concert of the Grand Conservatory of Music. But just two nights before (December 5th), the Amicitia Society made a bad failure, even though Blanche Stone Barton and Caryl Florio assisted. According to the Herald, the instrumentalists groped and fumbled, and the conductor merely beat time. Students' debuts were now in the air. Fanny Hunt's matinée, on December 8th, introduced Ellie Long, a contralto from Canada and a pupil of the once highly esteemed Clara Brinckerhoff. "The lady is studying for the concert and operatic stage," quoth the advertisement, "and being young, with a charming stage presence, is very likely to make a very favorable impression. Managers are invited to attend." I quote this killing notice merely for its human interest. Alas! Ellie never attained, at least under the name of Long. On the 9th, the Reverend Joseph Parker, of London, lectured on the Right Honourable William E. Gladstone, M.P., the Man, the Statesman, His Opponents and Allies. I should like to have heard that talk.

Instead, I go back, with dutiful interest, as with pleasure, to the permanently stationed Mendelssohn Glee Club, whose season's activities I shall, as usual, and perhaps reprehensibly, gather into a posy. On December 6th, they called to their help Gertrude Griswold and Teresina Tua, two women in a garden of mere men; on February 14th, they were assisted by Marie Gramm, Max Heinrich and Conrad Ansorge. In the bill, on that latter occasion, was Song in May, by Reinhold L. Herman (sic), to words by Lord Thurlow. Lilli Lehmann-Kalisch, so announced, sang on April 17th, in R. Pohl's Nordlicht, in a Chopin-Viardot Mazourka and in Mädchenlied, by

[544]

Meyer Helmund. I revert to the second concert of F. and H. Carri, which fell on December 13th; on the 14th, Max O'Rell read from his works, in French, before a small audience. And, on the 19th, Munczi Lajos, known to all frequenters of the Eden Musée, deserted the world of wax for a world of real people—if they attended.

The Rubinstein Club met, on December 15th, in concert, with Annie Louise Cary, Mrs. Stone Barton, Fannie Hirsch and Mrs. Barron Anderson in the chorus. The Beethoven String Quartet and Maud Morgan also appeared. The first concert of the second season of the Gounod Choral Society gave, on the 21st, Mendelssohn's Forty-second Psalm. Under the caption of Italian Activities will be found account of a concert on the 22nd, for the cholera victims in Messina; Tua and De Anna among the artists. On December 29th, the clock was set back so far that it seemed not to be able to strike. Ilma di Murska, that glittering songstress of the '70s, appeared in concert at Chickering Hall, assisted by some of the artists who had come to sing with poor Etelka Gerster; these were Bjorksten, Carbone, De Anna, Nettie Carpenter and Neuendorff. Eugenie de Roode (pianist) also was promised. According to the Herald review, Di Murska still was pretty good, though of course the glittering brilliancy of her prime was not in evidence.

During the autumn of 1887, the Reverend Dr. Maynard gave ten lectures, illustrated, on Norway and Sweden, Holland, Spain, the Holy Land, France, London, Rome and Scotland; the first of these occurred on October 5th. Today (1941) we can but wonder if some of those free countries ever existed.

From mid-December the National Conservatory of Music advertised that it had invited Henry T. Finck, musical critic of the then highly esteemed Evening Post, to give four lectures in Chickering Hall. Mr. Finck, who took himself and Wagner very seriously, was to speak (and did) on How Composers Work (January 7th); Chopin, the Greatest Genius of the Pianoforte (February 24th); Italian and German Vocal Style (March 14th); and Music and Morals (April 18th). These solemn conclaves I here dismiss with the notice now served on the reader. In Finck's day, though he frequently angered us, we nevertheless read his lucubrations, perhaps for the pleasure of disagreeing with him. On January 11th, George Becker lectured in this hall, on Sir Walter Raleigh—always a fruitful theme. The third Carri concert was listed for January 17th. Mrs. Lawrence Brown, M.D., gave, on January 18th, "by request and free," a lecture on Christian Science. More musical, on the 21st, was a Scottish concert provided by Hattie J. Clapper, Mrs. J. McPherson, Francis Walker and Fred Jameson, with Andrew Carnegie presiding. The afternoon before, Charles Dickens, with a "magnificent audience," read from his father's works. A testimonial to Mrs. M. Appleton Baker, whose fame has not descended to 1941, re-

[545]

cruited, on January 23rd, the services of Anna Bulkley Hills, Alice J. Shaw (the whistler), Cappa's Seventh Regiment Band, Arthur Oswald and Miss Griswold (Gertrude?). Arthur Voorhis, on the 24th, played the piano, associates in the programme being Carlotta Pinner (soprano) and Van der Stucken's orchestra.

Chickering Hall now became very busy. Charles Dickens, the younger, read once more on January 27th (afternoon) and again on February 3rd. On the evening of the 27th, appeared Miss Sedohr Rhodes, a young lady from the far West, who, according to preliminary announcements, could "handle a rifle, and ride a mustang as well as she can sing an aria." She tried to shoot high notes brilliantly, in the *Caro Nome* and Eckert's Echo Song, without disturbing, as it proved, memories of Jenny Lind or Adelina Patti. She surrounded herself with genuine talent in Lizzie Macnichol, Albert King, Carl Dufft, the New York Beethoven String Quartet and Agramonte. On January 28th, Giuseppe di Grandi, not unknown to us, gave a concert, with C. Bologna, Klahre and others of but little note; and George Riddle read, on the afternoons of January 31st, February 2nd and 6th, a new sketch, Boston Fads, figuring in the programme. The evening of the 31st brought the second concert of the New York Vocal Union. On February 3rd (evening?) le Capitaine Voyer held his first concert, with Lizzie Macnichol and Van der Stucken's orchestra; he played the piano, and not so very well. The afternoon of February 7th found Master W. C. Macfarlane giving his fourth organ recital, Mrs. Thom (piano) and Mrs. Watson-Doty (singer) assisting. February 9th brought Henrietta Beebe and W. H. Lawton, whom she had recently married, in a programme of English songs, which they could render beautifully. Vocally, Mrs. Beebe-Lawton was declared to be the better half of the case. A February concert, at this time and place, presented W. A. Rabock (violin), Chr. Bareuther ('cello), John White (organ) and Caroline Schmidt (contralto), with Victor Schwarz (accompanist). Doubtless, then, as now (1941) regular concert-goers took anything, especially if it was free. On February 11th, Company F, Seventh Regiment, regaled itself with a minstrel show. Le Capitaine Voyer gave piano recitals, on February 10th and 14th. It would seem that Charles Dickens, if not so great a reader as was his famous father, must have had ability beyond what we have been tutored into believing he had; at any rate he advertised four more readings in Chickering Hall, on the afternoons of February 17th, March 2nd and 9th, and the evening of the 9th. At four o'clock, on the 24th of February, H. T. Finck lectured on Chopin, the Greatest Genius of the Pianoforte; in the evening of that day the Princeton Glee and Banjo Clubs gave an entirely different idea of musical genius.

For five Thursday afternoons, beginning on February 23rd, G. W. Morgan played the organ, and his daughter, Maud, beautifully played the harp. Holst Hansen assisted at the first recital; Alice Geraldine Koller, on March

[546]

8th; William Courtney on the 15th.   Marie Dausz, whom I had unchiv-
alrously forgotten, appeared with her pupils, on February 25th, in this tol-
erant hall.   As one who never thrilled to the twanging of a banjo, I record,
without enthusiasm, a banjo "tournament," which, on the 27th, enlisted
Reuben Brooks, the Columbia College Banjo Club, and many others.   Those
I have mentioned won the prizes—the Columbia Club by default—no com-
petitors.   Something stimulating to (dare I say?) a higher musical taste
came on March 2nd, with the first of three orchestral concerts conducted
by the very devotedly admired Anton Seidl.   Like Arturo Toscanini of years
later, Seidl desired to pass at times from the field of opera to that of the
concert-podium.   His programme for March 2nd embraced the "first and
only performance in America" (I suppose he meant up to that time) of
Wagner's Symphony; the overture and finale of Don Juan; and the Vorspiel
to Parsifal.   In the Don Juan (or Don Giovanni) selection were to appear
Lilli Lehmann, Frl. Brandt, Frau Seidl-Kraus, Emil Fischer and Paul
Kalisch (his début).   The illness of Frl. Brandt caused a substitution of the
useful, if never distinguished, Ida Klein.   The second of Seidl's concerts
provided (March 16th) Beethoven's Emperor Concerto (played with W. H.
Sherwood), Bruckner's Fourth Symphony ("first time in America"), and
the Tannhäuser music, as enlarged for the Paris opera, and with Kalisch
and Lilli Kalisch-Lehmann as soloists.   The Götterdämmerung Funeral
March commemorated the death of the Kaiser.   Frau Kalisch-Lehmann,
as indispensable for high-class concerts as for the opera of 1887–88, was
again prominent in Seidl's last concert (April 6th), along with Kalisch (who
ever trailed in the triumphal career of his great wife), Maud Powell and
Alexander Lambert.

In my desire to group these Seidl concerts, I have missed several smaller
functions to which I now dutifully return.   On March 7th, Paula Buchheim
(a pianist twelve years old), and L. G. Schmidt (violinist, also of twelve
years in this vale of tears), with the adult Lizzie Macnichol, held the hall
and, one hopes, an audience.   On the 8th, the Beethoven Quartet gave its
last concert, Adelaide Foresman (contralto) and W. H. Sherwood helping to
assuage the grief of parting.   Perhaps Lent interfered with concert-giving;
not till March 13th did music's sweet voice again call us to Chickering Hall,
and then for the not unusual ministrations of the Carri Brothers (their fifth
recital).   On the 23rd, we were called to the not overwhelming excitement
of Edwin Klahre's second piano recital.   On March 26th gathered in the
hall Charles Roberts, Jr., Francis Walker (bass), Gustave Schmidt (boy
violinist), and the Knickerbocker Quartet.   But the afternoon of April 5th
should have brought a flutter in the dove-cotes.   Major J. B. Pond, our
great provider of lecturers, announced, for that date, "the first and only lecture in America" by Mrs. Ashton W. Dilke, "best-known advocate of woman's
rights in Great Britain, editor of the Sunday Advocate, and most successful

business woman in London." Naturally she spoke on Women in Politics in England. After that outbreak of feminism, four men, doubtless of the Pond office, gave him a testimonial, on the afternoon of the 6th, the four purveyors of masculinity being Max O'Rell, J. Whitcomb Riley, George W. Cable and Bill Nye. On April 9th, Whitney Mockridge's concert enlisted Jennie Dutton, Emily Winant and Maud Powell, the last named replacing Ovide Musin, ill.

The Carri Brothers held the hall on April 10th. On the 11th, the Gounod Choral Society gave its second concert, singing By Babylon's Wave, Miss Le Clair, Mme. Salvotti, Colletti and Silbernagel assisting. The evening of the 16th was dedicated to Edward J. O'Mahoney's concert, with assistants in Minnie Dilthey, Jessamine Hallenbeck (soprano), Julia O'Connell and Inez Caresi (harpists), the Courtney Ladies' Quartet, Courtney and Elder (tenors), Loughran (baritone) and Victor Harris (accompanist). The Orpheus Glee Club was announced for April 19th, with the New York Philharmonic Club to assist. On the 28th, came an exhibition by Professor J. Hartl, "fencing champion of Austria and Germany," with nine Viennese "lady pupils." Soon, we remember, these prodigies were exhibiting in variety halls. Fanny Hunt, on April 30th, recited Richard II from memory, proving, I suppose, that it could be done; Ida Hall did something, in the same programme to uplift the public joy. On that same 30th, in a different session, a concert to benefit St. George's Seaside Home was enriched (April 30th) by the art of Nettie Carpenter, Gertrude Griswold, Virginia Rider, and Anna Bulkley Hills. On May 1st, Melton Prior, war artist of the Illustrated London News, spoke on the Soudan War, the Nile Expedition and the Defeat of Baker Pasha; 63 of his sketches were shown. The Yale Glee and Banjo Clubs, on May 4th, doubtless seemed wonderful to susceptible maidens; and, on the 8th, Giuseppe di Grandi's concert enlisted Maud Dixon, Frida Seitz-Meyer and Sofie Zorn. On the 11th, friendly lodges tendered a benefit to J. Leslie Gossin. May 9th, I forgot to note, found Biro de Marion, that failure in Metropolitan opera, again attempting the concert platform; with her were Minnie Strielsheimer, Walker (baritone) and Mrs. Coventry Walker (reciter). I wonder if any one bought tickets; and who paid expenses, including rent? And de Grandi is now di Grandi.

By a lapse in chronology I failed to record in proper sequence a concert on May 2nd, for the Homeopathic Medical College and Free Hospital, at which appeared Mrs. C. M. Raymond (Annie Louise Cary?), the Berkeley Quartet, the Schirmer Quartet, Francis F. Powers, Emily Winant, men from the Mendelssohn Glee Club, women from the Rubinstein Club, and Richard Hoffman. May 14th brought to Chickering Hall Philip Phillips with his illuminated Around the World in a Chariot of Song. He was to remain a week. In the afternoon of the 19th, Campanini and Eva Tetrazzini tried, in concert, to recuperate for the dreadful financial loss of Otello. The 22nd invited to the farewell of William Ludwig.   How the defeated opera singers had taken refuge in Chickering Hall!   In the Ludwig concert appeared Gertrude Griswold, Emily Winant, Charles Bassett, Vetta, M. Bauer, Hartdegen, McFarlane (*sic*) and Dulcken—a goodly list.   With the Ladies' Health Protective Association meeting there, on May 24th, I leave the hall for 1887–88; Judge Charles P. Daly was to preside on that serious occasion.

MUSIC AND MISCELLANY (NEW YORK), 1887–1888

Having exhausted the attraction of the beaches and other summer delights (1887), we are now ready for the incitement of indoor entertainments. Steinway and Chickering Halls have drawn the greatest stars and specialists, but churches and less ostentatious auditoriums were not without inducements of greater or less allure.

The panorama of The Merrimac and the Monitor was an inheritance from the summer, and lasted far into the winter.   Blind Tom, on Monday, September 26, 1887, gave the first of four concerts, "since his freedom." On October 2nd, Alexander Strakosch, in Irving Hall, recited the Marc Antony scene from Julius Cæsar; on October 12th, he rendered the first three acts of Hamlet; on the 10th, the park scene from Mary Stuart. Christ on Calvary, by Munkacsy, opened on October 14th, at the 23rd Street Tabernacle (once Salmi Morse's Temple), and drew admiring witnesses for weeks thereafter.   Charles Dickens, the younger, read, on October 29th, at the Metropolitan Opera House Concert Hall, selections from David Copperfield falling to his lure.

Religious or moral-religious art seemed to attract, at that time, in gay New York.   The Yandell Gallery, Fifth Avenue and 19th Street, opened, on November 9th, a protracted exhibition of Piloty's The Wise and Foolish Virgins.   On November 16th, the Reverend Sam S. Small, a Southern evangelist, gave a "suggestive" lecture on Christ on Calvary, at the 23rd Street Tabernacle.   More lively, doubtless, was the concert, on November 23rd, at Mendelssohn Hall (55th Street, near Fifth Avenue), of the Williams College Glee and Banjo Clubs; or the performances of Blind Tom, on December 1st, 2nd and 3rd, at Harlem Hall, 125th Street.   But Christ on Calvary and The Wise and Foolish Virgins were joined, on November 14th, by Otto Wolf's painting, Christ and the Adulteress, shown at 176 Fifth Avenue, and in early December, at the American Art Galleries, by Mackart's painting, Diana's Hunting Party; 16 East 14th Street, brought another, on January 2nd—Mackart's Five Senses.   Was Munich becoming psychopathic in art?   Let us forget this morbidity by attending, in Mendelssohn Hall, 55th Street, near Sixth Avenue, the jolly concert, on November 23rd, by the Williams College Glee and Banjo Clubs—nothing psychopathic there!

Christmas joy was rampant that year.   Frank A. Robbins's Circus began in the American Institute Building, verily a Christmas gift better than the contents of the Christmas stocking to good little boys; it was at first advertised as "a Winter Circus, with fifty beautiful lady artists." By January 2nd, Robbins was stressing Charles W. Fish, Mlle. Tournour, and Mlle. Alma ("Human Fly"), Mlle. de Granville ("rises to a giddy height, hanging by her teeth"), El Niño Eddie, and Mlle. Dubsky's Waltz in Mid-air.   Surely this is a list of aerial wonders, and I hope none of them came unexpectedly to the tanbark.   Robbins, whom I associate with his Railroad Circus, in summer, in Long Island retreats, continued at the American Institute well into January.   Philoppoteaux's panorama, The Battle of Gettysburg, began on December 24th, at Fourth Avenue and 19th Street, what was to prove a prodigiously lengthy stay, throughout the season of 1888–89. Let me take the reader into the great out-doors, on any afternoon or evening from the 24th, for fun on the Toboggan Slide at the New York Driving Club (Fleetwood Park, 165th Street and Jerome Avenue), in January, or for skating, on Van Cortlandt Lake, "only fifteen minutes from New York," at 155th Street.   And an American Winter Carnival, at Fleetwood Park, was advertised in the Herald (January 16th–21st), with tobogganing, skating, a sleigh race, dancing, electric lights and fun—surely enough to set the blood tingling, in 1888.   Returning to art, I may say that, on January 23rd, began the last two weeks of Diana's Hunting Party.   In that period Walter Damrosch gave, in the Metropolitan Opera House Assembly Rooms, a lecture at the piano—a thing he could do extremely well.   And, on January 30th, Daniel Dougherty, at Cooper Union, delivered a lecture on The Stage.   In those same Assembly Rooms of the Metropolitan, Jerome Hopkins, whom I had pleasantly forgotten, gave, on February 4th, a Young Philharmonic Concert.

I am taking the reader through a veritable hodge-podge.   With pleasure I call his attention to a series of free organ recitals, at the First Presbyterian Church, Fifth Avenue and 12th Street.   Beginning on February 13th, players would be R. Huntington Woodman, Gerrit Smith and Frank Taft; soloists promised were Mrs. Gerrit Smith, Bessie Grovesteen, Jennie Dutton, Francis F. Powers and T. J. Toedt, a veritable gift.   The Männerchor Society's dance, on February 22nd, at the Lexington Avenue Opera House, doubtless belongs to the German story, as, indeed, does the Purim Ball, on February 15th, at the Harlem Casino.   I had hoped that I should never again be exercised by walking matches.   Alas! here is a Twenty-four Hour Go as You Please, February 21st–22nd, at the American Institute; promised contestants were George Cartwright (champion of England), Daniel Herty (of Boston), D. Bennett (Toronto), George Noremac, Robert Vint, Archie Sinclair (ex-amateur champion of England), Sam Gay (of England), William G. Keefe (ex-amateur champion of America) and 31 others.   Gentler airs breathed through the concert at the New York College of Music, given, near the beginning of March, with Anna Lankow, Alexander Lambert, Gustav Dannreuther and A. Hartdegen.   And Gettysburg and Christ on Calvary were still here in March.   After a lapse of more than a year, the Amateur Comedy Club re-emerged, on February 28th, at the Berkeley Lyceum, with a double bill comprising John M. Morton's play, A Husband to Order, and the farce, A Little Savage.   In the former appeared Evert Jansen Wendell (I wish he were alive now, in 1941, to read his name in my book), H. Chauncey, Jr., Stephen G. Williams, T. V. Boynton, Frederic D. Phillips, Elita Proctor Otis and Georgie and Caroline Shippen; in the latter piece were Gabriel Gordon Cleather, Robert S. Minturn, Frederic R. Satterlee, Charles E. Boynton, Mrs. Charles A. Doremus and Elita Proctor Otis.   Again I feel as if I were reading in the Social Register of New York.

On March 5th, the Clan-na-Gael celebrated, at Cooper Institute, Robert Emmet's birthday; vocal and instrumental music made solemn the function. Kitty Berger, "harp and zither virtuoso," gave, on March 24th, a "soirée musicale," in the ballroom of the Hotel Brunswick.   On March 22nd, at 11 A. M., Harriet Webb read selections from Burns, at 12 East 23rd Street; in that same blustery period, Charles F. Underhill read in the Fourth Presbyterian Church, in 34th Street, scenes from David Copperfield, quite as if the son of the author had not done the same thing frequently in our vicinity. I rather dislike to call attention to the haphazard proceedings of April.   The 23rd Street Tabernacle, beginning on April 4th, exhibited Paul Philoppoteaux's Famous American Battles, Noted Places Abroad, and Scenes in General Grant's Life.   Rating pictures by size, the management assured us that each painting was 28 by 19 feet; as if, forsooth, one judged of the beauty of a statue by its weight.   On April 11th and 12th, Carl Marwig repeated, in the Metropolitan Opera House, his spectacle, A Fashing Thursday in Venice.   Amusing, I suspect, must have been something like The Taming of the Shrew, produced on April 5th, for the benefit of sick members of the National Guard, at the Ninth Regiment Armoury.   Francis G. Landon was Petruchio, George M. Boynton Baptista, and Edward Fales Coward Katharine, with, in other parts, W. D. Preston, W. P. Clagett, W. A. Dennison, J. Wray Cleveland, H. W. Banks, Jr., and Samuel W. Sterritt.   In the afternoon of the 5th, Columbia College and New York played baseball, all in youthful vigour vying.

We continue in the strain of youthful fooling.   We all like college boys and love to humour them in their fun-making; hence I chronicle with delight two contiguous presentations of that order.   On April 6th, at the Berkeley Lyceum the Class of '89, Columbia College (my own class, by the way) presented Captain Kidd, or, the Peerless Peeress and the Haughty Pirate, the cast embracing Robert Cornell Sands, Edwin M. Post, Frank Chickering Warren, Tracy Hyde Harris, Edward Fales Coward, Robert Lee Morrell, George Austin Morrison, Julian Gerard Buckley, Henry Brundage

Culver, Eugene J. O'Sullivan and Thomas Hugh Kelly. The ballet was led by O. H. P. La Farge, R. H. Hoadley, Theodore Havemeyer, Jr., J. B. and W. A. Stein and H. B. Taylor. It is a pleasure to write those names, so representative of New York and Columbia College, in 1888. The Harvard Hasty Pudding Club, on April 9th, presented at the Berkeley Lyceum, Constance, or, the Beau, the Belle and the Bandit. The Herald lists no actors, but enrolls for posterity a fashionable audience. An amateur performance of As You Like It, postponed from April 12th to the 27th, was to have had Edward Fales Coward as Orlando, Victoria Siddons (daughter of Mrs. Scott-Siddons, and "great-grand-daughter of Sarah Siddons") as Rosalind, J. K. Hackett as Touchstone, and Beverley Sitgreaves as Celia. After all, it was not given; the owners of the Berkeley Lyceum had not complied with the regulations about public buildings. On April 23rd, however, the Berkeley Lyceum was expected to open for the second annual "classic" banjo recital of A. D. Cammeyer, Theodor Bjorksten and the Madrigal Quartet assisting. I go back to April 18th, when, at Mendelssohn Hall, Lillie Berg's concert enlisted Anna Bulkley Hills, Mrs. Edward Lauterbach, Anna Winch, Ovide Musin, S. B. Mills, Arthur Oswald and Emilio Agramonte. Thus we approached the end of the season.

On April 21st, 27th and May 5th, Juliet Corson was to give, in the Assembly Rooms, Metropolitan Opera House, lectures on Cooking by Gas. By a kind of congruity, Jacob A. Riis, on May 10th, showed at Association Hall, How the Other Half Lives, calling on the stereopticon for proof of his points. Miss Corson travelled to West End Hall, 125th Street, there to show Harlem ladies, on May 26th, how to Cook by Gas.

The open air now summoned us. On May 30th, at Erastina, Staten Island, Buffalo Bill's Wild West began an all-summer séance. On that day, Gilmore and the 22nd Regiment Band marched, in New York, with the Regiment, and then returned to Manhattan Beach, for their nightly musical fanfare. There, too, Pain's fiery spectacle of 1666, The Great Fire of London, sent flaming rockets into the sky and thrills down the spines of susceptible onlookers. Baseball, then as now, led fanatic-religiose enthusiasts to the Polo Grounds. A Battery Park Concert, by Bayne's 69th Regiment Band, must not be overlooked, in planning for June 1st. And Sunday, June 10th, listed a concert at the West Brighton Beach Hotel (late Paul Bauer's). Levy was there, on June 16th and later. June 13th found Feldman mind-reading in the Free Baptist Church, West 25th Street. On June 23rd, Blondin, after twenty-seven years, did his dangerous exercises in air, at St. George, Staten Island. But, before that date, Mlle. Mathilde de Nogueiras, daughter of the late Portuguese minister, gave, on the afternoon of June 11th, a concert in the Hoffman House ball-room. Arthur Joseph wrestled with an Italian air or two, but went down in defeat.

At Madison Avenue and 59th Street was set up, in mid-June, a panorama of Jerusalem and the Crucifixion, causing us to wonder again at the religious tendency in so many pictures exhibited that year in New York. St. George, Staten Island, forges to the front. Beginning on June 25th, Imre Kiralfy's Nero, or, the Fall of Rome, caused wonder and amaze; a bad storm delayed the opening, from a date originally announced. Blondin continued on Tuesdays, Thursdays and Saturdays; and, of course, Erastina still boasted of Buffalo Bill's Wild West. Seidl, on June 30th, began nightly orchestral concerts at Brighton Beach, which then, as now, made me feel that he was cheapening his great fame; but a man must live, and the concerts were of fine quality. And we must not forget Gilmore, at Manhattan Beach, and the elaborate fiery Taking of New Orleans at Brighton Beach. Perhaps we may escape from this suburban activity by attending the June meeting (June 19th, 20th, 21st, 22nd, 23rd, 26th, 27th, 28th, 29th, 30th) of the Coney Island Jockey Club. And, periodically, one need go no further than Tompkins Square, where Eben's Military Band poured forth brazen defiance to the heat.

PHILHARMONIC SOCIETY, NEW YORK, 1887–1888

Our oldest, indeed our venerable, orchestra began, on November 18th and 19th, under the direction of Theodore Thomas, the scene of operations being the Metropolitan Opera House. Auditors were regaled with, in order, Eine Faust Overture (Wagner); Beethoven's Fifth Symphony (played two weeks earlier by the Symphony Society); Concerto for violin, op. 46 (Rubinstein), played by the returning Camilla Urso; and Festklänge (by Liszt). Thomas conducted the Fifth Symphony without a score. December 9th and 10th brought the rehearsal and the final performance, respectively, of Beethoven's Leonore Overture, No. 2; an aria from Euryanthe, sung by Emil Fischer; Brahms's Second Symphony; songs by Schumann, with Gertrude Griswold; and the overture to Die Meistersinger. For January 13th and 14th, the Philharmonic presented Suite in D major, by Bach; Symphonic Prologue to Othello, by Krug; Joseffy, in Tchaikowsky's Piano Concerto, opus 23; and Schumann's Symphony in D minor.

The fourth pair of concerts, February 10th and 11th, gave Bargiel's Prometheus; Emil Fischer in a recitative and aria from The Creation; Concerto for string orchestra, in G minor, by Bach; Schubert's Der Wanderer, sung by Fischer; and the Eroica of Beethoven. March 9th and 10th invited with Schumann's Manfred Overture; the Siegfried Idyl of Wagner; Adele Aus der Ohe, in Beethoven's Emperor concerto; and Dvorak's Symphony No. 1, in D major. The season closed (April 20th and 21st) with Beethoven's Pastoral Symphony; Recitative and Air, from Fidelio (sung by Lilli Lehmann); Symphonic Variations, op. 27, by Nicode; Gretchen am Spinnrad (sung by Lehmann); overture to Tannhäuser; and, in honour

[553]

of the recently deceased president of the society, Chopin's Funeral March, at the beginning of the concert.

THEODORE THOMAS CONCERTS, 1887–1888

The reader knows that Thomas could not confine his activities to the Philharmonic Society of New York and that of Brooklyn. Now that his connection with the National Opera Company had ceased, he devoted his attention to a larger number of concerts, with his orchestra, in the receptive auditorium of Steinway Hall.

The first of his symphony concerts, so called, fell on November 8th, preceded by a rehearsal, on the afternoon of November 3rd. A rich programme provided Beethoven's Coriolan overture; Symphonic Concerto, No. 1 in E minor (Chopin-Tausig) played by Joseffy; Introduction and closing scene, Tristan und Isolde; and Wagner's Kaisermarsch. The first Young People's Concert came on the afternoon of Saturday, November 12th. The second symphony concert (November 22nd) with the preceding rehearsal, on the 17th, gave compositions by Haydn, Mozart, J. K. Paine and Massenet, chief feature being the Romeo and Juliet of Berlioz; Gertrude Griswold was soloist. The third rehearsal (December 1st) had Emil Fischer as soloist, and furnished music by Schubert, Wagner, Chopin-Thomas, and Liszt. The concert came on the 6th. Victor Herbert was soloist at the third Young People's Concert, on December 10th. The fourth symphony rehearsal, on December 15th, with the concert on the 20th, enjoyed the skilful playing of Adele Aus der Ohe. I regret that I did not hear very many of these performances.

Matinées, on January 12th and 14th, provided the eminently satisfactory Emily Winant; the 14th was in the series for young people. The Thomas Symphony Concert, January 17th and 19th, included Preludio to Franchetti's Asrael, one day to be disastrously produced by the Metropolitan Opera; Mendelssohn's concerto for violin, Opus 64, played by Mme. Urso; Brahms's Fourth Symphony; Fantasia (Liebesnacht, by Philip Scharwenka); and Liszt's Tasso. Certainly 1887–88 heard some good music. For the rehearsal, on February 2nd, Carl Baermann was soloist. At the Symphony Concert on February 14th, Victor Herbert played Rubinstein's Concerto, No. 2, for 'cello. I wonder if Herbert had any vision of his future fame? On the 23rd, Mme. Herbert-Förster, wife, as we know, of Victor Herbert, and Conrad Ansorge were soloists. A request performance for March 10th presented numbers by Schubert, Moszkowski, Goldmark, Volkmann, Wagner and Liszt. On March 15th we had Giulia Valda and Michael Banner. On March 31st appeared Miss M. Beardsley and John Cheshire (harp). The twelfth and last public rehearsal of the Thomas orchestra came on the afternoon of April 5th; Mme. Fursch-Madi (with *Ah! perfido*) and Max Heinrich appeared, as they did on April 10th, when the concert was repeated for the season's farewell.

SYMPHONY SOCIETY, 1887–1888

Under the direction of the young, energetic and ambitious Walter Damrosch, the Symphony Society began its season with a rehearsal and concert, respectively, on November 4th and 5th, the Metropolitan Opera House still serving as haven.   The programme included Dvorak's dramatic overture, Husitska; a Concerto, No. 4, for piano and orchestra (Litolff), with Camille Gurikx (*sic*) as soloist; ballet music from Idomoneo (Mozart); songs, by Schubert and Schumann, with Johann Elmblad; and Beethoven's Fifth Symphony.   For November 25th and 26th, Damrosch treated us to Eugene d'Albert's Symphony, No. 1; an air from Don Giovanni, with Max Alvary, who utterly lacked the vocal elegance required for Mozart; Introduction and Serenade, from Namouna (Lalo); Ballade, Siegfried's Sword (by Leopold Damrosch), sung by Alvary; and three Romantic Overtures (Der Freischütz, The Flying Dutchman, and Berlioz's The Corsair)—certainly a fresh and interesting programme.   On December 16th and 17th, Brahms (evidently a favourite with Damrosch) was represented by his Third Symphony, and Dvorak by the first performance of a new Terzetto; Fannie Bloomfield Zeisler played a piano concerto by Henselt, and Beethoven's First Symphony closed the bill.   Even at that early stage of his career, Walter Damrosch was a remarkable programme maker.

For January 6th and 7th, he provided Schubert's Ninth Symphony (in C); Camilla Urso, in the Beethoven violin concerto; the March of the Pilgrims, from Berlioz's Harold Symphony; and La Russie, a symphonic poem by Rubinstein.   January 27th and 28th also provided a very interesting programme: Irish Symphony (by Stanford); Adagio and Le Rouet d'Omphale (by Saint-Saëns); Overture to a Comedy (Smeta—*sic*); Concerto for Piano and Orchestra (Rubinstein), played with Adele Aus der Ohe; and Goldmark's overture Sakuntala.   And the offering of February 24th and 25th, sounds attractive today, more than half a century later: Overture to King Lear (Berlioz); Liszt's O Salutaris, for female voices; Psalm for mezzo-soprano, female chorus, orchestra and organ (Liszt); and the Vorspiel to Die Meistersinger.   Marianne Brandt and the ladies' chorus of the Oratorio Society assisted.

ORATORIO SOCIETY, 1887–1888

The second of Walter Damrosch's interests, inherited from his father— the Oratorio Society—began its season, on November 30th–December 1st, with the usual rehearsal and final performance, respectively, of Mozart's

Requiem Mass, and the third part of Schumann's Faust; Ella Earle (a lovely singer), Marie Groebl, Minnie Dilthey, Charles Kaiser, von Milde and Elmblad assisted. Of course the Christmastide Messiah came to expectation. On December 28th and 29th, the soloists announced were Mme. Fursch-Madi, Gertrude Griswold, Sarah Barron Anderson (for the 28th) replaced (for the 29th) by Gertrude Edmands, Max Alvary and Max Heinrich. A terrible disappointment awaited those who hear music through the eyes; the handsome Alvary failed to appear, and the not over-pulchritudinous W. H. Lawton took his place. The St. Matthew Passion appropriately for the Lenten season, was heard, on March 7th and 8th, Ella Earle, Emily Winant, William Dennison, Emil Fischer and Max Heinrich seeming, to the Herald critic, to fall short of the nobility of the work.

New York Philharmonic Club, 1887–1888

The first concert of the season of the New York Philharmonic Club brought in, as assistants, Jennie Dutton and Richard Hoffman. November 22nd was the date, and Chickering Hall the place. On January 3rd, the assistants were S. B. Mills and Mrs. Emil Gramm. A new sextet by F. Gernsheim figured in the programme. The third concert fell, on February 7th, in the same hall; soloists were Nelly Stevens (piano), Whitney Mockridge, and Richard Arnold; and the fourth, in March, called in Francis Fischer Powers and William H. Sherwood. A zealous search through the Annals will find this organisation supporting concert-givers in both Manhattan and Brooklyn.

CHAPTER IX

BROOKLYN, WILLIAMSBURGH, GREENPOINT, QUEENS, STATEN ISLAND, 1887-1888

WE must honour the theatres of Brooklyn and Williamsburgh, even though visiting them will usually reward us only by repetition of plays and musical shows which we have seen to the point of tedium in one New York theatre after another.

Let us begin with Colonel Sinn's Park Theatre, which opened, on August 29, 1887, with a week of McNish, Johnson and Slavin's Minstrels. In subsequent weeks came Effie Ellsler (September 5th–10th) for three days each of Woman against Woman, and Egypt, or, a Daughter of the Nile; J. B. Polk, in Mixed Pickles (September 12th); Jim, the Penman (19th), with Ada Dyas, J. E. Whiting, H. M. Pitt, Evelyn Campbell, Jennie Eustace, and W. J. Ferguson (as Redwood); Thatcher, Primrose and West's Minstrels (26th), and Henry E. Dixey, in Adonis (October 3rd–8th). Mme. Rhea, who seldom reached Manhattan, but sometimes visited Brooklyn, came to the Park (October 10th) in Fairy Fingers (from Scribe and Legouvé's Les Doigts de Fée), with a support including Adelaide Fitz-Allen, Ella Wren, Marie Dantes, Belle Sutton, Edward Bell, W. R. Owen, Robert G. Wilson, Robert Gibbs, J. R. Armory (*sic*), Richard Hayden and C. N. Drew—certainly no glittering host. Later in the week she gave Camille, Pygmalion and Galatea and Frou-Frou. Herrmann's magic mystified in the week of October 17th–22nd. Held by the Enemy filled the week of October 24th.

Clara Morris, ever, as we know, a great favourite in Brooklyn, appeared for a week, in Renée de Moray (October 31st, November 2nd and 4th); Article 47 (November 1st and 3rd) and The New Magdalen (5th). Her company, for the matinées on the 2nd and 5th, offered Our Regiment. Frederick Warde filled the week of November 7th–12th with sturdy performances of Virginius, Richard III, Damon and Pythias and his new Gaston Cadol; in his support were Clarence Handyside, Eugenia Blair, Augusta Foster, Thomas Garrick and L. F. Rand, mostly from the ranks of the second-best. Minnie Palmer varied her nightly offering (November 14th–19th) of My Sweetheart with a Wednesday matinée of My Brother's Sister, "in which she wears her superb toilets and jewels." Minnie, this season, was much exercised about her jewellery; she published, in the Eagle, a letter of protest against unkind journalists who insinuated that her priceless gems, "the gifts of crowned heads," were in reality only false and pasty stuff—

[557]

the very idea! After this inflation of advertising, it was a relief to turn (November 21st–26th) to the black-face realities of McNish, Johnson and Slavin's Minstrels. And what a joy to welcome Joseph Jefferson and Mrs. John Drew, in The Rivals (November 28th, 29th, and matinée, 30th); Jefferson in The Cricket on the Hearth and Lend Me Five Shillings (evenings of the 30th and December 1st), and Rip Van Winkle (2nd and 3rd).

Robert Mantell, in Monbars (week of December 5th–10th) was supported by Eleanor Moretti, B. T. Ringgold, and the former Brooklyn favourite, F. Chippendale. The next week gave Annie Pixley, in the sentimental The Deacon's Daughter, a delectability that yielded both performances, on Saturday, the 17th, to the ever-desired M'liss. It is a pleasure to welcome Arthur Rehan's Company (December 19th–23rd) in the charming Love on Crutches, and for the matinée and evening, on the 24th, in Nancy and Company. The talented Carrie Turner headed the casts, which also included Harry Hotto and the historic Clara Fisher Maeder, these two in the Lewis — Mrs. Gilbert rôles, A. S. Lipman, George Parkes, Harold Russell, David Longworth, Adele Waters, Lily Vinton, Charline Weidman and Lizzie St. Quentin, a better aggregation than one usually found in Rehan's productions of Daly successes. Negro minstrelsy of the big, modern variety succeeded for Christmas festivities in the holiday week of December 26th–31st. This "art" had almost faded from regular residence in New York and its vicinity, but, in that time of Nanki-Poo and The Mikado, great bands of "wandering minstrels" were infesting the "legitimate" theatres, especially in church-going Brooklyn.

N. C. Goodwin started the New Year (January 2nd) with Turned Up and Lend Me Five Shillings. On the 9th, Fanny Davenport began a week of Fedora, with The Lady of Lyons serving for the Wednesday matinée. When Jim, the Penman, returned, on January 16th, the Herald condescendingly asserted of Ada Dyas that "she played in a manner which did not suffer much by comparison with Mrs. Booth." It is interesting to notice that for a number of years Miss Dyas had been seen in only two parts — Mrs. Dick Chetwyn and Nina Ralston — both triumphantly first played in New York by Agnes Booth. In the Brooklyn cast of Jim, the Penman were again H. M. Pitt and W. J. Ferguson. Mme. Cottrelly and accomplished associates, Marion Manola, Wilke, Hopper, De Angelis, Digby Bell and Annie Myers, filled the week of January 23rd, in The Begum. And Richard Mansfield devoted the week of January 30th–February 4th, to Dr. Jekyll and Mr. Hyde, except that, for the Wednesday matinée, he reverted to A Parisian Romance. Mr. and Mrs. Knight, in Rudolph, had the week beginning on February 6th. The Boston Ideal Opera Company, with Zélie de Lussan, fulfilled a busy week, with Carmen (February 13th and 17th), Victor, the Bluestocking (14th), The Elixir of Love (matinée, 15th), The Daughter of the Regiment (evening of the 15th and afternoon of the 18th),

[558]

NELLIE McHENRY
(THE TROUBADOURS)

CHARLES T. ELLIS

BURBECK—G. LYTTON
(A POSSIBLE CASE)

MINNA K. GALE

HELENA MODJESKA
AS IMOGEN

VIOLA ALLEN

ANNIE MYERS
(McCAULL OPERA)

DIGBY BELL AND
DE WOLF HOPPER

FRANK MAYO
(THE ROYAL GUARD)

The Bohemian Girl (16th) and Martha (evening of the 18th). Somehow the record of these artists rather chills me. Cora Tanner (February 20th) in Alone in London, reminds me of when I saw it at the Boston Park Theatre, in the early autumn of 1885; and Miss Tanner had played little else in all that time. Natural Gas, with Donnelly, Girard and John D. Gilbert, filled the week of February 27th–March 3rd, two months before it reached the Fifth Avenue Theatre.

Rosina Vokes managed to crowd into one week a large part of the repertoire that lasted her for six spring weeks at Daly's: Which Is Which?, The Circus Rider and The Pantomime Rehearsal (March 5th, 6th, 7th and 10th); In Honour Bound, My Milliner's Bill and A Double Lesson (8th and 9th); and The Widow's Device (not given at Daly's) and My Milliner's Bill (matinée, 10th). Evangeline became farcical again, in the week of the 12th. W. J. Scanlan sang and acted (March 19th–24th) in, successively, The Irish Minstrel and Shane-na-Lawn. Minnie Maddern also divided her week (March 26th–31st) between In Spite of All and Caprice. Lotta, who almost divided with Clara Morris the allegiance of Brooklyn, had the week of April 2nd, with Pawn Ticket No. 210. A worthy week followed, with Modjeska, supported by Eben Plympton, in Much Ado about Nothing (April 9th) and, in this order, for following nights, Measure for Measure, As You Like It, Cymbeline, Camille (by request) and Romeo and Juliet. E. H. Sothern, in The Highest Bidder, held the week of April 16th–21st, and The Corsair, fresh from the Bijou Opera House, that of the 23rd–28th. Mansfield returned, with Dr. Jekyll and Mr. Hyde, for the major part of the week beginning on April 30th, relieving the strain with Monsieur, for the Wednesday matinée, and with A Parisian Romance for Thursday night and Saturday afternoon.

Dolores came for the week of May 7th and seems to have remained a fortnight. On May 21st, the aging Boucicault acted the youthful Conn, the Shaughraun. The Pearl of Pekin (May 28th–June 2nd); seems to have ended what was, all in all, an interesting season at Sinn's Park Theatre. Today (1941) Brooklyn citizens must go to Manhattan, if they would see a play with living actors. To such a state have the modern inventions of the cinema and the subway reduced Americans of Brooklyn.

BROOKLYN THEATRE, 1887–1888

The Dominie's Daughter, that *quasi*-success of Wallack's at the end of the preceding season, and visible in the People's Theatre in the week of August 29th, 1887, was at the Brooklyn Theatre for the week of September 5th–7th, with Marion Booth, Thomas L. Coleman, Hardy Vernon and Edward McWall, not a striking array. Robert Downing entered, on the 12th, in The Gladiator. And Rosedale, rather pretentiously revived, filled the week beginning on the 19th with Joseph Haworth as Eliot, Miss Sydney Armstrong as Rosa, Helen Leigh as Lady May, Sidney Drew as Bunbury Cobb, Mark Lynch as Matthew Leigh, John Sutherland as Colonel May, and James E. Jackson as Myles McKenna. Emmet, in Fritz, Our Cousin German, held the stage from September 26th to October 1st, inclusive. Hoodman Blind (October 3rd–8th) lured with promise of Frederic De Belleville and the advancing Viola Allen.

A Hole in the Ground made bright the week of October 10th, with Flora Walsh and Julian Mitchell. On the 17th, Lagardère, with J. H. Gilmour succeeding Maurice Barrymore in the title-rôle, still had Helen Tracy, Marie (sic) Floyd and Helen Sedgwick in chief support. Allan Dare, on the 24th, presented F. B. Conway and Mabel Bert in prominent parts; Conway, son of the popular Conways of the last decade or two in Brooklyn, seldom graces our later narrative. This season of 1887–88 brought his sister, Minnie (Mrs. Osmond Tearle) for scattering performances at Wallack's; and Lillian was in the hinterland of cheaper theatredom.

Harbour Lights may have brightened the weeks of October 31st–November 12th; a biweekly engagement would promise so much. Aladdin had an interesting cast (November 14th–19th), with Loie Fuller in the title-rôle, in association with Lena Merville, Richard Golden and William Gill. Mrs. James Brown Potter, that pretty woman of society, an excellent amateur turned into a rather poor actress of the real theatre, came, under H. C. Miner's management, to this, his Brooklyn playhouse, in a week (November 21st–26th) devoted to equal division between Mlle. de Bressier and Loyal Love — offerings which had not set New York afire. A spectacular Macbeth, arranged by McKee Rankin, was not quite ready for a promised production on November 28th, and waited, perforce, till Tuesday, November 29th, when Rankin revealed himself, according to the Eagle, as a too portly Thane, with a voice "full of whiskers." Mabel Bert, whom Rankin was trying to turn into a great actress (and she became a fairly good one) was Lady Macbeth, Kate Molony was Lady Macduff, John L. Burleigh Macduff, and Frank Evans Banquo. Second-rate persons are always murdering Macbeth; I have seen in recent years (1930–40) some dreary, appalling performances of the great tragedy.

Mrs. Langtry, in As in a Looking Glass, proved, I believe, in the week of December 5th–10th, that, though she also had been an amateur, she had become more professional, in bearing and style, than Mrs. Potter showed signs of becoming. Jefferson, Taylor and Nugent's A Dark Secret flooded the stage (December 12th–17th) with enough water to float the much-advertised scene of the Henley Regatta; Mrs. McKee Rankin (Kitty Blanchard) came, without McKee, for a week (December 19th–24th) of The Golden Giant. A Bunch of Keys (December 26th–31st) closed the year 1887.

[560]

J. K. Emmet, ever popular, was here again, on January 2nd, for another week of Fritz, Our Cousin German. A Dark Secret, with its water tank and its exciting boat race, filled the week of January 9th. The J. C. Duff Opera Company presented Dorothy for the week of the 16th. Let us wing our way rapidly through the winter nights with A Tin Soldier, with Eugene Canfield (January 23rd); Jim, the Penman (January 30th–February 4th), with a great cast, including Charles Coghlan, H. M. Pitt, Alexander Salvini, Myron Calice (Redwood), Walden Ramsay (now in Massen's former rôle of Lord Drelincourt), Harry Woodruff, grown up into a good-looking blond youth (in Ramsay's earlier part of Jack Ralston), and with Agnes Booth and Maud Harrison (in the characters they had sustained all the preceding season at the Madison Square Theatre) — a cast far superior to that seen a short time before at Sinn's Park Theatre, and here rendered possible because so many of Palmer's great company were out of the current bill at the home theatre; She, whom the public did not obey in great numbers (February 6th); The Lights o' London, ever flickering from theatre to theatre (February 13th); Frank Daniels, in Little Puck (20th); A Rag Baby, with Charles Reed and Georgie Parker (27th); and Charles Erin Verner, in Shamus O'Brien (March 5th–10th). Friday afternoon, March 2nd, staged a benefit for the Elks.

The great blizzard of March 12th closed the Brooklyn Theatre till Wednesday, March 14th, when Frank Mayo began, in The Royal Guard, with Alice Fischer as Lady de Winter. J. H. Taylor, who was to have played Richelieu did not (possibly could not) appear, and Roberts, of Brooklyn, read the part. Harbour Lights, on March 19th, found the snow of the devastating blizzard somewhat removed from busy Brooklyn streets. On March 26th, we began a week of Check 44, or, Tobogganing, with W. A. Mestayer, Theresa Vaughn, Gus Bruno, Fred Matthews, Sol Aiken, Marion Russell, &c. April 2nd–7th brought back Hoodman Blind, with De Belleville, Viola Allen and Harry Braham. On the 9th, a play by Mark Price, On the Rio Grande, had a cast including the author (as Del Paso), Harry Hawk, Ettie Baker, Florence Roberts and Amy Stone.

On April 16th, Lost in New York, which had been seen in Manhattan, came to the Brooklyn Theatre, with Patrice as Jenny Nelson and Miss Lindemann as Queen of the Blackmailers. It promised a "fine" scene of the harbour, at the opening of the second act, with the Elks Quartet, in a boat, singing The Lighthouse by the Sea — surely an affecting bit for auditors whose daily sight was of waters of the Sound, the East River and all shapes and size of water-craft. Daniel Sully in Daddy Nolan filled the week of the 23rd, and Monroe and Rice, in My Aunt Bridget, that of the 30th. Corinne, in Arcadia, moved in, for the week of May 7th–12th, and followed, in the next week, with Monte Cristo, Jr. True Irish Hearts (May

[561]

21st–26th) was advertised with "same prices," 15, 20, 30, and 50 cents' admission.

If the reader notes a sharp drop in artistic quality, in the offerings of the last few weeks, he may attribute it to the fact that H. R. Jacobs, shut out of the Third Avenue Theatre, had laid his hand on the Brooklyn Theatre, as well as on the Thalia Theater, then deserted by Amberg and his Germans. The Brooklyn house was advertised, on May 28th, as Jacobs' Brooklyn Theatre, when The Silver King showed virtue triumphing over villainy; Ethel Greybrooke and G. Morton Price accomplished the difficult feat. Frankie Kemble, on June 4th, brought Sybil, as seen at the Third Avenue, before the stern arm of the law forced that purveyor of thrills to close. With the aid of heat she seems, with this play, to have closed the season at the Brooklyn Theatre.

Grand Opera House, Brooklyn, 1887–1888

The week of September 5th–10th, introduced May Newman and Ida Jeffreys, in The White Slave. Patti Rosa, in Bob, was the challenging call of the 12th. Beacon Lights had (September 19th–24th) not very powerful interpreters in Gracie Emmett, T. J. Herndon, Neva Wharton, Tony Williams, J. E. Germon and others. Kate Claxton, accompanied, as usual, by her husband, Charles A. Stevenson, was here for the week of September 26th–October 1st. Harry Lacy, the fire engine and the noble steeds appertaining thereto were the lure for October 3rd–8th.

On October 10th, Lacy started a second week of The Still Alarm, and Lost in New York found another haven, on the 17th, in hospitable Brooklyn. Joseph Murphy, assisted by Stella Teuton, began, on the 24th, in Shaun Rhue, but shifted, on the 26th, to The Donagh, newer, though not better. Hanlons' Fantasma, trying many theatres in that season, came, on October 31st, for a magical week in the Grand Opera House. Shadows of a Great City darkened the week of November 7th–12th; but Denman Thompson, in The Old Homestead, began six nights of cheer, on the 14th.

More negro minstrelsy filled the stage, on November 21st–26th, led by Billy Rice, Frank Cushman and Billy Sweatnam — to balance McNish, Johnson and Slavin, that week at the Park. I cannot be specific about W. H. Powers and Company, in The Ivy Leaf (November 28–December 3rd); in good sooth I never found a word about it. But every one knows that Evans and Hoey's A Parlour Match (December 5th–10th) was very, very funny. Hanlons' Le Voyage en Suisse was break-neck and magical, for December 12th–17th. The next week (December 19th–26th) welcomed Frederic Bryton, in his perennial Forgiven; and Roland Reed ended 1887, with Humbug (December 26th–31st). Roland Reed remained a second week, presenting his customary Cheek, for the week of January 2nd–7th. W. J.

[562]

Florence, as Cap'n Cuttle, began the week of January 9th, a sketch, Husband Hunting included in the bill.   The Eagle thought his company might have been better.   On January 16th, Jeffreys Lewis, once a favourite, but seldom seen of late, began a week in Forget-Me-Not, Harry Mainhall playing Sir Horace Welby and Eleanor Barry the harassed Alice Verney.   Later in the week, Miss Lewis offered La Belle Russe, a play, as we know, very similar in theme.   Charles Erin Verner, in Shamus O'Brien, veered, on the 23rd, to the opposite pole of art.   On the 30th, Gus Williams, in Keppler's Fortunes, was assisted by Charles Tingay, Frank Girard and Mattie Ferguson — a rather good group.   February 6th brought Milton Nobles, in his own melo-drama, From Sire to Son; on the 13th, Kate Claxton and Stevenson presented their new The World against Her.   And, on the 20th, that sorrowful tale was offset by the fun of the Dalys, in Upside Down.   Herrmann's magic and black art held us for the week of February 27th–March 3rd.   C. T. Ellis, in Casper, the Yodler, attracted on the 5th of March, and The White Slave, ever on the move, brought tears of pity for the week of the 12th.   Laughter and romance of Irish pattern prevailed in the week of March 19th–24th, when Joseph Murphy appeared in, successively, The Kerry Gow, Shaun Rhue and his new play, The Donagh.   The Main Line, during the last week in March (26th–31st) brought its accustomed thrills.

On April 2nd, the Hanlons gave us all the magic and dance and panto-mime of Fantasma; Fanny Janauschek, a fading star, enacted, on the 9th, Meg Merrilies, and, on the afternoon of the 14th, Mother and Son.   And Brooklyn must have rejoiced, on the 16th, when Denman Thompson came back, in The Old Homestead, perhaps the most loved play of its time and most representative of the big heart of America.   Kellar, on the 23rd, brought his art both magical and musical, to confuse and mystify and de-light.   Edward Harrigan, expected ever in Brooklyn, after the close of his New York season, came to the Grand Opera House, on May 7th, in Old Lavender, following, for the week of May 14th, with his very successful Pete.   His Brooklyn admirers, like his New York followers, may have noticed how different these plays were from the usual Mulligan series.   Our journeys to the Brooklyn Grand Opera House are ended for 1887–88.

PROCTOR'S CRITERION THEATRE, 1887–1888

The Criterion Theatre, which had begun in rather high feather, sank considerably in offerings, for 1887–88; in fact, its standards differed but slightly from those of Proctor's other theatre, the Novelty, in Williamsburgh. The attraction for September 5th–10th was the Emily Soldene Burlesque and Novelty Company, featuring Zara and Geneviève de Brabant, seen this season in Bowery halls of "Variety."   Ezra Kendall, in A Pair of Kids, filled the following week; The Kindergarden (sic) educated downward for the week of September 19th–24th. Clio boasted (September 26th–October 1st) of specialty performers in Gail Forrest, Angie Griffiths and Rosina Astegani (*sic*).

Charles A. Gardner, in The New Karl, started October 3rd–8th, on the autumnal course; the Starr Opera Company tried to make October 10th–15th interesting, with The Mascot and Olivette. On October 17th, A Night Off began a week, with Ernest Bertram, C. J. Burridge, E. A. Eberle, John Flood, Robert Edeson, Ethel Barrington, Kate Carlyon and Alice Evans, an array in no wise comparable to the incomparable cast at Daly's. Mam'zelle, with the Kimball Musical Comedy Company, enlisted (October 24th–29th) Kate Foley, Mlle. Ottilie and Harry C. Clarke. The Starr Opera Company filled the week of October 31st–November 5th with, in succession, The Mascot, Billee Taylor, A Surprise (which proved to be Erminie of a sort) and Toilers of Paris; the company included Charles Osborne, Frank Deshon (these two played the rogues in the Erminie affair), Louise Neville and Agnes Hallock. Pat and Katie Rooney and their New York Star Company carried the week of November 7th–12th, yielding the stage, on the 14th, to more "Variety," in Tony Pastor, Rose Julian, Keating and Flynn, Musical Dale, and Albert Clives and his little dog. Alice Harrison, no longer so young as she had been twenty years earlier, was the star (November 21st–26th) in Photos, her support including Dickie Martinez, E. J. Connelly, W. C. Mandeville and Richard Morosco.

A much bepuffed pretty girl, Marian Fleming, was depended on to beautify the week of November 28th–December 3rd. H. R. Jacobs's Company, headed by Thomas F. McCabe and Miss Wardell, showed, for December 5th–10th, The Wages of Sin (seen, the following week, at Proctor's Novelty). December 12th–17th provided the thrills of J. H. Wallick, in the very familiar The Cattle King. Under the Gaslight, that undying melodrama, piled up more thrills for December 19th–24th; I hope the destroying railroad engine worked without a hitch.

The new year began (January 2nd–7th) with R. L. Scott and Harry Mills, in A Chip of the Old Block, an attraction that makes me feel as if I were wandering in a small country town. Zitka, with May Wheeler, on January 9th, reminds us of the same piece, at that time, in Proctor's Novelty. The Mountain Pink (January 16th–21st) reminds us of something lost to consciousness in our New York Chronicle. Keep It Dark, contemptuously set down by the Eagle as a "horse" play, advertised, for January 23rd–28th, Julia Wilson (once so essential to the success of Joshua Whitcomb), Bryant and Richmond, James Bevins and George Parsons; these last two never dinted the forehead of the age. The Silver King, with Charles Haswin, awakened faint memories for January 30th–February 4th. Michael Strogoff (February 6th–11th); Florence (Baby) Bindley, in Excitement (13th–18th); True Irish Hearts (20th–25th); A Heroine in Rags (February 27th–

March 3rd), with Hettie Bernard Chase; A Hoop of Gold (March 5th–10th) —these things carry me without comment from the Eagle, to the Great Blizzard of March 12th. On that snow-blanketed evening, Casper, the Yodler, was to have begun a week's engagement. When, later in the week, the drifts were mastered, the play carried through its appointed career.

A change for the better came in the following week (March 19th–24th) when Edmund Collier essayed, successively, Virginius, Damon, Jack Cade and Richard III, trying, like Frederick Warde, to persuade the public that the old Forrest-McCullough order had not changed. The answer came, next week, with King of the Mines. The cryptic notice of the Eagle concerning Nuggets (April 2nd–7th), which might have been dug from the Mines of the previous week, leaves me helpless in my desire to instruct my readers; I really am ignorant of the size or the value, theatrically, of those Nuggets. The Eagle carries no advertisements for Proctor's theatres, and I am left helpless by the short notes it generously gives, weekly, to the non-advertising Criterion. In view of this uncertainty, it is a pleasure to welcome (April 9th–14th) Tony Pastor and his good company; one knows what to expect from him and his clever cohorts.

Young Henry T. Chanfrau, for April 16th–21st, tried to revive interest in his lamented father's former success, Kit, the Arkansas Traveller. Frank Frayne returned, on April 23rd; Peck's Bad Boy was pretty bad, on the 30th; and what the irritable Eagle calls "that dreary dime novel in dialogue," Only a Farmer's Daughter, tried to affect tear-ducts, for May 7th–12th. The Eagle had had too much, during a long season; its satire takes a bitter turn on Sunday, May 13th. "The lofty intellectuality that the author of Muggs' Landing imbued that work with, will," it says, "be exhibited to the satisfaction of the Criterion's patrons this week." Ada Gray, rather above the usual run of Criterion stars, devoted the week of May 21st to her eternal East Lynne. On the 28th, Martin Hayden, who, according to the atrabiliar Eagle, "escapes being an infant prodigy by several years," began a week, in The Boy Hero. George Learock filled an exciting week (June 4th–9th) in the venerable appeal of The Corsican Brothers. Over the Garden Wall, without the Knights, who had made it tolerable, allows me to jump to safety from the Criterion, for 1887–88. I wonder if I owe the reader an apology for troubling him with this list of mediocre attractions; I almost feel that I owe the Novelty Theatre an apology for likening the Criterion's offerings to those of the Novelty. I cannot imagine what had happened to both houses; I can only suspect that there were too many theatres in Brooklyn, east and west.

ACADEMY OF MUSIC, BROOKLYN, 1887–1888

As frequently in past years, John L. Stoddard had the honour of opening the stately Academy for the new season. On September 29, 1887, he
began a series of illustrated lectures, two of which bore the attractive titles
of, respectively, Julius Cæsar and Byron; others were simply devoted to
Constantinople and other haunts of travel. On October 4th, a drive for
funds for a statue to Brooklyn's own Henry Ward Beecher promised a eulogy
on the great preacher by the Reverend Dr. Parker, of City Temple, London;
two nights previously the Kings County Henry George Land Club possessed the auditorium. On October 14th, for the benefit of Montauk Lodge,
Adelaide Thornton acted, for that night only, The Galley Slave. And
Charles Dickens, the younger, was to read, on October 26th, his father's
Dr. Marigold, and Scenes from the Pickwick Papers.

The Philharmonic concerts began on November 12th, but those I shall
chronicle under their own caption. Meantime, the avalanche of amateur
theatricals began its descent, on November 9th, when the respected Amaranth Society presented Everybody's Friend, with Alfred Young as Felix
Featherly, Frederick Bowne as Icebrook, Percy G. Williams as Major Wellington De Boots, John Littleton as Trap, Ella G. Greene as Mrs. Featherly,
Mrs. Charles Bellows, Jr., as Mrs. De Boots, Ada Woodruff as Mrs. Swansdown, and Annette Sterner as Fanny. Cappa's Seventh Regiment Band
somehow fitted in; the Amaranth always did things in style. The Charity
Ball of the Hebrew Orphan Asylum, on the 16th, made dancing a duty.
And Uncle Tom's Cabin was another kind of duty in the week of November
21st–26th. Meantime, the Kemble Society, on November 15th, played
Ours, with Annie B. Phelps, Mrs. Georgen, Miss Lyman and Messrs. Gardner, Montgomery and Platt.

The ambitious Walter Damrosch gave the first concert, on December
6th, of the Symphony Society of Brooklyn, Alvary and Frl. Brandt assisting.
For his later concerts (January 3rd and 31st) were promised Lilli Lehmann
and Adele Aus der Ohe.

The Amaranth again invited to the Academy for a performance, on
December 7th, of The Silver King, with Alfred Young as Wilfred Denver,
Helen Dayton as the sorrowing Nellie, Sterner as Jaikes, B. R. Throck-
morton as the Spider, Virgil Lopez as Sam Baxter, William Phelps Macfarlane as Elijah Combe, Albert Meafoy as Harry Corkett, Lizzie Wallace as
a Newsboy, Ada Woodruff as Olive Skinner, and May Halbert as Tabitha.
On the 9th, the wonderful child, Josef Hofmann, appeared at the Academy,
repeating the experiment on the 16th, supported by Helene Hastreiter, De
Anna, Nettie Carpenter and Ferrari. And, on the 12th, the superb Boston
Symphony Orchestra, directed by Wilhelm Gericke, gave the first of three
subscription concerts, the others being listed for February 9th and March

[566]

12th. The last date, being the day of the Great Blizzard, found the orchestra in piles of snow, somewhere between Boston and Brooklyn and necessitated a postponement to later March. On December 13th, according to the Brooklyn Times, the Kemble amateurs gave The Shaughraun, with Deane Pratt as Conn, Thomas C. Bell as Harvey Duff, Elita Proctor Otis as Claire, and Ida Waller as Moya.

The Amphion Society Concert, on December 15th, availed itself of aid from Jennie Dutton and H. A. Foresman. Before a "fashionable audience, mainly from the Hill"— I am quoting the Brooklyn Times — the Amateur Opera Association presented (December 20th) The Mascot, with a cast including Mrs. M. C. Boynton, Miss Edgeworth Starritt (her name frequently will greet us), Wallace Macreery (seemingly demoted from the professional stage), J. Williams Macy (a very busy amateur), S. L. Swazey (the handsome young singer), F. M. Brook and L. W. Forbell. Josef Hofmann appeared at a matinée, on the 21st. For seven nights and four matinées, beginning on December 26th, The Main Line, that Lyceum "success," spread Christmas cheer, with Etta Hawkins, a clever soubrette, Myron Leffingwell, E. F. Gilpin, Ernest Sterner, John Daly, Nellie Leffingwell, John Daly and Miss Forrester — not an overwhelming gift, *me judice*. And here again, on January 4th, are the indefatigable Amaranths, presenting French Flats, with Percy G. Williams as Blondeau, Harry T. Hill as Bonay, Albert Meafoy as Vallay, Alfred Young, a versatile soul, as Rifflardini, Thomas T. Hayden as Barrameda, Frederick Bowne as Billardo, Elsie Louis as the Marchioness, Annette Sterner as Anna, Ida Williams as Mme. Blondeau, &c.

Something professional brightened the week of January 9th–14th, no less a public joy than Erminie, with almost the original cast — Pauline Hall, Marie Jansen, Kitty Cheatham, Louise Sylvester, Francis Wilson, W. S. Daboll, Henry Hallam, George Olmi, Charles Plunkett, A. W. Maflin and Murry Woods, with Jesse Williams as musical director. And Josef Hofmann gave another matinée, on the 13th, and an evening concert on the 19th, with Mme. Hastreiter, De Anna and Adolf Neuendorff's orchestra. The Kemble Society, for which I found but little in the Eagle for 1887–88, was here, on January 17th, with Sheridan's The Critic; in it appeared A. J. Macaulay as Dangle, Frank Thonger as Sneer, Ernest Jacobson as Sir Fretful Plagiary, Douglas Montgomery as Puff, H. R. Graham as the Prompter, Mattie Brown as Mrs. Dangle, John Russell as Burleigh, John Smithson as the Governor of Tilbury Fort, Frank Cuddy as Leicester, F. D. Maltby as Raleigh, Thomas Platt as Sir Christopher, A. C. Munn as Whiskerandos, Madge Baron as Tilburina and Mrs. G. H. Parkhurst and Ella Georgen as the Confidants. That cast consumes more paper than I can afford.

The Emerald Association Ball was featly danced, on February 1st, to the strains of Gilmore's Band; a benefit for the Roman Catholic Orphan

Asylum. The Brooklyn Firemen's Association held their ball here, on the 6th; and the Brooklyn Sängerbund masquerade made jolly the night of the 13th. Eva Cummings announced, for January 23rd, a "grand operatic performance," consisting of the first two acts of The Barber of Seville, the third act of Faust, and a scene from Rigoletto; Arencibia (tenor), Orlandini, Bologna, Gangno and Fanciulli were to assist. This delight the lady postponed to February 11th, without, I fancy, causing Brooklyn to break its heart with disappointment. On February 9th, Campanini, Scalchi, Bocchetti, Elvira Repetto, Galassi, Corsini and Nannetti appeared in concert. It is sad to read, in the Brooklyn Times of the 10th that Campanini's voice was "but a shadow of its former self. The flexibility is gone and the tones are dry that once were brilliant." Yet "the compass is really surprising." He took a high C (weak, to be sure) in the *Salve dimora*. "To hear his voice is not an unmixed pleasure"; Scalchi sang the *Ah! quel giorno*, from Semiramide. "When she sings carelessly, as she did last night, her notes are often lamentably wanting in purity. But her method is always a compensation." This is the first of the adverse criticisms that, a few years later, were to meet the great contralto. The Kemble Society, on February 15th, gave The Captain of the Watch and Slasher and Crasher; Douglas Montgomery was Viscount de Ligny, one of Lester Wallack's best rôles.

I pass to February 16th, for a performance of The Pearl of Bagdad, by Edwin F. De Nyse and John M. Loretz, brought out by the Amateur Opera Association of Brooklyn, with a cast including T. H. Barry, John T. Brennan, J. Williams Macy, Georgia Weld, Miss Edgeworth Starritt, E. Berdu, Jr., Sadie Eubricken, L. W. Forbell and others. The McCaull Opera Company divided the week of February 20th–25th between Falka and Boccaccio, the casts including Mme. Cottrelly, Marion Manola, Laura Joyce Bell, Annie Myers, Josephine Knapp, Hubert Wilke, De Wolf Hopper, Digby Bell, Edwin Hoff and Jeff De Angelis.

The busy Amaranths devoted the evening of March 7th to the poor play of Belle Lamar, trusting in Ada Woodruff, Ella Greene, Lizzie Wallace, Ida Williams, Alfred Young, Frederick Bowne, George F. Barrett, Percy G. Williams and Albert Meafoy to stir the embers of their hopes. The almost defunct National Opera Company announced three performances — Tannhäuser (March 12th); Faust (13th); and The Queen of Sheba (15th). The Great Blizzard snowed under their ambition, and it was not till March 26th, 27th and 28th that the operas were given; and then Faust supplanted Tannhäuser. The company included Bertha Pierson, Emma Juch, Sophie Traubmann, Clara Poole, Amanda Fabris, Attalie Claire, Eloi Sylva, Barton McGuckin, Charles Bassett, William Ludwig, A. E. Stoddard and Frank Vetta, really too good a group to disband. I fear that Emma Juch was not, in late March, in the force. While we lament their failure we may consider Imre Kiralfy's Mazulm, the feature of March 19th–24th, with specialties

[568]

by the Braatz Brothers, the Vaidis Sisters, the Dare Brothers, Monsieur Arnold, Mlle. Franconi and Frl. Newman. The week of April 2nd–7th presented Easter joy, in Rudolph Aronson's Casino Company, with James T. Powers, Mark Smith, Lillian Grubb and Bertha Ricci; they devoted three nights to Madelon and three to The Marquis. For the National Guard and Soldiers' Ward of the Brooklyn Home for Consumptives, Co. I of the 7th Regiment presented Katharine, a travesty on The Taming of the Shrew, which we saw in New York. A sad evening was that of April 12th, when poor Etelka Gerster appeared in concert, with Louise Meisslinger, Michael Banner, Emil Steger, Henri Ducenzi, and F. Dulcken (director). She attempted *Ah! non credea* and other specialties of her great days — the de Beriot Andante and Valse, and the soprano part of the quartet from Rigoletto. She gave the impression of one labouring to reach the goal of high notes — nothing of the limpid ease of former times was heard. I was present and sat in sorrow before the wreck of a great art. What caused Gerster's early artistic decline?

The busy Amateur Operatic Association gave, on April 19th, The Beggar Student, with Edgeworth Starritt, Mrs. E. J. Grant, Mrs. M. C. Boynton, Wallace Macreery, John T. Brennan, J. Williams Macy, M. Berdu, Jr., and Bessie Rathbun. "Grand" Minstrel Entertainment by members of the De Long Council No. 725, Royal Arcanum, was featured on April 21st. And what one might unkindly call another ministrel show began on May 1st, with James Owen O'Conor, fresh from his fiasco in New York, devoting five nights to his absurd "rendition" of the classics — Hamlet, Richelieu, Richard III, Damon and Pythias, The Merchant of Venice, and The Lady of Lyons. A May Festival and Fair, for charity, held the Academy on May 10th, 11th, 12th and 13th.

Hyde and Behman's, 1887–1888

In scanning the programmes of Brooklyn's leading vaudeville house, one might imagine himself in front of the London Theatre, Bowery, or one of Harry Miner's "Variety" theatres. Visiting combinations in the Manhattan fastnesses almost invariably journeyed in time to Hyde and Behman's.

Hyde's Specialty Company, in the Brooklyn demesne, for September 5th–10th, included the Vidocqs, Byrnes and Helene, Kitty O'Neil, Kelly and Murphy, Sam Devere, Dick Carroll and Sharpley and West (in Doglets), veritably kings and queens of the craft. Sheffer and Blakely's Company was composed (September 12th–17th) of familiar faces in Mme. Quitsch (living pictures), Wylie and Sanford, Conroy and Dempsey, the Inman Sisters, Sheffer and Blakely (of course), Layman (of the contortion face), Adolf Seeman (who "hung a woman up in the atmosphere"), Pavillio and Rousillion, Hilda Thomas, and Kelly and Ryan.

[569]

The Rentz-Santley Combination (September 26th–October 1st) comprised, among many other flowerets of "Variety," Georgie Blake, Sanford and Wilson, Smith and Bloodgood, Lillian Markham, Capitola Forrest and George Murphy and Katie Wells. John and Harry Kernell were bright stars of eve and two matinées (October 3rd–8th), accompanying scintillants including the Luciers, Harry (*sic*) and Lizzie Smith, Solano (*sic*) and Fonti, Mlle. Eichlerette and Jennie Miaco. Reilly and Wood's Big Show, well-known in New York, made Brooklyn glad (October 10th–15th) with Florence Miller, the Four Emperors of Music, Mlle. Fogardus (*sic*), the Nelsons, and D'Alvini (with his "Birth of the Butterfly"). The Howard Athenæum Specialty Company, revered by certain Bostonians and alert Harvard boys, came for the week of October 17th–22nd, with an offering of Carl Hertz (magic), Foreman and Ida Meredith, the Fonti Boni Brothers, Sweeney and Ryland, Lizzie Daly, Rezene and Robini (trapeze) and James F. Hoey and Pete Dailey (that funny pair). The Night Owls Novelty and Burlesque Company catered to the rising addicts of the female form more or less divine, with exploitation of Victoria North, May Howard and Harry Morris. I did not disinter the others.

It is pleasing to pass (October 31st–November 5th) to Austin's Great Australian Novelty Company, with Harry Le Clair and W. J. Russell, Aimée and Rose Austin, Emilie Peare, Ramza and Arno and Edward Leslie. I may be wrong in assuming that this was one of the brightest aggregations in vaudeville. Davene's European Novelty and Specialty Company held the stage for November 7th–12th, featuring the Electric Three, the perennial Fannie Beane and Charles Gilday, Mlle. Lotto and William Davene. A special feature for November 14th–19th was the rope-walking of Fontaine, in wooden shoes, on roller skates, etc., other contributors to the joy of spectators being the Lawrence Sisters, Imro Fox and Frank H. and Lillian White. A "Knockabout Wench," during the next week, was kicked about the stage, doubtless to the edification of the patrons of art; other specialists in the bill were the Morello Brothers, Ada Burnett, Alna Don Janata (with her charming snakes), Pickert and Mayon and Kelly and Ashley.

Hyde and Behman's Own Company came home (December 5th–10th) in persons of William Carroll, Walter and Stanton, the Dare Brothers, the Winstanleys, Byrnes and Helene, Thomas and Watson, and Wylie and Sanford. For the 12th–17th, the particular stars were eight seals, who scratched banjos, beat drums and behaved generally as no well-bred seals should do. One, on the opening night galumphed (to quote Lewis Carroll) into the audience, and was captured with some difficulty. I wonder how one "captures" a slippery seal? This exhibition was part of Lester and Allen's show, The Early Birds. After seals, what? William Muldoon, with a "prize" of fifty dollars to be given to "any wrestler whom Muldoon cannot beat." Of course volunteers (December 19th–24th) were few. Other features of the bill were Ferguson and Mack, J. B. Wills and May Adams, Fannie Lewis, David S. Foster, Thomas and Watson and the American Four, a dazzling array for vaudeville enthusiasts. Christmas week (26th–31st) was rich in promise of Andy and Annie Hughes, Clives, Harry Kennedy, Lewis and Martin, the Glenroy Brothers, Dick Carroll and Nellie Parker. Humpty Dumpty, with Tony Denier, seems suitable for the new year (January 2nd–7th); other entertainers were Millis (ventriloquist), Madge Aiston, the Ashton Brothers (acrobats), and Marie Gilchrist (dancer).

The Sheffer and Blakely Company of January 9th–14th was somewhat changed since it was here in September; the personnel now included Billy and Alice Payne, Nellie and Pearl Inman, George H. Wood, Hilda Thomas, Castor and Currier (pole balancing), and Signor Zano (slack wire). Hyman's Big Specialty Company was rendered glorious by participation of Jack McAuliffe (champion lightweight boxer), who was to appear on the afternoon of Tuesday, January 17th, and at all other performances of the week. This exploitation of boxers and sluggers was a growing device in "Variety." Colonel Wagner's Big Boom operated for January 23rd–28th, especially featuring "Chevalier" Ira Paine, the big shot of the world, Emerson and Clark, the National Four and Pavanelli. From this bluster it is a relief to welcome (January 30th–February 4th) Gus Hill's World of Novelties, one of the best combinations, with Alberta and Hill (on the ceiling or wherever their feet would stick), C. W. Williams (ventriloquist), Conroy and Thompson, Swift and Chase (musical comedians), Lou Sanford, the Rices (acrobats), Weber and Fields, Dan Hart (and his "purp"), the Sheerans, and Gus Hill (in his famous act of club-swinging). Reilly and Wood's Show (February 6th–11th) now included the Nelson Family (five in number), Bobby Gaylor, "Professor" Harry Deaves, Twelve Roman Gladiators, the Four Emperors of Music, Mlle. Fogardus (sic), Florence Miller and Pat Reilly.

Harry and John Kernell returned (February 27th–March 3rd), also with a slightly changed personnel — Harry Kennedy, the California Four, De Witt and Armstrong, Marlow and Regan, Bloodgood and Smith, Solani (sic) and Fonti and Larry (sic) and Lizzie Smith. The Rentz-Santley Company featured, for March 5th–10th, their Tobogganing and Adam and Eve — also Sorakichi (Japanese wrestler) and a host of shapely females. On March 12th began a week of Marinelli, declared by the Eagle to be "the most serpentine of human serpents," who "coiled and twisted himself, put his head on the floor and ran around it, bent backward until he looked out between his knees, and wandered about in that attitude." In view of such abnormal procedure, the audience may have thought Johnny Reagan and Jack Files, fellows in the bill, rather ordinary men. March 26th–31st again exalted physical development in a contest between Jack Dempsey and Denny Costigan; obviously the human form divine, male or female, was a growing feature in "Variety." For the Dempsey week, however, Hyde and Behman's also stressed the Electric Three, the La Rose (*sic*) Brothers and the Horseshoe Four. The Howard Athenæum Specialty Company, returning (April 2nd–7th), still featured James F. Hoey and Pete Dailey, the Brothers Fonti-Boni, Lizzie Daly, and Carl Hertz, and added Adams, Casey and Howard, and the delightful Irwin Sisters.

Austin's Australian Novelty Company returned, on April 9th, for a week. The Eagle becomes bitterly sarcastic. Baldwin and Daly, in a Zulu act, "clad in little more than paint, came out of low straw huts, mumbled and contortioned themselves"; Marie McNeil played the cornet; Joe McNeil and John McCabe "kicked each other around the stage and walked on each other, in the name of refined comedy." Miss St. George Hussey, "who weighs about 200 pounds, impersonated an Irishman and sang in a loud voice." Those escaping the censure of the Eagle were Will Vidocq and Lottie Gilson (these not entirely escaping), the Austin Sisters, the Southern Quartet, R. G. Knowles and Edward Leslie. Lilly Clay's Colossal Gaiety Company whirls us back (April 16th–21st) to the realm of burlesque, with "Thirty Lovely Ladies — Novelty's Crowning Diadem." The choice morsel was Apollo in Eden, or, the Little Devil's Revel. This stuff we found in New York bills. Hyde's own company again allured (April 23rd–28th) with Sam Devere, Richmond and Glenroy, Kelly and Murphy (sluggers), Keating and Ardell, Harry and Clara Pierce, Heffernan and McDonald, William McMahon, Nellie Parker, Polly Cusick, Charles J. Newton (mimic), J. W. Hampton (with his dogs, monkeys, cats and geese), and (lo! the trail of the serpent in vaudeville's classic domain) Jack McAuliffe ("light weight pugilist"). And Parson Davies' Sluggers and Wrestlers and William Muldoon and his company of gladiators, including Evan Lewis, turned the Hyde and Behman stage of April 30th–May 5th, into a sort of Roman arena. And so addicted to such exhibitions had the patrons become that, when on May 7th, Sheffer and Blakely's Company began a third week-visit, they specially stressed George La Blanche and Patsy Kerrigan (sluggers). Otherwise the bill was human, with the Tills, Hilda Thomas, Hugh Dougherty, Conroy and Dempsey, Edward Kerwan (*sic*), Harrigan, and Master McCue. May 14th–19th brought the Early Birds, including Franks (*sic*) and Marion, Jolly Nash, Helene Mora (woman baritone), Tatali, the King Sisters, Flynn and Zitella and George Wood and twelve women. Monday, May 21st, gave a benefit to Henry W. Behman, treasurer, and a benefit to the reader and me, since that closed the season.

Standard Museum, 1887–1888

If visits to the Criterion force us to lower our standards, what shall we say of a history of the Standard Museum? Of course our only excuse is that history makes no distinctions; it must chronicle all and be thankful for the smallest details.

With that useful and soothing platitude, I pick up the record, on September 5, 1887, when A Box of Cash began a week with Edward M. Favor and Edith Sinclair.   John A. Stevens's play, Passion's Slave, worried through the ensuing week, to be followed (September 19th–24th) by a frequently recurring A Checkered Life.   Under the Gaslight was the dazzling novelty for September 26th–October 1st.   Again I state that tiny notices in the Eagle prevent my being specific in detail.   With this excuse I pass to Grogan's Elevation (October 3rd–8th) and (10th–15th) Alfred Miaco, in The Magic Talisman, described by the Eagle as "witches, ghosts, clowns, imps, apes, fairies, dudes, farmers, peasants, belles, spiders, policemen, grandmothers and tradespeople."

Zitka, on the 17th, somehow by name suggests a warning to stay away. October 24th presented the familiar Lottie Church for a week of shifting values in Papeto, River Pirates, etc.   October 31st–November 5th offered Kit, with H. T. Chanfrau, "a clever young man," according to the Eagle. The Blackthorn (November 7th–12th) presented J. J. Sullivan, Mary (sic) and Carrie Wallace, Alfred Wallace, Spencer Pritchard, and John, Annie and Lea Peasley, a cast almost entirely recruited from "Variety."   The Molly Maguires, with Arthur Sprague, was pretty exciting for November 14th–19th, and, according to the Eagle, Arizona Joe, choice offering for November 21st–26th, "filled the theater [sic] with yells, applause, barkings and gunpowder smoke."   From that noise and tumult we dropped (November 28th–December 3rd) to the comfortable inanities of Moran and Thomas's San Francisco Minstrels, with Thomas and Foy, Dave Foy and Karoly Ordey. Jesse James made thrilling the week of December 5th–10th, with Tex Bender, Pauline Parker and Henry Belmer as executants.   I suppose boys and men of a lesser culture like outlaws for the same reason that women of their class like pretty Hollywood actors; it mitigates the dulness of their own lives.

The Pavements of Paris were trod during the week of December 12th–17th; the following week offered One of the Bravest, with Charles McCarthy, Lottie Blair and William Cronin, a trio not unknown in halls of "Variety." Christmas week (December 26th–31st) made us sad, with Thrown on the World.   Thus we turn, without dread, to the offering of January 2nd–7th — Kelly, in The Shadow Detective.   A group familiar to "Variety" audiences presented (January 9th–14th) Paul and Macy's three-act comedy, C. O. D., with Stanley Macy, Tillie McHenry, George Bruening and Gus Bruno.   The Stranglers of Paris, for January 16th–21st, thrilled with Frank A. Tannehill, Emma Chase, Ella Russland and Edward Blackwell, all, except one, strangers to my omniscient pen.   Under the Lash, doubtless, was painful for January 23rd–28th.   The cast of Lucky Ranch (January 30th) contained J. J. Lessenger, W. C. Matthews, Nellie Harris, and, according to the Eagle, "one

[573]

horse, one jackass and two bull-dogs." One sees in theatres like the Standard the origin of our Wild West and animal films of 1941. According to the very quotable Eagle, Master N. S. Wood, who came, on February 6th, in Waifs of New York, was "getting to be a big boy now." The reader must classify for himself the miscellaneous offerings of February 13th–18th — the Westons (Sam and Morris), the French Troupe Davene, Happy Jack Sutton's New Wild West, Two Black Johns, and Señorita Donna Emilia (the Prairie Pearl).

One of the Bravest, a "fire" piece, illuminated the wintry stage of February 20th–25th; and Life in a Great City, with May Estelle and William Cattell, doubtless was illuminating in another way from February 27th to March 3rd. Uncle Tom's Cabin was bound to arrive here, and did so for the week of March 5th–10th. Sid C. France was listed for March 12th, in what play the Eagle does not state; since that was the night of the Great Blizzard, it may have been postponed for a night or more, in hope of more propitious weather. The Black Flag waved ominously for March 19th–24th. A Checkered Life, to me one of the season's puzzles, returned for the week of March 26th–31st; McEvoy's Hibernicon fitted into the scheme for April 2nd–7th. A Hoop of Gold, another contrivance that leaves me in the dark, enlightened auditors (perhaps) for April 9th–14th. Minnie Oscar Gray and W. T. Stephens, whom we have not recently met, gave three plays, all in the week of April 16th–21st. Storm Beaten practically ended showery April in the week of the 23rd–28th. The Two Orphans and A Celebrated Case were very emotional in dividing the week of April 30th–May 5th. Passion's Slave, with T. H. Winnett's Company, kept us alert from the 7th of May to the 12th. Harry Webber, in Nip and Tuck (May 14th–19th), and Michael Strogoff (21st–26th) led the way to Gus Williams's former success, One of the Finest (May 28th–June 2nd), of course without Williams, but with Daniel Mason, L. P. Hicks, Edward Chrissie, Frank Girard, Jr., Belle Barron, Frank Wayne, Jr., Hattie Haynes and Marion Gray. The season closed, on June 4th, with a benefit to Business Manager Isham and Treasurer Turner, who probably had had a busy season.

Zipp's Casino, 1887–1888

Zipp's Casino, Elm Place and Fulton Street, is almost too humble to be included in our stately procession. Entertainment there was provided (September 12th–17th) by Della Torra, Maud Vincent, the Geistinger Double Quartet and Minnie Schult. Miss Schult I may dismiss with the remark that she remained at Zipp's throughout the season; habitués must have liked her. Assisting factors till October 29th were Ned Hanson and Mamie Hayman, Alma De Linna, the Acme Quartet (O'Keefe, Martin, Hibbard, Davis), Lillie Larkelle, Carl Eschert, Adolph Kirchner's Orchestra (this band also

[574]

remained through the better part of the season), Maggie Webb, Rittmeyer, Annie Walsh, Meuselbach (*sic*)—of course many of them for only a week each. The week of October 31st–November 5th stressed, besides Miss Schult, the Little German Rose, Emery and Russell and Emil Müller.

I gathered no more from the Eagle till December 8th when many volunteers carried through a benefit for the Liquor Dealers' Mutual Benefit Fund. Stars of December were Hanson and Hayman, Bertha Reigle (*sic*), Lillian Granger, Harry and Lizzie Roth, Lynch and Griffin, Nand'l Hofer, and a Tyrolean Trio; there probably were more, whom my eye failed to catch in the terribly difficult columns of the Eagle. January 9th–14th richly provided J. M. Myers (*sic*), Emma Meyer (*sic*), Armand Veazey, C. Eschert, Meuschbach (*sic*), and the ever remaining Minnie Schult and Kirchner's Orchestra. The patiently abiding Miss Schult had, on January 30th, the benefit due to her claims. Paucity of notes in the Eagle carries me to February 27th, when Miss Schult, Veazey, George Scobie and Hanson and Hayman were feathers dropped from that paper, on the wings of night. Eliza (*sic*) and Harry Roth, Little Rosina and Ada Melville greeted the visitors of April 16th–21st. Schwarz and Weiss (surely a "made-up" firm name), Miss A. Dagmar, Frank Gay, J. M. Woods, A. Meusenbach (*sic*) and Alfred Rado carried through the week of April 30th–May 5th. Alexandra Dagmar (contralto and "jodler") headed, for May 7th–12th, a list that included Fred Roberts, Annie Wildemuth, Ellen Valleys (*sic*), Alfred Rado and Augustus Meusebach (*sic*). Of course Minnie Schult and Kirchner's Orchestra always supplied the comfort of the familiar.

The Morells, Edward Figuere (*sic*), Maggie Webb, Harry Plant, Minnie Schult, Ellen Valleys, H. Wuestenberg, A Meusebach (*sic*) and the Kirchner Orchestra made an imposing array for May 14th–19th. There my scrip runs out for Zipp's, in Elm Place, for the year of the Great Blizzard.

ATHENÆUM, 1887–1888

I fear the reader may grow weary of visits to the busy Athenæum, in the year now investigated; the offerings were largely of amateur acting. The deluge began, on October 13th, with an entertainment and concert, under direction of St. Francis Xavier Academy, with F. V. Beggs, J. H. Stubbs, Ella Kelly, Mr. and Mrs. Nickolds, E. C. Fitzgerald and Annie Kemp. The Arcadian Club (or Society?) wasted the evening of October 25th, with Leah, the Forsaken. Pop's Foibles, a new American comedy, graced the night of November 14th, presented by a "mixed" company of amateurs, before an audience, saith the Eagle, "meagre but enthusiastic." The "mixed" perpetrators were Wilby Frampton, George Duryea, W. H. Kay, W. Sperry, James Quin, Paul Revere, Lizzie Gowrie, Marguerite Merton and many more. I confess that I find no familiar name in all that mixture, now "eternised"

[575]

in our record. But every one had heard of Blind Tom, who appeared on November 24th, 25th and 26th. In that week the Confraternity of the Sacred Heart (St. Patrick's Parish) gave a performance of The Stolen Will.

Lectures and demonstrations on the Treatment of Chronic Diseases were advertised to be given every morning from 10 to 11 o'clock, beginning on November 29th. Dr. Greene's Free Illustrated Lectures were to fall on December 12th, 13th, 14th, 15th and 16th, on subjects so exhilarating as (a) Health; (b) The Nervous System; (c) Physical and Mental Culture. One afternoon was to be "for gentlemen only," with stereopticon illustration; another "for ladies only."

Dismissing these delicate discussions, we return to normal, with the Davenport's first appearance of the year. On December 14th they gave Nevada, or, the Lost Mine, depending for verisimilitude on G. F. Holmes, Benjamin Ryer, G. W. McEvoy, H. Murphy, J. Demorest, E. D. Osgood, E. Q. Baker, Fred Cuthbert, Mamie Gardner, Hortense Booth, and Agnes Butcher — again a group to me unknown. December 21st (or 20th, according to the Times) found the Arcadian Dramatic Society once more on the stricken field, with A Celebrated Case; Henry Mason appeared as Jean, J. H. Connellan as Aubeterre, S. G. Frost as O'Rourke, Hortense Booth as the Chanoinesse, Stella Elmore as Madeleine and Valentine, Ella Greene as Adrienne, J. C. Costello as Raoul, and J. J. Breen as the wicked Lazare. On January 5th, St. Paul's Lyceum gave a benefit to J. J. Crowley, who acted Othello, to the Iago of Adam Dove, the Desdemona of Alice Shepard, and the Emilia of Stella Elmore. J. D. Billings and George Becks directed. The Arcadian Association came, on January 23rd, in a double bill of Withered Leaves and Checkmate, introducing Charles Bellows, Jr., J. C. Costello, B. R. Throckmorton, Stella Elmore, Ella Greene, J. J. Breen, M. H. Lindeman and Annie Smith.

For January 25th the Eagle announces a performance by the La Salle Dramatic Association, of The Lost Heiress, acted by Joseph N. Graham, E. J. François, J. A. McNeeley, Charles F. Willemin, John F. Heath, Fanny Rorke, Grace Lawrence, Flora Dayton and many others. I hope the reader may restrain his enthusiasm over the repetition, on January 30th, of The Mascot, given by F. Irving Crane's Vocal Chorus. The contribution of the Booth Society, on an evening in mid-February was At Folly's Feet, interpreted by William F. Wells, Thomas F. Young, James Miniter, Thomas T. Hayden, Edith Elwood and Mamie Maginn. February 21st found Pauline Schneider trying to show how good she was, in Act I of Fanchon, Act IV of Romeo and Juliet, and Act V of Adrienne Lecouvreur. Frederick Bowne and W. F. Wells, from the heart of amateurism, supported her in the ordeal; the Eagle seemed to think she wasn't so bad.

The Davenport was at it again, on February 29th, this time with Robert Macaire: why not in this time of Erminie, derived from that old play? The

[576]

Brooklyn Times announced, for April 2nd, a performance of Camille, by the Arcadians, with Matilda Davis in the title-rôle, with J. C. Costello as Armand, J. J. Breen as the elder Duval, Alice Butcher as Prudence, H. Lindeman as Gaston, and E. O. Jacobson as de Varville. On the 6th, this same affecting drama served Ada Austin as a medium of expression, her Camille, according to the Eagle, being supported by Thomas T. Hayden (Armand), William F. Wells, Albert Meafoy (Gaston), T. F. Young, G. T. M. Janvrin, Lizzie Wallace, Pauline Schneider (the ambitious débutante of February 21st — as Nanine) and Edith Elwood — a picked band of amateurs. Some time during the week of April 16th–23rd, the Lyceum Association essayed Partners for Life. And the Booth Dramatic Society, on May 7th, did Our Boys, with William J. Moran, James Miniter, William J. McCaull, John T. Nicholson, Lizzie Wallace, Libbie Healey, Miriam Smithson and Fannie (*sic*) Rorke. The Melpomene, which escaped me for the earlier months, closed its season, on May 14th, with May Blossom, presenting the much-engaged Lizzie Wallace in the title-rôle, Ernest O. Jacobson as Tom Blossom, Thomas T. Hayden as Steve Harland, Frank J. Oliver as Richard Ashcroft, Mamie Sloat as Deborah, William M. Campbell as Owen Hathaway, Albert Meafoy as Eph, William J. Moran as Hiram Sloane, Maud Sterner as Lulu, and Annette Sterner as Millie. This ends the onslaught of amateur acting in the Athenæum, for 1887–88. It remains merely to record a May Festival (on the 17th) for the benefit of the Kindergarten of St. Peter's Catholic Church. The children executed a grand floral march and a something-or-other called The Berry Pickers. I'll wager that every little boy and every little girl in the show felt very, very important. On May 22nd, Gabriel Harrison and his pupils gave an entertainment; Harrison was institutional in Brooklyn.

Historical Hall, 1887–1888

Dramatic exhibitions, amateur or professional, we shall not look for in Historical Hall, nestled as it was in the building of the staid Long Island Historical Society, at Pierrepont and Clinton Streets. I shall first invite the reader, on October 20th, for a concert of the gifted Teresina Tua, assisted by Henri Duzensi (*sic* — tenor), Alexander Lambert, and William Thaule (musical director). A second Tua concert followed, on the 25th, Max Heinrich co-operating. On October 27th, August Walter gave a piano recital, with two of his pupils, Josie Biggs and Helen Bunker, also performing. Those names suggest the desirability of swelling patronymics for artists who would win world applause. October 29th gave a talk on Mental Healing, by Mrs. Mary H. Plunkett, of the Christian Science faith.

Here follows matter of related import. In November, Mrs. Longshore Potts (speaking of patronymics!), M. D. from London, lectured to both sexes, on the 2nd, 4th, 7th and 11th (evenings), and to women only on the afternoons of November 9th, 11th, 12th, 14th and 15th. Comparing these health talks with those of Dr. Greene at the Athenæum, I cannot but wonder what had made Brooklyn so nervously apprehensive about its physical condition. Leaving that question as for the moment unanswerable, I pass, on November 19th, to the first pianoforte recital of A. Victor Benham. On February 20th, 27th and March 5th, Harry Brandon provided three Lenten concerts. Laura B. Phelps, not unknown to our chronicle, gave, on March 20th, a concert, in which her assistants were Harry Brandon (boy soprano), Mattie Dorlon (contralto), J. H. Stubbs (tenor), Perlee V. Jervis (pianist), the Hatton Quartet, and Minnie C. Dorlon.

April 4th provided a concert by the Yale Glee and Banjo Clubs. Lizzie Douglass's pupils were here on the 18th. On the 19th, Paul Tidden played the piano, his associates being Max Bendix (violin), John C. Rietzel (viola), Michael Brand ('cello) and Robert Thallon (accompanist). Zippora Monteith (of the intriguing name), soprano in Dr. Storrs's church, came forth, on April 30th, in concert, along with Perlee V. Jervis (also of an arresting name), Mrs. Whitney McKnight, Harry Rowe Shelley and the Hatton Quartet. Helen Maigille, on an evening as May died in June, was at Historical Hall, assisted by Francis Fischer Powers, Averick Parry (contralto), Clara Thoms (pianist), Harry Rowe Shelley, and Clifford Schmidt (violin).

Association (Y.M.C.A.) Hall (Brooklyn), 1887–1888

The Philharmonic Club of New York shall have the honour of opening for our research the Y.M.C.A. Hall, at Broadway and Bond Street. On October 22nd, with Richard Hoffman at the piano, it rendered compositions by Schumann, Wagner, Boccherini, Corven, Rubinstein, Wollenhaupt, &c. The Club appeared again on the 29th, and on November 12th. On November 11th, Aunt Polly Bassett's Singin' Skewl was funny to the easily amused. And Max O'Rell, on the 16th, delivered his famous John Bull and Jacques Bonhomme. Professor Robert Spice (*sic*) lectured, on November 19th, before the Brooklyn Assembly Agassiz Association, with Reverend Charles H. Hall presiding. And the Eagle informs us that, at Association Hall, on November 25th, would be rendered The Harvest Cantata, recently given in the Garden City Cathedral and in St. Luke's Church, Brooklyn; seventy boys and men were in it. War-correspondent Williams, of the London Chronicle, gave, on December 14th, Scenes from Six Campaigns and How the English Lost Gordon.

Robert J. Burdette was to have lectured on January 31st; he was forced to leave town, and George W. Cable took his place, reading from his own works. An interesting concert, on Saturday afternoon, March 3rd, was devoted to Chopin only, Richard Hoffman, Gustav Dannreuther and Adolf Hartdegen interpreting. The Brooklyn Choral Society made May 16th

[578]

(evening) musical; Carrie Hun-King, Dudley Buck, A. Hartdegen and Frank Treat Southwick (pianist) contributed to the bill of musical fare. On the 18th, a Memorial Concert of the Charles R. Doane Post enlisted Mr. and Mrs. Gerrit Smith, Charles Roberts, Jr., A. D. Woodruff and Francis Fischer Powers, all for an admission fee of 50 cents—"no reserved seats." Surely this was a good aggregation.

Brooklyn Music and Miscellany, 1887–1888

Much of the entertainment of Brooklyn has already been listed under heading of the halls where it occurred; it will now be our stern duty to pursue it to minor halls and to church pulpits.

I begin with a function of the Brooklyn Turn-Verein, held at Piper's Club House, 198–202 Court Street, on September 5th. On September 17th, the Fifth Avenue Casino, Fifth Avenue, between Union and President Streets, opened under new management, with 20 billiard tables, 16 bowling alleys, shuffle-boards, and a concert "all evening." Toward mid-October, the young men from St. Paul's Lyceum were moved to present David Garrick, inciting to their purpose J. J. Crowley, W. J. Loughlin, W. H. Briordy, T. J. Mannioun (sic), P. A. Goss, J. E. Quinn, C. J. Kinsella, R. Jason, Lizzie Healey, Annie Smith and Miss O. Martin, whose modest obituaries I hereby chronicle. On October 17th, the Centennial Baptist Church permitted Leland T. Powers to illustrate North Ca'liny Ways, and transform himself from Jekyll to Hyde, doubtless to the delight of the congregation. Abby Sage Richardson began, on November 15th, in the Parlours of the Brooklyn Woman's Club, 80 Willoughby Street, a series of morning lectures on Novels and Novelists; at the same club, on the afternoon of the 14th, Gabriel Harrison spoke feelingly on The Drama of Old Times. Evidently Brooklyn ladies of that remote era preluded Town Hall ladies of 1941, in New York. With this sage reflection, we pass, on October 24th, to Sängerbund Hall, there to hear the Lessing Quartet, Annie Louise Tanner and the New York Philharmonic Club.

Warner Institute, Broadway and Willoughby Street, now enters the record, with a minstrel performance, on November 14th, by the Lexington Amateurs. On the 15th, Dell Thompson (elocutionist) and a chorus of twenty were at the Franklin Avenue Presbyterian Church; on the 24th, Mme. de Fere's pupils gave the first of several concerts at her Conservatory of Music. And Remsen Hall, Court and Remsen Streets, clamours for admission to the record, with the reception and musicale, on November 30th, of the Amateur Opera Association; Alfred Young, J. Williams Macy, W. T. Cameron, Mrs. Macy and the De Witt Clinton Quintet did what they could to amuse the guests. In latest November, the Sängerbund, in their hall, had assistance from Anna Bulkley Hills, F. Remmertz and Harry Brandon (boy soprano). December dawned brightly, on the 1st, with the Reverend A. B. Kendig lecturing, at the Simpson M. E. Church, on The Model Woman.

Fly as we may, we cannot avoid amateur actors, especially in Brooklyn. At Warner Institute, on December 6th, the Leonardis Dramatic Association, of the St. Leonard Academy, enacted Esmeralda, with M. J. McKenna as Elbert Rogers, Mamie Courter as Lydia Ann, Mamie Cavney as Esmeralda, J. J. Moran, Jr., as Dave, M. J. Colligan as Estabrook, Katie Leibold as Nora and Maggie McKenna as Kate. On the same busy 6th, at Bedford Hall, Tompkins Avenue, near Fulton Street, for the bare price of 25 cents, one could have heard the Irving Dramatic Society, in the equally innocuous Caste. Or, if desired, on that same fateful evening, one might have wended his way to the Simpson M. E. Church, Clermont and Willoughby "Avenues," there to hear T. De Witt Talmage expound The Bright Side of Life. On the 8th, at the Central Congregational Church, Hancock Street, the Columbia College Glee and Banjo Clubs delighted many more than three little maids from school. A Japanese Bazar and Supper, on December 8th and 9th, at the Parsonage, 205 Carroll Street, was perhaps too private for an incursion of noisy non-parishioners; yet churches always need money.

Mrs. Scott-Siddons, who is slowly fading from the scene, and her daughter, Victoria Siddons, gave joint readings at 117 State Street: Henry VIII (in earliest December), King John (December 8th), and Julius Cæsar (13th). On December 13th, also, the Aurora Gratis Cathedral, Bedford Avenue and Madison Street, gave, under the auspices of the Scottish Rite Bodies (this sounds like a morgue) of Brooklyn, a concert involving Jules Levy, Stella Levy (soprano), Lulu Klein (contralto), Enrico (*sic*) Ducenzi (*sic*), Lithgow James (baritone), and Paul Steindorff (pianist). Variety was subserved, on the 14th, by polo, at the Palace Rink, Clermont Avenue, with the Brooklyns opposing the Newarks (their "first appearance in this city"); roller skating was to precede and follow the game. On the 15th, at the Nostrand Avenue M. E. Church appeared the Meigs Sisters, Giuseppe Vitale (violin) and Helen Ottolengui (reciter). The delightful Meigs Sisters were at the Church of the Messiah, Greene and Clermont, on December 22nd, their associates then being Eva Duffy (violin), John G. Hill (tenor), Belle Elliott (soprano), Alfred D. Cammeyer (banjo) and William Scott Fennell (baritone). On the 26th of December, the second annual tournament for singles exercised the 23rd Regiment Tennis Club.

The elusive Warner Institute opened, on December 26th (or 29th, the Eagle and the Times conflicting), for School, performed by the pretentiously named Friendship Dramatic Society, with a cast involving M. B. Schmidt, I. S. Moag, I. B. Schmidt, Abe Strauss, Ben Rice, and several young ladies with names German or Jewish—Schmidt, Levy, Strauss, Lustig, Michels, Medler, Hoffman, Blum and Schilberg. January 10th introduced, at Plymouth Church, a curious Rock Harmonicon, which one Till and his sons had worked, in eleven years of labour, from solid rock; Miss Till and Annie Till sang to the best of their ability. If this device did not attract, one could have gone, on that same 10th, to Bedford Hall, where the Dramatic Committee of the Contemporary Club presented, not only Meg's Diversion, but In Cap and Bells, by E. F. Cole, a member of the Club. Whichever diversion one chose, for the 10th, he could have assuaged, on the 11th, with a lecture, at the Chapel of the Central Congregational Church, Hancock Street; in that, the Reverend Dr. Jackson Wray, of Whitfield Chapel, London, spoke of Rare Old Æsop, a theme which he may have adapted to needs of 1888. Ivan Panin lectured, on January 16th, at Brooklyn Heights Seminary, on Russian Literature. On January 17th, Minnie Dorlon, at 81 Johnson Street, read from Dickens for those who could not themselves read Dickens; Miss M. S. Dorlon mitigated the intellectual asperities by flights (I hope) of song. The Duryea Presbyterian Church (Clermont Avenue, near Atlantic) opened, on January 18th, for the charming Meigs Sisters, with Louise Johnson (reader), George Kilmer (baritone) and Master Bethune Jones (another precocious violinist). And the Reverend Jackson Wray moved, on January 19th, to the Summerfield M. E. Church, Greene and Washington "Avenues," there to speak on Wycliffe, or, Old England 500 Years Ago. January 19th was a much used date: at Unity Church, Gates Avenue and Irving Place, R. J. De Cordova expounded Courtship and Marriage; and, on the same evening, at the North Reformed Church, Clermont Avenue, between Myrtle and Willoughby, Philip Phillips, the "Singing Pilgrim," began a three-nights visit. Far different, in significance and intent, was the evening of the Amaranth, as January was finishing its course; it held a third informal reception, at which appeared Edith Dow (soprano), Master Fred Frankel (violin), Minnie C. Dorlon (elocutionist) and N. Mott, Jr. Those last nights of January found G. W. Leitsche at the Cumberland Avenue Presbyterian Church, lecturing on Life, Habits and Religion of the Hindoos; and the Thespian Dramatic Society exhibiting itself at Rivers Academy, 1586 Fulton Street.

At the Nostrand Avenue M. E. Church, the Wesleyan Literary Society, on February 1st, allowed William B. Perry, George D. Perry, J. Williams Macy, and Blanche and Marion Bender to give account of their talents, leaving me guessing (1941) as to whether this was the Blanche Bender who supported Joseph Jefferson, some years later, in Rip Van Winkle. But my mind is a blank concerning those members of the St. Agnes Young Men's Literary Association, of St. Agnes Church, who, on the same night, played Parted, with Thomas H. Millard, William C. Crolius, James F. Connelly, Maggie Dalton, Fanny Herko and Marion Smithson, though two of these names awaken a faint chime in my memory. On February 2nd, far over Canarsie way, the Excelsior Musical and Literary Association provided

[581]

(February 2nd) at Liebow's Hall (Fulton and Schenck "Avenues") an entertainment including a farce, A Little More Cider. I comply with my omnivorous reader's demand and supply the participants in the programme (copied religiously, from the Brooklyn Times)— E W. Smith, E. R. Wyatt, P. Webb, F. E. Hastings, C. F. Moadinger, Jr., Mrs. A. E. D. Van Sicle, Miss E. J. Wyatt, and Mrs. L. F. Moadinger. I cannot vouch for the accuracy of the Brooklyn Times in transcribing the initials of those misguided (?) Excelsiors. To be "excelsior," one should have a magnificent rhythmical name. I pass, in early February, to Labour Lyceum (I confess I don't know the way there) for the singing of the La Salle Männerchor.

The busy Central Congregational Church promised, for February 16th, the historic Camilla Urso, with Maud Morgan, Charles Herbert Clarke (tenor), Harry Foreman (sic—baritone) and the Schumann Male Quartet. Washington's Birthday was duly and variously celebrated: a "Grand Musicale," at the Church of Our Father, Lefferts Place, promised Edith Wendell (soprano), Mrs. Peter Bell (contralto), Atherton Furlong (tenor), and Charles T. Catlin (elocutionist). The Graham Celebration of the day presented Seth Low, in an address on The Life and Character of George Washington. And, possibly best of all, the Tabernacle advertised Jennie Dutton, Mrs. J. W. Macy, Laura Sedgwick Collins (reciter), Mrs. E. L. Simmelkaier (sic) and Harry Foresman (sic). The Euphonia concert, on February 24th, at Sängerbund Hall, was to provide Enrico Duzensi (sic), Dora Friedel, Master A. Edwin Farmer, Mrs. L. F. Sheville, Marie Prox, and Wilhelm and Edward H. Müller.

Lent may have confined the exuberance of Brooklyn; at any rate, not till March 12th were we invited to buy tickets for an entertainment. Then, at the Hanson Place M. E. Church, a testimonial to Henry Camp was to enlist Zippora Monteith, Anna Holbrook Rosan (soprano), Annie Webb (contralto), Laura B. Phelps (violin), T. J. Toedt, Walter C. Low (bass) and Harry Rowe Shelley. Alas! the only entertainment Brooklyn had, on March 12th, was hovering in warm homes, safe from the Great Blizzard; the Camp concert was postponed to March 22nd. March 20th opened the New Home for Aged Men, Classon Avenue and Park Place, for concerts, afternoon and evening, directed by John Hyatt Brewer, and involving Marie Van and H. O. C. Kortheuer. March 21st found Minnie C. Dorlon reading at her home, 81 Johnson Street, from Nicholas Nickleby; this was the fourth in a series of private readings by that determined elocutionist. A ball of the Società di Mutuo Soccorso, Principe di Napoli, scheduled for March 14th, at Sängerbund Hall, was postponed, perhaps because of the blizzard, to April 9th.

A banjo concert, as testimonial to the Dore Brothers, was listed for April 9th, at the Everett Assembly Rooms. On the 13th, in the York Street M. E. Church, John Q. Hoyt delivered his well-known Around the World in Eighty Minutes. A hint to seek open spaces came with notice that Paul Bauer's West Brighton Beach Hotel would give a concert, on Sunday, April 15th. But April 18th refused to take the hint, offering three concerts of note. In Plymouth Church, on that date, the Seventh Regiment Band of New York was to play in full uniform, and T. De Witt Talmage was to read from his own works. On the 18th, also, in St. Ann's Church, Clinton and Livingston Streets, Master L. Schmidt, boy violin virtuoso, showed his talent, others including Blanche Taylor (soprano), Miss Macnichol (contralto), Walter Brill (bass), Charles Battell Loomis (elocutionist), and Paolo Giorza (pianist). Finally, that same evening found Blind Tom at the Herkimer Street Baptist Church. At St. Mark's Hall, Adelphi Street, a date contiguous to the busy 18th provided a musical entertainment, with Emily Winant to assist. In the week of April 16th–21st, the Lyceum Amateurs acted Partners for Life, and, since Lester Wallack would not allow them to play Rosedale (see the Herald) the Gilbert amateurs played Our Boys — but where?

I approach April 23rd with something like awe, not, of course, because Ridgewood Council 678, Royal Arcanum, gave, at Warner Institute, Everybody's Friend and The Champion of Her Sex; nor, indeed, because, at Sängerbund Hall, the Lessing Quartet (Alexander Rihm conducting), Marie Gramm and the New York Philharmonic Club appeared in musical accord; but because, beginning on that day, Barnum and the London United Shows led Brooklyn captive for a blissful week, at Sumner and Putnam Avenues.

I pass with pleasure into flowery May. On the 8th and 9th of that presumably balmy month, Philip Phillips, at the Marcy Avenue Baptist Church, corner of Monroe Street, rolled Around the World in a Chariot of Song. On the 17th, the Sängerbund closed its season, with the Mitwirkung of Lube, Rank, and Damen Schatz and Hartmann of Thalia renown. On May 18th, the Green Collegiate Institute Scholars gave The Sleeping Beauty; on the same evening the Young Athletic Baseball Club of the pupils in the Grammar Grade of Public School No. 15 gave an entertainment in Bradbury Hall. In that year of the visit of Henry Irving and Ellen Terry and of the Great Blizzard, these last two events seem to me overwhelmingly unimportant. But very attractive seems the testimonial to William T. Angel, on May 21st, at the First Baptist Church, Pierrepont Street; excellent singers were provided in Ella Earle, Emily Winant, Charles Herbert Clarke, Whitney Mockridge and Francis Fischer Powers; in addition were promised Gustave Schmidt (violin), Harry Rowe Shelley, Helen Ludington (contralto) and Albert Gerard Theis. This big affair ended it; thereafter we could see Buffalo Bill's Wild West at Erastina, Pain's 1666 fireworks at Manhattan Beach, or Nero at Staten Island; or hear Gilmore's Band, at Manhattan Beach, or the 32nd Regiment Band. at the West Brighton Beach Hotel (late Paul Bauer's), or Seidl's good concerts at Brighton Beach. Or eat strawberries at festivals in June, or try to avoid ants at picnics or sail away to far-off shores on Long Island or up the Hudson! A merry world? This record for the Miscellany of 1887–88 seems hardly to repay the labour of collecting it from the huge, ragged pages of the files of the Brooklyn Eagle, in the New York Public Library. From the file of the Progresso Italo-Americano I gathered account of the visit of the Società Italiane Unite di Brooklyn, on September 20th, to the New York Schützen Park — a visit more fully allocated under the caption of Italian Activities.

BROOKLYN PHILHARMONIC, 1887–1888

The strongly entrenched Philharmonic began the new season on November 11th and 12th, with Theodore Thomas conducting Schubert's Ninth Symphony, in C major; Dvorak's overture, Husitzka; and the Vorspiel to Die Meistersinger. Helene Hastreiter was soloist. The second concert, on December 17th, of course with the customary rehearsal, on the 16th, was devoted to Beethoven, with all three of the Leonore overtures, the fifth concerto for piano (with Adele Aus der Ohe), and the Seventh Symphony. The first of three popular matinées fell on December 8th. For January 20th and 21st, Thomas provided Bach's Fugue in A minor; Schumann's Third Symphony; a Scene and Air from Euryanthe (with Emil Fischer); the Eine Faust Overture of Wagner; Schubert's Der Wanderer (with Fischer); and (first time) Morceau Symphonique, La Russie (by Rubinstein).

On February 17th, the orchestra played works by Haydn, Bruch, J. K. Paine (a symphonic poem on The Tempest), and Berlioz. The evening of the 18th produced Elijah, with Clementine Lasar, Emily Winant, Minnie Dilthey, Miss M. B. Campbell (alto), T. J. Toedt and D. M. Babcock. March 16th and 17th proffered an interesting programme in Beethoven's Eighth Symphony; a concerto for 'cello, by Raff (played by Victor Herbert); Aria, Der Dæmon (sung by Giulia Valda); and Richard Strauss's new Symphonic Fantasia, Italy. The April concerts allowed us to enjoy the overture to Tannhäuser; the Siegfried Idyll; Concerto No. 3, in E minor, Chopin-Tausig (with Joseffy at the piano), and Goldmark's Rustic Wedding.

LEE AVENUE ACADEMY, 1887–1888

I now invite the reader to Williamsburgh, for a season's activities in the Lee Avenue Academy. The term began on September 5th, with Stricken Blind, a thriller by Conquest and Pettitt, with Nina (sic) Crolius, J. Scott Spirey (sic), Mr. Evelyn Evans, Master James N. Gleason and others of equal lack of distinction. Lillian Olcott, as the harassing Theodora, filled the week of September 12th–17th, with Hudson Liston as Justinian, and Kellerd as Adrian.

[584]

Harry Lacy, on September 19th, began a week, in his recent great success, The Still Alarm. The Dominie's Daughter, a feebly striving infant, was here for the week of September 26th. October 3rd launched She, as dramatised by F. (sic) H. Glenney. Dixey, in Adonis (October 10th), James O'Neill, in Monte Cristo (17th), the Herrmanns, in black art (24th), and Thatcher, Primrose and West's Minstrels (31st) in a different style of black art, carry us expeditiously to November 7th, when Forgiven introduced Frederic Bryton, Fanny Reeves, Harry Harwood, Charles Titus and Louise St. Julian.

Two weeks of Charles H. Hoyt's popular nothingness gave us A Hole in the Ground (November 14th–19th) and A Bunch of Keys (21st–26th). In the former appeared George Richards, Frank Lawrence, Julian Mitchell and Flora Walsh (Mrs. Hoyt). For November 28th–December 3rd similar edification came, for the "tired business man," with McNish, Johnson and Slavin's Minstrels, and, for December 5th–10th, with the very funny Frank Daniels, in Little Puck. Mantell, in Monbars, was serious enough for the week of December 12th–17th; and Dorothy brought pre-Christmas cheer (December 19th–24th) with its really metropolitan cast — Eugene Oudin, Lillian Russell, Harry Paulton, Rose Leighton, John Brand and Agnes Stone. A Dark Secret seems a gloomy gift as herald for the new year (December 26th–31st), but the Henley Regatta scene may have led to thoughts of a trip abroad in the coming summer.

This brings us to January 2nd, when Jim, the Penman, began a week with the customary good cast, headed by Ada Dyas, Joseph E. Whiting and H. M. Pitt. A Rag Baby came (January 9th) with Charlie Reed as Old Sport, T. J. Cronin, Mark Sullivan and Jessie Jenkins (these in Three Little Tramps from Jail), Georgie Parker, Edith Jennesse, &c. Sweatnam, Rice and Fagan's Minstrels (16th), Evans and Hoey, in A Parlour Match (23rd), Scanlan, in Shane-na-Lawn (30th), carry us to February 6th, when Annie Pixley began a week divided between The Deacon's Daughter and M'liss. Maggie Mitchell, an actress of similar art, but superior, held the week of February 13th–18th, with, in rapid succession, The Pearl of Savoy, Lorle, Maggie, the Midget, Jane Eyre, Little Barefoot and Fanchon — a week's work that would utterly dishearten a modern star (1941). A Tin Soldier (February 20th) and Nat Goodwin, in Turned Up and Lend Me Five Shillings (27th) carried Williamsburgh into windy March.

The lure for March 5th was Cora Tanner in Alone in London, and, for the 12th–17th, Hoodman Blind, with F. de Belleville and Viola Allen. On the 19th, Held by the Enemy appealed, with Block, Marshall, Arthur, May Mills and Hattie Schell, none of whom dints my memory. For the week of the 26th, Deacon Brodie made us serious, and Harbour Lights brightened our outlook on April 2nd.

This brings us to April 9th, with Minnie Palmer, sprightly, though not

[585]

a great artist, dividing the week of April 9th–14th equally between My Brother's Sister and My Sweetheart. With her were Ben Hendrick, Virginia Buchanan and C. A. Matthews. On the 16th, Lotta, rival of the more youthful Miss Palmer and prototype of the style Miss Palmer adopted, entered, in her new piece, Pawn Ticket No. 210. Her good company included G. C. Boniface, Jr., P. Aug. Anderson and Cyril Scott. The Little Tycoon, on the 23rd, led to a similar manifestation, Evangeline, on the 30th. Louis James and Marie Wainwright began, on May 7th, in Virginius, and treated us to a week of the "legitimate," with that play, Othello, the "new Faust" (Gretchen) and Ingomar. But Vernona Jarbeau, in Starlight, on May 14th, immediately called us down from the exalted realm of the preceding week. The Old Oak, on the 21st, was supported by Henrietta Vaders, Charles Bradshaw, George S. Fleming, and Julius Kahn. Lost in New York fitted the week of May 28th–June 2nd. Here I leave the Lee Avenue Academy, for 1887–88, wondering if the large, new Amphion Academy may not have been crowding it to the rearward. Certainly the Amphion, as we shall see, had been providing some remarkable stars and novelties in plays. A benefit restrains my flight. On June 5th, a testimonial to Laurent Howard gave Mr. and Mrs. J. S. Berger in The Toodles, and several variety people.

AMPHION ACADEMY, 1888

This new and important theatre, at Bedford Avenue, near Broadway, was imposingly opened on Friday, January 27, 1888, with the struggling National Opera Company, in The Queen of Sheba. Thereafter they sang Aïda (matinée, 28th), Nero (evening, 28th), Tannhäuser (30th), Faust (31st), Queen of Sheba (matinée, February 1st), and Lohengrin (evening, February 1st) — certainly an ambitious programme. On Saturday afternoon, the Amphion carried on its good work with a concert by Josef Hofmann, Helene Hastreiter, Nettie Carpenter, Mme. Sacconi and Adolf Neuendorff's orchestra. The Amphion Musical Society whose name evidently was used for the new house, gave a concert there, with Blanche Stone Barton and Michael Banner.

The week of February 6th–11th brought the Madison Square actors, in Elaine, with Annie Russell, Minnie Seligman, Charles Overton, Alexander Salvini, William Davidge, Myron Calice and Walden Ramsay — this lasting for three days. The remaining days of the week (9th–11th) provided a very strong cast in Jim, the Penman — Agnes Booth, Maud Harrison, Mathilde Madison, Charles Coghlan, Alexander Salvini and Walden Ramsay. With so many of Palmer's great company thus absent from home, one might ask who were left in Madison Square; a glance at the cast of Heart of Hearts then on the home stage will answer that question. I may

[586]

say that, when this Jim, the Penman, was seen a few days earlier at the Brooklyn Theatre, the Brooklyn Times (January 31st) says that Coghlan as Ralston was "disappointing to many who had seen Mr. Fred Robinson in the part. He was vapid where he should have been strong." I can account for this estimate only by stating my own feeling that Ralston was entirely "out of the line" of Coghlan's art; as a matter of fact, I was never enthusiastic about Robinson in that or any other rôle.

James C. Roach, in Dan Darcy (February 13th–18th) may have been good entertainment, though I doubt it; but lovers of minstrelsy could have revelled in the offering of February 20th–25th — Thatcher, Primrose and West's Minstrels. The changeability of bills in even the best combination houses is exemplified in this paragraph. That big blackface offering was succeeded (February 27th–March 3rd) by Margaret Mather, with Milnes Levick, Frederick Paulding and Mrs. Sol Smith, in her classic and neo-classic repertoire, and she, in turn (March 5th–10th), by Robson and Crane, in The Henrietta ("with the original cast"). And they, on March 12th, by Imre Kiralfy's Mazulm! D. E. Bandmann, capitalising on Mansfield's success, filled the week of March 19th–24th with his version of Dr. Jekyll and Mr. Hyde, Louise Beaumont (sic) supporting as Sybil, and T. J. Herndon as Poole. The Brooklyn Times, which had preferred Robinson's James Ralston to Charles Coghlan's, now showed its independence by rating Bandmann's Jekyll-Hyde above Mansfield's, as "less exaggerated, but horrible." The Amphion was developing critical judgment.

Sydney Rosenfeld's play, A Possible Case, getting ready for a New York opening, spent two weeks (March 26th–April 7th) at the Amphion, the striking cast including M. A. Kennedy, Henry Miller, Robert Hilliard, George De Vere, W. H. Thompson, Edward Tannehill, Daniel Leeson, James H. Browne, R. V. Percy, A. H. Arnold, Edward Hughes, Genevieve Lytton, Daisy (Dorothy) Dorr, Louise Rial, Leila Wolstan, Kate Oesterle and Carrie Jackson. The reader knows how this cast compares with that in New York. The Amphion, after that flurry of novelty, settled down, for April 9th–14th, to Hanlons' New Fantasma. And more novelty came on the 16th — The Mystery of a Hansom Cab, "produced under the auspices of A. M. Palmer" (this surprises me), with Henry Lee, E. J. Henley, Wilton Lackaye, E. D. Lyons, Charles W. Butler, Bijou Heron, Carrie Jamison, Carrie Neville, Rose Snyder and Clara Lipman — a very good cast. Is this our third meeting with Miss Lipman? Perhaps the theatre offered no play for April 23rd–28th; my pilgrim scrip provides merely (for the 23rd) a concert by the Cæcilia Ladies' Vocal Society and the Amphion Society, with C. Mortimer Wiske directing. E. H. Sothern, in The Highest Bidder, also brought (April 30th–May 5th) a very good company — C. B. Bishop, Herbert Archer, Rowland Buckstone, W. B. Royston, Belle Archer, Fanny Addison and Ethelyn Friend — practically the group that had launched the play on its successful career. Barry and Fay were at the Amphion (May 7th–12th), in McKenna's Flirtation. And a glorious week followed with Booth and Barrett in Julius Cæsar (May 14th), Macbeth (15th), Hamlet (16th), King Lear (17th), The Merchant of Venice, the entire play (18th) Othello (matinée, 19th) and Julius Cæsar (evening, 19th). Glorious, I call this offering, yet Barrett, very middle-aged, was obliged to play some youthful parts, in which Irving's handsome Terriss and Alexander had accustomed us to more visual reasonableness. The Brooklyn Times speaks of the failure in nervous force now apparent, at times, in Booth's Hamlet. It also informs us (May 19th) that the Booth-Barrett tour of forty weeks, ending in Brooklyn on May 19th, was "the most phenomenally successful starring tour on record." The receipts had averaged from $15,000 to $20,000 a week, and, at the lower figure, the season would yield at least $600,000. I am pleased to learn this, in that day of the craze for operetta and extravaganza. The reader, if he is like me, will also be pleased to learn that Booth was to pass his summer in Newport and Boston, while Barrett was to go to Deerfoot Farm, near Southborough, Massachusetts.

His Lordship, by Edwin Atwell, had a first performance, on Tuesday, May 22nd. Frank Mayo divided the week of May 28th–June 2nd between The Royal Guard and Nordeck. Another "try-out" was The Parvenus, by S. M. Monroe, participants including Nellie Donald, Leffing-well, John W. Jennings, William E. Stafford, James L. Edwards, and Marie Hartley, decidedly a diminished host. Its departure allows me to leave the Amphion for 1887–88, quite convinced that the new theatre will open for us interesting vistas in months to come. Yet I must chronicle, for June 18th, a testimonial to C. Mortimer Wiske, become almost the Jerome Hopkins of his time, in activity and in demands on the public. A good group came to his aid—William Courtney, Carl Martin, and the New York Madrigal Quartet (Emma Henry Thomas, Clara Stutsman, George S. Sturgis and W. Thomas).

F. F. Proctor's (Novelty) Theatre, 1887–1888

If we attend the lately careful Novelty, in the season under review, we shall need to explain to fastidious friends our reasons for going; it will hardly suffice to say that, to students of the theatre, all shows are worth exploiting.

The Eagle was assuredly rather supercilious, on September 6th, in its description of Frank I. Frayne, as a "tamer of lions, rider of horses, marks-man, and something of an actor"; the evening before, he had begun a week, in Mardo, the Hunter. Bartley Campbell's exciting Clio followed, on the 12th. Arcadia, with Little Corinne, was, doubtless, interesting (September 19th) to lovers of youthful prodigies. Personally I should have preferred

Hallen and Hart's First Prize Ideals (September 26th), with Isabella Ward (xylophone and bell solos), Joe Hart, Ralph Terry's shadow pictures, Wilton (twenty-one-foot somersault), Ella Wesner and Frank Bush. Charles T. Ellis, in William Carleton's Casper, the Yodler, filled the week of October 3rd–8th; doubtless innocuous, and amusing withal.   Zitka, also by the late William Carleton, filled the week of October 10th–15th.   Insha-vogue was thoroughly Irish — stage Irish — for the 17th–22nd.   The Wilbur Opera Company began a week, on the 24th, with the everlasting The Mascot. And Edwin Arden, in Eagle's Nest, was also a very familiar offering for October 31st–November 5th.

Hearts of Oak was strong matter for November 7th–12th, and George C. Boniface, in The Streets of New York, for November 14th–19th.   The Eagle is so scant in information for minor theatres that, often, I can supply merely names of plays and stars.   Charles Gardner, in Karl, was the not-over-exciting lure for November 21st–26th.   And Ada Gray, in East Lynne, could have been a novelty to no one, for November 28th–December 3rd. On December 5th, we veered to "Variety," for a week of Austin's Australian Novelty Company, for ingredients of which I refer the reader to Hyde and Behman's.   The Wages of Sin moved from Proctor's other theatre, the Criterion, for the week of the 12th, at the Novelty.   The Old Oaken Bucket was drawn from the well of public estimate, for the week of December 19th–24th; and Peck's Bad Boy distributed post-Christmas joy, be-ginning on December 26th.

It is hard to see why the Novelty had sunk so low; 10 cents and 20 cents admitted to its offerings.   George H. Adams, in Zo-Zo, the Magic Queen, filled the week of January 2nd–7th, the New Year gift of Sunday, January 1st, being John Q. Hoyt's Dissolving Views.   Nobody's Claim introduced (January 9th–14th) Joseph J. Dowling and Sadie Hasson, supported by Clifford Dempsey, A. W. Purcelle, Nellie Pierce and Addie Eaton.   The next week brought the Kimball Musical Comedy Company, in Mam'zelle. Thenceforth we travelled a hard-worn path with (January 23rd–28th) James H. Wallick in The Cattle King and The Bandit King, for three days each; and (January 30th–February 4th) McKee Rankin and Mabel Bert, in The New Danites.   During this latter engagement, "any purchaser of a 50 cents or a 75 cents ticket will be presented with an order for a town lot 25 x 100 feet."   This sounds like long ago in our Annals.   Those free lots were still promised for February 6th–11th, when Phosa McAllister was to show Taken from Life.   J. C. (Fattie) Stewart's The Two Johns Com-pany made more or less gay the week of February 13th–18th, and Her Atonement thrilling and sad that of the 20th–25th.

Under the Gaslight made the week of March 5th–10th luridly bright, and Pat Rooney, in Pat's Wardrobe, distributed fun for March 12th–17th. The following week saw the return of Joseph J. Dowling, with Addie Eaton,

Clifford Dempsey and Nellie Page, in Never Say Die. Sunday, March 18th, was dedicated to Frank Oakes Rose's lecture, Through London with Dickens. Dan McCarthy's True Irish Hearts was very much of its time, in the week of March 25th–30th. Proctor's, now definitely located at South Fourth and Driggs Streets, carried through April with (2nd–7th), Michael Strogoff; C. T. Ellis, in Casper, the Yodler (9th–14th); Daniel Sully (16th–21st) in, for three nights each, The Corner Grocery and Daddy Nolan; and Tony Pastor's Combination (23rd–28th). A Great Wrong may have been righted in the week of April 30th–May 5th. N. S. Wood followed (May 7th–12th) in The Waifs of New York, The Silver King spreading the triumph of virtue over the stage of May 14th–19th. Muggs' Landing, with Carlotta, began a week, on May 21st, and A Chip of the Old Block another, on the 28th. The Cawthorn (sic) Brothers, for June 4th–9th, tested the value of The Little Nugget. The last week of the season (June 11th–16th) brought the shivers of The Boy Tramp, or, the Maniac Mother, with Mme. Neuville and Augustin, her son.

On June 25th, the last performance of the season was tendered by Proctor to Allen and Wogler; promised to appear were Pat Rooney, John and James Russell, Benny Grinnell, George S. Knight, Victory Bateman, Harry Kennedy, the Julians, "Professor" Henry J. Campbell and several more. I am sufficiently skeptical to wonder how many of them appeared.

PEOPLE'S THEATRE, WILLIAMSBURGH, 1887–1888

The "New" People's Theatre began its season on Saturday, September 3rd, with a surprisingly dignified offering — Mrs. D. P. Bowers, supported by Henry Aveling, in The Czarina. This piece was repeated twice on the 5th (Labour Day); on the 6th and 7th, the star returned to her institutional Lady Audley's Secret, and, on the 8th, revealed her impressive Queen Elizabeth. For the 9th and twice on the 10th she essayed a new Mme. Crœsus. The Eastern District must have been surprised to find orchestra chairs held at $1.25. John F. Ward, as Higgins, in The Doctor, leaves me, for the week of September 12th, quite ignorant as to the star and his vehicle, though Beverly Turner and Ida Ward supported; but I know J. B. Polk and Mixed Pickles, served in the week of the 19th–24th. Phillips seems to have left the establishment, and Stubel and Fabiani were announced as managers.

Prices were reduced to 75 cents and 25 cents, when, on September 26th, The Magic Talisman, with Miaco, began a hopeful week. Thenceforward the house went its provincial way with Beacon Lights, starring George Learock (October 3rd–8th); with Frederick Warde in a week (October 10th–15th) divided between Richard III, Virginius, The Gladiator and Gaston Cadol, orchestra seats now selling at 50 cents and 35 cents; The Two Johns

(17th–22nd); Pete Baker (once of Baker and Farron), with Lulie (?) Miller as Lena, in Chris and Lena (October 24th–29th); and (October 31st–November 5th) Reilly and Wood's Mammoth Congress of International Stars, including the Nelson Family of six, D'Alvini, Bobby Gaylor, Mlle. Forgardis (*sic*), the Emperors of Music, Florence Miller, Adele Wilson, Reno and Reilly and Pat Reilly.

November's falling leaves included Kate Castleton, in Crazy Patch (7th–12th); Edwin Mayo, in Davy Crockett (14th–19th); Kate Claxton and Charles A. Stevenson, in The Two Orphans, at a top-price of 50 cents, (21st–26th); and William Cullington, in For Congress (28th–December 3rd). This array of talent surprises me. December allowed the year to die merrily, with Frank Howard, in Sam'l of Posen (5th–10th); Jennie Yeamans, in Our Jennie (12th–17th); Katie Hart, in The Quaker Club (19th–24th); and Robert McWade, in Rip Van Winkle (26th–31st). Surely the "New" People's was offering interesting matter for a low entrance fee. The Arthur Rehan Company of Comedians divided the week of January 2nd–7th between Love in Harness and Nancy and Company — plays associated with his sister's fame at Daly's.

For January 9th–14th J. S. Murphy, in The Kerry Gow, was supported by Virginia Marlowe, Harold Courtenay, Harry Sinclair and Ada Shattuck. James M. Hardie and Sara Von Leer followed (16th–21st), in their well-known On the Frontier. The Moran and Thomas San Francisco Minstrels, a name the reader will sadly recall from a then departed past, was quite contemporary (January 23rd–28th), with Frank Moran, Ned Thomas, Dave Fox, Pickert and Mayon, Harrington and Johnson, Karoly Ordey, J. M. Woods, Dave Christy, J. F. Davis, J. J. Dougherty, and William Blakeney and his band. Surely this list is more suggestive of vaudeville than of minstrelsy. A German Dramatic and Operatic Season for the Hospital Fund of the Altdeutsches Volksfest Verein und Hospital Gesellschaft gave us Inspector Bräsig (January 30th and 31st); Die Pfarrer's Küchen (February 1st and 2nd); and Der Freischütz (3rd and 4th). I did not discover the purveyors of this Teutonic feast.

Hettie Bernard Chase introduced us (February 6th–11th) to Rags, the Wildcat, and similarly removed from centres of culture was the offering of the following week (13th–18th) — Scouts of the Yellowstone, with three companies. Back to the better known Gus Williams lured us (February 20th–25th), with his popular Keppler's Fortunes. And Thrown upon the World was very tearful from February 27th to March 3rd. Mattie Vickers, who always interests me, divided the week of March 5th–10th between her accustomed offerings — Jacquine and Cherub. The West, more or less wild, seemed to be in the ascendant; for March 12th–17th Kate Purssell (*sic*) gave us Calamity Jane, or, the Queen of the Plains, a title very suggestive of a kind of thing at that time to be read in the popular weekly

[591]

story papers. Uncle Tom's Cabin (March 19th–24th) presented the well-known Harry Woodson as Uncle Tom, with J. E. Lewis as George Harris, and Little Charlotte Bardolph as Eva. March ended (26th–31st) with W. M. Paul, in Lucky Ranch.

Dan A. Kelly started April (2nd–7th) with After Seven Years, and very exciting must have been (April 9th–14th) Blanche Miller, in King of the Mines, with "the entire stage in flames." Emily Soldene, reduced from her higher estate in the '70s, brought (April 16th–21st) that Burlesque and Novelty Company she had presented in the Bowery; Harry Melville was with her, and Mlle. Zara, who, it was solemnly declared, "kicks her way into favour." After that, the Foryman (*sic*) and Martin Combination of April 23rd–28th may have seemed a bit tame — no kick in it. Only a Farmer's Daughter, that had outlived many city maidens of the stage, was the vehicle of Marion Abbott for the week beginning on April 30th. Austin's Australian Novelty Company, one of the best-liked, carried the People's from May 7th to 12th; Edith Sinclair and Edward M. Favor, in A Box of Cash, had a propitious title for May 14th–19th. It seems to have closed the season at the People's; summer theatres were now abloom in open spaces.

Grand Theatre, Brooklyn, E.D., 1887–1888

That second theatre of the outskirts, the Grand, re-opened, on August 27th, with Grau's Opera Company, in Olivette. Across the Continent, with Howard Coveney, filled the week of September 5th–10th, and Shadowed Crime and Returned to Life divided, equally, between them, the following week. The Early Birds Company of September 19th–24th caught the Ginger Snaps Company of September 26th–October 1st. The Brooklyn Times now advertises for the place "new management, increasing popularity. Parquet, not reserved, 25 cents, orchestra seats, reserved, 35 cents." Let us see.

Richard Scott, in Thrown upon the World, was the saddening output for October 3rd–8th; but Joe J. Sullivan, in The Black Thorn was, possibly, a sharp counter-irritant for October 10th–15th. Gus Hill's Combination, always good, brought variety in the next week, and, for October 24th–29th, Henry T. Chanfrau presented his father's perennial Kit, the Arkansas Traveller. A Brave Woman (October 31st–November 5th) leaves me helpless as to her claims; but I can guess the nature of the next week's show — Florence Wood's Autumn Leaves and the Three Comets Specialty and Burlesque Company, or, indeed, that of the offering of November 14th–19th — Arizona Joe, in The Wild West Dramatised, or, Life of Arizona Joe. Under the Lash may have been a hit for November 21st–26th. November 28th–December 3rd allowed William Thompson to produce successively three plays—The Gold King, For a Life, and The Convict, an interesting progression of titles. Lillie (*sic*) Hall's Burlesque Company, William M. Davene's Allied Attractions and Hasson and Haymon's Royal Japanese Troupe filled to overflowing the cup of joy for December 5th–10th. J. Z. Little, in The World (12th–17th); T. J. Farron, in A Soap Bubble (December 26th–31st); One of the Bravest (January 2nd–7th); Daniel Kelly (January 9th–14th); the Mignani-Siegrist Star Specialty Company (16th–21st); Lester and Allen's Specialty Company and the She Burlesque Company (January 23rd–28th) and William Cattell, in Micaliz (January 30th, 31st, and February 1st) and in Marteau, the Carpenter of Rouen (February 2nd, 3rd, 4th) get me well on in the winter of my discontent at the feeble offerings I have transcribed. But, after all, what can one expect at a top-price of 35 cents?

I am cheered by Gus Hill's World of Novelties (February 6th–11th); even by Lester, Williams, Wood and Sheppard and Howard's Show No. 2, visible and audible during the following week. The Grand had plunged into "Variety." For February 20th–25th, another heavily entitled combination employed T. F. Thomas and George W. Watson's Comedy Company, William M. Davene's Allied Attractions (they seem to have allied themselves with any convenient group) and Happy Jack Sutton's Wild West. Sam'l of Posen was single in the field for February 27th–March 3rd. March went on with The Black Flag (5th–10th); Rosner and Seeman's Electric Sensations (12th–17th); Sid C. France (19th–24th); and Parson Davies' Big Show, headed by William Muldoon and Strangler Lewis (26th–31st). Quite decidedly "Variety" ruled the stage. The Rentz-Santley group entered on April 2nd, for a usual ebullient week, and on the 9th, the London Specialty Company began another. After a week (April 16th–21st) of Edith Crolius and George E. Atkins, in A Checkered Life, the Silbon Show and Jack Dempsey filled the week of the 23rd–28th. A numerous host, for April 30th, embraced Jack McAuliffe, the Zanfretta Family, Minnie Lee, Heffernan and McDonald, Kelly and Murphy, Joseph A. Kelly, Ramza and Arno, Edward Leslie and Jenny (*sic*) Nelson—decidedly an interesting array. Aladdin, with his lamp, for May 7th–12th, lighted the dancing of Rosina Astegrano. Lottie Church, always to be expected in minor houses, made a belated visit (May 14th–19th) in three plays—Papeto (*sic*), The Dark Side of New York, and the inevitable Unknown. The Sheffer and Blakely Company specially stressed (May 21st–26th) James McAvoy, Moulton and Dashway, Alice Thompson and Conroy and Dempsey, all familiar to my pen.

Ten Great Japanese and Muldoon's Picnic Company formed the odd combination for June 4th–9th; and, for June 11th–16th, we were encouraged to learn that James Owen O'Conor and Professor A. A. Denton would "positively appear in Hamlet." The Fitz and Webster Comedy

Company was the last proponent I found for 1887–88 in this over-zealous Grand Theatre. As a research addict I regret that I could not discover more definite detail about some of its offerings; as a mere human being I can bear my loss.

PHILLIPS'S SUMMER THEATRE, 1888

The tented ecstasy at Montrose and Union Avenues proudly asserted, in mid-May, "The Place belongs to the People. Open with vaudeville and a tribe of Pawnee Indians." A Flying Man outside the theatre gave, every evening, a free exhibition. Assuredly this was "Variety" with a vengeance. As the People's Summer Theatre, it proclaimed itself, on May 14th, "the only real summer theatre in America," offering Nip and Tuck to prove its claim. There was certainly a sly wink in the "You know!" with which May Adams's Company was advertised for June 4th–9th. The Leonzo Brothers filled the following week. Joseph J. Sullivan and Muldoon, the Solid Man, figured in latest June. I found no further record for this place in the summer issues of the Brooklyn Times; I can only conjecture as to the cause.

FRIDAY'S PAVILION, 1888

But Friday's Pavilion, Broadway and Reid Avenue, opened, on May 28th, with Grau's Opera Company, in the not startling novelty of The Bohemian Girl, followed, for June 4th–9th, by The Bells of Corneville, with Hattie Arnold, Alice Johnson, Harry Howard (as Gaspard) and Edward Webb. This sounds summery for provincial audiences, as indeed did the attraction of June 11th–16th, Alfred Miaco, in Humpty Dumpty. For June 18th–23rd a vaudeville troupe included the Delmanning Brothers, H. M. Parker and his dogs, John Daly and Annie Devere, George F. Kaine, Harry Edwards, Tommy Morrissey, and Rentz, the Wonder. June ended (25th–30th) with the Four Musical Kings and Weston Brothers' Way of the World (with no reference to Congreve).

That Boy Next Door was, I suppose, a nuisance to others, for July 2nd–7th, but it was listed as a "blizzard of comedy" for those who had lived through the great blizzard of March 12th, and Edgar L. Benn was That Boy. A Boy Hero gave the *allegro* of the theme, for July 9th–14th, set down as a "great nautical drama." The week of July 16th–21st was divided between A Hoop of Gold and A Brave Woman. Then the inevitable Uncle Tom's Cabin brought tears and Topsy for July 23rd–28th. Sam Erwin Ryan (July 30th–August 4th) appeared as Moneypenny, in The Long Strike — another aging manifestation; but Dockstader's Minstrels and Dockstader's Lawn Party doubtless dried our tears, in the week of August 6th–11th. Mr. and Mrs. William M. Paul and their acting bull-dog, appropriately

[594]

named Nip, held the week of August 13th–18th, in Lucky Ranch. Ten Nights in a Bar-Room, which one might call the heavenly twin to Uncle Tom's Cabin, made very tearful the week of August 20th–25th, thereby bringing down the summer curtain for 1888.

WILLIAMSBURGH MISCELLANY, 1887–1888

We may begin this record with the Swabian Cannstatter Volksfest occupying Ridgewood Park, on September 11th, 12th, 13th, and 14th. That function duly celebrated, we wait eagerly for the joys of the future.

Not until late October did entertainments wing their way to advertisements in the Brooklyn Times. On the 25th and 26th of that charming month, a Harvest Home Festival filled the Lecture Room of Calvary Church, Marcy Avenue and South 9th Street, with cheerfulness and brotherly love. The ever-hospitable Lee Avenue Congregational Church received, on the 27th, the Schubert Double Quartet. Another evening in late October found in this same church Sauahbrah, Mrs. Edward Bausher (soprano) and George Dainty, Jr. (elocutionist, whose name always makes me feel like writing some humorous verses). November 1st opened Knickerbocker Hall for the ministrations of the St. Cæcilia Ladies' Vocal Society. And Belva Lockwood, who once ran for President, lectured, on the 4th, at St. Luke's M. E. Church, Marcy Avenue and Penn Street. I will not deceive the reader; this is a poor harvest. The German Fifth Regiment of the Eastern District, held a reception and ball, in early November, at Baumgärtner's Military Hall.

In early November, also, Joseph and His Brethren was sung in Knickerbocker Hall, by twenty young ladies, directed by W. A. Buckley. Portentous as this sounds, it probably gave pleasure to some. Reassurance of that kind may be bestowed on the Young People's Entertainment, musical and literary, carried through on November 9th, in the New England Congregational Church. The first United Presbyterian Church, South First and Rodney Streets, provided, on November 15th, Humour and Music, contributors being Mr. and Mrs. Clarke, Miss Mullen, George Duryea and Miss Evans. November 24th (Thanksgiving) flooded Williamsburgh with festivity, not that, in that decorous precinct, joy was wholly unconfined. Alfred E. Pearsall was at the Lee Avenue Congregational Church; at the Ainslie Street Presbyterian Church Carrie Louise Ray, Perry J. Averill (baritone), and Lawrence Bogert (accompanist) did their best; and the Williamsburgh Plattdeutscher Club were at the Eastern District Palace Hall. In that innocent, gladsome time, the Lee Avenue Congregational Church presented a Fair, Our "Ajeeb," an Oriental Booth, and Elmer P. Ransom (prestidigitateur). Blind Tom played, November 28th, 29th and 30th, at Knickerbocker Hall.

[595]

Thus we arrive at December 6th, to find Reverend Henry A. Powell lecturing at the Lee Avenue Congregational Church, on Fortunes and Fortune Tellers. In St. John's M. E. Sunday School Hall, in earlier December, Van Phou Lee, "of Yale College," gave an illustrated lecture on Chinese Manners and Customs. He was to wear Chinese costume and sing a Chinese song. Fairs and entertainments were running up large gas bills in various churches. In the First Presbyterian Church, the second of a series of entertainments promised, for December 13th, Blanche Bender (soprano), Marion Bender (alto), Charles H. Little (humourist), and the Perry Brothers (bellringers and violinists). A Blanche Bender, some years later, played Meenie, as I have stated, to Joseph Jefferson's Rip Van Winkle.

The holiday season, as usual, stopped all entertainments except Christmas celebrations in churches. On January 11th, however, the annual reception of Continental Congress, No. 308, A. L. of H., forgot its imposing title and initials at Grand Army Hall; the South Third Street M. E. Church, on an evening contiguous, opened welcoming doors for Pearl Whitney (violin), May Whitney (contralto), Mrs. C. Whitney (piano), Kolehest (violin) and Carrie Couch (elocutionist); this seems, in Shaw's phrase, too true to be good. Colonel L. F. Copeland finished the series of entertainments at the First United Presbyterian Church, lecturing (January 16th) on Snobs and Snobbery, a topic one had thought to be sacred to Thackeray alone. January 17th brought to Grand Army Hall the reception of the Seawanhaka Boat Club. The Columbia College Glee and Banjo Clubs were, on January 23rd, in the Chapel of St. John's M. E. Church, merry and bright as college boys could then be; and Aunt Polly Bassett's Singin' Skewl struck the pitch (I hope), on January 26th, at the Lee Avenue Congregational Church. The Turn-Verein Masquerade fell, in their own hall, on Sunday, January 29th. And the Liederkranz of the town was at this same hall, on February 8th (or was it the 9th?—records differ).

February 9th awoke us with clarion call for A. P. Burbank, at the Ainslie Street Church—an edifice near Williamsburgh, if not actually in it. On the same evening, St. Paul's Relief Society held an entertainment at Turn Hall, and the Lee Avenue Congregational Church projected a "Grand Valentine Entertainment," confirming the belief of those who solve, for the 8th, the perplexity at the end of the last paragraph. Either this Lee Avenue church was always in need of raising money, or the congregation found most of its pleasure in the church precincts. On February 11th, Mrs. Scott-Siddons and Victoria Siddons gave Shakespearian Readings, at 167 Taylor Street, without altering the course of the stars. A valentine of February 14th was the Peasants' Masquerade held, at Turn Hall, by the Schwäbischer Sängerbund. On February 15th, the First Reformed Church, Bedford Avenue, presented James S. Burdett and A. G. Waring (magician). I pass by Martha Washington Teas in churches, though I have no doubt the young ladies in their colonial dresses were very pretty. Such economy allows me to reach, on February 21st, the Arion masquerade, at the new Arion Club House, and also to present John M. Young's musical and humorous evening, on the 22nd, at Grand Army Hall. My faithful guide, the Brooklyn Times, leaves me perplexed. It states that, on Washington's Birthday, the first annual performance of the Clarendon Association took place in the parlours of 106 Clymer Street; yet, on March 2nd, unless my eyes deceived me, this band presented The Sleeping Beauty ("their first dramatic performance"), with a cast including Walter H. Young, Minnie Pond, Lottie, Edith and Florence Atwater, Norman Willis, Pembroke Chrysler (an impressive name), Henry W. Lobb (*sic*) and Blanche Chrysler. At Parish Hall, on February 22nd, the St. Anthony Young Men's Union gave the play, Battery B, entrusting leading rôles to James J. Simpson, J. J. and M. O'Gara, James and Joseph Woods and P. H. Malone. At this time New York's hypercritical were beginning to laugh at the prevailing epidemic of amateur acting in Brooklyn; one professional critic went so far as to say that the young ladies were in the casts merely to add social distinction; and, if they showed the slightest degree of dramatic talent, they were eyed with suspicion. These annals of ours are really serviceable in showing the prevalence of the epidemic in the City of Churches. After all, the "craze" was no more reprehensible than the night-club madness of 1941 that allows grinning young men and maidens to inflict their flatness on the desert air of public indifference.

I trust we may escape easily from the gales of March. The first evening of that blustery month installed the Reverend Edward P. Ingersoll in the First Baptist Church, Lee Avenue and Keap Street, there to discuss Saddle and Tent Life in Palestine. And, on March 5th, the Clan-na-Gael commemorated, in Grand Army Hall, the hundred-and-eleventh anniversary of Robert Emmet. The same evening found, in St. John's M. E. Church, Leland T. Powers, a Chariot Race, Katharine (*sic*) Cavannah and E. W. Van de Right (organist). The Eureka Peak Sisters, on the 6th, were at Eureka Hall, 378 Bedford Avenue, and, on the 8th, the First Reformed Church, Bedford Avenue and Clymer Street, held a Leap Year Entertainment, possibly forcing bachelors into the imminent deadly breach of Yea or Nay. Then, because of Lenten seriousness, and the blizzard, our narrative is forced to leap to March 19th, for nutriment, finding, at Central Baptist Church, a concert postponed to that date, with the attractive Meigs Sisters, J. Williams Macy, Signor Fanelli and "Professor" J. W. Fink. On the 25th the Church of the Transfiguration essayed the Rossini Stabat Mater.

April also furnishes something like a Barmecide Feast. Aunt Polly Bassett's Singin' Skewl ran true to form, on April 4th and 5th, at Trinity

Baptist Church, Patchen and Greene Avenues; on the 10th, the Sunday School-Room of the Lee Avenue Congregational Church staged a Feast of Days and a Grand Doll Drill, doubtless pleasing to parents. And "the greatest of American Elocutionists" was the tag, on April 23rd, for Professor J. W. Churchill, of Andover, Massachusetts; Mrs. Joshua Youngs (soprano) assisted. The closing soirée, on the 24th, at Turn Hall, also closes our scant April miscellany. And not till the 15th can I begin the May record, and then only with the offering at the New England Congregational Church of James S. Burdett, the Berkelee Mandolin Trio and P. Altman (violin). In May, also, a Memorial Concert for the Charles R. Doane Post must have been interesting, with Charles Roberts, Jr., Francis F. Powers and Mr. and Mrs. Gerrit Smith (pianist and soprano, respectively). The swan song may have been rendered on May 28th, at the Bedford Avenue Tabernacle, at South Third Street, when Mabel Stephenson, George Dainty, Jr., and Nelson Mott (humourist) united in oral delivery. But let us note, on that same fruitful 28th, at Arion Hall, Wall Street near Broadway, the Ladies Temple Association and its offering of Michael Banner, Mrs. Martha Flocken (née Spitzer) and William B. Green (humorous reader).

Greenpoint; Adelphi Theatre, 1887–1888

I expressed a wish, at the conclusion of my Greenpoint record for the preceding season, that the place might establish a theatre of some sort to brighten the monotonous tale of its struggles toward real drama. And here, at the beginning of the new season is actually an answer to my prayer, in the Adelphi Theatre, corner of Meserole Avenue and Lorimer Street, with F. DeBarrie and Company as proprietors and our old friend, George France, as manager. The Long Island Star supplies but scant information, but it serves.

The House opened, on September 12th, for a week of the Hall and Devoy Combination, in Fun in a Boarding School. Kate Holly and Henry Belmer filled the next week with Jesse James (September 19th, 20th, 21st and 22nd) and Calamity Jane, or, the Queen of the West (September 23rd and 24th). With the reader's permission, I will carry this Adelphi venture through to its early closing. The week of September 26th–October 1st introduced us to Bart W. Wallace as Pierce O'Brien, in An Irish Exile; Louise Ripley supported, and specialties included Earle and Miles (pipers and dancers) and Billy McGonigle (jig and reel dancer). After a perusal of these attractions, the sagacious reader realises that the Adelphi was a very cheap playhouse. The impression is strengthened by the offering of October 3rd–8th, the Davis All Fun Specialty Company. Fayette Welch's Minstrels, October 10th–15th, promised, besides Welch, himself, Catherine Nelson (magician), Layman ("the man of 100 faces"), George W. Woods, G. C. Ardray and Kittie Leonard (jig dancer). The Benn Comedy Company filled the week of October 17th–22nd with Peck's Bad Boy. For October 24th–29th, Yarber's Coloured Minstrels were really "coloured," embracing Joseph Holkom (pedestal clog dancer), Billy Wilson (mimic), the Southern Quartet (Moon, Wright, Green and Murshak), Charles Pope, ("king of old men impersonators"), William Goss ("only coloured female impersonator") and Charles Patterson ("sentimental songs").

I fear the first act of the play ends here. The Star carries no further mention of the new theatre till December 26th, when the house re-opened, with Frank L. Girard as proprietor, and Richard Hunt as manager. For the modest admission-fees of 10 cents, 20 cents and 30 cents — what old timers describe as "tents, twents, thirts" — one could have heard Harry Rich's All-Star Minstrels. January 2nd–7th proffered Lulu Rice's Comedy and Burlesque Company — "35 Artists in a refined and moral entertainment," a statement that leaves me, with my study of "burlesque" female companies of that time, somewhat skeptical. The Boston Elite Specialty Company, in the week of January 9th–14th, included our old friend, Nellie Sandford, along with John Lindsay and Luke Filan (song, dance, clog), "Professor" Henry ("magic and fun"), and Parker and Reed (society sketch, songs and dances). The Woodbury Theatre Company, for the week of January 16th–21st, presented, in succession, a decidedly mixed *menu*, with Esmeralda, A Gold Mine and Richelieu. On Sunday, the 15th, Happy Jack Sutton's Mirror of the Plains employed stereopticon effects. I found no more for this bold but unhappy venture. Perhaps the People's Theatre was sufficiently near to satisfy all demands of the inhabitants of Greenpoint; and the offerings were decidedly superior.

GREENPOINT MISCELLANY, 1887–1888

Let us dance into the new season with the opening ball, on October 10th, at Eckford Hall; or would it be more seemly to start at the Noble Street Baptist Church, with, in early October, the Reverend H. M. Gallaher's lecture on America and the Americans? While debating this important question, we could examine, with edification and unction, the very attractive list of ten entertainments to be given by the Greenpoint Y.M.C.A., in Bartholdi Hall. In succession were to come M. P. Wilder, D. W. Robertson (tumbleronicon) and H. B. (*sic*) Schmalix (zither) — this on October 20th; Edward Caswell's lecture on Laughter (October 27th); Alfred E. Pearsall (November 3rd); Professor C. E. Bolton's illustrated lecture, Re-united Germany and Heroic Louise; December 1st offered the Columbia College Glee Club, and December 15th H. J. Littlefield's lecture on Abraham Lincoln. On a following date, which I cannot supply, were to be combined the magic and mystery of Frederick H. Chase and the hand and sleigh bell ringing of the Perry Brothers. A. P. Burbank was due to follow, on January 27th, and Colonel L. F. Copeland (with his Snobs and Snobbery), on February 16th. The series was to end, on March 1st, with a concert by the New York Philharmonic Club.

I return to November 14th, 16th, 21st and 23rd, when Professor Nelson Sizer lectured, at the Christian Church of the Evangel, on Phrenology. The ever-active St. Anthony's Young Men's Union gave, on November 21st and 22nd, at Parish Hall, a usual musical and dramatic entertainment. The 22nd also allowed the Mt. Ararat Union to hold, in Bartholdi Hall, an entertainment and *soirée*, with the Continental Glee Club assisting. Thanksgiving (November 24th) allowed us to be grateful for three offerings: A "grand" orchestral concert and readings, at the First M. E. Sunday School, Prof. Wernig ("formerly leader of the 7th Regiment Band") directing a band; a musical and literary entertainment at the M. E. Tabernacle Church; and a concert sponsored by the Young People's Association, at the Noble Street Baptist Church, with the Courtney Ladies' Quartet, William Courtney, and Mabel Stephenson (humourist and bird-warbler).

The obscurity that had recently clouded the record, in the Brooklyn Times, for Greenpoint, broke, in the winter of this term, to send us a few enlightening items. The Greenpoint and Astoria Bowling Clubs contended, on December 10th, in Germania Hall, with the Greenpointers winning. At Eckford Hall, on December 21st, the Greenpoint Social Club held a show with varied talent embracing Murphy and Conlin (black face), Willie Rooney (club swinging), William Sherwood (comedian), Weidman, Henry and Schreck (musical trio), Evans and King (lightning changes), and John Peckenham (imitations). Again, not much in value — but a welcome signal from Greenpoint. In early January I learn from the Long Island City Star, the Silver Lake Quartet appeared, in concert, in Association Hall.

St. Anthony's Council, No. 101, C. B. L., gave a ball, on January 18th, at Bartholdi Hall. Something more germane to our story was the concert, on March 1st, in this same hall, by the New York Philharmonic Club, Eugene Weiner winning special praise from the Times, for his flute-playing. The Star lights our way, on March 8th, 9th, and 10th, to Association Hall for the Cosmoramic Views of Professor L. Schultz.

The fulness of the April items in the Brooklyn Times brings regret for the silence of other months. April 2nd found Nathan Hale Council, No. 2, Jr., O. V. A. M., Grand Army of the Republic, at Republic Hall, Calyer Street, Greenpoint, with Evans and King (lightning changes), Ella Earl (songs), Viola Henline (violinist), Bob Wylie (negro acts), the Lyceum Zither Quartet, Sparten Brothers (sword duets), Arthur Clash (elocutionist), and Thomas Walters (musket drill). And the E. J. Reagan Association, on that same busy 2nd of April, danced out its ball, in Smithsonian Hall; the

Shamrock Coterie on the same evening was at Bartholdi Hall, with Bayne's 69th Regiment Band to cheer it on its way. The same over-busy 2nd of April opened Eckford Hall for a dance of the Violet Social Club, footing its way to the strains of "Professor" Nolan's orchestra.

And April 3rd carried on the gayety. At Smithsonian Hall the concert of Richard Bäuchlen (pianist) brought in the aid of Zachary Taylor (violinist), E. Zeiner (pianist), F. Felix (baritone), W. Taylor (eight-year-old violinist) and Annie Mooney Burch (soprano). This caused the dance of the Oakland Club, at Bartholdi Hall, on the 3rd, to "pale its ineffectual fires"—at least for us; even that of the Eckford Association, in the same hall, on the 4th. In Eckford Hall, in the first week of April, the Social Quartet Club had a dance, preceded by a farce, Zwei Todte auf Reisen, with Charles Berger, Mrs. F. Schmidt, Josephine Stassen, August Wendel, L. Hartner, F. Hellmuth, Mrs. A. Kelm, J. Standermann and Julius Kurtz among the Germans involved. The Noble Street Baptist Church opened, on April 9th, for a programme rendered by Grace Haskell (soprano), Carrie Couch (elocutionist), Mabel Stephenson (humourist), Clarence Worrall (cornetist), Master Joseph Meyer (pianist), and H. E. H. Benedict and Kate Worrall (accompanists). And, on an evening in early April, the St. Anthony Choral Union gave, in Parish Hall, Greenpoint, the undying mirth and melody of The Pirates of Penzance, the cast including Joseph McKeever as Richard, Charles P. O'Neill as Frederick, Louis Reynolds as Major-General Stanley, Mary O'Neill as Mabel, Rose Dempsey as Kate, Minnie O'Connor as Edith, Maggie Mulhall as Isabel, and Minnie Campbell as Ruth—an Irish group to balance the German Social Quartet Club in our supposedly American city.

The Brooklyn Times now lapses into silence regarding its good neighbour, Greenpoint. From the Long Island City Star I gather an interesting item in the entertainment given by the Anti-Dyspeptics, at Smithsonian Hall, on April 25th, all for the benefit of the building fund of the Greenpoint Y.M.C.A. After a concert provided by May Fulton, Mrs. R. H. Tiebout, H. N. Dougherty, Dora Mooney, Jessie Mooney, Anne Mooney-Burch and C. R. Burch (largely, one sees, a nice family affair), we passed to what must always appeal to students of American drama, a farce by William Dean Howells—in this case the lively The Mouse Trap. In the cast (we must always cherish the cast, even of amateurs, in a Howells play), Dr. G. D. Hamlin was Willis Campbell and Jessie Mooney Mrs. Amy Somers, with Anna Logan as Mrs. Miller, Nellie Burch as Mrs. Bemis, Jennie Roberts as Mrs. Curwin, May Fenton as Mrs. Roberts, and Minnie Dougherty as Jane, the maid. The Anti-Dyspeptics were richly supplied with Mooneys, Burches and Doughertys, who, I trust, had no trouble with digestions. I thought, when I lighted on this entertainment, that the name, Anti-Dyspeptics, was a joke; in later years, I inclined to believe that it covered the purpose of the society really to ward off dyspepsia by inculcating a tendency toward the eating of digestible food. Perhaps I mistake, but the record of later years will show.

I pass to less perplexing problems. Yet May 9th brought to Bartholdi Hall that, at one time, great problem of orthodox Catholicism — the impetuous, but latterly amenable Reverend Dr. Edward McGlynn; he lectured on The Masses against the Classes, a topic with a tang of the life-conditions of a half-century later. On May 23rd, Dr. Isabelle Rankine entered the First M. E. Church with a lecture entitled So They Say, which leaves me guessing. Barbara Frietchie Post, No. 11, held G. A. R. Hall (116 Calyer Street), on May 28th, with a benefit for widows and orphans.

The Greenpoint Globe, having concealed from my eager eyes all news of a dramatic significance, bears notice of a wrestling match for $250 a side, waged in June between Sebastian Müller (who won) and Ernst Röder. Müller broke a heavy flint and ground the stones with his bare hands — more than I or my reader (I suspect) could do. Bartholdi Hall housed this exhibition. I can only marvel at the silence of the Globe as to amusements in Greenpoint; the chief excitement it found for these years was in running to the hare and hounds in Newtown, or in some festivity in Woodside.

Flatbush and Its Neighbours, 1887–88

In the section which, with loosely based topographical significance, I have thus named, I find, in latest February, a reception at the New Turn Hall, Sixteenth Street, near Fifth Avenue, a reception of the Gentlemen's Sons Social, of South Brooklyn; I leave to a future Ph.D. the research necessary to discover whether this name was adopted seriously or in a spirit of youthful fun. The South Brooklyn Turn-Verein had its masked ball there on February 13th. Flatbush itself was responsible, on February 27th, for a concert at the Town Hall, in that village; then and there the Second Reformed Dutch Church of Flatbush introduced to our over-laden caravan Messrs. Fritz and Wilhelm Gehringer, and A. Emmers, Mrs. C. Meyer, Lina Oberglock, Miss Henken and Miss Kuehn, names that to me sound far more German than Dutch. The Eighteenth Street M. E. Church, in late March, indulged in a concert by the Mozart Quintet, with May and Pearl Whitney to assist. Thetford Post, on May 14th, gave a concert at Turn Hall, South Brooklyn, for the benefit of W. M. Raynor, a war veteran in poor health; J. J. Breen, T. H. Hayden, J. J. Sullivan and Mrs. J. C. DeBoe appeared. On May 21st, occurred the May Festival of the South Brooklyn Turn-Verein, the scene of the joy being Koch's Bay View Park, Fifth Avenue and the City Line, Brooklyn. John Warth's Sommer-Garten advertised in June, its locale being Third Avenue and 65th Street, Brooklyn City Line, Bay Ridge.

LONG ISLAND CITY AND ITS NEIGHBOURS, 1887–1888

Again the Long Island City Star beacons to the town across the waters. Oliver W. Wren, as usual, stands in the forefront of the pleasures. On September 16, 1887, he was down for an entertainment in the Astoria Assembly Rooms, the John Allen Lodge, A. O. U. W., sponsoring. A "select" minstrel and variety entertainment fell, on Sunday evening, October 2nd, at Pete Hart's, Laurel Hill. But Arlington Hall was true Hunter's Point for the first annual entertainment, on October 31st, of Prospect Lodge, No. 47. I regret to say that the Star, in November, contributed nothing for our enlightenment, and, in December, only news of balls, masquerades, school entertainments and Christmas episodes in churches. This is so easy that it frightens my pen, ever on the alert for the veriest mouse in amusement.

I could not find a file of the Star for January, 1888, and in February still went groping through the numerous balls advertised in the paper. It is therefore cheering to learn that, on March 5th, the Astoria Männerchor masked and danced, at the Astoria Assembly Rooms; and that on the 10th, "Professor" Schultz had a very large audience for the last of a series of stereopticon entertainments. April 2nd found Bassett's Yankee Singin' Skewl, at the Reformed Church, Academy Street, Dutch Kills, and April 26th installed, in the Astoria Assembly Rooms, a dramatic entertainment (amateur) for the benefit of the Astoria Tennis Club.

May finally blossoms into something tangible. At Marra's Prospect Hall, Long Island City, the Gorilla Dramatic Social of New York City united, May 14th and 15th, with the Prospect Dramatic and Athletic Club of Long Island City to the end of perfect joy, at least for themselves. On the 14th, the farces of The Intelligence Office, and Scragg's Hotel enlisted Al and William Wagenheim, Gus Wall, Thomas O'Neill, Richard Langer, Albert Mutch, Helena and Joseph McInerny, Nellie McPhail, Otto Rechlin and John Ryan; on the 15th, Two Doctors and A Troublesome Servant exercised the talents of the devotees. On May 16th came duly forth in the long-suffering Assembly Rooms a musical and variety entertainment of the Holy Name Society. It remained for the Astoria Männerchor to stir the town to its centre and outskirts for three days of festivity, celebrating the Männerchor's twenty-fifth anniversary. On Saturday evening, May 19th, a torchlight parade through Astoria exhibited the Long Island City Singing Societies and the Long Island City Turn-Verein. On Sunday afternoon, May 20th, in the grounds of the Astoria Assembly Rooms, music was to be provided by 250 male voices and an orchestra under Professor Philip Stollwerck. May 21st was gladdened by a picnic at Kubasch's Astoria Schützen Park, with a parade of all the different societies through Astoria, Steinway and the German Settlement.

In my excitement over this Teutonic festival, I nearly forgot to chronicle

[603]

the lecture, on May 17th, in the Presbyterian Church, Astoria, of Colonel John Q. Hoyt, on the pleasing idea, Around the World in Eighty Minutes. I close for 1887–88, on June 11th, when a testimonial to Tom Cassidy, the wrestler, of Brooklyn, brought the "fancy" to Pete Hart's Concert Hall, Laurel Hill. Thenceforth, picnics, picnics, and excursions invited through July and August. But I am permitted to specialise on the Gran Festa Campestre of the Fratellanza San Felese and the Politica Calvellese held, on August 15th, at Roman Park, 74 and 76 Broadway, Astoria. By taking a steamer at 92nd Street, a New York investigator could have arrived "directly" in Astoria, near the Park — all this on the word of the advertisement in the Progresso Italo-Americano.

FLUSHING AND ITS NEIGHBOURS, 1887–1888

The Flushing Journal of September 10th states that W. R. Grace "will provide a vocal and instrumental concert for St. Mary's Church," but fails to give the date of performance. The Journal for October 15th says that the concert "took place recently." On that uncertain note I begin the Flushing chronicle for 1887–88, merely noting by the way that, according to the Journal, the Big All Company, at Knab's Hall, Whitestone, was "not so big, after all."

At the Opera House, an amateur minstrel show of the Flushing Athletic Club may have amused, on October 28th. The paper, on the 29th, assures us that "from now on till March 1st, there will be at least three entertainments a week in College Point"; and, on the same date, we are surprised to learn that Marshall P. Wilder is "in trouble with his townspeople at Jamaica, for making fun of them in a lecture recently at Glen Cove." Another popular entertainer, Sidney Woollett had an audience of great size, on November 30th, at the Flushing Opera House. By skipping lectures by indeterminate speakers, usually in churches or Opera-House, and church concerts by eager choirs, I arrive at January 3, 1888, only to be edified by Ten Nights in a Bar-Room, presented, in the Opera House, by the Fursman and Knapp Company, not of metropolitan repute.

The Journal of the 21st assures us that another company, unknown to New York, the Langdon Theatrical Combination, "has been playing to crowded houses" at the Opera House this week (January 16th–21st). More within our ken are Francis Fischer Powers and the Courtney Ladies' Quartet, at the Flushing Institute, on January 18th; and the Flushing Branch of the Church Choir Choral Union began its season, at the Baptist Church, on the 23rd, with W. A. Lafferty directing. More informal, possibly, was the stag party of the 17th Separate Company given in its armoury, on January 31st. In February, so far as I could learn from the Journal, Flushing simply danced or became "social." The Lend-a-Hand Club and the Pleasant Circle Social Club functioned; the last Assembly Ball of the season was danced, on the 10th, in the Opera House; and, on the 21st, the Grand Ball of Young America Hose Company carried through in the same hall.

March 17th finds the Journal recording a dismal failure for "the promised show at the Opera House. The few people who gathered . . . got their money back, which was one thing creditable that the management did. They tried to fill the Opera House without advertising, hence their failure to draw." This item will rejoice writers on "social significance." More village life comes to the front, on the 20th, with the drill of the 17th Regiment, in its armoury; and, on the 23rd, the Ball of the John J. Brennan Association, in the Opera House engaged "Professor" Pinkham for the dance music, with the Irish piper, John Eagan, to "fill in the intervals." Truly rural, this! And the issue of the Journal, for March 24th, is exciting with notes of balls of lodges and other congregations in the Opera House and elsewhere.

The Cheesman Flushing Band made its "first bow to a Flushing audience," on April 12th, at the Opera House, "Professor" Berge leading. The great big feature (I fall into rural ecstasy) was a violin and piano duet between "Professor" Kamper, leader of the Willets Point Band, and Master W. C. Steffens, "a rising young pianist of Whitestone." Also appeared Grant Moore (cornet), of the Jamaica Crescent Band, F. W. Lincoln (clarinet) and George Walsh ("Flushing's popular basso"). I hope the reader will forgive my irresistible desire to induct him into such harmless village episodes — harmless, if every musician kept the pitch. The very next night (April 13th) brought, at Poppenhusen Institute, College Point, the fourth concert of the pupils of Albert Steinfeld, Mrs. M. Ackerly-Drew giving the hyphenated dignity of her name and presence to the occasion. May 5th introduced, in Turn Hall, College Point, a dramatic entertainment by the Merry Companions; Foiled, or, a Struggle for Life and Liberty, was the intriguing title of their offering. So successful were these Merry Companions, a half-century before J. B. Priestley's Good Companions, that they gave another show, on May 19th. The same Turn Hall housed, on May 6th, the American Legion of Honour, in Er ist Baron; and opened again, on the 9th, for a concert of St. Fidelis Catholic Church, Rosa d'Erina assisting. Let us return to the Flushing Opera House for a testimonial, on May 30th, to the Reverend Mr. Reed. This must suffice till the week of July 23rd–28th, when the Langdon Dramatic Combination at the Opera House forced thinkers in Flushing to realise how provincial were the theatrical offerings of the town. Frank A. Robbins's Wild West Show performed twice, on August 6th; and a patriotic drama, Old Put, thrilled, perhaps, on August 27th, the Tom Barry Company providing the sinews of war. In later August, the Journal invites to excursions everywhere; the Kraekelia Singing

[605]

Society and the Alpenröschli going afloat in vessels weighted with the ballast of those names.

JAMAICA AND ITS NEIGHBOURS, 1887–1888

The Harvest Home, at Distler's, on September 15, 1887, warns of the end of summer. The issue of the Long Island Democrat for September 27th gives notice of autumn in the announcement that Dan Nash and his troupe would shortly appear in Jamaica. At Town Hall, on October 6th, a W. C. T. U. benefit introduced zealous ladies — Mrs. T. J. Armstrong, Laura Brenton, Laura Johnson, Mrs. P. J. Bernhard and Miss Remsen — without a perceptible rise in my artistic blood-pressure. Blind Tom was at the Jamaica Opera House, on November 16th, for two performances, admission being set at 50 cents and 75 cents, with, for children under twelve years of age, 25 cents. Ten Nights in a Bar-Room, on November 23rd, was the stale offering of Fursman and Knapp's Company, seen in January, at Flushing. The incitement for December 19th, in Town Hall, was Charles L. Hagedorn's Evidences of Creation; a short time before he had lectured, very *anti*, so to speak, on Darwinism.

The sole frost-bitten offering for January came, afternoon and evening of the 25th, with a Friends Odd Entertainment, in Hollis Chapel. But the Democrat bears hearty witness to wonderful sleighing in late January. February was more cordial. The Richmond Hill Comedy Club, on the 3rd, presented, in the Jamaica Town Hall, The Little Rebel and also Our Wife, or, the Rose of Amiens; participants were Messrs. Jones, Palmer, Vaughan, Kimball, Miles and Kimber, Mrs. Vaughan and Misses Sands, Hatfield, Miles and Graves. The same hall, on the 9th, housed a benefit to the Hospital for Temporary Patients. But think of the pleasure announced in the Journal for February 28th — three shows in the Jamaica Opera House for next week! Jacob Riis, of Richmond Hill, was down, on March 7th, for a lecture (illustrated by stereopticon) on The Other Half: How It Lives and Dies, in New York. There at least, is, a "song of social significance." All sorts of social clubs and their activities brightened the winter. Of course the most dramatic episode was the Great Blizzard of March 12th, burying Long Island under incredible masses of snow.

Forced to depend on weekly papers for these small communities, I have no doubt I failed to find interesting amusements that would have been chronicled in a daily journal. This deprivation makes blank the interval to May 18th, when the Baptist Church of Jamaica opened for a concert of the Hitchcock Sisters (three of them). On June 6th, the Crescent Cornet Band of Jamaica enlisted, as soloists, Grant Moore (cornet), Bessie Davenport (soprano) and Professor T. R. Davenport, who graces our chronicle for 1886–87. With the remark that the Democrat admits us to much baseball of local flavour (if baseball has a flavour), I reach, on July 3rd, a Mid-summer Night's Festival (Japanese) in the Chapel at Hollis. Not very thankful for this, I proceed to an operetta, The Sailor's Bride, by "Professor" Davenport, at the Lecture Room, on Clinton Avenue. Picnics and excursions abounded in July and August, and, on August 24th, Uncle Tom's Cabin, in the Jamaica Opera House, "enriched by a net profit of over forty dollars" Peck and Fursman, the proprietors; this on the word of the Long Island Democrat. Either on August 20th or 27th (the paper leaves me in doubt as to which), the Jamaica Sängerbund went to Distler's Atlantic Garden for a German festivity.

STATEN ISLAND, 1887–1888

Conscientious readers may tire of the constant ferrying to Staten Island; but I can spare them nothing. Fairlamb's Madrigal Boys begin, for us, a rather fruitful season, on September 13th, at the Pavilion Hotel. Staten Island, more and more Teutonic in tone, next summoned us, on October 12th, to a concert of the German Ladies' Society, in the well-known German Club Rooms; Selina Liliendahl assisted with harp-playing. These same rooms, on November 15th, presented Pinafore, with Joseph H. Moore's choir. In the German Club Rooms, also, on December 15th, a Minstrel and Dramatic Entertainment by the Staten Island and Manhattan Athletic Clubs should have attracted the young, with Tyndale's orchestra of fifty on the stage — "a pyramid of living souls," surely a phrasing that puts our prosaic generation to the blush. And, continuing the theme athletical, Knobloch's Turn Hall, Stapleton, was exhibiting, on December 17th, Sebastian Mull, "the strongest man in the world." The superlative degree had no terrors for that innocent age.

Roe's Hall, West New Brighton, was proud sanctuary, on January 16th, for Jedediah Bassett's Singin' Skewl. But, at that time, beginning on January 11th, H. H. Ragan was giving, in the German Club Rooms, a course of lectures which he called Illuminated Tours. And, on January 21st, John Stuart, of Hastings, England, spoke on Ireland, showing "how she is governed," and urging her "claims for home rule." I learn, from the Richmond County Sentinel, that he had spoken three times recently. With biting March, entertainments grew few in number. The Charity Ball, on February 13th, was a bright and dressy affair; more German, perhaps, was the twenty-first annual masquerade ball of the Staten Island Quartette Club, in the same rooms, on March 5th. After all that dancing, it is a welcome change to pass, on March 10th, to the clubhouse of the Staten Island Athletic Association, for a concert involving Mrs. E. V. Cæsar, Mrs. Thomas, and Messrs. Yuengling, Cammeyer, McGinnis, Elliott and Arthur Moore, Reuling, Fisher, Foot and George Phillips. And here, on April 7th, at Roe's Hall,

[607]

West Brighton, is something more germane to our theme — Rorke's Dramatic Company, with Alice Burroughs, in Nevada, or, the Lost Mine. The German Society, Erheiterung, on May 5th, gave Zehn Mädchen und kein Mann. At Odd Fellows' Hall, Broadway and Terrace, West New Brighton, "Professor" Regis Senac, the swordsman, and his pupils joined, on May 28th, with Tipaldi Brothers' mandolin quartet. Far better, on the 29th, at the German Club Rooms, was a concert by Emma Thursby. Both these events were for a "heroine of the blizzard" in Minnesota, who had saved her pupils but was now a cripple.

As with The Fall of Babylon of the previous year, Staten Island, in the summer of 1888, played with high stakes in an elaborate spectacle, Nero, employing, it asserted, 2,300 persons. Nero's Palace was declared to be 300 feet in length by 80 in depth. There were views of the Interior of the Palace and the Coliseum, and the show ended, of course, with the Burning of Rome. Blondin, the hero of Niagara, walked on a rope, 160 feet above the turf. The Sentinel of June 9th gives his history: in June, 1859, he walked, blindfolded, over Niagara, on a rope 1,100 feet long, 165 feet above the river. A month later, he walked across in a sack, and still later carried a man over on his back. On August 19, 1859, his human cargo was Harry Colcord, a Boston artist. In 1860, the Prince of Wales and the Duke of Newcastle saw him carry a man across. He was made a Chevalier of Queen Isabella of Spain. After that thrilling excitement, in 1888, it seems rather flat to find in St. Mary's Hall, Clifton, The Doctor of Alcantara, which walked no dizzy heights, carrying the burden of amateurism represented by Charles Barton, Charles Seale, J. Holmes Butler, Charles F. Post, J. B. Eccleston, Carrie Post, Marie Parmale and Gertrude Eccleston. The performance was for the benefit of St. Simon's Hospital.

My hope, expressed at the end of Volume XII, of including in the present volume the four years of my undergraduate life in Columbia College has been frustrated by limitations of space. The season of 1888–89 — the final goal of that ambition — presented many fine attractions, chief among which I should rank the engagement of Constant Coquelin, the elaborate Shakespearian revivals of Edwin Booth and Lawrence Barrett, Mary Anderson's beautiful production of The Winter's Tale, and the great performance of The Rivals, with Joseph Jefferson as Bob Acres, Mrs. John Drew as Mrs. Malaprop and John Gilbert as Sir Anthony Absolute. The scenes between that Mrs. Malaprop and that Sir Anthony are fixed in my memory as priceless examples of the lace-like finish of "old comedy" acting now gone, perhaps forever, from the stage. And, in 1888–89, the three stock companies — Daly's, Palmer's and Daniel Frohman's — offered many interesting new plays. The record of that season must wait till a new volume, haply, may continue the history of the New York theatre.

INDEX

INDEX

VOLUME XIII

INDEX

INDEX

INDEX

[621]

[625]

INDEX

[629]

INDEX

INDEX

[631]

INDEX

Cornalba, Adele, 35, 184
Corneille, French variety, 292
Cornelius, Miss M., 496
Corner Grocery, The, 53, 85, 183, 388, 590
Cornish, Miss Sylvester, 511
Cornu, Louis J., 191, 402
Cornucopia Lodge, 203
Correri, Mme., 306
Corsair, The, cast, etc., 456, 457; 559
Corsehair, The, or, the Northerland Sisters, 533
Corsi, parts, 303
Corsican Brothers, The, part cast, 54; 272, 372, 565
Corsini, concerts, 444, 540, 568
Corson, Juliet, lectures, 486, 552
Cort and Murphy, 88, 94, 110
Cortada, Ida, 126, 496
Corwin, Charles, 365
Cory, Ella, 394
Cosaque, La, 22, 23
Cosenza, Emilia, 540
Cosgrove, P. H., 172
Cosmi, parts, 305, 306
Cosmopolitan Hall, 349
Cosmopolitan Park, 65, 490
Cosmopolitan Skating Rink, 123
Cosmoramic Views, 398, 600
Cost of production, 79
Costa, Franz, 475 ff
Costello, J. C., amateur, 170, 172, 173, 199, 368, 376, 576, 577
Costello, Miss, 192
Costello, Mlle., 327, 332
Costello and Sheridan, Misses, clog, 369
Costigan, Denny, sparring, 473, 517, 571
Cotton, R. F., 426
Cottrelly, Mathilde, parts, etc., 1, 6, 14, 21, 43, 146, 213, 231, 414, 415, 431, 440, 478, 558, 568
Couch, Carrie, 399, 496, 601
Couldock, C. W., in The Willow Copse, 11; 17, 23; parts, 81, 157, 185; benefit, 233; parts. 262, 509
Coulson Sisters, 84, 94, 107, 113, 167, 510
Coulter, Frazer, 35, 148, 184, 454, 462
Country Girl, The, casts, 9, 10, 216
Country Store, A, 400
Country Visitor, The, 114
Courage, G., 313
Couran, Gertrude, 365
Courrier des États-Unis, 290 ff, 491 ff
Courtaine, Emma Grattan, 43
Courtaine, Harry, 249, 465, 474
Courter, Mamie, 376, 394, 580
Courtland, Helen, 163, 320
Courtney, Edna, 26, 272, 312, 467, 472
Courtney, Harold, 270
Courtney, Jr., concert, 131
Courtney, Mrs. William, 133, 348
Courtney, William, 126, 129, 180, 191, 348, 396, 541, 547, 548, 588, 600
Courtney Ladies' Quartet, 126, 128, 132, 191, 381, 395, 548, 600, 604

[632]

Courtright, William, 511
Courtship and Marriage, lecture, 539, 581
Cousin Dick, cast, 244
Coveney, Howard, 255, 267, 454, 592
Coward, Edward Fales, 12, 206, 218, 219, 224, 226, 346, 351, 353, 407, 427, 428, 551, 552
Cowboy Fiddler, 519, 524
Cowboy Pianist, 185
Cowell, Sarah, 137, 224, 348, 350, 383
Cowell, Sydney, parts, 157, 158, 261
Cowper, Archie, 17, 45, 152, 387, 443
Cowper, W. C., parts, 30, 46; author of Blackmail, 150; 263; his plays, 362, 387
Cox, Kenyon, drawings exhibited, 351
Cox, Louise, 214
Coyne (see Big Little Four)
Coyne, Joe (see Evans, Frank, and Coyne, Joe)
Coyne, M. (see Sheehan, John, and Coyne M.)
Craddock, P. F., 192
Craig, Charles G., 92, 267, 385
Craig, J. A., 399
Craigin (or Craigen), Maida, 14, 152, 184, 439
Crandall, H., 48
Crane, F. Irving, chorus, 576
Crane, Frank, 115, 361
Crane, Tillie, 179, 378
Crane, W., minor actor, 426
Crane, W. H., as Dromio, 18, 145, 263, 359; in The Henrietta, 436, 437, 455, 587; as Brutus, 500
Crane, W. S., concert, 406
Craven, Hawes, scenery, 430
Craven, Jean (or Joan), 190, 372
Crawford, Alice, 362
Crawford, Graham, 362
Crawford, Captain Jack, 177, 193, 194
Crawford, Roberta, 24
Crawford and McKission, 453
Crazy Patch, casts, 29, 146, 155; 183, 591
Crazy Quilt Show; prize, 134
Creese, Lizzie, 152
Cremorne Gardens, 124, 337
Creola, La, basis of The Commodore, 249
Creole, The (Article 47), cast, 89; 166
Crescent Athletic Club, 178
Crescent Band, Jamaica, 204, 205, 405, 606
Crescent City Quartette, 38, 117
Crescent Club, New York, 135
Crespi, tenor, 541
Crib Club, 121
Cricket on the Hearth, The, casts, 148, 230; 429, 508
Crimes of a Great City, cast, 166; 189, 316, 372
Crimes of Paris, 45
Crimmins Brothers (Mike and Danny), 96, 164
Crimmins and Doyle, 515
Crinkle, Nym (A. C. Wheeler), author of Pig Pony, 256
Cripps, Herbert A., 6, 214, 231, 415, 440
Crisp, Ada, 47

INDEX

Elise, Maggie (*see Petrie, Will O., and Elise, Maggie*)
Elixir of Love, The, 441, 454, 558
Elizabeth (Queen), with Mrs. Bowers, 247, 264
Elks, benefit, 42; ball, 78; benefits, 82, 145, 260, 360, 498, 561
Elks Quartet, 561
Ellani, Mlle., 174
Ellard, George. 171, 393
Elliot, W. G., 11, 29, 245, 367
Elliott, Arthur, 227
Elliott, Belle, 178, 580
Elliott, Lottie, 38, 87, 89, 92, 95, 97, 111, 310, 312, 316, 332, 325, 328
Elliott, W. A., 223, 229
Elliott Family (bicyclists), 186
Elliott and Odell's Roller Skating Rink, 195
Ellis, Cecilia (*sic*), as Pitti-Sing, 145
Ellis, Celie, parts, 6, 39, 145, 213, 214, 444
Ellis, Charles T., 105, 107, 108, 113, 115, 164, 182, 312, 324, 369, 371, 464, 563, 589, 590
Ellis, Sidney B., 270
Ellison, Clara, 236
Ellsler, Effie, parts, 31, 32, 44, 45, 51, 148, 183, 263, 267, 273, 359, 424, 425, 466, 557
Elm Park, Wendel's, 65, 68, 70
Elmblad, parts, 502 ff; 555, 556
Elmendorf, Dwight L., 404
Elmore, Florence, 182
Elmore. Julia. 149
Elmore, Marion, 30, 35. 82, 147, 233, 454
Elmore, Mrs., amateur, 173
Elmore, Stella, amateur, 170, 173, 576
Eloise, dancer, 467
Elsbach, Eduard, 54 ff, 275 ff, 475 ff
Elssner. Emma 169
Elton, William, parts. 3 ff, 22, 35, 37, 182
Elwood, Edith, 576, 577
Elwood Brothers, 375
Emerald Ball, Brooklyn, 161, 382, 567
Emerson, of Shannon and Emerson, 94
Emerson, Adelaide, 238
Emerson, Al, 525
Emerson, Harry. 94. 95; and George West, 114, 522
Emerson, Medora Henson, 140
Emerson, Mrs. F. M. G., 393
Emerson, Willis, and Clark, Morton, 331, 363, 516, 571
Emerson and Reynolds, 310
Emery, Irving Company, 430
Emery, D. B., and Russell, Laura, 106, 108, 114, 521, 535
Emery, Frank, 232
Emery, Winifred, 423, 431, 434
Emigration to America, cast, 313 ff; 529
Emile, violin, 494
Emmers, A., 602
Emmet, Harry W., 444
Emmet, J. K., parts, etc., 52, 151. 246, 261, 264, 273, 359, 463, 506, 560, 561
Emmet, Kathleen, amateur, 350
Emmet, Robert, birthday celebrated, 399, 551

Emmet, Robert, Association, 395
Emmett, Charles, 335, 531
Emmett, Florence, 107; with Fostelle, Al, 315, 329, 375
Emmett, Gracie, 269, 562
Emmons, J. Gordon, 468
Emperor William, lying in state, Eden Musée, 538
Empire City Colosseum, Jones Wood, 64, 70
Empire Hall, 290
Emrich, George, zither, 396
En Wagon, 120
Enchanted Clock, The, 334
Endlich hat er es gut gemacht, 281
Enelli, Regina, 536
Enemies, cast, 253
Engaged, 5; at Actors' Fund benefit, and at the Madison Square, cast, 13; at the Star cast, 23; 31, 52; casts, 151, 158; 186, 235, 267
Engel, actor, 41
Engel, Frl., 290
Engel, Jennie, 88, 117
Engel, Keila, 393
Engelliard, Mrs., 486
Engländer, Carola, 58, 475
Engle, Marie, 78, 133
English,, D. G., 228
English and McArthur, 527
Enlisted for the War, casts, 170, 197, 199
Enoch Arden, 198, 201, 202
Entrance of Italian troops into Naples and Rome, celebrated, 296
Entre Nous, reception, 161, 175, 366
Episodio, Un, della Rientrata di Guelfi in Firenze, 295
Er ist Baron, 605
Er ist taub, 283
Erastina, S. I., 195, 206, 353, 552
Erheiterung, S. I., 407
Erholung Concert Hall, 61
Erminic, lectures, 263
Erminie, cast, 34; 231, 249; revived, cast, 250; 300th and 450th performances, 251; changed cast, 250, 251; 305; in Brooklyn, 359; cast, in Williamsburgh, 386; 450; 500th time, 451; cast, 452; like A Surprise, 564; cast, 567; burlesqued, 319, 341, 371; as Our Minnie, 534
Ernani, 78
Ernestina, Mrs., 86
Ernestine, cast, 428
Errol, Lee, 90 (*see also Filson and Errol, Lee*)
Ervine, St. John, 208
Escaped from Sing Sing, 88; cast, 101, 102; 110, 162, 187, 269, 317; cast, 389
Eschenbach, Anna, 128
Eschenbach, Helen, 541
Eschert, concert, 67
Eschert, Albert, 119
Eschert, Charles (or Carl), concerts, 490, 574, 575
Escott, Frl., 297

[641]

[648]

INDEX

Goats, performing, 88, 96, 325, 326, 329, 331, 520, 521, 522, 526
Gobay, Joseph, 39
Göbel, Ferdinand, 486
Godowski, piano, 34
Godwin, Parke, 423
Goethe Society honours Henry Irving, 423, 430
Goetz's Taming of the Shrew, 79 ff
Going Back to Arkansaw, 110
Going It, 513
Going to the Masquerade, 90, 99, 115
Gold King, The, 167, 312, 317, 593
Gold Mine, A, 599
Gold Statues, 511, 516
Goldbeck, Robert, 129, 130, 176, 192, 346
Gold-Dust Dave, 315
Golden, Grace, 308
Golden, Richard, 415, 456, 463, 560
Golden and Drayton, 95
Golden Boom, The, 332
Golden Days, farce, 110
Golden Farmer, The, 377
Golden Giant, The, cast, 242; 255, 309, 360, 459, 463, 560
Golden Hen, The, 364
Goldene Kreutz, Das, cast, 298 ff
Goldfaden, Jewish playwright, 86, 313 ff, 317
Goldfische, cast, 477; 478 (see also Railroad of Love)
Goldie and Steele's World of Novelties, 186
Goldonkel, Der, 276, 288
Goldrich, Peter, 40, 41, 257, 258, 457, 458
Goldsby, Clara, 156
Goldstein, parts, 86
Goldstein, Mrs., 86, 87, 314, 530
Goldsticker, Carrie, 73 ff, 127, 140, 141
Goldthwaite, Dora, 52, 150, 498, 509
Goldthwaite, Fred, 149, 436
Goldzier, Julia, 365, 368
Goldzisher (sic), Mrs. M. M., 377
Golinas, Caccobatic, 369
Goma, Little, 337
Gomez, F. N., 193
Gonzales, Fanny, 510
Good as Gold, cast, 316; 392, 528
Good Friday, Lyceum closed, 428
Good Friday Spell, 385
Gooding, E. D., 94, 96, 98, 310 ff, 319 ff, 363
Goodrich, Mattie, 93, 117
Goodwin, Edwin F., parts, 29, 255, 256, 450
Goodwin, Myra, 24, 30, 212, 471
Goodwin, N. C., parts, 29, 43, 46, 51, 82, 145, 185, 231, 250; season at the Bijou, 255 ff; takes company to Boston, for benefit, 256; 259, 260, 299, 307, 338, 358, 367, 450, 461, 462, 498, 558, 585
Goodwin, Mrs. Robert, 383
Goodwin, Thomas, 222
Gordon, Jean, parts, 9, 150, 214 ff
Gordon, Joseph B., 152
Gordon, Robert, 458
Gordon and Grey, 163
Gordon and Lick, 319, 516

[650]

Gore, Alfredo, 444, 503
Gorham, J. H., 196
Gorilla Dramatic Social, 603
Gorman (see De Forrest and Gorman)
Gorman, Dick, 92, 108, 166, 391
Gorman Brothers, 100
Gormon (sic), ventriloquist, 107
Gosland, Josie, 336
Gosling, A. E., 203
Gosman, John, 402
Goss, P. A., 579
Goss, William, coloured female impersonator, 599
Gossin, J. Leslie, 197, 263, 349, 351, 548
Gotham Art Students, 126
Götterdämmerung, Die, promised, not given, 75; Lilli Lehmann sings finale, 353; production, cast, 506, 507
Gottheil, Richard, lecture, 351
Gotthold, Charles, 455
Gotthold, Newton, 49, 149, 182, 239, 249, 264, 360, 455
Göttich, Frau, 504
Gottschalk, Ferdinand, 420, 509
Gough, John B., 131, 175
Gould, Carrie, 122
Gould, Howard, 36, 464
Gounod Choral Society, 545, 548
Gourlay, of Harrison and Gourlay, 470
Gourlay, John, 144
Goutte, La, d'Eau, 120
Government Scout, The, 167
Go-won-go Mohawk, 467
Gowrie, Lizzie, 575
Grabber and Snapper, 94
Grace, Edmund, 182, 441
Grace, W. R., 604
Grace Church, 350
Gräf, Fritz W., 407
Gräf, Therese, amateur, 407
Graff, Jacob, 63, 127, 488
Graham, Irving's Company, 430
Graham, B. R., parts, 35, 148, 235, 428, 442, 459
Graham, Charles, 496
Graham, Charles J., 527
Graham, Donald De V., 136
Graham, Elsie, 29, 472
Graham, Frances, 425, 500
Graham, H. R., 567
Graham, Harry, 370
Graham, Joseph N., 576
Graham, R. E., parts, 28, 30, 39, 82, 85, 152, 184, 358
Grais, juggler, 331, 389, 511, 512, 520, 522, 523, 536
Gramm, Emil, 379
Gramm, Marie, 128, 343, 347, 541, 543, 544, 583
Gramm, Mrs. Emil, 345, 379, 556 (see supra)
Grand Army Hall, Williamsburgh, 193, 394, 396, 596 ff
Grand Casimir, Le, 2
Grand Conservatory of Music, 544

INDEX

Grizzly Adams, cast, 93; 117
Groebl, Edward, 129
Groebl, Marie, 78, 128, 129, 131, 132, 133, 141, 251, 306, 347, 355, 444, 501, 556
Grogan's Election, 373; Elevation, cast, 510; 573; Elevator, 405; Reception, 96, 116
Gronotski Brothers, 114
Groschel's Conservatory of Music, 176, 378
Groschel, W., 381
Grose-Graff, Emil, 119, 289
Gross, Margarethe, 338
Grosse, Bertha, 20, 121, 188
Grosse Wohlthäter, Der, 485
Grossmith, Weedon, 11, 29, 244, 245, 367
Groth, W. R., 170
Groux, Mons. F., 291
Grove Hill Park, 290
Grover, J. H., 88
Grover, Leonard, benefit, 81; 147, 385, 471
Grover, Leonard, Jr., 147
Groves, Charles, 209 ff, 409 ff
Groves, Laura, 161, 171, 179, 198, 367, 381, 382
Grovesteen, Bessie, 550
Growlers, The, or, the Adventures of a Fresh Young Man, 112
Grubb, Lillie (or Lillian), 31, 211, 256, 444, 451, 569
Grünbaum, Julius, 276
Grund-Idee in Wagner's Ring der Nibelungen, lecture, 489
Grundy, Sydney, his The Queen's Favourite, 228; his The Mouse Trap, 409, 410
Grunewald, Hedwig, 486
Grutli Männerchor, 63
Guardia Colombo, 70, 294, 495
Guardia Savoia, 496
Guardia Vittorio Emanuele II, 296, 496
Guernoy, opéra-bouffe, 429
Guidone, R., 295
Guild of St. Paul's P. E. Church, Brooklyn, 375
Guille, Albert, 250, 304, 306, 307
Guina, John, 513
Guinness, Charles, Company, 318, 375
Guion, Netta, 28, 30, 410 ff
Gulberson, W., 50
Gunn, Walter (sic), 192
Gunn, Wilbur (sic), 423
Gunter, A. C., his Prince Karl, 14; Two Nights in Rome, 90; Vendetta, 190; The Deacon's Daughter, 239; A Wall Street Bandit, 243; One against Many, 436
Gunther's Palm-Garten, 118, 119, 334, 335, 532
Gurickx, Camille, 503, 504, 555
Gurner, actor, 430
Gurney, Nellie, 376
Gute Michel, Der, 57, 277, 297
Guten Morgan, Herr Fischer, 59, 280
Guterding, J., Walhalla, 490
Guthrie, Francesca, 125
Guv'nor, The, revived, cast, 22, 37
Guzman, 202
Gwynette, Harry, parts, 4, 14, 156, 221, 222, 238, 356, 440

Gwynne's Oath, cast, 465
Gypsy Ball, 396
Gypsy Baron, The, at the Casino, 33; at Koster and Bial's, 122; Conried's Company, cast, 258, 259; 260, 264, 356, 360

Haack, Hermann, 433
Haan, Walter, 379
Haaren, J .H., 192, 394
Haase, Friedrich, 279
Habrich, Albertine, 55 ff, 275 ff, 283, 475 ff, 486
Habrich, Heinrich, 54 ff, 480, 486
Hackett, J. K., 552
Hadley, Miss, 215
Hadley, Nelson, drum-major, 325, 326, 334
Haff, Mrs., 201
Hagan, Charles T., 37
Hagan, J. F., 36, 439
Hagedorn, Charles L., 606
Hagedorn, Elisabeth, 54 ff, 480 ff
Hageman, Reverend Miller, on bird songs, 395
Hager's Great Republic, 160
Hagestolzen, Die, 278, 433
Haggard, Rider, She as a play, 453, 454
Hagger, Emma, 148, 245
Hague, actor, 264
Hague, Nellie, 106, 113, 186
Haines, May, 444
Haines, Nat, with American Four, 515; and Will Vidocq, 52, 93, 107, 114, 115, 319, 321, 328 (see also Four Diamonds)
Halbert, May, 368, 566
Halcyon Opera Association, 383
Hale, Carrie, 363
Hale, Edward Everett, reads, 177, 179; lectures on Washington, 382
Haley (see Big Four; also Electric Three)
Half-Way House, The, 84, 85, 94, 110, 113
Hall, Ada (Mrs. Dare), 513
Hall, Annetta, 214
Hall, Annie, 40, 41, 257
Hall, Carrie, 110, 111
Hall, Clinton, 373, 388
Hall, Daisy, 447
Hall, E. T., 464
Hall, Edith, 473
Hall, Elsie, 93
Hall, Grace, 223
Hall, Gustavus, 6, 44, 160, 259, 340
Hall, H. T., 173
Hall, Ida, 548
Hall, James and Frankie, 515
Hall, John G., 171
Hall, Josie, 242, 410, 456, 469
Hall, L. M., 21
Hall, Lillie, 100, 101, 118, 371; her Burlesque Company, 321, 322, 593; Lillie Hall and Fannie (sic) Bloodgood, 322, 323, 370, 389, 390
Hall, Lillie A., 528
Hall, Lillie May, 319, 512

[652]

INDEX

[654]

INDEX

INDEX

INDEX

McDonald, John G., 11
McDonald, Polly, 99, 105, 164, 167, 187, 327, 331, 335, 371, 510, 514, 516, 535
McDonough, Barney, 473
McDowell, Alfred, 388, 513 (*see also Watson, Henry and McDowell, Alfred*)
McDowell, E. A., parts, 442
MacDowell, E. A., music by, 543
McDowell, Melbourne, parts, 15, 23, 428, 443, 461
McDowell, Miss C., 193, 199
McElfatrick and Sons, 443
McEvoy, George, 170, 576
McEwen, Nettie, 198
McGill (*see Hearne and McGill*)
McGill, Sadie, of McGill and Hearne, 527
McGinnis, concert, 607
McGirr, Thomas F., 365
McGlynn, Rev. Dr. Edward, lectures, 175, 308, 369, 499, 524, 602
McGonigle, of Kerrigan and McGonigle, 517
McGonigle, Billy, 598
McGrath, J. H., 149
McGrath, J. W., 153
McGrath, Metcalf, 137
McGrath, Mrs. A. J., 137
McGreal, T. J., 172
McGregor, Genevieve, 396
McGuckin, Barton, 500, 541, 568
McHenry, Nellie, parts, 154, 231, 238, 456
McHenry, Tillie, as Katisha, 169; 473, 573
McHugh, of Ireland and McHugh, 328
McHugh, E. H., 107, 115
McInerny, 603
McIntyre and Heath, 92, 165, 370
McIntyre and Heath's Minstrels, 52, 164, 183
McIntyre, Robert, 468 (*see Clipper Quartet*)
McIntosh (*see Hunn and McIntosh*)
McIntosh, Burr, 82, 152, 158, 184
McKee, Andy, 320
McKeever, of Edwards and McKeever, 369
McKeever, J. P., 402
McKeever, Joseph, 601
McKelway, St. Clair, 543
McKenna, M. J., amateur, 170, 197, 376, 377, 392, 580
McKenna, Maggie, amateur, 376, 392, 394, 580
McKenna, Stanley, benefit, 209, 210
McKenna's Flirtation, 588
McKinstry, Kate, 18
McKission, of Crawford and McKission, 453
McKloskey (*sic*), C. J., 323
McKnight, Mrs. Whitney, 578
McLaughlin, James, presented with a diamond whip, 435
McMahon (*see Kelly, Murphy and Mc-Mahon*)
McMahon, William, 117, 321, 323, 329, 332, 518, 519, 521, 525, 572
McManus, C. A., 35, 148, 247, 385
McMullen Family, The, skit, 95
McNair, Robert, 312, 513
McNeely, J. A., amateur, 576

McNeil, Joe, and McCabe, John, 572
McNeil, Marie, 518, 522, 572
McNeill, Catharine, singer, 180
McNish, Frank E., 24, 356
McNish, Johnson and Slavin's Minstrels, 26, 37, 43, 145, 258, 356, 428, 448, 557, 558, 585
McNooney's Visit, cast, 257, 258; 308
McNoughton, J. H., his Onnalinda, 219
McPhail, Nellie, 603
McPherson, Mrs. J., 545
McShane, Charlie, 341
McShane, Thomas and Charles, 513
McShane, Thomas and Little Dixie, 311
McShane Brothers, midget acrobats, 84, 119, 163, 312, 371
McVickar, W. B., 407
McVicker, Sarah, 155, 312, 392
McWade, John, 211, 266
McWade, Joseph, minstrel, 340, 341
McWade, Robert, parts, 244, 263, 265
McWall, Edward, 559
Ma, Look at Him, 90, 92
Maas, James, 145
Maas, Louis, 128
Macaulay, 170, 368, 567
Macbeth, 28, 43; with Dixey and Mackay, 81; 148, 150, 160, 185, 247, 261, 265, 455; read by Mrs. Scott-Siddons, 542; 560, 588
Macbeth, Edward S. Kelley's music for, 348
Macbeth, Edwin Booth as, 28, 160, 588; T. W. Keene as, 148; Joseph Wheelock as, 247; McKee Rankin as, 560
Macdonough, Harry, 6; as Nanki-Poo, 145; 213, 214, 440
Macfarlane, Master W. C., 131, 343, 344, 345, 348, 546
Macfarlane, William Phelps, amateur, 170, 365, 368, 566
Macintosh, F. S., 402
Macintyre, R., 38
Mack, minstrel, 341
Mack (*see Ferguson and Mack*)
Mack, Charles A., 316
Mack, E. J., 54, 273, 472, 474
Mack, Harry, 227, 361
Mack, J. Herbert, and Raymond, Lizzie B., 528
Mack, Phil (*see Murphy, John E., and Mack, Phil*)
Mack, Rosa, 93
Mack, W. F., 263
Mack, Will J., 83, 263
Mack, William, parts, 447
Mack, William (*see California Quartet; also Muldoon Quartet*)
Mack and Curdy, 97
Mack and Holbrook, 165
Mackart's Diana's Hunting Party, also The Five Senses, 549
Mackay, Charles D., 442
Mackay, F. F., parts, 16, 48, 152, 213, 222; lectures on acting, 427, 428; parts, 454, 509
Mackay, John A., 6, 31; at 500th Adonis, 37; benefit, 81; 82, 149, 256, 358, 456

[673]

INDEX

Mitchell, William, and Lorraine, Claudia, 324, 330

Mitterwurzer, Friedrich, début, 20, 21; parts, 56, 59, 60

Mixed Ale, skit, 96

Mixed Mail, 107, 108, 111

Mixed Pickles, cast, 30; 143, 273, 274, 557, 590

M'liss, 42, 48, 145, 261, 385, 558, 585

Mlle. de Brass Ear, burlesque, 533 (*see infra*)

Mlle. de Bressier, cast, 439; 560

Mlle. Nitouche, with Judic, 1, 2; with Lotta, 29, 43, 149, 358

Moadinger, C. F., Jr., 582

Moadinger, Mrs. L. F., 582

Moag, I. S., amateur, 580

Möblirte Wohnung, Eine, 407

Mockridge, Whitney, 80, 129, 141, 149, 181, 348, 380, 383, 506, 548, 556, 583

Model Woman, The, lecture, 580

Modern Mother Goose, at Dockstader's, 533

Moderner Barbar, Ein, 484

Modjeska, Helena, as Rosalind, 19; parts, 21, 146, 235, 236, 299, 357, 449, 535, 559

Moglie, La, Deve Segnire il Marito, farce, 495

Mogulesko, 317; and Finkel, 282, 317

Mohican Club, 157

Molineux, Eloise, coloured actress, 125

Mollenhauer, Edward, pupils, concert, 126; The Passions, 127; 130, 239; violin recitals, 349, 352

Mollenhauer, Henry, 130, 161, 174, 383

Mollenhauer, Ida, 176, 383

Mollenhauer, Louis, 383

Molly Maguires, The, 573

Molony, Kate, 423, 438, 560

Molyneux, amateur, 407

Monbars, cast, 441, 442; 462; cast, 558; 585

Monde, Le, ou l'on s' Ennuie, as Our Society, 14

Money, cast, Wallack's, 413; 414

Monico, Louis, 467, 533

Monihan, Frank, 513

Monitor and Merrimac, 137

Monk, Minnie, 227, 254, 439, 462

Monkey Theatre, 436

Monkeys, performing, 105, 106, 113, 325, 331, 334, 370, 389, 436, 472, 511, 512, 522, 523, 536, 538, 572

Monroe, Carrie (*see Bruns, Harry, and Monroe, Carrie*)

Monroe, George W., 43, 145, 271, 389; and John C. Rice, 312, 561

Monroe, S. M., his play, The Parvenus, 588

Monsieur, casts, 221, 440; 559

Monsieur Bloison, comedy, 67

Monsieur Choufleuri, 338, 339, 494

Monsieur Hercules, 279

Montague, Alice, 82

Montague, Annis, 308

Montague, C. H., to expose Bishop's tricks, 341

Montague, Louise, 31, 147, 456

[680]

Montaine, Clarence, 432

Montant, A. P., 121, 494

Montauk Lodge, benefit, 566

Monte Cristo, cast, 36; 43, 47, 89; cast, 156; 167, 182, 190, 253, 261, 266, 359, 372, 461, 464; cast, 472; 585

Monte Cristo, Jr., 534, 561

Montecello, Monsignor, 491

Montefiore, Sir Moses, Fund, benefit, 125

Montefiore, Sir Moses, Under the Protection of, 529, 530

Montegriffo, A., as Nanki-Poo, 24

Montegriffo, Pauline, 465

Monteith, Zippora, 578, 582

Montgomery, Douglas, amateur, 170, 173, 365, 367, 368, 566 ff

Montgomery, H. W., parts, 159, 462

Montgomery Five, 316, 325

Monti, Luigi, 175

Monti, Mlle., 99

Monti, Signora, 118 (*see supra*)

Moody, Dwight L., and Sankey, Ira D., 175, 192

Moon, of Southern Quartet, 599

Mooney, Annie, 131, 196, 197, 199

Mooney, Dora, 601

Mooney, F. D., lecture on Ireland, 542

Mooney, Jessie, 601

Mooney, Misses, 196

Moonlight Masquerade, The, 164

Moor, Emanuel, pianist, 125, 126, 161, 284, 344, 346, 347, 349, 540

Moore, walker, 537

Moore, Adelaide, début, 17; parts, 158

Moore, Bella, 85, 154

Moore, Charles, and dogs, 90, 106

Moore, Charles and Carrie, skaters, 90, 106

Moore, Clara, 105, 107, 108, 113, 115, 164, 182, 312, 371, 464

Moore, Elliott and Arthur, 607

Moore, Estelle, 321

Moore, Eugene, 45

Moore, Flora, 82, 84, 85, 104, 107, 112, 122, 163, 259, 323, 371, 473, 518, 519, 521, 525

Moore, George F., "with 100 faces," 84, 100, 102, 104, 113, 327, 330, 331, 369

Moore, George T. (*sic*), 371

Moore, Grant, cornet, 606

Moore, Ira H., 170, 173, 375, 377

Moore, J. C., 106, 108, 114

Moore, J. H., 408, 607

Moore, J. W., lectures, 193

Moore, John, of Daly's, 9, 215

Moore, Laura, 353, 354, 384, 415

Moore, Maggie, 336

Moore, Preston, 152

Moore, William, 82 (*see Twilight Quartet*)

Moore and Sanford, 108, 114

Moores (*sic*), Ella, 376

Moorish Caravan, 537

Mora, Helene, 518, 572

Moral Crime, A, cast, 24; 49, 156

Moran, Frank, minstrel, 84, 374, 511, 513, 591

Moran, H. A., 15, 220

INDEX

Nelson, Marie, 95
Nelson, Mlle., 187
Nelson, Virginia, 245, 498
Nelson Brothers, 519, 520, 571
Nelson Family, acrobats, 327, 331, 369, 371, 519, 522, 570, 571, 591
Nelson and Lenton Pantomime, 392
Nelsoni, Japanese juggler, 85
Nelton, Egyptian juggler, 101, 467
Nero, by Rubinstein, cast, 302; 303, 368; cast, 500; 586
Nero, or, the Fall of Rome, at Staten Island, 553, 583; described, 608
Nethersole, J., amateur, 173
Neubauer, Mr. and Mrs. W. G., 402
Neuendorff, Adolf, 36; at Central Park Garden, 137; 231, 276; his Prinz Waldmeister, 281; and his orchestra, 342, 381, 485, 503 ff. 545, 567, 586
Neupert, Edmund, 125, 134, 161, 342, 346, 541
Neuville, Augustin, and Neuville, Mme., 85, 91, 590
Nevada, Emma, 129
Nevada, or, the Lost Mine, cast, 576; 608
Never Say Die, 388, 470, 590
Neville, Carrie, 587
Neville, Louise, 564
Neville, Sara, 46, 147, 185, 263
Nevins, Charles, 230
Nevins, H. R., 200
Nevins, R. Fletcher, testimonial, 200
New Adamless Eden, 94, 98, 100
New Brighton, S. I., 205
New Brooms Sweep Clean, 192
New Coachman, The, 103, 104, 106, 112
New Dorp, S. I., 408
New German Man, The, cast, 115
New Karl, The, cast, 513; 564, 589
New Magdalen, The, 36, 166, 265, 267, 364, 459, 557
New Men and Old Acres, 206
New Mexico, lecture on, 199
New Olympia, Forepaugh's, 353
New Orleans, Taking of, at Brighton Beach, 553
New Policeman, The, 99
New Shows Museum, 203
New Way to Pay Old Debts, A, 28
New World, The, cast, 316
New Year's Calls, 511
New Year's Eve, cantata, 398
New York Alderman, The, 91
New York as It Was, 273
New York Banks Glee Club, 133, 343, 344, 346, 540, 541, 542
New York College of Music, 550
New York Comedy Company, 404
New York Driving Club, 550
New York Harmonic Society, 130, 133
New York Madrigal Company, 539
New York Madrigal Quartet, 158, 159, 192, 193, 460, 588
New York Male Quartet, 308

[684]

New York Männerchor (see Männerchor, New York)
New York Museums, 532
New York Nowadays, 272
New York Operatic Club, 128
New York Philharmonic Club, 129, 130, 131, 135, 206, 345, 346, 347, 348, 365, 379, 548, 556, 578, 579, 583, 600
New York Press Club, 501
New York School of Acting, 225, 227, 427
New York Sing-Akadamie, 287
New York Sketch Club, 151
New York Star Company, 405
New York University Glee Club, 133, 179, 203, 381, 544
New York Vocal Society, 345
New York Vocal Union, 347, 348, 546
New York Zither Club (or Verein), 125, 284
Newark, 68
Newcomb, Ada, 510
Newcomb, Bobby, 94, 374
Newcomb, Harley, his opera, 297
Newcomb and Hassan, 84, 104, 105
Newcomb and Hamlin, 525
Newcomb Trio, dancers, 324, 371, 519, 526
Newcombe, Theresa, 389
Newell, Lizzie, 373
Newell, Major, 29
Newman (see Montgomery Five)
Newman, May, parts, 35, 36, 144, 185, 254, 265, 385, 446, 465, 562
Newman, Mlle., ballet, 253, 261, 499, 569
Newton, Alice, 92, 102
Newtown, L. I., 200, 201, 394
Newtown Association Hall, 200, 402; Choral Union, 200, 201, 402
Niagara, cast, 148
Nibbe, of Edegio, Campbelle and Nibbe, 511
Nibbe, M. E., and Vernon, May, 102
Nibelungen Ring, The, two cycles of, without Das Rheingold, 507
Niblo's Garden Theatre (1885-86), 35 ff; (1886-87), 252 ff; (1887-88), 453 ff
Nicholas, A. L., 243
Nicholas, G. W., 427, 428
Nicholls, Kate, 515
Nichols, C. A., 154
Nichols, C. T., 373, 388
Nichols, Hamilton, 118
Nicholson, John, 376, 577
Nicholson, W., 438
Nick of the Woods, 268
Nickolds, Mr. and Mrs., 575
Nicodemus, 511
Nicolai, Merry Wives of Windsor, 80 ff
Nicolaus Tyroleans, 61
Nicolini, sings with Patti, 305
Niemann, Albert, début, parts, success as Siegmund and Tristan, 297 ff; 342; parts, 502 ff
Niemann-Raabe, Hedwig, début, parts, 432, 433; 475, 499
Night, A, in Rome, cast, 187
Night of Terror, pantomime, 310, 312

[686]

[687]

INDEX

[690]

INDEX

[694]

INDEX

INDEX

[706]

INDEX

INDEX

INDEX

Walter Scott Loge, 287
Walters, of Somers and Walters, 325, 517, 518
Walters, Nellie, 516
Walters, Thomas, musket drill, 600
Walton, actor, 49
Walton, Charles, skater, 193
Walton, E. L., 151
Walton, Henry E., 24, 44, 50, 154, 155, 169, 237
Walzer König, Der, cast, 56
Wanamaker, Jeanie, coloured performer, 350
Wandell, concert, 394
Wandering Minstrel, The, cast, 309
Wanted, a Male Cook, 406
War to the Knife, 376
Ward, of Landis and Ward, 97
Ward, of West and Ward, 336
Ward, actor, 36
Ward, Ada Webster, 226
Ward, E. D., début, parts, 409 ff; 431
Ward, Eugene, footless dancer, 89, 332
Ward, F. F., parts, 38
Ward, F. T. (see Clipper Quartet)
Ward, Genevieve, parts, 228, 259, 260, 267, 274, 357
Ward, Hi Tom, 85, 100, 335, 370
Ward, Ida, 268, 390, 590
Ward, Isabel (or Isabella), 94, 106, 309, 310, 311, 320, 321, 322, 370, 388, 509, 512, 522, 523, 536, 589
Ward, James M., "first appearance in eleven years," 271, 275
Ward, John F., 465, 590
Ward, John T. (see Four Diamonds)
Ward, Thomas H., and Lynch, Con R., 87, 89, 98, 102, 104, 108, 110, 112, 328, 329, 330, 373, 388, 527 528
Ward, Tom, 99, 116, 164
Ward, Tom, and Mack, Eddie, 527
Ward and Lee, 99, 322
Warde, Carrie Clarke, 271
Warde, Frederick B., parts, 46, 50, 122, 147, 185, 186, 231, 259, 265, 269, 357, 385, 460, 466, 498, 557, 590
Wardell, Etelka, 359
Wardell, Miss, 564
Ware, Annie, 169, 237, 474
Ware, Josephine, 129, 345
Ware, Katherine, 44, 155
Wareing's Opera House, Hoboken, 275
Waring, A. G., magic, 197, 596
Waring, Harry F., amateur, 376
Warner, Charles Dudley, reads, 544
Warner, Colonel, his Big Boom, 571
Warner, Jessie, 336
Warner Institute, Brooklyn, 579, 580
Warren, actor, 229
Warren, A. H., 153, 245
Warren, Dolly, 82
Warren, E., 468
Warren, Edwin, 183
Warren, Frank C., 351, 407, 551
Warren, Fred, 152, 446
Warren, James E., 351
Warren, Lloyd, amateur, 351

Warren, Marion, 45, 270
Warren, R. H., 132
Warren, Samuel P., 175, 350, 543
Wartegg, G. von H., lecture, 63
Warth, John, Sommergarten, 602
Warwick, J. H., 395
Washburn, Clara, 114
Washburn, W., 392
Washington, Amy, 37
Washington, Billy and Charles, 115
Washington, George, lecture by Edward Everett Hale, 382; by Seth Low, 582
Washington, Martha, reception, 395; tea, 597
Washington Dramatic Association, 172
Washington Lodge (19), benefit, 352
Washington Park, 62 ff, 498
Wassman, Lena, 277
Watch Dog, The, 110, 331
Waterman, Edgar, 187
Waterman, Ida, 41, 42
Waters, Adele, 558
Watkins, Edward, 201
Watson, Alice, 114
Watson, Burt, of Kelly and Watson, 324, 327, 510, 523 (see also California Four)
Watson, G. W., 90, 91, 166, 167; benefit, 168 (see Thomas, T. F., and Watson, George W.)
Watson Henry, and McDowell, Alfred, 51, 106, 114
Watson, Mr. and Mrs. Harry, 83, 85, 102, 103, 110, 111, 163
Watson, Mrs. C., 442
Watson, Thomas F., 528
Watson and McDermott, 114
Watson, Quinlan and Cooper, 163
Watson-Doty, Mrs., 546
Watts (see Dalton and Watts)
Watts, Amelia, 46, 153, 182, 363, 467
Waugh, Amelia, 163
Waxworks, 532, 537, 538 (see Eden Musée)
Way of the World, The, 471
Way of the World, The, variety play, 515
Wayland, Charlotte, 152; Waylord, 273
Wayland, Miss, 45
Wayne, Dave (see Tierney, James and Wayne, Dave)
We, Us and Co., 30, 46, 48, 52, 149, 184, 264, 267, 386
Weathersby, Eliza (Mrs. N. C. Goodwin), dies, 256
Weathersby, Helen, 261, 267, 361, 459, 471
Weathersby, Jennie, 34, 250, 452
Weaver, Add, 514
Weaver, Affie, 36
Weaver, Blanche, 432, 442
Weaver, H. A., parts, 24, 25, 240, 243, 253, 421, 438
Weaver, H. A., Jr., 40, 247, 432, 468
Webb, Annie, 582
Webb, Edward, 594
Webb, Harriet, 127, 158, 172, 212, 551
Webb, Maggie, 575
Webb, P., 582

[717]

INDEX